Available with MyStatLab™ for Your Business Statistics Courses

MyStatLab is the market-leading online learning management program for learning and teaching business statistics.

Statistical Software Support

Built-in tutorial videos and functionality make using the most popular software solutions seamless and intuitive. Tutorial videos, study cards, and manuals (for select titles) are available within MyStatLab and accessible at the point of use. Easily launch exercise and eText data sets into Excel or StatCrunch, or copy and paste into any other software program.

Leverage the Power of StatCrunch

MyStatLab leverages the power of StatCrunch –powerful, web-based statistical software. In addition, access to the full online community allows users to take advantage of a wide variety of resources and applications at www.statcrunch.com.

Bring Statistics to Life

Virtually flip coins, roll dice, draw cards, and interact with animations on your mobile device with the extensive menu of experiments and applets in StatCrunch. Offering a number of ways to practice resampling procedures, such as permutation tests and bootstrap confidence intervals, StatCrunch is a complete and modern solution.

A ROADMAP FOR SELECTING A STATISTICAL METHOD

Data Analysis Task	For Numerical Variables	For Categorical Variables
Describing a group or several groups	Ordered array, stem-and-leaf display, frequency distribution, relative frequency distribution, percentage distribution, cumulative percentage distribution, histogram, polygon, cumulative percentage polygon, sparklines, gauges, treemaps **(Sections 2.2, 2.4, 2.6, 17.4)** Mean, median, mode, geometric mean, quartiles, range, interquartile range, standard deviation, variance, coefficient of variation, skewness, kurtosis, boxplot, normal probability plot **(Sections 3.1, 3.2, 3.3, 6.3)** Index numbers **(online Section 16.8)**	Summary table, bar chart, pie chart, doughnut chart, Pareto chart **(Sections 2.1 and 2.3)**
Inference about one group	Confidence interval estimate of the mean **(Sections 8.1 and 8.2)** t test for the mean **(Section 9.2)** Chi-square test for a variance or standard deviation **(online Section 12.7)**	Confidence interval estimate of the proportion **(Section 8.3)** Z test for the proportion **(Section 9.4)**
Comparing two groups	Tests for the difference in the means of two independent populations **(Section 10.1)** Wilcoxon rank sum test **(Section 12.4)** Paired t test **(Section 10.2)** F test for the difference between two variances **(Section 10.4)**	Z test for the difference between two proportions **(Section 10.3)** Chi-square test for the difference between two proportions **(Section 12.1)** McNemar test for two related samples **(online Section 12.6)**
Comparing more than two groups	One-way analysis of variance for comparing several means **(Section 11.1)** Kruskal-Wallis test **(Section 12.5)** Two-way analysis of variance **(Section 11.2)** Randomized block design **(online Section 11.3)**	Chi-square test for differences among more than two proportions **(Section 12.2)**
Analyzing the relationship between two variables	Scatter plot, time-series plot **(Section 2.5)** Covariance, coefficient of correlation **(Section 3.5)** Simple linear regression **(Chapter 13)** t test of correlation **(Section 13.7)** Time-series forecasting **(Chapter 16)** Sparklines **(Section 2.6)**	Contingency table, side-by-side bar chart, doughnut chart, PivotTables **(Sections 2.1, 2.3, 2.6)** Chi-square test of independence **(Section 12.3)**
Analyzing the relationship between two or more variables	Multiple regression **(Chapters 14 and 15)** Regression trees **(Section 17.5)**	Multidimensional contingency tables **(Section 2.6)** Drilldown and slicers **(Section 2.6)** Logistic regression **(Section 14.7)** Classification trees **(Section 17.5)**

Statistics for Managers Using Microsoft® Excel

8th Edition

David M. Levine

Department of Statistics and Computer Information Systems

Zicklin School of Business, Baruch College, City University of New York

David F. Stephan

Two Bridges Instructional Technology

Kathryn A. Szabat

Department of Business Systems and Analytics

School of Business, La Salle University

PEARSON

Boston Columbus Indianapolis New York San Francisco
Amsterdam Cape Town Dubai London Madrid Milan Munich Paris Montreal Toronto
Delhi Mexico City São Paulo Sydney Hong Kong Seoul Singapore Taipei Tokyo

Editorial Director: Chris Hoag
Editor in Chief: Deirdre Lynch
Acquisitions Editor: Suzanna Bainbridge
Senior Editorial Assistant: Justin Billing
Program Manager: Chere Bemelmans
Project Manager: Sherry Berg
Program Management Team Lead: Karen Wernholm
Project Management Team Lead: Peter Silvia
Media Producer: Jean Choe
TestGen Content Manager: John Flanagan
QA Manager, Assessment Content: Marty Wright
Senior MathXL Content Developer: Robert Carroll

Marketing Manager: Tiffany Bitzel
Field Marketing Manager: Adam Goldstein
Marketing Assistant: Jennifer Myers
Senior Author Support/Technology Specialist: Joe Vetere
Manager, Rights Management: Gina Cheselka
Senior Procurement Specialist: Carol Melville
Associate Director of Design: Andrea Nix
Program Design Lead and Cover Design: Barbara Atkinson
Text Design: Cenveo Publisher Services
Production Coordination, Composition, and Illustrations: Lumina Datamatics
Cover Image: Serp/Shutterstock

Library of Congress Cataloging-in-Publication Data

Levine, David M., 1946– author.
  Statistics for managers using Microsoft Excel / David M. Levine, David F. Stephan, Kathryn A. Szabat.—8th edition.
    pages cm
  Includes bibliographical references and index.
  ISBN 978-0-13-417305-4 (hardcover)
1. Microsoft Excel (Computer file) 2. Management—Statistical methods. 3. Commercial statistics. 4. Electronic spreadsheets.
    5. Management—Statistical methods—Computer programs. 6. Commercial statistics—Computer programs. I. Stephan,
    David F., author. II. Szabat, Kathryn A., author. III. Title.
  HD30.215.S73 2017
  519.50285'554—dc23

                                                                                              2015027139

www.pearsonhighered.com

ISBN-10:   0-13-417305-8
ISBN-13: 978-0-13-417305-4

To our spouses and children,
Marilyn, Sharyn, Mary, and Mark

and to our parents, in loving memory,
Lee, Reuben, Ruth, Francis, Mary, and William

About the Authors

Kathryn Szabat, David Levine, and David Stephan

David M. Levine, David F. Stephan, and Kathryn A. Szabat are all experienced business school educators committed to innovation and improving instruction in business statistics and related subjects.

David Levine, Professor Emeritus of Statistics and CIS at Baruch College, CUNY, is a nationally recognized innovator in statistics education for more than three decades. Levine has coauthored 14 books, including several business statistics textbooks; textbooks and professional titles that explain and explore quality management and the Six Sigma approach; and, with David Stephan, a trade paperback that explains statistical concepts to a general audience. Levine has presented or chaired numerous sessions about business education at leading conferences conducted by the Decision Sciences Institute (DSI) and the American Statistical Association, and he and his coauthors have been active participants in the annual DSI Making Statistics More Effective in Schools and Business (MSMESB) mini-conference. During his many years teaching at Baruch College, Levine was recognized for his contributions to teaching and curriculum development with the College's highest distinguished teaching honor. He earned B.B.A. and M.B.A. degrees from CCNY. and a Ph.D. in industrial engineering and operations research from New York University.

Advances in computing have always shaped **David Stephan's** professional life. As an undergraduate, he helped professors use statistics software that was considered advanced even though it could compute *only* several things discussed in Chapter 3, thereby gaining an early appreciation for the benefits of using software to solve problems (and perhaps positively influencing his grades). An early advocate of using computers to support instruction, he developed a prototype of a mainframe-based system that anticipated features found today in Pearson's MathXL and served as special assistant for computing to the Dean and Provost at Baruch College. In his many years teaching at Baruch, Stephan implemented the first computer-based *classroom*, helped redevelop the CIS curriculum, and, as part of a FIPSE project team, designed and implemented a multimedia learning environment. He was also nominated for teaching honors. Stephan has presented at the SEDSI conference and the DSI MSMESB mini-conferences, sometimes with his coauthors. Stephan earned a B.A. from Franklin & Marshall College and an M.S. from Baruch College, CUNY, and he studied instructional technology at Teachers College, Columbia University.

As Associate Professor of Business Systems and Analytics at La Salle University, **Kathryn Szabat** has transformed several business school majors into one interdisciplinary major that better supports careers in new and emerging disciplines of data analysis including analytics. Szabat strives to inspire, stimulate, challenge, and motivate students through innovation and curricular enhancements, and shares her coauthors' commitment to teaching excellence and the continual improvement of statistics presentations. Beyond the classroom she has provided statistical advice to numerous business, nonbusiness, and academic communities, with particular interest in the areas of education, medicine, and nonprofit capacity building. Her research activities have led to journal publications, chapters in scholarly books, and conference presentations. Szabat is a member of the American Statistical Association (ASA), DSI, Institute for Operation Research and Management Sciences (INFORMS), and DSI MSMESB. She received a B.S. from SUNY-Albany, an M.S. in statistics from the Wharton School of the University of Pennsylvania, and a Ph.D. degree in statistics, with a cognate in operations research, from the Wharton School of the University of Pennsylvania.

For all three coauthors, continuous improvement is a natural outcome of their curiosity about the world. Their varied backgrounds and many years of teaching experience have come together to shape this book in ways discussed in the Preface.

Brief Contents

Contents

3 Numerical Descriptive Measures 95

4 Basic Probability 141

8 Confidence Interval Estimation 237

9 Fundamentals of Hypothesis Testing: One-Sample Tests 270

13   Simple Linear Regression 427

14   Introduction to Multiple Regression 475

Preface

As business statistics evolves and becomes an increasingly important part of one's business education, how business statistics gets taught and what gets taught becomes all the more important.

We, the coauthors, think about these issues as we seek ways to continuously improve the teaching of business statistics. We actively participate in Decision Sciences Institute (DSI), American Statistical Association (ASA), and Making Statistics More Effective in Schools and Business (MSMESB) conferences. We use the ASA's Guidelines for Assessment and Instruction (GAISE) reports and combine them with our experiences teaching business statistics to a diverse student body at several universities. We also benefit from the interests and efforts of our past coauthors, Mark Berenson and Timothy Krehbiel.

Our Educational Philosophy

When writing for introductory business statistics students, five principles guide us.

Help students see the relevance of statistics to their own careers by using examples from the functional areas that may become their areas of specialization. Students need to learn statistics in the context of the functional areas of business. We present each statistics topic in the context of areas such as accounting, finance, management, and marketing and explain the application of specific methods to business activities.

Emphasize interpretation and analysis of statistical results over calculation. We emphasize the interpretation of results, the evaluation of the assumptions, and the discussion of what should be done if the assumptions are violated. We believe that these activities are more important to students' futures and will serve them better than focusing on tedious manual calculations.

Give students ample practice in understanding how to apply statistics to business. We believe that both classroom examples and homework exercises should involve actual or realistic data, using small and large sets of data, to the extent possible.

Familiarize students with the use of data analysis software. We integrate using Microsoft Excel into all statistics topics to illustrate how software can assist the business decision making process. (Using software in this way also supports our second point about emphasizing interpretation over calculation).

Provide clear instructions to students that facilitate their use of data analysis software. We believe that providing such instructions assists learning and minimizes the chance that the software will distract from the learning of statistical concepts.

What's New and Innovative in This Edition?

This eighth edition of *Statistics for Managers Using Microsoft Excel* contains these new and innovative features.

First Things First Chapter This new chapter provides an orientation that helps students start to understand the importance of business statistics and get ready to use Microsoft Excel even before they obtain a full copy of this book. Like its predecessor "Getting Started: Important Things to Learn First," this chapter has been developed and published to allow distribution online even before a first class meeting. Instructors teaching online or hybrid course sections may find this to be a particularly valuable tool to get students thinking about business statistics and learning the necessary foundational concepts.

Getting Ready to Analyze Data in the Future   This newly expanded version of Chapter 17 adds a second Using Statistics scenario that serves as an introduction to business analytics methods. That introduction, in turn, explains several advanced Excel features while familiarizing students with the fundamental concepts and vocabulary of business analytics. As such, the chapter provides students with a path for further growth and greater awareness about applying business statistics and analytics in their other courses and their business careers.

Expanded Excel Coverage   *Workbook* instructions replace the *In-Depth Excel* instructions in the Excel Guides and discuss more fully OS X Excel ("Excel for Mac") differences when they occur. Because the many current versions of Excel have varying capabilities, Appendix B begins by sorting through the possible confusion to ensure that students understand that not all Excel versions are alike.

In the Worksheet   Notes that help explain the worksheet illustrations that in-chapter examples use as model solutions.

Many More Exhibits   Stand-alone summaries of important procedures that serve as a review of chapter passages. Exhibits range from identifying best practices, such "Best Practices for Creating Visualizations" in Chapter 2, to serving as guides to data analysis such as the pair of "Questions to Ask" exhibits in Chapter 17.

New Visual Design   This edition uses a new visual design that better organizes chapter content and provides a more uncluttered, streamlined presentation.

Revised and Enhanced Content

This eighth edition of *Statistics for Managers Using Microsoft Excel* contains the following revised and enhanced content.

Revised End-of-Chapter Cases   The Managing Ashland MultiComm Services case that reoccurs throughout the book has several new or updated cases. The Clear Mountain State Student Survey case, also recurring, uses new data collected from a survey of undergraduate students to practice and reinforce statistical methods learned in various chapters.

Many New Applied Examples and Problems   Many of the applied examples throughout this book use new problems or revised data. Approximately 43% of the problems are new to this edition. Many of the new problems in the end-of-section and end-of-chapter problem sets contain data from *The Wall Street Journal*, *USA Today*, and other news media as well as from industry and marketing surveys from leading consultancies and market intelligence firms.

New or Revised Using Statistics Scenarios   This edition contains six all-new and three revised Using Statistics scenarios. Several of the scenarios form a larger narrative when considered together even as they can all be used separately and singularly.

New "Getting Started Learning Statistics" and "Preparing to Use Microsoft Excel for Statistics" sections   Included as part of the First Things First chapter, these new sections replace the "Making Best Use" section of the previous editions. The sections prepare students for learning with this book by discussing foundational statistics and Excel concepts together and explain the various ways students can work with Excel while learning business statistics with this book.

Revised Excel Appendices   These appendices review the foundational skills for using Microsoft Excel, review the latest technical and relevant setup information, and discuss optional but useful knowledge about Excel.

Software FAQ Appendix   This appendix provides answers to commonly-asked questions about PHStat and using Microsoft Excel and related software with this book.

Distinctive Features

This eighth edition of *Statistics for Managers Using Microsoft Excel* continues the use of the following distinctive features.

Using Statistics Business Scenarios   Each chapter begins with a Using Statistics scenario, an example that highlights how statistics is used in a functional area of business such as finance, information systems, management, and marketing. Every chapter uses its scenario throughout to provide an applied context for learning concepts. Most chapters conclude with a Using Statistics, Revisited section that reinforces the statistical methods and applications that a chapter discusses.

Emphasis on Data Analysis and Interpretation of Excel Results   Our focus emphasizes analyzing data by interpreting results while reducing emphasis on doing calculations. For example, in the coverage of tables and charts in Chapter 2, we help students interpret various charts and explain when to use each chart discussed. Our coverage of hypothesis testing in Chapters 9 through 12 and regression and multiple regression in Chapters 13–15 include extensive software results so that the *p*-value approach can be emphasized.

Student Tips   In-margin notes that reinforce hard-to-master concepts and provide quick study tips for mastering important details.

Other Pedagogical Aids   We use an active writing style, boxed numbered equations, set-off examples that reinforce learning concepts, problems divided into "Learning the Basics" and "Applying the Concepts," key equations, and key terms.

Digital Cases   These cases ask students to examine interactive PDF documents to sift through various claims and information and discover the data most relevant to a business case scenario. In doing so, students determine whether the data support the conclusions and claims made by the characters in the case as well as learn how to identify common misuses of statistical information. (Instructional tips for these cases and solutions to the Digital Cases are included in the Instructor's Solutions Manual.)

Answers   A special section at the end of this book provides answers to most of the even-numbered exercises of this book.

Flexibility Using Excel   For almost every statistical method discussed, students can use Excel Guide model workbook solutions with the *Workbook* instructions or the *PHStat* instructions to produce the worksheet solutions that the book discusses and presents. And, whenever possible, the book provides *Analysis ToolPak* instructions to create similar solutions.

Extensive Support for Using Excel   For readers using the *Workbook* instructions, this book explains operational differences among current Excel versions and provides alternate instructions when necessary.

PHStat   PHStat is the Pearson Education Statistics add-in that makes operating Excel as distraction-free as possible. PHStat executes for you the low-level menu selection and worksheet entry tasks that are associated with Excel-based solutions. Students studying statistics can focus solely on mastering statistical concepts and not worry about having to become expert Excel users simultaneously.

PHStat creates the "live," dynamic worksheets and chart sheets that match chapter illustrations and from which students can learn more about Excel. PHStat includes over 60 procedures including:

Descriptive Statistics: boxplot, descriptive summary, dot scale diagram, frequency distribution, histogram and polygons, Pareto diagram, scatter plot, stem-and-leaf display, one-way tables and charts, and two-way tables and charts

Probability and probability distributions: simple and joint probabilities, normal probability plot, and binomial, exponential, hypergeometric, and Poisson probability distributions

Sampling: sampling distributions simulation

Confidence interval estimation: for the mean, sigma unknown; for the mean, sigma known; for the population variance, for the proportion, and for the total difference

Sample size determination: for the mean and the proportion

One-sample tests: Z test for the mean, sigma known; t test for the mean, sigma unknown; chi-square test for the variance; and Z test for the proportion

Two-sample tests (unsummarized data): pooled-variance t test, separate-variance t test, paired t test, F test for differences in two variances, and Wilcoxon rank sum test

Two-sample tests (summarized data): pooled-variance t test, separate-variance t test, paired t test, Z test for the differences in two means, F test for differences in two variances, chi-square test for differences in two proportions, Z test for the difference in two proportions, and McNemar test

Multiple-sample tests: chi-square test, Marascuilo procedure Kruskal-Wallis rank test, Levene test, one-way ANOVA, Tukey-Kramer procedure, randomized block design, and two-way ANOVA with replication

Regression: simple linear regression, multiple regression, best subsets, stepwise regression, and logistic regression

Control charts: p chart, c chart, and R and *Xbar* charts

Decision-making: covariance and portfolio management, expected monetary value, expected opportunity loss, and opportunity loss

Data preparation: stack and unstack data

To learn more about PHStat, see Appendix C.

Visual Explorations   The Excel workbooks allow students to interactively explore important statistical concepts in the normal distribution, sampling distributions, and regression analysis. For the normal distribution, students see the effect of changes in the mean and standard deviation on the areas under the normal curve. For sampling distributions, students use simulation to explore the effect of sample size on a sampling distribution. For regression analysis, students fit a line of regression and observe how changes in the slope and intercept affect the goodness of fit.

Chapter-by-Chapter Changes Made for This Edition

As authors, we take pride in updating the content of our chapters *and* our problem sets. Besides incorporating the new and innovative features that the previous section discusses, each chapter of the eighth edition of *Statistics for Managers Using Microsoft Excel* contains specific changes that refine and enhance our past editions as well as many new or revised problems.

The new **First Things First** chapter replaces the seventh edition's Let's Get Started chapter, keeping that chapter's strength while immediately drawing readers into the changing face of statistics and business analytics with a new opening Using Statistics scenario. And like the previous edition's opening chapter, Pearson Education openly posts this chapter so students can get started learning business statistics even before they obtain their textbooks.

Chapter 1 builds on the opening chapter with a new Using Statistics scenario that offers a cautionary tale about the importance of defining and collecting data. Rewritten Sections 1.1 ("Defining Variables") and 1.2 ("Collecting Data") use lessons from the scenario to underscore important points. Over one-third of the problems in this chapter are new or updated.

Chapter 2 features several new or updated data sets, including a new data set of 407 mutual funds that illustrate a number of descriptive methods. The chapter now discusses doughnut charts and sparklines and contains a reorganized section on organizing and visualizing a mix of variables. Section 2.7 ("The Challenge in Organizing and Visualizing Variables") expands on previous editions' discussions that focused solely on visualization issues. This chapter uses an updated Clear Mountain State student survey as well. Over half of the problems in this chapter are new or updated.

Chapter 3 also uses the new set of 407 mutual funds and uses new or updated data sets for almost all examples that the chapter presents. Updated data sets include the restaurant meal cost samples and the NBA values data. This chapter also uses an updated Clear Mountain State student survey. Just under one-half of the problems in this chapter are new or updated.

Chapter 4 uses an updated Using Statistics scenario while preserving the best features of this chapter. The chapter now starts a section on Bayes' theorem which completes as an online section, and 43% of the problems in the chapter are new or updated.

Chapter 5 has been streamlined with the sections "Covariance of a Probability Distribution and Its Application in Finance" and "Hypergeometric Distribution" becoming online sections. Nearly 40% of the problems in this chapter are new or updated.

Chapter 6 features an updated Using Statistics scenario and the section "Exponential Distribution" has become an online section. This chapter also uses an updated Clear Mountain State student survey. Over one-third of the problems in this chapter are new or updated.

Chapter 7 now contains an additional example on sampling distributions from a larger population, and one-in-three problems are new or updated.

Chapter 8 has been revised to provide enhanced explanations of Excel worksheet solutions and contains a rewritten "Managing Ashland MultiComm Services" case. This chapter also uses an updated Clear Mountain State student survey, and new or updated problems comprise 39% of the problems.

Chapter 9 contains refreshed data for its examples and enhanced Excel coverage that provides greater details about the hypothesis test worksheets that the chapter uses. Over 40% of the problems in this chapter are new or updated.

Chapter 10 contains a new Using Statistics scenario that relates to sales of streaming video players and that connects to Using Statistics scenarios in Chapters 11 and 17. This chapter gains a new online section on effect size. The Clear Mountain State survey has been updated, and over 40% of the problems in this chapter are new or updated.

Chapter 11 expands on the Chapter 10 Using Statistics scenario that concerns the sales of mobile electronics. The Clear Mountain State survey has been updated. Over one-quarter of the problems in this chapter are new or updated.

Chapter 12 now incorporates material that was formerly part of the "Short Takes" for the chapter. The chapter also includes updated "Managing Ashland MultiComm Services" and Clear Mountain State student survey cases and 41% of the problems in this chapter are new or updated.

Chapter 13 features a brand new opening passage that better sets the stage for the discussion of regression that continues in subsequent chapters. Chapter 13 also features substantially revised and expanded Excel coverage that describes more fully the details of regression results worksheets. Nearly one-half of the problems in this chapter are new or updated.

Chapter 14 likewise contains expanded Excel coverage, with some Excel Guides sections completely rewritten. As with Chapter 13, nearly one-half of the problems in this chapter are new or updated.

Chapter 15 contains a revised opening passage, and the "Using Transformations with Regression Models" section has been greatly expanded with additional examples. Over 40% of the problems in this chapter are new or updated.

Chapter 16 contains updated chapter examples concerning movie attendance data and Cola-Cola Company and Wal-Mart Stores revenues. Two-thirds of the problems in this chapter are new or updated.

Chapter 17 has been retitled "Getting Ready to Analyze Data in the Future" and now includes sections on Business Analytics that return to issues that the First Things First Chapter scenario raises and that provide students with a path to future learning and application of business statistics. The chapter presents several Excel-based descriptive analytics techniques and illustrates how advanced statistical programs can work with worksheet data created in Excel. One-half of the problems in this chapter are new or updated.

A Note of Thanks

Creating a new edition of a textbook is a team effort, and we would like to thank our Pearson Education editorial, marketing, and production teammates: Suzanna Bainbridge, Chere Bemelmans, Sherry Berg, Tiffany Bitzel, Deirdre Lynch, Jean Choe, and Joe Vetere. We also thank our statistical readers and accuracy checkers James Lapp, Susan Herring, Dirk Tempelaar, Paul Lorczak, Doug Cashing, and Stanley Seltzer for their diligence in checking our work and Nancy Kincade of Lumina Datamatics. We also thank the following people for their helpful comments that we have used to improve this new edition: Anusua Datta, Philadelphia University; Doug Dotterweich, East Tennessee State University; Gary Evans, Purdue University; Chris Maurer, University of Tampa; Bharatendra Rai, University of Massachusetts Dartmouth; Joseph Snider and Keith Stracher, Indiana Wesleyan University; Leonie Stone, SUNY Geneseo; and Patrick Thompson, University of Florida.

We thank the RAND Corporation and the American Society for Testing and Materials for their kind permission to publish various tables in Appendix E, and to the American Statistical Association for its permission to publish diagrams from the *American Statistician*. Finally, we would like to thank our families for their patience, understanding, love, and assistance in making this book a reality.

Contact Us!

Please email us at **authors@davidlevinestatistics.com** or tweet us **@BusStatBooks** with your questions about the contents of this book. Please include the hashtag #SMUME8 in your tweet or in the subject line of your email. We also welcome suggestions you may have for a future edition of this book. And while we have strived to make this book as error-free as possible, we also appreciate those who share with us any perceived problems or errors that they encounter.

We are happy to answer all types of questions, but if you need assistance using Excel or PHStat, please contact your local support person or Pearson Technical Support at **247pearsoned .custhelp.com**. They have the resources to resolve and walk you through a solution to many technical issues in a way we do not.

We invite you to visit us at **smume8.davidlevinestatistics.com** (**bit.ly/1I8Lv2K**), where you will find additional information and support for this book that we furnish in addition to all the resources that Pearson Education offers you on our book's behalf (see pages xxiii and xxiv).

David M. Levine
David F. Stephan
Kathryn A. Szabat

Resources for Success

MyStatLab™ Online Course for Statistics for Managers Using Microsoft® Excel by Levine/Stephan/Szabat
(access code required)

MyStatLab is available to accompany Pearson's market leading text offerings. To give students a consistent tone, voice, and teaching method each text's flavor and approach is tightly integrated throughout the accompanying MyStatLab course, making learning the material as seamless as possible.

New! Launch Exercise Data in Excel

Students are now able to quickly and seamlessly launch data sets from exercises within MyStatLab into a Microsoft Excel spreadsheet for easy analysis. As always, students may also copy and paste exercise data sets into most other software programs.

Diverse Question Libraries

Build homework assignments, quizzes, and tests to support your course learning outcomes. From *Getting Ready* (GR) questions to the *Conceptual Question Library* (CQL), we have your assessment needs covered from the mechanics to the critical understanding of Statistics. The exercise libraries include technology-led instruction, including new Excel-based exercises, and learning aids to reinforce your students' success.

Technology Tutorials and Study Cards

Excel® tutorials provide brief video walkthroughs and step-by-step instructional study cards on common statistical procedures such as Confidence Intervals, ANOVA, Simple & Multiple Regression, and Hypothesis Testing. Tutorials will capture methods in Microsoft Windows Excel® 2010, 2013, and 2016 versions.

Resources for Success

Instructor Resources

Instructor's Solutions Manual, by Professor Pin Tian Ng of Northern Arizona University, includes solutions for end-of-section and end-of-chapter problems, answers to case questions, where applicable, and teaching tips for each chapter. The Instructor's Solutions Manual is available at the Instructor's Resource Center (**www .pearsonhighered.com/irc**) or in MyStatLab.

Lecture PowerPoint Presentations, by Professor Patrick Schur of Miami University (Ohio), are available for each chapter. The PowerPoint slides provide an instructor with individual lecture outlines to accompany the text. The slides include many of the figures and tables from the text. Instructors can use these lecture notes as is or can easily modify the notes to reflect specific presentation needs. The PowerPoint slides are available at the Instructor's Resource Center (**www.pearsonhighered.com /irc**) or in MyStatLab.

Test Bank, by Professor Pin Tian Ng of Northern Arizona University, contains true/false, multiple-choice, fill-in, and problem-solving questions based on the definitions, concepts, and ideas developed in each chapter of the text. New to this edition are specific test questions that use Excel datasets. The Test Bank is available at the Instructor's Resource Center (**www.pearsonhighered.com/irc**) or in MyStatLab.

TestGen® (**www.pearsoned.com/testgen**) enables instructors to build, edit, print, and administer tests using a computerized bank of questions developed to cover all the objectives of the text. TestGen is algorithmically based, allowing instructors to create multiple but equivalent versions of the same question or test with the click of a button. Instructors can also modify test bank questions or add new questions. The software and test bank are available for download from Pearson Education's online catalog.

Student Resources

Student's Solutions Manual, by Professor Pin Tian Ng of Northern Arizona University, provides detailed solutions to virtually all the even-numbered exercises and worked-out solutions to the self-test problems (ISBN-13: 978-0-13-417382-5).

Online resources

The complete set of online resources are discussed fully in Appendix C. For adopting instructors, the following resources are among those available at the Instructor's Resource Center (**www .pearsonhighered.com/irc**) or in MyStatLab.

First Things First

▼USING **STATISTICS**
"The Price of Admission"

It's the year 1900 and you are a promoter of theatrical productions, in the business of selling seats for individual performances. Using your knowledge and experience, you establish a selling price for the performances, a price you hope represents a good trade-off between maximizing revenues and avoiding driving away demand for your seats. You print up tickets and flyers, place advertisements in local media, and see what happens. After the event, you review your results and consider if you made a wise trade-off.

Tickets sold very quickly? Next time perhaps you can charge more. The event failed to sell out? Perhaps next time you could charge less or take out more advertisements to drive demand. If you lived over 100 years ago, that's about all you could do.

Jump ahead about 70 years. You're still a promoter but now using a computer system that allows your customers to buy tickets over the phone. You can get summary reports of advance sales for future events and adjust your advertising on radio and on TV and, perhaps, add or subtract performance dates using the information in those reports.

Jump ahead to today. You're still a promoter but you now have a fully computerized sales system that allows you to constantly adjust the price of tickets. You also can manage many more categories of tickets than just the near-stage and far-stage categories you might have used many years ago. You no longer have to wait until after an event to make decisions about changing your sales program. Through your sales system you have gained insights about your customers such as where they live, what other tickets they buy, and their appropriate demographic traits. Because you know more about your customers, you can make your advertising and publicity more efficient by aiming your messages at the types of people more likely to buy your tickets. By using social media networks and other online media, you can also learn almost immediately who is noticing and responding to your advertising messages. You might even run experiments online presenting your advertising in two different ways and seeing which way sells better.

Your current self has capabilities that allow you to be a more effective promoter than any older version of yourself. Just how much better? Turn the page.

OBJECTIVES

- Statistics is a way of thinking that can lead to better decision making

- Statistics requires analytics skills and is an important part of your business education

- Recent developments such as the use of business analytics and "big data" have made knowing statistics even more critical

- The DCOVA framework guides your application of statistics

- The opportunity business analytics represents for business students

1

Now Appearing on Broadway ... *and* Everywhere Else

In early 2014, Disney Theatrical Productions woke up the rest of Broadway when reports revealed that its *17*-year-old production of *The Lion King* had been the top-grossing Broadway show in 2013. How could such a long-running show, whose most expensive ticket was less than half the most expensive ticket on Broadway, earn so much while being so old? Over time, grosses for a show decline and, sure enough, weekly grosses for *The Lion King* had dropped about 25% by the year 2009. But, for 2013, grosses were up 67% from 2009 and weekly grosses for 2013 typically exceeded the grosses of opening weeks in 1997, adjusted for inflation!

Heavier advertising and some changes in ticket pricing helped, but the major reason for this change was something else: combining business acumen with the systematic application of *business statistics and analytics* to the problem of selling tickets. As a producer of the newest musical at the time said, "We make educated predictions on price. Disney, on the other hand, has turned this into a science" (see reference 3).

Disney had followed the plan of action that this book presents. It had collected its daily and weekly results, and summarized them, using techniques this book introduces in the next three chapters. Disney then analyzed those results by performing experiments and tests on the data collected (using techniques that later chapters introduce). In turn, those analyses were applied to a new interactive seating map that allowed customers to buy tickets for specific seats and permitted Disney to adjust the pricing of each seat for each performance. The whole system was constantly reviewed and refined, using the semiautomated methods to which Chapter 17 will introduce you. The end result was a system that outperformed the ticket-selling methods others used.

studentTIP
From other business courses, you may recognize that Disney's system uses dynamic pricing.

FTF.1 Think Differently About Statistics

The "Using Statistics" scenario suggests, and the Disney example illustrates, that modern-day information technology has allowed businesses to apply statistics in ways that could not be done years ago. This scenario and example reflect how this book teaches you about statistics. In these first two pages, you may notice

- the lack of calculation details and "math."
- the emphasis on enhancing business methods and management decision making.
- that none of this seems like the content of a middle school or high school statistics class you may have taken.

You may have had some prior knowledge or instruction in *mathematical statistics*. This book discusses *business statistics*. While the boundary between the two can be blurry, business statistics emphasizes business problem solving and shows a preference for using software to perform calculations.

One similarity that you might notice between these first two pages and any prior instruction is *data*. **Data** are the facts about the world that one seeks to study and explore. Some data are unsummarized, such as the facts about a single ticket-selling transaction, whereas other facts, such as weekly ticket grosses, are **summarized**, derived from a set of unsummarized data. While you may think of data as being numbers, such as the cost of a ticket or the percentage that weekly grosses have increased in a year, do not overlook that data can be non-numerical as well, such as ticket-buyer's name, seat location, or method of payment.

Statistics: A Way of Thinking

Statistics are the methods that allow you to work with data effectively. Business statistics focuses on interpreting the results of applying those methods. You interpret those results to help you enhance business processes and make better decisions. Specifically, business statistics provides you with a formal basis to summarize and visualize business data, reach conclusions about that data, make reliable predictions about business activities, and improve business processes.

You must apply this way of thinking correctly. Any "bad" things you may have heard about statistics, including the famous quote "there are lies, damned lies, and statistics" made famous by Mark Twain, speak to the errors that people make when either misusing statistical methods or mistaking statistics as a substitution for, and not an enhancement of, a decision-making process. (Disney Theatrical Productions' success was based on *combining* statistics with business acumen, not *replacing* that acumen.)

To minimize errors, you use a framework that organizes the set of tasks that you follow to apply statistics properly. The five tasks that comprise the **DCOVA framework** provide one such framework.

DCOVA Framework

- **D**efine the data that you want to study to solve a problem or meet an objective.
- **C**ollect the data from appropriate sources.
- **O**rganize the data collected, by developing tables.
- **V**isualize the data collected, by developing charts.
- **A**nalyze the data collected, to reach conclusions and present those results.

You must always do the **D**efine and **C**ollect tasks before doing the other three. The order of the other three varies and sometimes all three are done concurrently. In this book, you will learn more about the **D**efine and **C**ollect tasks in Chapter 1 and then be introduced to the **O**rganize and **V**isualize tasks in Chapter 2. Beginning with Chapter 3, you will learn methods that help complete the **A**nalyze task. Throughout this book, you will see specific examples that apply the DCOVA framework to specific business problems and examples.

Analytical Skills More Important than Arithmetic Skills

You have already read that business statistics shows a preference for using software to perform calculations. You can perform calculations *faster and more accurately* using software than you can if you performed those calculations by hand.

When you use software, you do more than just enter data. You need to review and modify, and possibly create, solutions. In Microsoft Excel, you use worksheet solutions that contain a mix of *organized* data and instructions that perform calculations on that data. Being able to review and modify worksheet solutions requires analytical skills more than arithmetic skills.

Allowing individuals to create new solutions from scratch in business can create risk. For example, in the aftermath of the 2012 "London Whale" trading debacle, JP Morgan Chase discovered a worksheet that could greatly miscalculate the volatility of a trading portfolio (see reference 4). To avoid this unnecessary risk, businesses prefer to use **templates**, *reusable* worksheet solutions that have been previously audited and verified.

When templates prove impractical, businesses seek to use *model worksheet solutions*. These solutions provide employees a basis for modification that is more extensive than changes one would make to a template. Whether you use the Excel Guide workbooks or PHStat with this book, you will reflect business practice by working with templates and model solutions as you use this book to learn statistics. You will not find many from-scratch construction tasks other than for the tasks of organizing and visualizing data in this book.

Statistics: An Important Part of Your Business Education

Until you read these pages, you may have seen a course in business statistics solely as a required course with little relevance to your overall business education. In just two pages, you have learned that statistics is a way of thinking that can help enhance your effectiveness in business—that is, applying statistics correctly is a fundamental, global skill in your business education.

In the current data-driven environment of business, you need the general analytical skills that allow you to work with data and interpret analytical results regardless of the discipline in which you work. No longer is statistics only for accounting, economics, finance, or other disciplines that directly work with numerical data. As the Disney example illustrates, the decisions you make will be increasingly based on data and not on your gut or intuition supported by past experience. Having a well-balanced mix of statistics, modeling, and basic technical skills as well as managerial skills, such as business acumen and problem-solving and communication skills, will best prepare you for the workplace today … *and* tomorrow (see reference 1).

FTF.2 Business Analytics: The Changing Face of Statistics

Of the recent changes that have made statistics an important part of your business education, the emergence of the set of methods collectively known as business analytics may be the most significant change of all. **Business analytics** combine traditional statistical methods with methods from management science and information systems to form an interdisciplinary tool that supports fact-based decision making. Business analytics include

- statistical methods to analyze and explore data that can uncover previously unknown or unforeseen relationships.
- information systems methods to collect and process data sets of all sizes, including very large data sets that would otherwise be hard to use efficiently.
- management science methods to develop optimization models that support all levels of management, from strategic planning to daily operations.

In the Disney Theatrical Productions example, statistical methods helped determine pricing factors, information systems methods made the interactive seating map and pricing analysis possible, and management science methods helped adjust pricing rules to match Disney's goal of sustaining ticket sales into the future. Other businesses use analytics to send custom mailings to their customers, and businesses such as the travel review site tripadvisor.com use analytics to help optimally price advertising as well as generate information that makes a persuasive case for using that advertising.

Generally, studies have shown that businesses that actively use business analytics and combine that use with data-guided management see increases in productivity, innovation, and competition (see reference 1). Chapter 17 introduces you to the statistical methods typically used in business analytics and shows how these methods are related to statistical methods that the book discusses in earlier chapters.

student TIP

Because you cannot "download" a big data collection, this book uses conventional structured (worksheet) files, both small and large, to demonstrate some of the principles and methods of business analytics in selected chapters, including Chapter 17, which introduce you to business analytics.

"Big Data"

Big data are collections of data that cannot be easily browsed or analyzed using traditional methods. *Big data* implies data that are being collected in huge *volumes*, at very fast rates or *velocities* (typically in near real time), and in a *variety* of forms other than the traditional structured forms such as data processing records, files, and tables and worksheets. These attributes of volume, velocity, and variety (see reference 5) distinguish big data from a set of data that contains a large number of similarly structured records or rows that you can place into a file or worksheet for browsing. In contrast, you cannot directly view big data; information system and statistical methods typically combine and summarize big data for you and then present the results of that processing.

Combined with business analytics and the basic statistical methods discussed in this book, big data presents opportunities to gain new management insights and extract value from the data resources of a business (see reference 8).

Structured Versus Unstructured Data

Statistics has traditionally used **structured data**, data that exist in repeating records or rows of similar format, such as the data found in the worksheet data files that this book describes in Appendix C. In contrast, **unstructured data** has very little or no repeating internal structure.

For example, to deeply analyze a group of companies, you might collect structured data in the form of published tables of financial data and the contents of fill-in-the-blank documents that record information from surveys you distributed. However, you might also collect unstructured data such as social media posts and tweets that do not have an internal repeating structure.

Typically, you preprocess or filter unstructured data before performing deep analysis. For example, to analyze social media posts you could use business analytics methods that determine whether the content of each post is a positive, neutral, or negative comment. The "type of comment" can become a new variable that can be inserted into a *structured* record, along with other attributes of the post, such as the number of words, and demographic data about the writer of the post.

Unstructured data can form part of a big data collection. When analyzed as part of a big data collection, you typically see the results of the preprocessing and not the unstructured data itself. Because unstructured data usually has some (external) structure, some authorities prefer to use the term *semistructured data*. If you are familiar with that term, undertand that this book's use of the phrase *unstructured data* incorporates that category.

FTF.3 Getting Started Learning Statistics

Learning the **operational definitions**, precise definitions and explanations that all can understand clearly, of several basic terms is a good way to get started learning statistics. Previously, you learned that *data* are the facts about the world that one seeks to study and explore. A related term, *variable of interest*, commonly shortened to *variable*, can be used to precisely define data in its statistical sense.

A **variable** defines a characteristic, or property, of an item or individual that can vary among the occurrences of those items or individuals. For example, for the item "book," variables would include title and number of chapters, as these facts can vary from book to book. For a given item, variables have a specific value. For this book, the value of the variable title would be "Statistics for Managers Using Microsoft Excel," and "17" would be the value for the variable number of chapters.

Using the definition of variable, you can state the definition of data, in its statistical sense, as the set of values associated with one or more variables. In statistics, each value for a specific variable is a single fact, not a list of facts. For example, what would be the value of the variable author when referring to this book? Without this rule, you might say that the single list "Levine, Stephan, Szabat" is the value. However, applying this rule, we say that the variable author has the three separate values: "Levine", "Stephan", and "Szabat". This distinction of using only *single-value data* has the practical benefit of simplifying the task of entering your data into a computer system for analysis.

Using the definitions of data and variable, you can restate the definition of statistics as the methods that analyze the data of the variables of interest. The methods that primarily help summarize and present data comprise **descriptive statistics**. Methods that use data collected from a small group to reach conclusions about a larger group comprise **inferential statistics**. Chapters 2 and 3 introduce descriptive methods, many of which are applied to support the inferential methods that the rest of the book presents.

Do not confuse this use of the word statistics with the noun *statistic*, the plural of which is, confusingly, *statistics*.

student TIP

Business analytics, discussed in Chapter 17, combine mostly inferential methods with methods from other disciplines.

Statistic

A **statistic** refers to a value that summarizes the data of a particular variable. (More about this in coming chapters.) In the Disney Theatrical Productions example, the statement "for 2013, weekly grosses were up 67% from 2009" cites a statistic that summarizes the variable weekly grosses using the 2013 data—all 52 values.

When someone warns you of a possible unfortunate outcome by saying, "Don't be a statistic!" you can always reply, "I can't be." *You* always represent one value and a *statistic* always summarizes multiple values. For the statistic "87% of our employees suffer a workplace accident," you, as an employee, will either have suffered or have not suffered a workplace accident.

The "have" or "have not" value contributes to the statistic but cannot be the statistic. A statistic can facilitate preliminary decision making. For example, would you immediately accept a position at a company if you learned that 87% of their employees suffered a workplace accident? (Sounds like this might be a dangerous place to work and that further investigation is necessary.)

Can Statistics (*pl.*, Statistic) Lie?

The famous quote "lies, damned lies, and statistics" actually refers to the plural form of *statistic* and does not refer to statistics, the field of study. Can any statistic "lie"? No, faulty, invalid statistics can be produced if any tasks in the DCOVA framework are applied incorrectly. As discussed in later chapters, many statistical methods are valid only if the data being analyzed have certain properties. To the extent possible, you test the assertion that the data have those properties, which in statistics are called *assumptions*. When an assumption is *violated*, shown to be invalid for the data being analyzed, the methods that require that assumption should not be used.

For the inferential methods discussed later in this book, you must always look for logical causality. **Logical causality** means that you can plausibly claim something directly causes something else. For example, you wear black shoes today and note that the weather is sunny. The next day, you again wear black shoes and notice that the weather continues to be sunny. The third day, you change to brown shoes and note that the weather is rainy. The fourth day, you wear black shoes again and the weather is again sunny. These four days seem to suggest a strong pattern between your shoe color choice and the type of weather you experience. You begin to think if you wear brown shoes on the fifth day, the weather will be rainy. Then you realize that your shoes cannot plausibly influence weather patterns, that your shoe color choice cannot *logically cause* the weather. What you are seeing is mere coincidence. (On the fifth day, you do wear brown shoes and it happens to rain, but that is just another coincidence.)

You can easily spot the lack of logical causality when trying to correlate shoe color choice with the weather, but in other situations the lack of logical causality may not be so easily seen. Therefore, relying on such correlations by themselves is a fundamental misuse of statistics. When you look for patterns in the data being analyzed, you must *always* be thinking of logical causes. Otherwise, you are misrepresenting your results. Such misrepresentations sometimes cause people to wrongly conclude that all statistics are "lies." Statistics (*pl.*, statistic) are not lies or "damned lies." They play a significant role in *statistics*, the way of thinking that can enhance your decision making and increase your effectiveness in business.

FTF.4 Preparing to Use Microsoft Excel for Statistics

As Section FTF.1 explains, the proper use of business statistics requires a framework to apply statistics correctly, analytic skills, and software to automate calculation. This book uses Microsoft Excel to demonstrate the integral role of software in applying statistics to decision making, and preparing to use Microsoft Excel is one of the first things you can do to prepare yourself to learn business statistics from this book.

Microsoft Excel is the data analysis component of Microsoft Office that evolved from earlier electronic spreadsheets used in accounting and financial applications. In Excel, you use **worksheets** (also known as spreadsheets) that organize data in tabular blocks as well as store **formulas**, instructions to process that data. You make entries in worksheet **cells** that are formed by the intersections of worksheet rows and columns. You refer to individual cells by their column letter and row number address, such as A1 for the uppermost left top cell (in column A and row 1). Into each cell, you place a single data value or a formula. With the proper design, worksheets can also present summaries of data and results of applying a particular statistical method.

"Excel files" are not single worksheets but **workbooks**, collections of one or more worksheets and **chart sheets**, sheets that display visualizations of data. Because workbooks contain collections, you can clearly present information in more than one way on different "slides" (sheets), much like a slide show. For example, you can present on separate sheets the summary table and appropriate chart for the data for a variable. (These tasks are discussed in Chapter 2.) When designing model solutions, workbooks allow you to segregate the parts of the solution that users may change frequently, such as problem-specific data. For example, the typical model solution files that this book uses and calls **Excel Guide workbooks** have a "Data" worksheet, one or more worksheets and chart sheets that present the results, and one or more worksheets that document the formulas that a template or model solution uses.

Reusability Through Recalculation

Earlier in this chapter, you learned that businesses prefer using templates and model worksheet solutions. You can reuse templates and model solutions, applying a previously constructed and verified worksheet solution to another, similar problem. When you work with templates, you never enter or edit formulas, thereby greatly reducing the chance that the worksheet will produce erroneous results. When you work with a model worksheet solution, you need only to edit or copy certain formulas. By not having to enter your own formulas from scratch, you also minimize the chance of errors. (Recall an analyst's entering of his own erroneous formulas was uncovered in the London Whale investigation mentioned on page 3.)

Templates and model solutions are reusable because worksheets are capable of recalculation. In worksheet **recalculation**, results displayed by formulas can automatically change as the data that the formulas use change, but only if the formulas properly refer to the cells that contain the data that might change.

Practical Matters: Skills You Need

To use Excel effectively with this book, you will need to know how to make cell entries, how to navigate to, or open to, a particular worksheet in a workbook, how to print a worksheet, and how to open and save files. If these skills are new to you, review the introduction to these skills that starts later in this chapter and continues in Appendix B.

You *may* need to modify model worksheet solutions, especially as you progress into the later chapters of this book. However, this book does not *require* you to learn this additional (information systems) skill. You can choose to use PHStat, which performs those modifications for you. By automating the necessary modifications, PHStat reduces your chance of making errors.

PHStat creates worksheet solutions that are identical to the solutions found in the Excel Guide workbooks and that are shown and annotated throughout this book. You will not learn anything less if you use PHStat, as you will be using and studying from the same solutions as those who decide not to use PHStat. If the information systems skill of modifying worksheets is one of your secondary goals, you can use PHStat to create solutions to several similar problems and then examine the modifications made in each solution.

PHStat uses a menu-driven interface and is an example of an **add-in**, a programming component designed to extend the abilities of Excel. Unlike add-ins such as the Data Analysis ToolPak that Microsoft packages with Excel, PHStat creates actual worksheets with working formulas. (The ToolPak and most add-ins produce a text-based report that is pasted into a worksheet.) Consider both PHStat and the set of Excel Guide workbooks as stand-ins for the template and model solution library that you would encounter in a well-run business.

Ways of Working with Excel

With this book, you can work with Excel by either using PHStat or making manual changes directly to the Excel Guide workbooks. Readers that are experienced Excel users may prefer making manual changes, and readers who use Excel in organizations that restrict the use of Microsoft Office add-ins may be forced to make such changes. Therefore, this book provides detailed instructions for using Excel with PHStat, which are labeled **PHStat**, *and* instructions for making manual changes to templates and model worksheet solutions, which are labeled **Workbook**.

In practice, if you face no restrictions on using add-ins, you may want to use a mix of both approaches if you have had some previous exposure to Excel. In this mix, you open the Excel Guide workbooks that contain the simpler templates and fill them in, and you use PHStat to modify the more complex solutions associated with statistical methods found in later chapters. You may also want to use PHStat when you construct charts, as PHStat automates the correction of chart formatting mistakes that Excel sometimes makes. (Making these corrections can be time-consuming and a distraction from learning statistics.)

This book also includes instructions for using the Data Analysis ToolPak, which is labeled **ToolPak**, for readers who prefer using this Microsoft-supplied add-in. Certain model worksheet solutions found in the Excel Guide workbooks, used by PHStat, and shown in this book mimic the appearance of ToolPak solutions to accommodate readers used to ToolPak results. Do not be fooled, though—while the worksheets mimic those solutions, the worksheets are fundamentally different, as they contain active formulas and not the pasted-in text of the ToolPak solutions.

Excel Guides

Excel Guides contain the detailed **PHStat**, **Workbook**, and, when applicable, **ToolPak** instructions. Guides present instructions by chapter section numbers, so, for example, Excel Guide Section EG2.3 provides instructions for the methods discussed in Section 2.3. Most Guide sections begin with a *key technique* that presents the most important or critical Excel feature that the templates and model solutions use and cite the *example* that the instructions that follow use. (The example is usually the example that has been worked out in the chapter section.)

For some methods, the Guides present separate instructions for summarized or unsummarized data. In such cases, you will see either **(summarized)** or **(unsummarized)** as part of the instruction label. When minor variations among current Excel versions affect the **Workbook** instructions, special sentences or separate instructions clarify the differences. (The minor variations do not affect either the **PHStat** or **ToolPak** instructions.)

Which Excel Version to Use?

Use a current version of Microsoft Excel for Microsoft Windows or (Mac) OS X when working with the examples, problems, and Excel Guide instructions in this book. A current version is a version that receives "mainstream support" from Microsoft that includes updates, refinements, and online support. As this book went to press, current versions included Microsoft Windows Excel 2016, 2013, and 2010, and the OS X Excel 2016 and 2011. If you have an Office 365 subscription, you always have access to the most current version of Excel.

If you use Microsoft Windows Excel 2007, you should know that Microsoft has already ended mainstream support and will end all (i.e., security update) support for this version during the expected in-print lifetime of this book. Excel 2007 does not include all of the features of Excel used in this book and has a number of significant differences that affect various worksheet solutions. (This is further explained in Appendix F.) Note that many Excel Guide workbooks contain special worksheet solutions for use with Excel 2007. If you use PHStat with Excel 2007, PHStat will produce these special worksheet solutions automatically.

If you use a mobile Excel version such as Excel for Android Tablets, you will need an Office 365 subscription to open, examine, edit, and save Excel Guide workbooks and data workbooks. (Without a subscription, you can only open and examine those workbooks.) As this book went to press, the current version of Excel for Android Tablets did not support all of the Excel features discussed or used in this book and did not support the use of add-ins such as PHStat.

Conventions Used

In both the annotated worksheet solutions shown as chapter figures and in the Excel Guide instructions, this book uses the following conventions:

- What to type as an entry and where to type the entry appear in boldface: Enter **450** in cell **B5**.
- Names of special keys appear capitalized and in boldface: Press **Enter**.

- For improved readability, Excel ribbon tabs appear in mixed case (File, Insert), not capitalized (FILE, INSERT) as they appear in certain Excel versions.
- Menu and ribbon selections appear in boldface, and sequences of consecutive selections are linked using the ➔ symbol: Select **File ➔ New**. Select **PHStat ➔ Descriptive Statistics ➔ Boxplot**.
- Key combinations, two or more keys that you press at the same time, are shown in boldface: Press **Ctrl+C**. Press **Command+Enter**.
- Names of specific Excel functions, worksheets, or workbooks appear in boldface.

Placeholders that express the general case appear in italics and boldface, such as **AVERAGE (*cell range of variable*)**. When you encounter a placeholder, you replace it with an actual value. For example, you would replace *cell range of variable* with an actual variable cell range. By special convention in this book, PHStat menu sequences always begin with **PHStat**, even though in some Excel versions you must first select the Add-Ins tab to display the PHStat menu.

▼ REFERENCES

1. Advani, D. "Preparing Students for the Jobs of the Future." *University Business* (2011), **bit.ly/1gNLTJm**.
2. Davenport, T., J. Harris, and R. Morison. *Analytics at Work.* Boston: Harvard Business School Press, 2010.
3. Healy, P. "Ticker Pricing Puts 'Lion King' atop Broadway's Circle of Life." *The New York Times, New York edition*, March 17, 2014, p. A1, and **nyti.ms.1zDkzki**.
4. JP Morgan Chase. "Report of JPMorgan Chase & Co. Management Task Force Regarding 2012 CIO Losses," **bit.ly/1BnQZzY**, as quoted in J. Ewok, "The Importance of Excel," *The Baseline Scenario*, **bit.ly/1LPeQUy**.
5. Laney, D. *3D Data Management: Controlling Data Volume, Velocity, and Variety.* Stamford, CT: META Group. February 6, 2001.
6. Levine, D., and D. Stephan. "Teaching Introductory Business Statistics Using the DCOVA Framework." *Decision Sciences Journal of Innovative Education* 9 (Sept. 2011): 393–398.
7. Liberatore, M., and W. Luo. "The Analytics Movement." *Interfaces* 40 (2010): 313–324.
8. "What Is Big Data?" IBM Corporation, **www.ibm.com/big-data/us/en/**.

▼ KEY TERMS

add-in   7
big data   4
cells   6
chart sheet   6
data   2
business analytics   4
DCOVA framework   3
descriptive statistics   5
formula   6

formula bar   10
inferential statistics   5
logical causality   6
operational definition   5
recalculation   7
statistic   5
statistics   2
structured data   4
summarized data   2

template   3
unstructured data   4
variable   5
workbook   6
worksheet   6

▼ EXCEL GUIDE

As explained earlier in this chapter, Excel Guides contain the detailed instructions for using Microsoft Excel with this book. Whether you choose to use the **PHStat**, **Workbook**, or, when applicable, **ToolPak** instructions (see page 8), you should know how to enter data for variables into a worksheet and how to review and inspect worksheets before applying them to a problem.

EG.1 ENTERING DATA

You should enter the data for variables using the style that the DATA worksheets of the Excel Guide workbooks and the Excel data files (see Appendix C) use. Those DATA worksheets use the business convention of entering the data for each variable in separate columns, and using the cell entry in the first row in each column as a heading to identify a variable by name. These worksheets also begin with column A, row 1 (cell A1) and do not skip any rows when entering data for a variable into a column.

To enter data in a specific cell, either use the cursor keys to move the cell pointer to the cell or use your mouse to select the cell directly. As you type, what you type appears in a space above the worksheet called the **formula bar**. Complete your data entry by pressing **Tab** or **Enter** or by clicking the checkmark button in the formula bar.

When you enter data, never skip any rows in a column, and as a general rule, also avoid skipping any columns. Also try to avoid using numbers as row 1 variable headings; if you cannot avoid their use, precede such headings with apostrophes. When you create a new data worksheet, begin the first entry in cell A1, as the sample below shows. Pay attention to special instructions in this book that note specific orderings of the columns that hold your variables. For some statistical methods, entering variables in a column order that Excel does not expect will lead to incorrect results.

	A	B	C	D	E	F	G	H	I	J	K	L
1	Fund Number	Market Cap	Type	Risk	Assets	Turnover Ratio(%)	SD	Sharpe Ratio	1YrReturn%	3YrReturn%	5YrReturn%	10YrReturn%
2	RF001	Large	Growth	Average	654.66	57.00	10.90	1.59	9.20	18.20	15.92	9.53
3	RF002	Large	Growth	Low	1999.02	0.00	9.44	1.32	13.31	12.75	12.27	9.70
4	RF003	Large	Growth	Average	97.70	29.00	10.50	1.28	8.18	13.79	13.83	6.93
5	RF004	Large	Growth	Average	1079.96	58.00	11.04	1.32	11.85	15.00	15.50	11.35
6	RF005	Large	Growth	Average	8861.25	103.00	9.88	1.45	13.07	14.81	14.59	9.20

student TIP

At the time this book went to press, some mobile versions of Excel could not display worksheets in formula view. If you are using such a version, you can select a cell and view the formula in the formula bar.

EG.2 REVIEWING WORKSHEETS

You should follow the best practice of reviewing worksheets before you use them to help solve problems. When you use a worksheet, what you see displayed in cells may be the result of either the recalculation of formulas or cell formatting. A cell that displays 4 might contain the value 4, might contain a formula calculation that results in the value 4, or might contain a value such as 3.987 that has been formatted to display as the nearest whole number.

To display and review all formulas, you press **Ctrl+`** (grave accent). Excel displays the *formula view* of the worksheet, revealing all formulas. (Pressing **Ctrl+`** a second time restores the worksheet to its normal display.) If you use the Excel Guide workbooks, you will discover that each workbook contains one or more FORMULAS worksheets that provide a second way of viewing all formulas.

Whether you use PHStat or the Excel Guide workbooks, you will notice cell formatting operations that change the background color of cells, change text attributes such as boldface of cell entries, and round values to a certain number of decimal places (typically four). Because cells in PHStat worksheets and Excel Guide workbooks have been already formatted for you, using this book does not require that you know how to apply these formatting operations. However, if you want to learn more about cell formatting, Appendix B includes a summary of common formatting operations, including those used in the worksheet solutions presented in this book.

EG.3 IF YOU PLAN TO USE THE *WORKBOOK* INSTRUCTIONS

The *Workbook* instructions in the Excel Guides help you to modify model worksheet solutions by directly operating a current version of Microsoft Excel. For most statistical methods, the *Workbook* instructions will be identical for all current versions. In some cases, especially in the instructions for constructing tabular and visual summaries discussed in Chapter 2, the *Workbook* instructions can greatly vary from one version to another. In those cases, the Excel Guides express instructions in the most universal way possible. Many instructions ask you to select (click on) an item from a gallery of items and identify that item by name. In some Excel versions, these names may be visible captions for the item; in other versions you will need to move the mouse over the image to pop up the image name.

Guides also use the word *display* to refer to either a task pane or a two-panel dialog box that contains similar or identical choices. A **task pane**, found in more recent versions, opens to the side of the worksheet and can remain onscreen indefinitely. Some parts of a pane may be initially hidden and you may need to click on an icon or label to reveal a hidden part to complete a command sequence. A **two-panel dialog box** opens over the worksheet and must be closed before you can continue your work. These dialog boxes contain one left panel, always visible, and a series of right panels, only one of which is visible at any given time. To reveal a hidden right panel, you click on a left panel entry, analogous to clicking an icon or label in a task pane. (To close either a task pane or a dialog box, click the system close button.)

Current Excel versions can vary in their command sequences. Excel Guide instructions show these variations as parenthetical phrases. For example, the command sequence, "select **Design** (or **Chart Design**) ➜ **Add Chart Element**" tells you to first select **Design** *or* **Chart Design** to begin the sequence and then to continue by selecting **Add Chart Element**. (Microsoft Windows Excels use Design and the current OS X Excel uses **Chart Design**.)

In some cases, OS X Excel 2016 instructions differ so much that an Excel Guide presents an alternate instruction using this color and font. In addition, OS X Excel 2011 has significantly different command sequences for creating visual and some tabular summaries. If you plan to use OS X Excel 2011 with this book, take note of the Student Tip to the left. If you must use this older OS X Excel, be sure to download and use the **OS X Excel 2011 Supplement** that provides notes and instructions for creating visual and tabular summaries in OS X Excel 2011. (For methods other than visual and tabular summaries, OS X Excel 2011 uses the same or similar sequences that other Excel versions use.)

Again, if only one set of *Workbook* instructions appears, that set applies to *all* current versions. You do not need to be concerned about command sequence differences if you use the *PHStat* (or *Analysis ToolPak*) instructions. Those instructions are always the same for all current versions.

student TIP

The authors discourage you from using OS X Excel 2011 if you plan to use the Chapter 2 *Workbook* instructions for creating visual summaries.

1

Defining and Collecting Data

OBJECTIVES

- Understand issues that arise when defining variables
- How to define variables
- Understand the different measurement scales
- How to collect data
- Identify the different ways to collect a sample
- Understand the issues involved in data preparation
- Understand the types of survey errors

▼ USING STATISTICS
Defining Moments

#1 You're the sales manager in charge of the best-selling beverage in its category. For years, your chief competitor has made sales gains, claiming a better tasting product. Worse, a new sibling product from your company, known for its good taste, has quickly gained significant market share at the expense of your product. Worried that your product may soon lose its number one status, you seek to improve sales by improving the product's taste. You experiment and develop a new beverage formulation. Using methods taught in this book, you conduct surveys and discover that people overwhelmingly like the newer formulation, and you decide to use that new formulation going forward, having statistically shown that people prefer the new taste formulation. *What could go wrong?*

#2 You're a senior airline manager who has noticed that your frequent fliers always choose another airline when flying from the United States to Europe. You suspect fliers make that choice because of the other airline's perceived higher quality. You survey those fliers,, using techniques taught in this book, and confirm your suspicions. You then design a new survey to collect detailed information about the quality of all components of a flight, from the seats to the meals served to the flight attendants' service. Based on the results of that survey, you approve a costly plan that will enable your airline to match the perceived quality of your competitor. *What could go wrong?*

In both cases, much did go wrong. Both cases serve as cautionary tales that if you choose the wrong variables to study, you may not end up with results that support making better decisions. Defining and collecting data, which at first glance can seem to be the simplest tasks in the DCOVA framework, can often be more challenging than people anticipate.

As the initial chapter notes, statistics is a way of thinking that can help fact-based decision making. But statistics, even properly applied using the DCOVA framework, can never be a substitute for sound management judgment. If you misidentify the business problem or lack proper insight into a problem, statistics cannot help you make a good decision. Case #1 retells the story of one of the most famous marketing blunders ever, the change in the formulation of Coca-Cola in the 1980s. In that case, Coke brand managers were so focused on the taste of Pepsi and the newly successful sibling Diet Coke that they decided only to define a variable and collect data about which drink tasters preferred in a blind taste test. When New Coke was preferred, even over Pepsi, managers rushed the new formulation into production. In doing so, those managers failed to reflect on whether the statistical results about a test that asked people to compare one-ounce samples of several beverages would demonstrate anything about beverage sales. After all, people were asked which beverage tasted better, not whether they would buy that better-tasting beverage in the future. New Coke was an immediate failure, and Coke managers reversed their decision a mere 77 days after introducing their new formulation (see reference 6).

Case #2 represents a composite story of managerial actions at several airlines. In some cases, managers overlooked the need to state operational definitions for quality factors about which fliers were surveyed. In at least one case, statistics was applied correctly, and an airline spent great sums on upgrades and was able to significantly improve quality. Unfortunately, their frequent fliers still chose the competitor's flights. In this case, no statistical survey about quality could reveal the managerial oversight that given the same level of quality between two airlines, frequent fliers will almost always choose the cheaper airline. While quality was a significant variable of interest, it was not the most significant.

Remember the lessons of these cases as you study the rest of this book. Due to the necessities of instruction, examples and problems presented in all chapters but the last one include preidentified business problems and defined variables. Identifying the business problem or objective to be considered is always a prelude to applying the DCOVA framework.

1.1 Defining Variables

When a proper business problem or objective has been identified, you can begin to define your data. You define data by defining variables. You assign an **operational definition** to each variable you identify and specify the type of variable and the *scale*, or type of measurement, the variable uses (the latter two concepts are discussed later in this section).

EXAMPLE 1.1

Defining Data at GT&M

You been hired by Good Tunes & More (GT&M), a local electronics retailer, to assist in establishing a fair and reasonable price for Whitney Wireless, a privately-held chain that GT&M seeks to acquire. You need data that would help to analyze and verify the contents of the wireless company's basic financial statements. A GT&M manager suggests that one variable you should use is monthly sales. What do you do?

SOLUTION Having first confirmed with the GT&M financial team that monthly sales is a relevant variable of interest, you develop an operational definition for this variable. Does this variable refer to sales per month for the entire chain or for individual stores? Does the variable refer to net or gross sales? Do the monthly sales data represent number of units sold or currency amounts? If the data are currency amounts, are they expressed in U.S. dollars? After getting answers to these and similar questions, you draft an operational definition for ratification by others working on this project.

Classifying Variables by Type

You need to know the type of data that a variable defines in order to choose statistical methods that are appropriate for that data. Broadly, all variables are either **numerical**, variables whose data represent a counted or measured quantity, or **categorical**, variables whose data represent categories. Gender with its categories male and female is a categorical variable, as is the variable preferred-New-Coke with its categories yes and no. In Example 1.1, the monthly sales variable is numerical because the data for this variable represent a quantity.

For some statistical methods, you must further specify numerical variables as either being *discrete* or *continuous*. **Discrete** numerical variables have data that arise from a counting process. Discrete numerical variables include variables that represent a "number of something," such as the monthly number of smartphones sold in an electronics store. **Continuous** numerical variables have data that arise from a measuring process. The variable "the time spent waiting on a checkout line" is a continuous numerical variable because its data represent timing measurements. The data for a continuous variable can take on any value within a continuum or an interval, subject to the precision of the measuring instrument. For example, a waiting time could be 1 minute, 1.1 minutes, 1.11 minutes, or 1.113 minutes, depending on the precision of the electronic timing device used.

For some data, you might define a numerical variable for one problem that you wish to study, but define the same data as a categorical variable for another. For example, a person's age might seem to always be a numerical variable, but what if you are interested in comparing the buying habits of children, young adults, middle-aged persons, and retirement-age people? In that case, defining age as categorical variable would make better sense.

Measurement Scales

You identify the **measurement scale** that the data for a variable represent, as part of defining a variable. The measurement scale defines the ordering of values and determines if differences among pairs of values for a variable are equivalent and whether you can express one value in terms of another. Table 1.1 presents examples of measurement scales, some of which are used in the rest of this section.

You define numerical variables as using either an **interval scale**, which expresses a difference between measurements that do not include a true zero point, or a **ratio scale**, an ordered scale that includes a true zero point. If a numerical variable has a ratio scale, you can characterize one value in terms of another. You can say that the item cost (ratio) $2 is twice as expensive as the item cost $1. However, because Fahrenheit temperatures use an interval scale, 2°F does not represent twice the heat of 1°F. For both interval and ratio scales, what the difference of 1 unit represents remains the same among pairs of values, so that the difference between $11 and $10 represents the same difference as the difference between $2 and $1 (and the difference between 11°F and 10°F represents the same as the difference between 2°F and 1°F).

Categorical variables use measurement scales that provide less insight into the values for the variable. For data measured on a **nominal scale**, category values express no order or ranking. For data measured on an **ordinal scale**, an ordering or ranking of category values is implied. Ordinal scales give you some information to compare values but not as much as interval or ratio scales. For example, the ordinal scale poor, fair, good, and excellent allows you to know that "good" is better than poor or fair and not better than excellent. But unlike interval and ratio scales, you do not know that the difference from poor to fair is the same as fair to good (or good to excellent).

TABLE 1.1

Examples of Different Scales and Types

Data	Scale, Type	Values
Cellular provider	nominal, categorical	AT&T, T-Mobile, Verizon, Other, None
Excel skills	ordinal, categorical	novice, intermediate, expert
Temperature (°F)	interval, numerical	−459.67°F or higher
SAT Math score	interval, numerical	a value between 200 and 800, inclusive
Item cost (in $)	ratio, numerical	$0.00 or higher

PROBLEMS FOR SECTION 1.1

LEARNING THE BASICS

1.1 Four different beverages are sold at a fast-food restaurant: soft drinks, tea, coffee, and bottled water.
a. Explain why the type of beverage sold is an example of a categorical variable.
b. Explain why the type of beverage is an example of a nominal-scaled variable.

1.2 U.S. businesses are listed by size: small, medium, and large. Explain why business size is an example of an ordinal-scaled variable.

1.3 The time it takes to download a video from the Internet is measured.
a. Explain why the download time is a continuous numerical variable.
b. Explain why the download time is a ratio-scaled variable.

APPLYING THE CONCEPTS

SELF TEST **1.4** For each of the following variables, determine whether the variable is categorical or numerical and determine its measurement scale. If the variable is numerical, determine whether the variable is discrete or continuous.
a. Number of cellphones in the household
b. Monthly data usage (in MB)
c. Number of text messages exchanged per month
d. Voice usage per month (in minutes)
e. Whether the cellphone is used for email

1.5 The following information is collected from students upon exiting the campus bookstore during the first week of classes.
a. Amount of time spent shopping in the bookstore
b. Number of textbooks purchased
c. Academic major
d. Gender

Classify each variable as categorical or numerical and determine its measurement scale.

1.6 For each of the following variables, determine whether the variable is categorical or numerical and determine its measurement scale. If the variable is numerical, determine whether the variable is discrete or continuous.
a. Name of Internet service provider
b. Time, in hours, spent surfing the Internet per week
c. Whether the individual uses a mobile phone to connect to the Internet

d. Number of online purchases made in a month
e. Where the individual uses social networks to find sought-after information

1.7 For each of the following variables, determine whether the variable is categorical or numerical and determine its measurement scale. If the variable is numerical, determine whether the variable is discrete or continuous.
a. Amount of money spent on clothing in the past month
b. Favorite department store
c. Most likely time period during which shopping for clothing takes place (weekday, weeknight, or weekend)
d. Number of pairs of shoes owned

1.8 Suppose the following information is collected from Robert Keeler on his application for a home mortgage loan at the Metro County Savings and Loan Association.
a. Monthly payments: $2,227
b. Number of jobs in past 10 years: 1
c. Annual family income: $96,000
d. Marital status: Married

Classify each of the responses by type of data and measurement scale.

1.9 One of the variables most often included in surveys is income. Sometimes the question is phrased "What is your income (in thousands of dollars)?" In other surveys, the respondent is asked to "Select the circle corresponding to your income level" and is given a number of income ranges to choose from.
a. In the first format, explain why income might be considered either discrete or continuous.
b. Which of these two formats would you prefer to use if you were conducting a survey? Why?

1.10 If two students score a 90 on the same examination, what arguments could be used to show that the underlying variable—test score—is continuous?

1.11 The director of market research at a large department store chain wanted to conduct a survey throughout a metropolitan area to determine the amount of time working women spend shopping for clothing in a typical month.
a. Indicate the type of data the director might want to collect.
b. Develop a first draft of the questionnaire needed in (a) by writing three categorical questions and three numerical questions that you feel would be appropriate for this survey.

1.2 Collecting Data

Collecting data using improper methods can spoil any statistical analysis. For example, Coca-Cola managers in the 1980s (see page 12) faced advertisements from their competitor publicizing the results of a "Pepsi Challenge" in which taste testers consistently favored Pepsi over Coke. No wonder—test recruiters deliberately selected tasters they thought would likely be more favorable to Pepsi and served samples of Pepsi chilled, while serving samples of Coke lukewarm (not a very fair comparison!). These introduced biases made the challenge anything but a proper scientific or statistical test. Proper data collection avoids introducing biases and minimizes errors.

Populations and Samples

You collect your data from either a population or a sample. A **population** contains all the items or individuals of interest that you seek to study. All of the GT&M sales transactions for a specific year, all of the full-time students enrolled in a college, and all of the registered voters in Ohio are examples of populations. A **sample** contains only a portion of a population of interest. You analyze a sample to estimate characteristics of an entire population. You might select a sample of 200 GT&M sales transactions, a sample of 50 full-time students selected for a marketing study, or a sample of 500 registered voters in Ohio in lieu of analyzing the populations identified in this paragraph.

You collect data from a sample when selecting a sample will be less time consuming or less cumbersome than selecting every item in the population or when analyzing a sample is less cumbersome or more practical than analyzing the entire population. Section FTF.3 defines *statistic* as a "value that summarizes the data of a specific variable." More precisely, a **statistic** summarizes the value of a specific variable for sample data. Correspondingly, a **parameter** summarizes the value of a population for a specific variable.

Data Sources

Data sources arise from the following activities:

- Capturing data generated by ongoing business activities
- Distributing data compiled by an organization or individual
- Compiling the responses from a survey
- Conducting a designed experiment and recording the outcomes of the experiment
- Conducting an observational study and recording the results of the study

When you perform the activity that collects the data, you are using a **primary data source**. When the data collection part of these activities is done by someone else, you are using a **secondary data source**.

Capturing data can be done as a byproduct of an organization's transactional information processing, such as the storing of sales transactions at a retailer such as GT&M, or as result of a service provided by a second party, such as customer information that a social media website business collects on behalf of another business. Therefore, such data capture may be either a primary or a secondary source.

Typically, organizations such as market research firms and trade associations distribute complied data, as do businesses that offer syndicated services, such as The Neilsen Company, known for its TV ratings. Therefore, this source of data is usually a secondary source. The other three sources are either primary or secondary, depending on whether you (your organization) are doing the activity. For example, if you oversee the distribution of a survey and the compilation of its results, the survey is a primary data source.

In both observational studies and designed experiments, researchers that collect data are looking for the effect of some change, called a **treatment**, on a variable of interest. In an observational study, the researcher collects data in a natural or neutral setting and has no direct control of the treatment. For example, in an observational study of the possible effects on theme park usage patterns (the variable of interest) that a new electronic payment method might cause, you would take a sample of visitors, identify those who use the new method and those who do not, and then "observe" if those who use the new method have different park usage patterns. In a designed experiment, you permit only those you select to use the new electronic payment method and then discover if the people you selected have different theme park usage patterns (from those who you did not select to use the new payment method). Choosing to use an observational study (or experiment) affects the statistical methods you apply and the decision-making processes that use the results of those methods, as later chapters (10, 11, and 17) will further explain.

learnMORE

Read the SHORT TAKES for Chapter 1 for a further discussion about data sources.

PROBLEMS FOR SECTION 1.2

APPLYING THE CONCEPTS

1.12 The American Community Survey (**www.census.gov/acs**) provides data every year about communities in the United States. Addresses are randomly selected, and respondents are required to supply answers to a series of questions.
a. Which of the sources of data best describe the American Community Survey?
b. Is the American Community Survey based on a sample or a population?

1.13 Visit the website of the Gallup organization at **www.gallup .com**. Read today's top story. What type of data source is the top story based on?

1.14 Visit the website of the Pew Research organization at **www .pewresearch.org**. Read today's top story. What type of data source is the top story based on?

1.15 Transportation engineers and planners want to address the dynamic properties of travel behavior by describing in detail the driving characteristics of drivers over the course of a month. What type of data collection source do you think the transportation engineers and planners should use?

1.16 Visit the home page of the Statistics Portal "Statista" at **statista.com**. Examine one of the "Popular infographic topics" in the Infographics section on that page. What type of data source is the information presented here based on?

1.3 Types of Sampling Methods

When you collect data by selecting a sample, you begin by defining the **frame**. The frame is a complete or partial listing of the items that make up the population from which the sample will be selected. Inaccurate or biased results can occur if a frame excludes certain groups, or portions of the population. Using different frames to collect data can lead to different, even opposite, conclusions.

Using your frame, you select either a nonprobability sample or a probability sample. In a **nonprobability sample**, you select the items or individuals without knowing their probabilities of selection. In a **probability sample**, you select items based on known probabilities. Whenever possible, you should use a probability sample as such a sample will allow you to make inferences about the population being analyzed.

Nonprobability samples can have certain advantages, such as convenience, speed, and low cost. Such samples are typically used to obtain informal approximations or as small-scale initial or pilot analyses. However, because the theory of statistical inference depends on probability sampling, nonprobability samples *cannot be used* for statistical inference and this more than offsets those advantages in more formal analyses.

Figure1.1 shows the subcategories of the two types of sampling. A nonprobability sample can be either a convenience sample or a judgment sample. To collect a **convenience sample**, you select items that are easy, inexpensive, or convenient to sample. For example, in a warehouse of stacked items, selecting only the items located on the tops of each stack and within easy reach would create a convenience sample. So, too, would be the responses to surveys that the websites of many companies offer visitors. While such surveys can provide large amounts of data quickly and inexpensively, the convenience samples selected from these responses will consist of self-selected website visitors. (Read the Consider This essay on page 24 for a related story.)

To collect a **judgment sample**, you collect the opinions of preselected experts in the subject matter. Although the experts may be well informed, you cannot generalize their results to the population.

FIGURE 1.1
Types of samples

The types of probability samples most commonly used include simple random, systematic, stratified, and cluster samples. These four types of probability samples vary in terms of cost, accuracy, and complexity, and they are the subject of the rest of this section.

Simple Random Sample

In a **simple random sample**, every item from a frame has the same chance of selection as every other item, and every sample of a fixed size has the same chance of selection as every other sample of that size. Simple random sampling is the most elementary random sampling technique. It forms the basis for the other random sampling techniques. However, simple random sampling has its disadvantages. Its results are often subject to more variation than other sampling methods. In addition, when the frame used is very large, carrying out a simple random sample may be time consuming and expensive.

With simple random sampling, you use n to represent the sample size and N to represent the frame size. You number every item in the frame from 1 to N. The chance that you will select any particular member of the frame on the first selection is $1/N$.

You select samples with replacement or without replacement. **Sampling with replacement** means that after you select an item, you return it to the frame, where it has the same probability of being selected again. Imagine that you have a fishbowl containing N business cards, one card for each person. On the first selection, you select the card for Grace Kim. You record pertinent information and replace the business card in the bowl. You then mix up the cards in the bowl and select a second card. On the second selection, Grace Kim has the same probability of being selected again, $1/N$. You repeat this process until you have selected the desired sample size, n.

Typically, you do not want the same item or individual to be selected again in a sample. **Sampling without replacement** means that once you select an item, you cannot select it again. The chance that you will select any particular item in the frame—for example, the business card for Grace Kim—on the first selection is $1/N$. The chance that you will select any card not previously chosen on the second selection is now 1 out of $N - 1$. This process continues until you have selected the desired sample of size n.

When creating a simple random sample, you should avoid the "fishbowl" method of selecting a sample because this method lacks the ability to thoroughly mix the cards and, therefore, randomly select a sample. You should use a more rigorous selection method.

learnMORE

Learn to use a table of random numbers to select a simple random sample in an online section of this chapter.

One such method is to use a **table of random numbers**, such as Table E.1 in Appendix E, for selecting the sample. A table of random numbers consists of a series of digits listed in a randomly generated sequence. To use a random number table for selecting a sample, you first need to assign code numbers to the individual items of the frame. Then you generate the random sample by reading the table of random numbers and selecting those individuals from the frame whose assigned code numbers match the digits found in the table. Because the number system uses 10 digits $(0, 1, 2, \ldots, 9)$, the chance that you will randomly generate any particular digit is equal to the probability of generating any other digit. This probability is 1 out of 10. Hence, if you generate a sequence of 800 digits, you would expect about 80 to be the digit 0, 80 to be the digit 1, and so on. Because every digit or sequence of digits in the table is random, the table can be read either horizontally or vertically. The margins of the table designate row numbers and column numbers. The digits themselves are grouped into sequences of five in order to make reading the table easier.

Systematic Sample

In a **systematic sample**, you partition the N items in the frame into n groups of k items, where

$$k = \frac{N}{n}$$

You round k to the nearest integer. To select a systematic sample, you choose the first item to be selected at random from the first k items in the frame. Then, you select the remaining $n - 1$ items by taking every kth item thereafter from the entire frame.

If the frame consists of a list of prenumbered checks, sales receipts, or invoices, taking a systematic sample is faster and easier than taking a simple random sample. A systematic sample is also a convenient mechanism for collecting data from membership directories, electoral registers, class rosters, and consecutive items coming off an assembly line.

To take a systematic sample of $n = 40$ from the population of $N = 800$ full-time employees, you partition the frame of 800 into 40 groups, each of which contains 20 employees. You then select a random number from the first 20 individuals and include every twentieth individual after the first selection in the sample. For example, if the first random number you select is 008, your subsequent selections are 028, 048, 068, 088, 108, . . . , 768, and 788.

Simple random sampling and systematic sampling are simpler than other, more sophisticated, probability sampling methods, but they generally require a larger sample size. In addition, systematic sampling is prone to selection bias that can occur when there is a pattern in the frame. To overcome the inefficiency of simple random sampling and the potential selection bias involved with systematic sampling, you can use either stratified sampling methods or cluster sampling methods.

Stratified Sample

learnMORE

Learn how to select a stratified sample in the online section of this chapter.

In a **stratified sample**, you first subdivide the N items in the frame into separate subpopulations, or **strata**. A stratum is defined by some common characteristic, such as gender or year in school. You select a simple random sample within each of the strata and combine the results from the separate simple random samples. Stratified sampling is more efficient than either simple random sampling or systematic sampling because you are ensured of the representation of items across the entire population. The homogeneity of items within each stratum provides greater precision in the estimates of underlying population parameters. In addition, stratified sampling enables you to reach conclusions about each strata in the frame. However, using a stratified sample requires that you can determine the variable(s) on which to base the stratification and can also be expensive to implement.

Cluster Sample

In a **cluster sample**, you divide the N items in the frame into clusters that contain several items. **Clusters** are often naturally occurring groups, such as counties, election districts, city blocks, households, or sales territories. You then take a random sample of one or more clusters and study all items in each selected cluster.

Cluster sampling is often more cost-effective than simple random sampling, particularly if the population is spread over a wide geographic region. However, cluster sampling often requires a larger sample size to produce results as precise as those from simple random sampling or stratified sampling. A detailed discussion of systematic sampling, stratified sampling, and cluster sampling procedures can be found in references 2, 4, and 5.

PROBLEMS FOR SECTION 1.3

LEARNING THE BASICS

1.17 For a population containing $N = 902$ individuals, what code number would you assign for
a. the first person on the list?
b. the fortieth person on the list?
c. the last person on the list?

1.18 For a population of $N = 902$, verify that by starting in row 05, column 01 of the table of random numbers (Table E.1), you need only six rows to select a sample of $N = 60$ *without* replacement.

1.19 Given a population of $N = 93$, starting in row 29, column 01 of the table of random numbers (Table E.1), and reading across the row, select a sample of $N = 15$
a. *without* replacement.
b. *with* replacement.

APPLYING THE CONCEPTS

1.20 For a study that consists of personal interviews with participants (rather than mail or phone surveys), explain why simple random sampling might be less practical than some other sampling methods.

1.21 You want to select a random sample of $n = 1$ from a population of three items (which are called A, B, and C). The rule for selecting the sample is as follows: Flip a coin; if it is heads, pick item A; if it is tails, flip the coin again; this time, if it is heads, choose B; if it is tails, choose C. Explain why this is a probability sample but not a simple random sample.

1.22 A population has four members (called A, B, C, and D). You would like to select a random sample of $n = 2$, which you decide to do in the following way: Flip a coin; if it is heads, the sample will be items A and B; if it is tails, the sample will be items C and D. Although this is a random sample, it is not a simple random sample. Explain why. (Compare the procedure described in Problem 1.21 with the procedure described in this problem.)

1.23 The registrar of a university with a population of $N = 4,000$ full-time students is asked by the president to conduct a survey to measure satisfaction with the quality of life on campus. The following table contains a breakdown of the 4,000 registered full-time students, by gender and class designation:

GENDER	CLASS DESIGNATION				
	Fr.	So.	Jr.	Sr.	Total
Female	700	520	500	480	2,200
Male	560	460	400	380	1,800
Total	1,260	980	900	860	4,000

The registrar intends to take a probability sample of $n = 200$ students and project the results from the sample to the entire population of full-time students.

a. If the frame available from the registrar's files is an alphabetical listing of the names of all $N = 4,000$ registered full-time students, what type of sample could you take? Discuss.

b. What is the advantage of selecting a simple random sample in (a)?

c. What is the advantage of selecting a systematic sample in (a)?

d. If the frame available from the registrar's files is a list of the names of all $N = 4,000$ registered full-time students compiled from eight separate alphabetical lists, based on the gender and class designation breakdowns shown in the class designation table, what type of sample should you take? Discuss.

e. Suppose that each of the $N = 4,000$ registered full-time students lived in one of the 10 campus dormitories. Each dormitory accommodates 400 students. It is college policy to fully integrate students by gender and class designation in each dormitory. If the registrar is able to compile a listing of all students by dormitory, explain how you could take a cluster sample.

✓ SELF TEST **1.24** Prenumbered sales invoices are kept in a sales journal. The invoices are numbered from 0001 to 5000.

a. Beginning in row 16, column 01, and proceeding horizontally in a table of random numbers (Table E.1), select a simple random sample of 50 invoice numbers.

b. Select a systematic sample of 50 invoice numbers. Use the random numbers in row 20, columns 05–07, as the starting point for your selection.

c. Are the invoices selected in (a) the same as those selected in (b)? Why or why not?

1.25 Suppose that 10,000 customers in a retailer's customer database are categorized by three customer types: 3,500 prospective buyers, 4,500 first time buyers, and 2,000 repeat (loyal) buyers. A sample of 1,000 customers is needed.

a. What type of sampling should you do? Why?

b. Explain how you would carry out the sampling according to the method stated in (a).

c. Why is the sampling in (a) not simple random sampling?

1.4 Data Preparation

studentTIP

Data preparation considerations are also critical when using business analytics, as Chapter 17 explains.

As you collect data, you may need to perform actions to help prepare the data for processing. This preparation both reviews the data for errors and inconsistencies as well as places the data into a format and structure required by the software you use to perform calculations (Microsoft Excel in this book).

Given the time constraints of the typical business statistics course, you will likely not practice data preparation tasks very much. With the exception of several examples designed for use with this section, data for the problems and examples in this book have already been properly "prepared" so that you can focus on the statistical concepts and methods that you are learning. That said, you should study these tasks for the occasions when you independently collect your own data and be generally knowledgeable about the importance of such tasks.

Data Cleaning

Perhaps the most critical data preparation task is **data cleaning**, the finding and possible fixing of irregularities in the data you collect. Irregularities that you find include undefined or impossible values as well as so-called **missing values**, data that were not able to be collected for a variable (and therefore not available for analysis).

For a categorical variable, an undefined value would be a category that is not one of the categories defined for the variable. For a numerical variable, an impossible value would be a value that falls outside a defined range of possible values for the variable. For a numerical variable without a defined range of possible values, you might also find **outliers**, values that seem excessively different from most of the other values. Such values may or may not be errors, but they demand a second review.

Missing values most frequently arise when you record a *nonresponse* to a survey question, but also occur with other data sources for a variety of reasons. Proper statistical analysis requires that you exclude missing values, and most specialized statistical software has ways of performing that exclusion, a type of data cleaning, for you. However, Microsoft Excel does not. When you use Excel, you must find and then exclude missing values manually as part of your data cleaning.

You may be able to fix some typographical irregularities that can occur with the data for a categorical variable. For example, given the variable gender with the defined categories male and female, data improperly recorded as mail or mael or as MALE or maLe can all be reasonably fixed to male, so long as you preserve a copy of the original data for later audit purposes. For other undefined or impossible values that you cannot fix, you may be tempted to exclude the data, but such exclusions violate proper sampling methods. Instead, unfixable irregularities should be recorded as missing values.

learnMORE

Excel Data Cleaning.pdf discusses techniques that you can use in Excel to clean data.

Data Formatting

You may need to reformat your data when you collect your data. Reformatting can mean rearranging the structure of the data or changing the electronic encoding of the data or both. For example, suppose that you seek to collect financial data about a sample of companies. You might find these data structured as tables of data, as the contents of standard forms, in a continuous stock ticker stream, or as messages or blog entries that appear on various websites. These data sources have various levels of structure which affect the ease of reformatting them for use.

Because tables of data are highly structured and are similar to the structure of a worksheet, tables would require the least reformatting. In the best case, you could make the rows and columns of a table the rows and columns of a worksheet. Unstructured data sources, such as messages and blog entries, often represent the worst case. You may have to paraphrase or characterize the message contents in a way that does not involve a direct transfer. As the use of business analytics grows (see Chapter 17), the use of automated ways to paraphrase or characterize these and other types of unstructured data grows, too.

Independent of the structure, the data you collect may exist in an electronic form that needs to be changed in order to be analyzed. For example, data presented as a digital picture of Excel worksheets would need to be changed into an actual Excel worksheet before that data could be analyzed. In this example, you are changing the electronic encoding of all the data, from a picture format such as jpeg to an Excel workbook format such as xlsx. Sometimes, individual numerical values that you have collected may need to changed, especially if you collect values that result from a computational process. You can demonstrate this issue in Excel by entering a formula that is equivalent to the expression $1 \times (0.5 - 0.4 - 0.1)$, which should evaluate as 0 but in Excel evaluates to a very small negative number. You would want to alter that value to 0 as part of your data cleaning.

Stacked and Unstacked Variables

When collecting data for a numerical variable, you sometimes want to subdivide that data into two or more groups for analysis. For example, if you were collecting data about the cost of a restaurant meal in an urban area, you might want to consider the cost of meals at restaurants in the center city district separately from the meal costs at metro area restaurants. When you want to consider two or more groups, you can arrange your data as either unstacked or stacked.

To use an **unstacked** arrangement, you create separate numerical variables for each group. In the example, you would create a center city meal cost variable and a second variable to hold the meal costs at metro area restaurants. To use a **stacked** arrangement format, you pair the single numerical variable meal cost with a second, categorical variable that contains two categories, such as center city and metro area. (The DATA and UNSTACKED worksheets of the Restaurants workbook present stacked and unstacked versions of the meal cost data that Chapter 2 uses for several examples.)

When you use software to analyze data, you may discover that a particular procedure requires data to be stacked (or unstacked). When such cases arise using Microsoft Excel, they are noted in the Excel Guide instructions. If you collect several numerical variables, each of which you want to subdivide in the same way, stacking your data will probably be the more efficient choice for you. Otherwise, it makes little difference whether your collected data is stacked or unstacked.

studentTIP

If you use PHStat, you can automate the stacking or unstacking of data as discussed in Section 1.4.

Recoding Variables

After you have collected data, you may need to reconsider the categories that you defined for a categorical variable or transform a numerical variable into a categorical variable by assigning the individual numeric values to one of several groups. In either case, you can define a **recoded variable** that supplements or replaces the original variable in your analysis.

For example, having already defined the variable class standing with the categories freshman, sophomore, junior, and senior, you decide that you want to investigate the differences between lowerclassmen (freshmen or sophomores) and upperclassmen (juniors or seniors). You can define a recoded variable UpperLower and assign the value Upper if a student is a junior or senior and assign the value Lower if the student is a freshman or sophomore.

When recoding variables, make sure that one and only one of the new categories can be assigned to any particular value being recoded and that each value can be recoded successfully by one of your new categories. You must ensure that your recoding has these properties of being **mutually exclusive** and **collectively exhaustive**.

When recoding numerical variables, pay particular attention to the operational definitions of the categories you create for the recoded variable, especially if the categories are not self-defining ranges. For example, while the recoded categories Under 12, 12–20, 21–34, 35–54, and 55-and-over are self-defining for age, the categories child, youth, young adult, middle aged, and senior each need to be further defined in terms of mutually exclusive and collectively exhaustive numerical ranges.

PROBLEMS FOR SECTION 1.4

APPLYING THE CONCEPTS

1.26 The cellphone brands owned by a sample of 20 respondents were:

Apple, Samsung, Appel, Nokia, Blackberry, HTC, Apple, , Samsung, HTC, LG, Blueberry, Samsung, Samsung, APPLE, Motorola, Apple, Samsun, Apple, Samsung

a. Clean these data and identify any irregularities in the data.
b. Are there any missing values in this set of 20 respondents? Identify the missing values.

1.27 The amount of monthly data usage by a sample of 10 cellphone users (in MB) was:

0.4, 2.7MB, 5.6, 4.3, 11.4, 26.8, 1.6, 1,079, 8.3, 4.2

Are there any potential irregularities in the data?

1.28 An amusement park company owns three hotels on an adjoining site. A guest relations manager wants to study the time it takes for shuttle buses to travel from each of the hotels to the amusement park entrance. Data were collected on a particular day that recorded the travel times in minutes.
a. Explain how the data could be organized in an unstacked format.
b. Explain how the data could be organized in a stacked format.

1.29 A hotel management company runs 10 hotels in a resort area. The hotels have a mix of pricing—some hotels have budget-priced rooms, some have moderate-priced rooms, and some have deluxe-priced rooms. Data are collected that indicate the number of rooms that are occupied at each hotel on each day of a month. Explain how the 10 hotels can be recoded into these three price categories.

1.5 Types of Survey Errors

When you collect data using the compiled responses from a survey, you must verify two things about the survey in order to make sure you have results that can be used in a decision-making process. You must evaluate the validity of the survey to make sure the survey does not lack objectivity or credibility. To do this, you evaluate the purpose of the survey, the reason the survey was conducted, and for whom the survey was conducted.

Having validated the objectivity and credibility of such a sample, you then determine if the survey was based on a probability sample (see Section 1.3). Surveys that use nonprobability samples are subject to serious biases that make their results useless for decision making purposes. In the case of the Coca-Cola managers concerned about the "Pepsi Challenge" results (see page 13), the managers failed to reflect on the subjective nature of the challenge as well as the nonprobability sample that this survey used. Had the mangers done so, they might not have been so quick to make the reformulation blunder that was reversed just weeks later.

Even when you verify these two things, surveys can suffer from any combination of the following types of survey errors: coverage error, nonresponse error, sampling error, or measurement error. Developers of well-designed surveys seek to reduce or minimize these types of errors, often at considerable cost.

Coverage Error

The key to proper sample selection is having an adequate frame. **Coverage error** occurs if certain groups of items are excluded from the frame so that they have no chance of being selected in the sample or if items are included from outside the frame. Coverage error results in a **selection bias**. If the frame is inadequate because certain groups of items in the population were not properly included, any probability sample selected will provide only an estimate of the characteristics of the frame, not the *actual* population.

Nonresponse Error

Not everyone is willing to respond to a survey. **Nonresponse error** arises from failure to collect data on all items in the sample and results in a **nonresponse bias**. Because you cannot always assume that persons who do not respond to surveys are similar to those who do, you need to follow up on the nonresponses after a specified period of time. You should make several attempts to convince such individuals to complete the survey and possibly offer an incentive to participate. The follow-up responses are then compared to the initial responses in order to make valid inferences from the survey (see references 2, 4, and 5). The mode of response you use, such as face-to-face interview, telephone interview, paper questionnaire, or computerized questionnaire, affects the rate of response. Personal interviews and telephone interviews usually produce a higher response rate than do mail surveys—but at a higher cost.

Sampling Error

When conducting a probability sample, chance dictates which individuals or items will or will not be included in the sample. **Sampling error** reflects the variation, or "chance differences," from sample to sample, based on the probability of particular individuals or items being selected in the particular samples.

When you read about the results of surveys or polls in newspapers or on the Internet, there is often a statement regarding a margin of error, such as "the results of this poll are expected to be within ± 4 percentage points of the actual value." This **margin of error** is the sampling error. You can reduce sampling error by using larger sample sizes. Of course, doing so increases the cost of conducting the survey.

Measurement Error

In the practice of good survey research, you design surveys with the intention of gathering meaningful and accurate information. Unfortunately, the survey results you get are often only a proxy for the ones you really desire. Unlike height or weight, certain information about behaviors and psychological states is impossible or impractical to obtain directly.

When surveys rely on self-reported information, the mode of data collection, the respondent to the survey, and or the survey itself can be possible sources of **measurement error**. Satisficing, social desirability, reading ability, and/or interviewer effects can be dependent on the mode of data collection. The social desirability bias or cognitive/memory limitations of a respondent can affect the results. And vague questions, double-barreled questions that ask about multiple issues but require a single response, or questions that ask the respondent to report something that occurs over time but fail to clearly define the extent of time about which the question asks (the reference period) are some of the survey flaws that can cause errors.

To minimize measurement error, you need to standardize survey administration and respondent understanding of questions, but there are many barriers to this (see references 1, 3, and 10).

Ethical Issues About Surveys

Ethical considerations arise with respect to the four types of survey error. Coverage error can result in selection bias and becomes an ethical issue if particular groups or individuals are purposely excluded from the frame so that the survey results are more favorable to the survey's sponsor. Nonresponse error can lead to nonresponse bias and becomes an ethical issue if the sponsor knowingly designs the survey so that particular groups or individuals are less likely than others to respond. Sampling error becomes an ethical issue if the findings are purposely presented without reference to sample size and margin of error so that the sponsor can promote a viewpoint that might otherwise be inappropriate. Measurement error can become an ethical issue in one of three ways: (1) a survey sponsor chooses leading questions that guide the respondent in a particular direction; (2) an interviewer, through mannerisms and tone, purposely makes a respondent obligated to please the interviewer or otherwise guides the respondent in a particular direction; or (3) a respondent willfully provides false information.

Ethical issues also arise when the results of nonprobability samples are used to form conclusions about the entire population. When you use a nonprobability sampling method, you need to explain the sampling procedures and state that the results cannot be generalized beyond the sample.

CONSIDER THIS

New Media Surveys/Old Survey Errors

Software company executives decide to create a "customer experience improvement program" to record how customers use the company's products, with the goal of using the collected data to make product enhancements. Product marketers decide to use social media websites to collect consumer feedback. These people risk making the same type of survey error that led to the quick demise of a very successful magazine nearly 80 years ago.

By 1935, "straw polls" conducted by the magazine *Literary Digest* had successfully predicted five consecutive U.S. presidential elections. For the 1936 election, the magazine

promised its largest poll ever and sent about 10 million ballots to people all across the country. After tabulating more than 2.3 million ballots, the *Digest* confidently proclaimed that Alf Landon would be an easy winner over Franklin D. Roosevelt. The actual results: FDR won in a landslide and Landon received the fewest electoral votes in U.S. history.

Being so wrong ruined the reputation of *Literary Digest* and it would cease publication less than two years after it made its erroneous claim. A review much later found that the low response rate (less than 25% of the ballots distributed were returned) and nonresponse error (Roosevelt voters were less likely to mail in a ballot than Landon voters) were significant reasons for the failure of the *Literary Digest* poll (see reference 9).

The *Literary Digest* error proved to be a watershed event in the history of sample surveys. First, the error disproved the assertion that the larger the sample is, the better the results will be—an assertion some people still mistakenly make today. The error paved the way for the modern methods of sampling discussed in this chapter and gave prominence to the more "scientific" methods that George Gallup and Elmo Roper both used to correctly predict the 1936 elections. (Today's Gallup Polls and Roper Reports remember those researchers.)

In more recent times, Microsoft software executives overlooked that experienced users could easily opt out of participating in their improvement program. This created another case of nonresponse error which may have led to the improved product (Microsoft Office) being so poorly received initially by experienced Office users who, by being more likely to opt out of the improvement program, biased the data that Microsoft used to determine Office "improvements."

And while those product marketers may be able to collect a lot of customer feedback data, those data also suffer from nonresponse error. In collecting data from social media websites, the marketers cannot know who chose *not* to leave comments. The marketers also cannot verify if the data collected suffer from a selection bias due to a coverage error

That you might use media newer than the mailed, dead-tree form that *Literary Digest* used does not mean that you automatically avoid the old survey errors. Just the opposite—the accessibility and reach of new media makes it much easier for unknowing people to commit such errors.

PROBLEMS FOR SECTION 1.5

APPLYING THE CONCEPTS

1.30 A survey indicates that the vast majority of college students own their own personal computers. What information would you want to know before you accepted the results of this survey?

1.31 A simple random sample of $n = 300$ full-time employees is selected from a company list containing the names of all $N = 5,000$ full-time employees in order to evaluate job satisfaction.

a. Give an example of possible coverage error.
b. Give an example of possible nonresponse error.
c. Give an example of possible sampling error.
d. Give an example of possible measurement error.

✓**SELF TEST** **1.32** Results of a 2015 Contact Solutions study reveal insights on perceptions and attitudes toward mobile shopping, providing direction to retailers for developing strategies for investing their dollars in the mobile app experience (**bit.ly/1OKdmqH**). Increased consumer interest in using shopping applications means retailers must adapt to meet the rising expectations for specialized mobile shopping experiences.

The results show that 23% of consumers indicate that in-app recommendations would drive them to add more items to their cart and that 33% would spend more time in the app. But shopper priorities change the moment they need help; they expect to get it immediately and effortlessly. If forced to stop what they're doing and leave the app to get help, 1 out of 4 shoppers would likely not make a purchase with the brand at all. The research is based on an online survey with a sample of 1,600 U.S. adults.

Identify *potential* concerns with coverage, nonresponse, sampling, and measurement errors.

1.33 A recent PwC survey of 1,322 CEOs in a wide range of industries representing a mix of company sizes from Asia, Europe, and the Americas indicated that CEOs no longer question the need to embrace technology at the core of their business in order to create value for customers (**pwc.to/1C5bG9D**). Eighty percent (80%) of CEOs see data mining and analysis as strategically important for their organization. Effectively leveraging data analytics tools, however, presents challenges for companies. Companies are not using analytics enough; there are issues about data quality, information overload, and a continuing lack of trust in the value of digital data. When companies do invest in digital technologies to deliver what customers want, that commitment would appear to pay off. CEOs are seeing the best return on digital investment in the area of operational efficiency; 88% percent think value has been created in this area.

What additional information would you want to know about the survey before you accepted the results for the study?

1.34 A recent survey points to growing consumer demand for state-of-the-art technology in vehicles. The 2015 KPMG Global Automotive Executive study found that automobile executives believe that consumers are still fixated on traditional product issues and not yet on innovative concepts and online services (**bit.ly/1GlkZ4Q**). Sixty-seven percent of executives rated fuel efficiency and 53% rated enhanced vehicle life span as extremely important to consumer vehicle purchases, while only 24% rated vehicle-bound connectivity and built-in technologies as extremely important. What additional information would you want to know about the survey before you accepted the results of the study?

▼ USING **STATISTICS**
Defining Moments, Revisited

The New Coke and airline quality cases illustrate missteps that can occur during the define and collect tasks of the DCOVA framework. To use statistics effectively, you must properly define a business problem or goal and then collect data that will allow you to make observations and reach conclusions that are relevant to that problem or goal.

In the New Coke case, managers failed to consider that data collected about a taste test would not necessary provide useful information about the sales issues they faced. The managers also did not realize that the test used improper sampling techniques, deliberately introduced biases, and were subject to coverage and nonresponse errors. Those mistakes invalidated the test, making the conclusion that New Coke tasted better than Pepsi an invalid claim.

In the airline quality case, no mistakes in defining and collecting data were made. The results that fliers like quality was a valid one, but decision makers overlooked that quality was not the most significant factor for people buying seats on transatlantic flights (price was). This case illustrates that no matter how well you apply statistics, if you do not properly analyze the business problem or goal being considered, you may end up with valid results that lead you to invalid management decisions.

▼ SUMMARY

In this chapter, you learned the details about the Define and Collect tasks of the DCOVA framework which are important first steps to applying statistics properly to decision making. You learned that defining variables means developing an operational definition that includes establishing the type of variable and the measurement scale that the variable uses. You learned important details about data collection as well some new basic vocabulary terms (sample, population, and parameter) and as a more precise definition of statistic. You specifically learned about sampling and the types of sampling methods available to you. Finally, you surveyed data preparation considerations and learned about the type of survey errors you can encounter.

▼ REFERENCES

1. Biemer, P. B., R. M. Graves, L. E. Lyberg, A. Mathiowetz, and S. Sudman. *Measurement Errors in Surveys*. New York: Wiley Interscience, 2004.
2. Cochran, W. G. *Sampling Techniques*, 3rd ed. New York: Wiley, 1977.
3. Fowler, F. J. *Improving Survey Questions: Design and Evaluation, Applied Special Research Methods Series*, Vol. 38, Thousand Oaks, CA: Sage Publications, 1995.
4. Groves R. M., F. J. Fowler, M. P. Couper, J. M. Lepkowski, E. Singer, and R. Tourangeau. *Survey Methodology*, 2nd ed. New York: John Wiley, 2009.
5. Lohr, S. L. *Sampling Design and Analysis*, 2nd ed. Boston, MA: Brooks/Cole Cengage Learning, 2010.
6. Polaris Marketing Research. "Brilliant Marketing Research or What? The New Coke Story." **bit.ly/1DofHSM**, posted 20 Sep 2011.
7. Rosenbaum, D. "The New Big Data Magic." CFO.com, 29 Aug 2011, **bit.ly/1DUMWzv**
8. Osbourne, J. *Best Practices in Data Cleaning*. Thousand Oaks, CA: Sage Publications, 2012.
9. Squire, P. "Why the 1936 *Literary Digest* Poll Failed." *Public Opinion Quarterly* 52 (1988): 125–133.
10. Sudman, S., N. M. Bradburn, and N. Schwarz. *Thinking About Answers: The Application of Cognitive Processes to Survey Methodology*. San Francisco, CA: Jossey-Bass, 1993.

▼ KEY TERMS

categorical variable   14
cluster   19
cluster sample   19

collectively exhaustive   22
continuous variable   14
convenience sample   17

coverage error   23
data cleaning   20
discrete variable   14

▼ CHECKING YOUR UNDERSTANDING

1.35 What is the difference between a sample and a population?

1.36 What is the difference between a statistic and a parameter?

1.37 What is the difference between a categorical variable and a numerical variable?

1.38 What is the difference between a discrete numerical variable and a continuous numerical variable?

1.39 What is the difference between a nominal scaled variable and an ordinal scaled variable?

1.40 What is the difference between an interval scaled variable and a ratio scaled variable?

1.41 What is the difference between probability sampling and nonprobability sampling?

1.42 What is the difference between a missing value and an outlier?

1.43 What is the difference between unstack and stacked variables?

▼ CHAPTER REVIEW PROBLEMS

1.44 Visit the official website for Microsoft Excel, **products .office.com/excel**. Review the features of Excel and then state the ways the program could be useful in statistical analysis.

1.45 Results of a 2015 Contact Solutions study reveal insights on perceptions and attitudes toward mobile shopping, providing direction to retailers for developing strategies for investing their dollars in the mobile app experience (**bit.ly/1OKdmqH**). Increased consumer interest in using shopping applications means retailers must adapt to meet the rising expectations for specialized mobile shopping experiences.

The study results show that 23% of consumers indicate that in-app recommendations would drive them to add more items to their cart and that 33% would spend more time in the app. But shopper priorities change the moment they need help; they expect to get it immediately and effortlessly. If forced to stop what they're doing and leave the app to get help, 1 out of 4 shoppers would likely not make a purchase with the brand at all. The research is based on an online survey with a sample of 1,600 U.S. adults who have made purchases via their mobile device.
a. Describe the population of interest.
b. Describe the sample that was collected.
c. Describe a parameter of interest.
d. Describe the statistic used to estimate the parameter in (c).

1.46 The Gallup organization releases the results of recent polls at its website, **www.gallup.com**. Visit this site and read an article of interest.
a. Describe the population of interest.
b. Describe the sample that was collected.
c. Describe a parameter of interest.
d. Describe the statistic used to estimate the parameter in (c).

1.47 A recent PwC survey of 1,322 CEOs in a wide range of industries representing a mix of company sizes from Asia, Europe, and the Americas indicated that CEOs no longer question the need to embrace technology at the core of their business in order to create value for customers (**pwc.to/1C5bG9D**). Eighty percent (80%) of CEOs see data mining and analysis as strategically important for their organization. Effectively leveraging data analytics tools, however, presents challenges for companies. Companies are not using analytics enough; there are issues about data quality, information overload, and a continuing lack of trust in the value of digital data.

When companies do invest in digital technologies to deliver what customers want, that commitment would appear to pay off. CEOs are seeing the best return on digital investment in the area of operational efficiency; 88% percent think value has been created in this area.

a. Describe the population of interest.
b. Describe the sample that was collected.

c. Describe a parameter of interest.

d. Describe the statistic used to estimate the parameter in (c).

1.48 The American Community Survey **www.census.gov/acs** provides data every year about communities in the United States. Addresses are randomly selected and respondents are required to supply answers to a series of questions.

a. Describe a variable for which data is collected.

b. Is the variable categorical or numerical?

c. If the variable is numerical, is it discrete or continuous?

1.49 Download and examine Zarca Interactive's *Association Salary Survey*, available on Zarca's "Sample Surveys, Online Survey Example, Sample Association Surveys, Sample Customer Service Survey" web page, **www.zarca.com/Online-Survey-Resource/Sample-Surveys.html**.

a. Give an example of a categorical variable included in the survey.

b. Give an example of a numerical variable included in the survey.

1.50 Three professors examined awareness of four widely disseminated retirement rules among employees at the University of Utah. These rules provide simple answers to questions about retirement planning (R. N. Mayer, C. D. Zick, and M. Glaittle, "Public Awareness of Retirement Planning Rules of Thumb," *Journal of Personal Finance*, 2011 10(1), 12–35). At the time of the investigation, there were approximately 10,000 benefited employees, and 3,095 participated in the study. Demographic data collected on these 3,095 employees included gender, age (years), education level (years completed), marital status, household income ($), and employment category.

a. Describe the population of interest.

b. Describe the sample that was collected.

c. Indicate whether each of the demographic variables mentioned is categorical or numerical.

1.51 Social media provides an enormous amount of data about the activities and habits of people using social platforms like Facebook and Twitter. The belief is that mining that data provides a treasure trove for those who seek to quantify and predict future human behavior. A marketer is planning a survey of Internet users in the United States to determine social media usage. The objective of the survey is to gain insight on these three items: key social media platforms used, frequency of social media usage, and demographics of key social media platform users.

a. For each of the three items listed, indicate whether the variables are categorical or numerical. If a variable is numerical, is it discrete or continuous?

b. Develop five categorical questions for the survey.

c. Develop five numerical questions for the survey.

CHAPTER 1

▾CASES

Managing Ashland MultiComm Services

Ashland MultiComm Services (AMS) provides high-quality telecommunications services in the Greater Ashland area. AMS traces its roots to a small company that redistributed the broadcast television signals from nearby major metropolitan areas but has evolved into a provider of a wide range of broadband services for residential customers.

AMS offers subscription-based services for digital cable television, local and long-distance telephone services, and high-speed Internet access. Recently, AMS has faced competition from other service providers as well as Internet-based, on demand streaming services that have caused many customers to "cut the cable" and drop their subscription to cable video services.

AMS management believes that a combination of increased promotional expenditures, adjustment in subscription fees, and improved customer service will allow AMS to successfully face these challenges. To help determine the proper mix of strategies to be taken, AMS management has decided to organize a research team to undertake a study.

The managers suggest that the research team examine the company's own historical data for number of subscribers, revenues, and subscription renewal rates for the past few years. They direct the team to examine year-to-date data as well, as the managers suspect that some of the changes they have seen have been a relatively recent phenomenon.

1. What type of data source would the company's own historical data be? Identify other possible data sources that the research team might use to examine the current marketplace for residential broadband services in a city such as Ashland.

2. What type of data collection techniques might the team employ?

3. In their suggestions and directions, the AMS managers have named a number of possible variables to study, but offered no operational definitions for those variables. What types of possible misunderstandings could arise if the team and managers do not first properly define each variable cited?

CardioGood Fitness

CardioGood Fitness is a developer of high-quality cardiovascular exercise equipment. Its products include treadmills, fitness bikes, elliptical machines, and e-glides. CardioGood Fitness looks to increase the sales of its treadmill products and has hired The AdRight Agency, a small advertising firm, to create and implement an advertising program. The AdRight Agency plans to identify particular market segments that are most likely to buy their clients' goods and services and then locate advertising outlets that will reach that market group. This activity includes collecting data on clients' actual sales and on the customers who make the purchases, with the goal of determining whether there is a distinct profile of the typical customer for a particular product or service. If a distinct profile emerges, efforts are made to match that profile to advertising outlets known to reflect the particular profile, thus targeting advertising directly to high-potential customers.

CardioGood Fitness sells three different lines of treadmills. The TM195 is an entry-level treadmill. It is as dependable as other models offered by CardioGood Fitness, but with fewer programs and features. It is suitable for individuals who thrive on minimal programming and the desire for simplicity to initiate their walk or hike. The TM195 sells for $1,500.

The middle-line TM498 adds to the features of the entry-level model two user programs and up to 15% elevation upgrade. The TM498 is suitable for individuals who are walkers at a transitional stage from walking to running or midlevel runners. The TM498 sells for $1,750.

The top-of-the-line TM798 is structurally larger and heavier and has more features than the other models. Its unique features include a bright blue backlit LCD console, quick speed and incline keys, a wireless heart rate monitor with a telemetric chest strap, remote speed and incline controls, and an anatomical figure that specifies which muscles are minimally and maximally activated. This model features a nonfolding platform base that is designed to handle rigorous, frequent running; the TM798 is therefore appealing to someone who is a power walker or a runner. The selling price is $2,500.

As a first step, the market research team at AdRight is assigned the task of identifying the profile of the typical customer for each treadmill product offered by CardioGood Fitness. The market research team decides to investigate whether there are differences across the product lines with respect to customer characteristics. The team decides to collect data on individuals who purchased a treadmill at a CardioGood Fitness retail store during the prior three months.

The team decides to use both business transactional data and the results of a personal profile survey that every purchaser completes as their sources of data. The team identifies the following customer variables to study: product purchased—TM195, TM498, or TM798; gender; age, in years; education, in years; relationship status, single or partnered; annual household income ($); mean number of times the customer plans to use the treadmill each week; mean number of miles the customer expects to walk/run each week; and self-rated fitness on a 1-to-5 scale, where 1 is poor shape and 5 is excellent shape. For this set of variables:

1. Which variables in the survey are categorical?
2. Which variables in the survey are numerical?
3. Which variables are discrete numerical variables?

Clear Mountain State Student Survey

The Student News Service at Clear Mountain State University (CMSU) has decided to gather data about the undergraduate students who attend CMSU. They create and distribute a survey

of 14 questions and receive responses from 111 undergraduates (stored in StudentSurvey).

Download (see Appendix C) and review the survey document **CMUndergradSurvey.pdf**. For each question asked in the survey, determine whether the variable is categorical or numerical. If you determine that the variable is numerical, identify whether it is discrete or continuous.

Learning with the Digital Cases

Identifying and preventing misuses of statistics is an important responsibility for all managers. The Digital Cases allow you to practice the skills necessary for this important task.

Each chapter's Digital Case tests your understanding of how to apply an important statistical concept taught in the chapter. As in many business situations, not all of the information you encounter will be relevant to your task, and you may occasionally discover conflicting information that you have to resolve in order to complete the case.

To assist your learning, each Digital Case begins with a learning objective and a summary of the problem or issue at hand. Each case directs you to the information necessary to reach your own conclusions and to answer the case questions. Many cases, such as the sample case worked out next, extend a chapter's Using Statistics scenario. You can download digital case files which are PDF format documents that may contain extended features as interactivity or data file attachments. Open these files with a current version of Adobe Reader, as other PDF programs may not support the extended features. (For more information, see Appendix C.)

To illustrate learning with a Digital Case, open the Digital Case file **WhitneyWireless.pdf** that contains summary information about the Whitney Wireless business. Apparently, from the claim on the title page, this business is celebrating its "best sales year ever."

Review the **Who We Are**, **What We Do**, and **What We Plan to Do** sections on the second page. Do these sections contain any useful information? What *questions* does this passage raise? Did you notice that while many facts are presented, no data that would support the claim of "best sales year ever" are presented? And were those mobile "mobilemobiles" used solely for promotion? Or did they generate any sales? Do you think that a talk-with-your-mouth-full event, however novel, would be a success?

Continue to the third page and the **Our Best Sales Year Ever!** section. How would you support such a claim? With a table of numbers? Remarks attributed to a knowledgeable source? Whitney Wireless has used a chart to present "two years ago" and "latest twelve months" sales data by category. Are there any problems with what the company has done? *Absolutely!*

Take a moment to identify and reflect on those problems. Then turn to pages 4 though 6 that present an annotated version of the first three pages and discusses some of the problems with this document.

In subsequent Digital Cases, you will be asked to provide this type of analysis, using the open-ended case questions as your guide. Not all the cases are as straightforward as this example, and some cases include perfectly appropriate applications of statistical methods. And none have annotated answers!

EG1.1 DEFINING VARIABLES

Classifying Variables by Type

Microsoft Excel infers the variable type from the data you enter into a column. If Excel discovers a column that contains numbers, it treats the column as a numerical variable. If Excel discovers a column that contains words or alphanumeric entries, it treats the column as a non-numerical (categorical) variable.

This imperfect method works most of the time, especially if you make sure that the categories for your categorical variables are words or phrases such as "yes" and "no." However, because you cannot explicitly define the variable type, Excel can mistakenly offer or allow you to do nonsensical things such as using a statistical method that is designed for numerical variables on categorical variables. If you must use coded values such as 1, 2, or 3, enter them preceded with an apostrophe, as Excel treats all values that begin with an apostrophe as non-numerical data. (You can check whether a cell entry includes a leading apostrophe by selecting a cell and viewing the contents of the cell in the formula bar.)

EG1.2 COLLECTING DATA

There are no Excel Guide instructions for this section.

EG1.3 TYPES OF SAMPLING METHODS

Simple Random Sample

Key Technique Use the **RANDBETWEEN**(*smallest integer, largest integer*) function to generate a random integer that can then be used to select an item from a frame.

Example 1 Create a simple random sample *with* replacement of size 40 from a population of 800 items.

Workbook Enter a formula that uses this function and then copy the formula down a column for as many rows as is necessary. For example, to create a simple random sample with replacement of size 40 from a population of 800 items, open to a new worksheet. Enter **Sample** in cell **A1** and enter the formula **=RANDBETWEEN(1, 800)** in cell **A2**. Then copy the formula down the column to cell **A41**.

Excel contains no functions to select a random sample *without* replacement. Such samples are most easily created using an add-in such as PHStat or the Analysis ToolPak, as described in the following paragraphs.

Analysis ToolPak Use **Sampling** to create a random sample *with replacement*.

For the example, open to the worksheet that contains the population of 800 items in column A and that contains a column heading in cell A1. Select **Data → Data Analysis**.

In the Data Analysis dialog box, select **Sampling** from the **Analysis Tools** list and then click **OK**. In the procedure's dialog box (shown below):

1. Enter **A1:A801** as the **Input Range** and check **Labels**.
2. Click **Random** and enter **40** as the **Number of Samples**.
3. Click **New Worksheet Ply** and then click **OK**.

Example 2 Create a simple random sample *without* replacement of size 40 from a population of 800 items.

PHStat Use **Random Sample Generation**.
For the example, select **PHStat → Sampling → Random Sample Generation**. In the procedure's dialog box (shown in next column):

1. Enter **40** as the **Sample Size**.
2. Click **Generate list of random numbers** and enter **800** as the **Population Size**.
3. Enter a **Title** and click **OK**.

Unlike most other PHStat results worksheets, the worksheet created contains no formulas.

Workbook Use the **COMPUTE worksheet** of the **Random workbook** as a template.

The worksheet already contains 40 copies of the formula **=RANDBETWEEN(1, 800)** in column B. Because the **RANDBETWEEN** function samples *with* replacement as discussed at the start of this section, you may need to add additional copies of the formula in new column B rows until you have 40 unique values.

If your intended sample size is large, you may find it difficult to spot duplicates. Read the SHORT TAKES for Chapter 1 to learn more about an advanced technique that uses formulas to detect duplicate values.

EG1.4 DATA PREPARATION
Recoding Variables

Key Technique To recode a categorical variable, you first copy the original variable's column of data and then use the find-and-replace function on the copied data. To recode a numerical variable, enter a formula that returns a recoded value in a new column.

Example Using the **DATA worksheet** of the **Recoded workbook**, create the recoded variable UpperLower from the categorical variable Class and create the recoded Variable Dean's List from the numerical variable GPA.

Workbook Use the **RECODED worksheet** of the **Recoded workbook** as a model.

The worksheet already contains UpperLower, a recoded version of Class that uses the operational definitions on page 22, and Dean's List, a recoded version of GPA, in which the value No recodes all GPA values less than 3.3 and Yes recodes all values 3.3 or greater than 3.3. The **RECODED_FORMULAS worksheet** in the same workbook shows how formulas in column I use the IF function to recode GPA as the Dean's List variable.

These recoded variables were created by first opening to the **DATA worksheet** in the same workbook and then following these steps:

1. Right-click column **D** (right-click over the shaded "D" at the top of column D) and click **Copy** in the shortcut menu.
2. Right-click column **H** and click the **first choice** in the **Paste Options** gallery.
3. Enter **UpperLower** in cell **H1**.
4. Select column **H**. With column H selected, click **Home → Find & Select → Replace**.

In the Replace tab of the Find and Replace dialog box:

5. Enter **Senior** as **Find what**, **Upper** as **Replace with**, and then click **Replace All**.
6. Click **OK** to close the dialog box that reports the results of the replacement command.
7. Still in the Find and Replace dialog box, enter **Junior** as **Find what** (replacing **Senior**), and then click **Replace All**.
8. Click **OK** to close the dialog box that reports the results of the replacement command.
9. Still in the Find and Replace dialog box, enter **Sophomore** as **Find what**, **Lower** as **Replace with**, and then click **Replace All**.
10. Click **OK** to close the dialog box that reports the results of the replacement command.
11. Still in the Find and Replace dialog box, enter **Freshman** as **Find what** and then click **Replace All**.
12. Click **OK** to close the dialog box that reports the results of the replacement command.

(This creates the recoded variable UpperLower in column H.)

13. Enter **Dean's List** in cell **I1**.
14. Enter the formula **=IF(G2 < 3.3, "No", "Yes")** in cell **I2**.
15. Copy this formula down the column to the last row that contains student data (row 63).

(This creates the recoded variable Dean's List in column I.)

The RECODED worksheet uses the **IF** function, discussed in Appendix F, to recode the numerical variable into two categories. Numerical variables can also be recoded into multiple categories by using the **VLOOKUP** function (see Appendix F).

2 Organizing and Visualizing Variables

OBJECTIVES

- How to organize and visualize categorical variables
- How to organize and visualize numerical variables
- How to summarize a mix of variables using special Excel features
- How to avoid making common errors when organizing and visualizing variables

▼ USING STATISTICS
"The Choice Is Yours"

Even though he is still in his 20s, Tom Sanchez realizes that you can never start too early to save for retirement. Based on research he has already done, Sanchez seeks to contribute to his 401(k) retirement plan by investing in one or more retirement funds.

Meanwhile, The Choice *Is* Yours investment service has been thinking about being better prepared to counsel younger investors such as Sanchez about retirement funds. To pursue this business objective, a company task force has already selected 407 retirement funds that may prove appropriate for younger investors. You have been asked to define, collect, organize, and visualize data about these funds in ways that could assist prospective clients making decisions about the funds in which they will invest. As a starting point, you think about the facts about each fund that would help customers compare and contrast funds.

You decide to begin by defining the variables for key characteristics of each fund, such as each fund's past performance. You also decide to define variables such as the amount of assets that a fund manages and whether the goal of a fund is to invest in companies whose earnings are expected to substantially increase in future years (a "growth" fund) or invest in companies whose stock price is undervalued, priced low relative to their earnings potential (a "value" fund).

You collect data from appropriate sources and organize the data as a worksheet, placing each variable in its own column. As you think more about your task, you realize that 407 rows of data, one for each fund in the sample, would be hard for prospective clients to review easily.

Is there something else you can do? Can you organize and present these data to prospective clients in a more helpful and comprehensible manner?

When using Microsoft Excel, you need to be aware of the type of errors Excel might make when visualizing your data.

The Excel functionality to implement these newer types of summaries are newer features of Excel, all added in recent years.

Defining your variables of interest and then collecting, preparing, and entering data into worksheets completes the **D**efine and **C**ollect **DCOVA** tasks. In the **DCOVA O**rganize task, you take that prepared data and create summaries that provide initial insights about your variables. These summaries guide you to further exploration of your data as well as sometimes directly facilitate decision making. For example, in the Choice *Is* Yours scenario, creating a summary of the retirement funds sample that would allow a prospective younger investor such as Tom Sanchez to quickly identify funds that were designed for growth and were identified as having moderate risk would be useful.

Methods you use during the Organize step create summaries in the form of various types of tables. Summaries can also take the form of visualizations. Visual summaries can facilitate the rapid review of larger amounts of data as well as show possible significant patterns to the data. For example, for the retirement funds sample, visualizing the 10-year rate of return and the management expense fees charged by each fund would help to identify the funds that would be charging you relatively little in fees for a "good" rate of return as well as the funds whose fees seem excessive given their modest or weak rates of return.

Because reviewing tabular *and* visual summaries together can lead to better insights and jumpstart analysis, the DCOVA **V**isualize task is often done concurrent to the **O**rganize task. For that reason, this chapter discusses methods to visualize variables after discussing methods that organize variables. Because the methods used to organize and visualize categorical variables differ from the methods used to organize and visualize numerical variables, this chapter discusses categorical and numerical methods in separate sections.

When you use methods to create tabular and visual summaries you risk making any number of common mistakes. These mistakes distort the information that those summaries present and undermine the usefulness of those summaries for decision making. Section 2.7 discusses the challenges you face in organizing and visualizing your variables. Because making mistakes when visualizing data is more common, the section includes a best practices for constructing visualizations.

As information technology evolves, more complex tabular and visual summaries become possible and these summaries can include a greater number of variables. As Section 2.6 discusses, some of these newer summaries present a mix of categorical *and* numerical variables and include interactive manipulation of those summaries. Section 2.6 also discusses the types of interactive manipulations you can do in Microsoft Excel, which vary but are similar to the type of manipulations you can do with specialized statistical software.

2.1 Organizing Categorical Variables

You organize a categorical variable by tallying the set of individual values for the variable by categories and placing the results in tables. Typically, you construct a summary table to organize the data for a single categorical variable and you construct a contingency table to organize the data from two or more categorical variables.

The Summary Table

A **summary table** tallies the set of individual values as frequencies or percentages for each category. A summary table helps you see the differences among the categories by displaying the frequency, amount, or percentage of items in a set of categories in a separate column. Table 2.1 presents a summary table that tallies responses to a recent survey that asked people how they paid for purchases and other transactions. From this table, stored in **Payment**, you can conclude that 40% paid with cash, 25% paid with a debit card, 17% paid with a credit card, and the remaining 18% paid by check, electronically, or by other means.

TABLE 2.1
How People Pay for Purchases and Other Transactions

Method	Percentage
Cash	40%
Debit card	25%
Credit card	17%
Check	7%
Online payment	7%
Other	4%

Source: Data extracted and adapted from "Paper beats Plastic," *USA Today*, December 26, 2014, p. 1A.

EXAMPLE 2.1

Summary Table of Levels of Risk of Retirement Funds

The sample of 407 retirement funds for The Choice *Is* Yours scenario (see page 32) includes the variable risk that has the defined categories Low, Average, and High. Construct a summary table of the retirement funds, categorized by risk.

SOLUTION From Table 2.2, you observe that more than 70% of the funds have average risk, while 10% of the funds have low risk and 17% of the funds have high risk.

TABLE 2.2
Frequency and Percentage Summary Table of Risk Level for 407 Retirement Funds

Fund Risk Level	Number of Funds	Percentage of Funds
Low	41	10.07%
Average	296	72.73%
High	70	17.20%
Total	407	100.00%

The Contingency Table

A **contingency table** cross-tabulates, or tallies jointly, the data of two or more categorical variables, allowing you to study patterns that may exist between the variables. Tallies can be shown as a frequency, a percentage of the overall total, a percentage of the row total, or a percentage of the column total, depending on the type of contingency table you use. Each tally appears in its own **cell**, and there is a cell for each **joint response**, a unique combination of values for the variables being tallied. In the simplest contingency table, one that contains only two categorical variables, the joint responses appear in a table such that the tallies of one variable are located in the rows and the tallies of the other variable are located in the columns.

For the sample of 407 retirement funds for The Choice *Is* Yours scenario, you might create a contingency table to examine whether there is any pattern between the fund type variable and the risk level variable. Because fund type has the defined categories Growth and Value and the risk level has the categories Low, Average, and High, there are six possible joint responses for this table. You could create the table by hand tallying the joint responses for each of the retirement funds in the sample. For example, for the first fund listed in the sample you would add to the tally in the cell that is the intersection of the Growth row and the Average column because the first fund is of type Growth and risk level Average. However, using one of the automated methods for creating contingency tables found in Sections EG2.1 of the Excel Guide would be a better choice.

In a contingency table, both the rows and the columns represent variables. Use the terms row variable and column variable to distinguish between the two variables.

Table 2.3 presents the completed contingency table after all 407 funds have been tallied. This table shows that there are 199 retirement funds that have the fund type Growth and risk level Average. In summarizing all six joint responses, the table reveals that Growth and Average is the most frequent joint response in the sample of 407 retirement funds.

TABLE 2.3

Contingency Table Displaying Fund Type and Risk Level

FUND TYPE	RISK LEVEL			Total
	Low	Average	High	
Growth	16	199	54	269
Value	25	97	16	138
Total	41	296	70	407

Contingency tables that display cell values as a percentage of a total can help show patterns between variables. Table 2.4 shows a contingency table that displays values as a percentage of the Table 2.3 overall total (407), Table 2.5 shows a contingency table that displays values as a percentage of the Table 2.3 row totals (269 and 138), and Table 2.6 shows a contingency table that displays values as a percentage of the Table 2.3 column totals (41, 296, and 70).

TABLE 2.4

Contingency Table Displaying Fund Type and Risk Level, Based on Percentage of Overall Total

FUND TYPE	RISK LEVEL			Total
	Low	Average	High	
Growth	3.93%	48.89%	13.27%	66.09%
Value	6.14%	23.83%	3.93%	33.91%
Total	10.07%	72.73%	17.20%	100.00%

TABLE 2.5

Contingency Table Displaying Fund Type and Risk Level, Based on Percentage of Row Total

FUND TYPE	RISK LEVEL			Total
	Low	Average	High	
Growth	5.95%	73.98%	20.07%	100.00%
Value	18.12%	70.29%	11.59%	100.00%
Total	10.07%	72.73%	17.20%	100.00%

TABLE 2.6

Contingency Table Displaying Fund Type and Risk Level, Based on Percentage of Column Total

FUND TYPE	RISK LEVEL			Total
	Low	Average	High	
Growth	39.02%	67.23%	77.14%	66.09%
Value	60.98%	32.77%	22.86%	33.91%
Total	100.00%	100.00%	100.00%	100.00%

Table 2.4 shows that 66.09% of the funds sampled are growth funds, 33.91% are value funds, and 3.93% are growth funds that have low risk. Table 2.5 shows that 5.95% of the growth funds have low risk, while 18.12% of the value funds have low risk. Table 2.6 shows that of the funds that have low risk, 39.02% are growth funds. From Tables 2.4 through 2.6, you see that growth funds are less likely than value funds to have low risk.

PROBLEMS FOR SECTION 2.1

LEARNING THE BASICS

2.1 A categorical variable has three categories, with the following frequencies of occurrence:

Category	Frequency
A	13
B	28
C	9

a. Compute the percentage of values in each category.
b. What conclusions can you reach concerning the categories?

2.2 The following data represent the responses to two questions asked in a survey of 40 college students majoring in business: What is your gender? (M = male; F = female) and What is your major? (A = Accounting; C = Computer Information Systems; M = Marketing):

Gender:	M	M	M	F	M	F	F	M	F	M
Major:	A	C	C	M	A	C	A	A	C	C

Gender:	F	M	M	M	M	F	F	M	F	F
Major:	A	A	A	M	C	M	A	A	A	C

Gender:	M	M	M	M	F	M	F	F	M	M
Major:	C	C	A	A	M	M	C	A	A	A

Gender:	F	M	M	M	M	F	M	F	M	M
Major:	C	C	A	A	A	A	C	C	A	C

a. Tally the data into a contingency table where the two rows represent the gender categories and the three columns represent the academic major categories.
b. Construct contingency tables based on percentages of all 40 student responses, based on row percentages and based on column percentages.

APPLYING THE CONCEPTS

2.3 The following table, stored in Smartphone Sales , represents the annual market share of smartphones, by type, for the years 2010, 2011, 2012, 2013, and 2014.

Type	2010	2011	2012	2013	2014
Android	23.3%	49.2%	69.0%	78.8%	81.5%
iOS	15.6%	18.8%	18.7%	15.1%	14.8%
Microsoft	4.9%	1.8%	2.5%	3.3%	2.7%
Blackberry	16.0%	10.3%	4.5%	1.9%	0.4%
OtherOS	40.2%	19.8%	5.4%	1.0%	0.6%

Source: Data extracted from **bit.ly/1JV5qRR**.

a. What conclusions can you reach about the market for smartphones in 2010, 2011, 2012, 2013, and 2014.
b. What differences are there in the market for smartphones in 2010, 2011, 2012, 2013, and 2014.

2.4 The **Edmunds.com** NHTSA Complaints Activity Report contains consumer vehicle complaint submissions by automaker, brand, and category (data extracted from **edmu.in/Ybmpuz**). The following table, stored in Automaker1 , represents complaints received by automaker for January 2013.

Automaker	Number
American Honda	169
Chrysler LLC	439
Ford Motor Company	440
General Motors	551
Nissan Motors Corporation	467
Toyota Motor Sales	332
Other	516

a. Compute the percentage of complaints for each automaker.
b. What conclusions can you reach about the complaints for the different automakers?

The following table, stored in Automaker2 , represents complaints received by category for January 2013.

Category	Number
Airbags and seatbelts	201
Body and glass	182
Brakes	163
Fuel/emission/exhaust system	240
Interior electronics/hardware	279
Powertrain	1,148
Steering	397
Tires and wheels	71

c. Compute the percentage of complaints for each category.
d. What conclusions can you reach about the complaints for different categories?

2.5 What factors are most important for a dream job? A survey of 1,006 people ages 40 through 59 revealed the following:

Most Important Factor	Percent
High pay	23
Good work-life balance	22
Low stress	15
Flexible schedule	12
Give back to community	10
Fun environment	9
Opportunities to learn or advance	9

What conclusions can you reach concerning the factors that are most important for a dream job?

SELF TEST

2.6 The following table represents world oil production in millions of barrels a day in 2013:

Region	Oil Production (millions of barrels a day)
Iran	2.69
Saudi Arabia	9.58
Other OPEC countries	17.93
Non-OPEC countries	51.99

Source: **opec.org**.

a. Compute the percentage of values in each category.
b. What conclusions can you reach concerning the production of oil in 2013?

2.7 Visier's 2014 Survey of Employers explores current workforce analytics and planning practices, investments, and future plans. U.S.-based employers were asked what they see as the most common technical barrier to workforce analytics. The responses, stored in Barriers , were as follows:

Barriers	Frequency
Data must be integrated from multiple sources	68
Lack of automation/repeatable process	51
Metrics need to be identified or defined	45
Production is cumbersome	42
Data quality is not reliable	36
Sharing findings is challenging	21
Analytic tools are too complex	17
Ensuring security and integrity of workforce data	17
Other	3

Source: Data extracted from *The State of Workforce Analytics and Planning, 2014 Survey Report*, available at **bit.ly/1zuM99Z**.

a. Compute the percentage of values for each response need.
b. What conclusions can you reach concerning technical barriers to workforce analytics?

2.8 A survey of 1,700 shoppers were asked, "Does social media influence your purchase decisions?" The results, available at **bit.ly/1JVaKoh**, indicated that 20.3% of females responded that their purchase decisions are influenced by social media compared to 10.5% of males. The sample sizes of males and females were not provided. Suppose that the results were as shown in the following table:

INFLUENCED	GENDER		Total
	Male	Female	
Yes	89	173	262
No	761	677	1,438
Total	850	850	1,700

a. Construct contingency tables based on total percentages, row percentages, and column percentages.
b. What conclusions can you reach from these analyses?

2.9 A study of selected Kickstarter projects showed that overall a majority were successful, achieving their goal and raising, at a minimum, the targeted amounts. In an effort to identify project types that influence success, selected projects were subdivided into project categories (Film & Video, Games, Music, and Technology). The results are as follows:

CATEGORY	OUTCOME		Total
	Successful	Not Successful	
Film & Video	17,024	26,857	43,881
Games	5,105	10,075	15,180
Music	19,275	17,050	36,325
Technology	2,556	8,770	11,326
Total	43,960	62,752	106,712

Source: **Kickstarter.com, kickstarter.com/help/stats**.

a. Construct contingency tables based on total percentages, row percentages, and column percentages.
b. Which type of percentage—row, column, or total—do you think is most informative for these data? Explain.
c. What conclusions concerning the pattern of successful Kickstarter projects can you reach?

2.10 Do social recommendations increase ad effectiveness? A study of online video viewers compared viewers who arrived at an advertising video for a particular brand by following a social media recommendation link to viewers who arrived at the same video by web browsing. Data were collected on whether the viewer could correctly recall the brand being advertised after seeing the video. The results were:

ARRIVAL METHOD	CORRECTLY RECALLED THE BRAND	
	Yes	No
Recommendation	407	150
Browsing	193	91

Source: Data extracted from "Social Ad Effectiveness: An Unruly White Paper," **www.unrulymedia.com**, January 2012, p. 3.

What do these results tell you about social recommendations?

2.2 Organizing Numerical Variables

You create ordered arrays and distribution tables to organize numerical variables. Unless the number of values to organize is very large, you always begin with an **ordered array** that arranges the data for a numerical variable in rank order, from the smallest to the largest value. An ordered array helps you get a better sense of the range of values in your data and is particularly useful when you have more than a few values.

When organizing a numerical variable, you sometimes want to group the data by the value of a categorical variable. For example, in collecting meal cost data as part of a study that reviews the travel and entertainment costs that a business incurs in a major city, you might want to determine if the cost of meals at restaurants located in the center city district differ from the cost at restaurants in the surrounding metropolitan area. As you collect meal cost data for this study, you also note the restaurant location, center city or metro area.

Table 2.7A contains the meal cost data collected from a sample of 50 center city restaurants and 50 metro area restaurants. Table 2.7B presents these two lists of data as two ordered arrays. Note that the ordered arrays in Table 2.7B allow you to make some quick observations about the meal cost data. Using Table 2.7B, you can much more easily see meal costs at center city restaurants range from $22 to $99 and that meal costs at metro area restaurants range from $14 to $68.

TABLE 2.7A
Meal Cost Data for 50 Center City and 50 Metro Area Restaurants

Meal Costs at Center City Restaurants
29 29 88 58 29 62 64 65 54 29 36 78 45 40 67 49 33 83 76 63 29 32 60 22 40
63 45 56 76 64 50 99 48 56 34 59 69 53 71 69 35 56 40 75 43 93 46 72 95 57

Meal Costs at Metro Area Restaurants
63 62 30 51 58 47 36 26 14 25 38 43 22 44 44 23 39 32 29 25 52 47 44 59 21
31 43 53 53 25 52 54 26 49 48 29 31 36 31 54 29 41 26 21 36 24 33 50 68 37

TABLE 2.7B
Ordered Array of Meal Costs at 50 Center City and 50 Metro Area Restaurants

Center City Restaurant Meal Costs
22 29 29 29 29 29 32 33 34 35 36 40 40 40 43 45 45 46 48 49 50 53 54 56 56
56 57 58 59 60 62 63 63 64 64 65 67 69 69 71 72 75 76 76 78 83 88 93 95 99

Metro Area Restaurant Meal Costs
14 21 21 22 23 24 25 25 25 26 26 26 29 29 29 30 31 31 31 32 33 36 36 36 37
38 39 41 43 43 44 44 44 47 47 48 49 50 51 52 52 53 53 54 54 58 59 62 63 68

In using Excel with this book, you will have occasions to use both stacked and unstacked arrangements of data.

When you collect data for a numerical variable that you intend to group, as is done in the previous example for the meal cost variable, you must decide whether you will prepare your data in stacked or unstacked arrangement, as first discussed in Section 1.4. The file Restaurants stores the Table 2.7A data in *both* stacked and unstacked arrangements, so you can compare both arrangements. As Section 1.4 notes, requirements of specific software procedures often dictate the choice of stacked or unstacked.

When a numerical variable contains a large number of values, using an ordered array to make quick observation or reach conclusions about the data can be difficult. For such a variable, constructing a distribution table would be a better choice. Frequency, relative frequency, percentage, and cumulative distributions are among the types of distribution tables commonly used.

The Frequency Distribution

A **frequency distribution** tallies the values of a numerical variable into a set of numerically ordered **classes**. Each class groups a mutually exclusive range of values, called a **class interval**. Each value can be assigned to only one class, and every value must be contained in one of the class intervals.

To create a useful frequency distribution, you must consider how many classes would be appropriate for your data as well as determine a suitable *width* for each class interval. In general, a frequency distribution should have at least 5 and no more than 15 classes because having too few or too many classes provides little new information. To determine the **class interval width** (see Equation [2.1]), you subtract the lowest value from the highest value and divide that result by the number of classes you want the frequency distribution to have.

DETERMINING THE CLASS INTERVAL WIDTH

$$\text{Interval width} = \frac{\text{highest value} - \text{lowest value}}{\text{number of classes}} \qquad \textbf{(2.1)}$$

For the center city restaurant meal cost data shown in Tables 2.7A and 2.7B, between 5 and 10 classes are acceptable, given the size (50) of that sample. From the center city restaurant meal costs ordered array in Table 2.7B, the difference between the highest value of $99 and the lowest value of $22 is $77. Using Equation (2.1), you approximate the class interval width as follows:

$$\frac{77}{10} = 7.7$$

This result suggests that you should choose an interval width of $7.70. However, your width should always be an amount that simplifies the reading and interpretation of the frequency distribution. In this example, such an amount would be either $5 or $10, and you should choose $10, which creates 9 classes, and not $5, which creates 18 classes, too many for the sample size of 50.

Having chosen a class interval, you examine your data to establish **class boundaries** that properly and clearly define each class. In setting class boundaries, you are looking to establish classes that are simple to interpret and include all values being summarized. With the meal cost data, having decided on $10 as the class interval, you note that the cost of a center city meal ranges from $22 to $99 and the cost of a metro area meal ranges from $14 to $68. You then conclude that the lower class boundary of the first class must be no more than $14 and that the upper boundary of the last class must include $99. You set the lower class boundary of the first class to $10 (for ease of readability) and define the first class as $10 but less than $20, the second class as $20 but less than $30, and so on, ending with the class $90 but less than $100. Table 2.8 uses these class intervals to present frequency distributions for the sample of 50 center city restaurant meal costs and the sample of 50 metro area restaurant meal costs.

Frequency distributions allow you to more easily make observation about your data that support preliminary conclusions about your data. For example, Table 2.8 shows that the cost of center city restaurant meals is concentrated between $40 and $70, while the cost of metro area restaurant meal is concentrated between $20 nd $60.

TABLE 2.8
Frequency Distributions for Cost of a Meal at 50 Center City Restaurants and 50 Metro Area Restaurants

Meal Cost ($)	Center City Frequency	Metro Area Frequency
10 but less than 20	0	1
20 but less than 30	6	14
30 but less than 40	5	12
40 but less than 50	9	10
50 but less than 60	9	10
60 but less than 70	10	3
70 but less than 80	6	0
80 but less than 90	2	0
90 but less than 100	3	0
Total	50	50

studentTIP

The total of the frequency column must always equal the number of values.

For some charts discussed later in this chapter, class intervals are identified by their **class midpoints**, the values that are halfway between the lower and upper boundaries of each class. For the frequency distributions shown in Table 2.8, the class midpoints are $15, $25, $35, $45, $55, $65, $75, $85 and $95. Note that well-chosen class intervals lead to class midpoints that are simple to read and interpret, as in this example.

If the data you have collected do not contain a large number of values, different sets of class intervals can create different impressions of the data. Such perceived changes will diminish as you collect more data. Likewise, choosing different lower and upper class boundaries can also affect impressions.

EXAMPLE 2.2

Frequency Distributions of the One-Year Return Percentages for Growth and Value Funds

As a member of the company task force in The Choice *Is* Yours scenario (see page 32), you are examining the sample of 407 retirement funds stored in Retirement Funds . You want to compare the numerical variable 1YrReturn%, the one-year percentage return of a fund, for the two subgroups that are defined by the categorical variable Type (Growth and Value). You construct separate frequency distributions for the growth funds and the value funds.

SOLUTION The one-year percentage returns for both the growth and value funds are concentrated between 5 and 15 (see Table 2.9).

TABLE 2.9
Frequency Distributions of the One-Year Return Percentage for Growth and Value Funds

One-Year Return Percentage	Growth Frequency	Value Frequency
−15 but less than −10	3	1
−10 but less than −5	2	3
−5 but less than 0	20	5
0 but less than 5	55	21
5 but less than 10	96	49
10 but less than 15	76	55
15 but less than 20	16	4
20 but less than 25	1	0
Total	269	138

In the solution for Example 2.2, the total frequency is different for each group (269 and 138). When such totals differ among the groups being compared, you cannot compare the distributions directly as was done in Table 2.8 because of the chance that the table will be misinterpreted. For example, the frequencies for the class interval "−5 but less than 0" for growth and "0 but less than 5" for value look similar—20 and 21—but represent two very different parts of a whole: 20 out of 269 and 21 out of 138 or 7.43% and 15.22%, respectively. When the total frequency differs among the groups being compared, you construct either a relative frequency distribution or a percentage distribution.

Classes and Excel Bins

Microsoft Excel creates distribution tables using *bins* rather than classes. A **bin** is a range of values defined by a bin number, the upper boundary of the range. Unlike a class, the lower boundary is not explicitly stated but is deduced by the bin number that defines the preceding bin. Consider the bins defined by the bin numbers 4.99, 9.99, and 14.99. The first bin represents all values up to 4.99, the second bin all values greater than 4.99 (the preceding bin number) through 9.99, and the third bin all values greater than 9.99 (the preceding bin number) through 14.99.

Note that when using bins, the lower boundary of the first bin will always be negative infinity, as that bin has no explicit lower boundary. That makes the first Excel bin always much larger than the rest of the bins and violates the rule having equal-sized classes. When you translate classes to bins to make use of certain Excel features, you must include an extra bin number as the first bin number. This extra bin number will always be a value slightly less than the lower boundary of your first class.

You translate your classes into a set of bin numbers that you enter into a worksheet column in ascending order. Tables 2.8 through 2.12 use classes stated in the form "*valueA* but less than *valueB*." For such classes, you create a set of bin numbers that are slightly lower than each *valueB* to approximate each class. For example, you translate the Table 2.9 classes on page 40 as the set of bin numbers −15.01 (the "extra" first bin number that is slightly lower than −15, the lower boundary value of the first class), −10.01 (slightly less than −10, the *valueB* of the first class), −5.01, −0.01, 4.99, 9.99, 14.99, 19.99, and 24.99 (slightly less than 25, the *valueB* of the eighth class).

For classes stated in the form "all values from *valueA* to *valueB*," you can approximate classes by choosing a bin number slightly more than each *valueB*. For example, you can translate the classes stated as 0.0 through 4.9, 5.0 through 9.9, 10.0 through 14.9, and 15.0 through 19.9, as the bin numbers: −0.01 (the extra first bin number), 4.99 (slightly more than 4.9), 9.99, 14.99, and 19.99 (slightly more than 19.9).

The Relative Frequency Distribution and the Percentage Distribution

Relative frequency and percentage distributions present tallies in ways other than as frequencies. A **relative frequency distribution** presents the relative frequency, or proportion, of the total for each group that each class represents. A **percentage distribution** presents the percentage of the total for each group that each class represents. When you compare two or more groups, knowing the proportion (or percentage) of the total for each group better facilitates comparisons than a table of frequencies for each group would. For example, for comparing meal costs, using Table 2.10 is better than using Table 2.8 on page 39, which displays frequencies.

TABLE 2.10
Relative Frequency Distributions and Percentage Distributions of the Meal Costs at Center City and Metro Area Restaurants

| | CENTER CITY | | METRO AREA | |
| | Relative | | Relative | |
MEAL COST ($)	Frequency	Percentage	Frequency	Percentage
10 but less than 20	0.00	0%	0.02	2%
20 but less than 30	0.12	12%	0.28	28%
30 but less than 40	0.10	10%	0.24	24%
40 but less than 50	0.18	18%	0.20	20%
50 but less than 60	0.18	18%	0.20	20%
60 but less than 70	0.20	20%	0.06	6%
70 but less than 80	0.12	12%	0.00	0%
80 but less than 90	0.04	4%	0.00	0%
90 but less than 100	0.06	6%	0.00	0%
Total	1.00	100.0%	1.00	100.0%

studentTIP

The total of the relative frequency column must always be 1.00. The total of the percentage column must always be 100.

The **proportion**, or **relative frequency**, in each group is equal to the number of *values* in each class divided by the total number of values. The percentage in each group is its proportion multiplied by 100%.

COMPUTING THE PROPORTION OR RELATIVE FREQUENCY

The proportion, or relative frequency, is the number of *values* in each class divided by the total number of values:

$$\text{Proportion} = \text{relative frequency} = \frac{\text{number of values in each class}}{\text{total number of values}} \qquad (2.2)$$

If there are 80 values and the frequency in a certain class is 20, the proportion of values in that class is

$$\frac{20}{80} = 0.25$$

and the percentage is

$$0.25 \times 100\% = 25\%$$

You construct a relative frequency distribution by first determining the relative frequency in each class. For example, in Table 2.8 on page 39, there are 50 center city restaurants, and the cost per meal at 9 of these restaurants is between $50 and $60. Therefore, as shown in Table 2.10, the proportion (or relative frequency) of meals that cost between $50 and $60 at center city restaurants is

$$\frac{9}{50} = 0.18$$

You construct a percentage distribution by multiplying each proportion (or relative frequency) by 100%. Thus, the proportion of meals at center city restaurants that cost between $50 and $60 is 9 divided by 50, or 0.18, and the percentage is 18%. Table 2.10 on page 41 presents the relative frequency distribution and percentage distribution of the cost of meals at center city and metro area restaurants. From Table 2.10, you conclude that meal cost is higher at

---

EXAMPLE 2.3

Relative Frequency Distributions and Percentage Distributions of the One-Year Return Percentage for Growth and Value Funds

As a member of the company task force in The Choice *Is* Yours scenario (see page 32), you want to compare the one-year return percentages for the growth and value retirement funds. You construct relative frequency distributions and percentage distributions for these funds.

SOLUTION From Table 2.11, you conclude that the one-year return percentage for the growth funds is lower than the one-year return percentage for the value funds. For example, 7.43% of the growth funds have returns between −5 and 0, while 3.62% of the value funds have returns between −5 and 0. Of the growth funds, 28.25% have returns between 10 and 15 as compared to 39.86% of the value funds.

TABLE 2.11
Relative Frequency Distributions and Percentage Distributions of the One-Year Return Percentage for Growth and Value Funds

ONE-YEAR RETURN PERCENTAGE	GROWTH Relative Frequency	GROWTH Percentage	VALUE Relative Frequency	VALUE Percentage
−15 but less than −10	0.0112	1.12%	0.0072	0.72%
−10 but less than −5	0.0074	0.74%	0.0217	2.17%
−5 but less than 0	0.0743	7.43%	0.0362	3.62%
0 but less than 5	0.2045	20.45%	0.1522	15.22%
5 but less than 10	0.3569	35.69%	0.3551	35.51%
10 but less than 15	0.2825	28.25%	0.3986	39.86%
15 but less than 20	0.0595	5.95%	0.0290	2.90%
20 but less than 25	0.0037	0.37%	0.0000	0.00%
Total	1.0000	100.00%	1.0000	100.00%

center city restaurants than at metro area restaurants. You note that 20% of the center city restaurant meals cost between $60 and $70 as compared to 6% of the metro area restaurant meals and that 10% of the center city restaurant meals cost between $30 and $40 as compared to 24% of the metro area restaurant meals.

The Cumulative Distribution

The **cumulative percentage distribution** provides a way of presenting information about the percentage of values that are less than a specific amount. You use a percentage distribution as the basis to construct a cumulative percentage distribution.

For example, you might want to know what percentage of the center city restaurant meals cost less than $40 or what percentage cost less than $50. Starting with the Table 2.10 meal cost percentage distribution for center city restaurants on page 41, you combine the percentages of individual class intervals to form the cumulative percentage distribution. Table 2.12 presents the necessary calculations. From this table, you see that none (0%) of the meals cost less than $20, 12% of meals cost less than $30, 22% of meals cost less than $40 (because 10% of the meals cost between $30 and $40), and so on, until all 100% of the meals cost less than $100.

TABLE 2.12
Developing the Cumulative Percentage Distribution for Center City Restaurant Meal Costs

From Table 2.10:		Percentage of Meal Costs That Are Less Than the Class Interval Lower Boundary
Class Interval	**Percentage**	
20 but less than 30	12%	0 (there are no meals that cost less than 20)
30 but less than 40	10%	12% = 0 + 12
40 but less than 50	18%	22% = 12 + 10
50 but less than 60	18%	40% = 12 + 10 + 18
60 but less than 70	20%	58% = 12 + 10 + 18 + 18
70 but less than 80	12%	78% = 12 + 10 + 18 + 18 + 20
80 but less than 90	4%	90% = 12 + 10 + 18 + 18 + 20 + 12
90 but less than 100	6%	94% = 12 + 10 + 18 + 18 + 20 + 12 + 4
100 but less than 110	0%	100% = 12 + 10 + 18 + 18 + 20 + 12 + 4 + 6

Table 2.13 is the cumulative percentage distribution for meal costs that uses cumulative calculations for the center city restaurants (shown in Table 2.12) as well as cumulative calculations for the metro area restaurants (which are not shown). The cumulative distribution shows that the cost of metro area restaurant meals is lower than the cost of meals in center city restaurants. This distribution shows that 54% of the metro area restaurant meals cost less than $40 as compared to 22% of the meals at center city restaurants; 74% of the metro area restaurant meals cost less than $50, but only 40% of the center city restaurant meals do; and 94% of the metro area restaurant meals cost less than $60 as compared to 58% of such meals at the center city restaurants.

Unlike in other distributions, the rows of a cumulative distribution do not correspond to class intervals. (Recall that class intervals are mutually *exclusive*. The rows of cumulative distributions are not: The next row "down" *includes* all of the rows above it.) To identify a row, you use the lower class boundaries from the class intervals of the percentage distribution as is done in Table 2.13.

TABLE 2.13
Cumulative Percentage Distributions of the Meal Costs for Center City and Metro Area Restaurants

Meal Cost ($)	Percentage of Center City Restaurants Meals That Cost Less Than Indicated Amount	Percentage of Metro Area Restaurants Meals That Cost Less Than Indicated Amount
10	0	0
20	0	2
30	12	30
40	22	54
50	40	74
60	58	94
70	78	100
80	90	100
90	94	100
100	100	100

EXAMPLE 2.4

Cumulative Percentage Distributions of the One-Year Return Percentage for Growth and Value Funds

As a member of the company task force in The Choice *Is* Yours scenario (see page 32), you want to continue comparing the one-year return percentages for the growth and value retirement funds. You construct cumulative percentage distributions for the growth and value funds.

SOLUTION The cumulative distribution in Table 2.14 indicates that returns are lower for the growth funds than for the value funds. The table shows that 29.74% of the growth funds and 21.74% of the value funds have returns below 5%. The table also reveals that 65.43% of the growth funds have returns below 10 as compared to 57.25% of the value funds.

TABLE 2.14
Cumulative Percentage Distributions of the One-Year Return Percentages for Growth and Value Funds

One-Year Return Percentages	Growth Percentage Less Than Indicated Value	Value Percentage Less Than Indicated Value
−15	0.00%	0.00%
−10	1.12%	0.72%
−5	1.86%	2.90%
0	9.29%	6.52%
5	29.74%	21.74%
10	65.43%	57.25%
15	93.68%	97.10%
20	99.63%	100.00%
25	100.00%	100.00%

PROBLEMS FOR SECTION 2.2

LEARNING THE BASICS

2.11 Construct an ordered array, given the following data from a sample of $n = 7$ midterm exam scores in accounting:

68 94 63 75 71 88 64

2.12 Construct an ordered array, given the following data from a sample of midterm exam scores in marketing:

88 78 78 73 91 78 85

2.13 In December 2014, the National Small Business Association (NSBA) surveyed small business owners, both members and nonmembers of the NSBA, representing every industry in the nation. NSBA asked a host of questions on cybersecurity and found that half of all small businesses report they have been the victim of a cyberattack. Not only has the cost of dealing with these attacks skyrocketed, cyberattacks are taking more time to resolve today. The following frequency distribution summarizes the average time needed by small business owners to resolve a cyberattack on their businesses.

Average Time to Resolve Cyberattacks	Frequency
Less than 1 day	101
Between 1 and less than 3 days	115
Between 3 and less than 7 days	47
Between 7 and less than 14 days	30
14 days or more	44

Source: *NSBA 2014 Year-End Economic Report*, available at **bit.ly/1EUxx63**.

a. What percentage of small businesses took less than 3 days, on average, to resolve cyberattacks?
b. What percentage of small businesses took between 1 and less than 14 days, on average, to resolve cyberattacks?
c. What percentage of small businesses took 3 or more days, on average, to resolve cyberattacks?

2.14 Data were collected on the Facebook website about the most "liked" fast-food brands. The data values (the number of "likes" for each fast-food brand) for the brands named ranged from 1.0 million to 29.2 million.
a. If these values are grouped into six class intervals, indicate the class boundaries.
b. What class interval width did you choose?
c. What are the six class midpoints?

APPLYING THE CONCEPTS

2.15 The file NBACost contains the total cost ($) for four average-priced tickets, two beers, four soft drinks, four hot dogs, two game programs, two adult-sized caps, and one parking space at each of the 30 National Basketball Association arenas during the 2014–2015 season. These costs were:

```
246.39 444.16 404.60 212.40 477.32 271.74 312.20 322.50
261.20 336.52 369.86 232.44 435.72 541.00 223.92 468.20
325.85 281.06 221.80 676.42 295.40 263.10 278.90 341.90
317.08 280.28 340.60 289.71 275.74 258.78
```

Source: Data extracted from Team Marketing Report, *2014–15 NBA Fan Cost Index*, available at **bit.ly/1JEjYbO**.

a. Organize these costs as an ordered array.
b. Construct a frequency distribution and a percentage distribution for these costs.
c. Around which class grouping, if any, are the costs of attending a basketball game concentrated? Explain.

 2.16 The file Utility contains the following data about the cost of electricity (in $) during July 2015 for a random sample of 50 one-bedroom apartments in a large city.

```
 96  171  202  178  147  102  153  197  127   82
157  185   90  116  172  111  148  213  130  165
141  149  206  175  123  128  144  168  109  167
 95  163  150  154  130  143  187  166  139  149
108  119  183  151  114  135  191  137  129  158
```

a. Construct a frequency distribution and a percentage distribution that have class intervals with the upper class boundaries $99, $119, and so on.
b. Construct a cumulative percentage distribution.
c. Around what amount does the monthly electricity cost seem to be concentrated?

2.17 How much time do commuters living in or near cities spend waiting in traffic, and how much does this waiting cost them per year? The file Congestion contains the time spent waiting in traffic and the yearly cost associated with that waiting for commuters in 31 U.S. cities. (Source: Data extracted from "The High Cost of Congestion," *Time*, October 17, 2011, p. 18.) For both the time spent waiting in traffic and the yearly cost associated with that waiting data,
a. Construct a frequency distribution and a percentage distribution.
b. Construct a cumulative percentage distribution.
c. What conclusions can you reach concerning the time Americans living in or near cities spend sitting in traffic?
d. What conclusions can you reach concerning the cost of waiting in traffic per year?

2.18 How do the average credit scores of people living in different American cities differ? The data in Credit Scores is an ordered array of the average credit scores of 143 American cities. (Data extracted from **bit.ly/1Pb7V4m**.)
a. Construct a frequency distribution and a percentage distribution.
b. Construct a cumulative percentage distribution.
c. What conclusions can you reach concerning the average credit scores of people living in different American cities?

2.19 One operation of a mill is to cut pieces of steel into parts that will later be used as the frame for front seats in an automobile. The steel is cut with a diamond saw and requires the resulting parts to be within ±0.005 inch of the length specified by the automobile company. Data are collected from a sample of 100 steel parts and stored in Steel. The measurement reported is the difference in inches between the actual length of the steel part, as measured by a laser measurement device, and the specified length of the steel part. For example, the first value, −0.002, represents a steel part that is 0.002 inch shorter than the specified length.
a. Construct a frequency distribution and a percentage distribution.
b. Construct a cumulative percentage distribution.
c. Is the steel mill doing a good job meeting the requirements set by the automobile company? Explain.

2.20 A manufacturing company produces steel housings for electrical equipment. The main component of the housing is a steel trough that is made out of a 14-gauge steel coil. It is produced using a 250-ton progressive punch press with a wipe-down operation that puts two 90-degree forms in the flat steel to make the trough. The distance from one side of the form to the other is critical because of weatherproofing in outdoor applications. The company requires that the width of the trough be between 8.31 inches and 8.61 inches. The widths of the troughs, in inches, collected from a sample of 49 troughs and stored in Trough, are:

```
8.312  8.343  8.317  8.383  8.348  8.410  8.351  8.373
8.481  8.422  8.476  8.382  8.484  8.403  8.414  8.419
8.385  8.465  8.498  8.447  8.436  8.413  8.489  8.414
8.481  8.415  8.479  8.429  8.458  8.462  8.460  8.444
8.429  8.460  8.412  8.420  8.410  8.405  8.323  8.420
8.396  8.447  8.405  8.439  8.411  8.427  8.420  8.498
8.409
```

a. Construct a frequency distribution and a percentage distribution.
b. Construct a cumulative percentage distribution.

c. What can you conclude about the number of troughs that will meet the company's requirements of troughs being between 8.31 and 8.61 inches wide?

2.21 The manufacturing company in Problem 2.20 also produces electric insulators. If the insulators break when in use, a short circuit is likely to occur. To test the strength of the insulators, destructive testing in high-powered labs is carried out to determine how much *force* is required to break the insulators. Force is measured by observing how many pounds must be applied to the insulator before it breaks. The force measurements, collected from a sample of 30 insulators and stored in Force, are:

1,870 1,728 1,656 1,610 1,634 1,784 1,522 1,696
1,592 1,662 1,866 1,764 1,734 1,662 1,734 1,774
1,550 1,756 1,762 1,866 1,820 1,744 1,788 1,688
1,810 1,752 1,680 1,810 1,652 1,736

a. Construct a frequency distribution and a percentage distribution.
b. Construct a cumulative percentage distribution.
c. What can you conclude about the strength of the insulators if the company requires a force measurement of at least 1,500 pounds before the insulator breaks?

2.22 The file Bulbs contains the life (in hours) of a sample of forty 20-watt compact fluorescent light bulbs produced by Manufacturer A and a sample of forty 20-watt compact fluorescent light bulbs produced by Manufacturer B.

a. Construct a frequency distribution and a percentage distribution for each manufacturer, using the following class interval widths for each distribution:

Manufacturer A: 6,500 but less than 7,500; 7,500 but less than 8,500; and so on.
Manufacturer B: 7,500 but less than 8,500; 8,500 but less than 9,500; and so on.

b. Construct cumulative percentage distributions.
c. Which bulbs have a longer life—those from Manufacturer A or Manufacturer B? Explain.

2.23 The file Drink contains the following data for the amount of soft drink (in liters) in a sample of fifty 2-liter bottles:

2.109 2.086 2.066 2.075 2.065 2.057 2.052 2.044 2.036 2.038
2.031 2.029 2.025 2.029 2.023 2.020 2.015 2.014 2.013 2.014
2.012 2.012 2.012 2.010 2.005 2.003 1.999 1.996 1.997 1.992
1.994 1.986 1.984 1.981 1.973 1.975 1.971 1.969 1.966 1.967
1.963 1.957 1.951 1.951 1.947 1.941 1.941 1.938 1.908 1.894

a. Construct a cumulative percentage distribution.
b. On the basis of the results of (a), does the amount of soft drink filled in the bottles concentrate around specific values?

2.3 Visualizing Categorical Variables

Visualizing categorical variables involves making choices about how you seek to present your data. When you visualize a single categorical variable, you must think about what you want to highlight about your data and whether your data are concentrated in only a few of your categories. To highlight how categories directly compare to each other, you use a bar chart. To highlight how categories form parts of a whole, you use a pie or doughnut chart. (Figure 2.1 allows you to compare a bar and pie chart for the same data.) To present data that are concentrated in only a few of your categories, you use a Pareto chart.

You can visualize two categorical variables together, again thinking about what you want to highlight. To highlight direct comparisons, you use a side-by-side chart. To highlight how parts form a whole, you use a doughnut chart.

The Bar Chart

A **bar chart** visualizes a categorical variable as a series of bars, with each bar representing the tallies for a single category. In a bar chart, the length of each bar represents either the frequency or percentage of values for a category and each bar is separated by space, called a gap.

The left illustration in Figure 2.1 displays the bar chart for the Table 2.1 summary table on page 34 that tallies responses to a recent survey that asked people how they paid for purchases and other transactions. Reviewing Figure 2.1, you see that respondents are most likely to pay for purchases with cash followed by debit card. Very few people paid by check or electronically.

FIGURE 2.1

Excel bar chart (left) and pie chart (right) for how people paid for purchases and other transactions

---

Bar Chart of Levels of Risk of Retirement Funds

As a member of the company task force in The Choice Is Yours scenario (see page 32), you want to examine how the risk categories in Table 2.2 on page 34 directly compare to each other.

SOLUTION You construct the bar chart shown in Figure 2.2. You see that average risk is the largest category, followed by high risk. Very few of the funds have low risk.

FIGURE 2.2

Excel bar chart of the levels of risk of retirement funds

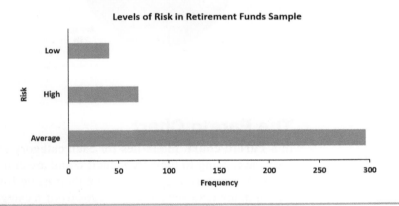

The Pie Chart and the Doughnut Chart

A **pie chart** and a **doughnut chart** both use parts of a circle to represent the tallies of each category of a categorical variable. The size of each part, or slice, varies according to the percentage in each category. To represent a category as a slice, you multiply the percentage of the whole that the category represents by 360 (the number of degrees in a circle) to get the size of the slice. For example, for the Table 2.1 how people pay data on page 34, the category cash represents 40% of the sample respondents. For this category, you would draw a slice that is 144 degrees (40 × 360). The category debit card represents 25% and for this category, you would draw a slice that is 90 degrees (25 × 360). (The Figure 2.1 pie chart shows these slices and the slices for the other Table 2.4 categories.)

Pie and doughnut charts differ only in that the latter has a center "hole," much like the hole found in a real doughnut, as shown in Figure 2.3. No consensus exists about which of these two types is the better choice. Most would agree that many pie charts presented together provide an overwhelming visual experience that should be avoided (see reference 2). In cases where you need to display multiple charts together, you should use doughnut charts. Doughnut charts can also be used to visualize two variables, as explained later in this section.

Multiple doughnut charts presented together are often seen in dashboards, discussed in Chapter 17.

While some suggest that neither pie nor doughnut charts should ever be used, all agree that pie and doughnut variations such as "3D" charts and "exploded" charts, in which one or more slices are pulled away from the center, introduce visual distortions and should be avoided. Be aware that 3D and exploded charts are among the wrong-headed chart types you can create using Excel.

EXAMPLE 2.6

Pie Chart and Doughnut Chart of Levels of Risk of Retirement Funds

As a member of the company task force in The Choice *Is* Yours scenario (see page 32), you want to examine how the risk categories in Table 2.2 on page 34 form parts of a whole.

SOLUTION You construct the pie or doughnut charts shown in Figure 2.3. You see that more than 70% of the funds are average risk, about 17% are high risk, and only about 10% are low risk.

FIGURE 2.3
Excel pie chart and doughnut chart of the risk of retirement funds

---

The Pareto Chart

In a **Pareto chart**, the tallies for each category are plotted as vertical bars in descending order, according to their frequencies, and are combined with a cumulative percentage line on the same chart. Pareto charts get their name from the **Pareto principle**, the observation that in many data sets, a few categories of a categorical variable represent the majority of the data, while many other categories represent a relatively small, or trivial, amount of the data.

Pareto charts help you to visually identify the "vital few" categories from the "trivial many" categories so that you can focus on the important categories. Pareto charts are also powerful tools for prioritizing improvement efforts, such as when data are collected that identify defective or nonconforming items.

The informal "80/20" rule, which states that often 80% of results are from 20% of some thing, such as "80% of the work is done by 20% of the employees," derives from the Pareto principle.

A Pareto chart presents the bars vertically, along with a cumulative percentage line. The cumulative line is plotted at the midpoint of each category, at a height equal to the cumulative percentage. In order for a Pareto chart to include all categories, even those with few defects, in some situations, you need to include a category labeled Other or Miscellaneous. If you include such a category, you place the bar that represents that category at the far end (to the right) of the *X* axis.

Using Pareto charts can be an effective way to visualize data for many studies that seek causes for an observed phenomenon. For example, consider a bank study team that wants to enhance the user experience of automated teller machines (ATMs). During this study, the team identifies incomplete ATM transactions as a significant issue and decides to collect data about the causes of such transactions. Using the bank's own processing systems as a primary data source, causes of incomplete transactions are collected, stored in ATM Transactions , and then organized in the Table 2.15 summary table.

TABLE 2.15
Summary Table of
Causes of Incomplete
ATM Transactions

Cause	Frequency	Percentage
ATM malfunctions	32	4.42%
ATM out of cash	28	3.87%
Invalid amount requested	23	3.18%
Lack of funds in account	19	2.62%
Card unreadable	234	32.32%
Warped card jammed	365	50.41%
Wrong keystroke	23	3.18%
Total	724	100.00%

Source: Data extracted from A. Bhalla, "Don't Misuse the Pareto Principle," *Six Sigma Forum Magazine*, May 2009, pp. 15–18.

To separate out the "vital few" causes from the "trivial many" causes, the bank study team creates the Table 2.16 summary table, in which the causes of incomplete transactions appear in descending order by frequency, as required for constructing a Pareto chart. The table includes the percentages and cumulative percentages for the reordered causes, which the team then uses to construct the Pareto chart shown in Figure 2.4. In Figure 2.4, the vertical axis on the left represents the percentage due to each cause and the vertical axis on the right represents the cumulative percentage.

TABLE 2.16
Ordered Summary
Table of Causes of
Incomplete ATM
Transactions

Cause	Frequency	Percentage	Cumulative Percentage
Warped card jammed	365	50.41%	50.41%
Card unreadable	234	32.32%	82.73%
ATM malfunctions	32	4.42%	87.15%
ATM out of cash	28	3.87%	91.02%
Invalid amount requested	23	3.18%	94.20%
Wrong keystroke	23	3.18%	97.38%
Lack of funds in account	19	2.62%	100.00%
Total	724	100.00%	

FIGURE 2.4
Excel Pareto chart
of incomplete ATM
transactions

Because the categories in a Pareto chart are ordered by decreasing frequency of occurrence, the team can quickly see which causes contribute the most to the problem of incomplete transactions. (Those causes would be the "vital few," and figuring out ways to avoid such causes would be, presumably, a starting point for improving the user experience of ATMs.) By following the cumulative percentage line in Figure 2.4, you see that the first two causes, warped card jammed (50.44%) and card unreadable (32.3%), account for 82.7% of the incomplete transactions. Attempts to reduce incomplete ATM transactions due to warped or unreadable cards should produce the greatest payoff.

EXAMPLE 2.7

Pareto Chart of the Main Reason for How People Pay for Purchases and Other Transactions

Construct a Pareto chart from Table 2.1 (see page 34), which summarizes how people pay for purchases and other transactions.

SOLUTION First, create a new table from Table 2.1 in which the categories are ordered by descending frequency and columns for percentages and cumulative percentages for the ordered categories are included (not shown). From that table, create the Pareto chart in Figure 2.5. From Figure 2.5, you observe that cash and debit card account for nearly two-thirds of the responses and that those two categories combined with credit card account for 82% of the responses.

FIGURE 2.5

Excel Pareto chart of how people pay for purchases and other transactions

Visualizing Two Categorical Variables

As when you visualize a single variable, visualizing two categorical variables requires making a choice about what you seek to highlight. To highlight how categories directly compare to each other, you use a side-by-side chart. To highlight how categories form parts of a whole, you use a doughnut chart.

The side-by-side chart   A **side-by-side chart** visualizes two categorical variables by showing the bars that represent the categories of one variable set grouped by the categories of the second variable. For example, the Figure 2.6 side-by-side chart visualizes the data for the levels of risk for growth and value funds shown in Table 2.3 on page 35. In Figure 2.6, you see that a substantial portion of the growth funds and the value funds have average risk. More of the growth funds have high risk than low risk, while more of the value funds have low risk than high risk.

The doughnut chart   Doughnut charts can visualize two as well as a single categorical variable. When visualizing two variables, the doughnut chart appears as two concentric rings, one inside the other, each ring containing the categories of one variable. In Figure 2.6, the doughnut chart of fund type and risk level highlights that the proportion of funds with average risk (darkest color) is approximately the same for growth and value funds, even as the ratio of high risk to low risk funds for both greatly differ.

FIGURE 2.6

Side-by-side bar chart and doughnut chart of fund type and risk level

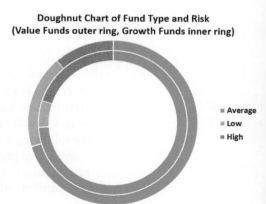

PROBLEMS FOR SECTION 2.3

APPLYING THE CONCEPTS

2.24 An online survey of CFA Institute members was conducted to gather feedback on market sentiment, performance, and market integrity issues in October 2014. Members were asked to indicate the most needed action to improve investor trust and market integrity. The survey results were as follows:

Most Needed Action	Percentage
Improved regulation and oversight of global systemic risk	28%
Improved transparency of financial reporting and other corporate disclosures	21%
Improved corporate governance practices	15%
Improved enforcement of existing laws and regulations	14%
Improved market trading rules on transparency and frequency of trades	15%
Improved auditing practices and standards	7%

Source: Data extracted from *Global Market Sentiment Survey 2015*, CFA Institute, 2014.

a. Construct a bar chart, a pie or doughnut chart, and a Pareto chart.
b. Which graphical method do you think is best for portraying these data?
c. What conclusions can you reach concerning the most needed action to improve investor trust and market integrity?

2.25 How much time doing what activities do college students spend using their cell phones? A 2014 Baylor University study showed college students spend an average of 9 hours a day using their cell phones for the following activities:

Cell Phone Activity	Percentage
Banking	2%
Checking Date and Time	8%
Listening to Music	12%
Playing Games	4%
Reading	3%
Sending Emails	9%
Social Media	18%
Surfing the Internet	7%
Taking Photos	3%
Talking	6%
Texting	18%
YouTube	2%
Other	8%

Source: Data extracted from "Cellphone Addiction Is 'an Increasingly Realistic Possibility,' Baylor Study of College Students Reveals," **bit.ly/1Ey3lKB**.

(Table data stored in Cell Phone Activity).
a. Construct a bar chart, a pie or doughnut chart, and a Pareto chart.
b. Which graphical method do you think is best for portraying these data?

c. What conclusions can you reach concerning how college students spend their time using cellphones?

2.26 The Energy Information Administration reported the following sources of electricity in the United States in 2013:

Source of Electricity	Percentage
Coal	39%
Hydro and renewables	13%
Natural gas	27%
Nuclear power	19%
Other	2%

Source: Energy Information Administration, 2014.

a. Construct a Pareto chart.
b. What percentage of power is derived from coal, nuclear power, or natural gas?
c. Construct a pie chart.
d. For these data, do you prefer using a Pareto chart or a pie chart? Why?

2.27 The **Edmunds.com** NHTSA Complaints Activity Report contains consumer vehicle complaint submissions by automaker, brand, and category (data extracted from **edmu.in/Ybmpuz**.) The following tables, stored in Automaker1 and Automaker2 , represent complaints received by automaker and complaints received by category for January 2013.

Automaker	Number
American Honda	169
Chrysler LLC	439
Ford Motor Company	440
General Motors	551
Nissan Motors Corporation	467
Toyota Motor Sales	332
Other	516

a. Construct a bar chart and a pie chart for the complaints received by automaker.
b. Which graphical method do you think is best for portraying these data?

Category	Number
Airbags and seatbelts	201
Body and glass	182
Brakes	63
Fuel/emission/exhaust system	240
Interior electronics/hardware	279
Powertrain	1,148
Steering	397
Tires and wheels	71

c. Construct a Pareto chart for the categories of complaints.
d. Discuss the "vital few" and "trivial many" reasons for the categories of complaints.

2.28 The following table indicates the percentage of residential electricity consumption in the United States, in a recent year organized by type of use.

Type of Use	Percentage %
Cooking	2%
Cooling	15%
Electronics	9%
Heating	15%
Lighting	13%
Refrigeration	10%
Water heating	10%
Wet cleaning	3%
Other	23%

Source: Department of Energy.

a. Construct a bar chart, a pie chart, and a Pareto chart.
b. Which graphical method do you think is best for portraying these data?
c. What conclusions can you reach concerning residential electricity consumption in the United States?

2.29 Visier's 2014 Survey of Employers explores current workforce analytics and planning practices, investments, and future plans. U.S.-based employers were asked what they see as the most common technical barrier to workforce analytics. The responses, stored in Barriers , were as follows:

Barriers	Frequency
Data must be integrated from multiple sources	68
Lack of automation/repeatable process	51
Metrics need to be identified or defined	45
Production is cumbersome	42
Data quality is not reliable	36
Sharing findings is challenging	21
Analytic tools are too complex	17
Ensuring security and integrity of workforce data	17
Other	3

Source: Data extracted from *The State of Workforce Analytics and Planning, 2014 Survey Report*, available at **bit.ly/1zuM99Z**.

a. Construct a bar chart and a pie chart.
b. What conclusions can you reach concerning technical barriers to workforce analytics?

2.30 For the companies in which they invest, pension fund managers seek to ensure the independence of the boards of directors. For one company, fund managers determine that the board had 7 inside directors, 5 independent (outside) directors, and 7 directors that the company labeled as independent, but whom officials consider to be insiders. Seeking more independence of this board, the fund managers ask for change. The company responds and fund managers evaluate the company's new board as having 5 inside directors, 10 independent directors, and 6 directors improperly labeled as independent.

Examine the two charts stored in BoardAnalysis that are based on these findings. If you were a corporate affairs officer at the company, would you choose Chart1 or Chart2 to highlight the changes in the composition of the board? If you were one of the pension fund managers seeking to ensure an independent board of directors, which chart would you choose? Explain your answer.

2.31 A study of selected Kickstarter projects showed that overall a majority were successful, achieving their goal and raising, at a minimum, the targeted amounts. In an effort to identify project types that influence success, selected projects were subdivided into project categories (Film & Video, Games, Music, and Technology). The results are as follows:

CATEGORY	OUTCOME		Total
	Successful	Not Successful	
Film & Video	17,024	26,857	43,881
Games	5,105	10,075	15,180
Music	19,275	17,050	36,325
Technology	2,556	8,770	11,326
Total	43,960	62,752	106,712

Source: **Kickstarter.com, kickstarter.com/help/stats**.

a. Construct a side-by-side bar chart and a doughnut chart of project outcome and category.
b. What conclusions concerning the pattern of successful Kickstarter projects can you reach?

2.32 Do social recommendations increase ad effectiveness? A study of online video viewers compared viewers who arrived at an advertising video for a particular brand by following a social media recommendation link to viewers who arrived at the same video by web browsing. Data were collected on whether the viewer could correctly recall the brand being advertised after seeing the video. The results were as follows:

ARRIVAL METHOD	CORRECTLY RECALLED THE BRAND	
	Yes	No
Recommendation	407	150
Browsing	193	91

Source: Data extracted from "Social Ad Effectiveness: An Unruly White Paper," **www.unrulymedia.com**, January 2012, p. 3.

a. Construct a side-by-side bar chart and a doughnut chart of the arrival method and whether the brand was promptly recalled.
b. What do these results tell you about the arrival method and brand recall?

2.4 Visualizing Numerical Variables

You visualize the data for a numerical variable through a variety of techniques that show the distribution of values. These techniques include the stem-and-leaf display, the histogram, the percentage polygon, and the cumulative percentage polygon (ogive), all discussed in this section, as well the boxplot, which requires descriptive summary measures as explained in Section 3.3.

The Stem-and-Leaf Display

A **stem-and-leaf display** visualizes data by presenting the data as one or more row-wise *stems* that represent a range of values. In turn, each stem has one or more *leaves* that branch out to the right of their stem and represent the values found in that stem. For stems with more than one leaf, the leaves are arranged in ascending order.

Stem-and-leaf displays allow you to see how the data are distributed and where concentrations of data exist. Leaves typically present the last significant digit of each value, but sometimes you round values. For example, suppose you collect the following meal costs (in $) for 15 classmates who had lunch at a fast-food restaurant (stored in FastFood):

7.42 6.29 5.83 6.50 8.34 9.51 7.10 6.80 5.90 4.89 6.50 5.52 7.90 8.30 9.60

To construct the stem-and-leaf display, you use whole dollar amounts as the stems and round the cents to one decimal place to use as the leaves. For the first value, 7.42, the stem is 7 and its leaf is 4. For the second value, 6.29, the stem is 6 and its leaf is 3. The completed stem-and-leaf display for these data is

4	9
5	589
6	3558
7	149
8	33
9	56

studentTIP

A stem-and-leaf display turned sideways looks like a histogram.

EXAMPLE 2.8

Stem-and-Leaf Display of the One-Year Return Percentage for the Value Funds

As a member of the company task force in The Choice *Is* Yours scenario (see page 32), you want to study the past performance of the value funds. One measure of past performance is the numerical variable 1YrReturn%, the one-year return percentage. Using the data from the 138 value funds, you want to visualize this variable as a stem-and-leaf display.

SOLUTION Figure 2.7 illustrates the stem-and-leaf display of the one-year return percentage for value funds.

FIGURE 2.7

Excel stem-and-leaf display of the one-year return percentage for value funds

```
Stem-and-Leaf Plot of One-Year Return Percentage
for Value Funds
Stem unit: 1

  -13 8
  -12
  -11
  -10
   -9
   -8
   -7 5
   -6 1
   -5 8
   -4 0
   -3
   -2 7
   -1 73
   -0 5
    0 28
    1 02
    2 5
    3 123379
    4 00145688
    5 0022457
    6 4779
    7 01233489
    8 0023455667788
    9 0011222344678888999
   10 011345789
   11 000113445566788999
   12 12555577789999
   13 22335578
   14 133555
   15 01
   16 4
   17 8
```

▶ *(continued)*

From Figure 2.7, you observe that:

- the lowest one-year return was −13.79.
- the highest one-year return was 17.75.
- the one-year returns were concentrated between 8 and 12.
- very few of the one-year returns were above 14.
- the distribution of the one-year return appears to have more very low values than very high values.

The Histogram

A **histogram** visualizes data as a vertical bar chart in which each bar represents a class interval from a frequency or percentage distribution. In a histogram, you display the numerical variable along the horizontal (X) axis and use the vertical (Y) axis to represent either the frequency or the percentage of values per class interval. There are never any gaps between adjacent bars in a histogram.

Figure 2.8 visualizes the data of Table 2.8 on page 39, meal costs at center city and metro area restaurants, as a pair of frequency histograms. The histogram for center city restaurants shows that the cost of meals is concentrated between approximately $40 and $70. Eleven meals at center city restaurants cost $70 or more. The histogram for metro area restaurants shows that the cost of meals is concentrated between $20 and $60. Very few meals at metro area restaurants cost more than $60.

FIGURE 2.8
Excel frequency histograms for meal costs at center city and metro area restaurants

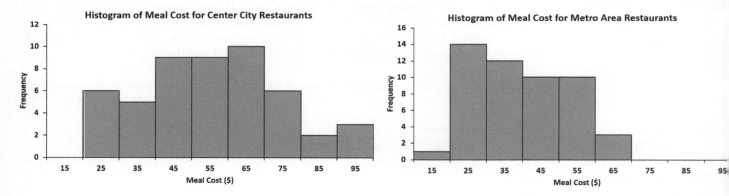

EXAMPLE 2.9

Histograms of the One-Year Return Percentages for the Growth and Value Funds

As a member of the company task force in The Choice *Is* Yours scenario (see page 32), you seek to compare the past performance of the growth funds and the value funds, using the one-year return percentage variable. Using the data from the sample of 407 funds, you construct histograms for the growth and the value funds to create a visual comparison.

SOLUTION Figure 2.9 on page 55 displays frequency histograms for the one-year return percentages for the growth and value funds.

Reviewing the histograms in Figure 2.9 leads you to conclude that the returns were lower for the growth funds than for value funds. The return for both the growth funds and the value funds is concentrated between 0 and 15, but the return for the value funds is more concentrated between 5 and 15 while the return for the growth funds is more concentrated between 0 and 15.

▶ *(continued)*

FIGURE 2.9

Excel frequency histograms for the one-year return percentages for the growth and value funds

The Percentage Polygon

When using a categorical variable to divide the data of a numerical variable into two or more groups, you visualize data by constructing a **percentage polygon**. This chart uses the midpoints of each class interval to represent the data of each class and then plots the midpoints, at their respective class percentages, as points on a line along the X axis. While you can construct two or more histograms, as was done in Figures 2.8 and 2.9, a percentage polygon allows you to make a direct comparison that is easier to interpret. (You cannot, of course, combine two histograms into one chart as bars from the two groups would overlap and obscure data.)

Figure 2.10 displays percentage polygons for the cost of meals at center city and metro area restaurants. You can make the same observations from this pair of charts as you made when examining the pair of histograms in Figure 2.8 on page 54. You again note that the center city meal cost is concentrated between $40 and $70 while the metro area meal cost is concentrated between $20 and $60. However, unlike the pair of histograms, the polygons allow you to more easily identify which class intervals have similar percentages for the two groups and which do not.

The polygons in Figure 2.10 have points whose values on the X axis represent the midpoint of the class interval. For example, look at the points plotted at X = 35 ($35). The point for meal costs at center city restaurants (the lower one) show that 10% of the meals cost between $30 and $40, while the point for the meal costs at metro area restaurants (the higher one) shows that 24% of meals at these restaurants cost between $30 and $40.

FIGURE 2.10

Excel percentage polygons of meal costs for center city and metro area restaurants

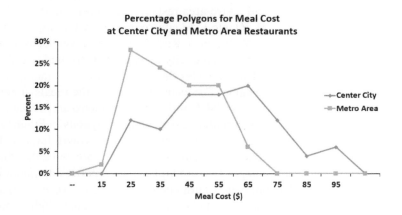

When you construct polygons or histograms, the vertical Y axis should include zero to avoid distorting the character of the data. The horizontal X axis does not need to show the zero point for the numerical variable, but a major portion of the axis should be devoted to the entire range of values for the variable.

EXAMPLE 2.10

Percentage Polygons of the One-Year Return Percentage for the Growth and Value Funds

As a member of the company task force in The Choice *Is* Yours scenario (see page 32), you seek to compare the past performance of the growth funds and the value funds using the one-year return percentage variable. Using the data from the sample of 407 funds, you construct percentage polygons for the growth and value funds to create a visual comparison.

SOLUTION Figure 2.11 displays percentage polygons of the one-year return percentage for the growth and value funds.

FIGURE 2.11
Excel percentage polygons of the one-year return percentages for the growth and value funds

Figure 2.11 shows that the value funds polygon is to the right of the growth funds polygon. This allows you to conclude that the one-year return percentage is higher for value funds than for growth funds. The polygons also show that the return for value funds is concentrated between 5 and 15, and the return for the growth funds is concentrated between 0 and 15.

The Cumulative Percentage Polygon (Ogive)

The **cumulative percentage polygon**, or **ogive**, uses the cumulative percentage distribution discussed in Section 2.2 to plot the cumulative percentages along the Y axis. Unlike the percentage polygon, the lower boundary of the class interval for the numerical variable are plotted, at their respective class percentages as points on a line along the X axis.

Figure 2.12 on page 57 shows cumulative percentage polygons of meal costs for center city and metro area restaurants. In this chart, the lower boundaries of the class intervals (10, 20, 30, 40, etc.) are approximated by the upper boundaries of the previous bins (9.99, 19.99, 29.99, 39.99, etc.). Reviewing the curves leads you to conclude that the curve of the cost of meals at the center city restaurants is located to the right of the curve for the metro area restaurants. This indicates that the center city restaurants have fewer meals that cost less than a particular value. For example, 40% of the meals at center city restaurants cost less than $50, as compared to 74% of the meals at metro area restaurants.

The cumulative percentage polygons in Figure 2.13 on page 57 show that the curve for the one-year return percentage for the growth funds is located slightly to the left of the curve for the value funds. This allows you to conclude that the growth funds have fewer one-year return percentages that are higher than a particular value. For example, 65.43% of the growth funds had one-year return percentages below 10, as compared to 57.25% of the value funds. You can conclude that, in general, the value funds slightly outperformed the growth funds in their one-year returns.

FIGURE 2.12
Excel cumulative percentage polygons of meal costs for center city and metro area restaurants

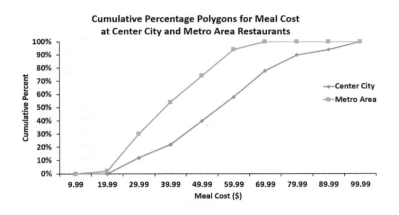

EXAMPLE 2.11

Cumulative Percentage Polygons of the One-Year Return Percentages for the Growth and Value Funds

As a member of the company task force in The Choice *Is* Yours scenario (see page 32), you seek to compare the past performance of the growth funds and the value funds using the one-year return percentage variable. Using the data from the sample of 407 funds, you construct cumulative percentage polygons for the growth and the value funds.

SOLUTION Figure 2.13 displays cumulative percentage polygons of the one-year return percentages for the growth and value funds.

FIGURE 2.13
Excel cumulative percentage polygons of the one-year return percentages for the growth and value funds

In Microsoft Excel, you approximate the lower boundary by using the upper boundary of the previous bin.

PROBLEMS FOR SECTION 2.4

LEARNING THE BASICS

2.33 Construct a stem-and-leaf display, given the following data from a sample of midterm exam scores in finance:

54 69 98 93 53 74

2.34 Construct an ordered array, given the following stem-and-leaf display from a sample of $n = 7$ midterm exam scores in information systems:

5	0
6	
7	446
8	19
9	2

APPLYING THE CONCEPTS

2.35 The following is a stem-and-leaf display representing the amount of gasoline purchased, in gallons (with leaves in tenths of gallons), for a sample of 25 cars that use a particular service station on the New Jersey Turnpike:

9	147
10	02238
11	125566777
12	223489
13	02

a. Construct an ordered array.
b. Which of these two displays seems to provide more information? Discuss.

c. What amount of gasoline (in gallons) is most likely to be purchased?

d. Is there a concentration of the purchase amounts in the center of the distribution?

✓ SELF TEST **2.36** The file **NBACost** contains the total cost (in $) for four average-priced tickets, two beers, four soft drinks, four hot dogs, two game programs, two adult-sized caps, and one parking space at each of the 30 National Basketball Association arenas during the 2014–2015 season. (Data extracted from Team Marketing Report, *2014–15 NBA Fan Cost Index,* available at **bit.ly/1JEjYbO.**)

a. Construct a stem-and-leaf display.

b. Around what value, if any, are the costs of attending a basketball game concentrated? Explain.

2.37 The file **Free Shipping** contains the minimum online order required to receive free shipping from 10 retailers. (Data extracted from E. Dwoskin, "That Free Shipping Is Going to Cost You," *The Wall Street Journal,* October 23, 2014, p. B1.)

a. Construct an ordered array.

b. Construct a stem-and-leaf display.

c. Does the ordered array or the stem-and-leaf display provide more information? Discuss.

d. Around what value, if any, is the minimum online order required to receive free shipping concentrated? Explain.

2.38 The file **Utility** contains the following data about the cost of electricity during July 2015 for a random sample of 50 one-bedroom apartments in a large city:

96	171	202	178	147	102	153	197	127	82
157	185	90	116	172	111	148	213	130	165
141	149	206	175	123	128	144	168	109	167
95	163	150	154	130	143	187	166	139	149
108	119	183	151	114	135	191	137	129	158

a. Construct a histogram and a percentage polygon.

b. Construct a cumulative percentage polygon.

c. Around what amount does the monthly electricity cost seem to be concentrated?

2.39 As player salaries have increased, the cost of attending baseball games has increased dramatically. The following histogram and cumulative percentage polygon visualizes the total cost (in $) for four tickets, two beers, four soft drinks, four hot dogs, two game programs, two baseball caps, and parking for one vehicle at each of the 30 Major League Baseball parks during the 2015 season that is stored in **BBCost2015**.

Cost of Attending a Baseball Game

Cumulative Percentage Polygon for the Cost of Attending a Baseball Game

What conclusions can you reach concerning the cost of attending a baseball game at different ballparks?

2.40 The following histogram and cumulative percentage polygon visualize the data about the property taxes per capita($) for the 50 states and the District of Columbia, stored in **Property Taxes**.

Histogram for Property Taxes Per Capita ($)

Cumulative Percentage Polygon for Property Taxes Per Capita

What conclusions can you reach concerning the property taxes per capita?

2.41 How much time do Americans living in or near cities spend waiting in traffic, and how much does waiting in traffic cost them per year? The data in the file **Congestion** include this cost for 31 cities. (Source: Data extracted from "The High Cost of Congestion," *Time,* October 17, 2011, p. 18.) For the time Americans living in or near cities spend waiting in traffic and the cost of waiting in traffic per year,

a. Construct a percentage histogram.

b. Construct a cumulative percentage polygon.

c. What conclusions can you reach concerning the time Americans living in or near cities spend waiting in traffic?

d. What conclusions can you reach concerning the cost of waiting in traffic per year?

2.42 How do the average credit scores of people living in various cities differ? The file Credit Scores contains an ordered array of the average credit scores of 143 American cities. (Data extracted from **bit.ly/1Pb7V4m**.)

a. Construct a percentage histogram.

b. Construct a cumulative percentage polygon.

c. What conclusions can you reach concerning the average credit scores of people living in different American cities?

2.43 One operation of a mill is to cut pieces of steel into parts that will later be used as the frame for front seats in an automobile. The steel is cut with a diamond saw and requires the resulting parts to be within ± 0.005 inch of the length specified by the automobile company. The data are collected from a sample of 100 steel parts and stored in Steel . The measurement reported is the difference in inches between the actual length of the steel part, as measured by a laser measurement device, and the specified length of the steel part. For example, the first value, −0.002, represents a steel part that is 0.002 inch shorter than the specified length.

a. Construct a percentage histogram.

b. Is the steel mill doing a good job meeting the requirements set by the automobile company? Explain.

2.44 A manufacturing company produces steel housings for electrical equipment. The main component of the housing is a steel trough that is made out of a 14-gauge steel coil. It is produced using a 250-ton progressive punch press with a wipe-down operation that puts two 90-degree forms in the flat steel to make the trough. The distance from one side of the form to the other is critical because of weatherproofing in outdoor applications. The company requires that the width of the trough be between 8.31 inches and 8.61 inches. The widths of the troughs, in inches, collected from a sample of 49 troughs, are stored in Trough .

a. Construct a percentage histogram and a percentage polygon.

b. Plot a cumulative percentage polygon.

c. What can you conclude about the number of troughs that will meet the company's requirements of troughs being between 8.31 and 8.61 inches wide?

2.45 The manufacturing company in Problem 2.44 also produces electric insulators. If the insulators break when in use, a short circuit is likely to occur. To test the strength of the insulators, destructive testing in high-powered labs is carried out to determine how much *force* is required to break the insulators. Force is measured by observing how many pounds must be applied to the insulator before it breaks. The force measurements, collected from a sample of 30 insulators, are stored in Force .

a. Construct a percentage histogram and a percentage polygon.

b. Construct a cumulative percentage polygon.

c. What can you conclude about the strengths of the insulators if the company requires a force measurement of at least 1,500 pounds before the insulator breaks?

2.46 The file Bulbs contains the life (in hours) of a sample of forty 20-watt compact fluorescent light bulbs produced by Manufacturer A and a sample of forty 20-watt compact fluorescent light bulbs produced by Manufacturer B.

Use the following class interval widths for each distribution:

Manufacturer A: 6,500 but less than 7,500; 7,500 but less than 8,500; and so on.
Manufacturer B: 7,500 but less than 8,500; 8,500 but less than 9,500; and so on.

a. Construct percentage histograms on separate graphs and plot the percentage polygons on one graph.

b. Plot cumulative percentage polygons on one graph.

c. Which manufacturer has bulbs with a longer life—Manufacturer A or Manufacturer B? Explain.

2.47 The data stored in Drink represents the amount of soft drink in a sample of fifty 2-liter bottles.

a. Construct a histogram and a percentage polygon.

b. Construct a cumulative percentage polygon.

c. On the basis of the results in (a) and (b), does the amount of soft drink filled in the bottles concentrate around specific values?

2.5 Visualizing Two Numerical Variables

Visualizing two numerical variables together can reveal possible relationships between two variables and serve as a basis for applying the methods discussed in Chapters 13 through 16. To visualize two numerical variables, you use a scatter plot. For the special case in which one of the two variables represents the passage of time, you use a time-series plot.

The Scatter Plot

A **scatter plot** explores the possible relationship between two numerical variables by plotting the values of one numerical variable on the horizontal, or X, axis and the values of a second numerical variable on the vertical, or Y, axis. For example, a marketing analyst could study the effectiveness of advertising by comparing advertising expenses and sales revenues of 50 stores by using the X axis to represent advertising expenses and the Y axis to represent sales revenues.

EXAMPLE 2.12

Scatter Plot for NBA Investment Analysis

Suppose that you are an investment analyst who has been asked to review the valuations of the 30 NBA professional basketball teams. You seek to know if the value of a team reflects its revenues. You collect revenue and valuation data (both in $millions) for all 30 NBA teams, organize the data as Table 2.17, and store the data in NBAValues.

To quickly visualize a possible relationship between team revenues and valuations, you construct a scatter plot as shown in Figure 2.14, in which you plot the revenues on the X axis and the value of the team on the Y axis.

TABLE 2.17
Revenues and Values for NBA Teams

Team Code	Revenue ($millions)	Value ($millions)	Team Code	Revenue ($millions)	Value ($millions)	Team Code	Revenue ($millions)	Value ($millions)
ATL	133	825	HOU	175	1250	OKC	152	930
BOS	173	1700	IND	149	830	ORL	143	875
BKN	212	1500	LAC	146	1600	PHI	125	700
CHA	130	725	LAL	293	2600	PHX	145	910
CHI	201	2000	MEM	135	750	POR	153	940
CLE	149	915	MIA	188	1175	SAC	125	800
DAL	168	1150	MIL	110	600	SAS	174	1000
DEN	136	855	MIN	128	625	TOR	151	920
DET	144	810	NOH	131	650	UTA	142	830
GSW	168	1300	NYK	278	2500	WAS	143	900

SOLUTION From Figure 2.14, you see that there appears to be a strong increasing (positive) relationship between revenues and the value of a team. In other words, teams that generate a smaller amount of revenues have a lower value, while teams that generate higher revenues have a higher value. This relationship has been highlighted by the addition of a linear regression prediction line that will be discussed in Chapter 13.

FIGURE 2.14
Scatter plot of revenue and value for NBA teams

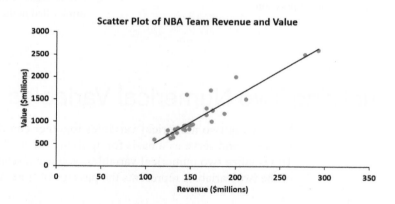

learnMORE

Read the SHORT TAKES for Chapter 2 for an example that illustrates a negative relationship.

Other pairs of variables may have a decreasing (negative) relationship in which one variable decreases as the other increases. In other situations, there may be a weak or no relationship between the variables.

The Time-Series Plot

A **time-series plot** plots the values of a numerical variable on the Y axis and plots the time period associated with each numerical value on the X axis. A time-series plot can help you visualize trends in data that occur over time.

EXAMPLE 2.13

Time-Series Plot for Movie Revenues

As an investment analyst who specializes in the entertainment industry, you are interested in discovering any long-term trends in movie revenues. You collect the annual revenues (in $billions) for movies released from 1995 to 2014, organize the data as Table 2.18, and store the data in Movie Revenues.

To see if there is a trend over time, you construct the time-series plot shown in Figure 2.15.

TABLE 2.18
Movie Revenues (in $billions) from 1995 to 2014

Year	Revenue ($billions)	Year	Revenue ($billions)	Year	Revenue ($billions)
1995	5.29	2002	9.19	2009	10.65
1996	5.59	2003	9.35	2010	10.54
1997	6.51	2004	9.11	2011	10.19
1998	6.79	2005	8.93	2012	10.83
1999	7.30	2006	9.25	2013	10.90
2000	7.48	2007	9.63	2014	10.36
2001	8.13	2008	9.95		

Source: Data extracted from **www.the-numbers.com/market**.

SOLUTION From Figure 2.15, you see that there was a steady increase in the annual movie revenues between 1995 and 2003, a leveling off from 2003 to 2006, followed by a further increase from 2007 to 2009, followed by another leveling off from 2010 to 2013, and then a decline in 2014 back to near the level of the revenue in 2011. During that time, the revenues increased from under $6 billion in 1995 to more than $10 billion in 2009 to 2014.

FIGURE 2.15
Time-series plot of movie revenues per year from 1995 to 2014

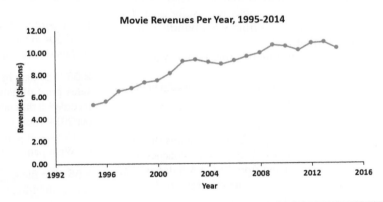

PROBLEMS FOR SECTION 2.5

LEARNING THE BASICS

2.48 The following is a set of data from a sample of $n = 11$ items:

X: 7 5 8 3 6 0 2 4 9 5 8

Y: 1 5 4 9 8 0 6 2 7 5 4

a. Construct a scatter plot.
b. Is there a relationship between X and Y? Explain.

2.49 The following is a series of annual sales (in $millions) over an 11-year period (2004 to 2014):

Year: 2004 2005 2006 2007 2008 2009 2010 2011 2012 2013 2014

Sales: 13.0 17.0 19.0 20.0 20.5 20.5 20.5 20.0 19.0 17.0 13.0

a. Construct a time-series plot.
b. Does there appear to be any change in annual sales over time? Explain.

APPLYING THE CONCEPTS

✓ SELF TEST **2.50** Movie companies need to predict the gross receipts of individual movies once a movie has debuted. The following results, stored in PotterMovies, are the first weekend gross, the U.S. gross, and the worldwide gross (in $millions) of the eight Harry Potter movies:

Title	First Weekend ($millions)	U.S. Gross ($millions)	Worldwide Gross ($millions)
Sorcerer's Stone	90.295	317.558	976.458
Chamber of Secrets	88.357	261.988	878.988
Prisoner of Azkaban	93.687	249.539	795.539
Goblet of Fire/	102.335	290.013	896.013
Order of the Phoenix	77.108	292.005	938.469
Half-Blood Prince	77.836	301.460	934.601
Deathly Hallows Part I	125.017	295.001	955.417
Deathly Hallows Part II	169.189	381.011	1,328.111

Source: Data extracted from **www.the-numbers.com/interactive/comp-Harry-Potter.php**.

a. Construct a scatter plot with first weekend gross on the X axis and U.S. gross on the Y axis.
b. Construct a scatter plot with first weekend gross on the X axis and worldwide gross on the Y axis.
c. What can you say about the relationship between first weekend gross and U.S. gross and first weekend gross and worldwide gross?

2.51 Data were collected on the typical cost of dining at American-cuisine restaurants within a 1-mile walking distance of a hotel located in a large city. The file Bundle contains the typical cost (a per transaction cost in $) as well as a Bundle score, a measure of overall popularity and customer loyalty, for each of 40 selected restaurants. (Data extracted from **www.bundle.com** via the link **on-msn.com/MnlBxo.**)

a. Construct a scatter plot with Bundle score on the X axis and typical cost on the Y axis.
b. What conclusions can you reach about the relationship between Bundle score and typical cost?

2.52 College football is big business, with coaches' pay in millions of dollars. The file College Football contains the 2013 total athletic department revenue and 2014 football coaches' total pay for 108 schools. (Data extracted from "NCAA Salaries" and "NCAA Finances," **usat.ly/1uws90v** and **usat.ly/1DOl0v3.**)

a. Do you think schools with higher total revenues also have higher total coaches' pay?
b. Construct a scatter plot with total revenue on the X axis and total coaches' pay on the Y axis.
c. Does the scatter plot confirm or contradict your answer to (a)?

2.53 A Pew Research Center survey found that social networking is popular, but Internet access is lacking in many nations around the world. The file GlobalSocialMedia contains the level of social media networking, measured as the percentage of Internet users polled who use social networking sites, and the file GlobalInternetUsage contains the level of Internet usage, measured as the percentage of adults polled who use Internet at least occasionally, as well as the GDP at purchasing power parity (PPP) per capita (in current international $) for each of 31 emerging and developing countries. (Data extracted from Pew Research Center, "Internet Seen as Positive Influence on Education but Negative on Morality in Emerging and Developing Nations," March 19, 2015, **bit.ly/1GASqhp**).

a. Construct a scatter plot with GDP (PPP) per capita on the X axis and social media usage on the Y axis.
b. What conclusions can you reach about the relationship between GDP and social media usage?
c. Construct a scatter plot with GDP (PPP) per capita on the X axis and Internet usage on the Y axis.
d. What conclusions can you reach about the relationship between GDP and Internet usage?

2.54 How have stocks performed in the past? The following table presents the data stored in Stock Performance and shows the performance of a broad measure of stocks (by percentage) for each decade from the 1830s through the 2000s:

Decade	Perf (%)	Decade	Perf (%)
1830s	2.8	1920s	13.3
1840s	12.8	1930s	−2.2
1850s	6.6	1940s	9.6
1860s	12.5	1950s	18.2
1870s	7.5	1960s	8.3
1880s	6.0	1970s	6.6
1890s	5.5	1980s	16.6
1900s	10.9	1990s	17.6
1910s	2.2	2000s*	−0.5

*Through December 15, 2009.

Source: Data extracted from T. Lauricella, "Investors Hope the '10s Beat the '00s," *The Wall Street Journal*, December 21, 2009, pp. C1, C2.

a. Construct a time-series plot of the stock performance from the 1830s to the 2000s.
b. Does there appear to be any pattern in the data?

2.55 The data in NewHomeSales represent number and median sales price of new single-family houses sold in the United States recorded at the end of each month from January 2000 through December 2014. (Data extracted from **www.census.gov**, February 28, 2015.)

a. Construct a time-series plot of new home sales prices.
b. What pattern, if any, is present in the data?

2.56 The file Movie Attendance contains the yearly movie attendance (in billions) from 2001 through 2014.

Year	Attendance (bill)	Year	Attendance (bill)
2001	1.44	2008	1.39
2002	1.58	2009	1.42
2003	1.55	2010	1.34
2004	1.47	2011	1.28
2005	1.39	2012	1.36
2006	1.41	2013	1.15
2007	1.40	2014	1.27

Source: Data extracted from **boxofficemojo.com/yearly**.

a. Construct a time-series plot for the movie attendance (in billions).

b. What pattern, if any, is present in the data?

2.57 The file Audits contains the number of audits of corporations with assets of more than $250 million conducted by the

Internal Revenue Service between 2001 and 2013. (Data extracted from **www.irs.gov**.)

a. Construct a time-series plot.

b. What pattern, if any, is present in the data?

2.6 Organizing and Visualizing a Mix of Variables

The changing face and increased application of statistics to decision making discussed in the First Things First chapter have created relatively new methods to create tabular and visual summaries for a mix of variables. These newer methods can discover patterns and relationships to your data that simpler tables and charts would not make apparent. In highlighting such patterns, these methods tend to produce less precise results than the methods discussed previously, so consider these newer methods supplemental to and not replacements for the other methods in this chapter.

Some of these Excel features illustrate underlying principles of business analytics, even though the features are not, by the strictest definition, business analytics methods.

Some of these newer methods illustrate **data discovery** methods that enable you to manipulate interactive tabular and visual summaries. Because data discovery represents one aspect of information systems methods that retrieve and manipulate data, you may discover Excel features in this section that you have previously used in an information systems course. That might better illustrate for you the "changing face of statistics" that business analytics represents better than anything written in the initial chapter of this book.

While you *could* use any number of variables with these methods, using more than three or four variables at once, or a categorical variable with many categories, will produce results that will be hard to comprehend and interpret. As Section 2.7 discusses, avoiding obscuring data is one of the challenges you always face when organizing and visualizing variables.

Multidimensional Contingency Table

A **multidimensional contingency table** tallies the data of three or more categorical variables. In Excel, you implement such a table as a **PivotTable**. PivotTables summarize a set of variables and allow you to interactively change the mix of variables and the level of summarization, and the formatting of the variables. When you use three categorical variables, each cell in a PivotTable contains the tallies of the third variable, organized by the subgroups represented by the categories of the other two variables, the row and column variables.

For example, return to the Table 2.4 contingency table on page 35 that jointly tallies the type and risk variables for the sample of 407 retirement funds as percentages of the overall total. From this table, repeated below at left in Figure 2.16, you observe that the growth funds contain relatively more high risk funds than the value funds groups (not unexpected), and there are many more growth and value funds of average risk than of low or high risk.

FIGURE 2.16

Retirement funds sample PivotTables showing percentage of the overall total

Type	Risk			
	Low	Average	High	Grand Total
Growth	3.93%	48.89%	13.27%	66.09%
Value	6.14%	23.83%	3.93%	33.91%
Grand Total	10.07%	72.73%	17.20%	100.00%

Type	Risk			
	Low	Average	High	Grand Total
⊟Growth	3.93%	48.89%	13.27%	66.09%
Large	3.19%	26.54%	1.47%	31.20%
Mid-Cap	0.74%	17.69%	3.44%	21.87%
Small	0.00%	4.67%	8.35%	13.02%
⊟Value	6.14%	23.83%	3.93%	33.91%
Large	5.65%	14.50%	0.25%	20.39%
Mid-Cap	0.49%	6.39%	0.49%	7.37%
Small	0.00%	2.95%	3.19%	6.14%
Grand Total	10.07%	72.73%	17.20%	100.00%

Adding the categorical variable market cap with the categories small, mid, and large produces the PivotTable shown at right in Figure 2.16. This multidimensional PivotTable reveals the following patterns that cannot be seen in the other table:

- Most of the low-risk funds of either type are large-cap funds.
- Large-cap growth funds have a higher proportion (26.54/31.20 = 85%) of average risk funds than large-cap value funds (14.50/20.39 = 71%).
- Small-cap funds of either type are disproportionally high risk when compared to other market cap categories.

These results suggest that market cap is a **lurking variable**, a variable that affects the summary results for the type and risk variables. Including market cap in the second PivotTable reveals that the (not unexpected) observation that growth funds contain relatively more high risk funds than the value funds is mostly due to the effect of small market cap growth funds than due to any quality inherit to all growth funds.

Adding a Numerical Variable to a Multidimensional Contingency Table

When you add a numerical variable to a multidimensional contingency table, the table display changes from a display of counts or percentages of the various group to a display of a summary measure of the numerical variable for that group. Typically, you use one of the numerical descriptive statistics that Sections 3.1 and 3.2 discuss as the summary measure. For example, Figure 2.17 presents PivotTables for the categorical variables type, risk, and market cap and the added numerical variable 10-year return percentage. Each cell displays the *mean* 10-year return percentage for each of the groups formed by the type, risk, and market-cap categories. The two cells for small cap funds with low risk are blank, as no mean can be calculated for those groups because the sample does not include any funds that are small cap and low risk (note 0.00% for the two cells in the table at right in Figure 2.16.)

The left table in Figure 2.17 has the market cap categories collapsed, or hidden from view. This table highlights that growth funds have higher mean 10-year return percentages than the value funds in every risk category. Similar to the Figure 2.16 example, displaying the market cap categories reveals the following patterns that cannot be seen in the left, collapsed table:

- Large cap, high risk *growth* funds have the highest mean 10-year return percentage, while large cap, high risk *value* funds have the lowest mean 10-year return percentage.
- Mid-cap, low risk growth funds have the second-best mean 10-year return percentage.
- Mid-cap growth funds have the best mean 10-year return percentage of any market cap and type group.

FIGURE 2.17
PivotTable of type, risk, and market cap showing mean 10-year return percentage

Mean 10YrReturn%	Risk ▼			
Type ▼	Low	Average	High	Grand Total
Growth	7.59	8.07	7.63	7.95
Value	6.48	6.93	7.02	6.86
Grand Total	6.91	7.70	7.49	7.58

Mean 10YrReturn%	Risk ▼			
Type ▼	Low	Average	High	Grand Total
⊟Growth	7.59	8.07	7.63	7.95
Large	7.35	7.83	10.14	7.89
Mid-Cap	8.61	8.49	7.41	8.32
Small		7.91	7.27	7.50
⊟Value	6.48	6.93	7.02	6.86
Large	6.52	6.46	4.10	6.45
Mid-Cap	6.05	7.84	7.28	7.68
Small		7.24	7.21	7.22
Grand Total	6.91	7.70	7.49	7.58

Drill Down

Patterns that you review when exploring multidimensional contingency tables, such as the patterns revealed in Figure 2.17 (right), may cause you to further investigate those patterns. To further investigate, you can **drill down** to reveal the data underlying a summary measure. In a PivotTable, double-clicking a cell drills down and causes Excel to display the underlying data in a new worksheet. You can then observe the data for patterns or apply additional statistical methods to that data without disturbing the original PivotTable.

For example, clicking the cell for large cap growth funds with high risk that displays the mean value 10.14 produces the new worksheet shown in Figure 2.18 that lists the five funds that are large cap growth funds with high risk. Examining the data shows that these funds have very different one-year return percentages and the fund with the best 10-year return percentage also is the only five-star rated fund in the group.

FIGURE 2.18
Results of drilling down to the details about large cap growth funds with high risk

	F	G	H	I	J	K	L	M	N
1	Turnover Ratio(%)	SD	Sharpe Ratio	1YrReturn%	3YrReturn%	5YrReturn%	10YrReturn%	Expense Ratio	Star Rating
2	49	16.94	1.01	0.53	16.18	15.16	9.50	1.3	Three
3	146	13.05	1.23	8.73	16.39	12.80	8.11	0.98	Two
4	39	14.51	1.17	2.90	17.23	17.02	11.13	1.27	Three
5	21	13.17	1.19	5.65	15.95	15.44	9.71	1.22	Two
6	31	13.62	1.35	6.42	19.02	18.05	10.26	0.96	Four
7	106	14.07	1.42	14.70	20.80	19.36	12.14	0.77	Five

Excel Slicers

Many newer business analytics methods start with many variables and allow you to *filter* your data by exploring specific combinations of categorical values or numerical ranges. In Excel, you use *slicers* to mimic this filtering operation. In its simplest form, a **slicer** is a panel of clickable buttons that appears superimposed over a worksheet. Each slicer panel corresponds to one of the variables of interest, and each button in the variable's slicer panel represents a unique value of the variable that is found in the data. You create a slicer for any variable that has been *associated* with a PivotTable, not only for the variables that you have physically inserted into such a table. This allows you to work with many variables at once in a way that avoids creating an overly complex multidimensional contingency table that would be hard to comprehend and interpret.

By clicking buttons in the slicer panels, you ask questions about your data. This is in contrast with the methods described earlier in this chapter, which allow you to observe data relationships but do not give you the opportunity to look for the presence of specific relationships. Because a set of slicers can give you a "heads-up" about your data, using a set of slicers mimics a function of a descriptive analytics dashboard, discussed in Chapter 17.

For example, the Figure 2.19 worksheet shows a PivotTable that has been associated with the variables stored in the DATA worksheet of the Retirement Funds workbook. The Pivot-Table summarizes the variables type and risk; slicers for the variables type, market cap, star rating, and expense ratio have been added to the worksheet.

FIGURE 2.19
PivotTable and slicers for the retirement funds sample data

With the four slicers, you can ask questions such as:

1. What are the attributes of the fund(s) with the lowest expense ratio?
2. Which fund(s) in the sample have the highest expense ratio?
3. What are the expense ratios associated with mid-cap funds that have a star rating of five?

Figure 2.20 on page 66 contains the slicer displays that answer questions 1 and 3. Excel dims, or disables, the buttons representing values that the current data filtering excludes, allowing you to visually see the answer to a question. For example, the answer to question 1 is a growth fund with a large market cap and a five-star rating; from the associated PivotTable, not shown

FIGURE 2.20
Slicer displays for answers to questions 1 (left) and 3 (right)

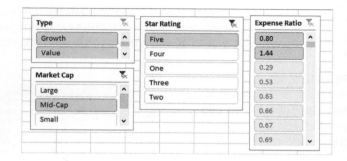

in Figure 2.19, you discover that there is only one such fund. For question 3, you observe that 0.88 and 1.44 are the expense ratios associated with mid-cap funds that have a star rating of five. (And from the PivotTable, not shown, you observe that there are 2 funds with those attributes.)

More complex displays are also possible. Figure 2.21 shows a seven-slicer panel in which the five highest turnover ratio percentages have been selected to reveal the identity and the attributes of the funds associated with those percentages.

FIGURE 2.21
Seven-slicer panel that identifies the retirement funds with the five highest turnover ratio percentages

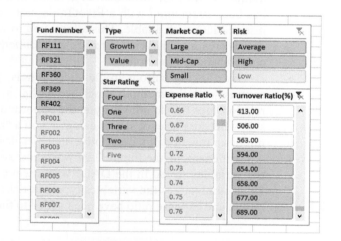

PivotChart

A **PivotChart** allows you to filter your data by exploring specific combinations of categorical values in a purely visual way. While more limited than the tabular Excel slicer, you can use a PivotChart to pull out and chart specific categories from a PivotTable source in a way that would otherwise be hard to do. For example, Figure 2.22 (left) displays a side-by-side PivotChart based on the Figure 2.17 (right) PivotTable. Unlike an Excel slicer, you can filter only the categorical variables. Filtering the chart to display the mean 10-year return percentages for only high risk funds (Figure 2.22 right), the PivotChart highlights that large-cap growth funds have the highest mean value.

Sparklines

Sparklines are compact time-series visualizations of numerical variables. This compact form allows you to view all the visualizations together, which can aid in making comparisons among the variables. Sparklines highlight the trends of the plots over the precise graphing of points found in a time-series plot. Although typically used to plot several independent numerical variables, such as several different business indicators, sparklines can also be used to plot time-series data using smaller time units than a time-series plot to reveal patterns that the time-series plot may not.

FIGURE 2.22

PivotCharts based on the Figure 2.17 PivotTable of type, risk, and market cap showing mean 10-year return percentage

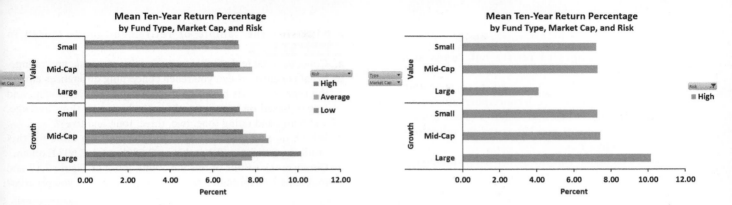

For example, Figure 2.23 (top) contains a time-series plot of annual movie revenues (in $billions) from 2005 through 2014, a subset of the data used in Example 2.13 on page 61. Figure 2.23 (bottom) contains a set of sparklines that plot movie revenues for each month of specific years. The sparklines reveal that movie revenues for the months of February and September do not vary much from year to year, while the monthly revenues for July and November 2014 seem to have caused most of the decline in 2014 revenues that can be seen on the time-series plot.

FIGURE 2.23

Time-series plot of movie revenues per year from 2005 to 2014 (top) and sparklines for movie revenues per month for the same time period (bottom)

PROBLEMS FOR SECTION 2.6

APPLYING THE CONCEPTS

2.58 Using the sample of retirement funds stored in RetirementFunds :
a. Construct a table that tallies type, market cap, and rating.
b. What conclusions can you reach concerning differences among the types of retirement funds (growth and value), based on market cap (small, mid-cap, and large) and the rating (one, two, three, four, and five)?
c. Construct a table that computes the average three-year return for each type, market cap, and rating.
d. Drill down to examine the large cap growth funds with a rating of three. How many funds are there? What conclusions can you reach about these funds?

2.59 Using the sample of retirement funds stored in RetirementFunds :
a. Construct a table that tallies market cap, risk, and rating.
b. What conclusions can you reach concerning differences among the funds based on market cap (small, mid-cap, and large), risk (low, average, and high), and the rating (one, two, three, four, and five)?
c. Construct a table that computes the average three-year return for each market cap, risk, and rating.
d. Drill down to examine the large cap funds that are high risk with a rating of three. How many funds are there? What conclusions can you reach about these funds?

2.60 Using the sample of retirement funds stored in RetirementFunds :
a. Construct a table that tallies type, risk, and rating.
b. What conclusions can you reach concerning differences among the types of retirement funds (growth and value), based on the risk (low, average, and high), and the rating (one, two, three, four, and five)?
c. Construct a table that computes the average three-year return for each type, risk, and rating.
d. Drill down to examine the growth funds with high risk with a rating of three. How many funds are there? What conclusions can you reach about these funds?

2.61 Using the sample of retirement funds stored in RetirementFunds :
a. Construct a table that tallies type, market cap, risk, and rating.
b. What conclusions can you reach concerning differences among the types of funds based on market cap (small, mid-cap, and large), based on type (growth and value), risk (low, average, and high), and rating (one, two, three, four, and five)?
c. Which do you think is easier to interpret: the table for this problem or the ones for problems 2.58 through 2.60? Explain.
d. Compare the results of this table with those of Figure 2.17 and problems 2.58 through 2.60. What differences can you observe?

2.62 In the sample of 407 retirement funds (RetirementFunds), what are the attributes of the fund with the highest five-year return?

2.63 In the sample of 407 retirement funds (RetirementFunds), what five-year returns are associated with small market cap funds that have a rating of five stars?

2.64 In the sample of 407 retirement funds (RetirementFunds), which funds in the sample have the lowest five-year return?

2.65 In the sample of 407 retirement funds (RetirementFunds), what is the type and market cap of the five-star fund with the highest five-year return?

2.66 In the sample of 407 retirement funds (RetirementFunds), what characteristics are associated with the funds that have the lowest five-year return?

2.67 The file Smartphone Sales contains the market share of smartphones by type from 2010 to 2014. (Data extracted from "Android and iOS Squeeze the Competition…," **bit.ly/1JV5qRR**).
a. Construct sparklines of smartphone sales by type.
b. What conclusions can you reach concerning smartphone sales from 2010 to 2014?

2.68 The file StockIndex contains the annual return for various stock indexes from 2009 to 2013.
a. Construct sparklines of each stock index.
b. What conclusions can you reach concerning the annual return of the stock indexes from 2009 to 2014?

2.7 The Challenge in Organizing and Visualizing Variables

The tabular and visual summaries that you create when you organize and visualize your variables of interest can jumpstart the analysis of the variables. However, you must be careful not to produce results that will be hard to comprehend and interpret or to present your data in ways that undercut the usefulness of the methods discussed in this chapter. You can too easily create summaries that obscure the data or create false impressions that would lead to misleading or unproductive analysis. The challenge in organizing and visualizing variables is to avoid these complications.

Obscuring Data

Management specialists have long known that information overload, presenting too many details, can obscure data and hamper decision making (see reference 4). Both tabular summaries and visualizations can suffer from this problem. For example, consider the Figure 2.24

FIGURE 2.24
Side-by-side bar chart for the retirement funds sample showing percentage of overall total for fund type, market cap, risk, and star rating

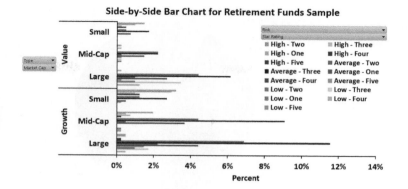

Side-by-Side Bar Chart for Retirement Funds Sample

side-by-side bar chart that shows percentages of the overall total for subgroups formed from combinations of fund type, market cap, risk, and star rating. While this chart highlights that there are more large-cap retirement funds with low risk and a three-star rating than any other combination of risk and star rating, other details about the retirement funds sample are less obvious. The overly complex legend obscures as well, even for people who do not suffer from color perception problems.

Creating False Impressions

As you organize and visualize variables, you must be careful not to create false impressions that could affect preliminary conclusions about the data. Selective summarizations and improperly constructed visualizations often create false impressions.

A *selective summarization* is the presentation of only part of the data that have been collected. Frequently, selective summarization occurs when data collected over a long period of time are summarized as percentage changes for a shorter period. For example, Table 2.19 (left) presents the one-year difference in sales of seven auto industry companies for the month of April. The selective summarization tells a different story, particularly for company G, than does Table 2.19 (right) that shows the year-to-year differences for a three-year period that included the 2008 economic downturn.

TABLE 2.19
Left: One-Year Percentage Change in Year-to-Year Sales for the Month of April; Right: Percentage Change for Three Consecutive Years

Company	Change from Prior Year
A	+7.2
B	+24.4
C	+24.9
D	+24.8
E	+12.5
F	+35.1
G	+29.7

Company	Change from Prior Year		
	Year 1	Year 2	Year 3
A	−22.6	−33.2	+7.2
B	−4.5	−41.9	+24.4
C	−18.5	−31.5	+24.9
D	−29.4	−48.1	+24.8
E	−1.9	−25.3	+12.5
F	−1.6	−37.8	+35.1
G	+7.4	−13.6	+29.7

Improperly constructed charts can also create false impressions. Figure 2.25 on page 70 shows two pie charts that display the market shares of companies in two industries. How quickly did you notice that both pie charts summarize identical data?

Because of their relative positions and colorings, many people will perceive the dark blue pie slice on the left chart to have a smaller market share than the dark red pie chart on the right chart even though both pie slices represent the company that has 27% market share. In this case, both the ordering of pie slices and the different colorings of the two pie charts contribute to creating the false impression. With other types of charts, improperly scaled axes or a *Y* axis that either does not begin at the origin or is a "broken" axis that is missing intermediate values are other common mistakes that create false impressions.

studentTIP

Order pie or doughnut slices from the largest to the smallest slice and color pie and doughnut charts meant for comparison in the same way.

FIGURE 2.25
Market shares of
companies in "two"
industries

*If you want to verify that
the two pie charts visualize
the same data, open the*
TwoPies worksheet *in the*
Challenging workbook.

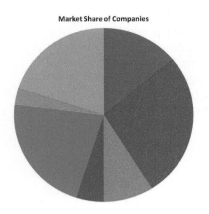

Chartjunk

Seeking to construct a visualization that can more effectively convey an important point, some people add decorative elements to enhance or replace the simple bar and line shapes of the visualizations discussed in this chapter. While judicious use of such elements may aid in the memorability of a chart (see reference 1), most often such elements either obscure the data or, worse, create a false impression of the data. Such elements are called **chartjunk**.

Figure 2.26 visualizes the market share for selected soft drink brands. The chartjunk version fails to convey any more information than a simple bar or pie chart would, and the soft drink bottle tops included on the chart obscure and distort the data. The side-by-side bar chart at right shows how the market shares as represented by the height of the "fizzy" elements overstate the actual market shares of the five lesser brands, using the height of the first bottle and fizz to represent 20%.

FIGURE 2.26
Two visualizations of market share of soft drinks

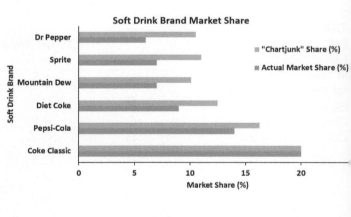

Source: Left illustration adapted from Anne B. Carey and Sam Ward, "Coke Still Has Most Fizz," *USA Today*, May 10, 2000, p. 1B.

Figure 2.27 visualizes Australian wine exports to the United States for four years. The chartjunk version on the left uses wine glasses in a histogram-like display in lieu of a proper time-series plot, such as the one shown on the right. Because the years between measurements are not equally spaced, the four wine glasses create a false impression about the ever-increasing

FIGURE 2.27

Two visualizations of Australian wine exports to the United States, in millions of gallons

Left illustration adapted from S. Watterson, "Liquid Gold—Australians Are Changing the World of Wine. Even the French Seem Grateful," *Time*, November 22, 1999, p. 68.

trend in wine exports. The wine glasses also distort the data by using an object with a three-dimensional volume. (While the height of wine in the 1997 glass is a bit more than six times the height of the 1989 glass, the volume of that filled 1997 wine glass would be much more than the almost empty 1989 glass.)

Figure 2.28 presents another visual used in the same magazine article. This visualization illustrates mistakes that are common ways of creating chartjunk unintentionally. The grapevine with its leaves and bunch of grapes adds to the clutter of decoration without conveying any useful information. The chart inaccurately shows the 1949–1950 measurement (135,326 acres) at a *higher* point on the Y axis than larger values such as the 1969–1970 measurement, 150,300 acres. The inconsistent scale of the X axis distorts the time variable. (The last two measurements, eight years apart, are drawn about as far apart as the 30-year gap between 1959 and 1989.) All of these errors create a very wrong impression that obscures the important trend of accelerating growth of land planted in the 1990s.

FIGURE 2.28

Two visualizations of the amount of land planted with grapes for the wine industry

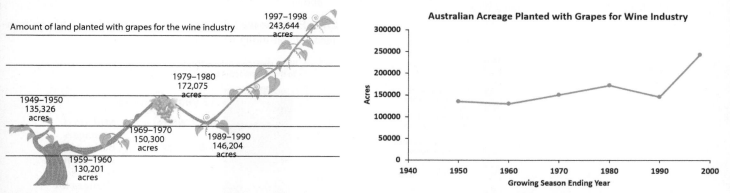

Adapted from S. Watterson, "Liquid Gold—Australians Are Changing the World of Wine. Even the French Seem Grateful," *Time*, November 22, 1999, pp. 68–69.

To help you produce results that will not be hard to comprehend and interpret and that avoid distortions in your data, Exhibit 2.1 summarizes the best practices for creating visualizations. When you use Excel, be aware that Excel may tempt you to use uncommon chart types and may produce charts that violate some of the best practices listed in the exhibit.

EXHIBIT 2.1

Best Practices for Creating Visualizations

- Use the simplest possible visualization
- Include a title and label all axes
- Include a scale for each axis if the chart contains axes
- Begin the scale for a vertical axis at zero and use a constant scale
- Avoid 3D or "exploded" effects and the use of chartjunk
- Use consistent colorings in charts meant to be compared
- Avoid using uncommon chart types including radar, surface, bubble, cone, and pyramid charts

---

PROBLEMS FOR SECTION 2.7

APPLYING THE CONCEPTS

2.69 (Student Project) Bring to class a chart from a website, newspaper, or magazine published recently that you believe to be a poorly drawn representation of a numerical variable. Be prepared to submit the chart to the instructor with comments about why you believe it is inappropriate. Do you believe that the intent of the chart is to purposely mislead the reader? Also, be prepared to present and comment on this in class.

2.70 (Student Project) Bring to class a chart from a website, newspaper, or magazine published this month that you believe to be a poorly drawn representation of a categorical variable. Be prepared to submit the chart to the instructor with comments about why you consider it inappropriate. Do you believe that the intent of the chart is to purposely mislead the reader? Also, be prepared to present and comment on this in class.

2.71 Examine the following visualization, adapted from one that appeared in a post in a digital marketing blog.

a. Describe at least one good feature of this visual display.
b. Describe at least one bad feature of this visual display.
c. Redraw the graph, using the guidelines above.

2.72 Examine the following visualization, adapted from one that appeared in the post "Who Are the Comic Book Fans on Facebook?" on February 2, 2013, as reported by **graphicspolicy.com**.

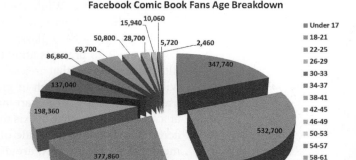

a. Describe at least one good feature of this visual display.
b. Describe at least one bad feature of this visual display.
c. Redraw the graph, by using best practices given in Exhibit 2.1 above.

2.73 Examine the following visualization, adapted from a management consulting white paper.

a. Describe at least one good feature of this visual display.
b. Describe at least one bad feature of this visual display.
c. Redraw the graph, by using the Exhibit 2.1 guidelines.

2.74 Professor Deanna Oxender Burgess of Florida Gulf Coast University conducted research on annual reports of corporations (see D. Rosato, "Worried About the Numbers? How About the Charts?" *The New York Times*, September 15, 2002, p. B7). Burgess found that even slight distortions in a chart changed readers' perception of the information. Using online or library sources, select a corporation and study its most recent annual report. Find at least one chart in the report that you think needs improvement and develop an improved version of the chart. Explain why you believe the improved chart is better than the one included in the annual report.

2.75 Figure 2.1 shows a bar chart and a pie chart for how people paid for purchases and other transactions (see page 47).

a. Create an exploded pie chart, a cone chart, or a pyramid chart that shows how people paid for purchases and other transactions.
b. Which graphs either seen in Figure 2.1 or created in (a), do you prefer? Explain.

2.76 Figures 2.2 and 2.3 show a bar chart and a pie chart for the risk level for the retirement fund data (see pages 47–48).
a. Create an exploded pie chart, a doughnut chart, a cone chart, and a pyramid chart that show the risk level of retirement funds.
b. Which graphs, either seen in Figures 2.2 and 2.3 or created in (a), do you prefer? Explain.

▼ USING **STATISTICS**
The Choice Is *Yours, Revisited*

In The Choice *Is* Yours scenario, you were hired to define, collect, organize, and visualize data about a sample of 407 retirement funds in ways that could assist prospective clients to make investment choices. Having verified that each of the 13 variables in the sample were properly defined, you had to consider which tabular and visual summaries were appropriate for each variable and how specific mixes of variables might be used to gain insights about the 407 funds.

From summaries of the risk variable, you learned that nearly three-quarters of the funds were of average risk and there are many more high risk funds than low risk funds. From contingency tables of the fund type and risk, you observed that high risk funds were proportionally a larger category for growth funds than for value funds. From histograms and percentage polygons of the one-year return percentages, you were able to observe that the one-year returns were lower for the growth funds than for the value funds and that returns for both groups were concentrated between 0% and 15%, with returns for the value funds more concentrated between 5 and 15 than the growth funds.

From various multidimensional contingency tables, you discovered more complex relationships. For example, from a table that summarizes fund type, risk, and market cap, you discovered that small cap funds for both the growth and value fund type categories were disproportionly high risk. From a table that added a summary measure of the 10-year return percentage variable, you discovered that large cap, high risk growth funds had the highest mean 10-year return percentage while large cap, high risk *value* funds had the lowest mean.

You used Excel slicers to answer interactive questions that prospective investors might have, such as: Which funds in the sample had the highest expense ratios? With the insights gained and the interactive exploratory tools you created, you can help prospective clients make better informed choices. Of course, the past performance of a fund does not guarantee its future performance. You might also want to use organize and visualize methods to analyze other variables. For example, you might want to examine the differences in return in the past 3 years, in the past 5 years, and the past 10 years to see how the growth funds, the value funds, and the small, mid-cap, and large market cap funds performed.

▼ SUMMARY

You organize and visualize variables by making tabular and visual summaries. The methods you use vary by the type of variable, as well as the number of variables you seek to organize and visualize at the same time. Table 2.20 summarizes these methods by type of variable and the number of variables being summarized.

Using the appropriate methods to organize and visualize your data allows you to reach preliminary conclusions about the data. In several different chapter examples, tabular and visual summaries helped you reach conclusions about the primary way people pay for purchases and other transactions, the cost of meals at center city and metro area restaurants, and some of the differences among the 407 funds in a retirement fund sample.

Using the appropriate tabular and visual summaries can provide initial insights about your variables and cause you to ask additional questions about your data. Those questions may cause you to use interactive techniques to further explore your data or perform additional analysis at a later time.

Organize and visualize methods can be misused, thereby undermining the usefulness of the tabular and visual summaries those methods create. Following best practices when making visual summaries (see Exhibit 2.1) can minimize common mistakes that lead to displays that obscure data or create a false or misleading impression of data collected.

For numerical variables, there are many additional ways to summarize data that involve computing sample statistics or population parameters. The most common examples of these *numerical descriptive measures* are the subject of Chapter 3.

TABLE 2.20
Methods to Organize and Visualize Variables

Categorical variables	
Organize	Summary table, contingency table (Section 2.1)
Visualize one variable	Bar chart, pie chart, doughnut chart, Pareto chart (Section 2.3)
Visualize two variables	Side-by-side chart, doughnut chart, sparklines (Sections 2.3 and 2.6)
Numerical variables	
Organize	Ordered array, frequency distribution, relative frequency distribution, percentage distribution, cumulative percentage distribution (Section 2.2)
Visualize one variable	Stem-and-leaf display, histogram, percentage polygon, cumulative percentage polygon (ogive) (Section 2.4)
Visualize two variables	Scatter plot, time-series plot (Section 2.5)
Mix of variables	
Organize	Multidimensional tables (Section 2.6)
Visualize	Excel PivotCharts, Excel slicers (section 2.6)

▼ REFERENCES

1. Batemen, S., R. Mandryk, C. Gutwin, A. Genest, D. McDine, and C. Brooks. "Useful Junk? The Effects of Visual Embellishment on Comprehension and Memorability of Charts." **bit.ly/1HMDnpc**.
2. edwardtutfe.com, "Edward Tufte forum: Pie Charts." **bit.ly/1E3l1Pb**.
3. Few, S. *Displaying Data for At-a-Glance Monitoring*, Second ed. Burlingame, CA: Analytics Press, 2013.
4. Gross, B. *The Managing of Organizations: The Administrative Struggle*, Vols. I & II. New York: The Free Press of Glencoe, 1964.
5. Huff, D. *How to Lie with Statistics*. New York: Norton, 1954.
6. Tufte, E. R. *Beautiful Evidence*. Cheshire, CT: Graphics Press, 2006.
7. Tufte, E. R. *The Visual Display of Quantitative Information*, 2nd ed. Cheshire, CT: Graphics Press, 2002.
8. Wainer, H. *Visual Revelations: Graphical Tales of Fate and Deception from Napoleon Bonaparte to Ross Perot*. New York: Copernicus/Springer-Verlag, 1997.

▼ KEY EQUATIONS

Determining the Class Interval Width

$$\text{Interval width} = \frac{\text{highest value} - \text{lowest value}}{\text{number of classes}} \quad (2.1)$$

Computing the Proportion or Relative Frequency

$$\text{Proportion} = \text{relative frequency} = \frac{\text{number of values in each class}}{\text{total number of values}} \quad (2.2)$$

▼ KEY TERMS

bar chart 46	doughnut chart 47	pie chart 47
bins 40	drill down 64	PivotChart 66
cell 34	frequency distribution 38	PivotTable 63
chartjunk 70	histogram 53	proportion 41
class boundaries 39	joint response 34	relative frequency 41
class interval 38	lurking variables 64	relative frequency distribution 41
class interval width 39	multidimensional contingency table 63	scatter plot 59
class midpoints 40	ogive (cumulative percentage polygon) 56	side-by-side bar chart 50
classes 38	ordered array 37	slicer 65
contingency table 34	Pareto chart 48	sparklines 66
cumulative percentage distribution 42	Pareto principle 48	stem-and-leaf display 53
cumulative percentage polygon (ogive) 56	percentage distribution 41	summary table 33
data discovery 63	percentage polygon 54	time-series plot 61

▼ CHECKING YOUR UNDERSTANDING

2.77 How do histograms and polygons differ in construction and use?

2.78 Why would you construct a summary table?

2.79 What are the advantages and disadvantages of using a bar chart, a pie chart, a doughnut chart, and a Pareto chart?

2.80 Compare and contrast the bar chart for categorical data with the histogram for numerical data.

2.81 What is the difference between a time-series plot and a scatter plot?

2.82 Why is it said that the main feature of a Pareto chart is its ability to separate the "vital few" from the "trivial many"?

2.83 What are the three different ways to break down the percentages in a contingency table?

2.84 How can a multidimensional table differ from a two-variable contingency table?

2.85 What type of insights can you gain from a contingency table that contains three variables that you cannot gain from a contingency table that contains two variables?

2.86 What is the difference between a drill-down and a slicer?

2.87 What is the difference between a time-series plot and sparklines?

▼ CHAPTER REVIEW PROBLEMS

2.88 The following summary table presents the breakdown of the price of a new college textbook:

Revenue Category	Percentage (%)	
Publisher	64.8	
Manufacturing costs		32.3
Marketing and promotion		15.4
Administrative costs and taxes		10.0
After-tax profit		7.1
Bookstore	22.4	
Employee salaries and benefits		11.3
Operations		6.6
Pretax profit		4.5
Author	11.6	
Freight	1.2	

Source: Data extracted from **www.nacs.org/LinkClick.aspx?file ticket=_Jz-tFOW7oM%3D**.

a. Using the four categories of publisher, bookstore, author, and freight, construct a bar chart, a pie chart, and a Pareto chart.

b. Using the four subcategories of publisher and three subcategories of bookstore, along with the author and freight categories, construct a Pareto chart.

c. Based on the results of (a) and (b), what conclusions can you reach concerning who gets the revenue from the sales of new college textbooks? Do any of these results surprise you? Explain.

2.89 The following table represents the market share (in number of movies, gross in millions of dollars, and millions of tickets sold) of each type of movie in 2014:

Type	Number	Gross ($millions)	Tickets (millions)
Original screenplay	386	3,405.7	416.9
Based on fiction book/short story	75	1,740.1	213.0
Based on comic/ graphic novel	14	1,468.1	179.7
Based on real-life events	198	336.9	41.2
Based on factual book/article	19	693.5	84.9
Based on folk tale/ fairy tale	6	286.7	35.1
Based on TV	9	711.5	87.1
Remake	7	569.7	69.7
Based on toy	1	257.8	35.1
Spin-off	5	417.9	51.2

Source: Data extracted from www.the-numbers.com/market/2014/summary.

a. Construct a bar chart, a pie chart, a doughnut chart, and a Pareto chart for the number of movies, gross (in $millions), and number of tickets sold (in millions).
b. What conclusions can you reach about the market shares of the different types of movies in 2014?

2.90 A survey was completed by senior-level marketers on marketer expectations and perspectives going into the next year for such things as marketing spending levels, media usage, and new business activities. Marketers were asked about how they most often find out about new marketing agencies for hire and the value they are placing on marketing agencies that specialize in their industry. The results are presented in the following tables:

Most often Way to Find out About New Marketing Agencies	Percentage (%)
Calls/emails from agencies	32%
Social outreach	6%
Searching on Google, Bing	7%
Referrals from friends, colleagues	48%
Agency search consultants	7%

Source: Data extracted from "2014 RSW/US New Year Outlook Report," bit.ly/1fVZTj5.

a. Construct a bar chart, a pie chart, a doughnut chart, and a Pareto chart.
b. Which graphical method do you think is best for portraying these data?

Importance of Marketing Agency Specializing in Marketer's Industry	Percentage (%)
Very important	43%
Somewhat important	45%
Not at all important	12%

Source: Data extracted from "2014 RSW/US New Year Outlook Report," bit.ly/1fVZTj5.

c. Construct a bar chart, a pie chart, a doughnut chart, and a Pareto chart.
d. Which graphical method do you think is best for portraying these data?
e. What conclusions can you reach concerning marketers' perspective on new marketing agencies?

2.91 The owner of a restaurant that serves Continental-style entrées has the business objective of learning more about the patterns of patron demand during the Friday-to-Sunday weekend time period. Data were collected from 630 customers on the type of entrée ordered and were organized in the following table (and stored in Entree):

Type of Entrée	Number Ordered
Beef	187
Chicken	103
Mixed	30
Duck	25
Fish	122
Pasta	63
Shellfish	74
Veal	26
Total	630

a. Construct a percentage summary table for the types of entrées ordered.
b. Construct a bar chart, a pie chart, doughnut chart, and a Pareto chart for the types of entrées ordered.
c. Do you prefer using a Pareto chart or a pie chart for these data? Why?
d. What conclusions can the restaurant owner reach concerning demand for different types of entrées?

2.92 Suppose that the owner of the restaurant in Problem 2.91 also wants to study the demand for dessert during the same time period. She decides that in addition to studying whether a dessert was ordered, she will also study the gender of the individual and whether a beef entrée was ordered. Data were collected from 630 customers and organized in the following contingency tables:

DESSERT ORDERED	GENDER Male	Female	Total
Yes	50	96	146
No	250	234	484
Total	300	330	630

DESSERT ORDERED	BEEF ENTRÉE		
	Yes	No	Total
Yes	74	68	142
No	123	365	488
Total	197	433	630

a. For each of the two contingency tables, construct contingency tables of row percentages, column percentages, and total percentages.
b. Which type of percentage (row, column, or total) do you think is most informative for each gender? For beef entrée? Explain.
c. What conclusions concerning the pattern of dessert ordering can the restaurant owner reach?

2.93 The following data represent the pounds per capita of fresh food and packaged food consumed in the United States, Japan, and Russia in a recent year:

	COUNTRY		
FRESH FOOD	United States	Japan	Russia
Eggs, nuts, and beans	88	94	88
Fruit	124	126	88
Meat and seafood	197	146	125
Vegetables	194	278	335
PACKAGED FOOD			
Bakery goods	108	53	144
Dairy products	298	147	127
Pasta	12	32	16
Processed, frozen, dried, and chilled food, and ready-to-eat meals	183	251	70
Sauces, dressings, and condiments	63	75	49
Snacks and candy	47	19	24
Soup and canned food	77	17	25

Source: Data extracted from H. Fairfield, "Factory Food," *The New York Times*, April 4, 2010, p. BU5.

a. For the United States, Japan, and Russia, construct a bar chart, a pie or doughnut chart, and a Pareto chart for different types of fresh foods consumed.
b. For the United States, Japan, and Russia, construct a bar chart, a pie or doughnut chart, and a Pareto chart for different types of packaged foods consumed.
c. What conclusions can you reach concerning differences between the United States, Japan, and Russia in the fresh foods and packaged foods consumed?

2.94 The Air Travel Consumer Report, a monthly product of the Department of Transportation's Office of Aviation Enforcement and Proceedings (OAEP), is designed to assist consumers with information on the quality of services provided by airlines. The report includes a summary of consumer complaints by industry group and by complaint category. A breakdown of 910 November

2014 consumer complaints based on industry group is given in the following table:

Industry Group	Number of Consumer Complaints
Airlines	876
Travel agents	19
Miscellaneous	15
Industry total	910

Source: Data extracted from "The Travel Consumer Report," Office of Aviation Enforcement and Proceedings, November 2014.

a. Construct a Pareto chart for the number of complaints by industry group. What industry group accounts for most of the complaints?

The 910 consumer complaints against airlines are summarized by type in the following table:

Complaint Category	Complaints
Flight problems	253
Oversales	39
Reservation/ticketing/boarding	116
Fares	78
Refunds	73
Baggage	162
Customer service	119
Disability	43
Advertising	9
Discrimination	2
Other	16
Total	910

b. Construct pie charts and doughnut charts to display the percentage of complaints by type.

2.95 One of the major measures of the quality of service provided by an organization is the speed with which the organization responds to customer complaints. A large family-held department store selling furniture and flooring, including carpet, had undergone a major expansion in the past several years. In particular, the flooring department had expanded from 2 installation crews to an installation supervisor, a measurer, and 15 installation crews. A business objective of the company was to reduce the time between when the complaint is received and when it is resolved. During a recent year, the company received 50 complaints concerning carpet installation. The number of days between the receipt of the complaint and the resolution of the complaint for the 50 complaints, stored in **Furniture**, are:

54	5	35	137	31	27	152	2	123	81	74	27
11	19	126	110	110	29	61	35	94	31	26	5
12	4	165	32	29	28	29	26	25	1	14	13
13	10	5	27	4	52	30	22	36	26	20	23
33	68										

a. Construct a frequency distribution and a percentage distribution.
b. Construct a histogram and a percentage polygon.

c. Construct a cumulative percentage distribution and plot a cumulative percentage polygon (ogive).

d. On the basis of the results of (a) through (c), if you had to tell the president of the company how long a customer should expect to wait to have a complaint resolved, what would you say? Explain.

2.96 The file DomesticBeer contains the percentage alcohol, number of calories per 12 ounces, and number of carbohydrates (in grams) per 12 ounces for 158 of the best selling domestic beers in the United States.

Source: Data extracted from **www.beer100.com/beercalories.htm**, February 3, 2015.

a. Construct a percentage histogram for percentage alcohol, number of calories per 12 ounces, and number of carbohydrates (in grams) per 12 ounces.

b. Construct three scatter plots: percentage alcohol versus calories, percentage alcohol versus carbohydrates, and calories versus carbohydrates.

c. Discuss what you learned from studying the graphs in (a) and (b).

2.97 The file CigaretteTax contains the state cigarette tax ($) for each state as of January 1, 2015.

a. Construct an ordered array.

b. Plot a percentage histogram.

c. What conclusions can you reach about the differences in the state cigarette tax between the states?

2.98 The file CDRate contains the yields for one-year certificates of deposit (CDs) and for five-year CDs for 25 banks in the United States, as of April 29, 2015.

Source: Data extracted and compiled from **www.Bankrate.com**, April 29, 2015.

a. Construct a stem-and-leaf display for one-year CDs and five-year CDs.

b. Construct a scatter plot of one-year CDs versus five-year CDs.

c. What is the relationship between the one-year CD rate and the five-year CD rate?

2.99 The file CEO2013 includes the total compensation (in $millions) for CEOs of 200 large public companies and the investment return in 2013. (Data extracted from "Millions by Millions, CEO Pay Goes Up," **usat.ly/1jhbypl**) For total compensation:

a. Construct a frequency distribution and a percentage distribution.

b. Construct a histogram and a percentage polygon.

c. Construct a cumulative percentage distribution and plot a cumulative percentage polygon (ogive).

d. Based on (a) through (c), what conclusions can you reach concerning CEO compensation in 2013?

e. Construct a scatter plot of total compensation and investment return in 2013.

f. What is the relationship between the total compensation and investment return in 2013?

2.100 Studies conducted by a manufacturer of Boston and Vermont asphalt shingles have shown product weight to be a major factor in customers' perception of quality. Moreover, the weight represents the amount of raw materials being used and is therefore very important to the company from a cost standpoint. The last stage of the assembly line packages the shingles before the packages are placed on wooden pallets. The variable of interest is the weight in pounds of the pallet, which for most brands holds 16 squares of shingles. The company expects pallets of its Boston brand-name shingles to weigh at least 3,050 pounds but less than 3,260 pounds. For the company's Vermont brand-name shingles, pallets should weigh at least 3,600 pounds but less than 3,800. Data, collected from a sample of 368 pallets of Boston shingles and 330 pallets of Vermont shingles, are stored in Pallet .

a. For the Boston shingles, construct a frequency distribution and a percentage distribution having eight class intervals, using 3,015, 3,050, 3,085, 3,120, 3,155, 3,190, 3,225, 3,260, and 3,295 as the class boundaries.

b. For the Vermont shingles, construct a frequency distribution and a percentage distribution having seven class intervals, using 3,550, 3,600, 3,650, 3,700, 3,750, 3,800, 3,850, and 3,900 as the class boundaries.

c. Construct percentage histograms for the Boston and Vermont shingles.

d. Comment on the distribution of pallet weights for the Boston and Vermont shingles. Be sure to identify the percentages of pallets that are underweight and overweight.

2.101 What was the average price of a room at two-star, three-star, and four-star hotels around the world during the first half of 2014? The file HotelPrices contains the prices in English pounds (about US$1.70 as of July 2015). (Data extracted from "Hotels. com Hotel Price Index," **bit.ly/1E0TZUr**.) Complete the following for the two-star, three-star, and four-star hotels:

a. Construct a frequency distribution and a percentage distribution.

b. Construct a histogram and a percentage polygon.

c. Construct a cumulative percentage distribution and plot a cumulative percentage polygon (ogive).

d. What conclusions can you reach about the cost of two-star, three-star, and four-star hotels?

e. Construct separate scatter plots of the cost of two-star hotels versus three-star hotels, two-star hotels versus four-star hotels, and three-star hotels versus four-star hotels.

f. What conclusions can you reach about the relationship of the price of two-star, three-star, and four-star hotels?

2.102 The file Protein contains calorie and cholesterol information for popular protein foods (fresh red meats, poultry, and fish).

Source: U.S. Department of Agriculture.

a. Construct a percentage histogram for the number of calories.

b. Construct a percentage histogram for the amount of cholesterol.

c. What conclusions can you reach from your analyses in (a) and (b)?

2.103 The file NaturalGas contains the monthly average commercial and residential prices for natural gas (dollars per thousand cubic feet) in the United States from January 1, 2008, to January 1, 2015. (Data extracted from "U.S. Natural Gas Prices," **1.usa.gov/1I2qMjg**, March 1, 2015.) For the commercial price and the residential price:

a. Construct a time-series plot.

b. What pattern, if any, is present in the data?

c. Construct a scatter plot of the commercial price and the residential price.

d. What conclusion can you reach about the relationship between the commercial price and the residential price?

2.104 The following data (stored in Drink) represent the amount of soft drink in a sample of 50 consecutively filled 2-liter bottles. The results are listed horizontally in the order of being filled:

2.109 2.086 2.066 2.075 2.065 2.057 2.052 2.044 2.036 2.038
2.031 2.029 2.025 2.029 2.023 2.020 2.015 2.014 2.013 2.014

2.012 2.012 2.012 2.010 2.005 2.003 1.999 1.996 1.997 1.992
1.994 1.986 1.984 1.981 1.973 1.975 1.971 1.969 1.966 1.967
1.963 1.957 1.951 1.951 1.947 1.941 1.941 1.938 1.908 1.894

a. Construct a time-series plot for the amount of soft drink on the Y axis and the bottle number (going consecutively from 1 to 50) on the X axis.

b. What pattern, if any, is present in these data?

c. If you had to make a prediction about the amount of soft drink filled in the next bottle, what would you predict?

d. Based on the results of (a) through (c), explain why it is important to construct a time-series plot and not just a histogram, as was done in Problem 2.47 on page 59.

2.105 The file **Currency** contains the exchange rates of the Canadian dollar, the Japanese yen, and the English pound from 1980 to 2014, where the Canadian dollar, the Japanese yen, and the English pound are expressed in units per U.S. dollar.

a. Construct time-series plots for the yearly closing values of the Canadian dollar, the Japanese yen, and the English pound.

b. Explain any patterns present in the plots.

c. Write a short summary of your findings.

d. Construct separate scatter plots of the value of the Canadian dollar versus the Japanese yen, the Canadian dollar versus the English pound, and the Japanese yen versus the English pound.

e. What conclusions can you reach concerning the value of the Canadian dollar, Japanese yen, and English pound in terms of the U.S. dollar?

2.106 A/B testing allows businesses to test a new design or format for a web page to determine if the new web page is more effective than the current one. Web designers decide to create a new call-to-action button for a web page. Every visitor to the web page was randomly shown either the original call-to-action button (the control) or the new variation. The metric used to measure success was the download rate: the number of people who downloaded the file divided by the number of people who saw that particular call-to-action button. Results of the experiment yielded the following:

Variations	Downloads	Visitors
Original call to action button	351	3,642
New call to action button	485	3,556

a. Compute the percentage of downloads for the original call-to-action button and the new call-to-action button.

b. Construct a bar chart of the percentage of downloads for the original call-to-action button and the new call-to-action button.

c. What conclusions can you reach concerning the original call-to-action button and the new call-to-action button?

Web designers then create a new page design for a web page. Every visitor to the web page was randomly shown either the original web design (the control) or the new variation. The metric used to measure success was the download rate: the number of people who downloaded the file divided by the number of people who saw that particular web design. Results of the experiment yielded the following:

Variations	Downloads	Visitors
Original web design	305	3,427
New web design	353	3,751

d. Compute the percentage of downloads for the original web design and the new web design.

e. Construct a bar chart of the percentage of downloads for the original web design and the new web design.

f. What conclusions can you reach concerning the original web design and the new web design?

g. Compare your conclusions in (f) with those in (c).

Web designers next test two factors simultaneously—the call-to-action button and the new page design. Every visitor to the web page was randomly shown one of the following:

> Old call-to-action button with original page design
> New call-to-action button with original page design
> Old call-to-action button with new page design
> New call-to-action button with new page design

Again, the metric used to measure success was the download rate: the number of people who downloaded the file divided by the number of people who saw that particular call-to-action button and web design. Results of the experiment yielded the following:

Call-to-Action Button	Page Design	Downloaded	Declined	Total
Original	Original	83	917	1,000
New	Original	137	863	1,000
Original	New	95	905	1,000
New	New	170	830	1,000
Total		485	3,515	4,000

h. Compute the percentage of downloads for each combination of call-to-action button and web design.

i. What conclusions can you reach concerning the original call to action button and the new call to action button and the original web design and the new web design?

j. Compare your conclusions in (i) with those in (c) and (g).

2.107 (Class Project) Have each student in the class respond to the question "Which carbonated soft drink do you most prefer?" so that the instructor can tally the results into a summary table.

a. Convert the data to percentages and construct a Pareto chart.

b. Analyze the findings.

2.108 (Class Project) Cross-classify each student in the class by gender (male, female) and current employment status (yes, no), so that the instructor can tally the results.

a. Construct a table with either row or column percentages, depending on which you think is more informative.

b. What would you conclude from this study?

c. What other variables would you want to know regarding employment in order to enhance your findings?

REPORT WRITING EXERCISES

2.109 Referring to the results from Problem 2.100 page 78 concerning the weights of Boston and Vermont shingles, write a report that evaluates whether the weights of the pallets of the two types of shingles are what the company expects. Be sure to incorporate tables and charts into the report.

▼CASES

Managing Ashland MultiComm Services

Recently, Ashland MultiComm Services has been criticized for its inadequate customer service in responding to questions and problems about its telephone, cable television, and Internet services. Senior management has established a task force charged with the business objective of improving customer service. In response to this charge, the task force collected data about the types of customer service errors, the cost of customer service errors, and the cost of wrong billing errors. It found the following data:

Types of Customer Service Errors

Type of Errors	Frequency
Incorrect accessory	27
Incorrect address	42
Incorrect contact phone	31
Invalid wiring	9
On-demand programming error	14
Subscription not ordered	8
Suspension error	15
Termination error	22
Website access error	30
Wrong billing	137
Wrong end date	17
Wrong number of connections	19
Wrong price quoted	20
Wrong start date	24
Wrong subscription type	33
Total	448

Cost of Customer Service Errors in the Past Year

Type of Errors	Cost ($thousands)
Incorrect accessory	17.3
Incorrect address	62.4
Incorrect contact phone	21.3
Invalid wiring	40.8
On-demand programming errors	38.8
Subscription not ordered	20.3
Suspension error	46.8
Termination error	50.9
Website access errors	60.7
Wrong billing	121.7
Wrong end date	40.9
Wrong number of connections	28.1
Wrong price quoted	50.3
Wrong start date	40.8
Wrong subscription type	60.1
Total	701.2

Type and Cost of Wrong Billing Errors

Type of Wrong Billing Errors	Cost ($thousands)
Declined or held transactions	7.6
Incorrect account number	104.3
Invalid verification	9.8
Total	121.7

1. Review these data (stored in AMS2-1). Identify the variables that are important in describing the customer service problems. For each variable you identify, construct the graphical representation you think is most appropriate and explain your choice. Also, suggest what other information concerning the different types of errors would be useful to examine. Offer possible courses of action for either the task force or management to take that would support the goal of improving customer service.

2. As a follow-up activity, the task force decides to collect data to study the pattern of calls to the help desk (stored in AMS2-2). Analyze these data and present your conclusions in a report.

Digital Case

In the Using Statistics scenario, you were asked to gather information to help make wise investment choices. Sources for such information include brokerage firms, investment counselors, and other financial services firms. Apply your knowledge about the proper use of tables and charts in this Digital Case about the claims of foresight and excellence by an Ashland-area financial services firm.

Open **EndRunGuide.pdf**, which contains the EndRun Financial Services "Guide to Investing." Review the guide, paying close attention to the company's investment claims and supporting data and then answer the following.

1. How does the presentation of the general information about EndRun in this guide affect your perception of the business?

2. Is EndRun's claim about having more winners than losers a fair and accurate reflection of the quality of its investment service? If you do not think that the claim is a fair and accurate one, provide an alternate presentation that you think is fair and accurate.

3. Review the discussion about EndRun's "Big Eight Difference" and then open and examine the attached sample of mutual funds. Are there any other relevant data from that file that could have been included in the Big Eight table? How would the new data alter your perception of EndRun's claims?

4. EndRun is proud that all Big Eight funds have gained in value over the past five years. Do you agree that EndRun should be proud of its selections? Why or why not?

CardioGood Fitness

The market research team at AdRight is assigned the task to identify the profile of the typical customer for each treadmill product offered by CardioGood Fitness. The market research team decides to investigate whether there are differences across the product lines with respect to customer characteristics. The team decides to collect data on individuals who purchased a treadmill at a CardioGood Fitness retail store during the prior three months. The data are stored in the `CardioGood Fitness` file. The team identifies the following customer variables to study: product purchased, TM195, TM498, or TM798; gender; age, in years; education, in years; relationship status, single or partnered; annual household income ($); average number of times the customer plans to use the treadmill each week; average number of miles the customer expects to walk/run each week; and self-rated fitness on an 1-to-5 ordinal scale, where 1 is poor shape and 5 is excellent shape.

1. Create a customer profile for each CardioGood Fitness treadmill product line by developing appropriate tables and charts.

2. Write a report to be presented to the management of CardioGood Fitness detailing your findings.

The Choice *Is* Yours Follow-Up

Follow up the Using Statistics Revisited section on page 73 by analyzing the differences in 3-year return percentages, 5-year return percentages, and 10-year return percentages for the sample of 407 retirement funds stored in `Retirement Funds`. In your analysis, examine differences between the growth and value funds as well as the differences among the small, mid-cap, and large market cap funds.

Clear Mountain State Student Survey

The student news service at Clear Mountain State University (CMSU) has decided to gather data about the undergraduate students that attend CMSU. They create and distribute a survey of 14 questions and receive responses from 111 undergraduates (stored in `StudentSurvey`). For each question asked in the survey, construct all the appropriate tables and charts and write a report summarizing your conclusions.

▾EXCEL GUIDE

EG2.1 ORGANIZING CATEGORICAL VARIABLES

The Summary Table

Key Technique Use the PivotTable feature to create a summary table from the set of untallied values for a variable.

Example Create a frequency and percentage summary table similar to Table 2.2 on page 34.

PHStat Use **One-Way Tables & Charts**.

For the example, open to the **DATA worksheet** of the **Retirement Funds workbook**. Select **PHStat ➜ Descriptive Statistics ➜ One-Way Tables & Charts**. In the procedure's dialog box (shown below):

1. Click **Raw Categorical Data**.
2. Enter **D1:D408** as the **Raw Data Cell Range** and check **First cell contains label**.
3. Enter a **Title**, check **Percentage Column**, and click **OK**.

PHStat creates a PivotTable summary table on a new worksheet. For problems with tallied data, click **Table of Frequencies** in step 1. Then, in step 2, enter the cell range of the tabular summary as the **Freq. Table Cell Range** (edit box name changes from Raw Data Cell Range).

In the PivotTable, risk categories appear in alphabetical order and not in the order low, average, and high as would normally be expected. To change to the expected order, use steps 14 and 15 of the *Workbook* instructions but change all references to cell A6 to cell A7 and drop the Low label over cell A5, not cell A4.

Workbook (untallied data) Use the **Summary Table workbook** as a model.

For the example, open to the **DATA worksheet** of the **Retirement Funds workbook** and select **Insert ➜ Pivot-Table** (**Data ➜ PivotTable** in Excel 2011). In the Create PivotTable dialog box (shown at top in right column):

1. Click **Select a table or range** and enter **D1:D408** as the **Table/Range** cell range.
2. Click **New Worksheet** and then click **OK**.

In the PivotTable fields (PivotTable Builder in OS X Excel, PivotTable Field List in older versions) display (shown below):

3. Drag **Risk** in the **Choose fields to add to report** box and drop it in the **Rows** (or **Row Labels**) box.
4. **Drag Risk in the Choose fields to add to report** box a second time and drop it in the Σ **Values** box. This second label changes to **Count of Risk to** indicate that a count, or tally, of the risk categories will be displayed in the PivotTable.

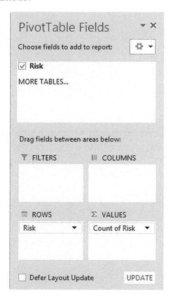

In the PivotTable being created:

5. Enter **Risk** in cell **A3** to replace the heading Row Labels.
6. Right-click cell **A3** and then click **PivotTable Options** in the shortcut menu that appears.

In the PivotTable Options dialog box (Windows version shown below):

7. Click the **Layout & Format** tab. Check **For empty cells show** and enter **0** as its value. Leave all other settings unchanged.
(*OS X*) Click the **Display** tab. Check **Empty cells as** and enter **0** as its value.

8. Click **OK** to complete the PivotTable.

To add a column for the percentage frequency:

9. Enter **Percentage** in cell **C3**. Enter the formula =B4/B$7 in cell **C4** and copy it down through **row 7**.
10. Select cell range **C4:C7**, right-click, and select **Format Cells** in the shortcut menu.
11. In the **Number** tab of the Format Cells dialog box, select **Percentage** as the **Category** and click **OK**.
12. Adjust the worksheet formatting, if appropriate (see Appendix B) and enter a title in cell **A1**.

In the PivotTable, risk categories appear in alphabetical order and not in the order low, average, and high, as would normally be expected. To change to the expected order:

13. Click the **Low** label in cell **A6** to highlight cell A6. Move the mouse pointer to the top edge of the cell until the mouse pointer changes to a four-way arrow (hand icon in OS X).
14. Drag the **Low** label and drop the label over cell **A4**. The risk categories now appear in the order Low, Average, and High in the summary table.

Workbook (tallied data) Use the **SUMMARY_ SIMPLE worksheet** of the **Summary Table workbook** as a model for creating a summary table.

The Contingency Table

Key Technique Use the PivotTable feature to create a contingency table from the set of individual values for a variable.

Example Construct a contingency table displaying fund type and risk level similar to Table 2.3 on Page 35.

PHStat (untallied data) Use **Two-Way Tables & Charts**. For the example, open to the **DATA worksheet** of the **Retirement Funds workbook**. Select **PHStat ➔ Descriptive Statistics ➔ Two-Way Tables & Charts**. In the procedure's dialog box (shown below):

1. Enter **C1:C408** as the **Row Variable Cell Range**.
2. Enter **D1:D408** as the **Column Variable Cell Range**.
3. Check **First cell in each range contains label**.
4. Enter a **Title** and click **OK**.

In the PivotTable, risk categories appear in alphabetical order and not in the order low, average, and high as would normally be expected. To change the expected order, use steps 13 and 14 of the *Workbook* instructions in the left column.

Workbook (untallied data) Use the **Contingency Table workbook** as a model.

For the example, open to the **DATA worksheet** of the **Retirement Funds workbook**. Select **Insert ➔ PivotTable**. In the Create PivotTable dialog box:

1. Click **Select a table or range** and enter **A1:N408** as the **Table/Range** cell range.
2. Click **New Worksheet** and then click **OK**.

In the PivotTable Fields (PivotTable Field List in some versions) task pane:

3. Drag **Type** from **Choose fields to add to report** and drop it in the **Rows** (or **Row Labels**) box.
4. Drag **Risk** from **Choose fields to add to report** and drop it in the **Columns** (or **Column Labels**) box.
5. Drag **Type** from **Choose fields to add to report** a second time and drop it in the Σ **Values** box. (**Type** changes to **Count of Type**.)

In the PivotTable being created:

6. Select cell **A3** and enter a **space character** to clear the label **Count of Type**.
7. Enter **Type** in cell **A4** to replace the heading Row Labels.
8. Enter **Risk** in cell **B3** to replace the heading Column Labels.
9. Click the **Low** label in cell **D4** to highlight cell D4. Move the mouse pointer to the left edge of the cell

until the mouse pointer changes to a four-way arrow (hand icon in OS X).

10. Drag the **Low** label to the left and drop the label between columns A and B. The Low label appears in B4 and column B now contains the low risk tallies.

11. Right-click over the PivotTable and then click **PivotTable Options** in the shortcut menu that appears.

In the PivotTable Options dialog box:

12. Click the **Layout & Format** tab. Check **For empty cells show** and enter **0** as its value. Leave all other settings unchanged.
    (*OS X*) Click the **Display** tab. Check **Empty cells as** and enter **0** as its value. Skip to step 15.

13. Click the **Total & Filters** tab.

14. Check **Show grand totals for columns** and **Show grand totals for rows**.

15. Click **OK** to complete the table.

[Separate Excel 2011 instructions are available online (see Appendix C).]

Workbook (tallied data) Use the **CONTINGENCY_SIMPLE worksheet** of the **Contingency Table workbook** as a model for creating a contingency table.

EG2.2 ORGANIZING NUMERICAL VARIABLES

Stacked and Unstacked Data

PHStat Use **Stack Data** or **Unstack Data**.
For example, to unstack the 1YrReturn% variable by the Type variable in the retirement funds sample, open to the **DATA worksheet** of the **Retirement Funds workbook**.
Select **PHStat → Data Preparation → Unstack Data**. In the procedure's dialog box:

1. Enter **C1:C408** as the **Grouping Variable Cell Range** (the Type variable).
2. Enter **J1:J408** as the **Stacked Data Cell Range** (the 3YrReturn% variable).
3. Check **First cells in both ranges contain label** and click **OK**.

The unstacked data appear on a new worksheet.

The Ordered Array

Workbook To create an ordered array, first select the numerical variable to be sorted. Then select **Home → Sort & Filter** (in the Editing group) and in the drop-down menu click **Sort Smallest to Largest**. (You will see **Sort A to Z** as the first drop-down choice if you did not select a cell range of *numerical* data.)

The Frequency Distribution

Key Technique Establish bins (see on page 40) and then use the **FREQUENCY** (untallied data cell range, bins cell

range) array function to tally data. (Appendix Section B.3 discusses how array functions differ from other functions.)

Example Create a frequency, percentage, and cumulative percentage distribution for the restaurant meal cost data that contain the information found in Tables 2.8, 2.10, and 2.13, in Section 2.2.

PHStat (untallied data) Use **Frequency Distribution**. If you plan to construct a histogram or polygon and a frequency distribution, use **Histogram & Polygons** (discussed in Section EG2.4).

For the example, open to the **DATA worksheet** of the **Restaurants workbook**. This worksheet contains the meal cost data in stacked format in column B and a set of bin numbers appropriate for those data in column I. Select **PHStat → Descriptive Statistics → Frequency Distribution**. In the procedure's dialog box (shown below):

1. Enter **B1:B101** as the **Variable Cell Range**, enter **I1:I11** as the **Bins Cell Range**, and check **First cell in each range contains label**.
2. Click **Multiple Groups - Stacked** and enter **A1:A101** as the **Grouping Variable Cell Range** (the Location variable.)
3. Enter a **Title** and click **OK**.

Frequency distributions for the two groups appear on separate worksheets. To display both distributions on the same worksheet, select the cell range **B3:D13** on one of the worksheets. Right-click that range and click **Copy** in the shortcut menu. Open to the other worksheet. In that other worksheet, right-click cell **E3** and click **Paste Special** in the shortcut menu. In the Paste Special dialog box, click **Values and numbers format** and click **OK**. Adjust the worksheet title and headings. (Appendix B further explains the Paste Special command.)

Click **Single Group Variable** in step 2 to construct a distribution from a single group. Click **Multiple Groups - Unstacked** in step 2 if the **Variable Cell Range** contains two or more columns of unstacked data.

Workbook (untalled data) Use the **Distributions workbook** as a model.
For the example, open to the **UNSTACKED worksheet** of the **Restaurants workbook**. This worksheet contains the

meal cost data unstacked in columns A and B and a set of bin numbers appropriate for those data in column D. Click the **insert worksheet icon** (the plus sign icon to the right of the sheet tabs, below the bottom of the worksheet) to insert a new worksheet.

In the new worksheet:

1. Enter a title in cell **A1**, **Bins** in cell **A3**, and **Frequency** in cell **B3**.

2. Copy the bin number list in the cell range **D2:D11** of the **UNSTACKED worksheet** and paste this list into cell **A4** of the new worksheet.

3. Select the cell range **B4:B13** that will hold the array formula.

4. Type, but do not press the **Enter** or **Tab** key, the formula =**FREQUENCY(UNSTACKED!$A$1:$A$51, $A$4:$A$13)**. Then, while holding down the **Ctrl** and **Shift** keys, press the **Enter** key to enter the array formula into the cell range **B4:B13**.

5. Adjust the worksheet formatting as necessary.

Note that in step 4, you enter the cell range as **UNSTACKED! $A$1:$A$51** and not as **$A$1:$A$51** because the untallied data are located on a separate worksheet (UNSTACKED). This is an example of an absolute cell reference, explained in Appendix Section B.3.

Steps 1 through 5 construct a frequency distribution for the meal costs at center city restaurants. To construct a frequency distribution for the meal costs at metro area restaurants, insert another worksheet and repeat steps 1 through 5, entering =**FREQUENCY(UNSTACKED!$B$1:$B$51, $A$4:$A$13)** as the array formula in step 4.

To display both distributions on the same worksheet, select the cell range **B3:B13** on one of the worksheets. Right-click that range and click **Copy** in the shortcut menu. Open to the other worksheet. In that other worksheet, right-click cell **C3** and click **Paste Special** in the shortcut menu. In the Paste Special dialog box, click **Values and numbers format** and click **OK**. Adjust the worksheet title and headings. (Appendix B further explains the Paste Special command.)

Analysis ToolPak (untallied data) Use **Histogram**. For the example, open to the **UNSTACKED worksheet** of the **Restaurants workbook**. This worksheet contains the meal cost data unstacked in columns A and B and a set of bin numbers appropriate for those data in column D. Then:

1. Select **Data ➔ Data Analysis**. In the Data Analysis dialog box, select **Histogram** from the **Analysis Tools** list and then click **OK**.

In the Histogram dialog box (shown in right column):

1. Enter **A1:A51** as the **Input Range** and enter **D1:D11** as the **Bin Range**. (If you leave **Bin Range** blank, the procedure creates a set of bins that will not be as well formed as the ones you can specify.)

2. Check **Labels** and click **New Worksheet Ply**.

3. Click **OK** to create the frequency distribution on a new worksheet.

In the new worksheet:

1. Select **row 1**. Right-click this row and click **Insert** in the shortcut menu. Repeat. (This creates two blank rows at the top of the worksheet.)

2. Enter a title in cell **A1**.

The ToolPak creates a frequency distribution that contains an improper bin labeled **More**. Correct this error by using these general instructions:

1. Manually add the frequency count of the **More** row to the frequency count of the preceding row. (For the example, the **More** row contains a zero for the frequency, so the frequency of the preceding row does not change.)

2. Select the worksheet row (for this example, row 14) that contains the More row.

3. Right-click that row and click **Delete** in the shortcut menu.

Steps 1 through 9 construct a frequency distribution for the meal costs at center city restaurants. To construct a frequency distribution for the meal costs at metro area restaurants, repeat these nine steps but in step 2 enter **B1:B51** as the **Input Range**.

The Relative Frequency, Percentage, and Cumulative Distributions

Key Technique Add columns that contain formulas for the relative frequency or percentage and cumulative percentage to a previously constructed frequency distribution.

Example Create a distribution that includes the relative frequency or percentage as well as the cumulative percentage information found in Tables 2.10 (relative frequency and percentage) and 2.13 (cumulative percentage) in Section 2.2 for the restaurant meal cost data.

PHStat (untallied data) Use **Frequency Distribution**. For the example, use the *PHStat* "The Frequency Distribution" instructions to construct a frequency distribution. PHStat constructs a frequency distribution that also includes columns for the percentages and cumulative percentages. To change the column of percentages to a column of relative frequencies, reformat that column. For example, open to the new worksheet that contains the center city restaurant frequency distribution and:

1. Select the cell range **C4:C13**, right-click, and select **Format Cells** from the shortcut menu.
2. In the **Number** tab of the Format Cells dialog box, select **Number** as the **Category** and click **OK**.

Then repeat these two steps for the new worksheet that contains the metro area restaurant frequency distribution.

Workbook (untallied data) Use the **Distributions workbook** as a model.

For the example, first construct a frequency distribution created using the *Workbook* "The Frequency Distribution" instructions. Open to the new worksheet that contains the frequency distribution for the center city restaurants and:

1. Enter **Percentage** in cell **C3** and **Cumulative Pctage** in cell **D3**.
2. Enter **=B4/SUM($B$4:$B$13)** in cell **C4** and copy this formula down through row **13**.
3. Enter **=C4** in cell **D4**.
4. Enter **=C5+D4** in cell **D5** and copy this formula down through row **13**.
5. Select the cell range **C4:D13**, right-click, and click **Format Cells** in the shortcut menu.
6. In the **Number** tab of the Format Cells dialog box, click **Percentage** in the **Category** list and click **OK**.

Then open to the worksheet that contains the frequency distribution for the metro area restaurants and repeat steps 1 through 6.

If you want column C to display relative frequencies instead of percentages, enter **Rel. Frequencies** in cell **C3**. Select the cell range **C4:C12**, right-click, and click **Format Cells** in the shortcut menu. In the **Number** tab of the Format Cells dialog box, click **Number** in the **Category** list and click **OK**.

Analysis ToolPak Use **Histogram** and then modify the worksheet created.

For the example, first construct the frequency distributions using the *Analysis ToolPak* instructions in "The Frequency Distribution." Then use the *Workbook* instructions to modify those distributions.

EG2.3 VISUALIZING CATEGORICAL VARIABLES

Many of the *Workbook* instructions in the rest of this Excel Guide refer to the numbered labels shown in the next column. Two Charts groups are shown: the left is the Microsoft Windows Excel display and the right is the OS X Excel display. (The Chart groups of older versions have

labeled icons that are similar to the ones in the illustrations below.)

The Bar Chart and the Pie (or Doughnut) Chart

Key Technique Use the Excel bar, pie, or doughnut chart feature with a tabular summary of the variable. If necessary, use the Sec-tion EG2.1 "The Summary Table" to first create that summary.

Example Construct a bar or pie (or doughnut) chart from a summary table similar to Table 2.3 on page 35.

PHStat Use **One-Way Tables & Charts**.

For the example, use the Section EG1 "The Summary Table" *PHStat* instructions, but in step 3, check either **Bar Chart** or **Pie Chart** (or both) in addition to entering a **Title**, checking **Percentage Column**, and clicking **OK**.

Workbook Use the **Summary Table workbook** as a model.

For the example, open to the **OneWayTable worksheet** of the **Summary Table workbook**. (The PivotTable in this worksheet was constructed using the Section EG2.1 "The Summary Table" instructions.) To construct a bar chart:

1. Select cell range **A4:B6**. (Begin your selection at cell B6 and not at cell A4, as you would normally do.)
2. Select **Insert → Bar** (#2 in the labeled Charts groups) and select the **Clustered Bar** gallery item.
3. Right-click the **Risk** drop-down button in the chart and click **Hide All Field Buttons** on Chart. (Does not apply to OS X Excel.)
4. Select **Design** (or **Chart Design**) → **Add Chart Element→ Axis Titles → Primary Horizontal**. In older Excel, select **Layout → Axis Titles → Primary Horizontal Axis Title → Title Below Axis**.
5. Select the words "Axis Title" and enter **Frequency** as the new axis title.
6. Relocate the chart to a chart sheet and turn off the chart legend and gridlines by using the instructions in Appendix Section B.6.

For other problems, the horizontal axis may not begin at 0. If this occurs, right-click the horizontal axis and click **Format Axis** in the shortcut menu. In the Format Axis display, click **Axis Options**. In the Axis Options, enter **0** as the **Minimum** and then close the display. In Excels with two-panel dialog boxes, in the Axis Options right pane, click the first **Fixed** (for **Minimum**), enter **0** as the value, and then click **Close**.

To construct a pie or doughnut chart, replace steps 2, 4, and 6 with these:

2. Select **Insert → Pie** (#4 in the labeled Charts groups) and select the **Pie** gallery item (or the **Doughnut** item).

4. Select **Design** (or **Chart Design**) **→ Add Chart Element → Data Labels → More Data Label Options**. In the Format Data Labels display, click **Label Options**. In the Label Options, check **Category Name** and **Percentage** and clear the other Label Contains check boxes. Click **Outside End** under Label Position (pie chart only) and close the display.

6. Relocate the chart to a chart sheet and turn off the chart legend and gridlines by using the instructions in Appendix Section B.6.

To see the Label Options in step 4 in the newest versions of Excel, you may need to first click the chart (fourth) icon at the top of the display. In older versions of Excel, select **Layout → Data Labels → More Data Label Options** in step 4. To construct a doughnut chart in those Excels, select **Insert → Other Charts** and then the **Doughnut** item in step 2.

The Pareto Chart

Key Technique Use the Excel chart feature with a modified summary table.

Example Construct a Pareto chart of the incomplete ATM transactions equivalent to Figure 2.4 on page 49.

PHStat Use **One-Way Tables & Charts**.
For the example, open to the **DATA worksheet** of the **ATM Transactions workbook**. Select **PHStat → Descriptive Statistics → One-Way Tables & Charts**. In the procedure's dialog box:

1. Click **Table of Frequencies** (because the worksheet contains tallied data).
2. Enter **A1:B8** as the **Freq. Table Cell Range** and check **First cell contains label**.
3. Enter a **Title**, check **Pareto Chart**, and click **OK**.

Workbook Use the **Pareto workbook** as a model.
For the example, open to the **ATMTable worksheet** of the **ATM Transactions workbook**. Begin by sorting the modified table by decreasing order of frequency:

1. Select row **11** (the Total row), right-click, and click **Hide** in the shortcut menu. (This prevents the total row from getting sorted.)
2. Select cell **B4** (the first frequency), right-click, and select **Sort → Sort Largest to Smallest**.
3. Select rows **10** and **12** (there is no row 11 visible), right-click, and click **Unhide** in the shortcut menu to restore row 11.

Next, add a column for cumulative percentage:

4. Enter **Cumulative Pct.** in cell **D3**. Enter **= C4** in cell **D4**. Enter **=D4 + C5** in cell **D5** and copy this formula down through **row 10**.
5. Adjust the formatting of column D as necessary.

Next, create the Pareto chart:

6. Select the cell range **A3:A10** and while holding down the **Ctrl** key also select the cell range **C3:D10**.
7. Select **Insert → Column** (#1 in the labeled Charts groups on page 86), and select the **Clustered Column** gallery item.
8. Select **Format**. In the Current Selection group, select **Series "Cumulative Pct."** from the drop-down list and then click **Format Selection**.
Select **Series "Cumulative Pct."** from the drop-down list at left and then click **More Formats**.
9. In the Format Data Series display, click **Series Options**. (To see the Series Options, you may have to first click the chart [third] icon near the top of the task pane.) In the Series Options, click **Secondary Axis**, and then close the display.
10. With the "Cumulative Pct." series still selected, select **Design → Change Chart Type**. In the Change Chart Type display, click **Combo** in the **All Charts** tab. In the Cumulative Pct. drop-down list, select the **Line with Markers** gallery item. Check **Secondary Axis** for the Cumulative Pct. and click **OK**.
With the "Cumulative Pct." series still selected, select **Chart Design → Change Chart Type → Line → Line with Markers**.

In older Excels, in step 10, select the **Line with Markers** gallery item in the Change Chart Type display and click **OK**. *(As first explained on page 11, instructions in this color and font are the alternate instructions for OS X Excel.)*

Next, set the maximum value of the primary and secondary (left and right) *Y* axis scales to 100%. For each *Y* axis:

11. Right-click on the axis and click **Format Axis** in the shortcut menu.
12. In the Format Axis display, click **Axis Options**. In Axis Options, enter **1** as the **Maximum**. (To see the Axis Options, you may have to first click the chart [fourth] icon near the top of the task pane.) Click **Tick Marks**, select **Outside** from the **Major type** drop-down list, and close the display. In Excel versions with two-panel dialog boxes, in the Axis Options right pane, click **Fixed** for **Maximum**, enter **1** as the value, and then click **Close**.
13. Relocate the chart to a chart sheet, turn off the chart legend and gridlines, and add chart and axis titles by using the instructions in Appendix Section B.6.

If you use a PivotTable as a summary table, replace steps 1 through 6 with these steps:

1. Add a percentage column in column C, using steps 9 through 12 of the *Workbook* "The Summary Table" instructions on page 82.
2. Add a cumulative percentage column in column D. Enter **Cumulative Pctage** in cell **D3**.
3. Enter **=C4** in cell **D4**. Enter **=C5+D4** in cell **D5**, and copy the formula down through all the rows in the PivotTable.
4. Select the total row, right-click, and click **Hide** in the shortcut menu. (This prevents the total row from getting sorted.)
5. Right-click the cell that contains the first frequency (cell B4 in the example) and select **Sort → Sort Largest to Smallest**.
6. Select the cell range of only the percentage and cumulative percentage columns (the equivalent of the cell range C3:D10 in the example).

When you construct a Pareto chart from a PivotTable using these steps, the categories will not have proper category labels. To correct the labels:

1. Right-click on the chart and click **Select Data** in the shortcut menu.
2. In the Select Data Source display, click **Edit** that appears under **Horizontal (Category) Axis Labels**. In the Axis Labels display, drag the mouse to select and enter the axis labels cell range (A4:A10 in the example) and then click **OK**.
   In the Select Data Source display, click the icon inside the **Horizontal (Category) axis labels** box and drag the mouse to select and enter the axis labels cell range.
3. Click **OK** to close the display.

Do not type the axis label cell range in step 2 as you would otherwise do for the reasons explained in Appendix Section B.7.

The Side-by-Side Chart

Key Technique Use an Excel bar chart that is based on a contingency table.

Example Construct a side-by-side chart that displays the fund type and risk level, similar to Figure 2.6 on page 50.

PHStat Use **Two-Way Tables & Charts**.
For the example, use the Section EG2.1 "The Contingency Table" *PHStat* instructions on page 83, but in step 4, check **Side-by-Side Bar Chart** in addition to entering a **Title** and clicking **OK**.

Workbook Use the **Contingency Table workbook** as a model.

For the example, open to the **TwoWayTable worksheet** of the **Contingency Table workbook** and:

1. Select cell **A3** (or any other cell inside the PivotTable).
2. Select **Insert → Bar** and select the **Clustered Bar** gallery item.
3. Right-click the **Risk** drop-down button in the chart and click **Hide All Field Buttons on Chart**. (Does not apply to OS X Excel.)
4. Relocate the chart to a chart sheet, turn off the gridlines, and add chart and axis titles by using the instructions in Appendix Section B.6.

When creating a chart from a contingency table that is not a PivotTable, select the cell range of the contingency table, including row and column headings, but excluding the total row and total column, as step 1.

To switch the row and column variables in a side-by-side chart, right-click the chart and then click **Select Data** in the shortcut menu. In the Select Data Source dialog box, click **Switch Row/Column** and then click **OK**.

EG2.4 VISUALIZING NUMERICAL VARIABLES

The Stem-and-Leaf Display

Key Technique Enter leaves as a string of digits that begin with the ' (apostrophe) character.

Example Construct a stem-and-leaf display of the one-year return percentage for the value retirement funds, similar to Figure 2.7 on page 54.

PHStat Use **Stem-and-Leaf Display**.
For the example, open to the **UNSTACKED worksheet** of the **Retirement Funds workbook**. Select **PHStat → Descriptive Statistics → Stem-and-Leaf Display**. In the procedure's dialog box (shown in the next column):

1. Enter **B1:B139** as the **Variable Cell Range** and check **First cell contains label**.
2. Click **Set stem unit as** and enter **10** in its box.
3. Enter a **Title** and click **OK**.

When creating other displays, use the **Set stem unit as** option sparingly and only if Autocalculate stem unit creates a display that has too few or too many stems. (Stem units you specify must be a power of 10.)

Workbook

Manually construct the stems and leaves on a new worksheet to create a stem-and-leaf display. Adjust the column width of the column that holds the leaves as necessary.

The Histogram

Key Technique Modify an Excel column chart.

Example Construct histograms for the one-year return percentages for the growth and value retirement funds, similar to Figure 2.9 on page 55.

PHStat Use **Histogram & Polygons**.
For the example, open to the **DATA worksheet** of the **Retirement Funds workbook**. Select **PHStat → Descriptive Statistics → Histogram & Polygons**. In the procedure's dialog box (shown below):

1. Enter **I1: I408** as the **Variable Cell Range**, **P1:P10** as the **Bins Cell Range**, **Q1:Q9** as the **Midpoints Cell Range**, and check **First cell in each range contains label**.
2. Click **Multiple Groups - Stacked** and enter **C1:C408** as the **Grouping Variable Cell Range**. (In the DATA worksheet, the one-year return percentages are stacked. The column C values allow PHStat to unstack the values into growth and value groups.)
3. Enter a **Title**, check **Histogram**, and click **OK**.

PHStat inserts two new worksheets, each of which contains a frequency distribution and a histogram. To relocate the histograms to their own chart sheets, use the instructions in Appendix Section B.6.

Because you cannot define an explicit lower boundary for the first bin, so the first bin (see Section 2.2), there can be no midpoint defined for that bin. Therefore, the **Midpoints Cell Range** you enter must have one fewer cell than the **Bins Cell Range**. PHStat uses the first midpoint for the second bin and uses "—" as the label for the first bin.

The example uses the workaround discussed in "Classes and Excel Bins" on page 40. When you use this workaround, the histogram bar labeled—will *always* be a zero bar. Appendix Section B.8 explains how you can delete this unnecessary bar from the histogram, as was done for the examples shown in Section 2.4.

Workbook Use the **Histogram workbook** as a model. For the example, first construct frequency distributions for the growth and value funds. Open to the **UNSTACKED worksheet** of the **Retirement Funds workbook**. This worksheet contains the retirement funds data unstacked in columns A and B and a set of bin numbers and midpoints appropriate for those variables in columns D and E. Click the **insert worksheet icon** to insert a new worksheet.
In the new worksheet:

1. Enter a title in cell **A1**, Bins in cell **A3**, **Frequency** in cell **B3**, and **Midpoints** in cell **C3**.
2. Copy the bin number list in the cell range **D2:D10** of the **UNSTACKED worksheet** and paste this list into cell **A4** of the new worksheet.
3. Enter '**--** in cell **C4**. Copy the midpoints list in the cell range **E2:E9** of the **UNSTACKED worksheet** and paste this list into cell **C5** of the new worksheet.
4. Select the cell range **B4:B12** that will hold the array formula.
5. Type, but do not press the **Enter** or **Tab** key, the formula **=FREQUENCY(UNSTACKED!$A$2: $A$270, $A$4: $A$12)**. Then, while holding down the **Ctrl** and **Shift** keys, press the **Enter** key to enter the array formula into the cell range **B4:B12**.
6. Adjust the worksheet formatting as necessary.

Steps 1 through 6 construct a frequency distribution for the growth retirement funds. To construct a frequency distribution for the value retirement funds, insert another worksheet and repeat steps 1 through 6, entering **=FREQUENCY (UNSTACKED!$B$1: $B$139, $A$4: $A$12)** as the array formula in step 5.
Having constructed the two frequency distributions, continue by constructing the two histograms. Open to the worksheet that contains the frequency distribution for the growth funds and:

1. Select the cell range **B3:B12** (the cell range of the frequencies).
2. Select **Insert → Column** (#3 in the in the labeled Charts groups on page 86) and select the **Clustered Column** gallery item.

3. Right-click the chart and click **Select Data** in the short-cut menu.

In the Select Data Source display:

4. Click **Edit** under the **Horizontal (Categories) Axis Labels** heading. In the Axis Labels display, drag the mouse to select and enter the midpoints cell range (C4:C14) and click **OK**.
   In the Select Data Source display, click the icon inside the **Horizontal (Category) axis labels** box and drag the mouse to select and enter the midpoints cell range (C4:C14).

5. Click **OK**.

In the chart:

6. Right-click inside a bar and click **Format Data Series** in the shortcut menu.

7. In the Format Data Series display, click **Series Options**. In the Series Options, click **Series Options**, enter **0** as the **Gap Width** and then close the display. (To see the second Series Options, you may have to first click the chart [third] icon near the top of the task pane.)
   In OS X Excel, there is only one Series Options label, and the Gap Width setting is displayed without having to click Series Options.

8. Relocate the chart to a chart sheet, turn off the chart legend and gridlines, add axis titles, and modify the chart title by using the instructions in Appendix Section B.6.

Do not type the axis label cell range in step 4 as you would otherwise do for the reasons explained in Appendix Section B.7. In older versions of Excel, in step 7, click **Series Options** in the left pane, and in the Series Options right pane, change the **Gap Width** slider to **No Gap** and then click **Close**.

This example uses the workaround discussed in "Classes and Excel Bins" on page 40. When you use this workaround, the histogram bar labeled—will *always* be a zero bar. Appendix Section B.8 explains how you can delete this unnecessary bar from the histogram, as was done for the examples shown in Section 2.4.

Analysis ToolPak Use Histogram. For the example, open to the **UNSTACKED worksheet** of the **Retirement Funds workbook** and:

1. Select **Data ➔ Data Analysis**. In the Data Analysis dialog box, select **Histogram** from the **Analysis Tools** list and then click **OK**.

In the Histogram dialog box:

2. Enter **A1:A270** as the **Input Range** and enter **D1:D10** as the **Bin Range**.

3. Check **Labels**, click **New Worksheet Ply**, and check **Chart Output**.

4. Click **OK** to create the frequency distribution and histogram on a new worksheet.

In the new worksheet:

5. Follow steps 5 through 9 of the *Analysis ToolPak* instructions in "The Frequency Distribution" on page 85.

These steps construct a frequency distribution and histogram for the growth funds. To construct a frequency distribution and histogram for the value funds, repeat the nine steps but in step 2 enter **B1:B139** as the **Input Range**. You will need to correct several formatting errors that Excel makes to the histograms it constructs. For each histogram, first change the gap widths between bars to 0. Follow steps 6 and 7 of the Workbook instructions of this section, noting the special instructions that appear after step 8.

Histogram bars are labeled by bin numbers. To change the labeling to midpoints, open to each of the new worksheets and:

1. Enter **Midpoints** in cell **C3** and '-- in cell **C4**. Copy the cell range **E2:E9** of the **UNSTACKED worksheet** and paste this list into cell **C5** of the new worksheet.

2. Right-click the histogram and click **Select Data**.

In the Select Data Source display:

3. Click **Edit** under the **Horizontal (Categories) Axis Labels** heading. In the Axis Labels display, drag the mouse to select and enter the cell range **C4:C12** and click **OK**.
   In the Select Data Source display, click the icon inside the **Horizontal (Category) axis labels** box and drag the mouse to select and enter the cell range **C4:C12**.

4. Click **OK**.

5. Relocate the chart to a chart sheet, turn off the chart legend, and modify the chart title by using the instructions in Appendix Section B.6.

Do not type the axis label cell range in step 3 as you would otherwise do for the reasons explained in Appendix Section B.7.

This example uses the workaround discussed on page 40, "Classes and Excel Bins." Appendix Section B.8 explains how you can delete this unnecessary bar from the histogram, as was done for the examples shown in Section 2.4.

The Percentage Polygon and the Cumulative Percentage Polygon (Ogive)

Key Technique Modify an Excel line chart that is based on a frequency distribution.

Example Construct percentage polygons and cumulative percentage polygons for the one-year return percentages for the growth and value retirement funds, similar to Figure 2.11 on page 56 and Figure 2.12 on page 57.

PHStat Use **Histogram & Polygons**.

For the example, use the *PHStat* instructions for creating a histogram on page 89 but in step 3 of those instructions, also check **Percentage Polygon** and **Cumulative Percentage Polygon (Ogive)** before clicking **OK**.

Workbook Use the **Polygons workbook** as a model.

For the example, open to the **UNSTACKED worksheet** of the **Retirement Funds workbook** and follow steps 1 through 6 of the *Workbook* "The Histogram" instructions on page 89 to construct a frequency distribution for the growth funds. Repeat the steps to construct a frequency distribution for the value funds using the instructions that immediately follow step 6. Open to the worksheet that contains the growth funds frequency distribution and:

1. Select column **C**. Right-click and click **Insert** in the shortcut menu. Right-click and click **Insert** in the shortcut menu a second time. (The worksheet contains new, blank columns C and D and the midpoints column is now column E.)
2. Enter **Percentage** in cell **C3** and **Cumulative Pctage.** in cell **D3**.
3. Enter **=B4/SUM($B$4:$B$12)** in cell **C4** and copy this formula down through **row 12**.
4. Enter **=C4** in cell **D4**.
5. Enter **=C5 + D4** in cell **D5** and copy this formula down through row **12**.
6. Select the cell range **C4:D12**, right-click, and click **Format Cells** in the shortcut menu.
7. In the **Number** tab of the Format Cells dialog box, click **Percentage** in the **Category** list and click **OK**.

Open to the worksheet that contains the value funds frequency distribution and repeat steps 1 through 7. To construct the percentage polygons, open to the worksheet that contains the growth funds distribution and:

1. Select cell range **C4:C12**.
2. Select **Insert ➔ Line** (#4 in the labeled Charts groups on page 86), and select the **Line with Markers** gallery item.
3. Right-click the chart and click **Select Data** in the shortcut menu.

In the Select Data Source display:

4. Click **Edit** under the **Legend Entries (Series)** heading. In the Edit Series dialog box, enter the *formula* **="Growth Funds"** as the **Series name** and click **OK**.
   Enter the *formula* ="Growth Funds" as the **Name**.
5. Click **Edit** under the **Horizontal (Categories) Axis Labels** heading. In the Axis Labels display, drag the mouse to select and enter the cell range **E4:E12** and click **OK**.

In the Select Data Source display, click the icon inside the **Horizontal (Category) axis labels** box and drag the mouse to select and enter the cell range **E4:E12**.

6. Click **OK**.
7. Relocate the chart to a chart sheet, turn off the chart gridlines, add axis titles, and modify the chart title by using the instructions in Appendix Section B.6.

In the new chart sheet:

8. Right-click the chart and click **Select Data** in the shortcut menu.

In the Select Data Source display:

9. Click **Add** under the **Legend Entries (Series)** heading. In the Edit Series dialog box, enter the *formula* **="Value Funds"** as the **Series name** and press **Tab**.
   Click the "+" icon below the **Legend entries (Series)** list. Enter the *formula* ="Value Funds" as the **Name**.
10. With the placeholder value in **Series values** highlighted, click the sheet tab for the worksheet that contains the value funds distribution. In that worksheet, drag the mouse to select and enter the cell range **C4:C12** and click **OK**.
    Click the icon in the **Y** values box. Click the sheet tab for the worksheet that contains the value funds distribution and, in that worksheet, drag the mouse to select and enter the cell range **C4:C12**.
11. Click **Edit** under the **Horizontal (Categories) Axis Labels** heading. In the Axis Labels display, drag the mouse to select and enter the cell range **E4:E12** and click **OK**.
    In the Select Data Source display, click the icon inside the **Horizontal (Category) axis labels** box and drag the mouse to select and enter the cell range **E4:E12**.
    Click **OK**.

Do not type the axis label cell range in steps 10 and 11 as you would otherwise do for the reasons explained in Appendix Section B.7.

To construct the cumulative percentage polygons, open to the worksheet that contains the growth funds distribution and repeat steps 1 through 12, but in step 1, select the cell range **D4:D12**; in step 5, drag the mouse to select and enter the cell range **A4:A12**; and in step 11, drag the mouse to select and enter the cell range **D4:D12**.

If the *Y* axis of the cumulative percentage polygon extends past 100%, right-click the axis and click **Format Axis** in the shortcut menu. In the Format Axis display, click **Axis Options**. In the Axis Options, enter **0** as the **Minimum** and then close the display. In Excels with two-panel dialog boxes, in the Axis Options right pane, click the first **Fixed** (for **Minimum**), enter **0** as the value, and then click **Close**.

EG2.5 VISUALIZING TWO NUMERICAL VARIABLES

The Scatter Plot

Key Technique Use the Excel scatter chart.

Example Construct a scatter plot of revenue and value for NBA teams, similar to Figure 2.14 on page 60.

PHStat Use **Scatter Plot**.

For the example, open to the **DATA worksheet** of the **NBAValues workbook**. Select **PHStat → Descriptive Statistics → Scatter Plot**. In the procedure's dialog box (shown below):

1. Enter **D1:D31** as the **Y Variable Cell Range**.
2. Enter **C1:C31** as the **X Variable Cell Range**.
3. Check **First cells in each range contains label**.
4. Enter a **Title** and click **OK**.

To add a superimposed line like the one shown in Figure 2.14, click the chart and use step 3 of the *Workbook* instructions.

Workbook Use the **Scatter Plot workbook** as a model.

For the example, open to the **DATA worksheet** of the **NBAValues workbook** and:

1. Select the cell range **C1:D31**.
2. Select **Insert → Scatter (X, Y) or Bubble Chart** (#5 in the labeled Charts groups on page 86) and select the **Scatter** gallery item. (OS X Excel labels the #5 icon as **X Y (Scatter)**).
3. Select **Design** (or **Chart Design**) **→ Add Chart Element → Trendline → Linear**.

In older Excels, select **Scatter** in the Charts group in step 2 and **Layout → Trendline → Linear Trendline** in step 3.

4. Relocate the chart to a chart sheet, turn off the chart legend and gridlines, add axis titles, and modify the chart title by using the instructions in Appendix Section B.6.

When constructing Excel scatter charts with other variables, make sure that the *X* variable column precedes (is to the left of) the *Y* variable column. (If the worksheet is arranged *Y* then *X*, cut and paste so that the *Y* variable column appears to the right of the *X* variable column.)

The Time-Series Plot

Key Technique Use the Excel scatter chart.

Example Construct a time-series plot of movie revenue per year from 1995 to 2014, similar to Figure 2.15 on page 61.

Workbook Use the **Time Series workbook** as a model.

For the example, open to the **DATA worksheet** of the **Movie Revenues workbook** and:

1. Select the cell range **A1:B21**.
2. Select **Insert → Scatter (X, Y) or Bubble Chart** (#5 in the labeled Charts groups on page 86) and select the **Scatter with Straight Lines and Markers** gallery item. (OS X Excel labels the #5 icon as **X Y (Scatter)**, and older versions of Excel label the icon **Scattter**.)
3. Relocate the chart to a chart sheet, turn off the chart legend and gridlines, add axis titles, and modify the chart title by using the instructions in Appendix Section B.6.

When constructing time-series charts with other variables, make sure that the *X* variable column precedes (is to the left of) the *Y* variable column. (If the worksheet is arranged *Y* then *X*, cut and paste so that the *Y* variable column appears to the right of the *X* variable column.)

EG2.6 ORGANIZING AND VISUALIZING A SET OF VARIABLES

Multidimensional Contingency Tables

Key Technique Use the Excel PivotTable feature.

Example Construct a PivotTable showing percentage of overall total for fund type, risk, and market cap for the retirement funds sample, similar to the one shown at the right in Figure 2.16 on page 63.

Workbook Use the **MCT workbook** as a model.

For the example, open to the **DATA worksheet** of the **Retirement Funds workbook** and:

1. Select **Insert → PivotTable**.

In the Create PivotTable display:

2. Click **Select a table or range** and enter **A1: N408** as the **Table/Range**.
3. Click **New Worksheet** and then click **OK**.

In the PivotTable Fields (PivotTable Builder in OS X Excel, PivotTable Field List in older versions) display (partially shown below):

4. Drag **Type** in the **Choose fields to add to report** box and drop it in the **Rows** (or **Row** Labels) box.
5. Drag **Market Cap** in the **Choose fields to add to report** box and drop it in the **Rows** (or **Row Labels**) box.
6. Drag **Risk** in the **Choose fields to add to report** box and drop it in the **Columns** (or **Column Labels**) box.

7. Drag **Type** in the **Choose fields to add to report** box a second time and drop it in the Σ **Values** box. The dropped label changes to **Count of Type**.

8. Click (not right-click) the dropped label **Count of Type** and then click **Value Field Settings** in the shortcut menu. In the Value Field Settings display, click the **Show Values As** tab and select **% of Grand Total** from the **Show values as** drop-down list (shown below).
   Click the "*i*" icon to the right of the dropped label **Count of Type**. In the PivotTable Field display, click the **Show data as** tab and select **% of total** from the drop-down list.

9. Click **OK**.

In the PivotTable:

10. Enter a title in cell **A1**.
11. Follow steps 6 through 10 of the *Workbook* "The Contingency Table" instructions on page 83 that relabel the rows and columns and rearrange the order of the risk category columns.

Adding a Numerical Variable to a Multidimensional Contingency Table

Key Technique Alter the contents of the Σ Values box in the PivotTable Field List pane.

Example Construct a PivotTable of fund type, risk, and market cap, showing the mean three-year return percentage for the retirement funds sample, similar to the one shown in Figure 2.17 on page 64.

Workbook Use the **MCT workbook** as a model.
For the example, first construct the PivotTable showing percentage of overall total for fund type, risk, and market cap

for the retirement funds sample using the 11-step instructions of the "Multidimensional Contingency Table" *Workbook* instructions that begins on the previous page. Then continue with these steps:

12. If the PivotTable Field List pane is not visible, right-click cell **A3** and click **Show Field List** in the shortcut menu.
    If the PivotTable Builder (or PivotTable Field List) display is not visible, select **PivotTable Analyze → Field List**.

In the display:

13. Drag the blank label (changed from *Count of Type* in a prior step) in the Σ **Values** box and drop it outside the display to delete. In the PivotTable, all of the percentages disappear.
14. Drag **10YrReturn%** in the **Choose fields to add to report** box and drop it in the Σ **Values** box. The dropped label changes to *Sum of 10YrReturn%*.
15. Click (not right-click) **Sum of 10YrReturn%** and then click **Value Field Settings** in the shortcut menu. In the Value Field Settings display, click the **Summarize Values By** tab and select **Average** from the **Summarize value field by** drop-down list.
    Click the "*i*" icon to the right of the label **Sum of 10YrReturn%**. In the PivotTable Field display, click the **Summarize by** tab and select **Average** from the list.
16. Click **OK**. The label in the Σ **Values** box changes to *Average of 10YrReturn%*.

In the PivotTable:

17. Select cell range **B5:E13**, right-click, and click **Format Cells** in the shortcut menu. In the **Number** tab of the Format Cells dialog box, click Number, set the **Decimal places** to **2**, and click **OK**.

Excel Slicers

Key Technique Use the Excel slicer feature with a previously constructed PivotTable.

Example Construct slicers for type, market cap, star rating, and expense ratio to use with a PivotTable of fund type and risk, similar to the Figure 2.19 slicers on page 65.

Workbook Use the **Slicers workbook** as a model.
For the example, first construct a PivotTable using the *Workbook* "The Contingency Table" instructions on page 83. Then:

1. Click cell **A3** in the PivotTable.
2. Select **Insert → Slicer**.

In the Insert Slicers dialog box (shown on page 94):

3. Check **Market Cap**, **Type**, **Expense Ratio**, and **Star Rating**.
4. Click **OK**.

In the worksheet, drag the slicers to reposition them. If necessary, resize slicer panels as you would resize a window. Click the value buttons in the slicers to explore the data. For example, to create the display shown in the left illustration of Figure 2.20 on page 66 that answers question 1, click **0.29** in the **Expense Ratio** slicer.

When you click a value button, the icon at the top right of the slicer changes to include a red X [as can be seen in the expense ratio slicer in Figure 2.20 (left)]. Click this X icon to reset the slicer. When you click a value button, value buttons in other slicers may become dimmed [as have buttons such as Value, Mid-Cap, Small, Four, One, Three, and Two in Figure 2.20 (left)]. Dimmed buttons represent values that are not found in the currently "sliced" data.

PivotChart

Key Technique Use the PivotChart feature with a previously constructed PivotTable. (The PivotChart feature is not available in OS X Excel.)

Example Construct the PivotChart based on the Figure 2.17 PivotTable of type, risk, and market cap showing mean 10-year return percentage, shown in Figure 2.22 on page 67.

Workbook Use the **MCT workbook** as a model. For the example, open to the **MCT worksheet** of the **MCT workbook** and:

1. Select cell **A3** (or any other cell inside the PivotTable).
2. Select **Insert → PivotChart**.
3. In the Insert Chart display, click **Bar** in the **All Charts** tab and then select the **Clustered Bar** gallery item.

4. Relocate the chart to a chart sheet, turn off the gridlines, and add chart and axis titles by using the instructions in Appendix Section B.6.

In the PivotTable, collapse the **Growth** and **Value** categories, hiding the **Market Cap** categories. Note that contents of PivotChart changes to reflect changes made to the PivotTable.

Sparklines

Key Technique Use the sparklines feature.

Example Construct the sparklines for movie revenues per month for the period 2005 to 2014, shown in Figure 2.23 on page 67.

Workbook Use the **Sparklines workbook** as a model. For the example, open to the **DATA worksheet** of the **MCT workbook** and:

1. Select **Insert → Line Sparkline**.
2. In the Create Sparklines dialog box (shown below), enter **B2:K13** as the **Data Range** and **M2:M13** as the **Location Range**.
3. Click **OK**.

With the sparklines selected:

4. Select **Design → Axis → Same for All Sparklines** (under Vertical Axis Minimum Value Options). Select **Design → Axis → Same for All Sparklines** (under Vertical Axis Maximum Value Options).
5. Select rows 2 through 13. Right-click and click **Row Height** in the shortcut menu. In the Row height dialog box, enter **30** (**0.85** in OS X Excel) as the **Row Height** and click **OK**.

Optionally, insert one or more rows at top of worksheet for a title and copy the month values in column A to column L for easier reference.

Numerical Descriptive Measures

OBJECTIVES

- Describe the properties of central tendency, variation, and shape in numerical variables
- Construct and interpret a boxplot
- Compute descriptive summary measures for a population
- Compute the covariance and the coefficient of correlation

▼USING STATISTICS
More Descriptive Choices

As a member of a Choice *Is* Yours investment service task force, you helped organize and visualize the variables found in a sample of 407 retirement funds. Now, several weeks later, prospective clients are asking for more information on which they can base their investment decisions. In particular, they would like to compare the results of an individual retirement fund to the results of similar funds.

For example, while the earlier work your team did shows how the one-year return percentages are distributed, prospective clients would like to know how the value for a particular mid-cap growth fund compares to the one-year returns of all mid-cap growth funds. They also seek to understand the variation among the returns. Are all the values relatively similar? And does any variable have outlier values that are either extremely small or extremely large?

While doing a complete search of the retirement funds data could lead to answers to the preceding questions, you wonder if there are better ways than extensive searching to uncover those answers. You also wonder if there are other ways of being more *descriptive* about the sample of funds—providing answers to questions not yet raised by prospective clients. If you can help the Choice *Is* Yours investment service provide such answers, prospective clients will be better able to evaluate the retirement funds that your firm features.

T he prospective clients in the More Descriptive Choices scenario have begun asking questions about numerical variables such as how the one-year return percentages vary among the individual funds that comprise the sample of 407 retirement funds. You also need to apply methods that help describe the central tendency, variation, and shape of such variables.

Central tendency is the extent to which the values of a numerical variable group around a typical, or central, value. **Variation** measures the amount of dispersion, or scattering, away from a central value that the values of a numerical variable show. The **shape** of a variable is the pattern of the distribution of values from the lowest value to the highest value.

This chapter describes ways you can compute these numerical descriptive measures as you begin to analyze your data within the DCOVA framework. The chapter also discusses the covariance and the coefficient of correlation, measures that can help show the strength of the association between two numerical variables. Computing the descriptive measures discussed in this chapter would be one way to help prospective clients of the Choice *Is* Yours service find the answers they seek.

3.1 Central Tendency

Most variables show a distinct tendency to group around a central value. When people talk about an "average value" or the "middle value" or the "most frequent value," they are talking informally about the mean, median, and mode—three measures of central tendency.

The Mean

The **arithmetic mean** (typically referred to as the **mean**) is the most common measure of central tendency. The mean can suggest a typical or central value and serves as a "balance point" in a set of data, similar to the fulcrum on a seesaw. The mean is the only common measure in which all the values play an equal role. You compute the mean by adding together all the values and then dividing that sum by the number of values in the data set.

The symbol $\overline{X}$, called *X-bar*, is used to represent the mean of a sample. For a sample containing n values, the equation for the mean of a sample is written as

$$\overline{X} = \frac{\text{sum of the values}}{\text{number of values}}$$

Using the series $X_1, X_2, \ldots, X_n$ to represent the set of n values and n to represent the number of values in the sample, the equation becomes

$$\overline{X} = \frac{X_1 + X_2 + \cdots + X_n}{n}$$

By using summation notation (discussed in Appendix A), you replace the numerator $X_1 + X_2 + \cdots + X_n$ with the term $\displaystyle\sum_{i=1}^{n} X_i$, which means sum all the X_i values from the first X value, X_1, to the last X value, X_n, to form Equation (3.1), a formal definition of the sample mean.

SAMPLE MEAN

The **sample mean** is the sum of the values in a sample divided by the number of values in the sample:

$$\overline{X} = \frac{\displaystyle\sum_{i=1}^{n} X_i}{n} \tag{3.1}$$

where

$$\overline{X} = \text{sample mean}$$
$$n = \text{number of values or sample size}$$
$$X_i = i\text{th value of the variable } X$$

$$\sum_{i=1}^{n} X_i = \text{summation of all } X_i \text{ values in the sample}$$

Because all the values play an equal role, a mean is greatly affected by any value that is very different from the others. When you have such extreme values, you should avoid using the mean as a measure of central tendency.

For example, if you knew the typical time it takes you to get ready in the morning, you might be able to arrive at your first destination every day in a more timely manner. Using the DCOVA framework, you first define the time to get ready as the time from when you get out of bed to when you leave your home, rounded to the nearest minute. Then, you collect the times for 10 consecutive workdays and organize and store them in Times .

Using the collected data, you compute the mean to discover the "typical" time it takes for you to get ready. For these data:

Day:	1	2	3	4	5	6	7	8	9	10
Time (minutes):	39	29	43	52	39	44	40	31	44	35

the mean time is 39.6 minutes, computed as follows:

$$\overline{X} = \frac{\text{sum of the values}}{\text{number of values}} = \frac{\sum_{i=1}^{n} X_i}{n}$$

$$\overline{X} = \frac{39 + 29 + 43 + 52 + 39 + 44 + 40 + 31 + 44 + 35}{10}$$

$$= \frac{396}{10} = 39.6$$

Even though no individual day in the sample had a value of 39.6 minutes, allotting this amount of time to get ready in the morning would be a reasonable decision to make. The mean is a good measure of central tendency in this case because the data set does not contain any exceptionally small or large values.

To illustrate how the mean can be greatly affected by any value that is very different from the others, imagine that on Day 3, a set of unusual circumstances delayed you getting ready by an extra hour, so that the time for that day was 103 minutes. This extreme value causes the mean to rise to 45.6 minutes, as follows:

$$\overline{X} = \frac{\text{sum of the values}}{\text{number of values}} = \frac{\sum_{i=1}^{n} X_i}{n}$$

$$\overline{X} = \frac{39 + 29 + 103 + 52 + 39 + 44 + 40 + 31 + 44 + 35}{10}$$

$$\overline{X} = \frac{456}{10} = 45.6$$

The one extreme value has increased the mean by 6 minutes. The extreme value also moved the position of the mean relative to all the values. The original mean, 39.6 minutes, had a middle, or *central*, position among the data values: 5 of the times were less than that mean and 5 were greater than that mean. In contrast, the mean using the extreme value is greater than 9 of the 10 times, making the new mean a poor measure of central tendency.

EXAMPLE 3.1

The Mean Calories in Cereals

Nutritional data about a sample of seven breakfast cereals (stored in `Cereals`) includes the number of calories per serving:

Cereal	Calories
Kellogg's All Bran	80
Kellogg's Corn Flakes	100
Wheaties	100
Nature's Path Organic Multigrain Flakes	110
Kellogg's Rice Krispies	130
Post Shredded Wheat Vanilla Almond	190
Kellogg's Mini Wheats	200

Compute the mean number of calories in these breakfast cereals.

SOLUTION The mean number of calories is 130, computed as follows:

$$\overline{X} = \frac{\text{sum of the values}}{\text{number of values}} = \frac{\sum_{i=1}^{n} X_i}{n} = \frac{910}{7} = 130$$

The Median

The **median** is the middle value in an ordered array of data that has been ranked from smallest to largest. Half the values are smaller than or equal to the median, and half the values are larger than or equal to the median. The median is not affected by extreme values, so you can use the median when extreme values are present.

To compute the median for a set of data, you first rank the values from smallest to largest and then use Equation (3.2) to compute the rank of the value that is the median.

MEDIAN

$$\text{Median} = \frac{n + 1}{2} \text{ ranked value} \tag{3.2}$$

You compute the median by following one of two rules:

- **Rule 1**   If the data set contains an *odd* number of values, the median is the measurement associated with the middle-ranked value.
- **Rule 2**   If the data set contains an *even* number of values, the median is the measurement associated with the average of the two middle-ranked values.

To further analyze the sample of 10 times to get ready in the morning, you can compute the median. To do so, you rank the daily times as follows:

studentTIP

Remember that you must rank the values in order from the smallest to the largest to compute the median.

Ranked values:	29	31	35	39	39	40	43	44	44	52
Ranks:	1	2	3	4	5	6	7	8	9	10

$$\uparrow$$
Median = 39.5

Because the result of dividing $n + 1$ by 2 for this sample of 10 is $(10 + 1)/2 = 5.5$, you must use Rule 2 and average the measurements associated with the fifth and sixth ranked values, 39 and 40. Therefore, the median is 39.5. The median of 39.5 means that for half the days, the time to get ready is less than or equal to 39.5 minutes, and for half the days, the time to get ready is greater than or equal to 39.5 minutes. In this case, the median time to get ready of 39.5 minutes is very close to the mean time to get ready of 39.6 minutes.

EXAMPLE 3.2

Computing the Median from an Odd-Sized Sample

Nutritional data about a sample of seven breakfast cereals (stored in Cereals) includes the number of calories per serving (see Example 3.1 on page 98). Compute the median number of calories in breakfast cereals.

SOLUTION Because the result of dividing $n + 1$ by 2 for this sample of seven is $(7 + 1)/2 = 4$, using Rule 1, the median is the measurement associated with the fourth-ranked value. The number of calories per serving values are ranked from the smallest to the largest:

Ranked values:	80	100	100	110	130	190	200
Ranks:	1	2	3	4	5	6	7

Median = 110

The median number of calories is 110. Half the breakfast cereals have 110 or less than 110 calories per serving, and half the breakfast cereals have 110 or more than 110 calories per serving.

The Mode

The **mode** is the value that appears most frequently. Like the median and unlike the mean, extreme values do not affect the mode. For a particular variable, there can be several modes or no mode at all. For example, for the sample of 10 times to get ready in the morning:

$$29 \quad 31 \quad 35 \quad 39 \quad 39 \quad 40 \quad 43 \quad 44 \quad 44 \quad 52$$

there are two modes, 39 minutes and 44 minutes, because each of these values occurs twice. However, for this sample of seven smartphone prices offered by a cellphone provider (stored in Smartphones):

$$80 \quad 150 \quad 200 \quad 230 \quad 280 \quad 370 \quad 595$$

there is no mode. None of the values is "most typical" because each value appears the same number of times (once) in the data set.

EXAMPLE 3.3

Determining the Mode

A systems manager in charge of a company's network keeps track of the number of server failures that occur in a day. Determine the mode for the following data, which represent the number of server failures per day for the past two weeks:

$$1 \quad 3 \quad 0 \quad 3 \quad 26 \quad 2 \quad 7 \quad 4 \quad 0 \quad 2 \quad 3 \quad 3 \quad 6 \quad 3$$

SOLUTION The ordered array for these data is

$$0 \quad 0 \quad 1 \quad 2 \quad 2 \quad 3 \quad 3 \quad 3 \quad 3 \quad 3 \quad 4 \quad 6 \quad 7 \quad 26$$

▶ *(continued)*

Because 3 occurs five times, more times than any other value, the mode is 3. Thus, the systems manager can say that the most common occurrence is having three server failures in a day. For this data set, the median is also equal to 3, and the mean is equal to 4.5. The value 26 is an extreme value. For these data, the median and the mode are better measures of central tendency than the mean.

The Geometric Mean

When you want to measure the rate of change of a variable over time, you need to use the geometric mean instead of the arithmetic mean. Equation (3.3) defines the geometric mean.

GEOMETRIC MEAN

The **geometric mean** is the nth root of the product of n values:

$$\bar{X}_G = (X_1 \times X_2 \times \cdots \times X_n)^{1/n} \tag{3.3}$$

The **geometric mean rate of return** measures the mean percentage return of an investment per time period. Equation (3.4) defines the geometric mean rate of return.

GEOMETRIC MEAN RATE OF RETURN

$$\bar{R}_G = [(1 + R_1) \times (1 + R_2) \times \cdots \times (1 + R_n)]^{1/n} - 1 \tag{3.4}$$

where

$$R_i = \text{rate of return in time period } i$$

To illustrate these measures, consider an investment of \$100,000 that declined to a value of \$50,000 at the end of Year 1 and then rebounded back to its original \$100,000 value at the end of Year 2. The rate of return for this investment per year for the two-year period is 0 because the starting and ending value of the investment is unchanged. however, the arithmetic mean of the yearly rates of return of this investment is

$$\bar{X} = \frac{(-0.50) + (1.00)}{2} = 0.25 \text{ or } 25\%$$

because the rate of return for Year 1 is

$$R_1 = \left(\frac{50,000 - 100,00}{100,000}\right) = -0.50 \text{ or } -50\%$$

and the rate of return for Year 2 is

$$R_2 = \left(\frac{100,000 - 50,000}{50,000}\right) = 1.00 \text{ or } 100\%$$

Using equation (3.4), the geometric mean rate of return per year for the two years is

$$\begin{aligned}
\bar{R}_G &= [(1 + R_1) \times (1 + R_2)]^{1/n} - 1 \\
&= [(1 + (-0.50)) \times (1 + (1.0))]^{1/2} - 1 \\
&= [(0.50) \times (2.0)]^{1/2} - 1 \\
&= [1.0]^{1/2} - 1 \\
&= 1 - 1 = 0
\end{aligned}$$

Using the geometric mean rate of return more accurately reflects the (zero) change in the value of the investment per year for the two-year period than does the arithmetic mean.

EXAMPLE 3.4

Computing the
Geometric Mean
Rate of Return

The percentage change in the Russell 2000 Index of the stock prices of 2,000 small companies was 37.0% in 2013 and 3.5% in 2014. Compute the geometric rate of return.

SOLUTION Using equation (3.4), the geometric mean rate of return in the Russell 2000 Index for the two years is

$$
\begin{aligned}
\overline{R}_G &= [(1 + R_1) \times (1 + R_2)]^{1/n} - 1 \\
&= [(1 + (0.37)) \times (1 + (0.035))]^{1/2} - 1 \\
&= [(1.37) \times (1.035)]^{1/2} - 1 \\
&= (1.41795)^{1/2} - 1 \\
&= 1.1908 - 1 = 0.1908
\end{aligned}
$$

The geometric mean rate of return in the Russell 2000 Index for the two years is 19.08% per year.

3.2 Variation and Shape

In addition to central tendency, every variable can be characterized by its variation and shape. Variation measures the **spread**, or **dispersion**, of the values. One simple measure of variation is the range, the difference between the largest and smallest values. More commonly used in statistics are the standard deviation and variance, two measures explained later in this section. The shape of a variable represents a pattern of all the values, from the lowest to highest value. As you will learn later in this section, many variables have a pattern that looks approximately like a bell, with a peak of values somewhere in the middle.

The Range

The **range** is the difference between the largest and smallest value and is the simplest descriptive measure of variation for a numerical variable.

RANGE

The range is equal to the largest value minus the smallest value.

$$
\text{Range} = X_{\text{largest}} - X_{\text{smallest}} \tag{3.5}
$$

To further analyze the sample of 10 times to get ready in the morning, you can compute the range. To do so, you rank the data from smallest to largest:

$$29 \quad 31 \quad 35 \quad 39 \quad 39 \quad 40 \quad 43 \quad 44 \quad 44 \quad 52$$

Using Equation (3.5), the range is $52 - 29 = 23$ minutes. The range of 23 minutes indicates that the largest difference between any two days in the time to get ready in the morning is 23 minutes.

EXAMPLE 3.5

Computing the
Range in the
Calories in Cereals

Nutritional data about a sample of seven breakfast cereals (stored in Cereals) includes the number of calories per serving (see Example 3.1 on page 98). Compute the range of the number of calories for the cereals.

SOLUTION Ranked from smallest to largest, the calories for the seven cereals are

80   100   100   110   130   190   200

Therefore, using Equation (3.5), the range $= 200 - 80 = 120$. The largest difference in the number of calories between any two cereals is 120.

The range measures the *total spread* in the set of data. Although the range is a simple measure of the total variation of the variable, it does not take into account *how* the values are distributed between the smallest and largest values. In other words, the range does not indicate whether the values are evenly distributed, clustered near the middle, or clustered near one or both extremes. Thus, using the range as a measure of variation when at least one value is an extreme value is misleading.

The Variance and the Standard Deviation

Being a simple measure of variation, the range does not consider how the values distribute or cluster between the extremes. Two commonly used measures of variation that account for how all the values are distributed are the **variance** and the **standard deviation**. These statistics measure the "average" scatter around the mean—how larger values fluctuate above it and how smaller values fluctuate below it.

A simple measure of variation around the mean might take the difference between each value and the mean and then sum these differences. However, if you did that, you would find that these differences sum to zero because the mean is the balance point for *every* numerical variable. A measure of variation that *differs* from one data set to another *squares* the difference between each value and the mean and then sums these squared differences. The sum of these squared differences, known as the **sum of squares** (SS), is then used to compute the sample variance (S^2) and the sample standard deviation (S).

The **sample variance (S^2)** is the sum of squares divided by the sample size minus 1. The **sample standard deviation (S)** is the square root of the sample variance. Because the sum of squares can never be a negative value, the variance and the standard deviation will always be a non-negative value and, in virtually all cases, the variance and standard deviation will be greater than zero. (Both the variance and standard deviation will be zero, meaning no variation, only for the special case in which every value in a sample is the same value).

For a sample containing n values, $X_1, X_2, X_3, \ldots, X_n$, the sample variance ($S^2$) is

$$S^2 = \frac{(X_1 - \overline{X})^2 + (X_2 - \overline{X})^2 + \cdots + (X_n - \overline{X})^2}{n - 1}$$

Equations (3.6) and (3.7) define the sample variance and sample standard deviation using summation notation. The term $\sum_{i=1}^{n}(X_i - \overline{X})^2$ represents the sum of squares.

SAMPLE VARIANCE

The sample variance is the sum of the squared differences around the mean divided by the sample size minus 1:

$$S^2 = \frac{\sum_{i=1}^{n}(X_i - \overline{X})^2}{n - 1} \tag{3.6}$$

where

$$\overline{X} = \text{sample mean}$$
$$n = \text{sample size}$$
$$X_i = i\text{th value of the variable } X$$

$$\sum_{i=1}^{n}(X_i - \overline{X})^2 = \text{summation of all the squared differences between the } X_i \text{ values and } \overline{X}$$

SAMPLE STANDARD DEVIATION

The sample standard deviation is the square root of the sum of the squared differences around the mean divided by the sample size minus 1:

$$S = \sqrt{S^2} = \sqrt{\frac{\sum_{i=1}^{n}(X_i - \overline{X})^2}{n-1}} \tag{3.7}$$

Note that in both equations, the sum of squares is divided by the sample size minus 1, $n - 1$. The value is used for reasons related to statistical inference and the properties of sampling distributions, a topic discussed in Section 7.2 on page 217. For now, observe that the difference between dividing by n and by $n - 1$ becomes smaller as the sample size increases.

Because the sample standard deviation will always be a value expressed in the same units as the original sample data, you will most likely use this statistic as your measure of variation. (The sample variance is a squared quantity that may have no real-world meaning.) For almost all samples, the majority of the values in a sample will be within an interval of plus and minus 1 standard deviation above and below the mean. Therefore, computing the sample mean and the sample standard deviation typically helps define where the majority of the values are clustering.

You can manually calculate the sample variance, S^2, and sample standard deviation, S, using the five steps listed in Exhibit 3.1.

studentTIP

Remember, neither the variance nor the standard deviation can ever be negative.

EXHIBIT 3.1

Manually Calculating the Sample Variance, S^2, and Sample Standard Deviation, S

Step 1 Calculate the difference between each value and the mean.
Step 2 Square each difference.
Step 3 Sum the squared differences.
Step 4 Divide this total by $n - 1$ to compute the sample variance.
Step 5 Take the square root of the sample variance to compute the sample standard deviation.

The mean ($\overline{X}$) equal to 39.6 was calculated previously using the method discussed on page 97.

Table 3.1 illustrates the four steps for calculating the variance for the sample of 10 times to get ready in the morning. The second column of the table corresponds to step 1, and third column corresponds to step 2. The sum of the third column corresponds to step 3, and dividing that sum by 9 (i. e. 10 − 1) to get the sample variance of 45.82 corresponds to step 4.

TABLE 3.1
Computing the Variance
of the Getting-Ready
Times

	Time (X)	Step 1: ($X_i - \bar{X}$)	Step 2: ($X_i - \bar{X}$)^2
	39	−0.60	0.36
	29	−10.60	112.36
	43	3.40	11.56
	52	12.40	153.76
$n = 10$	39	−0.60	0.36
$\bar{X} = 39.6$	44	4.40	19.36
	40	0.40	0.16
	31	−8.60	73.96
	44	4.40	19.36
	35	−4.60	21.16
		Step 3: Sum	412.40
		Step 4: Divide by ($n - 1$)	45.82

You can also compute the variance by substituting values for the terms in Equation (3.6):

$$S^2 = \frac{\sum_{i=1}^{n}(X_i - \bar{X})^2}{n-1}$$
$$= \frac{(39-39.6)^2 + (29-39.6)^2 + \cdots + (35-39.6)^2}{10-1}$$
$$= \frac{412.4}{9} = 45.82$$

Because the variance is in squared units (in squared minutes, for these data), to compute the standard deviation, you take the square root of the variance. Using Equation (3.7) on page 103, the sample standard deviation, S, is

$$S = \sqrt{S^2} = \sqrt{\frac{\sum_{i=1}^{n}(X_i - \bar{X})^2}{n-1}} = \sqrt{45.82} = 6.77$$

This indicates that the getting-ready times in this sample are clustering within 6.77 minutes around the mean of 39.6 minutes (i.e., clustering between $\bar{X} - 1S = 32.83$ and $\bar{X} + 1S = 46.37$). In fact, 7 out of 10 getting-ready times lie within this interval.

Using the second column of Table 3.1, you can also compute the sum of the differences between each value and the mean to be zero. For any set of data, this sum will always be zero:

$$\sum_{i=1}^{n}(X_i - \bar{X}) = 0 \text{ for all sets of data}$$

This property is one of the reasons that the mean is used as the most common measure of central tendency.

EXAMPLE 3.6

Computing the Variance and Standard Deviation of the Number of Calories in Cereals

Nutritional data about a sample of seven breakfast cereals (stored in Cereals) includes the number of calories per serving (see Example 3.1 on page 98). Compute the variance and standard deviation of the calories in the cereals.

SOLUTION Table 3.2 illustrates the computation of the variance and standard deviation for the calories in the cereals.

▶ (continued)

TABLE 3.2
Computing the
Variance of
the Calories in
the Cereals

	Calories	Step 1: $(X_i - \overline{X})$	Step 2: $(X_i - \overline{X})^2$
	80	−50	2,500
	100	−30	900
	100	−30	900
$n = 7$	110	−20	400
$\overline{X} = 130$	130	0	0
	190	60	3,600
	200	70	4,900
		Step 3: Sum	13,200
		Step 4: Divide by $(n - 1)$	2,220

Using Equation (3.6) on page 102:

$$S^2 = \frac{\sum_{i=1}^{n}(X_i - \overline{X})^2}{n - 1}$$

$$= \frac{(80 - 130)^2 + (100 - 130)^2 + \cdots + (200 - 130)^2}{7 - 1}$$

$$= \frac{13,200}{6} = 2,200$$

Using Equation (3.7) on page 103, the sample standard deviation, S, is

$$S = \sqrt{S^2} = \sqrt{\frac{\sum_{i=1}^{n}(X_i - \overline{X})^2}{n - 1}} = \sqrt{2,200} = 46.9042$$

The standard deviation of 46.9042 indicates that the calories in the cereals are clustering within ± 46.9042 around the mean of 130 (i.e., clustering between $\overline{X} - 1S = 83.0958$ and $\overline{X} + 1S = 176.9042$). In fact, 57.1% (four out of seven) of the calories lie within this interval.

The Coefficient of Variation

The coefficient of variation is equal to the standard deviation divided by the mean, multiplied by 100%. Unlike the measures of variation presented previously, the **coefficient of variation (CV)** measures the scatter in the data relative to the mean. The coefficient of variation is a *relative measure* of variation that is always expressed as a percentage rather than in terms of the units of the particular data. Equation (3.8) defines the coefficient of variation.

studentTIP

The coefficient of variation is always expressed as a percentage, not in the units of the variables.

COEFFICIENT OF VARIATION

The coefficient of variation is equal to the standard deviation divided by the mean, multiplied by 100%.

$$CV = \left(\frac{S}{\overline{X}}\right)100\% \tag{3.8}$$

where

S = sample standard deviation
$\overline{X}$ = sample mean

For the sample of 10 getting-ready times, because $\overline{X} = 39.6$ and $S = 6.77$, the coefficient of variation is

$$CV = \left(\frac{S}{\overline{X}}\right)100\% = \left(\frac{6.77}{39.6}\right)100\% = 17.10\%$$

For the getting-ready times, the standard deviation is 17.1% of the size of the mean.

The coefficient of variation is especially useful when comparing two or more sets of data that are measured in different units, as Example 3.6 illustrates.

EXAMPLE 3.7

Comparing Two Coefficients of Variation When the Two Variables Have Different Units of Measurement

Which varies more from cereal to cereal—the number of calories or the amount of sugar (in grams)?

SOLUTION Because calories and the amount of sugar have different units of measurement, you need to compare the relative variability in the two measurements.

For calories, using the mean and variance computed in Examples 3.1 and 3.6 on pages 98 and 104, the coefficient of variation is

$$CV_{\text{Calories}} = \left(\frac{46.9042}{130}\right)100\% = 36.08\%$$

For the amount of sugar in grams, the values for the seven cereals are

$$6 \quad 2 \quad 4 \quad 4 \quad 4 \quad 11 \quad 10$$

For these data, $\overline{X} = 5.8571$ and $S = 3.3877$. Therefore, the coefficient of variation is

$$CV_{\text{Sugar}} = \left(\frac{3.3877}{5.8571}\right)100\% = 57.84\%$$

You conclude that relative to the mean, the amount of sugar is much more variable than the calories.

Z Scores

The **Z score** of a value is the difference between that value and the mean, divided by the standard deviation. A Z score of 0 indicates that the value is the same as the mean. If a Z score is a positive or negative number, it indicates whether the value is above or below the mean and by how many standard deviations.

Z scores help identify **outliers**, the values that seem excessively different from most of the rest of the values (see Section 1.4). Values that are very different from the mean will have either very small (negative) Z scores or very large (positive) Z scores. As a general rule, a Z score that is less than -3.0 or greater than $+3.0$ indicates an outlier value.

Z SCORE

The Z score for a value is equal to the difference between the value and the mean, divided by the standard deviation:

$$Z = \frac{X - \overline{X}}{S} \tag{3.9}$$

To further analyze the sample of 10 times to get ready in the morning, you can compute the Z scores. Because the mean is 39.6 minutes, the standard deviation is 6.77 minutes, and the time to get ready on the first day is 39.0 minutes, you compute the Z score for Day 1 by using Equation (3.7):

$$Z = \frac{X - \overline{X}}{S}$$

$$= \frac{39.0 - 39.6}{6.77}$$

$$= -0.09$$

The Z score of -0.09 for the first day indicates that the time to get ready on that day is very close to the mean. Table 3.3 presents the Z scores for all 10 days.

TABLE 3.3
Z Scores for the 10 Getting-Ready Times

	Time (X)	Z Score
	39	−0.09
	29	−1.57
	43	0.50
	52	1.83
$\overline{X} = 39.6$	39	−0.09
$S = 6.77$	44	0.65
	40	0.06
	31	−1.27
	44	0.65
	35	−0.68

The largest Z score is 1.83 for Day 4, on which the time to get ready was 52 minutes. The lowest Z score is -1.57 for Day 2, on which the time to get ready was 29 minutes. Because none of the Z scores are less than -3.0 or greater then $+3.0$, you conclude that the getting-ready times include no apparent outliers.

EXAMPLE 3.8

Computing the Z Scores of the Number of Calories in Cereals

Nutritional data about a sample of seven breakfast cereals (stored in [Cereals]) includes the number of calories per serving (see Example 3.1 on page 98). Compute the Z scores of the calories in breakfast cereals.

SOLUTION Table 3.4 presents the Z scores of the calories for the cereals. The largest Z score is 1.49, for a cereal with 200 calories. The lowest Z score is -1.07, for a cereal with 80 calories. There are no apparent outliers in these data because none of the Z scores are less than -3.0 or greater than $+3.0$.

TABLE 3.4
Z Scores of the Number of Calories in Cereals

	Calories	Z Scores
	80	−1.07
	100	−0.64
	100	−0.64
$\overline{X} = 130$	110	−0.43
$S = 46.9042$	130	0.00
	190	1.28
	200	1.49

Shape: Skewness

Skewness measures the extent to which the data values are not **symmetrical** around the mean. The three possibilities are:

- **Mean < median**: negative, or **left-skewed distribution**
- **Mean = median**: symmetrical distribution (zero skewness)
- **Mean > median**: positive, or **right-skewed distribution**

In a *symmetrical* distribution, the values below the mean are distributed in exactly the same way as the values above the mean, and the skewness is zero. In a **skewed** distribution, there is an imbalance of data values below and above the mean, and the skewness is a nonzero value (less than zero for a left-skewed distribution, greater than zero for a right-skewed distribution). Figure 3.1 visualizes these possibilities.

FIGURE 3.1
The shapes of three data distributions

Panel A	Panel B	Panel C
Negative, or left-skewed	Symmetrical	Positive, or right-skewed

Panel A displays a left-skewed distribution. In a left-skewed distribution, most of the values are in the upper portion of the distribution. Some extremely small values cause the long tail and distortion to the left and cause the mean to be less than the median. Because the skewness statistic for such a distribution will be less than zero, some use the term *negative skew* to describe this distribution.

Panel B displays a symmetrical distribution. In a symmetrical distribution, values are equally distributed in the upper and lower portions of the distribution. This equality causes the portion of the curve below the mean to be the mirror image of the portion of the curve above the mean and makes the mean equal to the median.

Panel C displays a right-skewed distribution. In a right-skewed distribution, most of the values are in the lower portion of the distribution. Some extremely large values cause the long tail and distortion to the right and cause the mean to be greater than the median. Because the skewness statistic for such a distribution will be greater than zero, some use the term *positive skew* to describe this distribution.

Shape: Kurtosis

Kurtosis measures the peakedness of the curve of the distribution—that is, how sharply the curve rises approaching the center of the distribution. Kurtosis compares the shape of the peak to the shape of the peak of a bell-shaped normal distribution (see Chapter 6), which, by definition, has a kurtosis of zero.[1] A distribution that has a sharper-rising center peak than the peak of a normal distribution has *positive* kurtosis, a kurtosis value that is greater than zero, and is called **lepokurtic**. A distribution that has a slower-rising (flatter) center peak than the peak of a normal distribution has *negative* kurtosis, a kurtosis value that is less than zero, and is called **platykurtic**. A lepokurtic distribution has a higher concentration of values near the mean of the distribution compared to a normal distribution, while a platykurtic distribution has a lower concentration compared to a normal distribution.

In affecting the shape of the central peak, the relative concentration of values near the mean also affects the ends, or *tails*, of the curve of a distribution. A lepokurtic distribution has *fatter* tails, many more values in the tails, than a normal distribution has. If decision making about a set of data mistakenly assumes a normal distribution, when, in fact, the data forms a lepokurtic distribution, then that decision making will underestimate the occurrence of extreme values (values that are very different from the mean). Such an observation has been a basis for several explanations about the unanticipated reverses and collapses that financial markets have experienced in the recent past. (See reference 4 for an example of such an explanation.)

[1] Several different operational definitions exist for kurtosis. The definition here, used by Excel, is sometimes called *excess kurtosis* to distinguish it from other definitions. Read the SHORT TAKES for Chapter 3 to learn how excel calculates kurtosis (and skewness).

EXAMPLE 3.9

Descriptive Statistics for Growth and Value Funds

In the More Descriptive Choices scenario, you are interested in comparing the past performance of the growth and value funds from a sample of 407 funds. One measure of past performance is the one-year return percentage variable. Compute descriptive statistics for the growth and value funds.

SOLUTION Figure 3.2 presents descriptive summary measures for the two types of funds. The results include the mean, median, mode, minimum, maximum, range, variance, standard deviation, coefficient of variation, skewness, kurtosis, count (the sample size), and standard error. The standard error, discussed in Section 7.2, is the standard deviation divided by the square root of the sample size.

FIGURE 3.2
Descriptive statistics worksheet for the one-year return percentages for the growth and value funds

	A	B	C	
1	Descriptive Statistics for 1YrReturn%			
2				
3		Growth	Value	Growth
4	Mean	7.49	8.45	=AVERAGE(UNSTACKED!A:A)
5	Median	8.76	9.41	=MEDIAN(UNSTACKED!A:A)
6	Mode	8.97	12.53	=MODE(UNSTACKED!A:A)
7	Minimum	-14.05	-13.79	=MIN(UNSTACKED!A:A)
8	Maximum	21.70	17.75	=MAX(UNSTACKED!A:A)
9	Range	35.75	31.54	=B8 - B7
10	Variance	31.5032	25.4402	=VAR.S(UNSTACKED!A:A)
11	Standard Deviation	5.6128	5.0438	=STDEV.S(UNSTACKED!A:A)
12	Coeff. of Variation	74.96%	59.69%	=B11/B4
13	Skewness	-0.6779	-1.4311	=SKEW(UNSTACKED!A:A)
14	Kurtosis	0.6741	3.0125	=KURT(UNSTACKED!A:A)
15	Count	269	138	=COUNT(UNSTACKED!A:A)
16	Standard Error	0.3422	0.4294	=B11/SQRT(B15)

In the Worksheet

The worksheet uses a number of Excel functions and short arithmetic formulas to calculate descriptive statistics. (Only the formulas for the Growth column are shown.)

In examining the results, you see that there are some differences in the one-year return for the growth and value funds. The growth funds had a mean one-year return of 7.49 and a median return of 8.76. This compares to a mean of 8.45 and a median of 9.41 for the value funds. The medians indicate that half of the growth funds had one-year returns of 8.76 or better, and half the value funds had one-year returns of 9.41 or better. You conclude that the value funds had a higher return than the growth funds.

The growth funds had a higher standard deviation than the value funds (5.6128, as compared to 5.0438). Both the growth funds and the value funds showed left or negative skewness, as the skewness of the growth funds was −0.6779 and the skewness of the value funds was −1.4311. The kurtosis of the growth funds was somewhat positive, indicating a distribution that was more peaked than a normal distribution. The kurtosis of the value funds was very positive indicating a distribution that was much more peaked than a normal distribution.

EXAMPLE 3.10

Descriptive Statistics Using Multidimensional Contingency Tables

Continuing with the More Descriptive Choices scenario, you wish to explore the effects of each combination of type, market cap, and risk on measures of past performance. One measure of past performance is the three-year return percentage. Compute the mean three-year return percentage for each combination of type, market cap, and risk.

SOLUTION Compute the mean for each combination by adding the numerical variable three-year return percentage to a multidimensional contingency table. The Excel results are:

FIGURE 3.3
PivotTable display for the mean three-year return percentages for each combination of type, market cap, and risk

Mean 3YrReturn%	Risk			
Type	Low	Average	High	Grand Total
⊟ Growth	15.36	15.43	14.06	15.15
Large	14.96	16.31	17.60	16.24
Mid-Cap	17.09	14.60	13.40	14.49
Small		13.52	13.71	13.64
⊟ Value	13.79	15.91	12.61	15.14
Large	13.68	15.75	1.89	15.01
Mid-Cap	15.12	17.35	13.97	16.97
Small		13.57	13.23	13.39
Grand Total	14.40	15.58	13.73	15.15

In the Worksheet

Instructions in Section EG2.6 (Excel Guide for Chapter 2) describe how to add a numerical variable to a multidimensional contingency table.

▶ (continued)

Analyzing each combination of type, market cap, and risk reveals patterns that would not be seen if the mean of the three-year return percentage had been computed for only the growth and value funds (similar to what is done in Example 3.9). Empty cells, such as those for small growth and value funds with low risk, represent combinations that do not exist in the sample of 407 funds.

PROBLEMS FOR SECTIONS 3.1 AND 3.2

LEARNING THE BASICS

3.1 The following set of data is from a sample of $n = 5$:

7 4 9 8 2

a. Compute the mean, median, and mode.
b. Compute the range, variance, standard deviation, and coefficient of variation.
c. Compute the Z scores. Are there any outliers?
d. Describe the shape of the data set.

3.2 The following set of data is from a sample of $n = 6$:

7 4 9 7 3 12

a. Compute the mean, median, and mode.
b. Compute the range, variance, standard deviation, and coefficient of variation.
c. Compute the Z scores. Are there any outliers?
d. Describe the shape of the data set.

3.3 The following set of data is from a sample of $n = 7$:

12 7 4 9 0 7 3

a. Compute the mean, median, and mode.
b. Compute the range, variance, standard deviation, and coefficient of variation.
c. Compute the Z scores. Are there any outliers?
d. Describe the shape of the data set.

3.4 The following set of data is from a sample of $n = 5$:

7 −5 −8 7 9

a. Compute the mean, median, and mode.
b. Compute the range, variance, standard deviation, and coefficient of variation.
c. Compute the Z scores. Are there any outliers?
d. Describe the shape of the data set.

3.5 Suppose that the rate of return for a particular stock during the past two years was 10% for one of the years and 30% for the other year. Compute the geometric rate of return per year. (*Note:* A rate of return of 10% is recorded as 0.10, and a rate of return of 30% is recorded as 0.30.)

3.6 Suppose that the rate of return for a particular stock during the past two years was 20% for one of the years and −30% for the other year. Compute the geometric rate of return per year.

APPLYING THE CONCEPTS

3.7 *Wired*, a magazine that delivers a glimpse into the future of business, culture, innovation, and science, reported the following summary for the household incomes of its two types of subscribers, the print reader and the digital reader.

Audience	Median
Wired reader	$91,083
Wired.com user	80,108

Source: Data extracted from "WIRED Media Kit," **condenast.com/brands/wired/media-kit**.

Interpret the median household income for the *Wired* readers and the Wired.com users.

3.8 The operations manager of a plant that manufactures tires wants to compare the actual inner diameters of two grades of tires, each of which is expected to be 575 millimeters. A sample of five tires of each grade was selected, and the results representing the inner diameters of the tires, ranked from smallest to largest, are as follows:

Grade X	Grade Y
568 570 575 578 584	573 574 575 577 578

a. For each of the two grades of tires, compute the mean, median, and standard deviation.
b. Which grade of tire is providing better quality? Explain.
c. What would be the effect on your answers in (a) and (b) if the last value for grade Y was 588 instead of 578? Explain.

3.9 According to the U.S. Census Bureau (**census.gov**), in 2014, the median sales price of new houses was $282,800 and the mean sales price was $345,800.
a. Interpret the median sales price.
b. Interpret the mean sales price.
c. Discuss the shape of the distribution of the price of new houses.

✓ SELF TEST **3.10** The file MobileLoyalty contains spending on products ($) during a three-month period by a sample of 15 customers receiving incentives through a mobile loyalty program.

55.35	22.90	67.50	46.10	57.45	108.25	50.75	35.20
78.30	50.65	63.00	59.70	41.55	56.65	52.60	

a. Compute the mean and median.
b. Compute the variance, standard deviation, range, and coefficient of variation.
c. Are the data skewed? If so, how?
d. Based on the results of (a) through (c), what conclusions can you reach concerning spending on products by customers receiving incentives through a mobile loyalty program?

3.11 The file Sedans contains the overall miles per gallon (MPG) of 2015 midsized sedans:

26 38 26 30 24 26 28 28 24 26 24 39
32 23 22 24 28 37 31 40 25 25 33 30

Source: Data extracted from "Which Car Is Right for You," *Consumer Reports*, April 2015, pp. 40–41.

a. Compute the mean, median, and mode.
b. Compute the variance, standard deviation, range, coefficient of variation, and Z scores.
c. Are the data skewed? If so, how?
d. Compare the results of (a) through (c) to those of Problem 3.12 (a) through (c) that refer to the miles per gallon of small SUVs.

3.12 The file SUV contains the overall miles per gallon (MPG) of 2015 small SUVs:

26 22 24 22 26 21 24 25 28 24
22 21 22 21 24 23 23 22 21 22

Source: Data extracted from "Which Car Is Right for You," *Consumer Reports*, April 2015, pp. 60–61.

a. Compute the mean, median, and mode.
b. Compute the variance, standard deviation, range, coefficient of variation, and Z scores.
c. Are the data skewed? If so, how?
d. Compare the results of (a) through (c) to those of Problem 3.11 (a) through (c) that refer to the MPG of midsized sedans.

3.13 The file AccountingPartners contains the number of partners in a cohort of rising accounting firms that have been tagged as "firms to watch." The firms have the following numbers of partners:

16 21 27 11 33 20 30 27 31 15 21 20 28 34 23 17 29
13 16 16 13 16 21 17 10 19 10 10 20 25 11 14 13 16

Source: Data extracted from *2015 Top 100 Firms*, Bloomberg BNA, **accountingtoday.com**.

a. Compute the mean, median, and mode.
b. Compute the variance, standard deviation, range, coefficient of variation, and Z scores. Are there any outliers? Explain.
c. Are the data skewed? If so, how?
d. Based on the results of (a) through (c), what conclusions can you reach concerning the number of partners in rising accounting firms?

3.14 The file MobileCommerce contains the following mobile commerce penetration values, the percentage of the country population that bought something online via a mobile phone in the past month, for 28 of the world's economies:

17 15 15 13 27 12 20 23 9 9 16 6 19 14
11 14 8 15 23 11 37 17 11 19 27 18 18 15

Source: Data extracted from **www.slideshare.net/wearesocialsg/digital-social-mobile-in-2015**.

a. Compute the mean and median.
b. Compute the variance, standard deviation, range, coefficient of variation, and Z scores. Are there any outliers? Explain.

c. Are the data skewed? If so, how?
d. Based on the results of (a) through (c), what conclusions can you reach concerning mobile commerce population penetration?

3.15 Is there a difference in the variation of the yields of different types of investments? The file CD Rate contains the yields for one-year certificates of deposit (CDs) and five-year CDs for 25 banks in the United States, as of April 15, 2015.

Source: Data extracted from **www.Bankrate.com**, April 15, 2015.

a. For one-year and five-year CDs, separately compute the variance, standard deviation, range, and coefficient of variation.
b. Based on the results of (a), do one-year CDs or five-year CDs have more variation in the yields offered? Explain.

3.16 The file HotelAway contains the average room price (in US$) paid by various nationalities while traveling abroad (away from their home country) in 2014:

174 161 167 171 163 141 147 154

Source: Data extracted from "5. Prices paid at Home and Away," **bit.ly/1QNxDyv**.

a. Compute the mean, median, and mode.
b. Compute the range, variance, and standard deviation.
c. Based on the results of (a) and (b), what conclusions can you reach concerning the room price (in US$) in 2014?

3.17 A bank branch located in a commercial district of a city has the business objective of developing an improved process for serving customers during the noon-to-1:00 P.M. lunch period. The waiting time, in minutes, is defined as the time the customer enters the line to when he or she reaches the teller window. Data collected from a sample of 15 customers during this hour are stored in Bank1:

4.21 5.55 3.02 5.13 4.77 2.34 3.54 3.20
4.50 6.10 0.38 5.12 6.46 6.19 3.79

a. Compute the mean and median.
b. Compute the variance, standard deviation, range, coefficient of variation, and Z scores. Are there any outliers? Explain.
c. Are the data skewed? If so, how?
d. As a customer walks into the branch office during the lunch hour, she asks the branch manager how long she can expect to wait. The branch manager replies, "Almost certainly less than five minutes." On the basis of the results of (a) through (c), evaluate the accuracy of this statement.

3.18 Suppose that another bank branch, located in a residential area, is also concerned with the noon-to-1:00 P.M. lunch hour. The waiting time, in minutes, collected from a sample of 15 customers during this hour, are stored in Bank2:

9.66 5.90 8.02 5.79 8.73 3.82 8.01 8.35
10.49 6.68 5.64 4.08 6.17 9.91 5.47

a. Compute the mean and median.
b. Compute the variance, standard deviation, range, coefficient of variation, and Z scores. Are there any outliers? Explain.
c. Are the data skewed? If so, how?
d. As a customer walks into the branch office during the lunch hour, he asks the branch manager how long he can expect to wait. The branch manager replies, "Almost certainly less than five minutes." On the basis of the results of (a) through (c), evaluate the accuracy of this statement.

3.19 General Electric (GE) is one of the world's largest companies; it develops, manufactures, and markets a wide range of products, including medical diagnostic imaging devices, jet engines, lighting products, and chemicals. In 2013, the stock price rose 33.54%, and in 2014, the stock price declined 9.8%. (Data extracted from **finance.yahoo.com**, May 5, 2015.)

a. Compute the geometric mean rate of return per year for the two-year period 2013–2014. (Hint: Denote an increase of 33.54% as $R_2 = 0.3354$.)
b. If you purchased $1,000 of GE stock at the start of 2013, what was its value at the end of 2014?
c. Compare the result of (b) to that of Problem 3.20 (b).

✓SELF TEST **3.20** Facebook's stock price in 2013 increased by 105.3%, and in 2014, it increased by 42.8%. (Data extracted from **finance.yahoo.com**, May 5, 2015.)

a. Compute the geometric mean rate of return per year for the two-year period 2013–2014. (Hint: Denote an increase of 42.8% as $R_1 = 0.4280$.)
b. If you purchased $1,000 of Facebook stock at the start of 2013, what was its value at the end of 2014?
c. Compare the result of (b) to that of Problem 3.19 (b).

3.21 The file **Indices** contains data that represent the total rate of return percentage for the Dow Jones Industrial Average (DJIA), the Standard & Poor's 500 (S&P 500), and the technology-heavy NASDAQ Composite (NASDAQ) from 2011 through 2014. These data are:

Year	DJIA	S&P 500	NASDAQ
2011	5.5	0.0	−1.8
2012	7.3	13.4	15.9
2013	26.5	29.6	38.3
2014	7.5	11.4	13.4

Source: Data extracted from **finance.yahoo.com**, May 5, 2015.

a. Compute the geometric mean rate of return per year for the DJIA, S&P 500, and NASDAQ from 2011 through 2014.
b. What conclusions can you reach concerning the geometric mean rates of return per year of the three market indices?
c. Compare the results of (b) to those of Problem 3.22 (b).

3.22 In 2011 through 2014, the value of precious metals fluctuated dramatically. The data in the following table (stored in **Metals**) represent the total rate of return (in percentage) for platinum, gold, and silver from 2011 through 2014:

Year	Platinum	Gold	Silver
2011	−21.1	10.2	−9.8
2012	8.68	0.1	7.1
2013	−11.7	6.08	7.13
2014	−0.72	−28.65	−26.65

Source: Data extracted from **finance.yahoo.com**, May 5, 2015.

a. Compute the geometric mean rate of return per year for platinum, gold, and silver from 2011 through 2014.
b. What conclusions can you reach concerning the geometric mean rates of return of the three precious metals?
c. Compare the results of (b) to those of Problem 3.21 (b).

3.23 Using the one-year return percentage variable in **Retirement Funds**:
a. Construct a table that computes the mean for each combination of type, market cap, and risk.
b. Construct a table that computes the standard deviation for each combination of type, market cap, and risk.
c. What conclusions can you reach concerning differences among the types of retirement funds (growth and value), based on market cap (small, mid-cap, and large) and the risk (low, average, and high)?

3.24 Using the one-year return percentage variable in **Retirement Funds**:
a. Construct a table that computes the mean for each combination of type, market cap, and rating.
b. Construct a table that computes the standard deviation for each combination of type, market cap, and rating.
c. What conclusions can you reach concerning differences among the types of retirement funds (growth and value), based on market cap (small, mid-cap, and large) and the rating (one, two, three, four, and five)?

3.25 Using the one-year return percentage variable in **Retirement Funds**:
a. Construct a table that computes the mean for each combination of market cap, risk, and rating.
b. Construct a table that computes the standard deviation for each combination of market cap, risk, and rating.
c. What conclusions can you reach concerning differences based on the market cap (small, mid-cap, and large), risk (low, average, and high), and rating (one, two, three, four, and five)?

3.26 Using the one-year return percentage variable in **Retirement Funds**:
a. Construct a table that computes the mean for each combination of type, risk, and rating.
b. Construct a table that computes the standard deviation for each combination of type, risk, and rating.
c. What conclusions can you reach concerning differences among the types of retirement funds (growth and value), based on the risk (low, average, and high) and the rating (one, two, three, four, and five)?

3.3 Exploring Numerical Data

Sections 3.1 and 3.2 discuss measures of central tendency, variation, and shape. You can also visualize the distribution of the values for a numerical variable by computing the quartiles and the five-number summary and constructing a boxplot.

Quartiles

Quartiles split the values into four equal parts—the **first quartile (Q_1)** divides the smallest 25.0% of the values from the other 75.0% that are larger. The **second quartile (Q_2)** is the median; 50.0% of the values are smaller than or equal to the median, and 50.0% are larger than or equal to the median. The **third quartile (Q_3)** divides the smallest 75.0% of the values from the largest 25.0%. Equations (3.10) and (3.11) define the first and third quartiles.

FIRST QUARTILE, Q_1

25.0% of the values are smaller than or equal to Q_1, the first quartile, and 75.0% are larger than or equal to the first quartile, Q_1:

$$Q_1 = \frac{n + 1}{4} \text{ ranked value} \tag{3.10}$$

THIRD QUARTILE, Q_3

75.0% of the values are smaller than or equal to the third quartile, Q_3, and 25.0% are larger than or equal to the third quartile, Q_3:

$$Q_3 = \frac{3(n + 1)}{4} \text{ ranked value} \tag{3.11}$$

---

studentTIP

As is the case when you compute the median, you must rank the values in order from smallest to largest before computing the quartiles.

To manually compute quartiles, you first rank the values from smallest to largest value. Then you apply the three rules of Exhibit 3.2.

EXHIBIT 3.2

Rules for Calculating the Quartiles from a Set of Ranked Values

Rule 1 If the ranked value is a whole number, the quartile is equal to the measurement that corresponds to that ranked value. For example, if the sample size $n = 7$, the first quartile, Q_1, is equal to the measurement associated with the $(7 + 1)/4 =$ second ranked value.

Rule 2 If the ranked value is a fractional half (2.5, 4.5, etc.), the quartile is equal to the measurement that corresponds to the average of the measurements corresponding to the two ranked values involved. For example, if the sample size $n = 9$, the first quartile, Q_1, is equal to the $(9 + 1)/4 = 2.5$ ranked value, halfway between the second ranked value and the third ranked value.

Rule 3 If the ranked value is neither a whole number nor a fractional half, you round the result to the nearest integer and select the measurement corresponding to that ranked value. For example, if the sample size $n = 10$, the first quartile, Q_1, is equal to the $(10 + 1)/4 = 2.75$ ranked value. Round 2.75 to 3 and use the third ranked value.

For example, to compute the quartiles for the sample of 10 times to get ready in the morning, you first rank the data from smallest to largest:

Ranked values:	29	31	35	39	39	40	43	44	44	52
Ranks:	1	2	3	4	5	6	7	8	9	10

The first quartile is the $(n + 1)/4 = (10 + 1)/4 = 2.75$ ranked value. Using Rule 3, you round up to the third ranked value. The third ranked value for the getting-ready data is 35 minutes. You interpret the first quartile of 35 to mean that on 25% of the days, the time to get ready is less than or equal to 35 minutes, and on 75% of the days, the time to get ready is greater than or equal to 35 minutes.

The third quartile is the $3(n + 1)/4 = 3(10 + 1)/4 = 8.25$ ranked value. Using Rule 3 for quartiles, you round this down to the eighth ranked value. The eighth ranked value is 44 minutes. Thus, on 75% of the days, the time to get ready is less than or equal to 44 minutes, and on 25% of the days, the time to get ready is greater than or equal to 44 minutes.

Percentiles   Related to quartiles are **percentiles** that split a variable into 100 equal parts. By this definition, the first quartile is equivalent to the 25th percentile, the second quartile to the 50th percentile, and the third quartile to the 75th percentile.

EXAMPLE 3.11

Computing the Quartiles

Nutritional data about a sample of seven breakfast cereals (stored in [Cereals]) includes the number of calories per serving (see Example 3.1 on page 98). Compute the first quartile (Q_1) and third quartile (Q_3) of the number of calories for the cereals.

SOLUTION   Ranked from smallest to largest, the number of calories for the seven cereals are as follows:

Ranked values:	80	100	100	110	130	190	200
Ranks:	1	2	3	4	5	6	7

For these data

$$Q_1 = \frac{(n + 1)}{4} \text{ ranked value}$$

$$= \frac{7 + 1}{4} \text{ ranked value} = \text{2nd ranked value}$$

Therefore, using Rule 1, Q_1 is the second ranked value. Because the second ranked value is 100, the first quartile, Q_1, is 100.

To compute the third quartile, Q_3,

$$Q_3 = \frac{3(n + 1)}{4} \text{ ranked value}$$

$$= \frac{3(7 + 1)}{4} \text{ ranked value} = \text{6th ranked value}$$

Therefore, using Rule 1, Q_3 is the sixth ranked value. Because the sixth ranked value is 190, Q_3 is 190.

The first quartile of 100 indicates that 25% of the cereals contain 100 calories or fewer per serving and 75% contain 100 or more calories. The third quartile of 190 indicates that 75% of the cereals contain 190 calories or fewer per serving and 25% contain 190 or more calories.

The Interquartile Range

The **interquartile range** (also called the **midspread**) measures the difference in the center of a distribution between the third and first quartiles.

INTERQUARTILE RANGE

The interquartile range is the difference between the third quartile and the first quartile:

$$\text{Interquartile range} = Q_3 - Q_1 \qquad (3.12)$$

The interquartile range measures the spread in the middle 50% of the values. Therefore, it is not influenced by extreme values. To further analyze the sample of 10 times to get ready in the morning, you can compute the interquartile range. You first order the data as follows:

$$29 \quad 31 \quad 35 \quad 39 \quad 39 \quad 40 \quad 43 \quad 44 \quad 44 \quad 52$$

You use Equation (3.12) and the earlier results on page 114, $Q_1 = 35$ and $Q_3 = 44$:

$$\text{Interquartile range} = 44 - 35 = 9 \text{ minutes}$$

Therefore, the interquartile range in the time to get ready is 9 minutes. The interval 35 to 44 is often referred to as the *middle fifty*.

EXAMPLE 3.12

Computing the Interquartile Range for the Number of Calories in Cereals

Nutritional data about a sample of seven breakfast cereals (stored in `Cereals`) includes the number of calories per serving (see Example 3.1 on page 98). Compute the interquartile range of the number of calories in cereals.

SOLUTION Ranked from smallest to largest, the number of calories for the seven cereals are as follows:

$$80 \quad 100 \quad 100 \quad 110 \quad 130 \quad 190 \quad 200$$

Using Equation (3.12) and the earlier results from Example 3.11 on page 114, $Q_1 = 100$ and $Q_3 = 190$:

$$\text{Interquartile range} = 190 - 100 = 90$$

Therefore, the interquartile range of the number of calories in cereals is 90 calories.

Because the interquartile range does not consider any value smaller than Q_1 or larger than Q_3, it cannot be affected by extreme values. Descriptive statistics such as the median, Q_1, Q_3, and the interquartile range, which are not influenced by extreme values, are called **resistant measures**.

The Five-Number Summary

The **five-number summary** for a variable consists of the smallest value (X_{smallest}), the first quartile, the median, the third quartile, and the largest value (X_{largest}).

FIVE-NUMBER SUMMARY

$$X_{\text{smallest}} \quad Q_1 \quad \text{Median} \quad Q_3 \quad X_{\text{largest}}$$

The five-number summary provides a way to determine the shape of the distribution for a set of data. Table 3.5 explains how relationships among these five statistics help to identify the shape of the distribution.

TABLE 3.5
Relationships Among the Five-Number Summary and the Type of Distribution

| | TYPE OF DISTRIBUTION | | |
COMPARISON	Left-Skewed	Symmetrical	Right-Skewed
The distance from $X_{smallest}$ to the median versus the distance from the median to $X_{largest}$.	The distance from $X_{smallest}$ to the median is greater than the distance from the median to $X_{largest}$.	The two distances are the same.	The distance from $X_{smallest}$ to the median is less than the distance from the median to $X_{largest}$.
The distance from $X_{smallest}$ to Q_1 versus the distance from Q_3 to $X_{largest}$.	The distance from $X_{smallest}$ to Q_1 is greater than the distance from Q_3 to $X_{largest}$.	The two distances are the same.	The distance from $X_{smallest}$ to Q_1 is less than the distance from Q_3 to $X_{largest}$.
The distance from Q_1 to the median versus the distance from the median to Q_3.	The distance from Q_1 to the median is greater than the distance from the median to Q_3.	The two distances are the same.	The distance from Q_1 to the median is less than the distance from the median to Q_3.

To further analyze the sample of 10 times to get ready in the morning, you can compute the five-number summary. For these data, the smallest value is 29 minutes, and the largest value is 52 minutes (see page 98). Calculations done on pages 99 and 114 show that the median = 39.5, Q_1 = 35, and Q_3 = 44. Therefore, the five-number summary is as follows:

$$29 \quad 35 \quad 39.5 \quad 44 \quad 52$$

The distance from $X_{smallest}$ to the median ($39.5 - 29 = 10.5$) is slightly less than the distance from the median to $X_{largest}$ ($52 - 39.5 = 12.5$). The distance from $X_{smallest}$ to Q_1 ($35 - 29 = 6$) is slightly less than the distance from Q_3 to $X_{largest}$ ($52 - 44 = 8$). The distance from Q_1 to the median ($39.5 - 35 = 4.5$) is the same as the distance from the median to Q_3($44 - 39.5 = 4.5$). Therefore, the getting-ready times are slightly right-skewed.

EXAMPLE 3.13

Computing the Five-Number Summary of the Number of Calories in Cereals

Nutritional data about a sample of seven breakfast cereals (stored in `Cereals`) includes the number of calories per serving (see Example 3.1 on page 98). Compute the five-number summary of the number of calories in cereals.

SOLUTION From previous computations for the number of calories in cereals (see pages 99 and 114), you know that the median = 110, Q_1 = 100, and Q_3 = 190.
In addition, the smallest value in the data set is 80, and the largest value is 200. Therefore, the five-number summary is as follows:

$$80 \quad 100 \quad 110 \quad 190 \quad 200$$

The three comparisons listed in Table 3.5 are used to evaluate skewness. The distance from $X_{smallest}$ to the median ($110 - 80 = 30$) is less than the distance ($200 - 110 = 90$) from the median to $X_{largest}$. The distance from $X_{smallest}$ to Q_1 ($100 - 80 = 20$) is greater than the distance from Q_3 to $X_{largest}$ ($200 - 190 = 10$). The distance from Q_1 to the median ($110 - 100 = 10$) is less than the distance from the median to Q_3 ($190 - 110 = 80$). Two comparisons indicate a right-skewed distribution, whereas the other indicates a left-skewed distribution. Therefore, given the small sample size and the conflicting results, the shape cannot be clearly determined.

The Boxplot

The **boxplot** uses a five-number summary to visualize the shape of the distribution for a variable. Figure 3.4 contains a boxplot for the sample of 10 times to get ready in the morning.

FIGURE 3.4
Boxplot for the getting-ready times

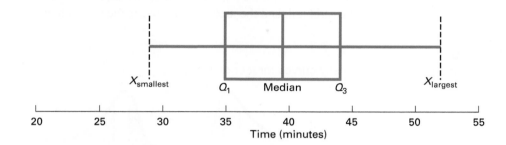

The vertical line drawn within the box represents the median. The vertical line at the left side of the box represents the location of Q_1, and the vertical line at the right side of the box represents the location of Q_3. Thus, the box contains the middle 50% of the values. The lower 25% of the data are represented by a line connecting the left side of the box to the location of the smallest value, $X_{smallest}$. Similarly, the upper 25% of the data are represented by a line connecting the right side of the box to $X_{largest}$.

The Figure 3.4 boxplot for the getting-ready times shows a slight right-skewness: The distance between the median and the highest value is slightly greater than the distance between the lowest value and the median, and the right tail is slightly longer than the left tail.

EXAMPLE 3.14

Boxplots of the One-Year Returns for the Growth and Value Funds

In the More Descriptive Choices scenario, you are interested in comparing the past performance of the growth and value funds from a sample of 407 funds. One measure of past performance is the one-year return percentage variable. Construct the boxplots for this variable for the growth and value funds.

SOLUTION Figure 3.5 contains the five-number summary worksheet and boxplot for the one-year return percentages for the growth and value funds. The five-number summary for the growth funds associated with these boxplots is $X_{smallest} = -14.05$, $Q_1 = 3.695$, median $= 8.76$, $Q_3 = 11.55$, and $X_{largest} = 21.7$. The five-number summary for the value funds associated with these boxplots is $X_{smallest} = -13.79$, $Q_1 = 5.71$, median $= 9.405$, $Q_3 = 11.88$, and $X_{largest} = 17.75$.

FIGURE 3.5
Five-number summary worksheet and boxplot for the one-year return percentage variable

	A	B	C
1	Five-Number Summary for 1YrReturn%		
2			
3		Growth	Value
4	Minimum	-14.05	-13.79
5	First Quartile	3.695	5.71
6	Median	8.76	9.405
7	Third Quartile	11.55	11.88
8	Maximum	21.7	17.75

The median return, the quartiles, and the minimum returns are higher for the value funds than for the growth funds. Both the growth and value funds are left-skewed. These results are consistent with the statistics computed in Figure 3.2 on page 109.

Figure 3.6 demonstrates the relationship between the boxplot and the density curve for four different types of distributions. The area under each density curve is split into quartiles corresponding to the five-number summary for the boxplot.

The distributions in Panels A and D of Figure 3.6 are symmetrical. In these distributions, the mean and median are equal. In addition, the length of the left tail is equal to the length of the right tail, and the median line divides the box in half.

FIGURE 3.6
Boxplots and corresponding density curves for four distributions

Panel A
Bell-shaped distribution

Panel B
Left-skewed distribution

Panel C
Right-skewed distribution

Panel D
Rectangular distribution

studentTIP

A long tail on the left side of the boxplot indicates a left-skewed distribution. A long tail on the right side of the boxplot indicates a right-skewed distribution.

The distribution in Panel B of Figure 3.6 is left-skewed. The few small values distort the mean toward the left tail. For this left-skewed distribution, there is a heavy clustering of values at the high end of the scale (i.e., the right side); 75% of all values are found between the left edge of the box (Q_1) and the end of the right tail $(X_{largest})$. There is a long left tail that contains the smallest 25% of the values, demonstrating the lack of symmetry in this data set.

The distribution in Panel C of Figure 3.6 is right-skewed. The concentration of values is on the low end of the scale (i.e., the left side of the boxplot). Here, 75% of all values are found between the beginning of the left tail and the right edge of the box (Q_3). There is a long right tail that contains the largest 25% of the values, demonstrating the lack of symmetry in this data set.

PROBLEMS FOR SECTION 3.3

LEARNING THE BASICS

3.27 The following is a set of data from a sample of $n = 7$:

$$12 \quad 7 \quad 4 \quad 9 \quad 0 \quad 7 \quad 3$$

a. Compute the first quartile (Q_1), the third quartile (Q_3), and the interquartile range.
b. List the five-number summary.
c. Construct a boxplot and describe its shape.
d. Compare your answer in (c) with that from Problem 3.3 (d) on page 110. Discuss.

3.28 The following is a set of data from a sample of $n = 6$:

$$7 \quad 4 \quad 9 \quad 7 \quad 3 \quad 12$$

a. Compute the first quartile (Q_1), the third quartile (Q_3), and the interquartile range.
b. List the five-number summary.
c. Construct a boxplot and describe its shape.
d. Compare your answer in (c) with that from Problem 3.2 (d) on page 110. Discuss.

3.29 The following is a set of data from a sample of $n = 5$:

$$7 \quad 4 \quad 9 \quad 8 \quad 2$$

a. Compute the first quartile (Q_1), the third quartile (Q_3), and the interquartile range.

b. List the five-number summary.
c. Construct a boxplot and describe its shape.
d. Compare your answer in (c) with that from Problem 3.1 (d) on page 110. Discuss.

3.30 The following is a set of data from a sample of $n = 5$:

$$7 \quad -5 \quad -8 \quad 7 \quad 9$$

a. Compute the first quartile (Q_1), the third quartile (Q_3), and the interquartile range.
b. List the five-number summary.
c. Construct a boxplot and describe its shape.
d. Compare your answer in (c) with that from Problem 3.4 (d) on page 110. Discuss.

APPLYING THE CONCEPTS

3.31 The file AccountingPartners contains the number of partners in a cohort of rising accounting firms that have been tagged as "firms to watch." The firms have the following number of partners:

16 21 27 11 33 20 30 27 31 15 21 20 28 34 23 17 29

13 16 16 13 16 21 17 10 19 10 10 20 25 11 14 13 16

Source: Data extracted from *2015 Top 100 Firms*, Bloomberg BNA, **accountingtoday.com**.

a. Compute the first quartile (Q_1), the third quartile (Q_3), and the interquartile range.

b. List the five-number summary.

c. Construct a boxplot and describe its shape.

3.32 The file MobileCommerce contains the following mobile commerce penetration values, the percentage of the country population that bought something online via a mobile phone in the past month, for twenty-eight of the world's economies:

17 15 15 13 27 12 20 23 9 9 16 6 19 14
11 14 8 15 23 11 37 17 11 19 27 18 18 15

Source: Data extracted from www. slideshare.net/wearesocialsg/digital-social-mobile-in-2015.

a. Compute the first quartile (Q_1), the third quartile (Q_3), and the interquartile range.

b. List the five-number summary.

c. Construct a boxplot and describe its shape.

3.33 The file HotelAway contains the average room price (in US$) paid by various nationalities while traveling abroad (away from their home country) in 2014:

174 161 167 171 163 141 147 154

Source: Data extracted from "5. Prices paid at Home and Away," bit.ly/1QNxDyv.

a. Compute the first quartile (Q_1), the third quartile (Q_3), and the interquartile range.

b. List the five-number summary.

c. Construct a boxplot and describe its shape.

3.34 The file SUV contains the overall MPG of 2015 small SUVs:

26 22 24 22 26 21 24 25 28 24
22 21 22 21 24 23 23 22 21 22

Source: Data extracted from "Which Car Is Right for You," *Consumer Reports*, April 2015, pp. 60–61.

a. Compute the first quartile (Q_1), the third quartile (Q_3), and the interquartile range.

b. List the five-number summary.

c. Construct a boxplot and describe its shape.

3.35 The file CD Rate contains the yields for one-year CDs and five-year CDs, for 5 banks in the United States, as of April 15, 2015.

Source: Data extracted from www.Bankrate.com, April 15, 2015.

For each type of account:

a. Compute the first quartile (Q_1), the third quartile (Q_3), and the interquartile range.

b. List the five-number summary.

c. Construct a boxplot and describe its shape.

✓SELF TEST **3.36** A bank branch located in a commercial district of a city has the business objective of developing an improved process for serving customers during the noon-to-1:00 P.M. lunch period. The waiting time, in minutes, is defined as the time the customer enters the line to when he or she reaches the teller window. Data are collected from a sample of 15 customers during this hour. The file Bank1 contains the results, which are listed below:

4.21 5.55 3.02 5.13 4.77 2.34 3.54 3.20
4.50 6.10 0.38 5.12 6.46 6.19 3.79

Another bank branch, located in a residential area, is also concerned with the noon-to-1:00 P.M. lunch hour. The waiting times, in minutes, collected from a sample of 15 customers during this hour, are contained in the file Bank2 and listed here:

9.66 5.90 8.02 5.79 8.73 3.82 8.01 8.35
10.49 6.68 5.64 4.08 6.17 9.91 5.47

a. List the five-number summaries of the waiting times at the two bank branches.

b. Construct boxplots and describe the shapes of the distributions for the two bank branches.

c. What similarities and differences are there in the distributions of the waiting times at the two bank branches?

3.4 Numerical Descriptive Measures for a Population

Sections 3.1 and 3.2 discuss the statistics that can be computed to describe the properties of central tendency and variation for a sample. When you collect data from an entire population (see Section 1.2), you compute and analyze population *parameters* for these properties, including the population mean, population variance, and population standard deviation.

To help illustrate these parameters, consider the population of stocks for the 10 companies in the Dow Jones Industrial Average (DJIA) that form the "Dogs of the Dow," the 10 stocks in the DJIA whose dividend is the highest fraction of their price in the previous year. (An alternative investment scheme popularized by Michael O'Higgins uses these "dogs.") Table 3.6 on page 120 contains the 2014 one-year returns (excluding dividends) for the 10 "Dow Dog" stocks of 2013. These data, stored in DowDogs, will be used to illustrate the population parameters discussed in this section.

TABLE 3.6
One-Year Return for the "Dogs of the Dow"

Stock	One-Year Return%	Stock	One-Year Return%
AT&T	2.28	McDonald's	0.54
Chevron	−5.96	Merck	17.75
Cisco System	10.92	Microsoft	33.7
GE	−4.3	Pfizer	5.17
Intel	49.33	Verizon	1.65

Source: Data extracted from **dogsofthedow.com**.

The Population Mean

The **population mean** is the sum of the values in the population divided by the population size, N. This parameter, represented by the Greek lowercase letter mu, μ, serves as a measure of central tendency. Equation (3.13) defines the population mean.

POPULATION MEAN

The population mean is the sum of the values in the population divided by the population size, N.

$$\mu = \frac{\sum_{i=1}^{N} X_i}{N} \tag{3.13}$$

where
μ = population mean
X_i = ith value of the variable X
$\sum_{i=1}^{N} X_i$ = summation of all X_i values in the population
N = number of values in the population

To compute the mean one-year return for the population of "Dow Dog" stocks in Table 3.6, use Equation (3.13):

$$\mu = \frac{\sum_{i=1}^{N} X_i}{N}$$

$$= \frac{2.28 + (-5.96) + 10.92 + (-4.30) + 49.33 + 0.54 + 17.75 + 33.70 + 5.17 + 1}{10}$$

$$= \frac{111.08}{10} = 11.11$$

Thus, the mean one-year return for the "Dow Dog" stocks is 11.11.

The Population Variance and Standard Deviation

The population variance and the population standard deviation parameters measure variation in a population. The **population variance** is the sum of the squared differences around the population mean divided by the population size, N, and the **population standard deviation** is the square root of the population variance. In practice, you will most likely use the population standard deviation because, unlike the population variance, the standard deviation will always be a number expressed in the same units as the original population data.

The lowercase Greek letter sigma, σ, represents the population standard deviation, and sigma squared, σ^2, represents the population variance. Equations (3.14) and (3.15) define these parameters. The denominators for the right-side terms in these equations use N and not the $(n-1)$ term that is found in Equations (3.6) and (3.7) on pages 102 and 103 that define the sample variance and standard deviation.

POPULATION VARIANCE

$$\sigma^2 = \frac{\sum_{i=1}^{N} (X_i - \mu)^2}{N} \tag{3.14}$$

where

$$\mu = \text{population mean}$$
$$X_i = i\text{th value of the variable } X$$

$$\sum_{i=1}^{N} (X_i - \mu)^2 = \text{summation of all the squared differences between the } X_i \text{ values and } \mu$$

POPULATION STANDARD DEVIATION

$$\sigma = \sqrt{\frac{\sum_{i=1}^{N} (X_i - \mu)^2}{N}} \tag{3.15}$$

To compute the population variance for the data of Table 3.6, you use Equation (3.14):

$$\sigma^2 = \frac{\sum_{i=1}^{N} (X_i - \mu)^2}{N}$$

$$= \frac{\begin{array}{c}77.9336 + 291.3166 + 0.0353 + 237.4065 + 1{,}460.9213 + \\ 111.6826 + 44.1162 + 510.3985 + 35.2598 + 89.4538\end{array}}{10}$$

$$= \frac{2{,}858.5242}{10} = 285.85$$

From Equation (3.15), the population sample standard deviation is

$$\sigma = \sqrt{\sigma^2} = \sqrt{\frac{\sum_{i=1}^{N} (X_i - \mu)^2}{N}} = \sqrt{\frac{2{,}858.5242}{10}} = 16.91$$

Therefore, the typical percentage return differs from the mean of 11.11 by approximately 16.91. This large amount of variation suggests that the "Dow Dog" stocks produce results that differ greatly.

The Empirical Rule

In most data sets, a large portion of the values tend to cluster somewhere near the mean. In right-skewed data sets, this clustering occurs to the left of the mean—that is, at a value less than the mean. In left-skewed data sets, the values tend to cluster to the right of the mean—that is, greater than the mean. In symmetrical data sets, where the median and mean are the same, the values often tend to cluster around the median and mean, producing a bell-shaped normal distribution (discussed in Chapter 6).

The **empirical rule** states that for population data from a symmetric mound-shaped distribution such as the normal distribution, the following are true:

- Approximately 68% of the values are within ± 1 standard deviation from the mean.
- Approximately 95% of the values are within ± 2 standard deviations from the mean.
- Approximately 99.7% of the values are within ± 3 standard deviations from the mean.

The empirical rule helps you examine variability in a population as well as identify outliers. The empirical rule implies that in a normal distribution, only about 1 out of 20 values will be beyond 2 standard deviations from the mean in either direction. As a general rule, you can consider values not found in the interval $\mu \pm 2\sigma$ as potential outliers. The rule also implies that only about 3 in 1,000 will be beyond 3 standard deviations from the mean. Therefore, values not found in the interval $\mu \pm 3\sigma$ are almost always considered outliers.

EXAMPLE 3.15	
Using the Empirical Rule	A population of 2-liter bottles of cola is known to have a mean fill-weight of 2.06 liters and a standard deviation of 0.02 liter. The population is known to be bell-shaped. Describe the distribution of fill-weights. Is it very likely that a bottle will contain less than 2 liters of cola?

SOLUTION

$$\mu \pm \sigma = 2.06 \pm 0.02 = (2.04, 2.08)$$
$$\mu \pm 2\sigma = 2.06 \pm 2(0.02) = (2.02, 2.10)$$
$$\mu \pm 3\sigma = 2.06 \pm 3(0.02) = (2.00, 2.12)$$

Using the empirical rule, you can see that approximately 68% of the bottles will contain between 2.04 and 2.08 liters, approximately 95% will contain between 2.02 and 2.10 liters, and approximately 99.7% will contain between 2.00 and 2.12 liters. Therefore, it is highly unlikely that a bottle will contain less than 2 liters.

Chebyshev's Theorem

For heavily skewed sets of data and data sets that do not appear to be normally distributed, you should use Chebyshev's theorem instead of the empirical rule. **Chebyshev's theorem** (see reference 2) states that for any data set, regardless of shape, the percentage of values that are found within distances of k standard deviations from the mean must be at least

$$\left(1 - \frac{1}{k^2}\right) \times 100\%$$

You can use this rule for any value of k greater than 1. For example, consider $k = 2$. Chebyshev's theorem states that at least $[1 - (1/2)^2] \times 100\% = 75\%$ of the values must be found within ± 2 standard deviations of the mean.

Section EG3.4 describes the VE-Variability workbook that allows you to explore the empirical rule and Chebyshev's theorem.

Chebyshev's theorem is very general and applies to any distribution. The theorem indicates *at least* what percentage of the values fall within a given distance from the mean. However, if the data set is approximately bell-shaped, the empirical rule will more accurately reflect the greater concentration of data close to the mean. Table 3.7 compares Chebyshev's theorem to the empirical rule.

TABLE 3.7
How Data Vary
Around the Mean

	% of Values Found in Intervals Around the Mean	
Interval	**Chebyshev's Theorem (any distribution)**	**Empirical Rule (normal distribution)**
$(\mu - \sigma, \mu + \sigma)$	At least 0%	Approximately 68%
$(\mu - 2\sigma, \mu + 2\sigma)$	At least 75%	Approximately 95%
$(\mu - 3\sigma, \mu + 3\sigma)$	At least 88.89%	Approximately 99.7%

EXAMPLE 3.16

Using the
Chebyshev Rule

As in Example 3.15, a population of 2-liter bottles of cola is known to have a mean fill-weight of 2.06 liter and a standard deviation of 0.02 liter. However, the shape of the population is unknown, and you cannot assume that it is bell-shaped. Describe the distribution of fill-weights. Is it very likely that a bottle will contain less than 2 liters of cola?

SOLUTION

$$\mu \pm \sigma = 2.06 \pm 0.02 = (2.04, 2.08)$$
$$\mu \pm 2\sigma = 2.06 \pm 2(0.02) = (2.02, 2.10)$$
$$\mu \pm 3\sigma = 2.06 \pm 3(0.02) = (2.00, 2.12)$$

Because the distribution may be skewed, you cannot use the empirical rule. Using Chebyshev's theorem, you cannot say anything about the percentage of bottles containing between 2.04 and 2.08 liters. You can state that at least 75% of the bottles will contain between 2.02 and 2.10 liters and at least 88.89% will contain between 2.00 and 2.12 liters. Therefore, between 0 and 11.11% of the bottles will contain less than 2 liters.

You use Chebyshev's theorem and the empirical rules to understand how data are distributed around the mean when you have sample data. With each, you use the value you computed for $\overline{X}$ in place of μ and the value you computed for S in place of σ. The results you compute using the sample statistics are *approximations* because you used sample statistics $(\overline{X}, S)$ and not population parameters (μ, σ).

PROBLEMS FOR SECTION 3.4

LEARNING THE BASICS

3.37 The following is a set of data for a population with $N = 10$:

        7   5   11   8   3   6   2   1   9   8

a. Compute the population mean.
b. Compute the population standard deviation.

3.38 The following is a set of data for a population with $N = 10$:

        7   5   6   6   6   4   8   6   9   3

a. Compute the population mean.
b. Compute the population standard deviation.

APPLYING THE CONCEPTS

3.39 The file McDonaldsStores contains the number of McDonald's stores located in each of the 50 U.S. states and the District of Columbia, as of December 31, 2014:

Source: Data extracted from "US McDonald's Locations," **bit.ly/1GaK5VR**.

a. Compute the mean, variance, and standard deviation for this population.
b. What percentage of the 50 states have McDonald's stores within ± 1, ± 2, or ± 3 standard deviations of the mean?
c. Compare your findings with what would be expected on the basis of the empirical rule. Are you surprised at the results in (b)?

3.40 Consider a population of 1,024 mutual funds that primarily invest in large companies. You have determined that μ, the mean one-year total percentage return achieved by all the funds, is 8.20 and that σ, the standard deviation, is 2.75.

a. According to the empirical rule, what percentage of these funds is expected to be within ± 1 standard deviation of the mean?
b. According to the empirical rule, what percentage of these funds is expected to be within ± 2 standard deviations of the mean?
c. According to Chebyshev's theorem, what percentage of these funds is expected to be within ± 1, ± 2, or ± 3 standard deviations of the mean?

d. According to Chebyshev's theorem, at least 93.75% of these funds are expected to have one-year total returns between what two amounts?

3.41 The file CigaretteTax contains the state cigarette tax (in $) for each of the 50 states as of January 1, 2015.
a. Compute the population mean and population standard deviation for the state cigarette tax.
b. Interpret the parameters in (a).

✓ **SELF TEST** **3.42** The file Energy contains the per capita energy consumption, in million BTUs, for each of the 50 states and the District of Columbia during a recent year.
a. Compute the mean, variance, and standard deviation for the population.
b. What proportion of these states has per capita energy consumption within ±1 standard deviation of the mean, within ±2

standard deviations of the mean, and within ±3 standard deviations of the mean?
c. Compare your findings with what would be expected based on the empirical rule. Are you surprised at the results in (b)?

3.43 Thirty companies comprise the DJIA. Just how big are these companies? One common method for measuring the size of a company is to use its market capitalization, which is computed by multiplying the number of stock shares by the price of a share of stock. On May 6, 2015, the market capitalization of these companies ranged from Traveler's $32.6 billion to Apple's $724.7 billion. The entire population of market capitalization values is stored in DowMarketCap .

Source: Data extracted from **money.cnn.com**, May 6, 2015.

a. Compute the mean and standard deviation of the market capitalization for this population of 30 companies.
b. Interpret the parameters computed in (a).

3.5 The Covariance and the Coefficient of Correlation

This section presents two measures of the relationship between two numerical variables: the covariance and the coefficient of correlation.

The Covariance

The **covariance** measures the strength of the linear relationship between two numerical variables (X and Y). Equation (3.16) defines the **sample covariance**, and Example 3.17 illustrates its use.

SAMPLE COVARIANCE

$$\text{cov}(X, Y) = \frac{\sum_{i=1}^{n} (X_i - \overline{X})(Y_i - \overline{Y})}{n - 1} \tag{3.16}$$

EXAMPLE 3.17

Computing the Sample Covariance

NBA team revenue and NBA values were used to construct a scatter plot that showed the relationship between those two variables. Now, you want to measure the association between the annual revenue and value of a team by determining the sample covariance.

SOLUTION Figure 3.7 contains two worksheets that together compute the covariance of revenue and value of 30 NBA teams.

From the result in cell B9 of the covariance worksheet, or by using Equation (3.16) directly (shown below), you determine that the covariance is 19,582.2414:

$$\text{cov}(X, Y) = \frac{567,885.0000}{30 - 1}$$
$$= 19,582.2414$$

▶ *(continued)*

FIGURE 3.7
Excel data and covariance worksheets for the revenue and value for the 30 NBA teams

	A	B	C	D
1	Revenue	Value	(X-XBar)	(Y-YBar)
2	133	825	-27.00	-280.50
3	173	1700	13.00	594.50
4	212	1500	52.00	394.50
5	130	725	-30.00	-380.50
6	201	2000	41.00	894.50
7	149	915	-11.00	-190.50
8	168	1150	8.00	44.50
9	136	855	-24.00	-250.50
10	144	810	-16.00	-295.50
11	168	1300	8.00	194.50
12	175	1250	15.00	144.50
13	149	830	-11.00	-275.50
14	146	1600	-14.00	494.50
15	293	2600	133.00	1494.50
16	135	750	-25.00	-355.50

	A	B	C	D
1	Revenue	Value	(X-XBar)	(Y-YBar)
17	188	1175	28.00	69.50
18	110	600	-50.00	-505.50
19	128	625	-32.00	-480.50
20	131	650	-29.00	-455.50
21	278	2500	118.00	1394.50
22	152	930	-8.00	-175.50
23	143	875	-17.00	-230.50
24	125	700	-35.00	-405.50
25	145	910	-15.00	-195.50
26	153	940	-7.00	-165.50
27	125	800	-35.00	-305.50
28	174	1000	14.00	-105.50
29	151	920	-9.00	-185.50
30	142	830	-18.00	-275.50
31	143	900	-17.00	-205.50

	A	B	
1	Covariance Analysis of Revenue and Value		
2			
3	Intermediate Calculations		
4	XBar	160.0000	=AVERAGE(DATA!A:A)
5	YBar	1105.5000	=AVERAGE(DATA!B:B)
6	Σ(X-XBar)(Y-YBar)	567885.0000	=SUMPRODUCT(DATA!C:C, DATA!D:D)
7	n-1	29	=COUNT(DATA!A:A) - 1
8			
9	Covariance	19582.2414	=COVARIANCE.S(DATA!A:A, DATA!B:B)

The covariance has a major flaw as a measure of the linear relationship between two numerical variables. Because the covariance can have any value, you cannot use it to determine the relative strength of the relationship. In Example 3.17, you cannot tell whether the value 19,582.2414 indicates a strong relationship or a weak relationship between revenue and value. To better determine the relative strength of the relationship, you need to compute the coefficient of correlation.

The Coefficient of Correlation

The **coefficient of correlation** measures the relative strength of a linear relationship between two numerical variables. The values of the coefficient of correlation range from −1 for a perfect negative correlation to +1 for a perfect positive correlation. *Perfect* in this case means that if the points were plotted on a scatter plot, all the points could be connected with a straight line.

When dealing with population data for two numerical variables, the Greek letter ρ (*rho*) is used as the symbol for the coefficient of correlation. Figure 3.8 illustrates three different types of association between two variables.

FIGURE 3.8
Types of association between variables

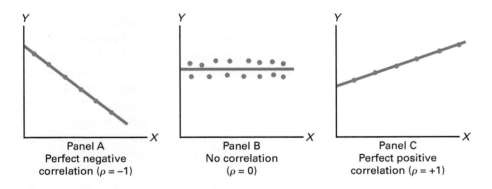

In Panel A of Figure 3.8, there is a perfect negative linear relationship between X and Y. Thus, the coefficient of correlation, ρ, equals −1, and when X increases, Y decreases in a perfectly predictable manner. Panel B shows a situation in which there is no relationship between X and Y. In this case, the coefficient of correlation, ρ, equals 0, and as X increases, there is no tendency for Y to increase or decrease. Panel C illustrates a perfect positive relationship where ρ equals $+1$. In this case, Y increases in a perfectly predictable manner when X increases.

Correlation alone cannot prove that there is a causation effect—that is, that the change in the value of one variable caused the change in the other variable. A strong correlation can be produced by chance; by the effect of a **lurking variable**, a third variable not considered in the calculation of the correlation; or by a cause-and-effect relationship. You would need to perform additional analysis to determine which of these three situations actually produced the correlation. Therefore, you can say that *causation implies correlation, but correlation alone does not imply causation.*

Equation (3.17) defines the **sample coefficient of correlation (r)**.

SAMPLE COEFFICIENT OF CORRELATION

$$r = \frac{\text{cov}(X, Y)}{S_X S_Y} \tag{3.17}$$

where

$$\text{cov}(X, Y) = \frac{\sum_{i=1}^{n} (X_i - \overline{X})(Y_i - \overline{Y})}{n - 1}$$

$$S_X = \sqrt{\frac{\sum_{i=1}^{n} (X_i - \overline{X})^2}{n - 1}}$$

$$S_Y = \sqrt{\frac{\sum_{i=1}^{n} (Y_i - \overline{Y})^2}{n - 1}}$$

When you have sample data, you can compute the sample coefficient of correlation, r. When using sample data, you are unlikely to have a sample coefficient of correlation of exactly $+1, 0$, or -1. Figure 3.9 on page 127 presents scatter plots along with their respective sample coefficients of correlation, r, for six data sets, each of which contains 100 X and Y values.

In Panel A, the coefficient of correlation, r, is -0.9. You can see that for small values of X, there is a very strong tendency for Y to be large. Likewise, the large values of X tend to be paired with small values of Y. The data do not all fall on a straight line, so the association between X and Y cannot be described as perfect. The data in Panel B have a coefficient of correlation equal to -0.6, and the small values of X tend to be paired with large values of Y. The linear relationship between X and Y in Panel B is not as strong as that in Panel A. Thus, the coefficient of correlation in Panel B is not as negative as that in Panel A. In Panel C, the linear relationship between X and Y is very weak, $r = -0.3$, and there is only a slight tendency for the small values of X to be paired with the large values of Y.

Panels D through F depict data sets that have positive coefficients of correlation because small values of X tend to be paired with small values of Y, and large values of X tend to be associated with large values of Y. Panel D shows weak positive correlation, with $r = 0.3$. Panel E shows stronger positive correlation, with $r = 0.6$. Panel F shows very strong positive correlation, with $r = 0.9$.

FIGURE 3.9

Six scatter plots and their sample coefficients of correlation, r

Panel A

Panel B

Panel C

Panel D

Panel E

Panel F

EXAMPLE 3.18

Computing the Sample Coefficient of Correlation

In Example 3.17 on page 124, you computed the covariance of the revenue and value for the 30 NBA teams. Now, you want to measure the relative strength of a linear relationship between the revenue and value by determining the sample coefficient of correlation.

SOLUTION By using Equation (3.17) directly (shown below) or from cell B14 in the coefficient of correlation worksheet (shown in Figure 3.10), you determine that the sample coefficient of correlation is 0.9246:

$$r = \frac{\text{cov}(X, Y)}{S_X S_Y}$$

$$= \frac{19{,}582.2414}{(41.1725)(514.4253)}$$

$$= 0.9246$$

FIGURE 3.10

Excel worksheet to compute the sample coefficient of correlation between revenue and value

This worksheet uses the Figure 3.7 data worksheet shown on page 124.

	A	B	
1	Coefficient of Correlation Analysis		
2			
3	Intermediate Calculations		
4	XBar	160.0000	=AVERAGE(DATA!A:A)
5	YBar	1105.5000	=AVERAGE(DATA!B:B)
6	$\Sigma(X\text{-}XBar)^2$	49160.0000	=DEVSQ(DATA!A:A)
7	$\Sigma(Y\text{-}YBar)^2$	7674367.5000	=DEVSQ(DATA!B:B)
8	$\Sigma(X\text{-}XBar)(Y\text{-}YBar)$	567885.0000	=SUMPRODUCT(DATA!C:C, DATA!D:D)
9	n-1	29	=COUNT(DATA!A:A) - 1
10	Covariance	19582.2414	=COVARIANCE.S(DATA!A:A, DATA!B:B)
11	S_x	41.1725	=SQRT(B6/B9)
12	S_y	514.4253	=SQRT(B7/B9)
13			
14	r	0.9246	=CORREL(DATA!A:A, DATA!B:B)

In the Worksheet

The worksheet uses two advanced functions, DEVSQ and SUMPRODUCT, both of which are explained in Appendix F.

The value and revenue of the NBA teams are very highly correlated. The teams with the lowest revenues have the lowest values. The teams with the highest revenues have the highest values. This relationship is very strong, as indicated by the coefficient of correlation, $r = 0.9246$.

In general, you cannot assume that just because two variables are correlated, changes in one variable caused changes in the other variable. However, for this example, it makes sense to conclude that changes in revenue would tend to cause changes in the value of a team.

In summary, the coefficient of correlation indicates the linear relationship, or association, between two numerical variables. When the coefficient of correlation gets closer to +1 or −1, the linear relationship between the two variables is stronger. When the coefficient of correlation is near 0, little or no linear relationship exists. The sign of the coefficient of correlation indicates whether the data are positively correlated (i.e., the larger values of X are typically paired with the larger values of Y) or negatively correlated (i.e., the larger values of X are typically paired with the smaller values of Y). The existence of a strong correlation does not imply a causation effect. It only indicates the tendencies present in the data.

PROBLEMS FOR SECTION 3.5

LEARNING THE BASICS

3.44 The following is a set of data from a sample of $n = 11$ items:

X	7	5	8	3	6	10	12	4	9	15	18
Y	21	15	24	9	18	30	36	12	27	45	54

a. Compute the covariance.
b. Compute the coefficient of correlation.
c. How strong is the relationship between X and Y? Explain.

APPLYING THE CONCEPTS

3.45 A study of 1,649 college students suggests a link between Facebook use and grade point average. Freshmen reporting a higher use of Facebook had lower grade point averages than freshmen reporting a lower use of Facebook. (Data extracted from R. Junco, "Student class standing, Facebook use, and academic performance," *Journal of Applied Developmental Psychology*, 2015.)

a. Does the study suggest that use of Facebook and grade point average are positively correlated or negatively correlated?
b. Do you think that there might be a cause-and-effect relationship between use of Facebook and grade point average? Explain.

 3.46 The file Cereals lists the calories and sugar, in grams, in one serving of seven breakfast cereals:

Cereal	Calories	Sugar
Kellogg's All Bran	80	6
Kellogg's Corn Flakes	100	2
Wheaties	100	4
Nature's Path Organic Multigrain Flakes	110	4
Kellogg's Rice Krispies	130	4
Post Shredded Wheat Vanilla Almond	190	11
Kellogg's Mini Wheats	200	10

a. Compute the covariance.
b. Compute the coefficient of correlation.
c. Which do you think is more valuable in expressing the relationship between calories and sugar—the covariance or the coefficient of correlation? Explain.
d. Based on (a) and (b), what conclusions can you reach about the relationship between calories and sugar?

3.47 Movie companies need to predict the gross receipts of individual movies once a movie has debuted. The data, shown below and stored in PotterMovies , are the first weekend gross, the U.S. gross, and the worldwide gross (in $ millions) of the eight Harry Potter movies:

a. Compute the covariance between first weekend gross and U.S. gross, first weekend gross and worldwide gross, and U.S. gross and worldwide gross.
b. Compute the coefficient of correlation between first weekend gross and U.S. gross, first weekend gross and worldwide gross, and U.S. gross and worldwide gross.

Title	First Weekend	U.S. Gross	Worldwide Gross
Sorcerer's Stone	90.295	317.558	976.458
Chamber of Secrets	88.357	261.988	878.988
Prisoner of Azkaban	93.687	249.539	795.539
Goblet of Fire	102.335	290.013	896.013
Order of the Phoenix	77.108	292.005	938.469
Half-Blood Prince	77.836	301.460	934.601
Deathly Hallows Part 1	125.017	295.001	955.417
Deathly Hallows Part 2	169.189	381.011	1,328.111

Source: Data extracted from **www.the-numbers.com/interactive/comp-Harry-Potter.php**.

c. Which do you think is more valuable in expressing the relationship between first weekend gross, U.S. gross, and worldwide gross—the covariance or the coefficient of correlation? Explain.
d. Based on (a) and (b), what conclusions can you reach about the relationship between first weekend gross, U.S. gross, and worldwide gross?

3.48 College football is big business, with coaches' pay in millions of dollars. The file College Football contains the 2013 total athletic department revenue and 2014 football coaches' total pay for 108 schools. (Data extracted from **usat.ly/1uws90v** and **usat .ly/1DOl0v3**.)
a. Compute the covariance.
b. Compute the coefficient of correlation.
c. Based on (a) and (b), what conclusions can you reach about the relationship between coaches' total pay and athletic department revenues?

3.49 A Pew Research Center survey found that social networking is popular but Internet access is lacking in many nations around the world. The file GlobalSocialMedia contains the level of social media networking, measured as the percentage of Internet users polled who use social networking sites, and the file GlobalInternetUsage contains the level of Internet usage, measured as the percentage of adults polled who use the Internet at least occasionally, and the GDP at purchasing power parity (PPP, current international $) per capita for each of 31 emerging and developing countries. (Data extracted from Pew Research Center, "Internet Seen as Positive Influence on Education but Negative on Morality in Emerging and Developing Nations," March 19, 2015, **bit.ly/1GASqhp**.)

For the relationship between percentage of Internet users polled who use social networking sites, and GDP and the relationship between the percentage of adults polled who use the Internet at least occasionally and GDP,
a. Compute the covariance.
b. Compute the coefficient of correlation.
c. Based on (a) and (b), what conclusions can you reach about the relationship between the GDP and social media use and the relationship between the percentage of adults polled who use the Internet at least occasionally and GDP?

3.6 Statistics: Pitfalls and Ethical Issues

This chapter describes how a set of numerical data can be characterized by the statistics that measure the properties of central tendency, variation, and shape. In business, descriptive statistics such as the ones discussed in this chapter are frequently included in summary reports that are prepared periodically.

The volume of information available from online, broadcast, or print media has produced much skepticism in the minds of many about the objectivity of data. When you are reading information that contains descriptive statistics, you should keep in mind the quip often attributed to the famous nineteenth-century British statesman Benjamin Disraeli: "There are three kinds of lies: lies, damned lies, and statistics."

For example, in examining statistics, you need to compare the mean and the median. Are they similar, or are they very different? Or is only the mean provided? The answers to these questions will help you determine whether the data are skewed or symmetrical and whether the median might be a better measure of central tendency than the mean. In addition, you should look to see whether the standard deviation or interquartile range for a very skewed set of data has been included in the statistics provided. Without this, it is impossible to determine the amount of variation that exists in the data.

Ethical considerations arise when you are deciding what results to include in a report. You should document both good and bad results. In addition, in all presentations, you need to report results in a fair, objective, and neutral manner. Unethical behavior occurs when you selectively fail to report pertinent findings that are detrimental to the support of a particular position.

▼ USING **STATISTICS**
More Descriptive Choices, Revisited

In the More Descriptive Choices scenario, you were hired by the Choice *Is* Yours investment company to assist investors interested in stock mutual funds. A sample of 407 stock mutual funds included 269 growth funds and 138 value funds. By comparing these two categories, you were able to provide investors with valuable insights.

The one-year returns for both the growth funds and the value funds were left-skewed, as the Figure 3.5 boxplot on page 117 reveals. The descriptive statistics (see Figure 3.2 on page 109) allowed you to compare the central tendency, variability, and shape of the returns of the growth funds and the value funds. The mean indicated that the growth funds returned a mean of 7.49, and the median indicated that half of the growth funds had returns of 8.76 or more. The value funds' central tendencies were slightly higher than those of the growth funds—they had a mean of 8.45, and half the

funds had one-year returns above 9.41. The growth funds showed slightly more variability than the value funds, with a standard deviation of 5.6128 as compared to 5.0438. The kurtosis of value funds was very positive, indicating a distribution that was much more peaked than a normal distribution. Although past performance is no assurance of future performance, the value funds slightly outperformed the growth funds in 2014. (You can examine other variables in Retirement Funds to see if the value funds outperformed the growth funds for the 3-year period 2012–2014, for the 5-year period 2010–2014 and for the 10-year period 2005–2014.)

▼ SUMMARY

In this chapter, you studied descriptive statistics—how you can organize data through tables, visualize data through charts, and how you can use various statistics to help analyze the data and reach conclusions. In this chapter, you learned how descriptive statistics such as the mean, median, quartiles, range, and standard deviation describe the characteristics of central tendency, variability, and shape. In addition, you constructed boxplots to visualize the distribution of the data. You also learned how the coefficient of correlation describes the relationship between two numerical variables. Table 3.8 summarizes the methods discussed in this chapter.

You also learned several concepts about variation in data. These concepts are:

- The greater the spread or dispersion of the data, the larger the range, variance, and standard deviation.

- The smaller the spread or dispersion of the data, the smaller the range, variance, and standard deviation.
- If the values are all the same (no variation in the data), the range, variance, and standard deviation will all equal zero.
- Measures of variation (the range, variance, and standard deviation) are never negative.

TABLE 3.8
Chapter 3 Descriptive
Statistics Methods

Type of Analysis	Methods
Central tendency	Mean, median, mode (Section 3.1)
Variation and shape	Quartiles, range, interquartile range, variance, standard deviation, coefficient of variation, Z scores, boxplot (Sections 3.2 through 3.4)
Describing the relationship between two numerical variables	Covariance, coefficient of correlation (Section 3.5)

▼ REFERENCES

1. Booker, J., and L. Ticknor. "A Brief Overview of Kurtosis." www.osti.gov/bridge/purl.cover.jsp?purl=/677174-zdulqk/webviewable/677174.pdf.
2. Kendall, M. G., A. Stuart, and J. K. Ord. *Kendall's Advanced Theory of Statistics, Volume 1: Distribution Theory*, 6th ed. New York: Oxford University Press, 1994.
3. Taleb, N. *The Black Swan*, 2nd ed. New York: Random House, 2010.

▼ KEY EQUATIONS

Sample Mean

$$\overline{X} = \frac{\sum_{i=1}^{n} X_i}{n} \tag{3.1}$$

Median

$$\text{Median} = \frac{n+1}{2} \text{ ranked value} \tag{3.2}$$

Geometric Mean

$$\overline{X}_G = (X_1 \times X_2 \times \cdots \times X_n)^{1/n} \tag{3.3}$$

Geometric Mean Rate of Return

$$\overline{R}_G = [(1 + R_1) \times (1 + R_2) \times \cdots \times (1 + R_n)]^{1/n} - 1 \tag{3.4}$$

Range

$$\text{Range} = X_{\text{largest}} - X_{\text{smallest}} \tag{3.5}$$

Sample Variance

$$S^2 = \frac{\sum_{i=1}^{n} (X_i - \overline{X})^2}{n-1} \tag{3.6}$$

Sample Standard Deviation

$$S = \sqrt{S^2} = \sqrt{\frac{\sum_{i=1}^{n} (X_i - \overline{X})^2}{n-1}} \tag{3.7}$$

Coefficient of Variation

$$CV = \left(\frac{S}{\overline{X}}\right)100\% \tag{3.8}$$

Z Score

$$Z = \frac{X - \overline{X}}{S} \tag{3.9}$$

First Quartile, Q_1

$$Q_1 = \frac{n+1}{4} \text{ ranked value} \qquad (3.10)$$

Third Quartile, Q_3

$$Q_3 = \frac{3(n+1)}{4} \text{ ranked value} \qquad (3.11)$$

Interquartile Range

$$\text{Interquartile range} = Q_3 - Q_1 \qquad (3.12)$$

Population Mean

$$\mu = \frac{\sum_{i=1}^{N} X_i}{N} \qquad (3.13)$$

Population Variance

$$\sigma^2 = \frac{\sum_{i=1}^{N} (X_i - \mu)^2}{N} \qquad (3.14)$$

Population Standard Deviation

$$\sigma = \sqrt{\frac{\sum_{i=1}^{N} (X_i - \mu)^2}{N}} \qquad (3.15)$$

Sample Covariance

$$\text{cov}(X, Y) = \frac{\sum_{i=1}^{n} (X_i - \overline{X})(Y_i - \overline{Y})}{n-1} \qquad (3.16)$$

Sample Coefficient of Correlation

$$r = \frac{\text{cov}(X, Y)}{S_X S_Y} \qquad (3.17)$$

▼KEY TERMS

▼CHECKING YOUR UNDERSTANDING

3.50 What are the properties of a set of numerical data?

3.51 What is meant by the property of central tendency?

3.52 What are the differences among the mean, median, and mode, and what are the advantages and disadvantages of each?

3.53 How do you interpret the first quartile, median, and third quartile?

3.54 What is meant by the property of variation?

3.55 What does the Z score measure?

3.56 What are the differences among the various measures of variation, such as the range, interquartile range, variance, standard deviation, and coefficient of variation, and what are the advantages and disadvantages of each?

3.57 How does the empirical rule help explain the ways in which the values in a set of numerical data cluster and distribute?

3.58 How do the empirical rule and the Chebyshev rule differ?

3.59 What is meant by the property of shape?

3.60 What is the difference between skewness and kurtosis?

3.61 What is the difference between the arithmetic mean and the geometric mean?

3.62 How do the covariance and the coefficient of correlation differ?

▼CHAPTER REVIEW PROBLEMS

3.63 The American Society for Quality (ASQ) conducted a salary survey of all its members. ASQ members work in all areas of manufacturing and service-related institutions, with a common theme of an interest in quality. Manager and quality engineer were the most frequently reported job titles among the valid responses. Master Black Belt, a person who takes a leadership role as the keeper of the Six Sigma process (see Section 18.6) and Green Belt, someone who works on Six Sigma projects part time, were among the other job titles cited. Descriptive statistics concerning salaries for these four titles are given in the following table:

Job Title	Sample Size	Minimum	Maximum	Standard Deviation	Mean	Median
Green Belt	29	37,000	156,000	25,503	77,514	76,000
Manager	1,415	30,000	750,400	34,896	94,279	90,700
Quality Engineer	944	28,000	196,000	21,921	79,152	77,000
Master Black Belt	67	78,645	195,000	27,865	123,091	120,000

Source: Data extracted from M. Hansen, "QP Salary Survey," *Quality Progress*, December 2014, p. 27.

Compare the salaries of Green Belts, managers, quality engineers, and Master Black Belts.

3.64 In certain states, savings banks are permitted to sell life insurance. The approval process consists of underwriting, which includes a review of the application, a medical information bureau check, possible requests for additional medical information and medical exams, and a policy compilation stage, in which the policy pages are generated and sent to the bank for delivery. The ability to deliver approved policies to customers in a timely manner is critical to the profitability of this service to the bank. Using the DCOVA framework you define the variable of interest as the total processing time in days. You collect the data by selecting a random sample of 27 approved policies during a period of one month. You organize the data collected in a worksheet and store them in Insurance :

```
73  19  16  64  28  28  31  90  60  56  31  56  22  18
45  48  17  17  17  91  92  63  50  51  69  16  17
```

a. Compute the mean, median, first quartile, and third quartile.
b. Compute the range, interquartile range, variance, standard deviation, and coefficient of variation.
c. Construct a boxplot. Are the data skewed? If so, how?

d. What would you tell a customer who enters the bank to purchase this type of insurance policy and asks how long the approval process takes?

3.65 One of the major measures of the quality of service provided by an organization is the speed with which it responds to customer complaints. A large family-held department store selling furniture and flooring, including carpet, had undergone a major expansion in the past several years. In particular, the flooring department had expanded from 2 installation crews to an installation supervisor, a measurer, and 15 installation crews. The business objective of the company was to reduce the time between when a complaint is received and when it is resolved. During a recent year, the company received 50 complaints concerning carpet installation. The data from the 50 complaints, organized in Furniture , represent the number of days between the receipt of a complaint and the resolution of the complaint:

54	5	35	137	31	27	152	2	123	81	74	27	11
19	126	110	110	29	61	35	94	31	26	5	12	4
165	32	29	28	29	26	25	1	14	13	13	10	5
27	4	52	30	22	36	26	20	23	33	68		

a. Compute the mean, median, first quartile, and third quartile.
b. Compute the range, interquartile range, variance, standard deviation, and coefficient of variation.
c. Construct a boxplot. Are the data skewed? If so, how?
d. On the basis of the results of (a) through (c), if you had to tell the president of the company how long a customer should expect to wait to have a complaint resolved, what would you say? Explain.

3.66 A manufacturing company produces steel housings for electrical equipment. The main component part of the housing is a steel trough that is made of a 14-gauge steel coil. It is produced using a 250-ton progressive punch press with a wipe-down operation and two 90-degree forms placed in the flat steel to make the trough. The distance from one side of the form to the other is critical because of weatherproofing in outdoor applications. The company requires that the width of the trough be between 8.31 inches and 8.61 inches. Data are collected from a sample of 49 troughs and stored in Trough , which contains these widths of the troughs, in inches:

```
8.312  8.343  8.317  8.383  8.348  8.410  8.351  8.373  8.481  8.422
8.476  8.382  8.484  8.403  8.414  8.419  8.385  8.465  8.498  8.447
8.436  8.413  8.489  8.414  8.481  8.415  8.479  8.429  8.458  8.462
8.460  8.444  8.429  8.460  8.412  8.420  8.410  8.405  8.323  8.420
8.396  8.447  8.405  8.439  8.411  8.427  8.420  8.498  8.409
```

a. Compute the mean, median, range, and standard deviation for the width. Interpret these measures of central tendency and variability.

b. List the five-number summary.

c. Construct a boxplot and describe its shape.

d. What can you conclude about the number of troughs that will meet the company's requirement of troughs being between 8.31 and 8.61 inches wide?

3.67 The manufacturing company in Problem 3.66 also produces electric insulators. If the insulators break when in use, a short circuit is likely to occur. To test the strength of the insulators, destructive testing is carried out to determine how much force is required to break the insulators. Force is measured by observing how many pounds must be applied to an insulator before it breaks. Data are collected from a sample of 30 insulators. The file Force contains the strengths, as follows:

1,870 1,728 1,656 1,610 1,634 1,784 1,522 1,696 1,592 1,662
1,866 1,764 1,734 1,662 1,734 1,774 1,550 1,756 1,762 1,866
1,820 1,744 1,788 1,688 1,810 1,752 1,680 1,810 1,652 1,736

a. Compute the mean, median, range, and standard deviation for the force needed to break the insulators.

b. Interpret the measures of central tendency and variability in (a).

c. Construct a boxplot and describe its shape.

d. What can you conclude about the strength of the insulators if the company requires a force of at least 1,500 pounds before breakage?

3.68 Data were collected on the typical cost of dining at American-cuisine restaurants within a 1-mile walking distance of a hotel located in a large city. The file Bundle contains the typical cost (a per transaction cost in $) as well as a Bundle score, a measure of overall popularity and customer loyalty, for each of 40 selected restaurants. (Data extracted from www.bundle.com via the link **on-msn.com/MnlBxo**.)

a. For each variable, compute the mean, median, first quartile, and third quartile.

b. For each variable, compute the range, interquartile range, variance, standard deviation, and coefficient of variation.

c. For each variable, construct a boxplot. Are the data skewed? If so, how?

d. Compute the coefficient of correlation between Bundle score and typical cost.

e. What conclusions can you reach concerning Bundle score and typical cost?

3.69 A quality characteristic of interest for a tea-bag-filling process is the weight of the tea in the individual bags. If the bags are underfilled, two problems arise. First, customers may not be able to brew the tea to be as strong as they wish. Second, the company may be in violation of the truth-in-labeling laws. For this product, the label weight on the package indicates that, on average, there are 5.5 grams of tea in a bag. If the mean amount of tea in a bag exceeds the label weight, the company is giving away product. Getting an exact amount of tea in a bag is problematic because of variation in the temperature and humidity inside the factory, differences in the density of the tea, and the extremely fast filling operation of the machine (approximately 170 bags per minute). The file Teabags contains these weights, in grams, of a sample of 50 tea bags produced in one hour by a single machine:

5.65 5.44 5.42 5.40 5.53 5.34 5.54 5.45 5.52 5.41
5.57 5.40 5.53 5.54 5.55 5.62 5.56 5.46 5.44 5.51

5.47 5.40 5.47 5.61 5.53 5.32 5.67 5.29 5.49 5.55
5.77 5.57 5.42 5.58 5.58 5.50 5.32 5.50 5.53 5.58
5.61 5.45 5.44 5.25 5.56 5.63 5.50 5.57 5.67 5.36

a. Compute the mean, median, first quartile, and third quartile.

b. Compute the range, interquartile range, variance, standard deviation, and coefficient of variation.

c. Interpret the measures of central tendency and variation within the context of this problem. Why should the company producing the tea bags be concerned about the central tendency and variation?

d. Construct a boxplot. Are the data skewed? If so, how?

e. Is the company meeting the requirement set forth on the label that, on average, there are 5.5 grams of tea in a bag? If you were in charge of this process, what changes, if any, would you try to make concerning the distribution of weights in the individual bags?

3.70 The manufacturer of Boston and Vermont asphalt shingles provides its customers with a 20-year warranty on most of its products. To determine whether a shingle will last as long as the warranty period, accelerated-life testing is conducted at the manufacturing plant. Accelerated-life testing exposes a shingle to the stresses it would be subject to in a lifetime of normal use via an experiment in a laboratory setting that takes only a few minutes to conduct. In this test, a shingle is repeatedly scraped with a brush for a short period of time, and the shingle granules removed by the brushing are weighed (in grams). Shingles that experience low amounts of granule loss are expected to last longer in normal use than shingles that experience high amounts of granule loss. In this situation, a shingle should experience no more than 0.8 gram of granule loss if it is expected to last the length of the warranty period. The file Granule contains a sample of 170 measurements made on the company's Boston shingles and 140 measurements made on Vermont shingles.

a. List the five-number summaries for the Boston shingles and for the Vermont shingles.

b. Construct side-by-side boxplots for the two brands of shingles and describe the shapes of the distributions.

c. Comment on the ability of each type of shingle to achieve a granule loss of 0.8 gram or less.

3.71 The file Restaurants contains the cost per meal and the ratings of 50 center city and 50 metro area restaurants on their food, décor, and service (and their summated ratings). (Data extracted from *Zagat Survey 2015 New York City Restaurants*.) Complete the following for the center city and metro area restaurants:

a. Construct the five-number summary of the cost of a meal.

b. Construct a boxplot of the cost of a meal. What is the shape of the distribution?

c. Compute and interpret the correlation coefficient of the summated rating and the cost of a meal.

d. What conclusions can you reach about the cost of a meal at center city and metro area restaurants?

3.72 The file Protein contains calories, protein, and cholesterol of popular protein foods (fresh red meats, poultry, and fish).
Source: U.S. Department of Agriculture.

a. Compute the correlation coefficient between calories and protein.

b. Compute the correlation coefficient between calories and cholesterol.

c. Compute the correlation coefficient between protein and cholesterol.

d. Based on the results of (a) through (c), what conclusions can you reach concerning calories, protein, and cholesterol?

3.73 What was the mean price of a room at two-star, three-star, and four-star hotels in the major cities of the world during the first half of 2014? The file HotelPrices contains the mean prices in English pounds, approximately US$1.57 as of May 2015, for the three categories of hotels. (Data extracted from "Average room prices by star ratings," **bit.ly/1Hlp1xy**.) Do the following for two-star, three-star, and four-star hotels:

a. Compute the mean, median, first quartile, and third quartile.
b. Compute the range, interquartile range, variance, standard deviation, and coefficient of variation.
c. Interpret the measures of central tendency and variation within the context of this problem.
d. Construct a boxplot. Are the data skewed? If so, how?
e. Compute the covariance between the mean price at two-star and three-star hotels, between two-star and four-star hotels, and between three-star and four-star hotels.
f. Compute the coefficient of correlation between the mean price at two-star and three-star hotels, between two-star and four-star hotels, and between three-star and four-star hotels.
g. Which do you think is more valuable in expressing the relationship between the mean price of a room at two-star, three-star, and four-star hotels—the covariance or the coefficient of correlation? Explain.
h. Based on (f), what conclusions can you reach about the relationship between the mean price of a room at two-star, three-star, and four-star hotels?

3.74 The file PropertyTaxes contains the property taxes per capita for the 50 states and the District of Columbia.

a. Compute the mean, median, first quartile, and third quartile.
b. Compute the range, interquartile range, variance, standard deviation, and coefficient of variation.
c. Construct a boxplot. Are the data skewed? If so, how?
d. Based on the results of (a) through (c), what conclusions can you reach concerning property taxes per capita for each state and the District of Columbia?

3.75 Have you wondered how Internet download speed varies around the globe? The file DownloadSpeed contains the mean download speed Mbps for various countries. (Data extracted from **www.netindex.com/download/allcountries/**.)

a. Compute the mean, median, first quartile, and third quartile.
b. Compute the range, interquartile range, variance, standard deviation, and coefficient of variation.
c. Construct a boxplot. Are the data skewed? If so, how?
d. Based on the results of (a) through (c), what conclusions can you reach concerning the download speed around the globe?

3.76 311 is Chicago's web and phone portal for government information and nonemergency services. 311 serves as a comprehensive one-stop shop for residents, visitors, and business owners; therefore, it is critical that 311 representatives answer calls and respond to requests in a timely and accurate fashion. The target response time for answering 311 calls is 45 seconds. Agent abandonment rate is one of several call center metrics tracked by 311 officials. This metric tracks the percentage of callers who hang up after the target response time of 45 seconds has elapsed. The file 311CallCenter contains the agent abandonment rate for 22 weeks of call center operation during the 7:00 A.M.–3:00 P.M. shift.

a. Compute the mean, median, first quartile, and third quartile.
b. Compute the range, interquartile range, variance, standard deviation, and coefficient of variation.

c. Construct a boxplot. Are the data skewed? If so, how?
d. Compute the correlation coefficient between day and agent abandonment rate.
e. Based on the results of (a) through (c), what conclusions might you reach concerning 311 call center performance operation?

3.77 How much time do Americans living in or near cities spend waiting in traffic, and how much does waiting in traffic cost them per year? The file Congestion includes this cost for 31 cities. (Source: Data extracted from "The High Cost of Congestion," *Time*, October 17, 2011, p. 18.) For the time Americans living in or near cities spend waiting in traffic and the cost of waiting in traffic per year:

a. Compute the mean, median, first quartile, and third quartile.
b. Compute the range, interquartile range, variance, standard deviation, and coefficient of variation.
c. Construct a boxplot. Are the data skewed? If so, how?
d. Compute the correlation coefficient between the time spent sitting in traffic and the cost of sitting in traffic.
e. Based on the results of (a) through (c), what conclusions might you reach concerning the time spent waiting in traffic and the cost of waiting in traffic.

3.78 How do the mean credit scores of people living in various American cities differ? The file Credit Scores is an ordered array of the average credit scores of people living in 143 American cities. (Data extracted from **experian.com/live-credit-smart/state-of-credit-2014.html**.)

a. Compute the mean, median, first quartile, and third quartile.
b. Compute the range, interquartile range, variance, standard deviation, and coefficient of variation.
c. Construct a boxplot. Are the data skewed? If so, how?
d. Based on the results of (a) through (c), what conclusions might you reach concerning the average credit scores of people living in various American cities?

3.79 You are planning to study for your statistics examination with a group of classmates, one of whom you particularly want to impress. This individual has volunteered to use Microsoft Excel to generate the needed summary information, tables, and charts for a data set that contains several numerical and categorical variables assigned by the instructor for study purposes. This person comes over to you with the printout and exclaims, "I've got it all—the means, the medians, the standard deviations, the boxplots, the pie charts—for all our variables. The problem is, some of the output looks weird—like the boxplots for gender and for major and the pie charts for grade point average and for height. Also, I can't understand why Professor Szabat said we can't get the descriptive stats for some of the variables; I got them for everything! See, the mean for height is 68.23, the mean for grade point average is 2.76, the mean for gender is 1.50, the mean for major is 4.33." What is your reply?

REPORT WRITING EXERCISES

3.80 The file DomesticBeer contains the percentage alcohol, number of calories per 12 ounces, and number of carbohydrates (in grams) per 12 ounces for 158 of the best-selling domestic beers in the United States. (Data extracted from **bit.ly/1A4E6AF**, February 3, 2015.) Write a report that includes a complete descriptive evaluation of each of the numerical variables—percentage of alcohol, number of calories per 12 ounces, and number of carbohydrates (in grams) per 12 ounces. Append to your report all appropriate tables, charts, and numerical descriptive measures.

CHAPTER

3

▼CASES

Managing Ashland MultiComm Services

For what variable in the Chapter 2 "Managing Ashland Multi-Comm Services" case (see page 80) are numerical descriptive measures needed?

1. For the variable you identify, compute the appropriate numerical descriptive measures and construct a boxplot.
2. For the variable you identify, construct a graphical display. What conclusions can you reach from this other plot that cannot be made from the boxplot?
3. Summarize your findings in a report that can be included with the task force's study.

Digital Case

Apply your knowledge about the proper use of numerical descriptive measures in this continuing Digital Case.

Open **EndRunGuide.pdf**, the EndRun Financial Services "Guide to Investing." Reexamine EndRun's supporting data for the "More Winners Than Losers" and "The Big Eight Difference" and then answer the following:

1. Can descriptive measures be computed for any variables? How would such summary statistics support EndRun's claims? How would those summary statistics affect your perception of EndRun's record?
2. Evaluate the methods EndRun used to summarize the results presented on the "Customer Survey Results" page. Is there anything you would do differently to summarize these results?
3. Note that the last question of the survey has fewer responses than the other questions. What factors may have limited the number of responses to that question?

CardioGood Fitness

Return to the CardioGood Fitness case first presented on page 28. Using the data stored in CardioGoodFitness :

1. Compute descriptive statistics to create a customer profile for each CardioGood Fitness treadmill product line.
2. Write a report to be presented to the management of CardioGood Fitness, detailing your findings.

More Descriptive Choices Follow-up

Follow up the Using Statistics Revisited section on page 130 by computing descriptive statistics to analyze the differences in 3-year return percentages, 5-year return percentages, and 10-year return percentages for the sample of 407 retirement funds stored in Retirement Funds . In your analysis, examine differences between the growth and value funds as well as the differences among the small, mid-cap, and large market cap funds.

Clear Mountain State Student Survey

The student news service at Clear Mountain State University (CMSU) has decided to gather data about the undergraduate students who attend CMSU. They create and distribute a survey of 14 questions and receive responses from 111 undergraduates (stored in StudentSurvey). For each numerical variable included in the survey, compute all the appropriate descriptive statistics and write a report summarizing your conclusions.

▾EXCEL GUIDE

EG3.1 CENTRAL TENDENCY

The Mean, Median, and Mode

Key Technique Use the **AVERAGE(***variable cell range***)**, **MEDIAN(***variable cell range***)**, and **MODE(***variable cell range***)** functions to compute these measures.

Example Compute the mean, median, and mode for the sample of getting-ready times introduced in Section 3.1.

PHStat Use **Descriptive Summary**.

For the example, open to the **DATA worksheet** of the **Times workbook**. Select **PHStat → Descriptive Statistics → Descriptive Summary**. In the procedure's dialog box (shown below):

1. Enter **A1:A11** as the **Raw Data Cell Range** and check **First cell contains label**.
2. Click **Single Group Variable**.
3. Enter a **Title** and click **OK**.

PHStat inserts a new worksheet that contains various measures of central tendency, variation, and shape discussed in Sections 3.1 and 3.2. This worksheet is similar to the CompleteStatistics worksheet of the Descriptive workbook.

Workbook Use the **CentralTendency worksheet** of the **Descriptive workbook** as a model.

For the example, open the **Times workbook**, insert a new worksheet (see Section B.2), and:

1. Enter a title in cell **A1**.
2. Enter **Get-Ready Times** in cell **B3**, **Mean** in cell **A4**, **Median** in cell **A5**, and **Mode** in cell **A6**.
3. Enter the formula **=AVERAGE(DATA!A:A)** in cell **B4**, the formula **=MEDIAN(DATA!A:A)** in cell **B5**, and the formula **=MODE(DATA!A:A)** in cell **B6**.

For these functions, the *variable cell range* includes the name of the DATA worksheet because the data being summarized appears on the separate DATA worksheet. For another problem, paste the data for the problem into column A of the DATA worksheet, overwriting the existing getting-ready times.

Analysis ToolPak Use **Descriptive Statistics**.

For the example, open to the **DATA worksheet** of the **Times workbook** and:

1. Select **Data → Data Analysis**.
2. In the Data Analysis dialog box, select **Descriptive Statistics** from the **Analysis Tools** list and then click **OK**.

In the Descriptive Statistics dialog box (shown below):

1. Enter **A1:A11** as the **Input Range**. Click **Columns** and check **Labels in first row**.
2. Click **New Worksheet Ply** and check **Summary statistics**, **Kth Largest**, and **Kth Smallest**.
3. Click **OK**.

The ToolPak inserts a new worksheet that contains various measures of central tendency, variation, and shape discussed in Sections 3.1 and 3.2.

The Geometric Mean

Key Technique Use the **GEOMEAN((1 + (***R1***)),** **(1 + (***R2***)), . . . (1 + (***Rn***))) − 1** function to compute the geometric mean rate of return.

Example Compute the geometric mean rate of return in the Russell 2000 Index for the two years as shown in Example 3.4 on page 101.

Workbook Enter the formula **=GEOMEAN((1 +** **(0.37)), (1 + (−0.035))) − 1** in any cell.

EG3.2 VARIATION and SHAPE

The Range

Key Technique   Use the **MIN(*variable cell range*)** and **MAX(*variable cell range*)** functions to help compute the range.

Example   Compute the range for the sample of getting-ready times first introduced in Section 3.1.

PHStat   Use **Descriptive Summary** (see Section EG3.1).

Workbook   Use the **Range worksheet** of the **Descriptive workbook** as a model.

For the example, open the worksheet constructed in the *Workbook* "The Mean, Median, and Mode" instructions. Enter **Minimum** in cell **A7**, **Maximum** in cell **A8**, and **Range** in cell **A9**. Enter the formula **=MIN(DATA!A:A)** in cell **B7**, the formula **=MAX(DATA!A:A)** in cell **B8**, and the formula **=B8 − B7** in cell **B9**.

The Variance, Standard Deviation, Coefficient of Variation, and *Z* Scores

Key Technique   Use the **VAR.S(*variable cell range*)** and **STDEV.S(*variable cell range*)** functions to compute the sample variance and the sample standard deviation, respectively. Use the AVERAGE and STDEV.S functions for the coefficient of variation. Use the **STANDARDIZE(*value, mean, standard deviation*)** function to compute *Z* scores.

Example   Compute the variance, standard deviation, coefficient of variation, and *Z* scores for the sample of getting-ready times first introduced in Section 3.1.

PHStat   Use **Descriptive Summary** (see Section EG3.1).

Workbook   Use the **Variation** and **ZScores worksheets** of the **Descriptive workbook** as models.

For the example, the Variation and ZScores worksheets already compute these statistics using the getting-ready times in the DATA worksheet. To compute the variance, standard deviation, and coefficient of variation for another problem, paste the data for the problem into column A of the DATA worksheet, overwriting the existing getting-ready times.

To compute the *Z* scores for another problem, copy the updated DATA worksheet. In the new, copied worksheet, enter **Z Score** in cell **B1**. Enter the formula **=STANDARDIZE(A2, Variation!$B$4, Variation!$B$11)** in cell **B2** and copy the formula down through row **11**. If you use an Excel version older than Excel 2010, enter **Variation_OLDER!$B$4** and **Variation_OLDER!$B$11** as the cell references in the formula.

Analysis ToolPak   Use **Descriptive Statistics** (see Section EG3.1). This procedure does not compute *Z* scores.

Shape: Skewness and Kurtosis

Key Technique   Use the **SKEW(*variable cell range*)** and the **KURT(*variable cell range*)** functions to compute these measures.

Example   Compute the skewness and kurtosis for the sample of getting-ready times first introduced in Section 3.1.

PHStat   Use **Descriptive Summary** (see Section EG3.1).

Workbook   Use the **Shape worksheet** of the **Descriptive workbook** as a model.

For the example, the Shape worksheet already computes the skewness and kurtosis using the getting-ready times in the DATA worksheet. To compute these statistics for another problem, paste the data for the problem into column A of the DATA worksheet, overwriting the existing getting-ready times.

Analysis ToolPak   Use **Descriptive Statistics** (see Section EG3.1).

EG3.3 EXPLORING NUMERICAL DATA

Quartiles

Key Technique   Use the MEDIAN and COUNT, and SMALL, INT, FLOOR, CEILING, and IF functions (all discussed in Appendix F) to compute the quartiles. Avoid using any of the Excel quartile functions because they do not use the Section 3.3 rules to calculate quartiles.

Example   Compute the quartiles for the sample of getting-ready times first introduced in Section 3.1.

PHStat   Use **Boxplot** (discussed later on this page).

Workbook   Use the **COMPUTE worksheet** of the **Quartiles workbook** as a model.

For the example, the COMPUTE worksheet already computes the quartiles for the getting-ready times. To compute the quartiles for another problem, paste the data into column A of the DATA worksheet, overwriting the existing getting-ready times.

The COMPUTE worksheet uses a number of arithmetic and logical formulas that use the IF function to produce results consistent to the Section 3.3 rules. Open to the **COMPUTE_FORMULAS worksheet** to review these formulas and read the SHORT TAKES for Chapter 3 for a detailed explanation of those formulas.

The COMPUTE worksheet avoids using any of the current Excel QUARTILE functions because none of them calculate quartiles using the Section 3.3 rules. The **COMPARE** worksheet compares the COMPUTE worksheet results to the quartiles calculated by the Excel QUARTILE.EXC and QUARTILE.INC functions.

The Interquartile Range

Key Technique Use a formula to subtract the first quartile from the third quartile.

Example Compute the interquartile range for the sample of getting-ready times first introduced in Section 3.1.

Workbook Use the **COMPUTE worksheet** of the **Quartiles workbook** (introduced in the previous section) as a model.

For the example, the interquartile range is already computed in cell B19 using the formula **=B18 − B16**.

The Five-Number Summary and the Boxplot

Key Technique Plot a series of line segments on the same chart to construct a boxplot. (Most Excel versions do not include a boxplot chart type and those that do use a type of boxplot different than the one described in Section 3.3.)

Example Compute the five-number summary and construct the boxplots of the one-year return percentage variable for the growth and value funds used in Example 3.14 on page 117.

PHStat Use **Boxplot**.
For the example, open to the **DATA worksheet** of the **Retirement Funds workbook**. Select **PHStat → Descriptive Statistics → Boxplot**. In the procedure's dialog box (shown below):

1. Enter **I1:I408** as the **Raw Data Cell Range** and check **First cell contains label**.
2. Click **Multiple Groups - Stacked** and enter **C1:C408** as the **Grouping Variable Cell Range**.
3. Enter a **Title**, check **Five-Number Summary**, and click **OK**.

The boxplot appears on its own chart sheet, separate from the worksheet that contains the five-number summary.

Workbook Use the worksheets of the **Boxplot workbook** as templates.

For the example, use the **PLOT_DATA worksheet** which already shows the five-number summary and boxplot for the value funds. To compute the five-number summary and construct a boxplot for the growth funds, copy the

growth funds from **column A** of the **UNSTACKED worksheet** of the **Retirement Funds workbook** and paste into **column A** of the **DATA worksheet** of the **Boxplot workbook**.

For other problems, use the **PLOT_SUMMARY worksheet** as the template if the five-number summary has already been determined; otherwise, paste your unsummarized data into column A of the DATA worksheet and use the PLOT_DATA worksheet as was done for the example.

The worksheets creatively misuse Excel line charting features to construct a boxplot. Read the SHORT TAKES for Chapter 3 for an explanation of this "misuse."

EG3.4 NUMERICAL DESCRIPTIVE MEASURES for a POPULATION

The Population Mean, Population Variance, and Population Standard Deviation

Key Technique Use AVERAGE(*variable cell range*), VAR.P(*variable cell range*), and STDEV.P(*variable cell range*) to compute these measures.

Example Compute the population mean, population variance, and population standard deviation for the "Dow Dogs" population data of Table 3.6 on page 120.

Workbook Use the **Parameters workbook** as a model. For the example, the **COMPUTE worksheet** of the **Parameters workbook** already computes the three population parameters for the "Dow Dogs."

The Empirical Rule and Chebyshev's Theorem

Use the **COMPUTE worksheet** of the **VE-Variability workbook** to explore the effects of changing the mean and standard deviation on the ranges associated with ±1 standard deviation, ±2 standard deviations, and ±3 standard deviations from the mean. Change the mean in cell **B4** and the standard deviation in cell **B5** and then note the updated results in rows 9 through 11.

EG3.5 THE COVARIANCE and the COEFFICIENT of CORRELATION

The Covariance

Key Technique Use the **COVARIANCE.S(*variable 1 cell range, variable 2 cell range*)** function to compute this measure.

Example Compute the sample covariance for the NBA team revenue and value shown in Figure 3.7 on page 125.

Workbook Use the **Covariance workbook** as a model. For the example, the revenue and value have already been placed in columns A and B of the DATA worksheet and the COMPUTE worksheet displays the computed covariance in cell B9. For other problems, paste the data for two variables into columns A and B of the DATA worksheet, overwriting the revenue and value data.

Read the SHORT TAKES for Chapter 3 for an explanation of the formulas found in the DATA and COMPUTE worksheets. If you use an Excel version older than Excel 2010, use the COMPUTE_OLDER worksheet that computes the covariance without using the COVARIANCE.S function that was introduced in Excel 2010.

The Coefficient of Correlation

Key Technique Use the **CORREL(*variable 1 cell range, variable 2 cell range*)** function to compute this measure.

Example Compute the coefficient of correlation for the NBA team revenue and value data of Example 3.18 on page 128.

Workbook Use the **Correlation workbook** as a model. For the example, the revenue and value have already been placed in columns A and B of the DATA worksheet and the COMPUTE worksheet displays the coefficient of correlation in cell B14. For other problems, paste the data for two variables into columns A and B of the DATA worksheet, overwriting the revenue and value data.

The COMPUTE worksheet that uses the COVARIANCE.S function to compute the covariance (see the previous section) and also uses the DEVSQ, COUNT, and SUMPRODUCT functions discussed in Appendix F. Open to the **COMPUTE_FORMULAS worksheet** to examine the use of all these functions.

Basic Probability

CONTENTS

OBJECTIVES

- Understand basic probability concepts
- Understand conditional probability

▼USING **STATISTICS**
Possibilities at M&R Electronics World

As the marketing manager for M&R Electronics World, you are analyzing the results of an intent-to-purchase study. The heads of 1,000 households were asked about their intentions to purchase a large TV (screen size of at least 60 inches, measured diagonally) sometime during the next 12 months. As a follow-up, you plan to survey the same people 12 months later to see whether they purchased a large TV. For households that did purchase a large TV, you would like to know whether the television they purchased had a faster refresh rate (240 Hz or higher) or a standard refresh rate (60 or 120 Hz), whether they also purchased a streaming media player in the past 12 months, and whether they were satisfied with their purchase of the large TV.

You plan to use the results of this survey to form a new marketing strategy that will enhance sales and better target those households likely to purchase multiple or more expensive products. What questions can you ask in this survey? How can you express the relationships among the various intent-to-purchase responses of individual households?

The principles of probability help bridge the worlds of descriptive statistics and inferential statistics. Probability principles are the foundation for the probability distributions, the concept of mathematical expectation, and the binomial and Poisson distributions. In this chapter, you will learn about probability to answer questions such as the following:

- What is the probability that a household is planning to purchase a large TV in the next year?
- What is the probability that a household will actually purchase a large TV?
- What is the probability that a household is planning to purchase a large TV and actually purchases the television?
- Given that the household is planning to purchase a large TV, what is the probability that the purchase is made?
- Does knowledge of whether a household *plans* to purchase a large TV change the likelihood of predicting whether the household *will* purchase a large TV?
- What is the probability that a household that purchases a large TV will purchase a television with a faster refresh rate?
- What is the probability that a household that purchases a large TV with a faster refresh rate will also purchase a streaming media player?
- What is the probability that a household that purchases a large TV will be satisfied with the purchase?

With answers to questions such as these, you can begin to form a marketing strategy. You can consider whether to target households that have indicated an intent to purchase or to focus on selling televisions that have faster refresh rates or both. You can also explore whether households that purchase large TVs with faster refresh rates can be easily persuaded to also purchase streaming media players.

4.1 Basic Probability Concepts

What is meant by the word *probability*? A **probability** is the numerical value representing the chance, likelihood, or possibility that a particular event will occur, such as the price of a stock increasing, a rainy day, a defective product, or the outcome five dots in a single toss of a die. In all these instances, the probability involved is a proportion or fraction whose value ranges between 0 and 1, inclusive. An event that has no chance of occurring (the **impossible event**) has a probability of 0. An event that is sure to occur (the **certain event**) has a probability of 1.

There are three types of probability:

- *A priori*
- Empirical
- Subjective

In the simplest case, where each outcome is equally likely, the chance of occurrence of the event is defined in Equation (4.1).

PROBABILITY OF OCCURRENCE

$$\text{Probability of occurrence} = \frac{X}{T} \tag{4.1}$$

where

X = number of ways in which the event occurs

T = total number of possible outcomes

In *a priori* probability, the probability of an occurrence is based on prior knowledge of the process involved. Consider a standard deck of cards that has 26 red cards and 26 black cards. The probability of selecting a black card is $26/52 = 0.50$ because there are $X = 26$ black cards and $T = 52$ total cards. What does this probability mean? If each card is replaced after it is selected, does it mean that 1 out of the next 2 cards selected will be black? No, because you cannot say for certain what will happen on the next several selections. However, you can say that in the long run, if this selection process is continually repeated, the proportion of black cards selected will approach 0.50. Example 4.1 shows another example of computing an *a priori* probability.

EXAMPLE 4.1 Finding *A Priori* Probabilities	A standard six-sided die has six faces. Each face of the die contains either one, two, three, four, five, or six dots. If you roll a die, what is the probability that you will get a face with five dots? **SOLUTION** Each face is equally likely to occur. Because there are six faces, the probability of getting a face with five dots is 1/6.

The preceding examples use the *a priori* probability approach because the number of ways the event occurs and the total number of possible outcomes are known from the composition of the deck of cards or the faces of the die.

In the **empirical probability** approach, the probabilities are based on observed data, not on prior knowledge of a process. Surveys are often used to generate empirical probabilities. Examples of this type of probability are the proportion of individuals in the Using Statistics scenario who actually purchase a large TV, the proportion of registered voters who prefer a certain political candidate, and the proportion of students who have part-time jobs. For example, if you take a survey of students, and 60% state that they have part-time jobs, then there is a 0.60 probability that an individual student has a part-time job.

The third approach to probability, **subjective probability**, differs from the other two approaches because subjective probability differs from person to person. For example, the development team for a new product may assign a probability of 0.60 to the chance of success for the product, while the president of the company may be less optimistic and assign a probability of 0.30. The assignment of subjective probabilities to various outcomes is usually based on a combination of an individual's past experience, personal opinion, and analysis of a particular situation. Subjective probability is especially useful in making decisions in situations in which you cannot use *a priori* probability or empirical probability.

Events and Sample Spaces

The basic elements of probability theory are the individual outcomes of a variable under study. You need the following definitions to understand probabilities.

studentTIP

Events are represented by letters of the alphabet.

EVENT
Each possible outcome of a variable is referred to as an **event**.
A **simple event** is described by a single characteristic.

For example, when you toss a coin, the two possible outcomes are heads and tails. Each of these represents a simple event. When you roll a standard six-sided die in which the six faces of the die contain either one, two, three, four, five, or six dots, there are six possible simple events. An event can be any one of these simple events, a set of them, or a subset of all of them. For example, the event of an *even number of dots* consists of three simple events (i.e., two, four, or six dots).

JOINT EVENT

A **joint event** is an event that has two or more characteristics.

Getting two heads when you toss a coin twice is an example of a joint event because it consists of heads on the first toss and heads on the second toss.

COMPLEMENT

The **complement** of event *A* (represented by the symbol *A'*) includes all events that are not part of *A*.

The complement of a head is a tail because that is the only event that is not a head. The complement of five dots on a die is not getting five dots. Not getting five dots consists of getting one, two, three, four, or six dots.

SAMPLE SPACE

The collection of all the possible events is called the **sample space**.

The sample space for tossing a coin consists of heads and tails. The sample space when rolling a die consists of one, two, three, four, five, and six dots. Example 4.2 demonstrates events and sample spaces.

EXAMPLE 4.2

Events and Sample Spaces

The Using Statistics scenario on page 141 concerns M&R Electronics World. Table 4.1 presents the results of the sample of 1,000 households in terms of purchase behavior for large TVs.

TABLE 4.1
Purchase Behavior for Large TVs

PLANNED TO PURCHASE	ACTUALLY PURCHASED		
	Yes	No	Total
Yes	200	50	250
No	100	650	750
Total	300	700	1,000

What is the sample space? Give examples of simple events and joint events.

SOLUTION The sample space consists of the 1,000 respondents. Simple events are "planned to purchase," "did not plan to purchase," "purchased," and "did not purchase." The complement of the event "planned to purchase" is "did not plan to purchase." The event "planned to purchase and actually purchased" is a joint event because in this joint event, the respondent must plan to purchase the television *and* actually purchase it.

Contingency Tables

There are several ways in which you can view a particular sample space. The method used in this book involves using a **contingency table** (see Section 2.1) such as the one displayed in Table 4.1. You get the values in the cells of the table by subdividing the sample space of 1,000 households according to whether someone planned to purchase and actually purchased a large TV. For example, 200 of the respondents planned to purchase a large TV and subsequently did purchase the large TV.

Simple Probability

Now you can answer some of the questions posed in the Using Statistics scenario. Because the results are based on data collected in a survey (refer to Table 4.1), you can use the empirical probability approach.

As stated previously, the most fundamental rule for probabilities is that they range in value from 0 to 1. An impossible event has a probability of 0, and an event that is certain to occur has a probability of 1.

Simple probability refers to the probability of occurrence of a simple event, $P(A)$. A simple probability in the Using Statistics scenario is the probability of planning to purchase a large TV. How can you determine the probability of selecting a household that planned to purchase a large TV? Using Equation (4.1) on page 142:

$$\text{Probability of occurrence} = \frac{X}{T}$$

$$P(\text{Planned to purchase}) = \frac{\text{Number who planned to purchase}}{\text{Total number of households}}$$

$$= \frac{250}{1,000} = 0.25$$

Thus, there is a 0.25 (or 25%) chance that a household planned to purchase a large TV.

Example 4.3 illustrates another application of simple probability.

EXAMPLE 4.3

Computing the Probability That the Large TV Purchased Had a Faster Refresh Rate

In the Using Statistics follow-up survey, additional questions were asked of the 300 households that actually purchased large TVs. Table 4.2 indicates the consumers' responses to whether the television purchased had a faster refresh rate and whether they also purchased a streaming media player in the past 12 months.

Find the probability that if a household that purchased a large TV is randomly selected, the television purchased had a faster refresh rate.

TABLE 4.2
Purchase Behavior About Purchasing a Faster Refresh Rate Television and a Streaming Media Player

REFRESH RATE OF TELEVISION PURCHASED	STREAMING MEDIA PLAYER		
	Yes	No	Total
Faster	38	42	80
Standard	70	150	220
Total	108	192	300

(continued)

SOLUTION   Using the following definitions:

$$A = \text{purchased a television with a faster refresh rate}$$
$$A' = \text{purchased a television with a standard refresh rate}$$
$$B = \text{purchased a streaming media player}$$
$$B' = \text{did not purchase a streaming media player}$$

$$P(\text{Faster refresh rate}) = \frac{\text{Number of faster refresh rate televisions purchased}}{\text{Total number of televisions}}$$

$$= \frac{80}{300} = 0.267$$

There is a 26.7% chance that a randomly selected large TV purchased has a faster refresh rate.

Joint Probability

Whereas simple probability refers to the probability of occurrence of simple events, **joint probability** refers to the probability of an occurrence involving two or more events. An example of joint probability is the probability that you will get heads on the first toss of a coin and heads on the second toss of a coin.

In Table 4.1 on page 144, the group of individuals who planned to purchase and actually purchased a large TV consist only of the outcomes in the single cell "yes—planned to purchase *and* yes—actually purchased." Because this group consists of 200 households, the probability of picking a household that planned to purchase *and* actually purchased a large TV is

$$P(\text{Planned to purchase and actually purchased}) = \frac{\text{Planned to purchase and actually purchased}}{\text{Total number of respondents}}$$

$$= \frac{200}{1,000} = 0.20$$

Example 4.4 also demonstrates how to determine joint probability.

EXAMPLE 4.4

Determining the Joint Probability That a Household Purchased a Large TV with a Faster Refresh Rate and Purchased a Streaming Media Box

In Table 4.2 on page 145, the purchases are cross-classified as having a faster refresh rate or having a standard refresh rate and whether the household purchased a streaming media player. Find the probability that a randomly selected household that purchased a large TV also purchased a television that had a faster refresh rate and purchased a streaming media player.

SOLUTION   Using Equation (4.1) on page 142,

$$P\left(\begin{array}{c}\text{TV with a faster refresh rate} \\ \text{and streaming media player}\end{array}\right) = \frac{\begin{array}{c}\text{Number that purchased a TV with a faster refresh} \\ \text{rate and purchased a streaming media player}\end{array}}{\text{Total number of large TV purchasers}}$$

$$= \frac{38}{300} = 0.127$$

Therefore, there is a 12.7% chance that a randomly selected household that purchased a large TV purchased a television that had a faster refresh rate and purchased a streaming media player.

Marginal Probability

The **marginal probability** of an event consists of a set of joint probabilities. You can determine the marginal probability of a particular event by using the concept of joint probability just discussed. For example, if B consists of two events, B_1 and B_2, then $P(A)$, the probability of event A, consists of the joint probability of event A occurring with event B_1 and the joint probability of event A occurring with event B_2. You use Equation (4.2) to compute marginal probabilities.

MARGINAL PROBABILITY

$$P(A) = P(A \text{ and } B_1) + P(A \text{ and } B_2) + \cdots + P(A \text{ and } B_k) \qquad (4.2)$$

where $B_1, B_2, \ldots, B_k$ are k mutually exclusive and collectively exhaustive events, defined as follows:

Two events are **mutually exclusive** if both the events cannot occur simultaneously.
A set of events is **collectively exhaustive** if one of the events must occur.

Heads and tails in a coin toss are mutually exclusive events. The result of a coin toss cannot simultaneously be a head and a tail. Heads and tails in a coin toss are also collectively exhaustive events. One of them must occur. If heads does not occur, tails must occur. If tails does not occur, heads must occur. Being male and being female are mutually exclusive and collectively exhaustive events. No person is both (the two are mutually exclusive), and everyone is one or the other (the two are collectively exhaustive).

You can use Equation (4.2) to compute the marginal probability of "planned to purchase" a large TV:

$$P(\text{Planned to purchase}) = P(\text{Planned to purchase } and \text{ purchased})$$
$$+ P(\text{Planned to purchase } and \text{ did not purchase})$$
$$= \frac{200}{1,000} + \frac{50}{1,000} = \frac{250}{1,000} = 0.25$$

You get the same result if you add the number of outcomes that make up the simple event "planned to purchase."

General Addition Rule

How do you find the probability of event "*A or B*"? You need to consider the occurrence of either event A or event B or both A and B. For example, how can you determine the probability that a household planned to purchase *or* actually purchased a large TV?

The event "planned to purchase *or* actually purchased" includes all households that planned to purchase and all households that actually purchased a large TV. You examine each cell of the contingency table (Table 4.1 on page 144) to determine whether it is part of this event. From Table 4.1, the cell "planned to purchase *and* did not actually purchase" is part of the event because it includes respondents who planned to purchase. The cell "did not plan to purchase *and* actually purchased" is included because it contains respondents who actually purchased. Finally, the cell "planned to purchase *and* actually purchased" has both characteristics of interest. Therefore, one way to calculate the probability of "planned to purchase *or* actually purchased" is

$$P(\text{Planned to purchase } or \text{ actually purchased}) = P(\text{Planned to purchase } and \text{ did not actually purchase}) + P(\text{Did not plan to purchase } and \text{ actually purchased}) + P(\text{Planned to purchase } and \text{ actually purchased})$$

$$= \frac{50}{1,000} + \frac{100}{1,000} + \frac{200}{1,000}$$

$$= \frac{350}{1,000} = 0.35$$

Often, it is easier to determine $P(A \text{ or } B)$, the probability of the event $A \text{ or } B$, by using the **general addition rule**, defined in Equation (4.3).

GENERAL ADDITION RULE

The probability of $A \text{ or } B$ is equal to the probability of A plus the probability of B minus the probability of $A \text{ and } B$.

$$P(A \text{ or } B) = P(A) + P(B) - P(A \text{ and } B) \qquad (4.3)$$

Applying Equation (4.3) to the previous example produces the following result:

$$\begin{aligned} P(\text{Planned to purchase } or \text{ actually purchased}) &= P(\text{Planned to purchase}) \\ &\quad + P(\text{Actually purchased}) - P(\text{Planned to purchase } and \text{ actually purchased}) \\ &= \frac{250}{1,000} + \frac{300}{1,000} - \frac{200}{1,000} \\ &= \frac{350}{1,000} = 0.35 \end{aligned}$$

The general addition rule consists of taking the probability of A and adding it to the probability of B and then subtracting the probability of the joint event $A \text{ and } B$ from this total because the joint event has already been included in computing both the probability of A and the probability of B. Referring to Table 4.1 on page 144, if the outcomes of the event "planned to purchase" are added to those of the event "actually purchased," the joint event "planned to purchase *and* actually purchased" has been included in each of these simple events. Therefore, because this joint event has been included twice, you must subtract it to compute the correct result. Example 4.5 illustrates another application of the general addition rule.

EXAMPLE 4.5

Using the General Addition Rule for the Households That Purchased Large TVs

In Example 4.3 on page 145, the purchases were cross-classified in Table 4.2 as televisions that had a faster refresh rate or televisions that had a standard refresh rate and whether the household purchased a streaming media player. Find the probability that among households that purchased a large TV, they purchased a television that had a faster refresh rate or purchased a streaming media player.

SOLUTION Using Equation (4.3),

$$\begin{aligned} P(\text{Television had a faster refresh} &= P(\text{Television had a faster refresh rate}) \\ \text{rate } or \text{ purchased a streaming media player}) &\quad + P(\text{purchased a streaming media player}) \\ &\quad - P(\text{Television had a faster refresh rate } and \\ &\quad \text{purchased a streaming media player}) \end{aligned}$$

▶ *(continued)*

$$= \frac{80}{300} + \frac{108}{300} - \frac{38}{300}$$

$$= \frac{150}{300} = 0.50$$

Therefore, of households that purchased a large TV, there is a 50% chance that a randomly selected household purchased a television that had a faster refresh rate or purchased a streaming media player.

PROBLEMS FOR SECTION 4.1

LEARNING THE BASICS

4.1 Two coins are tossed.
a. Give an example of a simple event.
b. Give an example of a joint event.
c. What is the complement of a head on the first toss?
d. What does the sample space consist of?

4.2 An urn contains 12 red balls and 8 white balls. One ball is to be selected from the urn.
a. Give an example of a simple event.
b. What is the complement of a red ball?
c. What does the sample space consist of?

4.3 Consider the following contingency table:

	B	B'
A	10	20
A'	20	40

What is the probability of event
a. A?
b. A'?
c. A and B?
d. A or B?

4.4 Consider the following contingency table:

	B	B'
A	10	30
A'	25	35

What is the probability of event
a. A'?
b. A and B?
c. A' and B'?
d. A' or B'?

APPLYING THE CONCEPTS

4.5 For each of the following, indicate whether the type of probability involved is an example of *a priori* probability, empirical probability, or subjective probability.
a. The next toss of a fair coin will land on heads.
b. Italy will win soccer's World Cup the next time the competition is held.

c. The sum of the faces of two dice will be seven.
d. The train taking a commuter to work will be more than 10 minutes late.

4.6 For each of the following, state whether the events created are mutually exclusive and whether they are collectively exhaustive.
a. Undergraduate business students were asked whether they were sophomores or juniors.
b. Each respondent was classified by the type of car he or she drives: sedan, SUV, American, European, Asian, or none.
c. People were asked, "Do you currently live in (i) an apartment or (ii) a house?"
d. A product was classified as defective or not defective.

4.7 Which of the following events occur with a probability of zero? For each, state why or why not.
a. A company is listed on the New York Stock Exchange and NASDAQ.
b. A consumer owns a smartphone and a tablet.
c. A cellphone is a Motorola and a Samsung.
d. An automobile is a Toyota and was manufactured in the United States.

4.8 Do males or females feel more tense or stressed out at work? A survey of employed adults conducted online by Harris Interactive on behalf of the American Psychological Association revealed the following:

GENDER	FELT TENSE OR STRESSED OUT AT WORK	
	Yes	No
Male	244	495
Female	282	480

Source: Data extracted from "The 2013 Work and Well-Being Survey," American Psychological Association and Harris Interactive, March 2013, p. 5, **bit.ly/11JGcPf.**

a. Give an example of a simple event.
b. Give an example of a joint event.
c. What is the complement of "Felt tense or stressed out at work"?
d. Why is "Male and felt tense or stressed out at work" a joint event?

4.9 Referring to the contingency table in Problem 4.8, if an employed adult is selected at random, what is the probability that
a. the employed adult felt tense or stressed out at work?
b. the employed adult was a male who felt tense or stressed out at work?
c. the employed adult was a male *or* felt tense or stressed out at work?
d. Explain the difference in the results in (b) and (c).

4.10 How will marketers change their social media use in the near future? A survey by Social Media Examiner reported that 77% of B2B marketers (marketers that focus primarily on attracting businesses) plan to increase their use of LinkedIn, as compared to 54% of B2C marketers (marketers that primarily target consumers). The survey was based on 1,184 B2B marketers and 1,703 B2C marketers. The following table summarizes the results:

INCREASE USE OF LINKEDIN?	BUSINESS FOCUS		
	B2B	B2C	Total
Yes	912	920	1,832
No	272	783	1,055
Total	1,184	1,703	2,887

Source: Data extracted from "2014 Social Media Marketing Industry Report," **socialmediaexaminer.com.**

a. Give an example of a simple event.
b. Give an example of a joint event.
c. What is the complement of a marketer who plans to increase use of LinkedIn?
d. Why is a marketer who plans to increase use of LinkedIn and is a B2C marketer a joint event?

4.11 Referring to the contingency table in Problem 4.10, if a marketer is selected at random, what is the probability that
a. he or she plans to increase use of LinkedIn?
b. he or she is a B2C marketer?
c. he or she plans to increase use of LinkedIn *or* is a B2C marketer?
d. Explain the difference in the results in (b) and (c).

✓SELF TEST **4.12** What business and technical skills are critical for today's business intelligence/analytics and information management professionals? As part of InformationWeek's 2014 U.S. IT Salary Survey, business intelligence/analytics and data integration/warehousing professionals, both staff and managers, were asked to indicate what business and technical skills are critical to their job. The list of business and technical skills included *Analyzing Data*. The following table summarizes the responses to this skill:

ANALYZING DATA	PROFESSIONAL POSITION		
	Staff	Management	Total
Critical	324	255	579
Not critical	86	81	167
Total	410	336	746

Source: Data extracted from "2014 Salary Survey: BI & Analytics," InformationWeek Reports, May 2014, p. 35, **reports.informationweek.com.**

If a professional is selected at random, what is the probability that he or she
a. indicates analyzing data as critical to his or her job?
b. is a manager?

c. indicates analyzing data as critical to his or her job *or* is a manager?
d. Explain the difference in the results in (b) and (c).

4.13 Do Americans prefer name-brand milk or store brand milk? A survey was conducted by Harris Poll Interactive, Inc. in November 2014. Suppose the results, based on 1,138 females and 1,138 males, were as follows:

PREFERENCE	GENDER		
	Male	Female	Total
Name-Brand Milk	319	341	660
Store Brand Milk	717	649	1,366
Something Else	102	148	250
Total	1,138	1,138	2,276

Source: Data extracted from Harris Interactive, "Do Americans Prefer Name-Brands or Store Brands? Well, That Depends," **bit.ly/1Fpa0KI.**

If an American is selected at random, what is the probability that he or she
a. prefers name-brand milk?
b. is male *and* prefers name-brand milk?
c. is male *or* prefers name-brand milk?
d. Explain the difference in the results in (b) and (c).

4.14 A survey of 1,700 shoppers asked, "Does social media influence your purchase decisions?" The results indicated that 20.3% of females responded that their purchase decisions are influenced by social media compared to 10.5% of males. (Data extracted from "The Myth of the Mansumer...," **bit.ly/1JVaKoh.**) The sample sizes of males and females were not provided. Suppose that the results indicated that of 850 males, 89 answered yes. Of 850 females, 173 answered yes. Construct a contingency table to evaluate the probabilities. What is the probability that a respondent chosen at random
a. indicates that social media does influence his/her purchase decisions?
b. is a female *and* indicates that social media does influence his/her purchase decisions?
c. is a female *or* is a person whose purchase decisions are influenced by social media?
d. is a male *or* a female?

4.15 Each year, ratings are compiled concerning the performance of new cars during the first 90 days of use. Suppose that the cars have been categorized according to whether a car needs warranty-related repair (yes or no) and the country in which the company manufacturing a car is based (United States or not United States). Based on the data collected, the probability that the new car needs a warranty repair is 0.04, the probability that the car was manufactured by a U.S.-based company is 0.60, and the probability that the new car needs a warranty repair *and* was manufactured by a U.S.-based company is 0.025. Construct a contingency table to evaluate the probabilities of a warranty-related repair. What is the probability that a new car selected at random
a. needs a warranty repair?
b. needs a warranty repair *and* was manufactured by a U.S.-based company?
c. needs a warranty repair *or* was manufactured by a U.S.-based company?
d. needs a warranty repair *or* was not manufactured by a U.S.-based company?

4.2 Conditional Probability

Each example in Section 4.1 involves finding the probability of an event when sampling from the entire sample space. How do you determine the probability of an event if you know certain information about the events involved?

Computing Conditional Probabilities

Conditional probability refers to the probability of event A, given information about the occurrence of another event, B.

> ### CONDITIONAL PROBABILITY
>
> The probability of A given B is equal to the probability of A and B divided by the probability of B.
>
> $$P(A\,|\,B) = \frac{P(A\ and\ B)}{P(B)} \qquad \text{(4.4a)}$$
>
> The probability of B given A is equal to the probability of A and B divided by the probability of A.
>
> $$P(B\,|\,A) = \frac{P(A\ and\ B)}{P(A)} \qquad \text{(4.4b)}$$
>
> where
>
> $$P(A\ and\ B) = \text{joint probability of } A \text{ and } B$$
> $$P(A) = \text{marginal probability of } A$$
> $$P(B) = \text{marginal probability of } B$$

Referring to the Using Statistics scenario involving the purchase of large TVs, suppose you were told that a household planned to purchase a large TV. Now, what is the probability that the household actually purchased the television?

In this example, the objective is to find $P($Actually purchased $|$ Planned to purchase$)$. Here you are given the information that the household planned to purchase the large TV. Therefore, the sample space does not consist of all 1,000 households in the survey. It consists of only those households that planned to purchase the large TV. Of 250 such households, 200 actually purchased the large TV. Therefore, based on Table 4.1 on page 144, the probability that a household actually purchased the large TV given that they planned to purchase is

$$P(\text{Actually purchased} \,|\, \text{Planned to purchase}) = \frac{\text{Planned to purchase } and \text{ actually purchased}}{\text{Planned to purchase}}$$

$$= \frac{200}{250} = 0.80$$

You can also use Equation (4.4b) to compute this result:

$$P(B\,|\,A) = \frac{P(A\ and\ B)}{P(A)}$$

where

$$A = \text{planned to purchase}$$
$$B = \text{actually purchased}$$

then

$$P(\text{Actually purchased} \,|\, \text{Planned to purchase}) = \frac{200/1,000}{250/1,000} = \frac{200}{250} = 0.80$$

Example 4.6 further illustrates conditional probability.

Table 4.2 on page 145 is a contingency table for whether a household purchased a television with a faster refresh rate and whether the household purchased a streaming media player. If a household purchased a television with a faster refresh rate, what is the probability that it also purchased a streaming media player?

SOLUTION Because you know that the household purchased a television with a faster refresh rate, the sample space is reduced to 80 households. Of these 80 households, 38 also purchased a streaming media player. Therefore, the probability that a household purchased a streaming media player, given that the household purchased a television with a faster refresh rate, is

$$P(\text{Purchased streaming media player} \mid \text{Purchased television with faster refresh rate}) = \frac{\text{Number purchasing television with faster refresh rate } and \text{ streaming media pla}}{\text{Number purchasing television with faster refresh rate}}$$

$$= \frac{38}{80} = 0.475$$

Using Equation (4.4b) on page 151 and the following definitions:

   A = purchased a television with a faster refresh rate

   B = purchased a streaming media player

then

$$P(B \mid A) = \frac{P(A \text{ and } B)}{P(A)} = \frac{38/300}{80/300} = 0.475$$

Therefore, given that the household purchased a television with a faster refresh rate, there is a 47.5% chance that the household also purchased a streaming media player. You can compare this conditional probability to the marginal probability of purchasing a streaming media player, which is 108/300 = 0.36, or 36%. These results tell you that households that purchased televisions with a faster refresh rate are more likely to purchase a streaming media player than are households that purchased large TVs that have a standard refresh rate.

Decision Trees

In Table 4.1 on page 144, households are classified according to whether they planned to purchase and whether they actually purchased large TVs. A **decision tree** is an alternative to the contingency table. Figure 4.1 represents the decision tree for this example.

FIGURE 4.1
Decision tree for planned
to purchase and actually
purchased

In Figure 4.1, beginning at the left with the entire set of households, there are two "branches" for whether or not the household planned to purchase a large TV. Each of these branches has two subbranches, corresponding to whether the household actually purchased or did not actually purchase the large TV. The probabilities at the end of the initial branches represent the marginal probabilities of A and A'. The probabilities at the end of each of the four subbranches represent the joint probability for each combination of events A and B. You compute the conditional probability by dividing the joint probability by the appropriate marginal probability.

For example, to compute the probability that the household actually purchased, given that the household planned to purchase the large TV, you take P(Planned to purchase *and* actually purchased) and divide by P(Planned to purchase). From Figure 4.1,

$$P(\text{Actually purchased} \mid \text{Planned to purchase}) = \frac{200/1{,}000}{250/1{,}000}$$

$$= \frac{200}{250} = 0.80$$

Example 4.7 illustrates how to construct a decision tree.

EXAMPLE 4.7

Constructing the Decision Tree for the Households That Purchased Large TVs

Using the cross-classified data in Table 4.2 on page 145, construct the decision tree. Use the decision tree to find the probability that a household purchased a streaming media player, given that the household purchased a television with a faster refresh rate.

SOLUTION The decision tree for purchased a streaming media player and a television with a faster refresh rate is displayed in Figure 4.2.

FIGURE 4.2
Decision tree for purchased a television with a faster refresh rate and a streaming media player

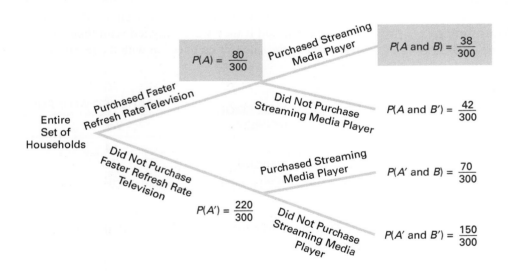

Using Equation (4.4b) on page 151 and the following definitions:

    A = purchased a television with a faster refresh rate

    B = purchased a streaming media player

then

$$P(B \mid A) = \frac{P(A \text{ and } B)}{P(A)} = \frac{38/300}{80/300} = 0.475$$

Independence

In the example concerning the purchase of large TVs, the conditional probability is $200/250 = 0.80$ that the selected household actually purchased the large TV, given that the household planned to purchase. The simple probability of selecting a household that actually purchased is $300/1,000 = 0.30$. This result shows that the prior knowledge that the household planned to purchase affected the probability that the household actually purchased the television. In other words, the outcome of one event is *dependent* on the outcome of a second event.

When the outcome of one event does *not* affect the probability of occurrence of another event, the events are said to be independent. **Independence** can be determined by using Equation (4.5).

INDEPENDENCE

Two events, A and B, are independent if and only if

$$P(A|B) = P(A) \qquad (4.5)$$

where

$$P(A|B) = \text{conditional probability of } A \text{ given } B$$
$$P(A) = \text{marginal probability of } A$$

Example 4.8 demonstrates the use of Equation (4.5).

EXAMPLE 4.8

Determining Independence

In the follow-up survey of the 300 households that actually purchased large TVs, the households were asked if they were satisfied with their purchases. Table 4.3 cross-classifies the responses to the satisfaction question with the responses to whether the television had a faster refresh rate.

TABLE 4.3
Satisfaction with Purchase of Large TVs

TELEVISION REFRESH RATE	SATISFIED WITH PURCHASE?		
	Yes	No	Total
Faster	64	16	80
Standard	176	44	220
Total	240	60	300

Determine whether being satisfied with the purchase and the refresh rate of the television purchased are independent.

SOLUTION For these data,

$$P(\text{Satisfied} | \text{Faster refresh rate}) = \frac{64/300}{80/300} = \frac{64}{80} = 0.80$$

which is equal to

$$P(\text{Satisfied}) = \frac{240}{300} = 0.80$$

Thus, being satisfied with the purchase and the refresh rate of the television purchased are independent. Knowledge of one event does not affect the probability of the other event.

Multiplication Rules

The **general multiplication rule** is derived using Equation (4.4a) on page 151:

$$P(A \mid B) = \frac{P(A \text{ and } B)}{P(B)}$$

and solving for the joint probability $P(A \text{ and } B)$.

GENERAL MULTIPLICATION RULE

The probability of A and B is equal to the probability of A given B times the probability of B.

$$P(A \text{ and } B) = P(A \mid B)P(B) \tag{4.6}$$

Example 4.9 demonstrates the use of the general multiplication rule.

EXAMPLE 4.9

Using the General Multiplication Rule

Consider the 80 households that purchased televisions that had a faster refresh rate. In Table 4.3 on page 154, you see that 64 households are satisfied with their purchase, and 16 households are dissatisfied. Suppose 2 households are randomly selected from the 80 households. Find the probability that both households are satisfied with their purchase.

SOLUTION Here you can use the multiplication rule in the following way. If

$$A = \text{second household selected is satisfied}$$
$$B = \text{first household selected is satisfied}$$

then, using Equation (4.6),

$$P(A \text{ and } B) = P(A \mid B)P(B)$$

The probability that the first household is satisfied with the purchase is $64/80$. However, the probability that the second household is also satisfied with the purchase depends on the result of the first selection. If the first household is not returned to the sample after the satisfaction level is determined (i.e., sampling without replacement), the number of households remaining is 79. If the first household is satisfied, the probability that the second is also satisfied is $63/79$ because 63 satisfied households remain in the sample. Therefore,

$$P(A \text{ and } B) = \left(\frac{63}{79}\right)\left(\frac{64}{80}\right) = 0.6380$$

There is a 63.80% chance that both of the households sampled will be satisfied with their purchase.

The **multiplication rule for independent events** is derived by substituting $P(A)$ for $P(A \mid B)$ in Equation (4.6).

MULTIPLICATION RULE FOR INDEPENDENT EVENTS

If A and B are independent, the probability of A and B is equal to the probability of A times the probability of B.

$$P(A \text{ and } B) = P(A)P(B) \tag{4.7}$$

If this rule holds for two events, A and B, then A and B are independent. Therefore, there are two ways to determine independence:

1. Events A and B are independent if, and only if, $P(A|B) = P(A)$.
2. Events A and B are independent if, and only if, $P(A \text{ and } B) = P(A)P(B)$.

Marginal Probability Using the General Multiplication Rule

In Section 4.1, marginal probability was defined using Equation (4.2) on page 147. You can state the equation for marginal probability by using the general multiplication rule. If

$$P(A) = P(A \text{ and } B_1) + P(A \text{ and } B_2) + \cdots + P(A \text{ and } B_k)$$

then, using the general multiplication rule, Equation (4.8) defines the marginal probability.

MARGINAL PROBABILITY USING THE GENERAL MULTIPLICATION RULE

$$P(A) = P(A|B_1)P(B_1) + P(A|B_2)P(B_2) + \cdots + P(A|B_k)P(B_k) \quad \textbf{(4.8)}$$

where $B_1, B_2, \ldots, B_k$ are k mutually exclusive and collectively exhaustive events.

To illustrate Equation (4.8), refer to Table 4.1 on page 144. Let

$$P(A) = \text{probability of planned to purchase}$$
$$P(B_1) = \text{probability of actually purchased}$$
$$P(B_2) = \text{probability of did not actually purchase}$$

Then, using Equation (4.8), the probability of planned to purchase is

$$P(A) = P(A|B_1)P(B_1) + P(A|B_2)P(B_2)$$
$$= \left(\frac{200}{300}\right)\left(\frac{300}{1,000}\right) + \left(\frac{50}{700}\right)\left(\frac{700}{1,000}\right)$$
$$= \frac{200}{1,000} + \frac{50}{1,000} = \frac{250}{1,000} = 0.25$$

PROBLEMS FOR SECTION 4.2

LEARNING THE BASICS

4.16 Consider the following contingency table:

	B	B'
A	10	20
A'	20	40

What is the probability of
a. $A|B$?
b. $A|B'$?
c. $A'|B'$?
d. Are events A and B independent?

4.17 Consider the following contingency table:

	B	B'
A	10	30
A'	25	35

What is the probability of
a. $A|B$?
b. $A'|B'$?
c. $A|B'$?
d. Are events A and B independent?

4.18 If $P(A \text{ and } B) = 0.4$ and $P(B) = 0.8$, find $P(A|B)$.

4.19 If $P(A) = 0.7$, $P(B) = 0.6$, and A and B are independent, find $P(A \text{ and } B)$.

4.20 If $P(A) = 0.3$, $P(B) = 0.4$, and $P(A \text{ and } B) = 0.2$, are A and B independent?

APPLYING THE CONCEPTS

4.21 Do males or females feel more tense or stressed out at work? A survey of employed adults conducted online by Harris Interactive on behalf of the American Psychological Association revealed the following:

	FELT TENSE OR STRESSED OUT AT WORK	
GENDER	Yes	No
Male	244	495
Female	282	480

Source: Data extracted from "The 2013 Work and Well-Being Survey," American Psychological Association and Harris Interactive, March 2013, p. 5, **bit.ly/11JGcPf.**

a. Given that the employed adult felt tense or stressed out at work, what is the probability that the employed adult was a male?
b. Given that the employed adult is male, what is the probability that he felt tense or stressed out at work?
c. Explain the difference in the results in (a) and (b).
d. Is feeling tense or stressed out at work and gender independent?

4.22 How will marketers change their social media use in the near future? A survey by Social Media Examiner of B2B marketers (marketers that focus primarily on attracting businesses) and B2C marketers (marketers that primarily target consumers) was based on 1,184 B2B marketers and 1,703 B2C marketers. The following table summarizes the results:

INCREASE USE OF LINKEDIN?	BUSINESS FOCUS		
	B2B	B2C	Total
Yes	912	920	1,832
No	272	783	1,055
Total	1,184	1,703	2,887

Source: Data extracted from "2014 Social Media Marketing Industry Report," **socialmediaexaminer .com.**

a. Suppose you know that the marketer is a B2B marketer. What is the probability that he or she plans to increase use of LinkedIn?
b. Suppose you know that the marketer is a B2C marketer. What is the probability that he or she plans to increase use of LinkedIn?
c. Are the two events, increase use of LinkedIn and business focus, independent? Explain.

4.23 Do Americans prefer name-brand milk or store brand milk? A survey was conducted by Harris Poll Interactive, Inc. in November 2014. Suppose the results, based on 1,138 females and 1,138 males, were as follows:

	GENDER		
PREFERENCE	Male	Female	Total
Name-Brand Milk	319	341	660
Store Brand Milk	717	649	1,366
Something Else	102	148	250
Total	1,138	1,138	2,276

Source: Data extracted from Harris Interactive, "Do Americans Prefer Name-Brands or Store Brands? Well, That Depends," **bit.ly/1Fpa0KI.**

a. Given that an American is a male, what is the probability that he prefers name-brand milk?
b. Given that an American is a female, what is the probability that she prefers name-brand milk?
c. Is preference independent of gender? Explain.

SELF TEST **4.24** What business and technical skills are critical for today's business intelligence/analytics and information management professionals? As part of InformationWeek's 2014 U.S. IT Salary Survey, business intelligence/analytics and data integration/warehousing professionals, both staff and managers, were asked to indicate what business and technical skills are critical to their job. The list of business and technical skills included *Analyzing Data*. The following table summarizes the responses to this skill:

	PROFESSIONAL POSITION		
ANALYZING DATA	Staff	Management	Total
Critical	324	255	579
Not critical	86	81	167
Total	410	336	746

Source: Data extracted from "2014 Salary Survey: BI & Analytics," *InformationWeek Reports*, May 2014, p. 35, **reports.informationweek .com.**

a. Given that a professional is staff, what is the probability that the professional indicates analyzing data as critical to his or her job?
b. Given that a professional is staff, what is the probability that the professional does not indicate analyzing data as critical to his or her job?
c. Given that a professional is a manager, what is the probability that the professional indicates analyzing data as critical to his or her job?
d. Given that a professional is a manager, what is the probability that the professional does not indicate analyzing data as critical to his or her job?

4.25 A survey of 1,700 shoppers asked, "Does social media influence your purchase decisions?" The results indicated that 20.3% of females responded that their purchase decisions are influenced by social media compared to 10.5% of males. (Data extracted from "The myth of the mansumer…," **bit.ly/1JVaKoh.**) The sample sizes of males and females were not provided. Suppose that the results indicated that of 850 males, 89 answered yes. Of 850 females, 173 answered yes.

a. Suppose that the respondent chosen is a female. What is the probability that her purchase decisions are influenced by social media?

b. Suppose that the respondent chosen does indicate that his/her purchase decisions are influenced by social media. What is the probability that the individual is a male?

c. Are influence of purchase decisions by social media and the gender of the individual independent? Explain.

4.26 Each year, ratings are compiled concerning the performance of new cars during the first 90 days of use. Suppose that the cars have been categorized according to whether a car needs warranty-related repair (yes or no) and the country in which the company manufacturing a car is based (United States or not United States). Based on the data collected, the probability that the new car needs a warranty repair is 0.04, the probability that the car is manufactured by a U.S.-based company is 0.60, and the probability that the new car needs a warranty repair *and* was manufactured by a U.S.-based company is 0.025.

a. Suppose you know that a company based in the United States manufactured a particular car. What is the probability that the car needs a warranty repair?

b. Suppose you know that a company based in the United States did not manufacture a particular car. What is the probability that the car needs a warranty repair?

c. Are need for a warranty repair and location of the company manufacturing the car independent?

4.27 In 42 of the 64 years from 1950 through 2014 (in 2011 there was virtually no change), the S&P 500 finished higher after the first five days of trading. In 37 out of 42 years, the S&P 500 finished higher for the year. Is a good first week a good omen for the upcoming year? The following table gives the first-week and annual performance over this 64-year period:

FIRST WEEK	S&P 500'S ANNUAL PERFORMANCE	
	Higher	Lower
Higher	37	5
Lower	11	11

a. If a year is selected at random, what is the probability that the S&P 500 finished higher for the year?

b. Given that the S&P 500 finished higher after the first five days of trading, what is the probability that it finished higher for the year?

c. Are the two events "first-week performance" and "annual performance" independent? Explain.

d. Look up the performance after the first five days of 2015 and the 2015 annual performance of the S&P 500 at **finance.yahoo.com**. Comment on the results.

4.28 A standard deck of cards is being used to play a game. There are four suits (hearts, diamonds, clubs, and spades), each having 13 faces (ace, 2, 3, 4, 5, 6, 7, 8, 9, 10, jack, queen, and king), making a total of 52 cards. This complete deck is thoroughly mixed, and you will receive the first 2 cards from the deck, without replacement (the first card is not returned to the deck after it is selected).

a. What is the probability that both cards are queens?

b. What is the probability that the first card is a 10 and the second card is a 5 or 6?

c. If you were sampling with replacement (the first card is returned to the deck after it is selected), what would be the answer in (a)?

d. In the game of blackjack, the face cards (jack, queen, king) count as 10 points, and the ace counts as either 1 or 11 points. All other cards are counted at their face value. Blackjack is achieved if 2 cards total 21 points. What is the probability of getting blackjack in this problem?

4.29 A box of nine iPhone 6C cellphones (the iPhone "for the colorful") contains two gold cellphones and seven silver cellphones.

a. If two cellphones are randomly selected from the box, without replacement (the first cellphone is not returned to the box after it is selected), what is the probability that both cellphones selected will be gold?

b. If two cellphones are randomly selected from the box, without replacement (the first cellphone is not returned to the box after it is selected), what is the probability that there will be one gold cellphone and one silver cellphone selected?

c. If three cellphones are selected, with replacement (the cellphones are returned to the box after they are selected), what is the probability that all three will be gold?

d. If you were sampling with replacement (the first cellphone is returned to the box after it is selected), what would be the answers to (a) and (b)?

4.3 Ethical Issues and Probability

Ethical issues can arise when any statements related to probability are presented to the public, particularly when these statements are part of an advertising campaign for a product or service. Unfortunately, many people are not comfortable with numerical concepts (see reference 5) and tend to misinterpret the meaning of the probability. In some instances, the misinterpretation is not intentional, but in other cases, advertisements may unethically try to mislead potential customers.

One example of a potentially unethical application of probability relates to advertisements for state lotteries. When purchasing a lottery ticket, the customer selects a set of numbers (such as 6) from a larger list of numbers (such as 54). Although virtually all participants know that they are unlikely to win the lottery, they also have very little idea of how unlikely it is for them to select all 6 winning numbers from the list of 54 numbers. They have even less of an idea of the probability of not selecting any winning numbers.

Given this background, you might consider a recent commercial for a state lottery that stated, "We won't stop until we have made everyone a millionaire" to be deceptive and possibly unethical. Do you think the state has any intention of ever stopping the lottery, given the fact that the state relies on it to bring millions of dollars into its treasury? Is it possible that the lottery can make everyone a millionaire? Is it ethical to suggest that the purpose of the lottery is to make everyone a millionaire?

Another example of a potentially unethical application of probability relates to an investment newsletter promising a 90% probability of a 20% annual return on investment. To make the claim in the newsletter an ethical one, the investment service needs to (a) explain the basis on which this probability estimate rests, (b) provide the probability statement in another format, such as 9 chances in 10, and (c) explain what happens to the investment in the 10% of the cases in which a 20% return is not achieved (e.g., is the entire investment lost?).

These are serious ethical issues. If you were going to write an advertisement for the state lottery that ethically describes the probability of winning a certain prize, what would you say? If you were going to write an advertisement for the investment newsletter that ethically states the probability of a 20% return on an investment, what would you say?

4.4 Bayes' Theorem

Developed by Thomas Bayes in the eighteenth century (see references 1, 2, 3, and 6), **Bayes' theorem** is an extension of what you previously learned about conditional probability. Bayes' theorem revises previously calculated probabilities using additional information and forms the basis for Bayesian analysis.

In recent years, Bayesian analysis has gained new prominence for its application to and in analyzing big data using predictive analytics (discussed in Chapter 17). Bayesian analysis does not require big data and can be used in a variety of problems to better determine the *revised probability* of certain events. The **Bayesian Analysis online topic** contains examples that apply Bayes' theorem to a marketing problem and a diagnostic problem and presents a set of additional study problems. The following *Consider This* feature also explores an application of Bayes' theorem that you may unknowingly be using every day.

CONSIDER THIS

Divine Providence and Spam

Would you ever guess that the essays *Divine Benevolence: Or, An Attempt to Prove That the Principal End of the Divine Providence and Government Is the Happiness of His Creatures* and *An Essay Towards Solving a Problem in the Doctrine of Chances* were written by the same person? Probably not, and in doing so, you illustrate a modern-day application of Bayesian statistics: spam, or junk mail filters.

In not guessing correctly, you probably looked at the words in the titles of the essays and concluded that they were talking about two different things. An implicit rule you used was that word frequencies vary by subject matter. A statistics essay would very likely contain the word *statistics* as well as words such as *chance*, *problem*, and *solving*. An eighteenth-century essay about theology and religion would be more likely to contain the uppercase forms of *Divine* and *Providence*.

Likewise, there are words you would guess to be very unlikely to appear in either book, such as technical terms from finance, and words that are most likely to appear in both—common words such as *a*, *and*, and *the*. That words would be either likely or unlikely suggests an application of probability theory. Of course, likely and unlikely are fuzzy concepts, and we might occasionally misclassify an essay if we kept things too simple, such as relying solely on the occurrence of the words *Divine* and *Providence*.

For example, a profile of the late Harris Milstead, better known as *Divine*, the star of *Hairspray* and other films, visiting Providence (Rhode Island), would most certainly not be an essay about theology. But if we widened the number of words we examined and found such words as movie or the name John Waters (Divine's director in many films), we probably would quickly realize the essay had something to

(continued)

do with twentieth-century cinema and little to do with theology and religion.

We can use a similar process to try to classify a new email message in your in-box as either spam or a legitimate message (called "ham," in this context). We would first need to add to your email program a "spam filter" that has the ability to track word frequencies associated with spam and ham messages as you identify them on a day-to-day basis. This would allow the filter to constantly update the prior probabilities necessary to use Bayes' theorem. With these probabilities, the filter can ask, "What is the probability that an email is spam, given the presence of a certain word?"

Applying the terms of Equation (4.9), discussed in the **Bayesian Analysis online topic**, such a Bayesian spam filter would multiply the probability of finding the word in a spam email, $P(A|B)$, by the probability that the email is spam, $P(B)$, and then divide by the probability of finding the word in an email, the denominator in Equation (4.9). Bayesian spam filters also use shortcuts by focusing on a small set of words that have a high probability of being found in a spam message as well as on a small set of other words that have a low probability of being found in a spam message.

As spammers (people who send junk email) learned of such new filters, they tried to outfox them. Having learned that Bayesian filters might be assigning a high $P(A|B)$ value to words commonly found in spam, such as Viagra, spammers thought they could fool the filter by misspelling the word as Vi@gr@ or V1agra. What they overlooked was that the misspelled variants were even more likely to be found in a spam message than the original word. Thus, the misspelled variants made the job of spotting spam easier for the Bayesian filters.

Other spammers tried to fool the filters by adding "good" words, words that would have a low probability of being found in a spam message, or "rare" words, words not frequently encountered in any message. But these spammers overlooked the fact that the conditional probabilities are constantly updated and that words once considered "good" would be soon discarded from the good list by the filter as their $P(A|B)$, value increased. Likewise, as "rare" words grew more common in spam and yet stayed rare in ham, such words acted like the misspelled variants that others had tried earlier.

Even then, and perhaps after reading about Bayesian statistics, spammers thought that they could "break" Bayesian filters by inserting random words in their messages. Those random words would affect the filter by causing it to see many words whose $P(A|B)$, value would be low. The Bayesian filter would begin to label many spam messages as ham and end up being of no practical use. Spammers again overlooked that conditional probabilities are constantly updated.

Other spammers decided to eliminate all or most of the words in their messages and replace them with graphics so that Bayesian filters would have very few words with which to form conditional probabilities. But this approach failed, too, as Bayesian filters were rewritten to consider things other than words in a message. After all, Bayes' theorem concerns events, and "graphics present with no text" is as valid an event as "some word, X, present in a message." Other future tricks will ultimately fail for the same reason. (By the way, spam filters use non-Bayesian techniques as well, which makes spammers' lives even more difficult.)

Bayesian spam filters are an example of the unexpected way that applications of statistics can show up in your daily life. You will discover more examples as you read the rest of this book. By the way, the author of the two essays mentioned earlier was Thomas Bayes, who is a lot more famous for the second essay than the first essay, a failed attempt to use mathematics and logic to prove the existence of God.

4.5 Counting Rules

In many cases there are a large number of possible outcomes, and determining the exact number of outcomes can be difficult. In these situations, rules have been developed for counting the exact number of possible outcomes. The **Section 4.5 online topic** discusses these rules and illustrates their use.

▼USING **STATISTICS**
Possibilities at M&R Electronics World, Revisited

As the marketing manager for M&R Electronics World, you analyzed the survey results of an intent-to-purchase study. This study asked the heads of 1,000 households about their intentions to purchase a large TV sometime during the next 12 months, and as a follow-up, M&R surveyed the same people 12 months later to see whether such a television was purchased. In addition, for households purchasing large TVs, the survey asked whether the television they purchased had a faster refresh rate, whether they also purchased a streaming media player in the past 12 months, and whether they were satisfied with their purchase of the large TV.

By analyzing the results of these surveys, you were able to uncover many pieces of valuable information that will help you plan a marketing strategy to enhance sales and better target those households likely to purchase multiple or more expensive products. Whereas only 30% of the households actually purchased a large TV, if a household indicated that it planned to purchase a large TV in the next 12 months, there was an 80% chance that the household actually made the purchase. Thus the marketing strategy should target those households that have indicated an intention to purchase.

You determined that for households that purchased a television that had a faster refresh rate, there was a 47.5% chance that the household also purchased a streaming media player. You then compared this conditional probability to the marginal probability of purchasing a streaming media player, which was 36%. Thus, households that purchased televisions that had a faster refresh rate are more likely to purchase a streaming media player than are households that purchased large TVs that have a standard refresh rate.

▼SUMMARY

This chapter began by developing the basic concepts of probability. You learned that probability is a numeric value from 0 to 1 that represents the chance, likelihood, or possibility that a particular event will occur. In addition to simple probability, you learned about conditional probabilities and independent events. Throughout the chapter, contingency tables and decision trees were used to display information.

▼REFERENCES

1. Anderson-Cook, C. M. "Unraveling Bayes' Theorem." *Quality Progress*, March 2014, p. 52–54.
2. Bellhouse, D. R. "The Reverend Thomas Bayes, FRS: A Biography to Celebrate the Tercentenary of His Birth." *Statistical Science*, 19 (2004), 3–43.
3. Hooper, W. "Probing Probabilities." *Quality Progress*, March 2014, pp. 18–22.
4. Lowd, D., and C. Meek. "Good Word Attacks on Statistical Spam Filters." Presented at the Second Conference on Email and Anti-Spam, 2005.
5. Paulos, J. A. *Innumeracy*. New York: Hill and Wang, 1988.
6. Silberman, S. "The Quest for Meaning," *Wired 8.02*, February 2000.
7. Zeller, T. "The Fight Against V1@gra (and Other Spam)." *The New York Times*, May 21, 2006, pp. B1, B6.

▼KEY EQUATIONS

Probability of Occurrence

$$\text{Probability of occurrence} = \frac{X}{T} \qquad (4.1)$$

Marginal Probability

$$P(A) = P(A \text{ and } B_1) + P(A \text{ and } B_2) \\ + \cdots + P(A \text{ and } B_k) \qquad (4.2)$$

General Addition Rule

$$P(A \text{ or } B) = P(A) + P(B) - P(A \text{ and } B) \qquad (4.3)$$

Conditional Probability

$$P(A|B) = \frac{P(A \text{ and } B)}{P(B)} \qquad (4.4a)$$

$$P(B|A) = \frac{P(A \text{ and } B)}{P(A)} \qquad (4.4b)$$

Independence

$$P(A|B) = P(A)$$ **(4.5)**

General Multiplication Rule

$$P(A \text{ and } B) = P(A|B)P(B)$$ **(4.6)**

Multiplication Rule for Independent Events

$$P(A \text{ and } B) = P(A)P(B)$$ **(4.7**

Marginal Probability Using the General Multiplication Rule

$$P(A) = P(A|B_1)P(B_1) + P(A|B_2)P(B_2) + \cdots + P(A|B_k)P(B_k)$$ **(4.8**

▼ KEY TERMS

▼ CHECKING YOUR UNDERSTANDING

4.30 What are the differences between *a priori* probability, empirical probability, and subjective probability?

4.31 What is the difference between a simple event and a joint event?

4.32 How can you use the general addition rule to find the probability of occurrence of event *A* or *B*?

4.33 What is the difference between mutually exclusive event and collectively exhaustive events?

4.34 How does conditional probability relate to the concept o independence?

4.35 How does the multiplication rule differ for events that ar and are not independent?

▼ CHAPTER REVIEW PROBLEMS

4.36 A survey by Accenture indicated that 68% of "millennials" are likely to ask for a pay raise, as compared to 45% of "baby boomers." (Data extracted from *#ListenLearnLead Global Research 2015*, Accenture, 2015, p. 13.) Suppose that the survey was based on 500 respondents from each of the two generation groups.
a. Construct a contingency table.
b. Give an example of a simple event and a joint event.
c. What is the probability that a randomly selected respondent is likely to ask for a pay raise?
d. What is the probability that a randomly selected respondent is likely to ask for a pay raise *and* is a baby boomer?
e. Are the events "generation group" and "likely to ask for a pay raise" independent? Explain.

4.37 SHL Americas provides a unique, global perspective of how talent is measured in its Global Assessment Trends Report. The report presents the results of an online survey conducted in early 2014 with HR professionals from companies headquartered

throughout the world. The authors were interested in examining differences between respondents in *emerging economies* and thos in *established economies* to provide relevant information for read ers who may be creating assessment programs for organization with global reach; one area of focus was on HR professionals response to two statements: "My organization views HR as a stra tegic function" and "My organization uses talent information t make business decisions." The results are as follows:

	ORGANIZATION VIEWS HR AS A STRATEGIC FUNCTION		
ECONOMY	Yes	No	Total
Established	847	320	1,167
Emerging	179	60	239
Total	1,026	380	1,406

ORGANIZATION USES INFORMATION ABOUT TALENT TO MAKE BUSINESS DECISIONS			
ECONOMY	Yes	No	Total
Established	607	560	1,167
Emerging	120	119	239
Total	727	679	1,406

What is the probability that a randomly chosen HR professional
a. is from an established economy?
b. is from an established economy *or* agrees to the statement "My organization uses information about talent to make business decisions?"
c. does not agree with the statement "My organization views HR as a strategic function" *and* is from an emerging economy?
d. does not agree with the statement "My organization views HR as a strategic function" *or* is from an emerging economy?
e. Suppose the randomly chosen HR professional does not agree with the statement "My organization views HR as a strategic function." What is the probability that the HR professional is from an emerging economy?
f. Are "My organization views HR as a strategic function" and the type of economy independent?
g. Is "My organization uses information about talent to make business decisions" independent of the type of economy?

4.38 Sustainable Brand Index takes a closer look at today's sustainable consumers based on how consumers act in different situations and the underlying structures in their attitudes. Sustainable Brand Index has identified four behaviors that consumers show in relation to sustainability and brands: *Ego*, do not care about sustainability; *Moderate*, believe that sustainability can be a bit interesting; *Smart*, curious about as well as interested in sustainability; and *Dedicated*, zealous and well prepared regarding sustainability.

Suppose a sample of 200 consumers, 100 males and 100 females, were categorized into the consumer behavioral groups with the following results:

BEHAVIORAL GROUP	GENDER		
	Male	Female	Total
Ego	35	29	64
Moderate	45	53	98
Smart	15	13	28
Dedicated	5	5	10
Total	100	100	200

Source: Data extracted from *Official Report: Sustainable Brand Index 2015*, Sustainable Brand Insight, 2015, p. 12.

If a consumer is selected at random, what is the probability that he or she
a. is classified as smart?
b. is classified as smart *or* dedicated?
c. is a male *or* is classified as moderate?
d. is a male *and* is classified as moderate?
e. Given that the consumer selected is a female, what is the probability that she is classified as ego?

4.39 Content Marketing Institute provides insights on the content marketing habits of nonprofit professionals representing a broad range of nonprofit agencies and organizations. A survey of nonprofit marketers conducted by the Content Marketing Institute indicated that 35% of nonprofit marketers rated themselves *highly* in terms of use of content marketing effectiveness. Furthermore, of the nonprofit marketers who rated themselves *highly* in terms of use of content marketing effectiveness, 42% reported having a documented content strategy. Of the nonprofit marketers who did not rate themselves *highly* in terms of use of content marketing effectiveness, 13% reported having a documented content strategy. (Data extracted from "2015 Nonprofit Content Marketing," **bit.ly/1bVhSpx**.)

If a nonprofit marketer is known to have a documented content strategy, what is the probability that the nonprofit marketer rates himself or herself *highly* in terms of use of content marketing effectiveness?

4.40 The CMO Survey collects and disseminates the opinions of top marketers in order to *predict* the future of markets, *track* marketing excellence, and *improve* the value of marketing in firms and in society. Part of the survey explores how companies are using marketing analytics to drive decision making in acquisition and promotion decisions. The following findings, based on responses from 204 senior marketers within B2B firms and 84 senior marketers within B2C firms, summarize those findings. (Data extracted from *CMO Survey Report: Results by Firm & Industry Characteristics*, The CMO Survey, February 2015, p. 134.)

DRIVES CUSTOMER ACQUISITION DECISIONS			
FIRM	Yes	No	Total
B2B	68	136	204
B2C	41	43	84
Total	109	179	288

DRIVES PROMOTION STRATEGY DECISIONS			
FIRM	Yes	No	Total
B2B	35	169	204
B2C	28	56	84
Total	63	225	288

a. What is the probability that a randomly selected senior marketer indicates that marketing analytics is used to drive decision making in customer acquisition?
b. Given that a randomly selected senior marketer is within a B2B firm, what is the probability that the senior marketer indicates that marketing analytics is used to drive decision making in customer acquisition?
c. Given that a randomly selected senior marketer is within a B2C firm, what is the probability that the senior marketer indicates that marketing analytics is used to drive decision making in customer acquisition?
d. What is the probability that a randomly selected senior marketer indicates that marketing analytics is used to drive decision making in promotion strategy?

e. Given that a randomly selected senior marketer is within a B2B firm, what is the probability that the senior marketer indicates that marketing analytics is used to drive decision making in promotion strategy?

f. Given that a randomly selected senior marketer is within a B2C firm, what is the probability that the senior marketer indicates

that marketing analytics is used to drive decision making in promotion strategy?

g. Comment on the results in (a) through (f).

CHAPTER 4

▾CASES

Digital Case

Apply your knowledge about contingency tables and the proper application of simple and joint probabilities in this continuing Digital Case from Chapter 3.

Open **EndRunGuide.pdf**, the EndRun Financial Services "Guide to Investing," and read the information about the Guaranteed Investment Package (GIP). Read the claims and examine the supporting data. Then answer the following questions:

How accurate is the claim of the probability of success for EndRun's GIP? In what ways is the claim misleading? How would you calculate and state the probability of having an annual rate of return not less than 15%?

1. Using the table found under the "Show Me the Winning Probabilities" subhead, compute the proper probabilities for the group of investors. What mistake was made in reporting the 7% probability claim?

2. Are there any probability calculations that would be appropriate for rating an investment service? Why or why not?

CardioGood Fitness

1. For each CardioGood Fitness treadmill product line (see CardioGoodFitness), construct two-way contingency tables of gender, education in years, relationship status, and self-rated fitness. (There will be a total of six tables for each treadmill product.)

2. For each table you construct, compute all conditional and marginal probabilities.

3. Write a report detailing your findings to be presented to the management of CardioGood Fitness.

The Choice *Is* Yours Follow-Up

1. Follow up the "Using Statistics: The Choice Is Yours Revisited" on page 73 by constructing contingency tables of market cap and type, market cap and risk, market cap and rating, type and risk, type and rating, and risk and rating for the sample of 407 retirement funds stored in Retirement Funds .

2. For each table you construct, compute all conditional and marginal probabilities.

3. Write a report summarizing your conclusions.

Clear Mountain State Student Survey

The Student News Service at Clear Mountain State University (CMSU) has decided to gather data about the undergraduate students that attend CMSU. CMSU creates and distributes a survey of 14 questions and receive responses from 111 undergraduates (stored in StudentSurvey).

For these data, construct contingency tables of gender and major, gender and graduate school intention, gender and employment status, gender and computer preference, class and graduate school intention, class and employment status, major and graduate school intention, major and employment status, and major and computer preference.

1. For each of these contingency tables, compute all the conditional and marginal probabilities.

2. Write a report summarizing your conclusions.

▼EXCEL GUIDE

EG4.1 BASIC PROBABILITY CONCEPTS

Simple Probability, Joint Probability, and the General Addition Rule

Key Technique Use Excel arithmetic formulas.

Example Compute simple and joint probabilities for the Table 4.1 on page 144 purchase behavior data.

PHStat Use **Simple & Joint Probabilities**.

For the example, select **PHStat → Probability & Prob. Distributions → Simple & Joint Probabilities**. In the new template, similar to the worksheet shown below, fill in the **Sample Space** area with the data.

Workbook Use the **COMPUTE worksheet** of the **Probabilities workbook** as a template.

The worksheet (shown below) already contains the Table 4.1 purchase behavior data. For other problems, change the sample space table entries in the cell ranges **C3:D4** and **A5:D6**. As you change the event names in cells, B5, B6, C5, and C5, the column A row labels for simple and joint probabilities and the addition rule change as well. These column A labels are *formulas* that use the concatenation operator (&) to form row labels from the event names you enter. For example, the cell A10 formula **= " P ("& B5 & ")"** combines the two characters **P(** with the value in cell B5 (**Yes**) with the character **)** to form the label **P(Yes)**. To examine all of the COMPUTE worksheet formulas not shown below, open to the COMPUTE_FORMULAS worksheet.

	A	B	C	D	E
1	Probabilities				
2					
3	Sample Space		Actually Purchased		
4			Yes	No	Totals
5	Planned to Purchase	Yes	200	50	250
6		No	100	650	750
7		Totals	300	700	1000
8					
9	Simple Probabilities				
10	P(Yes)	0.25	=E5/E7		
11	P(No)	0.75	=E6/E7		
12	P(Yes)	0.30	=C7/E7		
13	P(No)	0.70	=D7/E7		
14					
15	Joint Probabilities				
16	P(Yes and Yes)	0.20	=C5/E7		
17	P(Yes and No)	0.05	=D5/E7		
18	P(No and Yes)	0.10	=C6/E7		
19	P(No and No)	0.65	=D6/E7		
20					
21	Addition Rule				
22	P(Yes or Yes)	0.35	=B10 + B12 - B16		
23	P(Yes or No)	0.90	=B10 + B13 - B17		
24	P(No or Yes)	0.95	=B11 + B12 - B18		
25	P(No or No)	0.80	=B11 + B13 - B19		

EG4.4 BAYES' THEOREM

Key Technique Use Excel arithmetic formulas.

Example Apply Bayes' theorem to the television marketing example in the **Bayesian Analysis** online topic.

Workbook Use the **COMPUTE worksheet** of the **Bayes workbook** as a template.

The worksheet (shown below) already contains the probabilities for the online section example. For other problems, change those probabilities in the cell range **B5:C6**.

	A	B	C	D	E
1	Bayes' Theorem Computations				
2					
3			Probabilities		
4	Event	Prior	Conditional	Joint	Revised
5	S	0.4	0.8	0.32	0.64
6	S'	0.6	0.3	0.18	0.36
7			Total:	0.5	

Joint	Revised
=B5 * C5	=D5/$D$7
=B6 * C6	=D6/$D$7
=D5 + D6	

Open to the **COMPUTE_FORMULAS worksheet** to examine the arithmetic formulas that compute the probabilities, which are also shown as an inset to the worksheet.

5

Discrete Probability Distributions

CONTENTS

OBJECTIVES

- Learn the properties of a probability distribution
- Compute the expected value and variance of a probability distribution
- Compute probabilities from the binomial and Poisson distributions
- Use the binomial and Poisson distributions to solve business problems

▼USING **STATISTICS**
Events of Interest at Ricknel Home Centers

Like most other large businesses, Ricknel Home Centers, LLC, a regional home improvement chain, uses an accounting information system (AIS) to manage its accounting and financial data. The Ricknel AIS collects, organizes, stores, analyzes, and distributes financial information to decision makers both inside and outside the firm.

One important function of the Ricknel AIS is to continuously audit accounting information, looking for errors or incomplete or improbable information. For example, when customers submit orders online, the Ricknel AIS reviews the orders for possible mistakes. Any questionable invoices are tagged and included in a daily *exceptions report*. Recent data collected by the company show that the likelihood is 0.10 that an order form will be tagged.

As a member of the AIS team, you have been asked by Ricknel management to determine the likelihood of finding a certain number of tagged forms in a sample of a specific size. For example, what would be the likelihood that none of the order forms are tagged in a sample of four forms? That one of the order forms is tagged?

How could you determine the solution to this type of probability problem?

This chapter introduces you to the concept and characteristics of probability distributions. You will learn how the binomial and Poisson distributions can be applied to help solve business problems. In the Rickel Home Centers scenario, you could use a *probability distribution* as a mathematical model, or small-scale representation, that approximates the process. By using such an approximation, you could make inferences about the actual order process including the likelihood of finding a certain number of tagged forms in a sample.

5.1 The Probability Distribution for a Discrete Variable

Recall from Section 1.1 that *numerical* variables are variables that have values that represent quantities, such as the cost of a restaurant meal or the number of social media sites to which you belong. Some numerical variables are *discrete*, having numerical values that arise from a counting process, while others are *continuous*, having numerical values that arise from a measuring process (e.g., the one-year return of growth and value funds that were the subject of the Using Statistics scenario in Chapters 2 and 3). This chapter deals with probability distributions that represent a discrete numerical variable, such as the number of social media sites to which you belong.

> **PROBABILITY DISTRIBUTION FOR A DISCRETE VARIABLE**
> A **probability distribution for a discrete variable** is a mutually exclusive list of all the possible numerical outcomes along with the probability of occurrence of each outcome.

For example, Table 5.1 gives the distribution of the number of interruptions per day in a large computer network. The list in Table 5.1 is collectively exhaustive because all possible outcomes are included. Thus, the probabilities sum to 1. Figure 5.1 is a graphical representation of Table 5.1.

TABLE 5.1
Probability Distribution of the Number of Interruptions per Day

Interruptions per Day	Probability
0	0.35
1	0.25
2	0.20
3	0.10
4	0.05
5	0.05

FIGURE 5.1
Probability distribution of the number of interruptions per day

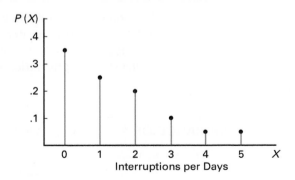

Expected Value of a Discrete Variable

The **expected value** of a discrete variable is the population mean, μ, of its probability distribution. To calculate the expected value, you multiply each possible outcome, x_i, by its corresponding probability, $P(X = x_i)$, and then sum these products.

EXPECTED VALUE, μ, OF A DISCRETE VARIABLE

$$\mu = E(X) = \sum_{i=1}^{N} x_i P(X = x_i) \qquad (5.1)$$

where

$$x_i = \text{the } i\text{th value of the discrete variable } X$$
$$P(X = x_i) = \text{probability of occurrence of the ith value of } X$$

For the probability distribution of the number of interruptions per day in a large computer network (Table 5.1), the expected value is computed as follows, using Equation (5.1), and is also shown in Table 5.2:

$$\mu = E(X) = \sum_{i=1}^{N} x_i P(X = x_i)$$
$$= (0)(0.35) + (1)(0.25) + (2)(0.20) + (3)(0.10) + (4)(0.05) + (5)(0.05)$$
$$= 0 + 0.25 + 0.40 + 0.30 + 0.20 + 0.25$$
$$= 1.40$$

TABLE 5.2
Computing the
Expected Value
of the Number of
Interruptions per Day

Interruptions per Day (x_i)	$P(X = x_i)$	$x_i P(X = x_i)$
0	0.35	$(0)(0.35) = 0.00$
1	0.25	$(1)(0.25) = 0.25$
2	0.20	$(2)(0.20) = 0.40$
3	0.10	$(3)(0.10) = 0.30$
4	0.05	$(4)(0.05) = 0.20$
5	0.05	$(5)(0.05) = 0.25$
	1.00	$\mu = E(X) = 1.40$

The expected value is 1.40. The expected value of 1.40 interruptions per day is not a possible result because the actual number of interruptions on a given day must be an integer value. The expected value represents the *mean* number of interruptions per day.

Variance and Standard Deviation of a Discrete Variable

You compute the variance of a probability distribution by multiplying each possible squared difference $[x_i - E(X)]^2$ by its corresponding probability, $P(X = x_i)$, and then summing the resulting products. Equation (5.2) defines the **variance of a discrete variable**, and Equation (5.3) defines the **standard deviation of a discrete variable**.

VARIANCE OF A DISCRETE VARIABLE

$$\sigma^2 = \sum_{i=1}^{N} [x_i - E(X)]^2 P(X = x_i) \qquad (5.2)$$

where

$$x_i = \text{the ith value of the discrete variable } X$$
$$P(X = x_i) = \text{probability of occurrence of the ith value of } X$$

STANDARD DEVIATION OF A DISCRETE VARIABLE

$$\sigma = \sqrt{\sigma^2} = \sqrt{\sum_{i=1}^{N}[x_i - E(X)]^2 P(X = x_i)} \qquad (5.3)$$

The variance and the standard deviation of the number of interruptions per day are computed as follows and in Table 5.3, using Equations (5.2) and (5.3):

$$\sigma^2 = \sum_{i=1}^{N}[x_i - E(X)]^2 P(X = x_i)$$

$$= (0 - 1.4)^2(0.35) + (1 - 1.4)^2(0.25) + (2 - 1.4)^2(0.20) + (3 - 1.4)^2(0.10)$$
$$+ (4 - 1.4)^2(0.05) + (5 - 1.4)^2(0.05)$$

$$= 0.686 + 0.040 + 0.072 + 0.256 + 0.338 + 0.648$$

$$= 2.04$$

and

$$\sigma = \sqrt{\sigma^2} = \sqrt{2.04} = 1.4283$$

TABLE 5.3
Computing the Variance and Standard Deviation of the Number of Interruptions per Day

Interruptions per Day (x_i)	$P(X = x_i)$	$x_i P(X = x_i)$	$[x_i - E(X)]^2$	$[x_i - E(X)]^2 P(X = x_i)$
0	0.35	0.00	$(0 - 1.4)^2 = 1.96$	$(1.96)(0.35) = 0.686$
1	0.25	0.25	$(1 - 1.4)^2 = 0.16$	$(0.16)(0.25) = 0.040$
2	0.20	0.40	$(2 - 1.4)^2 = 0.36$	$(0.36)(0.20) = 0.072$
3	0.10	0.30	$(3 - 1.4)^2 = 2.56$	$(2.56)(0.10) = 0.256$
4	0.05	0.20	$(4 - 1.4)^2 = 6.76$	$(6.76)(0.05) = 0.338$
5	0.05	0.25	$(5 - 1.4)^2 = 12.96$	$(12.96)(0.05) = 0.648$
	1.00	$\mu = E(X) = 1.40$		$\sigma^2 = 2.04$
				$\sigma = \sqrt{\sigma^2} = 1.4283$

Thus, the mean number of interruptions per day is 1.4, the variance is 2.04, and the standard deviation is approximately 1.43 interruptions per day.

PROBLEMS FOR SECTION 5.1

LEARNING THE BASICS

5.1 Given the following probability distributions:

Distribution A		Distribution B	
x_i	$P(X = x_i)$	x_i	$P(X = x_i)$
0	0.50	0	0.05
1	0.20	1	0.10
2	0.15	2	0.15
3	0.10	3	0.20
4	0.05	4	0.50

a. Compute the expected value for each distribution.
b. Compute the standard deviation for each distribution.
c. Compare the results of distributions A and B.

APPLYING THE CONCEPTS

✓ SELF TEST **5.2** The following table contains the probability distribution for the number of traffic accidents daily in a small town:

Number of Accidents Daily (X)	$P(X = x_i)$
0	0.10
1	0.20
2	0.45
3	0.15
4	0.05
5	0.05

a. Compute the mean number of accidents per day.
b. Compute the standard deviation.

5.3 Recently, a regional automobile dealership sent out fliers to perspective customers indicating that they had already won one of three different prizes: an automobile valued at $25,000, a $100 gas card, or a $5 Walmart shopping card. To claim his or her prize, a prospective customer needed to present the flier at the dealership's showroom. The fine print on the back of the flier listed the probabilities of winning. The chance of winning the car was 1 out of 31,478, the chance of winning the gas card was 1 out of 31,478, and the chance of winning the shopping card was 31,476 out of 31,478.

a. How many fliers do you think the automobile dealership sent out?
b. Using your answer to (a) and the probabilities listed on the flier, what is the expected value of the prize won by a prospective customer receiving a flier?
c. Using your answer to (a) and the probabilities listed on the flier, what is the standard deviation of the value of the prize won by a prospective customer receiving a flier?
d. Do you think this is an effective promotion? Why or why not?

5.4 In the carnival game Under-or-Over-Seven, a pair of fair dice is rolled once, and the resulting sum determines whether the player wins or loses his or her bet. For example, the player can bet $1 that the sum will be under 7—that is, 2, 3, 4, 5, or 6. For this bet, the player wins $1 if the result is under 7 and loses $1 if the outcome equals or is greater than 7. Similarly, the player can bet $1 that the sum will be over 7—that is, 8, 9, 10, 11, or 12. Here, the player wins $1 if the result is over 7 but loses $1 if the result is 7 or under. A third method of play is to bet $1 on the outcome 7. For this bet, the player wins $4 if the result of the roll is 7 and loses $1 otherwise.

a. Construct the probability distribution representing the different outcomes that are possible for a $1 bet on under 7.
b. Construct the probability distribution representing the different outcomes that are possible for a $1 bet on over 7.
c. Construct the probability distribution representing the different outcomes that are possible for a $1 bet on 7.
d. Show that the expected long-run profit (or loss) to the player is the same, no matter which method of play is used.

5.5 The number of arrivals per minute at a bank located in the central business district of a large city was recorded over a period of 200 minutes, with the following results:

Arrivals	Frequency
0	14
1	31
2	47
3	41
4	29
5	21
6	10
7	5
8	2

a. Compute the expected number of arrivals per minute.
b. Compute the standard deviation.

5.6 The manager of the commercial mortgage department of a large bank has collected data during the past two years concerning the number of commercial mortgages approved per week. The results from these two years (104 weeks) are as follows:

Number of Commercial Mortgages Approved	Frequency
0	13
1	25
2	32
3	17
4	9
5	6
6	1
7	1

a. Compute the expected number of mortgages approved per week.
b. Compute the standard deviation.

5.7 You are trying to develop a strategy for investing in two different stocks. The anticipated annual return for a $1,000 investment in each stock under four different economic conditions has the following probability distribution:

Probability	Economic Condition	Returns Stock X	Stock Y
0.1	Recession	−50	−100
0.3	Slow growth	20	50
0.4	Moderate growth	100	130
0.2	Fast growth	150	200

Compute the
a. expected return for stock X and for stock Y.
b. standard deviation for stock X and for stock Y.
c. Would you invest in stock X or stock Y? Explain.

5.8 You plan to invest $1,000 in a corporate bond fund or in a common stock fund. The following table presents the annual return (per $1,000) of each of these investments under various economic conditions and the probability that each of those economic conditions will occur. Compute the

Probability	Economic Condition	Corporate Bond Fund	Common Stock Fund
0.01	Extreme recession	−200	−999
0.09	Recession	−70	−300
0.15	Stagnation	30	−100
0.35	Slow growth	80	100
0.30	Moderate growth	100	150
0.10	High growth	120	350

a. expected return for the corporate bond fund and for the common stock fund.
b. standard deviation for the corporate bond fund and for the common stock fund.
c. Would you invest in the corporate bond fund or the common stock fund? Explain.
d. If you chose to invest in the common stock fund in (c), what do you think about the possibility of losing $999 of every $1,000 invested if there is an extreme recession?

5.2 Binomial Distribution

This is the first of two sections that considers mathematical models. A **mathematical model** is a mathematical expression that represents a variable of interest. When a mathematical model exists, you can compute the exact probability of occurrence of any particular value of the variable. For discrete variables, the mathematical model is a **probability distribution function**.

The **binomial distribution** is an important mathematical model used in many business situations. You use the binomial distribution when the discrete variable is the number of events of interest in a sample of n observations. The binomial distribution has four important properties.

studentTIP

Do not confuse this use of the Greek letter pi, π, to represent the probability of an event of interest with the constant that is the ratio of the circumference to a diameter of a circle—approximately 3.14159.

PROPERTIES OF THE BINOMIAL DISTRIBUTION
- The sample consists of a fixed number of observations, n.
- Each observation is classified into one of two mutually exclusive and collectively exhaustive categories.
- The probability of an observation being classified as the event of interest, π, is constant from observation to observation. Thus, the probability of an observation being classified as not being the event of interest, $1 - \pi$, is constant over all observations.
- The value of any observation is independent of the value of any other observation.

Returning to the Ricknel Home Improvement scenario presented on page 166 concerning the accounting information system, suppose the event of interest is defined as a tagged order form. You want to determine the number of tagged order forms in a given sample of orders.

What results can occur? If the sample contains four orders, there could be none, one, two, three, or four tagged order forms. No other value can occur because the number of tagged order forms cannot be more than the sample size, n, and cannot be less than zero. Therefore, the range of the binomial variable is from 0 to n.

Suppose that you observe the following result in a sample of four orders:

First Order	Second Order	Third Order	Fourth Order
Tagged	Tagged	Not tagged	Tagged

What is the probability of having three tagged order forms in a sample of four orders in this particular sequence? Because the historical probability of a tagged order is 0.10, the probability that each order occurs in the sequence is

First Order	Second Order	Third Order	Fourth Order
$\pi = 0.10$	$\pi = 0.10$	$1 - \pi = 0.90$	$\pi = 0.10$

Each outcome is essentially independent of the others because the order forms were selected from an extremely large or practically infinite population and each order form could only be selected once. Therefore, the probability of having this particular sequence is

$$\pi\pi(1 - \pi)\pi = \pi^3(1 - \pi)^1$$
$$= (0.10)^3(0.90)^1 = (0.10)(0.10)(0.10)(0.90)$$
$$= 0.0009$$

This result indicates only the probability of three tagged order forms (events of interest) from a sample of four order forms in a *specific sequence*. To find the number of ways of selecting x objects from n objects, *irrespective of sequence*, you use the **rule of combinations** given in Equation (5.4).

[1]On many scientific calculators, there is a button labeled $_nC_r$ that allows you to compute the number of combinations. On these calculators, the symbol r is used instead of x.

COMBINATIONS

The number of combinations of selecting x objects[1] out of n objects is given by

$$_nC_x = \frac{n!}{x!(n - x)!} \qquad (5.4)$$

where

$n! = (n)(n - 1) \cdots (1)$ is called n factorial. By definition, $0! = 1$.

With $n = 4$ and $x = 3$, there are

$$_nC_x = \frac{n!}{x!(n - x)!} = \frac{4!}{3!(4 - 3)!} = \frac{4 \times 3 \times 2 \times 1}{(3 \times 2 \times 1)(1)} = 4$$

such sequences. The four possible sequences are

Sequence 1 = (*tagged, tagged, tagged, not tagged*), with probability
$$\pi\pi\pi(1 - \pi) = \pi^3(1 - \pi)^1 = 0.0009$$
Sequence 2 = (*tagged, tagged, not tagged, tagged*), with probability
$$\pi\pi(1 - \pi)\pi = \pi^3(1 - \pi)^1 = 0.0009$$
Sequence 3 = (*tagged, not tagged, tagged, tagged*), with probability
$$\pi(1 - \pi)\pi\pi = \pi^3(1 - \pi)^1 = 0.0009$$
Sequence 4 = (*not tagged, tagged, tagged, tagged*), with probability
$$(1 - \pi)\pi\pi\pi = \pi^3(1 - \pi)^1 = 0.0009$$

Therefore, the probability of three tagged order forms is equal to

$$(\text{number of possible sequences}) \times (\text{probability of a particular sequence})$$
$$= (4) \times (0.0009) = 0.0036$$

You can make a similar, intuitive derivation for the other possible values of the variable—zero, one, two, and four tagged order forms. However, as n, the sample size, gets large, the computations involved in using this intuitive approach become time-consuming. Equation (5.5) is the mathematical model that provides a general formula for computing any probability from the binomial distribution with the number of events of interest, x, given n and π.

BINOMIAL DISTRIBUTION

$$P(X = x \mid n, \pi) = \frac{n!}{x!(n-x)!} \pi^x (1-\pi)^{n-x} \tag{5.5}$$

where

$P(X = x \mid n, \pi)$ = probability that $X = x$ events of interest, given n and π

n = number of observations

π = probability of an event of interest

$1 - \pi$ = probability of not having an event of interest

x = number of events of interest in the sample $(X = 0, 1, 2, \ldots, n)$

$\dfrac{n!}{x!(n-x)!}$ = number of combinations of x events of interest out of n observations

Equation (5.5) restates what was intuitively derived previously. The binomial variable X can have any integer value x from 0 through n. In Equation (5.5), the product

$$\pi^x (1-\pi)^{n-x}$$

represents the probability of exactly x events of interest from n observations in a *particular sequence*.

The term

$$\frac{n!}{x!(n-x)!}$$

is the number of *combinations* of the x events of interest from the n observations possible. Hence, given the number of observations, n, and the probability of an event of interest, π, the probability of x events of interest is

$$P(X = x \mid n, \pi) = (\text{number of combinations}) \times (\text{probability of a particular combination})$$
$$= \frac{n!}{x!(n-x)!} \pi^x (1-\pi)^{n-x}$$

Example 5.1 illustrates the use of Equation (5.5). Examples 5.2 and 5.3 show the computations for other values of X.

EXAMPLE 5.1

Determining
$P(X = 3)$, Given
$n = 4$ and $\pi = 0.1$

If the likelihood of a tagged order form is 0.1, what is the probability that there are three tagged order forms in the sample of four?

SOLUTION Using Equation (5.5), the probability of three tagged orders from a sample of four is

$$P(X = 3 \mid n = 4, \pi = 0.1) = \frac{4!}{3!(4-3)!}(0.1)^3(1-0.1)^{4-3}$$
$$= \frac{4!}{3!(1)!}(0.1)^3(0.9)^1$$
$$= 4(0.1)(0.1)(0.1)(0.9) = 0.0036$$

EXAMPLE 5.2

Determining
$P(X \geq 3)$, Given
$n = 4$ and $\pi = 0.1$

If the likelihood of a tagged order form is 0.1, what is the probability that there are three or more (i.e., at least three) tagged order forms in the sample of four?

SOLUTION In Example 5.1, you found that the probability of *exactly* three tagged order forms from a sample of four is 0.0036. To compute the probability of *at least* three tagged order forms, you need to add the probability of three tagged order forms to the probability of four tagged order forms. The probability of four tagged order forms is

studentTIP

Another way of saying "three or more" is "at least three."

$$P(X = 4 \mid n = 4, \pi = 0.1) = \frac{4!}{4!(4-4)!}(0.1)^4(1-0.1)^{4-4}$$
$$= \frac{4!}{4!(0)!}(0.1)^4(0.9)^0$$
$$= 1(0.1)(0.1)(0.1)(0.1)(1) = 0.0001$$

Thus, the probability of at least three tagged order forms is

$$P(X \geq 3) = P(X = 3) + P(X = 4)$$
$$= 0.0036 + 0.0001 = 0.0037$$

There is a 0.37% chance that there will be at least three tagged order forms in a sample of four.

EXAMPLE 5.3

Determining
$P(X < 3)$, Given
$n = 4$ and $\pi = 0.1$

If the likelihood of a tagged order form is 0.1, what is the probability that there are less than three tagged order forms in the sample of four?

SOLUTION The probability that there are less than three tagged order forms is

$$P(X < 3) = P(X = 0) + P(X = 1) + P(X = 2)$$

Using Equation (5.5) on page 173, these probabilities are

$$P(X = 0 \mid n = 4, \pi = 0.1) = \frac{4!}{0!(4-0)!}(0.1)^0(1-0.1)^{4-0} = 0.6561$$

$$P(X = 1 \mid n = 4, \pi = 0.1) = \frac{4!}{1!(4-1)!}(0.1)^1(1-0.1)^{4-1} = 0.2916$$

$$P(X = 2 \mid n = 4, \pi = 0.1) = \frac{4!}{2!(4-2)!}(0.1)^2(1-0.1)^{4-2} = 0.0486$$

▶ (continued)

Therefore, $P(X < 3) = 0.6561 + 0.2916 + 0.0486 = 0.9963$. $P(X < 3)$ could also be calculated from its complement, $P(X \geq 3)$, as follows:

$$P(X < 3) = 1 - P(X \geq 3)$$
$$= 1 - 0.0037 = 0.9963$$

Computing binomial probabilities become tedious as n gets large. Figure 5.2 shows an Excel worksheet that computes binomial probabilities for you. You can also look up binomial probabilities in a table of probabilities.

FIGURE 5.2
Excel worksheet for computing binomial probabilities with $n = 4$ and $\pi = 0.1$

	A	B
1	Binomial Probabilities	
2		
3	Data	
4	Sample size	4
5	Probability of an event of interest	0.1
6		
7	Statistics	
8	Mean	0.4 =B4 * B5
9	Variance	0.36 =B8 * (1 - B5)
10	Standard deviation	0.6 =SQRT(B9)
11		
12	Binomial Probabilities Table	
13	X	P(X)
14	0	0.6561 =BINOM.DIST(A14, $B$4, $B$5, FALSE)
15	1	0.2916 =BINOM.DIST(A15, $B$4, $B$5, FALSE)
16	2	0.0486 =BINOM.DIST(A16, $B$4, $B$5, FALSE)
17	3	0.0036 =BINOM.DIST(A17, $B$4, $B$5, FALSE)
18	4	0.0001 =BINOM.DIST(A18, $B$4, $B$5, FALSE)

learnMORE

The **Binomial Table online topic** contains binomial probabilities and cumulative binomial probabilities tables and explains how to use the tables to compute binomial and cumulative binomial probabilities.

The shape of a binomial probability distribution depends on the values of n and π. Whenever $\pi = 0.5$, the binomial distribution is symmetrical, regardless of how large or small the value of n. When $\pi \neq 0.5$, the distribution is skewed. The closer π is to 0.5 and the larger the number of observations, n, the less skewed the distribution becomes. For example, the distribution of the number of tagged order forms is highly right-skewed because $\pi = 0.1$ and $n = 4$ (see Figure 5.3).

FIGURE 5.3
Histogram of the binomial probability with $n = 4$ and $\pi = 0.1$

Binomial Probability Histogram

Observe from Figure 5.3 that unlike the histogram for continuous variables in Section 2.4, the bars for the values are very thin, and there is a large gap between each pair of values. That is because the histogram represents a discrete variable. (Theoretically, the bars should have no width. They should be vertical lines.)

The mean (or expected value) of the binomial distribution is equal to the product of n and π. Instead of using Equation (5.1) on page 168 to compute the mean of the probability distribution, you can use Equation (5.6) to compute the mean for variables that follow the binomial distribution.

MEAN OF THE BINOMIAL DISTRIBUTION

The mean, μ, of the binomial distribution is equal to the sample size, n, multiplied by the probability of an event of interest, π.

$$\mu = E(X) = n\pi \tag{5.6}$$

On the average, over the long run, you theoretically expect $\mu = E(X) = n\pi = (4)(0.1) = 0.4$ tagged order form in a sample of four orders.

The standard deviation of the binomial distribution can be calculated using Equation (5.7)

STANDARD DEVIATION OF THE BINOMIAL DISTRIBUTION

$$\sigma = \sqrt{\sigma^2} = \sqrt{Var(X)} = \sqrt{n\pi(1 - \pi)} \tag{5.7}$$

The standard deviation of the number of tagged order forms is

$$\sigma = \sqrt{4(0.1)(0.9)} = 0.60$$

You get the same result if you use Equation (5.3) on page 169.

Example 5.4 applies the binomial distribution to service at a fast-food restaurant.

EXAMPLE 5.4

Computing Binomial Probabilities for Service at a Fast-Food Restaurant

Accuracy in taking orders at a drive-through window is important for fast-food chains. Periodically, *QSR Magazine* publishes "The Drive-Thru Performance Study: Order Accuracy" that measures the percentage of orders that are filled correctly. In a recent month, the percentage of orders filled correctly at Wendy's was approximately 86.8%. Suppose that you go to the drive-through window at Wendy's and place an order. Two friends of yours independently place orders at the drive-through window at the same Wendy's. What are the probabilities that all three, that none of the three, and that at least two of the three orders will be filled correctly? What are the mean and standard deviation of the binomial distribution for the number of orders filled correctly?

SOLUTION Because there are three orders and the probability of a correct order is 0.868, $n = 3$, and $\pi = 0.868$, using Equation (5.5) on page 173,

$$P(X = 3 \,|\, n = 3, \pi = 0.868) = \frac{3!}{3!(3 - 3)!}(0.868)^3(1 - 0.868)^{3-3}$$

$$= \frac{3!}{3!(3 - 3)!}(0.868)^3(0.132)^0$$

$$= 1(0.868)(0.868)(0.868)(1) = 0.6540$$

$$P(X = 0 \,|\, n = 3, \pi = 0.868) = \frac{3!}{0!(3 - 0)!}(0.868)^0(1 - 0.868)^{3-0}$$

$$= \frac{3!}{0!(3 - 0)!}(0.868)^0(0.132)^3$$

$$= 1(1)(0.132)(0.132)(0.132) = 0.0023$$

▶ *(continued)*

$$P(X = 2 \mid n = 3, \pi = 0.868) = \frac{3!}{2!(3-2)!}(0.868)^2(1 - 0.868)^{3-2}$$

$$= \frac{3!}{2!(3-2)!}(0.868)^2(0.132)^1$$

$$= 3(0.868)(0.868)(0.132) = 0.2984$$

$$P(X \geq 2) = P(X = 2) + P(X = 3)$$

$$= 0.2984 + 0.6540$$

$$= 0.9524$$

Using Equations (5.6) and (5.7),

$$\mu = E(X) = n\pi = 3(0.868) = 2.604$$

$$\sigma = \sqrt{\sigma^2} = \sqrt{Var(X)} = \sqrt{n\pi(1 - \pi)}$$

$$= \sqrt{3(0.868)(0.132)}$$

$$= \sqrt{0.3437} = 0.5863$$

The mean number of orders filled correctly in a sample of three orders is 2.604, and the standard deviation is 0.5863. The probability that all three orders are filled correctly is 0.6540, or 65.4%. The probability that none of the orders are filled correctly is 0.0023 (0.23%). The probability that at least two orders are filled correctly is 0.9524 (95.24%).

PROBLEMS FOR SECTION 5.2

LEARNING THE BASICS

5.9 Determine the following:
a. For $n = 4$ and $\pi = 0.12$, what is $P(X = 0)$?
b. For $n = 10$ and $\pi = 0.40$, what is $P(X = 9)$?
c. For $n = 10$ and $\pi = 0.50$, what is $P(X = 8)$?
d. For $n = 6$ and $\pi = 0.83$, what is $P(X = 5)$?

5.10 Determine the mean and standard deviation of the variable X in each of the following binomial distributions:
a. $n = 4$ and $\pi = 0.10$
b. $n = 4$ and $\pi = 0.40$
c. $n = 5$ and $\pi = 0.80$
d. $n = 3$ and $\pi = 0.50$

APPLYING THE CONCEPTS

5.11 The increase or decrease in the price of a stock between the beginning and the end of a trading day is assumed to be an equally likely random event. What is the probability that a stock will show an increase in its closing price on five consecutive days?

5.12 According to Verto Analytics, Inc., 53% of 30- to-34-year-olds in the United States own tablets. (Data extracted from "The Impact of Income and Age on Device Ownership," **bit.ly/1yR21gL**.) Using the binomial distribution, what is the probability that in the next six 30- to-34-year-olds surveyed,
a. four will own a tablet?
b. all six will own a tablet?
c. at least four will own a tablet?

d. What are the mean and standard deviation of the number of 30- to-34-year-olds who will own a tablet in a survey of six?
e. What assumptions do you need to make in (a) through (c)?

5.13 A student is taking a multiple-choice exam in which each question has four choices. Assume that the student has no knowledge of the correct answers to any of the questions. She has decided on a strategy in which she will place four balls (marked A, B, C, and D) into a box. She randomly selects one ball for each question and replaces the ball in the box. The marking on the ball will determine her answer to the question. There are five multiple-choice questions on the exam. What is the probability that she will get
a. five questions correct?
b. at least four questions correct?
c. no questions correct?
d. no more than two questions correct?

5.14 A manufacturing company regularly conducts quality control checks at specified periods on the products it manufactures. Historically, the failure rate for LED light bulbs that the company manufactures is 5%. Suppose a random sample of 10 LED light bulbs is selected. What is the probability that
a. none of the LED light bulbs are defective?
b. exactly one of the LED light bulbs is defective?
c. two or fewer of the LED light bulbs are defective?
d. three or more of the LED light bulbs are defective?

5.15 Past records indicate that the probability of online retail orders that turn out to be fraudulent is 0.08. Suppose that, on a given day, 20 online retail orders are placed. Assume that the number of online retail orders that turn out to be fraudulent is distributed as a binomial random variable.

a. What are the mean and standard deviation of the number of on-line retail orders that turn out to be fraudulent?

b. What is the probability that zero online retail orders will turn out to be fraudulent?

c. What is the probability that one online retail order will turn out to be fraudulent?

d. What is the probability that two or more online retail orders will turn out to be fraudulent?

✓SELF TEST **5.16** In Example 5.4 on page 176, you and two friends decided to go to Wendy's. Now, suppose that instead you go to Burger King, which recently filled approximately 82.3% of orders correctly. What is the probability that

a. all three orders will be filled correctly?

b. none of the three will be filled correctly?

c. at least two of the three will be filled correctly?

d. What are the mean and standard deviation of the binomial distribution used in (a) through (c)? Interpret these values.

5.17 In Example 5.4 on page 176, you and two friends decided to go to Wendy's. Now, suppose that instead you go to McDonald's, which recently filled approximately 88.3% of the orders correctly. What is the probability that

a. all three orders will be filled correctly?

b. none of the three will be filled correctly?

c. at least two of the three will be filled correctly?

d. What are the mean and standard deviation of the binomial distribution used in (a) through (c)? Interpret these values.

e. Compare the result of (a) through (d) with those of Burger King in Problem 5.16 and Wendy's in Example 5.4 on page 176.

5.3 Poisson Distribution

Many studies are based on counts of the occurrences of a particular event in a fixed interval of time or space (often referred to as an *area of opportunity*). In such an **area of opportunity** there can be more than one occurrence of an event. The Poisson distribution can be used to compute probabilities in such situations. Examples of variables that follow the Poisson distribution are the surface defects on a new refrigerator, the number of network failures in a day, the number of people arriving at a bank, and the number of fleas on the body of a dog. You can use the **Poisson distribution** to calculate probabilities in situations such as these if the following properties hold:

- You are interested in counting the number of times a particular event occurs in a given area of opportunity. The area of opportunity is defined by time, length, surface area, and so forth.
- The probability that an event occurs in a given area of opportunity is the same for all the areas of opportunity.
- The number of events that occur in one area of opportunity is independent of the number of events that occur in any other area of opportunity.
- The probability that two or more events will occur in an area of opportunity approaches zero as the area of opportunity becomes smaller.

Consider the number of customers arriving during the lunch hour at a bank located in the central business district in a large city. You are interested in the number of customers who arrive each minute. Does this situation match the four properties of the Poisson distribution given earlier?

First, the *event* of interest is a customer arriving, and the *given area of opportunity* is defined as a one-minute interval. Will zero customers arrive, one customer arrive, two customers arrive, and so on? Second, it is reasonable to assume that the probability that a customer arrives during a particular one-minute interval is the same as the probability for all the other one-minute intervals. Third, the arrival of one customer in any one-minute interval has no effect on (i.e., is independent of) the arrival of any other customer in any other one-minute interval. Finally, the probability that two or more customers will arrive in a given time period approaches zero as the time interval becomes small. For example, the probability is virtually zero that two customers will arrive in a time interval of 0.01 second. Thus, you can use the Poisson distribution to determine probabilities involving the number of customers arriving at the bank in a one-minute time interval during the lunch hour.

The Poisson distribution has one parameter, called λ (the Greek lowercase letter *lambda*), which is the mean or expected number of events per unit. The variance of a Poisson distribution is also equal to λ, and the standard deviation is equal to $\sqrt{\lambda}$. The number of events, X, of the Poisson variable ranges from 0 to infinity (∞).

Equation (5.8) is the mathematical expression for the Poisson distribution for computing the probability of $X = x$ events, given that λ events are expected.

POISSON DISTRIBUTION

$$P(X = x \mid \lambda) = \frac{e^{-\lambda}\lambda^x}{x!} \qquad (5.8)$$

where

$P(X = x \mid \lambda)$ = probability that $X = x$ events in an area of opportunity given λ
λ = expected number of events per unit
e = mathematical constant approximated by 2.71828
x = number of events $(x = 0, 1, 2, \ldots)$

To illustrate an application of the Poisson distribution, suppose that the mean number of customers who arrive per minute at the bank during the noon-to-1 P.M. hour is equal to 3.0. What is the probability that in a given minute, exactly two customers will arrive? And what is the probability that more than two customers will arrive in a given minute?

Using Equation (5.8) and $\lambda = 3$, the probability that in a given minute exactly two customers will arrive is

$$P(X = 2 \mid \lambda = 3) = \frac{e^{-3.0}(3.0)^2}{2!} = \frac{9}{(2.71828)^3(2)} = 0.2240$$

To determine the probability that in any given minute more than two customers will arrive,

$$P(X > 2) = P(X = 3) + P(X = 4) + \cdots$$

Because in a probability distribution, all the probabilities must sum to 1, the terms on the right side of the equation $P(X > 2)$ also represent the complement of the probability that X is less than or equal to 2 [i.e., $1 - P(X \le 2)$]. Thus,

$$P(X > 2) = 1 - P(X \le 2) = 1 - [P(X = 0) + P(X = 1) + P(X = 2)]$$

Now, using Equation (5.8),

learnMORE

The **Poisson Table online topic** contains a table of Poisson probabilities and explains how to use the table to compute Poisson probabilities.

$$P(X > 2) = 1 - \left[\frac{e^{-3.0}(3.0)^0}{0!} + \frac{e^{-3.0}(3.0)^1}{1!} + \frac{e^{-3.0}(3.0)^2}{2!}\right]$$
$$= 1 - [0.0498 + 0.1494 + 0.2240]$$
$$= 1 - 0.4232 = 0.5768$$

Thus, there is a 57.68% chance that more than two customers will arrive in the same minute.

Computing Poisson probabilities can be tedious. Figure 5.4 on page 180 shows an Excel worksheet that computes Poisson probabilities for you. You can also look up Poisson probabilities in a table of probabilities.

FIGURE 5.4
Excel worksheet for
computing Poisson
probabilities with $\lambda = 3$

◢	A	B	C	D	E
1	Poisson Probabilities				
2					
3		Data			
4	Mean/Expected number of events of interest:		3		
5					
6	Poisson Probabilities Table				
7	X	P(X)			
8	0	0.0498	=POISSON.DIST(A8, $E$4, FALSE)		
9	1	0.1494	=POISSON.DIST(A9, $E$4, FALSE)		
10	2	0.2240	=POISSON.DIST(A10, $E$4, FALSE)		
11	3	0.2240	=POISSON.DIST(A11, $E$4, FALSE)		
12	4	0.1680	=POISSON.DIST(A12, $E$4, FALSE)		
13	5	0.1008	=POISSON.DIST(A13, $E$4, FALSE)		
14	6	0.0504	=POISSON.DIST(A14, $E$4, FALSE)		
15	7	0.0216	=POISSON.DIST(A15, $E$4, FALSE)		
16	8	0.0081	=POISSON.DIST(A16, $E$4, FALSE)		
17	9	0.0027	=POISSON.DIST(A17, $E$4, FALSE)		
18	10	0.0008	=POISSON.DIST(A18, $E$4, FALSE)		
19	11	0.0002	=POISSON.DIST(A19, $E$4, FALSE)		
20	12	0.0001	=POISSON.DIST(A20, $E$4, FALSE)		
21	13	0.0000	=POISSON.DIST(A21, $E$4, FALSE)		
22	14	0.0000	=POISSON.DIST(A22, $E$4, FALSE)		
23	15	0.0000	=POISSON.DIST(A23, $E$4, FALSE)		

EXAMPLE 5.5

Computing Poisson
Probabilities

The number of work-related injuries per month in a manufacturing plant is known to follow a Poisson distribution, with a mean of 2.5 work-related injuries a month. What is the probability that in a given month, no work-related injuries occur? That at least one work-related injury occurs?

SOLUTION Using Equation (5.8) on page 179 with $\lambda = 2.5$ (or Excel or a Poisson table lookup), the probability that in a given month no work-related injuries occur is

$$P(X = 0 \mid \lambda = 2.5) = \frac{e^{-2.5}(2.5)^0}{0!} = \frac{1}{(2.71828)^{2.5}(1)} = 0.0821$$

The probability that there will be no work-related injuries in a given month is 0.0821, or 8.21%. Thus,

$$P(X \geq 1) = 1 - P(X = 0)$$
$$= 1 - 0.0821 = 0.9179$$

The probability that there will be at least one work-related injury is 0.9179, or 91.79%.

PROBLEMS FOR SECTION 5.3

LEARNING THE BASICS

5.18 Assume a Poisson distribution.
a. If $\lambda = 2.5$, find $P(X = 2)$.
b. If $\lambda = 8.0$, find $P(X = 8)$.
c. If $\lambda = 0.5$, find $P(X = 1)$.
d. If $\lambda = 3.7$, find $P(X = 0)$.

5.19 Assume a Poisson distribution.
a. If $\lambda = 2.0$, find $P(X \geq 2)$.
b. If $\lambda = 8.0$, find $P(X \geq 3)$.
c. If $\lambda = 0.5$, find $P(X \leq 1)$.
d. If $\lambda = 4.0$, find $P(X \geq 1)$.
e. If $\lambda = 5.0$, find $P(X \leq 3)$.

5.20 Assume a Poisson distribution with $\lambda = 5.0$. What is the probability that
a. $X = 1$?
b. $X < 1$?
c. $X > 1$?
d. $X \leq 1$?

APPLYING THE CONCEPTS

5.21 Assume that the number of new visitors to a website in one minute is distributed as a Poisson variable. The mean number of new visitors to the website is 4.0 per minute. What is the probability that in any given minute
a. zero new visitors will arrive at the website?
b. exactly one new visitor will arrive at the website?
c. two or more new visitors will arrive at the website?
d. fewer than three new visitors will arrive at the website?

✓SELF TEST **5.22** The quality control manager of Marilyn's Cookies is inspecting a batch of chocolate-chip cookies that has just been baked. If the production process is in control, the mean number of chocolate-chip parts per cookie is 6.0. What is the probability that in any particular cookie being inspected
a. fewer than five chocolate-chip parts will be found?
b. exactly five chocolate-chip parts will be found?
c. five or more chocolate-chip parts will be found?
d. either four or five chocolate-chip parts will be found?

5.23 Refer to Problem 5.22. How many cookies in a batch of 100 should the manager expect to discard if company policy requires that all chocolate-chip cookies sold have at least four chocolate-chip parts?

5.24 The U.S. Department of Transportation maintains statistics for mishandled bags per 1,000 airline passengers. In 2013, Delta mishandled 2.19 bags per 1,000 passengers. What is the probability that in the next 1,000 passengers, Delta will have
a. no mishandled bags?
b. at least one mishandled bag?
c. at least two mishandled bags?

5.25 The U.S. Department of Transportation maintains statistics for involuntary denial of boarding. In July–September 2014, the American Airlines rate of involuntarily denying boarding was 0.58 per 10,000 passengers. What is the probability that in the next 10,000 passengers, there will be
a. no one involuntarily denied boarding?
b. at least one person involuntarily denied boarding?
c. at least two persons involuntarily denied boarding?

5.26 The Consumer Financial Protection Bureau's consumer response team hears directly from consumers about the challenges they face in the marketplace, brings their concerns to the attention of financial institutions, and assists in addressing their complaints. The consumer response team accepts complaints related to mortgages, bank accounts and services, private student loans, other consumer loans, and credit reporting. An analysis of complaints over time indicates that the mean number of credit reporting complaints registered by consumers is 3.30 per day. (Source: *Consumer Response Annual Report*, **1.usa.gov/1GnNDVG**.) Assume that the number of credit reporting complaints registered by consumers is distributed as a Poisson random variable. What is the probability that on a given day
a. no credit reporting complaints will be registered by consumers?
b. exactly one credit reporting complaint will be registered by consumers?
c. more than one credit reporting complaint will be registered by consumers?
d. fewer than two credit reporting complaints will be registered by consumers?

5.27 J.D. Power and Associates calculates and publishes various statistics concerning car quality. The dependability score measures problems experienced during the past 12 months by owners of vehicles (2015). For these models of cars, Ford had 1.88 problems per car and Toyota had 1.11 problems per car. (Data extracted from C. Woodyard, "Lexus Has Staying 'Power'," *USA Today*, February 26, 2015, p. 5B.) Let X be equal to the number of problems with a Ford.
a. What assumptions must be made in order for X to be distributed as a Poisson random variable? Are these assumptions reasonable?
Making the assumptions as in (a), if you purchased a Ford in the 2015 model year, what is the probability that in the past 12 months, the car had
b. zero problems?
c. two or fewer problems?
d. Give an operational definition for *problem*. Why is the operational definition important in interpreting the initial quality score?

5.28 Refer to Problem 5.27. If you purchased a Toyota in the 2015 model year, what is the probability that in the past 12 months the car had
a. zero problems?
b. two or fewer problems?
c. Compare your answers in (a) and (b) to those for the Ford in Problem 5.27 (b) and (c).

5.29 A toll-free phone number is available from 9 A.M. to 9 P.M. for your customers to register complaints about a product purchased from your company. Past history indicates that a mean of 0.8 calls is received per minute.
a. What properties must be true about the situation described here in order to use the Poisson distribution to calculate probabilities concerning the number of phone calls received in a one-minute period?
Assuming that this situation matches the properties discussed in (a), what is the probability that during a one-minute period
b. zero phone calls will be received?
c. three or more phone calls will be received?
d. What is the maximum number of phone calls that will be received in a one-minute period 99.99% of the time?

5.4 Covariance of a Probability Distribution and Its Application in Finance

Section 5.1 defines the expected value, variance, and standard deviation for the probability distribution of a *single* variable. The **Section 5.4 online topic** discusses covariance between *two* variables and explores how financial analysts apply this method as a tool for modern portfolio management.

5.5 Hypergeometric Distribution

The hypergeometric distribution determines the probability of *x* events of interest when sample data *without* replacement from a *finite* population has been collected. The **Section 5.5 online topic** discusses the hypergeometric distribution and illustrates its use.

▼USING **STATISTICS**
Events of Interest…, Revisited

In the Ricknel Home Centers scenario at the beginning of this chapter, you were an accountant for the Ricknel Home Centers, LLC. The company's accounting information system automatically reviews order forms from online customers for possible mistakes. Any questionable invoices are tagged and included in a daily exceptions report. Knowing that the probability that an order will be tagged is 0.10, you were able to use the binomial distribution to determine the chance of finding a certain number of tagged forms in a sample of size four. There was a 65.6% chance that none of the forms would be tagged, a 29.2% chance that one would be tagged, and a 5.2% chance that two or more would be tagged. You were also able to determine that, on average, you would expect 0.4 form to be tagged, and the standard deviation of the number of tagged order forms would be 0.6. Now that you have learned the mechanics of using the binomial distribution for a known probability of 0.10 and a sample size of four, you will be able to apply the same approach to any given probability and sample size. Thus, you will be able to make inferences about the online ordering process and, more importantly, evaluate any changes or proposed changes to the process.

▼SUMMARY

In this chapter, you have studied the probability distribution for a discrete variable and two important discrete probability distributions: the binomial and Poisson distributions. In the next chapter, you will study the normal and uniform distributions.

Use the following rules to select which discrete distribution to use for a particular situation:

- If there is a fixed number of observations, *n*, each of which is classified as an event of interest or not an event of interest, use the binomial distribution.
- If there is an area of opportunity, use the Poisson distribution.

▼REFERENCES

1. Hogg, R. V., J. T. McKean, and A. V. Craig. *Introduction to Mathematical Statistics*, 7th ed. New York: Pearson Education, 2013.

2. Levine, D. M., P. Ramsey, and R. Smidt. *Applied Statistics for Engineers and Scientists Using Microsoft Excel and Minitab.* Upper Saddle River, NJ: Prentice Hall, 2001.

▼KEY EQUATIONS

Expected Value, μ, of a Discrete Variable

$$\mu = E(X) = \sum_{i=1}^{N} x_i P(X = x_i) \qquad (5.1)$$

Variance of a Discrete Variable

$$\sigma^2 = \sum_{i=1}^{N} [x_i - E(X)]^2 P(X = x_i) \qquad (5.2)$$

Standard Deviation of a Discrete Variable

$$\sigma = \sqrt{\sigma^2} = \sqrt{\sum_{i=1}^{N}[x_i - E(X)]^2 P(X = x_i)} \quad (5.3)$$

Combinations

$$_nC_x = \frac{n!}{x!(n-x)!} \quad (5.4)$$

Binomial Distribution

$$P(X = x \mid n, \pi) = \frac{n!}{x!(n-x)!}\pi^x(1-\pi)^{n-x} \quad (5.5)$$

Mean of the Binomial Distribution

$$\mu = E(X) = n\pi \quad (5.6)$$

Standard Deviation of the Binomial Distribution

$$\sigma = \sqrt{\sigma^2} = \sqrt{\text{Var}(X)} = \sqrt{n\pi(1-\pi)} \quad (5.7)$$

Poisson Distribution

$$P(X = x \mid \lambda) = \frac{e^{-\lambda}\lambda^x}{x!} \quad (5.8)$$

▼ KEY TERMS

▼ CHECKING YOUR UNDERSTANDING

5.30 What is the meaning of the expected value of a variable?

5.31 What are the four properties that must be present in order to use the binomial distribution?

5.32 What are the four properties that must be present in order to use the Poisson distribution?

▼ CHAPTER REVIEW PROBLEMS

5.33 Darwin Head, a 35-year-old sawmill worker, won $1 million and a Chevrolet Malibu Hybrid by scoring 15 goals within 24 seconds at the Vancouver Canucks National Hockey League game (B. Ziemer, "Darwin Evolves into an Instant Millionaire," *Vancouver Sun*, February 28, 2008, p. 1). Head said he would use the money to pay off his mortgage and provide for his children, and he had no plans to quit his job. The contest was part of the Chevrolet Malibu Million Dollar Shootout, sponsored by General Motors Canadian Division. Did GM-Canada risk the $1 million? No! GM-Canada purchased event insurance from a company specializing in promotions at sporting events such as a half-court basketball shot or a hole-in-one giveaway at the local charity golf outing. The event insurance company estimates the probability of a contestant winning the contest, and for a modest charge, insures the event. The promoters pay the insurance premium but take on no added risk as the insurance company will make the large payout in the unlikely event that a contestant wins. To see how it works, suppose that the insurance company estimates that the probability a contestant would win a million-dollar shootout is 0.001 and that the insurance company charges $4,000.
a. Calculate the expected value of the profit made by the insurance company.

b. Many call this kind of situation a win–win opportunity for the insurance company and the promoter. Do you agree? Explain.

5.34 Between 1896—when the Dow Jones index was created—and 2014, the index rose in 67% of the years. (Sources: M. Hulbert, "What the Past Can't Tell Investors," *The New York Times*, January 3, 2010, p. BU2 and **bit.ly/100zwvT**.) Based on this information, and assuming a binomial distribution, what do you think is the probability that the stock market will rise
a. next year?
b. the year after next?
c. in four of the next five years?
d. in none of the next five years?
e. For this situation, what assumption of the binomial distribution might not be valid?

5.35 Smartphone adoption among American younger adults has increased substantially and mobile access to the Internet is pervasive. Fifteen percent of young adults, ages 18–29, who own a smartphone are "smartphone-dependent," meaning that they do not have home broadband service and have limited options for going online other than their mobile device. (Data extracted from

"U.S. Smartphone Use in 2015," Pew Research Center, April 1, 2015, **bit.ly/1JxYKNi.**)

If a sample of 10 American young adults is selected, what is the probability that

a. 3 are smartphone-dependent?

b. at least 3 are smartphone-dependent?

c. at most 6 are smartphone-dependent?

d. If you selected the sample in a particular geographical area and found that none of the 10 respondents are smartphone-dependent, what conclusions might you reach about whether the percentage of smartphone-dependent young adults in this area was 15%?

5.36 One theory concerning the Dow Jones Industrial Average is that it is likely to increase during U.S. presidential election years. From 1964 through 2012, the Dow Jones Industrial Average increased in 10 of the 13 U.S. presidential election years. Assuming that this indicator is a random event with no predictive value, you would expect that the indicator would be correct 50% of the time.

a. What is the probability of the Dow Jones Industrial Average increasing in 10 or more of the 13 U.S. presidential election years if the probability of an increase in the Dow Jones Industrial Average is 0.50?

b. What is the probability that the Dow Jones Industrial Average will increase in 10 or more of the 13 U.S. presidential election years if the probability of an increase in the Dow Jones Industrial Average in any year is 0.75?

5.37 Medical billing errors and fraud are on the rise. According to the MBAA website, 8 out of 10 times, the medical bills that you get are not right. (Source: "Accurate Medical Billing," **bit.ly/1lHKIu3**, April 2, 2014.) If a sample of 10 medical bills is selected, what is the probability that

a. 0 medical bills will contain errors?

b. exactly 5 medical bills will contain errors?

c. more than 5 medical bills will contain errors?

d. What are the mean and standard deviation of the probability distribution?

5.38 Refer to Problem 5.37. Suppose that a quality improvement initiative has reduced the percentage of medical bills containing errors to 40%. If a sample of 10 medical bills is selected, what is the probability that

a. 0 medical bills will contain errors?

b. exactly 5 medical bills will contain errors?

c. more than 5 medical bills contain errors?

d. What are the mean and standard deviation of the probability distribution?

e. Compare the results of (a) through (c) to those of Problem 5.37 (a) through (c).

5.39 Social log-ins involve recommending or sharing an article that you read online. According to Janrain, in the first quarter of 2015, 34% signed in via Facebook compared with 37% for Google. (Source: "Social Login Trends Across the Web: Q1 2015," **bit.ly/1F9ykdq**) If a sample of 10 social log-ins is selected, what is the probability that

a. more than 5 signed in using Facebook?

b. more than 5 signed in using Google?

c. none signed in using Facebook?

d. What assumptions did you have to make to answer (a) through (c)?

5.40 The Consumer Financial Protection Bureau's Consumer Response Team hears directly from consumers about the challenges they face in the marketplace, brings their concerns to the attention of financial institutions, and assists in addressing their complaints. Consumer Response accepts complaints related to mortgages, bank accounts and services, private student loans, other consumer loans, and credit reporting. Of the consumers who registered a bank account and service complaint, 47% cited "account management" as the type of complaint; these complaints are related to opening, closing, or managing the account and address issues such as confusing marketing, denial, fees, statements, and joint accounts. (Source: *Consumer Response Annual Report*, **1.usa.gov/ 1GnNDVG**.)

Consider a sample of 20 consumers who registered bank account and service complaints. Use the binomial model to answer the following questions:

a. What is the expected value, or mean, of the binomial distribution?

b. What is the standard deviation of the binomial distribution?

c. What is the probability that 10 of the 20 consumers cited "account management" as the type of complaint?

d. What is the probability that no more than 5 of the consumers cited "account management" as the type of complaint?

e. What is the probability that 5 or more of the consumers cited "account management" as the type of complaint?

5.41 Refer to Problem 5.40. In the same time period, 24% of the consumers registering a bank account and service compliant cited "deposit and withdrawal" as the type of complaint; these are issues such as transaction holds and unauthorized transactions.

a. What is the expected value, or mean, of the binomial distribution?

b. What is the standard deviation of the binomial distribution?

c. What is the probability that none of the 20 consumers cited "deposit and withdrawal" as the type of complaint?

d. What is the probability that no more than 2 of the consumers cited "deposit and withdrawal" as the type of complaint?

e. What is the probability that 3 or more of the consumers cited "deposit and withdrawal" as the type of complaint?

5.42 One theory concerning the S&P 500 Index is that if it increases during the first five trading days of the year, it is likely to increase during the entire year. From 1950 through 2014, the S&P 500 Index had these early gains in 42 years (in 2011 there was virtually no change). In 37 of these 42 years, the S&P 500 Index increased for the entire year. Assuming that this indicator is a random event with no predictive value, you would expect that the indicator would be correct 50% of the time. What is the probability of the S&P 500 Index increasing in 37 or more years if the true probability of an increase in the S&P 500 Index is

a. 0.50?

b. 0.70?

c. 0.90?

d. Based on the results of (a) through (c), what do you think is the probability that the S&P 500 Index will increase if there is an early gain in the first five trading days of the year? Explain.

5.43 *Spurious correlation* refers to the apparent relationship between variables that either have no true relationship or are related to other variables that have not been measured. One widely publicized stock market indicator in the United States that is an example of spurious correlation is the relationship between the winner of the National Football League Super Bowl and the performance of the Dow Jones Industrial Average in that year. The "indicator" states that when a team that existed before the National Football League merged with the American Football League wins the Super Bowl, the Dow Jones Industrial Average will increase in that year. (Of course, any correlation between these is spurious as one thing has absolutely nothing to do with the other!) Since the first Super Bowl was held in 1967 through 2014, the indicator has been correct 37 out of 48 times. Assuming that this indicator is a random event with no predictive value, you would expect that the indicator would be correct 50% of the time.

a. What is the probability that the indicator would be correct 37 or more times in 48 years?

b. What does this tell you about the usefulness of this indicator?

5.44 The United Auto Courts Reports blog notes that the National Insurance Crime Bureau says that Miami-Dade, Broward, and Palm Beach counties account for a substantial number of questionable insurance claims referred to investigators. Assume that the number of questionable insurance claims referred to investigators by Miami-Dade, Broward, and Palm Beach counties is distributed as a Poisson random variable with a mean of 7 per day.

a. What assumptions need to be made so that the number of questionable insurance claims referred to investigators by Miami-Dade, Broward, and Palm Beach counties is distributed as a Poisson random variable?

Making the assumptions given in (a), what is the probability that

b. 5 questionable insurance claims will be referred to investigators by Miami-Dade, Broward, and Palm Beach counties in a day?

c. 10 or fewer questionable insurance claims will be referred to investigators by Miami-Dade, Broward, and Palm Beach counties in a day?

d. 11 or more questionable insurance claims will be referred to investigators by Miami-Dade, Broward, and Palm Beach counties in a day?

▼ CASES

CHAPTER 5

Managing Ashland MultiComm Services

The Ashland MultiComm Services (AMS) marketing department wants to increase subscriptions for its *3-For-All* telephone, cable, and Internet combined service. AMS marketing has been conducting an aggressive direct-marketing campaign that includes postal and electronic mailings and telephone solicitations. Feedback from these efforts indicates that including premium channels in this combined service is a very important factor for both current and prospective subscribers. After several brainstorming sessions, the marketing department has decided to add premium cable channels as a no-cost benefit of subscribing to the *3-For-All* service.

The research director, Mona Fields, is planning to conduct a survey among prospective customers to determine how many premium channels need to be added to the *3-For-All* service in order to generate a subscription to the service. Based on past campaigns and on industry-wide data, she estimates the following:

Number of Free Premium Channels	Probability of Subscriptions
0	0.02
1	0.04
2	0.06
3	0.07
4	0.08
5	0.085

1. If a sample of 50 prospective customers is selected and no free premium channels are included in the *3-For-All* service offer, given past results, what is the probability that

a. fewer than 3 customers will subscribe to the *3-For-All* service offer?

b. 0 customers or 1 customer will subscribe to the *3-For-All* service offer?

c. more than 4 customers will subscribe to the *3-For-All* service offer?

d. Suppose that in the actual survey of 50 prospective customers, 4 customers subscribe to the *3-For-All* service offer. What does this tell you about the previous estimate of the proportion of customers who would subscribe to the *3-For-All* service offer?

2. Instead of offering no premium free channels as in Problem 1, suppose that two free premium channels are included in the *3-For-All* service offer. Given past results, what is the probability that

a. fewer than 3 customers will subscribe to the *3-For-All* service offer?

b. 0 customers or 1 customer will subscribe to the *3-For-All* service offer?

c. more than 4 customers will subscribe to the *3-For-All* service offer?

d. Compare the results of (a) through (c) to those of Problem 1.

e. Suppose that in the actual survey of 50 prospective customers, 6 customers subscribe to the *3-For-All* service offer. What does this tell you about the previous estimate of the proportion of customers who would subscribe to the *3-For-All* service offer?

f. What do the results in (e) tell you about the effect of offering free premium channels on the likelihood of obtaining subscriptions to the *3-For-All* service?

3. Suppose that additional surveys of 50 prospective customers were conducted in which the number of free premium channels was varied. The results were as follows:

Number of Free Premium Channels	Number of Subscriptions
1	5
3	6
4	6
5	7

How many free premium channels should the research director recommend for inclusion in the *3-For-All* service? Explain.

Digital Case

Apply your knowledge about expected value in this continuing Digital Case from Chapters 3 and 4.

Open **BullsAndBears.pdf**, a marketing brochure from EndRun Financial Services. Read the claims and examine the supporting data. Then answer the following:

1. Are there any "catches" about the claims the brochure makes for the rate of return of Happy Bull and Worried Bear funds?

2. What subjective data influence the rate-of-return analyses of these funds? Could EndRun be accused of making false and misleading statements? Why or why not?

3. The expected-return analysis seems to show that the Worried Bear fund has a greater expected return than the Happy Bull fund. Should a rational investor never invest in the Happy Bull fund? Why or why not?

▼EXCEL GUIDE

EG5.1 THE PROBABILITY DISTRIBUTION for a DISCRETE VARIABLE

Key Technique Use **SUMPRODUCT(***X cell range, P($X=x_1$) cell range***)** to compute the expected value. Use **SUMPRODUCT(***squared differences cell range, P($X=x_1$) cell range***)** to compute the variance.

Example Compute the expected value, variance, and standard deviation for the number of interruptions per day data of Table 5.1 on page 167.

Workbook Use the **Discrete Variable workbook** as a model.

For the example, open to the **DATA worksheet** of the **Discrete Variable workbook**. The worksheet already contains the column A and B entries needed to compute the expected value, variance, and standard deviation (shown in the COMPUTE worksheet) for the example. Unusual for a DATA worksheet in this book, columns C through E contain the intermediate calculations shown in Table 5.3 on page 169 (shown below). Column D calculates the squared differences using the expected value that the COMPUTE worksheet cell B4 (not shown) calculates.

	A	B	C	D	E
1	X	P(X)	X*P(X)	[X-E(X)]^2	[X-E(X)]^2*P(X)
2	0	0.35	=A2 * B2	=(A2 - COMPUTE!$B$4)^2	=D2 * B2
3	1	0.25	=A3 * B3	=(A3 - COMPUTE!$B$4)^2	=D3 * B3
4	2	0.20	=A4 * B4	=(A4 - COMPUTE!$B$4)^2	=D4 * B4
5	3	0.10	=A5 * B5	=(A5 - COMPUTE!$B$4)^2	=D5 * B5
6	4	0.05	=A6 * B6	=(A6 - COMPUTE!$B$4)^2	=D6 * B6
7	5	0.05	=A7 * B7	=(A7 - COMPUTE!$B$4)^2	=D7 * B7

For other problems, modify the DATA worksheet. Enter the probability distribution data into columns A and B and, if necessary, extend columns C through E, first selecting cell range C7:E7 and then copying that cell range down as many rows as necessary. If the probability distribution has fewer than six outcomes, select the rows that contain the extra, unwanted outcomes, right-click, and then click **Delete** in the shortcut menu.

Appendix F contains additional information about the SUMPRODUCT function, used in the COMPUTE worksheet to calculate the expected value and variance.

EG5.2 BINOMIAL DISTRIBUTION

Key Technique Use the **BINOM.DIST(***number of events of interest, sample size, probability of an event of interest, FALSE***)** function.

Example Compute the binomial probabilities for $n = 4$ and $\pi = 0.1$, and construct a histogram of that probability distribution, similar to Figures 5.2 and 5.3 on page 175.

PHStat Use **Binomial**.

For the example, select **PHStat → Probability & Prob. Distributions → Binomial**. In the procedure's dialog box (shown below):

1. Enter **4** as the **Sample Size**.
2. Enter **0.1** as the **Prob. of an Event of Interest**.
3. Enter **0** as the **Outcomes From** value and enter **4** as the (Outcomes) **To** value.
4. Enter a **Title**, check **Histogram**, and click **OK**.

Check **Cumulative Probabilities** before clicking **OK** in step 4 to have the procedure include columns for $P(\leq X), P(<X), P(>X)$, and $P(\geq X)$ in the binomial probabilities table.

Workbook Use the **Binomial workbook** as a template and model.

For the example, open to the **COMPUTE worksheet** of the **Binomial workbook**, shown in Figure 5.2 on page 175. The worksheet already contains the entries needed for the example. For other problems, change the sample size in cell B4 and the probability of an event of interest in cell B5. If necessary, extend the binomial probabilities table by first selecting cell range A18:B18 and then copying that cell range down as many rows as necessary. To construct a histogram of the probability distribution, use the Appendix Section B.9 instructions.

For problems that require cumulative probabilities, use the CUMULATIVE worksheet in the Binomial workbook. The SHORT TAKES for Chapter 5 explains and documents this worksheet.

EG5.3 POISSON DISTRIBUTION

Key Technique Use the **POISSON.DIST**(*number of events of interest, the average or expected number of events of interest,* **FALSE**) function.

Example Compute the Poisson probabilities for the customer arrival problem in which $\lambda = 3$, as is done in Figure 5.4 on page 180.

PHStat Use **Poisson**.
For the example, select **PHStat → Probability & Prob. Distributions → Poisson**. In this procedure's dialog box (shown below):

1. Enter **3** as the **Mean/Expected No. of Events of Interest**.
2. Enter a **Title** and click **OK**.

Check **Cumulative Probabilities** before clicking **OK** in step 2 to have the procedure include columns for $P(\leq X)$, $P(<X)$, $P(>X)$, and $P(\geq X)$ in the Poisson probabilities table. Check **Histogram** to construct a histogram of the Poisson probability distribution.

Workbook Use the **Poisson workbook** as a template. For the example, open to the **COMPUTE worksheet** of the **Poisson workbook**, shown in Figure 5.4 on page 180. The worksheet already contains the entries for the example. For other problems, change the mean or expected number of events of interest in cell E4. To construct a histogram of the probability distribution, use the Appendix Section B.9 instructions.

For problems that require cumulative probabilities, use the CUMULATIVE worksheet in the Binomial workbook. The Short Takes for Chapter 5 explains and documents this worksheet.

The Normal Distribution and Other Continuous Distributions

6

OBJECTIVES

- Compute probabilities from the normal distribution
- Use the normal distribution to solve business problems
- Use the normal probability plot to determine whether a set of data is approximately normally distributed
- Compute probabilities from the uniform distribution

▼ USING **STATISTICS**
Normal Load Times at MyTVLab

You are the vice president in charge of sales and marketing for MyTVLab, a web-based business that has evolved into a full-fledged, subscription-based streaming video service. To differentiate MyTVLab from the other companies that sell similar services, you decide to create a "Why Choose Us" web page to help educate new and prospective subscribers about all that MyTVLab offers.

As part of that page, you have produced a new video that samples the content MyTVLab streams as well as demonstrates the relative ease of setting up MyTVLab on many types of devices. You want this video to download with the page so that a visitor can jump to different segments immediately or view the video later, when offline.

You know from research (see reference 3) and past observations, Internet visitors will not tolerate waiting too long for a web page to load. One wait time measure is load time, the time in seconds that passes from first pointing a browser to a web page until the web page is fully loaded and content such as video is ready to be viewed. You have set a goal that the load time for the new sales page should rarely exceed 10 seconds (too long for visitors to wait) and, ideally, should rarely be less than 1 second (a waste of company Internet resources).

To measure this time, you point a web browser at the MyTVLab corporate test center to the new sales web page and record the load time. In your first test, you record a time of 6.67 seconds. You repeat the test and record a time of 7.52 seconds. Though consistent to your goal, you realize that two load times do not constitute strong proof of anything, especially as your assistant has performed his own test and recorded a load time of 8.83 seconds.

Could you use a method based on probability theory to ensure that most load times will be within the range you seek? MyTVLab has recorded past load times of a similar page with a similar video and determined the mean load time of that page is 7 seconds, the standard deviation of those times is 2 seconds, and that approximately two-thirds of the load times are between 5 and 9 seconds, and about 95% of the load times are between 3 and 11 seconds.

Could you use these facts to assure yourself that the load time goal you have set for the new sales page is likely to be met?

n Chapter 5 you learned how to use probability distributions for a *discrete* numerical variable. In the MyTVLab scenario, you are examining the load time, a *continuous* numerical variable. You are no longer considering a table of discrete (specific) values, but a continuous range of values. For example, the phrase "load times are between 5 and 9 seconds" includes *any* value between 5 and 9 and not just the values 5, 6, 7, 8, and 9. If you plotted the phrase on a graph, you would draw a *continuous* line from 5 to 9 and not just plot five specific points.

When you add information about the shape of the range of values, such as two-thirds of the load times are between 5 and 9 seconds or about 95% of the load times are between 3 and 11 seconds, you can visualize the plot of all values as an area under a curve. If that area under the curve follows the well-known pattern of certain continuous distributions, you can use the continuous probability distribution for that pattern to estimate the likelihood that a load time is within a range of values. In the MyTVLab scenario, the third bullet describes a pattern that conforms to the pattern associated with the normal distribution, the subject of Section 6.2. That would allow you, as the vice president for sales and marketing, to use the normal distribution with the statistics given in the first two bullets to determine if your load time goal is likely to be met.

6.1 Continuous Probability Distributions

Continuous probability distributions vary by the shape of the area under the curve. Figure 6.1 visualizes the normal, uniform, and exponential probability distributions.

FIGURE 6.1
Three continuous
probability distributions

Some distributions, including the normal and uniform distributions in Figure 6.1, show a symmetrical shape. Distributions such as the right-skewed exponential distribution are not. In symmetrical distributions the mean equals the median, whereas in a right-skewed distribution the mean is greater than the median. Each of the three distributions also has unique properties.

The **normal distribution** is not only symmetrical, but bell-shaped, a shape that (loosely) suggests the profile of a bell. Being bell-shaped means that most values of the continuous variable will cluster around the mean. Although the values in a normal distribution can range from negative infinity to positive infinity, the shape of the normal distribution makes it very unlikely that extremely large or extremely small values will occur.

The **uniform distribution**, also known as the rectangular distribution, contains values that are equally distributed in the range between the smallest value and the largest value. In a uniform distribution, every value is equally likely. The **exponential distribution** contains values from zero to positive infinity and is right-skewed, making the mean greater than the median. Its shape makes it unlikely that extremely large values will occur.

Besides visualizations such as those in Figure 6.1, a continuous probability distribution can be expressed mathematically as a *probability density function*. A **probability density function** for a specific continuous probability distribution defines the distribution of the values for a continuous variable and can be used as the basis for calculations that determine the likelihood or probability that a value will be within a certain range.

6.2 The Normal Distribution

The most commonly used continuous distribution, the normal distribution, plays an important role in statistics. You can use the normal distribution to approximate various discrete probability distributions and, because of its relationship to the Central Limit Theorem (see Section 7.2), the normal distribution provides the basis for classical statistical inference. In business, many continuous variables used in decision making have distributions that closely resemble the normal distribution, which allows this distribution to be used to estimate values for those variables.

Exhibit 6.1 presents the important theoretical properties of the normal distribution. In the normal distribution, you can calculate the probability that values occur within certain ranges or intervals. For example, you can determine the probability that the load time for the MyTVLab sales page is between 7 and 10 seconds, or the probability that the load time is between 8 and 9 seconds, or the probability that the load time is between 7.99 and 8.01 seconds. However, because you measure probability for continuous variables as an area under a curve, the probability of a *particular* value from a continuous distribution such as the normal distribution is always zero. Therefore, you would say that the probability that the load time is exactly 8.1 seconds (or any other value) is zero.

EXHIBIT 6.1

Normal Distribution Important Theoretical Properties

Symmetrical distribution. Its mean and median are therefore equal.

Bell-shaped. Values cluster around the mean.

Interquartile range is roughly 1.33 standard deviations. Therefore, the middle 50% of the values are contained within an interval that is approximately two-thirds of a standard deviation below and two-thirds of a standard deviation above the mean.

The distribution has an infinite range $(-\infty < X < \infty)$. Six standard deviations approximate this range (as explained on page 197).

In practice, many variables have distributions that closely resemble the important theoretical properties of the normal distribution. The Table 6.1 data represent the amount of soft drink in 10,000 1-liter bottles filled on a recent day. The continuous variable of interest, the amount of soft drink filled, can be *approximated* by the normal distribution. The measurements of the

TABLE 6.1
Amount of Fill in 10,000 Bottles of a Soft Drink

Amount of Fill (liters)	Relative Frequency
< 1.025	48/10,000 = 0.0048
1.025 < 1.030	122/10,000 = 0.0122
1.030 < 1.035	325/10,000 = 0.0325
1.035 < 1.040	695/10,000 = 0.0695
1.040 < 1.045	1,198/10,000 = 0.1198
1.045 < 1.050	1,664/10,000 = 0.1664
1.050 < 1.055	1,896/10,000 = 0.1896
1.055 < 1.060	1,664/10,000 = 0.1664
1.060 < 1.065	1,198/10,000 = 0.1198
1.065 < 1.070	695/10,000 = 0.0695
1.070 < 1.075	325/10,000 = 0.0325
1.075 < 1.080	122/10,000 = 0.0122
1.080 or above	48/10,000 = 0.0048
Total	1.0000

amount of soft drink in the 10,000 bottles cluster in the interval 1.05 to 1.055 liters and distribute symmetrically around that grouping, forming a bell-shaped pattern. Figure 6.2 visually summarizes that pattern as a relative frequency histogram and polygon (see Section 2.4).

FIGURE 6.2
Relative frequency histogram and polygon of the amount filled in 10,000 bottles of a soft drink

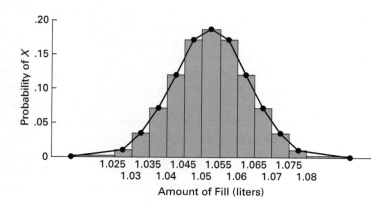

For these data, the first three theoretical properties of the normal distribution are approximately satisfied. However, the fourth one, having an infinite range, is not. The amount filled in a bottle cannot possibly be zero or below, nor can a bottle be filled beyond its capacity. From Table 6.1, you see that only 48 out of every 10,000 bottles filled are expected to contain 1.08 liters or more, and an equal number are expected to contain less than 1.025 liters.

The symbol $f(X)$ is used to represent a probability density function. The **probability density function for the normal distribution** is given in Equation (6.1).

NORMAL PROBABILITY DENSITY FUNCTION

$$f(X) = \frac{1}{\sqrt{2\pi}\sigma} e^{-(1/2)[(X-\mu)/\sigma]^2} \tag{6.1}$$

where

e = mathematical constant approximated by 2.71828
π = mathematical constant approximated by 3.14159
μ = mean
σ = standard deviation
X = any value of the continuous variable, where $-\infty < X < \infty$

---

studentTIP

There is a different normal distribution for each combination of the mean, μ, and the standard deviation, σ.

Although Equation (6.1) may look complicated, the probabilities of the variable X are dependent only on the mean, μ, and the standard deviation, σ, the two parameters of the normal distribution, because e and π are mathematical constants. There is a different normal distribution for each combination of the mean μ and the standard deviation σ. Figure 6.3 illustrates this principle. The distributions labeled A and B have the same mean (μ) but have different standard deviations. Distributions A and C have the same standard deviation (σ) but have different means. Distributions B and C have different values for both μ and σ.

Computing Normal Probabilities

To compute normal probabilities, you first convert a normally distributed variable, X, to a **standardized normal variable**, Z, using the **transformation formula**, shown in Equation (6.2). Applying this formula allows you to look up values in a normal probability table and avoid the tedious and complex computations that Equation (6.1) would otherwise require.

FIGURE 6.3
Three normal
distributions

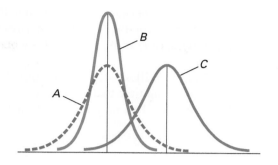

Z TRANSFORMATION FORMULA

The Z value is equal to the difference between X and the mean, μ, divided by the standard deviation, σ.

$$Z = \frac{X - \mu}{\sigma} \qquad\qquad (6.2)$$

The transformation formula computes a Z value that expresses the difference of the X value from the mean, μ, in standard deviation units (see Section 3.2 on page 106) called *standardized units*. While a variable, X, has mean, μ, and standard deviation, σ, the standardized variable, Z, always has mean $\mu = 0$ and standard deviation $\sigma = 1$.

Then you can determine the probabilities by using Table E.2, the **cumulative standardized normal distribution**. For example, recall from the MyTVLab scenario on page 189 that past data indicate that the sales page load time is normally distributed, with a mean $\mu = 7$ seconds and a standard deviation $\sigma = 2$ seconds. From Figure 6.4, you see that every measurement X has a corresponding standardized measurement Z, computed from Equation (6.2), the transformation formula.

FIGURE 6.4
Transformation of scales

Therefore, a load time of 9 seconds is equivalent to 1 standardized unit (1 standard deviation) above the mean because

$$Z = \frac{9 - 7}{2} = +1$$

A load time of 1 second is equivalent to -3 standardized units (3 standard deviations) below the mean because

$$Z = \frac{1 - 7}{2} = -3$$

In Figure 6.4, the standard deviation is the unit of measurement. In other words, a time of seconds is 2 seconds (1 standard deviation) higher, or *slower*, than the mean time of 7 seconds. Similarly, a time of 1 second is 6 seconds (3 standard deviations) lower, or *faster*, than the mean time.

To further illustrate the transformation formula, suppose that the technical support web page has a load time that is normally distributed, with a mean $\mu = 4$ seconds and a standard deviation $\sigma = 1$ second. Figure 6.5 shows this distribution.

FIGURE 6.5
A different transformation
of scales

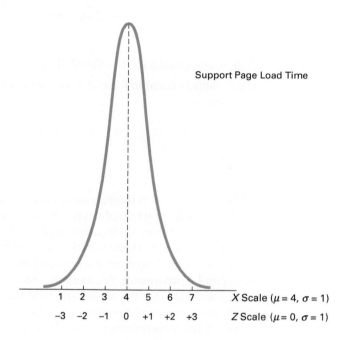

Support Page Load Time

| 1 | 2 | 3 | 4 | 5 | 6 | 7 | X Scale ($\mu = 4$, $\sigma = 1$) |
| -3 | -2 | -1 | 0 | +1 | +2 | +3 | Z Scale ($\mu = 0$, $\sigma = 1$) |

Comparing these results with those of the sales page, you see that a load time of 5 seconds is 1 standard deviation above the mean download time because

$$Z = \frac{5 - 4}{1} = +1$$

A time of 1 second is 3 standard deviations below the mean load time because

$$Z = \frac{1 - 4}{1} = -3$$

Having determined the Z value, you use a table of values from the cumulative standardized normal distribution to look up the normal probability. Suppose you wanted to find the probability that the load time for the MyTVLab sales page is less than 9 seconds. Recall from page 193 that transforming $X = 9$ to standardized Z units, given a mean $\mu = 7$ seconds and a standard deviation $\sigma = 2$ seconds, leads to a Z value of $+1.00$.

studentTIP

When discussing the normal or other continuous distributions, the word *area* has the same meaning as *probability*.

With this value, you use Table E.2 to find the cumulative area under the normal curve less than (to the left of) $Z = +1.00$. To read the probability or area under the curve less than $Z = +1.00$, you scan down the Z column in Table E.2 until you locate the Z value of interest (in 10ths) in the Z row for 1.0. Next, you read across this row until you intersect the column that contains the 100ths place of the Z value. Therefore, in the body of the table, the probability for $Z = 1.00$ corresponds to the intersection of the row $Z = 1.0$ with the column $Z = .00$. Table 6.2, which reproduces a portion of Table E.2, shows this intersection. The probability listed at the intersection is 0.8413, which means that there is an 84.13% chance that the download time will be less than 9 seconds. Figure 6.6 on page 195 graphically shows this probability.

However, for the other website, you see that a time of 5 seconds is 1 standardized unit above the mean time of 4 seconds. Thus, the probability that the load time will be less than 5 seconds is also 0.8413. Figure 6.7 shows that regardless of the value of the mean, μ, and

TABLE 6.2

Finding a Cumulative Area Under the Normal Curve

Source: Extracted from Table E.2.

					Cumulative Probabilities					
Z	.00	.01	.02	.03	.04	.05	.06	.07	.08	.09
0.0	.5000	.5040	.5080	.5120	.5160	.5199	.5239	.5279	.5319	.5359
0.1	.5398	.5438	.5478	.5517	.5557	.5596	.5636	.5675	.5714	.5753
0.2	.5793	.5832	.5871	.5910	.5948	.5987	.6026	.6064	.6103	.6141
0.3	.6179	.6217	.6255	.6293	.6331	.6368	.6406	.6443	.6480	.6517
0.4	.6554	.6591	.6628	.6664	.6700	.6736	.6772	.6808	.6844	.6879
0.5	.6915	.6950	.6985	.7019	.7054	.7088	.7123	.7157	.7190	.7224
0.6	.7257	.7291	.7324	.7357	.7389	.7422	.7454	.7486	.7518	.7549
0.7	.7580	.7612	.7642	.7673	.7704	.7734	.7764	.7794	.7823	.7852
0.8	.7881	.7910	.7939	.7967	.7995	.8023	.8051	.8078	.8106	.8133
0.9	.8159	.8186	.8212	.8238	.8264	.8289	.8315	.8340	.8365	.8389
1.0	.8413	.8438	.8461	.8485	.8508	.8531	.8554	.8577	.8599	.8621

FIGURE 6.6

Determining the area less than Z from a cumulative standardized normal distribution

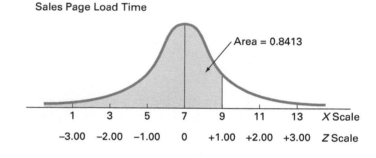

FIGURE 6.7

Demonstrating a transformation of scales for corresponding cumulative portions under two normal curves

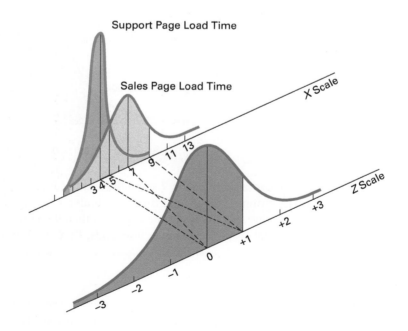

standard deviation, σ, of a normally distributed variable, Equation (6.2) can transform the X value to a Z value.

Now that you have learned to use Table E.2 with Equation (6.2), you can answer many questions related to the sales page load time, including whether achieving the load time goal is likely, using the normal distribution.

EXAMPLE 6.1

Finding $P(X > 9)$

What is the probability that the load time for the MyTVLab sales page will be more than 9 seconds?

SOLUTION The probability that the load time will be less than 9 seconds is 0.8413 (see Figure 6.6 on page 195). Thus, the probability that the load time will be more than 9 seconds is the *complement* of less than 9 seconds, $1 - 0.8413 = 0.1587$. Figure 6.8 illustrates this result.

FIGURE 6.8
Finding $P(X > 9)$

EXAMPLE 6.2

Finding $P(X < 7$ or $X > 9)$

What is the probability that the load time for the MyTVLab will be less than 7 seconds or more than 9 seconds?

SOLUTION To find this probability, you separately calculate the probability of a load time less than 7 seconds and the probability of a load time greater than 9 seconds and then add these two probabilities together. Figure 6.9 illustrates this result.

FIGURE 6.9
Finding
$P(X < 7$ or $X > 9)$

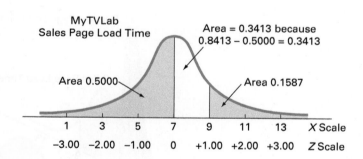

Because the mean is 7 seconds, and because the mean is equal to the median in a normal distribution, 50% of load times are under 7 seconds. From Example 6.1, you know that the probability that the load time is greater than 9 seconds is 0.1587. Therefore, the probability that a load time is under 7 or over 9 seconds, $P(X < 7$ or $X > 9)$, is $0.5000 + 0.1587 = 0.6587$.

EXAMPLE 6.3

Finding
$P(5 < X < 9)$

What is the probability that load time for the MyTVLab sales page will be between 5 and 9 seconds—that is, $P(5 < X < 9)$?

SOLUTION In Figure 6.10 on page 197, you can see that the area of interest is located between two values, 5 and 9.

▶ *(continued)*

FIGURE 6.10
Finding $P(5 < X < 9)$

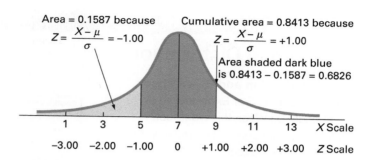

In Example 6.1 on page 196, you already found that the area under the normal curve less than 9 seconds is 0.8413. To find the area under the normal curve less than 5 seconds,

$$Z = \frac{5 - 7}{2} = -1.00$$

Using Table E.2, you look up $Z = -1.00$ and find 0.1587. Therefore, the probability that the load time will be between 5 and 9 seconds is $0.8413 - 0.1587 = 0.6826$, as displayed in Figure 6.10.

The result of Example 6.3 enables you to state that for any normal distribution, 68.26% of the values are within ± 1 standard deviation of the mean. From Figure 6.11, you can see that 95.44% of the values are within ± 2 standard deviations of the mean. Thus, 95.44% of the download times are between 3 and 11 seconds. From Figure 6.12, you can see that 99.73% of the values are within ± 3 standard deviations above or below the mean.

FIGURE 6.11
Finding $P(3 < X < 11)$

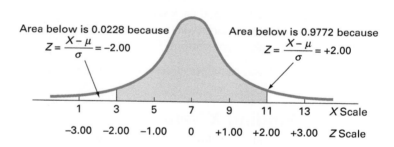

FIGURE 6.12
Finding $P(1 < X < 13)$

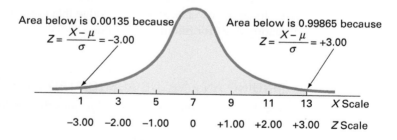

Thus, 99.73% of the load times are between 1 and 13 seconds. Therefore, it is unlikely (0.0027, or only 27 in 10,000) that a load time will be so fast or so slow that it will take less than 1 second or more than 13 seconds. In general, you can use 6σ (i.e., 3 standard deviations below the mean to 3 standard deviations above the mean) as a practical approximation of the range for normally distributed data.

Figures 6.10, 6.11, and 6.12 illustrate that for any normal distribution,

- Approximately 68.26% of the values fall within ± 1 standard deviation of the mean
- Approximately 95.44% of the values fall within ± 2 standard deviations of the mean
- Approximately 99.73% of the values fall within ± 3 standard deviations of the mean

This result is the justification for the empirical rule presented on page 122. The accuracy of the empirical rule increases the closer the variable follows the normal distribution.

VISUAL EXPLORATIONS

Exploring the Normal Distribution

Open the **VE-Normal Distribution add-in workbook** to explore the normal distribution. (For Excel technical requirements, see Appendix D.) When this workbook opens properly, it adds a Normal Distribution menu in the Add-ins tab (Apple menu in OS X Excel).

To explore the effects of changing the mean and standard deviation on the area under a normal distribution curve, select **Normal Distribution → Probability Density Function**. The add-in displays a normal curve for the MyTVLab website download example and a floating control panel (top right). Use the control panel spinner buttons to change the values for the mean, standard deviation, and *X* value and then note the effects of these changes on the probability of *X* < value and the corresponding shaded area under the curve. To see the normal curve labeled with *Z* values, click **Z Values**. Click **Reset** to reset the control panel values. Click **Finish** to finish exploring.

To create shaded areas under the curve for problems similar to Examples 6.2 and 6.3, select **Normal Distribution → Areas**. In the Areas dialog box (bottom right), enter values, select an Area Option, and click **OK**. The add-in creates a normal distribution curve with areas that are shaded according to the values you entered.

Finding *X* Values

Examples 6.1 through 6.3 require you to use the normal distribution Table E.2 to find an area under the normal curve that corresponds to a specific *X* value. For other situations, you may need to do the reverse: Find the *X* value that corresponds to a specific area. In general, you use Equation (6.3) for finding an *X* value.

> **FINDING AN *X* VALUE ASSOCIATED WITH A KNOWN PROBABILITY**
>
> The *X* value is equal to the mean, μ, plus the product of the *Z* value and the standard deviation, σ.
>
> $$X = \mu + Z\sigma \qquad\qquad \textbf{(6.3)}$$

To find a *particular* value associated with a known probability, follow these steps:

- Sketch the normal curve and then place the values for the mean and *X* on the *X* and *Z* scales.
- Find the cumulative area less than *X*.
- Shade the area of interest.
- Using Table E.2, determine the *Z* value corresponding to the area under the normal curve less than *X*.
- Using Equation (6.3), solve for *X*: $X = \mu + Z\sigma$

Examples 6.4 and 6.5 illustrate this technique demonstrate using the five-step procedure to find a particular value associated with a known probability.

EXAMPLE 6.4

Finding the X Value for a Cumulative Probability of 0.10

How much time (in seconds) will elapse before the fastest 10% of the MyTVLab sales pages load time occur?

SOLUTION Because 10% of the load times are expected to occur in under X seconds, the area under the normal curve less than this value is 0.1000. Using the body of Table E.2, you search for the area or probability of 0.1000. The closest result is 0.1003, as shown in Table 6.3 (which is extracted from Table E.2).

TABLE 6.3
Finding a Z Value Corresponding to a Particular Cumulative Area (0.10) Under the Normal Curve

Source: Extracted from Table E.2.

Cumulative Probabilities

Z	.00	.01	.02	.03	.04	.05	.06	.07	.08	.09
⋮	⋮	⋮	⋮	⋮	⋮	⋮	⋮	⋮	⋮	⋮
−1.5	.0668	.0655	.0643	.0630	.0618	.0606	.0594	.0582	.0571	.0559
−1.4	.0808	.0793	.0778	.0764	.0749	.0735	.0721	.0708	.0694	.0681
−1.3	.0968	.0951	.0934	.0918	.0901	.0885	.0869	.0853	.0838	.0823
−1.2	.1151	.1131	.1112	.1093	.1075	.0156	.0138	.1020	.1003	.0985

Working from this area to the margins of the table, you find that the Z value corresponding to the particular Z row (−1.2) and Z column (.08) is −1.28 (see Figure 6.13).

FIGURE 6.13
Finding Z to determine X

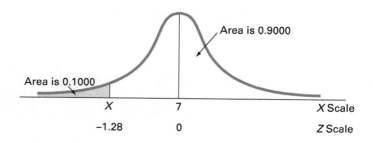

Once you find Z, you use Equation (6.3) on page 198 to determine the X value. Substituting $\mu = 7$, $\sigma = 2$, and $Z = -1.28$,

$$X = \mu + Z\sigma$$
$$X = 7 + (-1.28)(2) = 4.44 \text{ seconds}$$

Thus, 10% of the load times are 4.44 seconds or less.

EXAMPLE 6.5

Finding the *X* Values That Include 95% of the Download Times

What are the lower and upper values of *X*, symmetrically distributed around the mean, that include 95% of the load times for the MyTVLab sales page?

You need to find the lower value of *X* (called X_L). Then, you find the upper value of *X* (called X_U). Because 95% of the values are between X_L and X_U, and because X_L and X_U are equally distant from the mean, 2.5% of the values are below X_L (see Figure 6.14).

FIGURE 6.14

Finding *Z* to determine X_L

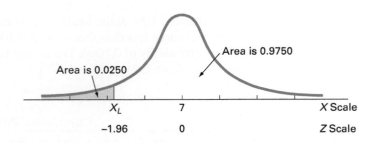

Although X_L is not known, you can find the corresponding *Z* value because the area under the normal curve less than this *Z* is 0.0250. Using the body of Table 6.4, you search for the probability 0.0250.

TABLE 6.4

Finding a *Z* Value Corresponding to a Cumulative Area of 0.025 Under the Normal Curve

Source: Extracted from Table E.2.

					Cumulative Area					
Z	.00	.01	.02	.03	.04	.05	.06	.07	.08	.09
⋮	⋮	⋮	⋮	⋮	⋮	⋮	⋮	⋮	⋮	⋮
−2.0	.0228	.0222	.0217	.0212	.0207	.0202	.0197	.0192	.0188	.0183
−1.9	.0287	.0281	.0274	.0268	.0262	.0256	.0250	.0244	.0239	.0233
−1.8	.0359	.0351	.0344	.0336	.0329	.0232	.0314	.0307	.0301	.0294

Working from the body of the table to the margins of the table, you see that the *Z* value corresponding to the particular *Z* row (−1.9) and *Z* column (.06) is −1.96.

Once you find *Z*, the final step is to use Equation (6.3) on page 198 as follows:

$$X = \mu + Z\sigma$$
$$= 7 + (-1.96)(2)$$
$$= 7 - 3.92$$
$$= 3.08 \text{ seconds}$$

You use a similar process to find X_U. Because only 2.5% of the load times take longer than X_U seconds, 97.5% of the load times take less than X_U seconds. From the symmetry of the normal distribution, you find that the desired *Z* value, as shown in Figure 6.15 on page 201, is +1.96 (because *Z* lies to the right of the standardized mean of 0). You can also extract this *Z* value from Table 6.5. You can see that 0.975 is the area under the normal curve less than the *Z* value of +1.96.

▶ *(continued)*

FIGURE 6.15
Finding Z to determine X_U

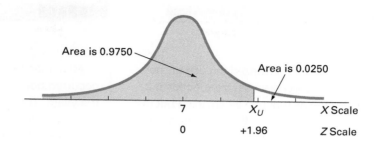

Area is 0.9750

Area is 0.0250

| | 7 | X_U | X Scale |
| | 0 | +1.96 | Z Scale |

TABLE 6.5
Finding a Z Value
Corresponding to
a Cumulative Area
of 0.975 Under the
Normal Curve

Source: Extracted from
Table E.2.

					Cumulative Area					
Z	**.00**	**.01**	**.02**	**.03**	**.04**	**.05**	**.06**	**.07**	**.08**	**.09**
⋮	⋮	⋮	⋮	⋮	⋮	⋮	⋮	⋮	⋮	⋮
+1.8	.9641	.9649	.9656	.9664	.9671	.9678	.9686	.9693	.9699	.9706
+1.9	.9713	.9719	.9726	.9732	.9738	.9744	.9750	.9756	.9761	.9767
+2.0	.9772	.9778	.9783	.9788	.9793	.9798	.9803	.9808	.9812	.9817

Using Equation (6.3) on page 198,

$$X = \mu + Z\sigma$$
$$= 7 + (+1.96)(2)$$
$$= 7 + 3.92$$
$$= 10.92 \text{ seconds}$$

Therefore, 95% of the load times are between 3.08 and 10.92 seconds.

Instead of looking up cumulative probabilities in a table, you can use Excel to compute normal probabilities. Figure 6.16 displays, in two parts, an Excel worksheet that computes normal probabilities and finds X values for problems similar to Examples 6.1 through 6.5. In this worksheet, NORM.DIST determines an area under a curve, STANDARDIZE performs the Z transformation [Equation (6.2) on page 192], NORM.S.INV performs the lookups that Tables 6.3 through 6.5 illustrate, and NORM.INV performs the X value calculation that Examples 6.4 and 6.5 on pages 199 and 200 illustrate.

FIGURE 6.16
Excel worksheet for
computing normal
probabilities and finding
X values (shown in two
parts)

CONSIDER THIS

What Is Normal?

Ironically, the statistician who popularized the use of "normal" to describe the distribution discussed in Section 6.2 was someone who saw the distribution as anything but the everyday, anticipated occurrence that the adjective *normal* usually suggests.

Starting with an 1894 paper, Karl Pearson argued that measurements of phenomena do not naturally, or "normally," conform to the classic bell shape. While this principle underlies much of statistics today, Pearson's point of view was radical to contemporaries who saw the world as standardized and normal. Pearson changed minds by showing that some populations are naturally *skewed* (coining that term in passing), and he helped put to rest the notion that the normal distribution underlies all phenomena.

Today, people still make the type of mistake that Pearson refuted. As a student, you are probably familiar with discussions about grade inflation, a real phenomenon at many schools. But have you ever realized that a "proof" of this inflation—that there are "too few" low grades because grades are skewed toward A's and B's—wrongly implies that grades should be "normally" distributed? Because college students represent small *nonrandom* samples, there are plenty of reasons to suspect that the distribution of grades would not be "normal."

Misunderstandings about the normal distribution have occurred both in business and in the public sector through the years. These misunderstandings have caused a number of business blunders and have sparked several public policy debates, including the causes of the collapse of large financial institutions in 2008. According to one theory, the investment banking industry's application of the normal distribution to assess risk may have contributed to the global collapse (see "A Finer Formula for Assessing Risks," *The New York Times*, May 11, 2010, p. B2 and reference 8). Using the normal distribution led these banks to overestimate the probability of having stable market conditions and underestimate the chance of unusually large market losses.

According to this theory, the use of other distributions that have less area in the middle of their curves, and, therefore, more in the "tails" that represent unusual market outcomes, may have led to less serious losses.

As you study this chapter, make sure you understand the assumptions that must hold for the proper use of the "normal" distribution, assumptions that were not explicitly verified by the investment bankers. And, most importantly, always remember that the name *normal distribution* does not mean normal in the everyday sense of the word.

PROBLEMS FOR SECTION 6.2

LEARNING THE BASICS

6.1 Given a standardized normal distribution (with a mean of 0 and a standard deviation of 1, as in Table E.2), what is the probability that
a. Z is less than 1.57?
b. Z is greater than 1.84?
c. Z is between 1.57 and 1.84?
d. Z is less than 1.57 or greater than 1.84?

6.2 Given a standardized normal distribution (with a mean of 0 and a standard deviation of 1, as in Table E.2), what is the probability that
a. Z is between −1.57 and 1.84?
b. Z is less than −1.57 or greater than 1.84?
c. What is the value of Z if only 2.5 percent of all possible Z values are larger?
d. Between what two values of Z (symmetrically distributed around the mean) will 68.26 percent of all possible Z values be contained?

6.3 Given a standardized normal distribution (with a mean of 0 and a standard deviation of 1, as in Table E.2), what is the probability that

a. Z is less than 1.08?
b. Z is greater than −0.21?
c. Z is less than −0.21 or greater than the mean?
d. Z is less than −0.21 or greater than 1.08?

6.4 Given a standardized normal distribution (with a mean of 0 and a standard deviation of 1, as in Table E.2), determine the following probabilities:
a. $P(Z > 1.08)$
b. $P(Z < -0.21)$
c. $P(-1.96 < Z < -0.21)$
d. What is the value of Z if only 15.87 percent of all possible Z values are larger?

6.5 Given a normal distribution with $\mu = 100$ and $\sigma = 10$, what is the probability that
a. $X > 75$?
b. $X < 70$?
c. $X < 80$ or $X > 110$?
d. Between what two X values (symmetrically distributed around the mean) are eighty percent of the values?

6.6 Given a normal distribution with $\mu = 50$ and $\sigma = 4$, what is the probability that
a. $X > 43$?
b. $X < 42$?
c. Five percent of the values are less than what X value?
d. Between what two X values (symmetrically distributed around the mean) are sixty percent of the values?

APPLYING THE CONCEPTS

6.7 In 2014, the per capita consumption of bottled water in the United States was reported to be 34 gallons. (Data extracted from **bottledwater.org/economics/bottled-water-market**.) Assume that the per capita consumption of bottled water in the United States is approximately normally distributed with a mean of 34 gallons and a standard deviation of 10 gallons.
a. What is the probability that someone in the United States consumed more than 33 gallons of bottled water in 2014?
b. What is the probability that someone in the United States consumed between 10 and 20 gallons of bottled water in 2014?
c. What is the probability that someone in the United States consumed less than 10 gallons of bottled water in 2014?
d. Ninety-nine percent of the people in the United States consumed less than how many gallons of bottled water?

✓ SELF TEST **6.8** Toby's Trucking Company determined that the distance traveled per truck per year is normally distributed, with a mean of 50 thousand miles and a standard deviation of 12 thousand miles.
a. What proportion of trucks can be expected to travel between 34 and 50 thousand miles in a year?
b. What percentage of trucks can be expected to travel either less than 30 or more than 60 thousand miles in a year?
c. How many miles will be traveled by at least eighty percent of the trucks?
d. What are your answers to (a) through (c) if the standard deviation is 10 thousand miles?

6.9 Consumers spent an average of $15.30 on a meal at a restaurant in 2014. (Data extracted from **bit.ly/1KVWWxT**) Assume that the amount spent on a restaurant meal is normally distributed and that the standard deviation is $2.
a. What is the probability that a randomly selected person spent more than $16?
b. What is the probability that a randomly selected person spent between $10 and $12?
c. Between what two values will the middle ninety-five percent of the amounts spent fall?

6.10 A set of final examination grades in an introductory statistics course is normally distributed, with a mean of 73 and a standard deviation of 8.
a. What is the probability that a student scored below 91 on this exam?

b. What is the probability that a student scored between 65 and 89?
c. The probability is five percent that a student taking the test scores higher than what grade?
d. If the professor grades on a curve (i.e., gives As to the top ten percent of the class, regardless of the score), are you better off with a grade of 81 on this exam or a grade of 68 on a different exam, where the mean is 62 and the standard deviation is 3? Show your answer statistically and explain.

6.11 A Nielsen study indicates that 18- to 24- year olds spend a mean of 174 minutes watching video on their smartphones per month. (Data extracted from **bit.ly/1HVOgkZ**.) Assume that the amount of time watching video on a smartphone per month is normally distributed and that the standard deviation is 15 minutes.
a. What is the probability that an 18- to 24-year-old spends less than 150 minutes watching video on his or her smartphone per month?
b. What is the probability that an 18- to 24-year-old spends between 150 and 198 minutes watching video on his or her smartphone per month?
c. What is the probability that an 18- to 24-year-old spends more than 198 minutes watching video on his or her smartphone per month?
d. One percent of all 18- to 24-year-olds will spend less than how many minutes watching video on his or her smartphone per month?

6.12 In 2014, the per capita consumption of soft drinks in the United States was reported to be 42.1 gallons. (Data extracted from beverage-digest.com/pdf/top-10_2015.pdf.). Assume that the per capita consumption of soft drinks in the United States is approximately normally distributed with a mean of 42.1 gallons and a standard deviation of 13 gallons.
a. What is the probability that someone in the United States consumed more than 60 gallons of soft drinks in 2014?
b. What is the probability that someone in the United States consumed between 15 and 30 gallons of soft drinks in 2014?
c. What is the probability that someone in the United States consumed less than 15 gallons of soft drinks in 2014?
d. Ninety-nine percent of the people in the United States consumed less than how many gallons of soft drinks?

6.13 Many manufacturing problems involve the matching of machine parts, such as shafts that fit into a valve hole. A particular design requires a shaft with a diameter of 22.000 mm, but shafts with diameters between 21.990 mm and 22.010 mm are acceptable. Suppose that the manufacturing process yields shafts with diameters normally distributed, with a mean of 22.002 mm and a standard deviation of 0.005 mm. For this process, what is
a. the proportion of shafts with a diameter between 21.99 mm and 22.00 mm?
b. the probability that a shaft is acceptable?
c. the diameter that will be exceeded by only two percent of the shafts?
d. What would be your answers in (a) through (c) if the standard deviation of the shaft diameters were 0.004 mm?

6.3 Evaluating Normality

Recall the important theoretical properties of the normal distribution that Exhibit 6.1 lists on page 191. As Section 6.2 notes, many continuous variables used in business closely follow a normal distribution. To determine whether a set of data can be approximated by the normal distribution, you either compare the characteristics of the data with the theoretical properties of the normal distribution or construct a normal probability plot.

Comparing Data Characteristics to Theoretical Properties

Many continuous variables have characteristics that approximate theoretical properties. However, other continuous variables are often neither normally distributed nor approximately normally distributed. For such variables, the descriptive characteristics of the data are inconsistent with the properties of a normal distribution. For such a variable, you can compare the observed characteristics of the variable with what you would expect to occur if the variable follows a normal distribution. To use this method:

- Construct charts and observe their appearance. For small- or moderate-sized data sets, create a stem-and-leaf display or a boxplot. For large data sets, in addition, plot a histogram or polygon.
- Compute descriptive statistics and compare these statistics with the theoretical properties of the normal distribution. Compare the mean and median. Is the interquartile range approximately 1.33 times the standard deviation? Is the range approximately 6 times the standard deviation?
- Evaluate how the values are distributed. Determine whether approximately two-thirds of the values lie between the mean and ± 1 standard deviation. Determine whether approximately four-fifths of the values lie between the mean and ± 1.28 standard deviations. Determine whether approximately 19 out of every 20 values lie between the mean and ± 2 standard deviations.

For example, you can use these techniques to determine whether the one-year returns discussed in Chapters 2 and 3 (stored in Retirement Funds) follow a normal distribution.

Table 6.6 presents the descriptive statistics and the five-number summary for the one-year return percentage variable. Figure 6.17 presents the Excel boxplot for the one-year return percentages.

TABLE 6.6
Descriptive Statistics and Five-Number Summary for the One-Year Return Percentages

Descriptive Statistics		Five-Number Summary	
Mean	7.81	Minimum	−14.05
Median	8.94	First quartile	4.59
Mode	8.97	Median	8.94
Minimum	−14.05	Third quartile	11.66
Maximum	21.70	Maximum	21.70
Range	35.75		
Variance	29.59		
Standard deviation	5.44		
Coeff. of variation	69.62%		
Skewness	−0.90		
Kurtosis	1.18		
Count	407		
Standard error	0.27		

FIGURE 6.17
Excel boxplot for the one-year return percentages

Boxplot for One-Year Return Percentage

One-Year Return Percentage

From Table 6.6, Figure 6.17, and from an ordered array of the returns (not shown here), you can make the following statements about the one-year returns:

- The mean of 7.81 is less than the median of 8.94. (In a normal distribution, the mean and median are equal.)
- The boxplot is left-skewed. (The normal distribution is symmetrical.)

- The interquartile range of 7.07 is approximately 1.30 standard deviations. (In a normal distribution, the interquartile range is 1.33 standard deviations.)
- The range of 35.75 is equal to 6.57 standard deviations. (In a normal distribution, the range is approximately 6 standard deviations.)
- 72.48% of the returns are within ± 1 standard deviation of the mean. (In a normal distribution, 68.26% of the values lie within ± 1 standard deviation of the mean.)
- 83.54% of the returns are within ± 1.28 standard deviations of the mean. (In a normal distribution, 80% of the values lie within ± 1.28 standard deviations of the mean.)
- 95.05% of the returns are within ± 2 standard deviations of the mean. (In a normal distribution, 95.44% of the values lie within ± 2 standard deviations of the mean.)
- The skewness statistic is -0.8961 and the kurtosis statistic is 1.183. (In a normal distribution, each of these statistics equals zero.)

Based on these statements and the criteria given on page 204, you can conclude that the one-year returns are left-skewed and have slightly more values within ± 1 standard deviation of the mean than expected. The skewness is negative, and the kurtosis indicates a distribution that is more peaked than a normal distribution. Thus, you can conclude that the data characteristics of the one-year returns differ somewhat from the theoretical properties of a normal distribution.

Constructing the Normal Probability Plot

A **normal probability plot** is a visual display that helps you evaluate whether the data are normally distributed. One common plot is called the **quantile–quantile plot**. To create this plot, you first transform each ordered value to a Z value. For example, if you have a sample of $n = 19$, the Z value for the smallest value corresponds to a cumulative area of

$$\frac{1}{n + 1} = \frac{1}{19 + 1} = \frac{1}{20} = 0.05$$

The Z value for a cumulative area of 0.05 (from Table E.2) is -1.65. Table 6.7 illustrates the entire set of Z values for a sample of $n = 19$.

TABLE 6.7
Ordered Values and Corresponding Z Values for a Sample of $n = 19$

Ordered Value	Z Value	Ordered Value	Z Value	Ordered Value	Z Value
1	-1.65	8	-0.25	14	0.52
2	-1.28	9	-0.13	15	0.67
3	-1.04	10	-0.00	16	0.84
4	-0.84	11	0.13	17	1.04
5	-0.67	12	0.25	18	1.28
6	-0.52	13	0.39	19	1.65
7	-0.39				

In a quantile–quantile plot, the Z values are plotted on the X axis, and the corresponding values of the variable are plotted on the Y axis. If the data are normally distributed, the values will plot along an approximately straight line. Figure 6.18 illustrates the typical shape of the

FIGURE 6.18
Normal probability plots for a left-skewed distribution, a normal distribution, and a right-skewed distribution

Left-skewed
Panel A

Normal
Panel B

Right-skewed
Panel C

quantile–quantile normal probability plot for a left-skewed distribution (Panel A), a normal distribution (Panel B), and a right-skewed distribution (Panel C). If the data are left-skewed the curve will rise more rapidly at first and then level off. If the data are normally distributed the points will plot along an approximately straight line. If the data are right-skewed, the data will rise more slowly at first and then rise at a faster rate for higher values of the variable being plotted.

Figure 6.19 shows an Excel (quantile–quantile) normal probability plot for the one-year returns. The Excel quantile–quantile plot shows several low values followed by the bulk of the points that approximately follow a straight line except for a few high values.

FIGURE 6.19
Excel (quantile–quantile) normal probability plot for the one-year returns

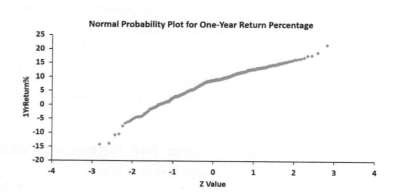

PROBLEMS FOR SECTION 6.3

LEARNING THE BASICS

6.14 Show that for a sample of $n = 39$, the smallest and largest Z values are -1.96 and $+1.96$, and the middle (i.e., 20th) Z value is 0.00.

6.15 For a sample of $n = 6$, list the six Z values.

APPLYING THE CONCEPTS

 6.16 The file SUV contains the overall miles per gallon (MPG) of 2015 small SUVs ($n = 20$):

26 22 24 22 26 21 24 25 28 24
22 21 22 21 24 23 23 22 21 22

Source: Data extracted from "Which Car Is Right for You," *Consumer Reports*, April 2015, pp. 60–61.

Decide whether the data appear to be approximately normally distributed by
a. comparing data characteristics to theoretical properties.
b. constructing a normal probability plot.

6.17 As player salaries have increased, the cost of attending basketball games has increased dramatically. The file NBACost contains the cost of four averaged-priced tickets, two beers, four soft drinks, four hot dogs, two game programs, two adult-sized caps, and one parking space at each of the 30 National Basketball Association arenas during the 2014–2015 season.

Source: Data extracted from *Team Marketing Report*, available at **bit.ly/1JEjYbO**.

Decide whether the data appear to be approximately normally distributed by
a. comparing data characteristics to theoretical properties.
b. constructing a normal probability plot.

6.18 The file Property Taxes contains the property taxes per capita for the 50 states and the District of Columbia. Decide whether the data appear to be approximately normally distributed by
a. comparing data characteristics to theoretical properties.
b. constructing a normal probability plot.

6.19 Thirty companies comprise the DJIA. How big are these companies? One common method for measuring the size of a company is to use its market capitalization, which is computed by multiplying the number of stock shares by the price of a share of stock. On May 6, 2015 the market capitalization of these companies ranged from Traveler's $32.6 billion to Apple's $724.7 billion. The entire population of market capitalization values is stored in DowMarketCap. (Data extracted from **money.cnn.com**, May 6, 2015.) Decide whether the market capitalization of companies in the DJIA appears to be approximately normally distributed by
a. comparing data characteristics to theoretical properties.
b. constructing a normal probability plot.
c. constructing a histogram.

6.20 One operation of a mill is to cut pieces of steel into parts that will later be used as the frame for front seats in an automotive plant. The steel is cut with a diamond saw, and the resulting parts must be within ± 0.005 inch of the length specified by the automobile company. The data come from a sample of 100 steel parts and are stored in Steel . The measurement reported is the difference, in inches, between the actual length of the steel part, as measured by a laser measurement device, and the specified length of the steel part. Determine whether the data appear to be approximately normally distributed by

a. comparing data characteristics to theoretical properties.
b. constructing a normal probability plot.

6.21 The file CD Rate contains the yields for a one-year certificate of deposit (CD) and a five-year CD for 25 banks in the United States, as of April 29, 2015. (Data extracted from **www.Bankrate.com**, April 29, 2015.) For each type of investment, decide whether the data appear to be approximately normally distributed by

a. comparing data characteristics to theoretical properties.
b. constructing a normal probability plot.

6.22 The file Utility contains the electricity costs, in dollars, during July 2015 for a random sample of 50 one-bedroom apartments in a large city:

96	171	202	178	147	102	153	197	127	82
157	185	90	116	172	111	148	213	130	165
141	149	206	175	123	128	144	168	109	167
95	163	150	154	130	143	187	166	139	149
108	119	183	151	114	135	191	137	129	158

Decide whether the data appear to be approximately normally distributed by

a. comparing data characteristics to theoretical properties.
b. constructing a normal probability plot.

6.4 The Uniform Distribution

In the **uniform distribution**, the values are evenly distributed in the range between the smallest value, a, and the largest value, b. Because of its shape, the uniform distribution is sometimes called the **rectangular distribution** (see Panel B of Figure 6.1 on page 190). Equation (6.4) defines the probability density function for the uniform distribution.

UNIFORM PROBABILITY DENSITY FUNCTION

$$f(X) = \frac{1}{b - a} \text{ if } a \leq X \leq b \text{ and 0 elsewhere} \tag{6.4}$$

where

$$a = \text{minimum value of } X$$
$$b = \text{maximum value of } X$$

Equation (6.5) defines the mean of the uniform distribution, and Equation (6.6) defines the variance and standard deviation of the uniform distribution.

MEAN OF THE UNIFORM DISTRIBUTION

$$\mu = \frac{a + b}{2} \tag{6.5}$$

VARIANCE AND STANDARD DEVIATION OF THE UNIFORM DISTRIBUTION

$$\sigma^2 = \frac{(b - a)^2}{12} \tag{6.6a}$$

$$\sigma = \sqrt{\frac{(b - a)^2}{12}} \tag{6.6b}$$

One of the most common uses of the uniform distribution is in the selection of random numbers. When you use simple random sampling (see Section 1.3), you assume that each random digit comes from a uniform distribution that has a minimum value of 0 and a maximum value of 9.

Figure 6.20 illustrates the uniform distribution with $a = 0$ and $b = 1$. The total area inside the rectangle is equal to the base (1.0) times the height (1.0). Thus, the resulting area of 1.0 satisfies the requirement that the area under any probability density function equals 1.0.

FIGURE 6.20
Probability density
function for a uniform
distribution with $a = 0$
and $b = 1$

In this uniform distribution, what is the probability of getting a random number between 0.10 and 0.30? The area between 0.10 and 0.30, depicted in Figure 6.21, is equal to the base (which is $0.30 - 0.10 = 0.20$) times the height (1.0). Therefore,

$$P(0.10 < X < 0.30) = (\text{Base})(\text{Height}) = (0.20)(1.0) = 0.20$$

FIGURE 6.21
Finding
$P(0.10 < X < 0.30)$ for a
uniform distribution with
$a = 0$ and $b = 1$

From Equations (6.5) and (6.6), the mean and standard deviation of the uniform distribution for $a = 0$ and $b = 1$ are computed as follows:

$$\mu = \frac{a + b}{2}$$
$$= \frac{0 + 1}{2} = 0.5$$

and

$$\sigma^2 = \frac{(b - a)^2}{12}$$
$$= \frac{(1 - 0)^2}{12}$$
$$= \frac{1}{12} = 0.0833$$
$$\sigma = \sqrt{0.0833} = 0.2887.$$

Thus, the mean is 0.5, and the standard deviation is 0.2887.

Example 6.6 provides another application of the uniform distribution.

EXAMPLE 6.6

Computing Uniform Probabilities

In the MyTVLab scenario on page 189, the load time of the new sales page was assumed to be normally distributed with a mean of 7 seconds. Suppose that the load time follows a uniform (instead of a normal) distribution between 4.5 and 9.5 seconds. What is the probability that a load time will take more than 9 seconds?

SOLUTION   The load time is uniformly distributed from 4.5 to 9.5 seconds. The area between 9 and 9.5 seconds is equal to 0.5 seconds, and the total area in the distribution is $9.5 - 4.5 = 5$ seconds. Therefore, the probability of a load time between 9 and 9.5 seconds is the portion of the area greater than 9, which is equal to $0.5/5.0 = 0.10$. Because 9.5 is the maximum value in this distribution, the probability of a load time above 9 seconds is 0.10. In comparison, if the load time is normally distributed with a mean of 7 seconds and a standard deviation of 2 seconds (see Example 6.1 on page 196), the probability of a load time above 9 seconds is 0.1587.

PROBLEMS FOR SECTION 6.4

LEARNING THE BASICS

6.23 Suppose you select one value from a uniform distribution with $a = 0$ and $b = 10$. What is the probability that the value will be
a. between 5 and 7?
b. between 2 and 3?
c. What is the mean?
d. What is the standard deviation?

APPLYING THE CONCEPTS

SELF TEST **6.24** The time between arrivals of customers at a bank during the noon-to-1 P.M. hour has a uniform distribution between 0 to 120 seconds. What is the probability that the time between the arrival of two customers will be
a. less than 20 seconds?
b. between 10 and 30 seconds?
c. more than 35 seconds?
d. What are the mean and standard deviation of the time between arrivals?

6.25 A study of the time spent shopping in a supermarket for a market basket of 20 specific items showed an approximately uniform distribution between 20 minutes and 40 minutes. What is the probability that the shopping time will be

a. between 25 and 30 minutes?
b. less than 35 minutes?
c. What are the mean and standard deviation of the shopping time?

6.26 How long does it take to download a two-hour movie from the iTunes store? According to Apple's technical support site, **support.apple.com/HT201587**, downloading such a movie using a 5 Mbit/s broadband connection should take 18 to 24 minutes. Assume that the download times are uniformly distributed between 18 and 24 minutes. If you download a two-hour movie, what is the probability that the download time will be
a. less than 19 minutes?
b. more than 23 minutes?
c. between 20 and 22 minutes?
d. What are the mean and standard deviation of the download times?

6.27 The scheduled commuting time on the Long Island Railroad from Glen Cove to New York City is 65 minutes. Suppose that the actual commuting time is uniformly distributed between 64 and 74 minutes. What is the probability that the commuting time will be
a. less than 70 minutes?
b. between 65 and 70 minutes?
c. greater than 65 minutes?
d. What are the mean and standard deviation of the commuting time?

6.5 The Exponential Distribution

The **exponential distribution** is a continuous distribution that is right-skewed and ranges from 0 to positive infinity (see Figure 6.1 on page 190). The **Section 6.5 online topic** discusses this distribution and illustrates its application.

6.6 The Normal Approximation to the Binomial Distribution

In many circumstances, the normal distribution can be used to approximate the binomial distribution, discussed in Section 5.2. The **Section 6.6 online topic** discusses this technique and illustrates its use.

▼ USING STATISTICS
Normal Load Times…, Revisited

In the Normal Downloading at MyTVLab scenario, you were the sales and marketing vice president for a web-based business. You sought to ensure that the load time for a new sales web page would be within a certain range. By running experiments in the corporate offices, you determined that the amount of time, in seconds, that passes from first pointing a browser to a web page until the web page is fully loaded is a bell-shaped distribution with a mean load time of 7 seconds and standard deviation of 2 seconds. Using the normal distribution, you were able to calculate that approximately 84% of the load times are 9 seconds or less, and 95% of the load times are between 3.08 and 10.92 seconds.

Now that you understand how to compute probabilities from the normal distribution, you can evaluate load times of similar sales web pages that use other designs. For example, if the standard deviation remained at 2 seconds, lowering the mean to 6 seconds would shift the entire distribution lower by 1 second. Thus, approximately 84% of the load times would be 8 seconds or less, and 95% of the load times would be between 2.08 and 9.92 seconds. Another change that could reduce long load times would be reducing the variation. For example, consider the case where the mean remained at the original 7 seconds but the standard deviation was reduced to 1 second. Again, approximately 84% of the load times would be 8 seconds or less, and 95% of the load times would be between 5.04 and 8.96 seconds.

▼ SUMMARY

In this and the previous chapter, you have learned about mathematical models called probability distributions and how they can be used to solve business problems. In Chapter 5, you used discrete probability distributions in situations where the values come from a counting process such as the number of social media sites to which you belong or the number of tagged order forms in a report generated by an accounting information system. In this chapter, you learned about continuous probability distributions where the values come from a measuring process such as your height or the download time of a video.

Continuous probability distributions come in various shapes, but the most common and most important in business is the normal distribution. The normal distribution is symmetrical; thus, its mean and median are equal. It is also

bell-shaped, and approximately 68.26% of its values are within ±1 standard deviation of the mean, approximately 95.44% of its values are within ±2 standard deviations of the mean, and approximately 99.73% of its values are within ±3 standard deviations of the mean. Although many variables in business are closely approximated by the normal distribution, do not think that all variables can be approximated by the normal distribution.

In Section 6.3, you learned about various methods for evaluating normality in order to determine whether the normal distribution is a reasonable mathematical model to use in specific situations. In Section 6.4, you learned about another continuous distribution, the uniform distribution, that was not normal. Chapter 7 uses the normal distribution to develop the subject of statistical inference.

▼ REFERENCES

1. Gunter, B. "Q-Q Plots." *Quality Progress* (February 1994): 81–86.
2. Hogg, R. V., J. T. McKean, and A. V. Craig. *Introduction to Mathematical Statistics*, 7th ed. New York: Pearson Education, 2013.
3. Kishnan, S. and R. Sitaraman. "Video stream quality impacts viewer behavior: inferring causality using quasi-experimental designs," in *Proceedings of the 2012 ACM conference on Internet measurement conference*: 211–224. New York: ACM.
4. Levine, D. M., P. Ramsey, and R. Smidt. *Applied Statistics for Engineers and Scientists Using Microsoft Excel and Minitab*. Upper Saddle River, NJ: Prentice Hall, 2001.
5. Miller, J. "Earliest Known Uses of Some of the Words of Mathematics." **jeff560.tripod.com/mathword.html**.
6. Pearl, R. "Karl Pearson, 1857–1936." *Journal of the American Statistical Association*, 31 (1936): 653–664.
7. Pearson, E. S. "Some Incidents in the Early History of Biometry and Statistics, 1890–94." *Biometrika* 52 (1965): 3–18.
8. Taleb, N. *The Black Swan*, 2nd ed. New York: Random House, 2010.
9. Walker, H. "The Contributions of Karl Pearson." *Journal of the American Statistical Association* 53 (1958): 11–22.

KEY EQUATIONS

Normal Probability Density Function

$$f(X) = \frac{1}{\sqrt{2\pi}\sigma}e^{-(1/2)[(X-\mu)/\sigma]^2} \qquad (6.1)$$

Transformation Formula

$$Z = \frac{X - \mu}{\sigma} \qquad (6.2)$$

Finding an X Value Associated with a Known Probability

$$X = \mu + Z\sigma \qquad (6.3)$$

Uniform Probability Density Function

$$f(X) = \frac{1}{b - a} \qquad (6.4)$$

Mean of the Uniform Distribution

$$\mu = \frac{a + b}{2} \qquad (6.5)$$

Variance and Standard Deviation of the Uniform Distribution

$$\sigma^2 = \frac{(b - a)^2}{12} \qquad (6.6a)$$

$$\sigma = \sqrt{\frac{(b - a)^2}{12}} \qquad (6.6b)$$

KEY TERMS

cumulative standardized normal distribution   193
exponential distribution   190
normal distribution   190
normal probability plot   205

probability density function   190
probability density function for the normal distribution   192
quantile–quantile plot   205
rectangular distribution   207

standardized normal variable   192
transformation formula   192
uniform distribution   190

CHECKING YOUR UNDERSTANDING

6.28 How do you find the area between two values under the normal curve?

6.29 How do you find the X value that corresponds to a given percentile of the normal distribution?

6.30 What are some of the distinguishing properties of a normal distribution?

6.31 How does the shape of the normal distribution differ from the shapes of the uniform and exponential distributions?

6.32 How can you use the normal probability plot to evaluate whether a set of data is normally distributed?

CHAPTER REVIEW PROBLEMS

6.33 An industrial sewing machine uses ball bearings that are targeted to have a diameter of 0.75 inch. The lower and upper specification limits under which the ball bearings can operate are 0.74 inch and 0.76 inch, respectively. Past experience has indicated that the actual diameter of the ball bearings is approximately normally distributed, with a mean of 0.753 inch and a standard deviation of 0.004 inch. What is the probability that a ball bearing is
a. between the target and the actual mean?
b. between the lower specification limit and the target?
c. above the upper specification limit?
d. below the lower specification limit?
e. Of all the ball bearings, 93% of the diameters are greater than what value?

6.34 The fill amount in 2-liter soft drink bottles is normally distributed, with a mean of 2.0 liters and a standard deviation of 0.05 liter. If bottles contain less than 95% of the listed net content (1.90 liters, in this case), the manufacturer may be subject to pen-

alty by the state office of consumer affairs. Bottles that have a net content above 2.10 liters may cause excess spillage upon opening. What proportion of the bottles will contain
a. between 1.90 and 2.0 liters?
b. between 1.90 and 2.10 liters?
c. below 1.90 liters or above 2.10 liters?
d. At least how much soft drink is contained in 99% of the bottles?
e. Ninety-nine percent of the bottles contain an amount that is between which two values (symmetrically distributed) around the mean?

6.35 In an effort to reduce the number of bottles that contain less than 1.90 liters, the bottler in Problem 6.34 sets the filling machine so that the mean is 2.02 liters. Under these circumstances, what are your answers in Problem 6.34 (a) through (e)?

6.36 Webrooming, researching products online before buying them in store, has become the new norm for today's connected consumers; this is in contrast to showrooming, researching products in a physical store before purchasing online. A recent study by Interactions reported that most shoppers have a specific spending limit in place while shopping online. Findings indicate that men spend a mean of $250 online before they decide to visit a store. (Data extracted from Retail Touchpoints, "88% of Shoppers Are Webrooming," **bit.ly/1JEcmqh**.) Assume that the spending limit is normally distributed and that the standard deviation is $20.

a. What is the probability that a male spent less than $210 online before deciding to visit a store?

b. What is the probability that a male spent between $270 and $300 online before deciding to visit a store?

c. Ninety percent of the amounts spent online by a male before deciding to visit a store are less than what value?

d. Eighty percent of the amounts spent online by a male before deciding to visit a store are between what two values symmetrically distributed around the mean?

6.37 The file DomesticBeer contains the percentage alcohol, number of calories per 12 ounces, and number of carbohydrates (in grams) per 12 ounces for 158 of the best-selling domestic beers in the United States. Determine whether each of these variables appears to be approximately normally distributed. Support your decision through the use of appropriate statistics and graphs. (Data extracted from **www.Beer100.com**, February 3, 2015.)

6.38 The evening manager of a restaurant was very concerned about the length of time some customers were waiting in line to be seated. She also had some concern about the seating times—that is, the length of time between when a customer is seated and the time he or she leaves the restaurant. Over the course of one week, 100 customers (no more than 1 per party) were randomly selected, and their waiting and seating times (in minutes) were recorded in Wait.

a. Think about your favorite restaurant. Do you think waiting times more closely resemble a uniform, an exponential, or a normal distribution?

b. Again, think about your favorite restaurant. Do you think seating times more closely resemble a uniform, an exponential, or a normal distribution?

c. Construct a histogram and a normal probability plot of the waiting times. Do you think these waiting times more closely resemble a uniform, an exponential, or a normal distribution?

d. Construct a histogram and a normal probability plot of the seating times. Do you think these seating times more closely resemble a uniform, an exponential, or a normal distribution?

6.39 The major stock market indexes had strong results in 2014. The mean one-year return for stocks in the S&P 500, a group of 500 very large companies, was +11.4%. The mean one-year return for the NASDAQ, a group of 3,200 small and medium-sized companies, was +13.4%. Historically, the one-year returns are approximately normally distributed, the standard deviation in the S&P 500 is approximately 20%, and the standard deviation in the NASDAQ is approximately 30%.

a. What is the probability that a stock in the S&P 500 gained value in 2014?

b. What is the probability that a stock in the S&P 500 gained 10% or more in 2014?

c. What is the probability that a stock in the S&P 500 lost 20% or more in 2014?

d. What is the probability that a stock in the S&P 500 lost 30% or more in 2014?

e. Repeat (a) through (d) for a stock in the NASDAQ.

f. Write a short summary on your findings. Be sure to include a discussion of the risks associated with a large standard deviation.

6.40 Interns report that when deciding on where to work, career growth, salary and compensation, location and commute, and company culture and values are important factors to them. According to reports by interns to Glassdoor, the mean monthly pay of interns at Intel is $5,988. (Data extracted from **read.bi/1T6rdwr**. Suppose that the intern monthly pay is normally distributed, with a standard deviation of $400. What is the probability that the monthly pay of an intern at Intel is

a. less than $5,900?

b. between $5,700 and $6,100?

c. above $6,500?

d. Ninety-nine percent of the intern monthly pays are higher than what value?

e. Ninety-five percent of the intern monthly pays are between what two values, symmetrically distributed around the mean?

6.41 According to the same Glassdoor source mentioned in Problem 6.40, the mean monthly pay for interns at Facebook is $6,058. Suppose that the intern monthly pay is normally distributed, with a standard deviation of $500. What is the probability that the monthly pay of an intern at Facebook is

a. less than $5,900?

b. between $5,700 and $6,100?

c. above $6,500?

d. Ninety-nine percent of the intern monthly pays are higher than what value?

e. Ninety-five percent of the intern monthly pays are between what two values, symmetrically distributed around the mean?

f. Compare the results for the Intel interns computed in Problem 6.40 to those of the Facebook interns.

6.42 (Class Project) One theory about the daily changes in the closing price of a stock is that these changes follow a *random walk*—that is, these daily events are independent of each other and move upward or downward in a random manner—and can be approximated by a normal distribution. To test this theory, use either a newspaper or the Internet to select one company traded on the NYSE, one company traded on the American Stock Exchange, and one company traded on the NASDAQ and then do the following:

1. Record the daily closing stock price of each of these companies for six consecutive weeks (so that you have 30 values per company).

2. Compute the daily changes in the closing stock price of each of these companies for six consecutive weeks (so that you have 30 values per company).

Note: The random-walk theory pertains to the daily changes in the closing stock price, not the daily closing stock price.

For each of your six data sets, decide whether the data are approximately normally distributed by

a. constructing the stem-and-leaf display, histogram or polygon and boxplot.

b. comparing data characteristics to theoretical properties.

c. constructing a normal probability plot.

d. Discuss the results of (a) through (c). What can you say about your three stocks with respect to daily closing prices and daily changes in closing prices? Which, if any, of the data sets are approximately normally distributed?

CHAPTER 6

▼CASES

Managing Ashland MultiComm Services

The AMS technical services department has embarked on a quality improvement effort. Its first project relates to maintaining the target upload speed for its Internet service subscribers. Upload speeds are measured on a standard scale in which the target value is 1.0. Data collected over the past year indicate that the upload speed is approximately normally distributed, with a mean of 1.005 and a standard deviation of 0.10. Each day, one upload speed is measured. The upload speed is considered acceptable if the measurement on the standard scale is between 0.95 and 1.05.

1. Assuming that the distribution of upload speed has not changed from what it was in the past year, what is the probability that the upload speed is
   a. less than 1.0?
   b. between 0.95 and 1.0?
   c. between 1.0 and 1.05?
   d. less than 0.95 or greater than 1.05?

2. The objective of the operations team is to reduce the probability that the upload speed is below 1.0. Should the team focus on process improvement that increases the mean upload speed to 1.05 or on process improvement that reduces the standard deviation of the upload speed to 0.075? Explain.

CardioGood Fitness

Return to the CardioGood Fitness case (stored in CardioGood Fitness) first presented on page 28.

1. For each CardioGood Fitness treadmill product line, determine whether the age, income, usage, and the number of miles the customer expects to walk/run each week can be approximated by the normal distribution.

2. Write a report to be presented to the management of CardioGood Fitness detailing your findings.

More Descriptive Choices Follow-up

Follow up the More Descriptive Choices Revisited Using Statistics scenario on page 136 by constructing normal probability plots for the 3-year return percentages, 5-year return percentages, and 10-year return percentages for the sample of 407 retirement funds stored in Retirement Funds . In your analysis, examine differences between the growth and value funds as well as the differences among the small, mid-cap, and large market cap funds.

Clear Mountain State Student Survey

The Student News Service at Clear Mountain State University (CMSU) has decided to gather data about the undergraduate students who attend CMSU. They create and distribute a survey of 14 questions and receive responses from 111 undergraduates (stored in StudentSurvey). For each numerical variable in the survey, decide whether the variable is approximately normally distributed by
   a. comparing data characteristics to theoretical properties.
   b. constructing a normal probability plot.
   c. writing a report summarizing your conclusions.

Digital Case

Apply your knowledge about the normal distribution in this Digital Case, which extends the Using Statistics scenario from this chapter.

To satisfy concerns of potential customers, the management of MyTVLab has undertaken a research project to learn how much time it takes users to load a complex video features page. The research team has collected data and has made some claims based on the assertion that the data follow a normal distribution.

Open **MTL_QRTStudy.pdf**, which documents the work of a quality response team at MyTVLab. Read the internal report that documents the work of the team and their conclusions. Then answer the following:

1. Can the collected data be approximated by the normal distribution?

2. Review and evaluate the conclusions made by the MyTVLab research team. Which conclusions are correct? Which ones are incorrect?

3. If MyTVLab could improve the mean time by 5 seconds, how would the probabilities change?

▾EXCEL GUIDE

EG6.1 CONTINUOUS PROBABILITY DISTRIBUTIONS

There are no Excel Guide instructions for this section.

EG6.2 THE NORMAL DISTRIBUTION

Key Technique Use the **NORM.DIST(***X value, mean, standard deviation,* **True**) function to compute normal probabilities and use the **NORM.S.INV(***percentage***)** function and the STANDARDIZE function (see Section EG3.2) to compute the Z value.

Example Compute the normal probabilities for Examples 6.1 through 6.3 on pages 196 and 197 and the X and Z values for Examples 6.4 and 6.5 on pages 199 and 200.

PHStat Use **Normal**.
For the example, select **PHStat → Probability & Prob. Distributions → Normal**. In this procedure's dialog box (shown below):

1. Enter **7** as the **Mean** and **2** as the **Standard Deviation**.
2. Check **Probability for: X <=** and enter **7** in its box.
3. Check **Probability for: X >** and enter **9** in its box.
4. Check **Probability for range** and enter **5** in the first box and **9** in the second box.
5. Check **X for Cumulative Percentage** and enter **10** in its box.
6. Check **X Values for Percentage** and enter **95** in its box.
7. Enter a **Title** and click **OK**.

Worksheet Use the **COMPUTE worksheet** of the **Normal workbook** as a template.
The worksheet already contains the data for solving the problems in Examples 6.1 through 6.5. For other problems, change the values for the **Mean, Standard Deviation, X**

Value, From X Value, To X Value, Cumulative Percentage, and/or **Percentage**.

Unlike most other Excel Guide COMPUTE worksheets, this worksheet uses formulas in column A to dynamically create labels based on the data values you enter. These formulas make extensive use of the ampersand operator (&) to construct the actual label. For example, the cell A10 formula **= "P(X< = "&B8&")"** results in the display of P(X<= 7) because the initial contents of cell B8, 7, is combined with "P(X<=" and ")". Changing the value in cell B8 to 9, changes the label in cell A10 to P(X<=9).

EG6.3 EVALUATING NORMALITY

Comparing Data Characteristics to Theoretical Properties

Use the Sections EG3.1 through EG3.3 instructions to compare data characteristics to theoretical properties.

Constructing the Normal Probability Plot

Key Technique Use an Excel Scatter (X, Y) chart with Z values computed using the NORM.S.INV function.

Example Construct the normal probability plot for the one-year return percentages for the sample of 407 retirement funds that is shown in Figure 6.19 on page 206.

PHStat Use **Normal Probability Plot**.
For the example, open to the **DATA worksheet** of the **Retirement Funds workbook**. Select **PHStat → Probability & Prob. Distributions → Normal Probability Plot**. In the procedure's dialog box (shown below):

1. Enter **I1:I408** as the **Variable Cell Range**.
2. Check **First cell contains label**.
3. Enter a **Title** and click **OK**.

In addition to the chart sheet containing the normal probability plot, the procedure creates a plot data worksheet identical to the PlotData worksheet discussed in the *Worksheet Excel* instructions.

Worksheet Use the worksheets of the **NPP workbook** as templates.

The **NormalPlot chart sheet** displays a normal probability plot using the rank, the proportion, the Z value, and the variable found in the **PLOT_DATA worksheet**. The PLOT_DATA worksheet already contains the one-year return percentages for the example.

To construct a plot for a different variable, paste the *sorted* values for that variable in **column D** of the **PLOT_DATA worksheet**. Adjust the number of ranks in **column A** and the divisor in the formulas in **column B** to compute cumulative percentages to reflect the quantity $n + 1$ (408 for the example). (Column C formulas use the NORM.S.INV function to compute the Z values for those cumulative percentages.)

If you have fewer than 407 values, delete rows from the bottom up. If you have more than 407 values, select row 408, right-click, click **Insert** in the shortcut menu, and copy down the formulas in columns B and C to the new rows. To create your own normal probability plot for the 1YrReturn% variable, open to the PLOT_DATA worksheet and select the cell range **C1:D408**. Then select **Insert → Scatter (X, Y) or Bubble Chart** (#5 in the labeled Charts groups) and select the **Scatter** gallery item. (OS X Excel labels the #5 icon as **X Y (Scatter)**).

Relocate the chart to a chart sheet, turn off the chart legend and gridlines, add axis titles, and modify the chart title.

7

Sampling Distributions

OBJECTIVES

- Learn about the concept of the sampling distribution
- Compute probabilities related to the sample mean and the sample proportion
- Understand the importance of the Central Limit Theorem

▼ USING STATISTICS
Sampling Oxford Cereals

The automated production line at the Oxford Cereals main plant fills thousands of boxes of cereal during each shift. As the plant operations manager, you are responsible for monitoring the amount of cereal placed in each box. To be consistent with package labeling, boxes should contain a mean of 368 grams of cereal. Because of the speed of the process, the cereal weight varies from box to box, causing some boxes to be underfilled and others to be overfilled. If the automated process fails to work as intended, the mean weight in the boxes could vary too much from the label weight of 368 grams to be acceptable.

Because weighing every single box is too time-consuming, costly, and inefficient, you must take a sample of boxes. For each sample you select, you plan to weigh the individual boxes and calculate a sample mean. You need to determine the probability that such a sample mean could have been randomly selected from a population whose mean is 368 grams. Based on your analysis, you will have to decide whether to maintain, alter, or shut down the cereal-filling process.

n Chapter 6, you used the normal distribution to study the distribution of load times for a MyTVLab web page. In this chapter, you need to make a decision about a cereal-filling process, based on the weights of a sample of cereal boxes packaged at Oxford Cereals. You will learn about sampling distributions and how to use them to solve business problems.

7.1 Sampling Distributions

In many applications, you want to make inferences that are based on statistics calculated from samples to estimate the values of population parameters. In the next two sections, you will learn about how the sample mean (a statistic) is used to estimate the population mean (a parameter) and how the sample proportion (a statistic) is used to estimate the population proportion (a parameter). Your main concern when making a statistical inference is reaching conclusions about a population, *not* about a sample. For example, a political pollster is interested in the sample results only as a way of estimating the actual proportion of the votes that each candidate will receive from the population of voters. Likewise, as plant operations manager for Oxford Cereals, you are only interested in using the mean weight calculated from a sample of cereal boxes to estimate the mean weight of a population of boxes.

In practice, you select a single random sample of a predetermined size from the population. Hypothetically, to use the sample statistic to estimate the population parameter, you could examine *every* possible sample of a given size that could occur. A **sampling distribution** is the distribution of the results if you actually selected all possible samples. The single result you obtain in practice is just one of the results in the sampling distribution.

7.2 Sampling Distribution of the Mean

In Chapter 3, several measures of central tendency, including the mean, median, and mode, were discussed. For several reasons, the mean is the most widely used measure of central tendency, and the sample mean is often used to estimate the population mean. The **sampling distribution of the mean** is the distribution of all possible sample means if you select all possible samples of a given size.

learnMORE

Learn more about the unbiased property of the sample in the SHORT TAKES for Chapter 7.

The Unbiased Property of the Sample Mean

The sample mean is **unbiased** because the mean of all the possible sample means (of a given sample size, n) is equal to the population mean, μ. A simple example concerning a population of four administrative assistants demonstrates this property. Each assistant is asked to apply the same set of updates to a human resources database. Table 7.1 presents the number of errors made by each of the administrative assistants. This population distribution is shown in Figure 7.1.

TABLE 7.1
Number of Errors Made by Each of Four Administrative Assistants

Administrative Assistant	Number of Errors
Ann	$X_1 = 3$
Bob	$X_2 = 2$
Carla	$X_3 = 1$
Dave	$X_4 = 4$

FIGURE 7.1
Number of errors made by a population of four administrative assistants

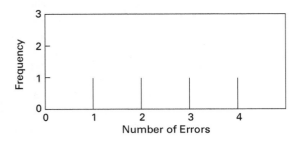

When you have data from a population, you compute the population mean by using Equation (7.1), and you compute the population standard deviation, σ, by using Equation (7.2).

Recall from Section 3.4 that the population mean is the sum of the values in the population divided by the population size, N.

POPULATION MEAN

$$\mu = \frac{\sum_{i=1}^{N} X_i}{N} \tag{7.1}$$

POPULATION STANDARD DEVIATION

$$\sigma = \sqrt{\frac{\sum_{i=1}^{N} (X_i - \mu)^2}{N}} \tag{7.2}$$

For the data of Table 7.1,

$$\mu = \frac{3 + 2 + 1 + 4}{4} = 2.5 \text{ errors}$$

and

$$\sigma = \sqrt{\frac{(3 - 2.5)^2 + (2 - 2.5)^2 + (1 - 2.5)^2 + (4 - 2.5)^2}{4}} = 1.12 \text{ errors}$$

If you select samples of two administrative assistants *with* replacement from this population, there are 16 possible samples ($N^n = 4^2 = 16$). Table 7.2 lists the 16 possible sample outcomes. If you average all 16 of these sample means, the mean of these values is equal to 2.5, which is also the mean of the population, μ.

TABLE 7.2

All 16 Samples of $n = 2$ Administrative Assistants from a Population of $N = 4$ Administrative Assistants When Sampling with Replacement

Sample	Administrative Assistants	Sample Outcomes	Sample Mean
1	Ann, Ann	3, 3	$\overline{X}_1 = 3$
2	Ann, Bob	3, 2	$\overline{X}_2 = 2.5$
3	Ann, Carla	3, 1	$\overline{X}_3 = 2$
4	Ann, Dave	3, 4	$\overline{X}_4 = 3.5$
5	Bob, Ann	2, 3	$\overline{X}_5 = 2.5$
6	Bob, Bob	2, 2	$\overline{X}_6 = 2$
7	Bob, Carla	2, 1	$\overline{X}_7 = 1.5$
8	Bob, Dave	2, 4	$\overline{X}_8 = 3$
9	Carla, Ann	1, 3	$\overline{X}_9 = 2$
10	Carla, Bob	1, 2	$\overline{X}_{10} = 1.5$
11	Carla, Carla	1, 1	$\overline{X}_{11} = 1$
12	Carla, Dave	1, 4	$\overline{X}_{12} = 2.5$
13	Dave, Ann	4, 3	$\overline{X}_{13} = 3.5$
14	Dave, Bob	4, 2	$\overline{X}_{14} = 3$
15	Dave, Carla	4, 1	$\overline{X}_{15} = 2.5$
16	Dave, Dave	4, 4	$\overline{X}_{16} = 4$
			$\mu_{\overline{X}} = 2.5$

Because the mean of the 16 sample means is equal to the population mean, the sample mean is an unbiased estimator of the population mean. Therefore, although you do not know how close the sample mean of any particular sample selected is to the population mean, you are assured that the mean of all the possible sample means that could have been selected is equal to the population mean.

Standard Error of the Mean

Figure 7.2 illustrates the variation in the sample means when selecting all 16 possible samples.

FIGURE 7.2
Sampling distribution of the mean, based on all possible samples containing two administrative assistants

Source: Data are from Table 7.2.

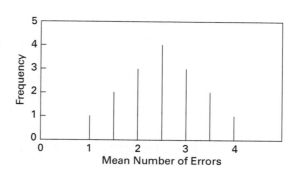

In this small example, although the sample means vary from sample to sample, depending on which two administrative assistants are selected, the sample means do not vary as much as the individual values in the population. That the sample means are less variable than the individual values in the population follows directly from the fact that each sample mean averages together all the values in the sample. A population consists of individual outcomes that can take on a wide range of values, from extremely small to extremely large. However, if a sample contains an extreme value, although this value will have an effect on the sample mean, the effect is reduced because the value is averaged with all the other values in the sample. As the sample size increases, the effect of a single extreme value becomes smaller because it is averaged with more values.

The value of the standard deviation of all possible sample means, called the **standard error of the mean**, expresses how the sample means vary from sample to sample. As the sample size increases, the standard error of the mean decreases by a factor equal to the square root of the sample size. Equation (7.3) defines the standard error of the mean when sampling *with* replacement or sampling *without* replacement from large or infinite populations.

STANDARD ERROR OF THE MEAN

The standard error of the mean, $\sigma_{\bar{X}}$, is equal to the standard deviation in the population, σ, divided by the square root of the sample size, n.

$$\sigma_{\bar{X}} = \frac{\sigma}{\sqrt{n}} \qquad (7.3)$$

Example 7.1 computes the standard error of the mean when the sample selected without replacement contains less than 5% of the entire population.

EXAMPLE 7.1

Computing the Standard Error of the Mean

▶ (continued)

Returning to the cereal-filling process described in the Using Statistics scenario on page 216, if you randomly select a sample of 25 boxes without replacement from the thousands of boxes filled during a shift, the sample contains a very small portion of the population. Given that the standard deviation of the cereal-filling process is 15 grams, compute the standard error of the mean.

SOLUTION Using Equation (7.3) with $n = 25$ and $\sigma = 15$ the standard error of the mean is

$$\sigma_{\bar{X}} = \frac{\sigma}{\sqrt{n}} = \frac{15}{\sqrt{25}} = \frac{15}{5} = 3$$

The variation in the sample means for samples of $n = 25$ is much less than the variation in the individual boxes of cereal (i.e., $\sigma_{\bar{X}} = 3$, while $\sigma = 15$).

Sampling from Normally Distributed Populations

Now that the concept of a sampling distribution has been introduced and the standard error of the mean has been defined, what distribution will the sample mean, $\bar{X}$, follow? If you are sampling from a population that is normally distributed with mean μ and standard deviation σ, then regardless of the sample size, n, the sampling distribution of the mean is normally distributed, with mean $\mu_{\bar{X}} = \mu$ and standard error of the mean $\sigma_{\bar{X}} = \sigma/\sqrt{n}$.

In the simplest case, if you take samples of size $n = 1$, each possible sample mean is a single value from the population because

$$\bar{X} = \frac{\sum\limits_{i=1}^{n} X_i}{n} = \frac{X_1}{1} = X_1$$

Therefore, if the population is normally distributed, with mean μ and standard deviation σ, the sampling distribution $\bar{X}$ for samples of $n = 1$ must also follow the normal distribution, with mean $\mu_{\bar{X}} = \mu$ and standard error of the mean $\sigma_{\bar{X}} = \sigma/\sqrt{1} = \sigma$. In addition, as the sample size increases, the sampling distribution of the mean still follows a normal distribution, with $\mu_{\bar{X}} = \mu$, but the standard error of the mean decreases so that a larger proportion of sample means are closer to the population mean. Figure 7.3 illustrates this reduction in variability. Note that 500 samples of size 1, 2, 4, 8, 16, and 32 were randomly selected from a normally

FIGURE 7.3
Sampling distributions of the mean from 500 samples of sizes $n = 1, 2, 4, 8, 16$, and 32 selected from a normal population

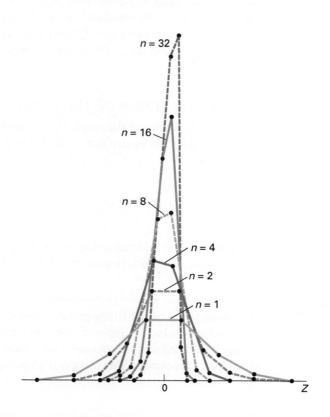

distributed population. From the polygons in Figure 7.3, you can see that, although the sampling distribution of the mean is approximately[1] normal for each sample size, the sample means are distributed more tightly around the population mean as the sample size increases.

To further examine the concept of the sampling distribution of the mean, consider the Using Statistics scenario described on page 216. The packaging equipment that is filling 368-gram boxes of cereal is set so that the amount of cereal in a box is normally distributed, with a mean of 368 grams. From past experience, you know the population standard deviation for this filling process is 15 grams.

If you randomly select a sample of 25 boxes from the many thousands that are filled in a day and the mean weight is computed for this sample, what type of result could you expect? For example, do you think that the sample mean could be 368 grams? 200 grams? 365 grams?

The sample acts as a miniature representation of the population, so if the values in the population are normally distributed, the values in the sample should be approximately normally distributed. Thus, if the population mean is 368 grams, the sample mean has a good chance of being close to 368 grams.

How can you determine the probability that the sample of 25 boxes will have a mean below 365 grams? From the normal distribution (Section 6.2), you know that you can find the area below any value X by converting to standardized Z values:

$$Z = \frac{X - \mu}{\sigma}$$

In the examples in Section 6.2, you studied how any single value, X, differs from the population mean. Now, in this example, you want to study how a sample mean, $\overline{X}$, differs from the population mean. Substituting $\overline{X}$ for X, $\mu_{\overline{X}}$ for μ, and $\sigma_{\overline{X}}$ for σ in the equation above results in Equation (7.4).

FINDING Z FOR THE SAMPLING DISTRIBUTION OF THE MEAN

The Z value is equal to the difference between the sample mean, $\overline{X}$, and the population mean, μ, divided by the standard error of the mean, $\sigma_{\overline{X}}$.

$$Z = \frac{\overline{X} - \mu_{\overline{X}}}{\sigma_{\overline{X}}} = \frac{\overline{X} - \mu}{\frac{\sigma}{\sqrt{n}}} \qquad (7.4)$$

To find the area below 365 grams, from Equation (7.4),

$$Z = \frac{\overline{X} - \mu_{\overline{X}}}{\sigma_{\overline{X}}} = \frac{365 - 368}{\frac{15}{\sqrt{25}}} = \frac{-3}{3} = -1.00$$

The area corresponding to $Z = -1.00$ in Table E.2 is 0.1587. Therefore, 15.87% of all the possible samples of 25 boxes have a sample mean below 365 grams.

The preceding statement is not the same as saying that a certain percentage of *individual* boxes will contain less than 365 grams of cereal. You compute that percentage as follows:

$$Z = \frac{X - \mu}{\sigma} = \frac{365 - 368}{15} = \frac{-3}{15} = -0.20$$

The area corresponding to $Z = -0.20$ in Table E.2 is 0.4207. Therefore, 42.07% of the *individual* boxes are expected to contain less than 365 grams. Comparing these results, you see that many more *individual boxes* than *sample means* are below 365 grams. This result is explained by the fact that each sample consists of 25 different values, some small and some large. The averaging process dilutes the importance of any individual value, particularly when the sample size is large. Therefore, the chance that the sample mean of 25 boxes is very different from the population mean is less than the chance that a *single* box is very different from the population mean.

Examples 7.2 and 7.3 show how these results are affected by using different sample sizes.

EXAMPLE 7.2 The Effect of Sample Size, *n*, on the Computation of $\sigma_{\overline{X}}$	How is the standard error of the mean affected by increasing the sample size from 25 to 100 boxes? **SOLUTION** If $n = 100$ boxes, then using Equation (7.3) on page 219, $$\sigma_{\overline{X}} = \frac{\sigma}{\sqrt{n}} = \frac{15}{\sqrt{100}} = \frac{15}{10} = 1.5$$ The fourfold increase in the sample size from 25 to 100 reduces the standard error of the mean by half—from 3 grams to 1.5 grams. This demonstrates that taking a larger sample results in less variability in the sample means from sample to sample.

EXAMPLE 7.3 The Effect of Sample Size, *n*, on the Clustering of Means in the Sampling Distribution	If you select a sample of 100 boxes, what is the probability that the sample mean is below 365 grams? **SOLUTION** Using Equation (7.4) on page 221, $$Z = \frac{\overline{X} - \mu_{\overline{X}}}{\sigma_{\overline{X}}} = \frac{365 - 368}{\dfrac{15}{\sqrt{100}}} = \frac{-3}{1.5} = -2.00$$ From Table E.2, the area less than $Z = -2.00$ is 0.0228. Therefore, 2.28% of the samples of 100 boxes have means below 365 grams, as compared with 15.87% for samples of 25 boxes.

Sometimes you need to find the interval that contains a specific proportion of the sample means. To do so, you determine a distance below and above the population mean containing a specific area of the normal curve. From Equation (7.4) on page 221,

$$Z = \frac{\overline{X} - \mu}{\dfrac{\sigma}{\sqrt{n}}}$$

Solving for $\overline{X}$ results in Equation (7.5).

FINDING $\overline{X}$ FOR THE SAMPLING DISTRIBUTION OF THE MEAN

$$\overline{X} = \mu + Z\frac{\sigma}{\sqrt{n}} \tag{7.5}$$

Example 7.4 illustrates the use of Equation (7.5).

EXAMPLE 7.4

Determining the
Interval That
Includes a Fixed
Proportion of the
Sample Means

In the cereal-filling example, find an interval symmetrically distributed around the population mean that will include 95% of the sample means, based on samples of 25 boxes.

SOLUTION If 95% of the sample means are in the interval, then 5% are outside the interval. Divide the 5% into two equal parts of 2.5%. The value of Z in Table E.2 corresponding to an area of 0.0250 in the lower tail of the normal curve is -1.96, and the value of Z corresponding to a cumulative area of 0.9750 (i.e., 0.0250 in the upper tail of the normal curve) is $+1.96$.

The lower value of $\overline{X}$ (called $\overline{X}_L$) and the upper value of $\overline{X}$ (called $\overline{X}_U$) are found by using Equation (7.5):

$$\overline{X}_L = 368 + (-1.96)\frac{15}{\sqrt{25}} = 368 - 5.88 = 362.12$$

$$\overline{X}_U = 368 + (1.96)\frac{15}{\sqrt{25}} = 368 + 5.88 = 373.88$$

Therefore, 95% of all sample means, based on samples of 25 boxes, are between 362.12 and 373.88 grams.

Sampling from Non-normally Distributed Populations— The Central Limit Theorem

So far in this section, only the sampling distribution of the mean for a normally distributed population has been considered. However, for many analyses, you will either be able to know that the population is not normally distributed or conclude that it would be unrealistic to assume that the population is normally distributed. An important theorem in statistics, the **Central Limit Theorem**, deals with these situations.

THE CENTRAL LIMIT THEOREM

As the sample size (the number of values in each sample) gets *large enough*, the sampling distribution of the mean is approximately normally distributed. This is true regardless of the shape of the distribution of the individual values in the population.

What sample size is *large enough*? As a general rule, statisticians have found that for many population distributions, when the sample size is at least 30, the sampling distribution of the mean is approximately normal. However, you can apply the Central Limit Theorem for even smaller sample sizes if the population distribution is approximately bell-shaped. In the case in which the distribution of a variable is extremely skewed or has more than one mode, you may need sample sizes larger than 30 to ensure normality in the sampling distribution of the mean.

Figure 7.4 illustrates that the Central Limit Theorem applies to all types of populations, regardless of their shape. In the figure, the effects of increasing sample size are shown for

- a normally distributed population in the left column.
- a uniformly distributed population, in which the values are evenly distributed between the smallest and largest values, in the center column.
- an exponentially distributed population, in which the values are heavily right-skewed, in the right column.

FIGURE 7.4
Sampling distribution of
the mean for samples of
$n = 2, 5,$ and 30, for three
different populations

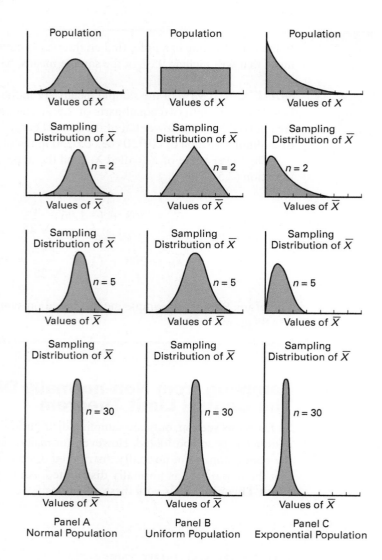

*Note: The mean of each of
the three sampling distributions shown in a column
is equal to the mean of
that column's population
because the sample mean
is an unbiased estimator of
the population mean.*

For the normally distributed population, the sampling distribution of the mean is always normally distributed, too. However, as the sample size increases, the variability of the sample means decreases resulting in a narrowing of the width of the graph.

For the other two populations, a *central limiting* effect causes the sample means to become more similar and the shape of the graphs to become more like a normal distribution. This effect happens initially more slowly for the heavily skewed exponential distribution than for the uniform distribution, but when the sample size is increased to 30, the sampling distributions of these two populations converge to the shape of the sampling distribution of the normal population. Using the results from all three distributions, you can reach the conclusions regarding the Central Limit Theorem that Exhibit 7.1 presents.

EXHIBIT 7.1

Normality and the Sampling Distribution of the Mean

For most distributions, regardless of shape of the population, the sampling distribution of the mean is approximately normally distributed if samples of at least size 30 are selected.

If the distribution of the population is fairly symmetrical, the sampling distribution of the mean is approximately normal for samples as small as size 5.

If the population is normally distributed, the sampling distribution of the mean is normally distributed, regardless of the sample size.

The Central Limit Theorem is of crucial importance in using statistical inference to reach conclusions about a population. It allows you to make inferences about the population mean without having to know the specific shape of the population distribution. Example 7.5 illustrates a sampling distribution for a skewed population.

EXAMPLE 7.5

Constructing a Sampling Distribution for a Skewed Population

Figure 7.5 shows the distribution of the time it takes to fill orders at a fast-food chain drive-through lane. Note that the probability distribution table is unlike Table 7.1 (page 217), which presents a population in which each value is equally likely to occur.

FIGURE 7.5

Probability distribution and histogram of the service time (in minutes) at a fast-food chain drive-through lane

Service Time (minutes)	Probability
1	0.10
2	0.40
3	0.20
4	0.15
5	0.10
6	0.05

Histogram of Probability Distribution of Service Time

Using Equation (5.1) on page 168, the population mean is computed as 2.9 minutes. Using Equation (5.3) on page 169, the population standard deviation is computed as 1.34. Select 100 samples of $n = 2, n = 15$, and $n = 30$. What conclusions can you reach about the sampling distribution of the service time (in minutes) at the fast-food chain drive-through lane?

SOLUTION Table 7.3 represents the mean service time (in minutes) at the fast-food chain drive-through lane for 100 different random samples of $n = 2$. The mean of these 100 sample means is 2.825 minutes, and the standard error of the mean is 0.883.

TABLE 7.3

Mean Service Times (in minutes) at a Fast-Food Chain Drive-Through Lane for 100 Different Random Samples of $n = 2$

3.5	2.5	3	3.5	4	3	2.5	2	2	2.5
3	3	2.5	2.5	2	2.5	2.5	2	3.5	1.5
2	3	2.5	3	3	2	3.5	3.5	2.5	2
4.5	3.5	4	2	2	4	3.5	2.5	2.5	3.5
3.5	3.5	2	1.5	2.5	2	3.5	3.5	2.5	2.5
2.5	3	3	3.5	2	3.5	2	1.5	5.5	2.5
3.5	3	3	2	1.5	3	2.5	2.5	2.5	2.5
3.5	1.5	6	2	1.5	2.5	3.5	2	3.5	5
2.5	3.5	4.5	3.5	3.5	2	4	2	3	3
4.5	1.5	2.5	2	2.5	2.5	2	2	2	4

Table 7.4 represents the mean service time (in minutes) at the fast-food chain drive-through lane for 100 different random samples of $n = 15$. The mean of these 100 sample means is 2.9313 minutes, and the standard error of the mean is 0.3458.

Table 7.5 represents the mean service time (in minutes) at the fast-food chain drive-through lane for 100 different random samples of $n = 30$. The mean of these 100 sample means is 2.9527 minutes, and the standard error of the mean is 0.2701.

▶ *(continued)*

TABLE 7.4
Mean Service Times (in minutes) at a Fast-Food Chain Drive-Through Lane for 100 Different Random Samples of $n = 15$

3.5333	2.8667	3.1333	3.6000	2.5333	2.8000	2.8667	3.1333	3.2667	3.3333
3.0000	3.3333	2.7333	2.6000	2.8667	3.0667	2.1333	2.5333	2.8000	3.1333
2.8000	2.7333	2.6000	3.1333	2.8667	3.4667	2.9333	2.8000	2.2000	3.0000
2.9333	2.6000	2.6000	3.1333	3.1333	3.1333	2.5333	3.0667	3.9333	2.8000
3.0000	2.7333	2.6000	2.4667	3.2000	2.4667	3.2000	2.9333	2.8667	3.4667
2.6667	3.0000	3.1333	3.1333	2.7333	2.7333	3.3333	3.4000	3.2000	3.0000
3.2000	3.0000	2.6000	2.9333	3.0667	2.8667	2.2667	2.5333	2.7333	2.2667
2.8000	2.8000	2.6000	3.1333	2.9333	3.0667	3.6667	2.6667	2.8667	2.6667
3.0000	3.4000	2.7333	3.6000	2.6000	2.7333	3.3333	2.6000	2.8667	2.8000
3.7333	2.9333	3.0667	2.6667	2.8667	2.2667	2.7333	2.8667	3.5333	3.2000

TABLE 7.5
Mean Service Times (in minutes) at a Fast-Food Chain Drive-Through Lane for 100 Different Random Samples of $n = 30$

3.0000	3.3667	3.0000	3.1333	2.8667	2.8333	3.2667	2.9000	2.7000	3.2000
3.2333	2.7667	3.2333	2.8000	3.4000	3.0333	2.8667	3.0000	3.1333	3.4000
2.3000	3.0000	3.0667	2.9667	3.0333	2.4000	2.8667	2.8000	2.5000	2.7000
2.7000	2.9000	2.8333	3.3000	3.1333	2.8667	2.6667	2.6000	3.2333	2.8667
2.7667	2.9333	2.5667	2.5333	3.0333	3.2333	3.0667	2.9667	2.4000	3.3000
2.8000	3.0667	3.2000	2.9667	2.9667	3.2333	3.3667	2.9000	3.0333	3.1333
3.3333	2.8667	2.8333	3.0667	3.3667	3.0667	3.0667	3.2000	3.1667	3.3667
3.0333	3.1667	2.4667	3.0000	2.6333	2.6667	2.9667	3.1333	2.8000	2.8333
2.9333	2.7000	3.0333	2.7333	2.6667	2.6333	3.1333	3.0667	2.5333	3.3333
3.1000	2.5667	2.9000	2.9333	2.9000	2.7000	2.7333	2.8000	2.6667	2.8333

Figure 7.6 Panels A through C show histograms of the mean service time (in minutes) at the fast-food chain drive-through lane for the three sets of 100 different random samples shown in Tables 7.3 through 7.5. Panel A, the histogram for the mean service time for 100 different random samples of $n = 2$, shows a skewed distribution, but a distribution that is not as skewed as the population distribution of service times shown in Figure 7.5.

FIGURE 7.6
Histograms of the mean service time (in minutes) at the fast-food chain drive-through lane of 100 different random samples of $n = 2$ (Panel A, left), 100 different random samples of $n = 15$ (Panel B, right), and 100 different random samples of $n = 30$ (Panel C, next page)

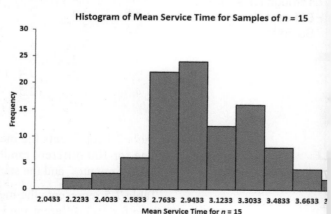

▶ (continued)

FIGURE 7.6
(continued)

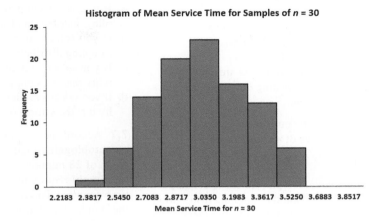

Panel B, the histogram for the mean service time for 100 different random samples of $n = 15$, shows a somewhat symmetrical distribution that contains a concentration of values in the center of the distribution. Panel C, the histogram for the mean service time for 100 different random samples of $n = 30$, shows a distribution that appears to be approximately bell-shaped with a concentration of values in the center of the distribution. The progression of the histograms from a skewed population toward a bell-shaped distribution as the sample size increases is consistent with the Central Limit Theorem.

VISUAL EXPLORATIONS

Exploring Sampling Distributions

Open the **VE-Sampling Distribution add-in work-book** to observe the effects of simulated rolls on the frequency distribution of the sum of two dice. (For Excel technical requirements, see Appendix D.) When this workbook opens properly, it adds a Sampling Distribution menu to the Add-ins tab (Apple menu in OS X Excel).

To observe the effects of simulated throws on the frequency distribution of the sum of the two dice, select **Sampling Distribution → Two Dice Simulation**. In the Sampling Distribution dialog box, enter the **Number of rolls per tally** and click **Tally**. Click **Finish** when done.

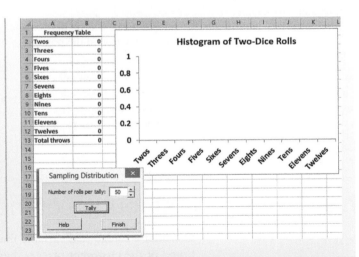

PROBLEMS FOR SECTION 7.2

LEARNING THE BASICS

7.1 Given a normal distribution with $\mu = 100$ and $\sigma = 10$, if you select a sample of $n = 25$, what is the probability that $\overline{X}$ is
a. less than 95?
b. between 95 and 97.5?
c. above 102.2?
d. There is a 65% chance that $\overline{X}$ is above what value?

7.2 Given a normal distribution with $\mu = 50$ and $\sigma = 5$, if you select a sample of $n = 100$, what is the probability that $\overline{X}$ is
a. less than 47?
b. between 47 and 49.5?
c. above 51.1?
d. There is a 35% chance that $\overline{X}$ is above what value?

APPLYING THE CONCEPTS

7.3 For each of the following three populations, indicate what the sampling distribution for samples of 25 would consist of:
a. Customer receipts for a supermarket for a year.
b. Insurance payouts in a particular geographical area in a year.
c. Call center logs of inbound calls tracking handling time for a credit card company during the year.

7.4 The following data represent the number of days absent per year in a population of six employees of a small company:

1 3 6 7 9 10

a. Assuming that you sample without replacement, select all possible samples of $n = 2$ and construct the sampling distribution of the mean. Compute the mean of all the sample means and also compute the population mean. Are they equal? What is this property called?
b. Repeat (a) for all possible samples of $n = 3$.
c. Compare the shape of the sampling distribution of the mean in (a) and (b). Which sampling distribution has less variability? Why?
d. Assuming that you sample with replacement, repeat (a) through (c) and compare the results. Which sampling distributions have the least variability—those in (a) or (b)? Why?

7.5 The diameter of a brand of tennis balls is approximately normally distributed, with a mean of 2.63 inches and a standard deviation of 0.03 inch. If you select a random sample of nine tennis balls,
a. what is the sampling distribution of the mean?
b. what is the probability that the sample mean is less than 2.61 inches?
c. what is the probability that the sample mean is between 2.62 and 2.64 inches?
d. The probability is 60% that the sample mean will be between what two values symmetrically distributed around the population mean?

7.6 The U.S. Census Bureau announced that the median sales price of new houses sold in 2014 was $282,800, and the mean sales price was $345,800 (**www.census.gov/newhomesales**, April 1, 2015). Assume that the standard deviation of the prices is $90,000.

a. If you select samples of $n = 4$, describe the shape of the sampling distribution of $\overline{X}$.
b. If you select samples of $n = 100$, describe the shape of the sampling distribution of $\overline{X}$.
c. If you select a random sample of $n = 100$, what is the probability that the sample mean will be less than $370,000?
d. If you select a random sample of $n = 100$, what is the probability that the sample mean will be between 350,000 and 365,000?

7.7 According to a social media blog, time spent on Tumblr, a microblogging platform and social networking website, has a mean of 28 minutes per visit. (Data extracted from "70+ Amazing Tumblr Statistics & Facts," **bit.ly/1FMioil**.) Assume that time spent on Tumblr per visit is normally distributed and that the standard deviation is 5 minutes. If you select a random sample of 25 visits,
a. what is the probability that the sample mean is between 27.5 and 28.5 minutes?
b. what is the probability that the sample mean is between 27 and 29 minutes?
c. If you select a random sample of 100 visits, what is the probability that the sample mean is between 27.5 and 28.5 minutes?
d. Explain the difference in the results of (a) and (c).

7.8 According to the National Survey of Student Engagement, the average student spends about 17 hours each week preparing for classes; preparation for classes includes homework, reading and any other assignments. (Data extracted from "How much do you study…," **usat.ly/1QrG1aj**.) Assume the standard deviation of time spent preparing for classes is 4 hours. If you select a random sample of 16 students,
a. What is the probability that the mean time spent preparing for classes is at least 16 hours per week?
b. There is an 85% chance that the sample mean is less than how many hours per week?
c. What assumption must you make in order to solve (a) and (b)?
d. If you select a random sample of 64 students, there is an 85% chance that the sample mean is less than how many hours per week?

7.3 Sampling Distribution of the Proportion

studentTIP

Do not confuse this use of the Greek letter pi, π, to represent the population proportion with the mathematical constant that uses the same letter to represent the ratio of the circumference to a diameter of a circle—approximately 3.14159.

Consider a categorical variable that has only two categories, such as the customer prefers your brand or the customer prefers the competitor's brand. You are interested in the proportion of items belonging to one of the categories—for example, the proportion of customers that prefer your brand. The population proportion, represented by π, is the proportion of items in the entire population with the characteristic of interest. The sample proportion, represented by p, is the proportion of items in the sample with the characteristic of interest. The sample proportion, a statistic, is used to estimate the population proportion, a parameter. To calculate the sample proportion, you assign one of two possible values, 1 or 0, to represent the presence or absence of the characteristic. You then sum all the 1 and 0 values and divide by n, the sample size. For example, if, in a sample of five customers, three preferred your brand and two did not, you have three 1s and two 0s. Summing the three 1s and two 0s and dividing by the sample size of 5 results in a sample proportion of 0.60.

SAMPLE PROPORTION

$$p = \frac{X}{n} = \frac{\text{Number of items having the characteristic of interest}}{\text{Sample size}} \qquad (7.6)$$

The sample proportion, p, will be between 0 and 1. If all items have the characteristic, you assign each a score of 1, and p is equal to 1. If half the items have the characteristic, you assign half a score of 1 and assign the other half a score of 0, and p is equal to 0.5. If none of the items have the characteristic, you assign each a score of 0, and p is equal to 0.

In Section 7.2, you learned that the sample mean, $\overline{X}$, is an unbiased estimator of the population mean, μ. Similarly, the statistic p is an unbiased estimator of the population proportion, π. By analogy to the sampling distribution of the mean, whose standard error is $\sigma_{\overline{X}} = \dfrac{\sigma}{\sqrt{n}}$, the **standard error of the proportion**, σ_p, is given in Equation (7.7).

STANDARD ERROR OF THE PROPORTION

$$\sigma_p = \sqrt{\frac{\pi(1 - \pi)}{n}} \qquad (7.7)$$

The **sampling distribution of the proportion** follows the binomial distribution, as discussed in Section 5.2, when sampling with replacement (or without replacement from extremely large populations). However, you can use the normal distribution to approximate the binomial distribution when $n\pi$ and $n(1 - \pi)$ are each at least 5. In most cases in which inferences are made about the population proportion, the sample size is substantial enough to meet the conditions for using the normal approximation (see reference 1). Therefore, in many instances, you can use the normal distribution to estimate the sampling distribution of the proportion.

Substituting p for $\overline{X}$, π for μ, and $\sqrt{\dfrac{\pi(1 - \pi)}{n}}$ for $\dfrac{\sigma}{\sqrt{n}}$ in Equation (7.4) on page 221 results in Equation (7.8).

FINDING Z FOR THE SAMPLING DISTRIBUTION OF THE PROPORTION

$$Z = \frac{p - \pi}{\sqrt{\dfrac{\pi(1 - \pi)}{n}}} \qquad (7.8)$$

To illustrate the sampling distribution of the proportion, a recent survey (C. Jones, "Top Reason for Picking a Hotel? It's Where It's At," *USA Today*, April 28, 2014, p. 3B) reported that 73% of business travelers stated that hotel location was most important when determining where to stay when on the road. Suppose that you select a random sample of 200 business travelers who have stayed at a specific hotel in the past year and you want to determine the probability that more than 80% of them stated that hotel location was most important when determining where to stay when on the road. Because $n\pi = 200(0.73) = 146 > 5$ and $n(1 - \pi) = 200(1 - 0.73) = 54 > 5$, the sample size is large enough to assume that the sampling distribution of the proportion is approximately normally distributed. Then, using the survey percentage of 73% as the population proportion, you can calculate the probability that more than 80% of the business travelers stated that hotel location was most important when determining where to stay when on the road by using Equation (7.8):

$$Z = \frac{p - \pi}{\sqrt{\frac{\pi(1-\pi)}{n}}}$$

$$= \frac{0.80 - 0.73}{\sqrt{\frac{(0.73)(0.27)}{200}}} = \frac{0.07}{\sqrt{\frac{0.1971}{200}}} = \frac{0.07}{0.0314}$$

$$= 2.23$$

Using Table E.2, the area under the normal curve greater than 2.23 is 0.0129. Therefore, if the population proportion is 0.73, the probability is 1.29% that more than 80% of the 200 business travelers in the sample will report that hotel location was most important when determining where to stay when on the road.

PROBLEMS FOR SECTION 7.3

LEARNING THE BASICS

7.9 In a random sample of 64 people, 48 are classified as "successful."
a. Determine the sample proportion, p, of "successful" people.
b. If the population proportion is 0.70, determine the standard error of the proportion.

7.10 A random sample of 50 households was selected for a phone (landline and cellphone) survey. The key question asked was, "Do you or any member of your household own an Apple product (iPhone, iPod, iPad, or Mac computer)?" Of the 50 respondents, 20 said yes and 30 said no.
a. Determine the sample proportion, p, of households that own an Apple product.
b. If the population proportion is 0.45, determine the standard error of the proportion.

7.11 The following data represent the responses (Y for yes and N for no) from a sample of 40 college students to the question "Do you currently own shares in any stocks?"

N N Y N N Y N Y N Y N N Y N Y Y N N N Y
N Y N N N N Y N N Y Y N N N Y N N Y N N

a. Determine the sample proportion, p, of college students who own shares of stock.
b. If the population proportion is 0.30, determine the standard error of the proportion.

APPLYING THE CONCEPTS

SELF TEST **7.12** A political pollster is conducting an analysis of sample results in order to make predictions on election night. Assuming a two-candidate election, if a specific candidate receives at least 55% of the vote in the sample, that candidate will be forecast as the winner of the election. If you select a random sample of 100 voters, what is the probability that a candidate will be forecast as the winner when

a. the population percentage of her vote is 50.1%?
b. the population percentage of her vote is 60%?
c. the population percentage of her vote is 49% (and she will actually lose the election)?
d. If the sample size is increased to 400, what are your answers to (a) through (c)? Discuss.

7.13 You plan to conduct a marketing experiment in which students are to taste one of two different brands of soft drink. Their task is to correctly identify the brand tasted. You select a random sample of 200 students and assume that the students have no ability to distinguish between the two brands. (Hint: If an individual has no ability to distinguish between the two soft drinks, then the two brands are equally likely to be selected.)
a. What is the probability that the sample will have between 50% and 60% of the identifications correct?
b. The probability is 90% that the sample percentage is contained within what symmetrical limits of the population percentage?
c. What is the probability that the sample percentage of correct identifications is greater than 65%?
d. Which is more likely to occur—more than 60% correct identifications in the sample of 200 or more than 55% correct identifications in a sample of 1,000? Explain.

7.14 What do workers around the world want in a job? An EY global study of full-time workers on work-life challenges found that one of the most important factors when seeking a job is flexibility, with 74% of workers saying that being able to work flexibly and still be on track for a promotion is important. (Data extracted from "Study highlights: people want flexibility," **bit.ly/1I7hOvW**.) Suppose you select a sample of 100 full-time workers.
a. What is the probability that in the sample fewer than 78% say that that being able to work flexibly and still be on track for a promotion is important?
b. What is the probability that in the sample between 70% and 78% say that being able to work flexibly and still be on track for a promotion is important?

c. What is the probability that in the sample more than 76% say that that being able to work flexibly and still be on track for a promotion is important?

d. If a sample of 400 is taken, how does this change your answers to (a) through (c)?

7.15 The goal of corporate sustainability is to manage the environmental, economic and social effects of a corporation's operations so it is profitable over the long-term while acting in a responsible manner to society. A Nielsen survey found that 55% of global respondents are willing to pay extra for products and services from companies that are committed to positive social and environmental impact. (Data extracted from *Doing Well by Doing Good*, Corporate **bit.ly/1TelF2U**.) Suppose you select a sample of 100 global respondents.

a. What is the probability that in the sample fewer than 55% are willing to pay extra for products and services from companies that are committed to positive social and environmental impact?

b. What is the probability that in the sample between 50% and 60% are willing to pay extra for products and services from companies that are committed to positive social and environmental impact?

c. What is the probability that in the sample more than 60% are willing to pay extra for products and services from companies that are committed to positive social and environmental impact?

d. If a sample of 400 is taken, how does this change your answers to (a) through (c)?

7.16 According to MSCI's *2014 Survey of Women on Boards*, the percentage of women on U.S. S&P 1500 boards has increased marginally since 2001, and now stands at 16%, well below the values for France and Italy. This study also reports that 17% of U.S. S&P 1500 companies have three or more female board directors. (Data extracted from **bit.ly/1MMiET1**). Suppose you select a random sample of 200 U.S. S&P 1500 companies.

a. What is the probability that the sample will have between 14% and 20% U.S. S&P 1500 companies that have three or more female board directors?

b. The probability is 90% that the sample percentage of companies that have three or more female board directors will be contained within what symmetrical limits of the population percentage?

c. The probability is 95% that the sample percentage of companies that have three or more female board directors will be contained within what symmetrical limits of the population percentage?

7.17 The Chartered Financial Analyst (CFA) Institute reported that 63% of its U.S. members indicate that lack of ethical culture within financial firms has contributed the most to the lack of trust in the financial industry. (Data extracted from *Global Market Sentiment Survey 2014*, **cfa.is/1dzvdF8**.) Suppose that you select a sample of 100 CFA members.

a. What is the probability that the sample percentage indicating that lack of ethical culture within financial firms has contributed the most to the lack of trust in the financial industry will be between 62% and 67%?

b. The probability is 90% that the sample percentage will be contained within what symmetrical limits of the population percentage?

c. The probability is 95% that the sample percentage will be contained within what symmetrical limits of the population percentage?

d. Suppose you selected a sample of 400 CFA members. How does this change your answers in (a) through (c)?

7.18 An IAB study on the state of original digital video showed that original digital video is becoming increasingly popular. Original digital video is defined as professionally produced video intended only for ad-supported online distribution and viewing. According to IAB data, 30% of American adults 18 or older watch original digital videos each month. (Data extracted from *IAB Original Digital Video Consumer Study: April 2015*, **bit.ly/1MtVhwL**.)

a. Suppose that you take a sample of 100 U.S. adults. If the population proportion of U.S. adults who watch original digital videos is 0.30, what is the probability that fewer than 25% in your sample will watch original digital videos?

b. Suppose that you take a sample of 500 U.S. adults. If the population proportion of U.S. adults who watch original digital videos is 0.30, what is the probability that fewer than 25% in your sample will watch original digital videos?

c. Discuss the effect of sample size on the sampling distribution of the proportion in general and the effect on the probabilities in (a) and (b).

▼ USING **STATISTICS**
Sampling Oxford Cereals, Revisited

A s the plant operations manager for Oxford Cereals, you were responsible for monitoring the amount of cereal placed in each box. To be consistent with package labeling, boxes should contain a mean of 368 grams of cereal. Because weighing each of the thousands of boxes produced each shift would be too time-consuming, costly, and inefficient, you selected a sample of boxes. Based on your analysis of this sample, you had to decide whether to maintain, alter, or shut down the process.

Using the concept of the sampling distribution of the mean, you were able to determine probabilities that such a sample mean could have been randomly selected from a population with a mean of 368 grams. Specifically, if a sample of size $n = 25$ is selected from a population with a mean of 368 and standard deviation of 15, you calculated the probability of selecting a sample with a mean of 365 grams or less to be 15.87%. If a larger sample size is selected, the sample mean should be closer to the population mean. This result was illustrated when you calculated the probability if the sample size were increased to $n = 100$. Using the larger sample size, you determined the probability of selecting a sample with a mean of 365 grams or less to be 2.28%.

▼ SUMMARY

You studied the sampling distribution of the sample mean and the sampling distribution of the sample proportion and their relationship to the Central Limit Theorem. You learned that the sample mean is an unbiased estimator of the population mean, and the sample proportion is an unbiased estimator of the population proportion. In the next five chapters, the techniques of confidence intervals and tests of hypotheses commonly used for statistical inference are discussed.

▼ REFERENCES

1. Cochran, W. G. *Sampling Techniques*, 3rd ed. New York: Wiley, 1977.

▼ KEY EQUATIONS

Population Mean

$$\mu = \frac{\sum_{i=1}^{N} X_i}{N} \tag{7.1}$$

Population Standard Deviation

$$\sigma = \sqrt{\frac{\sum_{i=1}^{N} (X_i - \mu)^2}{N}} \tag{7.2}$$

Standard Error of the Mean

$$\sigma_{\overline{X}} = \frac{\sigma}{\sqrt{n}} \tag{7.3}$$

Finding Z for the Sampling Distribution of the Mean

$$Z = \frac{\overline{X} - \mu_{\overline{X}}}{\sigma_{\overline{X}}} = \frac{\overline{X} - \mu}{\frac{\sigma}{\sqrt{n}}} \tag{7.4}$$

Finding $\overline{X}$ for the Sampling Distribution of the Mean

$$\overline{X} = \mu + Z\frac{\sigma}{\sqrt{n}} \tag{7.5}$$

Sample Proportion

$$p = \frac{X}{n} \tag{7.6}$$

Standard Error of the Proportion

$$\sigma_p = \sqrt{\frac{\pi(1 - \pi)}{n}} \tag{7.7}$$

Finding Z for the Sampling Distribution of the Proportion

$$Z = \frac{p - \pi}{\sqrt{\frac{\pi(1 - \pi)}{n}}} \tag{7.8}$$

▼ KEY TERMS

▼ CHECKING YOUR UNDERSTANDING

7.19 Why is the sample mean an unbiased estimator of the population mean?

7.20 Why does the standard error of the mean decrease as the sample size, n, increases?

7.21 Why does the sampling distribution of the mean follow a normal distribution for a large enough sample size, even though the population may not be normally distributed?

7.22 What is the difference between a population distribution and a sampling distribution?

7.23 Under what circumstances does the sampling distribution of the proportion approximately follow the normal distribution?

▼ CHAPTER REVIEW PROBLEMS

7.24 An industrial sewing machine uses ball bearings that are targeted to have a diameter of 0.75 inch. The lower and upper specification limits under which the ball bearing can operate are 0.74 inch (lower) and 0.76 inch (upper). Past experience has indicated that the actual diameter of the ball bearings is approximately normally distributed, with a mean of 0.753 inch and a standard deviation of 0.004 inch. If you select a random sample of 25 ball bearings, what is the probability that the sample mean is
a. between the target and the population mean of 0.753?
b. between the lower specification limit and the target?
c. greater than the upper specification limit?
d. less than the lower specification limit?
e. The probability is 93% that the sample mean diameter will be greater than what value?

7.25 The fill amount of bottles of a soft drink is normally distributed, with a mean of 2.0 liters and a standard deviation of 0.05 liter. If you select a random sample of 25 bottles, what is the probability that the sample mean will be
a. between 1.99 and 2.0 liters?
b. below 1.98 liters?
c. greater than 2.01 liters?
d. The probability is 99% that the sample mean amount of soft drink will be at least how much?
e. The probability is 99% that the sample mean amount of soft drink will be between which two values (symmetrically distributed around the mean)?

7.26 An orange juice producer buys oranges from a large orange grove that has one variety of orange. The amount of juice squeezed from these oranges is approximately normally distributed, with a mean of 4.70 ounces and a standard deviation of 0.40 ounce. Suppose that you select a sample of 25 oranges.
a. What is the probability that the sample mean amount of juice will be at least 4.60 ounces?
b. The probability is 70% that the sample mean amount of juice will be contained between what two values symmetrically distributed around the population mean?
c. The probability is 77% that the sample mean amount of juice will be greater than what value?

7.27 In Problem 7.26, suppose that the mean amount of juice squeezed is 5.0 ounces.
a. What is the probability that the sample mean amount of juice will be at least 4.60 ounces?
b. The probability is 70% that the sample mean amount of juice will be contained between what two values symmetrically distributed around the population mean?
c. The probability is 77% that the sample mean amount of juice will be greater than what value?

7.28 The stock market in Sweden reported strong returns in 2014. The population of stocks earned a mean return of 11.9% in 2014. (Data extracted from *The Wall Street Journal*, January 2, 2015, p. C5.) Assume that the returns for stocks on the Swedish stock market were distributed as a normal variable, with a mean of 11.9 and a standard deviation of 20. If you selected a random sample of 16 stocks from this population, what is the probability that the sample would have a mean return
a. less than 0 (i.e., a loss)?
b. between −10 and 10?
c. greater than 10?

7.29 The article mentioned in Problem 7.28 reported that the stock market in Germany had a mean return of 2.7% in 2014. Assume that the returns for stocks on the German stock market were distributed normally, with a mean of 2.7 and a standard deviation of 10. If you select an individual stock from this population, what is the probability that it would have a return
a. less than 0 (i.e., a loss)?
b. between −10 and −20?
c. greater than −5?
   If you selected a random sample of four stocks from this population, what is the probability that the sample would have a mean return
d. less than 0 (a loss)?
e. between −10 and −20?
f. greater than −5?
g. Compare your results in parts (d) through (f) to those in (a) through (c).

7.30 (Class Project) The table of random numbers is an example of a uniform distribution because each digit is equally likely to occur. Starting in the row corresponding to the day of the month in which you were born, use a table of random numbers (Table E.1) to take one digit at a time.

Select five different samples each of $n = 2$, $n = 5$, and $n = 10$. Compute the sample mean of each sample. Develop a frequency distribution of the sample means for the results of the entire class, based on samples of sizes $n = 2$, $n = 5$, and $n = 10$.

What can be said about the shape of the sampling distribution for each of these sample sizes?

7.31 (Class Project) Toss a coin 10 times and record the number of heads. If each student performs this experiment five times, a frequency distribution of the number of heads can be developed from the results of the entire class. Does this distribution seem to approximate the normal distribution?

7.32 (Class Project) The number of cars waiting in line at a car wash is distributed as follows:

Number of Cars	Probability
0	0.25
1	0.40
2	0.20
3	0.10
4	0.04
5	0.01

You can use a table of random numbers (Table E.1) to select samples from this distribution by assigning numbers as follows:

1. Start in the row corresponding to the day of the month in which you were born.
2. Select a two-digit random number.
3. If you select a random number from 00 to 24, record a length of 0; if from 25 to 64, record a length of 1; if from 65 to 84, record a length of 2; if from 85 to 94, record a length of 3; if from 95 to 98, record a length of 4; if 99, record a length of 5.

Select samples of $n = 2$, $n = 5$, and $n = 10$. Compute the mean for each sample. For example, if a sample of size 2 results in the random numbers 18 and 46, these would correspond to lengths 0 and 1, respectively, producing a sample mean of 0.5. If each student selects five different samples for each sample size, a frequency distribution of the sample means (for each sample size) can be developed from the results of the entire class. What conclusions can you reach concerning the sampling distribution of the mean as the sample size is increased?

7.33 (Class Project) Using a table of random numbers (Table E.1), simulate the selection of different-colored balls from a bowl, as follows:

1. Start in the row corresponding to the day of the month in which you were born.
2. Select one-digit numbers.
3. If a random digit between 0 and 6 is selected, consider the ball white; if a random digit is a 7, 8, or 9, consider the ball red.

Select samples of $n = 10$, $n = 25$, and $n = 50$ digits. In each sample, count the number of white balls and compute the proportion of white balls in the sample. If each student in the class selects five different samples for each sample size, a frequency distribution of the proportion of white balls (for each sample size) can be developed from the results of the entire class. What conclusions can you reach about the sampling distribution of the proportion as the sample size is increased?

7.34 (Class Project) Suppose that step 3 of Problem 7.33 uses the following rule: "If a random digit between 0 and 8 is selected, consider the ball to be white; if a random digit of 9 is selected, consider the ball to be red." Compare and contrast the results in this problem and those in Problem 7.33.

▼CASES

Managing Ashland MultiComm Services

Continuing the quality improvement effort first described in the Chapter 6 Managing Ashland MultiComm Services case, the target upload speed for AMS Internet service subscribers has been monitored. As before, upload speeds are measured on a standard scale in which the target value is 1.0. Data collected over the past year indicate that the upload speeds are approximately normally distributed, with a mean of 1.005 and a standard deviation of 0.10.

1. Each day, at 25 random times, the upload speed is measured. Assuming that the distribution has not changed from what it was in the past year, what is the probability that the mean upload speed is
   a. less than 1.0?
   b. between 0.95 and 1.0?
   c. between 1.0 and 1.05?
   d. less than 0.95 or greater than 1.05?
   e. Suppose that the mean upload speed of today's sample of 25 is 0.952. What conclusion can you reach about the mean upload speed today based on this result? Explain.

2. Compare the results of AMS Problem 1 (a) through (d) to those of AMS Problem 1 in Chapter 6 on page 213. What conclusions can you reach concerning the differences?

Digital Case

Apply your knowledge about sampling distributions in this Digital Case, which reconsiders the Oxford Cereals Using Statistics scenario.

The advocacy group Consumers Concerned About Cereal Cheaters (CCACC) suspects that cereal companies, including Oxford Cereals, are cheating consumers by packaging cereals at less than labeled weights. Recently, the group investigated the package weights of two popular Oxford brand cereals. Open **CCACC.pdf** to examine the group's claims and supporting data, and then answer the following questions:

1. Are the data collection procedures that the CCACC uses to form its conclusions flawed? What procedures could the group follow to make its analysis more rigorous?

2. Assume that the two samples of five cereal boxes (one sample for each of two cereal varieties) listed on the CCACC website were collected randomly by organization members. For each sample,
   a. calculate the sample mean.
   b. assuming that the standard deviation of the process is 15 grams and the population mean is 368 grams, calculate the percentage of all samples for each process that have a sample mean less than the value you calculated in (a).
   c. assuming that the standard deviation is 15 grams, calculate the percentage of individual boxes of cereal that have a weight less than the value you calculated in (a).

3. What, if any, conclusions can you form by using your calculations about the filling processes for the two different cereals?

4. A representative from Oxford Cereals has asked that the CCACC take down its page discussing shortages in Oxford Cereals boxes. Is this request reasonable? Why or why not?

5. Can the techniques discussed in this chapter be used to prove cheating in the manner alleged by the CCACC? Why or why not?

▾EXCEL GUIDE

There are no Excel Guide instructions for Section 7.1.

EG7.2 SAMPLING DISTRIBUTION of the MEAN

Key Technique Use an add-in procedure to create a simulated sampling distribution and use the **RAND**() function to create lists of random numbers.

Example Create a simulated sampling distribution that consists of 100 samples of $n = 30$ from a uniformly distributed population.

PHStat Use **Sampling Distributions Simulation**.
For the example, select **PHStat → Sampling → Sampling Distributions Simulation**. In the procedure's dialog box (shown below):

1. Enter **100** as the **Number of Samples**.
2. Enter **30** as the **Sample Size**.
3. Click **Uniform**.
4. Enter a **Title** and click **OK**.

The procedure inserts a new worksheet in which the sample means, overall mean, and standard error of the mean can be found starting in row 34.

Workbook Use the **SDS worksheet** of the **SDS workbook** as a model.
For the example, in a new worksheet, first enter a title in cell A1. Then enter the formula **=RAND()** in cell **A2** and then copy the formula down 30 rows and across 100

columns (through **column CV**). Then select this cell range (**A2:CV31**) and use **copy and paste values** as discussed in Appendix Section B.4.

Use the formulas that appear in rows 33 through 37 in the **SDS_FORMULAS worksheet** as models if you want to compute sample means, the overall mean, and the standard error of the mean.

Analysis ToolPak Use **Random Number Generation**.
For the example, select **Data → Data Analysis**. In the Data Analysis dialog box, select **Random Number Generation** from the **Analysis Tools** list and then click **OK**.
In the procedure's dialog box (shown below):

1. Enter **100** as the **Number of Variables**.
2. Enter **30** as the **Number of Random Numbers**.
3. Select **Uniform** from the **Distribution** drop-down list.
4. Keep the **Parameters** values as is.
5. Click **New Worksheet Ply** and then click **OK**.

If, for other problems, you select **Discrete** in step 3, you must be open to a worksheet that contains a cell range of X and $P(X)$ values. Enter this cell range as the **Value and Probability Input Range** (not shown when **Uniform** has been selected) in the **Parameters** section of the dialog box.

Use the formulas that appear in rows 33 through 37 in the **SDS_FORMULAS worksheet** of the **SDS workbook** as models if you want to compute sample means, the overall mean, and the standard error of the mean.

Confidence Interval Estimation

8

▼ USING **STATISTICS**
Getting Estimates at Ricknel Home Centers

A s a member of the AIS team at Ricknel Home Centers, you have already examined the probability of discovering questionable, or "tagged," invoices. Now you have been assigned the task of auditing the accuracy of the integrated inventory management and point of sale component of the firm's retail management system.

You could review the contents of each and every inventory and transactional record to check the accuracy of this system, but such a detailed review would be time-consuming and costly. Could you use statistical inference techniques to reach conclusions about the population of all records from a relatively small sample collected during an audit? At the end of each month, you could select a sample of the sales invoices to estimate population parameters such as

- The mean dollar amount listed on the sales invoices for the month
- The proportion of invoices that contain errors that violate the internal control policy of the company

If you used a sampling technique, how accurate would the results from the sample be? How would you use the results you generate? How could you be certain that the sample size is large enough to give you the information you need?

OBJECTIVES

- Construct and interpret confidence interval estimates for the mean and the proportion
- Determine the sample size necessary to develop a confidence interval estimate for the mean or proportion

n Section 7.2, you used the Central Limit Theorem and knowledge of the population distribution to determine the percentage of sample means that are within certain distances of the population mean. For instance, in the cereal-filling example used throughout Chapter 7 (see Example 7.4 on page 223), you can conclude that 95% of all sample means are between 362.12 and 373.88 grams. This is an example of *deductive* reasoning because the conclusion is based on taking something that is true in general (for the population) and applying it to something specific (the sample means).

Getting the results that Ricknel Home Centers needs requires *inductive* reasoning. Inductive reasoning lets you use some specifics to make broader generalizations. You cannot guarantee that the broader generalizations are absolutely correct, but with a careful choice of the specifics and a rigorous methodology, you can reach useful conclusions. As a Ricknel accountant, you need to use inferential statistics, which uses sample results (the "some specifics") to *estimate* (the making of "broader generalizations") unknown population parameters such as a population mean or a population proportion. Note that statisticians use the word *estimate* in the same sense of the everyday usage: something you are reasonably certain about but cannot flatly say is absolutely correct.

You estimate population parameters by using either point estimates or interval estimates. A **point estimate** is the value of a single sample statistic, such as a sample mean. A **confidence interval estimate** is a range of numbers, called an *interval*, constructed around the point estimate. The confidence interval is constructed such that the probability that the interval includes the population parameter is known.

Suppose you want to estimate the mean GPA of all the students at your university. The mean GPA for all the students is an unknown population mean, denoted by μ. You select a sample of students and compute the sample mean, denoted by $\overline{X}$, to be 2.80. As a *point estimate* of the population mean, μ, you ask how accurate is the 2.80 value as an estimate of the population mean, μ? By taking into account the variability from sample to sample (see Section 7.2, concerning the sampling distribution of the mean), you can construct a confidence interval estimate for the population mean to answer this question.

When you construct a confidence interval estimate, you indicate the confidence of correctly estimating the value of the population parameter, μ. This allows you to say that there is a specified confidence that μ is somewhere in the range of numbers defined by the interval.

After studying this chapter, you might find that a 95% confidence interval for the mean GPA at your university is $2.75 \le \mu \le 2.85$. You can interpret this interval estimate by stating that you are 95% confident that the interval that states that the mean GPA at your university is between 2.75 and 2.85 is an interval that includes the population mean.

In this chapter, you learn to construct a confidence interval for both the population mean and population proportion. You also learn how to determine the sample size that is necessary to construct a confidence interval of a desired width.

8.1 Confidence Interval Estimate for the Mean (σ Known)

In Section 7.2, you used the Central Limit Theorem and knowledge of the population distribution to determine the percentage of sample means that are within certain distances of the population mean. Suppose that in the cereal-filling example you wished to estimate the population mean, using the information from a single sample. Thus, rather than taking $\mu \pm (1.96)(\sigma/\sqrt{n})$ to find the upper and lower limits around μ, as in Section 7.2, you substitute the sample mean, $\overline{X}$, for the unknown μ and use $\overline{X} \pm (1.96)(\sigma/\sqrt{n})$ as an interval to estimate the unknown μ. Although in practice you select a single sample of n values and compute the mean, $\overline{X}$, in order to understand the full meaning of the interval estimate, you need to examine a hypothetical set of all possible samples of n values.

Suppose that a sample of $n = 25$ cereal boxes has a mean of 362.3 grams and a standard deviation of 15 grams. The interval developed to estimate μ is $362.3 \pm (1.96)(15)/(\sqrt{25})$, or 362.3 ± 5.88. The estimate of μ is

$$356.42 \le \mu \le 368.18$$

studentTIP
Remember, the confidence interval is for the population mean not the sample mean.

Because the population mean, μ (equal to 368), is included within the interval, this sample results in a correct statement about μ (see Figure 8.1).

FIGURE 8.1
Confidence interval estimates for five different samples of $n = 25$ taken from a population where $\mu = 368$ and $\sigma = 15$

To continue this hypothetical example, suppose that for a different sample of $n = 25$ boxes, the mean is 369.5. The interval developed from this sample is

$$369.5 \pm (1.96)(15)/(\sqrt{25})$$

or 369.5 $\pm$ 5.88. The estimate is

$$363.62 \le \mu \le 375.38$$

Because the population mean, μ (equal to 368), is also included within this interval, this statement about μ is correct.

Now, before you begin to think that correct statements about μ are always made by developing a confidence interval estimate, suppose a third hypothetical sample of $n = 25$ boxes is selected and the sample mean is equal to 360 grams. The interval developed here is $360 \pm (1.96)(15)/(\sqrt{25})$, or 360 $\pm$ 5.88. In this case, the estimate of μ is

$$354.12 \le \mu \le 365.88$$

This estimate is *not* a correct statement because the population mean, μ, is not included in the interval developed from this sample (see Figure 8.1). Thus, for some samples, the interval estimate for μ is correct, but for others it is incorrect. In practice, only one sample is selected, and because the population mean is unknown, you cannot determine whether the interval estimate is correct. To resolve this, you need to determine the proportion of samples producing intervals that result in correct statements about the population mean, μ. To do this, consider two other hypothetical samples: the case in which $\overline{X} = 362.12$ grams and the case in which $\overline{X} = 373.88$ grams. If $\overline{X} = 362.12$, the interval is $362.12 \pm (1.96)(15)/(\sqrt{25})$, or 362.12 $\pm$ 5.88. This leads to the following interval:

$$356.24 \le \mu \le 368.00$$

Because the population mean of 368 is at the upper limit of the interval, the statement is correct (see Figure 8.1).

When $\overline{X} = 373.88$, the interval is $373.88 \pm (1.96)(15)/(\sqrt{25})$, or 373.88 $\pm$ 5.88. The interval estimate for the mean is

$$368.00 \le \mu \le 379.76$$

In this case, because the population mean of 368 is included at the lower limit of the interval, the statement is correct.

In Figure 8.1, you see that when the sample mean falls somewhere between 362.12 and 373.88 grams, the population mean is included *somewhere* within the interval. In Example 7.4 on page 223, you found that 95% of the sample means are between 362.12 and 373.88 grams. Therefore, 95% of all samples of $n = 25$ boxes have sample means that will result in intervals that include the population mean.

Because, in practice, you select only one sample of size n, and μ is unknown, you never know for sure whether your specific interval includes the population mean. However, if you take all possible samples of n and compute their 95% confidence intervals, 95% of the intervals will include the population mean, and only 5% of them will not. In other words, you have 95% confidence that the population mean is somewhere in your interval.

Consider once again the first sample discussed in this section. A sample of $n = 25$ boxes had a sample mean of 362.3 grams. The interval constructed to estimate μ is

$$362.3 \pm (1.96)(15)/(\sqrt{25})$$
$$362.3 \pm 5.88$$
$$356.42 \le \mu \le 368.18$$

The interval from 356.42 to 368.18 is referred to as a *95% confidence interval*. The following contains an interpretation of the interval that most business professionals will understand. (For a technical discussion of different ways to interpret confidence intervals, see reference 4.)

"I am 95% confident that the interval that states that the mean amount of cereal in the population of boxes is somewhere between 356.42 and 368.18 grams is correct."

To help you understand the meaning of the confidence interval, consider the order-filling process at a website. Filling orders consists of several steps, including receiving an order, picking the parts of the order, checking the order, packing, and shipping the order. The file Order contains the time, in minutes, to fill orders for a population of $N = 200$ orders on a recent day. Although in practice the population characteristics are rarely known, for this population of orders, the mean, μ, is known to be equal to 69.637 minutes; the standard deviation, σ, is known to be equal to 10.411 minutes; and the population is normally distributed. To illustrate how the sample mean and sample standard deviation can vary from one sample to another, 20 different samples of $n = 10$ were selected from the population of 200 orders, and the sample mean and sample standard deviation (and other statistics) were calculated for each sample. Figure 8.2 shows these results.

FIGURE 8.2

Sample statistics and 95% confidence intervals for 20 samples of $n = 10$ randomly selected from the population of $N = 200$ orders

Sample	n	Mean	Std Dev	Minimum	Median	Maximum	Range	95% Conf. Int.
S01	10	74.15	13.39	56.10	76.85	97.70	41.60	(67.70, 80.60)
S02	10	61.10	10.60	46.80	61.35	79.50	32.70	(54.65, 67.55)
S03	10	74.36	6.50	62.50	74.50	84.00	21.50	(67.91, 80.81)
S04	10	70.40	12.80	47.20	70.95	84.00	36.80	(63.95, 76.85)
S05	10	62.18	10.85	47.10	59.70	84.00	36.90	(55.73, 68.63)
S06	10	67.03	9.68	51.10	69.60	83.30	32.20	(60.58, 73.48)
S07	10	69.03	8.81	56.60	68.85	83.70	27.10	(62.58, 75.48)
S08	10	72.30	11.52	54.20	71.35	87.00	32.80	(65.85, 78.75)
S09	10	68.18	14.10	50.10	69.95	86.20	36.10	(61.73, 74.63)
S10	10	66.67	9.08	57.10	64.65	86.10	29.00	(60.22, 73.12)
S11	10	72.42	9.76	59.60	74.65	86.10	26.50	(65.97, 78.87)
S12	10	76.26	11.69	50.10	80.60	87.00	36.90	(69.81, 82.71)
S13	10	65.74	12.11	47.10	62.15	86.10	39.00	(59.29, 72.19)
S14	10	69.99	10.97	51.00	73.40	84.60	33.60	(63.54, 76.44)
S15	10	75.76	8.60	61.10	75.05	87.80	26.70	(69.31, 82.21)
S16	10	67.94	9.19	56.70	67.70	87.80	31.10	(61.49, 74.39)
S17	10	71.05	10.48	50.10	71.15	86.20	36.10	(64.60, 77.50)
S18	10	71.68	7.96	55.60	72.35	82.60	27.00	(65.23, 78.13)
S19	10	70.97	9.83	54.40	70.05	84.00	30.20	(64.52, 77.42)
S20	10	74.48	8.80	62.00	76.25	85.70	23.70	(68.03, 80.93)

From Figure 8.2, you can see the following:

- The sample statistics differ from sample to sample. The sample means vary from 61.10 to 76.26 minutes, the sample standard deviations vary from 6.50 to 14.10 minutes, the sample medians vary from 59.70 to 80.60 minutes, and the sample ranges vary from 21.50 to 41.60 minutes.
- Some of the sample means are greater than the population mean of 69.637 minutes, and some of the sample means are less than the population mean.
- Some of the sample standard deviations are greater than the population standard deviation of 10.411 minutes, and some of the sample standard deviations are less than the population standard deviation.
- The variation in the sample ranges is much more than the variation in the sample standard deviations.

The variation of sample statistics from sample to sample is called *sampling error*. **Sampling error** is the variation that occurs due to selecting a single sample from the population. The size of the sampling error is primarily based on the amount of variation in the population and on the sample size. Large samples have less sampling error than small samples, but large samples cost more to select.

The last column of Figure 8.2 contains 95% confidence interval estimates of the population mean order-filling time, based on the results of those 20 samples of $n = 10$. Begin by examining the first sample selected. The sample mean is 74.15 minutes, and the interval estimate for the population mean is 67.70 to 80.60 minutes. In a typical study, you would not know for sure whether this interval estimate is correct because you rarely know the value of the population mean. However, for this population of orders, the population mean is known to be 69.637 minutes. If you examine the interval 67.70 to 80.60 minutes, you see that the population mean of 69.637 minutes is located *between* these lower and upper limits. Thus, the first sample provides a correct estimate of the population mean in the form of an interval estimate. Looking over the other 19 samples, you see that similar results occur for all the other samples *except* for samples 2, 5, and 12. For each of the intervals generated (other than samples 2, 5, and 12), the population mean of 69.637 minutes is located *somewhere* within the interval.

For sample 2, the sample mean is 61.10 minutes, and the interval is 54.65 to 67.55 minutes; for sample 5, the sample mean is 62.18, and the interval is between 55.73 and 68.63; for sample 12, the sample mean is 76.26, and the interval is between 69.81 and 82.71 minutes. The population mean of 69.637 minutes is *not* located within any of these intervals, and the estimate of the population mean made using these intervals is incorrect. Although 3 of the 20 intervals did not include the population mean, if you had selected all the possible samples of $n = 10$ from a population of $N = 200$, 95% of the intervals would include the population mean.

In some situations, you might want a higher degree of confidence of including the population mean within the interval (such as 99%). In other cases, you might accept less confidence (such as 90%) of correctly estimating the population mean. In general, the **level of confidence** is symbolized by $(1 - \alpha) \times 100\%$, where α is the proportion in the tails of the distribution that is outside the confidence interval. The proportion in the upper tail of the distribution is $\alpha/2$, and the proportion in the lower tail of the distribution is $\alpha/2$. You use Equation (8.1) to construct a $(1 - \alpha) \times 100\%$ confidence interval estimate for the mean with σ known.

CONFIDENCE INTERVAL FOR THE MEAN (σ KNOWN)

$$\bar{X} \pm Z_{\alpha/2}\frac{\sigma}{\sqrt{n}}$$

or

$$\bar{X} - Z_{\alpha/2}\frac{\sigma}{\sqrt{n}} \le \mu \le \bar{X} + Z_{\alpha/2}\frac{\sigma}{\sqrt{n}} \tag{8.1}$$

where

$Z_{\alpha/2}$ is the value corresponding to an upper-tail probability of $\alpha/2$ from the standardized normal distribution (i.e., a cumulative area of $1 - \alpha/2$).

The value of $Z_{\alpha/2}$ needed for constructing a confidence interval is called the **critical value** fo the distribution. 95% confidence corresponds to an α value of 0.05. The critical Z value co responding to a cumulative area of 0.975 is 1.96 because there is 0.025 in the upper tail of th distribution, and the cumulative area less than $Z = 1.96$ is 0.975.

There is a different critical value for each level of confidence, $1 - \alpha$. A level of conf dence of 95% leads to a Z value of 1.96 (see Figure 8.3). 99% confidence corresponds to an value of 0.01. The Z value is approximately 2.58 because the upper-tail area is 0.005 and th cumulative area less than $Z = 2.58$ is 0.995 (see Figure 8.4).

FIGURE 8.3
Normal curve for determining the Z value needed for 95% confidence

FIGURE 8.4
Normal curve for determining the Z value needed for 99% confidence

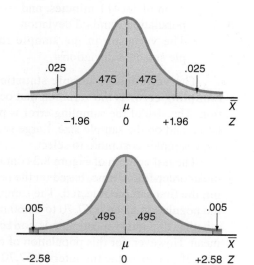

Now that various levels of confidence have been considered, why not make the confidenc level as close to 100% as possible? Before doing so, you need to realize that any increase i the level of confidence is achieved only by widening (and making less precise) the confidenc interval. There is no "free lunch" here. You would have more confidence that the population mean is within a broader range of values; however, this might make the interpretation of th confidence interval less useful. The trade-off between the width of the confidence interval an the level of confidence is discussed in greater depth in the context of determining the sampl size in Section 8.4. Example 8.1 illustrates the application of the confidence interval estimate.

EXAMPLE 8.1

Estimating the Mean Paper Length with 95% Confidence

A paper manufacturer has a production process that operates continuously throughout an entire production shift. The paper is expected to have a mean length of 11 inches, and the standard deviation of the length is 0.02 inch. At periodic intervals, a sample is selected to determine whether the mean paper length is still equal to 11 inches or whether something has gone wrong in the production process to change the length of the paper produced. You select a random sample of 100 sheets, and the mean paper length is 10.998 inches. Construct a 95% confidence interval estimate for the population mean paper length.

SOLUTION Using Equation (8.1) on page 241, with $Z_{\alpha/2} = 1.96$ for 95% confidence,

$$\bar{X} \pm Z_{\alpha/2}\frac{\sigma}{\sqrt{n}} = 10.998 \pm (1.96)\frac{0.02}{\sqrt{100}}$$

$$= 10.998 \pm 0.0039$$

$$10.9941 \leq \mu \leq 11.0019$$

Thus, with 95% confidence, you conclude that the population mean is between 10.9941 and 11.0019 inches. Because the interval includes 11, the value indicating that the production process is working properly, you have no reason to believe that anything is wrong with the production process.

Example 8.2 illustrates the effect of using a 99% confidence interval.

EXAMPLE 8.2

Estimating the Mean
Paper Length with
99% Confidence

Construct a 99% confidence interval estimate for the population mean paper length.

SOLUTION Using Equation (8.1) on page 241, with $Z_{\alpha/2} = 2.58$ for 99% confidence,

$$\overline{X} \pm Z_{\alpha/2}\frac{\sigma}{\sqrt{n}} = 10.998 \pm (2.58)\frac{0.02}{\sqrt{100}}$$

$$= 10.998 \pm 0.00516$$

$$10.9928 \leq \mu \leq 11.0032$$

Once again, because 11 is included within this wider interval, you have no reason to believe that anything is wrong with the production process.

As discussed in Section 7.2, the sampling distribution of the sample mean, $\overline{X}$, is normally distributed if the population for your characteristic of interest, X, follows a normal distribution. And if the population of X does not follow a normal distribution, the Central Limit Theorem almost always ensures that $\overline{X}$ is approximately normally distributed when n is large. However, when dealing with a small sample size and a population that does not follow a normal distribution, the sampling distribution of $\overline{X}$ is not normally distributed, and therefore the confidence interval discussed in this section is inappropriate. In practice, however, as long as the sample size is large enough and the population is not very skewed, you can use the confidence interval defined in Equation (8.1) to estimate the population mean when σ is known. To assess the assumption of normality, you can evaluate the shape of the sample data by constructing a histogram, stem-and-leaf display, boxplot, or normal probability plot.

Can You Ever Know the Population Standard Deviation?

studentTIP
Because understanding the confidence interval concept is very important when reading the rest of this book, review this section carefully to understand the underlying concept—even if you never have a practical reason to use the confidence interval estimate of the mean (σ known) method.

To use Equation (8.1), you must know the value for σ, the population standard deviation. To know σ implies that you know all the values in the entire population. (How else would you know the value of this population parameter?) If you knew all the values in the entire population, you could directly compute the population mean. There would be no need to use the *inductive* reasoning of inferential statistics to *estimate* the population mean. In other words, if you know σ, you really do not have a need to use Equation (8.1) to construct a confidence interval estimate of the mean (σ known).

More significantly, in virtually all real-world business situations, you would never know the standard deviation of the population. In business situations, populations are often too large to examine all the values. So why study the confidence interval estimate of the mean (σ known) at all? This method serves as an important introduction to the concept of a confidence interval because it uses the normal distribution, which has already been thoroughly discussed in Chapters 6 and 7. In the next section, you will see that constructing a confidence interval estimate when σ is not known requires another distribution (the t distribution) not previously mentioned in this book.

PROBLEMS FOR SECTION 8.1

LEARNING THE BASICS

8.1 If $\overline{X} = 85$, $\sigma = 8$, and $n = 64$, construct a 95% confidence interval estimate for the population mean, μ.

8.2 If $\overline{X} = 125$, $\sigma = 24$, and $n = 36$, construct a 99% confidence interval estimate for the population mean, μ.

8.3 Why is it not possible in Example 8.1 on page 242 to have 100% confidence? Explain.

8.4 Is it true in Example 8.1 on page 242 that you do not know for sure whether the population mean is between 10.9941 and 11.0019 inches? Explain.

APPLYING THE CONCEPTS

8.5 A market researcher selects a simple random sample of $n = 100$ Twitter users from a population of over 100 million Twitter registered users. After analyzing the sample, she states that she has 95% confidence that the mean time spent on the site per day is between 15 and 57 minutes. Explain the meaning of this statement.

8.6 Suppose that you are going to collect a set of data, either from an entire population or from a random sample taken from that population.
a. Which statistical measure would you compute first: the mean or the standard deviation? Explain.
b. What does your answer to (a) tell you about the "practicality" of using the confidence interval estimate formula given in Equation (8.1)?

8.7 Consider the confidence interval estimate discussed in Problem 8.5. Suppose the population mean time spent on the site is 36 minutes a day. Is the confidence interval estimate stated in Problem 8.5 correct? Explain.

8.8 You are working as an assistant to the dean of institutional research at your university. The dean wants to survey members of the alumni association who obtained their baccalaureate degrees five years ago to learn what their starting salaries were in their first full-time job after receiving their degrees. A sample of 100 alumni is to be randomly selected from the list of 2,500 graduates in that class. If the dean's goal is to construct a 95% confidence interval estimate for the population mean starting salary, why is it not possible that you will be able to use Equation (8.1) on page 241 for this purpose? Explain.

8.9 A bottled water distributor wants to estimate the amount of water contained in 1-gallon bottles purchased from a nationally known water bottling company. The water bottling company's specifications state that the standard deviation of the amount of water is equal to 0.02 gallon. A random sample of 50 bottles is selected, and the sample mean amount of water per 1-gallon bottle is 0.995 gallon.
a. Construct a 99% confidence interval estimate for the population mean amount of water included in a 1-gallon bottle.
b. On the basis of these results, do you think that the distributor has a right to complain to the water bottling company? Why?
c. Must you assume that the population amount of water per bottle is normally distributed here? Explain.
d. Construct a 95% confidence interval estimate. How does this change your answer to (b)?

SELF TEST **8.10** The operations manager at a compact fluorescent light bulb (CFL) factory needs to estimate the mean life of a large shipment of CFLs. The manufacturer's specifications are that the standard deviation is 1,000 hours. A random sample of 64 CFLs indicated a sample mean life of 7,500 hours.
a. Construct a 95% confidence interval estimate for the population mean life of compact fluorescent light bulbs in this shipment.
b. Do you think that the manufacturer has the right to state that the compact fluorescent light bulbs have a mean life of 8,000 hours? Explain.
c. Must you assume that the population compact fluorescent light bulb life is normally distributed? Explain.
d. Suppose that the standard deviation changes to 800 hours. What are your answers in (a) and (b)?

8.2 Confidence Interval Estimate for the Mean (σ Unknown)

In the previous section, you learned that in most business situations, you do not know σ, the population standard deviation. This section discusses a method of constructing a confidence interval estimate of μ that uses the sample statistic S as an estimate of the population parameter σ.

Student's t Distribution

At the start of the twentieth century, William S. Gosset was working at Guinness in Ireland, trying to help brew better beer less expensively (see reference 5). As he had only small samples to study, he needed to find a way to make inferences about means without having to know σ. Writing under the pen name "Student,"[1] Gosset solved this problem by developing what today is known as the **Student's t distribution**, or the t distribution.

If the variable X is normally distributed, then the following statistic:

$$t = \frac{\overline{X} - \mu}{\frac{S}{\sqrt{n}}}$$

[1]Guinness considered all research conducted to be proprietary and a trade secret. The firm prohibited its employees from publishing their results. Gosset circumvented this ban by using the pen name "Student" to publish his findings.

has a t distribution with $n - 1$ **degrees of freedom**. This expression has the same form as the Z statistic in Equation (7.4) on page 221, except that S is used to estimate the unknown σ.

Properties of the *t* Distribution

The *t* distribution is very similar in appearance to the standardized normal distribution. Both distributions are symmetrical and bell-shaped, with the mean and the median equal to zero. However, because *S* is used to estimate the unknown σ, the values of *t* are more variable than those for *Z*. Therefore, the *t* distribution has more area in the tails and less in the center than does the standardized normal distribution (see Figure 8.5).

FIGURE 8.5
Standardized normal distribution and *t* distribution for 5 degrees of freedom

- Standardized normal distribution
- *t* distribution for 5 degrees of freedom

The degrees of freedom, $n - 1$, are directly related to the sample size, *n*. The concept of *degrees of freedom* is discussed further on page 246. As the sample size and degrees of freedom increase, *S* becomes a better estimate of σ, and the *t* distribution gradually approaches the standardized normal distribution, until the two are virtually identical. With a sample size of about 120 or more, *S* estimates σ closely enough so that there is little difference between the *t* and *Z* distributions.

As stated earlier, the *t* distribution assumes that the variable *X* is normally distributed. In practice, however, when the sample size is large enough and the population is not very skewed, in most cases you can use the *t* distribution to estimate the population mean when σ is unknown. When dealing with a small sample size and a skewed population distribution, the confidence interval estimate may not provide a valid estimate of the population mean. To assess the assumption of normality, you can evaluate the shape of the sample data by constructing a histogram, stem-and-leaf display, boxplot, or normal probability plot. However, the ability of any of these graphs to help you evaluate normality is limited when you have a small sample size.

You find the critical values of *t* for the appropriate degrees of freedom from the table of the *t* distribution (see Table E.3). The columns of the table present the most commonly used cumulative probabilities and corresponding upper-tail areas. The rows of the table represent the degrees of freedom. The critical *t* values are found in the cells of the table. For example, with 99 degrees of freedom, if you want 95% confidence, you find the

TABLE 8.1
Determining the Critical Value from the *t* Table for an Area of 0.025 in Each Tail with 99 Degrees of Freedom

	\multicolumn{6}{c} Cumulative Probabilities					
	.75	.90	.95	.975	.99	.995
	\multicolumn{6}{c} Upper-Tail Areas					
Degrees of Freedom	.25	.10	.05	.025	.01	.005
1	1.0000	3.0777	6.3138	12.7062	31.8207	63.6574
2	0.8165	1.8856	2.9200	4.3027	6.9646	9.9248
3	0.7649	1.6377	2.3534	3.1824	4.5407	5.8409
4	0.7407	1.5332	2.1318	2.7764	3.7469	4.6041
5	0.7267	1.4759	2.0150	2.5706	3.3649	4.0322
⋮	⋮	⋮	⋮	⋮	⋮	⋮
96	0.6771	1.2904	1.6609	1.9850	2.3658	2.6280
97	0.6770	1.2903	1.6607	1.9847	2.3654	2.6275
98	0.6770	1.2902	1.6606	1.9845	2.3650	2.6269
99	0.6770	1.2902	1.6604	1.9842	2.3646	2.6264
100	0.6770	1.2901	1.6602	1.9840	2.3642	2.6259

Source: Extracted from Table E.3.

appropriate value of t, as shown in Table 8.1. The 95% confidence level means that 2.5% of the values (an area of 0.025) are in each tail of the distribution. Looking in the column for a cumulative probability of 0.975 and an upper-tail area of 0.025 in the row corresponding to 99 degrees of freedom gives you a critical value for t of 1.9842 (see Figure 8.6). Because t is a symmetrical distribution with a mean of 0, if the upper-tail value is +1.9842, the value for the lower-tail area (lower 0.025) is −1.9842. A t value of −1.9842 means that the probability that t is less than −1.9842 is 0.025, or 2.5%.

FIGURE 8.6

t distribution with
99 degrees of freedom

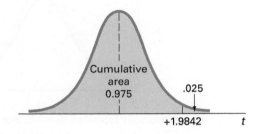

Note that for a 95% confidence interval, you will always have a cumulative probability of 0.975 and an upper-tail area of 0.025. Similarly, for a 99% confidence interval, you will have 0.995 and 0.005, and for a 90% confidence interval you will have 0.95 and 0.05.

The Concept of Degrees of Freedom

In Chapter 3, you learned that the numerator of the sample variance, S^2 requires the computation of the sum of squares around the sample mean:

$$\sum_{i=1}^{n} (X_i - \overline{X})^2$$

In order to compute S^2, you first need to know $\overline{X}$. Therefore, only $n - 1$ of the sample values are free to vary. This means that you have $n - 1$ degrees of freedom. For example, suppose a sample of five values has a mean of 20. How many values do you need to know before you can determine the remainder of the values? The fact that $n = 5$ and $\overline{X} = 20$ also tells you that

$$\sum_{i=1}^{n} X_i = 100$$

because

$$\frac{\sum_{i=1}^{n} X_i}{n} = \overline{X}$$

Thus, when you know four of the values, the fifth one is *not* free to vary because the sum must be 100. For example, if four of the values are 18, 24, 19, and 16, the fifth value must be 23, so that the sum is 100.

The Confidence Interval Statement

Equation (8.2) defines the $(1 - \alpha) \times 100\%$ confidence interval estimate for the mean with σ unknown.

> ## CONFIDENCE INTERVAL FOR THE MEAN (σ UNKNOWN)
>
> $$\overline{X} \pm t_{\alpha/2}\frac{S}{\sqrt{n}}$$
>
> or
>
> $$\overline{X} - t_{\alpha/2}\frac{S}{\sqrt{n}} \leq \mu \leq \overline{X} + t_{\alpha/2}\frac{S}{\sqrt{n}} \qquad (8.2)$$
>
> where
>
> $t_{\alpha/2}$ is the critical value corresponding to an upper-tail probability of $\alpha/2$ (i.e., a cumulative area of $1 - \alpha/2$) from the t distribution with $n - 1$ degrees of freedom.

To illustrate the application of the confidence interval estimate for the mean when the standard deviation is unknown, recall the Ricknel Home Centers scenario presented on page 237. Using the DCOVA steps first discussed on page 3, you define the variable of interest as the dollar amount listed on the sales invoices for the month. Your business objective is to estimate the mean dollar amount. Then you collect the data by selecting a sample of 100 sales invoices from the population of sales invoices during the month. Once you have collected the data, you organize the data in a worksheet. You can construct various graphs (not shown here) to better visualize the distribution of the dollar amounts. To analyze the data, you compute the sample mean of the 100 sales invoices to be equal to $110.27 and the sample standard deviation to be equal to $28.95. For 95% confidence, the critical value from the t distribution (as shown in Table 8.1 on page 245) is 1.9842. Using Equation (8.2),

$$\overline{X} \pm t_{\alpha/2}\frac{S}{\sqrt{n}}$$

$$= 110.27 \pm (1.9842)\frac{28.95}{\sqrt{100}}$$

$$= 110.27 \pm 5.74$$

$$104.53 \leq \mu \leq 116.01$$

Figure 8.7 shows the confidence interval estimate of the mean dollar amount worksheet.

FIGURE 8.7
Excel confidence interval estimate for the mean sales invoice amount worksheet results for the Ricknel Home Centers example

▲	A	B
1	Confidence Interval Estimate for the Mean	
2		
3	Data	
4	Sample Standard Deviation	28.95
5	Sample Mean	110.27
6	Sample Size	100
7	Confidence Level	95%
8		
9	Intermediate Calculations	
10	Standard Error of the Mean	2.895 =B4/SQRT(B6)
11	Degrees of Freedom	99 =B6 - 1
12	t Value	1.9842 =T.INV.2T(1 - B7, B11)
13	Interval Half Width	5.7443 =B12 * B10
14		
15	Confidence Interval	
16	Interval Lower Limit	104.53 =B5 - B13
17	Interval Upper Limit	116.01 =B5 + B13

In the Worksheet

The T.INV.2T function calculates the t critical value in cell B12 and is multiplied by the standard error of the mean in cell B10 to produce the interval half width in cell B13. In turn, that B13 value is subtracted from and added to the sample mean (cell B5) to calculate the lower and upper limits of the confidence interval in cells B16 and B17.

Thus, with 95% confidence, you conclude that the mean amount of all the sales invoices is between $104.53 and $116.01. The 95% confidence level indicates that if you selected all possible samples of 100 (something that is never done in practice), 95% of the intervals developed would include the population mean somewhere within the interval. The validity of this confidence interval estimate depends on the assumption of normality for the distribution of the amount of the sales invoices. With a sample of 100, the normality assumption is valid, and the use of the *t* distribution is likely appropriate. Example 8.3 further illustrates how you construct the confidence interval for a mean when the population standard deviation is unknown.

EXAMPLE 8.3

Estimating the Mean Processing Time of Life Insurance Applications

An insurance company has the business objective of reducing the amount of time it takes to approve applications for life insurance. The approval process consists of underwriting, which includes a review of the application, a medical information bureau check, possible requests for additional medical information and medical exams, and a policy compilation stage in which the policy pages are generated and sent for delivery. Using the DCOVA steps first discussed on page 3, you define the variable of interest as the total processing time in days. You collect the data by selecting a random sample of 27 approved policies during a period of one month. You organize the data collected in a worksheet. Table 8.2 lists the total processing time, in days, which are stored in Insurance . To analyze the data, you need to construct a 95% confidence interval estimate for the population mean processing time.

TABLE 8.2
Processing Time for Life Insurance Applications

| 73 | 19 | 16 | 64 | 28 | 28 | 31 | 90 | 60 | 56 | 31 | 56 | 22 | 18 |
| 45 | 48 | 17 | 17 | 17 | 91 | 92 | 63 | 50 | 51 | 69 | 16 | 17 | |

SOLUTION To visualize the data, you construct a boxplot of the processing time, as displayed in Figure 8.8, and a normal probability plot, as shown in Figure 8.9. To analyze the data, you construct the confidence interval estimate shown in Figure 8.10.

FIGURE 8.8
Excel boxplot for the processing time for life insurance applications

FIGURE 8.9
Excel normal probability plot for the processing time for life insurance applications

▶ (continued)

FIGURE 8.10

Excel confidence interval estimate for the mean processing time worksheet results for life insurance applications

	A	B
1	Processing Time for Life Insurance Applications	
2		
3	Data	
4	Sample Standard Deviation	25.28
5	Sample Mean	43.89
6	Sample Size	27
7	Confidence Level	95%
8		
9	Intermediate Calculations	
10	Standard Error of the Mean	4.8651
11	Degrees of Freedom	26
12	t Value	2.0555
13	Interval Half Width	10.0004
14		
15	Confidence Interval	
16	Interval Lower Limit	33.89
17	Interval Upper Limit	53.89

In the Worksheet

This worksheet solution shares the template that is used in Figure 8.7 Ricknel Home Centers example on page 247.

Figure 8.10 shows that the sample mean is $\bar{X} = 43.89$ days and the sample standard deviation is $S = 25.28$ days. Using Equation (8.2) on page 247 to construct the confidence interval, you need to determine the critical value from the t table, using the row for 26 degrees of freedom. For 95% confidence, you use the column corresponding to an upper-tail area of 0.025 and a cumulative probability of 0.975. From Table E.3, you see that $t_{\alpha/2} = 2.0555$. Thus, using $\bar{X} = 43.89$, $S = 25.28$, $n = 27$, and $t_{\alpha/2} = 2.0555$,

$$\bar{X} \pm t_{\alpha/2}\frac{S}{\sqrt{n}}$$

$$= 43.89 \pm (2.0555)\frac{25.28}{\sqrt{27}}$$

$$= 43.89 \pm 10.00$$

$$33.89 \le \mu \le 53.89$$

You conclude with 95% confidence that the mean processing time for the population of life insurance applications is between 33.89 and 53.89 days. The validity of this confidence interval estimate depends on the assumption that the processing time is normally distributed. From the boxplot displayed in Figure 8.8 and the normal probability plot shown in Figure 8.9, the processing time appears right-skewed. Thus, although the sample size is close to 30, you would have some concern about the validity of this confidence interval in estimating the population mean processing time. The concern is that a 95% confidence interval based on a small sample from a skewed distribution will contain the population mean less than 95% of the time in repeated sampling. In the case of small sample sizes and skewed distributions, you might consider the sample median as an estimate of central tendency and construct a confidence interval for the population median (see reference 2).

The interpretation of the confidence interval when σ is unknown is the same as when σ is known. To illustrate the fact that the confidence interval for the mean varies more when σ is unknown, return to the example concerning the order-filling times discussed in Section 8.1 on pages 240 and 241. Suppose that, in this case, you do *not* know the population standard deviation and instead use the sample standard deviation to construct the confidence interval estimate of the mean. Figure 8.11 shows the results for each of 20 samples of $n = 10$ orders.

FIGURE 8.11
Confidence interval
estimates of the mean
for 20 samples of $n = 10$
randomly selected from
the population of $N = 200$
orders with σ unknown

Sample	N	Mean	Std Dev	SE Mean	95% Conf. Int.
S01	10	71.64	7.58	2.40	(66.22, 77.06)
S02	10	67.22	10.95	3.46	(59.39, 75.05)
S03	10	67.97	14.83	4.69	(57.36, 78.58)
S04	10	73.90	10.59	3.35	(66.33, 81.47)
S05	10	67.11	11.12	3.52	(59.15, 75.07)
S06	10	68.12	10.83	3.43	(60.37, 75.87)
S07	10	65.80	10.85	3.43	(58.03, 73.57)
S08	10	77.58	11.04	3.49	(69.68, 85.48)
S09	10	66.69	11.45	3.62	(58.50, 74.88)
S10	10	62.55	8.58	2.71	(56.41, 68.69)
S11	10	71.12	12.82	4.05	(61.95, 80.29)
S12	10	70.55	10.52	3.33	(63.02, 78.08)
S13	10	65.51	8.16	2.58	(59.67, 71.35)
S14	10	64.90	7.55	2.39	(59.50, 70.30)
S15	10	66.22	11.21	3.54	(58.20, 74.24)
S16	10	70.43	10.21	3.23	(63.12, 77.74)
S17	10	72.04	6.25	1.96	(67.57, 76.51)
S18	10	73.91	11.29	3.57	(65.83, 81.99)
S19	10	71.49	9.76	3.09	(64.51, 78.47)
S20	10	70.15	10.84	3.43	(62.39, 77.91)

In Figure 8.11, observe that the standard deviation of the samples varies from 6.25 (sample 17) to 14.83 (sample 3). Thus, the width of the confidence interval developed varies from 8.94 in sample 17 to 21.22 in sample 3. Because you know that the population mean order time $\mu = 69.637$ minutes, you can see that the interval for sample 8 $(69.68 - 85.48)$ and the interval for sample 10 $(56.41 - 68.69)$ do not correctly estimate the population mean. All the other intervals correctly estimate the population mean. Once again, remember that in practice you select only one sample, and you are unable to know for sure whether your one sample provides a confidence interval that includes the population mean.

PROBLEMS FOR SECTION 8.2

LEARNING THE BASICS

8.11 If $\bar{X} = 75$, $S = 24$, and $n = 36$, and assuming that the population is normally distributed, construct a 95% confidence interval estimate for the population mean, μ.

8.12 Determine the critical value of t in each of the following circumstances:
a. $1 - \alpha = 0.95, n = 10$
b. $1 - \alpha = 0.99, n = 10$
c. $1 - \alpha = 0.95, n = 32$
d. $1 - \alpha = 0.95, n = 65$
e. $1 - \alpha = 0.90, n = 16$

8.13 Assuming that the population is normally distributed, construct a 95% confidence interval estimate for the population mean for each of the following samples:

   Sample A: 1 1 1 1 8 8 8 8

   Sample B: 1 2 3 4 5 6 7 8

Explain why these two samples produce different confidence intervals even though they have the same mean and range.

8.14 Assuming that the population is normally distributed, construct a 95% confidence interval for the population mean, based on the following sample of size $n = 7$:

   1 2 3 4 5 6 20

Change the value of 20 to 7 and recalculate the confidence interval. Using these results, describe the effect of an outlier (i.e., an extreme value) on the confidence interval.

APPLYING THE CONCEPTS

8.15 A marketing researcher wants to estimate the mean amount spent ($) on Amazon.com by Amazon Prime member shoppers. Suppose a random sample of 100 Amazon Prime member shoppers who recently made a purchase on Amazon.com yielded a mean of $1,500 and a standard deviation of $200.
a. Construct a 95% confidence interval estimate for the mean spending for all Amazon Prime member shoppers.
b. Interpret the interval constructed in (a).

✓ SELF TEST 8.16 A survey of nonprofit organizations showed that online fundraising has increased in the past year. Based on a random sample of 84 nonprofits, the mean one-time gift donation in the past year was $82, with a standard deviation of $9.
a. Construct a 95% confidence interval estimate for the population mean one-time gift donation.
b. Interpret the interval constructed in (a).

8.17 The U.S. Department of Transportation requires tire manufacturers to provide tire performance information on the sidewall of a tire to better inform prospective customers as they make purchasing decisions. One very important measure of tire performance is the tread wear index, which indicates the tire's resistance to tread wear compared with a tire graded with a base of 100. A tire with a grade of 200 should last twice as long, on average, as a tire graded with a base of 100. A consumer organization wants to estimate the actual tread wear index of a brand name of tires that claims "graded 200" on the sidewall of the tire. A random sample of $n = 18$ indicates a sample mean tread wear index of 195.3 and a sample standard deviation of 21.4.

a. Assuming that the population of tread wear indexes is normally distributed, construct a 95% confidence interval estimate for the population mean tread wear index for tires produced by this manufacturer under this brand name.

b. Do you think that the consumer organization should accuse the manufacturer of producing tires that do not meet the performance information provided on the sidewall of the tire? Explain.

c. Explain why an observed tread wear index of 210 for a particular tire is not unusual, even though it is outside the confidence interval developed in (a).

8.18 The file FastFood contains the amount that a sample of 15 customers spent for lunch ($) at a fast-food restaurant:

7.42 6.29 5.83 6.50 8.34 9.51 7.10 6.80 5.90
4.89 6.50 5.52 7.90 8.30 9.60

a. Construct a 95% confidence interval estimate for the population mean amount spent for lunch ($) at a fast-food restaurant, assuming a normal distribution.

b. Interpret the interval constructed in (a).

8.19 The file Sedans contains the overall miles per gallon (MPG) of 2015 midsized sedans:

26 38 26 30 24 26 28 28 24 26 24 39
32 23 22 24 28 37 31 40 25 25 33 30

Source: Data extracted from "Which Car Is Right for You," *Consumer Reports,* April 2015, pp. 40–41.

a. Construct a 95% confidence interval estimate for the population mean MPG of 2015 midsized sedans, assuming a normal distribution.

b. Interpret the interval constructed in (a).

c. Compare the results in (a) to those in Problem 8.20(a).

8.20 The file SUV contains the overall MPG of 2015 small SUVs:

26 22 24 22 26 21 24 25 28 24
22 21 22 21 24 23 23 22 21 22

Source: Data extracted from "Which Car Is Right for You," *Consumer Reports,* April 2015, pp. 60–61.

a. Construct a 95% confidence interval estimate for the population mean MPG of 2015 small SUVs, assuming a normal distribution.

b. Interpret the interval constructed in (a).

c. Compare the results in (a) to those in Problem 8.19(a).

8.21 Is there a difference in the yields of different types of investments? The file CDRate contains the yields for a one-year certificate of deposit (CD) and a five-year CD for 25 banks in the United States as of April 15, 2015. (Data extracted from **www.Bankrate.com**, April 15, 2015.)

a. Construct a 95% confidence interval estimate for the mean yield of one-year CDs.

b. Construct a 95% confidence interval estimate for the mean yield of five-year CDs.

c. Compare the results of (a) and (b).

8.22 One of the major measures of the quality of service provided by any organization is the speed with which the organization responds to customer complaints. A large family-held department store selling furniture and flooring, including carpet, had undergone a major expansion in the past several years. In particular, the flooring department had expanded from 2 installation crews to an installation supervisor, a measurer, and 15 installation crews. The store had the business objective of improving its response to complaints. The variable of interest was defined as the number of days between when the complaint was made and when it was resolved. Data were collected from 50 complaints that were made in the past year. The data, stored in Furniture, are as follows:

54 5 35 137 31 27 152 2 123 81 74 27
11 19 126 110 110 29 61 35 94 31 26 5
12 4 165 32 29 28 29 26 25 1 14 13
13 10 5 27   4 52 30 22 36 26 20 23
33 68

a. Construct a 95% confidence interval estimate for the population mean number of days between the receipt of a complaint and the resolution of the complaint.

b. What assumption must you make about the population distribution in order to construct the confidence interval estimate in (a)?

c. Do you think that the assumption needed in order to construct the confidence interval estimate in (a) is valid? Explain.

d. What effect might your conclusion in (c) have on the validity of the results in (a)?

8.23 A manufacturing company produces electric insulators. You define the variable of interest as the strength of the insulators. If the insulators break when in use, a short circuit is likely. To test the strength of the insulators, you carry out destructive testing to determine how much force is required to break the insulators. You measure force by observing how many pounds are applied to the insulator before it breaks. You collect the force data for 30 insulators selected for the experiment and organize and store these data in Force:

1,870 1,728 1,656 1,610 1,634 1,784 1,522 1,696
1,592 1,662 1,866 1,764 1,734 1,662 1,734 1,774
1,550 1,756 1,762 1,866 1,820 1,744 1,788 1,688
1,810 1,752 1,680 1,810 1,652 1,736

a. Construct a 95% confidence interval estimate for the population mean force.

b. What assumption must you make about the population distribution in order to construct the confidence interval estimate in (a)?

c. Do you think that the assumption needed in order to construct the confidence interval estimate in (a) is valid? Explain.

8.24 The file MobileCommerce contains mobile commerce penetration values, the percentage of the country population that bought something online via a mobile phone in the past month, for twenty-eight of the world's economies:

17 15 15 13 27 12 20 23 9 9
16 6 19 14 11 14 8 15 23 11
37 17 11 19 27 18 18 15

Source: Data extracted from "Digital, Social, and Mobile in 2015," **bit.ly/1yHE8vK**.

a. Construct a 95% confidence interval estimate for the population mean mobile commerce penetration.

b. What assumption do you need to make about the population to construct the interval in (a)?

c. Given the data presented, do you think the assumption needed in (a) is valid? Explain.

8.25 One operation of a mill is to cut pieces of steel into parts that are used in the frame for front seats in an automobile. The steel is cut with a diamond saw, and the resulting parts must be cut to be within ± 0.005 inch of the length specified by the automobile company. The measurement reported from a sample of 100 steel parts (stored in Steel) is the difference, in inches, between the actual length of the steel part, as measured by a laser measurement device, and the specified length of the steel part. For example, the first observation, -0.002, represents a steel part that is 0.002 inch shorter than the specified length.

a. Construct a 95% confidence interval estimate for the population mean difference between the actual length of the steel part and the specified length of the steel part.

b. What assumption must you make about the population distribution in order to construct the confidence interval estimate in (a)?

c. Do you think that the assumption needed in order to construct the confidence interval estimate in (a) is valid? Explain.

d. Compare the conclusions reached in (a) with those of Problem 2.43 on page 59.

8.3 Confidence Interval Estimate for the Proportion

studentTIP

As noted in Chapter 7, do not confuse this use of the Greek letter pi, π, to represent the population proportion with the mathematical constant pi.

The concept of a confidence interval also applies to categorical data. With categorical data, you want to estimate the proportion of items in a population having a certain characteristic of interest. The unknown population proportion is represented by the Greek letter π. The point estimate for π is the sample proportion, $p = X/n$, where n is the sample size and X is the number of items in the sample having the characteristic of interest. Equation (8.3) defines the confidence interval estimate for the population proportion.

CONFIDENCE INTERVAL ESTIMATE FOR THE PROPORTION

$$p \pm Z_{\alpha/2}\sqrt{\frac{p(1-p)}{n}}$$

or

$$p - Z_{\alpha/2}\sqrt{\frac{p(1-p)}{n}} \leq \pi \leq p + Z_{\alpha/2}\sqrt{\frac{p(1-p)}{n}} \quad \text{(8.3)}$$

where

$$p = \text{sample proportion} = \frac{X}{n} = \frac{\text{Number of items having the characteristic}}{\text{sample size}}$$

studentTIP

Remember, the sample proportion, p, must be between 0 and 1.

$\pi = \text{population proportion}$

$Z_{\alpha/2} = \text{critical value from the standardized normal distribution}$

$n = \text{sample size}$

Note: To use this equation for the confidence interval, the sample size n must be large enough to ensure that both X and $n - X$ are greater than 5.

You can use the confidence interval estimate for the proportion defined in Equation (8.3) to estimate the proportion of sales invoices that contain errors (see the Ricknel Home Centers scenario on page 237). Using the DCOVA steps, you define the variable of interest as whether the invoice contains errors (yes or no). Then, you collect the data from a sample of 100 sales invoices. The results, which you organize and store in a worksheet, show that 10 invoices contain errors. To analyze the data, you compute, for these data, $p = X/n = 10/100 = 0.10$. Since both $X = 10$ and $n - X = 100 - 10 = 90$ are > 5, using Equation (8.3) and $Z_{\alpha/2} = 1.96$, for 95% confidence,

$$p \pm Z_{\alpha/2}\sqrt{\frac{p(1-p)}{n}}$$

$$= 0.10 \pm (1.96)\sqrt{\frac{(0.10)(0.90)}{100}}$$

$$= 0.10 \pm (1.96)(0.03)$$

$$= 0.10 \pm 0.0588$$

$$0.0412 \le \pi \le 0.1588$$

Therefore, you have 95% confidence that the population proportion of all sales invoices containing errors is between 0.0412 and 0.1588. This means that you estimate that between 4.12% and 15.88% of all the sales invoices contain errors. Figure 8.12 shows a confidence interval estimate for this example.

FIGURE 8.12

Excel confidence interval estimate worksheet results for the proportion of sales invoices that contain errors

	A	B	
1	Proportion of In-Error Sales Invoices		
2			
3	Data		
4	Sample Size	100	
5	Number of Successes	10	
6	Confidence Level	95%	
7			
8	Intermediate Calculations		
9	Sample Proportion	0.1	=B5/B4
10	Z Value	-1.9600	=NORM.S.INV((1 - B6)/2)
11	Standard Error of the Proportion	0.03	=SQRT(B9 * (1 - B9)/B4)
12	Interval Half Width	0.0588	=ABS(B10 * B11)
13			
14	Confidence Interval		
15	Interval Lower Limit	0.0412	=B9 - B12
16	Interval Upper Limit	0.1588	=B9 + B12

In the Worksheet

The NORM.S.INV function calculates the Z value in cell B10 and is multiplied by the standard error of the proportion in cell B11 to produce the interval half width in cell B12. In turn, that B12 value is subtracted from and added to the sample proportion (cell B9) to calculate the lower and upper limits of the confidence interval in cells B16 and B17.

Example 8.4 illustrates another application of a confidence interval estimate for the proportion.

EXAMPLE 8.4

Estimating the Proportion of Nonconforming Newspapers Printed

The operations manager at a large newspaper wants to estimate the proportion of newspapers printed that have a nonconforming attribute. Using the DCOVA steps, you define the variable of interest as whether the newspaper has excessive rub-off, improper page setup, missing pages, or duplicate pages. You collect the data by selecting a random sample of $n = 200$ newspapers from all the newspapers printed during a single day. You organize the results in a worksheet, which shows that 35 newspapers contain some type of nonconformance. To analyze the data, you need to construct and interpret a 90% confidence interval estimate for the proportion of newspapers printed during the day that have a nonconforming attribute.

SOLUTION Using Equation (8.3),

$$p = \frac{X}{n} = \frac{35}{200} = 0.175, \text{ and with a 90\% level of confidence } Z_{\alpha/2} = 1.645$$

$$p \pm Z_{\alpha/2}\sqrt{\frac{p(1-p)}{n}}$$

$$= 0.175 \pm (1.645)\sqrt{\frac{(0.175)(0.825)}{200}}$$

$$= 0.175 \pm (1.645)(0.0269)$$

$$= 0.175 \pm 0.0442$$

$$0.1308 \le \pi \le 0.2192$$

You conclude with 90% confidence that the population proportion of all newspapers printed that day with nonconformities is between 0.1308 and 0.2192. This means you estimate that between 13.08% and 21.92% of the newspapers printed on that day have some type of nonconformance.

Equation (8.3) contains a Z statistic because you can use the normal distribution to approx
imate the binomial distribution when the sample size is sufficiently large. In Example 8.4, th
confidence interval using Z provides an excellent approximation for the population proportio
because both X and $n - X$ are greater than 5. However, if you do not have a sufficiently larg
sample size, you should use the binomial distribution rather than Equation (8.3) (see reference
1, 3, and 7). The exact confidence intervals for various sample sizes and proportions of item
of interest have been tabulated by Fisher and Yates (reference 3).

PROBLEMS FOR SECTION 8.3

LEARNING THE BASICS

8.26 If $n = 200$ and $X = 50$, construct a 95% confidence interval estimate for the population proportion.

8.27 If $n = 400$ and $X = 25$, construct a 99% confidence interval estimate for the population proportion.

APPLYING THE CONCEPTS

✓ SELF TEST **8.28** A cellphone provider has the business objective of wanting to estimate the proportion of subscribers who would upgrade to a new cellphone with improved features if it were made available at a substantially reduced cost. Data are collected from a random sample of 500 subscribers. The results indicate that 135 of the subscribers would upgrade to a new cell-phone at a reduced cost.
a. Construct a 99% confidence interval estimate for the population proportion of subscribers that would upgrade to a new cell-phone at a reduced cost.
b. How would the manager in charge of promotional programs use the results in (a)?

8.29 In a survey of 529 travelers, 386 said that location was very important and 323 said that room quality was very important in choosing a hotel. (Source: C. Jones, "Top Reason for Picking a Hotel? It's Where It's At," *USA Today*, April 28, 2014, p. 3B.)
a. Construct a 95% confidence interval estimate for the population proportion of travelers who said that location was very important for choosing a hotel.
b. Construct a 95% confidence interval estimate for the population proportion of travelers who said that room quality was very important in choosing a hotel.
c. Write a short summary of the information derived from (a) and (b).

8.30 Are you likely to purchase an item promoted by a celebrity on a social media site? According to a Brand Republic survey, 26% of social media users have made such a purchase (Source: "Celebrity endorsement on social media," **bit.ly/1o4yNHa**.)
a. Suppose that the survey had a sample size of $n = 1,000$. Con-struct a 95% confidence interval estimate for the population proportion of social media users that have purchased an item promoted by a celebrity on a social media site.
b. Based on (a), can you claim that more than a quarter of all social media users have purchased an item promoted by a celebrity on a social media site?

c. Repeat parts (a) and (b), assuming that the survey had a sample size of $n = 10,000$.
d. Discuss the effect of sample size on confidence interval estimation.

8.31 In a survey of 175 organizations, 77 responded that the top reason their HR function struggles with systematically using ana
lytics is a lack of people resources that understand how to interpre
analytics and turn them into actionable insight. (Data extracted from "HR Metrics, Measures, Data and Analytics, Oh My!" *Aber
deen Group Report*, May 2015, **bit.ly/1QT6ybi**.) Construct a 95% confidence interval estimate for the population proportion of orga
nizations that indicate the top reason their HR function struggle
with systematically using analytics is a lack of people resource
that understand how to interpret analytics and turn them into ac
tionable insight.

8.32 A Pew Research Center survey of online American adults included 1,074 Facebook users. Of these Facebook users, 935 are connected to friends from the past (such as high school or college classmates) while 419 of these Facebook users are connected to people they have never met in person. (Data extracted from "De
mographics of Key Social Networking Platforms," January, 9 2015, **bit.ly/1JKUD0o**.)
a. Construct a 95% confidence interval estimate for the popula-tion proportion of Facebook users who are connected to friends from the past.
b. Construct a 95% confidence interval estimate for the popula-tion proportion of Facebook users who are connected to people they have never met in person.
c. Compare the results of (a) and (b).

8.33 What are the digital technologies that tech CEOs believe are strategically important for their organization? In a survey by Price-waterhouseCoopers (PwC), 157 of 176 tech CEOs around the globe responded that cybersecurity is strategically important for their or-ganization, and 79 responded that robotics is strategically import-ant for their organization. (Data extracted from *One Global Village: Technology industry key findings*, February 2015, **pwc.to/1e9sl2F**.)
a. Construct a 95% confidence interval estimate for the popu-lation proportion of tech CEOs who indicate cybersecurity is strategically important for their organization.
b. Construct a 95% confidence interval estimate for the population proportion of tech CEOs who indicate robotics is strategically important for their organization.
c. Interpret the intervals in (a) and (b).

8.4 Determining Sample Size

In each confidence interval developed so far in this chapter, the sample size was reported along with the results, with little discussion of the width of the resulting confidence interval. In the business world, sample sizes are determined prior to data collection to ensure that the confidence interval is narrow enough to be useful in making decisions. Determining the proper sample size is a complicated procedure, subject to the constraints of budget, time, and the amount of acceptable sampling error. In the Ricknel Home Centers scenario, if you want to estimate the mean dollar amount of the sales invoices, you must determine in advance how large a sampling error to allow in estimating the population mean. You must also determine, in advance, the level of confidence (i.e., 90%, 95%, or 99%) to use in estimating the population parameter.

Sample Size Determination for the Mean

To develop an equation for determining the appropriate sample size needed when constructing a confidence interval estimate for the mean, recall Equation (8.1) on page 241:

$$\overline{X} \pm Z_{\alpha/2} \frac{\sigma}{\sqrt{n}}$$

In this context, some statisticians refer to *e* as the **margin of error**.

The amount added to or subtracted from $\overline{X}$ is equal to half the width of the interval. This quantity represents the amount of imprecision in the estimate that results from sampling error.[2] The sampling error, *e*, is defined as

$$e = Z_{\alpha/2} \frac{\sigma}{\sqrt{n}}$$

Solving for *n* gives the sample size needed to construct the appropriate confidence interval estimate for the mean. "Appropriate" means that the resulting interval will have an acceptable amount of sampling error.

SAMPLE SIZE DETERMINATION FOR THE MEAN

The sample size, *n*, is equal to the product of the $Z_{\alpha/2}$ value squared and the standard deviation, σ, squared, divided by the square of the sampling error, *e*.

$$n = \frac{Z_{\alpha/2}^2 \, \sigma^2}{e^2} \tag{8.4}$$

To compute the sample size, you must know three quantities:

- The desired confidence level, which determines the value of $Z_{\alpha/2}$, the critical value from the standardized normal distribution[3]
- The acceptable sampling error, *e*
- The standard deviation, σ

[3] You use Z instead of t because, to determine the critical value of t, you need to know the sample size, but you do not know it yet. For most studies, the sample size needed is large enough that the standardized normal distribution is a good approximation of the t distribution.

In some business-to-business relationships that require estimation of important parameters, legal contracts specify acceptable levels of sampling error and the confidence level required. For companies in the food and drug sectors, government regulations often specify sampling errors and confidence levels. In general, however, it is usually not easy to specify the three quantities needed to determine the sample size. How can you determine the level of confidence and sampling error? Typically, these questions are answered only by a subject matter expert (i.e., an individual very familiar with the variables under study). Although 95% is the most common confidence level used, if more confidence is desired, then 99% might be more appropriate; if less confidence is deemed acceptable, then 90% might be used. For the sampling error, you should think not of how much sampling error you would like to have (you really do not want any error) but of how much you can tolerate when reaching conclusions from the confidence interval.

In addition to specifying the confidence level and the sampling error, you need to estimate the standard deviation. Unfortunately, you rarely know the population standard deviation, σ. In some instances, you can estimate the standard deviation from past data. In other situations, you can make an educated guess by taking into account the range and distribution of the variable. For example, if you assume a normal distribution, the range is approximately equal to 6σ (i.e., $\pm 3\sigma$ around the mean) so that you estimate σ as the range divided by 6. If you cannot estimate σ in this way, you can conduct a small-scale study and estimate the standard deviation from the resulting data.

To explore how to determine the sample size needed for estimating the population mean, consider again the audit at Ricknel Home Centers. In Section 8.2, you selected a sample of 100 sales invoices and constructed a 95% confidence interval estimate for the population mean sales invoice amount. How was this sample size determined? Should you have selected a different sample size?

Suppose that, after consulting with company officials, you determine that a sampling error of no more than $\pm\$5$ is desired, along with 95% confidence. Past data indicate that the standard deviation of the sales amount is approximately \$25. Thus, $e = \$5$, $\sigma = \$25$, and $Z_{\alpha/2} = 1.96$ (for 95% confidence). Using Equation (8.4),

$$n = \frac{Z_{\alpha/2}^2\sigma^2}{e^2} = \frac{(1.96)^2(25)^2}{(5)^2}$$
$$= 96.04$$

Because the general rule is to slightly oversatisfy the criteria by rounding the sample size up to the next whole integer, you should select a sample of size 97. Thus, the sample of size $n = 100$ used on page 247 is slightly more than what is necessary to satisfy the needs of the company, based on the estimated standard deviation, desired confidence level, and sampling error. Because the calculated sample standard deviation is slightly higher than expected, \$28.95 compared to \$25.00, the confidence interval is slightly wider than desired. Figure 8.13 shows a worksheet for determining the sample size.

FIGURE 8.13
Excel worksheet for determining the sample size for estimating the mean sales invoice amount for the Ricknel Home Centers example

In the Worksheet

The NORM.S.INV function calculates the Z value that is used in the sample size calculation. The cell B13 ROUNDUP(B10, 0) function forces the calculated value in cell B10 to the next whole integer (96.0365 to 97).

Example 8.5 illustrates another application of determining the sample size needed to develop a confidence interval estimate for the mean.

EXAMPLE 8.5

Determining the Sample Size for the Mean

▶ (continued)

Returning to Example 8.3 on page 248, suppose you want to estimate, with 95% confidence, the population mean processing time to within ± 4 days. On the basis of a study conducted the previous year, you believe that the standard deviation is 25 days. Determine the sample size needed.

SOLUTION Using Equation (8.4) on page 255 and $e = 4$, $\sigma = 25$, and $Z_{\alpha/2} = 1.96$ for 95% confidence,

$$n = \frac{Z_{\alpha/2}^2 \sigma^2}{e^2} = \frac{(1.96)^2(25)^2}{(4)^2}$$
$$= 150.06$$

Therefore, you should select a sample of 151 applications because the general rule for determining sample size is to always round up to the next integer value in order to slightly oversatisfy the criteria desired. An actual sampling error larger than 4 will result if the sample standard deviation calculated in this sample of 151 is greater than 25 and smaller if the sample standard deviation is less than 25.

Sample Size Determination for the Proportion

So far in this section, you have learned how to determine the sample size needed for estimating the population mean. Now suppose that you want to determine the sample size necessary for estimating a population proportion.

To determine the sample size needed to estimate a population proportion, π, you use a method similar to the method for a population mean. Recall that in developing the sample size for a confidence interval for the mean, the sampling error is defined by

$$e = Z_{\alpha/2} \frac{\sigma}{\sqrt{n}}$$

When estimating a proportion, you replace σ with $\sqrt{\pi(1-\pi)}$. Thus, the sampling error is

$$e = Z_{\alpha/2}\sqrt{\frac{\pi(1-\pi)}{n}}$$

Solving for n, you have the sample size necessary to develop a confidence interval estimate for a proportion.

SAMPLE SIZE DETERMINATION FOR THE PROPORTION

The sample size n is equal to the product of $Z_{\alpha/2}$ squared, the population proportion, π, and 1 minus the population proportion, π, divided by the square of the sampling error, e.

$$n = \frac{Z_{\alpha/2}^2 \pi(1-\pi)}{e^2} \qquad (8.5)$$

To determine the sample size, you must know three quantities:

- The desired confidence level, which determines the value of $Z_{\alpha/2}$, the critical value from the standardized normal distribution
- The acceptable sampling error (or margin of error), e
- The population proportion, π

In practice, selecting these quantities requires some planning. Once you determine the desired level of confidence, you can find the appropriate $Z_{\alpha/2}$ value from the standardized normal distribution. The sampling error, e, indicates the amount of error that you are willing to tolerate in estimating the population proportion. The third quantity, π, is actually the population parameter that you want to estimate! Thus, how do you state a value for what you are trying to determine?

Here you have two alternatives. In many situations, you may have past information or relevant experience that provides an educated estimate of π. If you do not have past information or relevant experience, you can try to provide a value for π that would never *underestimate* the sample size needed. Referring to Equation (8.5), you can see that the quantity $\pi(1 - \pi)$ appears in the numerator. Thus, you need to determine the value of π that will make the quantity $\pi(1 - \pi)$ as large as possible. When $\pi = 0.5$, the product $\pi(1 - \pi)$ achieves its maximum value. To show this result, consider the following values of π, along with the accompanying products of $\pi(1 - \pi)$:

When $\pi = 0.9$, then $\pi(1 - \pi) = (0.9)(0.1) = 0.09$.
When $\pi = 0.7$, then $\pi(1 - \pi) = (0.7)(0.3) = 0.21$.
When $\pi = 0.5$, then $\pi(1 - \pi) = (0.5)(0.5) = 0.25$.
When $\pi = 0.3$, then $\pi(1 - \pi) = (0.3)(0.7) = 0.21$.
When $\pi = 0.1$, then $\pi(1 - \pi) = (0.1)(0.9) = 0.09$.

Therefore, when you have no prior knowledge or estimate for the population proportion π, you should use $\pi = 0.5$ for determining the sample size. Using $\pi = 0.5$ produces the largest possible sample size and results in the narrowest and most precise confidence interval. This increased precision comes at the cost of spending more time and money for an increased sample size. Also, note that if you use $\pi = 0.5$ and the proportion is different from 0.5, you will overestimate the sample size needed, because you will get a confidence interval narrower than originally intended.

Returning to the Ricknel Home Centers scenario on page 237, suppose that the auditing procedures require you to have 95% confidence in estimating the population proportion of sales invoices with errors to within ± 0.07. The results from past months indicate that the largest proportion has been no more than 0.15. Thus, using Equation (8.5) with $e = 0.07$, $\pi = 0.15$, and $Z_{\alpha/2} = 1.96$ for 95% confidence,

$$n = \frac{Z_{\alpha/2}^2 \pi(1 - \pi)}{e^2}$$

$$= \frac{(1.96)^2 (0.15)(0.85)}{(0.07)^2}$$

$$= 99.96$$

Because the general rule is to round the sample size up to the next whole integer to slightly oversatisfy the criteria, a sample size of 100 is needed. Thus, the sample size needed to satisfy the requirements of the company, based on the estimated proportion, desired confidence level, and sampling error, is equal to the sample size taken on page 252. The actual confidence interval is narrower than required because the sample proportion is 0.10, whereas 0.15 was used for π in Equation (8.5). Figure 8.14 shows a worksheet for determining the sample size.

FIGURE 8.14

Excel worksheet for determining the sample size for estimating the proportion of in-error sales invoices for Ricknel Home Centers

	A	B	
1	For the Proportion of In-Error Sales Invoices		
2			
3	Data		
4	Estimate of True Proportion	0.15	
5	Sampling Error	0.07	
6	Confidence Level	95%	
7			
8	Intermediate Calculations		
9	Z Value	-1.9600	=NORM.S.INV((1 - B6) / 2)
10	Calculated Sample Size	99.9563	=(B9^2 * B4 * (1 - B4)) / B5^2
11			
12	Result		
13	Sample Size Needed	100	=ROUNDUP(B10, 0)

In the Worksheet

The NORM.S.INV function calculates the Z value that is used in the sample size calculation. The cell B13 ROUNDUP(B10, 0) function forces the calculated value in cell B10 to the next whole integer (99.9563 to 100).

Example 8.6 provides another application of determining the sample size for estimating the population proportion.

EXAMPLE 8.6

Determining the Sample Size for the Population Proportion

You want to have 90% confidence of estimating the proportion of office workers who respond to email within an hour to within ± 0.05. Because you have not previously undertaken such a study, there is no information available from past data. Determine the sample size needed.

SOLUTION Because no information is available from past data, assume that $\pi = 0.50$. Using Equation (8.5) on page 257 and $e = 0.05$, $\pi = 0.50$, and $Z_{a/2} = 1.645$ for 90% confidence,

$$n = \frac{Z_{\alpha/2}^2 \pi (1 - \pi)}{e^2}$$

$$= \frac{(1.645)^2 (0.50)(0.50)}{(0.05)^2}$$

$$= 270.6$$

Therefore, you need a sample of 271 office workers to estimate the population proportion to within ± 0.05 with 90% confidence.

PROBLEMS FOR SECTION 8.4

LEARNING THE BASICS

8.34 If you want to be 95% confident of estimating the population mean to within a sampling error of ± 5 and the standard deviation is assumed to be 15, what sample size is required?

8.35 If you want to be 99% confident of estimating the population mean to within a sampling error of ± 20 and the standard deviation is assumed to be 100, what sample size is required?

8.36 If you want to be 99% confident of estimating the population proportion to within a sampling error of ± 0.04, what sample size is needed?

8.37 If you want to be 95% confident of estimating the population proportion to within a sampling error of ± 0.02 and there is historical evidence that the population proportion is approximately 0.40, what sample size is needed?

APPLYING THE CONCEPTS

✓**SELF TEST** **8.38** A survey is planned to determine the mean annual family medical expenses of employees of a large company. The management of the company wishes to be 95% confident that the sample mean is correct to within $\pm \$50$ of the population mean annual family medical expenses. A previous study indicates that the standard deviation is approximately $\$400$.
a. How large a sample is necessary?
b. If management wants to be correct to within $\pm \$25$, how many employees need to be selected?

8.39 If the manager of a bottled water distributor wants to estimate, with 95% confidence, the mean amount of water in a 1-gallon bottle to within ± 0.004 gallon and also assumes that the standard deviation is 0.02 gallon, what sample size is needed?

8.40 If a light bulb manufacturing company wants to estimate, with 95% confidence, the mean life of compact fluorescent light bulbs to within ± 200 hours and also assumes that the population standard deviation is 1,000 hours, how many compact fluorescent light bulbs need to be selected?

8.41 If the inspection division of a county weights and measures department wants to estimate the mean amount of soft-drink fill in 2-liter bottles to within ± 0.01 liter with 95% confidence and also assumes that the standard deviation is 0.05 liter, what sample size is needed?

8.42 An advertising executive wants to estimate the mean weekly amount of time consumers spend watching television daily. Based on previous studies, the standard deviation is assumed to be 20 minutes. The executive wants to estimate, with 99% confidence, the mean weekly amount of time to within ± 5 minutes.
a. What sample size is needed?
b. If 95% confidence is desired, how many consumers need to be selected?

8.43 An advertising executive wants to estimate the mean amount of time that consumers spend with digital media daily. From past studies, the standard deviation is estimated as 45 minutes.
a. What sample size is needed if the executive wants to be 90% confident of being correct to within ± 5 minutes?
b. If 99% confidence is desired, how many consumers need to be selected?

8.44 A growing niche in the restaurant business is gourmet-casual breakfast, lunch, and brunch. Chains in this group include Panera Bread. Suppose that the mean per-person check for breakfast at Panera Bread is approximately $\$9.50$.
a. Assuming a standard deviation of $\$2.00$, what sample size is needed to estimate, with 95% confidence, the mean per-person check for Panera Bread to within $\pm \$0.25$?

b. Assuming a standard deviation of $2.50, what sample size is needed to estimate, with 95% confidence, the mean per-person check for Panera Bread to within ±$0.25?

c. Assuming a standard deviation of $3.00, what sample size is needed to estimate, with 95% confidence, the mean per-person check for Panera Bread to within ±$0.25?

d. Discuss the effect of variation on the sample size needed.

8.45 How do Millennials respond to content marketing? According to a NewsCred study, 31% of Millennials are more likely to buy if the brand delivers interesting content that teaches them something. (Data extracted from "Build brand loyalty with millennials with meaningful content," February 25, 2015, **bit.ly/1BbXLPP**.)

a. To conduct a follow-up study that would provide 95% confidence that the point estimate is correct to within ±0.04 of the population proportion, how large a sample size is required?

b. To conduct a follow-up study that would provide 99% confidence that the point estimate is correct to within ±0.04 of the population proportion, how many people need to be sampled?

c. To conduct a follow-up study that would provide 95% confidence that the point estimate is correct to within ±0.02 of the population proportion, how large a sample size is required?

d. To conduct a follow-up study that would provide 99% confidence that the point estimate is correct to within ±0.02 of the population proportion, how many people need to be sampled?

e. Discuss the effects on sample size requirements of changing the desired confidence level and the acceptable sampling error.

8.46 A Federal Reserve Board Report looked at how consumers are using mobile devices throughout their purchase journey. In response to a survey question about mobile device use while shopping, 47% of smartphone owners said they use their smartphone to comparison shop on the Internet while at a retail store, 33% said they use a barcode scanning application for price comparisons, and 42% said they use their smartphone to get product reviews or product information while shopping at a retail store. (Data extracted from "Consumers and mobile Financial Services, March 2015," **1.usa.gov/1QtSryc**.) Suppose the results are based on a survey of 300 smartphone owners. Construct a 95% confidence interval estimate of the population proportion of smartphone owners who said they use their mobile device while shopping to

a. comparison shop on the Internet while at a retail shop.

b. price compare with a barcode scanning application.

c. get product reviews or product information while shopping at a retail store.

d. You have been asked to update the results of this study. Determine the sample size necessary to estimate, with 95% confidence, the population proportions in (a) through (c) to within ±0.02.

8.47 In a study of 362 nonprofits nationwide, 98 indicated that the greatest employee retention challenge they face is an inability to pay competitively. (Data extracted from *2015 Nonprofit Employment Practices Survey*, Nonprofit HR, **bit.ly/1SbD0Ir**.)

a. Construct a 95% confidence interval for the population proportion of nonprofits that indicate inability to pay competitively as the greatest employee retention challenge at their organization.

b. Interpret the interval constructed in (a).

c. If you wanted to conduct a follow-up study to estimate the population proportion of nonprofits that indicate inability to pay competitively as the greatest employee retention challenge at their organization to within ±0.01 with 95% confidence, how many nonprofits would you survey?

8.48 Cybersecurity is a critical business issue that demands the attention of an institution's Chief Executive Officer and the Board of Directors. According to a PwC study, 33% of financial services institutions say their Board is involved in the review of security and privacy risks. (Data extracted from *Managing cyber risks in an interconnected world*, available at **pwc.to/1L3woHX**.)

a. If you conduct a follow-up study to estimate the population proportion of financial institutions with Boards involved in the review of security and privacy risks, would you use a π of 0.33 or 0.50 in the sample size formula?

b. Using you answer in part (a), find the sample size necessary to estimate, with 95% confidence, the population proportion to within ±0.03.

8.49 How do consumers feel about companies sharing and selling their personal data? A Bain & Company press release (**bit.ly/1FZ1QCH**) reports that a new survey they conducted found that 67% of consumers indicate that it should be illegal for companies to collect or use such data without getting prior consent.

a. To conduct a follow-up study that would provide 99% confidence that the point estimate is correct to within ±0.03 of the population proportion, how many consumers need to be sampled?

b. To conduct a follow-up study that would provide 99% confidence that the point estimate is correct to within ±0.05 of the population proportion, how many consumers need to be sampled?

c. Compare the results of (a) and (b).

8.5 Confidence Interval Estimation and Ethical Issues

The selection of samples and the inferences that accompany them raise several ethical issues. The major ethical issue concerns whether confidence interval estimates accompany point estimates. Failure to include a confidence interval estimate might mislead the user of the results into thinking that the point estimate is all that is needed to predict the population characteristic with certainty. Confidence interval limits (typically set at 95%), the sample size used, and an interpretation of the meaning of the confidence interval in terms that a person untrained in statistics can understand should always accompany point estimates.

When media outlets publicize the results of a political poll, they often overlook this type of information. Sometimes, the results of a poll include the sampling error, but the sampling error is often presented in fine print or as an afterthought to the story being reported. A fully ethical presentation of poll results would give equal prominence to the confidence levels, sample size, sampling error, and confidence limits of the poll.

When you prepare your own point estimates, always state the interval estimate in a *prominent* place and include a brief explanation of the meaning of the confidence interval. In addition, make sure you highlight the sample size and sampling error.

8.6 Application of Confidence Interval Estimation in Auditing

Auditing is the collection and evaluation of evidence about information related to an economic entity in order to determine and report on how well the information corresponds to established criteria. Auditing uses probability sampling methods to develop confidence interval estimates. The **Section 8.6 online topic** reviews three common applications of confidence interval estimation in auditing.

8.7 Estimation and Sample Size Estimation for Finite Populations

To develop confidence interval estimates for population parameters or determine sample sizes when estimating population parameters, you use the finite population correction factor when samples are selected without replacement from a finite population. The **Section 8.7 online topic** explains how to use the finite population correction factor for these purposes.

8.8 Bootstrapping

The confidence interval estimation procedures discussed in this chapter make assumptions that are often not valid, especially for small samples. Bootstrapping, the selection of an initial sample and repeated sampling from that initial sample, provides an alternative approach that does not rely on those assumptions. The **Section 8.8 online topic** explains this alternative technique.

▼USING **STATISTICS**
Getting Estimates ..., Revisited

In the Ricknel Home Centers scenario, you were an accountant for a distributor of home improvement supplies in the northeastern United States. You were responsible for the accuracy of the integrated inventory management and sales information system. You used confidence interval estimation techniques to draw conclusions about the population of all records from a relatively small sample collected during an audit.

At the end of the month, you collected a random sample of 100 sales invoices and made the following inferences:

- With 95% confidence, you concluded that the mean amount of all the sales invoices is between $104.53 and $116.01.

- With 95% confidence, you concluded that between 4.12% and 15.88% of all the sales invoices contain errors.

These estimates provide an interval of values that you believe contain the true population parameters. If these intervals are too wide (i.e., the sampling error is too large) for the types of decisions Ricknel Home Centers needs to make, you will need to take a larger sample. You can use the sample size formulas in Section 8.4 to determine the number of sales invoices to sample to ensure that the size of the sampling error is acceptable.

▼ SUMMARY

This chapter discusses confidence intervals for estimating the characteristics of a population, along with how you can determine the necessary sample size. You learned how to apply these methods to numerical and categorical data. Table 8.3 provides a list of topics covered in this chapter.

To determine what equation to use for a particular situation, you need to answer these questions:

- Are you constructing a confidence interval, or are you determining sample size?
- Do you have a numerical variable, or do you have a categorical variable?

TABLE 8.3
Summary of Topics in
Chapter 8

	TYPE OF DATA	
TYPE OF ANALYSIS	**Numerical**	**Categorical**
Confidence interval for a population parameter	Confidence interval estimate for the mean (Sections 8.1 and 8.2)	Confidence interval estimate for the proportion (Section 8.3)
Determining sample size	Sample size determination for the mean (Section 8.4)	Sample size determination for the proportion (Section 8.4)

▼ REFERENCES

1. Cochran, W. G. *Sampling Techniques*, 3rd ed. New York: Wiley, 1977.
2. Daniel, W. W. *Applied Nonparametric Statistics*, 2nd ed. Boston: PWS Kent, 1990.
3. Fisher, R. A., and F. Yates. *Statistical Tables for Biological, Agricultural and Medical Research*, 5th ed. Edinburgh: Oliver & Boyd, 1957.
4. Hahn, G., and W. Meeker. *Statistical Intervals: A Guide for Practitioners*. New York: John Wiley and Sons, Inc., 1991.
5. Kirk, R. E., ed. *Statistical Issues: A Reader for the Behavioral Sciences*. Belmont, CA: Wadsworth, 1972.
6. Larsen, R. L., and M. L. Marx. *An Introduction to Mathematical Statistics and Its Applications*, 5th ed. Upper Saddle River, NJ: Prentice Hall, 2012.
7. Snedecor, G. W., and W. G. Cochran. *Statistical Methods*, 7th ed. Ames, IA: Iowa State University Press, 1980.

▼ KEY EQUATIONS

Confidence Interval for the Mean (σ Known)

$$\bar{X} \pm Z_{\alpha/2}\frac{\sigma}{\sqrt{n}}$$

or

$$\bar{X} - Z_{\alpha/2}\frac{\sigma}{\sqrt{n}} \le \mu \le \bar{X} + Z_{\alpha/2}\frac{\sigma}{\sqrt{n}} \qquad (8.1)$$

Confidence Interval for the Mean (σ Unknown)

$$\bar{X} \pm t_{\alpha/2}\frac{S}{\sqrt{n}}$$

or

$$\bar{X} - t_{\alpha/2}\frac{S}{\sqrt{n}} \le \mu \le \bar{X} + t_{\alpha/2}\frac{S}{\sqrt{n}} \qquad (8.2)$$

Confidence Interval Estimate for the Proportion

$$p \pm Z_{\alpha/2}\sqrt{\frac{p(1-p)}{n}}$$

or

$$p - Z_{\alpha/2}\sqrt{\frac{p(1-p)}{n}} \le \pi \le p + Z_{\alpha/2}\sqrt{\frac{p(1-p)}{n}} \qquad (8.3)$$

Sample Size Determination for the Mean

$$n = \frac{Z_{\alpha/2}^2 \sigma^2}{e^2} \qquad (8.4)$$

Sample Size Determination for the Proportion

$$n = \frac{Z_{\alpha/2}^2 \pi(1-\pi)}{e^2} \qquad (8.5)$$

▼KEY TERMS

confidence interval estimate   238
critical value   242
degrees of freedom   244

level of confidence   241
margin of error   255
point estimate   238

sampling error   241
Student's *t* distribution   244

▼CHECKING YOUR UNDERSTANDING

8.50 Why can you never really have 100% confidence of correctly estimating the population characteristic of interest?

8.51 When should you use the *t* distribution to develop the confidence interval estimate for the mean?

8.52 Why is it true that for a given sample size, *n*, an increase in confidence is achieved by widening (and making less precise) the confidence interval?

8.53 Why is the sample size needed to determine the proportion smaller when the population proportion is 0.20 than when the population proportion is 0.50?

▼CHAPTER REVIEW PROBLEMS

8.54 A GlobalWebIndex study, as reported by TechCrunch (**tcrn.ch/1MPKLRf**), noted the percentage of adult Internet users that owned various devices. Suppose that a survey of 1,000 adult Internet users found the 910 adult users own a computer, 800 own a smartphone, 470 own a tablet, and 90 own a smart watch.
a. For each of the four devices, construct a 95% confidence interval estimate for the population proportion of the adult Internet users that own the device.
b. What conclusions can you reach concerning which devices adult Internet users have?

8.55 How do women try to save when shopping for groceries? A sample of 1,008 adult women in the U. S. revealed that 937 women buy store brands, 837 women use print coupons, 726 women plan meals around sale items, and 333 women buy groceries online. (Data extracted from "Grocery Savings Habits of the American Woman," *Consumer Reports*, October 2014, p. 11.)
a. For each way women try to save when shopping for groceries, construct a 95% confidence interval estimate of the population proportion.
b. What conclusions can you reach concerning how adult women in the U. S. try to save when shopping for groceries?

8.56 A market researcher for a consumer electronics company wants to study the media viewing behavior of residents of a particular area. A random sample of 40 respondents is selected, and each respondent is instructed to keep a detailed record of time spent engaged viewing content across all screens (traditional TV, DVD/Blu-ray, game console, Internet on a computer, video on a computer, video on a smartphone) in a particular week. The results are as follows:
Content viewing time per week: $\bar{X} = 51$ hours, $S = 3.5$ hours. 32 respondents have high definition (HD) on at least one television set.
a. Construct a 95% confidence interval estimate for the mean content viewing time per week in this area.
b. Construct a 95% confidence interval estimate for the population proportion of residents who have HD on at least one television set.

Suppose that the market researcher wants to take another survey in a different location. Answer these questions:

c. What sample size is required to be 95% confident of estimating the population mean content viewing time to within ±2 hours assuming that the population standard deviation is equal to 5 hours?
d. How many respondents need to be selected to be 95% confident of being within ±0.06 of the population proportion who have HD on at least one television set if no previous estimate is available?
e. Based on (c) and (d), how many respondents should the market researcher select if a single survey is being conducted?

8.57 An information technology (IT) consulting firm specializing in health care solutions wants to study communication deficiencies in the health care industry. A random sample of 70 health care clinicians reveals the following:
Time wasted in a day due to outdated communication technologies: $\bar{X} = 45$ minutes, $S = 10$ minutes.
Thirty-six health care clinicians cite inefficiency of pagers as the reason for the wasted time.
a. Construct a 99% confidence interval estimate for the population mean time wasted in a day due to outdated communication technologies.
b. Construct a 95% confidence interval estimate for the population proportion of health care clinicians who cite inefficiency of pagers as the reason for the wasted time.

8.58 The human resource (HR) director of a large corporation wishes to study absenteeism among its mid-level managers at its central office during the year. A random sample of 25 mid-level managers reveals the following:
Absenteeism: $\bar{X} = 6.2$ days, $S = 7.3$ days.
13 mid-level managers cite stress as a cause of absence.
a. Construct a 95% confidence interval estimate for the mean number of absences for mid-level managers during the year.
b. Construct a 95% confidence interval estimate for the population proportion of mid-level managers who cite stress as a cause of absence.

Suppose that the HR director wishes to administer a survey in one of its regional offices. Answer these questions:
c. What sample size is needed to have 95% confidence in estimating the population mean absenteeism to within ±1.5 days if the population standard deviation is estimated to be 8 days?

d. How many mid-level managers need to be selected to have 90% confidence in estimating the population proportion of mid-level managers who cite stress as a cause of absence to within ±0.075 if no previous estimate is available?

e. Based on (c) and (d), what sample size is needed if a single survey is being conducted?

8.59 A national association devoted to HR and workplace programs, practices, and training wants to study HR department practices and employee turnover of its member organizations. HR professionals and organization executives focus on turnover not only because it has significant cost implications but also because it affects overall business performance. A survey is designed to estimate the proportion of member organizations that have both talent and development programs in place to drive human-capital management as well as the member organizations' mean annual employee turnover cost (cost to fill a frontline employee position left vacant due to turnover). A random sample of 100 member organizations reveals the following:

Frontline employee turnover cost: $\overline{X} = \$12,500$, $S = \$1,000$. Thirty member organizations have both talent and development programs in place to drive human-capital management.

a. Construct a 95% confidence interval estimate for the population mean frontline employee turnover cost of member organizations.

b. Construct a 95% confidence interval estimate for the population proportion of member organizations that have both talent and development programs in place to drive human-capital management.

c. What sample size is needed to have 99% confidence of estimating the population mean frontline employee turnover cost to within ±\$250?

d. How many member organizations need to be selected to have 90% confidence of estimating the population proportion of organizations that have both talent and development programs in place to drive human-capital management to within ±0.045?

8.60 The financial impact of IT systems downtime is a concern of plant operations management today. A survey of manufacturers examined the satisfaction level with the reliability and availability of their manufacturing IT applications. The variables of focus are whether the manufacturer experienced downtime in the past year that affected one or more manufacturing IT applications, the number of downtime incidents that occurred in the past year, and the approximate cost of a typical downtime incident. The results from a sample of 200 manufacturers are as follows:

Sixty-two experienced downtime this year that affected one or more manufacturing applications.
Number of downtime incidents: $\overline{X} = 3.5$, $S = 2.0$
Cost of downtime incidents: $\overline{X} = \$18,000$, $S = \$3,000$.

a. Construct a 90% confidence interval estimate for the population proportion of manufacturers who experienced downtime in the past year that affected one or more manufacturing IT applications.

b. Construct a 95% confidence interval estimate for the population mean number of downtime incidents experienced by manufacturers in the past year.

c. Construct a 95% confidence interval estimate for the population mean cost of downtime incidents.

8.61 The branch manager of an outlet (Store 1) of a nationwide chain of pet supply stores wants to study characteristics of her cus-

tomers. In particular, she decides to focus on two variables: the amount of money spent by customers and whether the customers own only one dog, only one cat, or more than one dog and/or cat. The results from a sample of 70 customers are as follows:

- Amount of money spent: $\overline{X} = \$21.34$, $S = \$9.22$.
- Thirty-seven customers own only a dog.
- Twenty-six customers own only a cat.
- Seven customers own more than one dog and/or cat.

a. Construct a 95% confidence interval estimate for the population mean amount spent in the pet supply store.

b. Construct a 90% confidence interval estimate for the population proportion of customers who own only a cat.

The branch manager of another outlet (Store 2) wishes to conduct a similar survey in his store. The manager does not have access to the information generated by the manager of Store 1. Answer the following questions:

c. What sample size is needed to have 95% confidence of estimating the population mean amount spent in this store to within ±\$1.50 if the standard deviation is estimated to be \$10?

d. How many customers need to be selected to have 90% confidence of estimating the population proportion of customers who own only a cat to within ±0.045?

e. Based on your answers to (c) and (d), how large a sample should the manager take?

8.62 Scarlett and Heather, the owners of an upscale restaurant in Dayton, Ohio, want to study the dining characteristics of their customers. They decide to focus on two variables: the amount of money spent by customers and whether customers order dessert. The results from a sample of 60 customers are as follows:
Amount spent: $\overline{X} = \$38.54$, $S = \$7.26$.
Eighteen customers purchased dessert.

a. Construct a 95% confidence interval estimate for the population mean amount spent per customer in the restaurant.

b. Construct a 90% confidence interval estimate for the population proportion of customers who purchase dessert.

Jeanine, the owner of a competing restaurant, wants to conduct a similar survey in her restaurant. Jeanine does not have access to the information that Scarlett and Heather have obtained from the survey they conducted. Answer the following questions:

c. What sample size is needed to have 95% confidence of estimating the population mean amount spent in her restaurant to within ±\$1.50, assuming that the standard deviation is estimated to be \$8?

d. How many customers need to be selected to have 90% confidence of estimating the population proportion of customers who purchase dessert to within ±0.04?

e. Based on your answers to (c) and (d), how large a sample should Jeanine take?

8.63 The manufacturer of Ice Melt claims that its product will melt snow and ice at temperatures as low as 0° Fahrenheit. A representative for a large chain of hardware stores is interested in testing this claim. The chain purchases a large shipment of 5-pound bags for distribution. The representative wants to know, with 95% confidence and within ±0.05, what proportion of bags of Ice Melt perform the job as claimed by the manufacturer.

a. How many bags does the representative need to test? What assumption should be made concerning the population proportion? (This is called *destructive testing*; i.e., the product being tested is destroyed by the test and is then unavailable to be sold.)

b. Suppose that the representative tests 50 bags, and 42 of them do the job as claimed. Construct a 95% confidence interval estimate for the population proportion that will do the job as claimed.

c. How can the representative use the results of (b) to determine whether to sell the Ice Melt product?

8.64 Claims fraud (illegitimate claims) and buildup (exaggerated loss amounts) continue to be major issues of concern among automobile insurance companies. Fraud is defined as specific material misrepresentation of the facts of a loss; buildup is defined as the inflation of an otherwise legitimate claim. A recent study examined auto injury claims closed with payment under private passenger coverages. Detailed data on injury, medical treatment, claimed losses, and total payments, as well as claim-handling techniques, were collected. In addition, auditors were asked to review the claim files to indicate whether specific elements of fraud or buildup appeared in the claim and, in the case of buildup, to specify the amount of excess payment. The file InsuranceClaims contains data for 90 randomly selected auto injury claims. The following variables are included: CLAIM—Claim ID; BUILDUP—1 if buildup indicated, 0 if not; and EXCESSPAYMENT—excess payment amount, in dollars.

a. Construct a 95% confidence interval for the population proportion of all auto injury files that have exaggerated loss amounts.

b. Construct a 95% confidence interval for the population mean dollar excess payment amount.

8.65 A quality characteristic of interest for a tea-bag-filling process is the weight of the tea in the individual bags. In this example, the label weight on the package indicates that the mean amount is 5.5 grams of tea in a bag. If the bags are underfilled, two problems arise. First, customers may not be able to brew the tea to be as strong as they wish. Second, the company may be in violation of the truth-in-labeling laws. On the other hand, if the mean amount of tea in a bag exceeds the label weight, the company is giving away product. Getting an exact amount of tea in a bag is problematic because of variation in the temperature and humidity inside the factory, differences in the density of the tea, and the extremely fast filling operation of the machine (approximately 170 bags per minute). The following data (stored in Teabags) are the weights, in grams, of a sample of 50 tea bags produced in one hour by a single machine:

5.65 5.44 5.42 5.40 5.53 5.34 5.54 5.45 5.52 5.41
5.57 5.40 5.53 5.54 5.55 5.62 5.56 5.46 5.44 5.51
5.47 5.40 5.47 5.61 5.53 5.32 5.67 5.29 5.49 5.55
5.77 5.57 5.42 5.58 5.58 5.50 5.32 5.50 5.53 5.58
5.61 5.45 5.44 5.25 5.56 5.63 5.50 5.57 5.67 5.36

a. Construct a 99% confidence interval estimate for the population mean weight of the tea bags.

b. Is the company meeting the requirement set forth on the label that the mean amount of tea in a bag is 5.5 grams?

c. Do you think the assumption needed to construct the confidence interval estimate in (a) is valid?

8.66 A manufacturing company produces steel housings for electrical equipment. The main component part of the housing is a steel trough that is made from a 14-gauge steel coil. It is produced using a 250-ton progressive punch press with a wipe-down operation that puts two 90-degree forms in the flat steel to make the trough. The distance from one side of the form to the other is critical because of weatherproofing in outdoor applications. The widths (in inches), shown in the next column and stored in Trough , are from a sample of 49 troughs:

8.312 8.343 8.317 8.383 8.348 8.410 8.351 8.373 8.481

8.422 8.476 8.382 8.484 8.403 8.414 8.419 8.385 8.465

8.498 8.447 8.436 8.413 8.489 8.414 8.481 8.415 8.479

8.429 8.458 8.462 8.460 8.444 8.429 8.460 8.412 8.420

8.410 8.405 8.323 8.420 8.396 8.447 8.405 8.439 8.411

8.427 8.420 8.498 8.409

a. Construct a 95% confidence interval estimate for the mean width of the troughs.

b. Interpret the interval developed in (a).

c. Do you think the assumption needed to construct the confidence interval estimate in (a) is valid?

8.67 The manufacturer of Boston and Vermont asphalt shingles knows that product weight is a major factor in a customer's perception of quality. The last stage of the assembly line packages the shingles before they are placed on wooden pallets. Once a pallet is full (a pallet for most brands holds 16 squares of shingles), it is weighed, and the measurement is recorded. The file Pallet contains the weight (in pounds) from a sample of 368 pallets of Boston shingles and 330 pallets of Vermont shingles.

a. For the Boston shingles, construct a 95% confidence interval estimate for the mean weight.

b. For the Vermont shingles, construct a 95% confidence interval estimate for the mean weight.

c. Do you think the assumption needed to construct the confidence interval estimates in (a) and (b) is valid?

d. Based on the results of (a) and (b), what conclusions can you reach concerning the mean weight of the Boston and Vermont shingles?

8.68 The manufacturer of Boston and Vermont asphalt shingles provides its customers with a 20-year warranty on most of its products. To determine whether a shingle will last the entire warranty period, accelerated-life testing is conducted at the manufacturing plant. Accelerated-life testing exposes the shingle to the stresses it would be subject to in a lifetime of normal use via a laboratory experiment that takes only a few minutes to conduct. In this test, a shingle is repeatedly scraped with a brush for a short period of time, and the shingle granules removed by the brushing are weighed (in grams). Shingles that experience low amounts of granule loss are expected to last longer in normal use than shingles that experience high amounts of granule loss. In this situation, a shingle should experience no more than 0.8 grams of granule loss if it is expected to last the length of the warranty period. The file Granule contains a sample of 170 measurements made on the company's Boston shingles and 140 measurements made on Vermont shingles.

a. For the Boston shingles, construct a 95% confidence interval estimate for the mean granule loss.

b. For the Vermont shingles, construct a 95% confidence interval estimate for the mean granule loss.

c. Do you think the assumption needed to construct the confidence interval estimates in (a) and (b) is valid?

d. Based on the results of (a) and (b), what conclusions can you reach concerning the mean granule loss of the Boston and Vermont shingles?

REPORT WRITING EXERCISE

8.69 Referring to the results in Problem 8.66 concerning the width of a steel trough, write a report that summarizes your conclusions.

▾CASES

Managing Ashland MultiComm Services

Marketing Manager Lauren Adler seeks to increase the number of subscribers to the AMS *3-For-All* cable TV & Internet and smartphone service. Her staff has designed the following 10-question survey to help determine various characteristics of households who subscribe to AMS cable or cellphone services.

1. Does your household subscribe to smartphone service from Ashland?   (1) Yes   (2) No

2. Does your household subscribe to Internet service from Ashland?   (1) Yes   (2) No

3. How often do you watch streaming video on any device?
   (1) Every day   (2) Most days
   (3) Occasionally or never

4. What type of cable television service do you have?
   (1) Basic or none   (2) Enhanced

5. How often do you watch premium content that requires an extra fee?
   (1) Almost every day   (2) Several times a week
   (3) Rarely   (4) Never

6. Which method did you use to obtain your current AMS subscription?
   (1) AMS email/text offer   (4) In-store signup
   (2) AMS toll-free number   (5) MyTVLab promotion
   (3) AMS website

7. Would you consider subscribing to the *3-For-All* service for a trial period if a discount were offered?
   (1) Yes   (2) No
   (If no, skip to question 9.)

8. If purchased separately, cable TV and Internet and smartphone service would currently cost $160 per month. How much would you be willing to pay per month for the *3-For-All* service?

9. Does your household use another provider of cellphone services?   (1) Yes   (2) No

10. AMS may distribute vouchers good for one free smartphone for subscribers who agree to a two-year subscription contract to the *3-For-All* service. Would being eligible to receive a voucher cause you to agree to the two-year term?
   (1) Yes   (2) No

Of the 500 households selected that subscribe to cable television service from Ashland, 82 households either refused to participate, could not be contacted after repeated attempts, or had telephone numbers that were not in service. The summary results for the 418 households that were contacted are as follows:

Household Has AMS Smartphone Service	Frequency
Yes	83
No	335

Household Has AMS Internet Service	Frequency
Yes	262
No	156

Streams Video	Frequency
Every day	170
Most days	166
Occasionally or never	82

Type of Cable Service	Frequency
Basic or none	164
Enhanced	254

Watches Premium Content	Frequency
Almost every day	16
Several times a week	40
Almost never	179
Never	183

Method Used to Obtain Subscription	Frequency
AMS email/text offer	70
AMS toll-free number	64
AMS website	236
In-store signup	36
MyTVLab promotion	12

Would Consider Discounted Trial Offer	Frequency
Yes	40
No	378

Trial Monthly Rate ($) Willing to Pay (stored in AMS8)

100 79 114 50 91 106 67 110 70 113 90 115 98 75 119
100 90 60 89 105 65 91 86 91 84 92 95 85 80 108
 90 97 79 91 125 99 98 50 77 85

Uses Another Cellphone Provider	Frequency
Yes	369
No	49

Voucher for Two-Year Agreement	Frequency
Yes	38
No	380

Analyze the results of the survey of Ashland households that receive AMS cable television service. Write a report that discusses the marketing implications of the survey results for Ashland MultiComm Services.

Digital Case

Apply your knowledge about confidence interval estimation in this Digital Case, which extends the MyTVLab Digital Case from Chapter 6.

Among its other features, the MyTVLab website allows customers to purchase MyTVLab LifeStyles merchandise online. To handle payment processing, the management of MyTVLab has contracted with the following firms:

- **PayAFriend (PAF)**—This is an online payment system with which customers and businesses such as MyTVLab register in order to exchange payments in a secure and convenient manner, without the need for a credit card.
- **Continental Banking Company (Conbanco)**—This processing services provider allows MyTVLab customers to pay for merchandise using nationally recognized credit cards issued by a financial institution.

To reduce costs, management is considering eliminating one of these two payment systems. However, Lorraine Hildick of the sales department suspects that customers use the two forms of payment in unequal numbers and that customers display different buying behaviors when using the two forms of payment. Therefore, she would like to first determine the following:

- The proportion of customers using PAF and the proportion of customers using a credit card to pay for their purchases.
- The mean purchase amount when using PAF and the mean purchase amount when using a credit card.

Assist Ms. Hildick by preparing an appropriate analysis. Open **PaymentsSample.pdf**, read Ms. Hildick's comments, and use her random sample of 50 transactions as the basis for your analysis. Summarize your findings to determine whether Ms. Hildick's conjectures about MyTVLab LifeStyle customer purchasing behaviors are correct. If you want the sampling error to be no more than $3 when estimating the mean purchase amount, is Ms. Hildick's sample large enough to perform a valid analysis?

Sure Value Convenience Stores

You work in the corporate office for a nationwide convenience store franchise that operates nearly 10,000 stores. The per-store daily customer count has been steady, at 900, for some time

(i.e., the mean number of customers in a store in one day is 900). To increase the customer count, the franchise is considering cutting coffee prices. The 12-ounce size will now be $0.59 instead of $0.99, and the 16-ounce size will be $0.69 instead of $1.19. Even with this reduction in price, the franchise will have a 40% gross margin on coffee. To test the new initiative, the franchise has reduced coffee prices in a sample of 34 stores, where customer counts have been running almost exactly at the national average of 900. After four weeks, the sample stores stabilize at a mean customer count of 974 and a standard deviation of 96. This increase seems like a substantial amount to you, but it also seems like a pretty small sample. Is there some way to get a feel for what the mean per-store count in all the stores will be if you cut coffee prices nationwide? Do you think reducing coffee prices is a good strategy for increasing the mean number of customers?

CardioGood Fitness

Return to the CardioGood Fitness case first presented on page 28. Using the data stored in CardioGood Fitness :

1. Construct 95% confidence interval estimates to create a customer profile for each CardioGood Fitness treadmill product line.
2. Write a report to be presented to the management of CardioGood Fitness detailing your findings.

More Descriptive Choices Follow-Up

Follow up the More Descriptive Choices Revisited, Using Statistics scenario on page 136 by constructing 95% confidence intervals estimates of the three-year return percentages, five-year return percentages, and ten-year return percentages for the sample of growth and value funds and for the small, mid-cap, and large market cap funds (stored in Retirement Funds). In your analysis, examine differences between the growth and value funds as well as the differences among the small, mid-cap, and large market cap funds.

Clear Mountain State Student Survey

The Student News Service at Clear Mountain State University (CMSU) has decided to gather data about the undergraduate students that attend CMSU. They create and distribute a survey of 14 questions and receive responses from 62 undergraduates (stored in StudentSurvey). For each variable included in the survey, construct a 95% confidence interval estimate for the population characteristic and write a report summarizing your conclusions.

▼EXCEL GUIDE

EG8.1 CONFIDENCE INTERVAL ESTIMATE for the MEAN (σ KNOWN)

Key Technique Use the **NORM.S.INV(*cumulative percentage*)** to compute the Z value for one-half of the $(1 - \alpha)$ value and use the **CONFIDENCE(1 − *confidence level, population standard deviation*, *sample size*)** function to compute the half-width of a confidence interval.

Example Compute the confidence interval estimate for the mean for the Example 8.1 mean paper length problem on page 242.

PHStat Use **Estimate for the Mean, sigma known**. For the example, select **PHStat → Confidence Intervals → Estimate for the Mean, sigma known**. In the procedure's dialog box (shown below):

1. Enter **0.02** as the **Population Standard Deviation**.
2. Enter **95** as the **Confidence Level** percentage.
3. Click **Sample Statistics Known** and enter **100** as the **Sample Size** and **10.998** as the **Sample Mean**.
4. Enter a **Title** and click **OK**.

When using unsummarized data, click **Sample Statistics Unknown** and enter the **Sample Cell Range** in step 3.

Workbook Use the **COMPUTE worksheet** of the **CIE sigma known workbook** as a template.
The worksheet already contains the data for the example.

For other problems, change the **Population Standard Deviation, Sample Mean, Sample Size**, and **Confidence Level** values in cells B4 through B7.

EG8.2 CONFIDENCE INTERVAL ESTIMATE for the MEAN (σ UNKNOWN)

Key Technique Use the **T.INV.2T(1 − *confidence level, degrees of freedom*)** function to determine the critical value from the *t* distribution.

Example Compute the Figure 8.7 confidence interval estimate for the mean sales invoice amount show on page 247.

PHStat Use **Estimate for the Mean, sigma unknown**. For the example, select **PHStat → Confidence Intervals → Estimate for the Mean, sigma unknown**. In the procedure's dialog box (shown below):

1. Enter **95** as the **Confidence Level** percentage.
2. Click **Sample Statistics Known** and enter **100** as the **Sample Size**, **110.27** as the **Sample Mean**, and **28.95** as the **Sample Std. Deviation**.
3. Enter a **Title** and click **OK**.

When using unsummarized data, click **Sample Statistics Unknown** and enter the **Sample Cell Range** in step 2.

Workbook Use the **COMPUTE worksheet** of the **CIE sigma unknown workbook** as a template.
The worksheet already contains the data for the example.

For other problems, change the **Sample Standard Deviation, Sample Mean, Sample Size**, and **Confidence Level** values in cells B4 through B7.

EG8.3 CONFIDENCE INTERVAL ESTIMATE for the PROPORTION

Key Technique Use the **NORM.S.INV((1 − *confidence level*)/2)** function to compute the *Z* value.

Example Compute the Figure 8.12 confidence interval estimate for the proportion of in-error sales invoices shown on page 253.

PHStat Use **Estimate for the Proportion**.
For the example, select **PHStat → Confidence Intervals → Estimate for the Proportion**. In the procedure's dialog box (shown below):

1. Enter **100** as the **Sample Size**.
2. Enter **10** as the **Number of Successes**.
3. Enter **95** as the **Confidence Level** percentage.
4. Enter a **Title** and click **OK**.

Workbook Use the **COMPUTE worksheet** of the **CIE Proportion workbook** as a template.
The worksheet already contains the data for the example.

To compute confidence interval estimates for other problems, change the **Sample Size**, **Number of Successes**, and **Confidence Level** values in cells B4 through B6.

EG8.4 DETERMINING SAMPLE SIZE

Sample Size Determination for the Mean

Key Technique Use the **NORM.S.INV((1 − *confidence level*)/2)** function to compute the *Z* value and use the **ROUNDUP(*calculated sample size*, 0)** function to round up the computed sample size to the next higher integer.

Example Determine the sample size for the mean sales invoice amount example that is shown in Figure 8.13 on page 256.

PHStat Use **Determination for the Mean**.
For the example, select **PHStat → Sample Size → Determination for the Mean**. In the procedure's dialog box (shown at top right):

1. Enter **25** as the **Population Standard Deviation**.
2. Enter **5** as the **Sampling Error**.
3. Enter **95** as the **Confidence Level** percentage.
4. Enter a **Title** and click **OK**.

Workbook Use the **COMPUTE worksheet** of the **Sample Size Mean workbook** as a template.
The worksheet already contains the data for the example.

For other problems, change the **Population Standard Deviation**, **Sampling Error**, and **Confidence Level** values in cells B4 through B6.

Sample Size Determination for the Proportion

Key Technique Use the **NORM.S.INV** and **ROUNDUP** functions discussed previously to help determine the sample size needed for estimating the proportion.

Example Determine the sample size for the proportion of in-error sales invoices example that is shown in Figure 8.14 on page 258.

PHStat Use **Determination for the Proportion**.
For the example, select **PHStat → Sample Size → Determination for the Proportion**. In the procedure's dialog box (shown below):

1. Enter **0.15** as the **Estimate of True Proportion**.
2. Enter **0.07** as the **Sampling Error**.
3. Enter **95** as the **Confidence Level** percentage.
4. Enter a **Title** and click **OK**.

Workbook Use the **COMPUTE worksheet** of the **Sample Size Proportion workbook** as a template.
The worksheet already contains the data for the example.

To compute confidence interval estimates for other problems, change the **Estimate of True Proportion**, **Sampling Error**, and **Confidence Level** in cells B4 through B6.

9

Fundamentals of Hypothesis Testing: One-Sample Tests

CONTENTS

OBJECTIVES

- Learn the basic principles of hypothesis testing
- How to use hypothesis testing to test a mean or proportion
- Identify the assumptions of each hypothesis-testing procedure, how to evaluate them, and the consequences if they are seriously violated
- Become aware of the pitfalls and ethical issues involved in hypothesis testing
- How to avoid the pitfalls involved in hypothesis testing

▼ USING STATISTICS
Significant Testing at Oxford Cereals

As in Chapter 7, you again find yourself as plant operations manager for Oxford Cereals. Among other responsibilities, you are responsible for monitoring the amount in each cereal box filled. Company specifications require a mean weight of 368 grams per box. You must adjust the cereal-filling process when the mean fill-weight in the population of boxes differs from 368 grams. Adjusting the process requires shutting down the cereal production line temporarily, so you do not want to make unnecessary adjustments.

What decision-making method can you use to decide if the cereal-filling process needs to be adjusted? You decide to begin by selecting a random sample of 25 cereal boxes and weighing each box. From the weights collected, you compute a sample mean. How could that sample mean be used to help decide whether adjustment is necessary?

n Chapter 7, you learned methods to determine whether the value of a sample mean is consistent with a known population mean. In this Oxford Cereals scenario, you seek to use a sample mean to validate a claim about the population mean, a somewhat different problem. For this type of situation, you use the inferential method known as **hypothesis testing**. Hypothesis testing requires that you state a claim unambiguously. In this scenario, the claim is that the population mean is 368 grams. You examine a sample statistic to see if it better supports the stated claim, called the *null hypothesis*, or the mutually exclusive alternative hypothesis (for this scenario, that the population mean is not 368 grams).

In this chapter, you will learn several applications of hypothesis testing. You will learn how to make inferences about a population parameter by *analyzing differences* between the results observed, the sample statistic, and the results you would expect to get if an underlying hypothesis were actually true. For the Oxford Cereals scenario, hypothesis testing allows you to infer one of the following:

- The mean weight of the cereal boxes in the sample is a value consistent with what you would expect if the mean of the entire population of cereal boxes were 368 grams.
- The population mean is not equal to 368 grams because the sample mean is significantly different from 368 grams.

9.1 Fundamentals of Hypothesis-Testing Methodology

Hypothesis testing typically begins with a theory, a claim, or an assertion about a particular parameter of a population. For example, your initial hypothesis in the cereal example is that the process is working properly, so the mean fill is 368 grams, and no corrective action is needed.

The Null and Alternative Hypotheses

The hypothesis that the population parameter is equal to the company specification is referred to as the null hypothesis. A **null hypothesis** is often one of status quo and is identified by the symbol H_0. Here the null hypothesis is that the filling process is working properly, and therefore the mean fill is the 368-gram specification provided by Oxford Cereals. This is stated as

$$H_0 : \mu = 368$$

studentTIP

Remember, hypothesis testing reaches conclusions about parameters, not statistics.

Even though information is available only from the sample, the null hypothesis is stated in terms of the population parameter because your focus is on the population of all cereal boxes. You use the sample statistic to make inferences about the entire filling process. One inference may be that the results observed from the sample data indicate that the null hypothesis is false. If the null hypothesis is considered false, something else must be true.

Whenever a null hypothesis is specified, an alternative hypothesis is also specified, and it must be true if the null hypothesis is false. The **alternative hypothesis, H_1,** is the opposite of the null hypothesis, H_0. This is stated in the cereal example as

$$H_1 : \mu \neq 368$$

The alternative hypothesis represents the conclusion reached by rejecting the null hypothesis. In many research situations, the alternative hypothesis serves as the hypothesis that is the focus of the research being conducted. The null hypothesis is rejected when there is sufficient evidence from the sample data that the null hypothesis is false. In the cereal example, if the weights of the sampled boxes are sufficiently above or below the expected 368-gram mean specified by Oxford Cereals, you reject the null hypothesis in favor of the alternative hypothesis that the mean fill is different from 368 grams. You stop production and take whatever action is necessary to correct the problem. If the null hypothesis is not rejected, you should continue to believe that the process is working correctly and that no corrective action is necessary. In this second circumstance, you have not proven that the process is working correctly. Rather, you have failed to prove that it is working incorrectly, and therefore you continue your belief (although unproven) in the null hypothesis.

In hypothesis testing, you reject the null hypothesis when the sample evidence suggests that it is far more likely that the alternative hypothesis is true. However, failure to reject the null hypothesis is not proof that it is true. You can never prove that the null hypothesis is correct because the decision is based only on the sample information, not on the entire population. Therefore, if you fail to reject the null hypothesis, you can only conclude that there is insufficient evidence to warrant its rejection. The following key points summarize the null and alternative hypotheses:

- The null hypothesis, H_0, represents the current belief in a situation.
- The alternative hypothesis, H_1, is the opposite of the null hypothesis and represents a research claim or specific inference you would like to prove.
- If you reject the null hypothesis, you have statistical proof that the alternative hypothesis is correct.
- If you do not reject the null hypothesis, you have failed to prove the alternative hypothesis. The failure to prove the alternative hypothesis, however, does not mean that you have proven the null hypothesis.
- The null hypothesis, H_0, always refers to a specified value of the population parameter (such as μ), not a sample statistic (such as $\overline{X}$).
- The statement of the null hypothesis always contains an equal sign regarding the specified value of the population parameter (e.g., $H_0 : \mu = 368$ grams).
- The statement of the alternative hypothesis never contains an equal sign regarding the specified value of the population parameter (e.g., $H_1 : \mu \neq 368$ grams).

EXAMPLE 9.1

The Null and Alternative Hypotheses

You are the manager of a fast-food restaurant. You want to determine whether the waiting time to place an order has changed in the past month from its previous population mean value of 4.5 minutes. State the null and alternative hypotheses.

SOLUTION The null hypothesis is that the population mean has not changed from its previous value of 4.5 minutes. This is stated as

$$H_0 : \mu = 4.5$$

The alternative hypothesis is the opposite of the null hypothesis. Because the null hypothesis is that the population mean is 4.5 minutes, the alternative hypothesis is that the population mean is not 4.5 minutes. This is stated as

$$H_1 : \mu \neq 4.5$$

The Critical Value of the Test Statistic

Hypothesis testing uses sample data to determine how likely it is that the null hypothesis is true. In the Oxford Cereal Company scenario, the null hypothesis is that the mean amount of cereal per box in the entire filling process is 368 grams (the population parameter specified by the company). You select a sample of boxes from the filling process, weigh each box, and compute the sample mean $\overline{X}$. This sample statistic is an estimate of the corresponding parameter, the population mean, μ. Even if the null hypothesis is true, the sample statistic $\overline{X}$ is likely to differ from the value of the parameter (the population mean, μ) because of variation due to sampling.

You do expect the sample statistic to be close to the population parameter if the null hypothesis is true. If the sample statistic is close to the population parameter, you have insufficient evidence to reject the null hypothesis. For example, if the sample mean is 367.9 grams, you might conclude that the population mean has not changed (i.e., $\mu = 368$) because a sample mean of 367.9 grams is very close to the hypothesized value of 368 grams. Intuitively, you think that it is likely that you could get a sample mean of 367.9 grams from a population whose mean is 368.

However, if there is a large difference between the value of the sample statistic and the hypothesized value of the population parameter, you might conclude that the null hypothesis is false. For example, if the sample mean is 320 grams, you might conclude that the population mean is not 368 grams (i.e., $\mu \neq 368$) because the sample mean is very far from the hypothesized value of 368 grams. In such a case, you might conclude that it is very unlikely to get a sample mean of 320 grams if the population mean is really 368 grams. Therefore, it is more logical to conclude that the population mean is not equal to 368 grams. Here you reject the null hypothesis.

However, the decision-making process is not always so clear-cut. Determining what is "very close" and what is "very different" is arbitrary without clear definitions. Hypothesis-testing methodology provides clear definitions for evaluating differences. Furthermore, it enables you to quantify the decision-making process by computing the probability of getting a certain sample result if the null hypothesis is true. You calculate this probability by determining the sampling distribution for the sample statistic of interest (e.g., the sample mean) and then computing the particular **test statistic** based on the given sample result. Because the sampling distribution for the test statistic often follows a well-known statistical distribution, such as the standardized normal distribution or t distribution, you can use these distributions to help determine whether the null hypothesis is true.

Regions of Rejection and Nonrejection

The sampling distribution of the test statistic is divided into two regions, a **region of rejection** (sometimes called the critical region) and a **region of nonrejection** (see Figure 9.1). If the test statistic falls into the region of nonrejection, you do not reject the null hypothesis. In the Oxford Cereals scenario, you conclude that there is insufficient evidence that the population mean fill is different from 368 grams. If the test statistic falls into the rejection region, you reject the null hypothesis. In this case, you conclude that the population mean is not 368 grams.

FIGURE 9.1
Regions of rejection and nonrejection in hypothesis testing

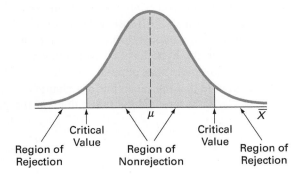

The region of rejection consists of the values of the test statistic that are unlikely to occur if the null hypothesis is true. These values are much more likely to occur if the null hypothesis is false. Therefore, if a value of the test statistic falls into this rejection region, you reject the null hypothesis because that value is unlikely if the null hypothesis is true.

To make a decision concerning the null hypothesis, you first determine the **critical value** of the test statistic. The critical value divides the nonrejection region from the rejection region. Determining the critical value depends on the size of the rejection region. The size of the rejection region is directly related to the risks involved in using only sample evidence to make decisions about a population parameter.

Risks in Decision Making Using Hypothesis Testing

Using hypothesis testing involves the risk of reaching an incorrect conclusion. You might wrongly reject a true null hypothesis, H_0, or, conversely, you might wrongly *not* reject a false null hypothesis, H_0. These types of risk are called Type I and Type II errors.

TYPE I AND TYPE II ERRORS

A **Type I error** occurs if you reject the null hypothesis, H_0, when it is true and should not be rejected. A Type I error is a "false alarm." The probability of a Type I error occurring is α.

A **Type II error** occurs if you do not reject the null hypothesis, H_0, when it is false and should be rejected. A Type II error represents a "missed opportunity" to take some corrective action. The probability of a Type II error occurring is β.

In the Oxford Cereals scenario, you would make a Type I error if you concluded that the population mean fill is *not* 368 grams when it *is* 368 grams. This error causes you to needlessly adjust the filling process (the "false alarm") even though the process is working properly. In the same scenario, you would make a Type II error if you concluded that the population mean fill *is* 368 grams when it is *not* 368 grams. In this case, you would allow the process to continue without adjustment, even though an adjustment is needed (the "missed opportunity").

Traditionally, you control the Type I error by determining the risk level, α (the lower-case Greek letter *alpha*), that you are willing to have of rejecting the null hypothesis when it is true. This risk, or probability, of committing a Type I error is called the *level of significance* (α). Because you specify the level of significance before you perform the hypothesis test, you directly control the risk of committing a Type I error. Traditionally, you select a level of 0.01, 0.05, or 0.10. The choice of a particular risk level for making a Type I error depends on the cost of making a Type I error. After you specify the value for α, you can then determine the critical values that divide the rejection and nonrejection regions. You know the size of the rejection region because α is the probability of rejection when the null hypothesis is true. From this, you can then determine the critical value or values that divide the rejection and nonrejection regions.

The probability of committing a Type II error is called the β *risk*. Unlike the Type I error, which you control through the selection of α, the probability of making a Type II error depends on the difference between the hypothesized and actual values of the population parameter. Because large differences are easier to find than small ones, if the difference between the hypothesized and actual values of the population parameter is large, β is small. For example, if the population mean is 330 grams, there is a small chance (β) that you will conclude that the mean has not changed from 368 grams. However, if the difference between the hypothesized and actual values of the parameter is small, β is large. For example, if the population mean is actually 367 grams, there is a large chance (β) that you will conclude that the mean is still 368 grams.

PROBABILITY OF TYPE I AND TYPE II ERRORS

The **level of significance** (α) of a statistical test is the probability of committing a Type I error.

The β **risk** is the probability of committing a Type II error.

The complement of the probability of a Type I error, $(1 - \alpha)$, is called the *confidence coefficient*. The confidence coefficient is the probability that you will not reject the null hypothesis, H_0, when it is true and should not be rejected. In the Oxford Cereals scenario, the confidence coefficient measures the probability of concluding that the population mean fill is 368 grams when it is actually 368 grams.

The complement of the probability of a Type II error, $(1 - \beta)$, is called the *power of a statistical test*. The power of a statistical test is the probability that you will reject the null hypothesis when it is false and should be rejected. In the Oxford Cereals scenario, the power of he test is the probability that you will correctly conclude that the mean fill amount is not 368 grams when it actually is not 368 grams.

COMPLEMENTS OF TYPE I AND TYPE II ERRORS

The **confidence coefficient**, $(1 - \alpha)$, is the probability that you will not reject the null hypothesis, H_0, when it is true and should not be rejected.

The **power of a statistical test**, $(1 - \beta)$, is the probability that you will reject the null hypothesis when it is false and should be rejected.

Table 9.1 illustrates the results of the two possible decisions (do not reject H_0 or reject H_0) that you can make in any hypothesis test. You can make a correct decision or make one of two types of errors.

TABLE 9.1
Hypothesis Testing and Decision Making

	ACTUAL SITUATION	
STATISTICAL DECISION	H_0 **True**	H_0 **False**
Do not reject H_0	Correct decision Confidence $= (1 - \alpha)$	Type II error $P(\text{Type II error}) = \beta$
Reject H_0	Type I error $P(\text{Type I error}) = \alpha$	Correct decision Power $= (1 - \beta)$

One way to reduce the probability of making a Type II error is by increasing the sample size. Large samples generally permit you to detect even very small differences between the hypothesized values and the actual population parameters. For a given level of α, increasing the sample size decreases β and therefore increases the power of the statistical test to detect that the null hypothesis, H_0, is false.

However, there is always a limit to your resources, and this affects the decision of how large a sample you can select. For any given sample size, you must consider the trade-offs between the two possible types of errors. Because you can directly control the risk of a Type I error, you can reduce this risk by selecting a smaller value for α. For example, if the negative consequences associated with making a Type I error are substantial, you could select $\alpha = 0.01$ instead of 0.05. However, when you decrease α, you increase β, so reducing the risk of a Type I error results in an increased risk of a Type II error. However, to reduce β, you could select a larger value for α. Therefore, if it is important to try to avoid a Type II error, you can select α of 0.05 or 0.10 instead of 0.01.

In the Oxford Cereals scenario, the risk of a Type I error occurring involves concluding that the mean fill amount has changed from the hypothesized 368 grams when it actually has not changed. The risk of a Type II error occurring involves concluding that the mean fill amount has not changed from the hypothesized 368 grams when it actually has changed. The choice of reasonable values for α and β depends on the costs inherent in each type of error. For example, if it is very costly to change the cereal-filling process, you would want to be very confident that a change is needed before making any changes. In this case, the risk of a Type I error occurring is more important, and you would choose a small α. However, if you want to be very certain of detecting changes from a mean of 368 grams, the risk of a Type II error occurring is more important, and you would choose a higher level of α.

Now that you have been introduced to hypothesis testing, recall that in the Oxford Cereals scenario on page 270, the business problem facing Oxford Cereals is to determine if the mean fill-weight in the population of boxes in the cereal-filling process differs from 368 grams. To make this determination, you select a random sample of 25 boxes, weigh each box, compute the sample mean, $\overline{X}$, and then evaluate the difference between this sample statistic and the hypothesized population parameter by comparing the sample mean weight (in grams) to the expected population mean of 368 grams specified by the company. The null and alternative hypotheses are:

$$H_0 : \mu = 368$$
$$H_1 : \mu \neq 368$$

Z Test for the Mean (σ Known)

When the standard deviation, σ, is known (which rarely occurs), you use the *Z* **test for the mean** if the population is normally distributed. If the population is not normally distributed, you can still use the *Z* test if the sample size is large enough for the Central Limit Theorem to take effect (see Section 7.2). Equation (9.1) defines the Z_{STAT} test statistic for determining the difference between the sample mean, $\overline{X}$, and the population mean, μ, when the standard deviation, σ, is known.

Z TEST FOR THE MEAN (σ KNOWN)

$$Z_{STAT} = \frac{\overline{X} - \mu}{\dfrac{\sigma}{\sqrt{n}}}$$

(9.1)

In Equation (9.1), the numerator measures the difference between the observed sample mean, $\overline{X}$, and the hypothesized mean, μ. The denominator is the standard error of the mean, so Z_{STAT} represents the difference between $\overline{X}$ and μ in standard error units.

Hypothesis Testing Using the Critical Value Approach

The critical value approach compares the value of the computed Z_{STAT} test statistic from Equation (9.1) to critical values that divide the normal distribution into regions of rejection and nonrejection. The critical values are expressed as standardized *Z* values that are determined by the level of significance.

For example, if you use a level of significance of 0.05, the size of the rejection region is 0.05. Because the null hypothesis contains an equal sign and the alternative hypothesis contains a not equal sign, you have a **two-tail test** in which the rejection region is divided into the two tails of the distribution, with two equal parts of 0.025 in each tail. For this two-tail test, a rejection region of 0.025 in each tail of the normal distribution results in a cumulative area of 0.025 below the lower critical value and a cumulative area of 0.975 $(1 - 0.025)$ below the upper critical value (which leaves an area of 0.025 in the upper tail). According to the cumulative standardized normal distribution table (Table E.2), the critical values that divide the rejection and nonrejection regions are -1.96 and $+1.96$. Figure 9.2 illustrates that if the mean is actually 368 grams, as H_0 claims, the values of the Z_{STAT} test statistic have a standardized normal distribution centered at $Z = 0$ (which corresponds to an $\overline{X}$ value of 368 grams). Values of Z_{STAT} greater than $+1.96$ and less than -1.96 indicate that $\overline{X}$ is sufficiently different from the hypothesized $\mu = 368$ that it is unlikely that such an $\overline{X}$ value would occur if H_0 were true.

studentTIP

Remember, first you determine the level of significance. This enables you to then determine the critical value. A different level of significance leads to a different critical value.

FIGURE 9.2
Testing a hypothesis about the mean (σ known) at the 0.05 level of significance

studentTIP

In a two-tail test, there is a rejection region in each tail of the distribution.

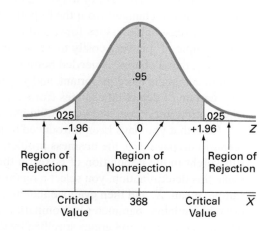

Therefore, the decision rule is

$$\text{reject } H_0 \text{ if } Z_{STAT} > +1.96$$
$$\text{or if } Z_{STAT} < -1.96;$$
$$\text{otherwise, do not reject } H_0.$$

Suppose that the sample of 25 cereal boxes indicates a sample mean, $\bar{X}$, of 372.5 grams, and the population standard deviation, σ, is 15 grams. Using Equation (9.1) on page 276,

studentTIP

Remember, the decision rule always concerns H_0. Either you reject H_0 or you do not reject H_0.

$$Z_{STAT} = \frac{\bar{X} - \mu}{\frac{\sigma}{\sqrt{n}}} - \frac{372.5 - 368}{\frac{15}{\sqrt{25}}} = +1.50$$

Because $Z_{STAT} = +1.50$ is greater than -1.96 and less than $+1.96$, you do not reject H_0 (see Figure 9.3).

You continue to believe that the mean fill amount is 368 grams. To take into account the possibility of a Type II error, you state the conclusion as "there is insufficient evidence that the mean fill is different from 368 grams."

FIGURE 9.3
Testing a hypothesis about the mean cereal weight (σ known) at the 0.05 level of significance

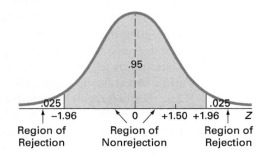

Exhibit 9.1 summarizes the critical value approach to hypothesis testing. Steps 1 and 2 are part of the Define task, step 5 combines the Collect and Organize tasks, and steps 3, 4, and 6 involve the Visualize and Analyze tasks of the DCOVA framework first introduced on page 3. Examples 9.2 and 9.3 apply the critical value approach to hypothesis testing to Oxford Cereals and to a fast-food restaurant.

EXHIBIT 9.1

The Critical Value Approach to Hypothesis Testing

Step 1 State the null hypothesis, H_0, and the alternative hypothesis, H_1.

Step 2 Choose the level of significance, α, and the sample size, n. The level of significance is based on the relative importance of the risks of committing Type I and Type II errors in the problem.

Step 3 Determine the appropriate test statistic and sampling distribution.

Step 4 Determine the critical values that divide the rejection and nonrejection regions.

Step 5 Collect the sample data, organize the results, and compute the value of the test statistic.

Step 6 Make the statistical decision, determine whether the assumptions are valid, and state the managerial conclusion in the context of the theory, claim, or assertion being tested. If the test statistic falls into the nonrejection region, you do not reject the null hypothesis. If the test statistic falls into the rejection region, you reject the null hypothesis.

EXAMPLE 9.2

Applying the Critical Value Approach to Hypothesis Testing at Oxford Cereals

State the critical value approach to hypothesis testing at Oxford Cereals.

SOLUTION

Step 1 State the null and alternative hypotheses. The null hypothesis, H_0, is always stated as a mathematical expression, using population parameters. In testing whether the mean fill is 368 grams, the null hypothesis states that μ equals 368. The alternative hypothesis, H_1, is also stated as a mathematical expression, using population parameters. Therefore, the alternative hypothesis states that μ is not equal to 368 grams.

Step 2 Choose the level of significance and the sample size. You choose the level of significance, α, according to the relative importance of the risks of committing Type I and Type II errors in the problem. The smaller the value of α, the less risk there is of making a Type I error. In this example, making a Type I error means that you conclude that the population mean is not 368 grams when it is 368 grams. Thus, you will take corrective action on the filling process even though the process is working properly. Here, $\alpha = 0.05$ is selected. The sample size, n, is 25.

Step 3 Select the appropriate test statistic. Because σ is known from information about the filling process, you use the normal distribution and the Z_{STAT} test statistic.

Step 4 Determine the rejection region. Critical values for the appropriate test statistic are selected so that the rejection region contains a total area of α when H_0 is true and the nonrejection region contains a total area of $1 - \alpha$ when H_0 is true. Because $\alpha = 0.05$ in the cereal example, the critical values of the Z_{STAT} test statistic are -1.96 and $+1.96$. The rejection region is therefore $Z_{STAT} < -1.96$ or $Z_{STAT} > +1.96$. The nonrejection region is $-1.96 \le Z_{STAT} \le +1.96$.

Step 5 Collect the sample data and compute the value of the test statistic. In the cereal example, $\overline{X} = 372.5$, and the value of the test statistic is $Z_{STAT} = +1.50$.

Step 6 State the statistical decision and the managerial conclusion. First, determine whether the test statistic has fallen into the rejection region or the nonrejection region. For the cereal example, $Z_{STAT} = +1.50$ is in the region of nonrejection because $-1.96 \le Z_{STAT} = +1.50 \le +1.96$. Because the test statistic falls into the nonrejection region, the statistical decision is to not reject the null hypothesis, H_0. The managerial conclusion is that insufficient evidence exists to prove that the mean fill is different from 368 grams. No corrective action on the filling process is needed.

EXAMPLE 9.3

Testing and Rejecting a Null Hypothesis

You are the manager of a fast-food restaurant. The business problem is to determine whether the population mean waiting time to place an order has changed in the past month from its previous population mean value of 4.5 minutes. From past experience, you can assume that the population is normally distributed, with a population standard deviation of 1.2 minutes. You select a sample of 25 orders during a one-hour period. The sample mean is 5.1 minutes. Use the six-step approach listed in Exhibit 9.1 on page 277 to determine whether there is evidence at the 0.05 level of significance that the population mean waiting time to place an order has changed in the past month from its previous population mean value of 4.5 minutes.

SOLUTION

Step 1 The null hypothesis is that the population mean has not changed from its previous value of 4.5 minutes:

$$H_0 : \mu = 4.5$$

The alternative hypothesis is the opposite of the null hypothesis. Because the null hypothesis is that the population mean is 4.5 minutes, the alternative hypothesis is that the population mean is not 4.5 minutes:

▶ (continued)

$$H_1 : \mu \ne 4.5$$

Step 2 You have selected a sample of $n = 25$. The level of significance is 0.05 (i.e., $\alpha = 0.05$).

Step 3 Because σ is assumed to be known, you use the normal distribution and the Z_{STAT} test statistic.

Step 4 Because $\alpha = 0.05$, the critical values of the Z_{STAT} test statistic are -1.96 and $+1.96$. The rejection region is $Z_{STAT} < -1.96$ or $Z_{STAT} > +1.96$. The nonrejection region is $-1.96 \leq Z_{STAT} \leq +1.96$.

Step 5 You collect the sample data and compute $\overline{X} = 5.1$. Using Equation (9.1) on page 276, you compute the test statistic:

$$Z_{STAT} = \frac{\overline{X} - \mu}{\dfrac{\sigma}{\sqrt{n}}} = \frac{5.1 - 4.5}{\dfrac{1.2}{\sqrt{25}}} = +2.50$$

Step 6 Because $Z_{STAT} = +2.50 > +1.96$, you reject the null hypothesis. You conclude that there is evidence that the population mean waiting time to place an order has changed from its previous value of 4.5 minutes. The mean waiting time for customers is longer now than it was last month. As the manager, you would now want to determine how waiting time could be reduced to improve service.

Hypothesis Testing Using the *p*-Value Approach

The ***p*-value** is the probability of getting a test statistic equal to or more extreme than the sample result, given that the null hypothesis, H_0, is true. The *p*-value is also known as the *observed level of significance*. Using the *p*-value to determine rejection and nonrejection is another approach to hypothesis testing.

The decision rules for rejecting H_0 in the *p*-value approach are

- If the *p*-value is greater than or equal to α, do not reject the null hypothesis.
- If the *p*-value is less than α, reject the null hypothesis.

studentTIP

A small (or low) *p*-value indicates a small probability that H_0 is true. A big or large *p*-value indicates a large probability that H_0 is true.

Many people confuse these rules, mistakenly believing that a high *p*-value is reason for rejection. You can avoid this confusion by remembering the following:

If the *p*-value is low, then H_0 must go.

To understand the *p*-value approach, consider the Oxford Cereals scenario. You tested whether the mean fill was equal to 368 grams. The test statistic resulted in a Z_{STAT} value of $+1.50$ and you did not reject the null hypothesis because $+1.50$ was less than the upper critical value of $+1.96$ and greater than the lower critical value of -1.96.

To use the *p*-value approach for the *two-tail test*, you find the probability that the test statistic Z_{STAT} is equal to or *more extreme than* 1.50 standard error units from the center of a standardized normal distribution. In other words, you need to compute the probability that the Z_{STAT} value is greater than $+1.50$ along with the probability that the Z_{STAT} value is less than -1.50. Table E.2 shows that the probability of a Z_{STAT} value below -1.50 is 0.0668. The probability of a value below $+1.50$ is 0.9332, and the probability of a value above $+1.50$ is $1 - 0.9332 = 0.0668$. Therefore, the *p*-value for this two-tail test is $0.0668 + 0.0668 = 0.1336$ (see Figure 9.4). Thus, the probability of a test statistic equal to or more extreme than the sample result is 0.1336. Because 0.1336 is greater than $\alpha = 0.05$, you do not reject the null hypothesis.

FIGURE 9.4

Finding a *p*-value for a two-tail test

In this example, the observed sample mean is 372.5 grams, 4.5 grams above the hypothesized value, and the *p*-value is 0.1336. Thus, if the population mean is 368 grams, there is a 13.36% chance that the sample mean differs from 368 grams by at least 4.5 grams (i.e., is ≥ 372.5 grams or ≤ 363.5 grams). Therefore, even though 372.5 grams is above the hypothesized value of 368 grams, a result as extreme as or more extreme than 372.5 grams is not highly unlikely when the population mean is 368 grams.

Unless you are dealing with a test statistic that follows the normal distribution, you will only be able to approximate the *p*-value from the tables of the distribution. However, Excel can compute the *p*-value for any hypothesis test, and this allows you to substitute the *p*-value approach for the critical value approach when you conduct hypothesis testing.

Figure 9.5 displays the Excel worksheet results for the cereal-filling example discussed beginning on page 277.

FIGURE 9.5

Excel *Z* test for the mean (σ known) worksheet results for the cereal-filling example

	A	B	
1	Z Test for the Mean		
2			
3	**Data**		
4	Null Hypothesis μ =	368	
5	Level of Significance	0.05	
6	Population Standard Deviation	15	
7	Sample Size	25	
8	Sample Mean	372.5	
9			
10	Intermediate Calculations		
11	Standard Error of the Mean	3	=B6/SQRT(B7)
12	Z Test Statistic	1.5	=(B8 - B4)/B11
13			
14	**Two-Tail Test**		
15	Lower Critical Value	-1.9600	=NORM.S.INV(B5/2)
16	Upper Critical Value	1.9600	=NORM.S.INV(1 - B5/2)
17	p-Value	0.1336	=2 * (1 - NORM.S.DIST(ABS(B12), TRUE))
18	Do not reject the null hypothesis		=IF(B17 < B5, "Reject the null hypothesis", "Do not reject the null hypothesis")

In the Worksheet

The NORM.S.INV functions in cells B15 and B16 perform a calculation equivalent to Equation (9.1). The NORM.S.DIST function performs the equivalent of a Table E.2 lookup and the rest of the formula in cell B17 performs the calculations explained at the bottom of page 279. The IF function (see Appendix F) in cell A18 determines which test message gets displayed in cell A18.

Exhibit 9.2 summarizes the *p*-value approach to hypothesis testing. Example 9.4 applies the *p*-value approach to the fast-food restaurant example.

EXHIBIT 9.2

The *p*-Value Approach to Hypothesis Testing

Step 1 State the null hypothesis, H_0, and the alternative hypothesis, H_1.

Step 2 Choose the level of significance, α, and the sample size, *n*. The level of significance is based on the relative importance of the risks of committing Type I and Type II errors in the problem.

Step 3 Determine the appropriate test statistic and the sampling distribution.

Step 4 Collect the sample data, compute the value of the test statistic, and compute the *p*-value.

Step 5 Make the statistical decision and state the managerial conclusion in the context of the theory, claim, or assertion being tested. If the *p*-value is greater than or equal to α, do not reject the null hypothesis. If the *p*-value is less than α, reject the null hypothesis.

EXAMPLE 9.4

Testing and Rejecting a Null Hypothesis Using the *p*-Value Approach

You are the manager of a fast-food restaurant. The business problem is to determine whether the population mean waiting time to place an order has changed in the past month from its previous value of 4.5 minutes. From past experience, you can assume that the population standard deviation is 1.2 minutes and the population waiting time is normally distributed. You select a sample of 25 orders during a one-hour period. The sample mean is 5.1 minutes. Use the five-step *p*-value approach of Exhibit 9.2 to determine whether there is evidence that the population mean waiting time to place an order has changed in the past month from its previous population mean value of 4.5 minutes.

SOLUTION

Step 1 The null hypothesis is that the population mean has not changed from its previous value of 4.5 minutes:

$$H_0 : \mu = 4.5$$

The alternative hypothesis is the opposite of the null hypothesis. Because the null hypothesis is that the population mean is 4.5 minutes, the alternative hypothesis is that the population mean is not 4.5 minutes:

$$H_1 : \mu \neq 4.5$$

Step 2 You have selected a sample of $n = 25$ and you have chosen a 0.05 level of significance (i.e., $\alpha = 0.05$).

Step 3 Select the appropriate test statistic. Because σ is assumed known, you use the normal distribution and the Z_{STAT} test statistic.

Step 4 You collect the sample data and compute $\overline{X} = 5.1$. Using Equation (9.1) on page 276, you compute the test statistic as follows:

$$Z_{STAT} = \frac{\overline{X} - \mu}{\dfrac{\sigma}{\sqrt{n}}} = \frac{5.1 - 4.5}{\dfrac{1.2}{\sqrt{25}}} = +2.50$$

To find the probability of getting a Z_{STAT} test statistic that is equal to or more extreme than 2.50 standard error units from the center of a standardized normal distribution, you compute the probability of a Z_{STAT} value greater than $+2.50$ along with the probability of a Z_{STAT} value less than -2.50. From Table E.2, the probability of a Z_{STAT} value below -2.50 is 0.0062. The probability of a value below $+2.50$ is 0.9938. Therefore, the probability of a value above $+2.50$ is $1 - 0.9938 = 0.0062$. Thus, the *p*-value for this two-tail test is $0.0062 + 0.0062 = 0.0124$.

Step 5 Because the *p*-value $= 0.0124 < \alpha = 0.05$, you reject the null hypothesis. You conclude that there is evidence that the population mean waiting time to place an order has changed from its previous population mean value of 4.5 minutes. The mean waiting time for customers is longer now than it was last month.

A Connection Between Confidence Interval Estimation and Hypothesis Testing

This chapter and Chapter 8 discuss confidence interval estimation and hypothesis testing, the two major elements of statistical inference. Although confidence interval estimation and hypothesis testing share the same conceptual foundation, they are used for different purposes. In Chapter 8, confidence intervals estimated parameters. In this chapter, hypothesis testing makes decisions about specified values of population parameters. Hypothesis tests are used when trying to determine whether a parameter is less than, more than, or not equal to a specified value. Proper interpretation of a confidence interval, however, can also indicate whether a parameter is less than, more than, or not equal to a specified value. For example, in this section, you tested whether the population mean fill amount was different from 368 grams by using Equation (9.1) on page 276:

$$Z_{STAT} = \frac{\overline{X} - \mu}{\dfrac{\sigma}{\sqrt{n}}}$$

Instead of testing the null hypothesis that $\mu = 368$ grams, you can reach the same conclusion by constructing a confidence interval estimate of μ. If the hypothesized value of $\mu = 368$ is contained within the interval, you do not reject the null hypothesis because 368 would not be considered an unusual value. However, if the hypothesized value does not fall into the interval, you reject the null hypothesis because $\mu = 368$ grams is then considered an unusual value. Using Equation (8.1) on page 241 and the following results:

$$\overline{X} \pm Z_{\alpha/2} \frac{\sigma}{\sqrt{n}}$$

$$n = 25, \overline{X} = 372.5 \text{ grams}, \sigma = 15 \text{ grams}$$

for a confidence level of 95% (i.e., $\alpha = 0.05$),

$$\overline{X} \pm Z_{\alpha/2} \frac{\sigma}{\sqrt{n}}$$

$$372.5 \pm (1.96) \frac{15}{\sqrt{25}}$$

$$372.5 \pm 5.88$$

so that

$$366.62 \leq \mu \leq 378.38$$

Because the interval includes the hypothesized value of 368 grams, you do not reject the null hypothesis. There is insufficient evidence that the mean fill amount for the entire filling process is not 368 grams. You reached the same decision by using a two-tail hypothesis test.

Can You Ever Know the Population Standard Deviation?

Section 8.1 concludes with the thought that you would be unlikely to use a confidence interval estimation method that required knowing σ, the population standard deviation, because if you knew the population standard deviation you could directly compute the population mean—you would not need to use a method to estimate that statistic!

Likewise, for most practical applications, you are unlikely to use a hypothesis-testing method that requires knowing σ. If you knew the population standard deviation, you would also know the population mean and therefore have no need to form and then test. A hypothesis about the mean **Then why study a hypothesis test of the mean which requires that σ is known?** Explaining the fundamentals of hypothesis testing is simpler when using such a test. With a known population standard deviation, you can use the normal distribution and compute p-values using the tables of the normal distribution.

Because it is important that you understand the concept of hypothesis testing when reading the rest of this book, review this section carefully—even if you anticipate never having a practical reason to use the test represented in Equation (9.1).

PROBLEMS FOR SECTION 9.1

LEARNING THE BASICS

9.1 If you use a 0.05 level of significance in a two-tail hypothesis test, what decision will you make if $Z_{STAT} = -0.76$?

9.2 If you use a 0.05 level of significance in a two-tail hypothesis test, what decision will you make if $Z_{STAT} = +2.21$?

9.3 If you use a 0.10 level of significance in a two-tail hypothesis test, what is your decision rule for rejecting a null hypothesis that the population mean equals 500 if you use the Z test?

9.4 If you use a 0.01 level of significance in a two-tail hypothesis test, what is your decision rule for rejecting $H_0 : \mu = 12.5$ if you use the Z test?

9.5 What is your decision in Problem 9.4 if $Z_{STAT} = -2.61$?

9.6 What is the p-value if, in a two-tail hypothesis test, $Z_{STAT} = +2.00$?

9.7 In Problem 9.6, what is your statistical decision if you test the null hypothesis at the 0.10 level of significance?

9.8 What is the p-value if, in a two-tail hypothesis test, $Z_{STAT} = -1.38$?

APPLYING THE CONCEPTS

9.9 In the U.S. legal system, a defendant is presumed innocent until proven guilty. Consider a null hypothesis, H_0, that a defendant is innocent, and an alternative hypothesis, H_1, that the defendant is guilty. A jury has two possible decisions: Convict the defendant (i.e., reject the null hypothesis) or do not convict the defendant (i.e., do not reject the null hypothesis). Explain the meaning of the risks of committing either a Type I or Type II error in this example.

9.10 Suppose the defendant in Problem 9.9 is presumed guilty until proven innocent. How do the null and alternative hypotheses differ from those in Problem 9.9? What are the meanings of the risks of committing either a Type I or Type II error here?

9.11 Many consumer groups feel that the U.S. Food and Drug Administration (FDA) drug approval process is too easy and, as a result, too many drugs are approved that are later found to be unsafe. On the other hand, a number of industry lobbyists have pushed for a more lenient approval process so that pharmaceutical companies can get new drugs approved more easily and quickly. Consider a null hypothesis that a new, unapproved drug is unsafe and an alternative hypothesis that a new, unapproved drug is safe.
a. Explain the risks of committing a Type I or Type II error.
b. Which type of error are the consumer groups trying to avoid? Explain.
c. Which type of error are the industry lobbyists trying to avoid? Explain.
d. How would it be possible to lower the chances of both Type I and Type II errors?

9.12 As a result of complaints from both students and faculty about lateness, the registrar at a large university is ready to undertake a study to determine whether the scheduled break

between classes should be changed. Until now, the registrar has believed that there should be 20 minutes between scheduled classes. State the null hypothesis, H_0, and the alternative hypothesis, H_1.

9.13 Do business seniors at your school prepare for class more than, less than, or about the same as business seniors at other schools? The National Survey of Student Engagement (NSSE) annual results, available at **bit.ly/1j3Ob7N**, found that business seniors spent a mean of 13 hours per week preparing for class.
a. State the null and alternative hypotheses to try to prove that the mean number of hours preparing for class by business seniors at your school is different from the 13-hour-per-week benchmark reported by the NSSE.
b. What is a Type I error for your test?
c. What is a Type II error for your test?

9.14 The quality-control manager at a compact fluorescent light bulb (CFL) factory needs to determine whether the mean life of a large shipment of CFLs is equal to 7,500 hours. The population standard deviation is 1,000 hours. A random sample of 64 CFLs indicates a sample mean life of 7,250 hours.
a. At the 0.05 level of significance, is there evidence that the mean life is different from 7,500 hours?
b. Compute the p-value and interpret its meaning.
c. Construct a 95% confidence interval estimate of the population mean life of the CFLs.
d. Compare the results of (a) and (c). What conclusions do you reach?

9.15 Suppose that in Problem 9.14, the standard deviation is 1,200 hours.
a. Repeat (a) through (d) of Problem 9.14, assuming a standard deviation of 1,200 hours.
b. Compare the results of (a) to those of Problem 9.14.

9.16 A bottled water distributor wants to determine whether the mean amount of water contained in 1-gallon bottles purchased from a nationally known water bottling company is actually 1 gallon. You know from the water bottling company specifications that the standard deviation of the amount of water per bottle is 0.02 gallon. You select a random sample of 50 bottles, and the mean amount of water per 1-gallon bottle is 0.995 gallon.
a. Is there evidence that the mean amount is different from 1.0 gallon? (Use $\alpha = 0.01$.)
b. Compute the p-value and interpret its meaning.
c. Construct a 99% confidence interval estimate of the population mean amount of water per bottle.
d. Compare the results of (a) and (c). What conclusions do you reach?

9.17 Suppose that in Problem 9.16, the standard deviation is 0.012 gallon.
a. Repeat (a) through (d) of Problem 9.16, assuming a standard deviation of 0.012 gallon.
b. Compare the results of (a) to those of Problem 9.16.

9.2 t Test of Hypothesis for the Mean (σ Unknown)

In virtually all hypothesis-testing situations concerning the population mean, μ, you do not know the population standard deviation, σ. However, you will always be able to know the sample standard deviation, S. If you assume that the population is normally distributed, then the sampling distribution of the mean will follow a t distribution with $n - 1$ degrees of freedom and you can use the **t test for the mean**. If the population is not normally distributed, you can still use the t test if the population is not too skewed and the sample size is not too small. Equation (9.2) defines the test statistic for determining the difference between the sample mean, $\overline{X}$, and the population mean, μ, when using the sample standard deviation, S.

t TEST FOR THE MEAN (σ UNKNOWN)

$$t_{STAT} = \frac{\overline{X} - \mu}{\dfrac{S}{\sqrt{n}}} \tag{9.2}$$

where the t_{STAT} test statistic follows a t distribution having $n - 1$ degrees of freedom.

To illustrate the use of the t test for the mean, return to the Chapter 8 Ricknel Home Centers scenario on page 237. The business objective is to determine whether the mean amount per sales invoice is unchanged from the $120 of the past five years. As an accountant for the company, you need to determine whether this amount has changed. In other words, the hypothesis test is used to try to determine whether the mean amount per sales invoice is increasing or decreasing.

The Critical Value Approach

To perform this two-tail hypothesis test, you use the six-step method listed in Exhibit 9.1 on page 277.

studentTIP

Remember, the null hypothesis uses an equal sign and the alternative hypothesis *never* uses an equal sign.

Step 1   You define the following hypotheses:

$$H_0 : \mu = 120$$
$$H_1 : \mu \neq 120$$

The alternative hypothesis contains the statement you are trying to prove. If the null hypothesis is rejected, then there is statistical evidence that the population mean amount per sales invoice is no longer $120. If the statistical conclusion is "do not reject H_0," then you will conclude that there is insufficient evidence to prove that the mean amount differs from the long-term mean of $120.

Step 2   You collect the data from a sample of $n = 12$ sales invoices. You decide to use $\alpha = 0.05$.

Step 3   Because σ is unknown, you use the t distribution and the t_{STAT} test statistic. You must assume that the population of sales invoices is approximately normally distributed in order to use the t distribution because the sample size is only 12. This assumption is discussed on page 286.

studentTIP

Since this is a two-tail test, the level of significance, $\alpha = 0.05$, is divided into two equal 0.025 parts, in each of the two tails of the distribution.

Step 4   For a given sample size, n, the test statistic t_{STAT} follows a t distribution with $n - 1$ degrees of freedom. The critical values of the t distribution with $12 - 1 = 11$ degrees of freedom are found in Table E.3, as illustrated in Table 9.2 and Figure 9.6. The alternative hypothesis, $H_1 : \mu \neq 120$, has two tails. The area in the rejection region of the t distribution's left (lower) tail is 0.025, and the area in the rejection region of the t distribution's right (upper) tail is also 0.025.

From the *t* table as given in Table E.3, a portion of which is shown in Table 9.2, the critical values are ± 2.2010. The decision rule is

$$\text{reject } H_0 \text{ if } t_{STAT} < -2.2010$$
$$\text{or if } t_{STAT} > +2.2010;$$
$$\text{otherwise, do not reject } H_0.$$

TABLE 9.2
Determining the Critical Value from the *t* Table for an Area of 0.025 in Each Tail, with 11 Degrees of Freedom

	Cumulative Probabilities					
	.75	.90	.95	.975	.99	.995
Degrees of Freedom	Upper-Tail Areas					
	.25	.10	.05	.025	.01	.005
1	1.0000	3.0777	6.3138	12.7062	31.8207	63.6574
2	0.8165	1.8856	2.9200	4.3027	6.9646	9.9248
3	0.7649	1.6377	2.3534	3.1824	4.5407	5.8409
4	0.7407	1.5332	2.1318	2.7764	3.7469	4.6041
5	0.7267	1.4759	2.0150	2.5706	3.3649	4.0322
6	0.7176	1.4398	1.9432	2.4469	3.1427	3.7074
7	0.7111	1.4149	1.8946	2.3646	2.9980	3.4995
8	0.7064	1.3968	1.8595	2.3060	2.8965	3.3554
9	0.7027	1.3830	1.8331	2.2622	2.8214	3.2498
10	0.6998	1.3722	1.8125	2.2281	2.7638	3.1693
11	0.6974	1.3634	1.7959	2.2010	2.7181	3.1058

Source: Extracted from Table E.3.

FIGURE 9.6
Testing a hypothesis about the mean (σ unknown) at the 0.05 level of significance with 11 degrees of freedom

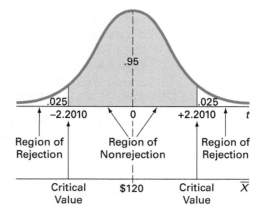

Region of Rejection — Region of Nonrejection — Region of Rejection

Critical Value — $120 — Critical Value — $\overline{X}$

Step 5 You organize and store the data from a random sample of 12 sales invoices in **Invoices**:

108.98	152.22	111.45	110.59	127.46	107.26
93.32	91.97	111.56	75.71	128.58	135.11

Using Equations (3.1) and (3.7) on pages 96 and 103,

$$\overline{X} = \$112.85 \text{ and } S = \$20.80$$

From Equation (9.2) on page 284,

$$t_{STAT} = \frac{\overline{X} - \mu}{\dfrac{S}{\sqrt{n}}} = \frac{112.85 - 120}{\dfrac{20.80}{\sqrt{12}}} = -1.1908$$

Step 6   Because $-2.2010 < t_{STAT} = -1.1908 < 2.2010$, you do not reject H_0. You have insufficient evidence to conclude that the mean amount per sales invoice differs from $120. The audit suggests that the mean amount per invoice has not changed.

Figure 9.7 displays the Excel worksheet results for this test of hypothesis for the mean amount per sales invoice.

FIGURE 9.7
Excel worksheet results for the sales invoices example *t* test

	A	B	
1	t Test for the Hypothesis of the Mean		
2			
3	**Data**		
4	Null Hypothesis μ=	120	
5	Level of Significance	0.05	
6	Sample Size	12	
7	Sample Mean	112.85	
8	Sample Standard Deviation	20.8	
9			
10	**Intermediate Calculations**		
11	Standard Error of the Mean	6.0044	=B8/SQRT(B6)
12	Degrees of Freedom	11	=B6 - 1
13	t Test Statistic	-1.1908	=(B7 - B4)/B11
14			
15	**Two-Tail Test**		
16	Lower Critical Value	-2.2010	=-T.INV.2T(B5, B12)
17	Upper Critical Value	2.2010	=T.INV.2T(B5, B12)
18	p-Value	0.2588	=T.DIST.2T(ABS(B13), B12)
19	Do not reject the null hypothesis		=IF(B18 < B5, "Reject the null hypothesis", "Do not reject the null hypothesis")

In the Worksheet

The T.INV.2T functions in cells B16 and B17 perform the equivalent of the table lookup that Table 9.2 illustrates. The T.DIST.2T function in cell B18 determines the *p*-value from the absolute value of the *t* test statistic and the degrees of freedom (cells B13 and B12).

The IF function (see Appendix F) in cell A19 determines which of two phrases cell A19 displays.

p-Value Approach

To perform this two-tail hypothesis test, you use the five-step method listed in Exhibit 9.2 on page 280.

Step 1–3   These steps are the same as in the critical value approach discussed on page 284.

Step 4   From the Figure 9.7 results, $t_{STAT} = -1.19$ and the *p*-value $= 0.2588$.

Step 5   Because the *p*-value of 0.2588 is greater than $\alpha = 0.05$, you do not reject H_0. The data provide insufficient evidence to conclude that the mean amount per sales invoice differs from $120. The audit suggests that the mean amount per invoice has not changed. The *p*-value indicates that if the null hypothesis is true, the probability that a sample of 12 invoices could have a sample mean that differs by $7.15 or more from the stated $120 is 0.2588. In other words, if the mean amount per sales invoice is truly $120, then there is a 25.88% chance of observing a sample mean below $112.85 or above $127.15.

In the preceding example, it is incorrect to state that there is a 25.88% chance that the null hypothesis is true. Remember that the *p*-value is a conditional probability, calculated by *assuming* that the null hypothesis is true. In general, it is proper to state the following:

If the null hypothesis is true, there is a $(p\text{-value}) \times 100\%$ chance of observing a test statistic at least as contradictory to the null hypothesis as the sample result.

Checking the Normality Assumption

You use the *t* test when the population standard deviation, σ, is not known and is estimated using the sample standard deviation, *S*. To use the *t* test, you assume that the data represent a random sample from a population that is normally distributed. In practice, as long as the sample size is not very small and the population is not very skewed, the *t* distribution provides a good approximation of the sampling distribution of the mean when σ is unknown.

There are several ways to evaluate the normality assumption necessary for using the *t* test. You can examine how closely the sample statistics match the normal distribution's theoretical properties. You can also construct a histogram, stem-and-leaf display, boxplot, or normal probability plot to visualize the distribution of the sales invoice amounts. For details on evaluating normality, see Section 6.3.

Figures 9.8 and 9.9 show the descriptive statistics, boxplot, and normal probability plot for the sales invoice data.

FIGURE 9.8

Descriptive statistics and Excel boxplot for the sales invoice data

	Invoice Amount
Mean	112.8508
Median	111.02
Mode	#N/A
Minimum	75.71
Maximum	152.22
Range	76.51
Variance	432.5565
Standard Deviation	20.7980
Coeff. of Variation	18.43%
Skewness	0.1336
Kurtosis	0.1727
Count	12
Standard Error	6.0039

FIGURE 9.9

Excel normal probability plot for the sales invoice data

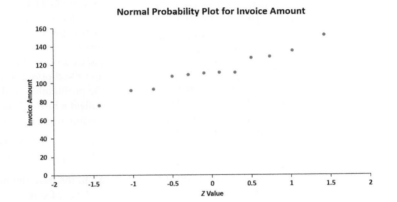

The mean is very close to the median, and the points on the normal probability plot appear to be increasing approximately in a straight line. The boxplot appears to be approximately symmetrical. Thus, you can assume that the population of sales invoices is approximately normally distributed. The normality assumption is valid, and therefore the auditor's results are valid.

The *t* test is a **robust** test. A robust test does not lose power if the shape of the population departs somewhat from a normal distribution, particularly when the sample size is large enough to enable the test statistic *t* to follow the *t* distribution. However, you can reach erroneous conclusions and can lose statistical power if you use the *t* test incorrectly. If the sample size, *n*, is small (i.e., less than 30) and you cannot easily make the assumption that the underlying population is at least approximately normally distributed, then *nonparametric* testing procedures are more appropriate (see references 2 and 3).

PROBLEMS FOR SECTION 9.2

LEARNING THE BASICS

9.18 If, in a sample of $n = 16$ selected from a normal population, $\overline{X} = 56$ and $S = 12$, what is the value of t_{STAT} if you are testing the null hypothesis $H_0 : \mu = 50$?

9.19 In Problem 9.18, how many degrees of freedom does the *t* test have?

9.20 In Problems 9.18 and 9.19, what are the critical values of *t* if the level of significance, α, is 0.05 and the alternative hypothesis, H_1, is $\mu \neq 50$?

9.21 In Problems 9.18, 9.19, and 9.20, what is your statistical decision if the alternative hypothesis, H_1, is $\mu \neq 50$?

9.22 If, in a sample of $n = 16$ selected from a left-skewed population, $\overline{X} = 65$, and $S = 21$, would you use the t test to test the null hypothesis $H_0 : \mu = 60$? Discuss.

9.23 If, in a sample of $n = 160$ selected from a left-skewed population, $\overline{X} = 65$, and $S = 21$, would you use the t test to test the null hypothesis $H_0 : \mu = 60$? Discuss.

APPLYING THE CONCEPTS

✓ SELF TEST **9.24** You are the manager of a restaurant for a fast-food franchise. Last month, the mean waiting time at the drive-through window for branches in your geographic region, as measured from the time a customer places an order until the time the customer receives the order, was 3.7 minutes. You select a random sample of 64 orders. The sample mean waiting time is 3.57 minutes, with a sample standard deviation of 0.8 minute.
a. At the 0.05 level of significance, is there evidence that the population mean waiting time is different from 3.7 minutes?
b. Because the sample size is 64, do you need to be concerned about the shape of the population distribution when conducting the t test in (a)? Explain.

9.25 A manufacturer of chocolate candies uses machines to package candies as they move along a filling line. Although the packages are labeled as 8 ounces, the company wants the packages to contain a mean of 8.17 ounces so that virtually none of the packages contain less than 8 ounces. A sample of 50 packages is selected periodically, and the packaging process is stopped if there is evidence that the mean amount packaged is different from 8.17 ounces. Suppose that in a particular sample of 50 packages, the mean amount dispensed is 8.159 ounces, with a sample standard deviation of 0.051 ounce.
a. Is there evidence that the population mean amount is different from 8.17 ounces? (Use a 0.05 level of significance.)
b. Determine the p-value and interpret its meaning.

9.26 A marketing researcher wants to estimate the mean amount spent ($) on Amazon.com by Amazon Prime member shoppers. Suppose a random sample of 100 Amazon Prime member shoppers who recently made a purchase on Amazon.com yielded a mean amount spent of $1,500 and a standard deviation of $200.
a. Is there evidence that the population mean amount spent on Amazon.com by Amazon Prime member shoppers is different from $1,475? (Use a 0.05 level of significance.)
b. Determine the p-value and interpret its meaning.

9.27 The U.S. Department of Transportation requires tire manufacturers to provide performance information on tire sidewalls to help prospective buyers make their purchasing decisions. One very important piece of information is the tread wear index, which indicates the tire's resistance to tread wear. A tire with a grade of 200 should last twice as long, on average, as a tire with a grade of 100.

A consumer organization wants to test the actual tread wear index of a brand name of tires that claims "graded 200" on the sidewall of the tire. A random sample of $n = 18$ indicates a sample mean tread wear index of 195.3 and a sample standard deviation of 21.4.
a. Is there evidence that the population mean tread wear index is different from 200? (Use a 0.05 level of significance.)
b. Determine the p-value and interpret its meaning.

9.28 The file **FastFood** contains the amount that a sample of fifteen customers spent for lunch ($) at a fast-food restaurant:

7.42 6.29 5.83 6.50 8.34 9.51 7.10 6.80 5.90
4.89 6.50 5.52 7.90 8.30 9.60

a. At the 0.05 level of significance, is there evidence that the mean amount spent for lunch is different from $6.50?
b. Determine the p-value in (a) and interpret its meaning.
c. What assumption must you make about the population distribution in order to conduct the t test in (a) and (b)?
d. Because the sample size is 15, do you need to be concerned about the shape of the population distribution when conducting the t test in (a)? Explain.

9.29 An insurance company has the business objective of reducing the amount of time it takes to approve applications for life insurance. The approval process consists of underwriting, which includes a review of the application, a medical information bureau check, possible requests for additional medical information and medical exams, and a policy compilation stage in which the policy pages are generated and sent for delivery. The ability to deliver approved policies to customers in a timely manner is critical to the profitability of this service. During a period of one month, you collect a random sample of 27 approved policies and the total processing time, in days, stored in **Insurance**, are:

73 19 16 64 28 28 31 90 60 56 31 56 22 18 45 48
17 17 17 91 92 63 50 51 69 16 17

a. In the past, the mean processing time was 45 days. At the 0.05 level of significance, is there evidence that the mean processing time has changed from 45 days?
b. What assumption about the population distribution is needed in order to conduct the t test in (a)?
c. Construct a boxplot or a normal probability plot to evaluate the assumption made in (b).
d. Do you think that the assumption needed in order to conduct the t test in (a) is valid? Explain.

9.30 The following data (in **Drink**) represent the amount of soft drink filled in a sample of 50 consecutive 2-liter bottles. The results, listed horizontally in the order of being filled, were:

2.109 2.086 2.066 2.075 2.065 2.057 2.052 2.044
2.036 2.038 2.031 2.029 2.025 2.029 2.023 2.020
2.015 2.014 2.013 2.014 2.012 2.012 2.012 2.010
2.005 2.003 1.999 1.996 1.997 1.992 1.994 1.986
1.984 1.981 1.973 1.975 1.971 1.969 1.966 1.967
1.963 1.957 1.951 1.951 1.947 1.941 1.941 1.938
1.908 1.894

a. At the 0.05 level of significance, is there evidence that the mean amount of soft drink filled is different from 2.0 liters?
b. Determine the p-value in (a) and interpret its meaning.
c. In (a), you assumed that the distribution of the amount of soft drink filled was normally distributed. Evaluate this assumption by constructing a boxplot or a normal probability plot.
d. Do you think that the assumption needed in order to conduct the t test in (a) is valid? Explain.
e. Examine the values of the 50 bottles in their sequential order, as given in the problem. Does there appear to be a pattern to the results? If so, what impact might this pattern have on the validity of the results in (a)?

9.31 One of the major measures of the quality of service provided by any organization is the speed with which it responds to customer complaints. A large family-held department store selling furniture and flooring, including carpet, had undergone a major expansion in the past several years. In particular, the flooring department had expanded from 2 installation crews to an installation supervisor, a measurer, and 15 installation crews. The store had the business objective of improving its response to complaints. The variable of interest was defined as the number of days between when the complaint was made and when it was resolved. Data were collected from 50 complaints that were made in the past year. These data, stored in Furniture , are:

```
54   5   35 137   31 27 152   2 123 81 74 27
11 19 126 110 110 29   61 35   94 31 26   5
12   4 165   32   29 28   29 26   25   1 14 13
13 10   5   27   4 52   30 22   36 26 20 23
33 68
```

a. The installation supervisor claims that the mean number of days between the receipt of a complaint and the resolution of the complaint is 20 days. At the 0.05 level of significance, is there evidence that the claim is not true (i.e., the mean number of days is different from 20)?
b. What assumption about the population distribution is needed in order to conduct the *t* test in (a)?
c. Construct a boxplot or a normal probability plot to evaluate the assumption made in (b).
d. Do you think that the assumption needed in order to conduct the *t* test in (a) is valid? Explain.

9.32 A manufacturing company produces steel housings for electrical equipment. The main component part of the housing is a steel trough that is made out of a 14-gauge steel coil. It is produced using a 250-ton progressive punch press with a wipe-down operation that puts two 90-degree forms in the flat steel to make the trough. The distance from one side of the form to the other is critical because of weatherproofing in outdoor applications. The company requires that the width of the trough be between 8.31 inches and 8.61 inches. The file Trough contains the widths of the troughs, in inches, for a sample of $n = 49$:

```
8.312 8.343 8.317 8.383 8.348 8.410 8.351 8.373 8.481 8.422
8.476 8.382 8.484 8.403 8.414 8.419 8.385 8.465 8.498 8.447
8.436 8.413 8.489 8.414 8.481 8.415 8.479 8.429 8.458 8.462
8.460 8.444 8.429 8.460 8.412 8.420 8.410 8.405 8.323 8.420
8.396 8.447 8.405 8.439 8.411 8.427 8.420 8.498 8.409
```

a. At the 0.05 level of significance, is there evidence that the mean width of the troughs is different from 8.46 inches?
b. What assumption about the population distribution is needed in order to conduct the *t* test in (a)?

c. Evaluate the assumption made in (b).
d. Do you think that the assumption needed in order to conduct the *t* test in (a) is valid? Explain.

9.33 One operation of a steel mill is to cut pieces of steel into parts that are used in the frame for front seats in an automobile. The steel is cut with a diamond saw and requires the resulting parts must be cut to be within ±0.005 inch of the length specified by the automobile company. The file Steel contains a sample of 100 steel parts. The measurement reported is the difference, in inches, between the actual length of the steel part, as measured by a laser measurement device, and the specified length of the steel part. For example, a value of −0.002 represents a steel part that is 0.002 inch shorter than the specified length.
a. At the 0.05 level of significance, is there evidence that the mean difference is different from 0.0 inches?
b. Construct a 95% confidence interval estimate of the population mean. Interpret this interval.
c. Compare the conclusions reached in (a) and (b).
d. Because $n = 100$, do you have to be concerned about the normality assumption needed for the *t* test and *t* interval?

9.34 In Problem 3.69 on page 134, you were introduced to a tea-bag-filling operation. An important quality characteristic of interest for this process is the weight of the tea in the individual bags. The file Teabags contains an ordered array of the weight, in grams, of a sample of 50 tea bags produced during an 8-hour shift.
a. Is there evidence that the mean amount of tea per bag is different from 5.5 grams? (Use $\alpha = 0.01$.)
b. Construct a 99% confidence interval estimate of the population mean amount of tea per bag. Interpret this interval.
c. Compare the conclusions reached in (a) and (b).

9.35 Experian Marketing Services reported that the typical American spends a mean of 144 minutes (2.4 hours) per day accessing the Internet via a mobile device. (Source: *The 2014 Digital Marketer,* available at **ex.pn/1kXJjfX.**) In order to test the validity of this statement, you select a sample of 30 friends and family. The results for the time spent per day accessing the Internet via mobile device (in minutes) are stored in InternetMobileTime .
a. Is there evidence that the population mean time spent per day accessing the Internet via mobile device is different from 144 minutes? Use the *p*-value approach and a level of significance of 0.05.
b. What assumption about the population distribution is needed in order to conduct the *t* test in (a)?
c. Make a list of the various ways you could evaluate the assumption noted in (b).
d. Evaluate the assumption noted in (b) and determine whether the test in (a) is valid.

9.3 One-Tail Tests

The examples of hypothesis testing in Sections 9.1 and 9.2 are called two-tail tests because the rejection region is divided into the two tails of the sampling distribution of the mean. In contrast, some hypothesis tests are one-tail tests because they require an alternative hypothesis that focuses on a *particular direction.*

One example of a one-tail hypothesis test would test whether the population mean is *less than* a specified value. One such situation involves the business problem concerning the service time at the drive-through window of a fast-food restaurant. According to a *QSR* magazine special report ("The Drive-Thru Study," October 2013, available at **bit.ly/1lU6Enz**), the speed with which customers are served is of critical importance to the success of the service. In that study, an audit of McDonald's drive-throughs had a mean service time of 189.49 seconds, which was slower than the drive-throughs of several other fast-food chains. Suppose that McDonald's began a quality improvement effort to reduce the service time by deploying an improved drive-through service process in a sample of 25 stores. Because McDonald's would want to institute the new process in all of its stores only if the test sample saw a *decreased* drive-through time, the entire rejection region is located in the lower tail of the distribution.

The Critical Value Approach

You wish to determine whether the new drive-through process has a mean that is less than 189.49 seconds. To perform this one-tail hypothesis test, you use the six-step method listed in Exhibit 9.1 on page 277:

Step 1 You define the null and alternative hypotheses:

$$H_0 : \mu \geq 189.49$$

$$H_1 : \mu < 189.49$$

studentTIP

The rejection region matches the direction of the alternative hypothesis. If the alternative hypothesis contains a < sign, the rejection region is in the lower tail. If the alternative hypothesis contains a > sign, the rejection region is in the upper tail.

The alternative hypothesis contains the statement for which you are trying to find evidence. If the conclusion of the test is "reject H_0," there is statistical evidence that the mean drive-through time is less than the drive-through time in the old process. This would be reason to change the drive-through process for the entire population of stores. If the conclusion of the test is "do not reject H_0," then there is insufficient evidence that the mean drive-through time in the new process is significantly less than the drive-through time in the old process. If this occurs, there would be insufficient reason to institute the new drive-through process in the population of stores.

Step 2 You collect the data by selecting a sample of $n = 25$ stores. You decide to use $\alpha = 0.05$.

Step 3 Because σ is unknown, you use the t distribution and the t_{STAT} test statistic. You need to assume that the drive-through time is normally distributed because a sample of only 25 drive-through times is selected.

Step 4 The rejection region is entirely contained in the lower tail of the sampling distribution of the mean because you want to reject H_0 only when the sample mean is significantly less than 189.49 seconds. When the entire rejection region is contained in one tail of the sampling distribution of the test statistic, the test is called a **one-tail test**, or **directional test**. If the alternative hypothesis includes the *less than* sign, the critical value of t is negative. As shown in Table 9.3 and Figure 9.10, because the entire rejection region is in the lower tail of the t distribution and contains an area of 0.05, due to the symmetry of the t distribution, the critical value of the t test statistic with $25 - 1 = 24$ degrees of freedom is -1.7109.

The decision rule is

$$\text{reject } H_0 \text{ if } t_{STAT} < -1.7109;$$

$$\text{otherwise, do not reject } H_0.$$

TABLE 9.3
Determining the Critical Value from the *t* Table for an Area of 0.05 in the Lower Tail, with 24 Degrees of Freedom

	Cumulative Probabilities					
	.75	.90	.95	.975	.99	.995
Degrees of Freedom	Upper-Tail Areas					
	.25	.10	.05	.025	.01	.005
1	1.0000	3.0777	6.3138	12.7062	31.8207	63.6574
2	0.8165	1.8856	2.9200	4.3027	6.9646	9.9248
3	0.7649	1.6377	2.3534	3.1824	4.5407	5.8409
⋮	⋮	⋮	⋮	⋮	⋮	⋮
23	0.6853	1.3195	1.7139	2.0687	2.4999	2.8073
24	0.6848	1.3178	1.7109	2.0639	2.4922	2.7969
25	0.6844	1.3163	1.7081	2.0595	2.4851	2.7874

Source: Extracted from Table E.3.

FIGURE 9.10
One-tail test of hypothesis for a mean (σ unknown) at the 0.05 level of significance

Step 5 From the sample of 25 stores you selected, you find that the sample mean service time at the drive-through equals 175.8 seconds and the sample standard deviation equals 21.3 seconds. Using $n = 25, \overline{X} = 175.8, S = 21.3$, and Equation (9.2) on page 284,

$$t_{STAT} = \frac{\overline{X} - \mu}{\dfrac{S}{\sqrt{n}}} = \frac{175.8 - 189.49}{\dfrac{21.3}{\sqrt{25}}} = -3.2136$$

Step 6 Because $t_{STAT} = -3.2136 < -1.7109$, you reject the null hypothesis (see Figure 9.10). You conclude that the mean service time at the drive-through is less than 189.49 seconds. There is sufficient evidence to change the drive-through process for the entire population of stores.

The *p*-Value Approach

Use the five steps listed in Exhibit 9.2 on page 280 to illustrate the *t* test for the drive-through time study using the *p*-value approach:

Step 1–3 These steps are the same as was used in the critical value approach on page 290.

Step 4 $t_{STAT} = -3.2136$ (see step 5 of the critical value approach). Because the alternative hypothesis indicates a rejection region entirely in the lower tail of the sampling distribution, to compute the *p*-value, you need to find the probability that the t_{STAT} test statistic will be less than -3.2136. Figure 9.11 shows that the *p*-value is 0.0019.

Step 5 The *p*-value of 0.0019 is less than $\alpha = 0.05$ (see Figure 9.12). You reject H_0 and conclude that the mean service time at the drive-through is less than 189.49 seconds. There is sufficient evidence to change the drive-through process for the entire population of stores.

FIGURE 9.11

Excel *t* test worksheet results for the drive-through time study

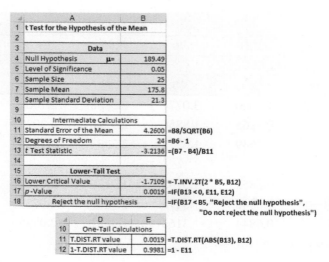

In the Worksheet

The T.INV.2T function in cell B16 performs the equivalent of the table lookup that Table 9.3 illustrates. The IF function in cell 17 determines which of the calculations in cells B11 and E12 to use to compute the *p*-value (E11 for this problem).

The IF function (see Appendix F) in cell A18 determines which of two phrases cell A18 displays.

FIGURE 9.12

Determining the *p*-value for a one-tail test

Example 9.5 illustrates a one-tail test in which the rejection region is in the upper tail.

EXAMPLE 9.5

A One-Tail Test for the Mean

A company that manufactures chocolate bars is particularly concerned that the mean weight of a chocolate bar is not greater than 6.03 ounces. A sample of 50 chocolate bars is selected; the sample mean is 6.034 ounces, and the sample standard deviation is 0.02 ounce. Using the $\alpha = 0.01$ level of significance, is there evidence that the population mean weight of the chocolate bars is greater than 6.03 ounces?

SOLUTION Using the critical value approach, listed in Exhibit 9.1 on page 277,

Step 1   First, you define the null and alternative hypotheses:

$$H_0 : \mu \leq 6.03$$
$$H_1 : \mu > 6.03$$

Step 2   You collect the data from a sample of $n = 50$. You decide to use $\alpha = 0.01$.

Step 3   Because σ is unknown, you use the *t* distribution and the t_{STAT} test statistic.

Step 4   The rejection region is entirely contained in the upper tail of the sampling distribution of the mean because you want to reject H_0 only when the sample mean is significantly greater than 6.03 ounces. Because the entire rejection region is in the upper tail of the *t* distribution and contains an area of 0.01, the critical value of the *t* distribution with $50 - 1 = 49$ degrees of freedom is 2.4049 (see Table E.3).

The decision rule is

$$\text{reject } H_0 \text{ if } t_{STAT} > 2.4049;$$
$$\text{otherwise, do not reject } H_0.$$

▶ *(continued)*

Step 5 From your sample of 50 chocolate bars, you find that the sample mean weight is 6.034 ounces, and the sample standard deviation is 0.02 ounces. Using $n = 50, \overline{X} = 6.034, S = 0.02$, and Equation (9.2) on page 284,

$$t_{STAT} = \frac{\overline{X} - \mu}{\dfrac{S}{\sqrt{n}}} = \frac{6.034 - 6.03}{\dfrac{0.02}{\sqrt{50}}} = 1.414$$

Step 6 Because $t_{STAT} = 1.414 < 2.4049$ or the p-value (from Excel) is $0.0818 > 0.01$, you do not reject the null hypothesis. There is insufficient evidence to conclude that the population mean weight is greater than 6.03 ounces.

To perform one-tail tests of hypotheses, you must properly formulate H_0 and H_1. Exhibit 9.3 summarizes the key points about the null and alternative hypotheses for one-tail tests.

EXHIBIT 9.3

The Null and Alternative Hypotheses in One-Tail Tests

The null hypothesis, H_0, represents the status quo or the current belief in a situation.

The alternative hypothesis, H_1, is the opposite of the null hypothesis and represents a research claim or specific inference you would like to prove.

If you reject the null hypothesis, you have statistical proof that the alternative hypothesis is correct.

If you do not reject the null hypothesis, you have failed to prove the alternative hypothesis. The failure to prove the alternative hypothesis, however, does not mean that you have proven the null hypothesis.

The null hypothesis always refers to a specified value of the *population parameter* (such as μ), not to a *sample statistic* (such as $\overline{X}$).

The statement of the null hypothesis *always* contains an equal sign regarding the specified value of the parameter (e.g., $H_0 : \mu \geq 189.49$).

The statement of the alternative hypothesis *never* contains an equal sign regarding the specified value of the parameter (e.g., $H_1 : \mu < 189.49$).

PROBLEMS FOR SECTION 9.3

LEARNING THE BASICS

9.36 In a one-tail hypothesis test where you reject H_0 only in the *upper* tail, what is the p-value if $Z_{STAT} = +2.00$?

9.37 In Problem 9.36, what is your statistical decision if you test the null hypothesis at the 0.05 level of significance?

9.38 In a one-tail hypothesis test where you reject H_0 only in the *lower* tail, what is the p-value if $Z_{STAT} = -1.38$?

9.39 In Problem 9.38, what is your statistical decision if you test the null hypothesis at the 0.01 level of significance?

9.40 In a one-tail hypothesis test where you reject H_0 only in the *lower* tail, what is the p-value if $Z_{STAT} = +1.38$?

9.41 In Problem 9.40, what is the statistical decision if you test the null hypothesis at the 0.01 level of significance?

9.42 In a one-tail hypothesis test where you reject H_0 only in the *upper* tail, what is the critical value of the t-test statistic with 10 degrees of freedom at the 0.01 level of significance?

9.43 In Problem 9.42, what is your statistical decision if $t_{STAT} = +2.39$?

9.44 In a one-tail hypothesis test where you reject H_0 only in the *lower* tail, what is the critical value of the t_{STAT} test statistic with 20 degrees of freedom at the 0.01 level of significance?

9.45 In Problem 9.44, what is your statistical decision if $t_{STAT} = -1.15$?

APPLYING THE CONCEPTS

9.46 The Los Angeles County Metropolitan Transportation Authority has set a bus mechanical reliability goal of 3,013 bus miles. Bus mechanical reliability is measured specifically as the number of bus miles between mechanical road calls. Suppose a sample of 64 buses resulted in a sample mean of 3,295 bus miles and a sample standard deviation of 825 bus miles.

a. Is there evidence that the population mean bus miles is greater than 3,013 bus miles? (Use a 0.05 level of significance.)

b. Determine the p-value and interpret its meaning.

9.47 *CarMD* reports that the cost of repairing a hybrid vehicle is falling even while typical repairs on conventional vehicles are getting more expensive. One of the most common hybrid repairs, replacing the hybrid inverter assembly, had a mean repair cost of $1,357 in 2014. (Data extracted from *2015 CarMD Vehicle Health Index,* available at **bitly.com/1Gd3tjg**.) Industry experts suspect that the cost will continue to decrease given the increase in the number of technicians who have gained expertise on fixing gas–electric engines in recent months. Suppose a sample of 100 hybrid inverter assembly repairs completed in the last month was selected. The sample mean repair cost was $1,280 with the sample standard deviation of $300.

a. Is there evidence that the population mean repair cost is less than $1,357? (Use a 0.05 level of significance.)

b. Determine the p-value and interpret its meaning.

✓SELF TEST **9.48** A quality improvement project was conducted with the objective of improving the wait time in a county health department (CHD) Adult Primary Care Unit (APCU). The evaluation plan included *waiting room time* as one key waiting time process measure. Waiting room time was defined as the time elapsed between requesting that the patient be seated in the waiting room and the time he or she was called to be placed in an exam room. Suppose that, initially, a targeted wait time goal of 25 minutes was set. After implementing an improvement framework and process, the quality improvement team collected data on a sample of 355 patients. In this sample, the mean wait time was 23.05 minutes, with a standard deviation of 16.83 minutes. (Data extracted from M. Michael, S. D. Schaffer, P. L. Egan, B. B. Little, and P. S. Pritchard, "Improving Wait Times and Patient Satisfaction in Primary Care," *Journal for Healthcare Quality,* 2013, 35(2), pp. 50–60.)

a. If you test the null hypothesis at the 0.01 level of significance, is there evidence that the population mean wait time is less than 25 minutes?

b. Interpret the meaning of the p-value in this problem.

9.49 You are the manager of a restaurant that delivers pizza to college dormitory rooms. You have just changed your delivery process in an effort to reduce the mean time between the order and completion of delivery from the current 25 minutes. A sample of 36 orders using the new delivery process yields a sample mean of 22.4 minutes and a sample standard deviation of 6 minutes.

a. Using the six-step critical value approach, at the 0.05 level of significance, is there evidence that the population mean delivery time has been reduced below the previous population mean value of 25 minutes?

b. At the 0.05 level of significance, use the five-step p-value approach.

c. Interpret the meaning of the p-value in (b).

d. Compare your conclusions in (a) and (b).

9.50 A survey of nonprofit organizations showed that online fundraising has increased in the past year. Based on a random sample of 84 nonprofit organizations, the mean one-time gift donation in the past year was $82, with a standard deviation of $9.

a. If you test the null hypothesis at the 0.01 level of significance, is there evidence that the mean one-time gift donation is greater than $80?

b. Interpret the meaning of the p-value in this problem.

9.51 The population mean waiting time to check out of a supermarket has been 4 minutes. Recently, in an effort to reduce the waiting time, the supermarket has experimented with a system in which infrared cameras use body heat and in-store software to determine how many lanes should be opened. A sample of 100 customers was selected, and their mean waiting time to check out was 3.25 minutes, with a sample standard deviation of 2.7 minutes.

a. At the 0.05 level of significance, using the critical value approach to hypothesis testing, is there evidence that the population mean waiting time to check out is less than 4 minutes?

b. At the 0.05 level of significance, using the p-value approach to hypothesis testing, is there evidence that the population mean waiting time to check out is less than 4 minutes?

c. Interpret the meaning of the p-value in this problem.

d. Compare your conclusions in (a) and (b).

9.4 *Z* Test of Hypothesis for the Proportion

studentTIP

Do not confuse this use of the Greek letter pi, π, to represent the population proportion with the mathematical constant that uses the same letter to represent the ratio of the circumference to a diameter of a circle—approximately 3.14159.

In some situations, you want to test a hypothesis about the proportion of events of interest in the population, π, rather than test the population mean. To begin, you select a random sample and compute the **sample proportion**, $p = X/n$. You then compare the value of this statistic to the hypothesized value of the parameter, π, in order to decide whether to reject the null hypothesis.

If the number of events of interest (X) and the number of events that are not of interest ($n - X$) are each at least five, the sampling distribution of a proportion approximately follows a normal distribution, and you can use the **Z test for the proportion**. Equation (9.3) defines this hypothesis test for the difference between the sample proportion, p, and the hypothesized population proportion, π.

Z TEST FOR THE PROPORTION

$$Z_{STAT} = \frac{p - \pi}{\sqrt{\dfrac{\pi(1 - \pi)}{n}}}$$ **(9.3)**

where

$$p = \text{sample proportion} = \frac{X}{n} = \frac{\text{number of events of interest in the sample}}{\text{sample size}}$$

$$\pi = \text{hypothesized proportion of events of interest in the population}$$

The Z_{STAT} test statistic approximately follows a standardized normal distribution when X and $(n - X)$ are each at least 5.

Alternatively, by multiplying the numerator and denominator by n, you can write the Z_{STAT} test statistic in terms of the number of events of interest, X, as shown in Equation (9.4).

Z TEST FOR THE PROPORTION IN TERMS OF THE NUMBER OF EVENTS OF INTEREST

$$Z_{STAT} = \frac{X - n\pi}{\sqrt{n\pi(1 - \pi)}}$$ **(9.4)**

The Critical Value Approach

In a survey of 792 Internet users, 681 said that they had taken steps to remove or mask their digital footprints. (Source: E. Dwoskin, "Give Me Back My Privacy," *The Wall Street Journal*, March 24, 2014, p. R2.) Suppose that a survey conducted in the previous year indicated that 80% of Internet users said that they had taken steps to remove or mask their digital footprints. Is there evidence that the proportion of Internet users who said that they had taken steps to remove or mask their digital footprints has changed from the previous year? To investigate this question, the null and alternative hypotheses are as follows:

$H_0 : \pi = 0.80$ (i.e., the proportion of Internet users who said that they had taken steps to remove or mask their digital footprints has not changed from the previous year)

$H_1 : \pi \neq 0.80$ (i.e., the proportion of Internet users who said that they had taken steps to remove or mask their digital footprints has changed from the previous year)

Because you are interested in determining whether the population proportion of Internet users who said that they had taken steps to remove or mask their digital footprints has changed from 0.80 in the previous year, you use a two-tail test. If you select the $\alpha = 0.05$ level of significance, the rejection and nonrejection regions are set up as in Figure 9.13, and the decision rule is

reject H_0 if $Z_{STAT} < -1.96$ or if $Z_{STAT} > +1.96$;

otherwise, do not reject H_0.

Because 681 of the 792 Internet users said that they had taken steps to remove or mask their digital footprints,

$$p = \frac{681}{792} = 0.8598$$

FIGURE 9.13

Two-tail test of hypothesis for the proportion at the 0.05 level of significance

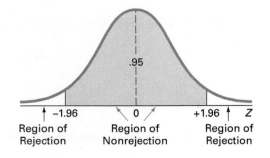

−1.96	0	+1.96	Z
Region of Rejection	Region of Nonrejection	Region of Rejection	

Since $X = 681$ and $n - X = 111$, each > 5, using Equation (9.3),

$$Z_{STAT} = \frac{p - \pi}{\sqrt{\dfrac{\pi(1 - \pi)}{n}}} = \frac{0.8598 - 0.80}{\sqrt{\dfrac{0.80(1 - 0.80)}{792}}} = \frac{0.0598}{0.0142} = 4.2107$$

or, using Equation (9.4),

$$Z_{STAT} = \frac{X - n\pi}{\sqrt{n\pi(1 - \pi)}} = \frac{681 - (792)(0.80)}{\sqrt{792(0.80)(0.20)}} = \frac{47.4}{11.257} = 4.2107$$

Because $Z_{STAT} = 4.2107 > 1.96$, you reject H_0. There is evidence that the population proportion of all Internet users who said that they had taken steps to remove or mask their digital footprints has changed from 0.80 in the previous year. Figure 9.14 presents the Excel worksheet results for these data.

FIGURE 9.14

Excel Z test worksheet results for whether the proportion of Internet users who said that they had taken steps to remove or mask their digital footprints has changed from 0.80 in the previous year

	A	B
1	Z Test of Hypothesis for the Proportion	
2		
3	**Data**	
4	**Null Hypothesis** π =	0.8
5	**Level of Significance**	0.05
6	**Number of Items of Interest**	681
7	**Sample Size**	792
8		
9	**Intermediate Calculations**	
10	Sample Proportion	0.8598 =B6/B7
11	Standard Error	0.0142 =SQRT(B4 * (1 - B4)/B7)
12	Z Test Statistic	4.2107 =(B10 - B4)/B11
13		
14	**Two-Tail Test**	
15	**Lower Critical Value**	-1.9600 =NORM.S.INV(B5/2)
16	**Upper Critical Value**	1.9600 =NORM.S.INV(1 - B5/2)
17	**p-Value**	0.0000 =2 * (1 - NORM.S.DIST(ABS(B12), TRUE))
18	**Reject the null hypothesis**	=IF(B17 < B5 ,"Reject the null hypothesis", "Do not reject the null hypothesis")

In the Worksheet

The NORM.S.INV functions in cells B15 and B16 determine the upper and lower critical values visualized in Figure 9.13. The NORM.S.DIST function helps calculates the p-value in cell B17. The IF function (see Appendix F) in cell A18 determines which of two phrases cell A18 displays.

The p-Value Approach

As an alternative to the critical value approach, you can compute the p-value. For this two-tail test in which the rejection region is located in the lower tail and the upper tail, you need to find the area below a Z value of −4.2107 and above a Z value of +4.2107. Figure 9.14 reports a p-value of 0.0000. Because this value is less than the selected level of significance $(\alpha = 0.05)$, you reject the null hypothesis.

Example 9.6 illustrates a one-tail test for a proportion.

EXAMPLE 9.6

Testing a Hypothesis for a Proportion

In addition to the business problem of the speed of service at the drive-through, fast-food chains want to fill orders correctly. The same audit that reported that McDonald's had a drive-through service time of 189.49 seconds also reported that McDonald's filled 88.3% of its drive-through orders correctly. Suppose that McDonald's begins a quality improvement effort to ensure that

▶ *(continued)*

orders at the drive-through are filled correctly. The business problem is defined as determining whether the new process can increase the percentage of orders filled correctly. Data are collected from a sample of 400 orders using the new process. The results indicate that 378 orders were filled correctly. At the 0.01 level of significance, can you conclude that the new process has increased the proportion of orders filled correctly?

SOLUTION The null and alternative hypotheses are

$H_0 : \pi \leq 0.883$ (i.e., the population proportion of orders filled correctly using the new process is less than or equal to 0.883)

$H_1 : \pi > 0.883$ (i.e., the population proportion of orders filled correctly using the new process is greater than 0.883)

Since $X = 378$ and $n - X = 22$, both > 5, using Equation (9.3) on page 295,

$$p = \frac{X}{n} = \frac{378}{400} = 0.945$$

$$Z_{STAT} = \frac{p - \pi}{\sqrt{\frac{\pi(1 - \pi)}{n}}} = \frac{0.945 - 0.883}{\sqrt{\frac{0.883(1 - 0.883)}{400}}} = \frac{0.063}{0.0161} = 3.8579$$

The p-value (computed by Excel) for $Z_{STAT} > 3.8579$ is 0.0001.

Using the critical value approach, you reject H_0 if $Z_{STAT} > 2.33$. Using the p-value approach, you reject H_0 if the p-value < 0.01. Because $Z_{STAT} = 3.8579 > 2.33$ or the p-value $= 0.0001 < 0.01$, you reject H_0. You have evidence that the new process has increased the proportion of correct orders above 0.883 or 88.3%. Therefore, McDonald's should institute the new process at all of its stores.

PROBLEMS FOR SECTION 9.4

LEARNING THE BASICS

9.52 If, in a random sample of 400 items, 88 are defective, what is the sample proportion of defective items?

9.53 In Problem 9.52, if the null hypothesis is that 20% of the items in the population are defective, what is the value of Z_{STAT}?

9.54 In Problems 9.52 and 9.53, suppose you are testing the null hypothesis $H_0 : \pi = 0.20$ against the two-tail alternative hypothesis $H_1 : \pi \neq 0.20$ and you choose the level of significance $\alpha = 0.05$. What is your statistical decision?

APPLYING THE CONCEPTS

9.55 According to a recent National Association of Colleges and Employers (NACE) report, 47% of college student internships are unpaid. (Data extracted from "Paid Interns More Likely to Get Hired," **bit.ly/1JTIYuA**.) A recent survey of 60 college interns at a local university found that 30 had unpaid internships.
a. Use the five-step p-value approach to hypothesis testing and a 0.05 level of significance to determine whether the proportion of college interns that had unpaid internships is different from 0.47.

b. Assume that the study found that 37 of the 60 college interns had unpaid internships and repeat (a). Are the conclusions the same?

9.56 The worldwide market share for the Chrome web browser was 26% in a recent month. (Data extracted from **netmarketshare .com**.) Suppose that you decide to select a sample of 100 students at your university and you find that 30 use the Chrome web browser.
a. Use the five-step p-value approach to determine whether there is evidence that the market share for the Chrome web browser at your university is greater than the worldwide market share of 26%. (Use the 0.05 level of significance.)
b. Suppose that the sample size is $n = 400$, and you find that 30% of the sample of students at your university (120 out of 400) use the Chrome web browser. Use the five-step p-value approach to try to determine whether there is evidence that the market share for the Chrome web browser at your university is greater than the worldwide market share of 26%. (Use the 0.05 level of significance.)
c. Discuss the effect that sample size has on hypothesis testing.
d. What do you think are your chances of rejecting any null hypothesis concerning a population proportion if a sample size of $n = 20$ is used?

9.57 One of the issues facing organizations is increasing diversity throughout an organization. One of the ways to evaluate an organization's success at increasing diversity is to compare the percentage of employees in the organization in a particular position with a specific background to the percentage in a particular position with that specific background in the general workforce. Recently, a large academic medical center determined that 9 of 17 employees in a particular position were female, whereas 55% of the employees for this position in the general workforce were female. At the 0.05 level of significance, is there evidence that the proportion of females in this position at this medical center is different from would be expected in the general workforce?

9.58 What are companies' biggest obstacles to attracting the best talent? Of 406 surveyed U.S. talent acquisition professionals, 215 reported that competition is the biggest obstacle at their company. (Source: LinkedIn Talent Solutions, *2015 Global Recruiting Trends*, **linkd.in/1KThkPp**.) At the 0.05 level of significance, is there evidence that the proportion of all talent acquisition professionals who report competition is the biggest obstacle to attracting the best talent at their company is different from 45%?

9.59 A cellphone provider has the business objective of wanting to determine the proportion of subscribers who would upgrade to a new cellphone with improved features if it were made available

at a substantially reduced cost. Data are collected from a random sample of 500 subscribers. The results indicate that 135 of the subscribers would upgrade to a new cellphone at a reduced cost.

a. At the 0.05 level of significance, is there evidence that more than 20% of the customers would upgrade to a new cellphone at a reduced cost?

b. How would the manager in charge of promotional programs concerning residential customers use the results in (a)?

9.60 Actuation Consulting conducted a global survey of product teams with the goal of better understanding the dynamics of product team performance and uncovering the practices that make these teams successful. One of the survey findings was that 42% of organizations consider the project manager role vital to successful completion of product development activities (Source: *The Study of Product Team Performance, 2014*, **bit.ly/1GHTT9M**.) Suppose another study is conducted to check the validity of this result, with the goal of proving that the percentage is less than 42%.

a. State the null and research hypotheses.

b. A sample of 100 organizations is selected, and results indicate that 40 consider the project manager role vital to successful completion of product development activities. Use either the six-step critical value hypothesis testing approach or the five-step *p*-value approach to determine at the 0.05 level of significance whether there is evidence that the percentage is less than 42%.

9.5 Potential Hypothesis-Testing Pitfalls and Ethical Issues

To this point, you have studied the fundamental concepts of hypothesis testing. You have used hypothesis testing to analyze differences between sample statistics and hypothesized population parameters in order to make business decisions concerning the underlying population characteristics. You have also learned how to evaluate the risks involved in making these decisions.

When planning to carry out a hypothesis test based on a survey, research study, or designed experiment, you must ask and answer the questions presented in Exhibit 9.4

EXHIBIT 9.4

Questions for the Planning Stage of Hypothesis Testing

1. What is the goal of the survey, study, or experiment? How can you translate the goal into a null hypothesis and an alternative hypothesis?
2. Is the hypothesis test a two-tail test or one-tail test?
3. Can you select a random sample from the underlying population of interest?
4. What types of data will you collect in the sample? Are the variables numerical or categorical?
5. At what level of significance should you conduct the hypothesis test?
6. Is the intended sample size large enough to achieve the desired power of the test for the level of significance chosen?
7. What statistical test procedure should you use and why?
8. What conclusions and interpretations can you reach from the results of the hypothesis test?

Failing to consider these questions early in the planning process can lead to biased or incomplete results. Proper planning can help ensure that the statistical study will provide objective information needed to make good business decisions.

Statistical Significance Versus Practical Significance

You need to make a distinction between the existence of a statistically significant result and its practical significance in a field of application. Sometimes, due to a very large sample size, you may get a result that is statistically significant but has little practical significance.

For example, suppose that prior to a national marketing campaign focusing on a series of expensive television commercials, you believe that the proportion of people who recognize your brand is 0.30. At the completion of the campaign, a survey of 20,000 people indicates that 6,168 recognized your brand. A one-tail test trying to prove that the proportion is now greater than 0.30 results in a p-value of 0.0048, and the correct statistical conclusion is that the proportion of consumers recognizing your brand name has now increased. Was the campaign successful? The result of the hypothesis test indicates a statistically significant increase in brand awareness, but is this increase practically important? The population proportion is now estimated at $6,168/20,000 = 0.3084 = 0.3084$ or 30.84%. This increase is less than 1% more than the hypothesized value of 30%. Did the large expenses associated with the marketing campaign produce a result with a meaningful increase in brand awareness? Because of the minimal real-world impact that an increase of less than 1% has on the overall marketing strategy and the huge expenses associated with the marketing campaign, you should conclude that the campaign was not successful. On the other hand, if the campaign increased brand awareness from 30% to 50%, you would be inclined to conclude that the campaign was successful.

Statistical *Insignificance* Versus Importance

In contrast to the issue of the practical significance of a statistically significant result is the situation in which an important result may not be statistically significant. In a recent case (see reference 1), the U.S. Supreme Court ruled that companies cannot rely solely on whether the result of a study is significant when determining what they communicate to investors.

In some situations (see reference 4), the lack of a large enough sample size may result in a nonsignificant result when in fact an important difference does exist. A study that compared male and female entrepreneurship rates globally and within Massachusetts found a significant difference globally but not within Massachusetts, even though the entrepreneurship rates for females and for males in the two geographic areas were similar (8.8% for males in Massachusetts as compared to 8.4% globally; 5% for females in both geographic areas). The difference was due to the fact that the global sample size was 20 times larger than the Massachusetts sample size.

Reporting of Findings

In conducting research, you should document both good and bad results. You should not just report the results of hypothesis tests that show statistical significance but omit those for which there is insufficient evidence in the findings. In instances in which there is insufficient evidence to reject H_0, you must make it clear that this does not prove that the null hypothesis is true. What the result indicates is that with the sample size used, there is not enough information to *disprove* the null hypothesis.

Ethical Issues

You need to distinguish between poor research methodology and unethical behavior. Ethical considerations arise when the hypothesis-testing process is manipulated. Some of the areas where ethical issues can arise include the use of human subjects in experiments, the data collection method, the type of test (one-tail or two-tail test), the choice of the level of significance, the cleansing and discarding of data, and the failure to report pertinent findings.

9.6 Power of the Test

The power of a hypothesis test is the probability that you correctly reject a false null hypothesis. The power of the test is affected by the level of significance, the sample size, and whether the test is one-tail or two-tail. The **Section 9.6 online topic** further explains the power of the test and illustrates its use.

▼USING **STATISTICS**
Significant Testing..., Revisited

As the plant operations manager for Oxford Cereals, you were responsible for the cereal-filling process. It was your responsibility to adjust the process when the mean fill-weight in the population of boxes deviated from the company specification of 368 grams. You chose to conduct a hypothesis test.

You determined that the null hypothesis should be that the population mean fill was 368 grams. If the mean weight of the sampled boxes was sufficiently above or below the expected 368-gram mean specified by Oxford Cereals, you would reject the null hypothesis in favor of the alternative hypothesis that the mean fill was different from 368 grams. If this happened, you would stop production and take whatever action was necessary to correct the problem. If the null hypothesis was not rejected, you would continue to believe in the status quo—that the process was working correctly—and therefore take no corrective action.

Before proceeding, you considered the risks involved with hypothesis tests. If you rejected a true null hypothesis, you would make a Type I error and conclude that the population mean fill was not 368 when it actually was 368 grams. This error would result in adjusting the filling process even though the process was working properly. If you did not reject a false null hypothesis, you would make a Type II error and conclude that the population mean fill was 368 grams when it actually was not 368 grams. Here, you would allow the process to continue without adjustment even though the process was not working properly.

After collecting a random sample of 25 cereal boxes, you used either the six-step critical value approach or the five-step *p*-value approach to hypothesis testing. Because the test statistic fell into the nonrejection region, you did not reject the null hypothesis. You concluded that there was insufficient evidence to prove that the mean fill differed from 368 grams. No corrective action on the filling process was needed.

▼SUMMARY

This chapter presented the foundation of hypothesis testing. You learned how to perform tests on the population mean and on the population proportion. The chapter developed both the critical value approach and the *p*-value approach to hypothesis testing.

In deciding which test to use, you should ask the following question: Does the test involve a numerical variable or a categorical variable? If the test involves a numerical variable, you use the *t* test for the mean. If the test involves a categorical variable, you use the *Z* test for the proportion. Table 9.4 lists the hypothesis tests covered in the chapter.

TABLE 9.4
Summary of Topics

TYPE OF ANALYSIS	TYPE OF DATA	
	Numerical	**Categorical**
Hypothesis test concerning a single parameter	*Z* test of hypothesis for the mean (Section 9.1) *t* test of hypothesis for the mean (Section 9.2)	*Z* test of hypothesis for the proportion (Section 9.4)

▼ REFERENCES

1. Bialik, C. "Making a Stat Less Significant." *The Wall Street Journal*, April 2, 2011, A5.
2. Bradley, J. V. *Distribution-Free Statistical Tests*. Upper Saddle River, NJ: Prentice Hall, 1968.
3. Daniel, W. *Applied Nonparametric Statistics*, 2nd ed. Boston: Houghton Mifflin, 1990.
4. Seaman, J., and E. Allen. "Not Significant, But Important?" *Quality Progress*, August 2011, 57–59.

▼ KEY EQUATIONS

Z Test for the Mean (σ Known)

$$Z_{STAT} = \frac{\overline{X} - \mu}{\frac{\sigma}{\sqrt{n}}} \tag{9.1}$$

t Test for the Mean (σ Unknown)

$$t_{STAT} = \frac{\overline{X} - \mu}{\frac{S}{\sqrt{n}}} \tag{9.2}$$

Z Test for the Proportion

$$Z_{STAT} = \frac{p - \pi}{\sqrt{\frac{\pi(1 - \pi)}{n}}} \tag{9.3}$$

Z Test for the Proportion in Terms of the Number of Events of Interest

$$Z_{STAT} = \frac{X - n\pi}{\sqrt{n\pi(1 - \pi)}} \tag{9.4}$$

▼ KEY TERMS

alternative hypothesis (H_1)   271
β risk   274
confidence coefficient   275
critical value   273
directional test   290
hypothesis testing   271
level of significance (α)   274
null hypothesis (H_0)   271
one-tail test   290
p-value   279
power of a statistical test   275
region of nonrejection   273
region of rejection   273
robust   287
sample proportion   294
t test for the mean   284
test statistic   273
two-tail test   276
Type I error   274
Type II error   274
Z test for the mean   276
Z test for the proportion   294

▼ CHECKING YOUR UNDERSTANDING

9.61 What is the difference between a null hypothesis, H_0, and an alternative hypothesis, H_1?

9.62 What is the difference between a Type I error and a Type II error?

9.63 What is meant by the power of a test?

9.64 What is the difference between a one-tail test and a two-tail test?

9.65 What is meant by a p-value?

9.66 How can a confidence interval estimate for the population mean provide conclusions for the corresponding two-tail hypothesis test for the population mean?

9.67 What is the six-step critical value approach to hypothesis testing?

9.68 What is the five-step p-value approach to hypothesis testing?

▼ CHAPTER REVIEW PROBLEMS

9.69 In hypothesis testing, the common level of significance is $\alpha = 0.05$. Some might argue for a level of significance greater than 0.05. Suppose that web designers tested the proportion of potential web page visitors with a preference for a new web design over the existing web design. The null hypothesis was that the population proportion of web page visitors preferring the new design was 0.50, and the alternative hypothesis was that it was not equal to 0.50. The p-value for the test was 0.20.

a. State, in statistical terms, the null and alternative hypotheses for this example.
b. Explain the risks associated with Type I and Type II errors in this case.
c. What would be the consequences if you rejected the null hypothesis for a p-value of 0.20?
d. What might be an argument for raising the value of α?
e. What would you do in this situation?
f. What is your answer in (e) if the p-value equals 0.12? What if it equals 0.06?

9.70 Financial institutions utilize prediction models to predict bankruptcy. One such model is the Altman Z-score model, which uses multiple corporate income and balance sheet values to measure the financial health of a company. If the model predicts a low Z-score value, the firm is in financial stress and is predicted to go bankrupt within the next two years. If the model predicts a moderate or high Z-score value, the firm is financially healthy and is predicted to be a non-bankrupt firm (see **pages.stern.nyu.edu/~ealtman/Zscores.pdf**). This decision-making procedure can be expressed in the hypothesis-testing framework. The null hypothesis is that a firm is predicted to be a non-bankrupt firm. The alternative hypothesis is that the firm is predicted to be a bankrupt firm.

a. Explain the risks associated with committing a Type I error in this case.
b. Explain the risks associated with committing a Type II error in this case.
c. Which type of error do you think executives want to avoid? Explain.
d. How would changes in the model affect the probabilities of committing Type I and Type II errors?

9.71 IAB conducted a study of U.S. online adults that included 416 tablet owners. The study found that 221 tablet owners use their tablet while watching TV. (Source: *The Changing TV Experience: Attitudes and Usage across Multiple Screens*, **bit.ly/1HL2lG8**.) The authors of the report imply that the survey proves that more than half of all tablet owners use their tablet while watching TV at least once per day.

a. Use the five-step p-value approach to hypothesis testing and a 0.05 level of significance to try to prove that more than half of all tablet owners use their tablet while watching TV at least once per day.
b. Based on your result in (a), is the claim implied by the authors valid?
c. Suppose the study found that 242 tablet owners use their tablet while watching TV at least once per day. Repeat parts (a) and (b).
d. Compare the results of (b) and (c).

9.72 The owner of a specialty coffee shop wants to study coffee purchasing habits of customers at her shop. She selects a random sample of 60 customers during a certain week, with the following results:
• The amount spent was $\overline{X} = \$7.25$, $S = \$1.75$.
• Thirty-one customers say they "definitely will" recommend the specialty coffee shop to family and friends.

a. At the 0.05 level of significance, is there evidence that the population mean amount spent was different from $6.50?
b. Determine the p-value in (a).
c. At the 0.05 level of significance, is there evidence that more than 50% of all the customers say they "definitely will" recommend the specialty coffee shop to family and friends?
d. What is your answer to (a) if the sample mean equals $6.25?
e. What is your answer to (c) if 39 customers say they "definitely will" recommend the specialty coffee shop to family and friends?

9.73 An auditor for a government agency was assigned the task of evaluating reimbursement for office visits to physicians paid by Medicare. The audit was conducted on a sample of 75 reimbursements, with the following results:
• In 12 of the office visits, there was an incorrect amount of reimbursement.
• The amount of reimbursement was $\overline{X} = \$93.70$, $S = \$34.55$.

a. At the 0.05 level of significance, is there evidence that the population mean reimbursement was less than $100?
b. At the 0.05 level of significance, is there evidence that the proportion of incorrect reimbursements in the population was greater than 0.10?
c. Discuss the underlying assumptions of the test used in (a).
d. What is your answer to (a) if the sample mean equals $90?
e. What is your answer to (b) if 15 office visits had incorrect reimbursements?

9.74 A bank branch located in a commercial district of a city has the business objective of improving the process for serving customers during the noon-to-1:00 p.m. lunch period. The waiting time (defined as the time the customer enters the line until he or she reaches the teller window) of a random sample of 15 customers is collected, and the results are organized and stored in `Bank1`. These data are:

4.21	5.55	3.02	5.13	4.77	2.34	3.54	3.20
4.50	6.10	0.38	5.12	6.46	6.19	3.79

a. At the 0.05 level of significance, is there evidence that the population mean waiting time is less than 5 minutes?
b. What assumption about the population distribution is needed in order to conduct the t test in (a)?
c. Construct a boxplot or a normal probability plot to evaluate the assumption made in (b).
d. Do you think that the assumption needed in order to conduct the t test in (a) is valid? Explain.
e. As a customer walks into the branch office during the lunch hour, she asks the branch manager how long she can expect to wait. The branch manager replies, "Almost certainly not longer than 5 minutes." On the basis of the results of (a), evaluate this statement.

.75 A manufacturing company produces electrical insulators. the insulators break when in use, a short circuit is likely to ccur. To test the strength of the insulators, destructive testing carried out to determine how much force is required to break e insulators. Force is measured by observing the number of ounds of force applied to the insulator before it breaks. The following data (stored in Force) are from 30 insulators subjected this testing:

1,870 1,728 1,656 1,610 1,634 1,784 1,522 1,696 1,592 1,662
1,866 1,764 1,734 1,662 1,734 1,774 1,550 1,756 1,762 1,866
1,820 1,744 1,788 1,688 1,810 1,752 1,680 1,810 1,652 1,736

. At the 0.05 level of significance, is there evidence that the population mean force required to break the insulator is greater than 1,500 pounds?
. What assumption about the population distribution is needed in order to conduct the *t* test in (a)?
. Construct a histogram, boxplot, or normal probability plot to evaluate the assumption made in (b).
. Do you think that the assumption needed in order to conduct the *t* test in (a) is valid? Explain.

.76 An important quality characteristic used by the manufacturer of Boston and Vermont asphalt shingles is the amount of moisture the shingles contain when they are packaged. Customers may feel that they have purchased a product lacking in quality if they find moisture and wet shingles inside the packaging. In some cases, excessive moisture can cause the granules attached to the shingles for texture and coloring purposes to fall off the shingles, resulting in appearance problems. To monitor the amount of moisture present, the company conducts moisture tests. A shingle is weighed and then dried. The shingle is then reweighed, and, based on the amount of moisture taken out of the product, the pounds of moisture per 100 square feet are calculated. The company would like to show that the mean moisture content is less than 0.35 pound per 100 square feet. The file Moisture includes 36 measurements in pounds per 100 square feet) for Boston shingles and 31 for Vermont shingles.
. For the Boston shingles, is there evidence at the 0.05 level of significance that the population mean moisture content is less than 0.35 pound per 100 square feet?
. Interpret the meaning of the *p*-value in (a).
. For the Vermont shingles, is there evidence at the 0.05 level of significance that the population mean moisture content is less than 0.35 pound per 100 square feet?
. Interpret the meaning of the *p*-value in (c).
. What assumption about the population distribution is needed in order to conduct the *t* tests in (a) and (c)?
. Construct histograms, boxplots, or normal probability plots to evaluate the assumption made in (a) and (c).
. Do you think that the assumption needed in order to conduct the *t* tests in (a) and (c) is valid? Explain.

9.77 Studies conducted by the manufacturer of Boston and Vermont asphalt shingles have shown product weight to be a major factor in the customer's perception of quality. Moreover, the weight represents the amount of raw materials being used and is therefore very important to the company from a cost standpoint. The last stage of the assembly line packages the shingles before the packages are placed on wooden pallets. Once a pallet is full (a pallet for most brands holds 16 squares of shingles), it is weighed, and the measurement is recorded. The file Pallet contains the weight (in pounds) from a sample of 368 pallets of Boston shingles and 330 pallets of Vermont shingles.
a. For the Boston shingles, is there evidence at the 0.05 level of significance that the population mean weight is different from 3,150 pounds?
b. Interpret the meaning of the *p*-value in (a).
c. For the Vermont shingles, is there evidence at the 0.05 level of significance that the population mean weight is different from 3,700 pounds?
d. Interpret the meaning of the *p*-value in (c).
e. In (a) through (d), do you have to be concerned with the normality assumption? Explain.

9.78 The manufacturer of Boston and Vermont asphalt shingles provides its customers with a 20-year warranty on most of its products. To determine whether a shingle will last through the warranty period, accelerated-life testing is conducted at the manufacturing plant. Accelerated-life testing exposes the shingle to the stresses it would be subject to in a lifetime of normal use in a laboratory setting via an experiment that takes only a few minutes to conduct. In this test, a shingle is repeatedly scraped with a brush for a short period of time, and the shingle granules removed by the brushing are weighed (in grams). Shingles that experience low amounts of granule loss are expected to last longer in normal use than shingles that experience high amounts of granule loss. The file Granule contains a sample of 170 measurements made on the company's Boston shingles and 140 measurements made on Vermont shingles.
a. For the Boston shingles, is there evidence at the 0.05 level of significance that the population mean granule loss is different from 0.30 grams?
b. Interpret the meaning of the *p*-value in (a).
c. For the Vermont shingles, is there evidence at the 0.05 level of significance that the population mean granule loss is different from 0.30 grams?
d. Interpret the meaning of the *p*-value in (c).
e. In (a) through (d), do you have to be concerned with the normality assumption? Explain.

REPORT WRITING EXERCISE

9.79 Referring to the results of Problems 9.76 through 9.78 concerning Boston and Vermont shingles, write a report that evaluates the moisture level, weight, and granule loss of the two types of shingles.

▼CASES

Managing Ashland MultiComm Services

Continuing its monitoring of the upload speed first described in the Chapter 6 Managing Ashland MultiComm Services case on page 213, the technical operations department wants to ensure that the mean target upload speed for all Internet service subscribers is at least 0.97 on a standard scale in which the target value is 1.0. Each day, upload speed was measured 50 times, with the following results (stored in AMS9).

0.854	1.023	1.005	1.030	1.219	0.977	1.044	0.778	1.122	1.114
1.091	1.086	1.141	0.931	0.723	0.934	1.060	1.047	0.800	0.889
1.012	0.695	0.869	0.734	1.131	0.993	0.762	0.814	1.108	0.805
1.223	1.024	0.884	0.799	0.870	0.898	0.621	0.818	1.113	1.286
1.052	0.678	1.162	0.808	1.012	0.859	0.951	1.112	1.003	0.972

1. Compute the sample statistics and determine whether there is evidence that the population mean upload speed is less than 0.97.
2. Write a memo to management that summarizes your conclusions.

Digital Case

Apply your knowledge about hypothesis testing in this Digital Case, which continues the cereal-fill-packaging dispute first discussed in the Digital Case from Chapter 7.

In response to the negative statements made by the Concerned Consumers About Cereal Cheaters (CCACC) in the Chapter 7 Digital Case, Oxford Cereals recently conducted an experiment concerning cereal packaging. The company claims that the results of the experiment refute the CCACC allegations that Oxford Cereals has been cheating consumers by packaging cereals at less than labeled weights.

Open **OxfordCurrentNews.pdf**, a portfolio of current new releases from Oxford Cereals. Review the relevant press release and supporting documents. Then answer the following questions

1. Are the results of the experiment valid? Why or why not? I you were conducting the experiment, is there anything yo would change?
2. Do the results support the claim that Oxford Cereals is no cheating its customers?
3. Is the claim of the Oxford Cereals CEO that many cerea boxes contain *more* than 368 grams surprising? Is it true?
4. Could there ever be a circumstance in which the results o the Oxford Cereals experiment *and* the CCACC's results are both correct? Explain.

Sure Value Convenience Stores

You work in the corporate office for a nationwide convenience store franchise that operates nearly 10,000 stores. The per-store daily customer count (i.e., the mean number of customers ir a store in one day) has been steady, at 900, for some time. To increase the customer count, the chain is considering cutting prices for coffee beverages. The small size will now be $0.59 instead of $0.99, and the medium size will be $0.69 instead of $1.19. Even with this reduction in price, the chain will have a 40% gross margin on coffee.

To test the new initiative, the chain has reduced coffee prices in a sample of 34 stores, where customer counts have been running almost exactly at the national average of 900. After four weeks, the stores sampled stabilize at a mean customer count of 974 and a standard deviation of 96. This increase seems like a substantial amount to you, but it also seems like a pretty small sample. Is there statistical evidence that reducing coffee prices is a good strategy for increasing the mean customer count? Be prepared to explain your conclusion.

EG9.1 FUNDAMENTALS of HYPOTHESIS-TESTING METHODOLOGY

Key Technique Use the **NORM.S.INV**(*level of significance/2*) and **NORM.S.INV**(1 – *level of significance/2*) functions to compute the lower and upper critical values. Use **NORM.S.DIST** (*absolute value of the Z test statistic*, **True**) as part of a formula to compute the *p*-value.

Example Perform the Figure 9.5 two-tail *Z* test for the mean for the cereal-filling example shown on page 280.

PHStat Use **Z Test for the Mean, sigma known**. For the example, select **PHStat → One-Sample Tests → Z Test for the Mean, sigma known**. In the procedure's dialog box (shown below):

1. Enter **368** as the **Null Hypothesis**.
2. Enter **0.05** as the **Level of Significance**.
3. Enter **15** as the **Population Standard Deviation**.
4. Click **Sample Statistics Known** and enter **25** as the **Sample Size** and **372.5** as the **Sample Mean**.
5. Click **Two-Tail Test**.
6. Enter a **Title** and click **OK**.

When using unsummarized data, click **Sample Statistics Unknown** in step 4 and enter the cell range of the unsummarized data as the **Sample Cell Range**.

Workbook Use the **COMPUTE worksheet** of the **Z Mean workbook** as a template.

The worksheet already contains the data for the example. For other problems, change the null hypothesis, level of significance, population standard deviation, sample size, and sample mean values in cells B4 through B8 as necessary.

EG9.2 *t* TEST of HYPOTHESIS for the MEAN (σ UNKNOWN)

Key Technique Use the **T.INV.2T**(*level of significance, degrees of freedom*) function to compute the lower and upper critical values and use **T.DIST.2T**(*absolute value of the t test statistic, degrees of freedom*) to compute the *p*-value.

Example Perform the Figure 9.7 two-tail *t* test for the mean for the sales invoices example shown on page 286.

PHStat Use **t Test for the Mean, sigma unknown**. For the example, select **PHStat → One-Sample Tests → t Test for the Mean, sigma unknown**. In the procedure's dialog box (shown below):

1. Enter **120** as the **Null Hypothesis**.
2. Enter **0.05** as the **Level of Significance**.
3. Click **Sample Statistics Known** and enter **12** as the **Sample Size**, **112.85** as the **Sample Mean**, and **20.8** as the **Sample Standard Deviation**.
4. Click **Two-Tail Test**.
5. Enter a **Title** and click **OK**.

When using unsummarized data, click **Sample Statistics Unknown** in step 3 and enter the cell range of the unsummarized data as the **Sample Cell Range**.

Workbook Use the **COMPUTE worksheet** of the **T mean workbook**, as a template.

The worksheet already contains the data for the example. For other problems, change the values in cells B4 through B8 as necessary.

EG9.3 | ONE-TAIL TESTS

Key Technique (Z test for the mean) Use the **NORM.S. INV**(*level of significance*) and **NORM.S.INV**(1 − *level of significance*) functions to compute the lower and upper critical values. Use the **NORM.S.DIST**(*Z test statistic*, **True**) and 1 − **NORM.S.DIST**(*Z test statistic*, **True**) to compute the lower-tail and upper-tail *p*-values.

Key Technique (t test for the mean) Use the −**T.INV .2T**(2 * *level of significance, degrees of freedom*) and **T.INV.2T**(2 * *level of significance, degrees of freedom*) functions to compute the lower and upper critical values. Use an IF function that tests the *t* test statistic to determine how **T.DIST.RT**(*absolute value of the t test statistic, degrees of freedom*) or 1 − **T.DIST.RT**(*absolute value of the t test statistic, degrees of freedom*) are used to compute the lower-tail and upper-tail *p*-values.

Example Perform the Figure 9.11 lower-tail *t* test for the mean for the drive-through time study example shown on page 292.

PHStat Click either **Lower-Tail Test** or **Upper-Tail Test** in the procedure dialog boxes discussed in Sections EG9.1 and EG9.2 to perform a one-tail test.
For the example, select **PHStat ➔ One-Sample Tests ➔ t Test for the Mean, sigma unknown**. In the procedure's dialog box (shown below):

1. Enter **189.49** as the **Null Hypothesis**.
2. Enter **0.05** as the **Level of Significance**.
3. Click **Sample Statistics Known** and enter **25** as the **Sample Size**, **175.8** as the **Sample Mean**, and **21.3** as the **Sample Standard Deviation**.
4. Click **Lower-Tail Test**.
5. Enter a **Title** and click **OK**.

Workbook Use the **COMPUTE_LOWER worksheet** or the **COMPUTE_UPPER worksheet** of the **Z Mean** and **T mean workbooks** as templates.
For the example, open to the **COMPUTE_LOWER worksheet** of the **T mean workbook**. For other problems

that require a *t* test, open to the appropriate worksheet and change the **Null Hypothesis, Level of Significance, Sample Size, Sample Mean**, and **Sample Standard Deviation** in the cell range B4:B8.

For other problems that require a *Z* test, open o the appropriate worksheet and change the **Null Hypothesis, Level of Significance, Population Standard Deviation, Sample Size**, and **Sample Mean** in the cell range B4:B8.

To see the all of the formulas used in the one-tail test worksheets, open to the **COMPUTE_ALL_FORMULAS** worksheet.

EG9.4 *Z* TEST of HYPOTHESIS for the PROPORTION

Key Technique Use the **NORM.S.INV**(*level of significance/2*) and **NORM.S.INV**(1 − *level of significance/2*) functions to compute the lower and upper critical values. Use **NORM.S.DIST**(*absolute value of the Z test statistic*, **True**) as part of a formula to compute the *p*-value.

Example Perform the Figure 9.14 two-tail *Z* test for the proportion of Internet users who said that they had taken steps to remove or mask their digital footprints shown on page 296.

PHStat Use *Z* Test for the Proportion.
For the example, select **PHStat ➔ One-Sample Tests ➔ Z Test for the Proportion**. In the procedure's dialog box (shown below):

1. Enter **0.8** as the **Null Hypothesis**.
2. Enter **0.05** as the **Level of Significance**.
3. Enter **681** as the **Number of Items of Interest**.
4. Enter **792** as the **Sample Size**.
5. Click **Two-Tail Test**.
6. Enter a **Title** and click **OK**.

Workbook Use the **COMPUTE worksheet** of the **Z Proportion workbook** as a template.
The worksheet already contains the data for the example. For other problems, change the null hypothesis, level of significance, population standard deviation, sample size, and sample mean values in cells B4 through B7 as necessary.

Use the COMPUTE_LOWER or COMPUTE_UPPER worksheets as templates for performing one-tail tests.

Two-Sample Tests

▼USING **STATISTICS**
Differing Means for Selling Streaming Media Players at Arlingtons?

To what extent does the location of products in a store affect sales? At Arlingtons, a general merchandiser that competes with discount and wholesale club retailers, management has been considering this question as part of a general review. Seeking to enhance revenues, managers have decided to create a new sales area at the front of the each Arlingtons store, near the checkout lanes. Management plans to charge product manufacturers a placement fee for placing specific products in this front area, but first need to demonstrate that the area would boost sales.

While some manufacturers refuse to pay such placement fees, Arlingtons has found a willing partner in Pierrsöhn Technologies. Pierrsöhn wants to introduce VLABGo, their new mobile streaming player, and is willing to pay a placement fee to be featured at the front of each Arlingtons store. However, Pierrsöhn management wants reassurance that the front of the store will be worth the placement fee. As the retail operations chief at Arlingtons, you have been asked to negotiate with Pierrsöhn. You propose a test that will involve 20 Arlingtons locations, all with similar storewide sales volumes and shopper demographics. You explain that you will randomly select 10 stores to sell the VLABGo player among other, similar items in the mobile electronics aisle in those Arlingtons stores. For the other 10 stores, you will place the VLABGo players in a special area at the front of the store.

At the end of the one month test period, the sales of VLABGo players from the two store samples will be recorded and compared. You wonder how you could determine whether the sales in the in-aisle stores are different from the sales in the stores where the VLABGo players appears in the special front area. You also would like to decide if the variability in sales from store to store is different for the two types of sales location. If you can demonstrate a difference in sales, you will have a stronger case for asking for a special front of the store placement fee from Pierrsöhn. What should you do?

CONTENTS

OBJECTIVES

- Compare the means of two independent populations
- Compare the means of two related populations
- Compare the proportions of two independent populations
- Compare the variances of two independent populations

307

n Chapter 9, you learned several hypothesis-testing procedures commonly used to test a single sample of data selected from a single population. In this chapter, you learn how to extend hypothesis testing to **two-sample tests** that compare statistics from samples selected from *two* populations. In the Arlingtons scenario one such test would be "Are the mean VLABGo player monthly sales at the special front location (one population) different from the mean VLABGo player monthly sales at the in-aisle location (a second population)?"

10.1 Comparing the Means of Two Independent Populations

In Sections 8.1 and 9.1, you learned that in almost all cases, you would not know the standard deviation of the population under study. Likewise, when you take a random sample from each of two independent populations, you almost always do not know the standard deviation of either population. In addition, when using a two-sample test that compares the means of samples selected from two populations, you must establish whether the assumption that the variances in the two populations are equal holds. The statistical method used to test whether the means of each population are different depends on whether the assumption holds or not.

Pooled-Variance t Test for the Difference Between Two Means

studentTIP

Whichever population is defined as population 1 in the null and alternative hypotheses must be defined as population 1 in Equation (10.1). Whichever population is defined as population 2 in the null and alternative hypotheses must be defined as population 2 in Equation (10.1).

If you assume that the random samples are independently selected from two populations and that the populations are normally distributed and have equal variances, you can use a **pooled-variance t test** to determine whether there is a significant difference between the means. If the populations do not differ greatly from a normal distribution, you can still use the pooled-variance t test, especially if the sample sizes are large enough (typically ≥ 30 for each sample).

Using subscripts to distinguish between the population mean of the first population, μ_1, and the population mean of the second population, μ_2, the null hypothesis of no difference in the means of two independent populations can be stated as

$$H_0: \mu_1 = \mu_2 \quad \text{or} \quad \mu_1 - \mu_2 = 0$$

and the alternative hypothesis, that the means are different, can be stated as

$$H_1: \mu_1 \neq \mu_2 \quad \text{or} \quad \mu_1 - \mu_2 \neq 0$$

[1]When the two sample sizes are equal (i.e., $n_1 = n_2$), the equation for the pooled variance can be simplified to

$$S_p^2 = \frac{S_1^2 + S_2^2}{2}$$

To test the null hypothesis, you use the pooled-variance t test statistic t_{STAT} shown in Equation (10.1). The pooled-variance t test gets its name from the fact that the test statistic pools, or combines, the two sample variances S_1^2 and S_2^2 to compute S_p^2, the best estimate of the variance common to both populations, under the assumption that the two population variances are equal.[1]

POOLED-VARIANCE t TEST FOR THE DIFFERENCE BETWEEN TWO MEANS

$$t_{STAT} = \frac{(\overline{X}_1 - \overline{X}_2) - (\mu_1 - \mu_2)}{\sqrt{S_p^2 \left(\frac{1}{n_1} + \frac{1}{n_2} \right)}}$$

(10.1)

where

$$S_p^2 = \frac{(n_1 - 1)S_1^2 + (n_2 - 1)S_2^2}{(n_1 - 1) + (n_2 - 1)}$$

and S_p^2 = pooled variance
$\overline{X}_1$ = mean of the sample taken from population 1
S_1^2 = variance of the sample taken from population 1
n_1 = size of the sample taken from population 1
$\overline{X}_2$ = mean of the sample taken from population 2
S_2^2 = variance of the sample taken from population 2
n_2 = size of the sample taken from population 2

The t_{STAT} test statistic follows a t distribution with $n_1 + n_2 - 2$ degrees of freedom.

For a given level of significance, α, in a two-tail test, you reject the null hypothesis if the computed t_{STAT} test statistic is greater than the upper-tail critical value from the t distribution or if the computed t_{STAT} test statistic is less than the lower-tail critical value from the t distribution. Figure 10.1 displays the regions of rejection.

FIGURE 10.1
Regions of rejection and nonrejection for the pooled-variance t test for the difference between the means (two-tail test)

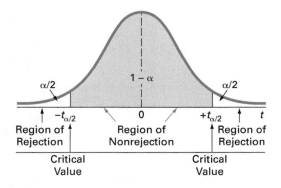

studentTIP

When *lower* or *less than* is used in an example, you have a lower-tail test. When *upper* or *more than* is used in an example, you have an upper-tail test. When *different* or *the same as* is used in an example, you have a two-tail test.

In a one-tail test in which the rejection region is in the lower tail, you reject the null hypothesis if the computed t_{STAT} test statistic is less than the lower-tail critical value from the t distribution. In a one-tail test in which the rejection region is in the upper tail, you reject the null hypothesis if the computed t_{STAT} test statistic is greater than the upper-tail critical value from the t distribution.

To demonstrate the pooled-variance t test, return to the Arlingtons scenario on page 307. Using the DCOVA problem-solving approach, you define the business objective as determining whether there is a difference in the mean VLABGo player monthly sales at the special front and in-aisle locations. There are two populations of interest. The first population is the set of all possible VLABGo player monthly sales at the special front location. The second population is the set of all possible VLABGo player monthly sales at the in-aisle location. You collect the data from a sample of 10 Arlingtons stores that have been assigned the special front location and another sample of 10 Arlingtons stores that have been assigned the in-aisle location. You organize the data as Table 10.1 and store the data in VLABGo .

TABLE 10.1
Comparing VLABGo player Sales from Two Different Locations

SALES LOCATION									
Special Front					**In-Aisle**				
224	189	248	285	273	192	236	164	154	189
160	243	215	280	317	220	261	186	219	202

The null and alternative hypotheses are

$$H_0: \mu_1 = \mu_2 \quad \text{or} \quad \mu_1 - \mu_2 = 0$$

$$H_1: \mu_1 \neq \mu_2 \quad \text{or} \quad \mu_1 - \mu_2 \neq 0$$

Assuming that the samples are from normal populations having equal variances, you can use the pooled-variance t test. The t_{STAT} test statistic follows a t distribution with $10 + 10 - 2 = 18$ degrees of freedom. Using an $\alpha = 0.05$ level of significance, you divide the rejection region into the two tails for this two-tail test (i.e., two equal parts of 0.025 each). Table E.3 shows that the critical values for this two-tail test are $+2.1009$ and -2.1009. As shown in Figure 10.2, the decision rule is

$$\text{Reject } H_0 \text{ if } t_{STAT} > +2.1009$$

$$\text{or if } t_{STAT} < -2.1009;$$

$$\text{otherwise, do not reject } H_0.$$

FIGURE 10.2

Two-tail test of hypothesis for the difference between the means at the 0.05 level of significance with 18 degrees of freedom

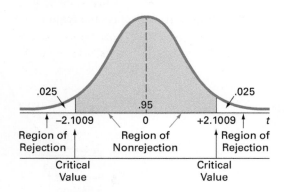

From Figure 10.3, the computed t_{STAT} test statistic for this test is 2.2510 and the p-value is 0.0371.

FIGURE 10.3

Excel pooled-variance t test worksheet with confidence interval estimate for the two different sales locations data

	A	B	
1	Pooled-Variance *t* Test for Differences in Two Means		
2	(assumes equal population variances)		
3	Data		
4	Hypothesized Difference	0	
5	Level of Significance	0.05	
6	Population 1 Sample		
7	Sample Size	10	=COUNT(DataCopy!$A:$A)
8	Sample Mean	243.4	=AVERAGE(DataCopy!$A:$A)
9	Sample Standard Deviation	47.7056	=STDEV.S(DataCopy!$A:$A)
10	Population 2 Sample		
11	Sample Size	10	=COUNT(DataCopy!$B:$B)
12	Sample Mean	202.3	=AVERAGE(DataCopy!$B:$B)
13	Sample Standard Deviation	32.5271	=STDEV.S(DataCopy!$B:$B)
14			
15	Intermediate Calculations		
16	Population 1 Sample Degrees of Freedom	9	=B7 - 1
17	Population 2 Sample Degrees of Freedom	9	=B11 - 1
18	Total Degrees of Freedom	18	=B16 + B17
19	Pooled Variance	1666.9167	=((B16 * B9^2) + (B17 * B13^2))/B18
20	Standard Error	18.2588	=SQRT(B19 * (1/B7 + 1/B11))
21	Difference in Sample Means	41.1	=B8 - B12
22	*t* Test Statistic	2.2510	=(B21 - B4)/B20
23			
24	Two-Tail Test		
25	Lower Critical Value	-2.1009	=-(T.INV.2T(B5, B18))
26	Upper Critical Value	2.1009	=T.INV.2T(B5, B18)
27	*p*-Value	0.0371	=T.DIST.2T(ABS(B22), B18)
28	Reject the null hypothesis		=IF(B27 < B5, "Reject the null hypothesis", "Do not reject the null hypothesis")

	D	E	
3	Confidence Interval Estimate		
4	for the Difference Between Two Means		
5			
6	Data		
7	Confidence Level	95%	
8			
9	Intermediate Calculations		
10	Degrees of Freedom	18	=B16 + B17
11	*t* Value	2.1009	=T.INV.2T(1 - E7, E10)
12	Interval Half Width	38.3603	=(E11 * SQRT(B19 * (1/B7 + 1/B11)))
13			
14	Confidence Interval		
15	Interval Lower Limit	2.7397	=B21 - E12
16	Interval Upper Limit	79.4603	=B21 + E12

Using Equation (10.1) on page 308 and the descriptive statistics provided in Figure 10.3,

$$t_{STAT} = \frac{(\bar{X}_1 - \bar{X}_2) - (\mu_1 - \mu_2)}{\sqrt{S_p^2 \left(\dfrac{1}{n_1} + \dfrac{1}{n_2}\right)}}$$

where

$$S_p^2 = \frac{(n_1 - 1)S_1^2 + (n_2 - 1)S_2^2}{(n_1 - 1) + (n_2 - 1)}$$

$$= \frac{9(47.7056)^2 + 9(32.5271)^2}{9 + 9} = 1,666.9167$$

Therefore,

$$t_{STAT} = \frac{(243.4 - 202.3) - 0.0}{\sqrt{1,666.9167 \left(\dfrac{1}{10} + \dfrac{1}{10}\right)}} = \frac{41.1}{\sqrt{333.3833}} = 2.2510$$

You reject the null hypothesis because $t_{STAT} = 2.2510 > 2.1009$ and the p-value is 0.0371. In other words, the probability that $t_{STAT} > 2.2510$ or $t_{STAT} < -2.2510$ is equal to 0.0371. This p-value indicates that if the population means are equal, the probability of observing a difference in the two sample means this large or larger is only 0.0371. Because the p-value is less than $\alpha = 0.05$, there is sufficient evidence to reject the null hypothesis. You can conclude that the mean sales are different for the special front and in-aisle locations. Because the t_{STAT} statistic is positive, you can conclude that the mean sales are higher for the special front location (and lower for the in-aisle location). This provides evidence to justify charging a placement fee for placing VLABGo players in the special in-front location.

In testing for the difference between the means, you assume that the populations are normally distributed, with equal variances. For situations in which the two populations have equal variances, the pooled-variance t test is **robust** (i.e., not sensitive) to moderate departures from the assumption of normality, provided that the sample sizes are large. In such situations, you can use the pooled-variance t test without serious effects on its power. However, if you cannot assume that both populations are normally distributed, you have two choices. You can use a nonparametric procedure, such as the Wilcoxon rank sum test (see Section 12.4), that does not depend on the assumption of normality for the two populations, or you can use a normalizing transformation (see reference 4) on each of the values and then use the pooled-variance t test.

To check the assumption of normality in each of the two populations, you can construct a boxplot of the sales for the two display locations shown in Figure 10.4. For these two small samples, there appears to be only slight departure from normality, so the assumption of normality needed for the t test is not seriously violated.

FIGURE 10.4

Excel boxplot for sales at the special front and in-aisle locations

Example 10.1 provides another application of the pooled-variance t test.

EXAMPLE 10.1

Testing for the Difference in the Mean Delivery Times

You and some friends have decided to test the validity of an advertisement by a local pizza restaurant, which says it delivers to the dormitories faster than a local branch of a national chain. Both the local pizza restaurant and national chain are located across the street from your college campus. You define the variable of interest as the delivery time, in minutes, from the time the pizza is ordered to when it is delivered. You collect the data by ordering 10 pizzas from the local pizza restaurant and 10 pizzas from the national chain at different times. You organize and store the data in PizzaTime. Table 10.2 shows the delivery times.

TABLE 10.2

Delivery Times (in minutes) for a Local Pizza Restaurant and a National Pizza Chain

Local		Chain	
16.8	18.1	22.0	19.5
11.7	14.1	15.2	17.0
15.6	21.8	18.7	19.5
16.7	13.9	15.6	16.5
17.5	20.8	20.8	24.0

At the 0.05 level of significance, is there evidence that the mean delivery time for the local pizza restaurant is less than the mean delivery time for the national pizza chain?

SOLUTION Because you want to know whether the mean is *lower* for the local pizza restaurant than for the national pizza chain, you have a one-tail test with the following null and alternative hypotheses:

H_0: $\mu_1 \geq \mu_2$ (The mean delivery time for the local pizza restaurant is equal to or greater than the mean delivery time for the national pizza chain.)

H_1: $\mu_1 < \mu_2$ (The mean delivery time for the local pizza restaurant is less than the mean delivery time for the national pizza chain.)

Figure 10.5 displays the results for the pooled-variance t test for these data.

FIGURE 10.5

Excel worksheet pooled-variance t test results for the pizza delivery time data

	A	B
1	Pooled-Variance t Test for Differences in Two Means	
2	(assumes equal population variances)	
3	**Data**	
4	Hypothesized Difference	0
5	Level of Significance	0.05
6	**Population 1 Sample**	
7	Sample Size	10
8	Sample Mean	16.7
9	Sample Standard Deviation	3.0955
10	**Population 2 Sample**	
11	Sample Size	10
12	Sample Mean	18.88
13	Sample Standard Deviation	2.8662
14		
15	**Intermediate Calculations**	
16	Population 1 Sample Degrees of Freedom	9
17	Population 2 Sample Degrees of Freedom	9
18	Total Degrees of Freedom	18
19	Pooled Variance	8.8986
20	Standard Error	1.3341
21	Difference in Sample Means	-2.18
22	t Test Statistic	-1.6341
23		
24	**Lower-Tail Test**	
25	Lower Critical Value	-1.7341
26	p-Value	0.0598
27	Do not reject the null hypothesis	

In the Worksheet

This is the COMPUTE_LOWER worksheet that is based on the COMPUTE worksheet shown in Figure 10.3.

▶ (continued)

To illustrate the computations, using Equation (10.1) on page 308,

$$t_{STAT} = \frac{(\overline{X}_1 - \overline{X}_2) - (\mu_1 - \mu_2)}{\sqrt{S_p^2\left(\dfrac{1}{n_1} + \dfrac{1}{n_2}\right)}}$$

where

$$S_p^2 = \frac{(n_1 - 1)S_1^2 + (n_2 - 1)S_2^2}{(n_1 - 1) + (n_2 - 1)}$$

$$= \frac{9(3.0955)^2 + 9(2.8662)^2}{9 + 9} = 8.8986$$

Therefore,

$$t_{STAT} = \frac{(16.7 - 18.88) - 0.0}{\sqrt{8.8986\left(\dfrac{1}{10} + \dfrac{1}{10}\right)}} = \frac{-2.18}{\sqrt{1.7797}} = -1.6341$$

You do not reject the null hypothesis because $t_{STAT} = -1.6341 > -1.7341$. The p-value (as computed in Figure 10.5) is 0.0598. This p-value indicates that the probability that $t_{STAT} < -1.6341$ is equal to 0.0598. In other words, if the population means are equal, the probability that the sample mean delivery time for the local pizza restaurant is at least 2.18 minutes faster than the national chain is 0.0598. Because the p-value is greater than $\alpha = 0.05$, there is insufficient evidence to reject the null hypothesis. Based on these results, there is insufficient evidence for the local pizza restaurant to make the advertising claim that it has a faster delivery time.

Confidence Interval Estimate for the Difference Between Two Means

Instead of, or in addition to, testing for the difference between the means of two independent populations, you can use Equation (10.2) to develop a confidence interval estimate of the difference in the means.

CONFIDENCE INTERVAL ESTIMATE FOR THE DIFFERENCE BETWEEN THE MEANS OF TWO INDEPENDENT POPULATIONS

$$(\overline{X}_1 - \overline{X}_2) \pm t_{\alpha/2}\sqrt{S_p^2\left(\frac{1}{n_1} + \frac{1}{n_2}\right)} \qquad \text{(10.2)}$$

or

$$(\overline{X}_1 - \overline{X}_2) - t_{\alpha/2}\sqrt{S_p^2\left(\frac{1}{n_1} + \frac{1}{n_2}\right)} \leq \mu_1 - \mu_2 \leq (\overline{X}_1 - \overline{X}_2) + t_{\alpha/2}\sqrt{S_p^2\left(\frac{1}{n_1} + \frac{1}{n_2}\right)}$$

where $t_{\alpha/2}$ is the critical value of the t distribution, with $n_1 + n_2 - 2$ degrees of freedom, for an area of $\alpha/2$ in the upper tail.

For the sample statistics pertaining to the two locations reported in Figure 10.3 on page 310, using 95% confidence, and Equation (10.2),

$\overline{X}_1 = 243.4$, $n_1 = 10$, $\overline{X}_2 = 202.3$, $n_2 = 10$, $S_p^2 = 1{,}666.9167$, and with $10 + 10 - 2$
$= 18$ degrees of freedom, $t_{0.025} = 2.1009$

$$(243.4 - 202.3) \pm (2.1009)\sqrt{1{,}666.9167\left(\frac{1}{10} + \frac{1}{10}\right)}$$

$$41.10 \pm (2.1009)(18.2588)$$

$$41.10 \pm 38.3603$$

$$2.7397 \leq \mu_1 - \mu_2 \leq 79.4603$$

Therefore, you are 95% confident that the difference in mean sales between the special front and in-aisle locations is between 2.7397 and 79.4603 VLABGo players sold. In other words, you can estimate, with 95% confidence, that the special front location has mean sales of between 2.7397 and 79.4603 more VLABGo players than the in-aisle location. From a hypothesis-testing perspective, using a two-tail test at the 0.05 level of significance, because the interval does not include zero, you reject the null hypothesis of no difference between the means of the two populations.

t Test for the Difference Between Two Means, Assuming Unequal Variances

If you can assume that the two independent populations are normally distributed but cannot assume that they have equal variances, you cannot pool the two sample variances into the common estimate S_p^2 and therefore cannot use the pooled-variance *t* test. Instead, you use the **separate-variance *t* test** developed by Satterthwaite that uses the two separate sample variances (see reference 3).

Figure 10.6 displays the separate-variance *t* test results for the two different sales locations data. Observe that the test statistic $t_{STAT} = 2.2510$ and the *p*-value is $0.0398 < 0.05$. Thus, the results for the separate-variance *t* test are nearly the same as those of the pooled-variance *t* test. The assumption of equality of population variances had no appreciable effect on the results. Sometimes, however, the results from the pooled-variance and separate-variance *t* tests conflict because the assumption of equal variances is violated. Therefore, it is important that you evaluate the assumptions and use those results as a guide in selecting a test procedure. In Section 10.4, the *F* test for the ratio of two variances is used to determine whether there is evidence of a difference in the two population variances. The results of that test can help you decide which of the *t* tests—pooled-variance or separate-variance—is more appropriate.

FIGURE 10.6

Excel separate-variance *t* test worksheet for the two different sales locations data

	A	B	
1	Separate-Variances *t* Test		
2	(assumes unequal population variances)		
3	**Data**		
4	Hypothesized Difference	0	
5	Level of Significance	0.05	
6	**Population 1 Sample**		
7	Sample Size	10	=COUNT(DataCopy2!$A:$A)
8	Sample Mean	243.4	=AVERAGE(DataCopy2!$A:$A)
9	Sample Standard Deviation	47.7056	=STDEV.S(DataCopy2!$A:$A)
10	**Population 2 Sample**		
11	Sample Size	10	=COUNT(DataCopy2!$B:$B)
12	Sample Mean	202.3	=AVERAGE(DataCopy2!$B:$B)
13	Sample Standard Deviation	32.5271	=STDEV.S(DataCopy2!$B:$B)
14			
15	**Intermediate Calculations**		
16	Numerator of Degrees of Freedom	111144.4469	=(E18 + E19)^2
17	Denominator of Degrees of Freedom	6998.6159	=(E18^2)/(B7 - 1) + (E19^2)/(B11 - 1)
18	Total Degrees of Freedom	15.8809	=B16/B17
19	Degrees of Freedom	15	=INT(B18)
20	Standard Error	18.2588	=SQRT(E18 + E19)
21	Difference in Sample Means	41.1000	=B8 - B12
22	Separate-Variance *t* Test Statistic	2.2510	=(B21 - B4)/B20
23			
24	**Two-Tail Test**		
25	Lower Critical Value	-2.1314	= -(T.INV.2T(B5, B19))
26	Upper Critical Value	2.1314	=T.INV.2T(B5, B19)
27	*p*-Value	0.0398	=T.DIST.2T(ABS(B22), B19)
28	Reject the null hypothesis		=IF(B27 < B5,"Reject the null hypothesis", "Do not reject the null hypothesis")

	D	E	
15	**Calculations Area**		
16	Pop. 1 Sample Variance	2275.8222	=B9^2
17	Pop. 2 Sample Variance	1058.0111	=B13^2
18	Pop. 1 Sample Var./Sample Size	227.5822	=E16/B7
19	Pop. 2 Sample Var./Sample Size	105.8011	=E17/B11
20	For one-tailed tests:		
21	T.DIST.RT value	0.0199	=T.DIST.RT(ABS(B22), B19)
22	1-T.DIST.RT value	0.9801	=1 - E21

CONSIDER THIS

Do People Really Do This?

Some question whether decision makers really use confirmatory methods, such as hypothesis testing, in this emerging era of big data. The following real case study, contributed by a former student of a colleague of the authors, reveals a role that confirmatory methods still play in business as well as answering another question: "Do businesses really monitor their customer service calls for quality assurance purposes as they sometime claim?"

In her first full-time job at a financial services company, a student was asked to improve a training program for new hires at a call center that handled customer questions about outstanding loans. For feedback and evaluation, she planned to randomly select phone calls received by each new employee and rate the employee on 10 aspects of the call, including whether the employee maintained a pleasant tone with the customer. When she presented her plan to her boss for approval, her boss wanted proof that her new training program would improve customer service. The boss, quoting a famous statistician, said "In God we trust; all others must bring data." Faced with this request, she called her business statistics professor. "Hello, Professor, you'll never believe why I called. I work for a large company, and in the project I am currently working on, I have to put some of the

statistics you taught us to work! Can you help?" Together they formulated this test:

- Randomly assign the 60 most recent hires to two training programs. Assign half to the preexisting training program and the other half to the new training program.
- At the end of the first month, compare the mean score for the 30 employees in the new training program against the mean score for the 30 employees in the preexisting training program.

She listened as her professor explained, "What you are trying to show is that the mean score from the new training program is higher than the mean score from the current program. You can make the null hypothesis that the means are equal and see if you can reject it in favor of the alternative that the mean score from the new program is higher."

"Or, as you used to say, 'if the *p*-value is low, H_o must go!'—yes, I do remember!" she replied. Her professor chuckled and added, "If you can reject H_o you will have the evidence to present to your boss." She thanked him for his help and got back to work, with the newfound confidence that she would be able to successfully apply the *t* test that compares the means of two independent populations.

PROBLEMS FOR SECTION 10.1

LEARNING THE BASICS

10.1 If you have samples of $n_1 = 12$ and $n_2 = 15$, in performing the pooled-variance *t* test, how many degrees of freedom do you have?

10.2 Assume that you have a sample of $n_1 = 8$, with the sample mean $\overline{X}_1 = 42$, and a sample standard deviation $S_1 = 4$, and you have an independent sample of $n_2 = 15$ from another population with a sample mean of $\overline{X}_2 = 34$ and a sample standard deviation $S_2 = 5$.
a. What is the value of the pooled-variance t_{STAT} test statistic for testing $H_0: \mu_1 = \mu_2$?
b. In finding the critical value, how many degrees of freedom are there?
c. Using the level of significance $\alpha = 0.01$, what is the critical value for a one-tail test of the hypothesis $H_0: \mu_1 \leq \mu_2$ against the alternative, $H_1: \mu_1 > \mu_2$?
d. What is your statistical decision?

10.3 What assumptions about the two populations are necessary in Problem 10.2?

10.4 Referring to Problem 10.2, construct a 95% confidence interval estimate of the population mean difference between μ_1 and μ_2.

10.5 Referring to Problem 10.2, if $n_1 = 5$ and $n_2 = 4$, how many degrees of freedom do you have?

10.6 Referring to Problem 10.2, if $n_1 = 5$ and $n_2 = 4$, at the 0.01 level of significance, is there evidence that $\mu_1 > \mu_2$?

APPLYING THE CONCEPTS

10.7 When people make estimates, they are influenced by anchors to their estimates. A study was conducted in which students were asked to estimate the number of calories in a cheeseburger. One group was asked to do this after thinking about a calorie-laden cheesecake. A second group was asked to do this after thinking about an organic fruit salad. The mean number of calories estimated in a cheeseburger was 780 for the group that thought about the cheesecake and 1,041 for the group that thought about the organic fruit salad. (Data extracted from "Drilling Down, Sizing Up a Cheeseburger's Caloric Heft," *The New York Times*, October 4, 2010, p. B2.) Suppose that the study was based on a sample of

20 people who thought about the cheesecake first and 20 people who thought about the organic fruit salad first, and the standard deviation of the number of calories in the cheeseburger was 128 for the people who thought about the cheesecake first and 140 for the people who thought about the organic fruit salad first.

a. State the null and alternative hypotheses if you want to determine whether the mean estimated number of calories in the cheeseburger is lower for the people who thought about the cheesecake first than for the people who thought about the organic fruit salad first.

b. In the context of this study, what is the meaning of the Type I error?

c. In the context of this study, what is the meaning of the Type II error?

d. At the 0.01 level of significance, is there evidence that the mean estimated number of calories in the cheeseburger is lower for the people who thought about the cheesecake first than for the people who thought about the organic fruit salad first?

10.8 A recent study (data extracted from E. J. Boyland et al., "Food Choice and Overconsumption: Effect of a Premium Sports Celebrity Endorser," *Journal of Pediatrics*, March 13, 2013, **bit.ly/16NR4Bi**) found that 51 children who watched a commercial for Walker Crisps (potato chips) featuring a long-standing sports celebrity endorser ate a mean of 36 grams of Walker Crisps as compared to a mean of 25 grams of Walker Crisps for 41 children who watched a commercial for an alternative food snack. Suppose that the sample standard deviation for the children who watched the sports celebrity–endorsed Walker Crisps commercial was 21.4 grams and the sample standard deviation for the children who watched the alternative food snack commercial was 12.8 grams.

a. Assuming that the population variances are equal and $\alpha = 0.05$, is there evidence that the mean amount of Walker Crisps eaten was significantly higher for the children who watched the sports celebrity–endorsed Walker Crisps commercial?

b. Assuming that the population variances are equal, construct a 95% confidence interval estimate of the difference between the mean amount of Walker Crisps eaten by children who watched the sports celebrity–endorsed Walker Crisps commercial and children who watched the alternative food snack commercial.

c. Compare and discuss the results of (a) and (b).

10.9 A problem with a phone line that prevents a customer from receiving or making calls is upsetting to both the customer and the telecommunications company. The file Phone contains samples of 20 problems reported to two different offices of a telecommunications company and the time to clear these problems (in minutes) from the customers' lines:

Central Office I Time to Clear Problems (minutes)

1.48	1.75	0.78	2.85	0.52	1.60	4.15	3.97	1.48	3.10
1.02	0.53	0.93	1.60	0.80	1.05	6.32	3.93	5.45	0.97

Central Office II Time to Clear Problems (minutes)

7.55	3.75	0.10	1.10	0.60	0.52	3.30	2.10	0.58	4.02
3.75	0.65	1.92	0.60	1.53	4.23	0.08	1.48	1.65	0.72

a. Assuming that the population variances from both offices are equal, is there evidence of a difference in the mean waiting time between the two offices? (Use $\alpha = 0.05$.)

b. Find the p-value in (a) and interpret its meaning.

c. What other assumption is necessary in (a)?

d. Assuming that the population variances from both offices are equal, construct and interpret a 95% confidence interval estimate of the difference between the population means in the two offices.

10.10 *Accounting Today* identified the top accounting firms in 10 geographic regions across the United States. All 10 regions reported growth in 2014. The Southeast and Gulf Coast regions reported growth of 12.36% and 5.8%, respectively. A characteristic description of the accounting firms in the Southeast and Gulf Coast regions included the number of partners in the firm. The file AccountingPartners2 contains the number of partners. (Data extracted from **bit.ly/1BoMzsv**)

a. At the 0.05 level of significance, is there evidence of a difference between Southeast region accounting firms and Gulf Coast accounting firms with respect to the mean number of partners?

b. Determine the p-value and interpret its meaning.

c. What assumptions do you have to make about the two populations in order to justify the use of the t test?

10.11 An important feature of tablets is battery life, the number of hours before the battery needs to be recharged. The file Tablets contains the battery life of 12 WiFi-only and 7 3G/4G/WiFi 9- through 12-inch tablets. (Data extracted from "Ratings and recommendations: Tablets," *Consumer Reports*, August 2013, p. 24.)

a. Assuming that the population variances from both types of tablets are equal, is there evidence of a difference in the mean battery life between the two types of tablets? (Use $\alpha = 0.05$.)

b. Determine the p-value in (a) and interpret its meaning.

c. Assuming that the population variances from both types of tablets are equal, construct and interpret a 95% confidence interval estimate of the difference between the population mean battery life of the two types of tablets.

10.12 A bank with a branch located in a commercial district of a city has the business objective of developing an improved process for serving customers during the noon-to-1 P.M. lunch period. Management decides to first study the waiting time in the current process. The waiting time is defined as the number of minutes that elapses from when the customer enters the line until he or she reaches the teller window. Data are collected from a random sample of 15 customers and stored in Bank1. These data are:

4.21	5.55	3.02	5.13	4.77	2.34	3.54	3.20
4.50	6.10	0.38	5.12	6.46	6.19	3.79	

Suppose that another branch, located in a residential area, is also concerned with improving the process of serving customers in the noon-to-1 p.m. lunch period. Data are collected from a random sample of 15 customers and stored in Bank2. These data are:

9.66	5.90	8.02	5.79	8.73	3.82	8.01	8.35
10.49	6.68	5.64	4.08	6.17	9.91	5.47	

a. Assuming that the population variances from both banks are equal, is there evidence of a difference in the mean waiting time between the two branches? (Use $\alpha = 0.05$.)

b. Determine the p-value in (a) and interpret its meaning.

c. In addition to equal variances, what other assumption is necessary in (a)?

d. Construct and interpret a 95% confidence interval estimate of the difference between the population means in the two branches.

10.13 Repeat Problem 10.12 (a), assuming that the population variances in the two branches are not equal. Compare these results with those of Problem 10.12 (a).

10.14 As a member of the international strategic management team in your company, you are assigned the task of exploring potential foreign market entry. As part of your initial investigation, you want to know if there is a difference between developed markets and emerging markets with respect to the time required to start a business. You select 15 developed countries and 15 emerging countries. The time required to start a business, defined as the number of days needed to complete the procedures to legally operate a business in these countries, is stored in ForeignMarket . (Data extracted from **data.worldbank.org**.)

a. Assuming that the population variances for developed countries and emerging countries are equal, is there evidence of a difference in the mean time required to start a business between developed countries and emerging countries? (Use $\alpha = 0.05$.)
b. Determine the *p*-value in (a) and interpret its meaning.
c. In addition to equal variances, what other assumption is necessary in (a)?
d. Construct a 95% confidence interval estimate of the difference between the population means of developed countries and emerging countries.

10.15 Repeat Problem 10.14 (a), assuming that the population variances from developed and emerging countries are not equal. Compare these results with those of Problem 10.14 (a).

10.16 Experian Marketing Services reported that the typical American spends 2.4 hours (144 minutes) per day accessing the Internet via a mobile device. (Source: *The 2014 Digital Marketer*, available at **ex.pn/1kXJjfX**.) You wonder if males and females spend differing amounts of time per day accessing the Internet through a mobile device.

You select a sample of 60 friends and family (30 males and 30 females), collect times spent per day accessing the Internet through a mobile device (in minutes), and store the data collected in InternetMobileTime2 .

a. Assuming that the variances in the population of times spent per day accessing the Internet via a mobile device are equal, is there evidence of a difference between males and females in the mean time spent per day accessing the Internet via a mobile device? (Use a 0.05 level of significance.)
b. In addition to equal variances, what other assumption is necessary in (a)?

10.17 Brand valuations are critical to CEOs, financial and marketing executives, security analysts, institutional investors, and others who depend on well-researched, reliable information needed for assessments, and comparisons in decision making. Millward Brown Optimor has developed the BrandZ Top 100 Most Valuable Global Brands for WPP, the world's largest communications services group. Unlike other studies, the BrandZ Top 100 Most Valuable Global Brands fuses consumer measures of brand equity with financial measures to place a financial value on brands. The file BrandZTechFin contains the brand values for the technology sector and the financial institution sector in the BrandZ Top 100 Most Valuable Global Brands for 2015 (Data extracted from **bit.ly/1BH8m5F**)

a. Assuming that the population variances are equal, is there evidence of a difference between the technology sector and the financial institutions sector with respect to mean brand value? (Use $\alpha = .05$.)
b. Repeat (a), assuming that the population variances are not equal.
c. Compare the results of (a) and (b).

10.2 Comparing the Means of Two Related Populations

The hypothesis-testing procedures presented in Section 10.1 enable you to examine differences between the means of two *independent* populations. In this section, you will learn about a procedure for examining the mean difference between two populations when you collect sample data from populations that are related—that is, when results of the first population are *not* independent of the results of the second population.

There are two situations that involve related data: when you take repeated measurements from the same set of items or individuals or when you match items or individuals according to some characteristic. In either situation, you are interested in the *difference between the two related values* rather than the *individual values* themselves.

When you take **repeated measurements** on the same items or individuals, you assume that the same items or individuals will behave alike if treated alike. Your objective is to show that any differences between two measurements of the same items or individuals are due to different treatments that have been applied to the items or individuals. For example, when performing an experiment comparing the retail prices of items from two different vendors, you would take the prices of identical items that the two vendors sell. (For each item, those two prices are the "repeated measurements" of the item.)

This technique allows you to answer questions such as "are new textbook prices at a local college bookstore different from the prices offered at a major online retailer?" By collecting the prices of the *same* new textbooks from both sellers, that is, by having two related samples, you can use a test that is more powerful than the tests discussed in Section 10.1. The Section 10.1 tests use two *independent* samples that mostly likely will not contain the same sample of text-books. That means that differences observed might be due to one sample having textbooks that are inherently costlier than the other. (Imagine one sample has very larger hardcover textbooks and the other has many trade paperback textbooks that publishers market at lower prices.)

Matched samples represent another type of related data between populations. In matched samples, items or individuals are paired together according to some characteristic of interest. For example, in test marketing a product in two different advertising campaigns, a sample of test markets can be *matched* on the basis of the test-market population size and/or demographic variables. By accounting for the differences in test-market population size and/or demographic variables, you are better able to measure the effects of the two different advertising campaigns.

Regardless of whether you have matched samples or repeated measurements, the objective is to study the difference between two measurements by reducing the effect of the variability that is due to the items or individuals themselves. Table 10.3 shows the differences between the individual values for two related populations. To read this table, let $X_{11}, X_{12}, \ldots, X_{1n}$ represent the n values from the first sample. And let $X_{21}, X_{22}, \ldots, X_{2n}$ represent either the corresponding n matched values from a second sample or the corresponding n repeated measurements from the initial sample. Then $D_1, D_2, \ldots, D_n$ will represent the corresponding set of n *difference scores* such that

$$D_1 = X_{11} - X_{21}, D_2 = X_{12} - X_{22}, \ldots, \text{and } D_n = X_{1n} - X_{2n}.$$

To test for the mean difference between two related populations, you treat the difference scores, each D_i, as values from a single sample.

TABLE 10.3
Determining the Difference Between Two Related Samples

Value	Sample 1	Sample 2	Difference
1	X_{11}	X_{21}	$D_1 = X_{11} - X_{21}$
2	X_{12}	X_{22}	$D_2 = X_{12} - X_{22}$
⋮	⋮	⋮	⋮
i	X_{1i}	X_{2i}	$D_i = X_{1i} - X_{2i}$
⋮	⋮	⋮	⋮
n	X_{1n}	X_{2n}	$D_n = X_{1n} - X_{2n}$

studentTIP

Which sample you define as sample 1 determines the type of one-tail test that would be appropriate to perform, if a one-tail test is needed.

Paired *t* Test

If you assume that the difference scores are randomly and independently selected from a population that is normally distributed, you can use the **paired *t* test for the mean difference** in related populations to determine whether there is a significant population mean difference. As with the one-sample *t* test developed in Section 9.2 [see Equation (9.2) on page 284], the paired *t* test statistic follows the *t* distribution with $n - 1$ degrees of freedom. Although the paired *t* test assumes that the population is normally distributed, since this test is robust, you can use this test as long as the sample size is not very small and the population is not highly skewed.

To test the null hypothesis that there is no difference in the means of two related populations:

$$H_0: \mu_D = 0 \ (\text{where } \mu_D = \mu_1 - \mu_2)$$

against the alternative that the means are not the same:

$$H_1: \mu_D \neq 0$$

you compute the t_{STAT} test statistic using Equation (10.3).

PAIRED t TEST FOR THE MEAN DIFFERENCE

$$t_{STAT} = \frac{\overline{D} - \mu_D}{\dfrac{S_D}{\sqrt{n}}} \qquad\qquad (10.3)$$

where

$$\mu_D = \text{hypothesized mean difference}$$

$$\overline{D} = \frac{\displaystyle\sum_{i=1}^{n} D_i}{n}$$

$$S_D = \sqrt{\frac{\displaystyle\sum_{i=1}^{n}(D_i - \overline{D})^2}{n-1}}$$

The t_{STAT} test statistic follows a t distribution with $n-1$ degrees of freedom.

For a two-tail test with a given level of significance, α, you reject the null hypothesis if the computed t_{STAT} test statistic is greater than the upper-tail critical value $t_{\alpha/2}$ from the t distribution, or, if the computed t_{STAT} test statistic is less than the lower-tail critical value $-t_{\alpha/2}$, from the t distribution. The decision rule is

$$\text{Reject } H_0 \text{ if } t_{STAT} > t_{\alpha/2}$$

$$\text{or if } t_{STAT} < -t_{\alpha/2};$$

$$\text{otherwise, do not reject } H_0.$$

You can use the paired t test for the mean difference to investigate a question raised earlier in this section: Are new textbook prices at a local college bookstore different from the prices offered at a major online retailer?

In this repeated-measurements experiment, you use one set of textbooks. For each textbook, you determine the price at the local bookstore and the price at the online retailer. By determining the two prices for the same textbooks, you can reduce the variability in the prices compared with what would occur if you used two independent sets of textbooks. This approach focuses on the differences between the prices of the same textbooks offered by the two retailers.

You collect data by conducting an experiment from a sample of $n = 16$ textbooks used primarily in business school courses during a recent semester at a local college. You determine the college bookstore price and the online price (which includes shipping costs, if any). You organize the data as Table 10.4 on page 320 and store the data in `BookPrices`. Notice that each row of the table shows the bookstore price and online retailer price for a specific book.

Your objective is to determine whether there is any difference between the mean textbook price at the college bookstore and at the online retailer. In other words, is there evidence that the mean price is different between the two textbook sellers? Thus, the null and alternative hypotheses are

$H_0: \mu_D = 0$ (There is no difference in the mean price between the college bookstore and the online retailer.)

$H_1: \mu_D \neq 0$ (There is a difference in the mean price between the college bookstore and the online retailer.)

TABLE 10.4
Prices of Textbooks at the College Bookstore and at the Online Retailer

Author	Title	Bookstore	Online
Bade	*Foundations of Microeconomics*	200.00	121.49
Brigham	*Financial Management*	304.00	235.88
Clauretie	*Real Estate Finance: Theory and Practice*	179.35	107.61
Foner	*Give Me Liberty! (Brief) Vol. 2*	72.00	59.99
Garrison	*Managerial Accounting*	277.15	146.99
Grewal	*M: Marketing*	73.75	63.49
Hill	*Global Business Today*	171.65	138.99
Lafore	*Object-Oriented Programming in C++*	65.00	42.26
Lank	*Modern Real Estate Practice*	47.45	65.99
Meyer	*Entrepreneurship*	106.00	37.83
Mitchell	*Public Affairs in the Nation and New York*	55.95	102.99
Pindyck	*Microeconomics*	224.40	144.99
Robbins	*Organizational Behavior*	223.20	179.39
Ross	*Fundamentals of Corporate Finance*	250.65	191.49
Schneier	*New York Politics: Tale of Two States*	34.95	28.66
Wilson	*American Government: The Essentials*	172.65	108.49

Choosing the level of significance $\alpha = 0.05$ and assuming that the differences are normally distributed, you use the paired t test [Equation (10.3)]. For a sample of $n = 16$ textbooks, there are $n - 1 = 15$ degrees of freedom. Using Table E.3, the decision rule is

$$\text{Reject } H_0 \text{ if } t_{STAT} > 2.1314$$

$$\text{or if } t_{STAT} < -2.1314;$$

$$\text{otherwise, do not reject } H_0.$$

For the $n = 16$ differences (calculated from the Table 10.4 data), the sample mean difference is

$$\overline{D} = \frac{\sum_{i=1}^{n} D_i}{n} = \frac{681.62}{16} = 42.6013$$

and

$$S_D = \sqrt{\frac{\sum_{i=1}^{n}(D_i - \overline{D})^2}{n - 1}} = 43.797$$

From Equation (10.3) on page 319,

$$t_{STAT} = \frac{\overline{D} - \mu_D}{\dfrac{S_D}{\sqrt{n}}} = \frac{42.6013 - 0}{\dfrac{43.797}{\sqrt{16}}} = 3.8908$$

Because $t_{STAT} = 3.8908 > 2.1314$, you reject the null hypothesis, H_0 (see Figure 10.7). There is evidence of a difference in the mean price of textbooks purchased at the college bookstore and the online retailer. You can conclude that the mean price is higher at the college bookstore than at the online retailer.

FIGURE 10.7
Two-tail paired t test at the 0.05 level of significance with 15 degrees of freedom

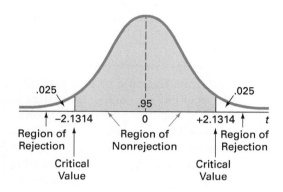

Figure 10.8 presents the results for this example, computing both the t test statistic and the p-value. Because the p-value $= 0.0014 < \alpha = 0.05$, you reject H_0. The p-value indicates that if the two sources for textbooks have the same population mean price, the probability that one source would have a sample mean \$42.60 more than the other is 0.0014. Because this probability is less than $\alpha = 0.05$, you conclude that there is evidence to reject the null hypothesis.

FIGURE 10.8
Excel paired t test worksheet for the textbook price data

	A	B	
1	Paired t Test		
2			
3	Data		
4	Hypothesized Mean Diff.	0	
5	Level of Significance	0.05	
6			
7	Intermediate Calculations		
8	Sample Size	16	=COUNT(PtCalcs!$A:$A)
9	DBar	42.6013	=AVERAGE(PtCalcs!$C:$C)
10	degrees of freedom	15	=B8 - 1
11	S_D	43.7970	=SQRT(DEVSQ(PtCalcs!C:C)/B10)
12	Standard Error	10.9493	=B11/SQRT(B8)
13	t Test Statistic	3.8908	=(B9 - B4)/B12
14			
15	Two-Tailed Test		
16	Lower Critical Value	-2.1314	=-T.INV.2T(B5, B10)
17	Upper Critical Value	2.1314	=T.INV.2T(B5, B10)
18	p-Value	0.0014	=T.DIST.2T(ABS(B13), B10)
19	Reject the null hypothesis		=IF(B18 < B5, "Reject the null hypothesis",)
			"Do not reject the null hypothesis")

In the Worksheet

In cell B11, the worksheet uses the DEVSQ function that computes the sum of the squares of the differences and simplifies the calculations of the worksheet.

To evaluate the validity of the assumption of normality, you construct a boxplot of the differences, as shown in Figure 10.9.

The Figure 10.9 boxplots show approximate symmetry and look similar to the boxplot for the normal distribution displayed in Figure 3.5 on page 117. Thus, the distribution of textbook

FIGURE 10.9
Excel boxplot for the textbook price differences

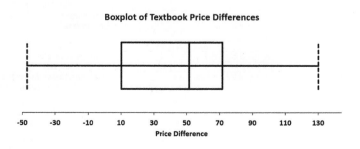

Boxplot of Textbook Price Differences

price differences does not greatly contradict the underlying assumption of normality. If a box plot, histogram, or normal probability plot reveals that the assumption of underlying normality in the population is severely violated, then the *t* test may be inappropriate, especially if the sample size is small. If you believe that the *t* test is inappropriate, you can use either a *non-parametric* procedure that does not make the assumption of underlying normality (see references 1 and 2) or make a data transformation (see reference 4) and then check the assumption again to determine whether you should use the *t* test.

EXAMPLE 10.2

Paired *t* Test of Pizza Delivery Times

Recall from Example 10.1 on page 327 that a local pizza restaurant situated across the street from your college campus advertises that it delivers to the dormitories faster than the local branch of a national pizza chain. In order to determine whether this advertisement is valid, you and some friends decided to order 10 pizzas from the local pizza restaurant and 10 pizzas from the national chain. In fact, each time you ordered a pizza from the local pizza restaurant, at the same time, your friends ordered a pizza from the national pizza chain. Therefore, you have matched samples (because each pair of pizzas was ordered at the same time). For each of the 10 times that pizzas were ordered, you have one measurement from the local pizza restaurant and one from the national chain. At the 0.05 level of significance, is the mean delivery time for the local pizza restaurant less than the mean delivery time for the national pizza chain?

SOLUTION Use the paired *t* test to analyze the Table 10.5 data (stored in PizzaTime). Figure 10.10 shows the paired *t* test results for the pizza delivery data.

TABLE 10.5
Delivery Times for Local Pizza Restaurant and National Pizza Chain

Time	Local	Chain	Difference
1	16.8	22.0	−5.2
2	11.7	15.2	−3.5
3	15.6	18.7	−3.1
4	16.7	15.6	1.1
5	17.5	20.8	−3.3
6	18.1	19.5	−1.4
7	14.1	17.0	−2.9
8	21.8	19.5	2.3
9	13.9	16.5	−2.6
10	20.8	24.0	−3.2
			−21.8

FIGURE 10.10
Excel paired *t* test results for the pizza delivery data

▶ (continued)

The null and alternative hypotheses are

$H_0: \mu_D \geq 0$ (Mean difference in the delivery time between the local pizza restaurant and the national pizza chain is greater than or equal to 0.)

$H_1: \mu_D < 0$ (Mean difference in the delivery time between the local pizza restaurant and the national pizza chain is less than 0.)

Choosing the level of significance $\alpha = 0.05$ and assuming that the differences are normally distributed, you use the paired t test [Equation (10.3) on page 319]. For a sample of $n = 10$ delivery times, there are $n - 1 = 9$ degrees of freedom. Using Table E.3, the decision rule is

$$\text{Reject } H_0 \text{ if } t_{STAT} < -t_{0.05} = -1.8331;$$

$$\text{otherwise, do not reject } H_0.$$

To illustrate the computations, for $n = 10$ differences (see Table 10.5), the sample mean difference is

$$\overline{D} = \frac{\sum\limits_{i=1}^{n} D_i}{n} = \frac{-21.8}{10} = -2.18$$

and the sample standard deviation of the difference is

$$S_D = \sqrt{\frac{\sum\limits_{i=1}^{n} (D_i - \overline{D})^2}{n - 1}} = 2.2641$$

From Equation (10.3) on page 319,

$$t_{STAT} = \frac{\overline{D} - \mu_D}{\dfrac{S_D}{\sqrt{n}}} = \frac{-2.18 - 0}{\dfrac{2.2641}{\sqrt{10}}} = -3.0448$$

Because $t_{STAT} = -3.0448$ is less than -1.8331, you reject the null hypothesis, H_0 (the p-value is $0.0070 < 0.05$). There is evidence that the mean delivery time is lower for the local pizza restaurant than for the national pizza chain.

This conclusion differs from the conclusion you reached on page 312 for Example 10.1 when you used the pooled-variance t test for these data. By pairing the delivery times, you are able to focus on the differences between the two pizza delivery services and not the variability created by ordering pizzas at different times of day. The paired t test is a more powerful statistical procedure that reduces the variability in the delivery time because you are controlling for the time of day the pizza was ordered.

Confidence Interval Estimate for the Mean Difference

Instead of, or in addition to, testing for the mean difference between two related populations, you can use Equation (10.4) on page 324 to construct a confidence interval estimate for the population mean difference.

CONFIDENCE INTERVAL ESTIMATE FOR THE MEAN DIFFERENCE

$$\overline{D} \pm t_{\alpha/2}\frac{S_D}{\sqrt{n}} \qquad (10.4)$$

or

$$\overline{D} - t_{\alpha/2}\frac{S_D}{\sqrt{n}} \le \mu_D \le \overline{D} + t_{\alpha/2}\frac{S_D}{\sqrt{n}}$$

where $t_{\alpha/2}$ is the critical value of the t distribution, with $n - 1$ degrees of freedom, for an area of $\alpha/2$ in the upper tail.

Recall the example comparing textbook prices on page 320. Using Equation (10.4), $\overline{D} = 42.6013$, $S_D = 43.797$, $n = 16$, and $t_{\alpha/2} = 2.1314$ (for 95% confidence and $n - 1 = 15$ degrees of freedom),

$$42.6013 \pm (2.1314)\frac{43.797}{\sqrt{16}}$$

$$42.6013 \pm 23.3373$$

$$19.264 \le \mu_D \le 65.9386$$

Thus, with 95% confidence, you estimate that the population mean difference in textbook prices between the college bookstore and the online retailer is between $19.26 and $65.94. Because the interval estimate does not contain zero, using the 0.05 level of significance and a two-tail test, you can conclude that there is evidence of a difference in the mean prices of textbooks at the college bookstore and the online retailer. Since both the lower and upper limits of the confidence interval are above 0, you can conclude that the mean price is higher at the college bookstore than the online retailer.

PROBLEMS FOR SECTION 10.2

LEARNING THE BASICS

10.18 An experimental design for a paired t test has 20 pairs of identical twins. How many degrees of freedom are there in this t test?

10.19 Fifteen volunteers are recruited to participate in an experiment. A measurement is made (such as blood pressure) before each volunteer is asked to read a particularly upsetting passage from a book and after each volunteer reads the passage from the book. In the analysis of the data collected from this experiment, how many degrees of freedom are there in the test?

APPLYING THE CONCEPTS

SELF TEST **10.20** Nine experts rated two brands of Colombian coffee in a taste-testing experiment. A rating on a 7-point scale (1 = extremely unpleasing, 7 = extremely pleasing) is given for each of four characteristics: taste, aroma, richness, and acidity. The following data stored in Coffee contain the ratings accumulated over all four characteristics:

	BRAND	
EXPERT	A	B
C.C.	24	26
S.E.	27	27
E.G.	19	22
B.L.	24	27
C.M.	22	25
C.N.	26	27
G.N.	27	26
R.M.	25	27
P.V.	22	23

a. At the 0.05 level of significance, is there evidence of a difference in the mean ratings between the two brands?
b. What assumption is necessary about the population distribution in order to perform this test?
c. Determine the p-value in (a) and interpret its meaning.
d. Construct and interpret a 95% confidence interval estimate of the difference in the mean ratings between the two brands.

10.21 How do the ratings of TV and Internet services compare? The file Telecom contains the rating of 14 different providers. (Data extracted from "Ratings: TV, Phone, and Internet Services," *Consumer Reports*, May 2014, pp. 28–29.)
a. At the 0.05 level of significance, is there evidence of a difference in the mean service rating between TV and Internet services?
b. What assumption is necessary about the population distribution in order to perform this test?
c. Use a graphical method to evaluate the validity of the assumption in (a).
d. Construct and interpret a 95% confidence interval estimate of the difference in the mean service rating between TV and Internet services.

10.22 Does the quality of cell service vary between providers? The file CellService provides the cellphone rating of AT&T and Verizon Wireless in 23 U. S. cities. (Data extracted from "Smart-Phone Shopping Guide," *Consumer Reports*, January 2014, pp. 30–31.)
a. At the 0.05 level of significance, is there evidence of a difference in the mean cell service rating between AT&T and Verizon Wireless?
b. What assumption about the cellphone rating is necessary to perform this test?
c. Use a graphical method to evaluate the assumption made in (a).
d. Construct and interpret a 95% confidence interval estimate of the difference in the mean cell service rating between AT&T and Verizon Wireless.

10.23 How do competing airline carrier fares compare? A frequent flyer investigated round-trip fares for nonstop travel from Philadelphia to 10 different U.S. destinations on Southwest Airlines and US Airways. Data was collected and stored the data in Airlines. (Data extracted from **bit.ly/1fIUhec** and **bit.ly/1eLoDwn**.)
a. At the 0.05 level of significance, is there evidence of a difference in the mean round-trip fare between Southwest Airlines and US Airways?
b. What assumption is necessary about the population distribution in order to perform this test?
c. Use a graphical method to evaluate the validity of the assumption in (b).

10.24 Multiple myeloma, or blood plasma cancer, is characterized by increased blood vessel formulation (angiogenesis) in the bone marrow that is a predictive factor in survival. One treatment approach used for multiple myeloma is stem cell transplantation with the patient's own stem cells. The data stored in Myeloma, and shown in the right column represent the bone marrow microvessel density for patients who had a complete response to the stem cell

transplant (as measured by blood and urine tests). The measurements were taken immediately prior to the stem cell transplant and at the time the complete response was determined.

Patient	Before	After
1	158	284
2	189	214
3	202	101
4	353	227
5	416	290
6	426	176
7	441	290

Data extracted from S. V. Rajkumar, R. Fonseca, T. E. Witzig, M. A. Gertz, and P. R. Greipp, "Bone Marrow Angiogenesis in Patients Achieving Complete Response After Stem Cell Transplantation for Multiple Myeloma," *Leukemia* 13 (1999): 469–472.

a. At the 0.05 level of significance, is there evidence that the mean bone marrow microvessel density is higher before the stem cell transplant than after the stem cell transplant?
b. Interpret the meaning of the *p*-value in (a).
c. Construct and interpret a 95% confidence interval estimate of the mean difference in bone marrow microvessel density before and after the stem cell transplant.
d. What assumption is necessary about the population distribution in order to perform the test in (a)?

10.25 To assess the effectiveness of a cola video ad, a random sample of 38 individuals from a target audience was selected to participate in a copy test. Participants viewed two ads, one of which was the ad being tested. Participants then answered a series of questions about how much they liked the ads. An adindex measure was created and stored in Adindex; the higher the adindex value, the more likeable the ad. Compute descriptive statistics and perform a paired *t* test. State your findings and conclusions in a report. (Use the 0.05 level of significance.)

10.26 The file Concrete1 contains the compressive strength, in thousands of pounds per square inch (psi), of 40 samples of concrete taken two and seven days after pouring. (Data extracted from O. Carrillo-Gamboa and R. F. Gunst, "Measurement- Error-Model Collinearities," *Technometrics*, 34 (1992): 454–464.)
a. At the 0.01 level of significance, is there evidence that the mean strength is lower at two days than at seven days?
b. What assumption is necessary about the population distribution in order to perform this test?
c. Find the *p*-value in (a) and interpret its meaning.

10.3 Comparing the Proportions of Two Independent Populations

Often, you need to make comparisons and analyze differences between two population proportions. You can perform a test for the difference between two proportions selected from independent populations by using two different methods. This section presents a procedure whose test statistic, Z_{STAT}, is approximated by a standardized normal distribution. In Section 12.1, a procedure whose test statistic, χ^2_{STAT}, is approximated by a chi-square distribution is used. As explained in the latter section, the results from these two tests are equivalent.

Z Test for the Difference Between Two Proportions

In evaluating differences between two population proportions, you can use a **Z test for the difference between two proportions**. The Z_{STAT} test statistic is based on the difference between two sample proportions $(p_1 - p_2)$. This test statistic, given in Equation (10.5), approximately follows a standardized normal distribution for large enough sample sizes.

Z TEST FOR THE DIFFERENCE BETWEEN TWO PROPORTIONS

$$Z_{STAT} = \frac{(p_1 - p_2) - (\pi_1 - \pi_2)}{\sqrt{\bar{p}(1 - \bar{p})\left(\dfrac{1}{n_1} + \dfrac{1}{n_2}\right)}} \tag{10.5}$$

where

$$\bar{p} = \frac{X_1 + X_2}{n_1 + n_2} \qquad p_1 = \frac{X_1}{n_1} \qquad p_2 = \frac{X_2}{n_2}$$

and

p_1 = proportion of items of interest in sample 1
X_1 = number of items of interest in sample 1
n_1 = sample size of sample 1
π_1 = proportion of items of interest in population 1
p_2 = proportion of items of interest in sample 2
X_2 = number of items of interest in sample 2
n_2 = sample size of sample 2
π_2 = proportion of items of interest in population 2
$\bar{p}$ = pooled estimate of the population proportion of items of interest

The Z_{STAT} test statistic approximately follows a standardized normal distribution.

studentTIP

Do not confuse this use of the Greek letter pi, π, to represent the population proportion with the mathematical constant that uses the same letter and is approximately 3.14159.

The null hypothesis in the Z test for the difference between two proportions states that the two population proportions are equal $(\pi_1 = \pi_2)$. Because the pooled estimate for the population proportion is based on the null hypothesis, you combine, or pool, the two sample proportions to compute $\bar{p}$, an overall estimate of the common population proportion. This estimate is equal to the number of items of interest in the two samples $(X_1 + X_2)$ divided by the total sample size from the two samples $(n_1 + n_2)$.

As shown in the following table, you can use this Z test for the difference between population proportions to determine whether there is a difference in the proportion of items of interest in the two populations (two-tail test) or whether one population has a higher proportion of items of interest than the other population (one-tail test):

Two-Tail Test	One-Tail Test	One-Tail Test
$H_0: \pi_1 = \pi_2$	$H_0: \pi_1 \geq \pi_2$	$H_0: \pi_1 \leq \pi_2$
$H_1: \pi_1 \neq \pi_2$	$H_1: \pi_1 < \pi_2$	$H_1: \pi_1 > \pi_2$

where

π_1 = proportion of items of interest in population 1
π_2 = proportion of items of interest in population 2

To test the null hypothesis that there is no difference between the proportions of two independent populations:

$$H_0: \pi_1 = \pi_2$$

against the alternative that the two population proportions are not the same:

$$H_1: \pi_1 \neq \pi_2$$

you use the Z_{STAT} test statistic, given by Equation (10.5). For a given level of significance, α, you reject the null hypothesis if the computed Z_{STAT} test statistic is greater than the upper-tail critical value from the standardized normal distribution or if the computed Z_{STAT} test statistic is less than the lower-tail critical value from the standardized normal distribution.

To illustrate the use of the Z test for the equality of the two proportions, recall the Chapter 6 Using Statistics scenario concerning MyTVLab. In overhauling its current website, MyTVLab is not only considering a new sales page, but a new signup page as well. Designers ponder whether this signup page should ask for many personal details or just a few. They decide to design both types of pages and devise an experiment. Every visitor going to the signup page will be randomly shown one of the two new designs. Effectiveness will be measured by whether the visitor clicks the signup button that appears on the page displayed. Using the DCOVA problem-solving approach, you define the business objective as determining if there is evidence of a significant difference in signups generated by the two pages. The results of the experiment showed that of 4,325 visitors to the signup page that asks only a few personal details, 387 clicked the signup button while of 4,639 visitors to the signup page that asks for many personal details, 283 clicked the signup button. At the 0.05 level of significance, is there evidence of a significant difference in signup between a signup page that asks only a few personal details and a signup page that asks for many personal details?

The null and alternative hypotheses are

$$H_0: \pi_1 = \pi_2 \quad \text{or} \quad \pi_1 - \pi_2 = 0$$
$$H_1: \pi_1 \neq \pi_2 \quad \text{or} \quad \pi_1 - \pi_2 \neq 0$$

Using the 0.05 level of significance, the critical values are -1.96 and $+1.96$ (see Figure 10.11), and the decision rule is

$$\text{Reject } H_0 \text{ if } Z_{STAT} < -1.96$$
$$\text{or if } Z_{STAT} > +1.96;$$
$$\text{otherwise, do not reject } H_0.$$

Using Equation (10.5) on page 326,

$$Z_{STAT} = \frac{(p_1 - p_2) - (\pi_1 - \pi_2)}{\sqrt{\bar{p}(1 - \bar{p})\left(\frac{1}{n_1} + \frac{1}{n_2}\right)}}$$

where

$$p_1 = \frac{X_1}{n_1} = \frac{387}{4,325} = 0.0895 \quad p_2 = \frac{X_2}{n_2} = \frac{283}{4,639} = 0.0610$$

and

$$\bar{p} = \frac{X_1 + X_2}{n_1 + n_2} = \frac{387 + 283}{4,325 + 4,639} = \frac{670}{8,964} = 0.0747$$

FIGURE 10.11

Regions of rejection and nonrejection when testing a hypothesis for the difference between two proportions at the 0.05 level of significance

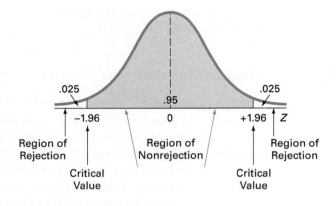

Region of Rejection   Critical Value   Region of Nonrejection   Critical Value   Region of Rejection

so that

$$Z_{STAT} = \frac{(0.0895 - 0.0610) - (0)}{\sqrt{0.0747(1 - 0.0747)\left(\dfrac{1}{4,325} + \dfrac{1}{4,639}\right)}}$$

$$= \frac{0.0285}{\sqrt{(0.06912)(0.0004467)}}$$

$$= \frac{0.0285}{\sqrt{0.000308}}$$

$$= \frac{0.0285}{0.00555} = +5.1228$$

Using the 0.05 level of significance, you reject the null hypothesis because $Z_{STAT} = +5.1228 > +1.96$. The p-value is 0.0000 (computed using Table E.2 or from Figure 10.12) and indicates that if the null hypothesis is true, the probability that a Z_{STAT} test statistic is less than -5.1228 is 0.0000, and, similarly, the probability that a Z_{STAT} test statistic is greater than $+5.1228$ is 0.0000. Thus, for this two-tail test, the p-value is 0.0000. Because $0.0000 < \alpha = 0.05$, you reject the null hypothesis. There is evidence to conclude that the two signup pages are significantly different with respect to signups. A greater proportion of visitors to the signup page that asks for fewer personal details have been willing to sign up. Therefore, MyTVLab should use the signup page that asks the fewest personal questions.

FIGURE 10.12

Excel Z test worksheet results for the difference between two proportions for the two signup pages problem

	A	B	
1	Z Test for Differences in Two Proportions		
2			
3	**Data**		
4	Hypothesized Difference	0	
5	Level of Significance	0.05	
6	**Group 1**		
7	Number of Successes	387	
8	Sample Size	4325	
9	**Group 2**		
10	Number of Successes	283	
11	Sample Size	4639	
12			
13	**Intermediate Calculations**		
14	Group 1 Proportion	0.0895	=B7/B8
15	Group 2 Proportion	0.0610	=B10/B11
16	Difference in Two Proportions	0.0285	=B14 - B15
17	Average Proportion	0.0747	=(B7 + B10)/(B8 + B11)
18	Z Test Statistic	5.1228	=(B16 - B4)/SQRT(B17 * (1 - B17) * (1/B8 + 1/B11))
19			
20	**Two-Tail Test**		
21	Lower Critical Value	-1.9600	=NORM.S.INV(B5/2)
22	Upper Critical Value	1.9600	=NORM.S.INV(1 - B5/2)
23	p-Value	0.0000	=2 * (1 - NORM.S.DIST(ABS(B18), TRUE))
24	Reject the null hypothesis		=IF(B23 < B5, "Reject the null hypothesis", "Do not reject the null hypothesis")

In the Worksheet

Cells B21 and B22 use the NORM.S.INC function to compute the lower and upper critical values. Cell B23 uses the NORM.S.DIST function in computing the p-value.

EXAMPLE 10.3

Testing for the
Difference Between
Two Proportions

Are men less likely than women to say that a major reason they use Facebook is to share with many people at once? A survey reported that 42% of men (193 out of 459 sampled) and 50% of women (250 out of 501 sampled) said that a major reason they use Facebook is to share with many people at once. (Source: "6 new facts about Facebook," **bit.ly/1kENZcA**.)

SOLUTION Because you want to know whether there is evidence that the proportion of men who say that a major reason they use Facebook is to share with many people at once is *less* than the proportion of women who say that a major reason they use Facebook is to share with many people at once, you have a one-tail test. The null and alternative hypotheses are

$H_0: \pi_1 \geq \pi_2$ (The proportion of men who say that a major reason they use Facebook is to share with many people at once is greater than or equal to the proportion of women who say that a major reason they use Facebook is to share with many people at once.)

$H_1: \pi_1 < \pi_2$ (The proportion of men who say that a major reason they use Facebook is to share with many people at once is less than the proportion of women who say that a major reason they use Facebook is to share with many people at once.)

Using the 0.05 level of significance, for the one-tail test in the lower tail, the critical value is +1.645. The decision rule is

Reject H_0 if $Z_{STAT} < -1.645$;

otherwise, do not reject H_0.

Using Equation (10.5) on page 326,

$$Z_{STAT} = \frac{(p_1 - p_2) - (\pi_1 - \pi_2)}{\sqrt{\bar{p}(1-\bar{p})\left(\frac{1}{n_1} + \frac{1}{n_2}\right)}}$$

where

$$p_1 = \frac{X_1}{n_1} = \frac{193}{459} = 0.4205 \quad p_2 = \frac{X_2}{n_2} = \frac{250}{501} = 0.4990$$

and

$$\bar{p} = \frac{X_1 + X_2}{n_1 + n_2} = \frac{193 + 250}{459 + 501} = \frac{443}{960} = 0.4615$$

so that

$$Z_{STAT} = \frac{(0.4205 - 0.4990) - (0)}{\sqrt{0.4615(1 - 0.4615)\left(\frac{1}{459} + \frac{1}{501}\right)}}$$

$$= \frac{-0.0785}{\sqrt{(0.2485)(0.0042)}}$$

$$= \frac{-0.0785}{\sqrt{0.0010437}}$$

$$= \frac{-0.0785}{0.0322} = -2.4379$$

Using the 0.05 level of significance, you reject the null hypothesis because $Z_{STAT} = -2.4379 < -1.645$. The p-value is 0.0074. Therefore, if the null hypothesis is true, the probability that a Z_{STAT} test statistic is less than −2.4379 is 0.0074 (which is less than $\alpha = 0.05$). You conclude that there is evidence that the proportion of men who say that a major reason they use Facebook is to share with many people at once is less than the proportion of women who say that a major reason they use Facebook is to share with many people at once.

Confidence Interval Estimate for the Difference Between Two Proportions

Instead of, or in addition to, testing for the difference between the proportions of two independent populations, you can construct a confidence interval estimate for the difference between the two proportions using Equation (10.6).

CONFIDENCE INTERVAL ESTIMATE FOR THE DIFFERENCE BETWEEN TWO PROPORTIONS

$$(p_1 - p_2) \pm Z_{\alpha/2}\sqrt{\frac{p_1(1 - p_1)}{n_1} + \frac{p_2(1 - p_2)}{n_2}} \tag{10.6}$$

or

$$(p_1 - p_2) - Z_{\alpha/2}\sqrt{\frac{p_1(1 - p_1)}{n_1} + \frac{p_2(1 - p_2)}{n_2}} \leq (\pi_1 - \pi_2)$$

$$\leq (p_1 - p_2) + Z_{\alpha/2}\sqrt{\frac{p_1(1 - p_1)}{n_1} + \frac{p_2(1 - p_2)}{n_2}}$$

To construct a 95% confidence interval estimate for the population difference between the proportion of visitors to the few details page who signed up and the proportion of visitors to the many details page who signed signed up, you use the results on page 327 or from Figure 10.12 on page 328:

$$p_1 = \frac{X_1}{n_1} = \frac{387}{4,325} = 0.0895 \quad p_2 = \frac{X_2}{n_2} = \frac{283}{4,639} = 0.0610$$

Using Equation (10.6),

$$(0.0895 - 0.0610) \pm (1.96)\sqrt{\frac{0.0895(1 - 0.0895)}{4,325} + \frac{0.0610(1 - 0.0610)}{4,639}}$$

$$0.0285 \pm (1.96)(0.0056)$$

$$0.0285 \pm 0.0109$$

$$0.0175 \leq (\pi_1 - \pi_2) \leq 0.0394$$

You have 95% confidence that the difference between the population proportion of visitors to the few details page who signed up and the population proportion of visitors to the many details page who signed up is between 0.0175 and 0.0394. In percentages, the difference is between 1.75% and 3.94%. Visitors are more likely to sign up if they are presented with a signup page that asks for fewer personal details.

PROBLEMS FOR SECTION 10.3

LEARNING THE BASICS

10.27 Let $n_1 = 100, X_1 = 50, n_2 = 100$, and $X_2 = 30$.
a. At the 0.05 level of significance, is there evidence of a significant difference between the two population proportions?
b. Construct a 95% confidence interval estimate for the difference between the two population proportions.

10.28 Let $n_1 = 100, X_1 = 45, n_2 = 50$, and $X_2 = 25$.
a. At the 0.01 level of significance, is there evidence of a significant difference between the two population proportions?
b. Construct a 99% confidence interval estimate for the difference between the two population proportions.

APPLYING THE CONCEPTS

10.29 An online survey asked 1,004 adults "If purchasing a used car made certain upgrades or features more affordable, what would be your preferred luxury upgrade?" The results indicated that 9% of the males and 14% of the females answered window tinting. (Source: Data extracted from Ipsos, "Safety Technology Tops the List of Most Desired Features Should They Be More Affordable when Purchasing a Used Car—Particularly Collision Avoidance," **bit.ly/1RCcc1L**.) The sample sizes of males and females were not provided. Suppose that both sample sizes were 502 and that 46 of 502 males and 71 of 502 females reported window tinting as their preferred luxury upgrade of choice.

a. Is there evidence of a difference between males and females in the proportion who said they prefer window tinting as a luxury upgrade at the 0.01 level of significance?

b. Find the *p*-value in (a) and interpret its meaning.

c. Construct and interpret a 99% confidence interval estimate for the difference between the proportion of males and females who said they prefer window tinting as a luxury upgrade.

d. What are your answers to (a) through (c) if 60 males said they prefer window tinting as a luxury upgrade?

10.30 Does Cable Video on Demand (VOD D4+) increase ad effectiveness? A 2015 VOD study compared general TV and VOD D4+ audiences after viewing a brand ad. Data were collected on whether the viewer indicated that the ad made them want to visit the brand website. The results were:

VIEWING AUDIENCE	MADE ME WANT TO VISIT THE BRAND WEBSITE	
	Yes	No
VOD D4+	147	103
General TV	35	166

Source: Data extracted from Canoe Ventures, *Understanding VOD Advertising Effectiveness*, **bit.ly/1JnmMup**.

a. Set up the null and alternative hypotheses to try to determine whether ad impact is stronger following VOD D4+ viewing than following general TV viewing.

b. Conduct the hypothesis test defined in (a), using the 0.05 level of significance.

c. Does the result of your test in (b) make it appropriate to claim that ad impact is stronger following VOD D4+ than following general TV viewing?

10.31 How often does work intrude during off hours? A survey of 1,000 office workers indicated that 53% of males and 41% of females had office intrusions while on vacation. (Data extracted from "Office Intrusions On the Off Hours," *USA Today Snapshots*, November 25, 2013, p. 1A.) Assume that the survey consisted of 500 males and 500 females.

a. At the 0.05 level of significance, is there evidence of a difference in the proportion of males and females who experience office intrusions while on vacation?

b. Find the *p*-values and interpret its meaning.

✓SELF TEST **10.32** The Society for Human Resource Management (SHRM) collaborated with Globoforce on a series of organizational surveys with the goal of identifying challenges that HR leaders face and what strategies help them conquer those challenges. A 2015 survey indicates that employee retention/turnover (40%) and employee engagement (39%) were cited as the most important organizational challenges currently faced by HR professionals. One strategy that may have an impact on employee retention, turnover and engagement, is a successful employee recognition program. Surveying both smaller organizations, those with 500 to 2,499 employees, and larger organizations, those with 2,500+ employees, SHRM and Globoforce showed that 278 (74%) of the 376 smaller organizations have employee recognition programs as compared to 316 (84%) of the 376 larger organizations. (Data extracted from *SHRM Survey Findings: Employee Recognition Programs—2015*, **bit.ly/1NltiQZ**.)

a. At the 0.01 level of significance, is there evidence of a significant difference between organizations with 500 to 2,499 employees and organizations with 2,500+ employees with respect to the proportion that have employee recognition programs?

b. Find the *p*-value in (a) and interpret its meaning.

c. Construct and interpret a 99% confidence interval estimate for the difference between organizations with 500 to 2,499 employees and organizations with 2,500+ employees with respect to the proportion that have employee recognition programs.

10.33 What social media tools do marketers commonly use? A survey by Social Media Examiner of B2B marketers, marketers that primarily target businesses, and B2C marketers, marketers that primarily target consumers, reported that 344 (88%) of B2B marketers and 373 (61%) of B2C marketers commonly use LinkedIn as a social media tool. The study also revealed that 239 (61%) of B2B marketers and 324 (53%) of B2C marketers commonly use Google+ as a social media tool. (Data extracted from *2014 Social Media Marketing Industry Report*, **bit.ly/1e896pD**.)

Suppose the survey was based on 390 B2B marketers and 610 B2C marketers.

a. At the 0.05 level of significance, is there evidence of a difference between B2B marketers and B2C marketers in the proportion that commonly use LinkedIn as a social media tool?

b. Find the *p*-value in (a) and interpret its value.

c. At the 0.05 level of significance, is there evidence of a difference between B2B marketers and B2C marketers in the proportion that commonly use Google+ as a social media tool?

10.34 Does co-browsing have positive effects on the customer experience? Co-browsing refers to the ability to have a contact center agent and customer jointly navigate an online document or mobile application on a real-time basis through the web. A study of businesses indicates that 81 of 129 co-browsing organizations use skills-based routing to match the caller with the *right* agent, whereas 65 of 176 non-co-browsing organizations use skills-based routing to match the caller with the *right* agent. (Source: *Cobrowsing Presents a 'Lucrative' Customer Service Opportunity*, available at **bit.ly/1wwALWr**.)

a. At the 0.05 level of significance, is there evidence of a difference between co-browsing organizations and non-co-browsing organizations in the proportion that use skills-based routing to match the caller with the *right* agent?

b. Find the *p*-value in (a) and interpret its meaning.

10.35 One of the most impressive, innovative advances in online fundraising over the past decade is the rise of crowd-funding websites. While features differ from site to site, crowd-funding sites are websites that allow you to set up an online fundraising campaign based around a fundraising page, and accept money directly from that page using the website's own credit card processor. Kickstarter, one crowd-funding website, reported that 49 of 233 *technology* crowd-funding projects were successfully launched in the past year and 291 of 767 *film and video* crowd-funding projects were successfully launched in the past year. (Data extracted from **kickstarter.com/help/stats**.)

a. Is there evidence of a significant difference in the proportion of *technology* crowd-funding projects and *film and*

video crowd-funding projects that were successful? (Use $\alpha = 0.05$.)

b. Determine the *p*-value in (a) and interpret its meaning.

c. Construct and interpret a 95% confidence interval estimate for the difference between the proportion of *technology* crowd-funding projects and *film and video* crowd-funding projects that are successful.

10.4 *F* Test for the Ratio of Two Variances

Often you need to determine whether two independent populations have the same variability. By testing variances, you can detect differences in the variability in two independent populations. One important reason to test for the difference between the variances of two populations is to determine whether to use the pooled-variance *t* test (which assumes equal variances) or the separate-variance *t* test (which does not assume equal variances) when comparing the means of two independent populations.

The test for the difference between the variances of two independent populations is based on the ratio of the two sample variances. If you assume that each population is normally distributed, then the sampling distribution of the ratio S_1^2/S_2^2 is distributed as an *F* distribution (see Table E.5). Unlike the normal and *t* distributions which are symmetric, the *F* distribution is right-skewed. The critical values of the **F distribution** in Table E.5 depend on the degrees of freedom in the two samples. In addition, the degrees of freedom in the numerator of the ratio are for the first sample, and the degrees of freedom in the denominator are for the second sample. The first sample taken from the first population is defined as the sample that has the *larger* sample variance. The second sample taken from the second population is the sample with the *smaller* sample variance. Equation (10.7) defines the **F test for the ratio of two variances**.

F TEST STATISTIC FOR TESTING THE RATIO OF TWO VARIANCES

The F_{STAT} test statistic is equal to the variance of sample 1 (the larger sample variance) divided by the variance of sample 2 (the smaller sample variance).

studentTIP

Since the numerator of Equation (10.7) contains the larger variance, the F_{STAT} statistic is always greater than or equal to 1.0.

$$F_{STAT} = \frac{S_1^2}{S_2^2} \qquad (10.7)$$

where

S_1^2 = variance of sample 1 (the larger sample variance)

S_2^2 = variance of sample 2 (the smaller sample variance)

n_1 = sample size selected from population 1

n_2 = sample size selected from population 2

$n_1 - 1$ = degrees of freedom from sample 1 (the numerator degrees of freedom)

$n_2 - 1$ = degrees of freedom from sample 2 (the denominator degrees of freedom)

The F_{STAT} test statistic follows an *F* distribution with $n_1 - 1$ and $n_2 - 1$ degrees of freedom.

For a given level of significance, α, to test the null hypothesis of equality of population variances:

$$H_0: \sigma_1^2 = \sigma_2^2$$

against the alternative hypothesis that the two population variances are not equal:

$$H_1: \sigma_1^2 \neq \sigma_2^2$$

you reject the null hypothesis if the computed F_{STAT} test statistic is greater than the upper-tail critical value, $F_{\alpha/2}$, from the *F* distribution, with $n_1 - 1$ degrees of freedom in the numerator and $n_2 - 1$ degrees of freedom in the denominator. Thus, the decision rule is

Reject H_0 if $F_{STAT} > F_{\alpha/2}$;

otherwise, do not reject H_0.

To illustrate how to use the *F* test to determine whether the two variances are equal, return to the Arlingtons scenario on page 307 concerning the sales of VLABGo players in two different sales locations. To determine whether to use the pooled-variance *t* test or the separate-variance *t* test in Section 10.1, you can test the equality of the two population variances. The null and alternative hypotheses are

$$H_0: \sigma_1^2 = \sigma_2^2$$
$$H_1: \sigma_1^2 \neq \sigma_2^2$$

Because you are defining sample 1 as the group with the larger sample variance, the rejection region in the upper tail of the *F* distribution contains $\alpha/2$. Using the level of significance $\alpha = 0.05$, the rejection region in the upper tail contains 0.025 of the distribution.

Because there are samples of 10 stores for each of the two sales locations, there are $10 - 1 = 9$ degrees of freedom in the numerator (the sample with the larger variance) and also in the denominator (the sample with the smaller variance). $F_{\alpha/2}$, the upper-tail critical value of the *F* distribution, is found directly from Table E.5, a portion of which is presented in Table 10.6. Because there are 9 degrees of freedom in the numerator and 9 degrees of freedom in the denominator, you find the upper-tail critical value, $F_{\alpha/2}$, by looking in the column labeled 9 and the row labeled 9. Thus, the upper-tail critical value of this *F* distribution is 4.03. Therefore, the decision rule is

Reject H_0 if $F_{STAT} > F_{0.025} = 4.03$;

otherwise, do not reject H_0.

TABLE 10.6
Finding the Upper-Tail Critical Value of *F* with 9 and 9 Degrees of Freedom for an Upper-Tail Area of 0.025

Denominator df_2	1	2	3	...	7	8	9
1	647.80	799.50	864.20	...	948.20	956.70	963.30
2	38.51	39.00	39.17	...	39.36	39.37	39.39
3	17.44	16.04	15.44	...	14.62	14.54	14.47
⋮	⋮	⋮	⋮	⋮	⋮	⋮	⋮
7	8.07	6.54	5.89	...	4.99	4.90	4.82
8	7.57	6.06	5.42	...	4.53	4.43	4.36
9	7.21	5.71	5.08	...	4.20	4.10	4.03

Cumulative Probabilities $= 0.975$ / Upper-Tail Area $= 0.025$ / Numerator df_1

Source: Extracted from Table E.5.

Using Equation (10.7) on page 332 and the VLABGo sales data (see Table 10.1 on page 309),

$$S_1^2 = (47.7056)^2 = 2,275.8222 \quad S_2^2 = (32.5271)^2 = 1,058.0111$$

so that

$$F_{STAT} = \frac{S_1^2}{S_2^2}$$

$$= \frac{2,275.8222}{1,058.0111} = 2.1510$$

Because $F_{STAT} = 2.1510 < 4.03$, you do not reject H_0. Figure 10.13 shows the results for this test, including the p-value, 0.2693. Because $0.2693 > 0.05$, you conclude that there is no evidence of a significant difference in the variability of the sales of the VLABGo players for the two sales locations.

FIGURE 10.13

Excel F test worksheet for the two different sales locations data

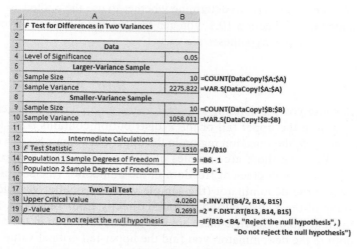

In the Worksheet

Cell B18 uses the F.INV.RT function to compute the upper critical value. Cell B19 uses the F.DIST.RT fiction in computing the p-value.

In testing for a difference between two variances using the F test, you assume that each of the two populations is normally distributed. The F test is very sensitive to the normality assumption. If boxplots or normal probability plots suggest even a mild departure from normality for either of the two populations, you should not use the F test. If this happens, you should use the Levene test (see Section 11.1) or a nonparametric approach (see references 1 and 2).

In testing for the equality of variances as part of assessing the validity of the pooled-variance t test procedure, the F test is a two-tail test with $\alpha/2$ in the upper tail. However, when you are interested in examining the variability in situations other than the pooled-variance t test, the F test is often a one-tail test. Example 10.4 illustrates a one-tail test.

EXAMPLE 10.4

A One-Tail Test for the Difference Between Two Variances

Waiting time is a critical issue at fast-food chains, which not only want to minimize the mean service time but also want to minimize the variation in the service time from customer to customer. One fast-food chain carried out a study to measure the variability in the waiting time (defined as the time in minutes from when an order was completed to when it was delivered to the customer) at lunch and breakfast at one of the chain's stores. The results were as follows:

$$\text{Lunch: } n_1 = 25 \quad S_1^2 = 4.4$$
$$\text{Breakfast: } n_2 = 21 \quad S_2^2 = 1.9$$

At the 0.05 level of significance, is there evidence that there is more variability in the service time at lunch than at breakfast? Assume that the population service times are normally distributed.

SOLUTION The null and alternative hypotheses are

$$H_0: \sigma_L^2 \leq \sigma_B^2$$
$$H_1: \sigma_L^2 > \sigma_B^2$$

▶ *(continued)*

The F_{STAT} test statistic is given by Equation (10.7) on page 332:

$$F_{STAT} = \frac{S_1^2}{S_2^2}$$

You use Table E.5 to find the upper critical value of the F distribution. With $n_1 - 1 = 25 - 1 = 24$ degrees of freedom in the numerator, $n_2 - 1 = 21 - 1 = 20$ degrees of freedom in the denominator, and $\alpha = 0.05$, the upper-tail critical value, $F_{0.05}$, is 2.08. The decision rule is

$$\text{Reject } H_0 \text{ if } F_{STAT} > 2.08;$$
$$\text{otherwise, do not reject } H_0.$$

From Equation (10.7) on page 332,

$$F_{STAT} = \frac{S_1^2}{S_2^2}$$

$$= \frac{4.4}{1.9} = 2.3158$$

Because $F_{STAT} = 2.3158 > 2.08$, you reject H_0. Using a 0.05 level of significance, you conclude that there is evidence that there is more variability in the service time at lunch than at breakfast.

PROBLEMS FOR SECTION 10.4

LEARNING THE BASICS

10.36 Determine the upper-tail critical values of F in each of the following two-tail tests.
a. $\alpha = 0.10, n_1 = 16, n_2 = 21$
b. $\alpha = 0.05, n_1 = 16, n_2 = 21$
c. $\alpha = 0.01, n_1 = 16, n_2 = 21$

10.37 Determine the upper-tail critical value of F in each of the following one-tail tests.
a. $\alpha = 0.05, n_1 = 16, n_2 = 21$
b. $\alpha = 0.01, n_1 = 16, n_2 = 21$

10.38 The following information is available for two samples selected from independent normally distributed populations:

Population A: $n_1 = 25$ $S_1^2 = 16$

Population B: $n_2 = 25$ $S_2^2 = 25$

a. Which sample variance do you place in the numerator of F_{STAT}?
b. What is the value of F_{STAT}?

10.39 The following information is available for two samples selected from independent normally distributed populations:

Population A: $n_1 = 25$ $S_1^2 = 161.9$

Population B: $n_2 = 25$ $S_2^2 = 133.7$

What is the value of F_{STAT} if you are testing the null hypothesis $H_0: \sigma_1^2 = \sigma_2^2$?

10.40 In Problem 10.39, how many degrees of freedom are there in the numerator and denominator of the F test?

10.41 In Problems 10.38 and 10.39, what is the upper-tail critical value for F if the level of significance, α, is 0.05 and the alternative hypothesis is $H_1: \sigma_1^2 \neq \sigma_2^2$?

10.42 In Problems 10.38 through 10.41, what is your statistical decision?

10.43 The following information is available for two samples selected from independent but very right-skewed populations:

Population A: $n_1 = 16$ $S_1^2 = 47.3$

Population B: $n_2 = 13$ $S_2^2 = 36.4$

Should you use the F test to test the null hypothesis of equality of variances? Discuss.

10.44 In Problem 10.43, assume that two samples are selected from independent normally distributed populations.
a. At the 0.05 level of significance, is there evidence of a difference between σ_1^2 and σ_2^2?
b. Suppose that you want to perform a one-tail test. At the 0.05 level of significance, what is the upper-tail critical value of F to determine whether there is evidence that $\sigma_1^2 > \sigma_2^2$? What is your statistical decision?

APPLYING THE CONCEPTS

10.45 A problem with a telephone line that prevents a customer from receiving or making calls is upsetting to both the customer and the telecommunications company. The file **Phone** contains samples of 20 problems reported to two different offices of a telecommunications company and the time to clear these problems (in minutes) from the customers' lines.

a. At the 0.05 level of significance, is there evidence of a difference in the variability of the time to clear problems between the two central offices?

b. Determine the p-value in (a) and interpret its meaning.

c. What assumption do you need to make in (a) about the two populations in order to justify your use of the F test?

d. Based on the results of (a) and (b), which t test defined in Section 10.1 should you use to compare the mean time to clear problems in the two central offices?

✓**SELF** **10.46** *Accounting Today* identified the top accounting
TEST firms in 10 geographic regions across the United States. All 10 regions reported growth in 2014. The Southeast and Gulf Coast regions reported growth of 12.36% and 5.8%, respectively. A characteristic description of the accounting firms in the Southeast and Gulf Coast regions included the number of partners in the firm. The file AccountingPartners2 contains the number of partners. (Data extracted from **bit.ly/1BoMzsv**.)

a. At the 0.05 level of significance, is there evidence of a difference in the variability in numbers of partners for Southeast region accounting firms and Gulf Coast accounting firms?

b. Determine the p-value in (a) and interpret its meaning.

c. What assumption do you have to make about the two populations in order to justify the use of the F test?

d. Based on (a) and (b), which t test defined in Section 10.1 should you use to test whether there is a significant difference in the mean number of partners for Southeast region accounting firms and Gulf Coast accounting firms?

10.47 A bank with a branch located in a commercial district of a city has the business objective of improving the process for serving customers during the noon-to-1 P.M. lunch period. To do so, the waiting time (defined as the number of minutes that elapses from when the customer enters the line until he or she reaches the teller window) needs to be shortened to increase customer satisfaction. A random sample of 15 customers is selected and the waiting times are collected and stored in Bank1 . These data are:

```
4.21   5.55   3.02   5.13   4.77   2.34   3.54   3.20
4.50   6.10   0.38   5.12   6.46   6.19   3.79
```

Suppose that another branch, located in a residential area, is also concerned with the noon-to-1 P.M. lunch period. A random sample of 15 customers is selected and the waiting times are collected and stored in Bank2 . These data are:

```
9.66    5.90   8.02   5.79   8.73   3.82   8.01   8.35
10.49   6.68   5.64   4.08   6.17   9.91   5.47
```

a. Is there evidence of a difference in the variability of the waiting time between the two branches? (Use $\alpha = 0.05$.)

b. Determine the p-value in (a) and interpret its meaning.

c. What assumption about the population distribution of each bank is necessary in (a)? Is the assumption valid for these data?

d. Based on the results of (a), is it appropriate to use the pooled-variance t test to compare the means of the two branches?

10.48 An important feature of tablets is battery life, the number of hours before the battery needs to be recharged. The file Tablets contains the battery life of 12 WiFi-only and 7 3G/4G/WiFi 9- through 12-inch tablets. (Data extracted from "Ratings and recommendations: Tablets," *Consumer Reports*, August 2013, p. 24.)

a. Is there evidence of a difference in the variability of the battery life between the two types of tablets? (Use $\alpha = 0.05$.)

b. Determine the p-value in (a) and interpret its meaning.

c. What assumption about the population distribution of the two types of tablets is necessary in (a)? Is the assumption valid for these data?

d. Based on the results of (a), which t test defined in Section 10.1 should you use to compare the mean battery life of the two types of tablets?

10.49 Experian Marketing Services reported that the typical American spends 144 minutes (2.4 hours) per day accessing the Internet through a mobile device. (Source: *The 2014 Digital Marketer*, available at **ex.pn/1kXJjfX**.) You wonder if males and females spend differing amounts of time per day accessing the Internet through a mobile device.

You select a sample of 60 friends and family (30 males and 30 females), collect times spent per day accessing the Internet through a mobile device (in minutes), and store the data collected in InternetMobileTime2 .

a. Using a 0.05 level of significance, is there evidence of a difference in the variances of time spent per day accessing the Internet via mobile device between males and females?

b. On the basis of the results in (a), which t test defined in Section 10.1 should you use to compare the means of males and females? Discuss.

10.50 Is there a difference in the variation of the 30-year mortgage rate in different cities? The file ThirtyYrRate contains the yields for a 30-year mortgage for ten banks in New York and 21 banks in West Palm Beach, Florida, as of June 24, 2015. (Data extracted from **www.Bankrate.com**, June 24, 2015.) At the 0.05 level of significance, is there evidence of a difference in the variance of the 30-year mortgage rates in the two cities? Assume that the population mortgage rates are normally distributed.

10.5 Effect Size

Section 9.5 discusses the issue of the practical significance of a statistically significant test and explains that when a very large sample is selected, a statistically significant result can be of limited importance. The **Section 10.5 online topic** shows how to measure the effect size of a statistical test.

▼USING **STATISTICS**
Differing Means for Selling..., Revisited

In the Arlingtons scenario, you sought to show that the sales location in a store could affect sales of a product. If you could show such an effect, you would have an argument for charging a placement fee for the better location. You designed an experiment that would sell the new VLABGo mobile streaming media player in one of two sales locations, at a special front of store location or in the mobile electronics aisle. You conducted an experiment in which 10 stores used the special front location to sell VLABGo players and 10 stores used the mobile electronics aisle.

Using a t test for the difference between two means, you were able to conclude that the mean sales using the special front location are higher than the mean sales for the in-aisle location. A confidence interval allowed you to infer with 95% confidence that population mean amount sold at the special front location was between 2.74 and 79.46 more than the in-aisle location. You also performed the F test for the difference between two variances to see if the store-to-store variability in sales in stores using the special front location differed from the store-to-store variability in sales in stores using the in-aisle location. You concluded that there was no significant difference in the variability of the sales of VLABGo players for the sales locations. That you now have evidence that sales are higher in the special front location, gives you one argument for charging manufacturers a placement fee for that location.

▼ SUMMARY

In this chapter, you were introduced to a variety of tests for two or more samples. For situations in which the samples are independent, you learned statistical test procedures for analyzing possible differences between means, proportions, and variances. In addition, you learned a test procedure that is frequently used when analyzing differences between the means of two related samples. Remember that you need to select the test that is most appropriate for a given set of conditions and to critically investigate the validity of the assumptions underlying each of the hypothesis-testing procedures.

Table 10.7 provides a list of topics covered in this chapter. The roadmap in Figure 10.14 illustrates the steps needed in determining which two-sample test of hypothesis to use. The following are the questions you need to consider:

1. What type of variables do you have? If you are dealing with categorical variables, use the Z test for the difference between two proportions. (This test assumes independent samples.)
2. If you have a numerical variable, determine whether you have independent samples or related samples. If you have related samples, and you can assume approximate normality, use the paired t test.
3. If you have independent samples, is your focus on variability or central tendency? If the focus is on variability, and you can assume approximate normality, use the F test.
4. If your focus is central tendency and you can assume approximate normality, determine whether you can assume that the variances of the two populations are equal. (This assumption can be tested using the F test.)
5. If you can assume that the two populations have equal variances, use the pooled-variance t test. If you cannot assume that the two populations have equal variances, use the separate-variance t test.

TABLE 10.7
Summary of Topics in Chapter 10

	TYPES OF DATA	
TYPE OF ANALYSIS	**Numerical**	**Categorical**
Compare two populations	t tests for the difference in the means of two independent populations (Section 10.1) Paired t test (Section 10.2) F test for the difference between two variances (Section 10.4)	Z test for the difference between two proportions (Section 10.3)

FIGURE 10.14
Roadmap for selecting a test of hypothesis for two or more samples

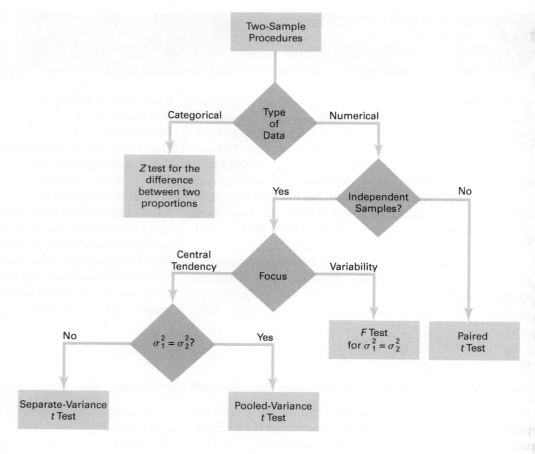

▼ REFERENCES

1. Conover, W. J. *Practical Nonparametric Statistics*, 3rd ed. New York: Wiley, 2000.
2. Daniel, W. *Applied Nonparametric Statistics*, 2nd ed. Boston: Houghton Mifflin, 1990.
3. Satterthwaite, F. E. "An Approximate Distribution of Estimates of Variance Components." *Biometrics Bulletin*, 2(1946): 110–114.
4. Snedecor, G. W., and W. G. Cochran. *Statistical Methods*, 8th ed. Ames, IA: Iowa State University Press, 1989.

▼ KEY EQUATIONS

Pooled-Variance *t* Test for the Difference Between Two Means

$$t_{STAT} = \frac{(\overline{X}_1 - \overline{X}_2) - (\mu_1 - \mu_2)}{\sqrt{S_p^2 \left(\frac{1}{n_1} + \frac{1}{n_2} \right)}} \qquad (10.1)$$

Confidence Interval Estimate for the Difference Between the Means of Two Independent Populations

$$(\overline{X}_1 - \overline{X}_2) \pm t_{\alpha/2} \sqrt{S_p^2 \left(\frac{1}{n_1} + \frac{1}{n_2} \right)} \qquad (10.2)$$

or

$$(\overline{X}_1 - \overline{X}_2) - t_{\alpha/2} \sqrt{S_p^2 \left(\frac{1}{n_1} + \frac{1}{n_2} \right)} \leq \mu_1 - \mu_2$$

$$\leq (\overline{X}_1 - \overline{X}_2) + t_{\alpha/2} \sqrt{S_p^2 \left(\frac{1}{n_1} + \frac{1}{n_2} \right)}$$

Paired *t* Test for the Mean Difference

$$t_{STAT} = \frac{\overline{D} - \mu_D}{\frac{S_D}{\sqrt{n}}} \qquad (10.3)$$

Confidence Interval Estimate for the Mean Difference

$$\overline{D} \pm t_{\alpha/2} \frac{S_D}{\sqrt{n}} \qquad (10.4)$$

or

$$\overline{D} - t_{\alpha/2} \frac{S_D}{\sqrt{n}} \leq \mu_D \leq \overline{D} + t_{\alpha/2} \frac{S_D}{\sqrt{n}}$$

Z Test for the Difference Between Two Proportions

$$Z_{STAT} = \frac{(p_1 - p_2) - (\pi_1 - \pi_2)}{\sqrt{\overline{p}(1 - \overline{p}) \left(\frac{1}{n_1} + \frac{1}{n_2} \right)}} \qquad (10.5)$$

Confidence Interval Estimate for the Difference Between Two Proportions

$$(p_1 - p_2) \pm Z_{\alpha/2}\sqrt{\left(\frac{p_1(1 - p_1)}{n_1} + \frac{p_2(1 - p_2)}{n_2}\right)} \quad (10.6)$$

or

$$(p_1 - p_2) - Z_{\alpha/2}\sqrt{\frac{p_1(1 - p_1)}{n_1} + \frac{p_2(1 - p_2)}{n_2}} \le (\pi_1 - \pi_2)$$

$$\le (p_1 - p_2) + Z_{\alpha/2}\sqrt{\frac{p_1(1 - p_1)}{n_1} + \frac{p_2(1 - p_2)}{n_2}}$$

F Test Statistic for Testing the Ratio of Two Variances

$$F_{STAT} = \frac{S_1^2}{S_2^2} \quad (10.7)$$

▼ KEY TERMS

F distribution   332
F test for the ratio of two variances   332
matched samples   318
paired t test for the mean difference   318

pooled-variance t test   308
repeated measurements   317
robust   311
separate-variance t test   314

two-sample tests   308
Z test for the difference between two proportions   326

▼ CHECKING YOUR UNDERSTANDING

10.51 What are some of the criteria used in the selection of a particular hypothesis-testing procedure?

10.52 Under what conditions should you use the pooled-variance t test to examine possible differences in the means of two independent populations?

10.53 Under what conditions should you use the F test to examine possible differences in the variances of two independent populations?

10.54 What is the distinction between two independent populations and two related populations?

10.55 What is the distinction between repeated measurements and matched items?

10.56 When you have two independent populations, explain the similarities and differences between the test of hypothesis for the difference between the means and the confidence interval estimate for the difference between the means.

10.57 Under what conditions should you use the paired t test for the mean difference between two related populations?

▼ CHAPTER REVIEW PROBLEMS

10.58 The American Society for Quality (ASQ) conducted a salary survey of all its members. ASQ members work in all areas of manufacturing and service-related institutions, with a common theme of an interest in quality. Two job titles are black belt and green belt. (See Section 18.6 for a description of these titles in a Six Sigma quality improvement initiative.) Descriptive statistics concerning salaries for these two job titles are given in the following table:

Job Title	Sample Size	Mean	Standard Deviation
Black belt	147	96,682	23,337
Green belt	29	77,514	25,503

Source: Data extracted from "QP Salary Survey," *Quality Progress*, December 2014, p. 27.

a. Using a 0.05 level of significance, is there a difference in the variability of salaries between black belts and green belts?
b. Based on the result of (a), which t test defined in Section 10.1 is appropriate for comparing mean salaries?
c. Using a 0.05 level of significance, is the mean salary of black belts greater than the mean salary of green belts?

10.59 How do private universities and public colleges compare with respect to debt at graduation incurred by students? The file **CollegeDebt** contains the average debt at graduation incurred by students for 100 private universities and 100 public colleges, as reported by Kiplinger. (Data extracted from "Kiplinger's Best College Values," bit.ly/1QT3L7l.)
a. At the 0.05 level of significance, is there a difference in the variance of average graduation debt incurred by students for private universities and public colleges?

b. Using the results of (a), which t test is appropriate for comparing mean debt at graduation incurred by students at private universities and public colleges?
c. At the 0.05 level of significance, conduct the test selected in (b).
d. Write a short summary of your findings.

10.60 Do males and females differ in the amount of time they spend online and the amount of time they spend playing games while online? A study reported that women spent a mean of 1,068 minutes per week online as compared to 1,398 minutes per week for men. (Data extracted from Ofcom, *Adults' Media Use and Attitudes Report, 2015*.) The sample sizes were not reported. Suppose that the sample sizes were 100 each for women and men and that the standard deviation for women was 50 minutes per week as compared to 75 minutes per week for men.
a. Using a 0.01 level of significance, is there evidence of a difference in the variances of the amount of time spent online between women and men?
b. To test for a difference in the mean online time of women and men, is it most appropriate to use the pooled-variance t test or the separate-variance t test? Use the most appropriate test to determine if there is a difference in the mean amount of time spent online between women and men.

The article also reported that women spent a mean of 276 minutes per week playing games while online compared to 396 minutes per week for men. Suppose that the standard deviation for women was 15 minutes per week compared to 20 minutes per week for men.
c. Using a 0.01 level of significance, is there evidence of a difference in the variances of the amount of time spent playing games while online per week by women and men?
d. Based on the results of (c), use the most appropriate test to determine, at the 0.01 level of significance, whether there is evidence of a difference in the mean amount of time spent playing games online per week by women and men.

10.61 The file Restaurants contains the ratings for food, décor, service, and the price per person for a sample of 50 restaurants located in a city and 50 restaurants located in a suburb. Completely analyze the differences between city and suburban restaurants for the variables food rating, décor rating, service rating, and cost per person, using $\alpha = 0.05$.
Source: Data extracted from *Zagat Survey 2013 New York City Restaurants* and *Zagat Survey 2012–2013 Long Island Restaurants*.

10.62 A computer information systems professor is interested in studying the amount of time it takes students enrolled in the Introduction to Computers course to write a program in VB.NET. The professor hires you to analyze the following results (in minutes), stored in VB, from a random sample of nine students:

10   13   9   15   12   13   11   13   12

a. At the 0.05 level of significance, is there evidence that the population mean time is greater than 10 minutes? What will you tell the professor?
b. Suppose that the professor, when checking her results, realizes that the fourth student needed 51 minutes rather than the recorded 15 minutes to write the VB.NET program. At the 0.05 level of significance, reanalyze the question posed in (a), using the revised data. What will you tell the professor now?
c. The professor is perplexed by these paradoxical results and requests an explanation from you regarding the justification for the difference in your findings in (a) and (b). Discuss.

d. A few days later, the professor calls to tell you that the dilemma is completely resolved. The original number 15 (the fourth data value) was correct, and therefore your findings in (a) are being used in the article she is writing for a computer journal. Now she wants to hire you to compare the results from that group of Introduction to Computers students against those from a sample of 11 computer majors in order to determine whether there is evidence that computer majors can write a VB.NET program in less time than introductory students. For the computer majors, the sample mean is 8.5 minutes, and the sample standard deviation is 2.0 minutes. At the 0.05 level of significance, completely analyze these data. What will you tell the professor?
e. A few days later, the professor calls again to tell you that a reviewer of her article wants her to include the p-value for the "correct" result in (a). In addition, the professor inquires about an unequal-variances problem, which the reviewer wants her to discuss in her article. In your own words, discuss the concept of p-value and also describe the unequal-variances problem. Then determine the p-value in (a) and discuss whether the unequal-variances problem had any meaning in the professor's study.

10.63 Do social shoppers differ from other online consumers with respect to spending behavior? A study of browser-based shopping sessions reported that social shoppers, consumers who click away from social networks to retail sites or share an item on a social network, spent a mean of $126.12 on a retail site in a 30-day period compared to other online shoppers who spent a mean of $115.55. (Data extracted from "Social shoppers spend 8% more than other online consumers," bit.ly/1FyyXP5.) Suppose that the study consisted of 500 social shoppers and 500 other online shoppers and the standard deviation of the order value was $40 for social shoppers and $10 for other online shoppers. Assume a level of significance of 0.05.
a. Is there evidence of a difference in the variances of the order values between social shoppers and other online shoppers?
b. Is there evidence of a difference in the mean order value between social shoppers and other online shoppers?
c. Construct a 95% confidence interval estimate for the difference in mean order value between social shoppers and other online shoppers.

10.64 The lengths of life (in hours) of a sample of 40 20-watt compact fluorescent light bulbs produced by manufacturer A and a sample of 40 20-watt compact fluorescent light bulbs produced by manufacturer B are stored in Bulbs. Completely analyze the differences between the lengths of life of the compact fluorescent light bulbs produced by the two manufacturers. (Use $\alpha = 0.05$.)

10.65 A hotel manager looks to enhance the initial impressions that hotel guests have when they check in. Contributing to initial impressions is the time it takes to deliver a guest's luggage to the room after check-in. A random sample of 20 deliveries on a particular day were selected in Wing A of the hotel, and a random sample of 20 deliveries were selected in Wing B. The results are stored in Luggage. Analyze the data and determine whether there is a difference between the mean delivery times in the two wings of the hotel. (Use $\alpha = 0.05$.)

10.66 The owner of a restaurant that serves Continental-style entrées has the business objective of learning more about the patterns of patron demand during the Friday-to-Sunday weekend time period. She decided to study the demand for dessert during this time period. In addition to studying whether a dessert was ordered, she will study the gender of the individual and whether a beef entrée was ordered. Data were collected from 630 customers and organized in the following contingency tables:

DESSERT ORDERED	GENDER		
	Male	Female	Total
Yes	50	96	146
No	250	234	484
Total	300	330	630

DESSERT ORDERED	BEEF ENTRÉE		
	Yes	No	Total
Yes	74	68	142
No	123	365	488
Total	197	433	630

a. At the 0.05 level of significance, is there evidence of a difference between males and females in the proportion who order dessert?

b. At the 0.05 level of significance, is there evidence of a difference in the proportion who order dessert based on whether a beef entrée has been ordered?

10.67 The manufacturer of Boston and Vermont asphalt shingles knows that product weight is a major factor in the customer's perception of quality. Moreover, the weight represents the amount of raw materials being used and is therefore very important to the company from a cost standpoint. The last stage of the assembly line packages the shingles before they are placed on wooden pallets. Once a pallet is full (a pallet for most brands holds 16 squares of shingles), it is weighed, and the measurement is recorded. The file Pallet contains the weight (in pounds) from a sample of 368 pallets of Boston shingles and 330 pallets of Vermont shingles.

Completely analyze the differences in the weights of the Boston and Vermont shingles, using $\alpha = 0.05$.

10.68 The manufacturer of Boston and Vermont asphalt shingles provides its customers with a 20-year warranty on most of its products. To determine whether a shingle will last as long as the warranty period, the manufacturer conducts accelerated-life testing. Accelerated-life testing exposes the shingle to the stresses it would be subject to in a lifetime of normal use in a laboratory setting via an experiment that takes only a few minutes to conduct. In this test, a shingle is repeatedly scraped with a brush for a short period of time, and the shingle granules removed by the brushing are weighed (in grams). Shingles that experience low amounts of granule loss are expected to last longer in normal use than shingles that experience high amounts of granule loss. In this situation, a shingle should experience no more than 0.8 grams of granule loss if it is expected to last the length of the warranty period. The file Granule contains a sample of 170 measurements made on the company's Boston shingles and 140 measurements made on Vermont shingles. Completely analyze the differences in the granule loss of the Boston and Vermont shingles, using $\alpha = 0.05$.

10.69 There are a very large number of mutual funds from which an investor can choose. Each mutual fund has its own mix of different types of investments. The data in BestFunds1 present the one-year return for the 10 best long-term bond funds and the 10 best world stock funds, according to the *U.S. News & World Report*. (Data extracted from **money.usnews.com/mutual-funds**.) Analyze the data and determine whether any differences exist between long-term bond funds and world stock funds. (Use the 0.05 level of significance.)

REPORT WRITING EXERCISE

10.70 Referring to the results of Problems 10.67 and 10.68 concerning the weight and granule loss of Boston and Vermont shingles, write a report that summarizes your conclusions.

CHAPTER 10

▼CASES

Managing Ashland MultiComm Services

Part 1 AMS communicates with customers who subscribe to telecommunications services through a special secured email system that sends messages about service changes, new features, and billing information to in-home digital set-top boxes for later display. To enhance customer service, the operations department established the business objective of reducing the amount of time to fully update each subscriber's set of messages. The department selected two candidate messaging systems and conducted an experiment in which 30 randomly chosen cable subscribers were assigned one of the two systems (15 assigned to each system). Update times were

measured, and the results are organized in Table AMS 10.1 and stored in AMS10.

1. Analyze the data in Table AMS 10.1 and write a report to the computer operations department that indicates your findings. Include an appendix in which you discuss the reason you selected a particular statistical test to compare the two independent groups of callers.

2. Suppose that instead of the research design described in the case, there were only 15 subscribers sampled, and the update process for each subscriber email was measured for each of the two messaging systems. Suppose that the results were organized in Table AMS 10.1—making each row in the table a pair of values for an individual subscriber. Using these suppositions, reanalyze

TABLE AMS 10.1
Update Times (in seconds) for Two Different
Email Interfaces

Email Interface 1	Email Interface 2
4.13	3.71
3.75	3.89
3.93	4.22
3.74	4.57
3.36	4.24
3.85	3.90
3.26	4.09
3.73	4.05
4.06	4.07
3.33	3.80
3.96	4.36
3.57	4.38
3.13	3.49
3.68	3.57
3.63	4.74

the Table AMS 10.1 data and write a report for presentation to the team that indicates your findings.

Digital Case

Apply your knowledge about hypothesis testing in this Digital Case, which continues the cereal-fill packaging dispute Digital Case from Chapters 7 and 9.

Even after the recent public experiment about cereal box weights, Consumers Concerned About Cereal Cheaters (CCACC) remains convinced that Oxford Cereals has misled the public. The group has created and circulated **MoreCheating.pdf**, a document in which it claims that cereal boxes produced at Plant Number 2 in Springville weigh less than the claimed mean of 368 grams. Review this document and then answer the following questions:

1. Do the CCACC's results prove that there is a statistically significant difference in the mean weights of cereal boxes produced at Plant Numbers 1 and 2?

2. Perform the appropriate analysis to test the CCACC's hypothesis. What conclusions can you reach based on the data?

Sure Value Convenience Stores

You continue to work in the corporate office for a nationwide convenience store franchise that operates nearly 10,000 stores. The per-store daily customer count (i.e., the mean number of customers in a store in one day) has been steady, at 900, for some time. To increase the customer count, the chain is considering cutting prices for coffee beverages. The small size will now be either $0.59 or $0.79 instead of $0.99. Even with this reduction in price, the chain will have a 40% gross margin on coffee.

The question to be determined is how much to cut prices to increase the daily customer count without reducing the gross margin on coffee sales too much. The chain decides to carry out an experiment in a sample of 30 stores where customer counts have been running almost exactly at the national

average of 900. In 15 of the stores, the price of a small coffee will now be $0.59 instead of $0.99, and in 15 other stores, the price of a small coffee will now be $0.79. After four weeks, the 15 stores that priced the small coffee at $0.59 had a mean daily customer count of 964 and a standard deviation of 88, and the 15 stores that priced the small coffee at $0.79 had a mean daily customer count of 941 and a standard deviation of 76. Analyze these data (using the 0.05 level of significance) and answer the following questions.

1. Does reducing the price of a small coffee to either $0.59 or $0.79 increase the mean per-store daily customer count?

2. If reducing the price of a small coffee to either $0.59 or $0.79 increases the mean per-store daily customer count, is there any difference in the mean per-store daily customer count between stores in which a small coffee was priced at $0.59 and stores in which a small coffee was priced at $0.79?

3. What price do you recommend for a small coffee?

CardioGood Fitness

Return to the CardioGood Fitness case first presented on page 28. Using the data stored in `CardioGood Fitness`:

1. Determine whether differences exist between males and females in their age in years, education in years, annual household income ($), mean number of times the customer plans to use the treadmill each week, and mean number of miles the customer expects to walk or run each week.

2. Write a report to be presented to the management of Cardio-Good Fitness detailing your findings.

More Descriptive Choices Follow-Up

Follow up the Using Statistics scenario "More Descriptive Choices, Revisited" on page 136.

Determine whether there is a difference in the 3-year return percentage, 5-year return percentages, and 10-year return percentages of the growth and value funds (stored in `Retirement Funds`).

Clear Mountain State Student Survey

The Student News Service at Clear Mountain State University (CMSU) has decided to gather data about the undergraduate students that attend CMSU. It creates and distributes a survey of 14 questions and receives responses from 111 undergraduates (stored in `StudentSurvey`).

1. At the 0.05 level of significance, is there evidence of a difference between males and females in grade point average, expected starting salary, number of social networking sites registered for, age, spending on textbooks and supplies, text messages sent in a week, and the wealth needed to feel rich?

2. At the 0.05 level of significance, is there evidence of a difference between students who plan to go to graduate school and those who do not plan to go to graduate school in grade point average, expected starting salary, number of social networking sites registered for, age, spending on textbooks and supplies, text messages sent in a week, and the wealth needed to feel rich?

▾EXCEL GUIDE

EG10.1 COMPARING the MEANS of TWO INDEPENDENT POPULATIONS

Pooled-Variance *t* Test for the Difference Between Two Means

Key Technique Use the **T.INV.2T**(*level of significance, total degrees of freedom*) function to compute the lower and upper critical values. Use the **T.DIST.2T**(*absolute value of the t test statistic, total degrees of freedom*) to compute the *p*-value.

Example Perform the Figure 10.3 pooled-variance *t* test for the Table 10.1 Arlingtons sales data for the two in-store sales locations.

PHStat Use **Pooled-Variance t Test**.

For the example, open to the **DATA worksheet** of the **VLABGo workbook**. Select **PHStat → Two-Sample Tests (Unsummarized Data) → Pooled-Variance t Test**. In the procedure's dialog box (shown below):

1. Enter **0** as the **Hypothesized Difference**.
2. Enter **0.05** as the **Level of Significance**.
3. Enter **A1:A11** as the **Population 1 Sample Cell Range**.
4. Enter **B1:B11** as the **Population 2 Sample Cell Range**.
5. Check **First cells in both ranges contain label**.
6. Click **Two-Tail Test**.
7. Enter a **Title** and click **OK.**

When using summarized data, select **PHStat → Two-Sample Tests (Summarized Data) → Pooled-Variance t Test**. In that procedure's dialog box, enter the hypothesized difference and level of significance, as well as the sample size, sample mean, and sample standard deviation for each sample.

Workbook Use the **COMPUTE worksheet** of the **Pooled-Variance T workbook** as a template.

The worksheet already contains the data and formulas to use the unsummarized data for the example. For other problems, use this worksheet with either unsummarized or summarized data.

For unsummarized data, paste the data in columns A and B in the **DataCopy** worksheet and keep the COMPUTE worksheet formulas that compute the sample size, sample mean, and sample standard deviation in the cell range B7:B13. For summarized data, replace the formulas in the cell range B7:B13 with the sample statistics and ignore the DataCopy worksheet.

Use the **COMPUTE_LOWER** or **COMPUTE_UPPER** worksheets in the same workbook as templates for performing one-tail pooled-variance *t* tests with either unsummarized or summarized data. For unsummarized data, paste the new data into the DataCopy worksheet. For summarized data, replace COMPUTE worksheet formulas with sample statistics.

Analysis ToolPak Use **t-Test: Two-Sample Assuming Equal Variances**.

For the example, open to the **DATA worksheet** of the **VLABGo workbook** and:

1. Select **Data → Data Analysis**.
2. In the Data Analysis dialog box, select **t-Test: Two-Sample Assuming Equal Variances** from the **Analysis Tools** list and then click **OK**.

In the procedure's dialog box (shown below):

3. Enter **A1:A11** as the **Variable 1 Range**
4. Enter **B1:B11** as the **Variable 2 Range**.
5. Enter **0** as the **Hypothesized Mean Difference**.
6. Check **Labels** and enter **0.05** as **Alpha**.
7. Click **New Worksheet Ply**.
8. Click **OK**.

Results (shown below) appear in a new worksheet that contains both two-tail and one-tail test critical values and *p*-values. Unlike the results shown in Figure 10.3, only the positive (upper) critical value is listed for the two-tail test.

	A	B	C
1	t-Test: Two-Sample Assuming Equal Variances		
2			
3		Front	In-Aisle
4	Mean	243.4	202.3
5	Variance	2275.8222	1058.0111
6	Observations	10	10
7	Pooled Variance	1666.9167	
8	Hypothesized Mean Difference	0	
9	df	18	
10	t Stat	2.2510	
11	P(T<=t) one-tail	0.0186	
12	t Critical one-tail	1.7341	
13	P(T<=t) two-tail	0.0371	
14	t Critical two-tail	2.1009	

Confidence Interval Estimate for the Difference Between Two Means

PHStat Modify the *PHStat* instructions for the pooled-variance *t* test. In step 7, check **Confidence Interval Estimate** and enter a **Confidence Level** in its box, in addition to entering a **Title** and clicking **OK**.

Workbook Use the *In-Depth Excel* instructions for the pooled-variance *t* test. The Pooled-Variance T workbook worksheets include a confidence interval estimate for the difference between two means in the cell range D3:E16.

t Test for the Difference Between Two Means, Assuming Unequal Variances

Key Technique Use the **T.INV.2T**(*level of significance, degrees of freedom*) function to compute the lower and upper critical values. Use the **T.DIST.2T**(*absolute value of the t test statistic, degrees of freedom*) to compute the *p*-value.

Example Perform the Figure 10.6 separate-variance *t* test for the two end-cap locations data shown on page 314.

PHStat Use **Separate-Variance t Test**.
For the example, open to the **DATA worksheet** of the **VLABGo workbook**. Select **PHStat → Two-Sample Tests (Unsummarized Data) → Separate-Variance t Test**. In the procedure's dialog box (shown in the right column):

1. Enter **0** as the **Hypothesized Difference**.
2. Enter **0.05** as the **Level of Significance**.
3. Enter **A1:A11** as the **Population 1 Sample Cell Range**.
4. Enter **B1:B11** as the **Population 2 Sample Cell Range**.
5. Check **First cells in both ranges contain label**.
6. Click **Two-Tail Test**.
7. Enter a **Title** and click **OK**.

When using summarized data, select **PHStat → Two-Sample Tests (Summarized Data) → Separate-Variance t Test**. In that procedure's dialog box, enter the hypothesized difference and the level of significance, as well as the sample size, sample mean, and sample standard deviation for each group.

Workbook Use the **COMPUTE worksheet** of the **Separate-Variance T workbook** as a template.
The worksheet already contains the data and formulas to use the unsummarized data for the example. For other problems, use this worksheet with either unsummarized or summarized data.

For unsummarized data, paste the data in columns A and B in the **DataCopy worksheet** and keep the COMPUTE worksheet formulas that compute the sample size, sample mean, and sample standard deviation in the cell range B7:B13. For summarized data, replace those formulas in the cell range B7:B13 with the sample statistics and ignore the DataCopy worksheet.

Use the **COMPUTE_LOWER** or **COMPUTE_UPPER worksheets** in the same workbook as templates for performing one-tail pooled-variance *t* tests with either unsummarized or summarized data. For unsummarized data, paste the new data into the DataCopy worksheet. For summarized data, replace the COMPUTE worksheet formulas with sample statistics.

Analysis ToolPak Use **t-Test: Two-Sample Assuming Unequal Variances**.
For the example, open to the **DATA worksheet** of the **Placements workbook** and:

1. Select **Data → Data Analysis**.
2. In the Data Analysis dialog box, select **t-Test: Two-Sample Assuming Unequal Variances** from the **Analysis Tools** list and then click **OK**.

In the procedure's dialog box (shown on page 345):

3. Enter **A1:A11** as the **Variable 1 Range**.
4. Enter **B1:B11** as the **Variable 2 Range**.
5. Enter **0** as the **Hypothesized Mean Difference**.
6. Check **Labels** and enter **0.05** as **Alpha**.

7. Click **New Worksheet Ply**.
8. Click **OK**.

Results (shown below) appear in a new worksheet that contains both two-tail and one-tail test critical values and *p*-values. Unlike the results shown in Figure 10.6, only the positive (upper) critical value is listed for the two-tail test. Because the Analysis ToolPak uses table lookups to approximate the critical values and the *p*-value, the results will differ slightly from the values shown in Figure 10.6.

	A	B	C
1	t-Test: Two-Sample Assuming Unequal Variances		
2			
3		Front	In-Aisle
4	Mean	243.4	202.3
5	Variance	2275.8222	1058.0111
6	Observations	10	10
7	Hypothesized Mean Difference	0	
8	df	16	
9	t Stat	2.2510	
10	P(T<=t) one-tail	0.0194	
11	t Critical one-tail	1.7459	
12	P(T<=t) two-tail	0.0388	
13	t Critical two-tail	2.1199	

EG10.2 COMPARING the MEANS of TWO RELATED POPULATIONS

Paired *t* Test

Key Technique Use the **T.INV.2T**(*level of significance, degrees of freedom*) function to compute the lower and upper critical values and use the **T.DIST.2T**(*absolute value of the t test statistic, degrees of freedom*) to compute the *p*-value.

Example Perform the Figure 10.8 paired *t* test for the textbook price data shown on page 321.

PHStat Use **Paired t Test**.

For the example, open to the **DATA worksheet** of the **BookPrices workbook**. Select **PHStat → Two-Sample Tests (Unsummarized Data) → Paired t Test**. In the procedure's dialog box (shown in the right column):

1. Enter **0** as the **Hypothesized Mean Difference**.
2. Enter **0.05** as the **Level of Significance**.

3. Enter **C1:C17** as the **Population 1 Sample Cell Range**.
4. Enter **D1:D17** as the **Population 2 Sample Cell Range**.
5. Check **First cells in both ranges contain label**.
6. Click **Two-Tail Test**.
7. Enter a **Title** and click **OK**.

The procedure creates two worksheets, one of which is similar to the PtCalcs worksheet discussed in the following Workbook section. When using summarized data, select **PHStat → Two-Sample Tests (Summarized Data) → Paired t Test**. In that procedure's dialog box, enter the hypothesized mean difference, the level of significance, and the differences cell range.

Workbook Use the **COMPUTE** and **PtCalcs worksheets** of the **Paired T workbook** as a template.

The COMPUTE and supporting PtCalcs worksheets already contain the textbook price data for the example. The PtCalcs worksheet also computes the differences that allow the COMPUTE worksheet to compute the S_D in cell B11.

For other problems, paste the unsummarized data into columns A and B of the PtCalcs worksheet. For sample sizes greater than 16, select cell C17 and copy the formula in that cell down through the last data row. For sample sizes less than 16, delete the column C formulas for which there are no column A and B values. If you know the sample size, $\overline{D}$, and S_D values, you can ignore the PtCalcs worksheet and enter the values in cells B8, B9, and B11 of the COMPUTE worksheet, overwriting the formulas that those cells contain.

Use the similar **COMPUTE_LOWER** and **COMPUTE_UPPER worksheets** in the same workbook as templates for performing one-tail tests. For unsummarized data, paste the new data into the DataCopy worksheet. For summarized data, replace COMPUTE worksheet formulas with sample statistics.

Analysis ToolPak Use **t-Test: Paired Two Sample for Means**.

For the example, open to the **DATA worksheet** of the **Book-Prices workbook** and:

1. Select **Data → Data Analysis**.
2. In the Data Analysis dialog box, select **t-Test: Paired Two Sample for Means** from the **Analysis Tools** list and then click **OK**.

In the procedure's dialog box (shown below):

3. Enter **C1:C17** as the **Variable 1 Range**.
4. Enter **D1:D17** as the **Variable 2 Range**.
5. Enter **0** as the **Hypothesized Mean Difference**.
6. Check **Labels** and enter **0.05** as **Alpha**.
7. Click **New Worksheet Ply**.
8. Click **OK**.

Results (shown below) appear in a new worksheet that contains both two-tail and one-tail test critical values and *p*-values. Unlike in Figure 10.8, only the positive (upper) critical value is listed for the two-tail test.

	A	B	C
1	t-Test: Paired Two Sample for Means		
2			
3		*Bookstore*	*Online*
4	Mean	153.6344	111.0331
5	Variance	7913.0962	3594.7263
6	Observations	16	16
7	Pearson Correlation	0.8990	
8	Hypothesized Mean Difference	0	
9	df	15	
10	t Stat	3.8908	
11	P(T<=t) one-tail	0.0007	
12	t Critical one-tail	1.7531	
13	P(T<=t) two-tail	0.0014	
14	t Critical two-tail	2.1314	

EG10.3 COMPARING the PROPORTIONS of TWO INDEPENDENT POPULATIONS

Z Test for the Difference Between Two Proportions

Key Technique Use the **NORM.S.INV** *(percentage)* function to compute the critical values and use the **NORM.S.DIST** *(absolute value of the Z test statistic, True)* function to compute the *p*-value.

Example Perform the Figure 10.12 *Z* test for the web signup page experiment.

PHStat Use *Z* **Test for Differences in Two Proportions**. For the example, select **PHStat → Two-Sample Tests (Summarized Data) → Z Test for Differences in Two Proportions**. In the procedure's dialog box (shown below):

1. Enter **0** as the **Hypothesized Difference**.
2. Enter **0.05** as the **Level of Significance**.
3. For the Population 1 Sample, enter **387** as the **Number of Items of Interest** and **4325** as the **Sample Size**.
4. For the Population 2 Sample, enter **283** as the **Number of Items of Interest** and **4639** as the **Sample Size**.
5. Click **Two-Tail Test**.
6. Enter a **Title** and click **OK**.

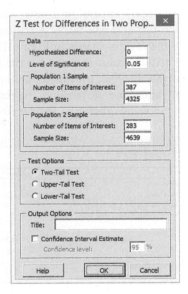

Workbook Use the **COMPUTE worksheet** of the **Z Two Proportions workbook** as a template.

The worksheet already contains data for the website signup survey. For other problems, change the hypothesized difference, the level of significance, and the number of items of interest and sample size for each group in the cell range B4:B11.

Use the similar **COMPUTE_LOWER** and **COMPUTE_UPPER worksheets** in the same workbook as templates for performing one-tail *Z* tests for the difference between two proportions. For unsummarized data, paste the new data into the DataCopy worksheet. For summarized data, replace COMPUTE worksheet formulas with sample statistics.

Confidence Interval Estimate for the Difference Between Two Proportions

PHStat Modify the *PHStat* instructions for the *Z* test for the difference between two proportions. In step 6, also check **Confidence Interval Estimate** and enter a **Confidence Level** in its box, in addition to entering a **Title** and clicking **OK**.

Workbook Use the *"Z Test for the Difference Between Two Proportions" Workbook* instructions in this section. The Z Two Proportions workbook worksheets include a confidence interval estimate for the difference between two means in the cell range D3:E16.

EG10.4 *F* TEST for the RATIO of TWO VARIANCES

Key Technique Use the **F.INV.RT**(*level of significance / 2, population 1 sample degrees of freedom, population 2 sample degrees of freedom*) function to compute the upper critical value and use the **F.DIST.RT**(*F test statistic, population 1 sample degrees of freedom, population 2 sample degrees of freedom*) function to compute the *p*-values.

Example Perform the Figure 10.13 *F* test for the ratio of two variances, for the Table 10.1 Arlingtons sales data for two in-store locations.

PHStat Use **F Test for Differences in Two Variances**. For the example, open to the **DATA worksheet** of the **VLABGo workbook**. Select **PHStat → Two-Sample Tests (Unsummarized Data) → F Test for Differences in Two Variances**. In the procedure's dialog box (shown below):

1. Enter **0.05** as the **Level of Significance**.
2. Enter **A1:A11** as the **Population 1 Sample Cell Range**.
3. Enter **B1:B11** as the **Population 2 Sample Cell Range**.
4. Check **First cells in both ranges contain label**.
5. Click **Two-Tail Test**.
6. Enter a **Title** and click **OK**.

When using summarized data, select **PHStat → Two-Sample Tests (Summarized Data) → F Test for Differences in Two Variances**. In that procedure's dialog box, enter the level of significance and the sample size and sample variance for each sample.

Workbook Use the **COMPUTE worksheet** of the **F Two Variances workbook** as a template.
The worksheet already contains the data and formulas for using the unsummarized data for the example. For

unsummarized data, paste the data in columns A and B in the **DataCopy worksheet** and keep the COMPUTE worksheet formulas that compute the sample size and sample variance for the two samples in cell range B4:B10. For summarized data, replace the COMPUTE worksheet formulas in cell ranges B4:B10 with the sample statistics and ignore the DataCopy worksheet.

Use the similar **COMPUTE_UPPER** worksheet in the same workbook as a template for performing the upper-tail test. For unsummarized data, paste the new data into the DataCopy worksheet. For summarized data, replace COMPUTE worksheet formulas with sample statistics.

Analysis ToolPak Use **F-Test Two-Sample for Variances**. For the example, open to the **DATA worksheet** of the **VALBGo workbook** and:

1. Select **Data → Data Analysis**.
2. In the Data Analysis dialog box, select **F-Test Two-Sample for Variances** from the **Analysis Tools** list and then click **OK**.

In the procedure's dialog box (shown below):

3. Enter **A1:A11** as the **Variable 1 Range** and enter **B1:B11** as the **Variable 2 Range**.
4. Check **Labels** and enter **0.05** as **Alpha**.
5. Click **New Worksheet Ply**.
6. Click **OK**.

Results (shown below) appear in a new worksheet and include only the one-tail test *p*-value (0.1347), which must be doubled for the two-tail test shown in Figure 10.13 on page 334.

	A	B	C
1	F-Test Two-Sample for Variances		
2			
3		Front	In-Aisle
4	Mean	243.4	202.3
5	Variance	2275.8222	1058.0111
6	Observations	10	10
7	df	9	9
8	F	2.1510	
9	P(F<=f) one-tail	0.1347	
10	F Critical one-tail	3.1789	

11

Analysis of Variance

OBJECTIVES

- Introduce the basic concepts of experimental design
- Learn to use the one-way analysis of variance to test for differences among the means of several groups
- Learn to use the two-way analysis of variance and interpret the interaction effect
- Learn to perform multiple comparisons in a one-way analysis of variance and a two-way analysis of variance

▼ USING **STATISTICS**
The Means to Find Differences at Arlingtons

Boosting sales of mobile electronics items is a key goal in a new strategic plan just issued by the senior management at the general merchandiser Arlingtons. Having helped to conduct an experiment that provided evidence that sales of a mobile streaming media player are higher in a special front location than in the mobile electronics aisle (see Chapter 10), you wonder if moving all mobile electronics items to another in-store location might also have an effect on sales.

The strategic plan also encourages managers to make better use of endcaps, the special end-of-aisle kiosk areas that face customers as customers enter aisles and suggests that managers create *expert counters*, positions that customers can visit to ask specially-trained staff questions about items for sale in a particular department, such as mobile electronics, or to see live demonstrations of particular items. Might these two in-store locations be combined with the two locations of the previous experiment (the special front location and the regular in-aisle location) into one larger experiment?

You suggest an experiment in which mobile electronics in selected Arlingtons stores will be sold at one of four in-store locations: the current in-aisle location, the special front of the store location, in a special endcap location, or at the expert counter position for mobile electronics. You propose to select 20 Arlingtons stores that have similar annual sales and divide the stores into four groups of five stores each. To each group, you assign a different in-store sales location for mobile electronics: current in-aisle, special front, endcap, or expert counter.

How would you determine if varying the locations had an effect on mobile electronics sales? As you consider this, another manager suggests that customers who use mobile payment methods might be more likely to buy mobile electronics items. If you also wanted to later explore the effects of permitting customers to use mobile payment methods to purchase mobile electronics items, could you design an experiment that examined this second factor while it was examining the effects of in-store location?

Comparing possible differences has been the subject of the statistical methods discussed in the previous two chapters. In the one-sample tests of Chapter 9, the comparison is to a standard, such as a certain mean weight for a cereal box being filled by a production line. In Chapter 10, the comparison is between samples taken from two populations. **Analysis of variance**, known by the acronym **ANOVA**, allows statistical comparison among samples taken from many populations.

In ANOVA, the comparison is typically the result of an experiment. For example, the management of a general merchandiser might be brainstorming ways of improving sales of mobile electronics items. At Arlingtons, the management decided to try selling those items in four different in-store locations and then observe what the sales would be in each of those locations. The basis for an ANOVA experiment is called the **factor**, which in the Arlingtons scenario is in-store location. The statistical use of the word "factor" complements the everyday usage, illustrated by a question such as "How much of a *factor* is in-store location in determining mobile electronics sales?"

The actual different locations (in-aisle, special front, endcap, and expert counter) are the **levels** of the factor. Levels of a factor are analogous to the categories of a categorical variable, but you call in-store location a *factor* and not a categorical variable because the variable under study is mobile electronics sales. Levels provide the basis of comparison by dividing the variable under study into **groups**. In the Arlingtons scenario, the groups are the stores selling the mobile electronics items in the mobile electronics aisle, the stores selling those items at the special front location, the stores selling those items at the endcap location, and the stores selling those items at the expert counter.

When performing ANOVA analysis, among the types of experiments that can be conducted are:

- Completely randomized design: An experiment with only one factor.
- Factorial design: An experiment in which more than one factor is considered. This chapter discusses two-way ANOVA that involves two factors as an example of this type of design. (Arlingtons considering the effects of allowing mobile payments while also experimenting with in-store location would be an example of a factorial design.)
- Randomized block design: An experiment in which the members of each group have been placed in blocks either by being matched or subjected to repeated measurements as was done with the two populations of a paired *t* test (see online Section 11.3).

Determining the type of design and the factor or factors the design uses becomes an additional step in the Define task of the DCOVA framework when performing ANOVA analysis.

While ANOVA literally does analyze variation, the purpose of ANOVA is to reach conclusions about possible differences among the *means* of each group, analogous to the hypothesis tests of the previous chapter. Every ANOVA design uses samples that represent each group and subdivides the total variation observed across all samples (all groups) toward the goal of analyzing possible differences among the means of each group. How this subdivision, called *partitioning*, works is a function of the design being used, but total variation, represented by the quantity **sum of squares total (SST)**, will always be the starting point. As with other statistical methods, ANOVA requires making assumptions about the populations that the groups represent. While these assumptions are discussed on page 356 as part of Section 11.1, the assumptions apply for all of the ANOVA methods discussed in this chapter.

studentTIP

ANOVA is also related to regression, a topic discussed later in this book. Because of ANOVA's special relationship with both hypothesis testing and regression, understanding the foundational concepts of ANOVA will prove very helpful in understanding other types of analysis presented in Chapters 13 through 17.

11.1 The Completely Randomized Design: One-Way ANOVA

The **completely randomized design** is the ANOVA method that analyzes a single factor. You execute this design using the statistical method **one-way ANOVA**. One-way ANOVA is a two-part process. You first determine if there is a significant difference among the group means. If you reject the null hypothesis that there is no difference among the means, you continue with a second method that seeks to identify the groups whose means are significantly different from the other group means.

Analyzing Variation in One-Way ANOVA

In one-way ANOVA, to analyze variation towards the goal of determining possible difference among the group means, you partition the total variation into variation that is due to difference among the groups and variation that is due to differences within the groups (see Figure 11.1). The **within-group variation (SSW)** measures random variation. The **among-group variation (SSA)** measures differences from group to group. The symbol n represents the number of values in all groups and the symbol c represents the number of groups.

FIGURE 11.1
Partitioning the total variation in a completely randomized design

Partitioning the Total Variation
$SST = SSA + SSW$

When using Excel, always organize multiple-sample data as unstacked data, one column per group. (See Section 1.4 for more information about unstacked data.)

Assuming that the c groups represent populations whose values are randomly and independently selected, follow a normal distribution, and have equal variances, the null hypothesis of no differences in the population means:

$$H_0: \mu_1 = \mu_2 = \cdots = \mu_c$$

is tested against the alternative that not all the c population means are equal:

$$H_1: \text{Not all } \mu_j \text{ are equal (where } j = 1, 2, \ldots, c\text{)}.$$

studentTIP

Another way of stating the alternative hypothesis, H_1, is that at least one population mean is different from the others.

To perform an ANOVA test of equality of population means, you subdivide the total variation in the values into two parts—that which is due to variation among the groups and that which is due to variation within the groups. The **total variation** is represented by the **sum of squares total (SST)**. Because the population means of the c groups are assumed to be equal under the null hypothesis, you compute the total variation among all the values by summing the squared differences between each individual value and the **grand mean, $\overline{\overline{X}}$**. The grand mean is the mean of all the values in all the groups combined. Equation (11.1) shows the computation of the total variation.

TOTAL VARIATION IN ONE-WAY ANOVA

$$SST = \sum_{j=1}^{c} \sum_{i=1}^{n_j} (X_{ij} - \overline{\overline{X}})^2 \qquad (11.1)$$

where

$$\overline{\overline{X}} = \frac{\sum_{j=1}^{c} \sum_{i=1}^{n_j} X_{ij}}{n} = \text{grand mean}$$

$X_{ij} = i$th value in group j

$n_j = $ number of values in group j

$n = $ total number of values in all groups combined
(that is, $n = n_1 + n_2 + \cdots + n_c$)

$c = $ number of groups

You compute the among-group variation, usually called the **sum of squares among groups (SSA)**, by summing the squared differences between the sample mean of each group, $\overline{X}_j$, and the grand mean, $\overline{\overline{X}}$, weighted by the sample size, n_j, in each group. Equation (11.2) shows the computation of the among-group variation.

AMONG-GROUP VARIATION IN ONE-WAY ANOVA

$$SSA = \sum_{j=1}^{c} n_j (\overline{X}_j - \overline{\overline{X}})^2 \qquad (11.2)$$

where

c = number of groups
n_j = number of values in group j
$\overline{X}_j$ = sample mean of group j
$\overline{\overline{X}}$ = grand mean

The within-group variation, usually called the **sum of squares within groups (SSW)**, measures the difference between each value and the mean of its own group and sums the squares of these differences over all groups. Equation (11.3) shows the computation of the within-group variation.

WITHIN-GROUP VARIATION IN ONE-WAY ANOVA

$$SSW = \sum_{j=1}^{c} \sum_{i=1}^{n_j} (X_{ij} - \overline{X}_j)^2 \qquad (11.3)$$

where

X_{ij} = ith value in group j
$\overline{X}_j$ = sample mean of group j

Because you are comparing c groups, there are $c - 1$ degrees of freedom associated with the sum of squares among groups. Because each of the c groups contributes $n_j - 1$ degrees of freedom, there are $n - c$ degrees of freedom associated with the sum of squares within groups. In addition, there are $n - 1$ degrees of freedom associated with the sum of squares total because you are comparing each value, X_{ij}, to the grand mean, $\overline{\overline{X}}$, based on all n values.

If you divide each of these sums of squares by its respective degrees of freedom, you have three variances, which in ANOVA are known as **mean squares**: MSA (mean square among), MSW (mean square within), and MST (mean square total).

MEAN SQUARES IN ONE-WAY ANOVA

$$MSA = \frac{SSA}{c - 1} \qquad (11.4a)$$

$$MSW = \frac{SSW}{n - c} \qquad (11.4b)$$

$$MST = \frac{SST}{n - 1} \qquad (11.4c)$$

F Test for Differences Among More Than Two Means

[1]As Section 10.4 discusses, the F distribution is right-skewed with a minimum valie of 0.

To determine if there is a significant difference among the group means, you use the F test for differences among more than two means.[1] If the null hypothesis is true and there are no differences among the c group means, MSA, MSW, and MST, will provide estimates of the overall variance in the population. Thus, to test the null hypothesis:

$$H_0: \mu_1 = \mu_2 = \cdots = \mu_c$$

against the alternative:

$$H_1: \text{Not all } \mu_j \text{ are equal (where } j = 1, 2, \ldots, c)$$

you compute the one-way ANOVA F_{STAT} test statistic as the ratio of MSA to MSW, as in Equation (11.5).

ONE-WAY ANOVA F_{STAT} TEST STATISTIC

$$F_{STAT} = \frac{MSA}{MSW} \tag{11.5}$$

The F_{STAT} test statistic follows an **F distribution**, with $c - 1$ degrees of freedom in the numerator and $n - c$ degrees of freedom in the denominator.

For a given level of significance, α, you reject the null hypothesis if the F_{STAT} test statistic computed in Equation (11.5) is greater than the upper-tail critical value, F_α, from the F distribution with $c - 1$ degrees of freedom in the numerator and $n - c$ in the denominator (see Table E.5). Thus, as shown in Figure 11.2, the decision rule is

$$\text{Reject } H_0 \text{ if } F_{STAT} > F_\alpha;$$

$$\text{otherwise, do not reject } H_0.$$

FIGURE 11.2
Regions of rejection and nonrejection when using ANOVA

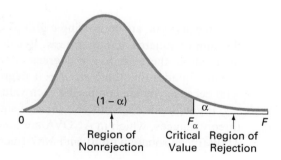

If the null hypothesis is true, the computed F_{STAT} test statistic is expected to be approximately equal to 1 because both the numerator and denominator mean square terms are estimating the overall variance in the population. If H_0 is false (and there are differences in the group means), the computed F_{STAT} test statistic is expected to be larger than 1 because the numerator, MSA, is estimating the differences among groups in addition to the overall variability in the values, while the denominator, MSW, is measuring only the overall variability in the values. Therefore, you reject the null hypothesis at a selected level of significance, α, only if the computed F_{STAT} test statistic is *greater than* F_α, the upper-tail critical value of the F distribution having $c - 1$ and $n - c$ degrees of freedom.

Table 11.1 presents the **ANOVA summary table** that is typically used to summarize the results of a one-way ANOVA. The table includes entries for the sources of variation (among groups, within groups, and total), the degrees of freedom, the sums of squares, the mean squares (the variances), and the computed F_{STAT} test statistic. The table may also include the *p*-value, the probability of having an F_{STAT} value as large as or larger than the one computed, given that the null hypothesis is true. The *p*-value allows you to reach conclusions about the null hypothesis without needing to refer to a table of critical values of the *F* distribution. If the *p*-value is less than the chosen level of significance, α, you reject the null hypothesis.

TABLE 11.1

ANOVA Summary Table

Source	Degrees of Freedom	Sum of Squares	Mean Square (Variance)	F
Among groups	$c - 1$	SSA	$MSA = \dfrac{SSA}{c - 1}$	$F_{STAT} = \dfrac{MSA}{MSW}$
Within groups	$n - c$	SSW	$MSW = \dfrac{SSW}{n - c}$	
Total	$n - 1$	SST		

To illustrate the one-way ANOVA *F* test, return to the Arlington's scenario (see page 348). You define the business problem as whether significant differences exist in the mobile electronics sales for the four different in-store locations, the four groups for the ANOVA analysis.

To test the comparative effectiveness of the four in-store locations, you conduct a 60-day experiment at 20 same-sized stores that have similar storewide net sales. You randomly assign five stores to use the current mobile electronics aisle (in-aisle), five stores to use the special front location (front), five stores to use the endcap location (endcap), and five stores to use the expert counter (expert). At the end of the experiment, you organize the mobile electronics sales data by group and store the data in unstacked format in Mobile Electronics . Figure 11.3 presents that unstacked data, along with the sample mean and the sample standard deviation for each group.

FIGURE 11.3

Mobile electronic sales ($000), sample means, and sample standard deviations for four different in-store locations

	In-aisle	Front	Kiosk	Expert
	30.06	32.22	30.78	30.33
	29.96	31.47	30.91	30.29
	30.19	32.13	30.79	30.25
	29.96	31.86	30.95	30.25
	29.74	32.29	31.13	30.55
Sample Mean	29.982	31.994	30.912	30.334
Sample Standard Deviation	0.165	0.335	0.143	0.125

Figure 11.3 shows differences among the sample means for the mobile electronics sales for the four in-store locations. For the original in-aisle location, mean sales were $29.982 thousands, whereas mean sales at the three new locations varied from $30.334 thousands ("expert" location) to $30.912 thousands ("endcap" location) to $31.994 thousands ("front" location).

Differences in the mobile electronic sales for the four in-store locations can also be presented visually. In Figure 11.4, the Excel scatter plot presents the mobile electronics sales at each store in each group, permitting you to observe differences *within* each location as well as among the four locations. (In this example, because the difference within each group is slight, the points for each group overlap and blur together.)

FIGURE 11.4
Excel scatter plot of
mobile electronics sales
for four in-store locations

*In the Excel scatter plot,
the locations in-aisle, front,
endcap, and expert were rela-
beled 1, 2, 3, and 4 in order
to use the scatter plot chart
type.*

If the sample sizes in
each group were larger,
you could construct
stem-and-leaf displays,
boxplots, and normal
probability plots as additional ways of visualizing
the sales data.

Having observed that the four sample means appear to be different, you use the F test for differences among more than two means to determine if these sample means are sufficiently different to conclude that the *population* means are not all equal. The null hypothesis states that there is no difference in the mean sales among the four in-store locations:

$$H_0: \mu_1 = \mu_2 = \mu_3 = \mu_4$$

The alternative hypothesis states that at least one of the in-store location mean sales differs from the other means:

$$H_1: \text{Not all the means are equal.}$$

To construct the ANOVA summary table, you first compute the sample means in each group (see Figure 11.3 on page 353). Then you compute the grand mean by summing all 20 values and dividing by the total number of values:

$$\overline{\overline{X}} = \frac{\displaystyle\sum_{j=1}^{c}\sum_{j=1}^{n_j} X_{ij}}{n} = \frac{616.12}{20} = 30.806$$

Then, using Equations (11.1) through (11.3) on pages 350–351, you compute the sum of squares:

$$SSA = \sum_{j=1}^{c} n_j (\overline{X}_j - \overline{\overline{X}})^2 = (5)(29.982 - 30.806)^2 + (5)(31.994 - 30.806)^2$$

$$+ (5)(30.912 - 30.806)^2 + (5)(30.334 - 30.806)^2$$

$$= 11.6217$$

$$SSW = \sum_{j=1}^{c}\sum_{i=1}^{n_j} (X_{ij} - \overline{X}_j)^2$$

$$= (30.06 - 29.982)^2 + \cdots + (29.74 - 29.982)^2 + (32.22 - 31.994)^2 + \cdots$$

$$+ (32.29 - 31.994)^2 + (30.78 - 30.912)^2 + \cdots + (31.13 - 30.912)^2$$

$$+ (30.33 - 30.334)^2 + \cdots + (30.55 - 30.334)^2$$

$$= 0.7026$$

$$SST = \sum_{j=1}^{c}\sum_{i=1}^{n_j} (X_{ij} - \overline{\overline{X}})^2$$

$$= (30.06 - 30.806)^2 + (29.96 - 30.806)^2 + \cdots + (30.55 - 30.806)^2$$

$$= 12.3243$$

You compute the mean squares by dividing the sum of squares by the corresponding degrees of freedom [see Equation (11.4) on page 351]. Because $c = 4$ and $n = 20$,

$$MSA = \frac{SSA}{c-1} = \frac{11.6217}{4-1} = 3.8739$$

$$MSW = \frac{SSW}{n-c} = \frac{0.7026}{20-4} = 0.0439$$

so that using Equation (11.5) on page 352,

$$F_{STAT} = \frac{MSA}{MSW} = \frac{3.8739}{0.0439} = 88.2186$$

Because you are trying to determine whether MSA is greater than MSW, you only reject H_0 if F_{STAT} is greater than the upper critical value of F. For a selected level of significance, α, you find the upper-tail critical value, F_α, from the F distribution using Table E.5. A portion of Table E.5 is presented in Table 11.2. In the in-store location sales experiment, there are 3 degrees of freedom in the numerator and 16 degrees of freedom in the denominator. F_α, the upper-tail critical value at the 0.05 level of significance, is 3.24.

TABLE 11.2
Finding the Critical Value of F with 3 and 16 Degrees of Freedom at the 0.05 Level of Significance

					Cumulative Probabilities $= 0.95$ Upper-Tail Area $= 0.05$ Numerator df_1				
Denominator df_2	**1**	**2**	**3**	**4**	**5**	**6**	**7**	**8**	**9**
⋮	⋮	⋮	⋮	⋮	⋮	⋮	⋮	⋮	⋮
11	4.84	3.98	3.59	3.36	3.20	3.09	3.01	2.95	2.90
12	4.75	3.89	3.49	3.26	3.11	3.00	2.91	2.85	2.80
13	4.67	3.81	3.41	3.18	3.03	2.92	2.83	2.77	2.71
14	4.60	3.74	3.34	3.11	2.96	2.85	2.76	2.70	2.65
15	4.54	3.68	3.29	3.06	2.90	2.79	2.71	2.64	2.59
16	4.49	3.63	3.24	3.01	2.85	2.74	2.66	2.59	2.54

Source: Extracted from Table E.5.

Because $F_{STAT} = 88.2186$ is greater than $F_\alpha = 3.24$, you reject the null hypothesis (see Figure 11.5). You conclude that there is a significant difference in the mean sales for the four in-store locations.

FIGURE 11.5
Regions of rejection and nonrejection for the one-way ANOVA at the 0.05 level of significance, with 3 and 16 degrees of freedom

Figure 11.6 shows the ANOVA results for the in-store location sales experiment, including the p-value. In Figure 11.6, what Table 11.1 (see page 353) labels Among Groups is labeled Between Groups in the Excel worksheet.

FIGURE 11.6

Excel ANOVA results for the in-store location sales experiment

	A	B	C	D	E	F	G
1	One-Way ANOVA (ANOVA: Single Factor)						
2							
3	SUMMARY						
4	*Groups*	*Count*	*Sum*	*Average*	*Variance*		
5	In-aisle	5	149.91	29.982	0.02722		
6	Front	5	159.97	31.994	0.11243		
7	Endcap	5	154.56	30.912	0.02032		
8	Expert	5	151.67	30.334	0.01568		
9							
10							
11	ANOVA						
12	*Source of Variation*	*SS*	*df*	*MS*	*F*	*P-value*	*F crit*
13	Between Groups	11.6217	3	3.8739	88.2186	0.0000	3.2389
14	Within Groups	0.7026	16	0.0439			
15							
16	Total	12.3243	19				
17						*Level of significance*	0.05

In the Worksheet

The worksheet uses the DEVSQ function (see Appendix F) to compute the sum of squares in cells B13 and B16. The worksheet uses the F.DIST.RT function to compute the *p*-value in cell F13 and the F.INV.RT function to compute the *F* test statistic in cell G13.

The *p*-value, or probability of getting a computed F_{STAT} statistic of 88.2186 or larger when the null hypothesis is true, is 0.0000. Because this *p*-value is less than the specified α of 0.05, you reject the null hypothesis. The *p*-value of 0.0000 indicates that there is a 0.00% chance of observing differences this large or larger if the population means for the four in-store locations are all equal. After performing the one-way ANOVA and finding a significant difference among the in-store locations, you still do not know *which* in-store locations differ. All you know is that there is sufficient evidence to state that the population means are not all the same. In other words, one or more population means are significantly different. To determine which in-store locations differ, you can use a multiple comparisons procedure such as the Tukey-Kramer procedure discussed on page 358.

One-Way ANOVA *F* Test Assumptions

To use the one-way ANOVA *F* test, you must make three assumptions about your data:

- **Randomness and independence** of the samples selected
- **Normality** of the *c* groups from which the samples are selected
- **Homogeneity of variance** (the variances of the *c* groups are equal)

studentTIP

To use the one-way ANOVA *F* test, the variable to be analyzed must either be interval or ratio scaled.

Most critical of all is the first assumption. The validity of any experiment depends on random sampling and/or the randomization process. To avoid biases in the outcomes, you need to select random samples from the *c* groups or use the randomization process to randomly assign the items to the *c* levels of the factor. Selecting a random sample or randomly assigning the levels ensures that a value from one group is independent of any other value in the experiment. Departures from this assumption can seriously affect inferences from the ANOVA. These problems are discussed more thoroughly in references 5 and 8.

As for the second assumption, **normality**, the one-way ANOVA *F* test is fairly robust against departures from the normal distribution. As long as the distributions are not extremely different from a normal distribution, the level of significance of the ANOVA *F* test is usually not greatly affected, particularly for large samples. You can assess the normality of each of the *c* samples by constructing a normal probability plot or a boxplot.

As for the third assumption, **homogeneity of variance**, if you have equal sample sizes in each group, inferences based on the *F* distribution are not seriously affected by unequal variances. However, if you have unequal sample sizes, unequal variances can have a serious effect on inferences from the ANOVA procedure. Thus, when possible, you should have equal sample sizes in all groups. You can use the Levene test for homogeneity of variance discussed on page 357, to test whether the variances of the *c* groups are equal.

When only the normality assumption is violated, you can use the Kruskal-Wallis rank test, a nonparametric procedure (see Section 12.5). When only the homogeneity-of-variance assumption is violated, you can use procedures similar to those used in the separate-variance test of Section 10.1 (see references 1 and 2). When both the normality and homogeneity-of-variance assumptions have been violated, you need to use an appropriate data transformation that both normalizes the data and reduces the differences in variances (see reference 6) or use a more general nonparametric procedure (see references 2 and 3).

Levene Test for Homogeneity of Variance

Although the one-way ANOVA F test is relatively robust with respect to the assumption of equal group variances, large differences in the group variances can seriously affect the level of significance and the power of the F test. One powerful yet simple procedure for testing the equality of the variances is the modified **Levene test** (see references 1 and 7). To test for the homogeneity of variance, you use the following null hypothesis:

$$H_0: \sigma_1^2 = \sigma_2^2 = \cdots = \sigma_c^2$$

studentTIP

Remember when performing the Levene test that you are conducting a one-way ANOVA on the absolute differences from the median in each group, not on the actual values themselves.

against the alternative hypothesis:

$$H_1: \text{Not all } \sigma_j^2 \text{ are equal}(j = 1, 2, 3, \ldots, c)$$

To test the null hypothesis of equal variances, you first compute the absolute value of the difference between each value and the median of the group. Then you perform a one-way ANOVA on these *absolute differences*. Most statisticians suggest using a level of significance of $\alpha = 0.05$ when performing the ANOVA. To illustrate the modified Levene test, return to the Figure 11.6 data and summary statistics on page 356 for the in-store location sales experiment. Table 11.3 summarizes the absolute differences from the median of each location.

TABLE 11.3
Absolute Differences from the Median Sales for Four Locations

In-Aisle (Median = 29.96)	Front (Median = 32.13)	Endcap (Median = 30.91)	Expert (Median = 30.29)
$\|30.06 - 29.96\| = 0.10$	$\|32.22 - 32.13\| = 0.09$	$\|30.78 - 30.91\| = 0.13$	$\|30.33 - 30.29\| = 0.04$
$\|29.96 - 29.96\| = 0.00$	$\|31.47 - 32.13\| = 0.66$	$\|30.91 - 30.91\| = 0.00$	$\|30.29 - 30.29\| = 0.00$
$\|30.19 - 29.96\| = 0.23$	$\|32.13 - 32.13\| = 0.00$	$\|30.79 - 30.91\| = 0.12$	$\|30.25 - 30.29\| = 0.04$
$\|29.96 - 29.96\| = 0.00$	$\|31.86 - 32.13\| = 0.27$	$\|30.95 - 30.91\| = 0.04$	$\|30.25 - 30.29\| = 0.04$
$\|29.74 - 29.96\| = 0.22$	$\|32.29 - 32.13\| = 0.16$	$\|31.13 - 30.91\| = 0.22$	$\|30.55 - 30.29\| = 0.26$

Using the absolute differences given in Table 11.3, you perform a one-way ANOVA shown in Figure 11.7 below. From those results, observe that $F_{STAT} = 1.0556$. (The Excel worksheet labels this value F.) Because $F_{STAT} = 1.0556 < 3.2389$ (or the p − value = 0.3953 > 0.05), you do not reject H_0. There is insufficient evidence of a significant difference among the four variances. In other words, it is reasonable to assume that the four in-store locations have an equal amount of variability in sales. Therefore, the homogeneity-of-variance assumption for the ANOVA procedure is justified.

FIGURE 11.7
Excel Levene test results for the absolute differences for the in-store location sales experiment

In the Worksheet

The Levene test shares the same COMPUTE worksheet template shown in Figure 11.6.

studentTIP

You have an α level of risk in the entire set of comparisons not just a single comparison.

Multiple Comparisons: The Tukey-Kramer Procedure

In the Arlingtons scenario on page 348, you used the one-way ANOVA F test to determine that there was a difference among the in-store locations. The next step is to construct **multiple comparisons** to test the null hypothesis that the differences in the means of all pairs of in-store locations are equal to 0.

Although many procedures are available (see references 5, 6, and 8), this text uses the **Tukey-Kramer multiple comparisons procedure for one-way ANOVA** to determine which of the c means are significantly different. This procedure enables you to simultaneously make comparisons between *all* pairs of groups. The procedure consists of the following four steps:

1. Compute the absolute mean differences, $|\overline{X}_j - \overline{X}_{j'}|$ (where j refers to group j, j' refers to group j', and $j \neq j'$), among all pairs of sample means [$c(c-1)/2$ pairs].
2. Compute the **critical range** for the Tukey-Kramer procedure, using Equation (11.6). If the sample sizes differ, compute a critical range for each pairwise comparison of sample means.

CRITICAL RANGE FOR THE TUKEY-KRAMER PROCEDURE

$$\text{Critical range} = Q_\alpha \sqrt{\frac{MSW}{2}\left(\frac{1}{n_j} + \frac{1}{n_{j'}}\right)} \tag{11.6}$$

where

n_j = the sample size in group j

$n_{j'}$ = the sample size in group j'

Q_α = the upper-tail critical value from a **Studentized range distribution** having c degrees of freedom in the numerator and $n - c$ degrees of freedom in the denominator.

studentTIP

Table E.7 contains the critical values for the Studentized range distribution.

3. Compare each of the $c(c-1)/2$ pairs of means against its corresponding critical range. Declare a specific pair significantly different if the absolute difference in the sample means, $|\overline{X}_j - \overline{X}_{j'}|$, is greater than the critical range.
4. Interpret the results.

In the mobile electronics sales example, there are four in-store locations. Thus, there are $4(4-1)/2 = 6$ pairwise comparisons. To apply the Tukey-Kramer multiple comparisons procedure, you first compute the absolute mean differences for all six pairwise comparisons:

1. $|\overline{X}_1 - \overline{X}_2| = |29.982 - 31.994| = 2.012$
2. $|\overline{X}_1 - \overline{X}_3| = |29.982 - 30.912| = 0.930$
3. $|\overline{X}_1 - \overline{X}_4| = |29.982 - 30.334| = 0.352$
4. $|\overline{X}_2 - \overline{X}_3| = |31.994 - 30.912| = 1.082$
5. $|\overline{X}_2 - \overline{X}_4| = |31.994 - 30.334| = 1.660$
6. $|\overline{X}_3 - \overline{X}_4| = |30.912 - 30.334| = 0.578$

You then compute only one critical range because the sample sizes in the four groups are equal. (Had the sample sizes in some of the groups been different, you would compute several critical ranges.) From the ANOVA summary table (Figure 11.6 on page 356), $MSW = 0.0439$ and $n_j = n_{j'} = 5$. From Table E.7, for $\alpha = 0.05$, $c = 4$, and $n - c = 20 - 4 = 16$, Q_α, the upper-tail critical value of the test statistic, is 4.05 (see Table 11.4).

TABLE 11.4

Finding the Studentized Range, Q_α, Statistic for $\alpha = 0.05$, with 4 and 16 Degrees of Freedom

	Cumulative Probabilities = 0.95 Upper-Tail Area = 0.05 Numerator df_1							
Denominator df_2	**2**	**3**	**4**	**5**	**6**	**7**	**8**	**9**
⋮	⋮	⋮	⋮	⋮	⋮	⋮	⋮	⋮
11	3.11	3.82	4.26	4.57	4.82	5.03	5.20	5.35
12	3.08	3.77	4.20	4.51	4.75	4.95	5.12	5.27
13	3.06	3.73	4.15	4.45	4.69	4.88	5.05	5.19
14	3.03	3.70	4.11	4.41	4.64	4.83	4.99	5.13
15	3.01	3.67	4.08	4.37	4.60	4.78	4.94	5.08
16	3.00	3.65	4.05	4.33	4.56	4.74	4.90	5.03

Source: Extracted from Table E.7.

From Equation (11.6),

$$\text{Critical range} = 4.05\sqrt{\left(\frac{0.0439}{2}\right)\left(\frac{1}{5}+\frac{1}{5}\right)} = 0.3795$$

Because the absolute mean difference for five pairs (1, 2, 4, 5, and 6) is greater than 0.3795, you can conclude that there is a significant difference between the mobile electronic sales means of those pairs. Because the absolute mean difference for pair 3 (in-aisle and expert locations) is 0.352, which is less than 0.3795, you conclude that there is no evidence of a difference in the means of those two locations. These results allow you to estimate that the population mean sales for mobile electronics items will be higher at the front location than any other location *and* that the population mean sales for mobile electronics items at endcap locations will be higher when compared to either the in-aisle or expert locations. As a member of Arlingtons management team, you conclude that selling mobile electronics items at the special front location would increase sales the most, but that selling those items at the endcap location would also improve sales. (These results also present additional evidence for charging a placement fee for the special front location, the subject of the Chapter 10 Using Statistics scenario.)

The formulas in the Excel results worksheet are not shown in Figure 11.6 but are discussed in Section EG11.1 and the Short Takes for Chapter 11.

Figure 11.8 presents the Excel results for the Tukey-Kramer procedure for the mobile electronics sales in-store location experiment. Note that by using $\alpha = 0.05$, you are able to make all six of the comparisons with an overall error rate of only 5%.

FIGURE 11.8

Excel Tukey-Kramer procedure results for the in-store location sales experiment

	A	B	C	D	E	F	G	H	I
1	Tukey Kramer Multiple Comparisons								
2									
3		Sample	Sample			Absolute	Std. Error	Critical	
4	Group	Mean	Size		Comparison	Difference	of Difference	Range	Results
5	1: In-aisle	29.982	5		Group 1 to Group 2	2.012	0.0937	0.3795	Means are different
6	2: Front	31.994	5		Group 1 to Group 3	0.93	0.0937	0.3795	Means are different
7	3: Endcap	30.912	5		Group 1 to Group 4	0.352	0.0937	0.3795	Means are not different
8	4: Expert	30.334	5		Group 2 to Group 3	1.082	0.0937	0.3795	Means are different
9					Group 2 to Group 4	1.66	0.0937	0.3795	Means are different
10	Other Data				Group 3 to Group 4	0.578	0.0937	0.3795	Means are different
11	Level of significance	0.05							
12	Numerator d.f.	4							
13	Denominator d.f.	16							
14	MSW	0.043913							
15	Q Statistic	4.05							

In the Worksheet

This worksheet transfers many values calculated in a one-way ANOVA worksheet template shown in Figure 11.6 and uses an IF function to determine which message is displayed in column I.

Example 11.1 illustrates another example of the one-way ANOVA.

EXAMPLE 11.1

ANOVA of the Speed of Drive-Through Service at Fast-Food Chains

For fast-food restaurants, the drive-through window is an important revenue source. The chain that offers the fastest service is likely to attract additional customers. Each year *QSR Magazine*, **www.qsrmagazine.com**, publishes its results of a survey of drive-through service times (from menu board to departure) at fast-food chains. In a recent year, the mean time was 133.83 seconds for Wendy's, 158.03 seconds for Taco Bell, 198.48 seconds for Burger King, 189.49 seconds for McDonald's, and 203.88 seconds for Chick-fil-A. Suppose the study was based on 20 customers for each fast-food chain. At the 0.05 level of significance, is there evidence of a difference in the mean drive-through service times of the five chains?

Table 11.5 contains the ANOVA table for this problem.

TABLE 11.5
ANOVA Summary Table of Drive-Through Service Times at Fast-Food Chains

Source	Degrees of Freedom	Sum of Squares	Mean Squares	F	p-value
Among chains	4	53,282.384	13,320.596	101.9954	0.0000
Within chains	95	12,407.00	130.60		

SOLUTION

$H_0: \mu_1 = \mu_2 = \mu_3 = \mu_4 = \mu_5$ where 1 = Wendy's, 2 = Taco Bell, 3 = Burger King, 4 = McDonald's, 5 = Chick-fil-A

H_1: Not all μ_j are equal   where $j = 1, 2, 3, 4, 5$

Decision rule: If the *p*-value < 0.05, reject H_0. Because the *p*-value is 0.0000, which is less than $\alpha = 0.05$, reject H_0. You have sufficient evidence to conclude that the mean drive-through times of the five chains are not all equal.

To determine which of the means are significantly different from one another, use the Tukey-Kramer procedure [Equation (11.6) on page 358] to establish the critical range:

Critical value of *Q* with 5 and 95 degrees of freedom ≈ 3.92

$$\text{Critical range} = Q_\alpha \sqrt{\left(\frac{MSW}{2}\right)\left(\frac{1}{n_j} + \frac{1}{n_{j'}}\right)} = (3.92)\sqrt{\left(\frac{130.6}{2}\right)\left(\frac{1}{20} + \frac{1}{20}\right)}$$

$$= 10.02$$

Any observed difference greater than 10.02 is considered significant. The mean drive-through service times are different between Wendy's (mean of 133.83 seconds) and Taco Bell, Burger King, McDonald's, and Chick-fil-A and also between Taco Bell (mean of 158.03) and Burger King, McDonald's, and Chick-fil-A. In addition, the mean drive-through service time is different between McDonald's and Chick-fil-A. Thus, with 95% confidence, you can conclude that the estimated population mean drive-through service time is faster for Wendy's than for Taco Bell. In addition, the population mean service time for Wendy's and for Taco Bell is faster than those of Burger King, McDonald's, and Chick-fil-A. Also, the population mean drive-through service time for McDonald's is faster than for Chick-Fil-A.

The Analysis of Means (ANOM)

The analysis of means (ANOM) provides an alternative approach that allows you to determine which, if any, of the *c* groups has a mean significantly different from the overall mean of all the group means combined. The **ANOM online topic** explains this alternative approach and illustrates its use.

PROBLEMS FOR SECTION 11.1

LEARNING THE BASICS

11.1 An experiment has a single factor with five groups and seven values in each group.
a. How many degrees of freedom are there in determining the among-group variation?
b. How many degrees of freedom are there in determining the within-group variation?
c. How many degrees of freedom are there in determining the total variation?

11.2 You are working with the same experiment as in Problem 11.1.
a. If $SSA = 60$ and $SST = 210$, what is SSW?
b. What is MSA?
c. What is MSW?
d. What is the value of F_{STAT}?

11.3 You are working with the same experiment as in Problems 11.1 and 11.2.
a. Construct the ANOVA summary table and fill in all values in the table.
b. At the 0.05 level of significance, what is the upper-tail critical value from the F distribution?
c. State the decision rule for testing the null hypothesis that all five groups have equal population means.
d. What is your statistical decision?

11.4 Consider an experiment with three groups, with seven values in each.
a. How many degrees of freedom are there in determining the among-group variation?
b. How many degrees of freedom are there in determining the within-group variation?
c. How many degrees of freedom are there in determining the total variation?

11.5 Consider an experiment with four groups, with eight values in each. For the ANOVA summary table below, fill in all the missing results:

Source	Degrees of Freedom	Sum of Squares	Mean Square (Variance)	F
Among groups	$c - 1 = ?$	$SSA = ?$	$MSA = 80$	$F_{STAT} = ?$
Within groups	$n - c = ?$	$SSW = 560$	$MSW = ?$	
Total	$n - 1 = ?$	$SST = ?$		

11.6 You are working with the same experiment as in Problem 11.5.
a. At the 0.05 level of significance, state the decision rule for testing the null hypothesis that all four groups have equal population means.
b. What is your statistical decision?
c. At the 0.05 level of significance, what is the upper-tail critical value from the Studentized range distribution?
d. To perform the Tukey-Kramer procedure, what is the critical range?

APPLYING THE CONCEPTS

11.7 *Accounting Today* identified the top accounting firms in 10 geographic regions across the United States. Even though all 10 regions reported growth in 2014, the Capital, Great Lakes, Mid-Atlantic, and New England regions reported combined growths of 6.22%, 9.75%, 7.28%, and 6.84%, respectively. A characteristic description of the accounting firms in the Capital, Great Lakes, Mid-Atlantic, and New England regions included the number of partners in the firm.
The file AccountingPartners4 contains the number of partners. (Data extracted from *2015 Top 100 Firms*, **bit.ly/1BoMzsv**.)
a. At the 0.05 level of significance, is there evidence of a difference among the Capital, Great Lakes, Mid-Atlantic, and New England region accounting firms with respect to the mean number of partners?
b. If the results in (a) indicate that it is appropriate to do so, use the Tukey-Kramer procedure to determine which regions differ in the mean number of partners. Discuss your findings.

✓SELF TEST **11.8** The more costly and time consuming it is to export and import, the more difficult it is for local companies to be competitive and to reach international markets. As part of an initial investigation exploring foreign market entry, 10 countries were selected from each of four global regions. The cost associated with importing a standardized cargo of goods by sea transport in these countries (in US$ per container) is stored in ForeignMarket2 . (Data extracted from **doingbusiness.org/data**.)
a. At the 0.05 level of significance, is there evidence of a difference in the mean cost of importing across the four global regions?
b. If appropriate, determine which global regions differ in mean cost of importing.
c. At the 0.05 level of significance, is there evidence of a difference in the variation in cost of importing among the four global regions?
d. Which global region(s) should you consider for foreign market entry? Explain.

11.9 A hospital conducted a study of the waiting time in its emergency room. The hospital has a main campus and three satellite locations. Management had a business objective of reducing waiting time for emergency room cases that did not require immediate attention. To study this, a random sample of 15 emergency room cases that did not require immediate attention at each location were selected on a particular day, and the waiting times (measured from check-in to when the patient was called into the clinic area) were collected and stored in ERWaiting .
a. At the 0.05 level of significance, is there evidence of a difference in the mean waiting times in the four locations?
b. If appropriate, determine which locations differ in mean waiting time.
c. At the 0.05 level of significance, is there evidence of a difference in the variation in waiting time among the four locations?

11.10 A manufacturer of pens has hired an advertising agency to develop an advertising campaign for the upcoming holiday season. To prepare for this project, the research director decides to initiate a study of the effect of advertising on product perception. An experiment is designed to compare five different advertisements. Advertisement *A* greatly undersells the pen's characteristics. Advertisement *B* slightly undersells the pen's characteristics. Advertisement *C* slightly oversells the pen's characteristics. Advertisement *D* greatly oversells the pen's characteristics. Advertisement *E* attempts to correctly state the pen's characteristics. A sample of 30 adult respondents, taken from a larger focus group, is randomly assigned to the five advertisements (so that there are 6 respondents to each advertisement). After reading the advertisement and developing a sense of "product expectation," all respondents unknowingly receive the same pen to evaluate. The respondents are permitted to test the pen and the plausibility of the advertising copy. The respondents are then asked to rate the pen from 1 to 7 (lowest to highest) on the product characteristic scales of appearance, durability, and writing performance. The *combined* scores of three ratings (appearance, durability, and writing performance) for the 30 respondents, stored in Pen , are as follows:

A	B	C	D	E
15	16	8	5	12
18	17	7	6	19
17	21	10	13	18
19	16	15	11	12
19	19	14	9	17
20	17	14	10	14

a. At the 0.05 level of significance, is there evidence of a difference in the mean rating of the pens following exposure to five advertisements?
b. If appropriate, determine which advertisements differ in mean ratings.
c. At the 0.05 level of significance, is there evidence of a difference in the variation in ratings among the five advertisements?
d. Which advertisement(s) should you use, and which advertisement(s) should you avoid? Explain.

11.11 *QSR* reports on the largest quick-serve and fast-casual brands in the United States. The file FastFoodChain contains the food segment (burger, chicken, pizza, or sandwich) and U.S. mean sales per unit ($ thousands) for each of 38 quick-service brands. (Data extracted from **bit.ly/16GJlEn.**)
a. At the 0.05 level of significance, is there evidence of a difference in the mean U.S. mean sales per unit ($ thousands) among the food segments?
b. At the 0.05 level of significance, is there a difference in the variation in U.S. average sales per unit ($ thousands) among the food segments?
c. What effect does your result in (b) have on the validity of the results in (a)?
d. If appropriate, determine which food segments differ in mean sales.

11.12 Researchers conducted a study to investigate the impact of resilience and key demographics on the transformational leadership behaviors demonstrated by frontline sales professionals.

The Leadership Practices Inventory (LPI) was used to assess transformational leadership; LPI scores range as high as 300, with 300 representing exemplary leadership. The initial analysis focused on the impact of education on transformational leadership. The researchers found the following:

Source	Degrees of Freedom	Sum of Squares	Mean Squares	F
Among groups	4	13,918.573		
Within groups	179	284,671.467		
Total	183	298,590.040		

Group	N	Mean
High School Degree	72	218.5689
Associate's/Technical Degree	44	216.8864
4-year College Degree	59	224.1559
Master's Degree	6	257.2250
Advanced Degree	3	183.0000

Source: Data Extracted from M. H. Sylvester, "The Impact of Resilience to Change on the Transformational Leadership Behaviors Demonstrated by Frontline Sales Professionals," *Journal of Management Research*, Vol. 7, No. 1 (2015): 107–129.

a. Complete the ANOVA summary table.
b. At the 0.05 level of significance, is there evidence of a difference in the mean LPI score across education levels?
c. If the results in (b) indicate that it is appropriate, use the Tukey-Kramer procedure to determine which groups differ in mean LPI score. Discuss your findings.

11.13 A pet food company has a business objective of expanding its product line beyond its current kidney and shrimp-based cat foods. The company developed two new products, one based on chicken liver and the other based on salmon. The company conducted an experiment to compare the two new products with its two existing ones, as well as a generic beef-based product sold at a supermarket chain.

For the experiment, a sample of 50 cats from the population at a local animal shelter was selected. Ten cats were randomly assigned to each of the five products being tested. Each of the cats was then presented with 3 ounces of the selected food in a dish at feeding time. The researchers defined the variable to be measured as the number of ounces of food that the cat consumed within a 10-minute time interval that began when the filled dish was presented. The results for this experiment are summarized in the table on page 363 and stored in CatFood .
a. At the 0.05 level of significance, is there evidence of a difference in the mean amount of food eaten among the various products?
b. If appropriate, determine which products appear to differ significantly in the mean amount of food eaten.
c. At the 0.05 level of significance, is there evidence of a difference in the variation in the amount of food eaten among the various products?
d. What should the pet food company conclude? Fully describe the pet food company's options with respect to the products.

Kidney	Shrimp	Chicken Liver	Salmon	Beef
2.37	2.26	2.29	1.79	2.09
2.62	2.69	2.23	2.33	1.87
2.31	2.25	2.41	1.96	1.67
2.47	2.45	2.68	2.05	1.64
2.59	2.34	2.25	2.26	2.16
2.62	2.37	2.17	2.24	1.75
2.34	2.22	2.37	1.96	1.18
2.47	2.56	2.26	1.58	1.92
2.45	2.36	2.45	2.18	1.32
2.32	2.59	2.57	1.93	1.94

11.14 A transportation strategist wanted to compare the traffic congestion levels across three continents: Asia, Europe, and North America. The file `CongestionLevel` contains congestion level, defined as the increase (%) in overall travel time when compared to a free flow situation (an uncongested situation) for 30 cities in each continent. (Data extracted from "TomTom Traffic Index," **bit.ly/1GNRRk1**.)

a. At the 0.05 level of significance, is there evidence of a difference in the mean congestion level across continents?

b. If the results in (a) indicate that it is appropriate to do so, use the Tukey-Kramer procedure to determine which continents differ in congestion level

c. What assumptions are necessary in (a)?

d. At the 0.05 level of significance, is there evidence of a difference in the variation of the congestion level across continents?

11.2 The Factorial Design: Two-Way ANOVA

In Section 11.1, you learned about the completely randomized design. In this section, the single-factor completely randomized design is extended to the **two-factor factorial design**, in which two factors are simultaneously evaluated. Each factor is evaluated at two or more levels. For example, in the Arlingtons scenario on page 348, the company faces the business problem of simultaneously evaluating four locations and the effectiveness of providing mobile payment to determine which location should be used and whether mobile payment should be made available. Although this section uses only two factors, you can extend factorial designs to three or more factors (see references 4, 5, 7, and 8).

To analyze data from a two-factor factorial design, you use **two-way ANOVA**. The following definitions are needed to develop the two-way ANOVA procedure:

r = number of levels of factor A

c = number of levels of factor B

n' = number of values (replicates) for each cell (combination of a particular level of factor A and a particular level of factor B)

n = number of values in the entire experiment (where $n = rcn'$)

X_{ijk} = value of the kth observation for level i of factor A and level j of factor B

$$\bar{\bar{X}} = \frac{\sum_{i=1}^{r}\sum_{j=1}^{c}\sum_{k=1}^{n'}X_{ijk}}{rcn'} = \text{grand mean}$$

$$\bar{X}_{i..} = \frac{\sum_{j=1}^{c}\sum_{k=1}^{n'}X_{ijk}}{cn'} = \text{mean of the } i\text{th level of factor } A \text{ (where } i = 1, 2, \ldots, r)$$

$$\bar{X}_{.j.} = \frac{\sum_{i=1}^{r}\sum_{k=1}^{n'}X_{ijk}}{rn'} = \text{mean of the } j\text{th level of factor } B \text{ (where } i = 1, 2, \ldots, c)$$

$$\bar{X}_{ij.} = \frac{\sum_{k=1}^{n'}X_{ijk}}{n'} = \text{mean of the cell } ij, \text{ the combination of the } i\text{th level of factor } A \text{ and the } j\text{th level of factor } B$$

Because of the complexity of these computations, you should only use computerized methods when performing this analysis. However, to help explain the two-way ANOVA, the decomposition of the total variation is illustrated. In this discussion, only cases in which there are an equal number of values (also called **replicates**) (sample sizes n') for each combination of the levels of factor A with those of factor B are considered. (See references 1, 6, and 8 for a discussion of two-factor factorial designs with unequal sample sizes.)

Factor and Interaction Effects

There is an **interaction** between factors A and B if the effect of factor A is different for various levels of factor B. Thus, when dividing the total variation into different sources of variation, you need to account for a possible interaction effect, as well as for factor A, factor B, and random variation. To accomplish this, the total variation (SST) is subdivided into sum of squares due to factor A (or SSA), sum of squares due to factor B (or SSB), sum of squares due to the interaction effect of A and B (or $SSAB$), and sum of squares due to random variation (or SSE). This decomposition of the total variation (SST) is displayed in Figure 11.9.

FIGURE 11.9
Partitioning the total variation in a two-factor factorial design

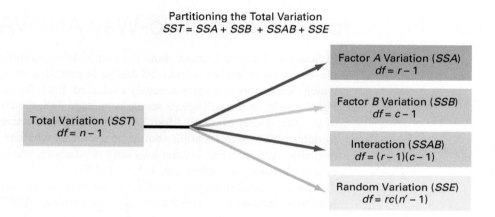

Partitioning the Total Variation
$SST = SSA + SSB + SSAB + SSE$

Total Variation (SST)
$df = n - 1$

Factor A Variation (SSA)
$df = r - 1$

Factor B Variation (SSB)
$df = c - 1$

Interaction ($SSAB$)
$df = (r - 1)(c - 1)$

Random Variation (SSE)
$df = rc(n' - 1)$

The sum of squares total (SST) represents the total variation among all the values around the grand mean. Equation (11.7) shows the computation for total variation.

TOTAL VARIATION IN TWO-WAY ANOVA

$$SST = \sum_{i=1}^{r} \sum_{j=1}^{c} \sum_{k=1}^{n'} (X_{ijk} - \overline{\overline{X}})^2 \qquad (11.7)$$

The **sum of squares due to factor A (SSA)** represents the differences among the various levels of factor A and the grand mean. Equation (11.8) shows the computation for factor A variation.

FACTOR A VARIATION

$$SSA = cn' \sum_{i=1}^{r} (\overline{X}_{i..} - \overline{\overline{X}})^2 \qquad (11.8)$$

The **sum of squares due to factor B (SSB)** represents the differences among the various levels of factor B and the grand mean. Equation (11.9) shows the computation for factor B variation.

FACTOR B VARIATION

$$SSB = rn' \sum_{j=1}^{c} (\overline{X}_{.j.} - \overline{\overline{X}})^2 \tag{11.9}$$

The **sum of squares due to interaction (SSAB)** represents the interacting effect of specific combinations of factor A and factor B. Equation (11.10) shows the computation for interaction variation.

INTERACTION VARIATION

$$SSAB = n' \sum_{i=1}^{r} \sum_{j=1}^{c} (\overline{X}_{ij.} - \overline{X}_{i..} - \overline{X}_{.j.} + \overline{\overline{X}})^2 \tag{11.10}$$

The **sum of squares error (SSE)** represents random variation—that is, the differences among the values within each cell and the corresponding cell mean. Equation (11.11) shows the computation for random variation.

RANDOM VARIATION IN TWO-WAY ANOVA

$$SSE = \sum_{i=1}^{r} \sum_{j=1}^{c} \sum_{k=1}^{n'} (X_{ijk} - \overline{X}_{ij.})^2 \tag{11.11}$$

Because there are r levels of factor A, there are $r - 1$ degrees of freedom associated with *SSA*. Similarly, because there are c levels of factor B, there are $c - 1$ degrees of freedom associated with *SSB*. Because there are n' replicates in each of the rc cells, there are $rc(n' - 1)$ degrees of freedom associated with the *SSE* term. Carrying this further, there are $n - 1$ degrees of freedom associated with the sum of squares total (*SST*) because you are comparing each value, X_{ijk}, to the grand mean, $\overline{\overline{X}}$, based on all n values. Therefore, because the degrees of freedom for each of the sources of variation must add to the degrees of freedom for the total variation (*SST*), you can calculate the degrees of freedom for the interaction component (*SSAB*) by subtraction. The degrees of freedom for interaction are $(r - 1)(c - 1)$.

If you divide each sum of squares by its associated degrees of freedom, you have the four variances or mean square terms (*MSA*, *MSB*, *MSAB*, and *MSE*). Equations (11.12a–d) give the mean square terms needed for the two-way ANOVA table.

studentTIP

Remember, *mean square* is another term for *variance*.

MEAN SQUARES IN TWO-WAY ANOVA

$$MSA = \frac{SSA}{r - 1}$$

(11.12a)

$$MSB = \frac{SSB}{c - 1}$$

(11.12b)

$$MSAB = \frac{SSAB}{(r - 1)(c - 1)}$$

(11.12c)

$$MSE = \frac{SSE}{rc(n' - 1)}$$

(11.12d)

Testing for Factor and Interaction Effects

There are three different tests to perform in a two-way ANOVA:

- A test of the hypothesis of no difference due to factor A
- A test of the hypothesis of no difference due to factor B
- A test of the hypothesis of no interaction of factors A and B

To test the hypothesis of no difference due to factor A:

$$H_0: \mu_{1..} = \mu_{2..} = \cdots = \mu_{r..}$$

against the alternative:

$$H_1: \text{Not all } \mu_{i..} \text{ are equal}$$

you use the F_{STAT} test statistic in Equation (11.13).

F TEST FOR FACTOR A EFFECT

$$F_{STAT} = \frac{MSA}{MSE}$$

(11.13)

You reject the null hypothesis at the α level of significance if

$$F_{STAT} = \frac{MSA}{MSE} > F_\alpha$$

where F_α is the upper-tail critical value from an F distribution with $r - 1$ and $rc(n' - 1)$ degrees of freedom.

To test the hypothesis of no difference due to factor B:

$$H_0: \mu_{.1.} = \mu_{.2.} = \cdots = \mu_{.c.}$$

against the alternative:

$$H_1: \text{Not all } \mu_{.j.} \text{ are equal}$$

you use the F_{STAT} test statistic in Equation (11.14).

F TEST FOR FACTOR B EFFECT

$$F_{STAT} = \frac{MSB}{MSE}$$

(11.14)

You reject the null hypothesis at the α level of significance if

$$F_{STAT} = \frac{MSB}{MSE} > F_\alpha$$

where F_α is the upper-tail critical value from an F distribution with $c - 1$ and $rc(n' - 1)$ degrees of freedom.

To test the hypothesis of no interaction of factors A and B:

H_0: The interaction of A and B is equal to zero

against the alternative:

H_1: The interaction of A and B is not equal to zero

you use the F_{STAT} test statistic in Equation (11.15).

F TEST FOR INTERACTION EFFECT

$$F_{STAT} = \frac{MSAB}{MSE} \qquad\qquad (11.15)$$

---

studentTIP

In each of these *F* tests, the denominator of the F_{STAT} statistic is *MSE*.

You reject the null hypothesis at the α level of significance if

$$F_{STAT} = \frac{MSAB}{MSE} > F_\alpha$$

where F_α is the upper-tail critical value from an F distribution with $(r - 1)(c - 1)$ and $rc(n' - 1)$ degrees of freedom.

Table 11.6 presents the entire two-way ANOVA table.

TABLE 11.6
Analysis of Variance Table for the Two-Factor Factorial Design

Source	Degrees of Freedom	Sum of Squares	Mean Square (Variance)	F
A	$r - 1$	SSA	$MSA = \dfrac{SSA}{r-1}$	$F_{STAT} = \dfrac{MSA}{MSE}$
B	$c - 1$	SSB	$MSB = \dfrac{SSB}{c-1}$	$F_{STAT} = \dfrac{MSB}{MSE}$
AB	$(r-1)(c-1)$	SSAB	$MSAB = \dfrac{SSAB}{(r-1)(c-1)}$	$F_{STAT} = \dfrac{MSAB}{MSE}$
Error	$rc(n'-1)$	SSE	$MSE = \dfrac{SSE}{rc(n'-1)}$	
Total	$n - 1$	SST		

To illustrate two-way ANOVA, return to the Arlingtons scenario on page 348. As a member of the sales team, you first explored how different in-store locations might affect the sales of mobile electronics items using one-way ANOVA. Now, to explore the effects of permitting mobile payment methods to buy mobile electronics items, you design an experiment that examines this second (B) factor as it studies the effects of in-store location (factor A) using two-way ANOVA. Two-way ANOVA will allow you to determine if there is a significant difference in mobile electronics sales among the four in-store locations *and* whether permitting mobile payment methods makes a difference.

To test the effects of the two factors, you conduct a 60-day experiment at 40 same-sized stores that have similar storewide net sales. You randomly assign ten stores to use the current in-aisle location, ten stores to use the special front location, ten stores to use the endcap location, and ten stores to use the expert counter. In five stores in each of the four groups, you permit mobile payment methods (for the other five in each group, mobile payment methods are not permitted). At the end of the experiment, you organize the mobile electronics sales data by group and store the data in Mobile Electronics2. Table 11.7 presents the data of the experiment.

TABLE 11.7
Mobile Electronics Sales at Four In-Store Locations with Mobile Payments Permitted and Not Permitted

MOBILE PAYMENTS	IN-STORE LOCATION			
	In-Aisle	**Front**	**Endcap**	**Expert**
No	30.06	32.22	30.78	30.33
No	29.96	31.47	30.91	30.29
No	30.19	32.13	30.79	30.25
No	29.96	31.86	30.95	30.25
No	29.74	32.29	31.13	30.55
Yes	30.66	32.81	31.34	31.03
Yes	29.99	32.65	31.80	31.77
Yes	30.73	32.81	32.00	30.97
Yes	30.72	32.42	31.07	31.43
Yes	30.73	33.12	31.69	30.72

Figure 11.10 presents the results for this example. In this worksheet, the *A*, *B*, and Error sources of variation in Table 11.6 on page 367 are labeled Sample, Columns, and Within, respectively.

FIGURE 11.10
Excel two-way ANOVA results for the in-store location sales and mobile payment experiment

	A	B	C	D	E	F	G
1	ANOVA: Two-Factor With Replication						
2							
3	SUMMARY	In-aisle	Front	Kiosk	Expert	Total	
4	No						
5	Count	5	5	5	5	20	
6	Sum	149.91	159.97	154.56	151.67	616.11	
7	Average	29.982	31.994	30.912	30.334	30.8055	
8	Variance	0.0272	0.1124	0.0203	0.0157	0.6486	
9							
10	Yes						
11	Count	5	5	5	5	20	
12	Sum	152.83	163.81	157.9	155.92	630.46	
13	Average	30.566	32.762	31.58	31.184	31.5230	
14	Variance	0.1045	0.0656	0.1387	0.1722	0.7773	
15							
16	Total						
17	Count	10	10	10	10		
18	Sum	302.74	323.78	312.46	307.59		
19	Average	30.274	32.378	31.246	30.759		
20	Variance	0.1533	0.2430	0.1946	0.2842		
21							
22							
23	ANOVA						
24	Source of Variation	SS	df	MS	F	P-value	F crit
25	Sample	5.1481	1	5.1481	62.7258	0.0000	4.1491
26	Columns	24.3664	3	8.1221	98.9631	0.0000	2.9011
27	Interaction	0.1009	3	0.0336	0.4100	0.7469	2.9011
28	Within	2.6263	32	0.0821			
29							
30	Total	32.2418	39				
31						Level of significance	0.05

In the Worksheet

The worksheet uses the F.DIST.RT function to compute the *p*-values in cell range F25:F27 and the F.INV.RT function to compute the *F* test statistics in cell range G25:G27.

Table E.5 does not provide the upper-tail critical values from the F distribution with 32 degrees of freedom in the denominator. When the desired degrees of freedom are not provided in the table, use the p-value computed by Excel.

To interpret the results, you start by testing whether there is an interaction effect between factor A (mobile payments) and factor B (in-store locations). If the interaction effect is significant, further analysis will focus on this interaction. If the interaction effect is not significant, you can focus on the **main effects**—the potential effect of permitting mobile payment (factor A) and the potential differences in in-store locations (factor B).

Using the 0.05 level of significance, to determine whether there is evidence of an interaction effect, you reject the null hypothesis of no interaction between mobile payments and in-store locations if the computed F_{STAT} statistic is greater than 2.9011, the upper-tail critical value from the F distribution, with 3 and 32 degrees of freedom (see Figures 11.10 and 11.11).[2]

Because $F_{STAT} = 0.4100 < 2.9011$ or the p-value $= 0.7469 > 0.05$, you do not reject H_0. You conclude that there is insufficient evidence of an interaction effect between mobile payment and in-store location. You can now focus on the main effects.

FIGURE 11.11

Regions of rejection and nonrejection at the 0.05 level of significance, with 3 and 32 degrees of freedom

Using the 0.05 level of significance and testing whether there is an effect due to mobile payment options (yes or no) (factor A), you reject the null hypothesis if the computed F_{STAT} test statistic is greater than 4.1491, the upper-tail critical value from the F distribution with 1 and 32 degrees of freedom (see Figures 11.10 and 11.12). Because $F_{STAT} = 62.7258 > 4.1491$ or the p-value $= 0.0000 < 0.05$, you reject H_0. You conclude that there is evidence of a difference in the mean sales when mobile payment methods are permitted as compared to when they are not. Because the mean sales when mobile payment methods are permitted is 31.523 and is 30.806 when they are not, you can conclude that permitting mobile payment methods has led to an increase in mean sales.

FIGURE 11.12

Regions of rejection and nonrejection at the 0.05 level of significance, with 1 and 32 degrees of freedom

Using the 0.05 level of significance and testing for a difference among the in-store locations (factor B), you reject the null hypothesis of no difference if the computed F_{STAT} test statistic is greater than 2.9011, the upper-tail critical value from the F distribution with 3 degrees of freedom in the numerator and 32 degrees of freedom in the denominator (see Figures 11.10 and 11.11). Because $F_{STAT} = 98.9631 > 2.9011$ or the p-value $= 0.0000 < 0.05$, you reject H_0. You conclude that there is evidence of a difference in the mean sales among the four in-store locations.

Multiple Comparisons: The Tukey Procedure

If one or both of the factor effects are significant and there is no significant interaction effect, when there are more than two levels of a factor, you can determine the particular levels that are significantly different by using the **Tukey multiple comparisons procedure for two-way ANOVA** (see references 6 and 8). Equation (11.16) gives the critical range for factor A.

CRITICAL RANGE FOR FACTOR A

$$\text{Critical range} = Q_\alpha \sqrt{\frac{MSE}{cn'}} \qquad\qquad (11.16)$$

where Q_α is the upper-tail critical value from a Studentized range distribution having r and $rc(n' - 1)$ degrees of freedom. (Values for the Studentized range distribution are found in Table E.7.)

Equation (11.17) gives the critical range for factor B.

CRITICAL RANGE FOR FACTOR B

$$\text{Critical range} = Q_\alpha \sqrt{\frac{MSE}{rn'}} \qquad\qquad (11.17)$$

where Q_α is the upper-tail critical value from a Studentized range distribution having c and $rc(n' - 1)$ degrees of freedom. (Values for the Studentized range distribution are found in Table E.7.)

To use the Tukey procedure, return to the mobile electronics sales data of Table 11.7 on page 368. In the ANOVA summary table in Figure 11.10 on page 368, the interaction effect is not significant. Because there are only two categories for mobile payment (yes and no), there are no multiple comparisons to be constructed. Using $\alpha = 0.05$, there is evidence of a significant difference among the four in-store locations that comprise factor B. Thus, you can use the Tukey multiple comparisons procedure to determine which of the four in-store locations differ.

Because there are four in-store locations, there are $4(4 - 1)/2 = 6$ pairwise comparisons. Using the calculations presented in Figure 11.10, the absolute mean differences are as follows:

1. $|\overline{X}_{.1.} - \overline{X}_{.2.}| = |30.274 - 32.378| = 2.104$
2. $|\overline{X}_{.1.} - \overline{X}_{.3.}| = |30.274 - 31.246| = 0.972$
3. $|\overline{X}_{.1.} - \overline{X}_{.4.}| = |30.274 - 30.759| = 0.485$
4. $|\overline{X}_{.2.} - \overline{X}_{.3.}| = |32.378 - 31.246| = 1.132$
5. $|\overline{X}_{.2.} - \overline{X}_{.4.}| = |32.378 - 30.759| = 1.619$
6. $|\overline{X}_{.3.} - \overline{X}_{.4.}| = |31.246 - 30.759| = 0.487$

To determine the critical range, refer to Figure 11.10 to find $MSE = 0.0821$, $r = 2$, $c = 4$, and $n' = 5$. From Table E.7 [for $\alpha = 0.05$, $c = 4$, and $rc(n' - 1) = 32$], Q_α, the upper-tail critical value of the Studentized range distribution with 4 and 32 degrees of freedom is approximately 3.84. Using Equation (11.17),

$$\text{Critical range} = 3.84 \sqrt{\frac{0.0821}{10}} = 0.3479$$

Because each of the six comparisons is greater than the critical range of 0.3479, you can conclude that the population mean sales is different for the four in-store locations. The front location is estimated to have higher mean sales than the other three in-store locations. The end-cap location is estimated to have higher mean sales than the in-aisle and expert locations. The expert location is estimated to have higher mean sales than the in-aisle location. Note that by using $\alpha = 0.05$, you are able to make all six comparisons with an overall error rate of only 5%. Consistent with the results of the one-factor experiment, you have additional evidence that selling mobile electronics items at the front location will increase sales the most. In addition, you now have evidence that enabling mobile payment will also lead to increased sales.

Visualizing Interaction Effects: The Cell Means Plot

You can get a better understanding of the interaction effect by plotting the **cell means**, the means of all possible factor-level combinations. Figure 11.13 presents a cell means plot that uses the cell means for the mobile payments permitted/in-store location combinations shown in Figure 11.10 on page 368. From the plot of the mean sales for each combination of mobile payments permitted and in-store location, observe that the two lines (representing the two levels of mobile payments, yes and no,) are roughly parallel. This indicates that the *difference* between the mean sales for stores that permit mobile payment methods and those that do not is virtually the same for the four in-store locations. In other words, there is no *interaction* between these two factors, as was indicated by the *F* test.

FIGURE 11.13
Excel cell means plots for mobile electronic sales based on mobile payments permitted and in-store location

Interpreting Interaction Effects

How do you interpret an interaction? When there is an interaction, some levels of factor *A* respond better with certain levels of factor *B*. For example, with respect to mobile electronics sales, suppose that some in-store locations were better when mobile payment methods were permitted and other in-store locations were better when mobile payment methods were not permitted. If this were true, the lines of Figure 11.13 would not be nearly as parallel, and the interaction effect might be statistically significant. In such a situation, the difference between whether mobile payment methods were permitted is no longer the same for all in-store locations. Such an outcome would also complicate the interpretation of the *main effects* because differences in one factor (whether mobile payment methods were permitted) would not be consistent across the other factor (the in-store locations).

Example 11.2 illustrates a situation with a significant interaction effect.

EXAMPLE 11.2

Interpreting Significant Interaction Effects

A nationwide company specializing in preparing students for college and graduate school entrance exams, such as the SAT, ACT, GRE, and LSAT, had the business objective of improving its ACT preparatory course. Two factors of interest to the company are the length of the course (a condensed 10-day period or a regular 30-day period) and the type of course (traditional classroom or online distance learning). The company collected data by randomly assigning 10 clients to each of the four cells that represent a combination of length of the course and type of course. The results are organized in the file ACT and presented in Table 11.8.

What are the effects of the type of course and the length of the course on ACT scores?

▶ *(continued)*

TABLE 11.8
ACT Scores for
Different Types and
Lengths of Courses

TYPE OF COURSE	LENGTH OF COURSE			
	Condensed		Regular	
Traditional	26	18	34	28
Traditional	27	24	24	21
Traditional	25	19	35	23
Traditional	21	20	31	29
Traditional	21	18	28	26
Online	27	21	24	21
Online	29	32	16	19
Online	30	20	22	19
Online	24	28	20	24
Online	30	29	23	25

SOLUTION The cell means plot presented in Figure 11.14 shows a strong interaction between the type of course and the length of the course. The nonparallel lines indicate that the effect of condensing the course depends on whether the course is taught in the traditional classroom or by online distance learning. The online mean score is higher when the course is condensed to a 10-day period, whereas the traditional mean score is higher when the course takes place over the regular 30-day period.

FIGURE 11.14
Excel cell means plot of
mean ACT scores

To verify the visual analysis provided by interpreting the cell means plot, you begin by testing whether there is a statistically significant interaction between factor A (length of course) and factor B (type of course). Using a 0.05 level of significance, you reject the null hypothesis because $F_{STAT} = 24.2569 > 4.1132$ or the p-value equals $0.0000 < 0.05$ (see Figure 11.15 on next page). Thus, the hypothesis test confirms the interaction evident in the cell means plot.

The existence of this significant interaction effect complicates the interpretation of the hypothesis tests concerning the two main effects. You cannot directly conclude that there is no effect with respect to length of course and type of course, even though both have p-values > 0.05.

Given that the interaction is significant, you can reanalyze the data with the two factors collapsed into four groups of a single factor rather than a two-way ANOVA with two levels of each of the two factors. You can reorganize the data as follows: Group 1 is traditional

▶ *(continued)*

FIGURE 11.15

Excel two-way ANOVA results for the ACT scores

	A	B	C	D
1	ANOVA: Two-Factor With Replication			
2				
3	SUMMARY	Condensed	Regular	Total
4	*traditional*			
5	Count	10	10	20
6	Sum	219	279	498
7	Average	21.9	27.9	24.9
8	Variance	11.2111	20.9889	24.7263
9				
10	*online*			
11	Count	10	10	20
12	Sum	270	213	483
13	Average	27	21.3	24.15
14	Variance	16.2222	8.0111	20.0289
15				
16	*Total*			
17	Count	20	20	
18	Sum	489	492	
19	Average	24.45	24.6	
20	Variance	19.8395	25.2000	
21				
22				

	A	B	C	D	E	F	G
23	ANOVA						
24	*Source of Variation*	SS	df	MS	F	P-value	F crit
25	Sample	5.6250	1	5.6250	0.3987	0.5318	4.1132
26	Columns	0.2250	1	0.2250	0.0159	0.9002	4.1132
27	Interaction	342.2250	1	342.2250	24.2569	0.0000	4.1132
28	Within	507.9000	36	14.1083			
29							
30	Total	855.9750	39				
31						Level of significance	0.05

In the Worksheet

The worksheet uses the F.DIST.RT function to compute the *p*-values in column *F* and the F.INV.RT function to compute the F test statistics in column G.

condensed, Group 2 is traditional, Group 3 is online condensed, and Group 4 is online regular. Figure 11.16 shows the results for these data, stored in ACT-OneWay .

From Figure 11.16, because $F_{STAT} = 8.2239 > 2.8663$ or *p*-value $= 0.0003 < 0.05$, there is evidence of a significant difference in the four groups (traditional condensed, traditional regular, online condensed, and online regular). Using the Tukey multiple comparisons procedure, traditional condensed is different from traditional regular and from online condensed. Traditional regular is also different from online regular, and online condensed is also different from online regular.

Therefore, whether condensing a course is a good idea depends on whether the course is offered in a traditional classroom or as an online distance learning course. To ensure the highest mean ACT scores, the company should use the traditional approach for courses that are given over a 30-day period but use the online approach for courses that are condensed into a 10-day period.

FIGURE 11.16

Excel one-way ANOVA and Tukey-Kramer results for the ACT scores

	A	B	C	D	E	F	G
1	One-Way ANOVA (ANOVA: Single Factor)						
2							
3	SUMMARY						
4	*Groups*	Count	Sum	Average	Variance		
5	Group 1	10	219	21.9	11.2111		
6	Group 2	10	279	27.9	20.9889		
7	Group 3	10	270	27	16.2222		
8	Group 4	10	213	21.3	8.0111		
9							
10							
11	ANOVA						
12	*Source of Variation*	SS	df	MS	F	P-value	F crit
13	Between Groups	348.0750	3	116.0250	8.2239	0.0003	2.8663
14	Within Groups	507.9000	36	14.1083			
15							
16	Total	855.9750	39				
17					Level of significance	0.05	

	A	B	C	D	E	F	G	H	I
1	Tukey Kramer Multiple Comparisons								
2									
3		Sample	Sample			Absolute	Std. Error	Critical	
4	Group	Mean	Size		Comparison	Difference	of Difference	Range	Results
5	1: Group 1	21.9	10		Group 1 to Group 2	6	1.1878	4.5373	Means are different
6	2: Group 2	27.9	10		Group 1 to Group 3	5.1	1.1878	4.5373	Means are different
7	3: Group 3	27	10		Group 1 to Group 4	0.6	1.1878	4.5373	Means are not different
8	4: Group 4	21.3	10		Group 2 to Group 3	0.9	1.1878	4.5373	Means are not different
9					Group 2 to Group 4	6.6	1.1878	4.5373	Means are different
10	Other Data				Group 3 to Group 4	5.7	1.1878	4.5373	Means are different
11	Level of significance	0.05							
12	Numerator d.f.	4							
13	Denominator d.f.	36							
14	MSW	14.10833							
15	Q Statistic	3.82							

PROBLEMS FOR SECTION 11.2

LEARNING THE BASICS

11.15 Consider a two-factor factorial design with three levels for factor A, three levels for factor B, and four replicates in each of the nine cells.
a. How many degrees of freedom are there in determining the factor A variation and the factor B variation?
b. How many degrees of freedom are there in determining the interaction variation?
c. How many degrees of freedom are there in determining the random variation?
d. How many degrees of freedom are there in determining the total variation?

11.16 Assume that you are working with the results from Problem 11.15, and $SSA = 120$, $SSB = 110$, $SSE = 270$, and $SST = 540$.
a. What is $SSAB$?
b. What are MSA and MSB?
c. What is $MSAB$?
d. What is MSE?

11.17 Assume that you are working with the results from Problems 11.15 and 11.16.
a. What is the value of the F_{STAT} test statistic for the interaction effect?
b. What is the value of the F_{STAT} test statistic for the factor A effect?
c. What is the value of the F_{STAT} test statistic for the factor B effect?
d. Form the ANOVA summary table and fill in all values in the body of the table.

11.18 Given the results from Problems 11.15 through 11.17,
a. at the 0.05 level of significance, is there an effect due to factor A?
b. at the 0.05 level of significance, is there an effect due to factor B?
c. at the 0.05 level of significance, is there an interaction effect?

11.19 Given a two-way ANOVA with two levels for factor A, five levels for factor B, and four replicates in each of the 10 cells, with $SSA = 18$, $SSB = 64$, $SSE = 60$, and $SST = 150$,
a. form the ANOVA summary table and fill in all values in the body of the table.
b. at the 0.05 level of significance, is there an effect due to factor A?
c. at the 0.05 level of significance, is there an effect due to factor B?
d. at the 0.05 level of significance, is there an interaction effect?

11.20 Given a two-factor factorial experiment and the ANOVA summary table that follows, fill in all the missing results:

Source	Degrees of Freedom	Sum of Squares	Mean Square (Variance)	F
A	$r - 1 = 2$	$SSA = ?$	$MSA = 80$	$F_{STAT} = ?$
B	$c - 1 = ?$	$SSB = 220$	$MSB = ?$	$F_{STAT} = 11.0$
AB	$(r-1)(c-1) = 8$	$SSAB = ?$	$MSAB = 10$	$F_{STAT} = ?$
Error	$rc(n'-1) = 30$	$SSE = ?$	$MSE = ?$	
Total	$n - 1 = ?$	$SST = ?$		

11.21 Given the results from Problem 11.20,
a. at the 0.05 level of significance, is there an effect due to factor A?
b. at the 0.05 level of significance, is there an effect due to factor B?
c. at the 0.05 level of significance, is there an interaction effect?

APPLYING THE CONCEPTS

11.22 An experiment was conducted to study the extrusion process of biodegradable packaging foam. Two of the factors considered for their effect on the unit density (mg/ml) were the die temperature (145° C vs. 155° C) and the die diameter (3 mm vs. 4 mm). The results are stored in PackagingFoam1 . (Data extracted from W. Y. Koh, K. M. Eskridge, and M. A. Hanna, "Supersaturated Split-Plot Designs," *Journal of Quality Technology*, 45, January 2013, pp. 61–72.)

At the 0.05 level of significance,
a. is there an interaction between die temperature and die diameter?
b. is there an effect due to die temperature?
c. is there an effect due to die diameter?
d. Plot the mean unit density for each die temperature for each die diameter.
e. What can you conclude about the effect of die temperature and die diameter on mean unit density?

11.23 Referring to Problem 11.22, the effect of die temperature and die diameter on the foam diameter was also measured and the results stored in PackagaingFoam2 .

At the 0.05 level of significance,
a. is there an interaction between die temperature and die diameter?
b. is there an effect due to die temperature?
c. is there an effect due to die diameter?
d. Plot the mean foam diameter for each die temperature and die diameter.
e. What conclusions can you reach concerning the importance of each of these two factors on the foam diameter?

✓ SELF TEST **11.24** A plastic injection molding process is often used in manufacturing because of its ability to mold complicated shapes. An experiment was conducted on the manufacture of a television remote part, and the warpage (mm) of the part was measured and stored in TVRemote . (Data extracted from M. A. Barghash and F. A. Alkaabneh, "Shrinkage and Warpage Detailed Analysis and Optimization for the Injection Molding Process Using Multistage Experimental Design," *Quality Engineering*, 26, 2014, pp. 319–334.) Two factors were to be considered, the filling time (1, 2, or 3 sec) and the mold temperature (60, 72.5, or 85° C).

At the 0.05 level of significance,
a. is there an interaction between filling time and mold temperature?
b. is there an effect due to filling time?
c. is there an effect due to mold temperature?
d. Plot the mean warpage for each filling time for each mold temperature.
e. Discuss the results of (a) through (d).

11.25 A metallurgy company wanted to investigate the effect of the percentage of ammonium and the stir rate on the density of the powder produced. The results (stored in Density) are as follows:

AMMONIUM (%)	STIR RATE	
	100	**150**
2	10.95	7.54
2	14.68	6.66
2	17.68	8.03
2	15.18	8.84
30	12.65	12.46
30	15.12	14.96
30	17.48	14.96
30	15.96	12.62

Source: Extracted from L. Johnson and K. McNeilly, "Results May Not Vary," *Quality Progress*, May 2011, pp. 41–48.

At the 0.05 level of significance,

a. is there an interaction between the percentage of ammonium and the stir rate?

b. is there an effect due to the percentage of ammonium?

c. is there an effect due to the stir rate?

d. Plot the mean density for each percentage of ammonium for each stir rate.

e. Discuss the results of (a) through (d).

11.26 An experiment was conducted to try to resolve a problem of brake discs overheating at high speed on construction equipment. Five different brake discs were measured by two different temperature gauges. The temperature of each brake disc and gauge combination was measured at eight different times and the results stored in Brakes .

Source: Data extracted from M. Awad, T. P. Erdmann, V. Shansal, and B. Barth, "A Measurement System Analysis Approach for Hard-to-Repeat Events," *Quality Engineering* 21 (2009): 300–305.

At the 0.05 level of significance,

a. is there an interaction between the brake discs and the gauges?

b. is there an effect due to brake discs?

c. is there an effect due to the gauges?

d. Plot the mean temperature for each brake disc for each gauge.

e. Discuss the results of (a) through (d).

11.3 The Randomized Block Design

Section 10.2 discusses how to use the paired *t* test to evaluate the difference between the means of two groups when you have repeated measurements or matched samples. The **randomized block design** evaluates differences among more than two groups that contain matched samples or repeated measures that have been placed in blocks. The **Section 11.3 online topic** discusses this method and illustrates its use.

11.4 Fixed Effects, Random Effects, and Mixed Effects Models

Sections 11.1 through 11.3 do not consider the distinction between how the levels of a factor were selected. The equation for the *F* test depends on whether the levels of a factor were specifically selected or randomly selected from a population. The **Section 11.4** online topic presents the appropriate *F* tests to use when the levels of a factor are either specifically selected or randomly selected from a population of levels.

▼USING **STATISTICS**
The Means to Find Differences at Arlingtons Revisited

In the Arlingtons scenario, you needed to determine whether there were differences in mobile electronics sales among four in-store locations as well as determine whether permitting mobile payments had an effect on those sales.

Using the one-way ANOVA, you determined that there was a difference in the mean sales for the four in-store locations. You then were able to conclude that the mean sales for the front location was higher than the current in-aisle or experimental end-cap or expert locations, that the endcap location mean sales were higher than the in-aisle or expert locations, and that there was no evidence of a difference between the mean sales for the in-aisle and expert locations. Using the two-way ANOVA, you determined that there was no interaction between in-store location and permitting mobile payment methods and that mean sales were higher when mobile payment methods were permitted than when such methods were not. In addition, you concluded that the population mean sales is different for the four in-store locations and reached these other conclusions:

- The front location is estimated to have higher mean sales than the other three locations.

- The endcap location is estimated to have higher mean sales than the current in-aisle location or expert location.
- The expert location is estimated to have higher mean sales than the current in-aisle location.

Your next step as a member of the sales team might be to further investigate the differences among the sales locations as well as examine other factors that could influence mobile electronics sale.

▼SUMMARY

In this chapter, various statistical procedures were used to analyze the effect of one or two factors of interest. The assumptions required for using these procedures were discussed in detail. Remember that you need to critically investigate the validity of the assumptions underlying the hypothesis-testing procedures. Table 11.9 summarizes the topics covered in this chapter.

TABLE 11.9
Summary of Chapter 11

Type of Analysis (numerical variables)	Type of Design
Comparing more than two groups	One-way analysis of variance (Section 11.1)
	Two-way analysis of variance (Section 11.2)
	Randomized block design (online Section 11.3)

▼REFERENCES

1. Berenson, M. L., D. M. Levine, and M. Goldstein. *Intermediate Statistical Methods and Applications: A Computer Package Approach*. Upper Saddle River, NJ: Prentice Hall, 1983.
2. Conover, W. J. *Practical Nonparametric Statistics*, 3rd ed. New York: Wiley, 2000.
3. Daniel, W. W. *Applied Nonparametric Statistics*, 2nd ed. Boston: PWS Kent, 1990.
4. Gitlow, H. S., R. Melnyck, and D. Levine. *A Guide to Six Sigma and Process Improvement for Practitioners and Students*, 2nd ed. Old Tappan, NJ: Pearson Education, 2015.
5. Hicks, C. R., and K. Turner. *Fundamental Concepts in the Design of Experiments*, 5th ed. New York: Oxford University Press, 1999.
6. Kutner, M., J. Neter, C. Nachtsheim, and W. Li. *Applied Linear Statistical Models*, 5th ed. New York: McGraw-Hill-Irwin, 2005.
7. Levine, D. *Statistics for Six Sigma Green Belts*. Upper Saddle River, NJ: Financial Times/Prentice Hall, 2006.
8. Montgomery, D. M. *Design and Analysis of Experiments*, 8th ed. New York: Wiley, 2013.

▼KEY EQUATIONS

Total Variation in One-Way ANOVA

$$SST = \sum_{j=1}^{c} \sum_{i=1}^{n_j} (X_{ij} - \overline{\overline{X}})^2 \qquad (11.1)$$

Among-Group Variation in One-Way ANOVA

$$SSA = \sum_{j=1}^{c} n_j(\overline{X}_j - \overline{\overline{X}})^2 \qquad (11.2)$$

Within-Group Variation in One-Way ANOVA

$$SSW = \sum_{j=1}^{c} \sum_{i=1}^{n_j} (X_{ij} - \overline{X}_j)^2 \qquad (11.3)$$

Mean Squares in One-Way ANOVA

$$MSA = \frac{SSA}{c-1} \qquad (11.4a)$$

$$MSW = \frac{SSW}{n-c} \qquad (11.4b)$$

$$MST = \frac{SST}{n-1} \qquad (11.4c)$$

One-Way ANOVA F_{STAT} Test Statistic

$$F_{STAT} = \frac{MSA}{MSW} \qquad (11.5)$$

Critical Range for the Tukey-Kramer Procedure

$$\text{Critical range} = Q_\alpha \sqrt{\frac{MSW}{2}\left(\frac{1}{n_j} + \frac{1}{n_{j'}}\right)} \quad (11.6)$$

Total Variation in Two-Way ANOVA

$$SST = \sum_{i=1}^{r}\sum_{j=1}^{c}\sum_{k=1}^{n'}(X_{ijk} - \overline{\overline{X}})^2 \quad (11.7)$$

Factor A Variation in Two-Way ANOVA

$$SSA = cn'\sum_{i=1}^{r}(\overline{X}_{i..} - \overline{\overline{X}})^2 \quad (11.8)$$

Factor B Variation in Two-Way ANOVA

$$SSB = rn'\sum_{j=1}^{c}(\overline{X}_{.j.} - \overline{\overline{X}})^2 \quad (11.9)$$

Interaction Variation in Two-Way ANOVA

$$SSAB = n'\sum_{i=1}^{r}\sum_{j=1}^{c}(\overline{X}_{ij.} - \overline{X}_{i..} - \overline{X}_{.j.} + \overline{\overline{X}})^2 \quad (11.10)$$

Random Variation in Two-Way ANOVA

$$SSE = \sum_{i=1}^{r}\sum_{j=1}^{c}\sum_{k=1}^{n'}(X_{ijk} - \overline{X}_{ij.})^2 \quad (11.11)$$

Mean Squares in Two-Way ANOVA

$$MSA = \frac{SSA}{r-1} \quad (11.12a)$$

$$MSB = \frac{SSB}{c-1} \quad (11.12b)$$

$$MSAB = \frac{SSAB}{(r-1)(c-1)} \quad (11.12c)$$

$$MSE = \frac{SSE}{rc(n'-1)} \quad (11.12d)$$

F Test for Factor A Effect

$$F_{STAT} = \frac{MSA}{MSE} \quad (11.13)$$

F Test for Factor B Effect

$$F_{STAT} = \frac{MSB}{MSE} \quad (11.14)$$

F Test for Interaction Effect

$$F_{STAT} = \frac{MSAB}{MSE} \quad (11.15)$$

Critical Range for Factor A

$$\text{Critical range} = Q_\alpha\sqrt{\frac{MSE}{cn'}} \quad (11.16)$$

Critical Range for Factor B

$$\text{Critical range} = Q_\alpha\sqrt{\frac{MSE}{rn'}} \quad (11.17)$$

▼ KEY TERMS

▼CHECKING YOUR UNDERSTANDING

11.27 In a one-way ANOVA, what is the difference between the among-groups variance MSA and the within-groups variance MSW?

11.28 What are the distinguishing features of the completely randomized design and two-factor factorial designs?

11.29 What are the assumptions of ANOVA?

11.30 Under what conditions should you use the one-way ANOVA F test to examine possible differences among the means of c independent populations?

11.31 When and how should you use multiple comparison procedures for evaluating pairwise combinations of the group means?

11.32 What is the difference between the one-way ANOVA F test and the Levene test?

11.33 Under what conditions should you use the two-way ANOVA F test to examine possible differences among the means of each factor in a factorial design?

11.34 What is meant by the concept of interaction in a two-factor factorial design?

11.35 How can you determine whether there is an interaction in the two-factor factorial design?

▼CHAPTER REVIEW PROBLEMS

11.36 You are the production manager at a parachute manufacturing company. Parachutes are woven in your factory using a synthetic fiber purchased from one of four different suppliers. The strength of these fibers is an important characteristic that ensures quality parachutes. You need to decide whether the synthetic fibers from each of your four suppliers result in parachutes of equal strength. Furthermore, to produce parachutes your factory uses two types of looms, the Jetta and the Turk. You need to determine if the parachutes woven on each type of loom are equally strong. You also want to know if any differences in the strength of the parachute can be attributed to the four suppliers are dependent on the type of loom used. You conduct an experiment in which five different parachutes from each supplier are manufactured on each of the two different looms and collect and store the data in ParachuteTwoWay .

At the 0.05 level of significance,
a. is there an interaction between supplier and loom?
b. is there an effect due to loom?
c. is there an effect due to supplier?
d. Plot the mean strength for each supplier for each loom.
e. If appropriate, use the Tukey procedure to determine differences between suppliers.
f. Repeat the analysis, using the Parachuteoneway file with suppliers as the only factor. Compare your results to those of (e).

11.37 Medical wires are used in the manufacture of cardiovascular devices. A study was conducted to determine the effect of several factors on the ratio of the load on a test specimen (YS) to the ultimate tensile strength (UTS). The file MedicalWires1 contains the study results, which examined factors including the machine (W95 vs. W96) and the reduction angle (narrow vs. wide). (Data extracted from B. Nepal, S. Mohanty, and L. Kay, "Quality Improvement of Medical Wire Manufacturing Process," *Quality Engineering* 25, 2013, pp. 151–163.)

At the 0.05 level of significance,
a. is there an interaction between machine type and reduction angle?
b. is there an effect due to machine type?
c. is there an effect due to reduction angle?

d. Plot the mean ratio of the load on a test specimen (YS) to the ultimate tensile strength (UTS) for each machine type for each reduction angle.
e. What can you conclude about the effects of machine type and reduction angle on the ratio of the load on a test specimen (YS) to the ultimate tensile strength (UTS)? Explain.
f. Repeat the analysis, using reduction angle as the only factor (see the MedicalWires2 file. Compare your results to those of (c) and (e).

11.38 An operations manager wants to examine the effect of air-jet pressure (in pounds per square inch [psi]) on the breaking strength of yarn. Three different levels of air-jet pressure are to be considered: 30 psi, 40 psi, and 50 psi. A random sample of 18 yarns are selected from the same batch, and the yarns are randomly assigned, 6 each, to the 3 levels of air-jet pressure. The breaking strength scores are stored in Yarn .
a. Is there evidence of a significant difference in the variances of the breaking strengths for the three air-jet pressures? (Use $\alpha = 0.05$.)
b. At the 0.05 level of significance, is there evidence of a difference among mean breaking strengths for the three air-jet pressures?
c. If appropriate, use the Tukey-Kramer procedure to determine which air-jet pressures significantly differ with respect to mean breaking strength. (Use $\alpha = 0.05$.)
d. What should the operations manager conclude?

11.39 Suppose that, when setting up the experiment in Problem 11.38, the operations manager is able to study the effect of side-to-side aspect in addition to air-jet pressure. Thus, instead of the one-factor completely randomized design in Problem 11.38, a two-factor factorial design was used, with the first factor, side-to-side aspect, having two levels (nozzle and opposite) and the second factor, air-jet pressure, having three levels (30 psi, 40 psi, and 50 psi). A sample of 18 yarns is randomly assigned, 3 to each of the 6 side-to-side aspect and pressure level combinations. The breaking-strength scores, stored in Yarn , are as follows:

SIDE-TO-SIDE ASPECT	AIR-JET PRESSURE		
	30 psi	40 psi	50 psi
Nozzle	25.5	24.8	23.2
Nozzle	24.9	23.7	23.7
Nozzle	26.1	24.4	22.7
Opposite	24.7	23.6	22.6
Opposite	24.2	23.3	22.8
Opposite	23.6	21.4	24.9

At the 0.05 level of significance,

a. is there an interaction between side-to-side aspect and air-jet pressure?
b. is there an effect due to side-to-side aspect?
c. is there an effect due to air-jet pressure?
d. Plot the mean yarn breaking strength for each level of side-to-side aspect for each level of air-jet pressure.
e. If appropriate, use the Tukey procedure to study differences among the air-jet pressures.
f. On the basis of the results of (a) through (e), what conclusions can you reach concerning yarn breaking strength? Discuss.
g. Compare your results in (a) through (f) with those from the completely randomized design in Problem 11.38. Discuss fully.

11.40 A hotel wanted to develop a new system for delivering room service breakfasts. In the current system, an order form is left on the bed in each room. If the customer wishes to receive a room service breakfast, he or she places the order form on the doorknob before 11 P.M. The current system requires customers to select a 15-minute interval for desired delivery time (6:30–6:45 A.M., 6:45–7:00 A.M., etc.). The new system is designed to allow the customer to request a specific delivery time. The hotel wants to measure the difference (in minutes) between the actual delivery time and the requested delivery time of room service orders for breakfast. (A negative time means that the order was delivered before the requested time. A positive time means that the order was delivered after the requested time.) The factors included were the menu choice (American or Continental) and the desired time period in which the order was to be delivered (Early Time Period [6:30–8:00 A.M.] or Late Time Period [8:00–9:30 A.M.]). Ten orders for each combination of menu choice and desired time period were studied on a particular day. The data, stored in Breakfast , are as follows:

TYPE OF BREAKFAST	DESIRED TIME	
	Early Time Period	Late Time Period
Continental	1.2	−2.5
Continental	2.1	3.0
Continental	3.3	−0.2
Continental	4.4	1.2
Continental	3.4	1.2
Continental	5.3	0.7
Continental	2.2	−1.3
Continental	1.0	0.2
Continental	5.4	−0.5
Continental	1.4	3.8

TYPE OF BREAKFAST	DESIRED TIME	
	Early Time Period	Late Time Period
American	4.4	6.0
American	1.1	2.3
American	4.8	4.2
American	7.1	3.8
American	6.7	5.5
American	5.6	1.8
American	9.5	5.1
American	4.1	4.2
American	7.9	4.9
American	9.4	4.0

At the 0.05 level of significance,

a. is there an interaction between type of breakfast and desired time?
b. is there an effect due to type of breakfast?
c. is there an effect due to desired time?
d. Plot the mean delivery time difference for each desired time for each type of breakfast.
e. On the basis of the results of (a) through (d), what conclusions can you reach concerning delivery time difference? Discuss.

11.41 Refer to the room service experiment in Problem 11.40. Now suppose that the results are as shown below and stored in Breakfast2 . Repeat (a) through (e), using these data, and compare the results to those of (a) through (e) of Problem 11.40.

TYPE OF BREAKFAST	DESIRED TIME	
	Early	Late
Continental	1.2	−0.5
Continental	2.1	5.0
Continental	3.3	1.8
Continental	4.4	3.2
Continental	3.4	3.2
Continental	5.3	2.7
Continental	2.2	0.7
Continental	1.0	2.2
Continental	5.4	1.5
Continental	1.4	5.8
American	4.4	6.0
American	1.1	2.3
American	4.8	4.2
American	7.1	3.8
American	6.7	5.5
American	5.6	1.8
American	9.5	5.1
American	4.1	4.2
American	7.9	4.9
American	9.4	4.0

11.42 A pet food company has the business objective of having the weight of a can of cat food come as close to the specified weight as possible. Realizing that the size of the pieces of meat contained in a can and the can fill height could impact the weight of a can, a team studying the weight of canned cat food wondered whether the current larger chunk size produced higher can weight and more variability. The team decided to study the effect on weight of a cutting size that was finer than the current size. In addition, the team slightly lowered the target for the sensing mechanism that determines the fill height in order to determine the effect of the fill height on can weight.

Twenty cans were filled for each of the four combinations of piece size (fine and current) and fill height (low and current). The contents of each can were weighed, and the amount above or below the label weight of 3 ounces was recorded as the variable coded weight. For example, a can containing 2.90 ounces was given a coded weight of −0.10. Results were stored in CatFood2.

Analyze these data and write a report for presentation to the team. Indicate the importance of the piece size and the fill height on the weight of the canned cat food. Be sure to include a recommendation for the level of each factor that will come closest to meeting the target weight and the limitations of this experiment, along with recommendations for future experiments that might be undertaken.

11.43 Brand valuations are critical to CEOs, financial and marketing executives, security analysts, institutional investors and others who depend on well-researched, reliable information needed for assessments and comparisons in decision making. Millward Brown Optimor has developed the BrandZ Top 100 Most Valuable Global Brands for WPP, the world's largest communications services group. Unlike other studies, the BrandZ Top 100 Most Valuable Global Brands fuses consumer measures of brand equity with financial measures to place a financial value on brands. The file BrandZTechFinTele contains the brand values for three sectors in the BrandZ Top 100 Most Valuable Global Brands for 2015 (Data extracted from **bit.ly/1BH8m5F**.)

a. At the 0.01 level of significance, is there evidence of a difference in mean brand value among the sectors?
b. What assumptions are necessary in order to complete (a)? Comment on the validity of these assumptions.
c. If appropriate, use the Tukey procedure to determine the sectors that differ in mean rating. (Use $\alpha = 0.01$.)

▾CASES

Managing Ashland MultiComm Services
PHASE 1

The computer operations department had a business objective of reducing the amount of time to fully update each subscriber's set of messages in a special secured email system. An experiment was conducted in which 24 subscribers were selected and three different messaging systems were used. Eight subscribers were assigned to each system, and the update times were measured. The results, stored in AMS11-1, are presented in Table AMS11.1.

TABLE AMS11.1
Update Times (in seconds) for Three Different Systems

System 1	System 2	System 3
38.8	41.8	32.9
42.1	36.4	36.1
45.2	39.1	39.2
34.8	28.7	29.3
48.3	36.4	41.9
37.8	36.1	31.7
41.1	35.8	35.2
43.6	33.7	38.1

1. Analyze the data in Table AMS11.1 and write a report to the computer operations department that indicates your findings. Include an appendix in which you discuss the reason you selected a particular statistical test to compare the three email interfaces.

DO NOT CONTINUE UNTIL THE PHASE 1 EXERCISE HAS BEEN COMPLETED.

PHASE 2

After analyzing the data in Table AMS11.1, the computer operations department team decided to also study the effect of the connection media used (cable or fiber).

The team designed a study in which a total of 30 subscribers were chosen. The subscribers were randomly assigned to one of the three messaging systems so that there were five subscribers in each of the six combinations of the two factors—messaging system and media used. Measurements were taken on the updated time. Table AMS11.2 summarizes the results that are stored in AMS11-2.

TABLE AMS11.2
Update Times (in seconds), Based on Messaging System and Media Used

MEDIA	INTERFACE		
	System 1	System 2	System 3
Cable	45.6	41.7	35.3
	49.0	42.8	37.7
	41.8	40.0	41.0
	35.6	39.6	28.7
	43.4	36.0	31.8
Fiber	44.1	37.9	43.3
	40.8	41.1	40.0
	46.9	35.8	43.1
	51.8	45.3	39.6
	48.5	40.2	33.2

2. Completely analyze these data and write a report to the team that indicates the importance of each of the two factors and/or the interaction between them on the update time. Include recommendations for future experiments to perform.

Digital Case

Apply your knowledge about ANOVA in this Digital Case, which continues the cereal-fill packaging dispute Digital Case from Chapters 7, 9, and 10.

After reviewing CCACC's latest document (see the Digital Case for Chapter 10 on page 342), Oxford Cereals has released **SecondAnalysis.pdf**, a press kit that Oxford Cereals has assembled to refute the claim that it is guilty of using selective data. Review the Oxford Cereals press kit and then answer the following questions.

1. Does Oxford Cereals have a legitimate argument? Why or why not?

2. Assuming that the samples Oxford Cereals has posted were randomly selected, perform the appropriate analysis to resolve the ongoing weight dispute.

3. What conclusions can you reach from your results? If you were called as an expert witness, would you support the claims of the CCACC or the claims of Oxford Cereals? Explain.

Sure Value Convenience Stores

You work in the corporate office for a nationwide convenience store franchise that operates nearly 10,000 stores. The per-store daily customer count (i.e., the mean number of customers in a store in one day) has been steady, at 900, for some time. To increase the customer count, the chain is considering cutting prices for coffee beverages. The question to be determined is how much to cut prices to increase the daily customer count without reducing the gross margin on coffee sales too much.

You decide to carry out an experiment in a sample of 24 stores where customer counts have been running almost exactly at the national average of 900. In 6 of the stores, the price of a small coffee will now be $0.59, in 6 stores the price of a small coffee will now be $0.69, in 6 stores, the price of a small coffee will now be $0.79, and in 6 stores, the price of a small coffee will now be $0.89. After four weeks of selling the coffee at the new price, the daily customer counts in the stores were recorded and stored in CoffeeSales.

1. Analyze the data and determine whether there is evidence of a difference in the daily customer count, based on the price of a small coffee.

2. If appropriate, determine which mean prices differ in daily customer counts.

3. What price do you recommend for a small coffee?

CardioGood Fitness

Return to the CardioGood Fitness case (stored in CardioGood Fitness) first presented on page 28.

1. Determine whether differences exist between customers based on the product purchased (TM195, TM498, TM798) in their age in years, education in years, annual household income ($), mean number of times the customer plans to use the treadmill each week, and mean number of miles the customer expects to walk or run each week.

2. Write a report to be presented to the management of CardioGood Fitness detailing your findings.

More Descriptive Choices Follow-Up

Follow up the Using Statistics scenario "More Descriptive Choices, Revisited" on page 136 by determining whether there is a difference between the small, mid-cap, and large market cap funds in the three-year return percentages, five-year return percentages, and ten-year return percentages (stored in Retirement Funds).

Clear Mountain State Student Survey

The Student News Service at Clear Mountain State University (CMSU) has decided to gather data about the undergraduate students who attend CMSU. They create and distribute a survey of 14 questions and receive responses from 111 undergraduates (stored in StudentSurvey).

1. At the 0.05 level of significance, is there evidence of a difference based on academic major in expected starting salary, number of social networking sites registered for, age, spending on textbooks and supplies, text messages sent in a week, and the wealth needed to feel rich?

2. At the 0.05 level of significance, is there evidence of a difference based on graduate school intention in grade point average, expected starting salary, number of social networking sites registered for, age, spending on textbooks and supplies, text messages sent in a week, and the wealth needed to feel rich?

EG11.1 The COMPLETELY RANDOMIZED DESIGN: ONE-WAY ANOVA

Analyzing Variation in One-Way ANOVA

Key Technique Use the Section EG2.5 instructions to construct scatter plots using stacked data. If necessary, change the levels of the factor to consecutive integers beginning with 1, as was done for Figure 11.4 the in-store location sales experiment data on page 354.

F Test for Differences Among More Than Two Means

Key Technique Use the **DEVSQ** (*cell range of data of all groups*) function to compute *SST* and uses an expression in the form *SST* – **DEVSQ** (*group 1 data cell range*) – **DEVSQ** (*group 2 data cell range*) ... – **DEVSQ** (*group n data cell range*) to compute *SSA*.

Example Perform the Figure 11.6 one-way ANOVA for the in-store location sales experiment shown on page 356.

PHStat Use **One-Way ANOVA**.
For the example, open to the **DATA worksheet** of the **Mobile Electronics workbook**. Select **PHStat → Multiple-Sample Tests → One-Way ANOVA**. In the procedure's dialog box (shown below):

1. Enter **0.05** as the **Level of Significance**.
2. Enter **A1:D6** as the **Group Data Cell Range**.
3. Check **First cells contain label**.
4. Enter a **Title**, clear the **Tukey-Kramer Procedure** check box, and click **OK**.

In addition to the worksheet shown in Figure 11.6, this procedure creates an **ASFData worksheet** to hold the data used for the test. See the following *Workbook* section for a complete description of this worksheet.

Workbook Use the **COMPUTE worksheet** of the **One-Way ANOVA workbook** as a template.
The COMPUTE worksheet uses the ASFDATA worksheet that already contains the data for the example. Modifying the COMPUTE worksheet for other problems involves

multiple steps and is more complex than template modifications discussed in earlier chapters.

To modify the One-Way ANOVA workbook for other problems, first paste the data for the new problem into the ASF-Data worksheet, overwriting the in-store locations sales data. Then, in the COMPUTE worksheet (shown in Figure 11.6):

1. Edit the *SST* formula **= DEVSQ(ASFData!A1:D6)** in cell B16 to use the cell range of the new data just pasted into the ASFData worksheet.
2. Edit the cell B13 *SSA* formula so there are as many **DEVSQ**(*group column cell range*) terms as there are groups.
3. Change the level of significance in cell G17, if necessary.
4. If the problem contains three groups, select **row 8**, right-click, and select **Delete** from the shortcut menu.

   If the problem contains more than four groups, select **row 8**, right-click, and click **Insert** from the shortcut menu. Repeat this step as many times as necessary.
5. If you inserted new rows, enter (not copy) the formulas for those rows, using the formulas in row 7 as models.
6. Adjust table formatting as necessary.

To see the arithmetic formulas that the COMPUTE worksheet uses, not shown in Figure 11.8, open to the COMPUTE_FORMULAS worksheet.

Analysis ToolPak Use **Anova: Single Factor**.
For the example, open to the **DATA worksheet** of the **Mobile Electronics workbook** and:

1. Select **Data → Data Analysis**.
2. In the Data Analysis dialog box, select **Anova: Single Factor** from the **Analysis Tools** list and then click **OK**.

In the procedure's dialog box (shown below):

3. Enter **A1:D6** as the **Input Range**.
4. Click **Columns**, check **Labels in First Row**, and enter **0.05** as **Alpha**.
5. Click **New Worksheet Ply**.
6. Click **OK**.

The Analysis ToolPak creates a worksheet that does not use formulas but is similar in layout to the Figure 11.6 worksheet on page 356.

Levene Test for Homogeneity of Variance

Key Technique Use the techniques for performing a one-way ANOVA.

Example Perform the Figure 11.7 Levene test for the in-store location sales experiment shown on page 357.

PHStat Use **Levene Test**.
For the example, open to the **DATA worksheet** of the **Mobile Electronics workbook**. Select **PHStat → Multiple-Sample Tests → Levene Test**. In the procedure's dialog box (shown below):

1. Enter **0.05** as the **Level of Significance**.
2. Enter **A1:D6** as the **Sample Data Cell Range**.
3. Check **First cells contain label**.
4. Enter a **Title** and click **OK**.

The procedure creates a worksheet that performs the Table 11.3 absolute differences computations (see page 357) as well as the Figure 11.7 worksheet. See the following *Workbook* section for a description of these worksheets.

Workbook Use the **COMPUTE worksheet** of the **Levene workbook** as a template.
The COMPUTE worksheet and the supporting AbsDiffs and DATA worksheets already contain the data for the example.

For other problems in which the absolute differences are already known, paste the absolute differences into the AbsDiffs worksheet. Otherwise, paste the problem data into the DATA worksheet, add formulas to compute the median for each group, and adjust the AbsDiffs worksheet as necessary. For example, for the in-store location sales experiment, the following steps 1 through 7 were done with the workbook open to the DATA worksheet:

1. Enter the label **Medians** in **cellA7**, the first empty cell in column A.
2. Enter the formula **= MEDIAN(A2:A6)** in **cellA8**. (Cell range A2:A6 contains the data for the first group, in-aisle.)
3. Copy the cell A8 formula across through column D.
4. Open to the **AbsDiffs worksheet**.

In the AbsDiffs worksheet:

5. Enter row 1 column headings **AbsDiff1**, **AbsDiff2**, **AbsDiff3**, and **AbsDiff4** in columns A through D.
6. Enter the formula **= ABS(DATA!A2 − DATA!A8)** in cell A2. Copy this formula down through row 6.
7. Copy the formulas now in cell range A2:A6 across through column D. Absolute differences now appear in the cell range A2:D6.

Analysis ToolPak Use **Anova: Single Factor** with absolute difference data to perform the Levene test. If the absolute differences have not already been calculated, first use the preceding *Workbook* instructions to compute those values.

Multiple Comparisons: The Tukey-Kramer Procedure

Key Technique Use arithmetic formulas to compute the absolute mean differences and use the **IF** function to compare pairs of means.

Example Perform the Figure 11.8 Tukey-Kramer procedure for the in-store location sales experiment shown on page 359.

PHStat Use **One-Way ANOVA** with the **Tukey-Kramer procedure** option.
For the example, use the Section EG11.1 "*F* Test…" PHStat instructions, checking, not clearing, the **Tukey-Kramer Procedure** check box in step 4.

With this option, the procedure creates a second worksheet that is identical to the Figure 11.8 worksheet on page 359, other than missing a proper *Q* statistic value. Use Table E.7 to look up and enter the missing Studentized range *Q* statistic (4.05, for the example) for the level of significance and the numerator and denominator degrees of freedom that are given in the worksheet. (The second worksheet that the option creates will be identical to one of the "TK" worksheets discussed in the following *Workbook* instructions.)

Workbook Use the appropriate **"TK" worksheet** in the **One-Way ANOVA workbook** and manually look up and enter the appropriate Studentized range *Q* statistic value.
For the example, the **TK4 worksheet**, shown in Figure 11.8 on page 359, already has the appropriate *Q* statistic value (4.05) entered in cell B15. To see the arithmetic formulas that the TK4 worksheet uses, not shown in Figure 11.8, open to the TK4_FORMULAS worksheet.

For other problems, first modify the COMPUTE worksheet using the Section EG11.1 *Workbook* "*F* Test…" instructions. Then, open to the appropriate "TK" worksheet: TK3 (three groups), TK4 (four groups), TK5 (five groups), TK6 (six groups), or TK7 (seven groups). Use Table E.7 to look up the proper value of the Studentized range *Q* statistic for the level of significance and the numerator and denominator degrees of freedom for the problem.

When using the TK5, TK6, or TK7 worksheets, you must also enter the name, sample mean, and sample size for the fifth and subsequent, if applicable, groups.

Analysis ToolPak   Modify the previous instructions to perform the Tukey-Kramer procedure in conjunction with using the **Anova: Single Factor** procedure. Transfer selected values from the Analysis ToolPak results worksheet to one of the TK worksheets in the **One-Way ANOVA workbook**. For the example:

1. Use the Analysis ToolPak "*F* Test…" instructions on page 382 to create a worksheet that contains ANOVA results for the in-store locations experiment.
2. Record the name, **sample size** (in the **Count** column), and **sample mean** (in the **Average** column) of each group. Also record the *MSW* value, found in the cell that is the intersection of the **MS** column and **Within Groups** row, and the **denominator degrees of freedom**, found in the cell that is the intersection of the **df** column and **Within Groups** row.
3. Open to the **TK4 worksheet** of the **One-Way ANOVA workbook**.

In the TK4 worksheet:

4. Overwrite the formulas in cell range **A5:C8** by entering the name, sample mean, and sample size of each group into that range.
5. Enter **0.05** as the **Level of significance** in cell **B11**.
6. Enter **4** as the **Numerator d.f.** (equal to the number of groups) in cell **B12**.
7. Enter **16** as the **Denominator d.f** in cell **B13**.
8. Enter **0.0439** as the **MSW** in cell **B14**.
9. Enter **4.05** as the **Q Statistic** in cell **B15**. (Use Table E.7 to look up the Studentized range *Q* statistic.)

EG11.2 The FACTORIAL DESIGN: TWO-WAY ANOVA

Key Technique   Use the **DEVSQ** function to compute *SSA*, *SSB*, *SSAB*, *SSE*, and *SST*.

Example   Perform the Figure 11.10 two-way ANOVA for the in-store location sales and mobile payment experiment shown on page 368.

PHStat   Use **Two-Way ANOVA with replication**. For the example, open to the **DATA worksheet** of the **Mobile Electronics2 workbook**. Select **PHStat → Multiple-Sample Tests → Two-Way ANOVA**. In the procedure's dialog box (shown in the right column):

1. Enter **0.05** as the **Level of Significance**.
2. Enter **A1:E11** as the **Sample Data Cell Range**.
3. Check **First cells contain label**.
4. Enter a **Title** and click **OK**.

This procedure requires that the labels that identify factor *A* appear stacked in column A, followed by columns for factor *B*.

Workbook   Use the **COMPUTE worksheet** of the **Two-Way ANOVA workbook** as a model. For the example, the COMPUTE worksheet uses the ATF-DATA worksheet that already contains the data to perform the test for the example.

For other problems in which $r = 2$ and $c = 4$, paste the data for the problem into the ATFData worksheet, overwriting the in-store location and mobile payments data and then adjust the factor level headings in the COMPUTE worksheet.

For problems with a different mix of factors and levels, consider using either the *PHStat* or *Analysis ToolPak* instructions. Modifying the COMPUTE worksheet for such problems requires inserting (or deleting) of both rows and columns as well as editing several lengthy formulas found in the ANOVA table portion of the worksheet, operations that can be error-prone. The SHORT TAKES for Chapter 11 includes the instructions for these operations, should you choose to make such manual modifications.

To see the arithmetic formulas that the COMPUTE worksheet uses, not shown in Figure 11.10, open to the COMPUTE_FORMULAS worksheet.

Analysis ToolPak   Use **Anova: Two-Factor With Replication**. For the example, open to the **DATA worksheet** of the Mobile Electronics2 workbook and:

1. Select **Data → Data Analysis**.
2. In the Data Analysis dialog box, select **Anova: Two-Factor With Replication** from the **Analysis Tools** list and then click **OK**.

In the procedure's dialog box (shown on page 385):

3. Enter **A1:E11** as the **Input Range**.
4. Enter **5** as the **Rows per sample**.
5. Enter **0.05** as **Alpha**.
6. Click **New Worksheet Ply**.
7. Click **OK**.

This procedure requires that the labels that identify factor *A* appear stacked in column A, followed by columns for factor *B*. The Analysis ToolPak creates a worksheet that does not use formulas but is similar in layout to the Figure 11.10 worksheet.

Visualizing Interaction Effects: The Cell Means Plot

Key Technique Use the **SUMPRODUCT(***cell range 1, cell range 2***)** function to compute the expected value and variance.

Example Construct the Figure 11.13 cell means plot for mobile electronics sales based on mobile payments permitted and in-store location on page 368.

PHStat Modify the *PHStat* instructions for the two-way ANOVA. In step 4, check **Cell Means Plot** before clicking **OK**.

Analysis ToolPak Use the *Workbook* instructions.

Workbook Create a cell means plot from a two-way ANOVA COMPUTE worksheet.

For the example, open to the **COMPUTE worksheet** of the **Two-Way ANOVA** workbook and:

1. Insert a new worksheet.
2. Copy cell range **B3:E3** of the COMPUTE worksheet (the factor *B* level names) to cell **B1** of the new worksheet, using the Paste Special **Values** option.
3. Copy the cell range **B7:E7** of the COMPUTE worksheet (the AVERAGE row for the factor *A* No level) and paste to cell **B2** of the new worksheet, using the Paste Special **Values** option.
4. Copy the cell range **B13:E13** of the COMPUTE worksheet (the AVERAGE row for the factor *A* Yes level) and paste to cell **B3** of a new worksheet, using the Paste Special **Values** option.
5. Enter **No** in cell **B3** and **Yes** in cell **A3** of the new worksheet as labels for the factor *A* levels.
6. Select the cell range **A1:E3**.
7. Select **Insert → Line** and select the **Line with Markers** gallery item.
8. Relocate the chart to a chart sheet, add axis titles, and modify the chart title by using the instructions in Appendix Section B.6.

For other problems, insert a new worksheet and first copy and paste the factor *B* level names to row 1 of the new worksheet and then copy and use Paste Special to transfer the values in the **Average** rows data for each factor *B* level to the new worksheet. (See Appendix B to learn more about the Paste Special command.)

12

Chi-Square and Nonparametric Tests

CONTENTS

OBJECTIVES

- Learn when to use the chi-square test for contingency tables
- Learn to use the Marascuilo procedure for determining pairwise differences when evaluating more than two proportions
- Learn to use nonparametric tests

▼ USING **STATISTICS**
Avoiding Guesswork About Resort Guests

You are the manager of T.C. Resort Properties, a collection of five upscale hotels located on two tropical islands. Guests who are satisfied with the quality of services during their stay are more likely to return on a future vacation and to recommend the hotel to friends and relatives. You have defined the business objective as improving the percentage of guests who choose to return to the hotels later. To assess the quality of services being provided by your hotels, your staff encourages guests to complete a satisfaction survey when they check out or via email after they check out.

You need to analyze the data from these surveys to determine the overall satisfaction with the services provided, the likelihood that the guests will return to the hotel, and the reasons some guests indicate that they will not return. For example, on one island, T.C. Resort Properties operates the Beachcomber and Windsurfer hotels. Is the perceived quality at the Beachcomber Hotel the same as at the Windsurfer Hotel? If there is a difference, how can you use this information to improve the overall quality of service at T.C. Resort Properties? Furthermore, if guests indicate that they are not planning to return, what are the most common reasons cited for this decision? Are the reasons cited unique to a certain hotel or common to all hotels operated by T.C. Resort Properties?

n the preceding three chapters, you used hypothesis-testing procedures to analyze both numerical and categorical data. Chapter 9 presented some one-sample tests, Chapter 10 developed several two-sample tests, and Chapter 11 discussed analysis of variance (ANOVA). This chapter extends hypothesis testing to analyze differences between population *proportions* based on two or more samples and to test the hypothesis of independence in the joint responses to two categorical variables. The chapter concludes with nonparametric tests as alternatives to several Chapter 10 and 11 hypothesis tests.

12.1 Chi-Square Test for the Difference Between Two Proportions

In Section 10.3, you studied the Z test for the difference between two proportions. In this section, the differences between two proportions are examined from a different perspective. The hypothesis-testing procedure uses a test statistic, whose sampling distribution is approximated by a chi-square (χ^2) distribution, a right-skewed distribution whose shape depends solely on the number of degrees of freedom. The results of this χ^2 test are equivalent to those of the Z test described in Section 10.3.

If you are interested in comparing the counts of categorical responses between two independent groups, you can develop a **two-way contingency table** to display the frequency of occurrence of items of interest and items not of interest for each group. (Contingency tables were first discussed in Section 2.1, and, in Chapter 4, contingency tables were used to define and study probability.)

To illustrate a contingency table, return to the Using Statistics scenario concerning T.C. Resort Properties. On one of the islands, T.C. Resort Properties has two hotels (the Beachcomber and the Windsurfer). You collect data from customer satisfaction surveys and focus on the responses to the single question "Are you likely to choose this hotel again?" You organize the results of the survey and determine that 163 of 227 guests at the Beachcomber responded yes to "Are you likely to choose this hotel again?" and 154 of 262 guests at the Windsurfer responded yes to "Are you likely to choose this hotel again?" You want to analyze the results to determine whether, at the 0.05 level of significance, there is evidence of a significant difference in guest satisfaction (as measured by likelihood to return to the hotel) between the two hotels.

The contingency table displayed in Table 12.1, which has two rows and two columns, is called a **2 × 2 contingency table**. The cells in the table indicate the frequency for each row-and-column combination.

TABLE 12.1
Layout of a 2 × 2 Contingency Table

ROW VARIABLE	COLUMN VARIABLE		
	Group 1	**Group 2**	**Totals**
Items of interest	X_1	X_2	X
Items not of interest	$n_1 - X_1$	$n_2 - X_2$	$n - X$
Totals	n_1	n_2	n

where

X_1 = number of items of interest in group 1

X_2 = number of items of interest in group 2

$n_1 - X_1$ = number of items that are not of interest in group 1

$n_2 - X_2$ = number of items that are not of interest in group 2

$X = X_1 + X_2$, the total number of items of interest

$n - X = (n_1 - X_1) + (n_2 - X_2)$, the total number of items that are not of interest

$$n_1 = \text{sample size in group 1}$$
$$n_2 = \text{sample size in group 2}$$
$$n = n_1 + n_2 = \text{total sample size}$$

Table 12.2 is the contingency table for the hotel guest satisfaction study. The contingency table has two rows, indicating whether the guests would return to the hotel or would not return to the hotel, and two columns, one for each hotel. The cells in the table indicate the frequency of each row-and-column combination. The row totals indicate the number of guests who would return to the hotel and the number of guests who would not return to the hotel. The column totals are the sample sizes for each hotel location.

TABLE 12.2
2 × 2 Contingency Table for the Hotel Guest Satisfaction Survey

CHOOSE HOTEL AGAIN?	HOTEL Beachcomber	Windsurfer	Total
Yes	163	154	317
No	64	108	172
Total	227	262	489

To test whether the population proportion of guests who would return to the Beachcomber, π_1, is equal to the population proportion of guests who would return to the Windsurfer, π_2, you can use the **chi-square (χ^2) test for the difference between two proportions**. To test the null hypothesis that there is no difference between the two population proportions:

$$H_0: \pi_1 = \pi_2$$

against the alternative that the two population proportions are not the same:

$$H_1: \pi_1 \neq \pi_2$$

you use the χ^2_{STAT} test statistic, shown in Equation (12.1). The sampling distribution of this test statistic follows the **chi-square (χ^2) distribution**, which is right-skewed and whose lowest value is 0, unlike the normal and t distributions discussed in earlier chapters. (Table E.4 contains the cumulative probabilities for the chi-square distribution.)

χ^2 TEST FOR THE DIFFERENCE BETWEEN TWO PROPORTIONS

The χ^2_{STAT} test statistic is equal to the squared difference between the observed and expected frequencies, divided by the expected frequency in each cell of the table, summed over all cells of the table.

$$\chi^2_{STAT} = \sum_{\text{all cells}} \frac{(f_o - f_e)^2}{f_e} \qquad (12.1)$$

where

f_o = **observed frequency** in a particular cell of a contingency table
f_e = **expected frequency** in a particular cell if the null hypothesis is true

The χ^2_{STAT} test statistic approximately follows a chi-square distribution with 1 degree of freedom.[1]

[1] In general, the degrees of freedom in a contingency table are equal to (number of rows −1) multiplied by (number of columns −1).

To compute the expected frequency, f_e, in any cell, you need to know that if the null hypothesis is true, the proportion of items of interest in the two populations will be equal. In such situations, the sample proportions you compute from each of the two groups would differ from each other only by chance. Each would provide an estimate of the common population parameter, π. A statistic that combines these two separate estimates together into one overall estimate of the population parameter provides more information than either of the two separate estimates could provide by itself. This statistic, given by the symbol $\bar{p}$, represents the estimated overall proportion of items of interest for the two groups combined (i.e., the total number of items of interest divided by the total sample size). The complement of $\bar{p}$, $1 - \bar{p}$, represents the estimated overall proportion of items that are not of interest in the two groups. Using the notation presented in Table 12.1 on page 387, Equation (12.2) defines $\bar{p}$.

COMPUTING THE ESTIMATED OVERALL PROPORTION FOR TWO GROUPS

$$\bar{p} = \frac{X_1 + X_2}{n_1 + n_2} = \frac{X}{n} \tag{12.2}$$

To compute the expected frequency, f_e, for cells that involve items of interest (i.e., the cells in the first row in the contingency table), you multiply the sample size (or column total) for a group by $\bar{p}$. To compute the expected frequency, f_e, for cells that involve items that are not of interest (i.e., the cells in the second row in the contingency table), you multiply the sample size (or column total) for a group by $1 - \bar{p}$.

The sampling distribution of the χ^2_{STAT} test statistic shown in Equation (12.1) on page 388 approximately follows a chi-square (χ^2) distribution with 1 degree of freedom. Using a level of significance α, you reject the null hypothesis if the computed χ^2_{STAT} test statistic is greater than χ^2_α, the upper-tail critical value from the χ^2 distribution with 1 degree of freedom. Thus, the decision rule is

$$\text{Reject } H_0 \text{ if } \chi^2_{STAT} > \chi^2_\alpha;$$
$$\text{otherwise, do not reject } H_0.$$

Figure 12.1 illustrates the decision rule.

FIGURE 12.1
Regions of rejection and nonrejection when using the chi-square test for the difference between two proportions, with level of significance α

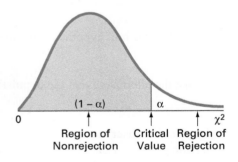

If the null hypothesis is true, the computed χ^2_{STAT} test statistic should be close to zero because the squared difference between what is actually observed in each cell, f_o, and what is theoretically expected, f_e, should be very small. If H_0 is false, then there are differences in the population proportions, and the computed χ^2_{STAT} test statistic is expected to be large. However, what is a large difference in a cell is relative. Because you are dividing by the expected frequencies, the same actual difference between f_o and f_e from a cell with a small number of expected frequencies contributes more to the χ^2_{STAT} test statistic than a cell with a large number of expected frequencies.

To illustrate the use of the chi-square test for the difference between two proportions, return to the Using Statistics scenario concerning T.C. Resort Properties on page 386 and the corresponding contingency table displayed in Table 12.2 on page 388. The null hypothesis

$(H_0: \pi_1 = \pi_2)$ states that there is no difference between the proportion of guests who are likely to choose either of these hotels again. To begin,

$$\bar{p} = \frac{X_1 + X_2}{n_1 + n_2} = \frac{163 + 154}{227 + 262} = \frac{317}{489} = 0.6483$$

$\bar{p}$ is the estimate of the common parameter π, the population proportion of guests who are likely to choose either of these hotels again if the null hypothesis is true. The estimated proportion of guests who are *not* likely to choose these hotels again is the complement of $\bar{p}$, $1 - 0.6483 = 0.3517$. Multiplying these two proportions by the sample size for the Beachcomber Hotel gives the number of guests expected to choose the Beachcomber again and the number not expected to choose this hotel again. In a similar manner, multiplying the two proportions by the Windsurfer Hotel's sample size yields the corresponding expected frequencies for that group.

EXAMPLE 12.1

Computing the Expected Frequencies

Compute the expected frequencies for each of the four cells of Table 12.2 on page 388.

SOLUTION

Yes—Beachcomber: $\bar{p} = 0.6483$ and $n_1 = 227$, so $f_e = 147.16$
Yes—Windsurfer: $\bar{p} = 0.6483$ and $n_2 = 262$, so $f_e = 169.84$
No—Beachcomber: $1 - \bar{p} = 0.3517$ and $n_1 = 227$, so $f_e = 79.84$
No—Windsurfer: $1 - \bar{p} = 0.3517$ and $n_2 = 262$, so $f_e = 92.16$

Table 12.3 presents these expected frequencies next to the corresponding observed frequencies.

TABLE 12.3
Comparing the Observed (f_o) and Expected (f_e) Frequencies

| | HOTEL | | | | |
| | Beachcomber | | Windsurfer | | |
CHOOSE HOTEL AGAIN?	Observed	Expected	Observed	Expected	Total
Yes	163	147.16	154	169.84	317
No	64	79.84	108	92.16	172
Total	227	227.00	262	262.00	489

To test the null hypothesis that the population proportions are equal:

$$H_0: \pi_1 = \pi_2$$

against the alternative that the population proportions are not equal:

$$H_1: \pi_1 \neq \pi_2$$

you use the observed and expected frequencies from Table 12.3 to compute the χ^2_{STAT} test statistic given by Equation (12.1) on page 388. Table 12.4 presents these calculations.

TABLE 12.4
Computing the χ^2_{STAT} Test Statistic for the Hotel Guest Satisfaction Survey

f_o	f_e	$(f_o - f_e)$	$(f_o - f_e)^2$	$(f_o - f_e)^2/f_e$
163	147.16	15.84	250.91	1.71
154	169.84	−15.84	250.91	1.48
64	79.84	−15.84	250.91	3.14
108	92.16	15.84	250.91	2.72
				9.05

You find the critical value for the χ^2 test from Table E.4, a portion of which is presented in Table 12.5.

TABLE 12.5

Finding the Critical Value from the Chi-Square Distribution with 1 Degree of Freedom, Using the 0.05 Level of Significance

		Cumulative Probabilities						
		.005	.01	...	.95	.975	.99	.995
		Upper-Tail Area						
Degrees of Freedom		.995	.99	...	.05	.025	.01	.005
1				... →	3.841	5.024	6.635	7.879
2		0.010	0.020	...	5.991	7.378	9.210	10.597
3		0.072	0.115	...	7.815	9.348	11.345	12.838
4		0.207	0.297	...	9.488	11.143	13.277	14.860
5		0.412	0.554	...	11.071	12.833	15.086	16.750

The values in Table 12.5 refer to selected upper-tail areas of the χ^2 distribution. A 2×2 contingency table has 1 degree of freedom because there are two rows and two columns. [The degrees of freedom are equal to the (number of rows -1)(number of columns -1).] Using $\alpha = 0.05$, with 1 degree of freedom, the critical value of χ^2 from Table 12.5 is 3.841. You reject H_0 if the computed χ^2_{STAT} test statistic is greater than 3.841 (see Figure 12.2). Because $\chi^2_{STAT} = 9.05 > 3.841$, you reject H_0. You conclude that the proportion of guests who would return to the Beachcomber is different from the proportion of guests who would return to the Windsurfer.

FIGURE 12.2

Regions of rejection and nonrejection when finding the χ^2 critical value with 1 degree of freedom, at the 0.05 level of significance

Figure 12.3 shows the Excel worksheet results for the Table 12.2 guest satisfaction contingency table on page 388.

FIGURE 12.3

Excel chi-square test worksheet results for the two-hotel guest satisfaction survey

▲	A	B	C	D	E	F	G
1	Chi-Square Test						
2							
3		Observed Frequencies					
4		Hotel				Calculations	
5	Choose Again?	Beachcomber	Windsurfer	Total		fo-fe	
6	Yes	163	154	317		15.8446	-15.8446
7	No	64	108	172		-15.8446	15.8446
8	Total	227	262	489			
9							
10		Expected Frequencies					
11		Hotel					
12	Choose Again?	Beachcomber	Windsurfer	Total		(fo-fe)^2/fe	
13	Yes	147.1554	169.8446	317		1.7060	1.4781
14	No	79.8446	92.1554	172		3.1442	2.7242
15	Total	227	262	489			
16							
17	Data						
18	Level of Significance	0.05					
19	Number of Rows	2					
20	Number of Columns	2					
21	Degrees of Freedom	1	=(B19 - 1) * (B20 - 1)				
22							
23	Results						
24	Critical Value	3.8415	=CHISQ.INV.RT(B18, B21)				
25	Chi-Square Test Statistic	9.0526	=SUM(F13:G14)				
26	p-Value	0.0026	=CHISQ.DIST.RT(B25, B21)				
27	Reject the null hypothesis		=IF(B26 < B18, "Reject the null hypothesis",				
28			"Do not reject the null hypothesis")				
29	Expected frequency assumption						
30	is met.		=IF(OR(B13 < 5, C13 < 5, B14 < 5, C14 < 5),				
			" is violated.", " is met.")				

In the Worksheet

This worksheet uses the CHISQ.INV.RT function to compute the critical value in cell B24 and uses the CHISQ.DIST.RT function to compute the p-value in cell B26.

The results of formulas that compute intermediate calculations in the first 15 rows provide the basis for computing the test statistic in cell B25. To see the formulas used in these rows, open to the COMPUTE_FORMULAS worksheet of the Chi-Square workbook.

In cell A30, an IF function that uses an embedded OR function (see Appendix F) checks to see if all expected frequencies are not less than 5.

These results include the expected frequencies, χ^2_{STAT}, degrees of freedom, and p-value. The computed χ^2_{STAT} test statistic is 9.0526, which is greater than the critical value of 3.8415 (or the p-value $= 0.0026 < 0.05$), so you reject the null hypothesis that there is no difference in guest satisfaction between the two hotels. The p-value, equal to 0.0026, is the probability of observing sample proportions as different as or more different from the actual difference between the Beachcomber and Windsurfer $(0.718 - 0.588 = 0.13)$ observed in the sample data, if the population proportions for the Beachcomber and Windsurfer hotels are equal. Thus, there is strong evidence to conclude that the two hotels are significantly different with respect to guest satisfaction, as measured by whether a guest is likely to return to the hotel again. From Table 12.3 on page 390 you can see that a greater proportion of guests are likely to return to the Beachcomber than to the Windsurfer.

For the χ^2 test to give accurate results for a 2×2 table, you must assume that each expected frequency is at least 5. If this assumption is not satisfied, you can use alternative procedures, such as Fisher's exact test (see references 1, 2, and 4).

In the hotel guest satisfaction survey, both the Z test based on the standardized normal distribution (see Section 10.3) and the χ^2 test based on the chi-square distribution lead to the same conclusion. You can explain this result by the interrelationship between the standardized normal distribution and a chi-square distribution with 1 degree of freedom. For such situations, the χ^2_{STAT} test statistic is the square of the Z_{STAT} test statistic.

For example, in the guest satisfaction study, using Equation (10.5) on page 326, the calculated Z_{STAT} test statistic is $+3.0088$, and the calculated χ^2_{STAT} test statistic is 9.0526. Except for rounding differences, this 9.0526 value is the square of $+3.0088$ [i.e., $(+3.0088)^2 \cong 9.0526$]. Also, if you compare the critical values of the test statistics from the two distributions, at the 0.05 level of significance, the χ^2 value of 3.841 with 1 degree of freedom is the square of the Z value of ± 1.96. Furthermore, the p-values for both tests are equal. Therefore, when testing the null hypothesis of equality of proportions:

$$H_0: \pi_1 = \pi_2$$

against the alternative that the population proportions are not equal:

$$H_1: \pi_1 \neq \pi_2$$

the Z test and the χ^2 test are equivalent. If you are interested in determining whether there is evidence of a *directional* difference, such as $\pi_1 > \pi_2$, you must use the Z test, with the entire rejection region located in one tail of the standardized normal distribution.

In Section 12.2, the χ^2 test is extended to make comparisons and evaluate differences between the proportions among more than two groups. However, you cannot use the Z test if there are more than two groups.

PROBLEMS FOR SECTION 12.1

LEARNING THE BASICS

12.1 Determine the critical value of χ^2 with 1 degree of freedom in each of the following circumstances:
a. $\alpha = 0.01$
b. $\alpha = 0.005$
c. $\alpha = 0.10$

12.2 Determine the critical value of χ^2 with 1 degree of freedom in each of the following circumstances:
a. $\alpha = 0.05$
b. $\alpha = 0.025$
c. $\alpha = 0.01$

12.3 Use the following contingency table:

	A	B	Total
1	20	30	50
2	30	45	75
Total	50	75	125

a. Compute the expected frequency for each cell.
b. Compare the observed and expected frequencies for each cell.
c. Compute χ^2_{STAT}. Is it significant at $\alpha = 0.05$?

12.4 Use the following contingency table:

	A	B	Total
1	20	30	50
2	30	20	50
Total	50	50	100

a. Compute the expected frequency for each cell.
b. Compute χ^2_{STAT}. Is it significant at $\alpha = 0.05$?

APPLYING THE CONCEPTS

12.5 An Ipsos poll asked 1,004 adults "If purchasing a used car made certain upgrades or features more affordable, what would be your preferred luxury upgrade?" The results indicated that 9% of the males and 14% of the females answered window tinting. (Source: Data extracted from "Safety Technology Tops the List of Most Desired Features Should They Be More Affordable when Purchasing a Used Car—Particularly Collision Avoidance," **bit.ly/1RCcc1L**.) The sample sizes of males and females were not provided. Suppose that both sample sizes were 502 and that 46 of 502 males and 71 of 502 females reported window tinting as their preferred luxury upgrade of choice.
a. Is there evidence of a difference between males and females in the proportion who said they prefer window tinting as a luxury upgrade at the 0.01 level of significance?
b. Find the p-value in (a) and interpret its meaning.
c. What are your answers to (a) and (b) if 60 males said they prefer window tinting as a luxury upgrade and 442 did not?
d. Compare the results of (a) through (c) to those of Problem 10.29 (a), (b), and (d) on page 331.

12.6 Does Cable Video on Demand (VOD D4+) increase ad effectiveness? A 2015 VOD study compared general TV and VOD D4+ audiences after viewing a brand ad. Whether the viewer indicated that the ad made them want to visit the brand website was collected and organized in the following table.

	MADE ME WANT TO VISIT THE BRAND WEBSITE	
VIEWING AUDIENCE	Yes	No
General TV	35	166
VOD D4+	147	103

Source: Data extracted from *Understanding VOD Advertising Effectiveness*, **bit.ly/1JnmMup**.

a. Set up the null and alternative hypotheses to try to determine whether there is difference in ad impact between general TV viewing and VOD D4+ viewing.
b. Conduct the hypothesis test defined in (a), using the 0.05 level of significance.
c. Compare the results of (a) and (b) to those of Problem 10.30 (a) and (b) on page 331.

12.7 Are males or females more satisfied with the growth and opportunities offered by their employer? A survey of employed adults conducted online by Harris Interactive on behalf of the American Psychological Association revealed the following:

	SATISFIED	
GENDER	Yes	No
Male	423	330
Feamle	377	422

Source: Data extracted from *The 2015 Work and Well-Being Survey*, American Psychological Association and Harris Interactive, 2015, **bit.ly/1HdJUbc**.

a. At the 0.05 level of significance, is there evidence of a difference between males and females in the proportion who are satisfied with the growth and opportunities offered by their employer?
b. Determine the p-value in (a) and interpret its meaning.

12.8 ✓SELF TEST The Society for Human Resource Management (SHRM) and Globoforce collaborated on a series of organizational surveys with the goal of identifying challenges that HR leaders face and what strategies help them conquer those challenges. In results published in 2015, employee retention/turnover (40%) and employee engagement (39%) were cited as the most important organizational challenges currently faced by HR professionals.
One strategy that may have an impact on employee retention, turnover, and engagement is a successful employee recognition program. As part of their surveys, SHRM and Globoforce showed that 278 (74%) of 376 organizations with 500 to 2,499 employees have employee recognition programs as compared to 316 (84%) of 376 organizations with 2,500+ employees. (Data extracted from *SHRM Survey Findings*, **bit.ly/1NltiQZ**).
a. At the 0.01 level of significance, is there evidence of a significant difference between organizations with 500 to 2,499 employees and organizations with 2,500+ employees with respect to the proportion that have employee recognition programs?
b. Determine the p-value in (a) and interpret is meaning.
c. Compare the results of (a) and (b) to those of Problem 10.32 on page 331.

12.9 How often does work intrude during off hours? A survey of 1,000 office workers indicated that 53% of males and 41% of females had office intrusions while on vacation. (Data extracted from "Office Intrusions on the Off Hours," *USA Today Snapshots*, November 25, 2013, p. 1A.) Assume that the survey consisted of 500 males and 500 females.
a. At the 0.05 level of significance, is there evidence of a difference in the proportion of males and females who had office intrusions while on vacation?
b. Find the p-value and interpret its meaning.

12.10 Does co-browsing have positive effects on the customer experience? Co-browsing refers to the ability to have a contact center agent and customer jointly navigate an application (e.g., web page, digital document, or mobile application) on a real time basis through the web. A study of businesses indicates that 81 of 129 co-browsing organizations use skills-based routing to match the caller with the *right* agent, whereas 65 of 176 non-co-browsing organizations use skills-based routing to match the caller with the *right* agent. (Data extracted from *Cobrowsing Presents a "Lucrative" Customer Service Opportunity,* **bit.ly/1wwALWr.**)

a. Construct a 2×2 contingency table.

b. At the 0.05 level of significance, is there evidence of a difference between co-browsing organizations and non-co-browsing organizations in the proportion that use skills-based routing to match the caller with the *right* agent?

c. Find the *p*-value in (a) and interpret its meaning.

d. Compare the results of (a) and (b) to those of Problem 10.34 on page 331.

12.2 Chi-Square Test for Differences Among More Than Two Proportions

In this section, the χ^2 test is extended to compare more than two independent populations. The letter c is used to represent the number of independent populations under consideration. Thus, the contingency table now has two rows and c columns. To test the null hypothesis that there are no differences among the c population proportions:

$$H_0: \pi_1 = \pi_2 = \cdots = \pi_c$$

against the alternative that not all the c population proportions are equal:

$$H_1: \text{Not all } \pi_j \text{ are equal (where } j = 1, 2, \ldots, c)$$

you use Equation (12.1) on page 388:

$$\chi^2_{STAT} = \sum_{\text{all cells}} \frac{(f_o - f_e)^2}{f_e}$$

where

f_o = observed frequency in a particular cell of a $2 \times c$ contingency table

f_e = expected frequency in a particular cell if the null hypothesis is true

If the null hypothesis is true and the proportions are equal across all c populations, the c sample proportions should differ only by chance. In such a situation, a statistic that combines these c separate estimates into one overall estimate of the population proportion, π, provides more information than any one of the c separate estimates alone. To expand on Equation (12.2) on page 389, the statistic $\bar{p}$ in Equation (12.3) represents the estimated overall proportion for all c groups combined.

> **COMPUTING THE ESTIMATED OVERALL PROPORTION FOR c GROUPS**
>
> $$\bar{p} = \frac{X_1 + X_2 + \cdots + X_c}{n_1 + n_2 + \cdots + n_c} = \frac{X}{n} \tag{12.3}$$

To compute the expected frequency, f_e, for each cell in the first row in the contingency table, multiply each sample size (or column total) by $\bar{p}$. To compute the expected frequency, f_e, for each cell in the second row in the contingency table, multiply each sample size (or column total) by $(1 - \bar{p})$. The sampling distribution of the test statistic shown in Equation (12.1) on page 388 approximately follows a chi-square distribution, with degrees of freedom equal to the number of rows in the contingency table minus 1, multiplied by the number of columns in the table minus 1. For a **$2 \times c$ contingency table**, there are $c - 1$ degrees of freedom:

$$\text{Degrees of freedom} = (2 - 1)(c - 1) = c - 1$$

Using the level of significance α, you reject the null hypothesis if the computed χ^2_{STAT} test statistic is greater than χ^2_α, the upper-tail critical value from a chi-square distribution with $c - 1$ degrees of freedom. Therefore, the decision rule is

$$\text{Reject } H_0 \text{ if } \chi^2_{STAT} > \chi^2_\alpha;$$

otherwise, do not reject H_0.

Figure 12.4 illustrates this decision rule.

FIGURE 12.4
Regions of rejection and nonrejection when testing for differences among c proportions using the χ^2 test

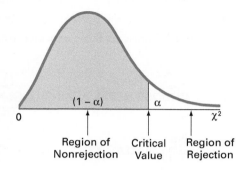

To illustrate the χ^2 test for equality of proportions when there are more than two groups, return to the Using Statistics scenario on page 386 concerning T.C. Resort Properties. Once again, you define the business objective as improving the quality of service, but this time, you are comparing three hotels located on a different island. Data are collected from customer satisfaction surveys at these three hotels. You organize the responses into the contingency table shown in Table 12.6.

TABLE 12.6
2 × 3 Contingency Table for Guest Satisfaction Survey

| | HOTEL | | | |
CHOOSE HOTEL AGAIN?	**Golden Palm**	**Palm Royale**	**Palm Princess**	**Total**
Yes	128	199	186	513
No	88	33	66	187
Total	216	232	252	700

Because the null hypothesis states that there are no differences among the three hotels in the proportion of guests who would likely return again, you use Equation (12.3) to calculate an estimate of π, the population proportion of guests who would likely return again:

$$\bar{p} = \frac{X_1 + X_2 + \cdots + X_c}{n_1 + n_2 + \cdots + n_c} = \frac{X}{n}$$

$$= \frac{(128 + 199 + 186)}{(216 + 232 + 252)} = \frac{513}{700}$$

$$= 0.733$$

The estimated overall proportion of guests who would *not* be likely to return again is the complement, $(1 - \bar{p})$, or 0.267. Multiplying these two proportions by the sample size for each hotel yields the expected number of guests who would and would not likely return.

EXAMPLE 12.2

Computing
the Expected
Frequencies

Compute the expected frequencies for each of the six cells in Table 12.6.

SOLUTION

Yes—Golden Palm: $\bar{p} = 0.733$ and $n_1 = 216$, so $f_e = 158.30$
Yes—Palm Royale: $\bar{p} = 0.733$ and $n_2 = 232$, so $f_e = 170.02$
Yes—Palm Princess: $\bar{p} = 0.733$ and $n_3 = 252$, so $f_e = 184.68$
No—Golden Palm: $1 - \bar{p} = 0.267$ and $n_1 = 216$, so $f_e = 57.70$
No—Palm Royale: $1 - \bar{p} = 0.267$ and $n_2 = 232$, so $f_e = 61.98$
No—Palm Princess: $1 - \bar{p} = 0.267$ and $n_3 = 252$, so $f_e = 67.32$

Table 12.7 presents these expected frequencies.

TABLE 12.7
Contingency Table of
Expected Frequencies
from a Guest Satisfaction Survey of Three
Hotels

CHOOSE HOTEL AGAIN?	HOTEL			Total
	Golden Palm	Palm Royale	Palm Princess	
Yes	158.30	170.02	184.68	513
No	57.70	61.98	67.32	187
Total	216.00	232.00	252.00	700

To test the null hypothesis that the proportions are equal:

$$H_0: \pi_1 = \pi_2 = \pi_3$$

against the alternative that not all three proportions are equal:

$$H_1: \text{Not all } \pi_j \text{ are equal (where } j = 1, 2, 3)$$

you use the observed frequencies from Table 12.6 and the expected frequencies from Table 12.7 to compute the χ^2_{STAT} test statistic [given by Equation (12.1) on page 388]. Table 12.8 presents the calculations.

TABLE 12.8
Computing the χ^2_{STAT}
Test Statistic for the
Three-Hotel Guest
Satisfaction Survey

f_o	f_e	$(f_o - f_e)$	$(f_o - f_e)^2$	$(f_o - f_e)^2/f_e$
128	158.30	−30.30	918.09	5.80
199	170.02	28.98	839.84	4.94
186	184.68	1.32	1.74	0.01
88	57.70	30.30	918.09	15.91
33	61.98	−28.98	839.84	13.55
66	67.32	−1.32	1.74	0.02
				40.23

You use Table E.4 to find the critical value of the χ^2 test statistic. In the guest satisfaction survey, because there are three hotels, there are $(2 - 1)(3 - 1) = 2$ degrees of freedom. Using $\alpha = 0.05$, the χ^2 critical value with 2 degrees of freedom is 5.991 (see Figure 12.5).

FIGURE 12.5
Regions of rejection and
nonrejection when testing
for differences in three
proportions at the 0.05
level of significance, with
2 degrees of freedom

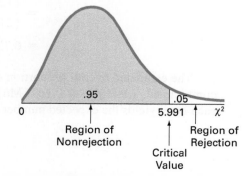

.95   .05

0   5.991 χ^2

Region of
Nonrejection

Region of
Rejection

Critical
Value

Because the computed χ^2_{STAT} test statistic is 40.23, which is greater than this critical value, you reject the null hypothesis. Figure 12.6 shows the Excel worksheet results for this problem. These results also report the p-value. Because the p-value is 0.0000, less than $\alpha = 0.05$, you reject the null hypothesis. Further, this p-value indicates that there is virtually no chance that there will be differences this large or larger among the three sample proportions, if the population proportions for the three hotels are equal. Thus, there is sufficient evidence to conclude that the hotel properties are different with respect to the proportion of guests who are likely to return.

FIGURE 12.6

Excel chi-square test worksheet results for the three-hotel guest satisfaction survey

	A	B	C	D	E	F	G	H	I
1	Chi-Square Test								
2									
3		Observed Frequencies							
4			Hotel					Calculations	
5	Choose Again?	Golden Palm	Palm Royale	Palm Princess	Total			fo - fe	
6	Yes	128	199	186	513		-30.2971	28.9771	1.32
7	No	88	33	66	187		30.2971	-28.9771	-1.32
8	Total	216	232	252	700				
9									
10		Expected Frequencies							
11			Hotel						
12	Choose Again?	Golden Palm	Palm Royale	Palm Princess	Total			(fo - fe)^2/fe	
13	Yes	158.2971	170.0229	184.68	513		5.7987	4.9386	0.0094
14	No	57.7029	61.9771	67.32	187		15.9077	13.5481	0.0259
15	Total	216	232	252	700				
16									
17	Data								
18	Level of Significance	0.05							
19	Number of Rows	2							
20	Number of Columns	3							
21	Degrees of Freedom	2	=(B19 - 1) * (B20 - 1)						
22									
23	Results								
24	Critical Value	5.9915	=CHISQ.INV.RT(B18, B21)						
25	Chi-Square Test Statistic	40.2284	=SUM(G13:I14)						
26	p-Value	0.0000	=CHISQ.DIST.RT(B25, B21)						
27	Reject the null hypothesis		=IF(B26 < B18, "Reject the null hypothesis",						
28			"Do not reject the null hypothesis")						
29	Expected frequency assumption								
30	is met.		=IF(OR(B13 < 1, C13 < 1, D13 < 1, B14 < 1, C14 < 1, D14 < 1),						
			" is violated.", " is met.")						

In the Worksheet

This worksheet is similar to the Figure 12.3 worksheet shown on page 391. The formulas in the first 15 rows are not shown at left but can be seen in the ChiSquare2x3_FORMULAS worksheet of the Chi-Square Worksheets workbook.

For the χ^2 test to give accurate results when dealing with $2 \times c$ contingency tables, all expected frequencies must be large. The definition of "large" has led to research among statisticians. Some statisticians (see reference 5) have found that the test gives accurate results as long as all expected frequencies are at least 0.5. Other statisticians believe that no more than 20% of the cells should contain expected frequencies less than 5, and no cells should have expected frequencies less than 1 (see reference 3). As a reasonable compromise between these points of view, to ensure the validity of the test, you should make sure that each expected frequency is at least 1. To do this, you may need to collapse two or more low-expected-frequency categories into one category in the contingency table before performing the test. If combining categories is undesirable, you can use one of the available alternative procedures (see references 1, 2, and 7).

The Marascuilo Procedure

Rejecting the null hypothesis in a χ^2 test of equality of proportions in a $2 \times c$ table allows you to only reach the conclusion that not all c population proportions are equal. To determine which proportions differ, you use a multiple-comparisons procedure such as the Marascuilo procedure.

The **Marascuilo procedure** enables you to make comparisons between all pairs of groups First, you compute the sample proportions. Then, you use Equation (12.4) to compute the critical ranges for the Marascuilo procedure. You compute a different critical range for each pairwise comparison of sample proportions.

CRITICAL RANGE FOR THE MARASCUILO PROCEDURE

$$\text{Critical range} = \sqrt{\chi_\alpha^2}\sqrt{\frac{p_j(1 - p_j)}{n_j} + \frac{p_{j'}(1 - p_{j'})}{n_{j'}}} \qquad \textbf{(12.4)}$$

where

p_j = proportion of items of interest in group j
$p_{j'}$ = proportion of items of interest in group j'
n_j = sample size in group j
$n_{j'}$ = sample size in group j'

---

studentTIP

You have an α level of risk in the entire set of comparisons not just a single comparison.

Then, you compare each of the $c(c - 1)/2$ pairs of sample proportions against its corresponding critical range. You declare a specific pair significantly different if the absolute difference in the sample proportions, $|p_j - p_{j'}|$, is greater than its critical range.

To apply the Marascuilo procedure, return to the three-hotel guest satisfaction survey. Using the χ^2 test, you concluded that there was evidence of a significant difference among the population proportions. From Table 12.6 on page 395, the three sample proportions are

$$p_1 = \frac{X_1}{n_1} = \frac{128}{216} = 0.5926$$

$$p_2 = \frac{X_2}{n_2} = \frac{199}{232} = 0.8578$$

$$p_3 = \frac{X_3}{n_3} = \frac{186}{252} = 0.7381$$

Next, you compute the absolute differences in sample proportions and their corresponding critical ranges. Because there are three hotels, there are $(3)(3 - 1)/2 = 3$ pairwise comparisons. Using Table E.4 and an overall level of significance of 0.05, the upper-tail critical value for a chi-square distribution having $(c - 1) = 2$ degrees of freedom is 5.991. Thus,

$$\sqrt{\chi_\alpha^2} = \sqrt{5.991} = 2.4477$$

The following displays the absolute differences and the critical ranges for each comparison.

Absolute Difference in Proportions	Critical Range
$\|p_j - p_{j'}\|$	$2.4477\sqrt{\dfrac{p_j(1 - p_j)}{n_j} + \dfrac{p_{j'}(1 - p_{j'})}{n_{j'}}}$
$\|p_1 - p_2\| = \|0.5926 - 0.8578\| = 0.2652$	$2.4477\sqrt{\dfrac{(0.5926)(0.4074)}{216} + \dfrac{(0.8578)(0.1422)}{232}} = 0.0992$
$\|p_1 - p_3\| = \|0.5926 - 0.7381\| = 0.1455$	$2.4477\sqrt{\dfrac{(0.5926)(0.4074)}{216} + \dfrac{(0.7381)(0.2619)}{252}} = 0.1063$
$\|p_2 - p_3\| = \|0.8578 - 0.7381\| = 0.1197$	$2.4477\sqrt{\dfrac{(0.8578)(0.1422)}{232} + \dfrac{(0.7381)(0.2619)}{252}} = 0.0880$

Figure 12.7 shows Excel worksheet results for this example.

FIGURE 12.7

Excel Marascuilo procedure worksheet results for the three-hotel guest satisfaction survey

	A	B	C	D
1	Marascuilo Procedure for Guest Satisfaction Analysis			
2				
3	Level of Significance	0.05	=ChiSquare2x3!B18	
4	Square Root of Critical Value	2.4477	=SQRT(ChiSquare2x3!B24)	
5				
6	Group Sample Proportions			
7	1: Golden Palm	0.5926	=ChiSquare2x3!B6/ChiSquare2x3!B8	
8	2: Palm Royale	0.8578	=ChiSquare2x3!C6/ChiSquare2x3!C8	
9	3: Palm Princess	0.7381	=ChiSquare2x3!D6/ChiSquare2x3!D8	
10				
11	MARASCUILO TABLE			
12	Proportions	Absolute Differences	Critical Range	
13	| Group 1 - Group 2 |	0.2652	0.0992	Significant
14	| Group 1 - Group 3 |	0.1455	0.1063	Significant
15				
16	| Group 2 - Group 3 |	0.1197	0.0880	Significant

In the Worksheet

This worksheet uses many of the results of the Figure 12.6 worksheet on page 397 as the basis for calculations. The formulas in rows 13, 14, and 16 that are not shown can be seen in the Marascuilo2x3_ FORMULAS worksheet of the Chi-Square Worksheets workbook.

As the final step, you compare the absolute differences to the critical ranges. If the absolute difference is greater than the critical range, the proportions are significantly different. At the 0.05 level of significance, you can conclude that guest satisfaction is higher at the Palm Royale ($p_2 = 0.858$) than at either the Golden Palm ($p_1 = 0.593$) or the Palm Princess ($p_3 = 0.738$) and that guest satisfaction is also higher at the Palm Princess than at the Golden Palm. These results clearly suggest that you should investigate possible reasons for these differences. In particular, you should try to determine why satisfaction is significantly lower at the Golden Palm than at the other two hotels.

The Analysis of Proportions (ANOP)

In many situations, you need to examine differences among several proportions. The analysis of proportions (ANOP) method provides a confidence interval approach that allows you to determine which, if any, of the c groups has a proportion significantly different from the overall mean of all the group proportions combined. The **ANOP online topic** discusses this method and illustrates its use.

PROBLEMS FOR SECTION 12.2

LEARNING THE BASICS

12.11 Consider a contingency table with two rows and five columns.
a. How many degrees of freedom are there in the contingency table?
b. Determine the critical value for $\alpha = 0.05$.
c. Determine the critical value for $\alpha = 0.01$.

12.12 Use the following contingency table:

	A	B	C	Total
1	10	30	50	90
2	40	45	50	135
Total	50	75	100	225

a. Compute the expected frequency for each cell.
b. Compute χ^2_{STAT}. Is it significant at $\alpha = 0.05$?

12.13 Use the following contingency table:

	A	B	C	Total
1	20	30	25	75
2	30	20	25	75
Total	50	50	50	150

a. Compute the expected frequency for each cell.
b. Compute χ^2_{STAT}. Is it significant at $\alpha = 0.05$?

APPLYING THE CONCEPTS

12.14 How common are financial cost or contractual constraints associated with smartphone ownership? A survey of smartphone owners found that 48% of the 18- to 29-year-olds, 38% of the 30- to 49-year-olds, 25% of the 50- to 64-year-olds, and 19% of those age 65 or older have reached the maximum amount of data they are allowed to use as part of their plan, at least on occasion. (Data extracted from *U.S. Smartphone Use 2015*, **bit.ly/1KL2WcW**.)

Suppose the survey was based on 200 smartphone owners in each of the four age groups: 18 to 29, 30 to 49, 50 to 64, and 65+.
a. At the 0.05 level of significance, is there evidence of a difference among the age groups in the proportion of smartphone owners who have reached the maximum amount of data they are allowed to use as part of their plan, at least on occasion?
b. Determine the *p*-value in (a) and interpret its meaning.
c. If appropriate, use the Marascuilo procedure and $\alpha = 0.05$ to determine which age groups differ.

12.15 Business sensor technology provides a way for companies to learn about their customers, employees, and operations; data captured from sensors can be used to improve engagement, sales, productivity, safety, and much more. A PwC survey of global business and IT executives found that 25% of automotive executives; 27% of energy, utilities, and mining executives; 30% of hospitality and leisure executives; 33% of industrial products executives; and 52% of retail and consumer executives say their companies are currently investing in business sensor technology. (Data extracted from *Three surprising digital bets for 2015*, pwc.to/1H8jcOY.)

Suppose these results were based on 500 business and IT executives in each of the five industries: Automotive; Energy, Utilities, and Mining; Hospitality and Leisure; Industrial Products; and Retail and Consumer.
a. At the 0.05 level of significance, is there evidence of a difference among the industries with respect to the proportion of executives that say their companies are currently investing in business sensor technology?
b. Compute the *p*-value and interpret its meaning.
c. If appropriate, use the Marascuilo procedure and $a = 0.05$ to determine which companies differ in their current investing in business sensor technology.

12.16 Most global organizations consider analytics and big data critical to success. However, is there a difference among North American, European, and Asian-Pacific organizations in the proportion of organizations that are investing heavily in analytics and big data technologies? A CSC study showed that 50% of North American, 66% of European, and 71% of Asian-Pacific organizations are investing heavily in analytics and big data technologies. (Data extracted from *CSC Global CIO Survey 2014–2015*, **bit.ly/1S6CLMQ**.)

Assume that 200 organization IT leaders within each global region were surveyed.
a. At the 0.05 level of significance, is there evidence of a difference among global regions with respect to the proportion of organizations that are investing heavily in analytics and big data technologies?
b. Determine the *p*-value in (a) and interpret its meaning.
c. If appropriate, use the Marascuilo procedure and $\alpha = 0.05$ to determine which global regions differ in the proportion of organizations that are investing heavily in analytics and big data technologies.

12.17 Repeat (a) and (b) of Problem 12.16, assuming that only 100 IT leaders within each global region were surveyed. Discuss the implications of sample size on the χ^2 test for differences among more than two populations.

12.18 Who uses a cellphone while watching TV? The Pew Research Center's Internet and American Life Project measured the prevalence of multiscreen viewing experiences by asking American adults who are cellphone owners whether they had used their phone to engage in several activities while watching TV. The study reported that 171 of 316 (54%) of urban American cellphone owners sampled, 516 of 993 (52%) of suburban American cellphone owners sampled, and 251 of 557 (45%) of rural American cellphone owners used their phone to engage in several activities while watching TV. (Data extracted from "The Rise of the Connected Viewer," Pew Research Center's Internet & American Life Project, July 17, 2012.)
a. Is there evidence of a significant difference among the urban, suburban, and rural American cellphone owners with respect to the proportion who use their phone to engage in several activities while watching TV? (Use $\alpha = 0.05$).
b. Determine the *p*-value and interpret its meaning.
c. If appropriate, use the Marascuilo procedure and $\alpha = 0.05$ to determine which groups differ.

12.19 An MSCI survey showed that there continues to be a slow increase in the overall percentage of women on boards of directors globally. The study reported that 7 of 22 (32%) Austrian companies sampled, 86 of 103 (83%) French companies sampled, 40 of 92 (43%) German companies sampled, 5 of 31 (16%) Irish companies sampled, and 37 of 55 (67%) Italian companies sampled have at least three female directors on their boards. (Data extracted from MSCI, *2014 Survey of Women on Boards*, **bit.ly/1MMiET1**.)
a. Is there evidence of a significant difference among the countries with respect to the proportion of companies who have at least three female directors on their boards? (Use $\alpha = 0.05$).
b. Determine the *p*-value and interpret its meaning.
c. If appropriate, use the Marascuilo procedure and $\alpha = 0.05$ to determine which countries differ.

12.3 Chi-Square Test of Independence

In Sections 12.1 and 12.2, you used the χ^2 test to evaluate potential differences among population proportions. For a contingency table that has *r* rows and *c* columns, you can generalize the χ^2 test as a *test of independence* for two categorical variables.

For a test of independence, the null and alternative hypotheses follow:

H_0: The two categorical variables are independent (i.e., there is no relationship between them).
H_1: The two categorical variables are dependent (i.e., there is a relationship between them).

Once again, you use Equation (12.1) on page 388 to compute the test statistic:

$$\chi^2_{STAT} = \sum_{\text{all cells}} \frac{(f_o - f_e)^2}{f_e}$$

You reject the null hypothesis at the α level of significance if the computed value of the χ^2_{STAT} test statistic is greater than χ^2_α, the upper-tail critical value from a chi-square distribution with $(r - 1)(c - 1)$ degrees of freedom (see Figure 12.8).

FIGURE 12.8
Regions of rejection and nonrejection when testing for independence in an $r \times c$ contingency table, using the χ^2 test

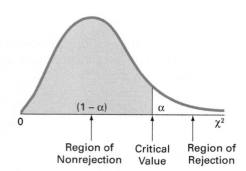

Thus, the decision rule is

$$\text{Reject } H_0 \text{ if } \chi^2_{STAT} > \chi^2_\alpha;$$

otherwise, do not reject H_0.

studentTIP

Remember that *independence* means no relationship, so you do not reject the null hypothesis. *Dependence* means there is a relationship, so you reject the null hypothesis.

The **chi-square (χ^2) test of independence** is similar to the χ^2 test for equality of proportions. The test statistics and the decision rules are the same, but the null and alternative hypotheses and conclusions are different. For example, in the guest satisfaction survey of Sections 12.1 and 12.2, there is evidence of a significant difference between the hotels with respect to the proportion of guests who would return. From a different viewpoint, you could conclude that there is a significant relationship between the hotels and the likelihood that a guest would return. However, the two types of tests differ in how the samples are selected.

In a test for equality of proportions, there is one factor of interest, with two or more levels. These levels represent samples selected from independent populations. The categorical responses in each group or level are classified into two categories, such as *an item of interest* and *not an item of interest*. The objective is to make comparisons and evaluate differences between the proportions of the *items of interest* among the various levels. However, in a test for independence, there are two factors of interest, each of which has two or more levels. You select one sample and tally the joint responses to the two categorical variables into the cells of a contingency table.

To illustrate the χ^2 test for independence, suppose that, in the three-hotel guest satisfaction survey, respondents who stated that they were not likely to return also indicated the primary reason for their unwillingness to return. Table 12.9 presents the resulting 4×3 contingency table.

TABLE 12.9
Contingency Table of Primary Reason for Not Returning and Hotel

PRIMARY REASON FOR NOT RETURNING	HOTEL			
	Golden Palm	Palm Royale	Palm Princess	Total
Price	23	7	37	67
Location	39	13	8	60
Room accommodation	13	5	13	31
Other	13	8	8	29
Total	88	33	66	187

In Table 12.9, observe that of the primary reasons for not planning to return to the hotel, 67 were due to price, 60 were due to location, 31 were due to room accommodation, and 29 were due to other reasons. In Table 12.6 on page 395, there were 88 guests at the Golden Palm, 33 guests at the Palm Royale, and 66 guests at the Palm Princess who were not planning to return. The observed frequencies in the cells of the 4 × 3 contingency table represent the joint tallies of the sampled guests with respect to primary reason for not returning and the hotel where they stayed. The null and alternative hypotheses are

H_0: There is no relationship between the primary reason for not returning and the hotel.

H_1: There is a relationship between the primary reason for not returning and the hotel.

To test this null hypothesis of independence against the alternative that there is a relationship between the two categorical variables, you use Equation (12.1) on page 398 to compute the test statistic:

$$\chi^2_{STAT} = \sum_{\text{all cells}} \frac{(f_o - f_e)^2}{f_e}$$

where

f_o = observed frequency in a particular cell of the $r \times c$ contingency table

f_e = expected frequency in a particular cell if the null hypothesis of independence is true

To compute the expected frequency, f_e, in any cell, you use the multiplication rule for independent events discussed on page 155 [see Equation (4.7)]. For example, under the null hypothesis of independence, the probability of responses expected in the upper-left-corner cell, representing primary reason of price for the Golden Palm is the product of the two separate probabilities $P(\text{Price})$ and $P(\text{Golden Palm})$. Here, the proportion of reasons that are due to price, $P(\text{Price})$, is $67/187 = 0.3583$, and the proportion of all responses from the Golden Palm, $P(\text{Golden Palm})$, is $88/187 = 0.4706$. If the null hypothesis is true, then the primary reason for not returning and the hotel are independent:

$$P(\text{Price } and \text{ Golden Palm}) = P(\text{Price}) \times P(\text{Golden Palm})$$
$$= (0.3583) \times (0.4706)$$
$$= 0.1686$$

The expected frequency is the product of the overall sample size, n, and this probability, $187 \times 0.1686 = 31.53$. The f_e values for the remaining cells are shown in Table 12.10.

TABLE 12.10

Contingency Table of Expected Frequencies of Primary Reason for Not Returning with Hotel

PRIMARY REASON FOR NOT RETURNING	HOTEL			
	Golden Palm	**Palm Royale**	**Palm Princess**	**Total**
Price	31.53	11.82	23.65	67
Location	28.24	10.59	21.18	60
Room accommodation	14.59	5.47	10.94	31
Other	13.65	5.12	10.24	29
Total	88.00	33.00	66.00	187

You can also compute the expected frequency by taking the product of the row total and column total for a cell and dividing this product by the overall sample size, as Equation (12.5) shows.

COMPUTING THE EXPECTED FREQUENCY

The expected frequency in a cell is the product of its row total and column total, divided by the overall sample size.

$$f_e = \frac{\text{Row total} \times \text{Column total}}{n} \qquad (12.5)$$

where

Row total = sum of the frequencies in the row
Column total = sum of the frequencies in the column
n = overall sample size

This alternate method results in simpler computations. For example, using Equation (12.5) for the upper-left-corner cell (price for the Golden Palm),

$$f_e = \frac{\text{Row total} \times \text{Column total}}{n} = \frac{(67)(88)}{187} = 31.53$$

and for the lower-right-corner cell (other reason for the Palm Princess),

$$f_e = \frac{\text{Row total} \times \text{Column total}}{n} = \frac{(29)(66)}{187} = 10.24$$

To perform the test of independence, you use the χ^2_{STAT} test statistic shown in Equation (12.1) on page 388. The sampling distribution of the χ^2_{STAT} test statistic approximately follows a chi-square distribution, with degrees of freedom equal to the number of rows in the contingency table minus 1, multiplied by the number of columns in the table minus 1:

$$\text{Degrees of freedom} = (r - 1)(c - 1)$$
$$= (4 - 1)(3 - 1) = 6$$

Table 12.11 presents the computations for the χ^2_{STAT} test statistic.

TABLE 12.11
Computing the χ^2_{STAT} Test Statistic for the Test of Independence

Cell	f_o	f_e	$(f_o - f_e)$	$(f_o - f_e)^2$	$(f_o - f_e)^2/f_e$
Price/Golden Palm	23	31.53	−8.53	72.76	2.31
Price/Palm Royale	7	11.82	−4.82	23.23	1.97
Price/Palm Princess	37	23.65	13.35	178.22	7.54
Location/Golden Palm	39	28.24	10.76	115.78	4.10
Location/Palm Royale	13	10.59	2.41	5.81	0.55
Location/Palm Princess	8	21.18	−13.18	173.71	8.20
Room/Golden Palm	13	14.59	−1.59	2.53	0.17
Room/Palm Royale	5	5.47	−0.47	0.22	0.04
Room/Palm Princess	13	10.94	2.06	4.24	0.39
Other/Golden Palm	13	13.65	−0.65	0.42	0.03
Other/Palm Royale	8	5.12	2.88	8.29	1.62
Other/Palm Princess	8	10.24	−2.24	5.02	0.49
					27.41

Using the $\alpha = 0.05$ level of significance, the upper-tail critical value from the chi-square distribution with 6 degrees of freedom is 12.592 (see Table E.4). Because $\chi^2_{STAT} = 27.41 > 12.592$, you reject the null hypothesis of independence (see Figure 12.9).

FIGURE 12.9
Regions of rejection and nonrejection when testing for independence in the three hotel guest satisfaction survey example at the 0.05 level of significance, with 6 degrees of freedom

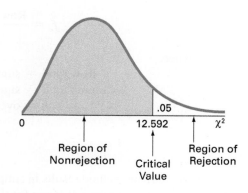

Figure 12.10 shows the Excel worksheet results for this test. Because $\chi^2_{STAT} = 27.410 > 12.592$, you reject the null hypothesis of independence. Using the p-value approach, you reject the null hypothesis of independence because the p-value $= 0.000 < 0.05$. The p-value indicates that there is virtually no chance of having a relationship this strong or stronger between the hotel and the primary reasons for not returning in a sample, if the primary reasons for not returning are independent of the specific hotels in the entire population. Thus, there is strong evidence of a relationship between the primary reason for not returning and the hotel.

FIGURE 12.10
Excel chi-square test worksheet results for the Table 12.9 primary reason for not returning to hotel data

	A	B	C	D	E	F	G	H	I
1	Chi-Square Test of Independence								
3		Observed Frequencies					Calculations		
4			Hotel						
5	Reason for Not Returning	Golden Palm	Palm Royale	Palm Princess	Total		fo - fe		
6	Price	23	7	37	67		-8.5294	-4.8235	13.3529
7	Location	39	13	8	60		10.7647	2.4118	-13.1765
8	Room accommodation	13	5	13	31		-1.5882	-0.4706	2.0588
9	Other	13	8	8	29		-0.6471	2.8824	-2.2353
10	Total	88	33	66	187				
12		Expected Frequencies							
14	Reason for Not Returning	Golden Palm	Palm Royale	Palm Princess	Total		(fo - fe)^2/fe		
15	Price	31.5294	11.8235	23.6471	67		2.3074	1.9678	7.5401
16	Location	28.2353	10.5882	21.1765	60		4.1040	0.5493	8.1987
17	Room accommodation	14.5882	5.4706	10.9412	31		0.1729	0.0405	0.3874
18	Other	13.6471	5.1176	10.2353	29		0.0307	1.6234	0.4882
19	Total	88	33	66	187				
21	Data								
22	Level of Significance	0.05							
23	Number of Rows	4							
24	Number of Columns	3							
25	Degrees of Freedom	6	=(B23 - 1) * (B24 - 1)						
27	Results								
28	Critical Value	12.5916	=CHISQ.INV.RT(B22, B25)						
29	Chi-Square Test Statistic	27.4104	=SUM(G15:I18)						
30	p-Value	0.0001	=CHISQ.DIST.RT(B29, B25)						
31	Reject the null hypothesis		=IF(B30 < B22, "Reject the null hypothesis",						
32			"Do not reject the null hypothesis")						
33	Expected frequency assumption								
34	is met.		=IF(OR(B15 < 1, C15 < 1, D15 < 1, B16 < 1, C16 < 1, D16 < 1,						
			B17 < 1, C17 < 1, D17 < 1, B18 < 1, C18 < 1, D18 < 1),							
			" is violated.", " is met.")						

In the Worksheet

This worksheet is similar to the Figure 12.6 worksheet on page 397. The formulas for the first 19 rows that are not shown can be seen in the ChiSquare4×3_FORMULAS worksheet of the Chi-Square Worksheets workbook.

Examination of the observed and expected frequencies (see Table 12.11 on page 403) reveals that price is underrepresented as a reason for not returning to the Golden Palm (i.e., $f_o = 23$ and $f_e = 31.53$) but is overrepresented at the Palm Princess. Guests are more satisfied with the price at the Golden Palm than at the Palm Princess. Location is overrepresented as a reason for not returning to the Golden Palm but greatly underrepresented at the Palm Princess. Thus, guests are much more satisfied with the location of the Palm Princess than with that of the Golden Palm.

To ensure accurate results, all expected frequencies need to be large in order to use the χ^2 test when dealing with $r \times c$ contingency tables. As in the case of $2 \times c$ contingency tables in Section 12.2, all expected frequencies should be at least 1. For contingency tables in which one or more expected frequencies are less than 1, you can use the chi-square test after collapsing two or more low-frequency rows into one row (or collapsing two or more low-frequency columns into one column). Merging rows or columns usually results in expected frequencies sufficiently large to ensure the accuracy of the χ^2 test.

PROBLEMS FOR SECTION 12.3

LEARNING THE BASICS

12.20 If a contingency table has three rows and four columns, how many degrees of freedom are there for the χ^2 test of independence?

12.21 When performing a χ^2 test of independence in a contingency table with r rows and c columns, determine the upper-tail critical value of the test statistic in each of the following circumstances:
a. $\alpha = 0.05, r = 4$ rows, $c = 5$ columns
b. $\alpha = 0.01, r = 4$ rows, $c = 5$ columns
c. $\alpha = 0.01, r = 4$ rows, $c = 6$ columns
d. $\alpha = 0.01, r = 3$ rows, $c = 6$ columns
e. $\alpha = 0.01, r = 6$ rows, $c = 3$ columns

APPLYING THE CONCEPTS

12.22 The owner of a restaurant serving Continental-style entrées has the business objective of learning more about the patterns of patron demand during the Friday-to-Sunday weekend time period. Data were collected from 630 customers on the type of entrée and dessert ordered and organized into the following table:

TYPE OF DESSERT	TYPE OF ENTRÉE				
	Beef	Poultry	Fish	Pasta	Total
Ice cream	13	8	12	14	47
Cake	98	12	29	6	145
Fruit	8	10	6	2	26
None	124	98	149	41	412
Total	243	128	196	63	630

At the 0.05 level of significance, is there evidence of a relationship between type of dessert and type of entrée?

12.23 An Australian Fair Work Commission survey of 1,134 employees across various industries gathered data on key drivers of job satisfaction. The most important aspect in determining employee satisfaction was collected by industry and organized into the table below. At the 0.05 level of significance, is there evidence of a significant relationship between the most important aspect in determining employee satisfaction and industry?

INDUSTRY	MOST IMPORTANT ASPECT IN DETERMINING EMPLOYEE SATISFACTION						
	Flexibility	Freedom	Total pay	Job security	Work itself	Hours worked	Total
Lodging and food services	61	19	25	21	25	14	165
Education/training	71	31	25	20	51	19	217
Financial services	30	9	10	14	15	4	82
Healthcare and social assistance	93	31	29	40	69	13	275
Communications	32	9	13	8	18	1	81
Retail trade	92	39	54	58	47	24	314
Total	379	138	156	161	225	75	1,134

Source: Data extracted from Fair Work Commission, "Key Drivers of Job Satisfaction," **bit.ly/1RiXIcw**.

12.24 How often do Facebook users post? A study by the Pew Research Center (data extracted from **bit.ly/1axbobZ**) revealed the following results:

FREQUENCY	AGE GROUP 18–22	23–35	36–49	50–65	65+	Total
Several times a day	20	22	9	2	1	54
About once a day	28	37	14	4	1	84
3–5 days per week	32	46	31	7	2	118
1–2 days per week	32	69	35	17	7	160
Every few weeks	22	66	47	28	6	169
Less often	16	59	56	61	18	210
Never	6	15	42	66	23	152
Total	156	314	234	185	58	947

At the 0.01 level of significance, is there evidence of a significant relationship between frequency of posting on Facebook and age?

12.25 Infusionsoft conducted a study to explore the attitudes, behaviors, and challenges that small businesses face related to sales and marketing. Small business owners were categorized by the amount they spend per month on marketing activities as well as the attitudinal segment to which they belong. Results were organized into the following table.

ATTITUDINAL SEGMENT	SPEND PER MONTH ON MARKETING ACTIVITIES Less than $200	$200–$1,000	$1000+	Total
Freedom Seekers	89	64	40	193
Passionate Creators	64	82	63	209
Struggling Survivors	87	66	48	201
Legacy Builders	122	63	49	234
Total	362	275	200	837

Source: Data extracted from *2015 Infusionsoft Small Business Market Research Sales & Marketing Report*, **bit.ly/1x8t9r2**.

At the 0.05 level of significance, is there evidence of a significant relationship between amount spent per month on marketing activities and attitudinal segment?

12.26 On a regular basis, PwC takes a closer look at what CEOs are looking for and are finding as new sources of value in their businesses and industries. Based on a 2014 Global CEO survey, CEOs are categorized by what they identified as the main opportunity for business growth in their company as well as the geographic region in which they are located. Survey results appear in the table below. At the 0.05 level of significance, is there evidence of a significant relationship between identified main opportunity and geographic region?

IDENTIFIED MAIN OPPORTUNITY	GEOGRAPHIC REGION United States	China and Hong Kong	Japan	Germany	Total
Product/service innovation	58	58	45	21	182
Increased share in existing markets	60	30	31	15	136
Mergers and acquisitions	23	10	12	4	49
New geographic markets	16	18	31	2	67
New joint ventures or alliances	5	18	8	3	34
Total	162	134	127	45	468

Source: Data extracted from PwC, "17th Annual Global CEO Survey," **pwc.to/1xHKtqe**.

12.4 Wilcoxon Rank Sum Test: A Nonparametric Method for Two Independent Populations

In Section 10.1, you used the *t* test for the difference between the means of two independent populations. If sample sizes are small and you cannot assume that the data in each sample are from normally distributed populations, you can choose to use the pooled-variance *t* test, following a *normalizing transformation* on the data (see reference 8), or use a nonparametric method that does not depend on the assumption of normality for the two populations.

Nonparametric methods require few or no assumptions about the populations from which data are obtained (see reference 4). The **Wilcoxon rank sum test** for testing whether there is a difference between two medians is one such method. You use this method when you cannot meet the assumptions that the pooled-variance and separate-variance *t* tests discussed in Section 10.1 require. In such conditions, the Wilcoxon rank sum test is likely to have more statistical power (see Section 9.6) than those *t* tests. (When assumptions can be met, the test has almost as much power as the *t* tests.) You can also use the Wilcoxon rank sum test when you have only ordinal data, as often happens in consumer behavior and marketing research.

To perform the Wilcoxon rank sum test, you replace the values in the two samples of sizes n_1 and n_2 with their combined ranks (unless the data contained the ranks initially). You begin by defining $n = n_1 + n_2$ as the total sample size. Next, you assign the ranks so that rank 1 is given to the smallest of the n combined values, rank 2 is given to the second smallest, and so on, until rank n is given to the largest. If several values are tied, you assign each value the average of the ranks that otherwise would have been assigned had there been no ties.

Whenever the two sample sizes are unequal, n_1 represents the smaller sample and n_2 the larger sample. The Wilcoxon rank sum test statistic, T_1, is defined as the sum of the ranks assigned to the n_1 values in the smaller sample. (For equal-sized samples, either sample may be used for determining T_1.) For any integer value n, the sum of the first n consecutive integers is $n(n + 1)/2$. Therefore, T_1 plus T_2, the sum of the ranks assigned to the n_2 items in the second sample, must equal $n(n + 1)/2$. You can use Equation (12.6) to check the accuracy of your rankings.

studentTIP
Remember that you combine the two groups before you rank the values.

studentTIP
Remember that the group that is defined as group 1 when computing the test statistic T_1 must also be defined as group 1 in the null and alternative hypotheses.

CHECKING THE RANKINGS

$$T_1 + T_2 = \frac{n(n + 1)}{2}$$ (12.6)

For a two-tail test shown in Figure 12.11, you reject the null hypothesis if the computed value of T_1 is greater than or equal to the upper critical value, or if T_1 is less than or equal to the lower critical value. Figure 12.11 also illustrates the two one-tail tests. For lower-tail tests which have the alternative hypothesis $H_1: M_1 < M_2$ that the median of population 1 (M_1) is less than the median of population 2 (M_2), you reject the null hypothesis if the observed value of T_1 is less than or equal to the lower critical value. For upper-tail tests which have the alternative hypothesis $H_1: M_1 > M_2$, you reject the null hypothesis if the observed value of T_1 equals or is greater than the upper critical value.

FIGURE 12.11
Regions of rejection and nonrejection using the Wilcoxon rank sum test

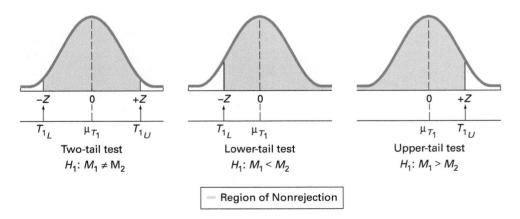

When n_1 and n_2 are each ≤ 10, you use Table E.6 to find the critical values of the test statistic T_1. For large sample sizes, the test statistic T_1 is approximately normally distributed, with the mean, μ_{T_1}, equal to

$$\mu_{T_1} = \frac{n_1(n + 1)}{2}$$

and the standard deviation, σ_{T_1}, equal to

$$\sigma_{T_1} = \sqrt{\frac{n_1 n_2 (n + 1)}{12}}$$

Therefore, Equation (12.7) defines the standardized Z test statistic for the Wilcoxon rank sum test.

LARGE-SAMPLE WILCOXON RANK SUM TEST

$$Z_{STAT} = \frac{T_1 - \dfrac{n_1(n + 1)}{2}}{\sqrt{\dfrac{n_1 n_2 (n + 1)}{12}}} \tag{12.7}$$

where the test statistic Z_{STAT} approximately follows a standardized normal distribution.

You use Equation (12.7) when the sample sizes are outside the range of Table E.6. Based on α, the level of significance selected, you reject the null hypothesis if the Z_{STAT} test statistic falls in the rejection region.

To study an application of the Wilcoxon rank sum test, recall the Chapter 10 Arlingtons scenario about VLABGo player monthly sales at the special front location and at the in-aisle location (stored in VLABGo). If you cannot assume that the populations are normally distributed, you can use the Wilcoxon rank sum test to evaluate possible differences in the median sales for the two display locations.[2] The VLABGo sales data and the combined ranks are shown in Table 12.12.

2 To test for differences in the median sales between the two locations, you must assume that the distributions of sales in both populations are identical except for differences in central tendency (i.e., the medians).

TABLE 12.12
Forming the Combined Rankings

Special Front ($n_1 = 10$)	Combined Ranking	In-Aisle ($n_2 = 10$)	Combined Ranking
224	12	192	7
189	5.5	236	13
248	15	164	3
285	19	154	1
273	17	189	5.5
160	2	220	11
243	14	261	16
215	9	186	4
280	18	219	10
317	20	202	8

Source: Data are taken from Table 10.1 on page 309.

Because you have not stated in advance which display location is likely to have a higher median, you use a two-tail test with the following null and alternative hypotheses:

$H_0: M_1 = M_2$ (the median sales are equal)

$H_1: M_1 \neq M_2$ (the median sales are not equal)

Next, you compute T_1, the sum of the ranks assigned to the *smaller* sample. When the sample sizes are equal, as in this example, you can define either sample as the group from which to compute T_1. Choosing the special front location as the first group,

$$T_1 = 12 + 5.5 + 15 + 19 + 17 + 2 + 14 + 9 + 18 + 20 = 131.5$$

As a check on the ranking procedure, you compute T_2 from

$$T_2 = 7 + 13 + 3 + 1 + 5.5 + 11 + 16 + 4 + 10 + 8 = 78.5$$

and then use Equation (12.6) on page 407 to show that the sum of the first $n = 20$ integers in the combined ranking is equal to $T_1 + T_2$:

$$T_1 + T_2 = \frac{n(n + 1)}{2}$$

$$131.5 + 78.5 = \frac{20(21)}{2} = 210$$

$$210 = 210$$

Next, you use Table E.6 to determine the lower- and upper-tail critical values for the test statistic T_1. From Table 12.13, a portion of Table E.6, observe that for a level of significance of 0.05, the critical values are 78 and 132. The decision rule is

Reject H_0 if $T_1 \leq 78$ or if $T_1 \geq 132$;

otherwise, do not reject H_0.

TABLE 12.13
Finding the Lower- and Upper-Tail Critical Values for the Wilcoxon Rank Sum Test Statistic, T_1, Where $n_1 = 10$, $n_2 = 10$, and $\alpha = 0.05$

n_2	One-tail α	Two-tail α	4	5	6	7	8	9	10
						(Lower, Upper)			
	.05	.10	16,40	24,51	33,63	43,76	54,90	66,105	
9	.025	.05	14,42	22,53	31,65	40,79	51,93	62,109	
	.01	.02	13,43	20,55	28,68	37,82	47,97	59,112	
	.005	.01	11,45	18,57	26,70	35,84	45,99	56,115	
	.05	.10	17,43	26,54	35,67	45,81	56,96	69,111	82,128
10	.025	.05	15,45	23,57	32,70	42,84	53,99	65,115	78,132
	.01	.02	13,47	21,59	29,73	39,87	49,103	61,119	74,136
	.005	.01	12,48	19,61	27,75	37,89	47,105	58,122	71,139

Source: Extracted from Table E.6.

Because the test statistic $T_1 = 131.5 < 132$, you do not reject H_0. There is insufficient evidence of a significant difference in the median sales for the two locations.

Figure 12.12 on page 410 shows the Wilcoxon rank sum test worksheet results for the VLABGo player monthly sales. These results include a warning to use a table such as Table E.6 because the small sample sizes in each group may violate the assumption of normality that is implicit in the worksheet calculations. The worksheet (wrongly) reports to reject the null hypothesis because the computed p-value is 0.0452, less than $\alpha = 0.05$. This worksheet example demonstrates the importance of heeding warnings issued by any software you might use to perform statistical computations.

FIGURE 12.12

Excel Wilcoxon rank sum test worksheet results for VLABGo player monthly sales for two different locations

	A	B
1	Wilcoxon Rank Sum Test	
2		
3	**Data**	
4	Level of Significance	0.05
5		
6	**Population 1 Sample**	
7	Sample Size	10 =COUNTIF(SortedRanks!A2:A21, "Special Front")
8	Sum of Ranks	131.5 =SUMIF(SortedRanks!A2:A21, "Special Front", SortedRanks!C2:C21)
9	**Population 2 Sample**	
10	Sample Size	10 =COUNTIF(SortedRanks!A2:A21, "In-aisle")
11	Sum of Ranks	78.5 =SUMIF(SortedRanks!A2:A21, "In-aisle", SortedRanks!C2:C21)
12		
13	**Intermediate Calculations**	
14	Total Sample Size	20 =B7 + B10
15	T_1 Test Statistic	131.5 =IF(B7 <= B10, B8, B11)
16	T_1 Mean	105 =IF(B7 <= B10, B7 * (B14 + 1)/2, B10 * (B14 + 1)/2)
17	Standard Error of T_1	13.2288 =SQRT(B7 * B10 * (B14 + 1)/12)
18	Z Test Statistic	2.0032 =(B15 - B16)/B17
19		
20	**Two-Tail Test**	
21	Lower Critical Value	-1.9600 =NORM.S.INV(B4/2)
22	Upper Critical Value	1.9600 =NORM.S.INV(1 - B4/2)
23	p-Value	0.0452 =2 * (1 - NORM.S.DIST(ABS(B18), TRUE))
24	Reject the null hypothesis	=IF(B23 < B4, "Reject the null hypothesis",
25		"Do not reject the null hypothesis")
26	Conclusion may be invalid due to sample sizes.	
27	Use table method to evaluate test statistic.	

In the Worksheet

This worksheet uses the Equation (12.7) large-sample approximation in computing the p-value. That value may be inaccurate when both sample sizes are less than or equal to 10 and the test statistic T_1 is less likely to be approximately normally distributed. Formulas in cells A26 and A27 (not shown) use the IF function and the expression **AND(B7 <= 10, B10 <= 10)** to determine if both sample sizes are 10 or fewer and to display a warning message if the condition holds.

See Appendix F to learn more about the AND function, and the COUNTIF and SUMIF functions that the worksheet uses to compute the sample sizes and sum of ranks from unsummarized data. To see all the formulas used in both two-tail *and* one-tail tests, open to the COMPUTE_ALL_FORMULAS worksheet in the Wilcoxon workbook.

Table E.6 shows the lower and upper critical values of the Wilcoxon rank sum test statistic, T_1, but only for situations in which both n_1 and n_2 are less than or equal to 10. If either one or both of the sample sizes are greater than 10, you *must* use the large-sample Z approximation formula [Equation (12.7) on page 408]. To demonstrate the large-sample Z approximation formula, consider the VLABGo player monthly sales data. Using Equation (12.7),

$$Z_{STAT} = \frac{T_1 - \dfrac{n_1(n+1)}{2}}{\sqrt{\dfrac{n_1 n_2(n+1)}{12}}}$$

$$= \frac{131.5 - \dfrac{(10)(21)}{2}}{\sqrt{\dfrac{(10)(10)(21)}{12}}}$$

$$= \frac{131.5 - 105}{13.2288} = 2.0032$$

studentTIP

If the assumption of normality is met, use the pooled-variance or separate-variance test as these tests are more powerful. Use the Wilcoxon rank sum test when you doubt the normality of the populations.

Because $Z_{STAT} = 2.0032 > 1.96$, the critical value of Z at the 0.05 level of significance (or p-value $= 0.0452 < 0.05$), you reject H_0. As with similar calculations in the Figure 12.12 worksheets, these calculations lead to an inaccurate conclusion. If you use the Z approximation formula with small sample sizes, consider using the table method discussed on pages 408–409 to verify your conclusion.

PROBLEMS FOR SECTION 12.4

LEARNING THE BASICS

12.27 Using Table E.6, determine the lower- and upper-tail critical values for the Wilcoxon rank sum test statistic, T_1, in each of the following two-tail tests:

a. $\alpha = 0.10, n_1 = 6, n_2 = 8$
b. $\alpha = 0.05, n_1 = 6, n_2 = 8$
c. $\alpha = 0.01, n_1 = 6, n_2 = 8$
d. Given the results in (a) through (c), what do you conclude regarding the width of the region of nonrejection as the selected level of significance, α, gets smaller?

12.28 Using Table E.6, determine the lower-tail critical value for the Wilcoxon rank sum test statistic, T_1, in each of the following one-tail tests:

a. $\alpha = 0.05, n_1 = 6, n_2 = 8$
b. $\alpha = 0.025, n_1 = 6, n_2 = 8$
c. $\alpha = 0.01, n_1 = 6, n_2 = 8$
d. $\alpha = 0.005, n_1 = 6, n_2 = 8$

12.29 The following information is available for two samples selected from independent populations:

Sample 1: $n_1 = 7$ **Assigned ranks:** 4 1 8 2 5 10 11
Sample 2: $n_2 = 9$ **Assigned ranks:** 7 16 12 9 3 14 13 6 15

What is the value of T_1 if you are testing the null hypothesis $H_0: M_1 = M_2$?

12.30 In Problem 12.29, what are the lower- and upper-tail critical values for the test statistic T_1 from Table E.6 if you use a 0.05 level of significance and the alternative hypothesis is $H_1: M_1 \neq M_2$?

12.31 In Problems 12.29 and 12.30, what is your statistical decision?

12.32 The following information is available for two samples selected from independent and similarly shaped right-skewed populations:

Sample 1: $n_1 = 5$ 1.1   2.3   2.9   3.6   14.7
Sample 2: $n_2 = 6$ 2.8   4.4   4.4   5.2   6.0   18.5

a. Replace the observed values with the corresponding ranks (where $1 =$ smallest value; $n = n_1 + n_2 = 11 =$ largest value) in the combined samples.
b. What is the value of the test statistic T_1?
c. Compute the value of T_2, the sum of the ranks in the larger sample.
d. To check the accuracy of your rankings, use Equation (12.6) on page 407 to demonstrate that $T_1 + T_2 = \dfrac{n(n+1)}{2}$

12.33 From Problem 12.32, at the 0.05 level of significance, determine the lower-tail critical value for the Wilcoxon rank sum test statistic, T_1, if you want to test the null hypothesis, $H_0: M_1 \geq M_2$, against the one-tail alternative, $H_1: M_1 < M_2$.

12.34 In Problems 12.32 and 12.33, what is your statistical decision?

APPLYING THE CONCEPTS

12.35 A vice president for marketing recruits 20 college graduates for management training. Each of the 20 individuals is randomly assigned to one of two groups (10 in each group). A "traditional" method of training (T) is used in one group, and an "experimental" method (E) is used in the other. After the graduates spend six months on the job, the vice president ranks them on the basis of their performance, from 1 (worst) to 20 (best), with the following results (stored in the file TestRank):

> **T:** 1 2 3 5 9 10 12 13 14 15
> **E:** 4 6 7 8 11 16 17 18 19 20

Is there evidence of a difference in the median performance between the two methods? (Use $\alpha = 0.05$.)

12.36 Wine experts Gaiter and Brecher use a six-category scale when rating wines: Yech, OK, Good, Very Good, Delicious, and Delicious! Suppose Gaiter and Brecher tested wines from a random sample of eight inexpensive California Cabernets and a random sample of eight inexpensive Washington Cabernets, where *inexpensive* means wines with a U.S. suggested retail price of less than $20, and assigned the following ratings:

> California—Good, Delicious, Yech, OK, OK, Very Good, Yech, OK
>
> Washington—Very Good, OK, Delicious!, Very Good, Delicious, Good, Delicious, Delicious!

The ratings were then ranked and the ratings and the rankings stored in Cabernet . (Data extracted from D. Gaiter and J. Brecher, "A Good U.S. Cabernet Is Hard to Find," *The Wall Street Journal*, May 19, 2006, p. W7.)

a. Are the data collected by rating wines using this scale nominal, ordinal, interval, or ratio?
b. Why is the two-sample t test defined in Section 10.1 inappropriate to test the mean rating of California Cabernets versus Washington Cabernets?
c. Is there evidence of a significant difference in the median rating of California Cabernets and Washington Cabernets? (Use $\alpha = 0.05$.)

12.37 A problem that prevents a customer from receiving or making phone calls is upsetting to both the customer and the company that provides the phone service. The file Phone contains samples of 20 problems reported to two different offices of a phone provider and the time (minutes) to clear these problems:

Office I Time to Clear Problems (Minutes)

> 1.48 1.75 0.78 2.85 0.52 1.60 4.15 3.97 1.48 3.10
> 1.02 0.53 0.93 1.60 0.80 1.05 6.32 3.93 5.45 0.97

Office II Time to Clear Problems (Minutes)

> 7.55 3.75 0.10 1.10 0.60 0.52 3.30 2.10 0.58 4.02
> 3.75 0.65 1.92 0.60 1.53 4.23 0.08 1.48 1.65 0.72

a. Is there evidence of a difference in the median time to clear problems between offices? (Use $\alpha = 0.05$.)
b. What assumptions must you make in (a)?
c. Compare the results of (a) with those of Problem 10.9(a) on page 316.

12.38 The management of a hotel has the business objective of increasing the return rate for hotel guests. One aspect of first impressions by guests relates to the time it takes to deliver a guest's luggage to the room after check-in to the hotel. A random sample of 20 deliveries on a particular day were selected in Wing A of the hotel, and a random sample of 20 deliveries were selected in Wing B. Delivery times were collected and stored in Luggage .
a. Is there evidence of a difference in the median delivery times in the two wings of the hotel? (Use $\alpha = 0.05$.)
b. Compare the results of (a) with those of Problem 10.65 on page 340.

12.39 The lengths of life (in hours) of a sample of 40 100-watt compact fluorescent light bulbs produced by Manufacturer A and a sample of 40 20-watt compact fluorescent light bulbs produced by Manufacturer B are stored in Bulbs .
a. Using a 0.05 level of significance, is there evidence of a difference in the median life of bulbs produced by the two manufacturers?
b. What assumptions must you make in (a)?
c. Compare the results of (a) with those of Problem 10.64 on page 340. Discuss.

12.40 Brand valuations are critical to CEOs, financial and marketing executives, security analysts, institutional investors, and others who depend on well-researched, reliable information for assessments and comparisons in decision making. WPP and Millward Brown annually publish the BrandZ Top 100 Most Valuable Global Brands. The BrandZ rankings combines consumer measures of brand equity with financial measures to establish a *brand value* for each brands. The file BrandZTechFin contains the 2015 brand values for the technology sector and the financial institutions sector. (Data extracted from BrandZ Top 1000 Most Valuable Global Brands 2015, **bit.ly/1FCLpz3**.)
a. Using a 0.05 level of significance, is there evidence of a difference in the median brand value between the two sectors?
b. What assumptions must you make in (a)?
c. Compare the results of (a) with those of Problem 10.17 on page 317. Discuss.

12.41 A bank with a branch located in a commercial district of a city has developed an improved process for serving customers during the noon-to-1 P.M. lunch period. The bank has the business objective of reducing the waiting time (defined as the number of minutes that elapse from when the customer enters the line until he or she reaches the teller window) to increase customer satisfaction. A random sample of 15 customers is selected and waiting times are collected and stored in Bank1 . These waiting times (in minutes) are:

4.21 5.55 3.02 5.13 4.77 2.34 3.54 3.20
4.50 6.10 0.38 5.12 6.46 6.19 3.79

Another branch, located in a residential area, is also concerned with the noon-to-1 P.M. lunch period. A random sample of 15 customers is selected and waiting times are collected and stored in Bank2 . These waiting times (in minutes) are:

9.66 5.90 8.02 5.79 8.73 3.82 8.01 8.35
10.49 6.68 5.64 4.08 6.17 9.91 5.47

a. Is there evidence of a difference in the median waiting time between the two branches? (Use $\alpha = 0.05$.)
b. What assumptions must you make in (a)?
c. Compare the results (a) with those of Problem 10.12 (a) on page 316. Discuss.

12.42 An important feature of tablets is battery life, the number of hours before the battery needs to be recharged. The file Tablets contains the battery life of 12 Wi-Fi-only and 7 3G/4G/Wi-Fi tablets. (Data extracted from "Ratings and Recommendations: Tablets," *Consumer Reports*, August 2013, p. 24.)
a. Is there evidence of a difference in the median battery life between Wi-Fi-only and 3G/4G/Wi-Fi tablets (Use $\alpha = 0.05$.)
b. What assumptions must you make in (a)?
c. Compare the results of (a) with those of Problem 10.11 (a) on page 316. Discuss.

12.5 Kruskal-Wallis Rank Test: A Nonparametric Method for the One-Way ANOVA

If the normality assumption of the one-way ANOVA F test is violated, you can use the Kruskal-Wallis rank test. The **Kruskal-Wallis rank test** for differences among c medians (where $c > 2$) is an extension of the Wilcoxon rank sum test for two independent populations, discussed in Section 12.4. The Kruskal-Wallis test has the same power relative to the one-way ANOVA F test that the Wilcoxon rank sum test has relative to the t test.

You use the Kruskal-Wallis rank test to test whether c independent groups have equal medians. The null hypothesis is

$$H_0: M_1 = M_2 = \cdots = M_c$$

and the alternative hypothesis is

$$H_1: \text{Not all } M_j \text{ are equal (where } j = 1, 2, \ldots, c).$$

To use the Kruskal-Wallis rank test, you first replace the values in the c samples with their combined ranks (if necessary). Rank 1 is given to the smallest of the combined values and rank n to the largest of the combined values (where $n = n_1 + n_2 + \cdots + n_c$). If any values are tied, you assign each of them the mean of the ranks they would have otherwise been assigned if ties had not been present in the data.

The Kruskal-Wallis test is an alternative to the one-way ANOVA F test. Instead of comparing each of the c group means against the grand mean, the Kruskal-Wallis test compares the mean rank in each of the c groups against the overall mean rank, based on all n combined values. Equation (12.8) defines the Kruskal-Wallis test statistic, H.

KRUSKAL-WALLIS RANK TEST FOR DIFFERENCES AMONG c MEDIANS

$$H = \left[\frac{12}{n(n+1)} \sum_{j=1}^{c} \frac{T_j^2}{n_j} \right] - 3(n+1) \qquad (12.8)$$

where

n = total number of values over the combined samples

n_j = number of values in the jth sample ($j = 1, 2, \ldots, c$)

T_j = sum of the ranks assigned to the jth sample

T_j^2 = square of the sum of the ranks assigned to the jth sample

c = number of groups

If there is a significant difference among the c groups, the mean rank differs considerably from group to group. In the process of squaring these differences, the test statistic H becomes large. If there are no differences present, the test statistic H is small because the mean of the ranks assigned in each group should be very similar from group to group.

As the sample sizes in each group get large (i.e., at least 5), the sampling distribution of the test statistic, H, approximately follows the chi-square distribution with $c - 1$ degrees of freedom. Thus, you reject the null hypothesis if the computed value of H is greater than the upper-tail critical value (see Figure 12.13). Therefore, the decision rule is

$$\text{Reject } H_0 \text{ if } H > \chi_\alpha^2;$$

otherwise, do not reject H_0.

FIGURE 12.13
Determining the rejection region for the Kruskal-Wallis test

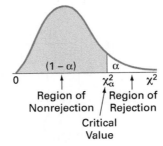

To illustrate the Kruskal-Wallis rank test for differences among c medians, return to the Arlington's scenario on page 348 that concerns the in-store sales location experiment. If you cannot assume that the mobile electronics sales are normally distributed in all c groups, you can use the Kruskal-Wallis rank test.

The null hypothesis is that the median mobile electronics sales from each of the four in-store locations are equal. The alternative hypothesis is that at least one of these medians differs from the others:

H_0: $M_1 = M_2 = M_3 = M_4$

H_1: Not all M_j are equal (where $j = 1, 2, 3, 4$).

Table 12.14 presents the data (stored in [Second Experiment]), along with the corresponding ranks of a second in-store location sales experiment at Arlington's.

TABLE 12.14

Mobile Electronics Sales and Rank for Four In-Store Locations for Second Experiment

IN-AISLE		FRONT		KIOSK		EXPERT	
Sales	**Rank**	**Sales**	**Rank**	**Sales**	**Rank**	**Sales**	**Rank**
29.60	2	33.21	20	31.23	14	29.83	6.5
29.59	1	31.80	17	31.14	13	29.69	4
30.11	9	30.54	11	30.04	8	29.61	3
29.83	6.5	31.39	15	30.87	12	29.72	5
30.32	10	33.05	18	33.08	19	31.41	16

In assigning ranks to the sales, the lowest sales, the second in-aisle sales in Table 12.4, is assigned the rank of 1 and the highest sales, the first front sales, is assigned the rank of 20. Because the fourth in-aisle sales and the first expert sales are tied for ranks 6 and 7, each is assigned the rank 6.5.

After all the ranks are assigned, you compute the sum of the ranks for each group:

$$\text{Rank sums: } T_1 = 28.5 \quad T_2 = 81 \quad T_3 = 66 \quad T_4 = 34.5$$

As a check on the rankings, recall from Equation (12.6) on page 407 that for any integer n, the sum of the first n consecutive integers is $n(n + 1)/2$. Therefore,

$$T_1 + T_2 + T_3 + T_4 = \frac{n(n + 1)}{2}$$

$$28.5 + 81 + 66 + 34.5 = \frac{(20)(21)}{2}$$

$$210 = 210$$

To test the null hypothesis of equal population medians, you calculate the test statistic H using Equation (12.8) on page 413:

$$H = \left[\frac{12}{n(n + 1)} \sum_{j=1}^{c} \frac{T_j^2}{n_j} \right] - 3(n + 1)$$

$$= \left\{ \frac{12}{(20)(21)} \left[\frac{(28.5)^2}{5} + \frac{(81)^2}{5} + \frac{(66)^2}{5} + \frac{(34.5)^2}{5} \right] \right\} - 3(21)$$

$$= \left(\frac{12}{420} \right)(2{,}583.9) - 63 = 10.8257$$

The test statistic H approximately follows a chi-square distribution with $c - 1$ degrees of freedom. Using a 0.05 level of significance, χ_α^2, the upper-tail critical value of the chi-square distribution with $c - 1 = 3$ degrees of freedom, is 7.815 (see Table 12.15). Because the computed value of the test statistic $H = 10.8257$ is greater than the critical value of 7.815, you reject the null hypothesis and conclude that the median mobile electronics sales is not the same for all the in-store locations.

TABLE 12.15
Finding χ_α^2, the Upper-Tail Critical Value for the Kruskal-Wallis Rank Test, at the 0.05 Level of Significance with 3 Degrees of Freedom

				Cumulative Area						
	.005	.01	.025	.05	.10	.25	.75	.90	.95	.975
					Upper-Tail Area					
Degrees of Freedom	.995	.99	.975	.95	.90	.75	.25	.10	.05	.025
1	—	—	0.001	0.004	0.016	0.102	1.323	2.706	3.841	5.024
2	0.010	0.020	0.051	0.103	0.211	0.575	2.773	4.605	5.991	7.378
3	0.072	0.115	0.216	0.352	0.584	1.213	4.108	6.251	7.815	9.348
4	0.207	0.297	0.484	0.711	1.064	1.923	5.385	7.779	9.488	11.143
5	0.412	0.554	0.831	1.145	1.610	2.675	6.626	9.236	11.071	12.833

Source: Extracted from Table E.4.

Figure 12.14 shows the Excel Kruskal-Wallis rank test worksheet results. From these results, you reject the null hypothesis because the p-value $= 0.0127 < 0.05$. At this point, you could simultaneously compare all pairs of locations to determine which ones differ (see reference 2).

FIGURE 12.14
Excel Kruskal-Wallis rank test worksheet results for the differences among the median mobile electronics sales for four in-store locations

In the Worksheet

This worksheet uses the **CHISQ.INV.RT** function in cell B13 to compute the critical value and uses the **CHISQ.DIST.RT** function to compute the p-value.

The columns D through G formulas that are not shown can be seen in the KruskalWallis4_FORMULAS worksheet of the Kruskal-Wallis Worksheets workbook.

Assumptions

To use the Kruskal-Wallis rank test, the following assumptions must be met:

- The c samples are randomly and independently selected from their respective populations.
- The underlying variable is continuous.
- The data provide at least a set of ranks, both within and among the c samples.
- The c populations have the same variability.
- The c populations have the same shape.

The Kruskal-Wallis procedure makes less stringent assumptions than does the F test. If you ignore the last two assumptions (variability and shape), you can still use the Kruskal-Wallis rank test to determine whether at least one of the populations differs from the other populations in some characteristic—such as central tendency, variation, or shape.

To use the F test, you must assume that the c samples are from normal populations that have equal variances. When the more stringent assumptions of the F test hold, you should use the F test instead of the Kruskal-Wallis test because it has slightly more power to detect significant differences among groups. However, if the assumptions of the F test do not hold, you should use the Kruskal-Wallis test.

PROBLEMS FOR SECTION 12.5

LEARNING THE BASICS

12.43 What is the upper-tail critical value from the chi-square distribution if you use the Kruskal-Wallis rank test for comparing the medians in six populations at the 0.01 level of significance?

12.44 For this problem, use the results of Problem 12.43.
a. State the decision rule for testing the null hypothesis that all six groups have equal population medians.
b. What is your statistical decision if the computed value of the test statistic H is 13.77?

APPLYING THE CONCEPTS

12.45 A pet food company has the business objective of expanding its product line beyond its current kidney and shrimp-based cat foods. The company developed two new products—one based on chicken livers and the other based on salmon. The company conducted an experiment to compare the two new products with its two existing ones, as well as a generic beef-based product sold at a supermarket chain.

For the experiment, a sample of 50 cats from the population at a local animal shelter was selected. Ten cats were randomly assigned to each of the five products being tested. Each of the cats was then presented with 3 ounces of the selected food in a dish at feeding time. The researchers defined the variable to be measured as the number of ounces of food that the cat consumed within a 10-minute time interval that began when the filled dish was presented. The results for this experiment are summarized in the table below and stored in CatFood .
a. At the 0.05 level of significance, is there evidence of a significant difference in the median amount of food eaten among the various products?
b. Compare the results of (a) with those of Problem 11.13 (a) on page 362.
c. Which test is more appropriate for these data: the Kruskal-Wallis rank test or the one-way ANOVA F test? Explain.

Kidney	Shrimp	Chicken Liver	Salmon	Beef
2.37	2.26	2.29	1.79	2.09
2.62	2.69	2.23	2.33	1.87
2.31	2.25	2.41	1.96	1.67
2.47	2.45	2.68	2.05	1.64
2.59	2.34	2.25	2.26	2.16
2.62	2.37	2.17	2.24	1.75
2.34	2.22	2.37	1.96	1.18
2.47	2.56	2.26	1.58	1.92
2.45	2.36	2.45	2.18	1.32
2.32	2.59	2.57	1.93	1.94

SELF TEST **12.46** A hospital conducted a study of the waiting time in its emergency room. The hospital has a main campus, along with three satellite locations. Management had a business objective of reducing waiting time for emergency room cases that did not require immediate attention. To study this, a random sample of 15 emergency room cases at each location were selected on a particular day, and the waiting time (recorded from check-in to when the patient was called into the clinic area) was measured. The results are stored in ERWaiting .
a. At the 0.05 level of significance, is there evidence of a difference in the median waiting times in the four locations?
b. Compare the results of (a) with those of Problem 11.9 (a) on page 361.

12.47 *QSR* magazine reports on the largest quick-serve and fast-casual brands in the United States. The file FastFoodChain contains the food segment (burger, chicken, sandwich, or snack) and U.S. mean sales per unit ($thousands). (Data extracted from "The QSR 50," **bit.ly/1sbeSrS**.)
a. At the 0.05 level of significance, is there evidence of a difference in the median U.S. average sales per unit ($thousands) among the food segments?
b. Compare the results of (a) with those of Problem 11.11 (a) on page 362.

12.48 An advertising agency has been hired by a manufacturer of pens to develop an advertising campaign for the upcoming holiday season. To prepare for this project, the research director decides to initiate a study of the effect of advertising on product perception. An experiment is designed to compare five different advertisements. Advertisement A greatly undersells the pen's characteristics. Advertisement B slightly undersells the pen's characteristics. Advertisement C slightly oversells the pen's characteristics. Advertisement D greatly oversells the pen's characteristics. Advertisement E attempts to correctly state the pen's characteristics.

A sample of 30 adult respondents, taken from a larger focus group, is randomly assigned to the five advertisements (so that there are six respondents to each). After reading the advertisement and developing a sense of product expectation, all respondents unknowingly receive the same pen to evaluate. The respondents are permitted to test the pen and the plausibility of the advertising copy. The respondents are then asked to rate the pen from 1 to 7 on the product characteristic scales of appearance, durability, and writing performance. The *combined* scores of three ratings (appearance, durability, and writing performance) for the 30 respondents are stored in Pen . These data are:

A	B	C	D	E
15	16	8	5	12
18	17	7	6	19
17	21	10	13	18
19	16	15	11	12
19	19	14	9	17
20	17	14	10	14

a. At the 0.05 level of significance, is there evidence of a difference in the median ratings of the five advertisements?
b. Compare the results of (a) with those of Problem 11.10 (a) on page 362.
c. Which test is more appropriate for these data: the Kruskal-Wallis rank test or the one-way ANOVA F test? Explain.

12.49 A transportation strategist wanted to compare the traffic congestion levels across three continents: Asia, Europe, and North America. The file CongestionLevel contains congestion level,

defined as the increase (%) in overall travel time when compared to a free flow situation (an uncongested situation) for 30 cities in each continent. (Data extracted from "TomTom Traffic Index," **bit.ly/1KvUAWM.**)
a. At the 0.05 level of significance, is there evidence of a difference in the median congestion levels across continents?
b. Compare the results of (a) with those of Problem 11.14 (a) on page 363.

12.50 The more costly and time consuming it is to export and import, the more difficult it is for local companies to be competitive and to reach international markets. As part of an initial investigation exploring foreign market entry, 10 countries were selected from each of four global regions. The cost associated with importing a standardized cargo of goods by sea transport in these countries (in US$ per container) is stored in ForeignMarket2 . (Data extracted from **doingbusiness.org/data**).
a. At the 0.05 level of significance, is there evidence of a difference in the median cost across the four global regions associated with importing a standardized cargo of goods by sea transport?
b. Compare the results in (a) to those in Problem 11.8 (a) on page 361.

12.6 McNemar Test for the Difference Between Two Proportions (Related Samples)

Tests such as chi-square test for the difference between two proportions discussed in Section 12.1 require independent samples from each population. However, sometimes when you are testing differences between the proportion of items of interest, the data are collected from repeated measurements or matched samples.

To test whether there is evidence of a difference between the proportions when the data have been collected from two related samples, you can use the McNemar test. The **Section 12.6 online topic** discusses this test and illustrates its use.

12.7 Chi-Square Test for the Variance or Standard Deviation

When analyzing numerical data, sometimes you need to test a hypothesis about the population variance or standard deviation. Assuming that the data are normally distributed, you use the χ^2 test for the variance or standard deviation to test whether the population variance or standard deviation is equal to a specified value. The **Section 12.7 online topic** discusses this test and illustrates its use.

▼USING **STATISTICS**
Avoiding Guesswork ..., Revisited

In the Using Statistics scenario, you were the manager of T.C. Resort Properties, a collection of five upscale hotels located on two tropical islands. To assess the quality of services being provided by your hotels, guests are encouraged to complete a satisfaction survey when they check out or via email after they check out. You analyzed the data from these surveys to determine the overall satisfaction with the services provided, the likelihood that the guests will return to the hotel, and the reasons given by some guests for not wanting to return.

On one island, T.C. Resort Properties operates the Beachcomber and Windsurfer hotels. You performed a chi-square test for the difference in two proportions and concluded that a greater proportion of guests are willing to return to the Beachcomber Hotel than to the Windsurfer. On the other island, T.C. Resort Properties operates the Golden Palm, Palm Royale, and Palm Princess hotels. To see if guest satisfaction was the same among the three hotels, you performed a chi-square test for the differences among more than two proportions. The test confirmed that the three proportions are not equal, and guests seem to be most likely to return to the Palm Royale and least likely to return to the Golden Palm.

In addition, you investigated whether the reasons given for not returning to the Golden Palm, Palm Royale, and Palm Princess were unique to a certain hotel or common to all three hotels. By performing a chi-square test of independence, you determined that the reasons given for wanting to return or not depended on the hotel where the guests had been staying. By examining the observed and expected frequencies, you concluded that guests were more satisfied with the price at the Golden Palm and were much more satisfied with the location of the Palm Princess. Guest satisfaction with room accommodations was not significantly different among the three hotels.

▼SUMMARY

Figure 12.15 presents a roadmap for this chapter. First, you used hypothesis testing for analyzing categorical data from two independent samples and from more than two independent samples. In addition, the rules of probability from Section 4.2 were extended to the hypothesis of independence in the joint responses to two categorical variables. You also studied two nonparametric tests. You used the Wilcoxon rank sum test when the assumptions of the t test for two independent samples were violated and the Kruskal-Wallis test when the assumptions of the one-way ANOVA F test were violated.

FIGURE 12.15
Roadmap of Chapter 12

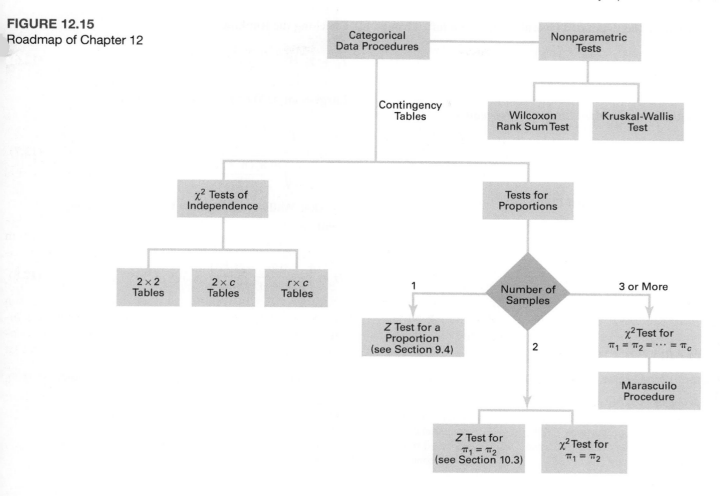

REFERENCES

1. Conover, W. J. *Practical Nonparametric Statistics*, 3rd ed. New York: Wiley, 2000.
2. Daniel, W. W. *Applied Nonparametric Statistics*, 2nd ed. Boston: PWS Kent, 1990.
3. Dixon, W. J., and F. J. Massey, Jr. *Introduction to Statistical Analysis*, 4th ed. New York: McGraw-Hill, 1983.
4. Hollander, M., D. A. Wolfe, and E. Chicken, *Nonparametric Statistical Methods*, 3rd ed. New York: Wiley, 2014.
5. Lewontin, R. C., and J. Felsenstein. "Robustness of Homogeneity Tests in 2 × n Tables," *Biometrics*, 21(March 1965): 19–33.
6. Marascuilo, L. A. "Large-Sample Multiple Comparisons," *Psychological Bulletin*, 65(1966): 280–290.
7. Marascuilo, L. A., and M. McSweeney. *Nonparametric and Distribution-Free Methods for the Social Sciences*. Monterey, CA: Brooks/Cole, 1977.
8. Winer, B. J., D. R. Brown, and K. M. Michels. *Statistical Principles in Experimental Design*, 3rd ed. New York: McGraw-Hill, 1989.

KEY EQUATIONS

χ^2 Test for the Difference Between Two Proportions

$$\chi^2_{STAT} = \sum_{\text{all cells}} \frac{(f_o - f_e)^2}{f_e} \qquad (12.1)$$

Computing the Estimated Overall Proportion for Two Groups

$$\bar{p} = \frac{X_1 + X_2}{n_1 + n_2} = \frac{X}{n} \qquad (12.2)$$

Computing the Estimated Overall Proportion for c Groups

$$\bar{p} = \frac{X_1 + X_2 + \cdots + X_c}{n_1 + n_2 + \cdots + n_c} = \frac{X}{n} \tag{12.3}$$

Critical Range for the Marascuilo Procedure

$$\text{Critical range} = \sqrt{\chi_\alpha^2}\sqrt{\frac{p_j(1 - p_j)}{n_j} + \frac{p_{j'}(1 - p_{j'})}{n_{j'}}} \tag{12.4}$$

Computing the Expected Frequency

$$f_e = \frac{\text{Row total} \times \text{Column total}}{n} \tag{12.5}$$

Checking the Rankings

$$T_1 + T_2 = \frac{n(n + 1)}{2} \tag{12.6}$$

Large-Sample Wilcoxon Rank Sum Test

$$Z_{STAT} = \frac{T_1 - \frac{n_1(n + 1)}{2}}{\sqrt{\frac{n_1 n_2(n + 1)}{12}}} \tag{12.7}$$

Kruskal-Wallis Rank Test for Differences Among c Medians

$$H = \left[\frac{12}{n(n + 1)}\sum_{j=1}^{c}\frac{T_j^2}{n_j}\right] - 3(n + 1) \tag{12.8}$$

▼ KEY TERMS

chi-square (χ^2) distribution   388
chi-square (χ^2) test for the difference between two proportions   388
chi-square (χ^2) test of independence   401
expected frequency (f_e)   388

Kruskal-Wallis rank test   402
Marascuilo procedure   388
nonparametric methods   407
observed frequency (f_o)   388
$2 \times c$ contingency table   394

2×2 contingency table   387
two-way contingency table   387
Wilcoxon rank sum test   387

▼ CHECKING YOUR UNDERSTANDING

12.51 Under what conditions should you use the χ^2 test to determine whether there is a difference between the proportions of two independent populations?

12.52 Under what conditions should you use the χ^2 test to determine whether there is a difference among the proportions of more than two independent populations?

12.53 Under what conditions should you use the χ^2 test of independence?

12.54 Under what conditions should you use the Wilcoxon rank sum test instead of the t test for the difference between the means?

12.55 Under what conditions should you use the Kruskal-Wallis rank test instead of the one-way ANOVA?

▼ CHAPTER REVIEW PROBLEMS

12.56 Undergraduate students at Miami University in Oxford, Ohio, were surveyed in order to evaluate the effect of gender and price on purchasing a pizza from Pizza Hut. Students were told to suppose that they were planning to have a large two-topping pizza delivered to their residence that evening. The students had to decide between ordering from Pizza Hut at a reduced price of $8.49 (the regular price for a large two-topping pizza from the Oxford Pizza Hut at the time was $11.49) and ordering a pizza from a different pizzeria. The results from this question are summarized in the following contingency table:

| | **PIZZERIA** | | |
GENDER	**Pizza Hut**	**Other**	**Total**
Female	4	13	17
Male	6	12	18
Total	10	25	35

a. Using a 0.05 level of significance, is there evidence of a difference between males and females in their pizzeria selection?
b. What is your answer to (a) if nine of the male students selected Pizza Hut and nine selected another pizzeria?

A subsequent survey evaluated purchase decisions at other prices. These results are summarized in the following contingency table:

PIZZERIA	PRICE			
	$8.49	**$11.49**	**$14.49**	**Total**
Pizza Hut	10	5	2	17
Other	25	23	27	75
Total	35	28	29	92

c. Using a 0.05 level of significance and using the data in the second contingency table, is there evidence of a difference in pizzeria selection based on price?

d. Determine the *p*-value in (c) and interpret its meaning.

12.57 What social media tools do marketers commonly use? The "2015 Social Media Marketing Industry Report" by Social Media Examiner (socialmediaexaminer.com) surveyed marketers who commonly use an indicated social media tool. Surveyed were both B2B marketers, marketers that focus primarily on attracting businesses, and B2C marketers, marketers that primarily target consumers. Suppose the survey was based on 500 B2B marketers and 500 B2C marketers and yielded the results in the following table. (Data extracted from **bit.ly /QmMxPa.**)

SOCIAL MEDIA TOOL	BUSINESS FOCUS	
	B2B	**B2C**
Facebook	88%	96%
Twitter	83%	77%
LinkedIn	88%	61%
Pinterest	39%	49%

For *each social media tool*, at the 0.05 level of significance, determine whether there is a difference between B2B marketers and B2C marketers in the proportion who used each social media tool.

12.58 A company is considering an organizational change involving the use of self-managed work teams. To assess the attitudes of employees of the company toward this change, a sample of 400 employees is selected and asked whether they favor the institution of self-managed work teams in the organization. Three responses are permitted: favor, neutral, or oppose. The results of the survey, cross-classified by type of job and attitude toward self-managed work teams, are summarized as follows:

TYPE OF JOB	SELF-MANAGED WORK TEAMS			
	Favor	**Neutral**	**Oppose**	**Total**
Hourly worker	108	46	71	225
Supervisor	18	12	30	60
Middle management	35	14	26	75
Upper management	24	7	9	40
Total	185	79	136	400

a. At the 0.05 level of significance, is there evidence of a relationship between attitude toward self-managed work teams and type of job?

The survey also asked respondents about their attitudes toward instituting a policy whereby an employee could take one additional vacation day per month without pay. The results, cross-classified by type of job, are as follows:

TYPE OF JOB	VACATION TIME WITHOUT PAY			
	Favor	**Neutral**	**Oppose**	**Total**
Hourly worker	135	23	67	225
Supervisor	39	7	14	60
Middle management	47	6	22	75
Upper management	26	6	8	40
Total	247	42	111	400

b. At the 0.05 level of significance, is there evidence of a relationship between attitude toward vacation time without pay and type of job?

12.59 Do Americans trust advertisements? A survey by YouGov asked Americans who view advertisements at least once a month how honest the advertisements that they see, read, and hear are. The results were:

HONEST?	GEOGRAPHIC REGION				
	Northeast	**Midwest**	**South**	**West**	**Total**
Yes	102	118	220	115	555
No	74	93	135	130	432
Total	176	211	355	245	987

Source: "Truth in advertising: 50% don't trust what they see, read and hear," **bit.ly/1ivIlLX.**

a. At the 0.05 level of significance, is there evidence of a difference in the proportion of Americans who say advertisements are honest on the basis of geographic region?

YouGov also asked Americans who view advertisements at least once a month how much they trust the advertisements that they see, read, and hear. The results were:

TRUST?	GEOGRAPHIC REGION				
	Northeast	**Midwest**	**South**	**West**	**Total**
Yes	88	108	202	93	491
No	88	103	153	152	496
Total	176	211	355	245	987

Source: "Truth in advertising: 50% don't trust what they see, read and hear," **bit.ly/1ivIlLX.**

b. At the 0.05 level of significance, is there evidence of a difference in the proportion of Americans who say they trust advertisements on the basis of geographic region?

▾CASES

Managing Ashland MultiComm Services
PHASE 1

Reviewing the results of its research, the marketing department team concluded that a segment of Ashland households might be interested in a discounted trial subscription to the AMS *3-For-All* service. The team decided to test various discounts before determining the type of discount to offer during the trial period. It decided to conduct an experiment using three types of discounts plus a plan that offered no discount during the trial period:

1. No discount for the *3-For-All* service. Subscribers would pay $99.99 per month for the *3-For-All* service during the trial period.

2. Moderate discount for the *3-For-All* service. Subscribers would pay $79.99 per month for the *3-For-All* service during the trial period.

3. Substantial discount for the *3-For-All* service. Subscribers would pay $59.99 per month for the *3-For-All* service during the trial period.

4. Discount restaurant card. Subscribers would be given a special card providing a discount of 15% at selected restaurants in Ashland during the trial period.

Each participant in the experiment was randomly assigned to a discount plan. A random sample of 100 subscribers to each plan during the trial period was tracked to determine how many would continue to subscribe to the *3-For-All* service after the trial period. Table AMS 12.1 summarizes the results.

TABLE AMS12.1
Number of Subscribers Who Continue Subscriptions After Trial Period with Four Discount Plans

CONTINUE SUBSCRIPTIONS AFTER TRIAL PERIOD	DISCOUNT PLANS				
	No Discount	Moderate Discount	Substantial Discount	Restaurant Card	Total
Yes	24	30	38	51	143
No	76	70	62	49	257
Total	100	100	100	100	400

1. Analyze the results of the experiment. Write a report to the team that includes your recommendation for which discount plan to use. Be prepared to discuss the limitations and assumptions of the experiment.

PHASE 2

The marketing department team discussed the results of the survey presented in Chapter 8, on pages 301–302. The team realized that the evaluation of individual questions was providing only limited information. In order to further understand the market for the *3-For-All* service, the data were organized in the following contingency tables:

HAS AMS SMARTPHONE	HAS AMS INTERNET SERVICE		
	Yes	No	Total
Yes	55	28	83
No	207	128	335
Total	262	156	418

TYPE OF SERVICE	DISCOUNT TRIAL		
	Yes	No	Total
Basic or none	8	156	164
Enhanced	32	222	254
Total	40	378	418

SERVICE	WATCHES PREMIUM CONTENT				
	Almost Every Day	Several Times a Week	Almost Never	Never	Total
Basic or none	2	5	30	127	164
Enhanced	14	35	149	56	254
Total	16	40	179	183	418

DISCOUNT	WATCHES PREMIUM CONTENT				
	Almost Every Day	Several Times a Week	Almost Never	Never	Total
Yes	5	6	16	13	40
No	11	34	163	170	378
Total	16	40	179	183	418

DISCOUNT	METHOD FOR CURRENT SUBSCRIPTION					
	Email/ Text	Toll-Free Number	AMS Website	In-store Signup	MyTVLab Promo	Tot
Yes	5	14	12	4	1	4
No	65	50	224	32	11	37
Total	70	64	236	36	12	41

GOLD CARD	METHOD FOR CURRENT SUBSCRIPTION					
	Email/ Text	Toll-Free Number	AMS Website	In-store Signup	MyTVLab Promo	Tot
Yes	4	12	12	4	11	3
No	66	54	224	32	11	38
Total	70	64	236	36	12	41

2. Analyze the results of the contingency tables. Write a report for the marketing department team, discussing the marketing implications of the results for Ashland MultiComm Services.

Digital Case

Apply your knowledge of testing for the difference between two proportions in this Digital Case, which extends the T.C. Resort Properties Using Statistics scenario of this chapter.

As T.C. Resort Properties seeks to improve its customer service, the company faces new competition from Sun-Low Resorts. SunLow has recently opened resort hotels on the islands where T.C. Resort Properties has its five hotels. SunLow is currently advertising that a random survey of 300 customers revealed that about 60% of the customers preferred its "Concierge Class" travel reward program over the T.C. Resorts "TCRewards Plus" program.

Open and review **ConciergeClass.pdf**, an electronic brochure that describes the Concierge Class program and compares it to the T.C. Resorts program. Then answer the following questions:

1. Are the claims made by SunLow valid?

2. What analyses of the survey data would lead to a more favorable impression about T.C. Resort Properties?

3. Perform one of the analyses identified in your answer to step 2.

4. Review the data about the T.C. Resort Properties customers presented in this chapter. Are there any other questions that you might include in a future survey of travel reward programs? Explain.

Sure Value Convenience Stores

You work in the corporate office for a nationwide convenience store franchise that operates nearly 10,000 stores. The per-store daily customer count (i.e., the mean number of customers in a store in one day) has been steady, at 900, for some time. To increase the customer count, the chain is considering cutting prices for coffee beverages. Management needs to determine how much prices can be cut in order to increase the daily customer count without reducing the gross margin on coffee sales too much. You decide to carry out an experiment in a sample of 24 stores where customer counts have been running almost exactly at the national average of 900. In 6 of the stores, a small coffee will be $0.59, in another 6 stores the price will be $0.69, in a third group of 6 stores, the price will be $0.79, and in a fourth group of 6 stores, the price will now be $0.89. After four weeks, the daily customer count in the stores is stored in CoffeeSales.

At the 0.05 level of significance, is there evidence of a difference in the median daily customer count based on the price of a small coffee? What price should the stores sell the coffee for?

CardioGood Fitness

Return to the CardioGood Fitness case first presented on page 28. The data for this case are stored in CardioGood Fitness.

1. Determine whether differences exist in the median age in years, education in years, annual household income ($), number of times the customer plans to use the treadmill each week, and the number of miles the customer expects to walk or run each week based on the product purchased (TM195, TM498, TM798).

2. Determine whether differences exist in the relationship status (single or partnered), and the self-rated fitness based on the product purchased (TM195, TM498, TM798).

3. Write a report to be presented to the management of Cardio-Good Fitness, detailing your findings.

More Descriptive Choices Follow-Up

Follow up the "Using Statistics: More Descriptive Choices, Revisited" on page 136 by using the data that are stored in Retirement Funds to:

1. Determine whether there is a difference between the growth and value funds in the median three-year return percentages, five-year return percentages, and ten-year return percentages.

2. Determine whether there is a difference between the small, mid-cap, and large market cap funds in the median three-year return percentages, five-year return percentages, and ten-year return percentages.

3. Determine whether there is a difference in risk based on market cap, a difference in rating based on market cap, a difference in risk based on type of fund, and a difference in rating based on type of fund.

4. Write a report summarizing your findings.

Clear Mountain State Student Survey

The Student News Service at Clear Mountain State University (CMSU) has decided to gather data about the undergraduate students that attend CMSU. It creates and distributes a survey of 14 questions and receives responses from 111 undergraduates, which it stores in StudentSurvey.

1. Construct contingency tables using gender, major, plans to go to graduate school, and employment status. (You need to construct six tables, taking two variables at a time.) Analyze the data at the 0.05 level of significance to determine whether any significant relationships exist among these variables.

2. At the 0.05 level of significance, is there evidence of a difference between males and females in median grade point average, expected starting salary, number of social networking sites registered for, age, spending on textbooks and supplies, text messages sent in a week, and the wealth needed to feel rich?

3. At the 0.05 level of significance, is there evidence of a difference between students who plan to go to graduate school and those who do not plan to go to graduate school in median grade point average, expected starting salary, number of social networking sites registered for, age, spending on textbooks and supplies.

▼EXCEL GUIDE

EG12.1 CHI-SQUARE TEST for the DIFFERENCE BETWEEN TWO PROPORTIONS

Key Technique Use the **CHISQ.INV.RT**(*level of significance, degrees of freedom*) function to compute the critical value and use the **CHISQ.DIST.RT**(*chi-square test statistic, degrees of freedom*) function to compute the *p*-value.

Example Perform the Figure 12.3 chi-square test for the two-hotel guest satisfaction data shown in Figure 12.3 on page 381.

PHStat Use **Chi-Square Test for Differences in Two Proportions**.

For the example, select **PHStat → Two-Sample Tests (Summarized Data) → Chi-Square Test for Differences in Two Proportions**. In the procedure's dialog box, enter **0.05** as the **Level of Significance**, enter a **Title**, and click **OK**. In the new worksheet:

1. Read the yellow note about entering values and then press the **Delete** key to delete the note.
2. Enter **Hotel** in cell **B4** and **Choose Again?** in cell **A5**.
3. Enter **Beachcomber** in cell **B5** and **Windsurfer** in cell **C5**.
4. Enter **Yes** in cell **A6** and **No** in cell **A7**.
5. Enter **163, 64, 154,** and **108** in cells **B6, B7, C6,** and **C7**, respectively.

Workbook Use the **COMPUTE worksheet** of the **Chi-Square workbook** as a template.
The worksheet already contains the Table 12.2 two-hotel guest satisfaction data. For other problems, change the **Observed Frequencies** cell counts and row and column labels in rows 4 through 7.

EG12.2 CHI-SQUARE TEST for DIFFERENCES AMONG MORE THAN TWO PROPORTIONS

Key Technique Use the **CHISQ.INV.RT** and **CHISQ.DIST.RT** functions to compute the critical value and the *p*-value, respectively.

Example Perform the Figure 12.6 chi-square test for the three-hotel guest satisfaction data shown in Figure 12.6 on page 397.

PHStat Use **Chi-Square Test**.
For the example, select **PHStat → Multiple-Sample Tests → Chi-Square Test**. In the procedure's dialog box (shown in right column):

1. Enter **0.05** as the **Level of Significance**.
2. Enter **2** as the **Number of Rows**.
3. Enter **3** as the **Number of Columns**.
4. Enter a **Title** and click **OK**.

In the new worksheet:

5. Read the yellow note instructions about entering values and then press the **Delete** key to delete the note.
6. Enter the Table 12.6 data (see page 395), including row and column labels, in rows 4 through 7. The **#DIV/0!** error messages will disappear when you finish entering all the table data.

Workbook Use the **ChiSquare2x3 worksheet** of the **Chi-Square Worksheets workbook** as a model.
The worksheet already contains the page 395 Table 12.6 guest satisfaction data. For other 2 × 3 problems, change the **Observed Frequencies** cell counts and row and column labels in rows 4 through 7. For 2 × 4 problems, use the **ChiSquare2x4 worksheet** and change the **Observed Frequencies** cell counts and row and column labels in that worksheet. For 2 × 5 problems, use the **ChiSquare2x5 worksheet** and change the **Observed Frequencies** cell counts and row and column labels in that worksheet.

The Marascuilo Procedure

Key Technique Use formulas to compute the absolute differences and the critical range.

Example Perform the Figure 12.7 Marascuilo procedure for the guest satisfaction survey shown on page 399.

PHStat Modify the *PHStat* instructions of the previous section. In step 4, check **Marascuilo Procedure** in addition to entering a **Title** and clicking **OK**.

Workbook Use the **Marascuilo2x3** of the **Chi-Square Worksheets workbook** as a template.

The worksheet requires no entries or changes to use. For 2 × 4 problems, use the **Marascuilo2x4 worksheet** and for 2 × 5 problems, use the **Marascuilo2x5 worksheet**.

Every Marascuilo worksheet uses values from the observed frequencies table in the companion ChiSquare worksheet to compute critical range values in the Marascuilo table area (rows 11 through 16 in Figure 12.7). In column D, the worksheet uses an IF function to compare the absolute difference to the critical range for each pair of groups and then displays either "Significant" or "Not Significant".

EG12.3 CHI-SQUARE TEST of INDEPENDENCE

Key Technique Use the **CHISQ.INV.RT** and **CHISQ. DIST.RT** functions to compute the critical value and the *p*-value, respectively.

Example Perform the Figure 12.10 chi-square test for the primary reason for not returning to hotel data that is shown in Figure 12.10 on page 404.

PHStat Use **Chi-Square Test**.

For the example, select **PHStat → Multiple-Sample Tests → Chi-Square Test**. In the procedure's dialog box (shown below):

1. Enter **0.05** as the **Level of Significance**.
2. Enter **4** as the **Number of Rows**.
3. Enter **3** as the **Number of Columns**.
4. Enter a **Title** and click **OK**.

In the new worksheet:

5. Read the yellow note about entering values and then press the **Delete** key to delete the note.
6. Enter the Table 12.9 data on page 401, including row and column labels, in rows 4 through 9. The **#DIV/0!** error messages will disappear when you finish entering all of the table data.

Workbook Use the **ChiSquare4x3 worksheet** of the **Chi-Square Worksheets workbook** as a model.

The worksheet already contains the page 401 Table 12.9 primary reason for not returning to hotel data. For other 4 × 3 problems, change the **Observed Frequencies** cell counts and row and column labels in rows 4 through 9. For problems that use an *r* × *c* contingency table of a different size, use the appropriate ChiSquare worksheets. For example, for 3 × 4 problems, use the **ChiSquare3x4 worksheet** and for 4 × 3 problems, use the **ChiSquare4x3 worksheet**. For each of these other worksheets, enter the contingency table data for the problem in the Observed Frequencies area.

EG12.4 WILCOXON RANK SUM TEST: A NONPARAMETRIC METHOD for TWO INDEPENDENT POPULATIONS

Key Technique Use the **NORM.S.INV**(*level of significance*) function to compute the upper and lower critical values and use **NORM.S.DIST**(*absolute value of the Z test statistic*) as part of a formula to compute the *p*-value.

For unsummarized data, use the **COUNTIF** and **SUMIF** functions (see Appendix Section F.4) to compute the sample size and the sum of ranks for each sample.

Example Perform the Figure 12.12 Wilcoxon rank sum test for the cola sales for the two different end-cap locations.

PHStat Use **Wilcoxon Rank Sum Test**.

For the example, open to the **DATA worksheet** of the **Mobile Electronics workbook**. Select **PHStat → Two-Sample Tests (Unsummarized Data) → Wilcoxon Rank Sum Test**. In the procedure's dialog box (shown below):

1. Enter **0.05** as the **Level of Significance**.
2. Enter **A1:A11** as the **Population 1 Sample Cell Range**.
3. Enter **B1:B11** as the **Population 2 Sample Cell Range**.
4. Check **First cells in both ranges contain label**.
5. Click **Two-Tail Test**.
6. Enter a **Title** and click **OK**.

The procedure creates a SortedRanks worksheet that contains the sorted ranks in addition to the worksheet shown in Figure 12.12. Both of these worksheets are discussed in the following *Workbook* instructions.

Workbook Use the **COMPUTE worksheet** of the **Wilcoxon workbook** as a template.
The worksheet already contains data and formulas to use the unsummarized data for the example. For other problems that use unsummarized data:

1. Open to the **SortedRanks worksheet**.
2. Enter the sorted values for both groups in stacked format, entering sample names in column A and sorted values in column B.
3. Assign a rank for each value and enter the ranks in column C.
4. If performing a two-tail test, open to the **COMPUTE worksheet**, otherwise open to the similar **COMPUTE_ALL worksheet** that includes the one-tail tests.
5. Edit the cell ranges in the formulas in cells **B7**, **B8**, **B10**, and **B11** to match the cell range of the new data.

For problems with summarized data, overwrite the formulas that compute the **Sample Size** and **Sum of Ranks** in the cell range **B7:B11**, with the values for these statistics.

EG12.5 KRUSKAL-WALLIS RANK TEST: A NONPARAMETRIC METHOD for the ONE-WAY ANOVA

Key Technique Use the **CHISQ.INV.RT**(*level of significance, number of groups - 1*) function to compute the critical value and use the **CHISQ.DIST.RT**(*H test statistic, number of groups - 1*) function to compute the *p*-value.

For unsummarized data, use the **COUNTIF** and **SUMIF** functions (see Appendix Section F.4) to compute the sample size and the sum of ranks for each sample.

Example Perform the Figure 12.14 Kruskal-Wallis rank test for differences among the median mobile electronics sales for four in-store locations that is shown on page 415.

PHStat Use **Kruskal-Wallis Rank Test**.
For the example, open to the **DATA worksheet** of the **Second Experiment workbook**. Select **PHStat ➜ Multiple-Sample Tests ➜ Kruskal-Wallis Rank Test**. In the procedure's dialog box (shown in right column):

1. Enter **0.05** as the **Level of Significance**.
2. Enter **A1:D6** as the **Sample Data Cell Range**.
3. Check **First cells contain label**.
4. Enter a **Title** and click **OK**.

The procedure creates a SortedRanks worksheet that contains sorted ranks in addition to the worksheet shown in Figure 12.14 on page 415. Both of these worksheets are discussed in the following *Workbook* instructions.

Workbook Use the **KruskalWallis4 worksheet** of the **Kruskal-Wallis Worksheets workbook** as a template.
The worksheet already contains the data and formulas to use the unsummarized data for the example. For other problems with four groups and unsummarized data:

1. Open to the **SortedRanks worksheet**
2. Enter the sorted values for both groups in stacked format, entering sample names in column A and sorted values in column B.
3. Assign a rank for each value and enter the ranks in column C.
4. Paste the unsummarized stacked data into this worksheet starting with Column E. (The first row of this pasted range should contain group names.)
5. Open to the **KruskalWallis4 worksheet** and edit the cell ranges in the formulas in columns **E** and **F**.

For other problems with four groups and summarized data, open to the KruskalWallis4 worksheet and overwrite the columns D, E, and F formulas with the name, sample size, and sum of ranks for each group.

For other problems with three groups, use the similar **KruskalWallis3 worksheet** and use the previous instructions for either unsummarized or summarized data, as appropriate.

Simple Linear Regression

13

CONTENTS

▼ USING **STATISTICS**
Knowing Customers at Sunflowers Apparel

Having survived recent economic slowdowns that have diminished their competitors, Sunflowers Apparel, a chain of upscale fashion stores for women, is in the midst of a companywide review that includes researching the factors that make their stores successful. Until recently, Sunflowers managers did not use data analysis to help select where to open stores, relying instead on subjective factors, such as the availability of an inexpensive lease or the perception that a particular location seemed ideal for one of their stores.

As the new director of planning, you have already consulted with marketing data firms that specialize in identifying and classifying groups of consumers. Based on such preliminary analyses, you have already tentatively discovered that the profile of Sunflowers shoppers may not only be the upper middle class long suspected of being the chain's clientele but may also include younger, aspirational families with young children, and, surprisingly, urban hipsters that set trends and are mostly single.

You seek to develop a systematic approach that will lead to making better decisions during the site-selection process. As a starting point, you have asked one marketing data firm to collect and organize data for the number of people in the identified groups of interest who live within a fixed radius of each store. You believe that the greater numbers of profiled customers contribute to store sales, and you want to explore the possible use of this relationship in the decision-making process. How can you use statistics so that you can forecast the annual sales of a proposed store based on the number of profiled customers that reside within a fixed radius of a Sunflowers store?

OBJECTIVES

- Learn to use regression analysis to predict the value of a dependent variable based on the value of an independent variable

- Understand the meaning of the regression coefficients b_0 and b_1

- Learn to evaluate the assumptions of regression analysis and what to do if the assumptions are violated
- Make inferences about the slope and correlation coefficient
- Estimate mean values and predict individual values

*Independent variables are also known as **predictor** or **explanatory variables** and dependent variables are also known as **response variables**.*

The preceding four chapters focus on hypothesis testing methods. Chapter 9 discusses methods that allow you to make inferences about a population parameter. Chapters 10, 11, and 12 present methods that look for differences among two or more populations. Beginning with this chapter, and continuing through Chapter 16, the focus shifts from examining differences among groups to predicting values of variables of interest.

Consider the data that a business generates as a by-product of ongoing operations, such as the Sunflowers sales data. How would you go about examining such data? You must go looking for possible relationships. **Regression analysis** techniques help uncover relationships between variables.

When you use regression analysis, you examine relationships by developing **models** that express how accurately one or more **independent variables** predict the value of a **dependent variable**. By convention, the symbol Y represents the dependent variable and the symbol X, subscripted, if necessary, represents the one or more independent variables. The mathematical relationship that a regression model identifies enables you to quantify the effect on the dependent Y variable that a change in the one or more X independent variables produces. Models also help you identify unusual values that may be outliers (see references 2, 3, and 4).

This chapter discusses **simple linear regression** models that use a single numerical independent variable, X, to predict a numerical dependent variable, Y. (Chapters 14 and 15 discuss multiple regression models that use several independent variables to predict the dependent variable.) In the Sunflowers scenario, your initial belief reflects a possible *linear* relationship between the single numerical independent X variable, the number of profiled customers, and the dependent Y variable, the annual sales of the store.

13.1 Types of Regression Models

Using a **scatter plot** (also known as **scatter diagram**) to visualize the X and Y variables, a technique introduced in Section 2.5 on page 59, can help suggest a starting point for regression analysis. The Figure 13.1 scatter plots illustrate six possible relationships between an X variable and a Y variable.

FIGURE 13.1
Six types of relationships found in scatter plots

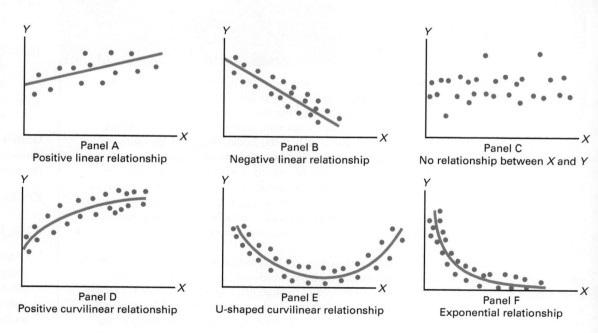

Panel A
Positive linear relationship

Panel B
Negative linear relationship

Panel C
No relationship between X and Y

Panel D
Positive curvilinear relationship

Panel E
U-shaped curvilinear relationship

Panel F
Exponential relationship

In Panel A, values of Y are generally increasing linearly as X increases. This panel is similar to Figure 13.3 on page 430, which shows a positive linear relationship between the number of profiled customers of the store and the store's annual sales for the Sunflowers Apparel women's clothing store chain.

Panel B illustrates a negative linear relationship. As X increases, the values of Y are generally decreasing. An example of this type of relationship might be the price of a particular product and the amount of sales. As the price charged for the product increases, the amount of sales may tend to decrease.

Panel C shows a set of data in which there is very little or no relationship between X and Y. High and low values of Y appear at each value of X.

Panel D illustrates a positive curvilinear relationship between X and Y. The values of Y increase as X increases, but this increase tapers off beyond certain values of X. An example of a positive curvilinear relationship might be the age and maintenance cost of a machine. As a machine gets older, the maintenance cost may rise rapidly at first but then level off beyond a certain number of years.

Panel E illustrates a U-shaped relationship between X and Y. As X increases, at first Y generally decreases; but as X continues to increase, Y then increases above its minimum value. An example of this type of relationship might be entrepreneurial activity and levels of economic development as measured by GDP per capita. Entrepreneurial activity occurs more in the least and most developed countries.

Panel F illustrates an exponential relationship between X and Y. In this case, Y decreases very rapidly as X first increases, but then it decreases much less rapidly as X continues to increase. An example of an exponential relationship could be the value of an automobile and its age. The value drops drastically from its original price in the first year, but it decreases much less rapidly in subsequent years.

Simple Linear Regression Models

Although scatter plots provide preliminary analysis, more sophisticated statistical procedures determine the most appropriate model for a set of variables. Simple linear regression models represent the simplest relationship of a straight-line or **linear relationship**. Figure 13.2 illustrates this relationship.

FIGURE 13.2
A straight-line relationship

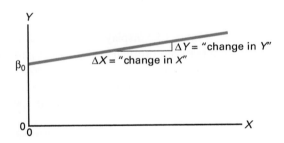

Equation (13.1) expresses this relationship mathematically by defining the simple linear regression model.

SIMPLE LINEAR REGRESSION MODEL

$$Y_i = \beta_0 + \beta_1 X_i + \varepsilon_i \qquad (13.1)$$

where

$\beta_0 = Y$ intercept for the population
$\beta_1 = $ slope for the population
$\varepsilon_i = $ random error in Y for observation i
$Y_i = $ dependent variable for observation i
$X_i = $ independent variable for observation i

The $Y_i = \beta_0 + \beta_1 X_i$ portion of the simple linear regression model expressed in Equation (13.1) is a straight line. The **slope** of the line, β_1, represents the expected change in Y per unit change in X. It represents the mean amount that Y changes (either positively or negatively) for a one-unit change in X. The **Y intercept**, β_0, represents the mean value of Y when X equals 0. The last component of the model, ε_i, represents the random error in Y for each observation, i. In other words, ε_i is the vertical distance of the actual value of Y_i above or below the expected value of Y_i on the line.

13.2 Determining the Simple Linear Regression Equation

In the Sunflowers Apparel scenario on page 427, the business objective of the director of planning is to forecast annual sales for all new stores, based on the number of profiled customers who live no more than 30 minutes from a Sunflowers store. To examine the relationship between the number of profiled customers (in millions) who live within a fixed radius from a Sunflowers store and its annual sales ($millions), data were collected from a sample of 14 stores. Table 13.1 shows the organized data, which are stored in SiteSelection .

TABLE 13.1
Number of Profiled Customers (in millions) and Annual Sales (in $millions) for a Sample of 14 Sunflowers Apparel Stores

Store	Profiled Customers (millions)	Annual Sales ($millions)	Store	Profiled Customers (millions)	Annual Sales ($millions)
1	3.7	5.7	8	3.1	4.7
2	3.6	5.9	9	3.2	6.1
3	2.8	6.7	10	3.5	4.9
4	5.6	9.5	11	5.2	10.7
5	3.3	5.4	12	4.6	7.6
6	2.2	3.5	13	5.8	11.8
7	3.3	6.2	14	3.0	4.1

Figure 13.3 displays the scatter plot for the data in Table 13.1. Observe the increasing relationship between profiled customers (X) and annual sales (Y). As the number of profiled customers increases, annual sales increase approximately as a straight line (superimposed on the scatter plot). Thus, you can assume that a straight line provides a useful mathematical model of this relationship. Now you need to determine the specific straight line that is the *best* fit to these data.

FIGURE 13.3
Scatter plot for the Sunflowers Apparel data

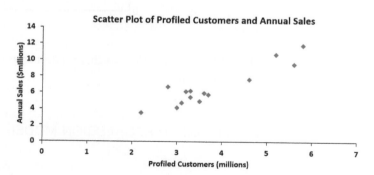

The Least-Squares Method

In the preceding section, a statistical model is hypothesized to represent the relationship between two variables—number of profiled customers and sales—in the entire population of Sunflowers Apparel stores. However, as shown in Table 13.1, the data are collected from a random sample of stores. If certain assumptions are valid (see Section 13.4), you can use the sample Y intercept, b_0, and the sample slope, b_1, as estimates of the respective population parameters, β_0 and β_1. Equation (13.2) uses these estimates to form the **simple linear regression equation**. This straight line is often referred to as the **prediction line**.

SIMPLE LINEAR REGRESSION EQUATION: THE PREDICTION LINE

The predicted value of Y equals the Y intercept plus the slope multiplied by the value of X.

$$\hat{Y}_i = b_0 + b_1 X_i \qquad (13.2)$$

where

$$\hat{Y}_i = \text{predicted value of } Y \text{ for observation } i$$
$$X_i = \text{value of } X \text{ for observation } i$$
$$b_0 = \text{sample } Y \text{ intercept}$$
$$b_1 = \text{sample slope}$$

Equation (13.2) requires you to determine two **regression coefficients**—b_0 (the sample Y intercept) and b_1 (the sample slope). The most common approach to finding b_0 and b_1 is using the least-squares method. This method minimizes the sum of the squared differences between the actual values (Y_i) and the predicted values ($\hat{Y}_i$), using the simple linear regression equation [i.e., the prediction line; see Equation (13.2)]. This sum of squared differences is equal to

$$\sum_{i=1}^{n} (Y_i - \hat{Y}_i)^2$$

Because $\hat{Y}_i = b_0 + b_1 X_i$,

$$\sum_{i=1}^{n} (Y_i - \hat{Y}_i)^2 = \sum_{i=1}^{n} [Y_i - (b_0 + b_1 X_i)]^2$$

Because this equation has two unknowns, b_0 and b_1, the sum of squared differences depends on the sample Y intercept, b_0, and the sample slope, b_1. The **least-squares method** determines the values of b_0 and b_1 that minimize the sum of squared differences around the prediction line. Any values for b_0 and b_1 other than those determined by the least-squares method result in a greater sum of squared differences between the actual values (Y_i) and the predicted values ($\hat{Y}_i$).

Figure 13.4 presents results for the simple linear regression model for the Sunflowers Apparel data. Excel labels b_0 as Intercept and labels b_1 as Profiled Customers.

FIGURE 13.4
Excel simple linear regression model worksheet results for the Sunflowers Apparel data

	A	B	C	D	E	F	G
1	Simple Linear Regression						
2							
3	*Regression Statistics*						
4	Multiple R	0.9208					
5	R Square	0.8479					
6	Adjusted R Square	0.8352					
7	Standard Error	0.9993					
8	Observations	14					
9							
10	ANOVA						
11		*df*	*SS*	*MS*	*F*	*Significance F*	
12	Regression	1	66.7854	66.7854	66.8792	0.0000	
13	Residual	12	11.9832	0.9986			
14	Total	13	78.7686				
15							
16		*Coefficients*	*Standard Error*	*t Stat*	*P-value*	*Lower 95%*	*Upper 95%*
17	Intercept	-1.2088	0.9949	-1.2151	0.2477	-3.3765	0.9588
18	Profiled Customers	2.0742	0.2536	8.1780	0.0000	1.5216	2.6268

In the Worksheet

The three methods in Section EG13.1 all create worksheets that *look like* this worksheet. Using the *PHStat* or *Workbook* instructions creates a worksheet that uses the LINEST function in column L and M formulas (not shown) to compute regression coefficients and statistics.

In Figure 13.4, observe that $b_0 = -1.2088$ and $b_1 = 2.0742$. Using Equation (13.2) on page 431, the prediction line for these data is

$$\hat{Y}_i = -1.2088 + 2.0742X_i$$

The slope, b_1, is $+2.0742$. This means that for each increase of 1 unit in X, the predicted mean value of Y is estimated to increase by 2.0742 units. In other words, for each increase of 1.0 million profiled customers within 30 minutes of the store, the predicted mean annual sales are estimated to increase by \$2.0742 million. Thus, the slope represents the portion of the annual sales that are estimated to vary according to the number of profiled customers.

The Y intercept, b_0, is -1.2088. The Y intercept represents the predicted value of Y when X equals 0. Because the number of profiled customers of the store cannot be 0, this Y intercept has little or no practical interpretation. Also, the Y intercept for this example is outside the range of the observed values of the X variable, and therefore interpretations of the value of b_0 should be made cautiously. Figure 13.5 displays the actual values and the prediction line.

FIGURE 13.5
Scatter plot and prediction line for Sunflowers Apparel data

Example 13.1 illustrates a situation in which there is a direct interpretation for the Y intercept, b_0.

EXAMPLE 13.1

Interpreting the Y Intercept, b_0, and the Slope, b_1

A statistics professor wants to use the number of absences from class during the semester (X) to predict the final exam score (Y). A regression model is fit based on data collected from a class during a recent semester, with the following results:

$$\hat{Y}_i = 85.0 - 5X_i$$

What is the interpretation of the Y intercept, b_0, and the slope, b_1?

SOLUTION The Y intercept $b_0 = 85.0$ indicates that when the student does not have any absences from class during the semester, the predicted mean final exam score is 85.0. The slope $b_1 = -5$ indicates that for each increase of one absence from class during the semester, the predicted change in the mean final exam score is -5.0. In other words, the final exam score is predicted to decrease by a mean of 5 points for each increase of one absence from class during the semester.

Return to the Sunflowers Apparel scenario on page 427. Example 13.2 illustrates how you use the prediction line to predict the annual sales.

EXAMPLE 13.2 Predicting Annual Sales Based on Number of Profiled Customers	Use the prediction line to predict the annual sales for a store with 4 million profiled customers. **SOLUTION** You can determine the predicted value of annual sales by substituting $X = 4$ (millions of profiled customers) into the simple linear regression equation: $$\hat{Y}_i = -1.2088 + 2.0742X_i$$ $$\hat{Y}_i = -1.2088 + 2.0742(4) = 7.0879 \text{ or } \$7,087,900$$ Thus, a store with 4 million profiled customers has predicted mean annual sales of $7,087,900.

Predictions in Regression Analysis: Interpolation Versus Extrapolation

When using a regression model for prediction purposes, you should consider only the **relevant range** of the independent variable in making predictions. This relevant range includes all values from the smallest to the largest X used in developing the regression model. Hence, when predicting Y for a given value of X, you can interpolate within this relevant range of the X values, but you should not extrapolate beyond the range of X values. When you use the number of profiled customers to predict annual sales, the number of profiled customers (in millions) varies from 2.2 to 5.8 (see Table 13.1 on page 430). Therefore, you should predict annual sales *only* for stores that have between 2.2 and 5.8 million profiled customers. Any prediction of annual sales for stores outside this range assumes that the observed relationship between sales and the number of profiled customers for stores that have between 2.2 and 5.8 million profiled customers is the same as for stores outside this range. For example, you cannot extrapolate the linear relationship beyond 5.8 million profiled customers in Example 13.2. It would be improper to use the prediction line to forecast the sales for a new store that has 8 million profiled customers because the relationship between sales and the number of profiled customers may have a point of diminishing returns. If that is true, as the number of profiled customers increases beyond 5.8 million, the effect on sales may become smaller and smaller.

Computing the Y Intercept, b_0 and the Slope, b_1

For small data sets, you can use a hand calculator to compute the least-squares regression coefficients. Equations (13.3) and (13.4) give the values of b_0 and b_1, which minimize

$$\sum_{i=1}^{n}(Y_i - \hat{Y}_i)^2 = \sum_{i=1}^{n}[Y_i - (b_0 + b_1X_i)]^2$$

COMPUTATIONAL FORMULA FOR THE SLOPE, b_1

$$b_1 = \frac{SSXY}{SSX} \tag{13.3}$$

where

$$SSXY = \sum_{i=1}^{n}(X_i - \bar{X})(Y_i - \bar{Y}) = \sum_{i=1}^{n}X_iY_i - \frac{\left(\sum_{i=1}^{n}X_i\right)\left(\sum_{i=1}^{n}Y_i\right)}{n}$$

$$SSX = \sum_{i=1}^{n}(X_i - \bar{X})^2 = \sum_{i=1}^{n}X_i^2 - \frac{\left(\sum_{i=1}^{n}X_i\right)^2}{n}$$

(continued)

COMPUTATIONAL FORMULA FOR THE Y INTERCEPT, b_0

$$b_0 = \bar{Y} - b_1\bar{X} \qquad (13.4)$$

where

$$\bar{Y} = \frac{\sum_{i=1}^{n} Y_i}{n}$$

$$\bar{X} = \frac{\sum_{i=1}^{n} X_i}{n}$$

EXAMPLE 13.3

Computing the Y Intercept, b_0, and the Slope, b_1

Compute the Y intercept, b_0, and the slope, b_1, for the Sunflowers Apparel data.

SOLUTION In Equations (13.3) and (13.4), five quantities need to be computed to determine b_1 and b_0. These are n, the sample size; $\sum_{i=1}^{n} X_i$, the sum of the X values; $\sum_{i=1}^{n} Y_i$, the sum of the Y values; $\sum_{i=1}^{n} X_i^2$, the sum of the squared X values; and $\sum_{i=1}^{n} X_i Y_i$, the sum of the product of X and Y. For the Sunflowers Apparel data, the number of profiled customers (X) is used to predict the annual sales (Y) in a store. Table 13.2 presents the computations of the sums needed for the site selection problem. The table also includes $\sum_{i=1}^{n} Y_i^2$, the sum of the squared Y values that will be used to compute SST in Section 13.3.

TABLE 13.2
Computations for the Sunflowers Apparel Data

Store	Profiled Customers (X)	Annual Sales (Y)	X^2	Y^2	XY
1	3.7	5.7	13.69	32.49	21.09
2	3.6	5.9	12.96	34.81	21.24
3	2.8	6.7	7.84	44.89	18.76
4	5.6	9.5	31.36	90.25	53.20
5	3.3	5.4	10.89	29.16	17.82
6	2.2	3.5	4.84	12.25	7.70
7	3.3	6.2	10.89	38.44	20.46
8	3.1	4.7	9.61	22.09	14.57
9	3.2	6.1	10.24	37.21	19.52
10	3.5	4.9	12.25	24.01	17.15
11	5.2	10.7	27.04	114.49	55.64
12	4.6	7.6	21.16	57.76	34.96
13	5.8	11.8	33.64	139.24	68.44
14	3.0	4.1	9.00	16.81	12.30
Totals	52.9	92.8	215.41	693.90	382.85

▶ *(continued)*

studentTIP

Coefficients computed manually with the assistance of handheld calculators may differ slightly because of rounding errors caused by the limited number of decimal places that your calculator might use.

Using Equations (13.3) and (13.4), you can compute b_0 and b_1:

$$SSXY = \sum_{i=1}^{n}(X_i - \overline{X})(Y_i - \overline{Y}) = \sum_{i=1}^{n}X_iY_i - \frac{\left(\sum_{i=1}^{n}X_i\right)\left(\sum_{i=1}^{n}Y_i\right)}{n}$$

$$= 382.85 - \frac{(52.9)(92.8)}{14} = 382.85 - 350.65142$$

$$= 32.19858$$

$$SSX = \sum_{i=1}^{n}(X_i - \overline{X})^2 = \sum_{i=1}^{n}X_i^2 - \frac{\left(\sum_{i=1}^{n}X_i\right)^2}{n}$$

$$= 215.41 - \frac{(52.9)^2}{14} = 215.41 - 199.88642$$

$$= 15.52358$$

With these values, compute b_1:

$$b_1 = \frac{SSXY}{SSX}$$

$$= \frac{32.19858}{15.52358}$$

$$= 2.07417$$

and:

$$\overline{Y} = \frac{\sum_{i=1}^{n}Y_i}{n} = \frac{92.8}{14} = 6.62857$$

$$\overline{X} = \frac{\sum_{i=1}^{n}X_i}{n} = \frac{52.9}{14} = 3.77857$$

With these values, compute b_0:

$$b_0 = \overline{Y} - b_1\overline{X}$$

$$= 6.62857 - 2.07417(3.77857)$$

$$= -1.2088265$$

VISUAL EXPLORATIONS

Exploring Simple Linear Regression Coefficients

Open the **VE-Simple Linear Regression add-in workbook** to explore the coefficients. (For Excel technical requirements, see Appendix D). When this workbook opens properly, it adds a **Simple Linear Regression** menu in either the Add-ins tab (Microsoft Windows) or the Apple menu bar (OS X).

To explore the effects of changing the simple linear regression coefficients, select **Simple Linear Regression → Explore Coefficients**. In the Explore Coefficients floating control panel (shown inset below),

click the spinner buttons for b_1 **slope** (the slope of the prediction line) and b_0 **intercept** (the Y intercept of the prediction line) to change the prediction line. Using the visual feedback of the chart, try to create a prediction line that is as close as possible to the prediction line defined by the least-squares estimates. In other words, try to make the **Difference from Target SSE** value as small as possible. (See page 439 for an explanation of *SSE*.)

At any time, click **Reset** to reset the b_1 and b_0 values or **Solution** to reveal the prediction line defined by the least-squares method. Click **Finish** when you are finished with this exercise.

Using Your Own Regression Data

Open to the worksheet that contains your data and uses row 1 for variable names. Select **Simple Linear Regression using your worksheet data** from the **Simple Linear Regression** menu. In the procedure's dialog box, enter the cell range of your Y variable as the **Y Variable Cell Range** and the cell range of your X variable as the **X Variable Cell Range**. Click **First cells in both ranges contain a label**, enter a **Title**, and click **OK**. After the scatter plot appears, continue with the Explore Coefficients floating control panel.

PROBLEMS FOR SECTION 13.2

LEARNING THE BASICS

13.1 Fitting a straight line to a set of data yields the following prediction line:

$$\hat{Y}_i = 2 + 5X_i$$

a. Interpret the meaning of the Y intercept, b_0.
b. Interpret the meaning of the slope, b_1.
c. Predict the value of Y for $X = 3$.

13.2 If the values of X in Problem 13.1 range from 2 to 25, should you use this model to predict the mean value of Y when X equals
a. 3?   **b.** −3?   **c.** 0?   **d.** 24?

13.3 Fitting a straight line to a set of data yields the following prediction line:

$$\hat{Y}_i = 16 - 0.5X_i$$

a. Interpret the meaning of the Y intercept, b_0.
b. Interpret the meaning of the slope, b_1.
c. Predict the value of Y for $X = 6$.

APPLYING THE CONCEPTS

 13.4 The production of wine is a multibillion-dollar worldwide industry. In an attempt to develop a model

of wine quality as judged by wine experts, data was collected from red wine variants of Portuguese "Vinho Verde" wine. (Data extracted from P. Cortez, Cerdeira, A., Almeida, F., Matos, T., and Reis, J., "Modeling Wine Preferences by Data Mining from Physiochemical Properties," *Decision Support Systems*, 47, 2009, pp. 547–553 and **bit.ly/9xKlEa**.) A sample of 50 wines is stored in VinhoVerde . Develop a simple linear regression model to predict wine quality, measured on a scale from 0 (very bad) to 10 (excellent), based on alcohol content (%).
a. Construct a scatter plot.
For these data, $b_0 = -0.3529$ and $b_1 = 0.5624$.
b. Interpret the meaning of the slope, b_1, in this problem.
c. Predict the mean wine quality for wines with a 10% alcohol content.
d. What conclusion can you reach based on the results of (a)–(c)?

13.5 Zagat's publishes restaurant ratings for various locations in the United States. The file Restaurants contains the Zagat rating for food, décor, service, and the cost per person for a sample of 100 restaurants located in the center of New York City and in an outlying area of New York City. Develop a regression model to predict the cost per person, based on a variable that represents the sum of the ratings for food, décor, and service.
Sources: Extracted from *Zagat Survey 2015, New York City*

a. Construct a scatter plot.
b. Assuming a linear relationship, use the least-squares method to compute the regression coefficients b_0 and b_1.
c. Interpret the meaning of the Y intercept, b_0, and the slope, b_1, in this problem.
d. Predict the mean cost per person for a restaurant with a summated rating of 50.
e. What should you tell the owner of a group of restaurants in this geographical area about the relationship between the summated rating and the cost of a meal?

13.6 Is an MBA a golden ticket? Pursuing an MBA is a major personal investment. Tuition and expenses associated with business school programs are costly, but the high costs come with hopes of career advancement and big salaries. A prospective MBA student would like to examine the factors that impact starting salary upon graduation and decides to develop a model that uses program per-year tuition as a predictor of starting salary. Data were collected for 37 full-time MBA programs offered at private universities. The data are stored in FTMBA . (Data extracted from "U.S. News Business School Compass," available at bit.ly/1k-T08Jg.)
a. Construct a scatter plot.
b. Assuming a linear relationship, use the least-squares method to determine the regression coefficients b_0 and b_1.
c. Interpret the meaning of the slope, b_1, in this problem.
d. Predict the mean starting salary upon graduation for a program that has a per-year tuition cost of $50,450.
e. What insights do you gain about the relationship between program per-year tuition and starting salary upon graduation?

13.7 Starbucks Coffee Co. uses a data-based approach to improving the quality and customer satisfaction of its products. When survey data indicated that Starbucks needed to improve its package-sealing process, an experiment was conducted to determine the factors in the bag-sealing equipment that might be affecting the ease of opening the bag without tearing the inner liner of the bag. (Data extracted from L. Johnson and S. Burrows, "For Starbucks, It's in the Bag," *Quality Progress*, March 2011, pp. 17–23.) One factor that could affect the rating of the ability of the bag to resist tears was the plate gap on the bag-sealing equipment. Data were collected on 19 bags in which the plate gap was varied. The results are stored in Starbucks .
a. Construct a scatter plot.
b. Assuming a linear relationship, use the least-squares method to determine the regression coefficients b_0 and b_1.
c. Interpret the meaning of the slope, b_1, in this problem.
d. Predict the mean tear rating when the plate gap is equal to 0.
e. What should you tell management of Starbucks about the relationship between the plate gap and the tear rating?

13.8 The value of a sports franchise is directly related to the amount of revenue that a franchise can generate. The file BBValues represents the value in 2014 (in $millions) and the annual revenue (in $millions) for the 30 Major League Baseball

franchises. (Data extracted from **www.forbes.com/mlb-valuations/list**.) Suppose you want to develop a simple linear regression model to predict franchise value based on annual revenue generated.
a. Construct a scatter plot.
b. Use the least-squares method to determine the regression coefficients b_0 and b_1.
c. Interpret the meaning of b_0 and b_1 in this problem.
d. Predict the mean value of a baseball franchise that generates $250 million of annual revenue.
e. What would you tell a group considering an investment in a major league baseball team about the relationship between revenue and the value of a team?

13.9 An agent for a residential real estate company in a suburb located outside of Washington, DC, has the business objective of developing more accurate estimates of the monthly rental cost for apartments. Toward that goal, the agent would like to use the size of an apartment, as defined by square footage to predict the monthly rental cost. The agent selects a sample of 48 one-bedroom apartments and collects and stores the data in RentSilverSpring .
a. Construct a scatter plot.
b. Use the least-squares method to determine the regression coefficients b_0 and b_1.
c. Interpret the meaning of b_0 and b_1 in this problem.
d. Predict the mean monthly rent for an apartment that has 800 square feet.
e. Why would it not be appropriate to use the model to predict the monthly rent for apartments that have 1,500 square feet?
f. Your friends Jim and Jennifer are considering signing a lease for a one-bedroom apartment in this residential neighborhood. They are trying to decide between two apartments, one with 800 square feet for a monthly rent of $1,130 and the other with 830 square feet for a monthly rent of $1,410. Based on (a) through (d), which apartment do you think is a better deal?

13.10 A company that holds the DVD distribution rights to movies previously released only in theaters has the business objective of developing estimates of the sales revenue of DVDs. Toward this goal, a company analyst plans to use box office gross to predict DVD sales revenue. For 38 movies, the analyst collects the box office gross (in $millions) in the year that they were released and the DVD revenue (in $millions) in the following year and stores these data in Movie . (Data extracted from "Annual Movie Chart–2013," bit.ly/1eXSP78 and "Top-Selling DVDs in the United States 2014," bit.ly/1TyHnOu.)

For these data,
a. Construct a scatter plot.
b. Assuming a linear relationship, use the least-squares method to determine the regression coefficients b_0 and b_1.
c. Interpret the meaning of the slope, b_1, in this problem.
d. Predict the mean sales revenue for a movie DVD that had a box office gross of $100 million.
e. What conclusions can you reach about predicting DVD revenue from movie gross?

13.3 Measures of Variation

When using the least-squares method to determine the regression coefficients you need to compute three measures of variation. The first measure, the **total sum of squares (SST)**, is a measure of variation of the Y_i values around their mean, $\bar{Y}$. The **total variation**, or total sum of squares, is subdivided into **explained variation** and **unexplained variation**. The explained variation, or **regression sum of squares (SSR)**, represents variation that is explained by the relationship between X and Y, and the unexplained variation, or **error sum of squares (SSE)**, represents variation due to factors other than the relationship between X and Y. Figure 13.6 shows the different measures of variation for a single Y_i value.

FIGURE 13.6
Measures of variation

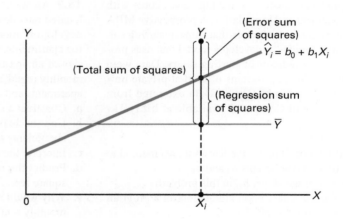

Computing the Sum of Squares

The regression sum of squares (SSR) is based on the difference between $\hat{Y}_i$ (the predicted value of Y from the prediction line) and $\bar{Y}$ (the mean value of Y). The error sum of squares (SSE) represents the part of the variation in Y that is not explained by the regression. It is based on the difference between Y_i and $\hat{Y}_i$. The total sum of squares (SST) is equal to the regression sum of squares (SSR) plus the error sum of squares (SSE). Equations (13.5), (13.6), (13.7), and (13.8) define these measures of variation and the total sum of squares (SST).

MEASURES OF VARIATION IN REGRESSION

The total sum of squares (SST) is equal to the regression sum of squares (SSR) plus the error sum of squares (SSE).

$$SST = SSR + SSE \tag{13.5}$$

TOTAL SUM OF SQUARES (SST)

The total sum of squares (SST) is equal to the sum of the squared differences between each observed value of Y and the mean value of Y.

$$SST = \text{Total sum of squares}$$

$$= \sum_{i=1}^{n} (Y_i - \bar{Y})^2 \tag{13.6}$$

REGRESSION SUM OF SQUARES (*SSR*)

The regression sum of squares (*SSR*) is equal to the sum of the squared differences between each predicted value of Y and the mean value of Y.

$$SSR = \text{Explained variation or regression sum of squares}$$

$$= \sum_{i=1}^{n}(\hat{Y}_i - \overline{Y})^2 \qquad (13.7)$$

ERROR SUM OF SQUARES (*SSE*)

The error sum of squares (*SSE*) is equal to the sum of the squared differences between each observed value of Y and the predicted value of Y.

$$SSE = \text{Unexplained variation or error sum of squares}$$

$$= \sum_{i=1}^{n}(Y_i - \hat{Y}_i)^2 \qquad (13.8)$$

Figure 13.7 shows the sum of squares portion of the Figure 13.4 results for the Sunflowers Apparel data. The total variation, *SST*, is equal to 78.7686. This amount is subdivided into the sum of squares explained by the regression (*SSR*), equal to 66.7854, and the sum of squares unexplained by the regression (*SSE*), equal to 11.9832. From Equation (13.5) on page 438:

$$SST = SSR + SSE$$
$$78.7686 = 66.7854 + 11.9832$$

FIGURE 13.7
Sum of squares portion of the Figure 13.4 worksheet

◢	A	B	C	D	E	F	G
10	ANOVA						
11		*df*	*SS*	*MS*	*F*	*Significance F*	
12	Regression	1	66.7854	66.7854	66.8792	0.0000	
13	Residual	12	11.9832	0.9986			
14	Total	13	78.7686				
15							
16		*Coefficients*	*Standard Error*	*t Stat*	*P-value*	*Lower 95%*	*Upper 95%*
17	Intercept	-1.2088	0.9949	-1.2151	0.2477	-3.3765	0.9588
18	Profiled Customers	2.0742	0.2536	8.1780	0.0000	1.5216	2.6268

The Coefficient of Determination

By themselves, *SSR*, *SSE*, and *SST* provide little information. However, the ratio of the regression sum of squares (*SSR*) to the total sum of squares (*SST*) measures the proportion of variation in Y that is explained by the linear relationship of the independent variable X with the dependent variable Y in the regression model. This ratio, called the coefficient of determination, r^2, is defined in Equation (13.9).

COEFFICIENT OF DETERMINATION

The coefficient of determination is equal to the regression sum of squares (i.e., explained variation) divided by the total sum of squares (i.e., total variation).

$$r^2 = \frac{\text{Regression sum of squares}}{\text{Total sum of squares}} = \frac{SSR}{SST} \qquad (13.9)$$

The **coefficient of determination** measures the proportion of variation in Y that is explained by the variation in the independent variable X in the regression model. The range of r^2 is from 0 to 1 and the greater the value, the more the variation in Y in the regression model can be explained by the variation in X.

For the Sunflowers Apparel data, with $SSR = 66.7854$, $SSE = 11.9832$, and $SST = 78.7686$,

$$r^2 = \frac{66.7854}{78.7686} = 0.8479$$

Therefore, 84.79% of the variation in annual sales is explained by the variability in the number of profiled customers. This large r^2 indicates a strong linear relationship between these two variables because the regression model has explained 84.79% of the variability in predicting annual sales. Only 15.21% of the sample variability in annual sales is due to factors other than what is accounted for by the linear regression model that uses the number of profiled customers.

Figure 13.8 presents the regression statistics table portion of the Figure 13.4 results for the Sunflowers Apparel data. This table contains the coefficient of determination.

FIGURE 13.8
Regression statistics portion of the Figure 13.4 worksheet

	A	B
3	**Regression Statistics**	
4	Multiple R	0.9208
5	R Square	0.8479
6	Adjusted R Square	0.8352
7	Standard Error	0.9993
8	Observations	14

EXAMPLE 13.4

Computing the Coefficient of Determination

Compute the coefficient of determination, r^2, for the Sunflowers Apparel data.

SOLUTION You can compute SST, SSR, and SSE, which are defined in Equations (13.6), (13.7), and (13.8) on pages 437 and 438, by using Equations (13.10), (13.11), and (13.12).

COMPUTATIONAL FORMULA FOR SST

$$SST = \sum_{i=1}^{n}(Y_i - \bar{Y})^2 = \sum_{i=1}^{n}Y_i^2 - \frac{\left(\sum_{i=1}^{n}Y_i\right)^2}{n} \tag{13.10}$$

COMPUTATIONAL FORMULA FOR SSR

$$SSR = \sum_{i=1}^{n}(\hat{Y}_i - \bar{Y})^2$$

$$= b_0\sum_{i=1}^{n}Y_i + b_1\sum_{i=1}^{n}X_iY_i - \frac{\left(\sum_{i=1}^{n}Y_i\right)^2}{n} \tag{13.11}$$

COMPUTATIONAL FORMULA FOR SSE

$$SSE = \sum_{i=1}^{n}(Y_i - \hat{Y}_i)^2 = \sum_{i=1}^{n}Y_i^2 - b_0\sum_{i=1}^{n}Y_i - b_1\sum_{i=1}^{n}X_iY_i \tag{13.12}$$

Using the summary results from Table 13.2 on page 434,

$$SST = \sum_{i=1}^{n}(Y_i - \bar{Y})^2 = \sum_{i=1}^{n}Y_i^2 - \frac{\left(\sum_{i=1}^{n}Y_i\right)^2}{n}$$

$$= 693.9 - \frac{(92.8)^2}{14}$$

▶ *(continued)*

$$= 693.9 - 615.13142$$

$$= 78.76858$$

$$SSR = \sum_{i=1}^{n}(\hat{Y}_i - \bar{Y})^2$$

Using something other than Excel to calculate these coefficients may lead to slightly different results. Those results will be consistent to the conclusion that there is a strong linear relationship between the two variables.

$$= b_0\sum_{i=1}^{n}Y_i + b_1\sum_{i=1}^{n}X_iY_i - \frac{\left(\sum_{i=1}^{n}Y_i\right)^2}{n}$$

$$= (-1.2088265)(92.8) + (2.07417)(382.85) - \frac{(92.8)^2}{14}$$

$$= 66.7854$$

$$SSE = \sum_{i=1}^{n}(Y_i - \hat{Y}_i)^2$$

$$= \sum_{i=1}^{n}Y_i^2 - b_0\sum_{i=1}^{n}Y_i - b_1\sum_{i=1}^{n}X_iY_i$$

$$= 693.9 - (-1.2088265)(92.8) - (2.07417)(382.85)$$

$$= 11.9832$$

Therefore,

$$r^2 = \frac{66.7854}{78.7686} = 0.8479$$

Standard Error of the Estimate

Although the least-squares method produces the line that fits the data with the minimum amount of prediction error, unless all the observed data points fall on a straight line, the prediction line is not a perfect predictor. Just as all data values cannot be expected to be exactly equal to their mean, neither can all the values in a regression analysis be expected to be located exactly on the prediction line. Figure 13.5 on page 432 illustrates the variability around the prediction line for the Sunflowers Apparel data. Notice that many of the observed values of Y fall near the prediction line, but none of the values are exactly on the line.

The **standard error of the estimate** measures the variability of the observed Y values from the predicted Y values in the same way that the standard deviation in Chapter 3 measures the variability of each value around the sample mean. In other words, the standard error of the estimate is the standard deviation *around* the prediction line, whereas the standard deviation in Chapter 3 is the standard deviation *around* the sample mean. Equation (13.13) defines the standard error of the estimate, represented by the symbol S_{YX}.

STANDARD ERROR OF THE ESTIMATE

$$S_{YX} = \sqrt{\frac{SSE}{n-2}} = \sqrt{\frac{\sum_{i=1}^{n}(Y_i - \hat{Y}_i)^2}{n-2}} \qquad \textbf{(13.13)}$$

where

$$Y_i = \text{observed value of } Y \text{ for a given } X_i$$
$$\hat{Y}_i = \text{predicted value of } Y \text{ for a given } X_i$$
$$SSE = \text{error sum of squares}$$

From Equation (13.8) and Figure 13.4 or Figure 13.7 on pages 431 or 439, $SSE = 11.9832$. Thus,

$$S_{YX} = \sqrt{\frac{11.9832}{14 - 2}} = 0.9993$$

This standard error of the estimate, equal to 0.9993 millions of dollars (i.e., \$999,300), is labeled Standard Error in the Figure 13.8 Excel results. The standard error of the estimate represents a measure of the variation around the prediction line. It is measured in the same units as the dependent variable Y. The interpretation of the standard error of the estimate is similar to that of the standard deviation. Just as the standard deviation measures variability around the mean, the standard error of the estimate measures variability around the prediction line. For Sunflowers Apparel, the typical difference between actual annual sales at a store and the predicted annual sales using the regression equation is approximately \$999,300.

PROBLEMS FOR SECTION 13.3

LEARNING THE BASICS

13.11 How do you interpret a coefficient of determination, r^2, equal to 0.80?

13.12 If $SSR = 36$ and $SSE = 4$, determine SST and then compute the coefficient of determination, r^2, and interpret its meaning.

13.13 If $SSR = 66$ and $SST = 88$, compute the coefficient of determination, r^2, and interpret its meaning.

13.14 If $SSE = 10$ and $SSR = 30$, compute the coefficient of determination, r^2, and interpret its meaning.

13.15 If $SSR = 120$, why is it impossible for SST to equal 110?

APPLYING THE CONCEPTS

✓SELF TEST **13.16** In Problem 13.4 on page 436, the percentage of alcohol was used to predict wine quality (stored in VinhoVerde). For those data, $SSR = 21.8677$ and $SST = 64.0000$.
a. Determine the coefficient of determination, r^2, and interpret its meaning.
b. Determine the standard error of the estimate.
c. How useful do you think this regression model is for predicting sales?

13.17 In Problem 13.5 on page 436, you used the summated rating to predict the cost of a restaurant meal (stored in Restaurants).
a. Determine the coefficient of determination, r^2, and interpret its meaning.
b. Determine the standard error of the estimate.
c. How useful do you think this regression model is for predicting the cost of a restaurant meal?

13.18 In Problem 13.6 on page 437, a prospective MBA student wanted to predict starting salary upon graduation, based on program per-year tuition (stored in FTMBA). Using the results of that problem,
a. determine the coefficient of determination, r^2, and interpret its meaning.
b. determine the standard error of the estimate.
c. How useful do you think this regression model is for predicting starting salary?

13.19 In Problem 13.7 on page 437, you used the plate gap on the bag-sealing equipment to predict the tear rating of a bag of coffee (stored in Starbucks). Using the results of that problem,
a. determine the coefficient of determination, r^2, and interpret its meaning.
b. determine the standard error of the estimate.
c. How useful do you think this regression model is for predicting the tear rating based on the plate gap in the bag-sealing equipment?

13.20 In Problem 13.8 on page 437, you used annual revenues to predict the value of a baseball franchise (stored in BBValues). Using the results of that problem,
a. determine the coefficient of determination, r^2, and interpret its meaning.
b. determine the standard error of the estimate.
c. How useful do you think this regression model is for predicting the value of a baseball franchise?

13.21 In Problem 13.9 on page 437, an agent for a real estate company wanted to predict the monthly rent for one-bedroom apartments, based on the size of the apartment (stored in Rent-SilverSpring). Using the results of that problem,
a. determine the coefficient of determination, r^2, and interpret its meaning.
b. determine the standard error of the estimate.
c. How useful do you think this regression model is for predicting the monthly rent?
d. Can you think of other variables that might explain the variation in monthly rent?

13.22 In Problem 13.10 on page 437, you used box office gross to predict DVD revenue (stored in Movie). Using the results of that problem,
a. determine the coefficient of determination, r^2, and interpret its meaning.
b. determine the standard error of the estimate.
c. How useful do you think this regression model is for predicting DVD revenue?
d. Can you think of other variables that might explain the variation in DVD revenue?

13.4 Assumptions of Regression

When hypothesis testing and the analysis of variance were discussed in Chapters 9 through 12, the importance of the assumptions to the validity of any conclusions reached was emphasized. The assumptions necessary for regression are similar to those of the analysis of variance because both are part of the general category of *linear models* (reference 4).

The four **assumptions of regression** (known by the acronym LINE) are:

- Linearity
- Independence of errors
- Normality of error
- Equal variance

The first assumption, **linearity**, states that the relationship between variables is linear. Relationships between variables that are not linear are discussed in reference 4.

The second assumption, **independence of errors**, requires that the errors (ε_i) be independent of one another. This assumption is particularly important when data are collected over a period of time. In such situations, the errors in a specific time period are sometimes correlated with those of the previous time period.

The third assumption, **normality**, requires that the errors (ε_i) be normally distributed at each value of X. Like the t test and the ANOVA F test, regression analysis is fairly robust against departures from the normality assumption. As long as the distribution of the errors at each level of X is not extremely different from a normal distribution, inferences about β_0 and β_1 are not seriously affected.

The fourth assumption, **equal variance**, or **homoscedasticity**, requires that the variance of the errors (ε_i) be constant for all values of X. In other words, the variability of Y values is the same when X is a low value as when X is a high value. The equal-variance assumption is important when making inferences about β_0 and β_1. If there are serious departures from this assumption, you can use either data transformations (see Section 15.2) or weighted least-squares methods (see reference 4).

13.5 Residual Analysis

Sections 13.2 and 13.3 developed a regression model using the least-squares method for the Sunflowers Apparel data. Is this the correct model for these data? Are the assumptions presented in Section 13.4 valid? **Residual analysis** visually evaluates these assumptions and helps you determine whether the regression model that has been selected is appropriate.

The **residual**, or estimated error value, e_i, is the difference between the observed (Y_i) and predicted ($\hat{Y}_i$) values of the dependent variable for a given value of X_i. A residual appears on a scatter plot as the vertical distance between an observed value of Y and the prediction line. Equation (13.14) defines the residual.

RESIDUAL

The residual is equal to the difference between the observed value of Y and the predicted value of Y.

$$e_i = Y_i - \hat{Y}_i \tag{13.14}$$

Evaluating the Assumptions

Recall from Section 13.4 that the four assumptions of regression (known by the acronym LINE) are linearity, independence, normality, and equal variance.

studentTIP

When there is no apparent pattern in the residual plot, the plot of the residuals will look like a random scattering of points.

Linearity To evaluate linearity, you plot the residuals on the vertical axis against the corresponding X_i values of the independent variable on the horizontal axis. If the linear model is appropriate for the data, you will not see any apparent pattern in the residual plot. However, if the linear model is not appropriate, in the residual plot, there will be a relationship between the X_i values and the residuals, e_i.

You can see such a pattern in the residuals in Figure 13.9. Panel A shows a situation in which, although there is an increasing trend in Y as X increases, the relationship seems curvilinear because the upward trend decreases for increasing values of X. This effect is even more apparent in Panel B, where there is a clear relationship between X_i and e_i. By removing the linear trend of X with Y, the residual plot has exposed the lack of fit in the simple linear model more clearly than the scatter plot in Panel A. For these data, a quadratic or curvilinear model (see Section 15.1) is a better fit and should be used instead of the simple linear model.

FIGURE 13.9
Studying the appropriateness of the simple linear regression model

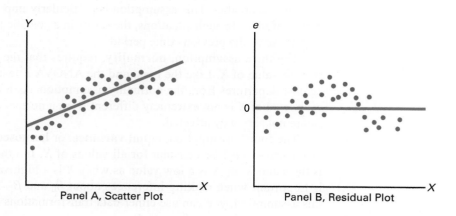

Panel A, Scatter Plot   Panel B, Residual Plot

To determine whether the simple linear regression model for the Sunflowers Apparel data is appropriate, you need to determine the residuals. Figure 13.10 displays the predicted annual sales values and residuals for the Sunflowers Apparel data.

FIGURE 13.10
Table of residuals for the Sunflowers Apparel data

	A	B	C	D	E
1	Observation	Profiled Customers	Predicted Annual Sales	Annual Sales	Residuals
2	1	3.7	6.4656	5.7	-0.7656
3	2	3.6	6.2582	5.9	-0.3582
4	3	2.8	4.5988	6.7	2.1012
5	4	5.6	10.4065	9.5	-0.9065
6	5	3.3	5.6359	5.4	-0.2359
7	6	2.2	3.3543	3.5	0.1457
8	7	3.3	5.6359	6.2	0.5641
9	8	3.1	5.2211	4.7	-0.5211
10	9	3.2	5.4285	6.1	0.6715
11	10	3.5	6.0508	4.9	-1.1508
12	11	5.2	9.5769	10.7	1.1231
13	12	4.6	8.3324	7.6	-0.7324
14	13	5.8	10.8214	11.8	0.9786
15	14	3	5.0137	4.1	-0.9137

In the Worksheet

Column C formulas compute the predicted Y values by multiplying the column B X values by the b_1 coefficient (Figure 13.4 worksheet cell B18) and then adding the b_0 coefficient (Figure 13.4 worksheet cell B17). Column E formulas compute residuals by subtracting the predicted Y values from the column D Y values.

To assess linearity, you plot the residuals against the independent variable (number of profiled customers, in millions) in Figure 13.11. Although there is widespread scatter in the residual plot, there is no clear pattern or relationship between the residuals and X_i. The residuals appear to be evenly spread above and below 0 for different values of X. You can conclude that the linear model is appropriate for the Sunflowers Apparel data.

FIGURE 13.11

Plot of residuals against the profiled customers of a store for the Sunflowers Apparel data

Independence You can evaluate the assumption of independence of the errors by plotting the residuals in the order or sequence in which the data were collected. If the values of Y are part of a time series (see Section 2.5), a residual may sometimes be related to the residual that precedes it. If this relationship exists between consecutive residuals (which violates the assumption of independence), the plot of the residuals versus the time variable will often show a cyclical pattern. If it does, you would then need to use the alternative approaches that reference 4 discusses. (Because the Sunflowers Apparel data are not time-series data, you do not need to evaluate the independence assumption in the Sunflowers Apparel problem.)

Normality You can evaluate the assumption of normality in the errors by constructing a histogram (see Section 2.4), using a stem-and-leaf display (see Section 2.4), a boxplot (see Section 3.3), or a normal probability plot (see Section 6.3). To evaluate the normality assumption for the Sunflowers Apparel data, Table 13.3 organizes the residuals into a frequency distribution and Figure 13.12 is a normal probability plot.

TABLE 13.3

Frequency Distribution of 14 Residual Values for the Sunflowers Apparel Data

Residuals	Frequency
−1.25 but less than −0.75	4
−0.75 but less than −0.25	3
−0.25 but less than +0.25	2
+0.25 but less than +0.75	2
+0.75 but less than +1.25	2
+1.25 but less than +1.75	0
+1.75 but less than +2.25	1
	14

Although the small sample size makes it difficult to evaluate normality, from the normal probability plot of the residuals in Figure 13.12, the data do not appear to depart substantially from a normal distribution. The robustness of regression analysis with modest departures from normality enables you to conclude that you should not be overly concerned about departures from this normality assumption in the Sunflowers Apparel data.

FIGURE 13.12

Excel normal probability plot of the residuals for the Sunflowers Apparel data

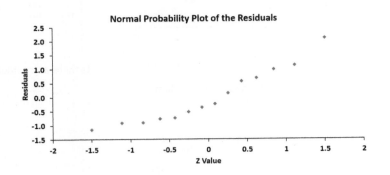

Equal Variance   You can evaluate the assumption of equal variance from a plot of the residuals with X_i. You examine the plot to see if there is approximately the same amount of variation in the residuals at each value of X. For the Sunflowers Apparel data of Figure 13.1 on page 445, there do not appear to be major differences in the variability of the residuals for different X_i values. Thus, you can conclude that there is no apparent violation in the assumption of equal variance at each level of X.

To examine a case in which the equal-variance assumption is violated, observe Figure 13.13, which is a plot of the residuals with X_i for a hypothetical set of data. This plot is fan shaped because the variability of the residuals increases dramatically as X increases. Because this plot shows unequal variances of the residuals at different levels of X, the equal-variance assumption is invalid and you would need to use the alternative approaches that reference 4 discusses.

FIGURE 13.13
Violation of equal variance

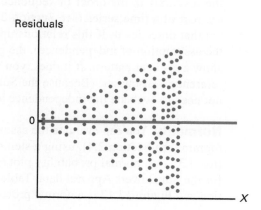

PROBLEMS FOR SECTION 13.5

LEARNING THE BASICS

13.23 The following results provide the X values, residuals, and a residual plot from a regression analysis:

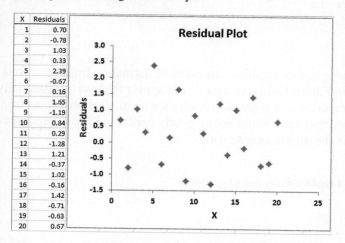

X	Residuals
1	0.70
2	-0.78
3	1.03
4	0.33
5	2.39
6	-0.67
7	0.16
8	1.65
9	-1.19
10	0.84
11	0.29
12	-1.28
13	1.21
14	-0.37
15	1.02
16	-0.16
17	1.42
18	-0.71
19	-0.63
20	0.67

Is there any evidence of a pattern in the residuals? Explain.

13.24 The following results show the X values, residuals, and a residual plot from a regression analysis:

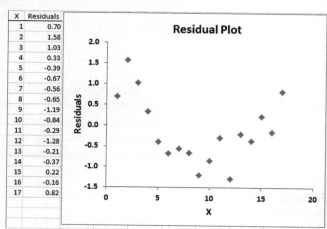

X	Residuals
1	0.70
2	1.58
3	1.03
4	0.33
5	-0.39
6	-0.67
7	-0.56
8	-0.65
9	-1.19
10	-0.84
11	-0.29
12	-1.28
13	-0.21
14	-0.37
15	0.22
16	-0.16
17	0.82

Is there any evidence of a pattern in the residuals? Explain.

APPLYING THE CONCEPTS

13.25 In Problem 13.5 on page 436, you used the summated rating to predict the cost of a restaurant meal. Perform a residual analysis for these data (stored in Restaurants). Evaluate whether the assumptions of regression have been seriously violated.

✓ **SELF TEST** **13.26** In Problem 13.4 on page 436, you used the percentage of alcohol to predict wine quality. Perform a residual analysis for these data (stored in VinhoVerde). Evaluate whether the assumptions of regression have been seriously violated.

13.27 In Problem 13.7 on page 437, you used the plate gap on the bag-sealing equipment to predict the tear rating of a bag of coffee. Perform a residual analysis for these data (stored in Starbucks). Based on these results, evaluate whether the assumptions of regression have been seriously violated.

13.28 In Problem 13.6 on page 437, a prospective MBA student wanted to predict starting salary upon graduation, based on program per-year tuition. Perform a residual analysis for these data (stored in FTMBA). Based on these results, evaluate whether the assumptions of regression have been seriously violated.

13.29 In Problem 13.9 on page 437, an agent for a real estate company wanted to predict the monthly rent for one-bedroom apartments, based on the size of the apartments. Perform a residual analysis for these data (stored in RentSilverSpring). Based on these results, evaluate whether the assumptions of regression have been seriously violated.

13.30 In Problem 13.8 on page 437, you used annual revenues to predict the value of a baseball franchise. Perform a residual analysis for these data (stored in BBValues). Based on these results, evaluate whether the assumptions of regression have been seriously violated.

13.31 In Problem 13.10 on page 437, you used box office gross to predict DVD revenue. Perform a residual analysis for these data (stored in Movie). Based on these results, evaluate whether the assumptions of regression have been seriously violated.

13.6 Measuring Autocorrelation: The Durbin-Watson Statistic

One of the basic assumptions of the regression model is the independence of the errors. This assumption is sometimes violated when data are collected over sequential time periods because a residual at any one time period sometimes is similar to residuals at adjacent time periods. This pattern in the residuals is called **autocorrelation**. When a set of data has substantial autocorrelation, the validity of a regression model is in serious doubt.

Residual Plots to Detect Autocorrelation

As mentioned in Section 13.5, one way to detect autocorrelation is to plot the residuals in time order. If a positive autocorrelation effect exists, there will be clusters of residuals with the same sign, and you will readily detect an apparent pattern. If negative autocorrelation exists, residuals will tend to jump back and forth from positive to negative to positive, and so on. Because negative autocorrelation is very rarely seen in regression analysis, the example in this section illustrates positive autocorrelation.

To illustrate positive autocorrelation, consider the case of a package delivery store manager who wants to be able to predict weekly sales. In approaching this problem, the manager has decided to develop a regression model to use the number of customers making purchases as an independent variable. She collects data for a period of 15 weeks and then organizes and stores these data in FifteenWeeks . Table 13.4 presents these data.

TABLE 13.4
Customers and Sales for a Period of 15 Consecutive Weeks

Week	Customers	Sales ($thousands)	Week	Customers	Sales ($thousands)
1	794	9.33	9	880	12.07
2	799	8.26	10	905	12.55
3	837	7.48	11	886	11.92
4	855	9.08	12	843	10.27
5	845	9.83	13	904	11.80
6	844	10.09	14	950	12.15
7	863	11.01	15	841	9.64
8	875	11.49			

Because the data are collected over a period of 15 consecutive weeks at the same store, you need to determine whether there is autocorrelation. First, you can develop the simple linear regression model you can use to predict sales based on the number of customers assuming there is no autocorrelation in the residuals. Figure 13.14 presents results for these data.

FIGURE 13.14
Excel regression worksheet results for the Table 13.4 package delivery store data

	A	B	C	D	E	F	G
1	Package Delivery Store Sales Analysis						
2							
3	*Regression Statistics*						
4	Multiple R	0.8108					
5	R Square	0.6574					
6	Adjusted R Square	0.6311					
7	Standard Error	0.9360					
8	Observations	15					
9							
10	ANOVA						
11		*df*	*SS*	*MS*	*F*	*Significance F*	
12	Regression	1	21.8604	21.8604	24.9501	0.0002	
13	Residual	13	11.3901	0.8762			
14	Total	14	33.2506				
15							
16		Coefficients	Standard Error	t Stat	P-value	Lower 95%	Upper 95%
17	Intercept	-16.0322	5.3102	-3.0192	0.0099	-27.5041	-4.5603
18	Customers	0.0308	0.0062	4.9950	0.0002	0.0175	0.0441

In the Worksheet

This worksheet uses the same template as the Figure 13.4 worksheet on page 431.

From Figure 13.14, observe that r^2 is 0.6574, indicating that 65.74% of the variation in sales is explained by variation in the number of customers. In addition, the Y intercept, b_0, is -16.0322 and the slope, b_1, is 0.0308. However, before using this model for prediction, you must perform a residual analysis. Because the data have been collected over a consecutive period of 15 weeks, in addition to checking the linearity, normality, and equal-variance assumptions, you must investigate the independence-of-errors assumption. To do this, you plot the residuals versus time in Figure 13.15 in order to examine whether a pattern in the residuals exists. In Figure 13.15, you can see that the residuals tend to fluctuate up and down in a cyclical pattern. This cyclical pattern provides strong cause for concern about the existence of autocorrelation in the residuals and, therefore, a violation of the independence-of-errors assumption.

FIGURE 13.15
Residual plot for the Table 13.4 package delivery store data

The Durbin-Watson Statistic

The **Durbin-Watson statistic** is used to measure autocorrelation. This statistic measures the correlation between each residual and the residual for the previous time period. Equation (13.15) defines the Durbin-Watson statistic.

DURBIN-WATSON STATISTIC

$$D = \frac{\sum_{i=2}^{n}(e_i - e_{i-1})^2}{\sum_{i=1}^{n}e_i^2}$$ (13.15)

where

e_i = residual at the time period i

In Equation (13.15), the numerator, $\sum_{i=2}^{n}(e_i - e_{i-1})^2$, represents the squared difference between two successive residuals, summed from the second value to the nth value and the denominator, $\sum_{i=1}^{n}e_i^2$, represents the sum of the squared residuals. This means that the value of the Durbin-Watson statistic, D, will approach 0 if successive residuals are positively autocorrelated. If the residuals are not correlated, the value of D will be close to 2. (If the residuals are negatively autocorrelated, D will be greater than 2 and could even approach its maximum value of 4.)

For the package delivery store data, the Durbin-Watson statistic, D, is 0.8830, as shown in Figure 13.16.

FIGURE 13.16
Excel Durbin-Watson statistic worksheet results for the package delivery store data

▲	A	B
1	**Durbin-Watson Statistic**	
2		
3	Sum of Squared Difference of Residuals	10.0575 =SUMXMY2(RESIDUALS!E3:E15, RESIDUALS!E2:E14)
4	Sum of Squared Residuals	11.3901 =SUMSQ(RESIDUALS!E2:E15)
5		
6	Durbin-Watson Statistic	0.8830 =B3/B4

In the Worksheet

The SUMXMY2 function computes the value of the numerator in Equation (13.15) and the SUMSQ function computes the value of the denominator in that equation. These functions use the residuals data which, in the Simple Linear Regression workbook, are in column E of the RESIDUALS worksheet.

You need to determine when the autocorrelation is large enough to conclude that there is significant positive autocorrelation. To do so, you compare D to the critical values of the Durbin-Watson statistic found in Table E.8, a portion of which is presented in Table 13.5. The critical values depend on α, the significance level chosen, n, the sample size, and k, the number of independent variables in the model (in simple linear regression, $k = 1$).

TABLE 13.5
Finding Critical Values of the Durbin-Watson Statistic

	$\alpha = .05$									
	$k = 1$		$k = 2$		$k = 3$		$k = 4$		$k = 5$	
n	d_L	d_U	d_L	d_U	d_L	d_U	d_L	d_U	d_L	d_U
15	1.08	1.36	.95	1.54	.82	1.75	.69	1.97	.56	2.21
16	1.10	1.37	.98	1.54	.86	1.73	.74	1.93	.62	2.15
17	1.13	1.38	1.02	1.54	.90	1.71	.78	1.90	.67	2.10
18	1.16	1.39	1.05	1.53	.93	1.69	.82	1.87	.71	2.06

In Table 13.5, two values are shown for each combination of α (level of significance), n (sample size), and k (number of independent variables in the model). The first value, d_L, represents the lower critical value. If D is below d_L, you conclude that there is evidence of positive autocorrelation among the residuals. If this occurs, the least-squares method used in this chap ter is inappropriate, and you should use alternative methods (see reference 4). The secon value, d_U, represents the upper critical value of D, above which you would conclude that ther is no evidence of positive autocorrelation among the residuals. If D is between d_L and d_U, yo are unable to arrive at a definite conclusion.

For the package delivery store data, with one independent variable ($k = 1$) and 15 value ($n = 15$), $d_L = 1.08$ and $d_U = 1.36$. Because $D = 0.8830 < 1.08$, you conclude that there i positive autocorrelation among the residuals. The least-squares regression analysis of the dat shown in Figure 13.14 on page 448 is inappropriate because of the presence of significant pos itive autocorrelation among the residuals. In other words, the independence-of-errors assump tion is invalid. You need to use alternative approaches, discussed in reference 4.

PROBLEMS FOR SECTION 13.6

LEARNING THE BASICS

13.32 The residuals for 10 consecutive time periods are as follows:

Time Period	Residual	Time Period	Residual
1	−5	6	+1
2	−4	7	+2
3	−3	8	+3
4	−2	9	+4
5	−1	10	+5

a. Plot the residuals over time. What conclusion can you reach about the pattern of the residuals over time?
b. Based on (a), what conclusion can you reach about the autocorrelation of the residuals?

13.33 The residuals for 15 consecutive time periods are as follows:

Time Period	Residual	Time Period	Residual
1	+4	9	+6
2	−6	10	−3
3	−1	11	+1
4	−5	12	+3
5	+2	13	0
6	+5	14	−4
7	−2	15	−7
8	+7		

a. Plot the residuals over time. What conclusion can you reach about the pattern of the residuals over time?
b. Compute the Durbin-Watson statistic. At the 0.05 level of significance, is there evidence of positive autocorrelation among the residuals?
c. Based on (a) and (b), what conclusion can you reach about the autocorrelation of the residuals?

APPLYING THE CONCEPTS

13.34 In Problem 13.7 on page 437 concerning the bag-sealing equipment at Starbucks, you used the plate gap to predict the tea rating.
a. Is it necessary to compute the Durbin-Watson statistic in thi case? Explain.
b. Under what circumstances is it necessary to compute the Durbin-Watson statistic before proceeding with the least squares method of regression analysis?

13.35 What is the relationship between the price of crude oil and the price you pay at the pump for gasoline? The file Oil & Gasoline contains the price ($) for a barrel of crude oi (Cushing, Oklahoma, spot price) and a gallon of gasoline (U.S average conventional spot price) for 287 weeks, ending June 26 2015. (Data extracted from **eia.doe.gov**.)
a. Construct a scatter plot with the price of oil on the horizonta axis and the price of gasoline on the vertical axis.
b. Use the least-squares method to develop a simple linear regres sion equation to predict the price of a gallon of gasoline usin the price of a barrel of crude oil as the independent variable.
c. Interpret the meaning of the slope, b_1, in this problem.
d. Plot the residuals versus the time period.
e. Compute the Durbin-Watson statistic.
f. At the 0.05 level of significance, is there evidence of positive autocorrelation among the residuals?
g. Based on the results of (d) through (f), is there reason to ques tion the validity of the model?
h. What conclusions can you reach concerning the relationship between the price of a barrel of crude oil and the price of a gal lon of gasoline?

✓ **SELF TEST** **13.36** A mail-order catalog business that sells personal computer supplies, software, and hardware maintains a centralized warehouse for the distribution of products ordered. Management is currently examining the process of distri bution from the warehouse and has the business objective of deter mining the factors that affect warehouse distribution costs. Currently, a handling fee is added to the order, regardless of the amount of the order. Data that indicate the warehouse distribution osts and the number of orders received have been collected over he past 24 months and are stored in Warecost .

. Assuming a linear relationship, use the least-squares method to find the regression coefficients b_0 and b_1.

. Predict the monthly warehouse distribution costs when the number of orders is 4,500.

. Plot the residuals versus the time period.

. Compute the Durbin-Watson statistic. At the 0.05 level of significance, is there evidence of positive autocorrelation among the residuals?

. Based on the results of (c) and (d), is there reason to question the validity of the model?

. What conclusions can you reach concerning the factors that affect distribution costs?

3.37 A freshly brewed shot of espresso has three distinct components: the heart, body, and crema. The separation of these three components typically lasts only 10 to 20 seconds. To use the espresso shot in making a latte, a cappuccino, or another drink, the shot must be poured into the beverage during the separation of the heart, body, nd crema. If the shot is used after the separation occurs, the drink ecomes excessively bitter and acidic, ruining the final drink. Thus, longer separation time allows the drink-maker more time to pour he shot and ensure that the beverage will meet expectations. An employee at a coffee shop hypothesized that the harder the espresso grounds were tamped down into the portafilter before brewing, he longer the separation time would be. An experiment using 24 observations was conducted to test this relationship. The independent variable Tamp measures the distance, in inches, between the espresso grounds and the top of the portafilter (i.e., the harder the amp, the greater the distance). The dependent variable Time is he number of seconds the heart, body, and crema are separated (i.e., he amount of time after the shot is poured before it must be used or the customer's beverage). The data are stored in Espresso .

a. Use the least-squares method to develop a simple regression equation with Time as the dependent variable and Tamp as the independent variable.

b. Predict the separation time for a tamp distance of 0.50 inch.

c. Plot the residuals versus the time order of experimentation. Are there any noticeable patterns?

d. Compute the Durbin-Watson statistic. At the 0.05 level of significance, is there evidence of positive autocorrelation among the residuals?

e. Based on the results of (c) and (d), is there reason to question the validity of the model?

f. What conclusions can you reach concerning the effect of tamping on the time of separation?

13.38 The owners of a chain of ice cream stores have the business objective of improving the forecast of daily sales so that staffing shortages can be minimized during the summer season. As a starting point, the owners decide to develop a simple linear regression model to predict daily sales based on atmospheric temperature. They select a sample of 21 consecutive days and store the results in IceCream . (Hint: Determine which are the independent and dependent variables.)

a. Assuming a linear relationship, use the least-squares method to compute the regression coefficients b_0 and b_1.

b. Predict the sales for a day in which the temperature is 83°F.

c. Plot the residuals versus the time period.

d. Compute the Durbin-Watson statistic. At the 0.05 level of significance, is there evidence of positive autocorrelation among the residuals?

e. Based on the results of (c) and (d), is there reason to question the validity of the model?

f. What conclusions can you reach concerning the relationship between sales and atmospheric temperature?

13.7 Inferences About the Slope and Correlation Coefficient

In Sections 13.1 through 13.3, regression was used solely for descriptive purposes. You learned how to determine the regression coefficients using the least-squares method and how to predict Y for a given value of X. In addition, you learned how to compute and interpret the standard error of the estimate and the coefficient of determination.

When residual analysis, as discussed in Section 13.5, indicates that the assumptions of a least-squares regression model are not seriously violated and that the straight-line model is appropriate, you can make inferences about the linear relationship between the variables in the population.

t Test for the Slope

To determine the existence of a significant linear relationship between the X and Y variables, you test whether β_1 (the population slope) is equal to 0. The null and alternative hypotheses are as follows:

$$H_0: \beta_1 = 0 \text{ [There is no linear relationship (the slope is zero).]}$$
$$H_1: \beta_1 \neq 0 \text{ [There is a linear relationship (the slope is not zero).]}$$

If you reject the null hypothesis, you conclude that there is evidence of a linear relationship. Equation (13.16) defines the test statistic for the slope, which is based on the sampling distribution of the slope.

TESTING A HYPOTHESIS FOR A POPULATION SLOPE, β_1, USING THE t TEST

The t_{STAT} test statistic equals the difference between the sample slope and hypothesized value of the population slope divided by S_{b_1}, the standard error of the slope.

$$t_{STAT} = \frac{b_1 - \beta_1}{S_{b_1}} \qquad (13.16)$$

where

$$S_{b_1} = \frac{S_{YX}}{\sqrt{SSX}}$$

$$SSX = \sum_{i=1}^{n} (X_i - \overline{X})^2$$

The t_{STAT} test statistic follows a t distribution with $n - 2$ degrees of freedom.

Return to the Sunflowers Apparel scenario on page 427. To test whether there is a significant linear relationship between the number of profiled customers and the annual sales at the 0.05 level of significance, refer to the t test results shown in Figure 13.17.

FIGURE 13.17

Excel t test for the slope worksheet results for the Sunflowers Apparel data

	A	B	C	D	E	F	G
16		Coefficients	Standard Error	t Stat	P-value	Lower 95%	Upper 95%
17	Intercept	-1.2088	0.9949	-1.2151	0.2477	-3.3765	0.9588
18	Profiled Customers	2.0742	0.2536	8.1780	0.0000	1.5216	2.6268

From Figure 13.4 or Figure 13.17,

$$b_1 = +2.0742 \quad n = 14 \quad S_{b_1} = 0.2536$$

and

$$t_{STAT} = \frac{b_1 - \beta_1}{S_{b_1}}$$

$$= \frac{2.0742 - 0}{0.2536} = 8.178$$

Using the 0.05 level of significance, the critical value of t with $n - 2 = 12$ degrees of freedom is 2.1788. Because $t_{STAT} = 8.178 > 2.1788$ or because the p-value is 0.0000, which is less than $\alpha = 0.05$, you reject H_0 (see Figure 13.18). Hence, you can conclude that there is a significant linear relationship between mean annual sales and the number of profiled customers.

FIGURE 13.18

Testing a hypothesis about the population slope at the 0.05 level of significance, with 12 degrees of freedom

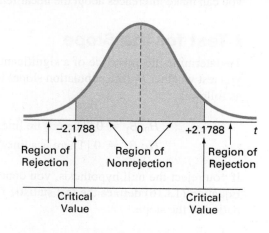

F Test for the Slope

As an alternative to the t test, in simple linear regression, you can use an F test to determine whether the slope is statistically significant. In previous chapters, Section 10.4 uses the F distribution to test the ratio of two variances and Sections 11.1 and 11.2 use the distribution as part of the analysis of variance. Equation (13.17) defines the F test for the slope as the ratio of the variance that is due to the regression (MSR) divided by the error variance ($MSE = S_{YX}^2$).

TESTING A HYPOTHESIS FOR A POPULATION SLOPE, β_1, USING THE F TEST

The F_{STAT} test statistic is equal to the regression mean square (MSR) divided by the mean square error (MSE).

$$F_{STAT} = \frac{MSR}{MSE} \qquad (13.17)$$

where

$$MSR = \frac{SSR}{1} = SSR$$

$$MSE = \frac{SSE}{n-2}$$

The F_{STAT} test statistic follows an F distribution with 1 and $n-2$ degrees of freedom.

Using a level of significance α, the decision rule is

Reject H_0 if $F_{STAT} > F_\alpha$;
otherwise, do not reject H_0.

Table 13.6 organizes the complete set of results into an analysis of variance (ANOVA) table.

TABLE 13.6
ANOVA Table for Testing the Significance of a Regression Coefficient

Source	df	Sum of Squares	Mean Square (variance)	F
Regression	1	SSR	$MSR = \dfrac{SSR}{1} = SSR$	$F_{STAT} = \dfrac{MSR}{MSE}$
Error	$n-2$	SSE	$MSE = \dfrac{SSE}{n-2}$	
Total	$n-1$	SST		

Figure 13.19, a completed ANOVA table for the Sunflowers sales data (extracted from Figure 13.4), shows that the computed F_{STAT} test statistic is 66.8792 and the p-value is 0.0000.

FIGURE 13.19
Excel F test worksheet results for the Sunflowers Apparel data

	A	B	C	D	E	F
10	ANOVA					
11		df	SS	MS	F	Significance F
12	Regression	1	66.7854	66.7854	66.8792	0.0000
13	Residual	12	11.9832	0.9986		
14	Total	13	78.7686			

Using a level of significance of 0.05, from Table E.5, the critical value of the F distribution, with 1 and 12 degrees of freedom, is 4.75 (see Figure 13.20). Because $F_{STAT} = 66.8792 > 4.75$ or because the p-value = 0.0000 < 0.05, you reject H_0 and conclude that there is a significant linear relationship between the number of profiled customers and annual sales. Because the

In simple linear regression, $t^2 = F$.

F test in Equation (13.17) on page 453 is equivalent to the t test in Equation (13.16) on page 452, you reach the same conclusion.

FIGURE 13.20
Regions of rejection and nonrejection when testing for the significance of the slope at the 0.05 level of significance, with 1 and 12 degrees of freedom

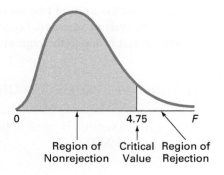

Confidence Interval Estimate for the Slope

In addition to testing for the existence of a linear relationship between the variables, you can construct a confidence interval estimate of β_1 using Equation (13.18).

CONFIDENCE INTERVAL ESTIMATE OF THE SLOPE, β_1

The confidence interval estimate for the population slope can be constructed by taking the sample slope, b_1, and adding and subtracting the critical t value multiplied by the standard error of the slope.

$$b_1 \pm t_{\alpha/2} S_{b_1}$$
$$b_1 - t_{\alpha/2} S_{b_1} \leq \beta_1 \leq b_1 + t_{\alpha/2} S_{b_1} \tag{13.18}$$

where

$t_{\alpha/2}$ = critical value corresponding to an upper-tail probability of $\alpha/2$ from the t distribution with $n - 2$ degrees of freedom (i.e., a cumulative area of $1 - \alpha/2$)

From the Figure 13.17 results on page 453,

$$b_1 = 2.0742 \quad n = 14 \quad S_{b_1} = 0.2536$$

To construct a 95% confidence interval estimate, $\alpha/2 = 0.025$, and from Table E.3, $t_{\alpha/2} = 2.1788$. Thus,

$$b_1 \pm t_{\alpha/2} S_{b_1} = 2.0742 \pm (2.1788)(0.2536)$$
$$= 2.0742 \pm 0.5526$$
$$1.5216 \leq \beta_1 \leq 2.6268$$

Therefore, you have 95% confidence that the population slope is between 1.5216 and 2.6268. The confidence interval indicates that for each increase of 1 million profiled customers, predicted annual sales are estimated to increase by at least \$1,521,600 but no more than \$2,626,800. Because both of these values are above 0, you have evidence of a significant linear relationship between annual sales and the number of profiled customers. Had the interval included 0, you would have concluded that there is no evidence of a significant linear relationship between the variables.

t Test for the Correlation Coefficient

In Section 3.5 on page 126, the strength of the relationship between two numerical variables was measured using the **correlation coefficient**, r. The values of the coefficient of correlation range from -1 for a perfect negative correlation to $+1$ for a perfect positive correlation. You can use the correlation coefficient to determine whether there is a statistically significant linear relationship between X and Y. To do so, you hypothesize that the population correlation coefficient, ρ, is 0. Thus, the null and alternative hypotheses are

$$H_0: \rho = 0 \text{ (no correlation)}$$
$$H_1: \rho \neq 0 \text{ (correlation)}$$

Equation (13.19) defines the test statistic for determining the existence of a significant correlation.

TESTING FOR THE EXISTENCE OF CORRELATION

$$t_{STAT} = \frac{r - \rho}{\sqrt{\dfrac{1 - r^2}{n - 2}}} \qquad \textbf{(13.19a)}$$

where

$$r = +\sqrt{r^2} \quad \text{if} \quad b_1 > 0$$
$$r = -\sqrt{r^2} \quad \text{if} \quad b_1 < 0$$

The t_{STAT} test statistic follows a t distribution with $n - 2$ degrees of freedom. r is calculated as in Equation (3.17) on page 126:

$$r = \frac{\text{cov}(X, Y)}{S_X S_Y} \qquad \textbf{(13.19b)}$$

where

$$\text{cov}(X, Y) = \frac{\displaystyle\sum_{i=1}^{n}(X_i - \bar{X})(Y_i - \bar{Y})}{n - 1}$$

$$S_X = \sqrt{\frac{\displaystyle\sum_{i=1}^{n}(X_i - \bar{X})^2}{n - 1}}$$

$$S_Y = \sqrt{\frac{\displaystyle\sum_{i=1}^{n}(Y_i - \bar{Y})^2}{n - 1}}$$

In the Sunflowers Apparel problem, $r^2 = 0.8479$ and $b_1 = +2.0742$ (see Figure 13.4 on page 431). Because $b_1 > 0$, the correlation coefficient for annual sales and profiled customers is the positive square root of r^2—that is, $r = +\sqrt{0.8479} = +0.9208$. You use Equation (13.19a) to test the null hypothesis that there is no correlation between these two variables. This results in the following t_{STAT} statistic:

$$t_{STAT} = \frac{r - 0}{\sqrt{\dfrac{1 - r^2}{n - 2}}}$$

$$= \frac{0.9208 - 0}{\sqrt{\dfrac{1 - (0.9208)^2}{14 - 2}}} = 8.178$$

Using the 0.05 level of significance, because $t_{STAT} = 8.178 > 2.1788$, you reject the null hypothesis. You conclude that there is a significant correlation between annual sales and the number of profiled customers. This t_{STAT} test statistic is equivalent to the t_{STAT} test statistic found when testing whether the population slope, β_1, is equal to zero.

PROBLEMS FOR SECTION 13.7

LEARNING THE BASICS

13.39 You are testing the null hypothesis that there is no linear relationship between two variables, X and Y. From your sample of $n = 10$, you determine that $r = 0.80$.
a. What is the value of the t test statistic t_{STAT}?
b. At the $\alpha = 0.05$ level of significance, what are the critical values?
c. Based on your answers to (a) and (b), what statistical decision should you make?

13.40 You are testing the null hypothesis that there is no linear relationship between two variables, X and Y. From your sample of $n = 18$, you determine that $b_1 = +4.5$ and $S_{b_1} = 1.5$.
a. What is the value of t_{STAT}?
b. At the $\alpha = 0.05$ level of significance, what are the critical values?
c. Based on your answers to (a) and (b), what statistical decision should you make?
d. Construct a 95% confidence interval estimate of the population slope, β_1.

13.41 You are testing the null hypothesis that there is no linear relationship between two variables, X and Y. From your sample of $n = 20$, you determine that $SSR = 60$ and $SSE = 40$.
a. What is the value of F_{STAT}?
b. At the $\alpha = 0.05$ level of significance, what is the critical value?
c. Based on your answers to (a) and (b), what statistical decision should you make?
d. Compute the correlation coefficient by first computing r^2 and assuming that b_1 is negative.
e. At the 0.05 level of significance, is there a significant correlation between X and Y?

APPLYING THE CONCEPTS

✓SELF TEST **13.42** In Problem 13.4 on page 436, you used the percentage of alcohol to predict wine quality. The data are stored in VinhoVerde. From the results of that problem, $b_1 = 0.5624$ and $S_{b_1} = 0.1127$.
a. At the 0.05 level of significance, is there evidence of a linear relationship between the percentage of alcohol and wine quality?
b. Construct a 95% confidence interval estimate of the population slope, β_1.

13.43 In Problem 13.5 on page 436, you used the summated rating of a restaurant to predict the cost of a meal. The data are stored in Restaurants.

a. At the 0.05 level of significance, is there evidence of a linear relationship between the summated rating of a restaurant and the cost of a meal?
b. Construct a 95% confidence interval estimate of the population slope, β_1.

13.44 In Problem 13.6 on page 437, a prospective MBA student wanted to predict starting salary upon graduation, based on program per-year tuition. The data are stored in FTMBA. Use the results of that problem.
a. At the 0.05 level of significance, is there evidence of a linear relationship between the starting salary upon graduation and program per-year tuition?
b. Construct a 95% confidence interval estimate of the population slope, β_1.

13.45 In Problem 13.7 on page 437, you used the plate gap in the bag-sealing equipment to predict the tear rating of a bag of coffee. The data are stored in Starbucks. Use the results of that problem.
a. At the 0.05 level of significance, is there evidence of a linear relationship between the plate gap of the bag-sealing machine and the tear rating of a bag of coffee?
b. Construct a 95% confidence interval estimate of the population slope, β_1.

13.46 In Problem 13.8 on page 437, you used annual revenues to predict the value of a baseball franchise. The data are stored in BBValues. Use the results of that problem.
a. At the 0.05 level of significance, is there evidence of a linear relationship between annual revenue and franchise value?
b. Construct a 95% confidence interval estimate of the population slope, β_1.

13.47 In Problem 13.9 on page 437, an agent for a real estate company wanted to predict the monthly rent for one-bedroom apartments, based on the size of the apartment. The data are stored in RentSilverSpring. Use the results of that problem.
a. At the 0.05 level of significance, is there evidence of a linear relationship between the size of the apartment and the monthly rent?
b. Construct a 95% confidence interval estimate of the population slope, β_1.

13.48 In Problem 13.10 on page 437, you used box office gross to predict DVD revenue. The data are stored in Movie. Use the results of that problem.
a. At the 0.05 level of significance, is there evidence of a linear relationship between box office gross and DVD revenue?
b. Construct a 95% confidence interval estimate of the population slope, β_1.

13.49 The volatility of a stock is often measured by its beta value. You can estimate the beta value of a stock by developing a simple linear regression model, using the percentage weekly change in the stock as the dependent variable and the percentage weekly change in a market index as the independent variable. The S&P 500 Index is a common index to use. For example, if you wanted to estimate the beta value for Disney, you could use the following model, which is sometimes referred to as a *market model*:

$$(\% \text{ weekly change in Disney}) = \beta_0$$
$$+ \beta_1 (\% \text{ weekly change in S \& P 500 index}) + \varepsilon$$

The least-squares regression estimate of the slope b_1 is the estimate of the beta value for Disney. A stock with a beta value of 1.0 tends to move the same as the overall market. A stock with a beta value of 1.5 tends to move 50% more than the overall market, and a stock with a beta value of 0.6 tends to move only 60% as much as the overall market. Stocks with negative beta values tend to move in the opposite direction of the overall market. The following table gives some beta values for some widely held stocks as of July 11, 2015:

Company	Ticker Symbol	Beta
Apple	AAPL	1.13
Disney	DIS	1.42
American Eagle Mines	AEM	−0.64
Marriott	MAR	1.50
Microsoft	MSFT	0.78
Procter & Gamble	PG	1.00

Source: Data extracted from finance.yahoo.com, July 11, 2015.

a. For each of the six companies, interpret the beta value.
b. How can investors use the beta value as a guide for investing?

13.50 Index funds are mutual funds that try to mimic the movement of leading indexes, such as the S&P 500 or the Russell 2000. The beta values (as described in Problem 13.49) for these funds are therefore approximately 1.0, and the estimated market models for these funds are approximately

$$(\% \text{ weekly change in index fund}) = 0.0 + 1.0$$
$$(\% \text{ weekly change in the index})$$

Leveraged index funds are designed to magnify the movement of major indexes. Direxion Funds is a leading provider of leveraged index and other alternative-class mutual fund products for investment advisors and sophisticated investors. Two of the company's funds are shown in the following table:

Name	Ticker Symbol	Description
Daily Small Cap Bull 3x Fund	TNA	300% of the Russell 2000 Index
Daily S&P Bear 3x Fund	SPXSX	300% of the S&P 500 Index

Source: Data extracted from **www.direxionfunds.com**.

The estimated market models for these funds are approximately

$$(\% \text{ daily change in TNA}) = 0.0 + 3.0$$
$$(\% \text{ daily change in the Russell 2000})$$
$$(\% \text{ daily change in SPXSX}) = 0.0 + 3.0$$
$$(\% \text{ daily change in the S\&P 500 Index})$$

Thus, if the Russell 2000 Index gains 10% over a period of time, the leveraged mutual fund TNA gains approximately 30%. On the downside, if the same index loses 20%, TNA loses approximately 60%.

a. The objective of the Direxion Funds Bull 3x Fund, SPXL, is 300% of the performance of the S&P 500 Index. What is its approximate market model?
b. If the S&P 500 Index gains 10% in a year, what return do you expect SPXL to have?
c. If the S&P 500 Index loses 20% in a year, what return do you expect SPXL to have?
d. What type of investors should be attracted to leveraged index funds? What type of investors should stay away from these funds?

13.51 The file **Cereals** contains the calories and sugar, in grams, in one serving of seven breakfast cereals:

Cereal	Calories	Sugar
Kellogg's All Bran	80	6
Kellogg's Corn Flakes	100	2
Wheaties	100	4
Nature's Path Organic Multigrain Flakes	110	4
Kellogg's Rice Krispies	130	4
Post Shredded Wheat Vanilla Almond	190	11
Kellogg's Mini Wheats	200	10

a. Compute and interpret the coefficient of correlation, r.
b. At the 0.05 level of significance, is there a significant linear relationship between calories and sugar?

13.52 Movie companies need to predict the gross receipts of an individual movie once the movie has debuted. The following results (stored in **PotterMovies**) are the first weekend gross, the U.S. gross, and the worldwide gross (in $millions) of the eight Harry Potter movies that debuted from 2001 to 2011:

Title	First Weekend	U.S. Gross	Worldwide Gross
Sorcerer's Stone	90.295	317.558	976.458
Chamber of Secrets	88.357	261.988	878.988
Prisoner of Azkaban	93.687	249.539	795.539
Goblet of Fire	102.335	290.013	896.013
Order of the Phoenix	77.108	292.005	938.469
Half-Blood Prince	77.836	301.460	934.601
Deathly Hallows Part I	125.017	295.001	955.417
Deathly Hallows Part II	169.189	381.001	1,328.11

Source: Data extracted from **www.the-numbers.com/interactive/comp-Harry-Potter.php**.

a. Compute the coefficient of correlation between first weekend gross and U.S. gross, first weekend gross and worldwide gross, and U.S. gross and worldwide gross.

b. At the 0.05 level of significance, is there a significant linear relationship between first weekend gross and U.S. gross, first weekend gross and worldwide gross, and U.S. gross and worldwide gross?

13.53 College football is big business, with coaches' salaries, revenues, and expenses in millions of dollars. The file College Football contains the coaches' pay and total athletic department revenue for college football at 108 schools. (Data extracted from "2014 NCAAF Coaches Salary," **usat.ly/1uws90v** and "NCAA Finances," **usat.ly/1PuEwoF**.)
a. Compute and interpret the coefficient of correlation, r.
b. At the 0.05 level of significance, is there a significant linear relationship between a coach's pay and revenue?

13.54 A survey by the Pew Research Center found that social networking is popular in many nations around the world. The file GlobalSocialMedia contains the level of social media networking (measured as the percent of individuals polled who use social networking sites) and the GDP per capita based on purchasing power parity (PPP) for each of 31 emerging and developing countries. (Data extracted from "2. Online Activities in Emerging and Developing Nations," **bit.ly/1GASqhp**.)
a. Compute and interpret the coefficient of correlation, r.
b. At the 0.05 level of significance, is there a significant linear relationship between GDP and social media usage?
c. What conclusions can you reach about the relationship between GDP and social media usage?

13.8 Estimation of Mean Values and Prediction of Individual Values

In Chapter 8, you studied the concept of the confidence interval estimate of the population mean. In Example 13.2 on page 433, you used the prediction line to predict the mean value of Y for a given X. The mean annual sales for stores that had 4 million profiled customers within a fixed radius was predicted to be 7.0879 millions of dollars ($7,087,900). This estimate, however, is a *point estimate* of the population mean. This section presents methods to develop a confidence interval estimate for the mean response for a given X and for developing a prediction interval for an individual response, Y, for a given value of X.

The Confidence Interval Estimate for the Mean Response

Equation (13.20) defines the **confidence interval estimate for the mean response** for a given X.

CONFIDENCE INTERVAL ESTIMATE FOR THE MEAN OF Y

$$\hat{Y}_i \pm t_{\alpha/2}S_{YX}\sqrt{h_i}$$

$$\hat{Y}_i - t_{\alpha/2}S_{YX}\sqrt{h_i} \leq \mu_{Y|X=X_i} \leq \hat{Y}_i + t_{\alpha/2}S_{YX}\sqrt{h_i} \qquad (13.20)$$

where

$$h_i = \frac{1}{n} + \frac{(X_i - \overline{X})^2}{SSX}$$

$\hat{Y}_i$ = predicted value of Y; $\hat{Y}_i = b_0 + b_1X_i$

S_{YX} = standard error of the estimate

n = sample size

X_i = given value of X

$\mu_{Y|X=X_i}$ = mean value of Y when $X = X_i$

$$SSX = \sum_{i=1}^{n}(X_i - \overline{X})^2$$

$t_{\alpha/2}$ = critical value corresponding to an upper-tail probability of $\alpha/2$ from the t distribution with $n - 2$ degrees of freedom (i.e., a cumulative area of $1 - \alpha/2$)

The width of the confidence interval in Equation (13.20) depends on several factors. Increased variation around the prediction line, as measured by the standard error of the estimate, results in a wider interval. As you would expect, increased sample size reduces the width of the interval. In addition, the width of the interval varies at different values of X. When you predict Y for values of X close to $\overline{X}$, the interval is narrower than for predictions for X values farther away from $\overline{X}$.

In the Sunflowers Apparel example, suppose you want to construct a 95% confidence interval estimate of the mean annual sales for the entire population of stores that have 4 million profiled customers $(X = 4)$. Using the simple linear regression equation,

$$\hat{Y}_i = -1.2088 + 2.0742X_i$$
$$= -1.2088 + 2.0742(4) = 7.0879 \text{ (millions of dollars)}$$

Also, given the following:

$$\overline{X} = 3.7786 \quad S_{YX} = 0.9993$$

$$SSX = \sum_{i=1}^{n}(X_i - \overline{X})^2 = 15.5236$$

From Table E.3, $t_{\alpha/2} = 2.1788$. Thus,

$$\hat{Y}_i \pm t_{\alpha/2}S_{YX}\sqrt{h_i}$$

where

$$h_i = \frac{1}{n} + \frac{(X_i - \overline{X})^2}{SSX}$$

so that

$$\hat{Y}_i \pm t_{\alpha/2}S_{YX}\sqrt{\frac{1}{n} + \frac{(X_i - \overline{X})^2}{SSX}}$$

$$= 7.0879 \pm (2.1788)(0.9993)\sqrt{\frac{1}{14} + \frac{(4 - 3.7786)^2}{15.5236}}$$

$$= 7.0879 \pm 0.5946$$

so

$$6.4932 \le \mu_{Y|X=4} \le 7.6825$$

Therefore, the 95% confidence interval estimate is that the population mean annual sales are between $6,493,200 and $7,682,500 for all stores with 4 million profiled customers.

The Prediction Interval for an Individual Response

In addition to constructing a confidence interval for the mean value of Y, you can also construct a prediction interval for an individual value of Y. Although the form of this interval is similar to that of the confidence interval estimate of Equation (13.20), the prediction interval is predicting an individual value, not estimating a mean. Equation (13.21) defines the **prediction interval for an individual response**, Y, at a given value, X_i, denoted by $Y_{X=X_i}$.

PREDICTION INTERVAL FOR AN INDIVIDUAL RESPONSE, Y

$$\hat{Y}_i \pm t_{\alpha/2}S_{YX}\sqrt{1 + h_i} \qquad \text{(13.21)}$$

$$\hat{Y}_i - t_{\alpha/2}S_{YX}\sqrt{1 + h_i} \le Y_{X=X_i} \le \hat{Y}_i + t_{\alpha/2}S_{YX}\sqrt{1 + h_i}$$

(continued)

where

$$Y_{X=X_i} = \text{future value of } Y \text{ when } X = X_i$$

$t_{\alpha/2}$ = critical value corresponding to an upper-tail probability of $\alpha/2$ from the t distribution with $n - 2$ degrees of freedom (i.e., a cumulative area of $1 - \alpha/2$)

In addition, h_i, $\hat{Y}_i$, S_{YX}, n, and X_i are defined as in Equation (13.20) on page 459.

To construct a 95% prediction interval of the annual sales for an individual store that has 4 million profiled customers $(X = 4)$, you first compute $\hat{Y}_i$. Using the prediction line:

$$\hat{Y}_i = -1.2088 + 2.0742X_i$$
$$= -1.2088 + 2.0742(4)$$
$$= 7.0879 \text{ (millions of dollars)}$$

Also, given the following:

$$\overline{X} = 3.7786 \quad S_{YX} = 0.9993$$

$$SSX = \sum_{i=1}^{n}(X_i - \overline{X})^2 = 15.5236$$

From Table E.3, $t_{\alpha/2} = 2.1788$. Thus,

$$\hat{Y}_i \pm t_{\alpha/2}S_{YX}\sqrt{1 + h_i}$$

where

$$h_i = \frac{1}{n} + \frac{(X_i - \overline{X})^2}{\sum_{i=1}^{n}(X_i - \overline{X})^2}$$

so that

$$\hat{Y}_i \pm t_{\alpha/2}S_{YX}\sqrt{1 + \frac{1}{n} + \frac{(X_i - \overline{X})^2}{SSX}}$$

$$= 7.0879 \pm (2.1788)(0.9993)\sqrt{1 + \frac{1}{14} + \frac{(4 - 3.7786)^2}{15.5236}}$$

$$= 7.0879 \pm 2.2570$$

so

$$4.8308 \le Y_{X=4} \le 9.3449$$

Therefore, with 95% confidence, you predict that the annual sales for an individual store with 4 million profiled customers is between $4,830,800 and $9,344,900.

If you compare the results of the confidence interval estimate and the prediction interval, you see that the width of the prediction interval for an individual store is much wider than the confidence interval estimate for the mean. Remember that there is much more variation in predicting an individual value than in estimating a mean value. Figure 13.21 on page 461 presents the Excel results for the confidence interval estimate and the prediction interval for the Sunflowers Apparel data.

FIGURE 13.21
Excel worksheet results
confidence interval esti-
mate and prediction
interval for the Sunflowers
Apparel data

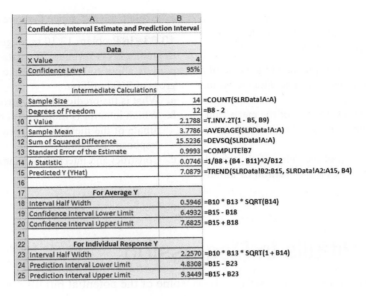

In the Worksheet

The T.INV.2T function
computes the *t* critical value
and the TREND function
computes the predicted *Y*
value from the regression
data and the specified *X* value
(in cell B4).

TREND, AVERAGE,
and DEVSQ, which
computes the *SSX*, all
use data from a SLRData
worksheet that contains the
data for the independent
variable in column A and
the data for the dependent
variable in column B.

PROBLEMS FOR SECTION 13.8

LEARNING THE BASICS

13.55 Based on a sample of $n = 20$, the least-squares method
was used to develop the following prediction line: $\hat{Y}_i = 5 + 3X_i$.
In addition,

$$S_{YX} = 1.0 \quad \overline{X} = 2 \quad \sum_{i=1}^{n}(X_i - \overline{X})^2 = 20$$

a. Construct a 95% confidence interval estimate of the population
mean response for $X = 2$.
b. Construct a 95% prediction interval of an individual response
for $X = 2$.

13.56 Based on a sample of $n = 20$, the least-squares method
was used to develop the following prediction line: $\hat{Y}_i = 5 + 3X_i$.
In addition,

$$S_{YX} = 1.0 \quad \overline{X} = 2 \quad \sum_{i=1}^{n}(X_i - \overline{X})^2 = 20$$

a. Construct a 95% confidence interval estimate of the population
mean response for $X = 4$.
b. Construct a 95% prediction interval of an individual response
for $X = 4$.
c. Compare the results of (a) and (b) with those of Problem 13.55
(a) and (b). Which intervals are wider? Why?

APPLYING THE CONCEPTS

13.57 In Problem 13.5 on page 436, you used the summated rating of a restaurant to predict the cost of a meal. The data are stored
in Restaurants .
a. Construct a 95% confidence interval estimate of the mean cost
of a meal for restaurants that have a summated rating of 50.
b. Construct a 95% prediction interval of the cost of a meal for an
individual restaurant that has a summated rating of 50.
c. Explain the difference in the results in (a) and (b).

✓ SELF TEST **13.58** In Problem 13.4 on page 436, you used the
percentage of alcohol to predict wine quality. The
data are stored in VinhoVerde . For these data, $S_{YX} = 0.9369$ and
$h_i = 0.024934$ when $X = 10$.
a. Construct a 95% confidence interval estimate of the mean wine
quality rating for all wines that have 10% alcohol.
b. Construct a 95% prediction interval of the wine quality rating
of an individual wine that has 10% alcohol.
c. Explain the difference in the results in (a) and (b).

13.59 In Problem 13.7 on page 437, you used the plate gap on the
bag-sealing equipment to predict the tear rating of a bag of coffee.
The data are stored in Starbucks .
a. Construct a 95% confidence interval estimate of the mean tear
rating for all bags of coffee when the plate gap is 0.
b. Construct a 95% prediction interval of the tear rating for an individual bag of coffee when the plate gap is 0.
c. Why is the interval in (a) narrower than the interval in (b)?

13.60 In Problem 13.6 on page 437, a prospective MBA student
wanted to predict starting salary upon graduation, based on program per-year tuition. The data are stored in FTMBA .
a. Construct a 95% confidence interval estimate of the mean starting salary upon graduation of an individual program with per-
year tuition cost of $50,450.
b. Construct a 95% prediction interval of the starting salary upon
graduation of an individual program with per-year tuition cost
of $50,450.
c. Why is the interval in (a) narrower than the interval in (b)?

13.61 In Problem 13.9 on page 437, an agent for a real estate
company wanted to predict the monthly rent for one-bedroom
apartments, based on the size of an apartment. The data are stored
in RentSilverSpring .
a. Construct a 95% confidence interval estimate of the mean
monthly rental for all one-bedroom apartments that are 800
square feet in size.

b. Construct a 95% prediction interval of the monthly rental for an individual one-bedroom apartment that is 800 square feet in size.

c. Explain the difference in the results in (a) and (b).

13.62 In Problem 13.8 on page 437, you predicted the value of a baseball franchise, based on current revenue. The data are stored in BBValues .

a. Construct a 95% confidence interval estimate of the mean value of all baseball franchises that generate $250 million of annual revenue.

b. Construct a 95% prediction interval of the value of an individual baseball franchise that generates $250 million of annual revenue.

c. Explain the difference in the results in (a) and (b).

13.63 In Problem 13.10 on page 437, you used box office gross to predict DVD revenue. The data are stored in Movie . The company is about to release a movie on DVD that had a box office gross of $100 million.

a. What is the predicted DVD revenue?

b. Which interval is more useful here, the confidence interval estimate of the mean or the prediction interval for an individual response? Explain.

c. Construct and interpret the interval you selected in (b).

13.9 Potential Pitfalls in Regression

When using regression analysis, some of the potential pitfalls are:

- Lacking awareness of the assumptions of least-squares regression
- Not knowing how to evaluate the assumptions of least-squares regression
- Not knowing what the alternatives are to least-squares regression if an assumption is violated
- Using a regression model without knowledge of the subject matter
- Omitting important variables from the regression model.
- Extrapolating outside the relevant range
- Concluding that a significant relationship identified always reflects a cause-and-effect relationship

You can avoid such pitfalls by using the six-step strategy in Exhibit 13.1.

EXHIBIT 13.1

Six Steps for Avoiding the Potential Pitfalls

1. Construct a scatter plot to observe the possible relationship between X and Y.

2. Perform a residual analysis to check the assumptions of regression (linearity, independence, normality, equal variance):

  a. Plot the residuals versus the independent variable to determine whether the linear model is appropriate and to check for equal variance.

  b. Construct a histogram, stem-and-leaf display, boxplot, or normal probability plot of the residuals to check for normality.

  c. Plot the residuals versus time to check for independence. (This step is necessary only if the data are collected over time.)

3. If there are violations of the assumptions, use alternative methods to least-squares regression or alternative least-squares models (see reference 4 and Section 15.2).

4. If there are no violations of the assumptions, carry out tests for the significance of the regression coefficients and develop confidence and prediction intervals.

5. Refrain from making predictions and forecasts outside the relevant range of the independent variable.

6. Remember that the relationships identified in observational studies may or may not be due to cause-and-effect relationships. (While causation implies correlation, correlation does not imply causation.)

Someone not familiar with the assumptions of regression or how to evaluate those assumptions may reach wrong conclusions about the data being analyzed. For example, the Table 13.7 data (stored in Anscombe) illustrate the importance of using scatter plots and residual analysis to complement the calculation of the Y intercept, the slope, and r^2.

TABLE 13.7
Four Sets of Artificial Data

Data Set A		Data Set B		Data Set C		Data Set D	
X_i	Y_i	X_i	Y_i	X_i	Y_i	X_i	Y_i
10	8.04	10	9.14	10	7.46	8	6.58
14	9.96	14	8.10	14	8.84	8	5.76
5	5.68	5	4.74	5	5.73	8	7.71
8	6.95	8	8.14	8	6.77	8	8.84
9	8.81	9	8.77	9	7.11	8	8.47
12	10.84	12	9.13	12	8.15	8	7.04
4	4.26	4	3.10	4	5.39	8	5.25
7	4.82	7	7.26	7	6.42	19	12.50
11	8.33	11	9.26	11	7.81	8	5.56
13	7.58	13	8.74	13	12.74	8	7.91
6	7.24	6	6.13	6	6.08	8	6.89

Source: Data extracted from F. J. Anscombe, "Graphs in Statistical Analysis," *The American Statistician*, 27 (1973), pp. 17–21.

Anscombe (reference 1) showed that all four data sets given in Table 13.7 have the following identical results:

$$\hat{Y}_i = 3.0 + 0.5X_i \quad S_{YX} = 1.237 \quad S_{b_1} = 0.118 \quad r^2 = 0.667$$
$$SSR = 27.51 \quad SSE = 13.76 \quad SST = 41.27$$

If you stopped the analysis at this point, you would fail to observe the important differences among the four data sets that scatter plots and residual plots can reveal. The Figure 13.22 scatter plots and residual plots show how different the four data sets are!

FIGURE 13.22
Scatter plots and residual plots for the data sets A, B, C, and D

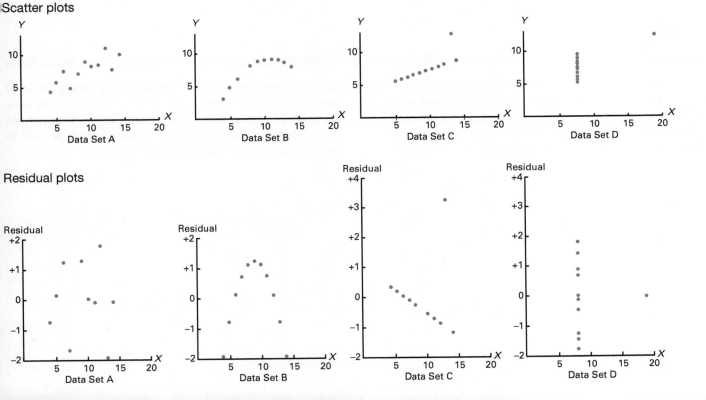

Scatter plots

Residual plots

Each data set has a different relationship between X and Y. The only data set that seems to approximately follow a straight line is data set A. The residual plot for data set A does not show any obvious patterns or outlying residuals. This is certainly not true for data sets B, C, and D. The scatter plot for data set B shows that a curvilinear regression model is more appropriate. This conclusion is reinforced by the residual plot for data set B. The scatter plot and the residual plot for data set C clearly show an outlying observation. In this case, one approach used is to remove the outlier and reestimate the regression model (see reference 4). The scatter plot for data set D represents a situation in which the model is heavily dependent on the outcome of a single data point ($X_8 = 19$ and $Y_8 = 12.50$). Any regression model with this characteristic should be used with caution.

▼USING **STATISTICS**
Knowing Customers . . . , Revisited

In the Knowing Customers at Sunflowers Apparel scenario, you were the director of planning for a chain of upscale clothing stores for women. Until now, Sunflowers managers selected sites based on factors such as the availability of a good lease or a subjective opinion that a location seemed like a good place for a store. To make more objective decisions, you used the more systematic DCOVA approach to identify and classify groups of consumers and developed a regression model to analyze the relationship between the number of profiled customers that live within a fixed radius of a Sunflowers store and the annual sales of the store. The model indicated that about 84.8% of the variation in sales was explained by the number of profiled customers that live within a fixed radius of a Sunflowers store. Furthermore, for each increase of 1 million profiled customers, mean annual sales were estimated to increase by $2.0742 million. You can now use your model to help make better decisions when selecting new sites for stores as well as to forecast sales for existing stores.

▼SUMMARY

This chapter develops the simple linear regression model and discusses the assumptions the model uses and how to evaluate them. Once you are assured that the model is appropriate, you can predict values by using the prediction line and test for the significance of the slope. Figure 13.23 provides a roadmap for navigating through the process of applying a simple linear regresssion model to a set of data. Chapters 14 and 15 extend regression analysis to situations in which more than one independent variable is used to predict the value of a dependent variable.

FIGURE 13.23
Roadmap for simple linear
regression

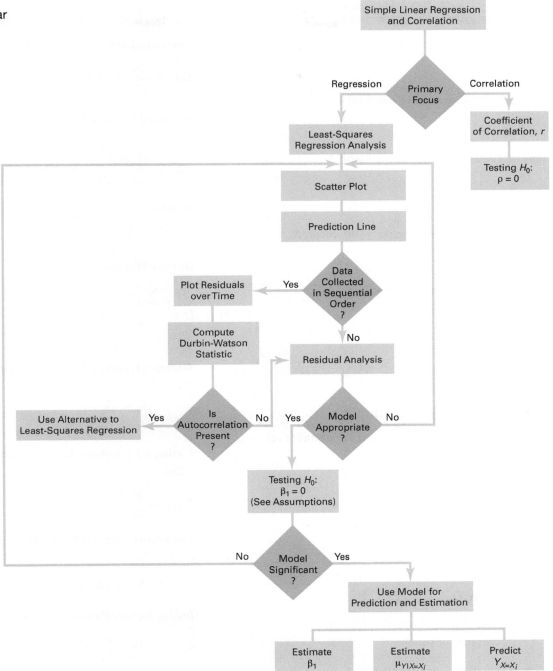

▼ REFERENCES

1. Anscombe, F. J. "Graphs in Statistical Analysis." *The American Statistician*, 27(1973): 17–21.

2. Hoaglin, D. C., and R. Welsch. "The Hat Matrix in Regression and ANOVA." *The American Statistician*, 32(1978): 17–22.

3. Hocking, R. R. "Developments in Linear Regression Methodology: 1959–1982." *Technometrics*, 25(1983): 219–250.

4. Kutner, M. H., C. J. Nachtsheim, J. Neter, and W. Li. *Applied Linear Statistical Models*, 5th ed. New York: McGraw-Hill/Irwin, 2005.

5. Montgomery, D. C., E. A. Peck, and G. G. Vining. *Introduction to Linear Regression Analysis*, 5th ed. New York, Wiley, 2012.

▼ KEY EQUATIONS

Simple Linear Regression Model

$$Y_i = \beta_0 + \beta_1 X_i + \varepsilon_i \tag{13.1}$$

Simple Linear Regression Equation: The Prediction Line

$$\hat{Y}_i = b_0 + b_1 X_i \tag{13.2}$$

Computational Formula for the Slope, b_1

$$b_1 = \frac{SSXY}{SSX} \tag{13.3}$$

Computational Formula for the Y Intercept, b_0

$$b_0 = \overline{Y} - b_1 \overline{X} \tag{13.4}$$

Measures of Variation in Regression

$$SST = SSR + SSE \tag{13.5}$$

Total Sum of Squares (SST)

$$SST = \text{Total sum of squares} = \sum_{i=1}^{n} (Y_i - \overline{Y})^2 \tag{13.6}$$

Regression Sum of Squares (SSR)

SSR = Explained variation or regression sum of squares

$$= \sum_{i=1}^{n} (\hat{Y}_i - \overline{Y})^2 \tag{13.7}$$

Error Sum of Squares (SSE)

SSE = Unexplained variation or error sum of squares

$$= \sum_{i=1}^{n} (Y_i - \hat{Y}_i)^2 \tag{13.8}$$

Coefficient of Determination

$$r^2 = \frac{\text{Regression sum of squares}}{\text{Total sum of squares}} = \frac{SSR}{SST} \tag{13.9}$$

Computational Formula for SST

$$SST = \sum_{i=1}^{n} (Y_i - \overline{Y})^2 = \sum_{i=1}^{n} Y_i^2 - \frac{\left(\sum_{i=1}^{n} Y_i\right)^2}{n} \tag{13.10}$$

Computational Formula for SSR

$$SSR = \sum_{i=1}^{n} (\hat{Y}_i - \overline{Y})^2$$

$$= b_0 \sum_{i=1}^{n} Y_i + b_1 \sum_{i=1}^{n} X_i Y_i - \frac{\left(\sum_{i=1}^{n} Y_i\right)^2}{n} \tag{13.11}$$

Computational Formula for SSE

$$SSE = \sum_{i=1}^{n} (Y_i - \hat{Y}_i)^2 = \sum_{i=1}^{n} Y_i^2 - b_0 \sum_{i=1}^{n} Y_i - b_1 \sum_{i=1}^{n} X_i Y_i \tag{13.12}$$

Standard Error of the Estimate

$$S_{YX} = \sqrt{\frac{SSE}{n-2}} = \sqrt{\frac{\sum_{i=1}^{n} (Y_i - \hat{Y}_i)^2}{n-2}} \tag{13.13}$$

Residual

$$e_i = Y_i - \hat{Y}_i \tag{13.14}$$

Durbin-Watson Statistic

$$D = \frac{\sum_{i=2}^{n} (e_i - e_{i-1})^2}{\sum_{i=1}^{n} e_i^2} \tag{13.15}$$

Testing a Hypothesis for a Population Slope, β_1, Using the t Test

$$t_{STAT} = \frac{b_1 - \beta_1}{S_{b_1}} \tag{13.16}$$

Testing a Hypothesis for a Population Slope, β_1, Using the F Test

$$F_{STAT} = \frac{MSR}{MSE} \tag{13.17}$$

Confidence Interval Estimate of the Slope, β_1

$$b_1 \pm t_{\alpha/2} S_{b_1}$$

$$b_1 - t_{\alpha/2} S_{b_1} \leq \beta_1 \leq b_1 + t_{\alpha/2} S_{b_1} \tag{13.18}$$

Testing for the Existence of Correlation

$$t_{STAT} = \frac{r - \rho}{\sqrt{\dfrac{1 - r^2}{n-2}}} \tag{13.19a}$$

$$r = \frac{\text{cov}(X, Y)}{S_X S_Y} \tag{13.19b}$$

Confidence Interval Estimate for the Mean of Y

$$\hat{Y}_i \pm t_{\alpha/2} S_{YX} \sqrt{h_i}$$

$$\hat{Y}_i - t_{\alpha/2} S_{YX} \sqrt{h_i} \leq \mu_{Y|X=X_i} \leq \hat{Y}_i + t_{\alpha/2} S_{YX} \sqrt{h_i} \tag{13.20}$$

Prediction Interval for an Individual Response, Y

$$\hat{Y}_i \pm t_{\alpha/2} S_{YX} \sqrt{1 + h_i}$$

$$\hat{Y}_i - t_{\alpha/2} S_{YX} \sqrt{1 + h_i} \leq Y_{X=X_i} \leq \hat{Y}_i + t_{\alpha/2} S_{YX} \sqrt{1 + h_i} \tag{13.21}$$

KEY TERMS

assumptions of regression 443
autocorrelation 447
coefficient of determination 440
confidence interval estimate for the mean response 458
correlation coefficient 455
dependent variable 428
Durbin-Watson statistic 448
equal variance 443
error sum of squares (SSE) 438
explained variation 438
explanatory variable 428
homoscedasticity 443
independence of errors 443

independent variable 428
least-squares method 431
linearity 443
linear relationship 429
model 428
normality 443
prediction interval for an individual response, Y 459
prediction line 430
regression analysis 428
regression coefficient 431
regression sum of squares (SSR) 438
relevant range 433
residual 443

residual analysis 443
response variable 428
scatter diagram 428
scatter plot 428
simple linear regression 428
simple linear regression equation 430
slope 430
standard error of the estimate 441
total sum of squares (SST) 438
total variation 438
unexplained variation 438
Y intercept 430

CHECKING YOUR UNDERSTANDING

13.64 What is the interpretation of the Y intercept and the slope in the simple linear regression equation?

13.65 What is the interpretation of the coefficient of determination?

13.66 When is the unexplained variation (i.e., error sum of squares) equal to 0?

13.67 When is the explained variation (i.e., regression sum of squares) equal to 0?

13.68 Why should you always carry out a residual analysis as part of a regression model?

13.69 What are the assumptions of regression analysis?

13.70 How do you evaluate the assumptions of regression analysis?

13.71 When and how do you use the Durbin-Watson statistic?

13.72 What is the difference between a confidence interval estimate of the mean response, $\mu_{Y|X=X_i}$, and a prediction interval of $Y_{X=X_i}$?

CHAPTER REVIEW PROBLEMS

13.73 Can you use Twitter activity to forecast box office receipts on the opening weekend? The following data (stored in **TwitterMovies**) indicate the Twitter activity ("want to see") and the receipts ($) per theater on the weekend a movie opened for seven movies:

Movie	Twitter Activity	Receipts ($)
The Devil Inside	219,509	14,763
The Dictator	6,405	5,796
Paranormal Activity 3	165,128	15,829
The Hunger Games	579,288	36,871
Bridesmaids	6,564	8,995
Red Tails	11,104	7,477
Act of Valor	9,152	8,054

Source: R. Dodes, "Twitter Goes to the Movies," *The Wall Street Journal*, August 3, 2012, pp. D1–D12.

a. Use the least-squares method to compute the regression coefficients b_0 and b_1.

b. Interpret the meaning of b_0 and b_1 in this problem.
c. Predict the mean receipts for a movie that has a Twitter activity of 100,000.
d. Should you use the model to predict the receipts for a movie that has a Twitter activity of 1,000,000? Why or why not?
e. Determine the coefficient of determination, r^2, and explain its meaning in this problem.
f. Perform a residual analysis. Is there any evidence of a pattern in the residuals? Explain.
g. At the 0.05 level of significance, is there evidence of a linear relationship between Twitter activity and receipts?
h. Construct a 95% confidence interval estimate of the mean receipts for a movie that has a Twitter activity of 100,000 and a 95% prediction interval of the receipts for a single movie that has a Twitter activity of 100,000.
i. Based on the results of (a)–(h), do you think that Twitter activity is a useful predictor of receipts on the first weekend a movie opens? What issues about these data might make you hesitant to use Twitter activity to predict receipts?

13.74 Management of a soft-drink bottling company has the business objective of developing a method for allocating delivery costs to customers. Although one cost clearly relates to travel time within a particular route, another variable cost reflects the time required to unload the cases of soft drink at the delivery point. To begin, management decided to develop a regression model to predict delivery time based on the number of cases delivered. A sample of 20 deliveries within a territory was selected. The delivery times and the number of cases delivered were organized in the following table and stored in Delivery .

Customer	Number of Cases	Delivery Time (minutes)	Customer	Number of Cases	Delivery Time (minutes)
1	52	32.1	11	161	43.0
2	64	34.8	12	184	49.4
3	73	36.2	13	202	57.2
4	85	37.8	14	218	56.8
5	95	37.8	15	243	60.6
6	103	39.7	16	254	61.2
7	116	38.5	17	267	58.2
8	121	41.9	18	275	63.1
9	143	44.2	19	287	65.6
10	157	47.1	20	298	67.3

a. Use the least-squares method to compute the regression coefficients b_0 and b_1.
b. Interpret the meaning of b_0 and b_1 in this problem.
c. Predict the mean delivery time for 150 cases of soft drink.
d. Should you use the model to predict the delivery time for a customer who is receiving 500 cases of soft drink? Why or why not?
e. Determine the coefficient of determination, r^2, and explain its meaning in this problem.
f. Perform a residual analysis. Is there any evidence of a pattern in the residuals? Explain.
g. At the 0.05 level of significance, is there evidence of a linear relationship between delivery time and the number of cases delivered?
h. Construct a 95% confidence interval estimate of the mean delivery time for 150 cases of soft drink and a 95% prediction interval of the delivery time for a single delivery of 150 cases of soft drink.
i. What conclusions can you reach from (a) through (h) about the relationship between the number of cases and delivery time?

13.75 Measuring the height of a California redwood tree is very difficult because these trees grow to heights of over 300 feet. People familiar with these trees understand that the height of a California redwood tree is related to other characteristics of the tree, including the diameter of the tree at the breast height of a person. The data in Redwood represent the height (in feet) and diameter (in inches) at the breast height of a person for a sample of 21 California redwood trees.

a. Assuming a linear relationship, use the least-squares method to compute the regression coefficients b_0 and b_1. State the regression equation that predicts the height of a tree based on the tree's diameter at breast height of a person.
b. Interpret the meaning of the slope in this equation.
c. Predict the mean height for a tree that has a breast height diameter of 25 inches.

d. Interpret the meaning of the coefficient of determination in this problem.
e. Perform a residual analysis on the results and determine the adequacy of the model.
f. Determine whether there is a significant relationship between the height of redwood trees and the breast height diameter at the 0.05 level of significance.
g. Construct a 95% confidence interval estimate of the population slope between the height of the redwood trees and breast height diameter.
h. What conclusions can you reach about the relationship of the diameter of the tree and its height?

13.76 You want to develop a model to predict the assessed value of homes based on their size. A sample of 30 single-family houses listed for sale in Silver Spring, Maryland, a suburb of Washington, DC, is selected to study the relationship between assessed value (in $thousands) and size (in thousands of square feet), and the data is collected and stored in SilverSpring . (Hint: First determine which are the independent and dependent variables.)
a. Construct a scatter plot and, assuming a linear relationship, use the least-squares method to compute the regression coefficients b_0 and b_1.
b. Interpret the meaning of the Y intercept, b_0, and the slope, b_1, in this problem.
c. Use the prediction line developed in (a) to predict the mean assessed value for a house whose size is 2,000 square feet.
d. Determine the coefficient of determination, r^2, and interpret its meaning in this problem.
e. Perform a residual analysis on your results and evaluate the regression assumptions.
f. At the 0.05 level of significance, is there evidence of a linear relationship between assessed value and size?
g. Construct a 95% confidence interval estimate of the population slope.
h. What conclusions can you reach about the relationship between the size of the house and its assessed value?

13.77 You want to develop a model to predict the taxes of houses, based on assessed value. A sample of 30 single-family houses listed for sale in Silver Spring, Maryland, a suburb of Washington, DC, is selected. The taxes (in $) and the assessed value of the houses (in $thousands) are recorded and stored in SilverSpring . (Hint: First determine which are the independent and dependent variables.)
a. Construct a scatter plot and, assuming a linear relationship, use the least-squares method to compute the regression coefficients b_0 and b_1.
b. Interpret the meaning of the Y intercept, b_0, and the slope, b_1, in this problem.
c. Use the prediction line developed in (a) to predict the mean taxes for a house whose assessed value is $400,000.
d. Determine the coefficient of determination, r^2, and interpret its meaning in this problem.
e. Perform a residual analysis on your results and evaluate the regression assumptions.
f. At the 0.05 level of significance, is there evidence of a linear relationship between taxes and assessed value?
g. What conclusions can you reach concerning the relationship between taxes and assessed value?

13.78 An analyst has the objective of predicting the return on equity (ROE) of banks. The analyst begins by using the leverage ratio, a financial measurement that looks at how much capital comes in the form of debt. A sample of 25 American banks is selected and stored in AmericanBanks . (Data extracted from K. Badenhausen, "Full List: America's Best and Worst Banks 2015," **onforb.es/1Cvw05F**.)

a. Construct a scatter plot and, assuming a linear relationship, use the least-squares method to compute the regression coefficients b_0 and b_1.
b. Interpret the meaning of the Y intercept, b_0, and the slope, b_1, in this problem.
c. Use the prediction line developed in (a) to predict the mean ROE for a bank with a leverage ratio of 9%.
d. Determine the coefficient of determination, r^2, and interpret its meaning in this problem.
e. Perform a residual analysis on your results and evaluate the regression assumptions.
f. At the 0.05 level of significance, is there evidence of a linear relationship between leverage ratio and ROE?
g. Construct a 95% confidence interval estimate of the mean ROE of banks with a leverage ratio of 9% and a 95% prediction interval of the ROE for a particular bank with a leverage ratio of 9%.
h. Construct a 95% confidence interval estimate of the population slope.
i. What conclusions can you reach concerning the relationship between leverage ratio and ROE?

13.79 An accountant for a large department store has the business objective of developing a model to predict the amount of time it takes to process invoices. Data are collected from the past 32 working days, and the number of invoices processed and completion time (in hours) are stored in Invoice . (Hint: First determine which are the independent and dependent variables.)

a. Assuming a linear relationship, use the least-squares method to compute the regression coefficients b_0 and b_1.
b. Interpret the meaning of the Y intercept, b_0, and the slope, b_1, in this problem.
c. Use the prediction line developed in (a) to predict the mean amount of time it would take to process 150 invoices.
d. Determine the coefficient of determination, r^2, and interpret its meaning.
e. Plot the residuals against the number of invoices processed and also against time.
f. Based on the plots in (e), does the model seem appropriate?
g. Based on the results in (e) and (f), what conclusions can you reach about the validity of the prediction made in (c)?
h. What conclusions can you reach about the relationship between the number of invoices and the completion time?

13.80 On January 28, 1986, the space shuttle *Challenger* exploded, and seven astronauts were killed. Prior to the launch, the predicted atmospheric temperature was for freezing weather at the launch site. Engineers for Morton Thiokol (the manufacturer of the rocket motor) prepared charts to make the case that the launch should not take place due to the cold weather. These arguments were rejected, and the launch tragically took place. Upon investigation after the tragedy, experts agreed that the disaster occurred because of leaky rubber O-rings that did not seal properly due to the cold temperature. Data indicating the atmospheric temperature at the time of 23 previous launches and the O-ring damage index are stored in O-Ring .

Note: Data from flight 4 is omitted due to unknown O-ring condition.

Sources: Data extracted from *Report of the Presidential Commission on the Space Shuttle Challenger Accident*, Washington, DC, 1986, Vol. II (H1–H3) and Vol. IV (664); and *Post-Challenger Evaluation of Space Shuttle Risk Assessment and Management*, Washington, DC, 1988, pp. 135–136.

a. Construct a scatter plot for the seven flights in which there was O-ring damage (O-ring damage index $\neq$ 0). What conclusions, if any, can you reach about the relationship between atmospheric temperature and O-ring damage?
b. Construct a scatter plot for all 23 flights.
c. Explain any differences in the interpretation of the relationship between atmospheric temperature and O-ring damage in (a) and (b).
d. Based on the scatter plot in (b), provide reasons why a prediction should not be made for an atmospheric temperature of 31°F, the temperature on the morning of the launch of the *Challenger*.
e. Although the assumption of a linear relationship may not be valid for the set of 23 flights, fit a simple linear regression model to predict O-ring damage, based on atmospheric temperature.
f. Include the prediction line found in (e) on the scatter plot developed in (b).
g. Based on the results in (f), do you think a linear model is appropriate for these data? Explain.
h. Perform a residual analysis. What conclusions do you reach?

13.81 A baseball analyst would like to study various team statistics for a recent season to determine which variables might be useful in predicting the number of wins achieved by teams during the season. He begins by using a team's earned run average (ERA), a measure of pitching performance, to predict the number of wins. He collects the team ERA and team wins for each of the 30 Major League Baseball teams and stores these data in Baseball . (Hint: First determine which are the independent and dependent variables.)

a. Assuming a linear relationship, use the least-squares method to compute the regression coefficients b_0 and b_1.
b. Interpret the meaning of the Y intercept, b_0, and the slope, b_1, in this problem.
c. Use the prediction line developed in (a) to predict the mean number of wins for a team with an ERA of 4.50.
d. Compute the coefficient of determination, r^2, and interpret its meaning.
e. Perform a residual analysis on your results and determine the adequacy of the fit of the model.
f. At the 0.05 level of significance, is there evidence of a linear relationship between the number of wins and the ERA?
g. Construct a 95% confidence interval estimate of the mean number of wins expected for teams with an ERA of 4.50.
h. Construct a 95% prediction interval of the number of wins for an individual team that has an ERA of 4.50.
i. Construct a 95% confidence interval estimate of the population slope.
j. The 30 teams constitute a population. In order to use statistical inference, as in (f) through (i), the data must be assumed to represent a random sample. What "population" would this sample be drawing conclusions about?

k. What other independent variables might you consider for inclusion in the model?

l. What conclusions can you reach concerning the relationship between ERA and wins?

13.82 Can you use the annual revenues generated by National Basketball Association (NBA) franchises to predict franchise values? Figure 2.14 on page 60 shows a scatter plot of revenue with franchise value, and Figure 3.10 on page 128, shows the correlation coefficient. Now, you want to develop a simple linear regression model to predict franchise values based on revenues. (Franchise values and revenues are stored in NBAValues .)

a. Assuming a linear relationship, use the least-squares method to compute the regression coefficients b_0 and b_1.

b. Interpret the meaning of the Y intercept, b_0, and the slope, b_1, in this problem.

c. Predict the mean value of an NBA franchise that generates $150 million of annual revenue.

d. Compute the coefficient of determination, r^2, and interpret its meaning.

e. Perform a residual analysis on your results and evaluate the regression assumptions.

f. At the 0.05 level of significance, is there evidence of a linear relationship between the annual revenues generated and the value of an NBA franchise?

g. Construct a 95% confidence interval estimate of the mean value of all NBA franchises that generate $150 million of annual revenue.

h. Construct a 95% prediction interval of the value of an individual NBA franchise that generates $150 million of annual revenue.

i. Compare the results of (a) through (h) to those of baseball franchises in Problems 13.8, 13.20, 13.30, 13.46, and 13.62 and European soccer teams in Problem 13.83.

13.83 In Problem 13.82 you used annual revenue to develop a model to predict the franchise value of National Basketball Association (NBA) teams. Can you also use the annual revenues generated by European soccer teams to predict franchise values? (European soccer team values and revenues are stored in SoccerValues .)

a. Repeat Problem 13.82 (a) through (h) for the European soccer teams.

b. Compare the results of (a) to those of baseball franchises in Problems 13.8, 13.20, 13.30, 13.46, and 13.62 and NBA franchises in Problem 13.82.

13.84 During the fall harvest season in the United States, pumpkins are sold in large quantities at farm stands. Often, instead of weighing the pumpkins prior to sale, the farm stand operator will just place the pumpkin in the appropriate circular cutout on the counter. When asked why this was done, one farmer replied, "I can tell the weight of the pumpkin from its circumference." To determine whether this was really true, the circumference and weight of each pumpkin from a sample of 23 pumpkins were determined and the results stored in Pumpkin .

a. Assuming a linear relationship, use the least-squares method to compute the regression coefficients b_0 and b_1.

b. Interpret the meaning of the slope, b_1, in this problem.

c. Predict the mean weight for a pumpkin that is 60 centimeters in circumference.

d. Do you think it is a good idea for the farmer to sell pumpkins by circumference instead of weight? Explain.

e. Determine the coefficient of determination, r^2, and interpret its meaning.

f. Perform a residual analysis for these data and evaluate the regression assumptions.

g. At the 0.05 level of significance, is there evidence of a linear relationship between the circumference and weight of a pumpkin?

h. Construct a 95% confidence interval estimate of the population slope, β_1.

13.85 Refer to the discussion of beta values and market models in Problem 13.49 on page 457. The S&P 500 Index tracks the overall movement of the stock market by considering the stock prices of 500 large corporations. The file StockPrices2014 contains 2014 weekly data for the S&P 500 and three companies. The following variables are included:

WEEK—Week ending on date given
S&P—Weekly closing value for the S&P 500 Index
GE—Weekly closing stock price for General Electric
DISCA—Weekly closing stock price for Discovery Communications
GOOG—Weekly closing stock price for Google

Source: Data extracted from **finance.yahoo.com**, June 27, 2015.

a. Estimate the market model for GE. (Hint: Use the percentage change in the S&P 500 Index as the independent variable and the percentage change in GE's stock price as the dependent variable.)

b. Interpret the beta value for GE.

c. Repeat (a) and (b) for Discovery Communications.

d. Repeat (a) and (b) for Google.

e. Write a brief summary of your findings.

13.86 The file CEO 2014 includes the total compensation (in $millions) for CEOs of 200 Standard & Poor's 500 companies and the investment return in 2014. (Data extracted from "Highest Paid Chiefs in 2014," **nyti.ms/1Hrapdm**.)

a. Compute the correlation coefficient between compensation and the investment return in 2014.

b. At the 0.05 level of significance, is the correlation between compensation and the investment return in 2014 statistically significant?

c. Write a short summary of your findings in (a) and (b). Do the results surprise you?

REPORT WRITING EXERCISE

13.87 In Problems 13.8, 13.20, 13.30, 13.46, 13.62, 13.82, and 13.83, you developed regression models to predict franchise value of major league baseball, NBA basketball, and soccer teams. Now, write a report based on the models you developed. Append to your report all appropriate charts and statistical information.

▾CASES

Managing Ashland MultiComm Services

To ensure that as many trial subscriptions to the *3-For-All* service as possible are converted to regular subscriptions, the marketing department works closely with the customer support department to accomplish a smooth initial process for the trial subscription customers. To assist in this effort, the marketing department needs to accurately forecast the monthly total of new regular subscriptions.

A team consisting of managers from the marketing and customer support departments was convened to develop a better method of forecasting new subscriptions. Previously, after examining new subscription data for the prior three months, a group of three managers would develop a subjective forecast of the number of new subscriptions. Livia Salvador, who was recently hired by the company to provide expertise in quantitative forecasting methods, suggested that the department look for factors that might help in predicting new subscriptions.

Members of the team found that the forecasts in the past year had been particularly inaccurate because in some months, much more time was spent on telemarketing than in other months. Livia collected data (stored in `AMS13`) for the number of new subscriptions and hours spent on telemarketing for each month for the past two years.

1. What criticism can you make concerning the method of forecasting that involved taking the new subscriptions data for the prior three months as the basis for future projections?

2. What factors other than number of telemarketing hours spent might be useful in predicting the number of new subscriptions? Explain.

3. **a.** Analyze the data and develop a regression model to predict the number of new subscriptions for a month, based on the number of hours spent on telemarketing for new subscriptions.

   b. If you expect to spend 1,200 hours on telemarketing per month, estimate the number of new subscriptions for the month. Indicate the assumptions on which this prediction is based. Do you think these assumptions are valid? Explain.

   c. What would be the danger of predicting the number of new subscriptions for a month in which 2,000 hours were spent on telemarketing?

Digital Case

Apply your knowledge of simple linear regression in this Digital Case, which extends the Sunflowers Apparel Using Statistics scenario from this chapter.

Leasing agents from the Triangle Mall Management Corporation have suggested that Sunflowers consider several locations in some of Triangle's newly renovated lifestyle malls that cater to shoppers with higher-than-mean disposable income. Although the locations are smaller than the typical Sunflowers location, the leasing agents argue that higher-than-mean disposable income in the surrounding community is a better predictor of higher sales than profiled customers. The leasing agents maintain that sample data from 14 Sunflowers stores prove that this is true.

Open **Triangle_Sunflower.pdf** and review the leasing agents' proposal and supporting documents. Then answer the following questions:

1. Should mean disposable income be used to predict sales based on the sample of 14 Sunflowers stores?

2. Should the management of Sunflowers accept the claims of Triangle's leasing agents? Why or why not?

3. Is it possible that the mean disposable income of the surrounding area is not an important factor in leasing new locations? Explain.

4. Are there any other factors not mentioned by the leasing agents that might be relevant to the store leasing decision?

Brynne Packaging

Brynne Packaging is a large packaging company, offering its customers the highest standards in innovative packaging solutions and reliable service. About 25% of the employees at Brynne Packaging are machine operators. The human resources department has suggested that the company consider using the Wesman Personnel Classification Test (WPCT), a measure of reasoning ability, to screen applicants for the machine operator job. In order to assess the WPCT as a predictor of future job performance, 25 recent applicants were tested using the WPCT; all were hired, regardless of their WPCT score. At a later time, supervisors were asked to rate the quality of the job performance of these 25 employees, using a 1-to-10 rating scale (where 1 = very low and 10 = very high). Factors considered in the ratings included the employee's output, defect rate, ability to implement continuous quality procedures, and contributions to team problem-solving efforts. The file `BrynnePackaging` contains the WPCT scores (WPCT) and job performance ratings (Ratings) for the 25 employees.

1. Assess the significance and importance of WPCT score as a predictor of job performance. Defend your answer.

2. Predict the mean job performance rating for all employees with a WPCT score of 6. Give a point prediction as well as a 95% confidence interval. Do you have any concerns using the regression model for predicting mean job performance rating given the WPCT score of 6?

3. Evaluate whether the assumptions of regression have been seriously violated.

▼EXCEL GUIDE

There are no Excel Guide instructions for Section 13.1.

EG13.2 DETERMINING the SIMPLE LINEAR REGRESSION EQUATION

Key Technique Use the **LINEST(*cell range of Y variable, cell range of X variable*, True, True)** array function to compute the b_1 and b_0 coefficients, the b_1 and b_0 standard errors, r^2 and the standard error of the estimate, the F test statistic and error df, and *SSR* and *SSE*.

Example Perform the Figure 13.4 analysis of the Sunflowers Apparel data on page 431.

PHStat Use **Simple Linear Regression**.
For the example, open to the **DATA worksheet** of the **Site-Selection workbook**. Select **PHStat → Regression → Simple Linear Regression**. In the procedure's dialog box (shown below):

1. Enter **C1:C15** as the **Y Variable Cell Range**.
2. Enter **B1:B15** as the **X Variable Cell Range**.
3. Check **First cells in both ranges contain label**.
4. Enter **95** as the **Confidence level for regression coefficients.**
5. Check **Regression Statistics Table** and **ANOVA and Coefficients Table**.
6. Enter a **Title** and click **OK**.

The procedure creates a worksheet that contains a copy of your data as well as the worksheet shown in Figure 13.4. For more information about these worksheets, read the following Workbook section.

To create a scatter plot that contains a prediction line and regression equation similar to Figure 13.5 on page 432, modify step 6 by checking **Scatter Plot** before clicking **OK**.

Workbook Use the **COMPUTE worksheet** of the **Simple Linear Regression workbook** as a template.
For the example, the worksheet uses the regression data already in the SLRData worksheet to perform the regression analysis.

Figure 13.4 does not include columns L through M. An array formula in the cell range L2:M6 uses the LINEST function to compute the b_1 and b_0 coefficients in cells L2 and M2, the b_1 and b_0 standard errors in cells L3 and M3, r^2 and the standard error of the estimate in cells L4 and M4, the F test statistic and error df in cells L5 and M5, and *SSR* and *SSE* in cells L6 and M6.

Cell L9 uses the expression **T.INV.2T(1 − *confidence level, Error degrees of freedom*)** to compute the critical value for the t test. To see all the formulas that the COMPUTE worksheet uses, open to the COMPUTE_FORMULAS worksheet.

To perform simple linear regression for other data, paste the regression data into the SLRData worksheet, using column A for the X variable data and column B for the Y variable data. Then, open to the COMPUTE worksheet and:

1. Enter the **confidence level** in cell **L8**.
2. Edit the *array formula* in the cell range **L2:M6** to reflect the cell range of the new regression data.

(To edit the array formula, first select L2:M6, then make changes to the formula, and then, while holding down the **Control** and **Shift** keys [or the **Command** key on a Mac], press the **Enter** key.)

To create a scatter plot that contains a prediction line and regression equation similar to Figure 13.5 on page 432, first use the Section EG2.5 *Workbook* scatter plot instructions with the Table 13.1 Sunflowers Apparel data to create a scatter plot. Then select the chart and:

1. Select **Design** (or **Chart Design**) → **Add Chart Element → Trendline → More Trendline Options**.

In the Format Trendline pane (parts of which are shown in the next two illustrations):

2. Click **Linear** (shown below).

3. Check the **Display Equation on chart** and **Display R-squared value on chart** check boxes near the bottom of the pane (shown below).

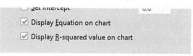

In older Excels, select **Layout → Trendline → More Trendline Options**. In the Format Trendline dialog box (similar to the Format Trendline pane), click **Trendline Options** in the left pane. In the Trendline Options right pane, click **Linear**, check **Display Equation on chart**, check **Display R-squared value on chart**, and then click **Close**.

For scatter plots of other data, if the X axis does not appear at the bottom of the plot, right-click the Y axis and click **Format Axis** from the shortcut menu. In the Format Axis pane, click **Axis Options** and then **Axis value**. In its box, enter the value shown in the **Minimum** box. In older Excels, you open the Format Axis dialog box, click **Axis Options** in the left pane to see the **Axis value** in a right pane, and click **Close** after entering the axis value.

Analysis ToolPak Use **Regression**.
For the example, open to the **DATA worksheet** of the **Site-Selection workbook** and:

1. Select **Data → Data Analysis**.
2. In the Data Analysis dialog box, select **Regression** from the **Analysis** Tools list and then click **OK**.

In the Regression dialog box (shown below):

3. Enter **C1:C15** as the **Input Y Range** and enter **B1:B15** as the **Input X Range**.
4. Check **Labels** and check **Confidence Level** and enter **95** in its box.
5. Click **New Worksheet Ply** and then click **OK**.

EG13.3 MEASURES of VARIATION

The measures of variation are computed as part of creating the simple linear regression worksheet using the Section EG13.2 instructions.

If you use either Section EG13.2 *PHStat* or *Workbook* instructions, COMPUTE worksheet formulas compute these measures. The formulas in cells B5, B7, B13, C12, C13, D12, and E12 copy values computed by the array formula in cell range L2:M6. In cell F12, the **F.DIST.RT(*F test statistic*, *regression degrees of freedom*, *error degrees of freedom*)** function computes the *p*-value for the *F* test for the slope that Section EG13.7 mentions.

EG13.4 ASSUMPTIONS of REGRESSION

There are no Excel Guide instructions for Section 13.4.

EG13.5 RESIDUAL ANALYSIS

Key Technique Use arithmetic formulas to compute the residuals. To evaluate assumptions, use the Section EG2.5 scatter plot instructions for constructing residual plots and the Section EG6.3 instructions for constructing normal probability plots.

Example Compute the residuals for the Table 13.1 Sunflowers Apparel shown in Figure 13.10 on page 444.

PHStat Use the Section EG12.2 *PHStat* instructions to compute the residuals. Use the Section EG6.3 *PHStat* instructions to construct a normal probability plot.
For the example, modify step 5 of the EG12.2 *PHStat* instructions by checking **Residuals Table** and **Residual Plot** in addition to checking the two other check boxes. PHStas creates a residual plot and a worksheet containing the residuals in addition to the COMPUTE worksheet described earlier.

To construct a normal probability plot, open to the residuals worksheet and modify the EG6.3 *PHStat* instructions by using the cell range of the residuals as the **Variable Cell Range** in step 1.

Workbook Use the **RESIDUALS worksheet** of the **Simple Linear Regression workbook** as a template.
The worksheet already computes the residuals for the example. For other problems, modify this worksheet by pasting the X values into column B and the Y values into column D. Then, for sample sizes smaller than 14, delete the extra rows. For sample sizes greater than 14, copy the column C and E formulas down through the row containing the last pair and X and Y values and add the new observation numbers in column A.

To construct a residual plot similar to Figure 13.11 on page 445, use the original X variable and the residuals (plotted as the Y variable) as the chart data and follow the Section EG2.5 scatter plot instructions. To construct a normal probability plot, follow the Section EG6.3 *Workbook* instructions, using the cell range of the residuals as the **Variable Cell Range**.

Analysis ToolPak Use the Section EG13.2 *Analysis Tool-Pak* instructions.

Modify step 5 by checking **Residuals** and **Residual Plots** before clicking **New Worksheet Ply** and then **OK**. To construct a residual plot or normal probability plot, use the *In-Depth Excel* instructions.

EG13.6 MEASURING AUTOCORRELATION: the DURBIN-WATSON STATISTIC

Key Technique Use the **SUMXMY2**(*cell range of the second through last residual*, *cell range of the first through the second-to-last residual*) function to compute the sum of squared difference of the residuals. Use the **SUMSQ**(*cell range of the residuals*) function to compute the sum of squared residuals.

Example Compute the Durbin-Watson statistic for the package delivery data shown in the Figure 13.16 on page 449.

PHStat Use the *PHStat* instructions at the beginning of Section EG13.2. Modify step 6 by checking the **Durbin-Watson Statistic** output option before clicking **OK**.

Workbook Use the **DURBIN_WATSON worksheet** of the **Simple Linear Regression** workbook as a template. The DURBIN_WATSON worksheet of the **Package Delivery workbook** already contains the proper cell formulas to compute the statistic for the example. (This workbook also uses the COMPUTE and RESIDUALS worksheet templates from the Simple Linear Regression workbook.)

To compute the Durbin-Watson statistic for other problems, first create the simple linear regression model and the residuals for the problem, using the Sections EG13.2 and EG13.5 *Workbook* instructions. Then open the DURBIN_WATSON worksheet and edit the formulas in cell B3 and B4 to point to the proper cell ranges of the new residuals.

EG13.7 INFERENCES ABOUT the SLOPE and CORRELATION COEFFICIENT

The t test for the slope and F test for the slope are included in the worksheet created by using the Section EG13.2 instructions. The t test computations in the worksheets created by using the *PHStat* and *Workbook* instructions are discussed in Section EG13.2. The F test computations are discussed in Section EG13.3.

EG13.8 ESTIMATION of MEAN VALUES and PREDICTION of INDIVIDUAL VALUES

Key Technique Use the **TREND**(*Y variable cell range, X variable cell range*, *X value*) function to compute the predicted Y value for the X value. Use the **DEVSQ**(*X variable cell range*) function to compute the SSX value.

Example Compute the Figure 13.21 confidence interval estimate and prediction interval for the Sunflowers Apparel data that is shown on page 461.

PHStat Use the Section EG13.2 *PHStat* instructions but replace step 6 with these steps 6 and 7:

1. Check **Confidence Int. Est. & Prediction Int. for X =** and enter **4** in its box. Enter **95** as the percentage for **Confidence level for intervals**.
2. Enter a **Title** and click **OK**.

The additional worksheet created is discussed in the following *Workbook* instructions.

Workbook Use the **CIEandPI worksheet** of the **Simple Linear Regression workbook**, as a template. The worksheet already contains the data and formulas for the example. To compute a confidence interval estimate and prediction interval for other problems:

1. Paste the regression data into the **SLRData worksheet**. Use column A for the X variable data and column B for the Y variable data.
2. Open to the **CIEandPI worksheet**.

In the CIEandPI worksheet:

3. Change values for the **X Value** and **Confidence Level**, as is necessary.
4. Edit the cell ranges used in the cell B15 formula that uses the TREND function to refer to the new cell ranges for the Y and X variables.

Introduction to Multiple Regression

14

▼USING **STATISTICS**
The Multiple Effects of OmniPower Bars

You are a marketing manager for OmniFoods, with oversight for nutrition bars and similar snack items. You seek to revive the sales of OmniPower, the company's primary product in this category. Originally marketed as a high-energy bar to runners, mountain climbers, and other athletes, OmniPower reached its greatest sales during an earlier time when high-energy bars were one of the most popular snack items with consumers. Now, you seek to reposition the product as a nutrition bar to benefit from the booming market for such bars.

Because the marketplace already contains several successful nutrition bars, you need to develop an effective marketing strategy. In particular, you need to determine the effect that price and in-store promotional expenses (special in-store coupons, signs, and displays as well as the cost of free samples) will have on sales of OmniPower. Before marketing the bar nationwide, you plan to conduct a test-market study of OmniPower sales, using a sample of 34 stores in a supermarket chain.

How can you extend the linear regression methods discussed in Chapter 13 to incorporate the effects of price *and* promotion into the same model? How can you use this model to improve the success of the nationwide introduction of OmniPower?

OBJECTIVES

- How to develop a multiple regression model
- How to interpret the regression coefficients
- How to determine which independent variables to include in the regression model
- How to determine which independent variables are most important in predicting a dependent variable

- How to use categorical independent variables in a regression model
- How to use logistic regression to predict a categorical dependent variable

hapter 13 discusses simple linear regression models that use *one* numerical independent variable, *X*, to predict the value of a numerical dependent variable, *Y*. Often you can make better predictions by using *more than one* independent variable. This chapter introduces you to **multiple regression models** that use two or more independent variables to predict the value of a dependent variable.

14.1 Developing a Multiple Regression Model

In the OmniPower Bars scenario, your business objective, to determine the effect that price and in-store promotional expenses will have on sales, calls for examining a multiple regression model in which the price of an OmniPower bar in cents (X_1) and the monthly budget for in-store promotional expenditures in dollars (X_2) are the independent variables and the number of OmniPower bars sold in a month (Y) is the dependent variable.

To develop this model, you collect data from a sample of 34 stores in a supermarket chain selected for a test-market study of OmniPower. You choose stores in a way to ensure that they all have approximately the same monthly sales volume. You organize and store the data collected in OmniPower. Table 14.1 presents these data.

TABLE 14.1
Monthly OmniPower Sales, Price, and Promotional Expenditures

Store	Sales	Price	Promotion	Store	Sales	Price	Promotion
1	4,141	59	200	18	2,730	79	400
2	3,842	59	200	19	2,618	79	400
3	3,056	59	200	20	4,421	79	400
4	3,519	59	200	21	4,113	79	600
5	4,226	59	400	22	3,746	79	600
6	4,630	59	400	23	3,532	79	600
7	3,507	59	400	24	3,825	79	600
8	3,754	59	400	25	1,096	99	200
9	5,000	59	600	26	761	99	200
10	5,120	59	600	27	2,088	99	200
11	4,011	59	600	28	820	99	200
12	5,015	59	600	29	2,114	99	400
13	1,916	79	200	30	1,882	99	400
14	675	79	200	31	2,159	99	400
15	3,636	79	200	32	1,602	99	400
16	3,224	79	200	33	3,354	99	600
17	2,295	79	400	34	2,927	99	600

Interpreting the Regression Coefficients

When there are several independent variables, you can extend the simple linear regression model of Equation (13.1) on page 429 by assuming a linear relationship between each independent variable and the dependent variable. For example, with *k* independent variables, the multiple regression model is expressed in Equation (14.1).

MULTIPLE REGRESSION MODEL WITH *k* INDEPENDENT VARIABLES

$$Y_i = \beta_0 + \beta_1 X_{1i} + \beta_2 X_{2i} + \beta_3 X_{3i} + \cdots + \beta_k X_{ki} + \varepsilon_i \qquad \textbf{(14.1)}$$

where

$\beta_0 = Y$ intercept

$\beta_1 =$ slope of Y with variable X_1, holding variables $X_2, X_3, \ldots, X_k$ constant

$\beta_2 =$ slope of Y with variable X_2, holding variables $X_1, X_3, \ldots, X_k$ constant

$\beta_3 =$ slope of Y with variable X_3, holding variables $X_1, X_2, \ldots, X_k$ constant

$\vdots$

$\beta_k =$ slope of Y with variable X_k holding variables $X_1, X_2, X_3, \ldots, X_{k-1}$ constant

$\varepsilon_i =$ random error in Y for observation i

Equation (14.2) defines the multiple regression model with two independent variables.

MULTIPLE REGRESSION MODEL WITH TWO INDEPENDENT VARIABLES

$$Y_i = \beta_0 + \beta_1 X_{1i} + \beta_2 X_{2i} + \varepsilon_i \qquad \textbf{(14.2)}$$

where

$\beta_0 =$ intercept

$\beta_1 =$ slope of Y with variable X_1, holding variable X_2 constant

$\beta_2 =$ slope of Y with variable X_2, holding variable X_1 constant

$\varepsilon_i =$ random error in Y for observation i

Compare the multiple regression model to the simple linear regression model [Equation (13.1) on page 429]:

$$Y_i = \beta_0 + \beta_1 X_i + \varepsilon_i$$

In the simple linear regression model, the slope, β_1, represents the change in the mean of Y per unit change in X and does not take into account any other variables. In the multiple regression model with two independent variables [Equation (14.2)], the slope, β_1, represents the change in the mean of Y per unit change in X_1, taking into account the effect of X_2.

As in the case of simple linear regression, you use the least-squares method to compute the sample regression coefficients b_0, b_1, and b_2 as estimates of the population parameters β_0, β_1, and β_2. Equation (14.3) defines the regression equation for a multiple regression model with two independent variables.

studentTIP

Use software to calculate multiple regression results due to the complexitity of those calculations.

MULTIPLE REGRESSION EQUATION WITH TWO INDEPENDENT VARIABLES

$$\hat{Y}_i = b_0 + b_1 X_{1i} + b_2 X_{2i} \qquad \textbf{(14.3)}$$

Figure 14.1 shows Excel worksheet results for the OmniPower sales data multiple regression model. In these results, the b_0 coefficient is labeled Intercept by Excel.

FIGURE 14.1
Excel worksheet results for the OmniPower sales multiple regression model

	A	B	C	D	E	F	G
1	OmniPower Sales Multiple Regression Model						
2							
3	*Regression Statistics*						
4	Multiple R	0.8705					
5	R Square	0.7577					
6	Adjusted R Square	0.7421					
7	Standard Error	638.0653					
8	Observations	34					
9							
10	ANOVA						
11		*df*	*SS*	*MS*	*F*	*Significance F*	
12	Regression	2	39472730.7730	19736365.3865	48.4771	0.0000	
13	Residual	31	12620946.6682	407127.3119			
14	Total	33	52093677.4412				
15							
16		*Coefficients*	*Standard Error*	*t Stat*	*P-value*	*Lower 95%*	*Upper 95%*
17	Intercept	5837.5208	628.1502	9.2932	0.0000	4556.3999	7118.6416
18	Price	-53.2173	6.8522	-7.7664	0.0000	-67.1925	-39.2421
19	Promotional Expenses	3.6131	0.6852	5.2728	0.0000	2.2155	5.0106

In the Worksheet

The three methods in Section EG14.1 all create worksheets that *look like* this worksheet. The *PHStat* and *Workbook* instructions create live worksheets that use the LINEST function in columns L through N formulas (not shown) to compute regression coefficients and statistics.

From Figure 14.1, the computed values of the three regression coefficients are

$$b_0 = 5,837.5208 \quad b_1 = -53.2173 \quad b_2 = 3.6131$$

Therefore, the multiple regression equation is

$$\hat{Y}_i = 5,837.5208 - 53.2173X_{1i} + 3.6131X_{2i}$$

where

$$\hat{Y}_i = \text{predicted monthly sales of OmniPower bars for store } i$$
$$X_{1i} = \text{price of OmniPower bar (in cents) for store } i$$
$$X_{2i} = \text{monthly in-store promotional expenditures (in \$) for store } i$$

The sample Y intercept ($b_0 = 5,837.5208$) estimates the number of OmniPower bars sold in a month if the price is \$0.00 and the total amount spent on promotional expenditures is also \$0.00. Because these values of price and promotion are outside the range of price and promotion used in the test-market study, and because they make no sense in the context of the problem, the value of b_0 has little or no practical interpretation.

The slope of price with OmniPower sales ($b_1 = -53.2173$) indicates that, for a given amount of monthly promotional expenditures, the predicted mean sales of OmniPower are estimated to decrease by 53.2173 bars per month for each 1-cent increase in the price. The slope of monthly promotional expenditures with OmniPower sales ($b_2 = 3.6131$) indicates that, for a given price, the predicted mean sales of OmniPower are estimated to increase by 3.6131 bars for each additional \$1 spent on promotions. These estimates allow you to better understand the likely effect that price and promotion decisions will have in the marketplace. For example, a 10-cent decrease in price is predicted to increase mean sales by 532.173 bars, with a fixed amount of monthly promotional expenditures. A \$100 increase in promotional expenditures is predicted to increase mean sales by 361.31 bars for a given price.

Regression coefficients in multiple regression are called **net regression coefficients**, and they estimate the predicted mean change in Y per unit change in a particular X, *holding constant the effect of the other X variables*. For example, in the study of OmniPower bar sales, for a store with a given amount of promotional expenditures, the mean sales are predicted to decrease by 53.2173 bars per month for each 1-cent increase in the price of an OmniPower bar. Another way to interpret this "net effect" is to think of two stores with an equal amount of promotional expenditures. If the first store charges 1 cent more than the other store, the net effect of this difference is that the first store is predicted to sell a mean of 53.2173 fewer bars per month than the second store. To interpret the net effect of promotional expenditures, you can consider two stores that are charging the same price. If the first store spends $1 more on promotional expenditures, the net effect of this difference is that the first store is predicted to sell a mean of 3.6131 more bars per month than the second store.

Predicting the Dependent Variable Y

You can use the multiple regression equation to predict values of the dependent variable. For example, what are the predicted mean sales for a store charging 79 cents during a month in which promotional expenditures are $400? Using the multiple regression equation,

$$\hat{Y}_i = 5,837.5208 - 53.2173X_{1i} + 3.6131X_{2i}$$

studentTIP

You should only predict within the range of the values of all the independent variables.

with $X_{1i} = 79$ and $X_{2i} = 400$,

$$\hat{Y}_i = 5,837.5208 - 53.2173(79) + 3.6131(400)$$
$$= 3,078.57$$

Thus, you predict that stores charging 79 cents and spending $400 in promotional expenditures will sell a mean of 3,078.57 OmniPower bars per month.

After you have developed the regression equation, done a residual analysis (see Section 14.3), and determined the significance of the overall fitted model (see Section 14.4), you can construct a confidence interval estimate of the mean value and a prediction interval for an individual value. Figure 14.2 presents an Excel worksheet that computes a confidence interval estimate and a prediction interval for the OmniPower sales data.

FIGURE 14.2
Excel confidence interval estimate and prediction interval worksheet for the OmniPower sales data

	A	B	C	D
1	Confidence Interval Estimate and Prediction Interval			
2				
3	**Data**			
4	Confidence Level	95%		
5		1		
6	Price given value	79		
7	Promotion given value	400		
8				
9	X'X	34	2646	13200
10		2646	214674	1018800
11		13200	1018800	6000000
12				
13	Inverse of X'X	0.9692	-0.0094	-0.0005
14		-0.0094	0.0001	0.0000
15		-0.0005	0.0000	0.0000
16				
17	X'G times Inverse of X'X	0.0121	0.0001	0.0000
18				
19	[X'G times Inverse of X'X] times XG	0.0298	=MMULT(B17:D17, B5:B7)	
20	t Statistic	2.0395	=T.INV.2T(1 - B4, COMPUTE!B13)	
21	Predicted Y (YHat)	3078.57	{=MMULT(TRANSPOSE(B5:B7), COMPUTE!B17:B19)}	
22				
23	**For Average Predicted Y (YHat)**			
24	Interval Half Width	224.50	=B20 * SQRT(B19) * COMPUTE!B7	
25	Confidence Interval Lower Limit	2854.07	=B21 - B24	
26	Confidence Interval Upper Limit	3303.08	=B21 + B24	
27				
28	**For Individual Response Y**			
29	Interval Half Width	1320.57	=B20 * SQRT(1 + B19) * COMPUTE!B7	
30	Prediction Interval Lower Limit	1758.01	=B21 - B29	
31	Prediction Interval Upper Limit	4399.14	=B21 + B29	

In the Worksheet

This worksheet uses the MMULT function in rows 9 through 11 and 17 to perform intermediate matrix calculations and uses the TRANSPOSE function to change a matrix column of data into a matrix row. Rows 13 through 15 use the MINVERSE function to compute the inverse of a matrix. Cell B21 contains an *array* formula that also uses the MMULT function to compute the predicted *Y* value.

See Appendix F for more information about these functions. (Formulas using these functions are not shown at left.)

The 95% confidence interval estimate of the mean OmniPower sales for all stores charging 79 cents and spending $400 in promotional expenditures is 2,854.07 to 3,303.08 bars. The prediction interval for an individual store is 1,758.01 to 4,399.14 bars.

PROBLEMS FOR SECTION 14.1

LEARNING THE BASICS

14.1 For this problem, use the following multiple regression equation:

$$\hat{Y}_i = 10 + 5X_{1i} + 3X_{2i}$$

a. Interpret the meaning of the slopes.
b. Interpret the meaning of the Y intercept.

14.2 For this problem, use the following multiple regression equation:

$$\hat{Y}_i = 50 - 2X_{1i} + 7X_{2i}$$

a. Interpret the meaning of the slopes.
b. Interpret the meaning of the Y intercept.

APPLYING THE CONCEPTS

14.3 A shoe manufacturer is considering developing a new brand of running shoes. The business problem facing the marketing analyst is to determine which variables should be used to predict durability (i.e., the effect of long-term impact). Two independent variables under consideration are X_1 (FOREIMP), a measurement of the forefoot shock-absorbing capability, and X_2 (MIDSOLE), a measurement of the change in impact properties over time. The dependent variable Y is LTIMP, a measure of the shoe's durability after a repeated impact test. Data are collected from a random sample of 15 types of currently manufactured running shoes, with the following results:

Variable	Coefficients	Standard Error	t Statistic	p-Value
Intercept	−0.02686	0.06905	−0.39	0.7034
FOREIMP	0.79116	0.06295	12.57	0.0000
MIDSOLE	0.60484	0.07174	8.43	0.0000

a. State the multiple regression equation.
b. Interpret the meaning of the slopes, b_1 and b_2, in this problem.
c. What conclusions can you reach concerning durability?

✓ SELF TEST **14.4** Profitability remains a challenge for banks and thrifts with less than $2 billion of assets. The business problem facing a bank analyst relates to the factors that affect return on assets (ROA), an indicator of how profitable a company is relative to its total assets. Data collected on a sample of 199 community banks and stored in CommunityBanks include the ROA (%), the efficiency ratio (%) as a measure of bank productivity, and total risk-based capital (%) as a measure of capital adequacy. (Data extracted from "What the Top 200 Publicly Traded Community Banks Do Better Than Peers," **bit.ly/1TLXbO0**.)
a. State the multiple regression equation.
b. Interpret the meaning of the slopes, b_1 and b_2, in this problem.
c. Predict the mean ROA when the efficiency ratio is 60% and the total risk-based capital is 15%.
d. Construct a 95% confidence interval estimate for the mean ROA when the efficiency ratio is 60% and the total risk-based capital is 15%.

e. Construct a 95% prediction interval for the ROA for a particular community bank when the efficiency ratio is 60% and the total risk-based capital is 15%.
f. Explain why the interval in (d) is narrower than the interval in (e).
g. What conclusions can you reach concerning ROA?

14.5 The production of wine is a multibillion-dollar worldwide industry. In an attempt to develop a model of wine quality as judged by wine experts, data was collected from red wine variants of Portuguese "Vinho Verde" wine. A sample of 50 wines is stored in VinhoVerde. (Data extracted from P. Cortez, Cerdeira, A., Almeida, F., Matos, T., and Reis, J., "Modeling Wine Preferences by Data Mining from Physiochemical Properties," *Decision Support Systems*, 47, 2009, pp. 547–553 and **bit.ly/9xKlEa**.) Develop a multiple linear regression model to predict wine quality, measured on a scale from 0 (very bad) to 10 (excellent) based on alcohol content (%) and the amount of chlorides.
a. State the multiple regression equation.
b. Interpret the meaning of the slopes, b_1 and b_2, in this problem.
c. Explain why the regression coefficient, b_0, has no practical meaning in the context of this problem.
d. Predict the mean wine quality rating for wines that have 10% alcohol and chlorides of 0.08.
e. Construct a 95% confidence interval estimate for the mean wine quality rating for wines that have 10% alcohol and chlorides of 0.08.
f. Construct a 95% prediction interval for the wine quality rating for an individual wine that has 10% alcohol and chlorides of 0.08.
g. What conclusions can you reach concerning this regression model?

14.6 Human resource managers face the business problem of assessing the impact of factors on full-time job growth. A human resource manager is interested in the impact of full-time voluntary turnover and total worldwide revenues on the number of full-time jobs added in the last year. Data are collected from a sample of 83 "best companies to work for." The total number of full-time jobs added in the past year, the full-time voluntary turnover in the past year (in %), and the total worldwide revenue (in $billions) are recorded and stored in BestCompanies. (Data extracted from *Best Companies to Work For, 2015*, **fortune.com/best-companies**.)
a. State the multiple regression equation.
b. Interpret the meaning of the slopes, b_1 and b_2, in this problem.
c. Interpret the meaning of the regression coefficient, b_0.
d. Which factor has the greatest effect on the number of full-time jobs added in the last year? Explain.

14.7 The business problem facing the director of broadcasting operations for a television station was the issue of standby hours (i.e., hours in which unionized graphic artists at the station are paid but are not actually involved in any activity) and what factors were related to standby hours. The study included the following variables:

Standby hours (Y)—Total number of standby hours in a week
Total staff present (X_1)—Weekly total of people-days
Remote hours (X_2)—Total number of hours worked by employees at locations away from the central plant

Data were collected for 26 weeks; these data are organized and stored in Standby .

a. State the multiple regression equation.

b. Interpret the meaning of the slopes, b_1 and b_2, in this problem.

c. Explain why the regression coefficient, b_0, has no practical meaning in the context of this problem.

d. Predict the mean standby hours for a week in which the total staff present have 310 people-days and the remote hours total 400.

e. Construct a 95% confidence interval estimate for the mean standby hours for weeks in which the total staff present have 310 people-days and remote hours total 400.

f. Construct a 95% prediction interval for the standby hours for a single week in which the total staff present have 310 people-days and the remote hours total 400.

g. What conclusions can you reach concerning standby hours?

14.8 Nassau County is located approximately 25 miles east of New York City. The data organized and stored in GlenCove include

the fair market value (in $thousands), land area of the property in acres, and age, in years, for a sample of 30 single-family homes located in Glen Cove, a small city in Nassau County. Develop a multiple linear regression model to predict the fair market value based on land area of the property and age, in years.

a. State the multiple regression equation.

b. Interpret the meaning of the slopes, b_1 and b_2, in this problem.

c. Explain why the regression coefficient, b_0, has no practical meaning in the context of this problem.

d. Predict the mean fair market value for a house that has a land area of 0.25 acre and is 55 years old.

e. Construct a 95% confidence interval estimate for the mean fair market value for houses that have a land area of 0.25 acre and are 55 years old.

f. Construct a 95% prediction interval estimate for the fair market value for an individual house that has a land area of 0.25 acre and is 55 years old.

14.2 r^2, Adjusted r^2, and the Overall F Test

This section discusses three methods you can use to evaluate the overall multiple regression model: the coefficient of multiple determination, r^2, the adjusted r^2, and the overall F test.

Coefficient of Multiple Determination

Recall from Section 13.3 that the coefficient of determination, r^2, measures the proportion of the variation in Y that is explained by the independent variable X in the simple linear regression model. In multiple regression, the **coefficient of multiple determination** represents the proportion of the variation in Y that is explained by all the independent variables. Equation (14.4) defines the coefficient of multiple determination for a multiple regression model with two or more independent variables.

COEFFICIENT OF MULTIPLE DETERMINATION

The coefficient of multiple determination is equal to the regression sum of squares (SSR) divided by the total sum of squares (SST).

$$r^2 = \frac{\text{Regression sum of squares}}{\text{Total sum of squares}} = \frac{SSR}{SST} \qquad (14.4)$$

In the OmniPower example, from Figure 14.1 on page 478, $SSR = 39{,}472{,}730.77$ and $SST = 52{,}093{,}677.44$. Thus,

$$r^2 = \frac{SSR}{SST} = \frac{39{,}472{,}730.77}{52{,}093{,}677.44} = 0.7577$$

studentTIP

r^2 in multiple regression represents the proportion of the variation in the dependent variable Y that is explained by all the independent X variables included in the model.

The coefficient of multiple determination ($r^2 = 0.7577$) indicates that 75.77% of the variation in sales is explained by the variation in the price and in the promotional expenditures. The coefficient of multiple determination also appears in the Figure 14.1 results on page 478, labeled R Square in the Excel results.

Adjusted r^2

When considering multiple regression models, some statisticians suggest that you should use the **adjusted r^2** to take into account both the number of independent variables in the model and the sample size. Because a model that has additional independent variables will always have

the same or higher regression sum of squares and r^2, using the adjusted r^2 provides a mor
appropriate interpretation when comparing models. Equation (14.5) defines the adjusted r^2.

ADJUSTED r^2

$$r_{adj}^2 = 1 - \left[(1 - r^2) \frac{n - 1}{n - k - 1} \right]$$

(14.5)

where

k is the number of independent variables in the regression equation.

Thus, for the OmniPower data, because $r^2 = 0.7577$, $n = 34$, and $k = 2$,

$$r_{adj}^2 = 1 - \left[(1 - 0.7577) \frac{34 - 1}{34 - 2 - 1} \right]$$

$$= 1 - \left[(0.2423) \frac{33}{31} \right]$$

$$= 1 - 0.2579$$

$$= 0.7421$$

Therefore, 74.21% of the variation in sales is explained by the multiple regression model—
adjusted for the number of independent variables and sample size. The adjusted r^2 also appears
in the Figure 14.1 worksheet on page 478, labeled, Adjusted R Square.

Test for the Significance of the Overall Multiple Regression Model

You use the **overall F test** to determine whether there is a significant relationship between the
dependent variable and the entire set of independent variables (the overall multiple regression
model). Because there is more than one independent variable, you use the following null and
alternative hypotheses:

H_0: $\beta_1 = \beta_2 = \cdots = \beta_k = 0$ (There is no linear relationship between the dependent
variable and the independent variables.)

H_1: At least one $\beta_j \neq 0, j = 1, 2, \cdots, k$ (There is a linear relationship between the
dependent variable and at least one of the
independent variables.)

If you fail to reject the null hypothesis, you conclude that the model fit is not appropriate.
If you reject the null hypothesis, you use methods that Sections 14.4 and 14.5 discuss to determine which independent variables should be included in the model. Equation (14.6) defines
the overall F test statistic. Table 14.2 presents the ANOVA summary table.

studentTIP

Remember that you are
testing whether at least
one independent variable
has a linear relationship
with the dependent
variable. If you reject H_0,
you are *not* concluding
that all the independent
variables have a linear
relationship with the
dependent variable, only
that *at least one* independent variable does.

OVERALL F TEST

The F_{STAT} test statistic is equal to the regression mean square (MSR) divided by the mean
square error (MSE).

$$F_{STAT} = \frac{MSR}{MSE}$$

(14.6)

The F_{STAT} test statistic follows an F distribution with k and $n - k - 1$ degrees of freedom, where k is the number of independent variables in the regression model.

TABLE 14.2
ANOVA Summary Table for the Overall F Test

Source	Degrees of Freedom	Sum of Squares	Mean Squares (Variance)	F
Regression	k	SSR	$MSR = \dfrac{SSR}{k}$	$F_{STAT} = \dfrac{MSR}{MSE}$
Error	$n - k - 1$	SSE	$MSE = \dfrac{SSE}{n - k - 1}$	
Total	$n - 1$	SST		

The decision rule is

$$\text{Reject } H_0 \text{ at the } \alpha \text{ level of significance if } F_{STAT} > F_{\alpha};$$
$$\text{otherwise, do not reject } H_0.$$

Using a 0.05 level of significance, the critical value of the F distribution with 2 and 31 degrees of freedom found in Table E.5 is approximately 3.32, shown in Figure 14.3. From Figure 14.1 on page 478, the F_{STAT} test statistic given in the ANOVA summary table is 48.4771. Because $48.4771 > 3.32$, or because the p-value $= 0.000 < 0.05$, you reject H_0 and conclude that at least one of the independent variables (price and/or promotional expenditures) is related to sales.

FIGURE 14.3
Testing for the significance of a set of regression coefficients at the 0.05 level of significance, with 2 and 31 degrees of freedom

---

PROBLEMS FOR SECTION 14.2

LEARNING THE BASICS

14.9 The following ANOVA summary table is for a multiple regression model with two independent variables:

Source	Degrees of Freedom	Sum of Squares	Mean Squares	F
Regression	2	60		
Error	18	120		
Total	20	180		

a. Determine the regression mean square (MSR) and the mean square error (MSE).
b. Compute the overall F_{STAT} test statistic.

c. Determine whether there is a significant relationship between Y and the two independent variables at the 0.05 level of significance.
d. Compute the coefficient of multiple determination, r^2, and interpret its meaning.
e. Compute the adjusted r^2.

14.10 The following ANOVA summary table is for a multiple regression model with two independent variables:

Source	Degrees of Freedom	Sum of Squares	Mean Squares	F
Regression	2	30		
Error	10	120		
Total	12	150		

a. Determine the regression mean square (MSR) and the mean square error (MSE).
b. Compute the overall F_{STAT} test statistic.
c. Determine whether there is a significant relationship between Y and the two independent variables at the 0.05 level of significance.
d. Compute the coefficient of multiple determination, r^2, and interpret its meaning.
e. Compute the adjusted r^2.

APPLYING THE CONCEPTS

14.11 A financial analyst engaged in business valuation obtained financial data on 72 drug companies (Industry Group SIC 3 code: 283). The file BusinessValuation contains the following variables:

COMPANY—Drug Company name
PB fye—Price-to-book-value ratio (fiscal year ending)
ROE—Return on equity
SGROWTH—Growth (GS5)

a. Develop a regression model to predict price-to-book-value ratio based on return on equity.
b. Develop a regression model to predict price-to-book-value ratio based on growth.
c. Develop a regression model to predict price-to-book-value ratio based on return on equity and growth.
d. Compute and interpret the adjusted r^2 for each of the three models.
e. Which of these three models do you think is the best predictor of price-to-book-value ratio?

SELF TEST **14.12** In Problem 14.3 on page 480, you predicted the durability of a brand of running shoe, based on the forefoot shock-absorbing capability and the change in impact properties over time. The regression analysis resulted in the following ANOVA summary table:

Source	Degrees of Freedom	Sum of Squares	Mean Squares	F	p-Value
Regression	2	12.61020	6.30510	97.69	0.0001
Error	12	0.77453	0.06454		
Total	14	13.38473			

a. Determine whether there is a significant relationship between durability and the two independent variables at the 0.05 level of significance.
b. Interpret the meaning of the p-value.
c. Compute the coefficient of multiple determination, r^2, and interpret its meaning.
d. Compute the adjusted r^2.

14.13 In Problem 14.5 on page 480, you used the percentage of alcohol and chlorides to predict wine quality (stored in VinhoVerde). Use the results from that problem to do the following:

a. Determine whether there is a significant relationship between wine quality and the two independent variables (percentage of alcohol and chlorides) at the 0.05 level of significance.
b. Interpret the meaning of the p-value.
c. Compute the coefficient of multiple determination, r^2, and interpret its meaning.
d. Compute the adjusted r^2.

14.14 In Problem 14.4 on page 480, you used efficiency ratio and total risk-based capital to predict ROA at a community bank (stored in CommunityBanks). Using the results from that problem,
a. a. determine whether there is a significant relationship between ROA and the two independent variables (efficiency ratio and total risk-based capital) at the 0.05 level of significance.
b. interpret the meaning of the p-value.
c. compute the coefficient of multiple determination, r^2, and interpret its meaning.
d. compute the adjusted r^2.

14.15 In Problem 14.7 on page 480, you used the total staff present and remote hours to predict standby hours (stored in Standby). Using the results from that problem,
a. determine whether there is a significant relationship between standby hours and the two independent variables (total staff present and remote hours) at the 0.05 level of significance.
b. interpret the meaning of the p-value.
c. compute the coefficient of multiple determination, r^2, and interpret its meaning.
d. compute the adjusted r^2.

14.16 In Problem 14.6 on page 480, you used full-time voluntary turnover (%) and total worldwide revenue ($billions) to predict number of full-time jobs added (stored in BestCompanies). Using the results from that problem,
a. determine whether there is a significant relationship between number of full-time jobs added and the two independent variables (full-time voluntary turnover and total worldwide revenue) at the 0.05 level of significance.
b. interpret the meaning of the p-value.
c. compute the coefficient of multiple determination, r^2, and interpret its meaning.
d. compute the adjusted r^2.

14.17 In Problem 14.8 on page 481, you used the land area of a property and the age of a house to predict the fair market value (stored in GlenCove). Using the results from that problem,
a. determine whether there is a significant relationship between fair market value and the two independent variables (land area of a property and age of a house) at the 0.05 level of significance.
b. interpret the meaning of the p-value.
c. compute the coefficient of multiple determination, r^2, and interpret its meaning.
d. compute the adjusted r^2.

14.3 Residual Analysis for the Multiple Regression Model

In Section 13.5, you used residual analysis to evaluate the fit of the simple linear regression model. For the multiple regression model with two independent variables, you need to construct and analyze the following residual plots:

- Residuals versus $\hat{Y}_i$
- Residuals versus X_{1i}
- Residuals versus X_{2i}
- Residuals versus time

studentTIP

A residual plot that does not contain any apparent patterns will look like a random scattering of points.

The first residual plot examines the pattern of residuals versus the predicted values of Y. If the residuals show a pattern for the predicted values of Y, there is evidence of a possible curvilinear effect (see Section 15.1) in at least one independent variable, a possible violation of the assumption of equal variance (see Figure 13.13 on page 446), and/or the need to transform the Y variable.

The second and third residual plots involve the independent variables. Patterns in the plot of the residuals versus an independent variable may indicate the existence of a curvilinear effect and, therefore, the need to add a curvilinear independent variable to the multiple regression model (see Section 15.1).

The fourth plot is used to investigate patterns in the residuals in order to validate the independence assumption when the data are collected in time order. Associated with this residual plot, as in Section 13.6, you can compute the Durbin-Watson statistic to determine the existence of positive autocorrelation among the residuals.

Figure 14.4 presents the residual plots for the OmniPower sales example. There is very little or no pattern in the relationship between the residuals and the predicted value of Y, the value of X_1 (price), or the value of X_2 (promotional expenditures). Thus, you can conclude that the multiple regression model is appropriate for predicting sales. There is no need to plot the residuals versus time because the data were not collected in time order.

FIGURE 14.4
Residual plots for the OmniPower sales data: residuals versus predicted Y, residuals versus price, and residuals versus promotional expenditures

PROBLEMS FOR SECTION 14.3

APPLYING THE CONCEPTS

14.18 In Problem 14.4 on page 480, you used efficiency ratio and total risk-based capital to predict ROA at a community bank (stored in CommunityBanks).
a. Plot the residuals versus $\hat{Y}_i$.
b. Plot the residuals versus X_{1i}.
c. Plot the residuals versus X_{2i}.
d. In the residual plots created in (a) through (c), is there any evidence of a violation of the regression assumptions? Explain.

14.19 In Problem 14.5 on page 480, you used the percentage of alcohol and chlorides to predict wine quality (stored in VinhoVerde).
a. Plot the residuals versus $\hat{Y}_i$
b. Plot the residuals versus X_{1i}.
c. Plot the residuals versus X_{2i}.
d. In the residual plots created in (a) through (c), is there any evidence of a violation of the regression assumptions? Explain.
e. Should you compute the Durbin-Watson statistic for these data? Explain.

14.20 In Problem 14.6 on page 480, you used full-time voluntary turnover (%), and total worldwide revenue ($billions) to predict number of full-time jobs added (stored in BestCompanies).
a. Perform a residual analysis on your results.
b. If appropriate, perform the Durbin-Watson test, using $\alpha = 0.05$.
c. Are the regression assumptions valid for these data?

14.21 In Problem 14.7 on page 480, you used the total staff present and remote hours to predict standby hours (stored in Standby).
a. Perform a residual analysis on your results.

b. If appropriate, perform the Durbin-Watson test, using $\alpha = 0.05$.
c. Are the regression assumptions valid for these data?

14.22 In Problem 14.8 on page 481, you used the land area of a property and the age of a house to predict the fair market value (stored in GlenCove).
a. Perform a residual analysis on your results.
b. If appropriate, perform the Durbin-Watson test, using $\alpha = 0.05$.
c. Are the regression assumptions valid for these data?

14.4 Inferences Concerning the Population Regression Coefficients

In Section 13.7, you tested the slope in a simple linear regression model to determine the significance of the relationship between X and Y. In addition, you constructed a confidence interval estimate of the population slope. This section extends those procedures to multiple regression.

Tests of Hypothesis

In a simple linear regression model, to test a hypothesis concerning the population slope, β_1, you used Equation (13.16) on page 452:

$$t_{STAT} = \frac{b_1 - \beta_1}{S_{b_1}}$$

Equation (14.7) generalizes this equation for multiple regression.

TESTING FOR THE SLOPE IN MULTIPLE REGRESSION

$$t_{STAT} = \frac{b_j - \beta_j}{S_{b_j}} \tag{14.7}$$

where

b_j = slope of variable j with Y, holding constant the effects of all other independent variables

S_{b_j} = standard error of the regression coefficient b_j

k = number of independent variables in the regression equation

β_j = hypothesized value of the population slope for variable j, holding constant the effects of all other independent variables

t_{STAT} = test statistic for a t distribution with $n - k - 1$ degrees of freedom

---

To determine whether variable X_2 (amount of promotional expenditures) has a significant effect on sales, after taking into account the effect of the price of OmniPower bars, the null and alternative hypotheses are

$$H_0: \beta_2 = 0$$
$$H_1: \beta_2 \neq 0$$

From Equation (14.7) and Figure 14.1 on page 478,

$$t_{STAT} = \frac{b_2 - \beta_2}{S_{b_2}}$$

$$= \frac{3.6131 - 0}{0.6852} = 5.2728$$

If you select a level of significance of 0.05, the critical values of t for 31 degrees of freedom from Table E.3 are -2.0395 and $+2.0395$ (see Figure 14.5).

FIGURE 14.5
Testing for significance of a regression coefficient at the 0.05 level of significance, with 31 degrees of freedom

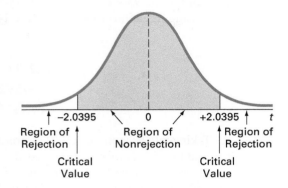

From Figure 14.1 on page 478, observe that the computed t_{STAT} test statistic is 5.2728. Because $t_{STAT} = 5.2728 > 2.0395$ or because p-value is 0.0000, you reject H_0 and conclude that there is a significant relationship between variable X_2 (promotional expenditures) and sales, taking into account the price, X_1. The extremely small p-value allows you to strongly reject the null hypothesis that there is no linear relationship between sales and promotional expenditures. Example 14.1 presents the test for the significance of β_1, the slope of sales with price.

EXAMPLE 14.1

Testing for the Significance of the Slope of Sales with Price

At the 0.05 level of significance, is there evidence that the slope of sales with price is different from zero?

SOLUTION From Figure 14.1 on page 478, $t_{STAT} = -7.7664 < -2.0395$ (the critical value for $\alpha = 0.05$) or the p-value $= 0.0000 < 0.05$. Thus, there is a significant relationship between price, X_1, and sales, taking into account the promotional expenditures, X_2.

As shown with these two independent variables, the test of significance for a specific regression coefficient in multiple regression is a test for the significance of adding that variable into a regression model, given that the other variable is included. In other words, the t test for the regression coefficient is actually a test for the contribution of each independent variable.

Confidence Interval Estimation

Instead of testing the significance of a population slope, you may want to estimate the value of a population slope. Equation (14.8) defines the confidence interval estimate for a population slope in multiple regression.

CONFIDENCE INTERVAL ESTIMATE FOR THE SLOPE

$$b_j \pm t_{\alpha/2} S_{b_j} \qquad \textbf{(14.8)}$$

where

$t_{\alpha/2}$ = the critical value corresponding to an upper-tail probability of $\alpha/2$ (a cumulative area of $1 - \alpha/2$) from the t distribution with $n - k - 1$ degrees of freedom

k = the number of independent variables

To construct a 95% confidence interval estimate of the population slope, β_1 (the effect of price, X_1, on sales, Y, holding constant the effect of promotional expenditures, X_2), the critical value of t at the 95% confidence level with 31 degrees of freedom is 2.0395 (see Table E.3). Then, using Equation (14.8) and Figure 14.1 on page 478,

$$b_1 \pm t_{\alpha/2}S_{b_1}$$
$$-53.2173 \pm (2.0395)(6.8522)$$
$$-53.2173 \pm 13.9752$$
$$-67.1925 \le \beta_1 \le -39.2421$$

Taking into account the effect of promotional expenditures, the estimated effect of a 1-cent increase in price is to reduce mean sales by approximately 39.2 to 67.2 bars. You have 95% confidence that this interval correctly estimates the relationship between these variables. From a hypothesis-testing viewpoint, because this confidence interval does not include 0, you conclude that the regression coefficient, β_1, has a significant effect.

Example 14.2 constructs and interprets a confidence interval estimate for the slope of sales with promotional expenditures.

EXAMPLE 14.2

Constructing a
Confidence Interval
Estimate for the
Slope of Sales
with Promotional
Expenditures

Construct a 95% confidence interval estimate of the population slope of sales with promotional expenditures.

SOLUTION The critical value of t at the 95% confidence level, with 31 degrees of freedom, is 2.0395 (see Table E.3). Using Equation (14.8) and Figure 14.1 on page 478,

$$b_2 \pm t_{\alpha/2}S_{b_2}$$
$$3.6131 \pm (2.0395)(0.6852)$$
$$3.6131 \pm 1.3975$$
$$2.2156 \le \beta_2 \le 5.0106$$

Thus, taking into account the effect of price, the estimated effect of each additional dollar of promotional expenditures is to increase mean sales by approximately 2.22 to 5.01 bars. You have 95% confidence that this interval correctly estimates the relationship between these variables. From a hypothesis-testing viewpoint, because this confidence interval does not include 0, you can conclude that the regression coefficient, β_2, has a significant effect.

PROBLEMS FOR SECTION 14.4

LEARNING THE BASICS

14.23 Use the following information from a multiple regression analysis:

$$n = 25 \quad b_1 = 5 \quad b_2 = 10 \quad S_{b_1} = 2 \quad S_{b_2} = 8$$

a. Which variable has the largest slope, in units of a t statistic?
b. Construct a 95% confidence interval estimate of the population slope, β_1.
c. At the 0.05 level of significance, determine whether each independent variable makes a significant contribution to the regression model. On the basis of these results, indicate the independent variables to include in this model.

14.24 Use the following information from a multiple regression analysis:

$$n = 20 \quad b_1 = 4 \quad b_2 = 3 \quad S_{b_1} = 1.2 \quad S_{b_2} = 0.8$$

a. Which variable has the largest slope, in units of a t statistic?
b. Construct a 95% confidence interval estimate of the population slope, β_1.
c. At the 0.05 level of significance, determine whether each independent variable makes a significant contribution to the regression model. On the basis of these results, indicate the independent variables to include in this model.

APPLYING THE CONCEPTS

14.25 In Problem 14.3 on page 480, you predicted the durability of a brand of running shoe, based on the forefoot shock-absorbing capability (FOREIMP) and the change in impact properties over time (MIDSOLE) for a sample of 15 pairs of shoes. Use the following results:

Variable	Coefficient	Standard Error	t Statistic	p-Value
Intercept	−0.02686	0.06905	−0.39	0.7034
FOREIMP	0.79116	0.06295	12.57	0.0000
MIDSOLE	0.60484	0.07174	8.43	0.0000

a. Construct a 95% confidence interval estimate of the population slope between durability and forefoot shock-absorbing capability.
b. At the 0.05 level of significance, determine whether each independent variable makes a significant contribution to the regression model. On the basis of these results, indicate the independent variables to include in this model.

✓**SELF TEST** **14.26** In Problem 14.4 on page 480, you used efficiency ratio and total risk-based capital to predict ROA at a community bank (stored in CommunityBanks). Using the results from that problem,
a. construct a 95% confidence interval estimate of the population slope between ROA and efficiency ratio.
b. at the 0.05 level of significance, determine whether each independent variable makes a significant contribution to the regression model. On the basis of these results, indicate the independent variables to include in this model.

14.27 In Problem 14.5 on page 480, you used the percentage of alcohol and chlorides to predict wine quality (stored in VinhoVerde). Using the results from that problem,

a. construct a 95% confidence interval estimate of the population slope between wine quality and the percentage of alcohol.
b. at the 0.05 level of significance, determine whether each independent variable makes a significant contribution to the regression model. On the basis of these results, indicate the independent variables to include in this model.

14.28 In Problem 14.6 on page 480, you used full-time voluntary turnover (%) and total worldwide revenue ($billions) to predict number of full-time jobs added (stored in BestCompanies). Using the results from that problem,
a. construct a 95% confidence interval estimate of the population slope between number of full-time jobs added and total worldwide revenue.
b. at the 0.05 level of significance, determine whether each independent variable makes a significant contribution to the regression model. On the basis of these results, indicate the independent variables to include in this model.

14.29 In Problem 14.7 on page 480, you used the total number of staff present and remote hours to predict standby hours (stored in Standby). Using the results from that problem,
a. construct a 95% confidence interval estimate of the population slope between standby hours and total number of staff present.
b. at the 0.05 level of significance, determine whether each independent variable makes a significant contribution to the regression model. On the basis of these results, indicate the independent variables to include in this model.

14.30 In Problem 14.8 on page 481, you used land area of a property and age of a house to predict the fair market value (stored in GlenCove). Using the results from that problem,
a. construct a 95% confidence interval estimate of the population slope between fair market value and land area of a property.
b. at the 0.05 level of significance, determine whether each independent variable makes a significant contribution to the regression model. On the basis of these results, indicate the independent variables to include in this model.

14.5 Testing Portions of the Multiple Regression Model

In developing a multiple regression model, you want to use only those independent variables that significantly reduce the error in predicting the value of a dependent variable. If an independent variable does not improve the prediction, you can delete it from the multiple regression model and use a model with fewer independent variables.

The **partial F test** is an alternative method to the t test discussed in Section 14.4 for determining the contribution of an independent variable. Using this method, you determine the contribution to the regression sum of squares made by each independent variable after all the other independent variables have been included in the model. The new independent variable is included only if it significantly improves the model.

To conduct partial F tests for the OmniPower sales example, you need to evaluate the contribution of promotional expenditures (X_2) after price (X_1) has been included in the model and also evaluate the contribution of price (X_1) after promotional expenditures (X_2) have been included in the model.

In general, if there are several independent variables, you determine the contribution of each independent variable by taking into account the regression sum of squares of a model that includes all independent variables except the one of interest, j. This regression sum of squares is denoted SSR (all Xs except j). Equation (14.9) determines the contribution of variable j, assuming that all other variables are already included.

DETERMINING THE CONTRIBUTION OF AN INDEPENDENT VARIABLE TO THE REGRESSION MODEL

$$SSR(X_j | \text{All } Xs \text{ except } j) = SSR(\text{All } Xs) - SSR(\text{All } Xs \text{ except } j) \quad \textbf{(14.9)}$$

If there are two independent variables, you use Equations (14.10a) and (14.10b) to determine the contribution of each variable.

CONTRIBUTION OF VARIABLE X_1, GIVEN THAT X_2 HAS BEEN INCLUDED

$$SSR(X_1 | X_2) = SSR(X_1 \text{ and } X_2) - SSR(X_2) \quad \textbf{(14.10a)}$$

CONTRIBUTION OF VARIABLE X_2, GIVEN THAT X_1 HAS BEEN INCLUDED

$$SSR(X_2 | X_1) = SSR(X_1 \text{ and } X_2) - SSR(X_1) \quad \textbf{(14.10b)}$$

The term $SSR(X_2)$ represents the sum of squares due to regression for a model that includes only the independent variable X_2 (promotional expenditures). Similarly, $SSR(X_1)$ represents the sum of squares due to regression for a model that includes only the independent variable X_1 (price). Figures 14.6 and 14.7 present results for these two models.

FIGURE 14.6
Excel results for the simple linear regression model of sales with promotional expenditures, $SSR(X_2)$

In the Worksheet

This worksheet uses the same template as the Figure 13.4 worksheet on page 431 uses.

From Figure 14.6, $SSR(X_2) = 14{,}915{,}814.10$ and from Figure 14.1 on page 478 $SSR(X_1$ and $X_2) = 39{,}472{,}730.77$. Then, using Equation (14.10a),

$$SSR(X_1 | X_2) = SSR(X_1 \text{ and } X_2) - SSR(X_2)$$
$$= 39{,}472{,}730.77 - 14{,}915{,}814.10$$
$$= 24{,}556{,}916.67$$

FIGURE 14.7
Excel results for the simple linear regression model of sales with price, $SSR(X_1)$

	A	B	C	D	E	F	G
1	Sales and Price Analysis						
2							
3	*Regression Statistics*						
4	Multiple R	0.7351					
5	R Square	0.5404					
6	Adjusted R Square	0.5261					
7	Standard Error	864.9457					
8	Observations	34					
9							
10	ANOVA						
11		*df*	*SS*	*MS*	*F*	*Significance F*	
12	Regression	1	28153486.1482	28153486.1482	37.6318	0.0000	
13	Residual	32	23940191.2930	748130.9779			
14	Total	33	52093677.4412				
15							
16		*Coefficients*	*Standard Error*	*t Stat*	*P-value*	*Lower 95%*	*Upper 95%*
17	Intercept	7512.3480	734.6189	10.2262	0.0000	6015.9796	9008.7164
18	Price	-56.7138	9.2451	-6.1345	0.0000	-75.5455	-37.8822

In the Worksheet

This worksheet uses the same template as the Figure 13.4 worksheet on page 431 uses.

To determine whether X_1 significantly improves the model after X_2 has been included, you divide the regression sum of squares into two component parts, as shown in Table 14.3.

TABLE 14.3
ANOVA Table Dividing the Regression Sum of Squares into Components to Determine the Contribution of Variable X_1

Source	Degrees of Freedom	Sum of Squares	Mean Square (Variance)	F
Regression	2	39,472,730.77	19,736,365.39	
$\begin{Bmatrix} X_2 \\ X_1 \mid X_2 \end{Bmatrix}$	$\begin{Bmatrix} 1 \\ 1 \end{Bmatrix}$	$\begin{Bmatrix} 14,915,814.10 \\ 24,556,916.67 \end{Bmatrix}$	24,556,916.67	60.32
Error	31	12,620,946.67	407,127.31	
Total	33	52,093,677.44		

The null and alternative hypotheses to test for the contribution of X_1 to the model are:

H_0: Variable X_1 does not significantly improve the model after variable X_2 has been included.
H_1: Variable X_1 significantly improves the model after variable X_2 has been included.

Equation (14.11) defines the partial F test statistic for testing the contribution of an independent variable.

PARTIAL F TEST STATISTIC

$$F_{STAT} = \frac{SSR(X_j \mid \text{All Xs } except\, j)}{MSE} \tag{14.11}$$

The partial F test statistic follows an F distribution with 1 and $n - k - 1$ degrees of freedom.

From Table 14.3,

$$F_{STAT} = \frac{24,556,916.67}{407,127.31} = 60.32$$

The partial F_{STAT} test statistic has 1 and $n - k - 1 = 34 - 2 - 1 = 31$ degrees of freedom. Using a level of significance of 0.05, the critical value from Table E.5 is approximately 4.17 (see Figure 14.8).

FIGURE 14.8
Testing for the contribution of a regression coefficient to a multiple regression model at the 0.05 level of significance, with 1 and 31 degrees of freedom

Because the computed partial F_{STAT} test statistic (60.32) is greater than this critical F value (4.17), you reject H_0. You conclude that the addition of variable X_1 (price) significantly improves a regression model that already contains variable X_2 (promotional expenditures).

To evaluate the contribution of variable X_2 (promotional expenditures) to a model in which variable X_1 (price) has been included, you need to use Equation (14.10b). First, from Figure 14.7 on page 491, observe that $SSR(X_1) = 28,153,486.15$. Second, from Table 14.3, observe that $SSR(X_1 \text{ and } X_2) = 39,472,730.77$. Then, using Equation (14.10b) on page 490,

$$SSR(X_2 | X_1) = 39,472,730.77 - 28,153,486.15 = 11,319,244.62$$

To determine whether X_2 significantly improves a model after X_1 has been included, you can divide the regression sum of squares into two component parts, as shown in Table 14.4.

TABLE 14.4
ANOVA Table Dividing the Regression Sum of Squares into Components to Determine the Contribution of Variable X_2

Source	Degrees of Freedom	Sum of Squares	Mean Square (Variance)	F
Regression	2	39,472,730.77	19,736,365.39	
$\left\{ \begin{array}{c} X_1 \\ X_2 \| X_1 \end{array} \right\}$	$\left\{ \begin{array}{c} 1 \\ 1 \end{array} \right\}$	$\left\{ \begin{array}{c} 28,153,486.15 \\ 11,319,244.62 \end{array} \right\}$	11,319,244.62	27.80
Error	31	12,620,946.67	407,127.31	
Total	33	52,093,677.44		

The null and alternative hypotheses to test for the contribution of X_2 to the model are:

H_0: Variable X_2 does not significantly improve the model after variable X_1 has been included.

H_1: Variable X_2 significantly improves the model after variable X_1 has been included.

Using Equation (14.11) and Table 14.4,

$$F_{STAT} = \frac{11,319,244.62}{407,127.31} = 27.80$$

In Figure 14.8, you can see that, using a 0.05 level of significance, the critical value of F, with 1 and 31 degrees of freedom, is approximately 4.17. Because the computed partial F_{STAT} test statistic (27.80) is greater than this critical value (4.17), you reject H_0. You can conclude that the addition of variable X_2 (promotional expenditures) significantly improves the multiple regression model already containing X_1 (price).

Thus, by testing for the contribution of each independent variable after the other independent variable has been included in the model, you determine that each of the two independent variables significantly improves the model. Therefore, the multiple regression model should include both price, X_1, and promotional expenditures, X_2.

The partial F test statistic developed in this section and the t test statistic of Equation (14.7) on page 486 are both used to determine the contribution of an independent variable to a multiple regression model. The hypothesis tests associated with these two statistics always result in the same decision (i.e., the p-values are identical). The t_{STAT} test statistics for the OmniPower regression model are -7.7664 and $+5.2728$, and the corresponding F_{STAT} test statistics are 60.32 and 27.80. Equation (14.12) states this relationship between t and F.[1]

RELATIONSHIP BETWEEN A t STATISTIC AND AN F STATISTIC

$$t_{STAT}^2 = F_{STAT} \qquad \text{(14.12)}$$

---

studentTIP

The coefficients of partial determination measure the proportion of the variation in the dependent variable explained by a specific independent variable, holding the other independent variables constant. They are different from the *coefficient of multiple determination* that measures the proportion of the variation in the dependent variable explained by the entire set of independent variables included in the model.

Coefficients of Partial Determination

Recall from Section 14.2 that the coefficient of multiple determination, r^2, measures the proportion of the variation in Y that is explained by variation in the independent variables. The **coefficients of partial determination** ($r_{Y1.2}^2$ and $r_{Y2.1}^2$) measure the proportion of the variation in the dependent variable that is explained by each independent variable while controlling for, or holding constant, the other independent variable. Equation (14.13) defines the coefficients of partial determination for a multiple regression model with two independent variables.

COEFFICIENTS OF PARTIAL DETERMINATION FOR A MULTIPLE REGRESSION MODEL CONTAINING TWO INDEPENDENT VARIABLES

$$r_{Y1.2}^2 = \frac{SSR(X_1 \mid X_2)}{SST - SSR(X_1 \text{ and } X_2) + SSR(X_1 \mid X_2)} \qquad \text{(14.13a)}$$

$$r_{Y2.1}^2 = \frac{SSR(X_2 \mid X_1)}{SST - SSR(X_1 \text{ and } X_2) + SSR(X_2 \mid X_1)} \qquad \text{(14.13b)}$$

where

$SSR(X_1 \mid X_2)$ = sum of squares of the contribution of variable X_1 to the regression model, given that variable X_2 has been included in the model

SST = total sum of squares for Y

$SSR(X_1 \text{ and } X_2)$ = regression sum of squares when variables X_1 and X_2 are both included in the multiple regression model

$SSR(X_2 \mid X_1)$ = sum of squares of the contribution of variable X_2 to the regression model, given that variable X_1 has been included in the model

---

For the OmniPower sales example,

$$r_{Y1.2}^2 = \frac{24{,}556{,}916.67}{52{,}093{,}677.44 - 39{,}472{,}730.77 + 24{,}556{,}916.67}$$

$$= 0.6605$$

$$r_{Y2.1}^2 = \frac{11{,}319{,}244.62}{52{,}093{,}677.44 - 39{,}472{,}730.77 + 11{,}319{,}244.62}$$

$$= 0.4728$$

The coefficient of partial determination, $r^2_{Y1.2}$, of variable Y with X_1 while holding X_2 constant is 0.6605. Thus, for a given (constant) amount of promotional expenditures, 66.05% of the variation in OmniPower sales is explained by the variation in the price. The coefficient of partial determination, $r^2_{Y2.1}$, of variable Y with X_2 while holding X_1 constant is 0.4728. Thus, for a given (constant) price, 47.28% of the variation in sales of OmniPower bars is explained by variation in the amount of promotional expenditures.

Equation (14.14) defines the coefficient of partial determination for the jth variable in a multiple regression model containing several (k) independent variables.

COEFFICIENT OF PARTIAL DETERMINATION FOR A MULTIPLE REGRESSION MODEL CONTAINING K INDEPENDENT VARIABLES

$$r^2_{Yj.(\text{All variables } except\,j)} = \frac{SSR(X_j|\text{All Xs } except\,j)}{SST - SSR(\text{All Xs}) + SSR(X_j|\text{All Xs } except\,j)} \quad (14.14)$$

PROBLEMS FOR SECTION 14.5

LEARNING THE BASICS

14.31 The following is the ANOVA summary table for a multiple regression model with two independent variables:

Source	Degrees of Freedom	Sum of Squares	Mean Squares	F
Regression	2	60		
Error	18	120		
Total	20	180		

If $SSR(X_1) = 45$ and $SSR(X_2) = 25$,
a. determine whether there is a significant relationship between Y and each independent variable at the 0.05 level of significance.
b. compute the coefficients of partial determination, $r^2_{Y1.2}$ and $r^2_{Y2.1}$, and interpret their meaning.

14.32 The following is the ANOVA summary table for a multiple regression model with two independent variables:

Source	Degrees of Freedom	Sum of Squares	Mean Squares	F
Regression	2	30		
Error	10	120		
Total	12	150		

If $SSR(X_1) = 20$ and $SSR(X_2) = 15$,
a. determine whether there is a significant relationship between Y and each independent variable at the 0.05 level of significance.
b. compute the coefficients of partial determination, $r^2_{Y1.2}$ and $r^2_{Y2.1}$, and interpret their meaning.

APPLYING THE CONCEPTS

14.33 In Problem 14.5 on page 480, you used alcohol percentage and chlorides to predict wine quality (stored in VinhoVerde). Using the results from that problem,
a. at the 0.05 level of significance, determine whether each independent variable makes a significant contribution to the regression model. On the basis of these results, indicate the most appropriate regression model for this set of data.
b. compute the coefficients of partial determination, $r^2_{Y1.2}$ and $r^2_{Y2.1}$, and interpret their meaning.

✓ SELF TEST 14.34 In Problem 14.4 on page 480, you used efficiency ratio and total risk-based capital to predict ROA at a community bank (stored in CommunityBanks). Using the results from that problem,
a. at the 0.05 level of significance, determine whether each independent variable makes a significant contribution to the regression model. On the basis of these results, indicate the most appropriate regression model for this set of data.
b. compute the coefficients of partial determination, $r^2_{Y1.2}$ and $r^2_{Y2.1}$, and interpret their meaning.

14.35 In Problem 14.7 on page 480, you used the total staff present and remote hours to predict standby hours (stored in Standby). Using the results from that problem,
a. at the 0.05 level of significance, determine whether each independent variable makes a significant contribution to the regression model. On the basis of these results, indicate the most appropriate regression model for this set of data.
b. compute the coefficients of partial determination, $r^2_{Y1.2}$ and $r^2_{Y2.1}$, and interpret their meaning.

14.36 In Problem 14.6 on page 480, you used full-time voluntary turnover (%), and total worldwide revenue ($billions) to predict

umber of full-time jobs added (stored in [BestCompanies]).
Using the results from that problem,
a. at the 0.05 level of significance, determine whether each independent variable makes a significant contribution to the regression model. On the basis of these results, indicate the most appropriate regression model for this set of data.
b. compute the coefficients of partial determination, $r^2_{Y1.2}$ and $r^2_{Y2.1}$, and interpret their meaning.

14.37 In Problem 14.8 on page 481, you used land area of a property and age of a house to predict the fair market value (stored in [GlenCove]). Using the results from that problem,
a. at the 0.05 level of significance, determine whether each independent variable makes a significant contribution to the regression model. On the basis of these results, indicate the most appropriate regression model for this set of data.
b. compute the coefficients of partial determination, $r^2_{Y1.2}$ and $r^2_{Y2.1}$, and interpret their meaning.

14.6 Using Dummy Variables and Interaction Terms in Regression Models

The multiple regression models discussed in Sections 14.1 through 14.5 assumed that each independent variable is a numerical variable. For example, in Section 14.1, you used price and promotional expenditures, two numerical independent variables, to predict the monthly sales of OmniPower nutrition bars. However, for some models, you need to examine the effect of a categorical independent variable. In such cases, you use a **dummy variable** to include a categorical independent variable in a regression model.

A dummy variable X_d recodes the categories of a categorical variable using the numeric values 0 and 1. In general, the number of dummy variables you need to define equals the number of categories − 1. If a categorical independent variable has only two categories, you define one dummy variable, X_d, and use the values 0 and 1 to represent the two categories. When the two categories represent the presence or absence of a characteristic, use 0 to represent the absence and 1 to represent the presence of the characteristic.

For example, to predict the monthly sales of the OmniPower bars, you might include the categorical variable location in the model to explore the possible effect on sales caused by displaying the OmniPower bars in the two different sales locations, a special front location and in the snack aisle, analogous to the locations used in the Chapter 10 Arlingtons scenario to sell streaming media players. In this case for the categorical variable location, the dummy variable, X_d, would have these values:

$$X_d = 0 \text{ if the observation is in first category (special front location)}$$
$$X_d = 1 \text{ if the observation is in second category (in-aisle location)}$$

To illustrate using dummy variables in regression, consider the business problem that seeks to develop a model for predicting the assessed value ($thousands) of houses in Silver Spring, Maryland, based on house size (in thousands of square feet) and whether the house has a fireplace. To include the categorical variable for the presence of a fireplace, the dummy variable X_2 is defined as

$$X_2 = 0 \text{ if the house does not have a fireplace}$$
$$X_2 = 1 \text{ if the house has a fireplace}$$

Assuming that the slope of assessed value with the size of the house is the same for houses that have and do not have a fireplace, the multiple regression model is

$$Y_i = \beta_0 + \beta_1 X_{1i} + \beta_2 X_{2i} + \varepsilon_i$$

where

Y_i = assessed value, in thousands of dollars, for house i
β_0 = Y intercept
X_{1i} = house size, in thousands of square feet, for house i
β_1 = slope of assessed value with house size, holding constant the presence or absence of a fireplace
X_{2i} = dummy variable that represents the absence or presence of a fireplace for house i
β_2 = net effect of the presence of a fireplace on assessed value, holding constant the house size
ε_i = random error in Y for house i

FIGURE 14.9
Excel worksheet results for the regression model that includes size of house and presence of fireplace

◢	A	B	C	D	E	F	G
1	Assessed Value Analysis						
2							
3		*Regression Statistics*					
4	Multiple R	0.5765					
5	R Square	0.3323					
6	Adjusted R Square	0.2829					
7	Standard Error	61.8788					
8	Observations	30					
9							
10	ANOVA						
11		*df*	*SS*	*MS*	*F*	*Significance F*	
12	Regression	2	51462.3960	25731.1980	6.7201	0.0043	
13	Residual	27	103382.7120	3828.9893			
14	Total	29	154845.1080				
15							
16		*Coefficients*	*Standard Error*	*t Stat*	*P-value*	*Lower 95%*	*Upper 95%*
17	Intercept	269.4185	33.5699	8.0256	0.0000	200.5388	338.2981
18	Size	49.8215	14.1326	3.5253	0.0015	20.8239	78.8191
19	FireplaceCoded	12.1623	27.0351	0.4499	0.6564	-43.3092	67.6339

In the Worksheet

This worksheet uses the same template as the Figure 14.1 worksheet on page 478 uses.

Figure 14.9 presents the regression results for this model, using a sample of 30 Silver Spring houses listed for sale that was extracted from trulia.com and stored in SilverSpring . In these results, the dummy variable X_2 is labeled as FireplaceCoded.

From Figure 14.9, the regression equation is

$$\hat{Y}_i = 269.4185 + 49.8215X_{1i} + 12.1623X_{2i}$$

For houses without a fireplace, you substitute $X_2 = 0$ into the regression equation:

$$\hat{Y}_i = 269.4185 + 49.8215X_{1i} + 12.1623X_{2i}$$
$$= 269.4185 + 49.8215X_{1i} + 12.1623(0)$$
$$= 269.4185 + 49.8215X_{1i}$$

For houses with a fireplace, you substitute $X_2 = 1$ into the regression equation:

$$\hat{Y}_i = 269.4185 + 49.8215X_{1i} + 12.1623X_{2i}$$
$$= 269.4185 + 49.8215X_{1i} + 12.1623(1)$$
$$= 281.5808 + 49.8215X_{1i}$$

In this model, the regression coefficients are interpreted as follows:

- Holding constant whether a house has a fireplace, for each increase of 1.0 thousand square feet in house size, the predicted mean assessed value is estimated to increase by 49.8215 thousand dollars (i.e., $49,821.50).
- Holding constant the house size, the presence of a fireplace is estimated to increase the predicted mean assessed value of the house by 12.1623 thousand dollars (i.e., $12,162.30).

In Figure 14.9, the t_{STAT} test statistic for the slope of house size with assessed value is 3.5253, and the p-value is 0.0015; the t_{STAT} test statistic for presence of a fireplace is 0.4499, and the p-value is 0.6564. Thus, using the 0.05 level of significance, since $0.0015 < 0.05$, the size of the house makes a significant contribution to the model. However, since $0.6564 > 0.05$, the presence of a fireplace does not make a significant contribution to the model. In addition, from Figure 14.9, observe that the coefficient of multiple determination indicates that 33.23% of the variation in assessed value is explained by variation in house size and whether the house has a fireplace. Thus, the variable fireplace does not make a significant contribution and should not be included in the model.

studentTIP

Remember that an independent variable does not always make a significant contribution to a regression model.

In some situations, the categorical independent variable has more than two categories. When this occurs, two or more dummy variables are needed. Example 14.3 illustrates such a situation.

EXAMPLE 14.3

Modeling a Three-Level Categorical Variable

Define a multiple regression model using sales as the dependent variable and package design and price as independent variables. Package design is a three-level categorical variable with designs A, B, or C.

SOLUTION To model the three-level categorical variable package design, two dummy variables, X_1 and X_2, are needed:

$$X_{1i} = 1 \text{ if package design } A \text{ is used in observation } i; 0 \text{ otherwise}$$
$$X_{2i} = 1 \text{ if package design } B \text{ is used in observation } i; 0 \text{ otherwise}$$

Thus, if observation i uses package design A, then $X_{1i} = 1$ and $X_{2i} = 0$; if observation i uses package design B, then $X_{1i} = 0$ and $X_{2i} = 1$; and if observation i uses package design C, then $X_{1i} = X_{2i} = 0$. Thus, package design C becomes the baseline category to which the effect of package design A and package design B is compared. A third independent variable is used for price:

$$X_{3i} = \text{price for observation } i$$

Thus, the regression model for this example is

$$Y_i = \beta_0 + \beta_1 X_{1i} + \beta_2 X_{2i} + \beta_3 X_{3i} + \varepsilon_i$$

where

$Y_i = $ sales for observation i

$\beta_0 = Y$ intercept

$\beta_1 = $ difference between the predicted sales of design A and the predicted sales of design C, holding price constant

$\beta_2 = $ difference between the predicted sales of design B and the predicted sales of design C, holding price constant

$\beta_3 = $ slope of sales with price, holding the package design constant

$\varepsilon_i = $ random error in Y for observation i

Interactions

In the regression models discussed so far, the effect an independent variable has on the dependent variable has been assumed to be independent of the other independent variables in the model. An **interaction** occurs if the effect of an independent variable on the dependent variable changes according to the *value* of a second independent variable. For example, it is possible that advertising will have a large effect on the sales of a product when the price of a product is low. However, if the price of the product is too high, increases in advertising will not dramatically change sales. In this case, price and advertising are said to interact. In other words, you cannot make general statements about the effect of advertising on sales. The effect that advertising has on sales is *dependent* on the price. You use an **interaction term** (sometimes referred to as a **cross-product term**) to model an interaction effect in a regression model.

To illustrate the concept of interaction and use of an interaction term, return to the example concerning the assessed values of homes discussed on pages 495–496. In the regression model, you assumed that the effect that house size has on the assessed value is independent of whether the house has a fireplace. In other words, you assumed that the slope of assessed value with house size is the same for all houses, regardless of whether the house contains a fireplace. If these two slopes are different, an interaction exists between the house size and the presence or absence of a fireplace.

To evaluate whether an interaction exists, you first define an interaction term that is the product of the independent variable X_1 (house size) and the dummy variable X_2 (Fireplace-Coded). You then test whether this interaction variable makes a significant contribution to the regression model. If the interaction is significant, you cannot use the original model for prediction. For these data you define the following:

$$X_3 = X_1 \times X_2$$

Figure 14.10 presents regression results for the model that includes the house size, X_1, the presence of a fireplace, X_2, and the interaction of X_1 and X_2 (defined as X_3 and labeled Size*Fireplace).

FIGURE 14.10
Excel worksheet results
for the regression model
that includes house size,
presence of fireplace, and
interaction of house size
and fireplace

	A	B	C	D	E	F	G
1	Assessed Value Analysis						
2							
3	*Regression Statistics*						
4	Multiple R	0.5885					
5	R Square	0.3464					
6	Adjusted R Square	0.2710					
7	Standard Error	62.3909					
8	Observations	30					
9							
10	ANOVA						
11		*df*	*SS*	*MS*	*F*	*Significance F*	
12	Regression	3	53636.8541	17878.9514	4.5930	0.0104	
13	Residual	26	101208.2539	3892.6252			
14	Total	29	154845.1080				
15							
16		*Coefficients*	*Standard Error*	*t Stat*	*P-value*	*Lower 95%*	*Upper 95%*
17	Intercept	226.8573	66.2454	3.4245	0.0021	90.6881	363.0266
18	Size	74.7987	36.3298	2.0589	0.0497	0.1216	149.4757
19	FireplaceCoded	63.8028	74.2760	0.8590	0.3982	-88.8737	216.4793
20	Size*Fireplace	-29.5183	39.4946	-0.7474	0.4615	-110.7006	51.6640

To test for the existence of an interaction, you use the null hypothesis:

$$H_0: \beta_3 = 0$$

versus the alternative hypothesis:

$$H_1: \beta_3 \neq 0.$$

studentTIP

It is possible that the
interaction between two
independent variables
will be significant even
though one of the inde-
pendent variables is not
significant.

In Figure 14.10, the t_{STAT} test statistic for the interaction of size and fireplace is -0.7474. Because $t_{STAT} = -0.7474 > -2.0555$ or the p-value $= 0.4615 > 0.05$, you do not reject the null hypothesis. Therefore, the interaction does not make a significant contribution to the model, given that house size and presence of a fireplace are already included. You can conclude that the slope of assessed value with size is the same for houses with fireplaces and houses without fireplaces.

Regression models can have several numerical independent variables along with a dummy variable. Example 14.4 illustrates a regression model in which there are two numerical independent variables and a categorical independent variable.

EXAMPLE 14.4

Studying a Regres-
sion Model That
Contains a Dummy
Variable and Two
Independent
Variables

The business problem facing a real estate developer involves predicting heating oil consumption in single-family houses. The independent variables considered are atmospheric temperature (°F), X_1, the amount of attic insulation (inches), X_2 and whether the house is ranch-style (X_3). Data are collected from a sample of 15 single-family houses. The data are organized and stored in HeatingOil. Develop and analyze an appropriate regression model, using these three independent variables X_1, X_2, and X_3.

SOLUTION Define X_3, a dummy variable for ranch-style house, as follows:

$$X_3 = 0 \text{ if the style is not ranch}$$

$$X_3 = 1 \text{ if the style is ranch}$$

▶ *(continued)*

Assuming that the slope between heating oil consumption and atmospheric temperature, X_1, and between heating oil consumption and the amount of attic insulation, X_2, is the same for both styles of houses, the regression model is

$$Y_i = \beta_0 + \beta_1 X_{1i} + \beta_2 X_{2i} + \beta_3 X_{3i} + \varepsilon_i$$

where
- Y_i = monthly heating oil consumption, in gallons, for house i
- β_0 = Y intercept
- β_1 = slope of heating oil consumption with atmospheric temperature, holding constant the effect of attic insulation and the style of the house
- β_2 = slope of heating oil consumption with attic insulation, holding constant the effect of atmospheric temperature and the style of the house
- β_3 = incremental effect of the presence of a ranch-style house, holding constant the effect of atmospheric temperature and attic insulation
- ε_i = random error in Y for house i

Figure 14.11 presents results for this regression model.

FIGURE 14.11
Excel worksheet results for the regression model that includes temperature, insulation, and style for the heating oil data

	A	B	C	D	E	F	G
1	Heating Oil Consumption Analysis						
3	Regression Statistics						
4	Multiple R	0.9942					
5	R Square	0.9884					
6	Adjusted R Square	0.9853					
7	Standard Error	15.7489					
8	Observations	15					
10	ANOVA						
11		df	SS	MS	F	Significance F	
12	Regression	3	233406.9094	77802.3031	313.6822	0.0000	
13	Residual	11	2728.3200	248.0291			
14	Total	14	236135.2293				
16		Coefficients	Standard Error	t Stat	P-value	Lower 95%	Upper 95%
17	Intercept	592.5401	14.3370	41.3295	0.0000	560.9846	624.0956
18	Temperature	-5.5251	0.2044	-27.0267	0.0000	-5.9751	-5.0752
19	Insulation	-21.3761	1.4480	-14.7623	0.0000	-24.5632	-18.1891
20	Ranch-style	-38.9727	8.3584	-4.6627	0.0007	-57.3695	-20.5759

From the results in Figure 14.11, the regression equation is

$$\hat{Y}_i = 592.5401 - 5.5251 X_{1i} - 21.3761 X_{2i} - 38.9727 X_{3i}$$

For houses that are not ranch style, because $X_3 = 0$, the regression equation reduces to

$$\hat{Y}_i = 592.5401 - 5.5251 X_{1i} - 21.3761 X_{2i}$$

For houses that are ranch style, because $X_3 = 1$, the regression equation reduces to

$$\hat{Y}_i = 553.5674 - 5.5251 X_{1i} - 21.3761 X_{2i}$$

In this model, the regression coefficients are interpreted as follows:

- Holding constant the attic insulation and the house style, for each additional 1°F increase in atmospheric temperature, you estimate that the predicted mean heating oil consumption decreases by 5.5251 gallons.
- Holding constant the atmospheric temperature and the house style, for each additional 1-inch increase in attic insulation, you estimate that the predicted mean heating oil consumption decreases by 21.3761 gallons.

▶ (continued)

- Holding constant the atmospheric temperature and attic insulation held, you estimate that the predicted mean heating oil consumption is 38.9727 gallons less for a ranch-style house than for a house that is not ranch style.

The three t_{STAT} test statistics representing the slopes for temperature, insulation, and ranch style are -27.0267, -14.7623, and -4.6627. Each of the corresponding p-values is extremely small (less than 0.001). Thus, each of the three variables makes a significant contribution to the model. In addition, the coefficient of multiple determination indicates that 98.84% of the variation in oil usage is explained by variation in temperature, insulation, and whether the house is ranch style.

Before you can use the model in Example 14.4, you need to determine whether the independent variables interact with each other. In Example 14.5, three interaction terms are added to the model.

EXAMPLE 14.5
Evaluating a Regression Model with Several Interactions

For the data of Example 14.4, determine whether adding interaction terms makes a significant contribution to the regression model.

SOLUTION To evaluate possible interactions between the independent variables, three interaction terms are constructed as follows: $X_4 = X_1 \times X_2$, $X_5 = X_1 \times X_3$, and $X_6 = X_2 \times X_3$. The regression model is now

$$Y_i = \beta_0 + \beta_1 X_{1i} + \beta_2 X_{2i} + \beta_3 X_{3i} + \beta_4 X_{4i} + \beta_5 X_{5i} + \beta_6 X_{6i} + \varepsilon_i$$

where X_1 is temperature, X_2 is insulation, X_3 is the dummy variable ranch style, X_4 is the interaction between temperature and insulation, X_5 is the interaction between temperature and ranch style, and X_6 is the interaction between insulation and ranch style. Figure 14.12 presents the results for this regression model.

FIGURE 14.12
Excel worksheet results for the regression model that includes temperature, X_1; insulation, X_2; the dummy variable ranch-style, X_3; the interaction of temperature and insulation, X_4; the interaction of temperature and ranch-style, X_5; and the interaction of insulation and ranch-style, X_6

▲	A	B	C	D	E	F	G
1	**Heating Oil Consumption Analysis**						
2							
3	*Regression Statistics*						
4	Multiple R	0.9966					
5	R Square	0.9931					
6	Adjusted R Square	0.9880					
7	Standard Error	14.2506					
8	Observations	15					
9							
10	**ANOVA**						
11		*df*	*SS*	*MS*	*F*	*Significance F*	
12	Regression	6	234510.5818	39085.0970	192.4607	0.0000	
13	Residual	8	1624.6475	203.0809			
14	Total	14	236135.2293				
15							
16		*Coefficients*	*Standard Error*	*t Stat*	*P-value*	*Lower 95%*	*Upper 95%*
17	Intercept	642.8867	26.7059	24.0728	0.0000	581.3027	704.4707
18	Temperature	-6.9263	0.7531	-9.1969	0.0000	-8.6629	-5.1896
19	Insulation	-27.8825	3.5801	-7.7882	0.0001	-36.1383	-19.6268
20	Style	-84.6088	29.9956	-2.8207	0.0225	-153.7788	-15.4389
21	Temperature * Insulation	0.1702	0.0886	1.9204	0.0911	-0.0342	0.3746
22	Temperature * Ranch-style	0.6596	0.4617	1.4286	0.1910	-0.4051	1.7242
23	Insulation * Ranch-style	4.9870	3.5137	1.4193	0.1936	-3.1156	13.0895

In the Worksheet

For problems with as many independent X variables as this model contains, use either the *PHStat* or *Analysis ToolPak* instructions to produce the regression results.

To test whether the three interactions significantly improve the regression model, you use the partial F test. The null and alternative hypotheses are

$$H_0: \beta_4 = \beta_5 = \beta_6 = 0 \text{ (There are no interactions among } X_1, X_2, \text{ and } X_3.)$$
$$H_1: \beta_4 \neq 0 \text{ and/or } \beta_5 \neq 0 \text{ and/or } \beta_6 \neq 0 \text{ } (X_1 \text{ interacts with } X_2,$$
$$\text{and/or } X_1 \text{ interacts with } X_3, \text{ and/or } X_2 \text{ interacts with } X_3.)$$

▶ *(continued)*

From Figure 14.12,

$$SSR(X_1, X_2, X_3, X_4, X_5, X_6) = 234{,}510.5818 \text{ with 6 degrees of freedom}$$

and from Figure 14.11 on page 499, $SSR\,(X_1, X_2, X_3) = 233{,}406.9094$ with 3 degrees of freedom. Thus,

$$SSR(X_1, X_2, X_3, X_4, X_5, X_6) - SSR(X_1, X_2, X_3) = 234{,}510.5818 - 233{,}406.9094 = 1{,}103.6724$$

The difference in degrees of freedom is $6 - 3 = 3$.

To use the partial F test for the simultaneous contribution of three variables to a model, you use an extension of Equation (14.11) on page 491.[2] The partial F_{STAT} test statistic is

$$F_{STAT} = \frac{[SSR(X_1, X_2, X_3, X_4, X_5, X_6) - SSR(X_1, X_2, X_3)]/3}{MSE(X_1, X_2, X_3, X_4, X_5, X_6)} = \frac{1{,}103.6724/3}{203.0809} = 1.8115$$

You compare the computed F_{STAT} test statistic to the critical F value for 3 and 8 degrees of freedom. Using a level of significance of 0.05, the critical F value from Table E.5 is 4.07. Because $F_{STAT} = 1.8115 < 4.07$, you conclude that the interactions do not make a significant contribution to the model, given that the model already includes temperature, X_1; insulation, X_2; and whether the house is ranch style, X_3. Therefore, the multiple regression model using X_1, X_2, and X_3 but no interaction terms is the better model. If you rejected this null hypothesis, you would then test the contribution of each interaction separately in order to determine which interaction terms to include in the model.

[2] In general, if a model has several independent variables and you want to test whether additional independent variables contribute to the model, the numerator of the F test is SSR (for all independent variables) minus SSR (for the initial set of variables) divided by the number of independent variables whose contribution is being tested.

PROBLEMS FOR SECTION 14.6

LEARNING THE BASICS

14.38 Suppose X_1 is a numerical variable and X_2 is a dummy variable with two categories and the regression equation for a sample of $n = 20$ is

$$\hat{Y}_i = 6 + 4X_{1i} + 2X_{2i}$$

a. Interpret the regression coefficient associated with variable X_1.
b. Interpret the regression coefficient associated with variable X_2.
c. Suppose that the t_{STAT} test statistic for testing the contribution of variable X_2 is 3.27. At the 0.05 level of significance, is there evidence that variable X_2 makes a significant contribution to the model?

APPLYING THE CONCEPTS

14.39 The chair of the accounting department plans to develop a regression model to predict the grade point average in accounting for those students who are graduating and have completed the accounting major, based on a student's SAT score and whether the student received a grade of B or higher in the introductory statistics course (0 = no and 1 = yes).
a. Explain the steps involved in developing a regression model for these data. Be sure to indicate the particular models you need to evaluate and compare.
b. Suppose the regression coefficient for the variable whether the student received a grade of B or higher in the introductory statistics course is +0.30. How do you interpret this result?

14.40 A real estate association in a suburban community would like to study the relationship between the size of a single-family

house (as measured by the number of rooms) and the selling price of the house (in $thousands). Two different neighborhoods are included in the study, one on the east side of the community (=0) and the other on the west side (=1). A random sample of 20 houses was selected, with the results stored in Neighbor . For (a) through (k), do not include an interaction term.
a. State the multiple regression equation that predicts the selling price, based on the number of rooms and the neighborhood.
b. Interpret the regression coefficients in (a).
c. Predict the mean selling price for a house with nine rooms that is located in an east-side neighborhood. Construct a 95% confidence interval estimate and a 95% prediction interval.
d. Perform a residual analysis on the results and determine whether the regression assumptions are valid.
e. Is there a significant relationship between selling price and the two independent variables (rooms and neighborhood) at the 0.05 level of significance?
f. At the 0.05 level of significance, determine whether each independent variable makes a contribution to the regression model. Indicate the most appropriate regression model for this set of data.
g. Construct and interpret a 95% confidence interval estimate of the population slope for the relationship between selling price and number of rooms.
h. Construct and interpret a 95% confidence interval estimate of the population slope for the relationship between selling price and neighborhood.
i. Compute and interpret the adjusted r^2.
j. Compute the coefficients of partial determination and interpret their meaning.

k. What assumption do you need to make about the slope of selling price with number of rooms?

l. Add an interaction term to the model and, at the 0.05 level of significance, determine whether it makes a significant contribution to the model.

m. On the basis of the results of (f) and (l), which model is most appropriate? Explain.

n. What conclusions can the real estate association reach about the effect of the number of rooms and neighborhood on the selling price of homes?

14.41 In Problem 14.5 on page 480, you developed a multiple regression model to predict wine quality for red wines. Now, you wish to determine whether there is an effect on wine quality due to whether the wine is white (0) or red (1). These data are organized and stored in RedandWhite. Develop a multiple regression model to predict wine quality based on the percentage of alcohol and the type of wine.

For (a) through (m), do not include an interaction term.

a. State the multiple regression equation that predicts wine quality based on the percentage of alcohol and the type of wine.

b. Interpret the regression coefficients in (a).

c. Predict the mean quality for a red wine that has 10% alcohol. Construct a 95% confidence interval estimate and a 95% prediction interval.

d. Perform a residual analysis on the results and determine whether the regression assumptions are valid.

e. Is there a significant relationship between wine quality and the two independent variables (percentage of alcohol and the type of wine) at the 0.05 level of significance?

f. At the 0.05 level of significance, determine whether each independent variable makes a contribution to the regression model. Indicate the most appropriate regression model for this set of data.

g. Construct and interpret 95% confidence interval estimates of the population slope for the relationship between wine quality and the percentage of alcohol and between wine quality and the type of wine.

h. Compare the slope in (b) with the slope for the simple linear regression model of Problem 13.4 on page 436. Explain the difference in the results.

i. Compute and interpret the meaning of the coefficient of multiple determination, r^2.

j. Compute and interpret the adjusted r^2.

k. Compare r^2 with the r^2 value computed in Problem 13.16 (a) on page 442.

m. Compute the coefficients of partial determination and interpret their meaning.

n. What assumption about the slope of type of wine with wine quality do you need to make in this problem?

o. Add an interaction term to the model and, at the 0.05 level of significance, determine whether it makes a significant contribution to the model.

p. On the basis of the results of (f) and (n), which model is most appropriate? Explain.

q. What conclusions can you reach concerning the effect of alcohol percentage and type of wine on wine quality?

14.42 In mining engineering, holes are often drilled through rock, using drill bits. As a drill hole gets deeper, additional rods are added to the drill bit to enable additional drilling to take place. It is expected that drilling time increases with depth. This in-

creased drilling time could be caused by several factors, including the mass of the drill rods that are strung together. The business problem relates to whether drilling is faster using dry drilling holes or wet drilling holes. Using dry drilling holes involves forcing compressed air down the drill rods to flush the cuttings and drive the hammer. Using wet drilling holes involves forcing water rather than air down the hole. Data have been collected from a sample of 50 drill holes that contains measurements of the time to drill each additional 5 feet (in minutes), the depth (in feet), and whether the hole was a dry drilling hole or a wet drilling hole. The data are organized and stored in Drill. (Data extracted from R. Penner and D. G. Watts, "Mining Information," *The American Statistician*, 45, 1991, pp. 4–9.) Develop a model to predict additional drilling time, based on depth and type of drilling hole (dry or wet). For (a) through (k) do not include an interaction term.

a. State the multiple regression equation.

b. Interpret the regression coefficients in (a).

c. Predict the mean additional drilling time for a dry drilling hole at a depth of 100 feet. Construct a 95% confidence interval estimate and a 95% prediction interval.

d. Perform a residual analysis on the results and determine whether the regression assumptions are valid.

e. Is there a significant relationship between additional drilling time and the two independent variables (depth and type of drilling hole) at the 0.05 level of significance?

f. At the 0.05 level of significance, determine whether each independent variable makes a contribution to the regression model. Indicate the most appropriate regression model for this set of data.

g. Construct a 95% confidence interval estimate of the population slope for the relationship between additional drilling time and depth.

h. Construct a 95% confidence interval estimate of the population slope for the relationship between additional drilling time and the type of hole drilled.

i. Compute and interpret the adjusted r^2.

j. Compute the coefficients of partial determination and interpret their meaning.

k. What assumption do you need to make about the slope of additional drilling time with depth?

l. Add an interaction term to the model and, at the 0.05 level of significance, determine whether it makes a significant contribution to the model.

m. On the basis of the results of (f) and (l), which model is most appropriate? Explain.

n. What conclusions can you reach concerning the effect of depth and type of drilling hole on drilling time?

14.43 The owner of a moving company typically has his most experienced manager predict the total number of labor hours that will be required to complete an upcoming move. This approach has proved useful in the past, but the owner has the business objective of developing a more accurate method of predicting labor hours. In a preliminary effort to provide a more accurate method, the owner has decided to use the number of cubic feet moved and whether there is an elevator in the apartment building as the independent variables and has collected data for 36 moves in which the origin and destination were within the borough of Manhattan in New York City and the travel time was an insignificant portion of the hours worked. The data are organized and stored in Moving. For (a) through (k), do not include an interaction term.

a. State the multiple regression equation for predicting labor hours, using the number of cubic feet moved and whether there is an elevator.
b. Interpret the regression coefficients in (a).
c. Predict the mean labor hours for moving 500 cubic feet in an apartment building that has an elevator and construct a 95% confidence interval estimate and a 95% prediction interval.
d. Perform a residual analysis on the results and determine whether the regression assumptions are valid.
e. Is there a significant relationship between labor hours and the two independent variables (cubic feet moved and whether there is an elevator in the apartment building) at the 0.05 level of significance?
f. At the 0.05 level of significance, determine whether each independent variable makes a contribution to the regression model. Indicate the most appropriate regression model for this set of data.
g. Construct a 95% confidence interval estimate of the population slope for the relationship between labor hours and cubic feet moved.
h. Construct a 95% confidence interval estimate for the relationship between labor hours and the presence of an elevator.
i. Compute and interpret the adjusted r^2.
j. Compute the coefficients of partial determination and interpret their meaning.
k. What assumption do you need to make about the slope of labor hours with cubic feet moved?
l. Add an interaction term to the model, and at the 0.05 level of significance, determine whether it makes a significant contribution to the model.
m. On the basis of the results of (f) and (l), which model is most appropriate? Explain.
n. What conclusions can you reach concerning the effect of the number of cubic feet moved and whether there is an elevator on labor hours?

✓ **SELF TEST** **14.44** In Problem 14.4 on page 480, you used efficiency ratio and total risk-based capital to predict ROA at a community bank (stored in CommunityBanks). Develop a regression model to predict ROA that includes efficiency ratio, total risk-based capital, and the interaction of efficiency ratio and total risk-based capital.
a. At the 0.05 level of significance, is there evidence that the interaction term makes a significant contribution to the model?
b. Which regression model is more appropriate, the one used in (a) or the one used in Problem 14.4? Explain.

14.45 Zagat's publishes restaurant ratings for various locations in the United States. The file Restaurants contains the Zagat rating for food, décor, service, and cost per person for a sample of 50 center city restaurants and 50 metro area restaurants. (Data extracted from *Zagat Survey 2015, New York City Restaurants*;.)

Develop a regression model to predict the cost per person, based on a variable that represents the sum of the ratings for food, décor, and service and a dummy variable concerning location (center city versus metro area). For (a) through (m), do not include an interaction term.
a. State the multiple regression equation.
b. Interpret the regression coefficients in (a).
c. Predict the mean cost for a center city restaurant with a summated rating of 60 and construct a 95% confidence interval estimate and a 95% prediction interval.

d. Perform a residual analysis on the results and determine whether the regression assumptions are satisfied.
e. Is there a significant relationship between price and the two independent variables (summated rating and location) at the 0.05 level of significance?
f. At the 0.05 level of significance, determine whether each independent variable makes a contribution to the regression model. Indicate the most appropriate regression model for this set of data.
g. Construct a 95% confidence interval estimate of the population slope for the relationship between cost and summated rating.
h. Compare the slope in (b) with the slope for the simple linear regression model of Problem 13.5 on page 436. Explain the difference in the results.
i. Compute and interpret the meaning of the coefficient of multiple determination.
j. Compute and interpret the adjusted r^2.
k. Compare r^2 with the r^2 value computed in Problem 13.17 (b) on page 442.
l. Compute the coefficients of partial determination and interpret their meaning.
m. What assumption about the slope of cost with summated rating do you need to make in this problem?
n. Add an interaction term to the model and, at the 0.05 level of significance, determine whether it makes a significant contribution to the model.
o. On the basis of the results of (f) and (n), which model is most appropriate? Explain.
p. What conclusions can you reach about the effect of the summated rating and the location of the restaurant on the cost of a meal?

14.46 In Problem 14.6 on page 480, you used full-time voluntary turnover (%), and total worldwide revenue ($billions) to predict number of full-time jobs added (stored in BestCompanies). Develop a regression model to predict the number of full-time jobs added that includes full-time voluntary turnover, total worldwide revenue, and the interaction of full-time voluntary turnover and total worldwide revenue.
a. At the 0.05 level of significance, is there evidence that the interaction term makes a significant contribution to the model?
b. Which regression model is more appropriate, the one used in this problem or the one used in Problem 14.6? Explain.

14.47 In Problem 14.5 on page 480, the percentage of alcohol and chlorides were used to predict the quality of red wines (stored in VinhoVerde). Develop a regression model that includes the percentage of alcohol, the chlorides, and the interaction of the percentage of alcohol and the chlorides to predict wine quality.
a. At the 0.05 level of significance, is there evidence that the interaction term makes a significant contribution to the model?
b. Which regression model is more appropriate, the one used in this problem or the one used in Problem 14.5? Explain.

14.48 In Problem 14.7 on page 480, you used total staff present and remote hours to predict standby hours (stored in Standby). Develop a regression model to predict standby hours that includes total staff present, remote hours, and the interaction of total staff present and remote hours.
a. At the 0.05 level of significance, is there evidence that the interaction term makes a significant contribution to the model?
b. Which regression model is more appropriate, the one used in this problem or the one used in Problem 14.7? Explain.

14.49 The director of a training program for a large insurance company has the business objective of determining which training method is best for training underwriters. The three methods to be evaluated are classroom, online, and courseware app. The 30 trainees are divided into three randomly assigned groups of 10. Before the start of the training, each trainee is given a proficiency exam that measures mathematics and computer skills. At the end of the training, all students take the same end-of-training exam. The results are organized and stored in Underwriting .

Develop a multiple regression model to predict the score on the end-of-training exam, based on the score on the proficiency exam and the method of training used. For (a) through (k), do not include an interaction term.

a. State the multiple regression equation.
b. Interpret the regression coefficients in (a).
c. Predict the mean end-of-training exam score for a student with a proficiency exam score of 100 who had courseware app-based training.
d. Perform a residual analysis on your results and determine whether the regression assumptions are valid.
e. Is there a significant relationship between the end-of-training exam score and the independent variables (proficiency score and training method) at the 0.05 level of significance?

f. At the 0.05 level of significance, determine whether each independent variable makes a contribution to the regression model. Indicate the most appropriate regression model for this set of data.
g. Construct and interpret a 95% confidence interval estimate of the population slope for the relationship between the end-of-training exam score and the proficiency exam score.
h. Construct and interpret 95% confidence interval estimates of the population slope for the relationship between the end-of-training exam score and type of training method.
i. Compute and interpret the adjusted r^2.
j. Compute the coefficients of partial determination and interpret their meaning.
k. What assumption about the slope of proficiency score with end-of-training exam score do you need to make in this problem?
l. Add interaction terms to the model and, at the 0.05 level of significance, determine whether any interaction terms make a significant contribution to the model.
m. On the basis of the results of (f) and (l), which model is most appropriate? Explain.

14.7 Logistic Regression

The discussion of the simple linear regression model in Chapter 13 and the multiple regression models in Sections 14.1 through 14.6 only considered *numerical* dependent variables. However, in many applications, the dependent variable is a *categorical* variable that takes on one of only two possible values, such as a customer purchases a product or a customer does not purchase a product. Using a categorical dependent variable violates the normality assumption of the least-squares method and can also result in predicted Y values that are impossible.

An alternative approach to least-squares regression originally applied to survival data in the health sciences (see reference 5), **logistic regression**, enables you to use regression models to predict the probability of a particular categorical response for a given set of independent variables. The logistic regression model uses the **odds ratio**, which represents the probability of an event of interest compared with the probability of not having an event of interest. Equation (14.15) defines the odds ratio.

ODDS RATIO

$$\text{Odds ratio} = \frac{\text{probability of an event of interest}}{1 - \text{probability of an event of interest}} \qquad (14.15)$$

Using Equation (14.15), if the probability of an event of interest is 0.50, the odds ratio is

$$\text{Odds ratio} = \frac{0.50}{1 - 0.50} = 1.0, \text{ or 1 to 1}$$

If the probability of an event of interest is 0.75, the odds ratio is

$$\text{Odds ratio} = \frac{0.75}{1 - 0.75} = 3.0, \text{ or 3 to 1}$$

The logistic regression model is based on the natural logarithm of the odds ratio, ln(odds ratio).

Equation (14.16) defines the logistic regression model for k independent variables.

LOGISTIC REGRESSION MODEL

$$\ln(\text{Odds ratio}) = \beta_0 + \beta_1 X_{1i} + \beta_2 X_{2i} + \cdots + \beta_k X_{ki} + \varepsilon_i \quad \textbf{(14.16)}$$

where

k = number of independent variables in the model
ε_i = random error in observation i

In Sections 13.2 and 14.1, the method of least squares was used to develop a regression equation. In logistic regression, a mathematical method called *maximum likelihood estimation* is typically used to develop a regression equation to predict the natural logarithm of this odds ratio. Equation (14.17) defines the logistic regression equation.

LOGISTIC REGRESSION EQUATION

$$\ln(\text{Estimated odds ratio}) = b_0 + b_1 X_{1i} + b_2 X_{2i} + \cdots + b_k X_{ki} \quad \textbf{(14.17)}$$

Once you have determined the logistic regression equation, you use Equation (14.18) to compute the estimated odds ratio.

ESTIMATED ODDS RATIO

$$\text{Estimated odds ratio} = e^{\ln(\text{Estimated odds ratio})} \quad \textbf{(14.18)}$$

Once you have computed the estimated odds ratio, you use Equation (14.19) to compute the estimated probability of an event of interest.

ESTIMATED PROBABILITY OF AN EVENT OF INTEREST

$$\text{Estimated probability of an event of interest} = \frac{\text{estimated odds ratio}}{1 + \text{estimated odds ratio}} \quad \textbf{(14.19)}$$

To illustrate the use of logistic regression, consider the case of the sales and marketing manager for the credit card division of a major financial company. The manager wants to conduct a campaign to persuade existing holders of the bank's standard credit card to upgrade, for a nominal annual fee, to the bank's platinum card. The manager wonders, "Which of the existing standard credit cardholders should we target for this campaign?"

The manager has access to the results from a sample of 30 cardholders who were targeted during a pilot campaign last year. These results have been organized as three variables and stored in CardStudy. The three variables are cardholder upgraded to a premium card, Y (0 = no, 1 = yes); and two independent variables: prior year's credit card purchases (in $thousands), X_1; and cardholder ordered additional credit cards for other authorized users, X_2 (0 = no, 1 = yes). Figure 14.13 presents the Excel results for the logistic regression model using these data.

FIGURE 14.13
Excel logistic regression results for the credit card pilot study data

▲	A	B	C	D	E
1	Logistic Regression				
2					
3	Predictor	Coefficients	SE Coef	Z	p-Value
4	Intercept	-6.9394	2.9471	-2.3547	0.0185
5	Purchases	0.1395	0.0681	2.0490	0.0405
6	Extra Cards:1	2.7743	1.1927	2.3261	0.0200
7					
8	Deviance	20.0769			

In the Worksheet

This worksheet uses the NORM.S.DIST function in column E to help compute the p-values. Columns G through N (not shown) contain intermediate calculations. Formulas in columns L and M use the IF function in ways much more complex than the other worksheets that this book features.

In this model, the regression coefficients are interpreted as follows:

- The regression constant, b_0, is –6.9394. This means that for a credit cardholder who did not charge any purchases last year and who does not have additional cards, the estimated natural logarithm of the odds ratio of purchasing the premium card is –6.9394.
- The regression coefficient, b_1, is 0.1395. This means that holding constant the effect of whether the credit cardholder has additional cards for members of the household, for each increase of $1,000 in annual credit card spending using the company's card, the estimated natural logarithm of the odds ratio of purchasing the premium card increases by 0.1395. Therefore, cardholders who charged more in the previous year are more likely to upgrade to a premium card.
- The regression coefficient, b_2, is 2.7743. This means that holding constant the annual credit card spending, the estimated natural logarithm of the odds ratio of purchasing the premium card increases by 2.7743 for a credit cardholder who has additional cards for members of the household compared with one who does not have additional cards. Therefore, cardholders possessing additional cards for other members of the household are much more likely to upgrade to a premium card.

The regression coefficients suggest that the credit card company should develop a marketing campaign that targets cardholders who tend to charge large amounts to their cards, and to households that possess more than one card.

As is the case with least-squares regression models, a main purpose of performing logistic regression analysis is to provide predictions of a dependent variable. For example, consider a cardholder who charged $36,000 last year and possesses additional cards for members of the household. What is the probability the cardholder will upgrade to the premium card during the marketing campaign? Using $X_1 = 36$, $X_2 = 1$, Equation (14.17) on page 505, and the results displayed in Figure 14.13 above,

$$\ln(\text{estimated odds of purchasing versus not purchasing}) = -6.9394 + (0.1395)(36) + (2.7743)(1)$$
$$= 0.8569$$

Then, using Equation (14.18) on page 505,

$$\text{estimated odds ratio} = e^{0.8569} = 2.3558$$

Therefore, the odds are 2.3558 to 1 that a credit cardholder who spent $36,000 last year and has additional cards will purchase the premium card during the campaign. Using Equation (14.19) on page 505, you can convert this odds ratio to a probability:

$$\text{estimated probability of purchasing premium card} = \frac{2.3558}{1 + 2.3558}$$
$$= 0.702$$

Thus, the estimated probability is 0.702 that a credit cardholder who spent $36,000 last year and has additional cards will purchase the premium card during the campaign. In other words, you predict 70.2% of such individuals will purchase the premium card.

Now that you have used the logistic regression model for prediction, you need to determine whether or not the model is a good-fitting model. The **deviance statistic** is frequently used to determine whether the current model provides a good fit to the data. This statistic measures the fit of the current model compared with a model that has as many parameters as there are data points (what is called a *saturated* model). The deviance statistic follows a chi-square distribution with $n - k - 1$ degrees of freedom. The null and alternative hypotheses are

H_0: The model is a good-fitting model.

H_1: The model is not a good-fitting model.

When using the deviance statistic for logistic regression, the null hypothesis represents a good-fitting model, which is the opposite of the null hypothesis when using the overall F test for the multiple regression model (see Section 14.2). Using the α level of significance, the decision rule is

$$\text{Reject } H_0 \text{ if deviance} > \chi_\alpha^2;$$
$$\text{otherwise, do not reject } H_o.$$

The critical value for a χ^2 statistic with $n - k - 1 = 30 - 2 - 1 = 27$ degrees of freedom is 40.113 (see Table E.4). From Figure 14.13 on page 506, the deviance = 20.0769 < 40.113. Thus, you do not reject H_0, and you conclude that there is insufficient evidence that the model is not a good-fitting one.

Now that you have concluded that the model is a good-fitting one, you need to evaluate whether each of the independent variables makes a significant contribution to the model in the presence of the others. As is the case with linear regression in Sections 13.7 and 14.4, the test statistic is based on the ratio of the regression coefficient to the standard error of the regression coefficient. In logistic regression, this ratio is defined by the **Wald statistic**, which approximately follows the normal distribution. From Figure 14.13, the Wald statistic (labeled Z) is 2.049 for X_1 and 2.3261 for X_2. Each of these is greater than the critical value of $+1.96$ of the normal distribution at the 0.05 level of significance (the p-values are 0.0405 and 0.02). You can conclude that each of the two independent variables makes a contribution to the model in the presence of the other. Therefore, you should include both these independent variables in the model.

PROBLEMS FOR SECTION 14.7

LEARNING THE BASICS

14.50 Interpret the meaning of a slope coefficient equal to 2.2 in logistic regression.

14.51 Given an estimated odds ratio of 2.5, compute the estimated probability of an event of interest.

14.52 Given an estimated odds ratio of 0.75, compute the estimated probability of an event of interest.

14.53 Consider the following logistic regression equation:

$$\ln(\text{Estimated odds ratio}) = 0.1 + 0.5X_{1i} + 0.2X_{2i}$$

a. Interpret the meaning of the logistic regression coefficients.
b. If $X_1 = 2$ and $X_2 = 1.5$, compute the estimated odds ratio and interpret its meaning.
c. On the basis of the results of (b), compute the estimated probability of an event of interest.

APPLYING THE CONCEPTS

14.54 Refer to Figure 14.13 on page 506.
a. Predict the probability that a cardholder who charged $36,000 last year and does not have

any additional credit cards for members of the household will purchase the platinum card during the marketing campaign.
b. Compare the results in (a) with those for a person with additional credit cards.
c. Predict the probability that a cardholder who charged $18,000 and does not have any additional credit cards for other authorized users will purchase the platinum card during the marketing campaign.
d. Compare the results of (a) and (c) and indicate what implications these results might have for the strategy for the marketing campaign.

14.55 A study was conducted to determine the factors involved in the rate of participation of discharged cardiac patients in a rehabilitation program. Data were collected from 516 treated patients (data extracted from F. Van Der Meulen, T. Vermaat, and P. Williams, "Case Study: An Application of Logistic Regression in a Six Sigma Project in Health Care," *Quality Engineering*, 2011, pp. 113–124). Among the variables used to predict participation (0 = no, 1 = yes) were the distance traveled to rehabilitation in kilometers, whether the person had a car (0 = no, 1 = yes), and the age of the person in years. The summarized data are:

	Estimate	Standard Error	Z Value	p-value
Intercept	5.7765	0.8619	6.702	0.0000
Distance	−0.0675	0.0111	−6.113	0.0000
Car	1.9369	0.2720	7.121	0.0000
Age	−0.0599	0.0119	−5.037	0.0000

a. State the logistic regression model.

b. Using the model in (a), predict the probability that a patient will participate in rehabilitation if he or she travels 20 km to rehabilitation, has a car, and is 65 years old.

c. Using the model in (a), predict the probability that a patient will participate in rehabilitation if he or she travels 20 km to rehabilitation, does not have a car, and is 65 years old.

d. Compare the results of (b) and (c).

e. At the 0.05 level of significance, is there evidence that the distance traveled, whether the patient has a car, and the age of the patient each make a significant contribution to the model?

f. What conclusions can you reach about the likelihood of a patient participating in the rehabilitation program?

14.56 Referring to Problem 14.41 on page 502, you have decided to analyze whether there are differences in fixed acidity, chlorides, and pH between white wines and red wines (0 = white 1 = red). Using the data stored in RedandWhite ,

a. Develop a logistic regression model to predict whether the wine is red based on the fixed acidity, chlorides, and pH.

b. Explain the meaning of the regression coefficients in the model developed in (a).

c. Predict the probability that a wine is red if it has a fixed acidity of 7.0, chlorides of 0.04, and pH of 3.5.

d. At the 0.05 level of significance, is there evidence that the logistic regression model developed in (a) is a good fitting model?

e. At the 0.05 level of significance, is there evidence that fixed acidity, chlorides, and pH each make a significant contribution to the model?

f. What conclusions concerning the probability of a wine selected being red can you reach?

14.57 Undergraduate students at Miami University in Oxford, Ohio, were surveyed in order to evaluate the effect of price on the purchase of a pizza from Pizza Hut. Students were first asked to imagine a situation in which they were planning to call and order for delivery a large two-topping pizza. Then they were asked to select from either Pizza Hut or another pizzeria of their choice. The price they would have to pay to get a Pizza Hut pizza differed from survey to survey. For example, some surveys used the price $11.49. Other prices investigated were $8.49, $9.49, $10.49, $12.49, $13.49, and $14.49. The dependent variable for this study is whether or not a student will select Pizza Hut. Possible independent variables are the price of a Pizza Hut pizza and the gender of the student. The file PizzaHut contains responses from 220 students and includes these three variables:

Gender: 1 = male, 0 = female
Price: 8.49, 9.49, 10.49, 11.49, 12.49, 13.49, or 14.49
Purchase: 1 = the student selected Pizza Hut, 0 = the student selected another pizzeria

a. Develop a logistic regression model to predict the probability that a student selects Pizza Hut based on the price of the pizza. Is price an important indicator of purchase selection?

b. Develop a logistic regression model to predict the probability that a student selects Pizza Hut based on the price of the pizza and the gender of the student. Is price an important indicator of purchase selection? Is gender an important indicator of purchase selection?

c. Compare the results from (a) and (b). Which model would you choose? Discuss.

d. Using the model selected in (c), predict the probability that a student will select Pizza Hut if the price is $8.99.

e. Using the model selected in (c), predict the probability that a student will select Pizza Hut if the price is $11.49.

f. Using the model selected in (c), predict the probability that a student will select Pizza Hut if the price is $13.99.

14.58 An automotive insurance company wants to predict which filed stolen vehicle claims are fraudulent, based on the mean number of claims submitted per year by the policy holder and whether the policy is a new policy, that is, is one year old or less (coded as 1 = yes, 0 = no). Data from a random sample of 98 automotive insurance claims, organized and stored in InsuranceFraud , show that 49 are fraudulent (coded as 1) and 49 are not (coded as 0). (Data extracted from A. Gepp *et al.*, "A Comparative Analysis of Decision Trees vis-à-vis Other Computational Data Mining Techniques in Automotive Insurance Fraud Detection," *Journal of Data Science*, 10 (2012), pp. 537–561.)

a. Develop a logistic regression model to predict the probability of a fraudulent claim, based on the number of claims submitted per year by the policy holder and whether the policy is new.

b. Explain the meaning of the regression coefficients in the model in (a).

c. Predict the probability of a fraudulent claim given that the policy holder has submitted a mean of one claim per year and holds a new policy.

d. At the 0.05 level of significance, is there evidence that a logistic regression model that uses the mean number of claims submitted per year by the policy holder and whether the policy is new to predict the probability of a fraudulent claim is a good fitting model?

e. At the 0.05 level of significance, is there evidence that the mean number of claims submitted per year by the policy holder and whether the policy is new each makes a significant contribution to the logistic model?

f. Develop a logistic regression model that includes only the number of claims submitted per year by the policy holder to predict the probability of a fraudulent claim.

g. Develop a logistic regression model that includes only whether the policy is new to predict a fraudulent claim.

h. Compare the models in (a), (f), and (g). Evaluate the differences among the models.

14.59 A marketing manager wants to predict customers with the risk of churning (switching their service contracts to another company) based on the number of calls the customer makes to the company call center and the number of visits the customer makes to the local service center. Data from a random sample of 30 customers, organized and stored in Churn show that 15 have churned (coded as 1) and 15 have not (coded as 0)

a. Develop a logistic regression model to predict the probability of churn, based on the number of calls the customer makes to the company call center and the number of visits the customer makes to the local service center.

b. Explain the meaning of the regression coefficients in the model in (a).

c. Predict the probability of churn for a customer who called the company call center 10 times and visited the local service center once.
d. At the 0.05 level of significance, is there evidence that a logistic regression model that uses the number of calls the customer makes to the company call center and the number of visits the customer makes to the local service center is a good fitting model?
e. At the 0.05 level of significance, is there evidence that the number of calls the customer makes to the company call center and the number of visits the customer makes to the local service center each make a significant contribution to the logistic model?
f. Develop a logistic regression model that includes only the number of calls the customer makes to the company call center to predict the probability of churn.
g. Develop a logistic regression model that includes only the number of visits the customer makes to the local service center to predict churn.
h. Compare the models in (a), (f), and (g). Evaluate the differences among the models.

14.60 A local supermarket manager wants to use two independent variables, customer age (in years) and whether the customer subscribes to the supermarket chain's health/wellness e-newsletters (coded as 1 = yes and 0 = no) to predict which customers are

likely to purchase a new line of organic products. Data from a random sample of 100 loyalty program customers, organized and stored in OrganicFood , show that 65 have purchased the organic products (coded as 1) and 35 have not (coded as 0).
a. Develop a logistic regression model to predict the probability that a customer purchases the organic products, based on age and whether the customer subscribes to the supermarket chain's health/wellness e-newsletters.
b. Explain the meaning of the regression coefficients in the model in (a).
c. Predict the probability of purchasing the organic products for a 35-year-old customer who subscribes to the supermarket chain's health/wellness e-newsletters.
d. At the 0.05 level of significance, is there evidence that a logistic regression model that uses customer age and whether the customer subscribes to the supermarket chain's health/wellness e-newsletters to predict the probability of purchasing the organic products is a good fitting model?
e. At the 0.05 level of significance, is there evidence that customer age and whether the customer subscribes to the supermarket chain's health/wellness e-newsletters each make a significant contribution to the logistic model?
f. What conclusions can you reach about which variables are affecting purchase of organic foods?

▼ USING **STATISTICS**
The Multiple Effects ..., Revisited

In the Using Statistics scenario, you were a marketing manager for OmniFoods, responsible for nutrition bars and similar snack items. You needed to determine the effect that price and in-store promotions would have on sales of OmniPower nutrition bars in order to develop an effective marketing strategy. A sample of 34 stores in a supermarket chain was selected for a test-market study. The stores charged between 59 and 99 cents per bar and were given an in-store promotion budget between $200 and $600.

At the end of the one-month test-market study, you performed a multiple regression analysis on the data. Two independent variables were considered: the price of an OmniPower bar and the monthly budget for in-store promotional expenditures. The dependent variable was the number of OmniPower bars sold in a month. The coefficient of determination indicated that 75.8% of the variation in sales was explained by knowing the price charged and the amount spent on in-store promotions. The model indicated that the predicted sales of OmniPower are estimated to decrease by 532 bars per

month for each 10-cent increase in the price, and the predicted sales are estimated to increase by 361 bars for each additional $100 spent on promotions.

After studying the relative effects of price and promotion, OmniFoods needs to set price and promotion standards for a nationwide introduction (obviously, lower prices and higher promotion budgets lead to more sales, but they do so at a lower profit margin). You determined that if stores spend $400 a month for in-store promotions and charge 79 cents, the 95% confidence interval estimate of the mean monthly sales is 2,854 to 3,303 bars. OmniFoods can multiply the lower and upper bounds of this confidence interval by the number of stores included in the nationwide introduction to estimate total monthly sales. For example, if 1,000 stores are in the nationwide introduction, then total monthly sales should be between 2.854 million and 3.308 million bars.

▼ SUMMARY

In this chapter, you learned how to develop and fit multiple regression models that use two or more independent variables to predict the value of a dependent variable. You also learned how to include categorical independent variables

and interaction terms in regression models and learned the logistic regression model that is used to predict a categorical dependent variable. Figure 14.14 summarizes how to apply a multiple regression model to a set of data.

FIGURE 14.14
Roadmap for multiple
regression

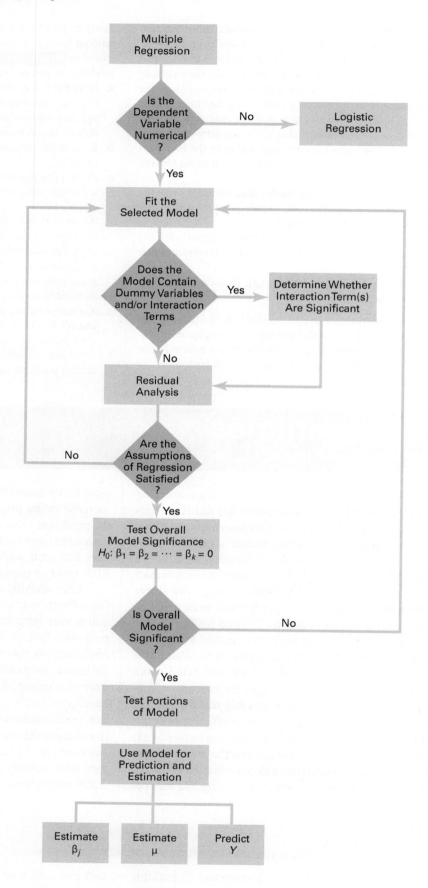

▼ REFERENCES

1. Andrews, D. F., and D. Pregibon. "Finding the Outliers that Matter." *Journal of the Royal Statistical Society* 40 (Ser. B., 1978): 85–93.
2. Atkinson, A. C. "Robust and Diagnostic Regression Analysis." *Communications in Statistics* 11 (1982): 2559–2572.
3. Belsley, D. A., E. Kuh, and R. Welsch. *Regression Diagnostics: Identifying Influential Data and Sources of Collinearity.* New York: Wiley, 1980.
4. Cook, R. D., and S. Weisberg. *Residuals and Influence in Regression.* New York: Chapman and Hall, 1982.
5. Hosmer, D. W., and S. Lemeshow. *Applied Logistic Regression*, 2nd ed. New York: Wiley, 2001.
6. Hoaglin, D. C., and R. Welsch. "The Hat Matrix in Regression and ANOVA," *The American Statistician*, 32, (1978), 17–22.
7. Kutner, M., C. Nachtsheim, J. Neter, and W. Li. *Applied Linear Statistical Models*, 5th ed. New York: McGraw-Hill/Irwin, 2005.
8. Montgomery, D. C., E. A. Peck, and G. G. Vining. *Introduction to Linear Regression Analysis*, 5th ed. New York: Wiley, 2012.

▼ KEY EQUATIONS

Multiple Regression Model with k Independent Variables

$$Y_i = \beta_0 + \beta_1 X_{1i} + \beta_2 X_{2i} + \beta_3 X_{3i} + \cdots + \beta_k X_{ki} + \varepsilon_i \quad (14.1)$$

Multiple Regression Model with Two Independent Variables

$$Y_i = \beta_0 + \beta_1 X_{1i} + \beta_2 X_{2i} + \varepsilon_i \quad (14.2)$$

Multiple Regression Equation with Two Independent Variables

$$\hat{Y}_i = b_0 + b_1 X_{1i} + b_2 X_{2i} \quad (14.3)$$

Coefficient of Multiple Determination

$$r^2 = \frac{\text{Regression sum of squares}}{\text{Total sum of squares}} = \frac{SSR}{SST} \quad (14.4)$$

Adjusted r^2

$$r^2_{\text{adj}} = 1 - \left[(1 - r^2)\frac{n-1}{n-k-1} \right] \quad (14.5)$$

Overall F Test

$$F_{STAT} = \frac{MSR}{MSE} \quad (14.6)$$

Testing for the Slope in Multiple Regression

$$t_{STAT} = \frac{b_j - \beta_j}{S_{b_j}} \quad (14.7)$$

Confidence Interval Estimate for the Slope

$$b_j \pm t_{\alpha/2}S_{b_j} \quad (14.8)$$

Determining the Contribution of an Independent Variable to the Regression Model

$$SSR(X_j | \text{All } Xs \text{ except } j) = SSR(\text{All } Xs) - SSR(\text{All } Xs \text{ except } j) \quad (14.9)$$

Contribution of Variable X_1, Given That X_2 Has Been Included

$$SSR(X_1 | X_2) = SSR(X_1 \text{ and } X_2) - SSR(X_2) \quad (14.10a)$$

Contribution of Variable X_2, Given That X_1 Has Been Included

$$SSR(X_2 | X_1) = SSR(X_1 \text{ and } X_2) - SSR(X_1) \quad (14.10b)$$

Partial F Test Statistic

$$F_{STAT} = \frac{SSR(X_j | \text{All } Xs \text{ except } j)}{MSE} \quad (14.11)$$

Relationship Between a t Statistic and an F Statistic

$$t^2_{STAT} = F_{STAT} \quad (14.12)$$

Coefficients of Partial Determination for a Multiple Regression Model Containing Two Independent Variables

$$r^2_{Y1.2} = \frac{SSR(X_1 | X_2)}{SST - SSR(X_1 \text{ and } X_2) + SSR(X_1 | X_2)} \quad (14.13a)$$

and

$$r^2_{Y2.1} = \frac{SSR(X_2 | X_1)}{SST - SSR(X_1 \text{ and } X_2) + SSR(X_2 | X_1)} \quad (14.13b)$$

Coefficient of Partial Determination for a Multiple Regression Model Containing k Independent Variables

$$r^2_{Yj.(\text{All variables except } j)} = \frac{SSR(X_j | \text{All } Xs \text{ except } j)}{SST - SSR(\text{All } Xs) + SSR(X_j | \text{All } Xs \text{ except } j)} \quad (14.14)$$

Odds Ratio

$$\text{Odds ratio} = \frac{\text{probability of an event of interest}}{1 - \text{probability of an event of interest}} \quad (14.15)$$

Logistic Regression Model

$$\ln(\text{Odds ratio}) = \beta_0 + \beta_1 X_{1i} + \beta_2 X_{2i} + \cdots + \beta_k X_{ki} + \varepsilon_i$$

$$(14.16)$$

Logistic Regression Equation

$$\ln(\text{Estimated odds ratio}) = b_0 + b_1 X_{1i} + b_2 X_{2i} + \cdots + b_k X_{ki}$$

$$(14.17)$$

Estimated Odds Ratio

$$\text{Estimated odds ratio} = e^{\ln(\text{Estimated odds ratio})} \qquad (14.18)$$

Estimated Probability of an Event of Interest

Estimated probability of an event of interest

$$= \frac{\text{estimated odds ratio}}{1 + \text{estimated odds ratio}} \qquad (14.19)$$

▼ KEY TERMS

▼ CHECKING YOUR UNDERSTANDING

14.61 What is the difference between r^2 and adjusted r^2?

14.62 How does the interpretation of the regression coefficients differ in multiple regression and simple linear regression?

14.63 How does testing the significance of the entire multiple regression model differ from testing the contribution of each independent variable?

14.64 How do the coefficients of partial determination differ from the coefficient of multiple determination?

14.65 Why and how do you use dummy variables?

14.66 How can you evaluate whether the slope of the dependent variable with an independent variable is the same for each level of the dummy variable?

14.67 Under what circumstances do you include an interaction term in a regression model?

14.68 When a dummy variable is included in a regression model that has one numerical independent variable, what assumption do you need to make concerning the slope between the dependent variable, Y, and the numerical independent variable, X?

14.69 When do you use logistic regression?

14.70 What is the difference between least squares regression and logistic regression?

▼ CHAPTER REVIEW PROBLEMS

14.71 Increasing customer satisfaction typically results in increased purchase behavior. For many products, there is more than one measure of customer satisfaction. In many, purchase behavior can increase dramatically with an increase in just one of the customer satisfaction measures. Gunst and Barry ("One Way to Moderate Ceiling Effects," *Quality Progress*, October 2003, pp. 83–85) consider a product with two satisfaction measures, X_1 and X_2, that range from the lowest level of satisfaction, 1, to the highest level of satisfaction, 7. The dependent variable, Y, is a measure of purchase behavior, with the highest value generating the most sales. Consider the regression equation:

$$\hat{Y}_i = -3.888 + 1.449 X_{1i} + 1.462 X_{2i} - 0.190 X_{1i} X_{2i}$$

Suppose that X_1 is the perceived quality of the product and X_2 is the perceived value of the product. (Note: If the customer thinks the product is overpriced, he or she perceives it to be of low value and vice versa.)

a. What is the predicted purchase behavior when $X_1 = 2$ and $X_2 = 2$?

b. What is the predicted purchase behavior when $X_1 = 2$ and $X_2 = 7$?

c. What is the predicted purchase behavior when $X_1 = 7$ and $X_2 = 2$?

d. What is the predicted purchase behavior when $X_1 = 7$ and $X_2 = 7$?

e. What is the regression equation when $X_2 = 2$? What is the slope for X_1 now?

f. What is the regression equation when $X_2 = 7$? What is the slope for X_1 now?

g. What is the regression equation when $X_1 = 2$? What is the slope for X_2 now?

h. What is the regression equation when $X_1 = 7$? What is the slope for X_2 now?

i. Discuss the implications of (a) through (h) in the context of increasing sales for this product with two customer satisfaction measures.

14.72 The owner of a moving company typically has his most experienced manager predict the total number of labor hours that will be required to complete an upcoming move. This approach has proved useful in the past, but the owner has the business objective of developing a more accurate method of predicting labor hours. In a preliminary effort to provide a more accurate method, the owner has decided to use the number of cubic feet moved and the number of pieces of large furniture as the independent variables and has collected data for 36 moves in which the origin and destination were within the borough of Manhattan in New York City and the travel time was an insignificant portion of the hours worked. The data are organized and stored in Moving .

a. State the multiple regression equation.

b. Interpret the meaning of the slopes in this equation.

c. Predict the mean labor hours for moving 500 cubic feet with two large pieces of furniture.

d. Perform a residual analysis on your results and determine whether the regression assumptions are valid.

e. Determine whether there is a significant relationship between labor hours and the two independent variables (the number of cubic feet moved and the number of pieces of large furniture) at the 0.05 level of significance.

f. Determine the p-value in (e) and interpret its meaning.

g. Interpret the meaning of the coefficient of multiple determination in this problem.

h. Determine the adjusted r^2.

i. At the 0.05 level of significance, determine whether each independent variable makes a significant contribution to the regression model. Indicate the most appropriate regression model for this set of data.

j. Determine the p-values in (i) and interpret their meaning.

k. Construct a 95% confidence interval estimate of the population slope between labor hours and the number of cubic feet moved.

l. Compute and interpret the coefficients of partial determination.

m. What conclusions can you reach concerning labor hours?

14.73 Professional basketball has truly become a sport that generates interest among fans around the world. More and more players come from outside the United States to play in the National Basketball Association (NBA). You want to develop a regression model to predict the number of wins achieved by each NBA team, based on field goal (shots made) percentage and three-point field goal percentage. The data are stored in NBA .

a. State the multiple regression equation.

b. Interpret the meaning of the slopes in this equation.

c. Predict the mean number of wins for a team that has a field goal percentage of 45% and a three-point field goal percentage of 35%.

d. Perform a residual analysis on your results and determine whether the regression assumptions are valid.

e. Is there a significant relationship between number of wins and the two independent variables (field goal percentage and three-point field goal percentage) at the 0.05 level of significance?

f. Determine the p-value in (e) and interpret its meaning.

g. Interpret the meaning of the coefficient of multiple determination in this problem.

h. Determine the adjusted r^2.

i. At the 0.05 level of significance, determine whether each independent variable makes a significant contribution to the regression model. Indicate the most appropriate regression model for this set of data.

j. Determine the p-values in (i) and interpret their meaning.

k. Compute and interpret the coefficients of partial determination.

l. What conclusions can you reach concerning field goal percentage and three-point field goal percentage in predicting the number of wins?

14.74 A sample of 30 houses recently listed for sale in Silver Spring, Maryland, was selected with the objective of developing a model to predict the assessed value (in $thousands), using the size of the house (in thousands of square feet) and age (in years). The results are stored in Silver Spring .

a. Fit a multiple regression model.

b. Interpret the meaning of the slopes in this model.

c. Predict the mean assessed value for a house that has 2,000 square feet and is 55 years old.

d. Perform a residual analysis on your results and determine whether the regression assumptions are valid.

e. Determine whether there is a significant relationship between assessed value and the two independent variables (house size and age) at the 0.05 level of significance.

f. Determine the p-value in (e) and interpret its meaning.

g. Interpret the meaning of the coefficient of multiple determination in this problem.

h. Determine the adjusted r^2.

i. At the 0.05 level of significance, determine whether each independent variable makes a significant contribution to the regression model. Indicate the most appropriate regression model for this set of data.

j. Determine the p-values in (i) and interpret their meaning.

k. Construct a 95% confidence interval estimate of the population slope between assessed value and the size of the house. How does the interpretation of the slope here differ from that in Problem 13.76 on page 468?

l. Compute and interpret the coefficients of partial determination.

m. What conclusions can you reach about the assessed value?

14.75 Measuring the height of a California redwood tree is very difficult because these trees grow to heights over 300 feet. People familiar with these trees understand that the height of a California redwood tree is related to other characteristics of the tree, including the diameter of the tree at the breast height of a person (in inches) and the thickness of the bark of the tree (in inches). The file Redwood contains the height, diameter at breast height of a person, and bark thickness for a sample of 21 California redwood trees.

a. State the multiple regression equation that predicts the height of a tree, based on the tree's diameter at breast height and the thickness of the bark.

b. Interpret the meaning of the slopes in this equation.

c. Predict the mean height for a tree that has a breast height diameter of 25 inches and a bark thickness of 2 inches.

d. Interpret the meaning of the coefficient of multiple determination in this problem.

e. Perform a residual analysis on the results and determine whether the regression assumptions are valid.

f. Determine whether there is a significant relationship between the height of redwood trees and the two independent variables (breast-height diameter and bark thickness) at the 0.05 level of significance.

g. Construct a 95% confidence interval estimate of the population slope between the height of redwood trees and breast-height diameter and between the height of redwood trees and the bark thickness.

h. At the 0.05 level of significance, determine whether each independent variable makes a significant contribution to the regression model. Indicate the independent variables to include in this model.

i. Construct a 95% confidence interval estimate of the mean height for trees that have a breast-height diameter of 25 inches and a bark thickness of 2 inches, along with a prediction interval for an individual tree.

j. Compute and interpret the coefficients of partial determination.

k. What conclusions can you reach concerning the effect of the diameter of the tree and the thickness of the bark on the height of the tree?

14.76 A sample of 30 houses recently listed for sale in Silver Spring, Maryland, was selected with the objective of developing a model to predict the taxes (in $) based on the assessed value of houses (in $thousands) and the age of the houses (in years) (stored in SilverSpring):

a. State the multiple regression equation.

b. Interpret the meaning of the slopes in this equation.

c. Predict the mean taxes for a house that has an assessed value of $400,000 and is 50 years old.

d. Perform a residual analysis on the results and determine whether the regression assumptions are valid.

e. Determine whether there is a significant relationship between taxes and the two independent variables (assessed value and age) at the 0.05 level of significance.

f. Determine the p-value in (e) and interpret its meaning.

g. Interpret the meaning of the coefficient of multiple determination in this problem.

h. Determine the adjusted r^2.

i. At the 0.05 level of significance, determine whether each independent variable makes a significant contribution to the regression model. Indicate the most appropriate regression model for this set of data.

j. Determine the p-values in (i) and interpret their meaning.

k. Construct a 95% confidence interval estimate of the population slope between taxes and assessed value. How does the interpretation of the slope here differ from that of Problem 13.77 on page 468?

l. Compute and interpret the coefficients of partial determination.

m. The real estate assessor's office has been publicly quoted as saying that the age of a house has no bearing on its taxes. Based on your answers to (a) through (l), do you agree with this statement? Explain.

14.77 A baseball analytics specialist wants to determine which variables are important in predicting a team's wins in a given season. He has collected data related to wins, earned run average (ERA), and runs scored per game for the 2014 season (stored in Baseball). Develop a model to predict the number of wins based on ERA and runs scored per game.

a. State the multiple regression equation.

b. Interpret the meaning of the slopes in this equation.

c. Predict the mean number of wins for a team that has an ERA of 4.50 and has scored 4.6 runs per game.

d. Perform a residual analysis on the results and determine whether the regression assumptions are valid.

e. Is there a significant relationship between the number of wins and the two independent variables (ERA and runs scored per game) at the 0.05 level of significance?

f. Determine the p-value in (e) and interpret its meaning.

g. Interpret the meaning of the coefficient of multiple determination in this problem.

h. Determine the adjusted r^2.

i. At the 0.05 level of significance, determine whether each independent variable makes a significant contribution to the regression model. Indicate the most appropriate regression model for this set of data.

j. Determine the p-values in (i) and interpret their meaning.

k. Construct a 95% confidence interval estimate of the population slope between wins and ERA.

l. Compute and interpret the coefficients of partial determination.

m. Which is more important in predicting wins—pitching, as measured by ERA, or offense, as measured by runs scored per game? Explain.

14.78 Referring to Problem 14.77, suppose that in addition to using ERA to predict the number of wins, the analytics specialist wants to include the league (0 = American, 1 = National) as an independent variable. Develop a model to predict wins based on ERA and league. For (a) through (k), do not include an interaction term.

a. State the multiple regression equation.

b. Interpret the slopes in (a).

c. Predict the mean number of wins for a team with an ERA of 4.50 in the American League.

d. Perform a residual analysis on the results and determine whether the regression assumptions are valid.

e. Is there a significant relationship between wins and the two independent variables (ERA and league) at the 0.05 level of significance?

f. At the 0.05 level of significance, determine whether each independent variable makes a contribution to the regression model. Indicate the most appropriate regression model for this set of data.

g. Construct a 95% confidence interval estimate of the population slope for the relationship between wins and ERA.

h. Construct a 95% confidence interval estimate of the population slope for the relationship between wins and league.

i. Compute and interpret the adjusted r^2.

j. Compute and interpret the coefficients of partial determination.

k. What assumption do you have to make about the slope of wins with ERA?

. Add an interaction term to the model and, at the 0.05 level of significance, determine whether it makes a significant contribution to the model.

n. On the basis of the results of (f) and (l), which model is most appropriate? Explain.

14.79 You are a real estate broker who wants to compare property values in Glen Cove and Roslyn (which are located approximately 8 miles apart). In order to do so, you will analyze the data in `GCRoslyn`, a file that includes samples of houses from Glen Cove and Roslyn. Making sure to include the dummy variable for location (Glen Cove or Roslyn), develop a regression model to predict fair market value, based on the land area of a property, the age of a house, and location. Be sure to determine whether any interaction terms need to be included in the model.

14.80 A recent article discussed a metal deposition process in which a piece of metal is placed in an acid bath and an alloy is layered on top of it. The business objective of engineers working on the process was to reduce variation in the thickness of the alloy layer. To begin, the temperature and the pressure in the tank holding the acid bath are to be studied as independent variables. Data are collected from 50 samples. The results are organized and stored in `Thickness`. (Data extracted from J. Conklin, "It's a Marathon, Not a Sprint," *Quality Progress*, June 2009, pp. 46–49.)

Develop a multiple regression model that uses temperature and the pressure in the tank holding the acid bath to predict the thickness of the alloy layer. Be sure to perform a thorough residual analysis. The article suggests that there is a significant interaction between the pressure and the temperature in the tank. Do you agree?

14.81 Starbucks Coffee Co. uses a data-based approach to improving the quality and customer satisfaction of its products. When survey data indicated that Starbucks needed to improve its package sealing process, an experiment was conducted to determine the factors in the bag-sealing equipment that might be affecting the ease of opening the bag without tearing the inner liner of the bag. (Data extracted from L. Johnson and S. Burrows, "For Starbucks, It's in the Bag," *Quality Progress*, March 2011, pp. 17–23.) Among the factors that could affect the rating of the ability of the bag to resist tears were the viscosity, pressure, and plate gap on the bag-sealing equipment.

Data were collected on 19 bags in which the plate gap was varied and stored in `Starbucks`. Develop a multiple regression model that uses the viscosity, pressure, and plate gap on the bag-sealing equipment to predict the tear rating of the bag. Be sure to perform a thorough residual analysis. Do you think that you need to use all three independent variables in the model? Explain.

14.82 An experiment was conducted to study the extrusion process of biodegradable packaging foam (data extracted from W. Y. Koh, K. M. Eskridge, and M. A. Hanna, "Supersaturated Split-Plot Designs," *Journal of Quality Technology*, 45, January 2013, pp. 61–72). Among the factors considered for their effect on the unit density (mg/ml) were the die temperature (145°C versus 155°C) and the die diameter (3 mm versus 4 mm). The results were stored in `PackagingFoam3`. Develop a multiple regression model that uses die temperature and die diameter to predict the unit density (mg/ml). Be sure to perform a thorough residual analysis. Do you think that you need to use both independent variables in the model? Explain.

14.83 Referring to Problem 14.82, instead of predicting the unit density, you now wish to predict the foam diameter from results stored in `PackagingFoam4`. Develop a multiple regression model that uses die temperature and die diameter to predict the foam diameter (mg/ml). Be sure to perform a thorough residual analysis. Do you think that you need to use both independent variables in the model? Explain.

CHAPTER

14

▾CASES

Managing Ashland MultiComm Services

In its continuing study of the *3-For-All* subscription solicitation process, a marketing department team wants to test the effects of two types of structured sales presentations (personal formal and personal informal) and the number of hours spent on telemarketing on the number of new subscriptions. The staff has recorded these data for the past 24 weeks in `AMS14`.

Analyze these data and develop a multiple regression model to predict the number of new subscriptions for a week, based on the number of hours spent on telemarketing and the sales presentation type. Write a report, giving detailed findings concerning the regression model used.

Digital Case

Apply your knowledge of multiple regression models in this Digital Case, which extends the OmniFoods Using Statistics scenario from this chapter.

To ensure a successful test marketing of its OmniPower energy bars, the OmniFoods marketing department has contracted with In-Store Placements Group (ISPG), a merchandising consulting firm. ISPG will work with the grocery store chain that is conducting the test-market study. Using the same 34-store sample used in the test-market study, ISPG claims that the choice of shelf location and the presence of in-store OmniPower coupon dispensers both increase sales of the energy bars.

Open **Omni_ISPGMemo.pdf** to review the ISPG claims and supporting data. Then answer the following questions:

1. Are the supporting data consistent with ISPG's claims? Perform an appropriate statistical analysis to confirm (or discredit) the stated relationship between sales and the two independent variables of product shelf location and the presence of in-store OmniPower coupon dispensers.

2. If you were advising OmniFoods, would you recommend using a specific shelf location and in-store coupon dispensers to sell OmniPower bars?

3. What additional data would you advise collecting in order to determine the effectiveness of the sales promotion techniques used by ISPG?

▾EXCEL GUIDE

EG14.1 DEVELOPING a MULTIPLE REGRESSION MODEL

Interpreting the Regression Coefficients

Key Technique Use the **LINEST**(*cell range of Y variable, cell range of X variables*, **True**, **True**) function to compute the regression coefficients and related values.

Example Develop the Figure 14.1 multiple regression model for the OmniPower sales data shown on page 478.

PHStat Use **Multiple Regression**.
For the example, open to the **DATA worksheet** of the **OmniPower workbook**. Select **PHStat → Regression → Multiple Regression**, and in the procedure's dialog box (shown below):

1. Enter **A1:A35** as the **Y Variable Cell Range**.
2. Enter **B1:C35** as the **X Variables Cell Range**.
3. Check **First cells in both ranges contain label**.
4. Enter **95** as the **Confidence level for regression coefficients**.
5. Check **Regression Statistics Table** and **ANOVA and Coefficients Table**.
6. Enter a **Title** and click **OK**.

The procedure creates a worksheet that contains a copy of your data in addition to the Figure 14.1 worksheet.

Workbook Use the **COMPUTE worksheet** of the **Multiple Regression workbook** as a template.
For the example, the COMPUTE worksheet already uses the OmniPower sales data in the MRData worksheet to perform the regression analysis.

To perform multiple regression analyses for other data with two independent variables, paste the regression data into the MRData worksheet, using column A for the *Y* variable data and subsequent columns, starting with B, for the *X* variable data. Then, open to the COMPUTE worksheet and:

1. Enter the **confidence level** in cell **L8**.
2. Edit the *array formula* in the cell range **L2:N6** to reflect the cell ranges of the data for the new *Y* and the new *X* variables.

Edited cell ranges for the new variable data should start with row 2 so as to exclude the row 1 variable names, an exception to the usual practice in this book. If you have more than two independent variables, select, in step 2, a range wider than L2:N6, adding a column for each independent variable in excess of two. For example, with three independent variables, you would select the cell range **L2:O6**.

3. Edit the labels in cells **K2** and **K3**.
4. Edit the ANOVA table formulas in columns **B** and **C**.
5. Select cell range **D18:I18**, right-click and select **Insert**. Repeat for as many times as necessary.
6. Select cell range **D17:I17** and copy down through all the rows of the ANOVA table (blank and nonblank).

To simplify your use of Excel, consider using the *PHStat* or *Analysis ToolPak* instructions when your problem includes many *X* independent variables.

Analysis ToolPak Use **Regression**.
For the example, open to the **DATA worksheet** of the **OmniPower workbook** and:

1. Select **Data → Data Analysis**.
2. In the Data Analysis dialog box, select **Regression** from the **Analysis Tools** list and then click **OK**.

In the Regression dialog box (shown on page 518):

3. Enter **A1:A35** as the **Input Y Range** and enter **B1:C35** as the **Input X Range**.
4. Check **Labels** and check **Confidence Level** and enter **95** in its box.
5. Click **New Worksheet Ply**.
6. Click **OK**.

Predicting the Dependent Variable Y

Key Technique Use the **MMULT** array function and the **T.INV.2T** function to help compute intermediate values that determine the confidence interval estimate and prediction interval.

Example Compute the Figure 14.2 confidence interval estimate and prediction interval for the OmniPower sales data shown on page 479.

PHStat Use the *PHStat* "Interpreting the Regression Coefficients" instructions but replace step 6 with the following steps 6 through 8:

6. Check **Confidence Interval Estimate & Prediction Interval** and enter **95** as the percentage for **Confidence level for intervals**.
7. Enter a **Title** and click **OK**.
8. In the new worksheet, enter **79** in cell **B6** and enter **400** in cell **B7**.

These steps create a new worksheet that is discussed in the following *Workbook* instructions.

Workbook Use the **CIEandPI worksheet** of the **Multiple Regression workbook** as a template.

The worksheet already contains the data and formulas for the example.

For other problems with two independent variables, paste the regression data for the independent variables into columns B and C of the **MRArray worksheet** and:

1. Adjust the number of entries in column A, all of which are 1, to match the number of rows of the new data.
2. Use the "Interpreting the Regression Coefficients" *Worksheet* instructions to edit the COMPUTE worksheet to reflect the new data.
3. Open to the CIEandPI worksheet and edit the array formula in cell range **B9:D11** and the labels in cells **A6** and **A7** to reflect the new data.

Cell ranges in the array formula should start with row 2 so as to exclude the row 1 variable names, an exception to the usual practice in this book.

To see the formulas that the CIEandPI worksheet uses that are not shown in Figure 14.4, open to the CIEandPI_FORMULAS worksheet.

EG14.2 r^2, ADJUSTED r^2, and the OVERALL *F* TEST

The coefficient of multiple determination, r^2, the adjusted r^2, and the overall *F* test are all computed as part of creating the multiple regression results worksheet using the Section EG14.1 instructions.

The *PHStat* or *Workbook* instructions use formulas to compute these results in the **COMPUTE worksheet**. Formulas in cells B5, B7, B13, C12, C13, D12, and E12 copy values computed by the array formula in cell range L2:N6. In cell F12, the expression **F.DIST.RT(*F test statistic*, 1, *error degrees of freedom*)** computes the *p*-value for the overall *F* test.

EG14.3 RESIDUAL ANALYSIS for the MULTIPLE REGRESSION MODEL

Key Technique Use arithmetic formulas and some results from the multiple regression COMPUTE worksheet to compute residuals.

Example Perform the residual analysis for the OmniPower sales data discussed in Section 14.3, starting on page 484.

PHStat Use the Section EG14.1 "Interpreting the Regression Coefficients" *PHStat* instructions. Modify step 5 by checking **Residuals Table** and **Residual Plots** in addition to checking **Regression Statistics Table** and **ANOVA and Coefficients Table.**

Workbook Use the **RESIDUALS worksheet** of the **Multiple Regression workbook** as a template. Then construct residual plots for the residuals and the predicted value of *Y* and for the residuals and each of the independent variables.

For the example, the RESIDUALS worksheet uses the OmniPower sales data already in the **MRData worksheet** to compute the residuals. To compute residuals for other data, first use the EG14.1 "Interpreting the Regression Coefficients" *Workbook* instructions to modify the MRData and COMPUTE worksheets. Then, open to the **RESIDUALS worksheet** and:

1. If the number of independent variables is greater than 2, select column D, right-click, and click **Insert** from the shortcut menu. Repeat this step as many times as necessary to create the additional columns to hold all the *X* variables.
2. Paste the data for the *X* variables into columns, starting with column B and paste the *Y* values into the second-to-last column (column E if there are two *X* variables).

3. For sample sizes smaller than 34, delete the extra rows. For sample sizes greater than 34, copy the predicted *Y* and residuals formulas down through the row containing the last pair of *X* and *Y* values. Also, add the new observation numbers in column A.

To construct the residual plots, open to the RESIDUALS worksheet and select pairs of columns and then use the EG2.5 "The Scatter Plot" *Workbook* instructions. For example, to construct the residual plot for the residuals and the predicted value of *Y*, select columns D and F. (See Appendix B for help in selecting a noncontiguous cell range.)

To see the formulas that the RESIDUAL worksheet uses, open to the RESIDUALS_FORMULAS worksheet.

Analysis ToolPak Use the Section EG14.1 *Analysis Tool-Pak* instructions. Modify step 5 by checking **Residuals** and **Residual Plots** before clicking **New Worksheet Ply** and then **OK**. The **Residuals Plots** option constructs residual plots only for each independent variable. To construct a plot of the residuals and the predicted value of *Y*, select the predicted and residuals cells (in the RESIDUAL OUTPUT area of the regression results worksheet) and then apply the Section EG2.5 *In-Depth Excel* "The Scatter Plot" instructions.

EG14.4 INFERENCES CONCERNING the POPULATION REGRESSION COEFFICIENTS

The regression results worksheets created by using the Section EG14.1 instructions include the information needed to make the inferences discussed in Section 14.4.

EG14.5 TESTING PORTIONS of the MULTIPLE REGRESSION MODEL

Key Technique Adapt the Section EG14.1 "Interpreting the Regression Coefficients" instructions.

Example Test portions of the multiple regression model for the OmniPower sales data as discussed in Section 14.5, starting on page 489.

PHStat Use the Section EG14.1 *PHStat* "Interpreting the Regression Coefficients" instructions but modify step 6 by checking **Coefficients of Partial Determination** before you click **OK**.

Workbook Use one of the **CPD worksheets** of the **Multiple Regression workbook** as a template.

For the example, the **CPD_2 worksheet** already contains the data to compute the coefficients of partial determination.

For other problems, first use the EG14.1 "Interpreting the Regression Coefficients" and EG13.2 *Worksheet* instructions to create all possible regression results worksheets. For example, if you have two independent variables, you perform three regression analyses: *Y* with X_1 and X_2, *Y* with X_1, and *Y* with X_2, to create three regression results worksheets. Then, open to the **CPD worksheet** for the number of independent variables and follow the instructions in the worksheet to transfer values from the regression results worksheets you just created.

EG14.6 USING DUMMY VARIABLES and INTERACTION TERMS in REGRESSION MODELS

Dummy Variables

Key Technique Use **Find and Replace** to create a dummy variable from a two-level categorical variable. Before using **Find and Replace**, copy and paste the categorical values to another column in order to preserve the original values.

Example From the two-level categorical variable Fireplace, create the dummy variable named FireplaceCoded that is used in the Figure 14.9 regression model on page 496.

Workbook For the example, open to the **DATA worksheet** of the **SilverSpring workbook** and:

1. Copy and paste the **Fireplace** values in column **I** to **column J** (the first empty column). Enter **FireplaceCoded** in **cell J1**.
2. Select **column J**.
3. Press **Ctrl+H** (the keyboard shortcut for **Find and Replace**).

In the Find and Replace dialog box:

4. Enter **Yes** in the **Find what** box and enter **1** in the **Replace with** box.
5. Click **Replace All**. If a message box to confirm the replacement appears, click **OK** to continue.
6. Enter **No** in the **Find what** box and enter **0** in the **Replace with** box.
7. Click **Replace All**. If a message box to confirm the replacement appears, click **OK** to continue.
8. Click **Close**.

Categorical variables that have more than two levels require the use of formulas in multiple columns. For example, to create the dummy variables for Example 14.3 on page 497, two columns are needed. Assume that the three-level categorical variable mentioned in the example is in Column D of the opened worksheet. A first new column that contains formulas in the form = **IF**(*column D cell* = *first level*, **1, 0**) and a second new column that contains formulas in the form = **IF**(*column D cell* = *second level*, **1, 0**) would properly create the two dummy variables that the example requires.

Interactions

To create an interaction term, add a column of formulas that multiply one independent variable by another. For example, if the first independent variable appeared in column B and the second independent variable appeared in column C, enter the formula = **B2 * C2** in the row 2 cell of an empty new column and then copy the formula down through all rows of data to create the interaction.

EG14.7 LOGISTIC REGRESSION

Key Technique Use an automated process that incorporates the use of the Solver add-in to develop a logistic regression analysis model.

Example Develop the Figure 14.13 logistic regression model for the credit card pilot study data shown on page 506.

PHStat Use **Logistic Regression**.
For the example, open to the **DATA worksheet** of the **Card-Study workbook**. Select **PHStat → Regression → Logistic Regression**, and in the procedure's dialog box:

1. Enter **A1:A31** as the **Y Variable Cell Range**.
2. Enter **B1:C31** as the **X Variables Cell Range**.
3. Check **First cells in both ranges contain label**.
4. Enter a **Title** and click **OK**.

If the Solver add-in is not installed (see Appendix Section D.6), PHStat will display an error message instead of the Logistic Regression dialog box.

Workbook Use the **Logistic Regression add-in workbook**. *The Excel Solver add-in must be installed before using this add-in workbook* (see Appendix D).

For the example, the **COMPUTE worksheet** of the **Logistic Model workbook** already contains the logistic regression model. For other problems:

1. Open to the worksheet that contains the data for the problem. The worksheet *must* be part of a workbook saved in the current **.xlsx** format (not the older **.xls** format).
2. Open the Logistic Regression add-in workbook (as you would open any other Excel file).

If the add-in workbook opens properly, it adds a Logistic Add-in menu to the Add-ins tab in Microsoft Windows Excel or to the Apple menu bar in OS X Excel.

3. Select **Logistic Add-in → Logistic Regression**.

In the Logistic Regression dialog box, identical to the PHStat dialog box shown in the left column, follow steps 1 through 4 of the *PHStat* instructions for this section.

Multiple Regression Model Building

OBJECTIVES

- How to use quadratic terms in a regression model

- How to use transformed variables in a regression model

- Measure the correlation among independent variables

- Build a regression model using either the step-wise or best-subsets approach

- Avoid the pitfalls involved in developing a multiple regression model

▼USING **STATISTICS**
Valuing Parsimony at WSTA-TV

Your job as the broadcast operations manager at local station WSTA-TV has proven more challenging of late, as you adjust to initiatives that have been announced by the station's new owners. To meet the new business objective of reducing expenses by 8% during the next fiscal year, you seek to investigate ways to reduce unnecessary labor expenses associated with the staff of graphic artists employed by the station. Currently, these graphic artists receive hourly pay for a significant number of *standby hours*, hours for which they are present at the station but not assigned any specific task to do.

You believe that an appropriate model will help you to predict the number of future standby hours, identify the root causes of excessive numbers of standby hours, and allow you to reduce the total number of future standby hours. You plan to first collect weekly data for the number of standby hours and these four variables: the number of graphic artists present, the number of remote hours, the number of Dubner (broadcast graphics) hours, and the total labor hours. Then, you seek to build a multiple regression model that will help determine which variables most heavily affect standby hours.

How do you build the model that has the most appropriate mix of independent variables? Are there statistical techniques that can help you identify a "best" model without having to consider all possible models?

The simple regression model and the multiple regression models that Chapters 13 and 14 discuss assume a linear relationship between the dependent Y variable and each independent X variable. As Section 13.1 notes, nonlinear relationships are possible, too. This chapter discusses nonlinear regression models and then presents the methods that help you efficiently develop the best model for any set of data. These methods are particularly useful when building a regression model for a set of data that has many independent variables, such as the data to be collected at WSTA-TV.

15.1 Quadratic Regression Model

The curvilinear relationship in which the value of the dependent Y variable increases (or decreases) at a *changing* rate as the value of X changes is one of the most common nonlinear relationships. Panels D and E in Figure 13.1 as examples of curvilinear relationships that also quadratic relationships. You use the quadratic regression model that Equation (15.1) defines to analyze such relationships between X and Y.

QUADRATIC REGRESSION MODEL

$$Y_i = \beta_0 + \beta_1 X_{1i} + \beta_2 X_{1i}^2 + \varepsilon_i \qquad (15.1)$$

where

$\beta_0 = Y$ intercept

$\beta_1 = $ coefficient of the linear effect on Y

$\beta_2 = $ coefficient of the quadratic effect on Y

$\varepsilon_i = $ random error in Y for observation i

The **quadratic regression model** is similar to the multiple regression model with two independent variables [see Equation (14.2) on page 477 defines. However, in a quadratic model, the second independent variable, called the **quadratic term**, is the square of the first independent variable. As with a multiple regression model, you use the least-squares method to compute sample regression coefficients (b_0, b_1, and b_2) as estimates of the population parameters (β_0, β_1, and β_2). Equation (15.2) defines the regression equation for the quadratic model with an independent variable (X_1) and a dependent variable (Y).

studentTIP

A quadratic regression model has an X term and an X squared term. Other curvilinear models can have additional X terms that might involve X cubed, X raised to the fourth power, and so on.

QUADRATIC REGRESSION EQUATION

$$\hat{Y}_i = b_0 + b_1 X_{1i} + b_2 X_{1i}^2 \qquad (15.2)$$

In Equation (15.2), the first regression coefficient, b_0, represents the Y intercept; the second regression coefficient, b_1, represents the linear effect; and the third regression coefficient, b_2, represents the quadratic effect.

Finding the Regression Coefficients and Predicting Y

To illustrate the quadratic regression model, consider a study that examined the business problem facing a concrete supplier of how adding fly ash affects the strength of concrete. (Fly ash is an inexpensive industrial waste by-product that can be used as a substitute for Portland cement, a more expensive ingredient of concrete.) Batches of concrete were prepared in which the percentage of fly ash ranged from 0% to 60%. Data were collected from a sample of 18 batches and organized and stored in FlyAsh . Table 15.1 summarizes the results.

TABLE 15.1
Fly Ash Percentage and Strength of 18 Batches of 28-Day-Old Concrete

Fly Ash %	Strength (psi)	Fly Ash %	Strength (psi)
0	4,779	40	5,995
0	4,706	40	5,628
0	4,350	40	5,897
20	5,189	50	5,746
20	5,140	50	5,719
20	4,976	50	5,782
30	5,110	60	4,895
30	5,685	60	5,030
30	5,618	60	4,648

By creating the scatter plot in Figure 15.1 to visualize these data, you will be better able to select the proper model for expressing the relationship between fly ash percentage and strength.

FIGURE 15.1
Scatter plot of fly ash percentage (X) and strength (Y)

Figure 15.1 indicates an initial increase in the strength of the concrete as the percentage of fly ash increases. The strength appears to level off and then drop after achieving maximum strength at about 40% fly ash. Strength for 50% fly ash is slightly below strength at 40%, but strength at 60% fly ash is substantially below strength at 50%. Therefore, you should fit a quadratic model, not a linear model, to estimate strength based on fly ash percentage.

From Figure 15.2, which shows the Excel results for these data, the regression coefficients are

$$b_0 = 4{,}486.3611 \quad b_1 = 63.0052 \quad b_2 = -0.8765$$

Therefore, the quadratic regression equation is

$$\hat{Y}_i = 4{,}486.3611 + 63.0052X_{1i} - 0.8765X_{1i}^2$$

where

$\hat{Y}_i$ = predicted strength for sample i

X_{1i} = percentage of fly ash for sample i

FIGURE 15.2

Excel multiple regression quadratic model worksheet results for the concrete strength data

	A	B	C	D	E	F	G
1	Concrete Strength Analysis						
2							
3	*Regression Statistics*						
4	Multiple R	0.8053					
5	R Square	0.6485					
6	Adjusted R Square	0.6016					
7	Standard Error	312.1129					
8	Observations	18					
9							
10	ANOVA						
11		*df*	*SS*	*MS*	*F*	*Significance F*	
12	Regression	2	2695473.4897	1347736.745	13.8351	0.0004	
13	Residual	15	1461217.0103	97414.4674			
14	Total	17	4156690.5000				
15							
16		*Coefficients*	*Standard Error*	*t Stat*	*P-value*	*Lower 95%*	*Upper 95%*
17	Intercept	4486.3611	174.7531	25.6726	0.0000	4113.8834	4858.8389
18	Fly Ash%	63.0052	12.3725	5.0923	0.0001	36.6338	89.3767
19	Fly Ash% ^2	-0.8765	0.1966	-4.4578	0.0005	-1.2955	-0.4574

In the Worksheet

This worksheet uses the same template as the Figure 14.1 worksheet on page 478. The three regression coefficients are in cells B17, B18, and B19.

Figure 15.3 is a scatter plot of this quadratic regression equation that shows the fit of the quadratic regression model to the original data.

FIGURE 15.3

Scatter plot showing the quadratic relationship between fly ash percentage and strength for the concrete data

Scatter Plot of Fly Ash % and Strength

$y = -0.8765x^2 + 63.005x + 4486.4$

From the quadratic regression equation and Figure 15.3, the Y intercept ($b_0 = 4,486.3611$) is the predicted strength when the percentage of fly ash is 0. To interpret the coefficients b_1 and b_2, observe that after an initial increase, strength decreases as fly ash percentage increases. This nonlinear relationship is further demonstrated by predicting the strength for fly ash percentages of 20, 40, and 60. Using the quadratic regression equation,

$$\hat{Y}_i = 4,486.3611 + 63.0052X_{1i} - 0.8765X_{1i}^2$$

for $X_{1i} = 20$,

$$\hat{Y}_i = 4,486.3611 + 63.0052(20) - 0.8765(20)^2 = 5,395.865$$

for $X_{1i} = 40$,

$$\hat{Y}_i = 4,486.3611 + 63.0052(40) - 0.8765(40)^2 = 5,604.169$$

and for $X_{1i} = 60$,

$$\hat{Y}_i = 4,486.3611 + 63.0052(60) - 0.8765(60)^2 = 5,111.273$$

Thus, the predicted concrete strength for 40% fly ash is 208.304 psi above the predicted strength for 20% fly ash, but the predicted strength for 60% fly ash is 492.896 psi below the predicted strength for 40% fly ash. The concrete supplier should consider using a fly ash percentage of 40% and not using fly ash percentages of 20% or 60% because those percentages lead to reduced concrete strength.

Testing for the Significance of the Quadratic Model

After you calculate the quadratic regression equation, you can test whether there is a significant overall relationship between strength, Y, and fly ash percentage, X_1. The null and alternative hypotheses are as follows:

$H_0: \beta_1 = \beta_2 = 0$ (There is no overall relationship between X_1 and Y.)
$H_1: \beta_1$ and/or $\beta_2 \neq 0$ (There is an overall relationship between X_1 and Y.)

Equation (14.6) on page 482 defines the overall F_{STAT} test statistic used for this test:

$$F_{STAT} = \frac{MSR}{MSE}$$

From the Figure 15.2 results on page 524,

$$F_{STAT} = \frac{MSR}{MSE} = \frac{1,347,736.745}{97,414.4674} = 13.8351$$

If you choose a level of significance of 0.05, from Table E.5, the critical value of the F distribution, with 2 and $18 - 2 - 1 = 15$ degrees of freedom, is 3.68 (see Figure 15.4). Because $F_{STAT} = 13.8351 > 3.68$, or because the p-value $= 0.0004 < 0.05$, you reject the null hypothesis (H_0) and conclude that there is a significant overall relationship between strength and fly ash percentage.

FIGURE 15.4
Testing for the existence of the overall relationship at the 0.05 level of significance, with 2 and 15 degrees of freedom

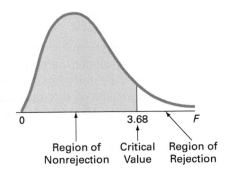

Testing the Quadratic Effect

In using a regression model to examine a relationship between two variables, you want to find not only the most accurate model but also the simplest model that expresses that relationship. Therefore, you need to examine whether there is a significant difference between the quadratic model:

$$Y_i = \beta_0 + \beta_1 X_{1i} + \beta_2 X_{1i}^2 + \varepsilon_i$$

and the linear model:

$$Y_i = \beta_0 + \beta_1 X_{1i} + \varepsilon_i$$

In Section 14.4, you used the t test to determine whether each independent variable makes a significant contribution to the regression model. To test the significance of the contribution of the quadratic effect, you use the following null and alternative hypotheses:

H_0: Including the quadratic effect does not significantly improve the model $(\beta_2 = 0)$.
H_1: Including the quadratic effect significantly improves the model $(\beta_2 \neq 0)$.

The standard error of each regression coefficient and its corresponding t_{STAT} test statistic are part of the regression results shown in Figure 15.2 on page 524. Equation (14.7) on page 480 defines the t_{STAT} test statistic:

$$t_{STAT} = \frac{b_2 - \beta_2}{S_{b_2}}$$

$$= \frac{-0.8765 - 0}{0.1966} = -4.4578$$

If you select the 0.05 level of significance, then from Table E.3, the critical values for the t distribution with 15 degrees of freedom are -2.1315 and $+2.1315$ (see Figure 15.5).

FIGURE 15.5

Testing for the contribution of the quadratic effect to a regression model at the 0.05 level of significance, with 15 degrees of freedom

-2.1315	0	$+2.1315$	t
Region of Rejection	Critical Value	Region of Nonrejection	Critical Value	Region of Rejection

Because $t_{STAT} = -4.4578 < -2.1315$ or because the p-value $= 0.0005 < 0.05$, you reject H_0 and conclude that the quadratic model is significantly better than the linear model for representing the relationship between strength and fly ash percentage.

Example 15.1 provides an additional illustration of a possible quadratic effect.

EXAMPLE 15.1

Studying the Quadratic Effect in a Multiple Regression Model

A real estate developer studying the business problem of estimating the consumption of heating oil by single-family houses has decided to examine the effect of atmospheric temperature and the amount of attic insulation on heating oil consumption. Data are collected from a random sample of 15 single-family houses. The data are organized and stored in **HeatingOil**. Figure 15.6 shows the regression results for a multiple regression model using the two independent variables: atmospheric temperature and attic insulation.

FIGURE 15.6

Excel multiple regression linear model worksheet results for predicting monthly consumption of heating oil

	A	B	C	D	E	F	G
1	**Heating Oil Consumption Analysis**						
2							
3	**Regression Statistics**						
4	Multiple R	0.9827					
5	R Square	0.9656					
6	Adjusted R Square	0.9599					
7	Standard Error	26.0138					
8	Observations	15					
9							
10	ANOVA						
11		*df*	*SS*	*MS*	*F*	*Significance F*	
12	Regression	2	228014.6263	114007.3132	168.4712	0.0000	
13	Residual	12	8120.6030	676.7169			
14	Total	14	236135.2293				
15							
16		*Coefficients*	*Standard Error*	*t Stat*	*P-value*	*Lower 95%*	*Upper 95%*
17	Intercept	562.1510	21.0931	26.6509	0.0000	516.1931	608.1089
18	Temperature	-5.4366	0.3362	-16.1699	0.0000	-6.1691	-4.7040
19	Insulation	-20.0123	2.3425	-8.5431	0.0000	-25.1162	-14.9084

The residual plot for attic insulation (not shown here) contained some evidence of a quadratic effect. Thus, the real estate developer reanalyzed the data by adding a quadratic term for attic insulation to the multiple regression model. At the 0.05 level of significance, is there evidence of a significant quadratic effect for attic insulation?

SOLUTION Figure 15.7 shows the results for this regression model.

FIGURE 15.7
Excel worksheet results for the multiple regression model with a quadratic term for attic insulation

	A	B	C	D	E	F	G
1	Quadratic Effect for Insulation Variable?						
2							
3	*Regression Statistics*						
4	Multiple R	0.9862					
5	R Square	0.9725					
6	Adjusted R Square	0.9650					
7	Standard Error	24.2938					
8	Observations	15					
9							
10	ANOVA						
11		*df*	*SS*	*MS*	*F*	*Significance F*	
12	Regression	3	229643.1645	76547.7215	129.7006	0.0000	
13	Residual	11	6492.0649	590.1877			
14	Total	14	236135.2293				
15							
16		*Coefficients*	*Standard Error*	*t Stat*	*P-value*	*Lower 95%*	*Upper 95%*
17	Intercept	624.5864	42.4352	14.7186	0.0000	531.1872	717.9856
18	Temperature	-5.3626	0.3171	-16.9099	0.0000	-6.0606	-4.6646
19	Insulation	-44.5868	14.9547	-2.9815	0.0125	-77.5019	-11.6717
20	Insulation ^2	1.8667	1.1238	1.6611	0.1249	-0.6067	4.3401

The multiple regression equation is

$$\hat{Y}_i = 624.5864 - 5.3626X_{1i} - 44.5868X_{2i} + 1.8667X_{2i}^2$$

To test for the significance of the quadratic effect:

H_0: Including the quadratic effect of insulation does not significantly improve the model $(\beta_3 = 0)$.

H_1: Including the quadratic effect of insulation significantly improves the model $(\beta_3 \neq 0)$.

From Figure 15.7 and Table E.3 with $15 - 3 - 1 = 11$ degrees of freedom, $-2.2010 < t_{STAT} = 1.6611 < 2.2010$ (or the p-value $= 0.1249 > 0.05$). Therefore, you do not reject the null hypothesis. You conclude that there is insufficient evidence that the quadratic effect for attic insulation is different from zero. In the interest of keeping the model as simple as possible, you should use the multiple regression equation shown in Figure 15.6:

$$\hat{Y}_i = 562.1510 - 5.4366X_{1i} - 20.0123X_{2i}$$

The Coefficient of Multiple Determination

studentTIP

For the case of quadratic regression, r^2 represents the proportion of the variation in the dependent variable Y that is explained by the linear term and the quadratic term.

In the multiple regression model, the coefficient of multiple determination, r^2 (see Section 14.2), represents the proportion of variation in Y that is explained by variation in the independent variables. Consider the quadratic regression model you used to predict the strength of concrete using fly ash and fly ash squared. You compute r^2 by using Equation (14.4) on page 481:

$$r^2 = \frac{SSR}{SST}$$

From Figure 15.2 on page 481,

$$SSR = 2,695,473.4897 \qquad SST = 4,156,690.5$$

Thus,

$$r^2 = \frac{SSR}{SST} = \frac{2,695,473.4897}{4,156,690.5} = 0.6485$$

This coefficient of multiple determination indicates that 64.85% of the variation in strength is explained by the quadratic relationship between strength and the percentage of fly ash. You should also compute r_{adj}^2 to account for the number of independent variables and the sample size. In the quadratic regression model, $k = 2$ because there are two independent variables, X_1 and X_1^2. Thus, using Equation (14.5) on page 482,

$$
\begin{aligned}
r_{adj}^2 &= 1 - \left[(1 - r^2)\frac{(n-1)}{(n-k-1)} \right] \\
&= 1 - \left[(1 - 0.6485)\frac{17}{15} \right] \\
&= 1 - 0.3984 \\
&= 0.6016
\end{aligned}
$$

PROBLEMS FOR SECTION 15.1

LEARNING THE BASICS

15.1 The following is the quadratic regression equation for a sample of $n = 25$:

$$\hat{Y}_i = 5 + 3X_{1i} + 1.5X_{1i}^2$$

a. Predict Y for $X_1 = 2$.
b. Suppose that the computed t_{STAT} test statistic for the quadratic regression coefficient is 2.35. At the 0.05 level of significance, is there evidence that the quadratic model is better than the linear model?
c. Suppose that the computed t_{STAT} test statistic for the quadratic regression coefficient is 1.17. At the 0.05 level of significance, is there evidence that the quadratic model is better than the linear model?
d. Suppose the regression coefficient for the linear effect is −3.0. Predict Y for $X_1 = 2$.

APPLYING THE CONCEPTS

15.2 Businesses actively recruit business students with well-developed higher-order cognitive skills (HOCS) such as problem identification, analytical reasoning, and content integration skills. Researchers conducted a study to see if improvement in students' HOCS was related to the students' GPA. (Data extracted from R. V. Bradley, C. S. Sankar, H. R. Clayton, V. W. Mbarika, and P. K. Raju, "A Study on the Impact of GPA on Perceived Improvement of Higher-Order Cognitive Skills," *Decision Sciences Journal of Innovative Education*, January 2007, 5(1), pp. 151–168.) The researchers conducted a study in which business students were taught using the case study method. Using data collected from 300 business students, the following quadratic regression equation was derived:

$$\text{HOCS} = -3.48 + 4.53(\text{GPA}) - 0.68(\text{GPA})^2$$

where the dependent variable HOCS measured the improvement in higher-order cognitive skills, with 1 being the lowest improvement in HOCS and 5 being the highest improvement in HOCS.
a. Construct a table of predicted HOCS, using GPA equal to 2.0, 2.1, 2.2, . . . , 4.0.
b. Plot the values in the table constructed in (a), with GPA on the horizontal axis and predicted HOCS on the vertical axis.

c. Discuss the curvilinear relationship between students' GPA and their predicted improvement in HOCS.
d. The researchers reported that the model had an r^2 of 0.07 and an adjusted r^2 of 0.06. What does this tell you about the scatter of individual HOCS scores around the curvilinear relationship plotted in (b) and discussed in (c)?

15.3 A study was conducted on automobile engines to examine the relationship between engine speed measured in revolutions per minute (RPM) and engine torque with the goal of predicting engine torque. (Data extracted from Y. Chen *et al.*, "Cluster-Based Profile Analysis in Phase I," *Journal of Quality Technology*, 47, January 2015, and stored in `Engines` .)
a. Construct a scatter plot for RPM and torque.
b. Fit a quadratic regression model and state the quadratic regression equation.
c. Predict the mean torque for an RPM of 3,000.
d. Perform a residual analysis on the results and determine whether the regression assumptions are valid.
e. At the 0.05 level of significance, is there a significant quadratic relationship between torque and RPM?
f. At the 0.05 level of significance, determine whether the quadratic model is a better fit than the linear model.
g. Interpret the meaning of the coefficient of multiple determination.
h. Compute the adjusted r^2.
i. What conclusions can you reach concerning the relationship between RPM and torque?

15.4 Is the number of calories in a beer related to the number of carbohydrates and/or the percentage of alcohol in the beer? Data concerning 158 of the best-selling domestic beers in the United States are stored in `DomesticBeer` . The values for three variables are included: the number of calories per 12 ounces, the alcohol percentage, and the number of carbohydrates (in grams) per 12 ounces. (Data extracted from **www.beer100.com/beercalories.htm**, February 3, 2015.)
a. Perform a multiple linear regression analysis, using calories as the dependent variable and percentage alcohol and number of carbohydrates as the independent variables.
b. Add quadratic terms for alcohol percentage and the number of carbohydrates.
c. Which model is better, the one in (a) or (b)?

d. What conclusions can you reach concerning the relationship between the number of calories in a beer and the alcohol percentage and number of carbohydrates?

15.5 In the production of printed circuit boards, errors in the alignment of electrical connections are a source of scrap. The data in the file RegistrationError-HighCost contains the registration error and the temperature used in the production of circuit boards in an experiment in which higher cost material was used. (Data extracted from C. Nachtsheim and B. Jones, "A Powerful Analytical Tool," *Six Sigma Forum Magazine*, August 2003, pp. 30–33.)
a. Construct a scatter plot for temperature and registration error.
b. Fit a quadratic regression model to predict registration error and state the quadratic regression equation.
c. Perform a residual analysis on the results and determine whether the regression model is valid.
d. At the 0.05 level of significance, is there a significant quadratic relationship between temperature and registration error?
e. At the 0.05 level of significance, determine whether the quadratic model is a better fit than the linear model.
f. Interpret the meaning of the coefficient of multiple determination.
g. Compute the adjusted r^2.
h. What conclusions can you reach concerning the relationship between registration error and temperature?

✓**SELF TEST** **15.6** An automotive sales manager wishes to examine the relationship between age (years) and sales price ($) for used Honda automobiles. The file HondaPrices contains data for a sample of Honda Civic LXs that were listed for sale at a car shopping website. (Data extracted from **cargurus.com**.)
a. Construct a scatter plot for age and price.
b. Fit a quadratic regression model to predict price and state the quadratic regression equation.
c. Predict the mean price of a Honda Civic LX that is five years old.
d. Perform a residual analysis on the results and determine whether the regression model is valid.
e. At the 0.05 level of significance, is there a significant quadratic relationship between age and price?
f. What is the *p*-value in (e)? Interpret its meaning.

g. At the 0.05 level of significance, determine whether the quadratic model is a better fit than the linear model.
h. What is the *p*-value in (g)? Interpret its meaning.
i. Interpret the meaning of the coefficient of multiple determination.
j. Compute the adjusted r^2.
k. What conclusions can you reach concerning the relationship between age and price?

15.7 Researchers wanted to investigate the relationship between employment and accommodation capacity in the European travel and tourism industry. The file EuroTourism contains a sample of 27 European countries. Variables included are the number of jobs generated in the travel and tourism industry in 2014 and the number of establishments that provide overnight accommodation for tourists. (Data extracted from **www.marketline.com**.)
a. Construct a scatter plot of the number of jobs generated in the travel and tourism industry in 2014 (Y) and the number of establishments that provide overnight accommodation for tourists (X).
b. Fit a quadratic regression model to predict the number of jobs generated and state the quadratic regression equation.
c. Predict the mean number of jobs generated in the travel and tourism industry for a country with 3,000 establishments that provide overnight accommodation for tourists.
d. Perform a residual analysis on the results and determine whether the regression model is valid.
e. At the 0.05 level of significance, is there a significant quadratic relationship between the number of jobs generated in the travel and tourism industry in 2014 and the number of establishments that provide overnight accommodation for tourists?
f. What is the *p*-value in (e)? Interpret its meaning.
g. At the 0.05 level of significance, determine whether the quadratic model is a better fit than the linear model.
h. Interpret the meaning of the coefficient of multiple determination.
i. Compute the adjusted r^2.
j. What conclusions can you reach concerning the relationship between the number of jobs generated in the travel and tourism industry in 2014 and the number of establishments that provide overnight accommodation for tourists?

15.2 Using Transformations in Regression Models

This section introduces regression models in which the independent variable, the dependent variable, or both are transformed in order to either overcome violations of the assumptions of regression or to make a model whose form is not linear into a linear model. Among the many transformations available (see references 1 and 2) are the square-root transformation and transformations involving the common logarithm (base 10) and the natural logarithm (base e).[1]

[1]For more information on logarithms, see Appendix Section A.3.

The Square-Root Transformation

The **square-root transformation** is often used to overcome violations of the normality and equal-variance assumptions as well as to transform a model whose form is not linear into a linear model. When the error term is normally distributed and the errors are equal for all values of X, you use a square root transformation of X to make the linear model appropriate. When the errors are not equal for all values of X or when the errors are not normally distributed, you use a square root transformation of Y (see reference 1).

Equation (15.3) shows a regression model that uses a square-root transformation of the dependent variable.

REGRESSION MODEL WITH A SQUARE-ROOT TRANSFORMATION

$$\sqrt{Y_i} = \beta_0 + \beta_1 X_{1i} + \varepsilon_i \tag{15.3}$$

Example 15.2 illustrates the use of a square-root transformation of the Y variable.

EXAMPLE 15.2

Using the Square-Root Transformation of the Y Variable

Given the following values for X and Y, use a square-root transformation for the Y variable:

X	Y	X	Y
1	57.3	3	87.9
1	70.0	4	124.4
2	92.5	4	96.1
2	77.4	5	141.3
3	114.7	5	111.1

Construct a scatter plot and a residual plot for these X and Y values, stored in Example 15-2 , and for X and the square root of Y.

SOLUTION Figures 15.8A and 15.8B display the four plots.

FIGURE 15.8A
Scatter plot and residual plot for the X and Y values

FIGURE 15.8B
Scatter plot and residual plot for X and the square root of Y

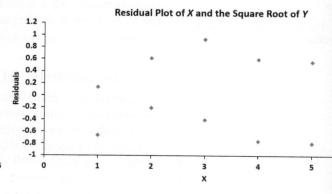

▶ *(continued)*

Figure 15.8A contains a scatter plot of X and Y that has been fit for a linear model in which $b_0 = 52.15$, $b_1 = 15.04$, and $r^2 = 0.7518$. The Figure 15.8A residual plot indicates the variation in the residuals in this model is much greater when $X = 3$, 4, and 5, than when $X = 1$ or 2. To overcome this lack of homogeneity of variance of the residuals, you need to use a square root transformation of the Y variable.

Figure 15.8B shows a scatter plot of X and the square root of Y that has been fit for a linear model in which $b_0 = 7.4536$, $b_1 = 0.7762$, and $r^2 = 0.7622$. The b_0 value $= 7.4536$ can be interpreted to mean that the predicted mean square root of Y when $X = 0$ is 7.4536. The b_1 value of 0.7762 can be interpreted to mean that for each increase of one unit of X, the predicted mean square root of Y increases by 0.7762. The Figure 15.8B residual plot shows much less variation in the residuals for different values of X, although the r^2 values of the two models are not very different. Because the residuals differ much less than the linear model to predict Y, the model that predicts the square root of Y is preferable to the model that predicts Y.

The Log Transformation

The **logarithmic transformation** is often used to overcome violations of the normality and equal-variance assumptions. You can also use the logarithmic transformation to change a nonlinear model into a linear model. Equation (15.4) shows a multiplicative model.

ORIGINAL MULTIPLICATIVE MODEL

$$Y_i = \beta_0 X_{1i}^{\beta_1} X_{2i}^{\beta_2} \varepsilon_i \tag{15.4}$$

By taking base 10 logarithms of both the dependent and independent variables, you can transform Equation (15.4) to the model shown in Equation (15.5).

TRANSFORMED MULTIPLICATIVE MODEL

$$\begin{aligned} \log Y_i &= \log(\beta_0 X_{1i}^{\beta_1} X_{2i}^{\beta_2} \varepsilon_i) \\ &= \log \beta_0 + \log(X_{1i}^{\beta_1}) + \log(X_{2i}^{\beta_2}) + \log \varepsilon_i \\ &= \log \beta_0 + \beta_1 \log X_{1i} + \beta_2 \log X_{2i} + \log \varepsilon_i \end{aligned} \tag{15.5}$$

Thus, Equation (15.5) is linear in the logarithms. Similarly, you can transform the exponential model shown in Equation (15.6) to a linear form by taking the natural logarithm of both sides of the equation. Equation (15.7) is the transformed model.

ORIGINAL EXPONENTIAL MODEL

$$Y_i = e^{\beta_0 + \beta_1 X_{1i} + \beta_2 X_{2i}} \varepsilon_i \tag{15.6}$$

TRANSFORMED EXPONENTIAL MODEL

$$\begin{aligned} \ln Y_i &= \ln(e^{\beta_0 + \beta_1 X_{1i} + \beta_2 X_{2i}} \varepsilon_i) \\ &= \ln(e^{\beta_0 + \beta_1 X_{1i} + \beta_2 X_{2i}}) + \ln \varepsilon_i \\ &= \beta_0 + \beta_1 X_{1i} + \beta_2 X_{2i} + \ln \varepsilon_i \end{aligned} \tag{15.7}$$

Example 15.3 illustrates the use of a natural log transformation.

EXAMPLE 15.3

Using the Natural Log Transformation

Given the following values for X and Y, use a natural logarithm transformation for the Y variable:

X	Y	X	Y
1	0.7	3	4.8
1	0.5	4	12.9
2	1.6	4	11.5
2	1.8	5	32.1
3	4.2	5	33.9

Construct a scatter plot and a residual plot for these X and Y values, stored in Example15-3, and for X and the natural logarithm of Y.

SOLUTION Figures 15.9A and 15.9B display the four plots.

FIGURE 15.9A

Scatter plot and residual plot for the X and Y values

FIGURE 15.9B

Scatter plot and residual plot for X and the natural logarithm of Y

Figure 15.9A contains a scatter plot of X and Y that has been fit for a linear model in which $b_0 = 12.19$, $b_1 = 7.53$, and $r^2 = 0.7854$ and shows an exponential relationship between X and Y. The Figure 15.9A residual plot shows a very clear curvilinear plot of the residuals. Therefore, you should use the natural log transformation of the Y variable.

▶ *(continued)*

Figure 15.9B contains a scatter plot of X and the natural log of Y that has been fit for a linear model in which $b_0 = -1.5035$, $b_1 = 1.0013$, and $r^2 = 0.9959$. The b_0 value $= -1.5035$ can be interpreted to mean that the predicted mean natural log of Y when $X = 0$ is -1.5035. The b_1 value of 1.0013 can be interpreted to mean that for each increase of one unit of X, the predicted mean natural log of Y increases by 1.0013. The Figure 15.9B residual plot does not show a pattern, although there is some difference in the variation when $X = 1$ and $X = 5$. In addition, the r^2 of this natural log model is 0.9959 as compared to an r^2 of 0.7854 for the simple linear model. This is another reason for preferring the natural log model over the linear model.

PROBLEMS FOR SECTION 15.2

LEARNING THE BASICS

15.8 Consider the following regression equation:

$$\log \hat{Y}_i = \log 3.07 + 0.9 \log X_{1i} + 1.41 \log X_{2i}$$

a. Predict the value of Y when $X_1 = 8.5$ and $X_2 = 5.2$.
b. Interpret the meaning of the regression coefficients b_0, b_1, and b_2.

15.9 Consider the following regression equation:

$$\ln \hat{Y}_i = 4.62 + 0.5X_{1i} + 0.7X_{2i}$$

a. Predict the value of Y when $X_1 = 8.5$ and $X_2 = 5.2$.
b. Interpret the meaning of the regression coefficients b_0, b_1, and b_2.

APPLYING THE CONCEPTS

 SELF TEST **15.10** Using the data of Problem 15.4 on page 528, stored in DomesticBeer , perform a square-root transformation on each of the independent variables (percentage alcohol and number of carbohydrates). Using calories as the dependent variable and the transformed independent variables, perform a multiple regression analysis.
a. State the regression equation.
b. Perform a residual analysis of the results and determine whether the regression model is valid.
c. At the 0.05 level of significance, is there a significant relationship between calories and the square root of the percentage of alcohol and the square root of the number of carbohydrates?
d. Interpret the meaning of the coefficient of determination, r^2, in this problem.
e. Compute the adjusted r^2.
f. Compare your results with those in Problem 15.4. Which model is better? Why?

15.11 Using the data of Problem 15.4 on page 528, stored in DomesticBeer , perform a natural logarithmic transformation of the dependent variable (calories). Using the transformed dependent variable and the percentage of alcohol and the number of carbohydrates as the independent variables, perform a multiple regression analysis.
a. State the regression equation.
b. Perform a residual analysis of the results and determine whether regression assumptions are valid.

c. At the 0.05 level of significance, is there a significant relationship between the natural logarithm of calories and the percentage of alcohol and the number of carbohydrates?
d. Interpret the meaning of the coefficient of determination, r^2, in this problem.
e. Compute the adjusted r^2.
f. Compare your results with those in Problems 15.4 and 15.10. Which model is best? Why?

15.12 Using the data of Problem 15.6 on page 529, stored in HondaPrices , perform a natural logarithm transformation of the dependent variable (price). Using the transformed dependent variable and the age as the independent variable, perform a regression analysis.
a. State the regression equation.
b. Predict the mean price for a five year old Honda Civic LX.
c. Perform a residual analysis of the results and determine whether the regression assumptions are valid.
d. At the 0.05 level of significance, is there a significant relationship between the natural logarithm of price and age?
e. Interpret the meaning of the coefficient of determination, r^2, in this problem.
f. Compute the adjusted r^2.
g. Compare your results with those in Problem 15.6. Which model is better? Why?

15.13 Using the data of Problem 15.6 on page 529, stored in HondaPrices , perform a square-root transformation of the dependent variable (price). Using the square root of price as the dependent variable, perform a regression analysis.
a. State the regression equation.
b. Predict the mean price for a five-year-old Honda Civic LX.
c. Perform a residual analysis of the results and determine whether the regression model is valid.
d. At the 0.05 level of significance, is there a significant relationship between the square root of price and age?
e. Interpret the meaning of the coefficient of determination, r^2, in this problem.
f. Compute the adjusted r^2.
g. Compare your results with those of Problems 15.6 and 15.12. Which model is best? Why?

15.3 Collinearity

One important problem in developing multiple regression models involves the possible **collinearity** of the independent variables. This condition refers to situations in which two or more of the independent variables are highly correlated with each other. In such situations, collinear variables do not provide unique information, and it becomes difficult to separate the effects of such variables on the dependent variable. When collinearity exists, the values of the regression coefficients for the correlated variables may fluctuate drastically, depending on which independent variables are included in the model.

One method of measuring collinearity is to determine the **variance inflationary factor** (**VIF**) for each independent variable. Equation (15.8) defines VIF_j, the variance inflationary factor for variable j.

VARIANCE INFLATIONARY FACTOR

$$VIF_j = \frac{1}{1 - R_j^2} \tag{15.8}$$

where R_j^2 is the coefficient of multiple determination for a regression model, using variable X_j as the dependent variable and all other X variables as independent variables.

If there are only two independent variables, R_1^2 is the coefficient of determination between X_1 and X_2. It is identical to R_2^2, which is the coefficient of determination between X_2 and X_1. If there are three independent variables, then R_1^2 is the coefficient of multiple determination of X_1 with X_2 and X_3; R_2^2 is the coefficient of multiple determination of X_2 with X_1 and X_3; and R_3^2 is the coefficient of multiple determination of X_3 with X_1 and X_2.

If a set of independent variables is uncorrelated, each VIF_j is equal to 1. If the set is highly correlated, then a VIF_j might even exceed 10. Snee (see reference 3) recommends using alternatives to least-squares regression if the maximum VIF_j exceeds 5.

You need to proceed with extreme caution when using a multiple regression model that has one or more large VIF values. And because the independent variables contain overlapping information, you should always avoid interpreting the regression coefficient estimates separately because there is no way to accurately estimate the individual effects of the independent variables. One solution to the problem is to delete the variable with the largest VIF value. The reduced model (i.e., the model with the independent variable with the largest VIF value deleted) is often free of collinearity problems. If you determine that all the independent variables are needed in the model, you can use methods discussed in reference 1.

In the OmniPower sales data (see Section 14.1), the correlation between the two independent variables, price and promotional expenditure, is -0.0968. Because there are only two independent variables in the model, from Equation (15.8):

$$VIF_1 = VIF_2 = \frac{1}{1 - (-0.0968)^2}$$
$$= 1.009$$

Thus, you can conclude that you should not be concerned with collinearity for the OmniPower sales data.

In models containing quadratic and interaction terms, collinearity is usually present. The linear and quadratic terms of an independent variable are usually highly correlated with each other, and an interaction term is often correlated with one or both of the independent variables making up the interaction. Thus, you cannot interpret individual regression coefficients separately. You need to interpret the linear and quadratic regression coefficients together in order to understand the nonlinear relationship. Likewise, you need to interpret an interaction regression coefficient in conjunction with the two regression coefficients associated with the variables comprising the interaction. In summary, large *VIF*s in quadratic or interaction models do not necessarily mean that the model is not a good one. They do, however, require you to carefully interpret the regression coefficients.

LEARNING THE BASICS

15.14 If the coefficient of determination between two independent variables is 0.20, what is the *VIF*?

15.15 If the coefficient of determination between two independent variables is 0.50, what is the *VIF*?

APPLYING THE CONCEPTS

✓ SELF TEST **15.16** Refer to Problem 14.4 on page 480. Perform a multiple regression analysis using the data in CommunityBanks and determine the *VIF* for each independent variable in the model. Is there reason to suspect the existence of collinearity?

15.17 Refer to Problem 14.5 on page 480. Perform a multiple regression analysis using the data in VinhoVerde and determine the *VIF* for each independent variable in the model. Is there reason to suspect the existence of collinearity?

15.18 Refer to Problem 14.6 on page 480. Perform a multiple regression analysis using the data in BestCompanies and determine the *VIF* for each independent variable in the model. Is there reason to suspect the existence of collinearity?

15.19 Refer to Problem 14.7 on page 480. Perform a multiple regression analysis using the data in Standby and determine the *VIF* for each independent variable in the model. Is there reason to suspect the existence of collinearity?

15.20 Refer to Problem 14.8 on page 481. Perform a multiple regression analysis using the data in GlenCove and determine the *VIF* for each independent variable in the model. Is there reason to suspect the existence of collinearity?

15.4 Model Building

This chapter and Chapter 14 have introduced you to many different topics in regression analysis, including quadratic terms, dummy variables, and interaction terms. In this section, you learn a structured approach to building the most appropriate regression model. As you will see, successful model building incorporates many of the topics you have studied so far.

To begin, refer to the WSTA-TV scenario introduced on page 521, in which four independent variables (total staff present, remote hours, Dubner hours, and total labor hours) are considered in the business problem that involves developing a regression model to predict standby hours of unionized graphic artists. Data are collected over a period of 26 weeks and organized and stored in Standby. Table 15.2 summarizes these data.

To develop a model to predict the dependent variable, standby hours in the WSTA-TV scenario, you need to be guided by a general problem-solving strategy, or *heuristic*. One heuristic appropriate for building regression models uses the principle of parsimony.

Parsimony guides you to select the regression model with the fewest independent variables that can predict the dependent variable adequately. Regression models with fewer independent variables are easier to interpret, particularly because they are less likely to be affected by collinearity problems (described in Section 15.3).

Developing an appropriate model when many independent variables are under consideration involves complexities that are not present with a model that has only two independent variables. The evaluation of all possible regression models is more computationally complex. And, although you can quantitatively evaluate competing models, there may not be a *uniquely* best model but several *equally appropriate* models.

To begin analyzing the standby-hours data, you compute the variance inflationary factors [see Equation (15.8) on page 521] to measure the amount of collinearity among the independent variables. The values for the four *VIF*s for this model appear in Figure 15.10, along with the results for the model that uses the four independent variables.

TABLE 15.2
Predicting Standby
Hours Based on Total
Staff Present, Remote
Hours, Dubner Hours,
and Total Labor Hours

Week	Standby Hours (Y)	Total Staff Present (X_1)	Remote Hours (X_2)	Dubner Hours (X_3)	Total Labor Hours (X_4)
1	245	338	414	323	2,001
2	177	333	598	340	2,030
3	271	358	656	340	2,226
4	211	372	631	352	2,154
5	196	339	528	380	2,078
6	135	289	409	339	2,080
7	195	334	382	331	2,073
8	118	293	399	311	1,758
9	116	325	343	328	1,624
10	147	311	338	353	1,889
11	154	304	353	518	1,988
12	146	312	289	440	2,049
13	115	283	388	276	1,796
14	161	307	402	207	1,720
15	274	322	151	287	2,056
16	245	335	228	290	1,890
17	201	350	271	355	2,187
18	183	339	440	300	2,032
19	237	327	475	284	1,856
20	175	328	347	337	2,068
21	152	319	449	279	1,813
22	188	325	336	244	1,808
23	188	322	267	253	1,834
24	197	317	235	272	1,973
25	261	315	164	223	1,839
26	232	331	270	272	1,935

FIGURE 15.10
Excel multiple regression
linear model worksheet
results for predicting
standby hours based on
four independent vari-
ables (with worksheets for
Durbin-Watson statistic
and *VIF*, inset)

Observe that all the *VIF* values in Figure 15.10 are relatively small, ranging from a high of
1.9993 for the total labor hours to a low of 1.2333 for remote hours. Thus, on the basis of the
criteria developed by Snee that all *VIF* values should be less than 5.0 (see reference 3), there is
little evidence of collinearity among the set of independent variables.

The Stepwise Regression Approach to Model Building

You continue your analysis of the standby-hours data by attempting to determine whether a subset of all independent variables yields an adequate and appropriate model. The first approach described here is **stepwise regression**, which attempts to find the "best" regression model without examining all possible models.

The first step of stepwise regression is to find the best model that uses one independent variable. The next step is to find the best of the remaining independent variables to add to the model selected in the first step. An important feature of the stepwise approach is that an independent variable that has entered into the model at an early stage may subsequently be removed after other independent variables are considered. Thus, in stepwise regression, variables are either added to or deleted from the regression model at each step of the model-building process. The t test for the slope (see Section 14.4) or the partial F_{STAT} test statistic (see Section 14.5) is used to determine whether variables are added or deleted. The stepwise procedure terminates with the selection of a best-fitting model when no additional variables can be added to or deleted from the last model evaluated. Figure 15.11 below shows the stepwise regression results worksheet that PHStat creates for the standby hours data.

FIGURE 15.11
Stepwise regression results worksheet for the standby-hours data

	A B	C	D	E	F	G	H
1	**Stepwise Analysis for Standby Hours**						
2	Table of Results for General Stepwise						
3							
4	Total Staff entered.						
5							
6		*df*	*SS*	*MS*	*F*	*Significance F*	
7	Regression	1	20667.3980	20667.3980	13.8563	0.0011	
8	Residual	24	35797.2174	1491.5507			
9	Total	25	56464.6154				
10							
11		*Coefficients*	*Standard Error*	*t Stat*	*P-value*	*Lower 95%*	*Upper 95%*
12	Intercept	-272.3816	124.2402	-2.1924	0.0383	-528.8008	-15.9625
13	Total Staff	1.4241	0.3826	3.7224	0.0011	0.6345	2.2136
14							
15							
16	Remote entered.						
17							
18		*df*	*SS*	*MS*	*F*	*Significance F*	
19	Regression	2	27662.5429	13831.2714	11.0450	0.0004	
20	Residual	23	28802.0725	1252.2640			
21	Total	25	56464.6154				
22							
23		*Coefficients*	*Standard Error*	*t Stat*	*P-value*	*Lower 95%*	*Upper 95%*
24	Intercept	-330.6748	116.4802	-2.8389	0.0093	-571.6322	-89.7175
25	Total Staff	1.7649	0.3790	4.6562	0.0001	0.9808	2.5490
26	Remote	-0.1390	0.0588	-2.3635	0.0269	-0.2606	-0.0173
27							
28							
29	No other variables could be entered into the model. Stepwise ends.						

In the Worksheet

This worksheet contains pasted results transferred from other regression results worksheets that PHStat created and examined.
This worksheet has no cell formulas, unlike most of the worksheets that this book features.

For this example, a significance level of 0.05 is used to enter a variable into the model or to delete a variable from the model. The first variable entered into the model is total staff, the variable that correlates most highly with the dependent variable standby hours. Because the cell F13 p-value $= 0.0011 < 0.05$, total staff is included in the regression model.

The next step involves selecting a second independent variable for the model. The second variable chosen is one that makes the largest contribution to the model, given that the first variable has been selected. For this model, the second variable is remote hours. Because the cell F26 p-value for remote hours $= 0.0269 < 0.05$, the remote hours variable is included in the regression model.

After the remote hours variable is entered into the model, the stepwise procedure determines whether total staff is still an important contributing variable or whether it can be eliminated from the model. Because the *p*-value of 0.0001 for total staff in cell F25 is less than 0.05, total staff remains in the regression model.

The next step involves selecting a third independent variable for the model. Because none of the other variables meets the 0.05 criterion for entry into the model, the stepwise procedure terminates with a model that includes total staff present and the number of remote hours.

This stepwise regression approach to model building was originally developed more than four decades ago, when regression computations on computers were time-consuming and costly. Although stepwise regression limited the evaluation of alternative models, the method was deemed a good trade-off between evaluation and cost.

Given the ability of today's computers to perform regression computations at very low cost and high speed, stepwise regression has been superseded to some extent by the best-subsets approach, discussed next, which evaluates a larger set of alternative models. Stepwise regression is not obsolete, however. Today, many businesses use stepwise regression as an exploratory approach that forms part of the *data mining* of big data (see Section 17.5).

The Best Subsets Approach to Model Building

The **best subsets approach** evaluates all possible regression models for a given set of independent variables. Figure 15.12 presents best subsets regression results of all possible regression models for the standby-hours data.

FIGURE 15.12
Best subsets regression results worksheet for the standby-hours data

In the Worksheet

This worksheet contains formulas that copy values from other regression results worksheets.

A criterion often used in model building is the adjusted r^2, which adjusts the r^2 of each model to account for the number of independent variables in the model as well as for the sample size (see Section 14.2). Because model building requires you to compare models with different numbers of independent variables, the adjusted r^2 is more appropriate than r^2. Referring to Figure 15.12, you see that the adjusted r^2 reaches a maximum value of 0.5513 when all four independent variables plus the intercept term (for a total of five estimated parameters) are included in the model.

A second criterion often used in the evaluation of competing models is the C_p **statistic** developed by Mallows (see reference 1). The C_p statistic, defined in Equation (15.9), measures the differences between a fitted regression model and a *true* model, along with random error.

C_P STATISTIC

$$C_p = \frac{(1 - R_k^2)(n - T)}{1 - R_T^2} - [n - 2(k + 1)] \tag{15.9}$$

where

k = number of independent variables included in a regression model

T = total number of parameters (including the intercept) to be estimated in the full regression model

R_k^2 = coefficient of multiple determination for a regression model that has k independent variables

R_T^2 = coefficient of multiple determination for a full regression model that contains all T estimated parameters

Using Equation (15.9) to compute C_p for the model containing total staff and remote hours,

$$n = 26 \quad k = 2 \quad T = 4 + 1 = 5 \quad R_k^2 = 0.4899 \quad R_T^2 = 0.6231$$

so that

$$C_p = \frac{(1 - 0.4899)(26 - 5)}{1 - 0.6231} - [26 - 2(2 + 1)]$$
$$= 8.4193$$

When a regression model with k independent variables contains only random differences from a *true* model, the mean value of C_p is $k + 1$, the number of parameters. Thus, in evaluating many alternative regression models, the goal is to find models whose C_p is close to or less than $k + 1$. In Figure 15.12, you see that only the model with all four independent variables considered contains a C_p value close to or below $k + 1$. Therefore, using the C_p criterion, you should choose that model.

Although it is not the case here, the C_p statistic often provides several alternative models for you to evaluate in greater depth. Moreover, the best model or models using the C_p criterion might differ from the model selected using the adjusted r^2 and/or the model selected using the stepwise procedure. (Note here that the model selected using stepwise regression has a C_p value of 8.4193, which is substantially above the suggested criterion of $k + 1 = 3$ for that model.) Remember that there may not be a uniquely best model, but there may be several equally appropriate models. Final model selection often involves using subjective criteria, such as parsimony, interpretability, and departure from model assumptions (as evaluated by residual analysis).

When you have finished selecting the independent variables to include in the model, you need to perform a residual analysis to evaluate the regression assumptions, and because the data were collected in time order, you also need to compute the Durbin-Watson statistic to determine whether there is autocorrelation in the residuals (see Section 13.6). From Figure 15.10 on page 536, you see that the Durbin-Watson statistic, D, is 2.2197. Because D is greater than 2.0, there is no indication of positive correlation in the residuals. Figure 15.13 on page 540 presents the plots used in the residual analysis.

None of the residual plots reveal apparent patterns. In addition, a plot of the residuals versus the predicted values of Y, shown in Figure 15.14, on page 540, does not show evidence of unequal variance. Therefore, using the Figure 15.10 regression model results, you state the regression equation as

$$\hat{Y}_i = -330.8318 + 1.2456X_{1i} - 0.1184X_{2i} - 0.2971X_{3i} + 0.1305X_{4i}$$

FIGURE 15.13
Residual plots for the standby-hours data

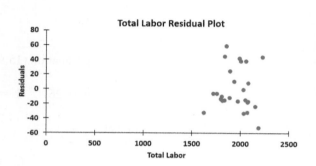

FIGURE 15.14
Scatter plot of the residuals versus the predicted
values of Y

Example 15.4 presents a situation in which there are several alternative models in which the C_p statistic is close to or less than $k + 1$.

EXAMPLE 15.4

Choosing Among
Alternative Regres-
sion Models

Table 15.3 shows results from a best-subsets regression analysis of a regression model with seven independent variables. Determine which regression model you would choose as the *best* model.

▶ (continued)

TABLE 15.3
Partial Results
from Best-Subsets
Regression

Number of Variables	r^2	Adjusted r^2	C_p	Variables Included
1	0.121	0.119	113.9	X_4
1	0.093	0.090	130.4	X_1
1	0.083	0.080	136.2	X_3
2	0.214	0.210	62.1	X_3, X_4
2	0.191	0.186	75.6	X_1, X_3
2	0.181	0.177	81.0	X_1, X_4
3	0.285	0.280	22.6	X_1, X_3, X_4
3	0.268	0.263	32.4	X_3, X_4, X_5
3	0.240	0.234	49.0	X_2, X_3, X_4
4	0.308	0.301	11.3	X_1, X_2, X_3, X_4
4	0.304	0.297	14.0	X_1, X_3, X_4, X_6
4	0.296	0.289	18.3	X_1, X_3, X_4, X_5
5	0.317	0.308	8.2	X_1, X_2, X_3, X_4, X_5
5	0.315	0.306	9.6	X_1, X_2, X_3, X_4, X_6
5	0.313	0.304	10.7	X_1, X_3, X_4, X_5, X_6
6	0.323	0.313	6.8	$X_1, X_2, X_3, X_4, X_5, X_6$
6	0.319	0.309	9.0	$X_1, X_2, X_3, X_4, X_5, X_7$
6	0.317	0.306	10.4	$X_1, X_2, X_3, X_4, X_6, X_7$
7	0.324	0.312	8.0	$X_1, X_2, X_3, X_4, X_5, X_6, X_7$

SOLUTION From Table 15.3, you need to determine which models have C_p values that are less than or close to $k + 1$. Two models meet this criterion. The model with six independent variables $(X_1, X_2, X_3, X_4, X_5, X_6)$ has a C_p value of 6.8, which is less than $k + 1 = 6 + 1 = 7$, and the full model with seven independent variables $(X_1, X_2, X_3, X_4, X_5, X_6, X_7)$ has a C_p value of 8.0.

One way you can choose among the two models is to select the model with the largest adjusted r^2—that is, the model with six independent variables. Another way to select a final model is to determine whether the models contain a subset of variables that are common. Then you test whether the contribution of the additional variables is significant. In this case, because the models differ only by the inclusion of variable X_7 in the full model, you test whether variable X_7 makes a significant contribution to the regression model, given that the variables $X_1, X_2, X_3, X_4, X_5,$ and X_6 are already included in the model. If the contribution is statistically significant, then you should include variable X_7 in the regression model. If variable X_7 does not make a statistically significant contribution, you should not include it in the model.

Model Validation

The final step in the model-building process is to validate the selected regression model. This step involves checking the model against data that were not part of the sample analyzed. The following are several ways of validating a regression model:

- Collect new data and compare the results.
- Compare the results of the regression model to previous results.
- If the data set is large, split the data into two parts and cross-validate the results.

Collecting new data is perhaps the best way of validating a regression model. If the results with new data are consistent with the selected regression model, you have strong reason to believe that the fitted regression model is applicable in a wide set of circumstances.

When collecting new data is impractical or impossible, for example, when working with very large data sets or big data, you can use cross-validation. **Cross-validation** first splits the existing data into two parts. You then use the first part of the data to *develop* the regression model and then use the second part of the data to *evaluate* the predictive ability of the model. Cross-validation is often used as a practical way of validating a model developed by predictive analytics methods (discussed in Section 17.5).

Figure 15.15 summarizes the model building process and Exhibit 15.1 lists the steps for successful model building.

FIGURE 15.15
The model building process

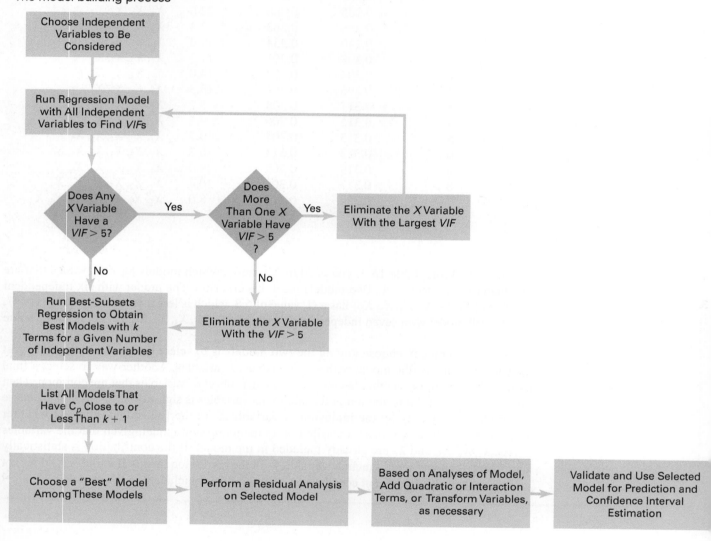

EXHIBIT   15.1

Steps for Successful Model Building

1. Choose the independent variables to be considered for the multiple regression model.
2. Develop a regression model that includes all of the independent variables.
3. Compute the VIF for each independent variable.

   If none of the independent variables has a $VIF > 5$, continue with step 4.

   If only one of the independent variables has a $VIF > 5$, eliminate that independent variable and continue with step 4.

   If more than one of the independent variables has a $VIF > 5$, eliminate the independent variable that has the highest VIF from the regression model and repeat step 2 with the remaining independent variables.

4. Perform a best-subsets regression with the remaining independent variables and compute the C_p statistic and/or the adjusted r^2 for each model.
5. List all models that have C_p close to or less than $k + 1$ and/or a high adjusted r^2.
6. From the models listed in step 4, choose a best model.
7. Perform a complete analysis of the model chosen, including a residual analysis.
8. Review the results of the residual analysis. If necessary, add quadratic and/or interaction terms, transform variables, and repeat steps 2 through 6. If no changes are necessary, continue with step 8.
9. Validate the regression model. If validated, use the regression model for prediction and inference.

PROBLEMS FOR SECTION 15.4

LEARNING THE BASICS

15.21 You are considering four independent variables for inclusion in a regression model. You select a sample of $n = 30$, with the following results:
1. The model that includes independent variables A and B has a C_p value equal to 4.6.
2. The model that includes independent variables A and C has a C_p value equal to 2.4.
3. The model that includes independent variables A, B, and C has a C_p value equal to 2.7.
   a. Which models meet the criterion for further consideration? Explain.
   b. How would you compare the model that contains independent variables A, B, and C to the model that contains independent variables A and B? Explain.

15.22 You are considering six independent variables for inclusion in a regression model. You select a sample of $n = 40$, with the following results:

$$k = 2 \quad T = 6 + 1 = 7 \quad R_k^2 = 0.274 \quad R_T^2 = 0.653$$

a. Compute the C_p value for this two-independent-variable model.
b. Based on your answer to (a), does this model meet the criterion for further consideration as the best model? Explain.

APPLYING THE CONCEPTS

15.23 The file FTMBA contains data from a sample of full-time MBA programs offered by private universities. The variables collected for this sample are average starting salary upon graduation ($), the percentage of applicants to the full-time program who were accepted, the average GMAT test score of students entering the program, program per-year tuition ($), and percent of students with job offers at time of graduation. (Data extracted from U.S. News & World Report Education, "Best Graduate Schools," **bit.ly/1qt0NXn**.)

Develop the most appropriate multiple regression model to predict the mean starting salary upon graduation. Be sure to include a thorough residual analysis. In addition, provide a detailed explanation of the results, including a comparison of the most appropriate multiple regression model to the best simple linear regression model.

✓ SELF TEST **15.24** You need to develop a model to predict the assessed value of houses in Silver Spring, Maryland, based on the size of the house, whether it has a fireplace, the number of bedrooms, and the number of bathrooms. A sample of 30 houses is selected and the results are stored in SilverSpring. Develop the most appropriate multiple regression model to predict assessed value. Be sure to perform a thorough residual analysis. In addition, provide a detailed explanation of the results.

15.25 *Accounting Today* identified top public accounting firms in ten geographic regions across the U.S. The file Accounting Partners6 contains data for public accounting firms in the Southeast, Gulf Coast, and Capital Regions. The variables are: revenue ($millions), number of partners in the firm, number of professionals in the firm, proportion of business dedicated to management advisory services (MAS%), whether the firm is located in the Southeast Region ($0 = $ no, $1 = $ yes), and whether the firm is located in the Gulf Coast Region ($0 = $ no, $1 = $ yes). (Data extracted from *2015 Top 100 Firms*, **bit.ly/1BoMzsv**.)

Develop the most appropriate multiple regression model to predict firm revenue. Be sure to perform a thorough residual analysis. In addition, provide a detailed explanation of the results.

15.5 Pitfalls in Multiple Regression and Ethical Issues

Pitfalls in Multiple Regression

Model building is an art as well as a science. Different individuals may not always agree on the best multiple regression model. To develop a good regression model, use the process summarized in Figure 15.15 and Exhibit 15.1 on pages 542 and 543. As you follow that process, you must avoid certain pitfalls that can interfere with the development of a useful model. Section 13.9 discussed pitfalls in simple linear regression and strategies for avoiding them. Multiple regression models require additional precautions. To avoid pitfalls in multiple regression, you also need to

- Interpret the regression coefficient for a particular independent variable from a perspective in which the values of all other independent variables are held constant.
- Evaluate residual plots for each independent variable.
- Evaluate interaction and quadratic terms.
- Compute the *VIF* for each independent variable before determining which independent variables to include in the model.
- Examine several alternative models, using best-subsets regression.
- Use logistic regression instead of least squares regression when the dependent variable is categorical.
- Validate the model before implementing it.

Ethical Issues

Ethical issues arise when a user who wants to make predictions manipulates the development process of the multiple regression model. The key here is intent. In addition to the situations discussed in Section 13.9, unethical behavior occurs when someone uses multiple regression analysis and *willfully fails* to remove from consideration independent variables that exhibit a high collinearity with other independent variables or *willfully fails* to use methods other than least-squares regression when the assumptions necessary for least-squares regression are seriously violated.

▼ USING **STATISTICS**
Valuing Parsimony . . . , Revisited

In the Using Statistics scenario, you were the WSTA-TV broadcast operations manager, who sought to reduce labor expenses. You needed to determine which variables have an effect on standby hours, the time during which graphic artists employed by the station are idle but getting paid. You collected data concerning standby hours and the total number of staff present, remote hours, Dubner hours, and total labor hours over a period of 26 weeks.

You performed a multiple regression analysis on the data. The coefficient of multiple determination indicated that 62.31% of the variation in standby hours can be explained by variation in the number of graphic artists present and the number of remote hours, Dubner hours, and total labor hours. The model indicated that standby hours are estimated to increase by 1.2456 hours for each additional staff member present, holding constant the other independent variables; to decrease by 0.1184 hour for each additional remote hour, holding constant the other independent variables; to decrease by 0.2971 hour for each additional Dubner hour, holding constant the other independent variables; and to increase by 0.1305 hour for each additional labor hour, holding constant the other independent variables. Each of the four independent variables had a significant effect on standby hours, holding constant the other independent variables. This regression model enables you to predict standby hours based on the total number of graphic artists present, remote hours, Dubner hours, and total labor hours. Any predictions developed by the model can then be carefully monitored, new data can be collected, and other variables may possibly be considered.

▼SUMMARY

Figure 15.16 summarizes the several topics associated with multiple regression model building and selection that this chapter discusses.

FIGURE 15.16
Roadmap for multiple regression

▼ REFERENCES

1. Kutner, M., C. Nachtsheim, J. Neter, and W. Li. *Applied Linear Statistical Models*, 5th ed. New York: McGraw-Hill/Irwin, 2005.
2. Montgomery, D. C., E. A. Peck, and G. G. Vining. *Introduction to Linear Regression Analysis*, 5th ed. New York: Wiley, 2012.
3. Snee, R. D. "Some Aspects of Nonorthogonal Data Analysis, Part I. Developing Prediction Equations." *Journal of Quality Technology* 5 (1973): 67–79.

▼ KEY EQUATIONS

Quadratic Regression Model

$$Y_i = \beta_0 + \beta_1 X_{1i} + \beta_2 X_{1i}^2 + \varepsilon_i \tag{15.1}$$

Quadratic Regression Equation

$$\hat{Y}_i = b_0 + b_1 X_{1i} + b_2 X_{1i}^2 \tag{15.2}$$

Regression Model with a Square-Root Transformation

$$\sqrt{Y_i} = \beta_0 + \beta_1 X_{1i} + \varepsilon_i \tag{15.3}$$

Original Multiplicative Model

$$Y_i = \beta_0 X_{1i}^{\beta_1} X_{2i}^{\beta_2} \varepsilon_i \tag{15.4}$$

Transformed Multiplicative Model

$$\log Y_i = \log(\beta_0 X_{1i}^{\beta_1} X_{2i}^{\beta_2} \varepsilon_i)$$
$$= \log \beta_0 + \log(X_{1i}^{\beta_1}) + \log(X_{2i}^{\beta_2}) + \log \varepsilon_i$$
$$= \log \beta_0 + \beta_1 \log X_{1i} + \beta_2 \log X_{2i} + \log \varepsilon_i \tag{15.5}$$

Original Exponential Model

$$Y_i = e^{\beta_0 + \beta_1 X_{1i} + \beta_2 X_{2i}} \varepsilon_i \tag{15.6}$$

Transformed Exponential Model

$$\ln Y_i = \ln(e^{\beta_0 + \beta_1 X_{1i} + \beta_2 X_{2i}} \varepsilon_i)$$
$$= \ln(e^{\beta_0 + \beta_1 X_{1i} + \beta_2 X_{2i}}) + \ln \varepsilon_i$$
$$= \beta_0 + \beta_1 X_{1i} + \beta_2 X_{2i} + \ln \varepsilon_i \tag{15.7}$$

Variance Inflationary Factor

$$VIF_j = \frac{1}{1 - R_j^2} \tag{15.8}$$

C_p Statistic

$$C_p = \frac{(1 - R_k^2)(n - T)}{1 - R_T^2} - [n - 2(k + 1)] \tag{15.9}$$

▼ KEY TERMS

best-subsets approach   538
C_p statistic   538
Collinearity   534
cross-validation   542
logarithmic transformation   531
parsimony   535
quadratic regression model   522
quadratic term   532
square-root transformation   529
stepwise regression   537
variance inflationary factor (*VIF*)   534

▼ CHECKING YOUR UNDERSTANDING

15.26 How can you evaluate whether collinearity exists in a multiple regression model?

15.27 What is the difference between stepwise regression and best-subsets regression?

15.28 How do you choose among models according to the C_p statistic in best-subsets regression?

▼ CHAPTER REVIEW PROBLEMS

15.29 A specialist in baseball analytics has expanded his analysis, presented in Problem 14.77 on page 514, of which variables are important in predicting a team's wins in a given baseball season. He has collected data in Baseball related to wins, ERA, saves, runs scored, batting average, home runs, and WHIP (hits and walks per inning) for the 2014 season.

Develop the most appropriate multiple regression model to predict a team's wins. Be sure to include a thorough residual analysis. In addition, provide a detailed explanation of the results.

15.30 In the production of printed circuit boards, errors in the alignment of electrical connections are a source of scrap. The file RegistrationError contains the registration error, the temperature, the pressure, and the cost of the material (low versus high) used in the production of circuit boards. (Data extracted from C. Nachtsheim and B. Jones, "A Powerful Analytical Tool," *Six Sigma Forum Magazine*, August 2003, pp. 30–33.) Develop the most appropriate multiple regression model to predict registration error.

15.31 Hemlock Farms is a community located in the Pocono Mountains area of eastern Pennsylvania. The file HemlockFarms contains information on homes that were recently for sale. The variables included were

List Price—Asking price of the house
Hot Tub—Whether the house has a hot tub, with 0 = No and 1 = Yes
Lake View—Whether the house has a lake view, with 0 = No and 1 = Yes
Bathrooms—Number of bathrooms
Bedrooms—Number of bedrooms
Loft/Den—Whether the house has a loft or den, with 0 = No and 1 = Yes
Finished basement—Whether the house has a finished basement, with 0 = No and 1 = Yes
Acres—Number of acres for the property

Develop the most appropriate multiple regression model to predict the asking price. Be sure to perform a thorough residual analysis. In addition, provide a detailed explanation of your results.

15.32 Nassau County is located approximately 25 miles east of New York City. The file GlenCove contains a sample of 30 single-family homes located in Glen Cove. Variables included are the fair market value, land area of the property (acres), interior size of the house (square feet), age (years), number of rooms, number of bathrooms, and number of cars that can be parked in the garage.
a. Develop the most appropriate multiple regression model to predict fair market value.
b. Compare the results in (a) with those of Problems 15.33 (a) and 15.34 (a).

15.33 Data similar to those in Problem 15.32 are available for homes located in Roslyn (approximately 8 miles from Glen Cove) and are stored in Roslyn.
a. Perform an analysis similar to that of Problem 15.32.
b. Compare the results in (a) with those of Problems 15.32 (a) and 15.34 (a).

15.34 Data similar to Problem 15.32 are available for homes located in Freeport (located approximately 20 miles from Roslyn) and are stored in Freeport.
a. Perform an analysis similar to that of Problem 15.32.
b. Compare the results in (a) with those of Problems 15.32 (a) and 15.33 (a).

15.35 You are a real estate broker who wants to compare property values in Glen Cove and Roslyn (which are located approximately 8 miles apart). Use the data in GCRoslyn. Make sure to include the dummy variable for location (Glen Cove or Roslyn) in the regression model.
a. Develop the most appropriate multiple regression model to predict fair market value.

b. What conclusions can you reach concerning the differences in fair market value between Glen Cove and Roslyn?

15.36 You are a real estate broker who wants to compare property values in Glen Cove, Freeport, and Roslyn. Use the data in GCFreeRoslyn.
a. Develop the most appropriate multiple regression model to predict fair market value.
b. What conclusions can you reach concerning the differences in fair market value between Glen Cove, Freeport, and Roslyn?

15.37 Financial analysts engage in business valuation to determine a company's value. A standard approach uses the multiple of earnings method: You multiply a company's profits by a certain value (average or median) to arrive at a final value. More recently, regression analysis has been demonstrated to consistently deliver more accurate predictions. A valuator has been given the assignment of valuing a drug company. She obtained financial data on 72 drug companies (Industry Group Standard Industrial Classification [SIC] 3 code 283), which included pharmaceutical preparation firms (SIC 4 code 2834), in vitro and in vivo diagnostic substances firms (SIC 4 code 2835), and biological products firms (SIC 4 2836). The file BusinessValuation2 contains these variables:
COMPANY—Drug company name
TS—Ticker symbol
SIC 3—Standard Industrial Classification 3 code (industry group identifier)
SIC 4—Standard Industrial Classification 4 code (industry identifier)
PB fye—Price-to-book value ratio (fiscal year ending)
PE fye—Price-to-earnings ratio (fiscal year ending)
NL Assets—Natural log of assets (as a measure of size)
ROE—Return on equity
SGROWTH—Growth (GS5)
DEBT/EBITDA—Ratio of debt to earnings before interest, taxes, depreciation, and amortization
D2834—Dummy variable indicator of SIC 4 code 2834 (1 if 2834, 0 if not)
D2835—Dummy variable indicator of SIC 4 code 2835 (1 if 2835, 0 if not)

Develop the most appropriate multiple regression model to predict the price-to-book value ratio. Perform a thorough residual analysis and provide a detailed explanation of your results.

15.38 A recent article (J. Conklin, "It's a Marathon, Not a Sprint," *Quality Progress*, June 2009, pp. 46–49) discussed a metal deposition process in which a piece of metal is placed in an acid bath and an alloy is layered on top of it. The key quality characteristic is the thickness of the alloy layer. The file Thickness contains the following variables:
Thickness—Thickness of the alloy layer
Catalyst—Catalyst concentration in the acid bath
pH—pH level of the acid bath
Pressure—Pressure in the tank holding the acid bath
Temp—Temperature in the tank holding the acid bath
Voltage—Voltage applied to the tank holding the acid bath

Develop the most appropriate multiple regression model to predict the thickness of the alloy layer. Be sure to perform a thorough residual analysis. The article suggests that there is a significant interaction between the pressure and the temperature in the tank. Do you agree?

15.39 A molding machine that contains different cavities is used in producing plastic parts. The product characteristics of interest are the product length (in.) and weight (g). The mold cavities were filled with raw material powder and then vibrated during the experiment. The factors that were varied were the vibration time (seconds), the vibration pressure (psi), the vibration amplitude (%), the raw material density (g/mL), and the quantity of raw material (scoops). The experiment was conducted in two different cavities on the molding machine. The data are stored in Molding. (Data extracted from M. Lopez and M. McShane-Vaughn, "Maximizing Product, Minimizing Costs," *Six Sigma Forum Magazine*, February 2008, pp. 18–23.)

a. Develop the most appropriate multiple regression model to predict the product length in cavity 1. Be sure to perform a thorough residual analysis. In addition, provide a detailed explanation of your results.
b. Repeat (a) for cavity 2.
c. Compare the results for length in the two cavities.
d. Develop the most appropriate multiple regression model to predict the product weight in cavity 1. Be sure to perform a thorough residual analysis. In addition, provide a detailed explanation of your results.
e. Repeat (d) for cavity 2.
f. Compare the results for weight in the two cavities.

15.40 The file HHIncome contains data from a sample of 25 U.S. cities. The variables collected for this sample are city median household income ($); unemployment rate (%); median home value ($); number of violent crimes per 100,000 residents; average commuter travel time (minutes); and livability score, a rating on a scale of 0 to 100 that rates the overall livability of the city. (Data extracted from "America's 50 Best Cities to Live," **bit.ly/1uGQIYh** and "Livability Index," **bit.ly/1Qbd6oj**.)

Develop the most appropriate multiple regression model to predict median city household income. Be sure to perform a thorough residual analysis and provide a detailed explanation of the results as part of your answer.

REPORT WRITING EXERCISE

15.41 In Problems 15.32–15.36 you developed multiple regression models to predict the fair market value of houses in Glen Cove, Roslyn, and Freeport. Now write a report based on the models you developed. Append all appropriate charts and statistical information to your report.

CHAPTER 15

▼CASES

The Mountain States Potato Company

Mountain States Potato Company sells a by-product of its potato-processing operation, called a filter cake, to area feedlots as cattle feed. The business problem faced by the feedlot owners is that the cattle are not gaining weight as quickly as they once were. The feedlot owners believe that the root cause of the problem is that the percentage of solids in the filter cake is too low.

Historically, the percentage of solids in the filter cakes ran slightly above 12%. Lately, however, the solids are running in the 11% range. What is actually affecting the solids is a mystery, but something has to be done quickly. Individuals involved in the process were asked to identify variables that might affect the percentage of solids. This review turned up the six variables (in addition to the percentage of solids) listed in the right column. Data collected by monitoring the process several times daily for 20 days are stored in Potato.

1. Thoroughly analyze the data and develop a regression model to predict the percentage of solids.

2. Write an executive summary concerning your findings to the president of the Mountain States Potato Company. Include specific recommendations on how to get the percentage of solids back above 12%.

Variable	Comments
SOLIDS	Percentage of solids in the filter cake.
PH	Acidity. This measure of acidity indicates bacterial action in the clarifier and is controlled by the amount of downtime in the system. As bacterial action progresses, organic acids are produced that can be measured using pH.
LOWER	Pressure of the vacuum line below the fluid line on the rotating drum.
UPPER	Pressure of the vacuum line above the fluid line on the rotating drum.
THICK	Filter cake thickness, measured on the drum.
VARIDRIV	Setting used to control the drum speed. May differ from DRUMSPD due to mechanical inefficiencies.
DRUMSPD	Speed at which the drum is rotating when collecting the filter cake. Measured with a stopwatch.

Sure Value Convenience Stores

You work in the corporate office for a nationwide convenience store franchise that operates nearly 10,000 stores. The per-store daily customer count (i.e., the mean number of customers in a store in one day) has been steady, at 900, for some time. To increase the customer count, the chain is considering cutting prices for coffee beverages. The question to be determined is how much prices should be cut to increase the daily customer count without reducing the gross margin on coffee sales too much. You decide to carry out an experiment in a sample of 24 stores where customer counts have been running almost exactly at the national average of 900. In six of the stores, the price of a small coffee will now be $0.59, in six stores the price of a small coffee will now be $0.69, in six stores, the price of a small coffee will now be $0.79, and in six stores, the price of a small coffee will now be $0.89. After four weeks at the new prices, the daily customer count in the stores is determined and is stored in CoffeeSales2 .

a. Construct a scatter plot for price and sales.
b. Fit a quadratic regression model and state the quadratic regression equation.
c. Predict the mean weekly sales for a small coffee priced at 79 cents.
d. Perform a residual analysis on the results and determine whether the regression model is valid.
e. At the 0.05 level of significance, is there a significant quadratic relationship between weekly sales and price?
f. At the 0.05 level of significance, determine whether the quadratic model is a better fit than the linear model.
g. Interpret the meaning of the coefficient of multiple determination.
h. Compute the adjusted r^2.
i. What price do you recommend the small coffee should be sold for?

Digital Case

Apply your knowledge of multiple regression model building in this Digital Case, which extends the Chapter 14 OmniPower Bars Using Statistics scenario.

Still concerned about ensuring a successful test marketing of its OmniPower bars, the marketing department of OmniFoods has contacted Connect2Coupons (C2C), another merchandising consultancy. C2C suggests that earlier analysis done by In-Store Placements Group (ISPG) was faulty because it did not use the correct type of data. C2C claims that its Internet-based viral marketing will have an even greater effect on OmniPower energy bar sales, as new data from the same 34-store sample will show. In response, ISPG says its earlier claims are valid and has reported to the OmniFoods marketing department that it can discern no simple relationship between C2C's viral marketing and increased OmniPower sales.

Open **OmniPowerForum15.pdf** to review all the claims made in a private online forum and chat hosted on the Omni-Foods corporate website. Then answer the following:

1. Which of the claims are true? False? True but misleading? Support your answer by performing an appropriate statistical analysis.
2. If the grocery store chain allowed OmniFoods to use an unlimited number of sales techniques, which techniques should it use? Explain.
3. If the grocery store chain allowed OmniFoods to use only one sales technique, which technique should it use? Explain.

The Craybill Instrumentation Company Case

The Craybill Instrumentation Company produces highly technical industrial instrumentation devices. The human resources (HR) director has the business objective of improving recruiting decisions concerning sales managers. The company has 45 sales regions, each headed by a sales manager. Many of the sales managers have degrees in electrical engineering, and due to the technical nature of the product line, several company officials believe that only applicants with degrees in electrical engineering should be considered.

At the time of their application, candidates are asked to take the Strong-Campbell Interest Inventory Test and the Wonderlic Personnel Test. Due to the time and money involved with the testing, some discussion has taken place about dropping one or both of the tests. To start, the HR director gathered information on each of the 45 current sales managers, including years of selling experience, electrical engineering background, and the scores from both the Wonderlic and Strong-Campbell tests. The HR director has decided to use regression modeling to predict a dependent variable of "sales index" score, which is the ratio of the regions' actual sales divided by the target sales. The target values are constructed each year by upper management, in consultation with the sales managers, and are based on past performance and market potential within each region. The file Managers contains information on the 45 current sales managers. The following variables are included:

Sales—Ratio of yearly sales divided by the target sales value for that region; the target values were mutually agreed-upon "realistic expectations"
Wonder—Score from the Wonderlic Personnel Test; the higher the score, the higher the applicant's perceived ability to manage
SC—Score on the Strong-Campbell Interest Inventory Test; the higher the score, the higher the applicant's perceived interest in sales
Experience—Number of years of selling experience prior to becoming a sales manager
Engineer—Dummy variable that equals 1 if the sales manager has a degree in electrical engineering and 0 otherwise

a. Develop the most appropriate regression model to predict sales.

b. Do you think that the company should continue administering both the Wonderlic and Strong-Campbell tests? Explain.

c. Do the data support the argument that electrical engineers outperform the other sales managers? Would you support the idea to hire only electrical engineers? Explain.

d. How important is prior selling experience in this case? Explain.

e. Discuss in detail how the HR director should incorporate the regression model you developed into the recruiting process.

More Descriptive Choices Follow-Up

Follow-up the Using Statistics scenario "More Descriptive Choices, Revisited" on page 136, by developing regression models to predict the one-year return, the three-year return, the five-year return, and the ten-year return based on the assets, turnover ratio, expense ratio, beta, standard deviation, type of fund (growth versus value), and risk (stored in Retirement Funds). (For this analysis, combine low and average risk into the new category "not high.") Be sure to perform a thorough residual analysis. Provide a summary report that explains your results in detail.

▼EXCEL GUIDE

EG15.1 The QUADRATIC REGRESSION MODEL

Finding the Regression Coefficients and Predicting Y

Key Technique Adapt Section EG14.1 and EG2.5 instructions to perform a regression analysis and construct a scatter plot that visualizes the quadratic relationship. Use the exponential operator (^) in a column of formulas to create the quadratic term.

Example Create the regression analysis and scatter plot for the concrete strength data shown in Figures 15.2 and 15.3 on page 524.

PHStat, Workbook, *and* **Analysis ToolPak** To complete the analysis requires these three steps:

A. Create the quadratic term in a new column in the worksheet that contains the regression data.

B. Perform a regression analysis that includes the quadratic term as an additional independent *X* variable.

C. Create a scatter plot that illustrates a nonlinear relationship that Excel calls polynomial.

For step A for the example, open to the **DATA worksheet** of the **FlyAsh workbook**, which contains the independent *Y* variable FlyAsh% in column A and the dependent *X* variable Strength(PSI) in column B and:

1. Select column B, right-click, and click **Insert** from the shortcut menu. This creates a new, blank column B, and changes Strength(PSI) to column C.

2. Enter the label **FlyAsh%^2** in cell **B1** and then enter the formula **=A2^2** in cell **B2**.

3. Copy this formula down column B through all the data rows (through row 19).

(Best practice dictates placing the quadratic term in a column that is contiguous to the columns of the other independent *X* variables.)

For step B for the example, perform a regression analysis using the EG14.1 "Developing a Multiple Regression Model" instructions on page 517. For *PHStat*, use **C1:C19** as the **Y Variable Cell Range** and **A1:A19** as the **X Variables Cell Range**. For *Worksheet*, use C2:C19 and A2:B19 in step 2 as the new cell ranges. For *Analysis ToolPak*, use **C1:C19** as the **Input Y Range** and **A1:B19** as the **Input X Range**.

For step C for the example, adapt the EG2.5 "The Scatter Plot" instructions. For *PHStat*, use **C1:C19** as the **Y Variable Cell Range** and **A1:B19** as the **X Variable Cell Range**. For *Worksheet*, select the noncontiguous cell range

A1:A19, C1:C19 in step 1 and skip step 3. (Appendix B explains how to select a noncontiguous cell range.) Select the scatter chart and then:

1. Select **Design** (or **Chart Design**) → **Add Chart Element** → **Trendline** → **More Trendline Options**.

In the Format Trendline pane (parts shown below),

2. Click **Polynomial** (shown below).

3. Check **Display Equation on chart** (shown below).

In older Excels, select **Layout** → **Trendline** → **More Trendline Options** in step 1 and in the Format Trendline dialog box, similar to the Format Trendline Pane, click **Trendline Options** in the left pane and in the Trendline Options right pane, click **Polynomial**, check **Display Equation on chart**, and click **OK**.

EG15.2 USING TRANSFORMATIONS in REGRESSION MODELS

The Square-Root Transformation

To the worksheet that contains your regression data, add a new column of formulas that computes the square root of the variable for which you want to create a square-root transformation. For example, to create a square root transformation in a blank column D for a variable in a column, enter the formula **=SQRT(C2)** in cell D2 of that worksheet and copy the formula down through all data rows.

If the column to the immediate right of the variable to be transformed is not empty, first select that column, right-click, and click **Insert** from the shortcut menu. Then place the transformation in the newly inserted blank column.

The Log Transformation

To the worksheet that contains your regression data, add a new column of formulas that computes the common (base 10) logarithm or natural logarithm (base *e*) of the dependent variable to create a log transformation. For example, to create a common logarithm transformation in a blank column D for a variable in a column C, enter the formula =**LOG(C2)** in cell D2 of that worksheet and copy the formula down through all data rows. To create a natural logarithm transformation in a blank column D for a variable in column C, enter the formula =**LN(C2)** in cell D2 of that worksheet and copy the formula down through all data rows.

If the dependent variable appears in a column to the immediate right of the independent variable being transformed, first select the dependent variable column, right-click, and click **Insert** from the shortcut menu and then place the transformation of the independent variable in that new column.

EG15.3 COLLINEARITY

PHStat To compute the variance inflationary factor (*VIF*), use the EG14.1 "Interpreting the Regression Coefficients" *PHStat* instructions on page 517, but modify step 6 by checking **Variance Inflationary Factor** (*VIF*) before you click **OK**. The *VIF* will appear in cell B9 of the regression results worksheet, immediately following the Regression Statistics area.

Workbook To compute the variance inflationary factor, first use the EG14.1 "Interpreting the Regression Coefficients" *Workbook* instructions on page 517 to create regression results worksheets for every combination of independent variables in which one serves as the dependent variable. Then, in each of the regression results worksheets, enter the label *VIF* in cell **A9** and enter the formula =**1/(1 − B5)** in cell **B9** to compute the *VIF*.

EG15.4 MODEL BUILDING

The Stepwise Regression Approach to Model Building

Key Technique Use PHStat to perform a stepwise analysis.

Example Perform the Figure 15.11 stepwise analysis for the standby-hours data that is shown on page 537.

PHStat Use **Stepwise Regression**.
For the example, open to the **DATA worksheet** of the **Standby workbook** and select **PHStat → Regression → Stepwise Regression**. In the procedure's dialog box (shown at the top of the right column):

1. Enter **A1:A27** as the **Y Variable Cell Range**.
2. Enter **B1:E27** as the **X Variables Cell Range**.
3. Check **First cells in both ranges contain label**.
4. Enter **95** as the **Confidence level for regression coefficients**.
5. Click **p values** as the **Stepwise Criteria**.
6. Click **General Stepwise** and keep the pair of **.05** values as the **p value to enter** and the **p value to remove**.

7. Enter a **Title** and click **OK**.

This procedure may take more than a few seconds to construct its results. The procedure finishes when the statement "Stepwise ends" is added to the stepwise regression results worksheet (shown in row 29 in Figure 15.11 on page 537).

The Best Subsets Approach to Model Building

Key Technique Use PHStat to perform a best subsets analysis.

Example Perform the Figure 15.12 best subsets analysis for the standby-hours data that is shown on page 538.

PHStat Use **Best Subsets**.
For the example, open to the **DATA worksheet** of the **Standby workbook**. Select **PHStat → Regression → Best Subsets**. In the procedure's dialog box (shown below):

1. Enter **A1:A27** as the **Y Variable Cell Range**.
2. Enter **B1:E27** as the **X Variables Cell Range**.
3. Check **First cells in each range contains label**.
4. Enter **95** as the **Confidence level for regression coefficients**.
5. Enter a **Title** and click **OK**.

This procedure constructs many regression results worksheets (that may be seen as a flickering in the Excel window) as it evaluates each subset of independent variables.

Time-Series Forecasting

OBJECTIVES

- Learn to construct different time-series forecasting models for annual and seasonal data
- Learn to choose the most appropriate time-series forecasting model

▼USING **STATISTICS**
Principled Forecasting

You are a financial analyst for The Principled, a large financial services company. You need to better evaluate investment opportunities for your clients. To assist in the forecasting, you have collected a time series for yearly movie attendance and the revenues of two large well-known companies, The Coca-Cola Company, and Wal-Mart Stores, Inc. Each time series has unique characteristics due to differences in business activities and growth patterns. You understand that you can choose among several different types of forecasting models. How do you decide which type of forecasting is best? How do you use the information gained from the forecasting models to evaluate investment opportunities for your clients?

n Chapters 13 through 15, you used regression analysis as a tool for model building and prediction. In this chapter, regression analysis and other statistical methodologies are applied to time-series data. A **time series** is a set of numerical data collected over time. Due to differences in the features of data for various investments described in the Using Statistics scenario, you need to consider several different approaches for forecasting time-series data.

This chapter begins with an introduction to the importance of business forecasting (see Section 16.1) and a description of the components of time-series models (see Section 16.2). The coverage of forecasting models begins with annual time-series data. Section 16.3 presents moving averages and exponential smoothing methods for smoothing a series. This is followed by least-squares trend fitting and forecasting in Section 16.4 and autoregressive modeling in Section 16.5. Section 16.6 discusses how to choose among alternative forecasting models. Section 16.7 develops models for monthly and quarterly time series.

16.1 The Importance of Business Forecasting

Forecasting involves monitoring changes that occur over time and predicting future business conditions. Managers must be able to develop *forecasts* to anticipate likely changes their businesses will face. For example, marketing executives at a retailer might forecast product demand, sales revenues, consumer preferences, and inventory, among other things, in order to make decisions regarding product promotions and strategic planning. Government officials forecast unemployment, inflation, industrial production, and revenues from income taxes in order to formulate economic policies. And college administrators need to forecast student enrollment in order to plan for facilities and personnel needs.

Two common approaches to forecasting are *qualitative* and *quantitative* forecasting. **Qualitative forecasting methods** are especially important when historical data are unavailable. Qualitative forecasting methods are considered to be highly subjective and judgmental. **Quantitative forecasting methods** make use of historical data. The goal of these methods is to use past data to predict future values.

Quantitative forecasting methods are subdivided into two types: *time series* and *causal*. **Time-series forecasting methods** involve forecasting future values based entirely on the past and present values of a variable. For example, the daily closing prices of a particular stock listed on the New York Stock Exchange constitute a time series. Other examples of economic or business time series are the consumer price index (CPI), the quarterly gross domestic product (GDP), and the annual sales revenues of a particular company.

Causal forecasting methods involve the determination of factors that relate to the variable you are trying to forecast. These include multiple regression analysis with lagged variables, econometric modeling, leading indicator analysis, and other economic barometers that are beyond the scope of this text (see references 2–5). The emphasis in this chapter is on time-series forecasting methods.

16.2 Component Factors of Time-Series Models

Time-series forecasting assumes that the factors that have influenced activities in the past and present will continue to do so in approximately the same way in the future. Time-series forecasting seeks to identify and isolate these component factors in order to make predictions. Typically, the following four factors are examined in time-series models:

- Trend
- Cyclical effect
- Irregular or random effect
- Seasonal effect

A **trend** is an overall long-term upward or downward movement in a time series. The **cyclical effect** involves the up-and-down swings or movements through the series. Cyclical movements vary in length, usually lasting from 2 to 10 years. They differ in intensity and are often correlated with a business cycle. In some time periods, the values are higher than would be predicted by a trend line (i.e., they are at or near the peak of a cycle). In other time periods, the values are lower than would be predicted by a trend line (i.e., they are at or near the bottom of a cycle). Any data that do not follow the trend modified by the cyclical component are considered part of the **irregular effect**, or **random effect**. When you have monthly or quarterly data, an additional component, the **seasonal effect**, is considered, along with the trend, cyclical, and irregular effects.

Your first step in a time-series analysis is to visualize the data and observe whether any patterns exist over time. You must determine whether there is a long-term upward or downward movement (a trend) in the series. If there is no obvious long-term upward or downward trend, then you can use moving averages or exponential smoothing to smooth the series (see Section 16.3). If a trend is present, you can consider several time-series forecasting methods. (See Sections 16.4 and 16.5 for forecasting annual data and Section 16.7 for forecasting monthly or quarterly time series.)

16.3 Smoothing an Annual Time Series

One of the investments considered in The Principled scenario is the entertainment industry. Table 16.1 presents the yearly U.S. and Canada movie attendance (in billions) from 2001 through 2014 (stored in Movie Attendance) and Figure 16.1 presents the time-series plot of these data.

TABLE 16.1
Movie Attendance from 2001 Through 2014

Year	Attendance (billions)	Year	Attendance (billions)	Year	Attendance (billions)
2001	1.44	2006	1.41	2011	1.28
2002	1.58	2007	1.40	2012	1.36
2003	1.55	2008	1.39	2013	1.15
2004	1.47	2009	1.42	2014	1.27
2005	1.39	2010	1.34		

Source: Data extracted from **boxofficemojo.com/yearly**.

FIGURE 16.1
Time-series plot of movie attendance from 2001 through 2014

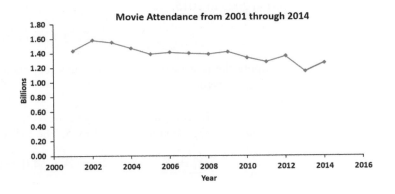

Figure 16.1 seems to show a slight downward trend in movie attendance between 2001 to 2014. However, when you examine annual data such as in Figure 16.1, your visual impression of the long-term trend in the series is sometimes obscured by the amount of variation from year to year. Often, you cannot judge whether any long-term upward or downward trend exists in the series. To get a better overall impression of the pattern of movement in the data over time, you can use the methods of *moving averages* or *exponential smoothing*.

Moving Averages

Moving averages for a time period of length L summarize L consecutive time-series values as a mean and associate that mean with the middle value in that group of values. Moving averages, represented by the symbol $MA(L)$, can be greatly affected by the value chosen for L, which should be an integer value that corresponds to, or is a multiple of, the estimated average length of a cycle in the time series.

For example, you decide to compute five-year moving averages from an annual series that has $n = 11$ years. Because $L = 5$, the five-year moving averages consist of a series of means computed by averaging consecutive sequences of five values. You compute the first five-year moving average by summing the values for the first five years in the series and dividing by 5:

$$MA(5) = \frac{Y_1 + Y_2 + Y_3 + Y_4 + Y_5}{5}$$

You compute the second five-year moving average by summing the values of years 2 through 6 in the series and then dividing by 5:

$$MA(5) = \frac{Y_2 + Y_3 + Y_4 + Y_5 + Y_6}{5}$$

You continue this process until you have computed the last of these five-year moving averages by summing the values of the last 5 years in the series (i.e., years 7 through 11) and then dividing by 5:

$$MA(5) = \frac{Y_7 + Y_8 + Y_9 + Y_{10} + Y_{11}}{5}$$

When you have annual time-series data, L should be an *odd* number of years. By following this rule, you are unable to compute any moving averages for the first $(L-1)/2$ years or the last $(L-1)/2$ years of the series. Thus, for a five-year moving average, you cannot make computations for the first two years or the last two years of the series.

When plotting moving averages, you plot each of the computed values against the middle year of the sequence of years used to compute it. If $n = 11$ and $L = 5$, the first moving average is centered on the third year, the second moving average is centered on the fourth year, and the last moving average is centered on the ninth year. Example 16.1 illustrates the computation of five-year moving averages.

studentTIP

Remember that you cannot compute moving averages at the beginning and at the end of the series.

EXAMPLE 16.1

Computing Five-Year Moving Averages

The following data represent total revenues (in $millions) for a fast-food store over the 11-year period 2005 to 2015:

4.0 5.0 7.0 6.0 8.0 9.0 5.0 7.0 7.5 5.5 6.5

Compute the five-year moving averages for this annual time series and plot the revenue and moving averages.

SOLUTION To compute the five-year moving averages, you first compute the total for the five years and then divide this total by 5. The first of the five-year moving averages is

$$MA(5) = \frac{Y_1 + Y_2 + Y_3 + Y_4 + Y_5}{5} = \frac{4.0 + 5.0 + 7.0 + 6.0 + 8.0}{5} = \frac{30.0}{5} = 6.0$$

The moving average is centered on the middle value—the third year of this time series. To compute the second of the five-year moving averages, you compute the total of the second through sixth years and divide this total by 5:

$$MA(5) = \frac{Y_2 + Y_3 + Y_4 + Y_5 + Y_6}{5} = \frac{5.0 + 7.0 + 6.0 + 8.0 + 9.0}{5} = \frac{35.0}{5} = 7.0$$

This moving average is centered on the new middle value—the fourth year of the time series. The remaining moving averages are

$$MA(5) = \frac{Y_3 + Y_4 + Y_5 + Y_6 + Y_7}{5} = \frac{7.0 + 6.0 + 8.0 + 9.0 + 5.0}{5} = \frac{35.0}{5} = 7.0$$

$$MA(5) = \frac{Y_4 + Y_5 + Y_6 + Y_7 + Y_8}{5} = \frac{6.0 + 8.0 + 9.0 + 5.0 + 7.0}{5} = \frac{35.0}{5} = 7.0$$

$$MA(5) = \frac{Y_5 + Y_6 + Y_7 + Y_8 + Y_9}{5} = \frac{8.0 + 9.0 + 5.0 + 7.0 + 7.5}{5} = \frac{36.5}{5} = 7.3$$

$$MA(5) = \frac{Y_6 + Y_7 + Y_8 + Y_9 + Y_{10}}{5} = \frac{9.0 + 5.0 + 7.0 + 7.5 + 5.5}{5} = \frac{34.0}{5} = 6.8$$

$$MA(5) = \frac{Y_7 + Y_8 + Y_9 + Y_{10} + Y_{11}}{5} = \frac{5.0 + 7.0 + 7.5 + 5.5 + 6.5}{5} = \frac{31.5}{5} = 6.3$$

These moving averages are centered on their respective middle values—the fifth, sixth, seventh, eighth, and ninth years in the time series. When you use the five-year moving averages, you are unable to compute a moving average for the first two or last two values in the time series.

Figure 16.2 plots the revenues and the five-year moving average for the fast-food store. Observe that the moving average exhibits much less variation than the revenues since they have smoothed the data.

FIGURE 16.2
Fast-food store revenue and five-year moving average

In practice, you can avoid the tedious computations by using Excel to compute moving averages. Figure 16.3 presents the annual movie attendance (in billions) from 2001 through 2014, the computations for three- and five-year moving averages, and a plot of the original data and the three-year and five-year moving averages.

FIGURE 16.3
Excel three- and five-year moving averages and plot for the movie attendance data

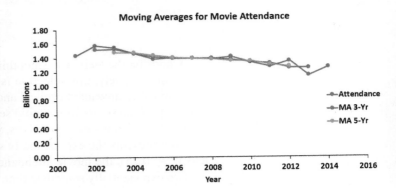

In Figure 16.3, there is no three-year moving average for the first year and the last year, and there is no five-year moving average for the first two years and last two years. Both the three-year and five-year moving averages have smoothed out the variation that exists in the movie attendance. Both the three-year and five-year moving average show a slight downward trend in movie attendance. The five-year moving average smooths the series more than the three-year moving average because the period length is longer. However, the longer the period, the smaller the number of moving averages you can compute. Therefore, selecting moving averages that are longer than five or seven years is usually undesirable because too many moving average values are missing at the beginning and end of the series.

The selection of L, the length of the period used for constructing the averages, is highly subjective. If cyclical fluctuations are present in the data, you should choose an integer value of L that corresponds to (or is a multiple of) the estimated length of a cycle in the series. For annual time-series data that has no obvious cyclical fluctuations, you should choose three years, five years, or seven years as the value of L, depending on the amount of smoothing desired and the amount of data available.

Exponential Smoothing

Exponential smoothing consists of a series of *exponentially weighted* moving averages. The weights assigned to the values change so that the most recent (the last) value receives the highest weight, the previous value receives the second-highest weight, and so on, with the first value receiving the lowest weight. Throughout the series, each exponentially smoothed value depends on all previous values, which often is an advantage of exponential smoothing over the method of moving averages. Exponential smoothing also allows you to compute short-term (one period into the future) forecasts when the presence and type of long-term trend in a time series is difficult to determine.

Equation (16.1) defines how to compute an exponentially smoothed value for any time period i. Note the special case that the smoothed value for time period 1 is the observed value for time period 1.

COMPUTING AN EXPONENTIALLY SMOOTHED VALUE IN TIME PERIOD i

$$E_1 = Y_1$$
$$E_i = WY_i + (1 - W)E_{i-1} \quad i = 2, 3, 4, \ldots \tag{16.1}$$

where

E_i = value of the exponentially smoothed series being computed in time period i
E_{i-1} = value of the exponentially smoothed series already computed in time period $i - 1$
Y_i = observed value of the time series in period i
W = subjectively assigned weight or smoothing coefficient, where $0 < W < 1$

studentTIP

Although W can approach 1.0, in virtually all business applications, $W \leq 0.5$.

Choosing the weight or smoothing coefficient W, that you assign to the time series is critical. Unfortunately, this selection is somewhat subjective. If your goal is to smooth a series by eliminating unwanted cyclical and irregular variations in order to see the overall long-term tendency of the series, you should select a small value for W (close to 0). If your goal is forecasting future short-term directions, you should choose a large value for W (close to 0.5). Figure 16.4 presents the exponentially smoothed values (with smoothing coefficients $W = 0.50$ and $W = 0.25$), the movie attendance from 2001 to 2014, and a plot of the original data and the two exponentially smoothed time series. Observe that exponential smoothing has smoothed out some of the variation in the movie attendance.

FIGURE 16.4

Exponentially smoothed series ($W = 0.50$ and $W = 0.25$) worksheet and plot for the movie attendance data

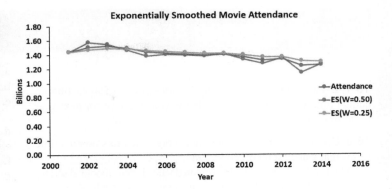

	A	B	C	D
1	Year	Attendance	ES(W=0.50)	ES(W=0.25)
2	2001	1.44	1.4400	1.4400
3	2002	1.58	1.5100	1.4750
4	2003	1.55	1.5300	1.4938
5	2004	1.47	1.5000	1.4878
6	2005	1.39	1.4450	1.4634
7	2006	1.41	1.4275	1.4500
8	2007	1.40	1.4138	1.4375
9	2008	1.39	1.4019	1.4256
10	2009	1.42	1.4109	1.4242
11	2010	1.34	1.3755	1.4032
12	2011	1.28	1.3277	1.3724
13	2012	1.36	1.3439	1.3693
14	2013	1.15	1.2469	1.3145
15	2014	1.27	1.2585	1.3033

To illustrate these exponential smoothing computations for a smoothing coefficient of $W = 0.25$, you begin with the initial value $Y_{2001} = 1.44$ as the first smoothed value ($E_{2001} = 1.44$). Then, using the value of the time series for 2002 ($Y_{2002} = 1.58$), you smooth the series for 2002 by computing

$$E_{2002} = WY_{2002} + (1 - W)E_{2001}$$
$$= (0.25)(1.58) + (0.75)(1.44) = 1.475$$

To smooth the series for 2003:

$$E_{2003} = WY_{2003} + (1 - W)E_{2002}$$
$$= (0.25)(1.55) + (0.75)(1.475) = 1.4938$$

To smooth the series for 2004:

$$E_{2004} = WY_{2004} + (1 - W)E_{2003}$$
$$= (0.25)(1.47) + (0.75)(1.4938) = 1.4878$$

You continue this process until you have computed the exponentially smoothed values for all 14 years in the series, as shown in Figure 16.4.

Exponential smoothing is a weighted average of all previous time periods. Therefore, when you use exponential smoothing for forecasting, you use the smoothed value in the current time period as the forecast of the value in the following period ($\hat{Y}_{i+1}$).

FORECASTING TIME PERIOD $i + 1$

$$\hat{Y}_{i+1} = E_i \qquad\qquad\qquad \textbf{(16.2)}$$

To forecast the movie attendance in 2015, using a smoothing coefficient of $W = 0.25$, you use the smoothed value for 2014 as its estimate.

$$\hat{Y}_{2014+1} = E_{2014}$$
$$\hat{Y}_{2015} = E_{2014}$$
$$\hat{Y}_{2015} = 1.3033$$

The exponentially smoothed forecast for 2015 is 1.3033 billion.

PROBLEMS FOR SECTION 16.3

LEARNING THE BASICS

16.1 If you are using exponential smoothing for forecasting an annual time series of revenues, what is your forecast for next year if the smoothed value for this year is $32.4 million?

16.2 Consider a nine-year moving average used to smooth a time series that was first recorded in 1984.
a. Which year serves as the first centered value in the smoothed series?
b. How many years of values in the series are lost when computing all the nine-year moving averages?

16.3 You are using exponential smoothing on an annual time series concerning total revenues (in $millions). You decide to use a smoothing coefficient of $W = 0.20$, and the exponentially smoothed value for 2015 is $E_{2013} = (0.20)(12.1) + (0.80)(9.4)$.
a. What is the smoothed value of this series in 2015?
b. What is the smoothed value of this series in 2016 if the value of the series in that year is $11.5 million?

APPLYING THE CONCEPTS

✓ SELF TEST **16.4** The data below (stored in DesktopLaptop) represent the hours per day spent by American desktop/laptop users from 2008 to 2014.

Year	Hours per Day	Year	Hours per Day
2008	2.2	2012	2.5
2009	2.3	2013	2.3
2010	2.4	2014	2.4
2011	2.6		

Source: Data extracted from E. C. Baig, "The Hottest Digital Trends," *USA Today*, May 26, 2015, p. B1.

a. Plot the time series.
b. Fit a three-year moving average to the data and plot the results.
c. Using a smoothing coefficient of $W = 0.50$, exponentially smooth the series and plot the results.
d. What is your exponentially smoothed forecast for 2015?
e. Repeat (c) and (d), using $W = 0.25$.
f. Compare the results of (d) and (e).
g. What conclusions can you reach about desktop/laptop use by American users?

16.5 The following data, stored in CoreAppliances provide the total number of shipments of core major household appliances in the U.S. from 2000 to 2014 (in millions).

Year	Shipments	Year	Shipments
2000	38.4	2008	39.8
2001	38.2	2009	36.5
2002	40.8	2010	38.2
2003	42.5	2011	36.0
2004	46.1	2012	35.8
2005	47.0	2013	39.2
2006	46.7	2014	41.5
2007	44.1		

Source: Data extracted from **www.statistica.com**.

a. Plot the time series.
b. Fit a three-year moving average to the data and plot the results.
c. Using a smoothing coefficient of $W = 0.50$, exponentially smooth the series and plot the results.
d. What is your exponentially smoothed forecast for 2015?
e. Repeat (c) and (d), using $W = 0.25$.
f. Compare the results of (d) and (e).
g. What conclusions can you reach concerning the total number of shipments of core major household appliances in the U.S. from 2000 to 2014 (in millions)?

16.6 How have stocks performed in the past? The following table presents the data stored in Stock Performance , which show the performance of a broad measure of stock performance (by percentage) for each decade from the 1830s through the 2000s:

Decade	Performance (%)	Decade	Performance (%)
1830s	2.8	1920s	13.3
1840s	12.8	1930s	−2.2
1850s	6.6	1940s	9.6
1860s	12.5	1950s	18.2
1870s	7.5	1960s	8.3
1880s	6.0	1970s	6.6
1890s	5.5	1980s	16.6
1900s	10.9	1990s	17.6
1910s	2.2	2000s*	−0.5

*Through December 15, 2009.

Source: T. Lauricella, "Investors Hope the '10s Beat the '00s," *The Wall Street Journal*, December 21, 2009, pp. C1, C2.

a. Plot the time series.
b. Fit a three-period moving average to the data and plot the results.
c. Using a smoothing coefficient of $W = 0.50$, exponentially smooth the series and plot the results.
d. What is your exponentially smoothed forecast for the 2010s?
e. Repeat (c) and (d), using $W = 0.25$.
f. Compare the results of (d) and (e).
g. What conclusions can you reach concerning how stocks have performed in the past?

16.7 The following data (stored in CoffeeExports) represent the coffee exports (in thousands of 60 kg bags) by Costa Rica from 2006 to 2013:

Year	Exports (thousands of 60 kg bags)
2006	1,310
2007	1.364
2008	1,440
2009	1,236
2010	1,200
2011	1,243
2012	1,374
2013	1,344

Source: International Coffee Organization, **www.ico.org**.

a. Plot the data.
b. Fit a three-year moving average to the data and plot the results.
c. Using a smoothing coefficient of $W = 0.50$, exponentially smooth the series and plot the results.
d. What is your exponentially smoothed forecast for 2014?
e. Repeat (c) and (d), using a smoothing coefficient of $W = 0.25$.
f. Compare the results of (d) and (e).
g. What conclusions can you reach about the exports of coffee in Costa Rica?

16.8 The file **Audits** contains the number of audits of corporations with assets of more than $250 million conducted by the Internal Revenue Service. (Data extracted from **www.irs.gov**.)

a. Plot the data.
b. Fit a three-year moving average to the data and plot the results.
c. Using a smoothing coefficient of $W = 0.50$, exponentially smooth the series and plot the results.
d. What is your exponentially smoothed forecast for 2014?
e. Repeat (c) and (d), using a smoothing coefficient of $W = 0.25$.
f. Compare the results of (d) and (e).
g. What conclusions can you reach concerning the number of audits of corporations with assets of more than $250 million conducted by the Internal Revenue Service?

16.4 Least-Squares Trend Fitting and Forecasting

Trend is the component factor of a time series most often used to make intermediate and long-range forecasts. To get a visual impression of the overall long-term movements in a time series, you construct a time-series plot. If a straight-line trend adequately fits the data, you can use a linear trend model [see Equation (16.3) and Section 13.2]. If the time-series data indicate some long-run downward or upward quadratic movement, you can use a quadratic trend model [see Equation (16.4) and Section 15.1]. When the time-series data increase at a rate such that the percentage difference from value to value is constant, you can use an exponential trend model [see Equation (16.5)].

The Linear Trend Model

The **linear trend model**:

$$Y_i = \beta_0 + \beta_1 X_i + \varepsilon_i$$

is the simplest forecasting model. Equation (16.3) defines the linear trend forecasting equation.

LINEAR TREND FORECASTING EQUATION

$$\hat{Y}_i = b_0 + b_1 X_i \qquad \textbf{(16.3)}$$

Recall that in linear regression analysis, you use the method of least squares to compute the sample slope, b_1, and the sample Y intercept, b_0. You then substitute the values for X into Equation (16.3) to predict Y.

When using the least-squares method for fitting trends in a time series, you can simplify the interpretation of the coefficients by assigning coded values to the X (time) variable. You assign consecutively numbered integers, starting with 0, as the coded values for the time periods. For example, in time-series data that have been recorded annually for 17 years, you assign the coded value 0 to the first year, the coded value 1 to the second year, the coded value 2 to the third year, and so on, concluding by assigning 16 to the seventeenth year.

In The Principled scenario on page 553, one of the companies of interest is The Coca-Cola Company. Founded in 1886 and headquartered in Atlanta, Georgia, Coca-Cola manufactures, distributes, and markets more than 500 beverage brands in over 200 countries worldwide. Brands include Coca-Cola, Diet Coke, Fanta, and Sprite, four of the world's top five nonalcoholic sparkling beverage products. According to The Coca-Cola Company's website, revenues in 2014 were almost $46 billion. Table 16.2 lists The Coca-Cola Company's gross revenues (in $billions) from 1998 to 2014 (stored in Coca-Cola).

TABLE 16.2
Revenues for The
Coca-Cola Company
(1998–2014)

Year	Revenues ($billions)	Year	Revenues ($billions)
1998	18.8	2007	28.9
1999	19.8	2008	31.9
2000	20.5	2009	31.0
2001	20.1	2010	35.1
2002	19.6	2011	46.5
2003	21.0	2012	48.0
2004	21.9	2013	46.7
2005	23.1	2014	45.9
2006	24.1		

Source: Data extracted from *Mergent's Handbook of Common Stocks*, 2006; and **www.thecoca-colacompany .com/investors/annual_other_reports.html**.

Figure 16.5 presents the regression results for the simple linear regression model that uses the consecutive coded values 0 through 16 as the X (coded year) variable. These results produce the following linear trend forecasting equation:

$$\hat{Y}_i = 13.5059 + 2.0096 X_i$$

where $X_1 = 0$ represents 1998.

FIGURE 16.5
Excel regression results
worksheet for the linear
trend model to forecast
revenues (in $billions) for
The Coca-Cola Company

	A	B	C	D	E	F	G
1	Linear Trend Model for The Coca-Cola Company Revenues						
2							
3	*Regression Statistics*						
4	Multiple R	0.9284					
5	R Square	0.8619					
6	Adjusted R Square	0.8526					
7	Standard Error	4.1961					
8	Observations	17					
9							
10	ANOVA						
11		*df*	*SS*	*MS*	*F*	*Significance F*	
12	Regression	1	1647.6373	1647.6373	93.5777	0.0000	
13	Residual	15	264.1074	17.6072			
14	Total	16	1911.7447				
15							
16		Coefficients	Standard Error	t Stat	P-value	Lower 95%	Upper 95%
17	Intercept	13.5059	1.9487	6.9305	0.0000	9.3522	17.6595
18	Coded Year	2.0096	0.2077	9.6736	0.0000	1.5668	2.4523

In the Worksheet

This worksheet uses the same template that the Figure 13.4 worksheet on page 431 uses.

You interpret the regression coefficients as follows:

- The Y intercept, $b_0 = 13.5059$, is the predicted mean revenues (in $billions) at The Coca-Cola Company during the origin, or base, year, 1998.
- The slope, $b_1 = 2.0096$, indicates that mean revenues are predicted to increase by $2.0096 billion per year.

To project the trend in the revenues at Coca-Cola to 2015, you substitute $X_{18} = 17$, the code for 2015 into the linear trend forecasting equation:

$$\hat{Y}_i = 13.5059 + 2.0096(17) = 47.6684 \text{ billions of dollars}$$

The trend line is plotted in Figure 16.6, along with the observed values of the time series. There is a strong upward linear trend, and r^2 is 0.8619, indicating that more than 86% of the variation in revenues is explained by the linear trend of the time series. However, you can observe that the early years are slightly above the trend line, but the middle years are below the trend line and the later years are also above the trend line. To investigate whether a different trend model might provide a better fit, a *quadratic* trend model and an *exponential* trend model can be fitted.

FIGURE 16.6
Plot of the linear trend forecasting equation for The Coca-Cola Company revenue data

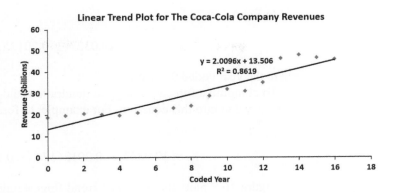

The Quadratic Trend Model

A **quadratic trend model**:

$$Y_i = \beta_0 + \beta_1 X_i + \beta_2 X_i^2 + \varepsilon_i$$

is a nonlinear model that contains a linear term and a curvilinear term in addition to a Y intercept. Using the least-squares method for a quadratic model described in Section 15.1, you can develop a quadratic trend forecasting equation, as presented in Equation (16.4).

QUADRATIC TREND FORECASTING EQUATION

$$\hat{Y}_i = b_0 + b_1 X_i + b_2 X_i^2 \tag{16.4}$$

where

b_0 = estimated Y intercept
b_1 = estimated *linear* effect on Y
b_2 = estimated *quadratic* effect on Y

Figure 16.7 presents the regression results for the quadratic trend model used to forecast revenues at The Coca-Cola Company.

FIGURE 16.7
Excel regression results worksheet for the quadratic trend model to forecast revenues (in $billions) for The Coca-Cola Company

	A	B	C	D	E	F	G
1	Quadratic Trend Model for The Coca-Cola Company Revenues						
2							
3	*Regression Statistics*						
4	Multiple R	0.9692					
5	R Square	0.9393					
6	Adjusted R Square	0.9306					
7	Standard Error	2.8799					
8	Observations	17					
9							
10	ANOVA						
11		df	SS	MS	F	Significance F	
12	Regression	2	1795.6320	897.8160	108.2519	0.0000	
13	Residual	14	116.1127	8.2938			
14	Total	16	1911.7447				
15							
16		Coefficients	Standard Error	t Stat	P-value	Lower 95%	Upper 95%
17	Intercept	19.0327	1.8710	10.1724	0.0000	15.0198	23.0456
18	Coded Year	-0.2012	0.5424	-0.3709	0.7163	-1.3645	0.9622
19	Coded Year Squared	0.1382	0.0327	4.2242	0.0008	0.0680	0.2083

In the Worksheet

This worksheet uses the same template that the Figure 14.2 worksheet on page 479 uses.

In Figure 16.7,

$$\hat{Y}_i = 19.0327 - 0.2012X_i + 0.1382X_i^2$$

where the year coded 0 is 1998.

To compute a forecast using the quadratic trend equation, you substitute the appropriate coded X value into this equation. For example, to forecast the trend in revenues for 2015 (i.e., $X = 17$),

$$\hat{Y}_i = 19.0327 - 0.2012(17) + 0.1382(17)^2 = 55.5521$$

Figure 16.8 plots the quadratic trend forecasting equation along with the time series for the actual data. This quadratic trend model provides a better fit (adjusted $r^2 = 0.9393$) to the time series than does the linear trend model. The t_{STAT} test statistic for the contribution of the quadratic term to the model is 4.2242 (p-value $= 0.0008$).

FIGURE 16.8
Plot of the quadratic trend forecasting equation for The Coca-Cola Company revenue data

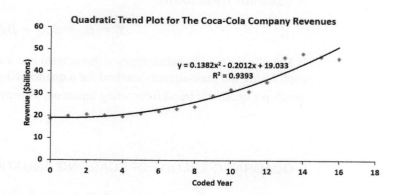

The Exponential Trend Model

When a time series increases at a rate such that the percentage difference from value to value is constant, an exponential trend is present. Equation (16.5) defines the **exponential trend model**.

EXPONENTIAL TREND MODEL

$$Y_i = \beta_0 \beta_1^{X_i} \varepsilon_i \qquad (16.5)$$

where

$$\beta_0 = Y \text{ intercept}$$
$$(\beta_1 - 1) \times 100\% = \text{annual compound growth rate (in \%)}$$

The model in Equation (16.5) is not in the form of a linear regression model. To transform this nonlinear model to a linear model, you use a base 10 logarithm transformation.[1] Taking the logarithm of each side of Equation (16.5) results in Equation (16.6).

[1]Alternatively, you can use base e logarithms. For more information on logarithms, see Section A.3 in Appendix A.

TRANSFORMED EXPONENTIAL TREND MODEL

$$\log(Y_i) = \log(\beta_0 \beta_1^{X_i} \varepsilon_i)$$
$$= \log(\beta_0) + \log(\beta_1^{X_i}) + \log(\varepsilon_i) \qquad (16.6)$$
$$= \log(\beta_0) + X_i \log(\beta_1) + \log(\varepsilon_i)$$

Equation (16.6) is a linear model you can estimate using the least-squares method, with $\log(Y_i)$ as the dependent variable and X_i as the independent variable. This results in Equation (16.7).

EXPONENTIAL TREND FORECASTING EQUATION

$$\log(\hat{Y}_i) = b_0 + b_1 X_i \tag{16.7a}$$

where

$$b_0 = \text{estimate of } \log(\beta_0) \text{ and thus } 10^{b_0} = \hat{\beta}_0$$
$$b_1 = \text{estimate of } \log(\beta_1) \text{ and thus } 10^{b_1} = \hat{\beta}_1$$

therefore,

$$\hat{Y}_i = \hat{\beta}_0 \hat{\beta}_1^{X_i} \tag{16.7b}$$

where

$(\hat{\beta}_1 - 1) \times 100\%$ is the estimated annual compound growth rate (in %)

Figure 16.9 shows the Excel regression results for an exponential trend model of revenues at The Coca-Cola Company.

Using Equation (16.7a) and the results from Figure 16.9,

$$\log(\hat{Y}_i) = 1.2159 + 0.0287X_i$$

where the year coded 0 is 1998.

FIGURE 16.9
Excel regression results worksheet for the exponential trend model to forecast revenues (in $billions) for The Coca-Cola Company

	A	B	C	D	E	F	G
1	Exponential Trend Model for The Coca-Cola Company Revenues						
2							
3	*Regression Statistics*						
4	Multiple R	0.9548					
5	R Square	0.9116					
6	Adjusted R Square	0.9057					
7	Standard Error	0.0465					
8	Observations	17					
9							
10	ANOVA						
11		*df*	*SS*	*MS*	*F*	*Significance F*	
12	Regression	1	0.3350	0.3350	154.6874	0.0000	
13	Residual	15	0.0325	0.0022			
14	Total	16	0.3675				
15							
16		*Coefficients*	*Standard Error*	*t Stat*	*P-value*	*Lower 95%*	*Upper 95%*
17	Intercept	1.2159	0.0216	56.2561	0.0000	1.1698	1.2620
18	Coded Year	0.0287	0.0023	12.4373	0.0000	0.0237	0.0336

You compute the values for $\hat{\beta}_0$ and $\hat{\beta}_1$ by taking the antilog of the regression coefficients (b_0 and b_1):

$$\hat{\beta}_0 = \text{antilog}(b_0) = \text{antilog}(1.2159) = 10^{1.2159} = 16.4399$$
$$\hat{\beta}_1 = \text{antilog}(b_1) = \text{antilog}(0.0287) = 10^{0.0287} = 1.0683$$

Thus, using Equation (16.7b), the exponential trend forecasting equation is

$$\hat{Y}_i = (16.4399)(1.0683)^{X_i}$$

where the year coded 0 is 1998.

The Y intercept, $\hat{\beta}_0 = 16.4399$ billions of dollars, is the revenue forecast for the base year 1998. The value $(\hat{\beta}_1 - 1) \times 100\% = 6.83\%$ is the annual compound growth rate in revenues at The Coca-Cola Company.

For forecasting purposes, you substitute the appropriate coded X values into either Equation (16.7a) or Equation (16.7b). For example, to forecast revenues for 2015 (i.e., $X = 17$) using Equation (16.7a),

$$\log(\hat{Y}_i) = 1.2159 + 0.0287(17) = 1.7038$$
$$\hat{Y}_i = \text{antilog}(1.7038) = 10^{1.7038} = 50.5592 \text{ billions of dollars}$$

Figure 16.10 plots the exponential trend forecasting equation, along with the time-series data. The adjusted r^2 for the exponential trend model (0.9057) is greater than the adjusted r^2 for the linear trend model (0.8619) but less than for the quadratic model (0.9393).

FIGURE 16.10

Plot of the exponential trend forecasting equation for The Coca-Cola Company revenue data

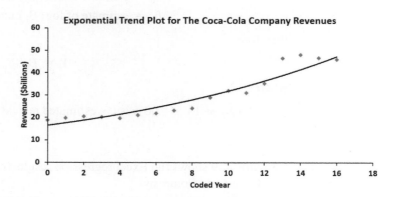

Model Selection Using First, Second, and Percentage Differences

You have used the linear, quadratic, and exponential models to forecast revenues for The Coca-Cola Company. How can you determine which of these models is the most appropriate model? In addition to visually inspecting time-series plots and comparing adjusted r^2 values, you can compute and examine first, second, and percentage differences. The identifying features of linear, quadratic, and exponential trend models are as follows:

- If a linear trend model provides a perfect fit to a time series, then the first differences are constant. Thus,

$$(Y_2 - Y_1) = (Y_3 - Y_2) = \cdots = (Y_n - Y_{n-1})$$

- If a quadratic trend model provides a perfect fit to a time series, then the second differences are constant. Thus,

$$[(Y_3 - Y_2) - (Y_2 - Y_1)] = [(Y_4 - Y_3) - (Y_3 - Y_2)] = \cdots = [(Y_n - Y_{n-1}) - (Y_{n-1} - Y_{n-2})]$$

- If an exponential trend model provides a perfect fit to a time series, then the percentage differences between consecutive values are constant. Thus,

$$\frac{Y_2 - Y_1}{Y_1} \times 100\% = \frac{Y_3 - Y_2}{Y_2} \times 100\% = \cdots = \frac{Y_n - Y_{n-1}}{Y_{n-1}} \times 100\%$$

Although you should not expect a perfectly fitting model for any particular set of time-series data, you can consider the first differences, second differences, and percentage differences as guides in choosing an appropriate model. Examples 16.2, 16.3, and 16.4 illustrate linear, quadratic, and exponential trend models that have perfect (or nearly perfect) fits to their respective data sets.

EXAMPLE 16.2

A Linear Trend Model with a Perfect Fit

The following time series represents the number of customers per year (in thousands) at a branch of a fast-food chain:

	Year									
	2006	2007	2008	2009	2010	2011	2012	2013	2014	2015
Customers Y	200	205	210	215	220	225	230	235	240	245

Using first differences, show that the linear trend model provides a perfect fit to these data.

SOLUTION The following table shows the solution:

	Year									
	2006	2007	2008	2009	2010	2011	2012	2013	2014	2015
Customers Y	200	205	210	215	220	225	230	235	240	245
First differences		5.0	5.0	5.0	5.0	5.0	5.0	5.0	5.0	5.0

The differences between consecutive values in the series are the same throughout. Thus, the number of customers at the branch of the fast-food chain shows a linear growth pattern.

EXAMPLE 16.3

A Quadratic Trend Model with a Perfect Fit

The following time series represents the number of customers per year (in thousands) at another branch of a fast-food chain:

	Year									
	2006	2007	2008	2009	2010	2011	2012	2013	2014	2015
Customers Y	200	201	203.5	207.5	213	220	228.5	238.5	250	263

Using second differences, show that the quadratic trend model provides a perfect fit to these data.

SOLUTION The following table shows the solution:

	Year									
	2006	2007	2008	2009	2010	2011	2012	2013	2014	2015
Customers Y	200	201	203.5	207.5	213	220	228.5	238.5	250	263
First differences		1.0	2.5	4.0	5.5	7.0	8.5	10.0	11.5	13.0
Second differences			1.5	1.5	1.5	1.5	1.5	1.5	1.5	1.5

The second differences between consecutive pairs of values in the series are the same throughout. Thus, the number of customers at the branch of the fast-food chain shows a quadratic growth pattern. Its rate of growth is accelerating over time.

EXAMPLE 16.4

An Exponential Trend Model with an Almost Perfect Fit

The following time series represents the number of customers per year (in thousands) for another branch of the fast-food chain:

	Year									
	2006	**2007**	**2008**	**2009**	**2010**	**2011**	**2012**	**2013**	**2014**	**2015**
Customers Y	200	206	212.18	218.55	225.11	231.86	238.82	245.98	253.36	260.96

Using percentage differences, show that the exponential trend model provides almost a perfect fit to these data.

SOLUTION The following table shows the solution:

	Year									
	2006	**2007**	**2008**	**2009**	**2010**	**2011**	**2012**	**2013**	**2014**	**2015**
Customers Y	200	206	212.18	218.55	225.11	231.86	238.82	245.98	253.36	260.96
Percentage differences		3.0	3.0	3.0	3.0	3.0	3.0	3.0	3.0	3.0

The percentage differences between consecutive values in the series are approximately the same throughout. Thus, this branch of the fast-food chain shows an exponential growth pattern. Its rate of growth is approximately 3% per year.

Figure 16.11 shows a worksheet that compares the first, second, and percentage differences for the revenues data at The Coca-Cola Company. Neither the first differences, second differences, nor percentage differences are constant across the series. Therefore, other models (including those considered in Section 16.5) may be more appropriate.

FIGURE 16.11

Excel worksheet that compares first, second, and percentage differences in revenues (in $billions) for The Coca-Cola Company

	A	B	C	D	E
1	Year	Revenues	First Difference	Second Difference	Percentage Difference
2	1998	18.8	#N/A	#N/A	#N/A
3	1999	19.8	1.0	#N/A	5.32%
4	2000	20.5	0.7	-0.3	3.54%
5	2001	20.1	-0.4	-1.1	-1.95%
6	2002	19.6	-0.5	-0.1	-2.49%
7	2003	21.0	1.4	1.9	7.14%
8	2004	21.9	0.9	-0.5	4.29%
9	2005	23.1	1.2	0.3	5.48%
10	2006	24.1	1.0	-0.2	4.33%
11	2007	28.9	4.8	3.8	19.92%
12	2008	31.9	3.0	-1.8	10.38%
13	2009	31.0	-0.9	-3.9	-2.82%
14	2010	35.1	4.1	5.0	13.23%
15	2011	46.5	11.4	7.3	32.48%
16	2012	48.0	1.5	-9.9	3.23%
17	2013	46.7	-1.3	-2.8	-2.71%
18	2014	45.9	-0.8	0.5	-1.71%

PROBLEMS FOR SECTION 16.4

LEARNING THE BASICS

16.9 If you are using the method of least squares for fitting trends in an annual time series containing 25 consecutive yearly values,
a. what coded value do you assign to X for the first year in the series?
b. what coded value do you assign to X for the fifth year in the series?
c. what coded value do you assign to X for the most recent recorded year in the series?
d. what coded value do you assign to X if you want to project the trend and make a forecast five years beyond the last observed value?

16.10 The linear trend forecasting equation for an annual time series containing 22 values (from 1994 to 2015) on total revenues (in \$millions) is

$$\hat{Y}_i = 4.0 + 1.5X_i$$

a. Interpret the Y intercept, b_0.
b. Interpret the slope, b_1.
c. What is the fitted trend value for the fifth year?
d. What is the fitted trend value for the most recent year?
e. What is the projected trend forecast three years after the last value?

16.11 The linear trend forecasting equation for an annual time series containing 42 values (from 1974 to 2015) on net sales (in \$billions) is

$$\hat{Y}_i = 1.2 + 0.5X_i$$

a. Interpret the Y intercept, b_0.
b. Interpret the slope, b_1.
c. What is the fitted trend value for the tenth year?
d. What is the fitted trend value for the most recent year?
e. What is the projected trend forecast two years after the last value?

APPLYING THE CONCEPTS

✓SELF TEST 16.12 There has been much publicity about bonuses paid to workers on Wall Street. Just how large are these bonuses? The file **Bonuses** contains the bonuses paid (in \$000) from 2000 to 2014. (Data extracted from K. McCoy, "Good job. Here's \$173K," *USA Today*, March 12, 2015, p. B1.)
a. Plot the data.
b. Compute a linear trend forecasting equation and plot the results.
c. Compute a quadratic trend forecasting equation and plot the results.
d. Compute an exponential trend forecasting equation and plot the results.
e. Using the forecasting equations in (b) through (d), what are your annual forecasts of the bonuses for 2015 and 2016?
f. How can you explain the differences in the three forecasts in (e)? What forecast do you think you should use? Why?

16.13 Gross domestic product (GDP) is a major indicator of a nation's overall economic activity. It consists of personal consumption expenditures, gross domestic investment, net exports of goods and services, and government consumption expenditures. The file **GDP** contains the GDP (in billions of current dollars) for the United States from 1980 to 2014. (Data extracted from Bureau of Economic Analysis, U.S. Department of Commerce, **www.bea.gov**.)
a. Plot the data.
b. Compute a linear trend forecasting equation and plot the trend line.
c. What are your forecasts for 2015 and 2016?
d. What conclusions can you reach concerning the trend in GDP?

16.14 The data in **FedReceipt** represent federal receipts from 1978 through 2014, in billions of current dollars, from individual and corporate income tax, social insurance, excise tax, estate and gift tax, customs duties, and federal reserve deposits. (Data extracted from "Historical Federal Receipt and Outlay Summary," Tax Policy Center, **tpc.io/1JMFKpo**.)
a. Plot the series of data.
b. Compute a linear trend forecasting equation and plot the trend line.
c. What are your forecasts of the federal receipts for 2015 and 2016?
d. What conclusions can you reach concerning the trend in federal receipts?

16.15 The file **HouseSales** contains the number of new, single-family houses sold in the U.S. from 1992 through 2014.
a. Plot the data.
b. Compute a linear trend forecasting equation and plot the trend line.
c. Compute a quadratic trend forecasting equation and plot the results.
d. Compute an exponential trend forecasting equation and plot the results.
e. Which model is the most appropriate?
f. Using the most appropriate model, forecast the number of new, single-family houses sold in the U.S. in 2015.

16.16 The data shown in the following table and stored in **Solar Power** represent the yearly amount of solar power generated by utilities (in millions of kWh) in the United States from 2002 through 2014:

Year	Solar Power Generated (millions of kWh)	Year	Solar Power Generated (millions of kWh)
2002	555	2008	864
2003	534	2009	891
2004	575	2010	1,212
2005	550	2011	1,818
2006	508	2012	4,327
2007	612	2013	9,253
		2014	18,321

Source: Data extracted from **en.wikipedia.org/wiki/Solar_power_in_the_United_States**.

a. Plot the data.
b. Compute a linear trend forecasting equation and plot the trend line.
c. Compute a quadratic trend forecasting equation and plot the results.
d. Compute an exponential trend forecasting equation and plot the results.
e. Using the models in (b) through (d), what are your annual trend forecasts of the yearly amount of solar power generated by utilities (in millions of kWh) in the United States in 2015 and 2016?

16.17 The file CarProduction contains the number of passenger cars produced in the U.S. (in thousands) from 1999 to 2014. (Data extracted from **www.statista.com**.)
a. Plot the data.
b. Compute a linear trend forecasting equation and plot the trend line.
c. Compute a quadratic trend forecasting equation and plot the results.
d. Compute an exponential trend forecasting equation and plot the results.
e. Which model is the most appropriate?
f. Using the most appropriate model, forecast the U.S. car production for 2015.

16.18 The average salary of Major League Baseball players on opening day from 2000 to 2015 is stored in BBSalaries and shown below.

Year	Salary ($millions)	Year	Salary ($millions)
2000	1.99	2008	3.13
2001	2.29	2009	3.26
2002	2.38	2010	3.27
2003	2.58	2011	3.32
2004	2.49	2012	3.38
2005	2.63	2013	3.62
2006	2.83	2014	3.81
2007	2.92	2015	4.25

Source: Data extracted from "Baseball Salaries," *USA Today*, April 6, 2009, p. 6C; and **mlb.com**.

a. Plot the data.
b. Compute a linear trend forecasting equation and plot the trend line.
c. Compute a quadratic trend forecasting equation and plot the results.
d. Compute an exponential trend forecasting equation and plot the results.
e. Which model is the most appropriate?
f. Using the most appropriate model, forecast the average salary for 2016.

16.19 The file Silver contains the following prices in London for an ounce of silver (in US$) on the last day of the year from 1999 to 2014:

Year	Price (US$/ounce)	Year	Price (US$/ounce)
1999	5.330	2007	14.760
2000	4.570	2008	10.790
2001	4.520	2009	16.990
2002	4.670	2010	30.630
2003	5.965	2011	28.180
2004	6.815	2012	29.950
2005	8.830	2013	19.500
2006	12.900	2014	15.970

Source: Data extracted from **bit.ly/1afifi**.

a. Plot the data.
b. Compute a linear trend forecasting equation and plot the trend line.
c. Compute a quadratic trend forecasting equation and plot the results.
d. Compute an exponential trend forecasting equation and plot the results.
e. Which model is the most appropriate?
f. Using the most appropriate model, forecast the price of silver at the end of 2015.

16.20 The data in CPI-U reflect the annual values of the consumer price index (CPI) in the United States over the 50-year period 1965 through 2014, using 1982 through 1984 as the base period. This index measures the average change in prices over time in a fixed "market basket" of goods and services purchased by all urban consumers, including urban wage earners (i.e., clerical, professional, managerial, and technical workers; self-employed individuals; and short-term workers), unemployed individuals, and retirees. (Data extracted from Bureau of Labor Statistics, U.S. Department of Labor, **www.bls.gov**.)
a. Plot the data.
b. Describe the movement in this time series over the 48-year period.
c. Compute a linear trend forecasting equation and plot the trend line.
d. Compute a quadratic trend forecasting equation and plot the results.
e. Compute an exponential trend forecasting equation and plot the results.
f. Which model is the most appropriate?
g. Using the most appropriate model, forecast the CPI for 2015 and 2016.

16.21 Although you should not expect a perfectly fitting model for any time-series data, you can consider the first differences, second differences, and percentage differences for a given series as guides in choosing an appropriate model.

Year	Series I	Series II	Series III
2003	10.0	30.0	60.0
2004	15.1	33.1	67.9
2005	24.0	36.4	76.1
2006	36.7	39.9	84.0
2007	53.8	43.9	92.2
2008	74.8	48.2	100.0
2009	100.0	53.2	108.0
2010	129.2	58.2	115.8
2011	162.4	64.5	124.1
2012	199.0	70.7	132.0
2013	239.3	77.1	140.0
2014	283.5	83.9	147.8

Year	Series I	Series II
2003	100.0	100.0
2004	115.2	115.2
2005	130.1	131.7
2006	144.9	150.8
2007	160.0	174.1
2008	175.0	200.0
2009	189.8	230.8
2010	204.9	266.1
2011	219.8	305.5
2012	235.0	351.8
2013	249.8	403.0
2014	264.9	469.2

For this problem, use each of the time series presented in the table above and stored in `Tsmodel1` :

a. Determine the most appropriate model.
b. Compute the forecasting equation.
c. Forecast the value for 2015.

16.22 A time-series plot often helps you determine the appropriate model to use. For this problem, use each of the time series presented in the following table and stored in `TsModel2` :

a. Plot the observed data (Y) over time (X) and plot the logarithm of the observed data $(\log Y)$ over time (X) to determine whether a linear trend model or an exponential trend model is more appropriate. (Hint: If the plot of log Y versus X appears to be linear, an exponential trend model provides an appropriate fit.)
b. Compute the appropriate forecasting equation.
c. Forecast the value for 2015.

16.5 Autoregressive Modeling for Trend Fitting and Forecasting

Frequently, the values of a time series at particular points in time are highly correlated with the values that precede and succeed them. This type of correlation is called *autocorrelation*. When the autocorrelation exists between values that are in consecutive periods in a time series, the time series displays **first-order autocorrelation**. When the autocorrelation exists between values that are two periods apart, the time series displays **second-order autocorrelation**. For the general case in which the autocorrelation exists between values that are p periods apart, the time series displays **pth-order autocorrelation**.

Autoregressive modeling is a technique used to forecast time series that display autocorrelation.[2] This type of modeling uses a set of *lagged predictor variables* to overcome the problems that autocorrelation causes with other models. A **lagged predictor variable** takes its value from the value of a predictor variable for another time period. For the general case of pth-order autocorrelation, you create a set of p lagged predictor variables such that the first lagged predictor variable takes its value from the value of a predictor variable that is one time period away, the *lag*; that the second lagged predictor variable takes its value from the value of a predictor variable that is two time periods away; and so on until the last, or pth, lagged predictor variable that takes its value from the value of a predictor variable that is p time periods away.

Equation (16.8) defines the **pth-order autoregressive model**. In the equation, $A_0, A_1, \ldots, A_p$ represent the parameters and $a_0, a_1, \ldots, a_p$ represent the corresponding regression coefficients. This is similar to the multiple regression model, Equation (14.1) on page 477, in which $\beta_0, \beta_1, \ldots, \beta_k$, represent the regression parameters and $b_0, b_1, \ldots, b_k$ represent the corresponding regression coefficients.

[2]The exponential smoothing model described in Section 16.3 and the autoregressive models described in this section are special cases of autoregressive integrated moving average (ARIMA) models developed by Box and Jenkins (see reference 2).

*p*TH-ORDER AUTOREGRESSIVE MODELS

$$Y_i = A_0 + A_1 Y_{i-1} + A_2 Y_{i-2} + \cdots + A_p Y_{i-p} + \delta_i \tag{16.8}$$

where

$$
\begin{aligned}
Y_i &= \text{observed value of the series at time i} \\
Y_{i-1} &= \text{observed value of the series at time } i - 1 \\
Y_{i-2} &= \text{observed value of the series at time } i - 2 \\
Y_{i-p} &= \text{observed value of the series at time } i - p \\
p &= \text{number of autoregression parameters (not including a } Y \text{ intercept)} \\
&\quad \text{to be estimated from least-squares regression analysis} \\
A_0, A_1, A_2, \ldots, A_p &= \text{autoregression parameters to be estimated from least-squares} \\
&\quad \text{regression analysis} \\
\delta_i &= \text{a nonautocorrelated random error component (with mean} = 0 \text{ and} \\
&\quad \text{constant variance)}
\end{aligned}
$$

studentTIP
δ is the Greek letter delta

Equations (16.9) and (16.10) define two specific autoregressive models. Equation (16.9) defines the **first-order autoregressive model** and is similar in form to the simple linear regression model, Equation (13.1) on page 429. Equation (16.10) defines the **second-order autoregressive model** and is similar to the multiple regression model with two independent variables, Equation (14.2) on page 477.

FIRST-ORDER AUTOREGRESSIVE MODEL

$$Y_i = A_0 + A_1 Y_{i-1} + \delta_i \tag{16.9}$$

SECOND-ORDER AUTOREGRESSIVE MODEL

$$Y_i = A_0 + A_1 Y_{i-1} + A_2 Y_{i-2} + \delta_i \tag{16.10}$$

Selecting an Appropriate Autoregressive Model

Selecting an appropriate autoregressive model can be complicated. You must weigh the advantages of using a simpler model against the concern of not taking into account important autocorrelation in the data. You also must be concerned with selecting a higher-order model that requires estimates of numerous parameters, some of which may be unnecessary, especially if n, the number of values in the series, is small. The reason for this concern is that when computing an estimate of A_p, you lose p out of the n data values when comparing each data value with the data value p periods earlier. Examples 16.5 and 16.6 illustrate this loss of data values.

EXAMPLE 16.5	Consider the following series of $n = 7$ consecutive annual values:

EXAMPLE 16.5
Comparison Schema for a First-Order Autoregressive Model

Consider the following series of $n = 7$ consecutive annual values:

				Year			
	1	**2**	**3**	**4**	**5**	**6**	**7**
Series	31	34	37	35	36	43	40

Show the comparisons needed for a first-order autoregressive model.

▶ *(continued)*

SOLUTION

Year i	First-Order Autoregressive Model (Lag1: Y_i versus Y_{i-1})
1	$31 \leftrightarrow \ldots$
2	$34 \leftrightarrow 31$
3	$37 \leftrightarrow 34$
4	$35 \leftrightarrow 37$
5	$36 \leftrightarrow 35$
6	$43 \leftrightarrow 36$
7	$40 \leftrightarrow 43$

Because Y_1 is the first value and there is no value prior to it, Y_1 is not used in the regression analysis. Therefore, the first-order autoregressive model would be based on six pairs of values.

EXAMPLE 16.6

Comparison Schema for a Second-Order Autoregressive Model

Consider the following series of $n = 7$ consecutive annual values:

				Year			
	1	**2**	**3**	**4**	**5**	**6**	**7**
Series	31	34	37	35	36	43	40

Show the comparisons needed for a second-order autoregressive model.

SOLUTION

Year i	Second-Order Autoregressive Model (Lag2: Y_i vs. Y_{i-1} and Y_i vs. Y_{i-2})
1	$31 \leftrightarrow \ldots$ and $31 \leftrightarrow \ldots$
2	$34 \leftrightarrow 31$ and $34 \leftrightarrow \ldots$
3	$37 \leftrightarrow 34$ and $37 \leftrightarrow 31$
4	$35 \leftrightarrow 37$ and $35 \leftrightarrow 34$
5	$36 \leftrightarrow 35$ and $36 \leftrightarrow 37$
6	$43 \leftrightarrow 36$ and $43 \leftrightarrow 35$
7	$40 \leftrightarrow 43$ and $40 \leftrightarrow 36$

Because no value is recorded prior to Y_1, the first two comparisons, each of which requires a value prior to Y_1, cannot be used when performing regression analysis. Therefore, the second-order autoregressive model would be based on five pairs of values.

Determining the Appropriateness of a Selected Model

After selecting a model and using the least-squares method to compute the regression coefficients, you need to determine the appropriateness of the model. Either you can select a particular pth-order autoregressive model based on previous experiences with similar data or start with a model that contains several autoregressive parameters and then eliminate the higher-order parameters that do not significantly contribute to the model. In this latter approach, you use a t test for the significance of A_p, the highest-order autoregressive parameter in the current model under consideration. The null and alternative hypotheses are:

$$H_0: A_p = 0$$

$$H_1: A_p \neq 0$$

Equation (16.11) defines the test statistic.

t TEST FOR SIGNIFICANCE OF THE HIGHEST-ORDER AUTOREGRESSIVE PARAMETER, A_p

$$t_{STAT} = \frac{a_p - A_p}{S_{a_p}}$$ (16.11)

where

A_p = hypothesized value of the highest-order parameter, A_p, in the autoregressive model

a_p = regression coefficient that estimates the highest-order parameter, A_p, in the autoregressive model

S_{a_p} = standard deviation of a_p

The t_{STAT} test statistic follows a *t* distribution with $n - 2p - 1$ degrees of freedom.

In addition to the degrees of freedom lost for each of the *p* population parameters you are estimating, *p* additional degrees of freedom are lost because there are *p* fewer comparisons to be made from the original *n* values in the time series.

For a given level of significance, α, you reject the null hypothesis if the t_{STAT} test statistic is greater than the upper-tail critical value from the *t* distribution or if the t_{STAT} test statistic is less than the lower-tail critical value from the *t* distribution. Thus, the decision rule is

$$\text{Reject } H_0 \text{ if } t_{STAT} < -t_{\alpha/2} \text{ or if } t_{STAT} > t_{\alpha/2};$$

otherwise, do not reject H_0.

Figure 16.12 illustrates the decision rule and regions of rejection and nonrejection.

FIGURE 16.12
Rejection regions for a two-tail test for the significance of the highest-order autoregressive parameter A_p

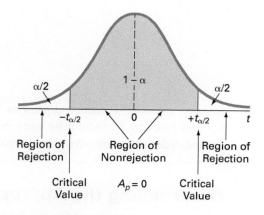

If you do not reject the null hypothesis that $A_p = 0$, you conclude that the selected model contains too many estimated autoregressive parameters. You then discard the highest-order term and develop an autoregressive model of order $p - 1$, using the least-squares method. You then repeat the test of the hypothesis that the new highest-order parameter is 0. This testing and modeling continues until you reject H_0. When this occurs, you can conclude that the remaining highest-order parameter is significant, and you can use that model for forecasting purposes.

Equation (16.12) defines the fitted *p*th-order autoregressive equation.

FITTED pTH-ORDER AUTOREGRESSIVE EQUATION

$$\hat{Y}_i = a_0 + a_1 Y_{i-1} + a_2 Y_{i-2} + \cdots + a_p Y_{i-p} \qquad \text{(16.12)}$$

where

$$\hat{Y}_i = \text{fitted values of the series at time } i$$
$$Y_{i-1} = \text{observed value of the series at time } i-1$$
$$Y_{i-2} = \text{observed value of the series at time } i-2$$
$$Y_{i-p} = \text{observed value of the series at time } i-p$$
$$p = \text{number of autoregression parameters (not including a } Y \text{ intercept) to}$$
$$\text{be estimated from least-squares regression analysis}$$
$$a_0, a_1, a_2, \ldots, a_p = \text{regression coefficients}$$

You use Equation (16.13) to forecast j years into the future from the current nth time period.

pTH-ORDER AUTOREGRESSIVE FORECASTING EQUATION

$$\hat{Y}_{n+j} = a_0 + a_1 \hat{Y}_{n+j-1} + a_2 \hat{Y}_{n+j-2} + \cdots + a_p \hat{Y}_{n+j-p} \qquad \text{(16.13)}$$

where

$$a_0, a_1, a_2, \ldots, a_p = \text{regression coefficients that estimate the parameters}$$
$$p = \text{number of autoregression parameters (not including a } Y \text{ intercept) to}$$
$$\text{be estimated from least-squares regression analysis}$$
$$j = \text{number of years into the future}$$
$$\hat{Y}_{n+j-p} = \text{forecast of } Y_{n+j-p} \text{ from the current year for } j-p > 0$$
$$\hat{Y}_{n+j-p} = \text{observed value for } Y_{n+j-p} \text{ for } j-p \leq 0$$

Thus, to make forecasts j years into the future, using a third-order autoregressive model, you need only the most recent $p = 3$ values (Y_n, Y_{n-1}, and Y_{n-2}) and the regression estimates a_0, a_1, a_2, and a_3.

To forecast one year ahead, Equation (16.13) becomes

$$\hat{Y}_{n+1} = a_0 + a_1 Y_n + a_2 Y_{n-1} + a_3 Y_{n-2}$$

To forecast two years ahead, Equation (16.13) becomes

$$\hat{Y}_{n+2} = a_0 + a_1 \hat{Y}_{n+1} + a_2 Y_n + a_3 Y_{n-1}$$

To forecast three years ahead, Equation (16.13) becomes

$$\hat{Y}_{n+3} = a_0 + a_1 \hat{Y}_{n+2} + a_2 \hat{Y}_{n+1} + a_3 Y_n$$

and so on.

Autoregressive modeling is a powerful forecasting technique for time series that have autocorrelation. Exhibit 16. 1 summarizes the steps to construct an autoregressive model.

EXHIBIT 16.1

Autoregressive Modeling Steps

1. Choose a value for p, the highest-order parameter in the autoregressive model to be evaluated, realizing that the t test for significance is based on $n - 2p - 1$ degrees of freedom.
2. Create a set of p lagged predictor variables. (See Figure 16.13 for an example.)

3. Perform a least-squares analysis of the multiple regression model containing all p lagged predictor variables using Excel.

4. Test for the significance of A_p, the highest-order autoregressive parameter in the model.

5. If you do not reject the null hypothesis, discard the pth variable and repeat steps 3 and 4. The test for the significance of the new highest-order parameter is based on a t distribution whose degrees of freedom are revised to correspond with the revised number of predictors.

If you reject the null hypothesis, select the autoregressive model with all p predictors for fitting [see Equation (16.12)] and forecasting [see Equation (16.13)].

To demonstrate the autoregressive modeling approach, return to the time series concerning the revenues for The Coca-Cola Company over the 17-year period 1998 through 2014. Figure 16.13 displays a worksheet that organizes the data for the first-order, second-order, and third-order autoregressive models.

FIGURE 16.13

Excel worksheet data for developing first-order, second-order, and third-order autoregressive models of the revenues for The Coca-Cola Company (1998–2014)

	A	B	C	D	E
1	Year	Revenues	Lag1	Lag2	Lag3
2	1998	18.8	#N/A	#N/A	#N/A
3	1999	19.8	18.8	#N/A	#N/A
4	2000	20.5	19.8	18.8	#N/A
5	2001	20.1	20.5	19.8	18.8
6	2002	19.6	20.1	20.5	19.8
7	2003	21.0	19.6	20.1	20.5
8	2004	21.9	21.0	19.6	20.1
9	2005	23.1	21.9	21.0	19.6
10	2006	24.1	23.1	21.9	21.0
11	2007	28.9	24.1	23.1	21.9
12	2008	31.9	28.9	24.1	23.1
13	2009	31.0	31.9	28.9	24.1
14	2010	35.1	31.0	31.9	28.9
15	2011	46.5	35.1	31.0	31.9
16	2012	48.0	46.5	35.1	31.0
17	2013	46.7	48.0	46.5	35.1
18	2014	45.9	46.7	48.0	46.5

The worksheet contains the lagged predictor variables Lag1, Lag2, and Lag3. Use all three lagged predictors to fit the third-order autoregressive model. Use only Lag1 and Lag2 to fit the second-order autoregressive model, and use only Lag1 to fit the first-order autoregressive models. Thus, out of $n = 17$ values, $p = 1, 2,$ or 3 values out of $n = 17$ are lost in the comparisons needed for developing the first-order, second-order, and third-order autoregressive models.

Selecting an autoregressive model that best fits the annual time series begins with the third-order autoregressive model shown in Figure 16.14.

FIGURE 16.14

Excel regression results worksheet for a third-order autoregressive model for The Coca-Cola Company revenues

	A	B	C	D	E	F	G
1	Third-Order Autoregressive Model for The Coca-Cola Company Revenues						
2							
3	*Regression Statistics*						
4	Multiple R	0.9668					
5	R Square	0.9347					
6	Adjusted R Square	0.9151					
7	Standard Error	3.1857					
8	Observations	14					
9							
10	ANOVA						
11		*df*	*SS*	*MS*	*F*	*Significance F*	
12	Regression	3	1453.0358	484.3453	47.7262	0.0000	
13	Residual	10	101.4842	10.1484			
14	Total	13	1554.5200				
15							
16		*Coefficients*	*Standard Error*	*t Stat*	*P-value*	*Lower 95%*	*Upper 95%*
17	Intercept	-0.0640	3.0786	-0.0208	0.9838	-6.9236	6.7956
18	Lag1	1.2899	0.2750	4.6899	0.0009	0.6771	1.9027
19	Lag2	-0.8690	0.4428	-1.9622	0.0781	-1.8557	0.1177
20	Lag3	0.6768	0.3714	1.8222	0.0984	-0.1508	1.5044

From Figure 16.14, the fitted third-order autoregressive equation is

$$\hat{Y}_i = -0.0640 + 1.2899Y_{i-1} - 0.8690Y_{i-2} + 0.6768Y_{i-3}$$

where the first year in the series is 2001.

Next, you test for the significance of A_3, the highest-order parameter. The highest-order regression coefficient, a_3, for the fitted third-order autoregressive model is 0.6768, with a standard error of 0.3714.

To test the null hypothesis:

$$H_0: A_3 = 0$$

against the alternative hypothesis:

$$H_1: A_3 \neq 0$$

using Equation (16.11) on page 574 and the worksheet results given in Figure 16.14,

$$t_{STAT} = \frac{a_3 - A_3}{S_{a_3}} = \frac{0.6768 - 0}{0.3714} = 1.8222$$

Using a 0.05 level of significance, the two-tail t test with $14 - 3 - 1 = 10$ degrees of freedom has critical values of ± 2.2281. Because $t_{STAT} = 1.8222 < 2.2281$ or because the p-value $= 0.0984 > 0.05$, you do not reject H_0. You conclude that the third-order parameter of the autoregressive model is not significant and should not remain in the model. You then fit a second-order autoregressive model using Excel (see Figure 16.15).

FIGURE 16.15

Excel regression results worksheet for the second-order autoregressive model for the Coca-Cola Company revenues data

	A	B	C	D	E	F	G
1	Second-Order Autoregressive Model for The Coca-Cola Company Revenues						
2							
3	*Regression Statistics*						
4	Multiple R	0.9583					
5	R Square	0.9183					
6	Adjusted R Square	0.9046					
7	Standard Error	3.3745					
8	Observations	15					
9							
10	ANOVA						
11		*df*	*SS*	*MS*	*F*	*Significance F*	
12	Regression	2	1534.9509	767.4755	67.3981	0.0000	
13	Residual	12	136.6464	11.3872			
14	Total	14	1671.5973				
15							
16		*Coefficients*	*Standard Error*	*t Stat*	*P-value*	*Lower 95%*	*Upper 9!*
17	Intercept	2.2422	2.7321	0.8207	0.4278	-3.7105	8.1!
18	X Variable 1	1.2345	0.2889	4.2726	0.0011	0.6050	1.8(
19	X Variable 2	-0.2689	0.3159	-0.8512	0.4113	-0.9571	0.4:

The fitted second-order autoregressive equation is

$$\hat{Y}_i = 2.2422 + 1.2345Y_{i-1} - 0.2689Y_{i-2}$$

where the first year of the series is 2000.

From Figure 16.15, the highest-order parameter estimate is $a_2 = -0.2689$, with a standard error of 0.3159.

To test the null hypothesis:

$$H_0: A_2 = 0$$

against the alternative hypothesis:

$$H_1: A_2 \neq 0$$

using Equation (16.11) on page 574,

$$t_{STAT} = \frac{a_2 - A_2}{S_{a_2}} = \frac{-0.2689 - 0}{0.3159} = -0.8512$$

Using the 0.05 level of significance, the two-tail t test with 12 degrees of freedom has critical values of ± 2.1788. Because $-2.1788 < t_{STAT} = -0.8512 < 2.1788$ or because the p-value $= 0.4113 > 0.05$, you do not reject H_0. You conclude that the second-order parameter of the autoregressive model is not significant and should be deleted from the model. You then fit a first-order autoregressive model using Excel (see Figure 16.16).

FIGURE 16.16
Excel regression results worksheet for the first-order autoregressive model for the Coca-Cola Company revenues data

	A	B	C	D	E	F	G
1	First-Order Autoregressive Model for the Coca-Cola Company Revenues						
2							
3	*Regression Statistics*						
4	Multiple R	0.9585					
5	R Square	0.9187					
6	Adjusted R Square	0.9129					
7	Standard Error	3.2225					
8	Observations	16					
9							
10	ANOVA						
11		*df*	*SS*	*MS*	*F*	*Significance F*	
12	Regression	1	1642.8400	1642.8400	158.2051	0.0000	
13	Residual	14	145.3794	10.3842			
14	Total	15	1788.2194				
15							
16		*Coefficients*	*Standard Error*	*t Stat*	*P-value*	*Lower 95%*	*Upper 95%*
17	Intercept	1.5712	2.4187	0.6496	0.5264	-3.6163	6.7588
18	X	1.0043	0.0798	12.5780	0.0000	0.8330	1.1755

The fitted first-order autoregressive equation is

$$\hat{Y}_i = 1.5712 + 1.0043 Y_{i-1}$$

where the first year of the series is 1999.

From Figure 16.16, the highest-order parameter estimate is $a_1 = 1.0043$, with a standard error of 0.0798.

To test the null hypothesis:

$$H_0: A_1 = 0$$

against the alternative hypothesis:

$$H_1: A_1 \neq 0$$

using Equation (16.11) on page 574,

$$t_{STAT} = \frac{a_2 - A_1}{S_{a_1}} = \frac{1.0043 - 0}{0.0798} = 12.5780$$

Using the 0.05 level of significance, the two-tail t test with 14 degrees of freedom has critical values of ± 2.1448. Because $t_{STAT} = 12.5780 > 2.1448$ or because the p-value $= 0.0000 < 0.05$, you reject H_0. You conclude that the first-order parameter of the autoregressive model is significant and should remain in the model.

The model-building approach has led to the selection of the first-order autoregressive model as the most appropriate for these data. Using the estimates $a_0 = 1.5712$, and $a_1 = 1.0043$, as well as the most recent data value $Y_{17} = 45.9$, the forecasts of revenues at the Coca-Cola Company for 2015 and 2016 from Equation (16.13) on page 575 are

$$\hat{Y}_{n+j} = 1.5712 + 1.0043 \hat{Y}_{n+j-1}$$

Therefore,

2015: 1 year ahead, $\hat{Y}_{18} = 1.5712 + 1.0043(45.9) = 47.6686$ billions of dollars
2016: 2 years ahead, $\hat{Y}_{19} = 1.5712 + 1.0043(47.6686) = 49.4448$ billions of dollars

Figure 16.17 displays the actual and predicted Y values from the first-order autoregressive model.

FIGURE 16.17

Plot of actual and predicted revenues from a first-order autoregressive model at the Coca-Cola Company

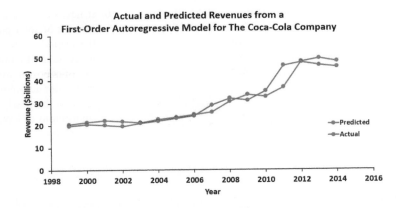

PROBLEMS FOR SECTION 16.5

LEARNING THE BASICS

16.23 You are given an annual time series with 40 consecutive values and asked to fit a fifth-order autoregressive model.
a. How many comparisons are lost in developing the autoregressive model?
b. How many parameters do you need to estimate?
c. Which of the original 40 values do you need for forecasting?
d. State the fifth-order autoregressive model.
e. Write an equation to indicate how you would forecast j years into the future.

16.24 A third-order autoregressive model is fitted to an annual time series with 17 values and has the following estimated parameters and standard errors:

$$a_0 = 4.50 \quad a_1 = 1.80 \quad a_2 = 0.80 \quad a_3 = 0.24$$
$$S_{a_1} = 0.50 \quad S_{a_2} = 0.30 \quad S_{a_3} = 0.10$$

At the 0.05 level of significance, test the appropriateness of the fitted model.

16.25 Refer to Problem 16.24. The three most recent values are

$$Y_{15} = 23 \quad Y_{16} = 28 \quad Y_{17} = 34$$

Forecast the values for the next year and the following year.

16.26 Refer to Problem 16.24. Suppose, when testing for the appropriateness of the fitted model, the standard errors are

$$S_{a_1} = 0.45 \quad S_{a_2} = 0.35 \quad S_{a_3} = 0.15$$

a. What conclusions can you reach?
b. Discuss how to proceed if forecasting is still your main objective.

APPLYING THE CONCEPTS

16.27 Using the data for Problem 16.15 on page 569 that represent the number of new, single-family houses sold in the U.S. from 1992 through 2014 (stored in HouseSales),
a. fit a third-order autoregressive model to the new single-family homes sold and test for the significance of the third-order autoregressive parameter. (Use $\alpha = 0.05$.)
b. if necessary, fit a second-order autoregressive model to the new single-family homes sold and test for the significance of the second-order autoregressive parameter. (Use $\alpha = 0.05$.)

c. if necessary, fit a first-order autoregressive model to the new single-family homes sold and test for the significance of the first-order autoregressive parameter. (Use $\alpha = 0.05$.)
d. if appropriate, forecast the new single-family homes sold in 2015.

✓**SELF TEST** **16.28** Using the data for Problem 16.12 on page 569 concerning the bonuses paid to workers on Wall Street from 2000 to 2014 (stored in Bonuses),
a. fit a third-order autoregressive model to the bonuses paid and test for the significance of the third-order autoregressive parameter. (Use $\alpha = 0.05$.)
b. if necessary, fit a second-order autoregressive model to the bonuses paid and test for the significance of the second-order autoregressive parameter. (Use $\alpha = 0.05$.)
c. if necessary, fit a first-order autoregressive model to the bonuses paid and test for the significance of the first-order autoregressive parameter. (Use $\alpha = 0.05$.)
d. if appropriate, forecast the bonuses paid in 2015 and 2016.

16.29 Using the data for Problem 16.17 on page 570 concerning the number of passenger cars produced in the United States from 1999 to 2014 (stored in CarProduction),
a. fit a third-order autoregressive model to the number of passenger cars produced in the United States and test for the significance of the third-order autoregressive parameter. (Use $\alpha = 0.05$.)
b. if necessary, fit a second-order autoregressive model to the number of passenger cars produced in the United States and test for the significance of the second-order autoregressive parameter. (Use $\alpha = 0.05$.)
c. if necessary, fit a first-order autoregressive model to the number of passenger cars produced in the United States and test for the significance of the first-order autoregressive parameter. (Use $\alpha = 0.05$.)
d. forecast the U.S. car production for 2015.

16.30 Using the average baseball salary from 2000 through 2015 data for Problem 16.18 on page 570 (stored in BBSalaries),
a. fit a third-order autoregressive model to the average baseball salary and test for the significance of the third-order autoregressive parameter. (Use $\alpha = 0.05$.)
b. if necessary, fit a second-order autoregressive model to the average baseball salary and test for the significance of the second-order autoregressive parameter. (Use $\alpha = 0.05$.)

c. if necessary, fit a first-order autoregressive model to the average baseball salary and test for the significance of the first- order autoregressive parameter. (Use $\alpha = 0.05$.)

d. forecast the average baseball salary for 2016.

16.31 Using the yearly amount of solar power generated by utilities (in millions of kWh) in the United States from 2002 through 2014 data for Problem 16.16 on page 569 (stored in SolarPower),

a. fit a third-order autoregressive model to the amount of solar power installed and test for the significance of the third-order autoregressive parameter. (Use $\alpha = 0.05$.)

b. if necessary, fit a second-order autoregressive model to the amount of solar power installed and test for the significance of the second-order autoregressive parameter. (Use $\alpha = 0.05$.)

c. if necessary, fit a first-order autoregressive model to the amount of solar power installed and test for the significance of the first-order autoregressive parameter. (Use $\alpha = 0.05$.)

d. forecast the yearly amount of solar power generated by utilities (in millions of kWh) in the United States in 2015 and 2016.

16.6 Choosing an Appropriate Forecasting Model

In Sections 16.4 and 16.5, you studied six time-series methods for forecasting: the linear trend model, the quadratic trend model, and the exponential trend model in Section 16.4; and the first-order, second-order, and *p*th-order autoregressive models in Section 16.5. Is there a *best* model? Among these models, which one should you select for forecasting? The following guidelines are provided for determining the adequacy of a particular forecasting model. These guidelines are based on a judgment of how well the model fits the data and assume that you can use past data to predict future values of the time series:

- Perform a residual analysis.
- Measure the magnitude of the residuals through squared differences.
- Measure the magnitude of the residuals through absolute differences.
- Use the principle of parsimony.

A discussion of these guidelines follows.

Performing a Residual Analysis

Recall from Sections 13.5 and 14.3 that residuals are the differences between observed and predicted values. After fitting a particular model to a time series, you plot the residuals over the *n* time periods. As shown in Figure 16.18 Panel A, if the particular model fits adequately, the residuals represent the irregular component of the time series. Therefore, they should be randomly distributed throughout the series. However, as illustrated in the three remaining panels of Figure 16.18, if the particular model does not fit adequately, the residuals may show a systematic pattern, such as a failure to account for trend (Panel B), a failure to account for cyclical variation (Panel C), or, with monthly or quarterly data, a failure to account for seasonal variation (Panel D).

FIGURE 16.18
Residual analysis for studying patterns of errors in regression models

Panel A
Randomly distributed forecast errors

Panel C
Cyclical effects not accounted for

Panel B
Trend not accounted for

Panel D
Seasonal effects not accounted for

Measuring the Magnitude of the Residuals Through Squared or Absolute Differences

If, after performing a residual analysis, you still believe that two or more models appear to fit the data adequately, you can use additional methods for model selection. Numerous measures based on the residuals are available (see references 1 and 4).

In regression analysis (see Section 13.3), you have already used the standard error of the estimate S_{YX} as a measure of variation around the predicted values. For a particular model, this measure is based on the sum of squared differences between the actual and predicted values in a time series. If a model fits the time-series data perfectly, then the standard error of the estimate is zero. If a model fits the time-series data poorly, then S_{YX} is large. Thus, when comparing the adequacy of two or more forecasting models, you can select the model with the smallest S_{YX} as most appropriate.

However, a major drawback to using S_{YX} when comparing forecasting models is that whenever there is a large difference between even a single Y_i and $\hat{Y}_i$, the value of S_{YX} becomes overly inflated because the differences between Y_i and $\hat{Y}_i$ are squared. For this reason, many statisticians prefer the **mean absolute deviation (MAD)**. Equation (16.14) defines the MAD as the mean of the absolute differences between the actual and predicted values in a time series.

MEAN ABSOLUTE DEVIATION

$$MAD = \frac{\sum_{i=1}^{n} |Y_i - \hat{Y}_i|}{n}$$

(16.14)

If a model fits the time-series data perfectly, the MAD is zero. If a model fits the time-series data poorly, the MAD is large. When comparing two or more forecasting models, you can select the one with the smallest MAD as the most appropriate model.

Using the Principle of Parsimony

If, after performing a residual analysis and comparing the S_{YX} and MAD measures, you still believe that two or more models appear to adequately fit the data, you can use the principle of parsimony for model selection. As first explained in Section 15.4, **parsimony** guides you to select the regression model with the fewest independent variables that can predict the dependent variable adequately. In general, the principle of parsimony guides you to select the least complex regression model. Among the six forecasting models studied in this chapter, most statisticians consider the least-squares linear and quadratic models and the first-order autoregressive model as simpler than the second- and pth-order autoregressive models and the least-squares exponential model.

A Comparison of Four Forecasting Methods

To illustrate the model selection process, you can compare four of the forecasting models used in Sections 16.4 and 16.5: the linear model, the quadratic model, the exponential model, and the first-order autoregressive model. Figure 16.19 shows the residual plots for the four models for The Coca-Cola Company revenues. In reaching conclusions from these residual plots, you must use caution because there are only 17 values for the linear model, the quadratic model, and the exponential model and only 16 values for the first-order autoregressive model.

In Figure 16.19, observe that the residuals in the linear model and exponential model are positive for the early years, negative for the intermediate years, and positive again for the latest years. For the quadratic and autoregressive models, the residuals do not exhibit any clear systematic pattern.

FIGURE 16.19

Residual plots for four forecasting models

To summarize, on the basis of the residual analysis of all four forecasting models, it appears that the quadratic and first-order autoregressive models are the most appropriate, and the linear and exponential models are not appropriate. For further verification, you can compare the magnitude of the residuals in the four models. Figure 16.20 shows the actual values (Y_i) along with the predicted values $\hat{Y}_i$, the residuals (e_i), the error sum of squares (*SSE*), the standard error of the estimate (S_{YX}), and the mean absolute deviation (*MAD*) for each of the four models.

For this time series, S_{YX} and *MAD* provide fairly similar results. A comparison of the S_{YX} and *MAD* clearly indicates that the linear model provides the poorest fit followed by the exponential model. The quadratic model provides the best fit followed by the first-order autoregressive model. Thus, you should choose the quadratic model as the best model.

After you select a particular forecasting model, you need to continually monitor and update the model. Once new data become available, you can use these data points to refine and improve the model. If large errors between forecasted and actual values occur, the underlying structure of the time series may have changed. Remember that the forecasting methods presented in this chapter assume that the patterns inherent in the past will continue into the future. Large forecasting errors are an indication that this assumption may no longer be true.

FIGURE 16.20

Comparison of four forecasting models using *SSE*, S_{YX}, and *MAD*

Year	Revenues	Linear Predicted	Linear Residual	Quadratic Predicted	Quadratic Residual	Exponential Predicted	Exponential Residual	First-Order AR Predicted	First-Order AR Residual
1998	18.8	13.5059	5.2941	19.0327	-0.2327	16.4399	2.3601	#N/A	#N/A
1999	19.8	15.5154	4.2846	18.9697	0.8303	17.5613	2.2387	20.4519	-0.6519
2000	20.5	17.5250	2.9750	19.1830	1.3170	18.7591	1.7409	21.4562	-0.9562
2001	20.1	19.5346	0.5654	19.6727	0.4273	20.0386	0.0614	22.1592	-2.0592
2002	19.6	21.5441	-1.9441	20.4388	-0.8388	21.4054	-1.8054	21.7575	-2.1575
2003	21.0	23.5537	-2.5537	21.4811	-0.4811	22.8654	-1.8654	21.2553	-0.2553
2004	21.9	25.5632	-3.6632	22.7998	-0.8998	24.4250	-2.5250	22.6613	-0.7613
2005	23.1	27.5728	-4.4728	24.3949	-1.2949	26.0910	-2.9910	23.5652	-0.4652
2006	24.1	29.5824	-5.4824	26.2663	-2.1663	27.8707	-3.7707	24.7703	-0.6703
2007	28.9	31.5919	-2.6919	28.4140	0.4860	29.7717	-0.8717	25.7746	3.1254
2008	31.9	33.6015	-1.7015	30.8381	1.0619	31.8023	0.0977	30.5952	1.3048
2009	31.0	35.6110	-4.6110	33.5385	-2.5385	33.9715	-2.9715	33.6081	-2.6081
2010	35.1	37.6206	-2.5206	36.5152	-1.4152	36.2887	-1.1887	32.7042	2.3958
2011	46.5	39.6301	6.8699	39.7683	6.7317	38.7638	7.7362	36.8218	9.6782
2012	48.0	41.6397	6.3603	43.2978	4.7022	41.4079	6.5921	48.2707	-0.2707
2013	46.7	43.6493	3.0507	47.1035	-0.4035	44.2322	2.4678	49.7771	-3.0771
2014	46.7	45.6588	0.2412	51.1857	-5.2857	47.2492	-1.3492	48.4715	-2.5715
		SSE	264.1074	*SSE*	116.1127	*SSE*	172.1227	*SSE*	145.3794
		S_{YX}	4.1961	S_{YX}	2.8799	S_{YX}	3.3875	S_{YX}	3.2225
		MAD	3.4872	*MAD*	1.8302	*MAD*	2.5079	*MAD*	2.0630

PROBLEMS FOR SECTION 16.6

LEARNING THE BASICS

16.32 The following residuals are from a linear trend model used to forecast sales:

  2.0 −0.5 1.5 1.0 0.0 1.0 −3.0 1.5 −4.5 2.0 0.0 −1.0

a. Compute S_{YX} and interpret your findings.
b. Compute the MAD and interpret your findings.

16.33 Refer to Problem 16.32. Suppose the first residual is 12.0 (instead of 2.0) and the last residual is −11.0 (instead of −1.0).
a. Compute S_{YX} and interpret your findings
b. Compute the MAD and interpret your findings.

APPLYING THE CONCEPTS

16.34 Using the yearly amount of solar power generated by utilities (in millions of kWh) in the United States data for Problem 16.16 on page 569 and Problem 16.31 on page 580 (stored in SolarPower),
a. perform a residual analysis.
b. compute the standard error of the estimate (S_{YX}).
c. compute the MAD.
d. On the basis of (a) through (c), and the principle of parsimony, which forecasting model would you select? Discuss.

16.35 Using the new, single-family house sales data for Problem 16.15 on page 569 and Problem 16.27 on page 579 (stored in HouseSales),
a. perform a residual analysis for each model.
b. compute the standard error of the estimate (S_{YX}) for each model.
c. compute the MAD for each model.
d. On the basis of (a) through (c) and the principle of parsimony, which forecasting model would you select? Discuss.

 16.36 Using the bonuses paid to workers on Wall Street data for Problem 16.12 on page 569 and Problem 16.28 on page 579 (stored in Bonuses),
a. perform a residual analysis for each model.
b. compute the standard error of the estimate (S_{YX}) for each model.
c. compute the MAD for each model.
d. On the basis of (a) through (c) and the principle of parsimony, which forecasting model would you select? Discuss.

16.37 Using the number of passenger cars produced in the U.S. data for Problem 16.17 on page 570 and Problem 16.29 on page 579 (stored in CarProduction),
a. perform a residual analysis for each model.
b. compute the standard error of the estimate (S_{YX}) for each model.
c. compute the MAD for each model.
d. On the basis of (a) through (c) and the principle of parsimony, which forecasting model would you select? Discuss.

16.38 Using the average baseball salary data for Problem 16.18 on page 570 and Problem 16.30 on page 579 (stored in BBSalaries),
a. perform a residual analysis for each model.
b. compute the standard error of the estimate (S_{YX}) for each model.
c. compute the MAD for each model.
d. On the basis of (a) through (c) and the principle of parsimony, which forecasting model would you select? Discuss.

16.39 Refer to the results for Problem 16.13 on page 569 that used the file GDP ,
a. perform a residual analysis.
b. compute the standard error of the estimate (S_{YX}).
c. compute the MAD.
d. On the basis of (a) through (c), are you satisfied with your linear trend forecasts in Problem 16.13? Discuss.

16.7 Time-Series Forecasting of Seasonal Data

So far, this chapter has focused on forecasting annual data. However, many time series are collected quarterly or monthly, and others are collected weekly, daily, and even hourly. When a time series is collected quarterly or monthly, you must consider the impact of seasonal effects. In this section, regression model building is used to forecast monthly or quarterly data.

One of the companies of interest in the Using Statistics scenario is Wal-Mart Stores, Inc. In 2015, according to the company's website, Wal-Mart Stores, Inc., operated nearly 11,000 retail units in 28 countries and had revenues of almost $500 billion. Walmart revenues are highly seasonal, and therefore you need to analyze quarterly revenues. The fiscal year for the company ends January 31. Thus, the fourth quarter of 2014 includes November and December 2013 as well as January 2014. Table 16.3 lists the quarterly revenues (in $billions) from 2010 to 2015 that are stored in Walmart . Figure 16.21 displays the time series.

TABLE 16.3
Quarterly Revenues (in $billions) for Wal-Mart Stores, Inc., 2010–2015

| | Year | | | | | |
Quarter	2010	2011	2012	2013	2014	2015
1	94.24	99.81	104.19	113.01	114.07	114.96
2	100.88	103.73	109.37	114.28	116.83	120.12
3	99.37	101.95	110.23	113.80	115.69	119.00
4	113.62	116.36	123.17	127.78	129.71	131.56

Source: Data extracted from **ycharts.com/companies/WMT/revenues**.

FIGURE 16.21
Plot of quarterly revenues ($billions) for Wal-Mart Stores, Inc., 2010–2015

Least-Squares Forecasting with Monthly or Quarterly Data

To develop a least-squares regression model that includes a seasonal component, the least-squares exponential trend fitting method used in Section 16.4 is combined with dummy variables to represent the quarters (see Section 14.6) to model the seasonal component.

Equation (16.15) defines the exponential trend model for quarterly data.

EXPONENTIAL MODEL WITH QUARTERLY DATA

$$Y_i = \beta_0 \beta_1^{X_i} \beta_2^{Q_1} \beta_3^{Q_2} \beta_4^{Q_3} \varepsilon_i \qquad (16.15)$$

where

$$X_i = \text{coded quarterly value, } i = 0, 1, 2, \ldots$$
$$Q_1 = 1 \text{ if first quarter, 0 if not first quarter}$$
$$Q_2 = 1 \text{ if second quarter, 0 if not second quarter}$$
$$Q_3 = 1 \text{ if third quarter, 0 if not third quarter}$$
$$\beta_0 = Y \text{ intercept}$$
$$(\beta_1 - 1) \times 100\% = \text{quarterly compound growth rate (in \%)}$$
$$\beta_2 = \text{multiplier for first quarter relative to fourth quarter}$$
$$\beta_3 = \text{multiplier for second quarter relative to fourth quarter}$$
$$\beta_4 = \text{multiplier for third quarter relative to fourth quarter}$$
$$\varepsilon_i = \text{value of the irregular component for time period } i$$

---

[3] Alternatively, you can use base e logarithms. For more information on logarithms, see Section A.3 in Appendix A.

The model in Equation (16.15) is not in the form of a linear regression model. To transform this nonlinear model to a linear model, you use a base 10 logarithmic transformation.[3] Taking the logarithm of each side of Equation (16.15) results in Equation (16.16).

TRANSFORMED EXPONENTIAL MODEL WITH QUARTERLY DATA

$$\log(Y_i) = \log(\beta_0 \beta_1^{X_i} \beta_2^{Q_1} \beta_3^{Q_2} \beta_4^{Q_3} \varepsilon_i) \qquad (16.16)$$
$$= \log(\beta_0) + \log(\beta_1^{X_i}) + \log(\beta_2^{Q_1}) + \log(\beta_3^{Q_2}) + \log(\beta_4^{Q_3}) + \log(\varepsilon_i)$$
$$= \log(\beta_0) + X_i \log(\beta_1) + Q_1 \log(\beta_2) + Q_2 \log(\beta_3) + Q_3 \log(\beta_4) + \log(\varepsilon_i)$$

Equation (16.16) is a linear model that you can estimate using least-squares regression. Performing the regression analysis using $\log(Y_i)$ as the dependent variable and $X_i, Q_1, Q_2,$ and Q_3 as the independent variables results in Equation (16.17).

EXPONENTIAL GROWTH WITH QUARTERLY DATA FORECASTING EQUATION

$$\log(\hat{Y}_i) = b_0 + b_1 X_i + b_2 Q_1 + b_3 Q_2 + b_4 Q_3 \tag{16.17}$$

where

$b_0 = $ estimate of $\log(\beta_0)$ and thus $10^{b_0} = \hat{\beta}_0$

$b_1 = $ estimate of $\log(\beta_1)$ and thus $10^{b_1} = \hat{\beta}_1$

$b_2 = $ estimate of $\log(\beta_2)$ and thus $10^{b_2} = \hat{\beta}_2$

$b_3 = $ estimate of $\log(\beta_3)$ and thus $10^{b_3} = \hat{\beta}_3$

$b_4 = $ estimate of $\log(\beta_4)$ and thus $10^{b_4} = \hat{\beta}_4$

Equation (16.18) is used for monthly data.

EXPONENTIAL MODEL WITH MONTHLY DATA

$$Y_i = \beta_0 \beta_1^{X_i} \beta_2^{M_1} \beta_3^{M_2} \beta_4^{M_3} \beta_5^{M_4} \beta_6^{M_5} \beta_7^{M_6} \beta_8^{M_7} \beta_9^{M_8} \beta_{10}^{M_9} \beta_{11}^{M_{10}} \beta_{12}^{M_{11}} \varepsilon_i \tag{16.18}$$

where

$X_i = $ coded monthly value, $i = 0, 1, 2, \ldots$

$M_1 = 1$ if January, 0 if not January

$M_2 = 1$ if February, 0 if not February

$M_3 = 1$ if March, 0 if not March

$\vdots$

$M_{11} = 1$ if November, 0 if not November

$\beta_0 = Y$ intercept

$(\beta_1 - 1) \times 100\% = $ monthly compound growth rate (in %)

$\beta_2 = $ multiplier for January relative to December

$\beta_3 = $ multiplier for February relative to December

$\beta_4 = $ multiplier for March relative to December

$\vdots$

$\beta_{12} = $ multiplier for November relative to December

$\varepsilon_i = $ value of the irregular component for time period i

The model in Equation (16.18) is not in the form of a linear regression model. To transform this nonlinear model into a linear model, you can use a base 10 logarithm transformation. Taking the logarithm of each side of Equation (16.18) results in Equation (16.19).

TRANSFORMED EXPONENTIAL MODEL WITH MONTHLY DATA

$$\begin{aligned}
\log(Y_i) &= \log\left(\beta_0 \beta_1^{X_i} \beta_2^{M_1} \beta_3^{M_2} \beta_4^{M_3} \beta_5^{M_4} \beta_6^{M_5} \beta_7^{M_6} \beta_8^{M_7} \beta_9^{M_8} \beta_{10}^{M_9} \beta_{11}^{M_{10}} \beta_{12}^{M_{11}} \varepsilon_i\right) \\
&= \log(\beta_0) + X_i \log(\beta_1) + M_1 \log(\beta_2) + M_2 \log(\beta_3) \\
&\quad + M_3 \log(\beta_4) + M_4 \log(\beta_5) + M_5 \log(\beta_6) + M_6 \log(\beta_7) \\
&\quad + M_7 \log(\beta_8) + M_8 \log(\beta_9) + M_9 \log(\beta_{10}) + M_{10} \log(\beta_{11}) \\
&\quad + M_{11} \log(\beta_{12}) + \log(\varepsilon_i)
\end{aligned} \tag{16.19}$$

Equation (16.19) is a linear model that you can estimate using the least-squares method. Performing the regression analysis using $\log(Y_i)$ as the dependent variable and $X_i, M_1, M_2, \ldots,$ and M_{11} as the independent variables results in Equation (16.20).

EXPONENTIAL GROWTH WITH MONTHLY DATA FORECASTING EQUATION

$$\log(\hat{Y}_i) = b_0 + b_1 X_i + b_2 M_1 + b_3 M_2 + b_4 M_3 + b_5 M_4 + b_6 M_5 + b_7 M_6 \\ + b_8 M_7 + b_9 M_8 + b_{10} M_9 + b_{11} M_{10} + b_{12} M_{11} \tag{16.20}$$

where

$$b_0 = \text{estimate of } \log(\beta_0) \text{ and thus } 10^{b_0} = \hat{\beta}_0$$
$$b_1 = \text{estimate of } \log(\beta_1) \text{ and thus } 10^{b_1} = \hat{\beta}_1$$
$$b_2 = \text{estimate of } \log(\beta_2) \text{ and thus } 10^{b_2} = \hat{\beta}_2$$
$$b_3 = \text{estimate of } \log(\beta_3) \text{ and thus } 10^{b_3} = \hat{\beta}_3$$
$$\vdots$$
$$b_{12} = \text{estimate of } \log(\beta_{12}) \text{ and thus } 10^{b_{12}} = \hat{\beta}_{12}$$

$Q_1, Q_2,$ and Q_3 are the three dummy variables needed to represent the four quarter periods in a quarterly time series. $M_1, M_2, M_3, \ldots, M_{11}$ are the 11 dummy variables needed to represent the 12 months in a monthly time series. In building the model, you use $\log(Y_i)$ instead of Y_i values and then find the regression coefficients by taking the antilog of the regression coefficients developed from Equations (16.17) and (16.20).

Although at first glance these regression models look imposing, when fitting or forecasting for any one time period, the values of all or all but one of the dummy variables in the model are equal to zero, and the equations simplify dramatically. In establishing the dummy variables for quarterly time-series data, the fourth quarter is the base period and has a coded value of zero for each dummy variable. With a quarterly time series, Equation (16.17) reduces as follows:

For any first quarter: $\log(\hat{Y}_i) = b_0 + b_1 X_i + b_2$
For any second quarter: $\log(\hat{Y}_i) = b_0 + b_1 X_i + b_3$
For any third quarter: $\log(\hat{Y}_i) = b_0 + b_1 X_i + b_4$
For any fourth quarter: $\log(\hat{Y}_i) = b_0 + b_1 X_i$

When establishing the dummy variables for each month, December serves as the base period and has a coded value of 0 for each dummy variable. For example, with a monthly time series, Equation (16.20) reduces as follows:

For any January: $\log(\hat{Y}_i) = b_0 + b_1 X_i + b_2$
For any February: $\log(\hat{Y}_i) = b_0 + b_1 X_i + b_3$
$$\vdots$$
For any November: $\log(\hat{Y}_i) = b_0 + b_1 X_i + b_{12}$
For any December: $\log(\hat{Y}_i) = b_0 + b_1 X_i$

To demonstrate the process of model building and least-squares forecasting with a quarterly time series, return to the Wal-Mart Stores, Inc., revenue data (in billions of dollars) originally displayed in Table 16.3 on page 583. The data are from the first quarter of 2010 through the last quarter of 2015. Figure 16.22 shows the Excel regression results for the quarterly exponential trend model.

From Figure 16.22, the model fits the data very well. The coefficient of determination $r^2 = 0.9642$, the adjusted $r^2 = 9.9566$, and the overall F test results in an F_{STAT} test statistic of 127.8418 (p-value $= 0.000$). At the 0.05 level of significance, each regression coefficient is

FIGURE 16.22

Excel regression results for the quarterly revenue data for Wal-Mart Stores, Inc.

	A	B	C	D	E	F	G
1	Quarterly Exponential Trend Model for Wal-Mart Stores, Inc., Revenues						
2							
3	*Regression Statistics*						
4	Multiple R	0.9819					
5	R Square	0.9642					
6	Adjusted R Square	0.9566					
7	Standard Error	0.0079					
8	Observations	24					
9							
10	ANOVA						
11		*df*	*SS*	*MS*	*F*	*Significance F*	
12	Regression	4	0.0323	0.0081	127.8418	0.0000	
13	Residual	19	0.0012	0.0001			
14	Total	23	0.0335				
15							
16		*Coefficients*	*Standard Error*	*t Stat*	*P-value*	*Lower 95%*	*Upper 95%*
17	Intercept	2.0397	0.0045	455.5936	0.0000	2.0304	2.0491
18	Coded Quarter	0.0040	0.0002	16.8477	0.0000	0.0035	0.0045
19	Q1	-0.0527	0.0046	-11.3554	0.0000	-0.0624	-0.0430
20	Q2	-0.0398	0.0046	-8.6228	0.0000	-0.0494	-0.0301
21	Q3	-0.0472	0.0046	-10.2836	0.0000	-0.0568	-0.0376

highly statistically significant and contributes to the model. The following summary includes the antilogs of all the regression coefficients:

Regression Coefficient	$b_i = \log \hat{\beta}_i$	$\hat{\beta}_i = \text{antilog}(b_i) = 10^{b_i}$
b_0: Y intercept	2.0397	109.5721
b_1: coded quarter	0.0040	1.0093
b_2: first quarter	-0.0527	0.8857
b_3: second quarter	-0.0398	0.9124
b_4: third quarter	-0.0472	0.8970

The interpretations for $\hat{\beta}_0$, $\hat{\beta}_1$, $\hat{\beta}_2$, $\hat{\beta}_3$, and $\hat{\beta}_4$ are as follows:

- The Y intercept, $\hat{\beta}_0 = 109.5721$ (in $billions), is the *unadjusted* forecast for quarterly revenues in the first quarter of 2010, the initial quarter in the time series. *Unadjusted* means that the seasonal component is not incorporated in the forecast.
- The value $(\hat{\beta}_1 - 1) \times 100\% = 0.0093$, or 0.93%, is the estimated *quarterly compound growth rate* in revenues, after adjusting for the seasonal component.
- $\hat{\beta}_2 = 0.8857$ is the seasonal multiplier for the first quarter relative to the fourth quarter; it indicates that there is $1 - 0.8857 = 11.43\%$ less revenue for the first quarter than for the fourth quarter.
- $\hat{\beta}_3 = 0.9124$ is the seasonal multiplier for the second quarter relative to the fourth quarter; it indicates that there is $1 - 0.9124 = 8.76\%$ less revenue for the second quarter than for the fourth quarter.
- $\hat{\beta}_4 = 0.8970$ is the seasonal multiplier for the third quarter relative to the fourth quarter; it indicates that there is $1 - 0.8970 = 10.30\%$ less revenue for the third quarter than for the fourth quarter. Thus, the fourth quarter, which includes the holiday shopping season, has the strongest sales.

Using the regression coefficients b_0, b_1, b_2, b_3, and b_4, and Equation (16.17) on page 585, you can make forecasts for selected quarters. As an example, to predict revenues for the fourth quarter of 2015 ($X_i = 23$),

$$\log(\hat{Y}_i) = b_0 + b_1 X_i$$
$$= 2.0397 + (0.0040)(23)$$
$$= 2.1317$$

Thus,

$$\log(\hat{Y}_i) = 10^{2.1317} = 135.4254$$

The predicted revenue for the fourth quarter of fiscal 2015 is \$135.4254 billion. To make a forecast for a future time period, such as the first quarter of fiscal 2016 ($X_i = 24, Q_1 = 1$),

$$\log(\hat{Y}_i) = b_0 + b_1 X_i + b_2 Q_1$$
$$= 2.0397 + (0.0040)(24) + (-0.0527)(1)$$
$$= 2.083$$

Thus,

$$\hat{Y}_i = 10^{2.083} = 121.0598$$

The predicted revenue for the first quarter of fiscal 2016 is \$121.0598 billion.

PROBLEMS FOR SECTION 16.7

LEARNING THE BASICS

16.40 In forecasting a monthly time series over a five-year period from January 2011 to December 2015, the exponential trend forecasting equation for January is

$$\log \hat{Y}_i = 2.0 + 0.01X_i + 0.10 \text{ (January)}$$

Take the antilog of the appropriate coefficient from this equation and interpret the
a. Y intercept, $\hat{b}_0$.
b. monthly compound growth rate.
c. January multiplier.

16.41 In forecasting daily time-series data, how many dummy variables are needed to account for the seasonal component day of the week?

16.42 In forecasting a quarterly time series over the five-year period from the first quarter of 2011 through the fourth quarter of 2015, the exponential trend forecasting equation is given by

$$\log \hat{Y}_i = 3.0 + 0.10X_i - 0.25Q_1 + 0.20Q_2 + 0.15Q_3$$

where quarter zero is the first quarter of 2011. Take the antilog of the appropriate coefficient from this equation and interpret the
a. Y intercept, $\hat{b}_0$.
b. quarterly compound growth rate.
c. second-quarter multiplier.

16.43 Refer to the exponential model given in Problem 16.42.
a. What is the fitted value of the series in the fourth quarter of 2013?
b. What is the fitted value of the series in the first quarter of 2013?
c. What is the forecast in the fourth quarter of 2015?
d. What is the forecast in the first quarter of 2016?

APPLYING THE CONCEPTS

✓SELF TEST **16.44** The data in `Toys R Us` are quarterly revenues (in \$millions) for Toys R Us from 1996-Q1 through 2015-Q1. (Data extracted from *Standard & Poor's Stock Reports*, November 1995, November 1998, and April 2002, and Toys R Us, Inc., **www.toysrus.com**.)
a. Do you think that the revenues for Toys R Us are subject to seasonal variation? Explain.
b. Plot the data. Does this chart support your answer in (a)?
c. Develop an exponential trend forecasting equation with quarterly components.

d. Interpret the quarterly compound growth rate.
e. Interpret the quarterly multipliers.
f. What are the forecasts for 2015-Q2, 2015-Q3, 2015-Q4, and all four quarters of 2016?

16.45 Are gasoline prices higher during the height of the summer vacation season than at other times? The file `GasPrices` contains the mean monthly prices (in \$/gallon) for unleaded gasoline in the United States from January 2006 to June 2015. (Data extracted from U.S. Energy Information Administration, **www.eia.gov/totalenergy/data/monthly/pdf/sec9_6.pdf**.)
a. Construct a time-series plot.
b. Develop an exponential trend forecasting equation with monthly components.
c. Interpret the monthly compound growth rate.
d. Interpret the monthly multipliers.
e. Write a short summary of your findings.

16.46 The file `Freezer` from January 2012 to December 2014 contains the number (in thousands) of freezer shipments in the United States from January 2012 to December 2014. (Data extracted from **www.statista.com**.)
a. Plot the time-series data.
b. Develop an exponential trend forecasting equation with monthly components.
c. What is the fitted value in December 2014?
d. What are the forecasts for the last four months of 2014?
e. Interpret the monthly compound growth rate.
f. Interpret the July multiplier.

16.47 The file `CallCenter` contains the monthly call volume for an existing product. (Data extracted from S. Madadevan and J. Overstreet, "Use of Warranty and Reliability Data to Inform Call Center Staffing," *Quality Engineering* 24 (2012): 386–399.)
a. Construct the time-series plot.
b. Describe the monthly pattern in the data.
c. In general, would you say that the overall call volume is increasing or decreasing? Explain.
d. Develop an exponential trend forecasting equation with monthly components.
e. Interpret the monthly compound growth rate.
f. Interpret the January multiplier.
g. What is the predicted call volume for month 60?
h. What is the predicted call volume for month 61?
i. How can this type of time-series forecasting benefit the call center?

16.48 The file Silver-Q contains the price in London for an ounce of silver (in US$) at the end of each quarter from 2004 through 2014. (Data extracted from **bit.ly/1afifi**.)
a. Plot the data.
b. Develop an exponential trend forecasting equation with quarterly components.
c. Interpret the quarterly compound growth rate.
d. Interpret the first quarter multiplier.
e. What is the fitted value for the last quarter of 2014?
f. What are the forecasts for all four quarters of 2015?
g. Are the forecasts in (f) accurate? Explain.

16.49 The file Gold contains the price in London for an ounce of gold (in US$) at the end of each quarter from 2004 through 2014. (Data extracted from **bit.ly/1afifi**.)
a. Plot the data.
b. Develop an exponential trend forecasting equation with quarterly components.
c. Interpret the quarterly compound growth rate.
d. Interpret the first quarter multiplier.
e. What is the fitted value for the last quarter of 2014?
f. What are the forecasts for all four quarters of 2015?
g. Are the forecasts in (f) accurate? Explain.

16.8 Index Numbers

An index number measures the value of an item (or group of items) at a particular point in time as a percentage of the value of an item (or group of items) at another point in time. The **Section 16.8 online topic** discusses this concept and illustrates its application.

CONSIDER THIS

Let the Model User Beware

When using a model, you must always review the assumptions built into the model and think about how novel or changing circumstances may render the model less useful.

Implicit in the time-series models developed in this chapter is that past data can be used to help predict the future. While using past data in this way is a legitimate application of time-series models, every so often, a crisis in financial markets illustrates that using models that rely on the past to predict the future is not without risk.

For example, during August 2007, many hedge funds suffered unprecedented losses. Apparently, many hedge fund managers used models that based their investment strategy on trading patterns over long time periods. These models did not—and could not—reflect trading patterns contrary to historical patterns (G. Morgenson, "A Week When Risk Came Home to Roost," *The New York Times*, August 12,

2007, pp. B1, B7). When fund managers in early August 2007 needed to sell stocks due to losses in their fixed income portfolios, stocks that were previously stronger became weaker, and weaker ones became stronger—the reverse of what the models expected. Making matters worse, many fund managers were using similar models and rigidly made investment decisions solely based on what those models said. These similar actions multiplied the effect of the selling pressure, an effect that the models had not considered and that therefore could not be seen in the models' results.

This example illustrates that using models does not absolve you of the responsibility of being a thoughtful decision maker. Go ahead and use models—when appropriately used, they will enhance your decision making. But always remember that no model can completely remove the risk involved in making a business decision.

▼USING **STATISTICS**
Principled Forecasting, Revisited

In the Using Statistics scenario, you were the financial analyst for The Principled, a large financial services company. You needed to forecast movie attendance, revenues for Coca-Cola, and for Walmart to better evaluate investment opportunities for your clients.

For movie attendance, you used moving averages and exponential smoothing methods to develop forecasts. You predicted that the movie attendance in 2015 would be 1.3033 billion.

For The Coca-Cola Company, you used least-squares linear, quadratic, and exponential models and autoregressive models to develop forecasts. You evaluated these alternative models and determined that the quadratic model gave the best forecast, according to several criteria. You predicted that the revenue of The Coca-Cola Company would be $55.5521 billion in 2015.

For Wal-Mart Stores, Inc., you used a least-squares regression model with seasonal components to develop forecasts. You predicted that Wal-Mart Stores would have revenues of $1121.0598 billion in the first quarter of fiscal 2016.

Given these forecasts, you now need to determine whether your clients should invest, and if so, how much they should invest in the movie industry or in The Coca-Cola Company or in Wal-Mart Stores, Inc.

▼ SUMMARY

In this chapter, you studied smoothing techniques, least-squares trend fitting, autoregressive models, and forecasting of seasonal data. Figure 16.23 summarizes the time-series methods discussed in this chapter.

When using time-series forecasting, you need to plot the time series and answer the following question: Is there a trend in the data? If there is a trend, then you can use the autoregressive model or the linear, quadratic, or exponential trend models. If there is no obvious trend in the time-series plot, then you should use moving averages or exponential smoothing to smooth out the effect of random effects and possible cyclical effects. After smoothing the data, if a trend is still not present, then you can use exponential smoothing to forecast short-term future values. If smoothing the data reveals a trend, then you can use the autoregressive model, or the linear, quadratic, or exponential trend models.

FIGURE 16.23
Summary chart of time-series forecasting methods

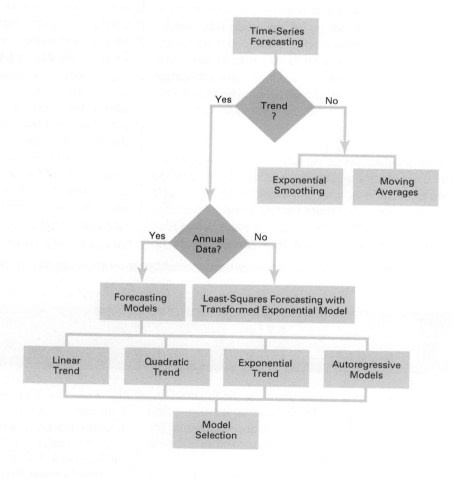

▼ REFERENCES

1. Bowerman, B. L., R. T. O'Connell, and A. Koehler. *Forecasting, Time Series, and Regression*, 4th ed. Belmont, CA: Duxbury Press, 2005.
2. Box, G. E. P., G. M. Jenkins, and G. C. Reinsel. *Time Series Analysis: Forecasting and Control*, 3rd ed. Upper Saddle River, NJ: Prentice Hall, 1994.
3. Frees, E. W. *Data Analysis Using Regression Models: The Business Perspective*. Upper Saddle River, NJ: Prentice Hall, 1996.
4. Hanke, J. E., D. W. Wichern, and A. G. Reitsch. *Business Forecasting*, 7th ed. Upper Saddle River, NJ: Prentice Hall, 2001.
5. Montgomery, D. C., C. L. Jenning, and M. Kulahci. *Introduction to Time Series Analysis and Forecasting*, 2nd ed. New York: Wiley, 2015.

▼ KEY EQUATIONS

Computing an Exponentially Smoothed Value in Time Period i

$$E_1 = Y_1$$
$$E_i = WY_i + (1 - W)E_{i-1} \quad i = 2, 3, 4, \ldots \qquad (16.1)$$

Forecasting Time Period $i + 1$

$$\hat{Y}_{i+1} = E_i \qquad (16.2)$$

Linear Trend Forecasting Equation

$$\hat{Y}_i = b_0 + b_1 X_i \qquad (16.3)$$

Quadratic Trend Forecasting Equation

$$\hat{Y}_i = b_0 + b_1 X_i + b_2 X_i^2 \qquad (16.4)$$

Exponential Trend Model

$$Y_i = \beta_0 \beta_1^{X_i} \varepsilon_i \qquad (16.5)$$

Transformed Exponential Trend Model

$$\begin{aligned} \log(Y_i) &= \log(\beta_0 \beta_1^{X_i} \varepsilon_i) \\ &= \log(\beta_0) + \log(\beta_1^{X_i}) + \log(\varepsilon_i) \\ &= \log(\beta_0) + X_i \log(\beta_1) + \log(\varepsilon_i) \end{aligned} \qquad (16.6)$$

Exponential Trend Forecasting Equation

$$\log(\hat{Y}_i) = b_0 + b_1 X_i \qquad (16.7a)$$
$$\hat{Y}_i = \hat{\beta}_0 \hat{\beta}_1^{X_i} \qquad (16.7b)$$

pth-Order Autoregressive Models

$$Y_i = A_0 + A_1 Y_{i-1} + A_2 Y_{i-2} + \cdots + A_p Y_{i-p} + \delta_i \qquad (16.8)$$

First-Order Autoregressive Model

$$Y_i = A_0 + A_1 Y_{i-1} + \delta_i \qquad (16.9)$$

Second-Order Autoregressive Model

$$Y_i = A_0 + A_1 Y_{i-1} + A_2 Y_{i-2} + \delta_i \qquad (16.10)$$

t Test for Significance of the Highest-Order Autoregressive Parameter, A_p

$$t_{STAT} = \frac{a_p - A_p}{S_{a_p}} \qquad (16.11)$$

Fitted pth-Order Autoregressive Equation

$$\hat{Y}_i = a_0 + a_1 Y_{i-1} + a_2 Y_{i-2} + \cdots + a_p Y_{i-p} \qquad (16.12)$$

pth-Order Autoregressive Forecasting Equation

$$\hat{Y}_{n+j} = a_0 + a_1 \hat{Y}_{n+j-1} + a_2 \hat{Y}_{n+j-2} + \cdots + a_p \hat{Y}_{n+j-p} \qquad (16.13)$$

Mean Absolute Deviation

$$MAD = \frac{\sum_{i=1}^{n} |Y_i - \hat{Y}_i|}{n} \qquad (16.14)$$

Exponential Model with Quarterly Data

$$Y_i = \beta_0 \beta_1^{X_i} \beta_2^{Q_1} \beta_3^{Q_2} \beta_4^{Q_3} \varepsilon_i \qquad (16.15)$$

Transformed Exponential Model with Quarterly Data

$$\begin{aligned} \log(Y_i) &= \log(\beta_0 \beta_1^{X_i} \beta_2^{Q_1} \beta_3^{Q_2} \beta_4^{Q_3} \varepsilon_i) \\ &= \log(\beta_0) + \log(\beta_1^{X_i}) + \log(\beta_2^{Q_1}) + \log(\beta_3^{Q_2}) \\ &\quad + \log(\beta_4^{Q_3}) + \log(\varepsilon_i) \\ &= \log(\beta_0) + X_i \log(\beta_1) + Q_1 \log(\beta_2) \\ &\quad + Q_2 \log(\beta_3) + Q_3 \log(\beta_4) + \log(\varepsilon_i) \end{aligned} \qquad (16.16)$$

Exponential Growth with Quarterly Data Forecasting Equation

$$\log(\hat{Y}_i) = b_0 + b_1 X_i + b_2 Q_1 + b_3 Q_2 + b_4 Q_3 \qquad (16.17)$$

Exponential Model with Monthly Data

$$Y_i = \beta_0 \beta_1^{X_i} \beta_2^{M_1} \beta_3^{M_2} \beta_4^{M_3} \beta_5^{M_4} \beta_6^{M_5} \beta_7^{M_6} \beta_8^{M_7} \beta_9^{M_8} \beta_{10}^{M_9} \beta_{11}^{M_{10}} \beta_{12}^{M_{11}} \varepsilon_i \qquad (16.18)$$

Transformed Exponential Model with Monthly Data

$$\begin{aligned} \log(Y_i) &= \log(\beta_0 \beta_1^{X_i} \beta_2^{M_1} \beta_3^{M_2} \beta_4^{M_3} \beta_5^{M_4} \beta_6^{M_5} \beta_7^{M_6} \beta_8^{M_7} \beta_9^{M_8} \beta_{10}^{M_9} \beta_{11}^{M_{10}} \beta_{12}^{M_{11}} \varepsilon_i) \\ &= \log(\beta_0) + X_i \log(\beta_1) + M_1 \log(\beta_2) + M_2 \log(\beta_3) \\ &\quad + M_3 \log(\beta_4) + M_4 \log(\beta_5) + M_5 \log(\beta_6) + M_6 \log(\beta_7) \\ &\quad + M_7 \log(\beta_8) + M_8 \log(\beta_9) + M_9 \log(\beta_{10}) \\ &\quad + M_{10} \log(\beta_{11}) + M_{11} \log(\beta_{12}) + \log(\varepsilon_i) \end{aligned} \qquad (16.19)$$

Exponential Growth with Monthly Data Forecasting Equation

$$\begin{aligned} \log(\hat{Y}_i) &= b_0 + b_1 X_i + b_2 M_1 + b_3 M_2 + b_4 M_3 + b_5 M_4 + b_6 M_5 \\ &\quad + b_7 M_6 + b_8 M_7 + b_9 M_8 + b_{10} M_9 + b_{11} M_{10} + b_{12} M_{11} \end{aligned} \qquad (16.19)$$

▼ KEY TERMS

autoregressive modeling   571
causal forecasting methods   554
cyclical effect   555
exponential smoothing   558
exponential trend model   564
first-order autocorrelation   571
first-order autoregressive model   572
forecasting   554
irregular effect   555

lagged predictor variable   571
linear trend model   561
mean absolute deviation (*MAD*)   581
moving averages   556
parsimony   581
*p*th-order autocorrelation   571
*p*th-order autoregressive model   571
quadratic trend model   563
qualitative forecasting method   554

quantitative forecasting method   554
random effect   555
seasonal effect   555
second-order autocorrelation   571
second-order autoregressive model   572
time series   554
time-series forecasting methods   554
trend   555

▼ CHECKING YOUR UNDERSTANDING

16.50   What is a time series?

16.51   What are the different components of a time-series model?

16.52   What is the difference between moving averages and exponential smoothing?

16.53   Under what circumstances is the exponential trend model most appropriate?

16.54   How does the least-squares linear trend forecasting model developed in this chapter differ from the least-squares linear regression model considered in Chapter 13?

16.55   How does autoregressive modeling differ from the other approaches to forecasting?

16.56   What are the different approaches to choosing an appropriate forecasting model?

16.57   What is the major difference between using S_{YX} and *MAD* for evaluating how well a particular model fits the data?

16.58   How does forecasting for monthly or quarterly data differ from forecasting for annual data?

▼ CHAPTER REVIEW PROBLEMS

16.59   The data in the following table, stored in `Polio`, represent the annual incidence rates (per 100,000 persons) of reported acute poliomyelitis recorded over five-year periods from 1915 to 1955:

Year	1915	1920	1925	1930	1935	1940	1945	1950	1955
Rate	3.1	2.2	5.3	7.5	8.5	7.4	10.3	22.1	17.6

Source: Data extracted from B. Wattenberg, ed., *The Statistical History of the United States: From Colonial Times to the Present*, ser. B303.

a. Plot the data.
b. Compute the linear trend forecasting equation and plot the trend line.
c. What are your forecasts for 1960, 1965, and 1970?
d. Using a library or the Internet, find the actually reported incidence rates of acute poliomyelitis for 1960, 1965, and 1970. Record your results.
e. Why are the forecasts you made in (c) not useful? Discuss.

16.60   The U.S. Department of Labor gathers and publishes statistics concerning the labor market. The file `Workforce` contains data on the size of the U.S. civilian noninstitutional population of people 16 years and over (in thousands) and the U.S. civilian noninstitutional workforce of people 16 years and over (in thousands) for 1984–2014. The workforce variable reports the number of people in the population who have a job or are actively looking for a job. (Data extracted from Bureau of Labor Statistics, U.S. Department of Labor, **www.bls.gov**.)

a. Plot the time series for the U.S. civilian noninstitutional population of people 16 years and older.

b. Compute the linear trend forecasting equation.
c. Forecast the U.S. civilian noninstitutional population of people 16 years and older for 2015 and 2016.
d. Repeat (a) through (c) for the U.S. civilian noninstitutional workforce of people 16 years and older.

16.61   The monthly commercial and residential prices for natural gas (dollars per thousand cubic feet) in the United States from January 2008 through December 2014 are stored in `Natural Gas`. (Data extracted from Energy Information Administration, U.S. Department of Energy, **www.eia.gov**, *Natural Gas Monthly*, March 1, 2015.)

   For the commercial price and the residential price,
a. do you think the price for natural gas has a seasonal component?
b. plot the time series. Does this chart support your answer in (a)?
c. compute an exponential trend forecasting equation for monthly data.
d. interpret the monthly compound growth rate.
e. interpret the monthly multipliers. Do the multipliers support your answers in (a) and (b)?
f. compare the results for the commercial prices and the residential prices.

16.62   The data stored in `McDonalds` represent the gross revenues (in billions of current dollars) of McDonald's Corporation from 1975 through 2014:
a. Plot the data.

b. Compute the linear trend forecasting equation.

c. Compute the quadratic trend forecasting equation.

d. Compute the exponential trend forecasting equation.

e. Determine the best-fitting autoregressive model, using $\alpha = 0.05$.

f. Perform a residual analysis for each of the models in (b) through (e).

g. Compute the standard error of the estimate (S_{YX}) and the *MAD* for each corresponding model in (f).

h. On the basis of your results in (f) and (g), along with a consideration of the principle of parsimony, which model would you select for purposes of forecasting? Discuss.

i. Using the selected model in (h), forecast gross revenues for 2015.

16.63 Teachers' Retirement System of the City of New York offers several types of investments for its members. Among the choices are investments with fixed and variable rates of return. There are several categories of variable-return investments. The Diversified Equity Fund consists of investments that are primarily made in stocks, and the Stable-Value Fund consists of investments in corporate bonds and other types of lower-risk instruments. The data in `TRSNYC` represent the value of a unit of each type of variable-return investment at the beginning of each year from 1984 to 2015. (Data extracted from "Historical Data-Unit Values, Teachers' Retirement System of the City of New York," **bit.ly/SESJF5**.)

For each of the two time series,

a. plot the data.

b. compute the linear trend forecasting equation.

c. compute the quadratic trend forecasting equation.

d. compute the exponential trend forecasting equation.

e. determine the best-fitting autoregressive model, using $\alpha = 0.05$.

f. Perform a residual analysis for each of the models in (b) through (e).

g. Compute the standard error of the estimate (S_{YX}) and the *MAD* for each corresponding model in (f).

h. On the basis of your results in (f) and (g), along with a consideration of the principle of parsimony, which model would you select for purposes of forecasting? Discuss.

i. Using the selected model in (h), forecast the unit values for 2016.

j. Based on the results of (a) through (i), what investment strategy would you recommend for a member of the Teachers' Retirement System of the City of New York? Explain.

REPORT WRITING EXERCISE

16.64 As a consultant to an investment company trading in various currencies, you have been assigned the task of studying long-term trends in the exchange rates of the Canadian dollar, the Japanese yen, and the English pound. Data from 1980 to 2014 are stored in `Currency`, where the Canadian dollar, the Japanese yen, and the English pound are expressed in units per U.S. dollar.

Develop a forecasting model for the exchange rate of each of these three currencies and provide forecasts for 2015 and 2016 for each currency. Write an executive summary for a presentation to be given to the investment company. Append to this executive summary a discussion regarding possible limitations that may exist in these models.

CHAPTER 16

▾ CASES

Managing Ashland MultiComm Services

As part of the continuing strategic initiative to increase subscribers to the *3-For-All* cable/phone/Internet services, the marketing department is closely monitoring the number of subscribers. To help do so, forecasts are to be developed for the number of subscribers in the future. To accomplish this task, the number of subscribers for the most recent 24-month period has been determined and is stored in `AMS16`.

1. Analyze these data and develop a model to forecast the number of subscribers. Present your findings in a report that includes the assumptions of the model and its limitations. Forecast the number of subscribers for the next four months.

2. Would you be willing to use the model developed to forecast the number of subscribers one year into the future? Explain.

3. Compare the trend in the number of subscribers to the number of new subscribers per month stored in `AMS13`. What explanation can you provide for any differences?

Digital Case

Apply your knowledge about time-series forecasting in this Digital Case.

The *Ashland Herald* competes for readers in the Tri-Cities area with the newer *Oxford Glen Journal* (*OGJ*). Recently, the circulation staff at the *OGJ* claimed that their newspaper's circulation and subscription base is growing faster than that of the *Herald* and that local advertisers would do better if they transferred their advertisements from the *Herald* to the *OGJ*. The circulation department of the *Herald* has complained to the Ashland Chamber of Commerce about *OGJ*'s claims and has asked the chamber to investigate, a request that was welcomed by *OGJ*'s circulation staff.

Open **ACC_Mediation216.pdf** to review the circulation dispute information collected by the Ashland Chamber of Commerce. Then answer the following:

1. Which newspaper would you say has the right to claim the fastest-growing circulation and subscription base? Support your answer by performing and summarizing an appropriate statistical analysis.

2. What is the single most positive fact about the *Herald*'s circulation and subscription base? What is the single most positive fact about the *OGJ*'s circulation and subscription base? Explain your answers.

3. What additional data would be helpful in investigating the circulation claims made by the staffs of each newspaper?

▾EXCEL GUIDE

There are no Excel Guide instructions for Sections 16.1 and 16.2.

EG16.3 SMOOTHING an ANNUAL TIME SERIES

Moving Averages

Key Technique Use the **AVERAGE**(*cell range of L consecutive values*) function to compute a moving average. Use the special value **#N/A** (not available) for time periods in which no moving average can be computed.

Example Calculate the Figure 16.3 three- and five-year moving averages for the movie attendance data that is shown in Figure 16.3 on page 557.

Worksheet Use the **COMPUTE worksheet** of the **Moving Averages workbook** as a template.

The worksheet already contains the data and formulas for the example. For other problems, paste the time-series data into columns A and B and:

1. For data that contain more than 14 time periods, copy the formulas in cell range **C13:D13** down through the new table rows; otherwise, delete rows as necessary.
2. Enter the special value #N/A in columns C and D for the first and last time periods.
3. Enter #N/A in the second and second-to-last time periods in column D.

To construct a moving average plot for other problems, open to the adjusted COMPUTE worksheet and:

1. Select the cell range of the time-series and the moving averages (**A1:D15** for the example).
2. Select **Insert → Scatter (X, Y) or Bubble Chart** and select the **Scatter** gallery item. [OS X Excel labels the icon as **X Y (Scatter)** and older Excels label the icon as **Scatter**.]
3. Relocate the chart to a chart sheet, turn off the gridlines, add axis titles, and modify the chart title by using the instructions in Appendix Section B.6.

Exponential Smoothing

Key Technique Use arithmetic formulas to compute exponentially smoothed values.

Example Calculate the Figure 16.4 exponentially smoothed series ($W = 0.50$ and $W = 0.25$) for the movie attendance data that is shown in Figure 16.4 on page 559.

Worksheet Use the **COMPUTE worksheet** of the **Exponential Smoothing workbook**, as a template.

The worksheet already contains the data and formulas for the example. In this worksheet, cells C2 and D2 contain the formula **=B2** that copies the initial value of the time series. The exponential smoothing begins in row 3, with cell C3 formula **=0.5 * B3 + 0.5 * C2**, and cell D3 formula **=0.25 * B3 + 0.75 * D2**. Note that in these formulas, the expression $1 - W$ in Equation (16.1) on page 558 has been simplified to the values 0.5 and 0.75, respectively.

For other problems, paste the time-series data into columns A and B and adjust the entries in columns C and D. For problems with fewer than 14 time periods, delete the excess rows. For problems with more than 14 time periods, select cell range **C15:D15** and copy down through the new table rows.

To construct a plot of exponentially smoothed values for other problems, open to the adjusted COMPUTE worksheet and:

1. Select the cell range of the time-series data and the exponentially smoothed values (**A1:D15** for the example).
2. Select **Insert → Scatter (X, Y)** or **Bubble Chart** and select the Scatter gallery item. [OS X Excel labels the icon as **X Y (Scatter)** and older Excels label the icon **Scatter**.]
3. Relocate the chart to a chart sheet, turn off the gridlines, add axis titles, and modify the chart title by using the instructions in Appendix Section B.6.

Analysis ToolPak Use **Exponential Smoothing**.
For the example, open to the **DATA worksheet** of the **Movie Attendance workbook** and:

1. Select **Data → Data Analysis**.
2. In the Data Analysis dialog box, select **Exponential Smoothing** from the **Analysis Tools** list and then click **OK**.

In the Exponential Smoothing dialog box (shown below):

3. Enter **B1:B15** as the **Input Range**.
4. Enter **0.5** as the **Damping factor**. (The damping factor is equal to $1 - W$.)

5. Check **Labels**, enter **C1** as the **Output Range**, and click **OK**.

In the new column C:

6. Copy the last formula in cell **C11** to cell **C12**.
7. Enter the column heading **ES(W = .50)** in cell **C1**, replacing the **#N/A** value.

To create the exponentially smoothed values that use a smoothing coefficient of $W = 0.25$, enter **0.75** as the **Damping factor** in step 4, enter **D1** as the **Output Range** in step 5, and enter **ES(W = .25)** as the column heading in step 7.

EG16.4 LEAST-SQUARES TREND FITTING and FORECASTING

The Linear Trend Model

Key Technique Modify the Section EG13.2 instructions (see page 472) to create a linear trend model. Use the cell range of the coded variable as the X variable cell range (called the **X Variable Cell Range** in the *PHStat* instructions, called the *cell range of X variable* in the *Worksheet* instructions, and called the **Input X Range** in the *Analysis ToolPak* instructions).

If you need to create coded values, enter them manually in a column. If you have many coded values, you can use **Home → Fill** (in the Editing group) → **Series** and in the Series dialog box, click **Columns** and **Linear**, and select appropriate values for **Step value** and **Stop value**.

The Quadratic Trend Model

Key Technique Modify the Section EG15.1 instructions (see page 551) to create a quadratic trend model. Use the cell range of the coded variable and the squared coded variable as the X variables cell range, called the **X Variables Cell Range** in the *PHStat* instructions and the **Input X Range** in the *Analysis ToolPak* instructions. Use the Sections EG15.2 and EG15.1 instructions to create the squared coded variable and to plot the quadratic trend.

The Exponential Trend Model

Key Technique Use the **POWER(10,** *predicted log(Y)*) function to compute the predicted Y values from the predicted $log(Y)$ results.

To create an exponential trend model, first convert the values of the dependent variable Y to $log(Y)$ values using the Section EG15.2 instructions on page 551. Then perform a simple linear regression analysis with residual analysis using the $log(Y)$ values. Modify theSection EG13.5 "Residual Analysis" instructions using the cell range of the $log(Y)$ values as the Y variable cell range and the cell range of the coded variable as the X variable cell range.

Note the Y and X variable cell ranges are called the **Y Variable Cell Range** and **X Variable Cell Range** in the *PHStat* instructions, the *cell range of Y variable* and *cell range of X variable* in the *Worksheet* instructions, and the **Input Y Range** and **Input X Range** in the *Analysis ToolPak* instructions.

If you use the *PHStat* or *Worksheet* instructions, residuals will appear in a residuals worksheet. If you use the Analysis ToolPak instructions, residuals will appear in the RESIDUAL OUTPUT area of the regression results worksheet. Because you use $log(Y)$ values for the regression, the predicted Y and residuals listed are *log values* that need to be converted. [The Analysis ToolPak incorrectly labels the new column for the logs of the residuals as *Residuals*, and not as *LOG(Residuals)*, as you might expect.]

In an empty column in the residuals worksheet (*PHStat* or *Worksheet*) or empty column ranges to the right of RESIDUALS OUTPUT area (*Analysis ToolPak*) to first add a column of formulas that use the POWER function to compute the predicted Y values. Then, add a second column that contains the original Y values. Finally, add a third new column that contains formulas in the form **=(** *revenue cell − predicted revenue cell***)** to compute the actual residuals.

Use columns G through I of the **RESIDUALS worksheet** of the **Exponential Trend workbook** as a model. The worksheet already contains the values and formulas needed to create the Figure 16.10 plot that fits an exponential trend forecasting equation for The Coca-Cola Company revenues (see page 566).

To construct an exponential trend plot, first select the cell range of the time-series data and then use the Section EG2.5 instructions to construct a scatter plot. (For The Coca-Cola Company revenue example, use the cell range is **B1:B18** in the **Data worksheet** of the **Coca-Cola workbook**.) Select the chart and

1. Select **Design** (or **Chart Design**) → **Add Chart Element** → **Trendline** → **More Trendline Options**.
2. In the Format Trendline pane, click **Exponential**.

In older Excels, select **Layout** → **Trendline** → **More Trendline Options**. In the Format Trendline dialog box, click **Trendline Options** in the left pane and in the Trendline Options right pane, click **Exponential** and click **OK**.

Model Selection Using First, Second, and Percentage Differences

Key Technique Use arithmetic formulas to compute the first, second, and percentage differences. Use division formulas to compute the percentage differences and use subtraction formulas to compute the first and second differences. Use the **COMPUTE worksheet** of the **Differences workbook**, shown in Figure 16.11 on page 568, as a model for developing a differences worksheet. (Open to the **COMPUTE_FORMULAS worksheet** to see all formulas used.)

EG16.5 AUTOREGRESSIVE MODELING for TREND FITTING and FORECASTING

Creating Lagged Predictor Variables

Key Technique Create lagged predictor variables by creating a column of formulas that refer to a previous row's (previous time period's) *Y* value. Enter the special worksheet value **#N/A** (not available) for the cells in the column to which lagged values do not apply.

Use the **COMPUTE worksheet** of the **Lagged Predictors workbook**, shown in Figure 16.13 on page 576 as a model for developing lagged predictor variables for the first-order, second-order, and third-order autoregressive models.

When specifying cell ranges for a lagged predictor variable, you include only rows that contain lagged values. Contrary to the usual practice in this book, you do not include rows that contain **#N/A**, nor do you include the row 1 column heading.

To see the formulas that the COMPUTE worksheet uses, not shown in Figure 16.13, open to the COMPUTE_FORMULAS worksheet.

Autoregressive Modeling

Key Technique Modify the Section EG14.1 instructions (see page 517) to create a third-order or second-order autoregressive model. Use the cell range of the first-order, second-order, and third-order lagged predictor variables as the *X* variables cell range for the third-order model. Use the cell range of the first-order and second-order lagged predictor variables as the *X* variables cell range for the second-order model.

If you use the *PHStat* instructions, modify step 3 to *clear* not *check* **First cells in both ranges contain label**. If using the *Worksheet* instructions, use the **COMPUTE3 worksheet** in lieu of the COMPUTE worksheet for the third-order model. If using the *Analysis ToolPak* instructions, do not check **Labels** in step 4.

Modify the Section EG13.2 instructions (see page 472) to create a first-order autoregressive model. Use the cell range of the first-order lagged predictor variable as the *X* variable cell range (called the **X Variable Cell Range** in the *PHStat* instructions, the *cell range of X variable* in the *Worksheet* instructions, and the **Input X Range** in the *Analysis ToolPak* instructions). If using the *PHStat* instructions, modify step 3 to *clear* not *check* **First cells in both ranges contain label**. If using the *Analysis ToolPak* instructions, do not check **Labels** in step 4.

EG16.6 CHOOSING an APPROPRIATE FORECASTING MODEL

Performing a Residual Analysis

To create residual plots for the linear trend model or the first-order autoregressive model, use the Section EG13.5 instructions on page 473. To create residual plots for the quadratic trend model or second-order autoregressive model, use the Section EG14.3 instructions on page 518. To create residual plots for the exponential trend model, use the instructions Section EG16.4 on page 595. To create residual plots for the third-order autoregressive model, use the Section EG14.3 instructions on page 518 but use the **RESIDUALS3** worksheet instead of the RESIDUALS worksheet if you use the *Worksheet* instructions.

Measuring the Magnitude of the Residuals Through Squared or Absolute Differences

Key Technique Use the function **SUMPRODUCT(ABS(*residuals cell range*)) / COUNT(*residuals cell range*)** to compute the mean asolute deviation (*MAD*).

To compute the mean absolute deviation (*MAD*), first perform a residual analysis. Then, in an empty cell, add the key technique formula. When entering the *residuals cell range,* do not include the column heading as is the standard practice in this book. (See Appendix Section F.4 to learn more about the application of **SUMPRODUCT** function in this formula.)

Cell I19 of the **RESIDUALS_FORMULAS** worksheet of the **Exponential Trend workbook** contains the *MAD* formula for The Coca-Cola Company revenues example.

A Comparison of Four Forecasting Methods

Key Technique Use the **COMPARE** worksheet of the **Forecasting Comparison workbook** as a model.

Construct a model comparison worksheet similar to the one shown in Figure 16.20 on page 582 by using **Paste Special values** (see Appendix Section B.4) to transfer results from the regression results worksheets. For the *SSE* values (row 20 in Figure 16.8), copy the regression results worksheet cell C13, the *SS* value for Residual in the ANOVA table. For the S_{YX} values (row), copy the regression results worksheet cell B7, labeled Standard Error, for all but the exponential trend model. For the *MAD* values, add formulas as discussed in the previous section.

For the S_{YX} value for the exponential trend model, enter a formula in the form =**SQRT(*exponential SSE cell* / (COUNT(*cell range of exponential residuals*) - 2))**. In the COMPARE worksheet, this formula is =**SQRT(H20/(COUNT(H3:H19) - 2))**.

Open to the **COMPARE_FORMULAS** worksheet to discover how the COMPARE worksheet uses the SUMSQ function as an alternate way of displaying the *SSE* values.

EG16.7 TIME-SERIES FORECASTING of SEASONAL DATA

Least-Squares Forecasting with Monthly or Quarterly Data

To develop a least-squares regression model for monthly or quarterly data, add columns of formulas that use the **IF** function (see Appendix F.4) to create dummy variables for the quarterly or monthly data. Enter all formulas in the form $= \mathbf{IF}(\mathit{comparison}, \mathbf{1}, \mathbf{0})$.

Shown at right are the first five rows of columns F through K of a data worksheet that contains dummy variables. In the first illustration, columns F, G, and H contain the quarterly dummy variables Q1, Q2, and Q3 that are based on column B coded quarter values (not shown). In

the second illustration, columns J and K contain the two monthly variables M1 and M6 that are based on column C month values (also not shown).

	F	G	H
1	Q1	Q2	Q3
2	=IF(B2 = 1, 1, 0)	=IF(B2 = 2, 1, 0)	=IF(B2 = 3, 1, 0)
3	=IF(B3 = 1, 1, 0)	=IF(B3 = 2, 1, 0)	=IF(B3 = 3, 1, 0)
4	=IF(B4 = 1, 1, 0)	=IF(B4 = 2, 1, 0)	=IF(B4 = 3, 1, 0)
5	=IF(B5 = 1, 1, 0)	=IF(B5 = 2, 1, 0)	=IF(B5 = 3, 1, 0)

	J	K
1	M1	M6
2	=IF(C2 ="January", 1, 0)	=IF(C2 = "June", 1, 0)
3	=IF(C3 ="January", 1, 0)	=IF(C3 = "June", 1, 0)
4	=IF(C4 ="January", 1, 0)	=IF(C4 = "June", 1, 0)
5	=IF(C5 ="January", 1, 0)	=IF(C5 = "June", 1, 0)

CONTENTS

OBJECTIVES

- Identify the questions to ask when choosing which statistical methods to use to conduct data analysis
- Generate rules for applying statistics in future studies and analyses
- Create descriptive analytics dashboard elements
- Understand fundamental business analytics concepts

▼USING **STATISTICS**
Mounting Future Analyses

Learning and applying business statistics methodology has some similarities with planning and executing a mountain climbing expedition. What might seem intimidating, or even overwhelming, at first can be conquered by applying methods and techniques using a framework that identifies and guides you through a series of tasks. In Section FTF.1, you first learned how the **DCOVA framework** can help apply statistical methods to business problems. After learning methods in early chapters to Define, Collect, and Organize data, you have spent most of your time studying ways to Visualize and Analyze data.

Determining which methods to use to organize, visualize, and analyze your data may have seemed straightforward when you worked out examples or problems from a particular chapter in which the data had already been defined and collected (and perhaps even organized) for you. The defined and possibly organized data gave clues about which methods to choose, as did the chapter itself. For example, while studying the descriptive statistics chapter, you could deduce properly that applying the inferential methods of other chapters would not be part of any example or problem.

But what should you do when you find yourself in new situations such as needing to analyze data for another course or to help solve a problem in a real business setting? You will not be studying a chapter of this book, so the methods to choose and apply will not necessarily be as obvious to you as they may have been when working out a specific problem from a specific chapter. How then can you guide yourself to choosing appropriate statistical methods as you seek to mount future analyses?

S electing the appropriate methods to use with data turns out to be the single most difficult thing you do when you apply business statistics to real situations. This is also the single most important task you face as well. Recall that when using the DCOVA approach, you first define the variables that you want to study in order to solve a business problem or meet a business objective. To do this, you identify the type of business problem, such as trying to describe a group or trying to make inferences about a group, and then determine the type of variable—*numerical* or *categorical*—you will be analyzing.

That act of defining a variable provides the starting point for selecting appropriate statistical methods to use. Once you know the type of variable, you can ask yourself a series of questions about what you seek to do with that variable. The questions can guide you to the appropriate methods to select as surely as a mountain guide can help you to the summit of a mountain. Therefore, the *answer* to the question "How can you guide yourself to choosing appropriate statistical methods as you seek to mount future analyses?" is "Ask more questions."

In the following two sections, this chapter presents two sets of questions, one for numerical variables and the other for categorical variables, that you can ask yourself once you have defined your variable. Unlike other chapters, this chapter introduces a Using Statistics scenario to raise a completely different type of question.

17.1 Analyzing Numerical Variables

To analyze a numerical variable, begin with the questions in Exhibit17.1.

EXHIBIT **17.1**

Questions to Ask When Analyzing Numerical Variables

Do you want to

- describe the characteristics of the variable (possibly broken down into several groups)?
- reach conclusions about the mean or the standard deviation of the variable in a population?
- determine whether the mean and/or standard deviation of the variable differs depending on the group?
- determine which factors affect the value of a variable?
- predict the value of the variable based on the values of other variables?
- determine whether the values of the variable are stable over time?

Answers to these questions appear next.

Describe the Characteristics of a Numerical Variable?

You develop tables and charts and compute descriptive statistics to describe characteristics such as central tendency, variation, and shape. Specifically, you can create a stem-and-leaf display, percentage distribution, histogram, polygon, boxplot, normal probability plot, gauge, and treemap (see Sections 2.2, 2.4, 3.3, 6.3, and 17.4), and you can compute statistics such as the mean, median, mode, quartiles, range, interquartile range, standard deviation, variance, coefficient of variation, skewness, and kurtosis (see Sections 3.1, 3.2, and 3.3).

Reach Conclusions About the Population Mean or the Standard Deviation?

You have several different choices, and you can use any combination of these choices. To estimate the mean value of the variable in a population, you construct a confidence interval estimate of the mean (see Section 8.2). To determine whether the population mean is equal to a specific value, you conduct a t test of hypothesis for the mean (see Section 9.2). To determine whether the population standard deviation or variance is equal to a specific value, you conduct a χ^2 test of hypothesis for the standard deviation or variance (see online Section 12.7).

Determine Whether the Mean and/or Standard Deviation Differs Depending on the Group?

When examining differences between groups, you first need to establish which categorical variable to use to divide your data into groups. You then need to know whether this grouping variable divides your data into two groups (such as male and female groups for a gender variable) or whether the variable divides your data into more than two groups (such as the four in-store locations for mobile electronics discussed in Section 11.1). Finally, you must ask whether your data set contains independent groups or whether your data set contains matched or repeated measurements.

If the Grouping Variable Defines Two Independent Groups and You Are Interested in Central Tendency   Which hypothesis tests you use depends on the assumptions you make about your data.

If you assume that your numerical variable is normally distributed and that the variances are equal, you conduct a pooled t test for the difference between the means (see Section 10.1). If you cannot assume that the variances are equal, you conduct a separate-variance t test for the difference between the means (see Section 10.1). In either case, if you believe that your numerical variables are not normally distributed, you can perform a Wilcoxon rank sum test (see Section 12.4) and compare the results of this test to those of the t test.

To evaluate the assumption of normality that the pooled t test and separate-variance t test include, you can construct boxplots and normal probability plots for each group.

If the Grouping Variable Defines Two Groups of Matched Samples or Repeated Measurements and You Are Interested in Central Tendency   If you can assume that the paired differences are normally distributed, you conduct a paired t test (see Section 10.2). If you cannot assume that the paired differences are normally distributed, you conduct a Wilcoxon signed rank test (see reference 2).

If the Grouping Variable Defines Two Independent Groups and You Are Interested in Variability   If you can assume that your numerical variable is normally distributed, you conduct an F test for the difference between two variances (see Section 10.4).

If the Grouping Variable Defines More Than Two Independent Groups and You Are Interested in Central Tendency   If you can assume that the values of the numerical variable are normally distributed, you conduct a one-way analysis of variance (see Section 11.1); otherwise, you conduct a Kruskal-Wallis rank test (see Section 12.5). You can use the Levene test (see Section 11.1) to test for the homogeneity of variance between the groups.

If the Grouping Variable Defines More Than Two Groups of Matched Samples or Repeated Measurements and You Are Interested in Central Tendency   Suppose that you have a design where the rows represent the blocks and the columns represent the levels of a factor. If you can assume that the values of the numerical variable are normally distributed, you conduct a randomized block design F test (see online Section 11.3). If you cannot assume that the paired differences are normally distributed, you conduct a Friedman rank test (see reference 2).

Determine Which Factors Affect the Value of a Variable?

If there are two factors to be examined to determine their effect on the values of a variable, you develop a two-factor factorial design (see Section 11.2).

Predict the Value of a Variable Based on the Values of Other Variables?

When predicting the values of a numerical dependent variable, you conduct least-squares regression analysis. The least-squares regression model you develop depends on the number of independent variables in your model. If there is only one independent variable being used to predict the numerical dependent variable of interest, you develop a simple linear regression model (see Chapter 13); otherwise, you develop a multiple regression model (see Chapters 14 and 15) and/or a regression tree (see Section 17.5).

If you have values over a period of time and you want to forecast the variable for future time periods, you can use moving averages, exponential smoothing, least-squares forecasting, and autoregressive modeling (see Chapter 16). If you want to visualize many variables simultaneously, you can use sparklines (see Section 2.6).

Determine Whether the Values of a Variable Are Stable Over Time?

If you are studying a process and have collected data on the values of a numerical variable over a time period, you construct R and $\overline{X}$ charts (see online Section 18.5). If you have collected data in which the values are counts of the number of nonconformities, you construct a c chart (see online Section 18.4).

17.2 Analyzing Categorical Variables

To analyze a categorical variable, begin with the questions in Exhibit17.2.

EXHIBIT 17.2

Questions to Ask When Analyzing Categorical Variables

Do you want to

- describe the proportion of items of interest in each category (possibly broken down into several groups)?
- reach conclusions about the proportion of items of interest in a population?
- determine whether the proportion of items of interest differs depending on the group?
- predict the proportion of items of interest based on the values of other variables?
- determine whether the proportion of items of interest is stable over time?

Answers to these questions appear next.

Describe the Proportion of Items of Interest in Each Category?

You create summary tables and use these charts: bar chart, pie chart, doughnut chart, Pareto chart, or side-by-side bar chart (see Sections 2.1 and 2.3).

Reach Conclusions About the Proportion of Items of Interest?

You have two different choices. You can estimate the proportion of items of interest in a population by constructing a confidence interval estimate of the proportion (see Section 8.3). Or, you can determine whether the population proportion is equal to a specific value by conducting a Z test of hypothesis for the proportion (see Section 9.4).

Determine Whether the Proportion of Items of Interest Differs Depending on the Group?

When examining this difference, you first need to establish the number of categories associated with your categorical variable and the number of groups in your analysis. If your data contain two groups, you must also ask if your data contain independent groups or if your data contain matched samples or repeated measurements.

For Two Categories and Two Independent Groups   You conduct either the Z test for the difference between two proportions (see Section 10.3) or the χ^2 test for the difference between two proportions (see Section 12.1).

For Two Categories and Two Groups of Matched or Repeated Measurements   You conduct the McNemar test (see online Section 12.6).

For Two Categories and More Than Two Independent Groups   You conduct a χ^2 test for the difference among several proportions (see Section 12.2).

For More Than Two Categories and More Than Two Groups   You develop contingency tables and use multidimensional contingency tables to drill down to examine relationships among two or more categorical variables (Sections 2.1, 2.6, and 17.4). When you have two categorical variables, you conduct a χ^2 test of independence (see Section 12.3).

Predict the Proportion of Items of Interest Based on the Values of Other Variables?

You develop a logistic regression model (see Section 14.7) or a classification tree (see Section 17.5).

Determine Whether the Proportion of Items of Interest Is Stable Over Time?

If you are studying a process and have collected data over a time period, you can create the appropriate control chart. If you have collected the proportion of items of interest over a time period, you develop a p chart (see online Section 18.2).

▼USING STATISTICS
Back to Arlingtons for the Future

Through sales experiments noted in the Using Statistics scenarios for Chapters 10 and 11, Arlingtons has discovered how the location of items in a store can affect the sales of those items. Increased sales and, in some cases, placement fees have enhanced revenues, but that increase has not done enough to help Arlingtons stay competitive.

When a private equity firm made an unsolicited bid for Arlingtons, senior management reluctantly agreed to a buyout. The new owners believe that with their knowledge of statistical analysis, along with the application of business analytics, they can grow the business, especially in the online marketplace where Arlingtons has been a weak competitor. Just as multiple regression allows consideration of several independent variables, they believe that predictive analytics methods will allow them to analyze many more relevant variables. They plan to track customer buying hab-

its—who were those customers that were most likely to buy VLABGo players from the special front of store sales location? What else could one expect those customers to buy at Arlingtons?

They believe that by using analytics, they will begin to start getting answers to such questions as well as more fundamental questions such as "Should we even be selling mobile electronics?" and "Should we invest more in online sales and less in brick-and-mortar (physical) stores?" Knowing that one needs to have a solid foundation in statistics to best understand the application of analytics, the new owners have hired you. If only there were something you could use as an orientation to analytics that would leverage what you learned in an introductory business statistics course to help you understand the basics of analytics. If only.......

17.3 Introduction to Business Analytics

Business statistics constantly evolves. Many inferential methods that were developed over a century ago awaited widespread use of sample data or the computerization of business to be practical. More recent advances have made practical the analysis of larger data sets (see Section FTF.2) and businesses now can summarize and analyze larger amounts of data faster, perhaps fast enough to *immediately* affect operational decision making. **Business analytics** are the methods that combine these advances with statistics and management science techniques.

Business analytics methods fall into one of three broad categories. **Descriptive analytics** explores business activities that have occurred or are occurring in the present moment. **Predictive analytics** identifies what is likely to occur in the near future and finds relationships in data that may not be readily apparent using descriptive analytics. **Prescriptive analytics** investigates what should occur and prescribes the best course of action for the future. Predictive and prescriptive analytics make practical the use of big data (see page 4) to support decision making. While typically used to analyze large data sets or big data, many methods also work with smaller sets of data, as some of the examples demonstrate.

Business analytics requires specialized software that goes beyond the data analysis capabilities of Microsoft Excel. However, Excel can be helpful in data preparation, preliminary analysis, and developing subsets from larger collections of data, and many of the methods that Chapter 2 discusses can be used directly or adapted for these purposes. Microsoft also offers online tools and additional add-ins that extend Excel to support these tasks and give analytics users the ability to display and interact with results in the form of worksheet tables. (Some of these extended capabilities are built into the latest versions of Excel, with more functionality expected in the years to come.)

Data Mining

Data mining is the process that extracts useful knowledge from huge repositories of data. This extraction is rarely simple and typically requires the application of statistical methods, computer science algorithms, and database-like search and retrieval operations. Data mining makes the application of predictive analytics to big data practical.

In terms of this book, data mining is akin to combining the regression techniques of Chapters 13 through 15 with the ability to summarize and selectively filter data that Section 2.6 discusses. However, unlike the regression results worksheets or the PivotTable or slicers, data mining can operate on more than one file and can combine data from multiple sources in multiple data formats.

Like regression analysis, data mining uncovers relationships among variables, but differs from the regression methods in these ways:

- Data mining examines a much greater number of variables at one time than regression techniques examine.
- Data mining is a semiautomated process that searches for possible independent variables from a much wider set of possible independent variables. Regression methods use a fixed list of previously-identified independent variables.
- Data mining makes extensive use of historical data sets.
- Data mining can increase the chance of encountering a regression pitfall (see Sections 13.9 and 15.5) when used in an unknowing manner.

In Excel 2013, Power Pivot features are part of the Microsoft-supplied PowerPivot add-in that you can download and install. In Excel 2016 for Windows, Power Pivot is a built-in feature.

Power Pivot

While there is no "data mining" command in Excel, Excel **Power Pivot** features can assist with data collection and preparation and review or serve as a convenient means to view the results of a data mining operation. Using formulas that you construct, Power Pivot can create new columns (variables) that can combine variables from multiple tables and files. In the simplest case, you can use Power Pivot to recode variables.

Section 14.6 discusses using dummy variables which recode a categorical variable as the numeric value 0 or 1. While you can use Power Pivot to do that, in lieu of using the Section

EG14.6 instructions, Power Pivot's real strength is in recoding numerical variables as categorical values. For instance, for the sample of 407 retirement funds that Chapter 2 introduces, you could recode the numeric variable expense ratio as a categorical variable with the defined values low (less than 1%), moderate (at least 1% but less than 2%), or high (2% or higher). In Figure 17.1, the partial Power Pivot window shows the partial results of using a formula to do this recoding. (In the formula visible in the formula bar, [Expense Ratio] refers to the column that contains the expense ratio.)

While recoding can be done with simple formulas, as Section EG16.7 discusses, recoded variables that Power Pivot creates can be used as PivotTable variables. The Figure 17.1 PivotTable uses the recoded expense ratio variable to reveal that value funds in the sample have proportionally more funds with a low expense ratio and the majority of both growth and value funds have a moderate expense ratio.

FIGURE 17.1
Using Power Pivot to create a PivotTable with a recoded numerical variable

17.4 Descriptive Analytics

Chapters 2 and 3 discuss descriptive methods that organize and visualize previously collected data. What if you could organize and visualize current data as it gets collected? That would change descriptive methods from being summaries of the status of a business at some point in the past into a tool that could be used for day-to-day, if not minute-by-minute, business monitoring. Giving decision makers this ability is one of the goals of descriptive analytics.

Descriptive analytics provide the means to monitor business activities in *near real time*, very quickly after a transaction or other business event has occurred. Being able to do this type of monitoring can be useful for a business that handles perishable inventory. As the First Things First Chapter Using Statistics scenario notes, empty seats on an airplane or in a concert hall or theater cannot be sold after a certain time. Descriptive analytics allows for a continuously updated display of the inventory, informing late-to-buy customers of the current availability of seats as well as visualizing patterns of sold and unsold seats for managers.

Descriptive analytics can help manage sets of interrelated flows of people or objects as those flows occur. For example, managers of large sports complexes use descriptive analytics to monitor the flow of cars in parking facilities, the flow of arriving patrons into the stadium, as well as the flow of patrons inside the stadium. Summaries generated by descriptive methods can highlight trends as they occur, such as points of growing congestion. By being provided with such information in a timely manner, stadium managers can redirect personnel to trouble spots in the complex and redirect patrons to entrances or facilities that are underutilized.

Dashboards

Dashboards are comprehensive summary displays that enable decision makers to monitor a business or business activity. Dashboards present the most important pieces of information, typically in a visual format that allows decision makers to quickly perceive the overall status of an activity. Dashboards present these key indicators in a way that provides drill-down abilities that can reveal progressive levels of detail interactively.

Dashboards can be of any size, from a single desktop computer display, to wall-mounted displays or even larger, such as the nearly 800-square-foot NASDAQ MarketSite Video Wall at Times Square which can be configured as a NASDAQ stock market dashboard that provides current stock market trends for passersby and viewers of financial programming (see reference 3).

While Excel does not create dashboards, various tabular and visual summaries can be placed on one worksheet to simulate a dashboard. Excel workbook files can also be used as the source data for programs that create more polished dashboards. One such program is Microsoft Power BI, a cloud-based (online) application that can import Excel workbooks and create various summaries, many of which look and act like the summaries that the Chapter 2 Excel Guide discusses.

Dashboard Elements

Dashboards can include any of the tabular and visual summaries that Chapter 2 discusses as well as word tiles that state important facts and novel forms of visual summaries. Some novel forms present more information in a small space, such as the sparklines that Section 2.6 discusses, while others such as gauges and treemaps summarize several variables together without creating a cluttered visual summary.

A **gauge** visualizes a numerical variable and an associated categorical variable as an analog dial. Figure 17.2 contains a set of gauges that might be included in a dashboard that displays the status of important attractions at an amusement park. The gauge combines the single numerical measure wait time with a categorical color that represents one of three categories: excellent, less than 20 minutes; acceptable, 20 to 70 minutes; and poor, more than 70 minutes. A **treemap** visualizes two or more variables, one of which is typically a categorical variable that is used to identify groups. In Figure 17.2, the treemap visualizes the number of social media comments (rectangle size) about park attractions as well as the favorability of those comments (rectangle color).

While older Excels cannot construct novel visual summaries, newer versions do either as a chart type or through an Office app that can be obtained by selecting Insert → My Apps in Excel while signed into the Microsoft Office store.

Some consider gauges as examples of chartjunk (see Section 2.7) and suggest bullet graphs as an alternative (see reference 2). Unfortunately, at the time of the publication of this book, bullet graphs could not be easily constructed in Excel.

FIGURE 17.2

Set of gauges and treemap that monitor amusement park attractions

As part of an amusement park dashboard, Figure 17.2 would highlight the problems with the *Inside TV 3D* attraction. Managers could increase the capacity of the ride or take other measures and watch if the negative comments are due more to the wait times than the attraction itself.

Figure 17.3 presents a Microsoft Power BI dashboard that managers at Arlingtons might use to monitor sales trends. The dashboard uses word tiles and clickable tabular summaries to track sales by department and several sales experiments, including the status of VLABGo player sales, the subject of the Chapter 10 Using Statistics scenario, and the mobile electronics sales experiment, the subject of the Chapter 11 Using Statistics scenario.

FIGURE 17.3
Sales dashboard for Arlingtons retail chain

17.5 Predictive Analytics

Predictive analytics are methods that determine what is likely to occur in the future. These methods fall into one of four categories:

- Prediction: Assigning a value to a target based on a model
- Classification: Assigning items in a collection to target categories or classes
- Clustering: Finding natural groupings in data
- Association: Finding items that tend to co-occur and specifying the rules that govern their co-occurrence

Earlier chapters have already discussed some prediction and classification methods including regression and correlation and logistic regression. Like regression model building, building models with predictive analytics requires validation, and that validation is typically done using the cross-validation technique (see page 542).

Table 17.1 summarizes several common predictive analytics methods that are used in business. While these methods are not currently available in Excel, worksheet data can often be used with other programs that perform these methods as the following section illustrates.

TABLE 17.1
Common Predictive Analytics Methods

METHOD	METHOD FOR			
	Prediction	Classification	Clustering	Association
Classification and Regression Trees	•	•		
Cluster Analysis			•	
Multidimensional Scaling		•		•

Classification and Regression Trees

Section 4.2 discusses decision trees, a visual alternative to contingency tables. **Classification and regression trees** are decision trees that split data into groups based on the values of independent (X) variables. This splitting determines which values of a specific independent (X) variable are useful in predicting the dependent (Y) variable. Classification and regression tree methods are not affected by the distribution of the variables that make up the data.

Using a *categorical* dependent Y variable results in a *classification tree*. Using a *numerical* dependent Y variable results in a *regression tree*. Classification and regression tree methods choose the independent variable that provides the best split of the data at each node in the tree, starting with the root. Splitting continues until no further gain in the fit occurs and may be followed by pruning, cutting back the tree by eliminating one or more nodes of the tree.

When using classification and regression tree methods, you perform cross-validation by splitting the original data into a training sample that is used to develop models for analysis and a validation sample that is used to determine the validity of the models developed in the training sample.

To illustrate a classification tree analysis, return to the Section 14.7 card study example on page 505 in which a logistic regression model was used to predict the proportion of credit card holders who would upgrade to a premium card. You can open and use the same worksheet data in JMP, the SAS Institute statistical program, to construct the classification tree shown in Figure 17.4.

In Figure 17.4, the root represents all the data. The Yes rate, 0.4333, reflects the 13 out of 30 cardholders who have upgraded to a premium card. (The No rate, 0.5667, reflects the 17 cardholders who have not upgraded.) The first split of the data is based on whether the cardholder has additional cards. In the Extra Cards(Yes) node that represents those cardholders who have extra cards, the Yes rate, 0.7857, represents the 11 of these 14 have upgraded. In the Extra Cards(No) node that represents those cardholders who do not have extra cards, the Yes rate, 0.125, represents the 2 out of 16 who have upgraded.

FIGURE 17.4
Classification tree results for predicting the proportion of credit card holders who would upgrade to a premium card

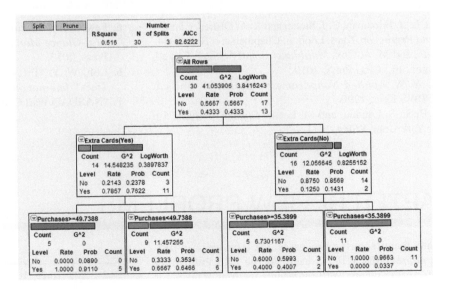

At the next level, the two nodes are split based on the amount of annual purchases. For the Extra Cards (Yes) node, the split is between those who charge more than $49,738.80 per year and those who charge less than $49,738.80 per year. For the Extra Cards(No) node, the split is between those who charge more than $35,389.90 per year and those who charge less than $35,389.90 per year.

These results show that customers who order extra cards are *more* likely to upgrade a premium card and that those customers in this group who charge extensively are *most* likely to upgrade. (Least likely to upgrade to a premium card are customers who have only a single charge card and have charged less than \$35,389.90.) Therefore, managers at the credit card company might want to make a special appeal to customers who charge extensively and have ordered extra cards while creating a broader marketing effort aimed at all those who have ordered extra cards.

The r^2 of 0.516, shown in the summary box below the plot, means that 51.6% of the variation in whether a cardholder upgrades can be explained by the variation in whether the cardholder has additional cards and the amount the cardholder charges per year.[12]

▼ USING **STATISTICS**
The Future to Be Visited

This chapter summarizes the statistical methods that the book discusses in previous chapters as exhibits that list questions that help you determine the appropriate methods with which to analyze your data. As the First Things First Chapter notes, business statistics is an important part of your business education. Your business statistics education cannot end with this page, but must continue to keep you abreast of new developments such as business analytics becoming the changing face of statistics, which the initial chapter also notes. Use Sections 17.3 through 17.5 as a starting point for keeping abreast of those developments. Expect to use Microsoft Excel with other, more specialized statistical and analytics software and to learn more about analytics as you advance through your studies, mount future analyses, and contemplate your business career.

▼ REFERENCES

1. Breiman, L., J. Friedman, C. J. Stone, and R. A. Olshen. *Classification and Regression Trees*. London: Chapman and Hall, 1984.
2. Cox, T. F., and M. A. Cox. *Multidimensional Scaling*, 2nd ed. Boca Raton, FL: CRC Press, 2010.
3. Daniel, W. W. *Applied Nonparametric Statistics*, 2nd ed. Boston: PWS Kent, 1990.
4. Everitt, B. S., S. Landau, and M. Leese. *Cluster Analysis*, 5th ed. New York: John Wiley, 2011.
5. Few, S. *Information Dashboard Design: Displaying Data for At-a-Glance Monitoring*, 2nd ed. Burlingame, CA: Analytics Press, 2013.
6. Loh, W. Y. "Fifty Years of Classification and Regression Trees." *International Statistical Review*, 2013.
7. "NASDAQ Wall Capabilities," bit.ly/1ubnLGQ.

▼ CHAPTER REVIEW PROBLEMS

17.1 In many manufacturing processes, the term *work-in-process* (often abbreviated WIP) is used. At the LSS Publishing book manufacturing plants, WIP represents the time it takes for sheets from a press to be folded, gathered, sewn, tipped on end sheets, and bound together to form a book, and the book placed in a packing carton. The operational definition of the variable of interest, processing time, is the number of days (measured in hundredths) from when the sheets come off the press to when the book is placed in a packing carton. The company has the business objective of determining whether there are differences in the WIP between plants. Data have been collected from samples of 20 books at each of two production plants. The data, stored in WIP, are as follows:

Plant A									
5.62	5.29	16.25	10.92	11.46	21.62	8.45	8.58	5.41	11.42
11.62	7.29	7.50	7.96	4.42	10.50	7.58	9.29	7.54	8.92

Plant B									
9.54	11.46	16.62	12.62	25.75	15.41	14.29	13.13	13.71	10.04
5.75	12.46	9.17	13.21	6.00	2.33	14.25	5.37	6.25	9.71

Completely analyze the data.

17.2 Many factors determine the attendance at Major League Baseball games. These factors can include when the game is played, the weather, the opponent, whether the team is having a good season, and whether a marketing promotion is held. Popular promotions during a recent season included the traditional hat days and poster days and the newer craze, bobble-heads of star players. (Data extracted from T. C. Boyd and T. C. Krehbiel, "An Analysis of the Effects of Specific Promotion Types on Attendance at Major League Baseball Games," *Mid-American Journal of Business*, 2006, 21, pp. 21–32.) The file BaseballTeams includes the following variables during a Major League Baseball season:

> TEAM—Kansas City Royals, Philadelphia Phillies, Chicago Cubs, or Cincinnati Reds
> ATTENDANCE—Paid attendance for the game
> TEMP—High temperature for the day
> WIN%—Team's winning percentage at the time of the game
> OPWIN%—Opponent team's winning percentage at the time of the game
> WEEKEND—1 if game played on Friday, Saturday, or Sunday; 0 otherwise
> PROMOTION—1 if a promotion was held; 0 if no promotion was held

You want to predict attendance and determine the factors that influence attendance. Completely analyze the data for the Kansas City Royals.

17.3 Repeat Problem 17.2 for the Philadelphia Phillies.

17.4 Repeat Problem 17.2 for the Chicago Cubs.

17.5 Repeat Problem 17.2 for the Cincinnati Reds.

17.6 The file EuroTourism2 contains a sample of 27 European countries. Variables included are the number of jobs generated in the travel and tourism industry in 2014, the spending on business travel within the country by residents and international visitors in 2014, the total number of international visitors who visited the country in 2014, and the number of establishments that provide overnight accommodation for tourists. (Data extracted from **www.marketline.com**.) You want to be able to predict the number of jobs generated in the travel and tourism industry. Completely analyze the data.

17.7 The file Philly contains a sample of 25 neighborhoods in Philadelphia. Variables included are neighborhood population, median sales price of homes in 2014, mean number of days homes were on the market in 2014, number of homes sold in 2014, median neighborhood household income, percentage of residents in the neighborhood with a bachelor's degree or higher, and whether the neighborhood is considered "hot" (coded as 1 = yes, 0 = no). (Data extracted from **bit.ly/13M7KuP**.) You want to be able to predict median sales price of homes. Completely analyze the data.

17.8 Professional basketball has truly become a sport that generates interest among fans around the world. More and more players come from outside the United States to play in the National Basketball Association (NBA). Many factors could impact the number of wins achieved by each NBA team. In addition to the number of wins, the file NBA contains team statistics for points per game (for team, opponent, and the dif-

ference between team and opponent), field goal (shots made) percentage (for team and opponent), turnovers (losing the ball before a shot is taken) per game, and rebounds per game. You want to be able to predict the number of wins. Completely analyze the data.

17.9 The data in UsedCars represent characteristics of cars that are currently part of an inventory of a used car dealership. The variables included are car, year, age, price ($), mileage, power (hp), and fuel (mpg).

You want to describe each of these variables, and you would like to predict the price of the used cars. Analyze the data.

17.10 A study was conducted to determine whether any gender bias existed in an academic science environment. Faculty from several universities were asked to rate candidates for the position of undergraduate laboratory manager based on their application. The gender of the applicant was given in the applicant's materials. The raters were from either biology, chemistry, or physics departments. Each rater was to give a competence rating to the applicant's materials on a seven point scale with 1 being the lowest and 7 being the highest. In addition, the rater supplied a starting salary that should be offered to the applicant. These data (which have been altered from an actual study to preserve the anonymity of the respondents) are stored in Candidate Assessment.

Analyze the data. Do you think that there is any gender bias in the evaluations? Support your point of view with specific references to your data analysis.

17.11 Zagat's publishes restaurant ratings for various locations in the United States. The file Restaurants2 contains the Zagat rating for food, décor, service, cost per person, and popularity index (popularity points the restaurant received divided by the number of people who voted for that restaurant) for various types of restaurants in New York City.

You want to study differences in the cost of a meal for the different types of cuisines and also want to be able to predict the cost of a meal. Completely analyze the data. (Data extracted from *Zagat Survey 2012 New York City Restaurants*).

17.12 The data in the file BankMarketing are from a direct marketing campaign conducted by a Portuguese banking institution (Data extracted from S. Moro, R. Laureano and P. Cortez, "Using Data Mining for Bank Direct Marketing: An Application of the CRISP-DM Methodology," in P. Novais et al. (Eds.), *Proceedings of the European Simulation and Modeling Conference—ESM'2011*, pp. 117–121.) The variables included were age, type of job, marital status, education, whether credit is in default, average yearly balance in account in Euros, whether there is a housing loan, whether there is a personal loan, last contact duration in seconds, number of contacts performed during this campaign, and has the client purchased a term deposit.

Analyze the data and assess the likelihood that the client will purchase a term deposit.

17.13 A mining company operates a large heap-leach gold mine in the western United States. The gold mined at this location consists of ore that is very low grade, having about 0.0032 ounce of gold in 1 ton of ore. The process of heap-leaching involves the mining, crushing, stacking, and leaching millions of tons of gold ore per year. In the process, ore is placed in a large heap on an impermeable pad. A weak chemical solution is sprinkled over the heap and is collected at the bottom after percolating through the ore. As the solution percolates through the ore, the gold is dissolved and is later recovered from the solution. This technology, which has been used for more than 30 years, has made the operation profitable. Due to the large amount of ore that is handled, the company is continually exploring ways to improve the process. As part of an expansion several years ago, the stacking process was automated with the construction of a computer controlled stacker. This stacker was designed to load 35,000 tons of ore per day at a cost that was less than the previous process that used manually operated trucks and bulldozers. However, since its installation, the stacker has not been able to achieve these results consistently. Data for a recent 35-day period that indicate the amount stacked (tons) and the downtime (minutes) are stored in the file Mining . Other data that indicate the causes for the downtime are stored in Mining2 .

Analyze the data, making sure to present conclusions about the daily amount stacked and the causes of the downtime. In addition, be sure to develop a model to predict the amount stacked based on downtime.

17.14 A survey was conducted on the characteristics of households in the United States. The data (which have been altered from an actual study to preserve the anonymity of the respondents) are stored in Households . The variables are gender, age, Hispanic origin, type of dwelling, age of dwelling in years, years living at dwelling, number of bedrooms, number of vehicles kept at dwelling, fuel type at dwelling, monthly cost of fuel at dwelling ($), U.S. citizenship, college degree, marital status, work for pay in previous week, mode of transportation to work, commuting time in minutes, hours worked per week, type of organization, annual earned income ($), and total annual income ($).

Analyze these data and prepare a report describing your conclusions.

17.15 The file HybridSales contains the number of domestic and imported hybrid vehicles sold in the United States from 1999 to 2014. (Data extracted from **bit.ly/17hJk9H**.) You want to be able to predict the number of domestic and imported hybrid vehicles sold in the United States in 2015 and 2016. Completely analyze the data.

▾EXCEL GUIDE

There are no Excel instructions for Sections 17.1, 17.2, and 17.3.

EG 17.3 INTRODUCTION TO BUSINESS ANALYTICS

Power Pivot

Key Technique Convert worksheet data into an Excel table and then use the Power Pivot feature.

Example Create the PivotTable of type and recoded expense ratio for the sample of 407 retirement funds.

Workbook For the example, open to the **DATA worksheet** of the **Retirement Funds workbook** and:

1. Select **Insert → Table**.

In the Create Table dialog box:

2. Enter **A1:N408** as the answer to **Where is the data for your table?**
3. Check **My table has headers** and click **OK**.

The worksheet format changes and pull-down lists for each variable appear as part of row 1 entries.

4. Select **Power Pivot** (**PowerPivot**) **→ Add to Data Model**.

In the Power Pivot for Excel window:

5. Select **Design → Insert Function**.
6. In the Insert Function dialog box, select **Logical** from the **Select a category** pull-down list, then select **IF** from the **Select a function** list and click **OK**.
7. Complete the function as **=IF([Expense Ratio] < 1, "Low", IF([Expense Ratio] < 2, "Moderate", "High"))**.

Click the Expense Ratio column heading to enter the characters **[Expense Ratio]**; you must use Insert Function to enter this formula. Power Pivot inserts a new calculated column.

8. Double-click the new column heading and enter **Recoded Expense Ratio** (as the name for the new column).
9. Select **Home → PivotTable → PivotTable**.
10. In the Create PivotTable dialog box, click **New Work-sheet** and click **OK**.

Power Pivot inserts a new worksheet with an empty PivotTable. In the PivotTable Fields (PivotTable Field List in older versions) display:

11. Drag **Type** in the **Choose fields to add to report** box and drop it in the **Rows** (or **Row Labels**) box.
12. Drag **Recoded Expense Ratio** in the **Choose fields to add to report** box and drop it in the **Columns** (or **Column Labels**) box.
13. Drag **Type** in the **Choose fields to add to report** box a second time and drop it in the **∑ Values** box. The dropped label changes to Count of Type.
14. In the PivotTable, click cell A3 and enter a space character to replace the label Count of Type.

Optionally, you can adapt Section EG2.1 *Workbook* instructions to make further changes to the PivotTable formatting and presentation.

EG 17.4 DESCRIPTIVE ANALYTICS

Gauge

Key Technique Use the Gauge Add-in (App) that requires being signed in to the Microsoft Office Store (see Appendix G).

Example Construct the Figure 17.2 set of four gauges

Workbook For the example, open to the **DATA worksheet** of the **Attractions workbook** and:

1. Select **Insert → My Add-ins** (or **My Apps**) and dou-ble-click **Gauge** from the gallery of add-ins (apps).
2. In the RE:VISION Gauge panel, click **Insert Gauges**.
3. In the Select Data dialog box, enter **C2:C5** and click **OK**.
4. Drag and resize the panel of four gauges until they can be easily read.

By default, gauges constructed by the Gauge App have a minimum value of 0 and a maximum of 100 and include three gauge zones: green, yellow, and red. To adjust the zones, click the **circular gear icon** at the top of panel. In the Settings panel:

5. Enter **20** as the Green Range **Max Value.**
6. Enter **20** as the Yellow Range **Min Value.**
7. Enter **70** as the Yellow Range **Max Value.**
8. Enter **70** as the Red Range **Min Value.**

Click the back (left-facing) arrow icon to return to the gauge display.

Gauges can also be simulated in any Excel version by overlaying a pie chart on a doughnut chart. In the pie chart, all slices of the pie chart are set to invisible except for the slice that represents the needle, and the background of the pie chart is also set to be invisible. In the doughnut chart, the lower half of the donut is made invisible to form an 180-degree arc that serves as the legend for the zones of the gauge.

A bullet graph, not discussed in this chapter but preferred by some as an alternate to gauges (see reference 5), can be simulated by overlaying a bar chart that has a transparent background with a bar graph that displays the colored zones (analogous to the colored zones on a gauge dial).

Treemap

Key Technique Use the Treemap chart (Excel 2016 for Windows) or the Excel 2013 Treemap App that requires being signed in to the Microsoft Office Store (see Appendix G).

Example Construct the Figure 17.2 treemap.

Workbook For the example, open to the **DATA worksheet** of the **Attractions workbook** and, if using Excel 2016 for Microsoft Windows:

1. Select cell range **A1:B9, D1:D9**.
2. **Insert → Hierarchy Chart → Treemap**.
3. Click **Chart Title** and enter a title.

The treemap that Excel 2016 constructs more accurately represents the relative number of social media comments for each ride than the Figure 17.2 (Excel 2013) treemap. However, this treemap (shown below) uses color to identify the town category and does not visualize a second numerical variable.

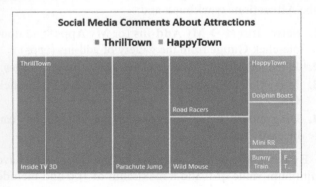

If using Excel 2013:

1. Select **Insert → My Apps** and double-click **Treemap** from the gallery of apps.

In the Treemap panel:

2. Click **Names Data** and, in the Select Data dialog box, enter **A2:B9** and click **OK**.
3. Click **Size Data** and, in the Select Data dialog box, enter **D2:D9** and click **OK**.
4. Click **Color Data** and, in the Select Data dialog box, enter **E2:E9** and click **OK**.

If the treemap displayed does not use the red-to-blue spectrum, click the **spectrum icon** (under Title) and click the red-to-blue (third) spectrum.

The Figure 17.2 treemap that Excel 2013 constructs inaccurately represents the relative number of social media comments. However, the treemap uses color to visualize a second numerical variable, rating, although the scale that the version of this app constructs inverts the scale (this error was corrected manually for Figure 17.2).

Appendices

Basic Math Concepts and Symbols

A.1 Rules for Arithmetic Operations

Rule	Example
1. $a + b = c$ and $b + a = c$	$2 + 1 = 3$ and $1 + 2 = 3$
2. $a + (b + c) = (a + b) + c$	$5 + (7 + 4) = (5 + 7) + 4 = 16$
3. $a - b = c$ but $b - a \neq c$	$9 - 7 = 2$ but $7 - 9 \neq 2$
4. $(a)(b) = (b)(a)$	$(7)(6) = (6)(7) = 42$
5. $(a)(b + c) = ab + ac$	$(2)(3 + 5) = (2)(3) + (2)(5) = 16$
6. $a \div b \neq b \div a$	$12 \div 3 \neq 3 \div 12$
7. $\dfrac{a + b}{c} = \dfrac{a}{c} + \dfrac{b}{c}$	$\dfrac{7 + 3}{2} = \dfrac{7}{2} + \dfrac{3}{2} = 5$
8. $\dfrac{a}{b + c} \neq \dfrac{a}{b} + \dfrac{a}{c}$	$\dfrac{3}{4 + 5} \neq \dfrac{3}{4} + \dfrac{3}{5}$
9. $\dfrac{1}{a} + \dfrac{1}{b} = \dfrac{b + a}{ab}$	$\dfrac{1}{3} + \dfrac{1}{5} = \dfrac{5 + 3}{(3)(5)} = \dfrac{8}{15}$
10. $\left(\dfrac{a}{b}\right)\left(\dfrac{c}{d}\right) = \left(\dfrac{ac}{bd}\right)$	$\left(\dfrac{2}{3}\right)\left(\dfrac{6}{7}\right) = \left(\dfrac{(2)(6)}{(3)(7)}\right) = \dfrac{12}{21}$
11. $\dfrac{a}{b} \div \dfrac{c}{d} = \dfrac{ad}{bc}$	$\dfrac{5}{8} \div \dfrac{3}{7} = \left(\dfrac{(5)(7)}{(8)(3)}\right) = \dfrac{35}{24}$

A.2 Rules for Algebra: Exponents and Square Roots

Rule	Example
1. $(X^a)(X^b) = X^{a+b}$	$(4^2)(4^3) = 4^5$
2. $(X^a)^b = X^{ab}$	$(2^2)^3 = 2^6$
3. $(X^a/X^b) = X^{a-b}$	$\dfrac{3^5}{3^3} = 3^2$
4. $\dfrac{X^a}{X^a} = X^0 = 1$	$\dfrac{3^4}{3^4} = 3^0 = 1$
5. $\sqrt{XY} = \sqrt{X}\sqrt{Y}$	$\sqrt{(25)(4)} = \sqrt{25}\sqrt{4} = 10$
6. $\sqrt{\dfrac{X}{Y}} = \dfrac{\sqrt{X}}{\sqrt{Y}}$	$\sqrt{\dfrac{16}{100}} = \dfrac{\sqrt{16}}{\sqrt{100}} = 0.40$

A.3 Rules for Logarithms

Base 10

Log is the symbol used for base-10 logarithms:

Rule	Example
1. $\log(10^a) = a$	$\log(100) = \log(10^2) = 2$
2. If $\log(a) = b$, then $a = 10^b$	If $\log(a) = 2$, then $a = 10^2 = 100$
3. $\log(ab) = \log(a) + \log(b)$	$\log(100) = \log[(10)(10)] = \log(10) + \log(10)$ $= 1 + 1 = 2$
4. $\log(a^b) = (b)\log(a)$	$\log(1{,}000) = \log(10^3) = (3)\log(10) = (3)(1) = 3$
5. $\log(a/b) = \log(a) - \log(b)$	$\log(100) = \log(1{,}000/10) = \log(1{,}000) - \log(10)$ $= 3 - 1 = 2$

EXAMPLE

Take the base-10 logarithm of each side of the following equation:

$$Y = \beta_0 \beta_1^X \varepsilon$$

SOLUTION Apply rules 3 and 4:

$$\log(Y) = \log(\beta_0 \beta_1^X \varepsilon)$$
$$= \log(\beta_0) + \log(\beta_1^X) + \log(\varepsilon)$$
$$= \log(\beta_0) + X\log(\beta_1) + \log(\varepsilon)$$

Base e

ln is the symbol used for base e logarithms, commonly referred to as natural logarithms. e is Euler's number, and $e \cong 2.718282$:

Rule	Example
1. $\ln(e^a) = a$	$\ln(7.389056) = \ln(e^2) = 2$
2. If $\ln(a) = b$, then $a = e^b$	If $\ln(a) = 2$, then $a = e^2 = 7.389056$
3. $\ln(ab) = \ln(a) + \ln(b)$	$\ln(100) = \ln[(10)(10)]$ $= \ln(10) + \ln(10) = 2.302585 + 2.302585 = 4.605170$
4. $\ln(a^b) = (b)\ln(a)$	$\ln(1{,}000) = \ln(10^3) = 3\ln(10) = 3(2.302585) = 6.907755$
5. $\ln(a/b) = \ln(a) - \ln(b)$	$\ln(100) = \ln(1{,}000/10) = \ln(1{,}000) - \ln(10)$ $= 6.907755 - 2.302585 = 4.605170$

616   APPENDICES

> **EXAMPLE**
>
> Take the base e logarithm of each side of the following equation:
>
> $$Y = \beta_0 \beta_1^X \varepsilon$$
>
> **SOLUTION** Apply rules 3 and 4:
>
> $$\begin{aligned}
> \ln(Y) &= \ln(\beta_0 \beta_1^X \varepsilon) \\
> &= \ln(\beta_0) + \ln(\beta_1^X) + \ln(\varepsilon) \\
> &= \ln(\beta_0) + X \ln(\beta_1) + \ln(\varepsilon)
> \end{aligned}$$

A.4 Summation Notation

The symbol Σ, the Greek capital letter sigma, represents "taking the sum of." Consider a set of n values for variable X. The expression $\sum_{i=1}^{n} X_i$ means to take the sum of the n values for variable X. Thus:

$$\sum_{i=1}^{n} X_i = X_1 + X_2 + X_3 + \cdots + X_n$$

The following problem illustrates the use of the symbol Σ. Consider five values of a variable X: $X_1 = 2, X_2 = 0, X_3 = -1, X_4 = 5$, and $X_5 = 7$. Thus:

$$\sum_{i=1}^{5} X_i = X_1 + X_2 + X_3 + X_4 + X_5 = 2 + 0 + (-1) + 5 + 7 = 13$$

In statistics, the squared values of a variable are often summed. Thus:

$$\sum_{i=1}^{n} X_i^2 = X_1^2 + X_2^2 + X_3^2 + \cdots + X_n^2$$

and, in the example above:

$$\sum_{i=1}^{5} X_i^2 = X_1^2 + X_2^2 + X_3^2 + X_4^2 + X_5^2$$

$$= 2^2 + 0^2 + (-1)^2 + 5^2 + 7^2$$
$$= 4 + 0 + 1 + 25 + 49$$
$$= 79$$

$\sum_{i=1}^{n} X_i^2$, the summation of the squares, is *not* the same as $\left(\sum_{i=1}^{n} X_i \right)^2$, the square of the sum:

$$\sum_{i=1}^{n} X_i^2 \neq \left(\sum_{i=1}^{n} X_i \right)^2$$

In the example given above, the summation of squares is equal to 79. This is not equal to the square of the sum, which is $13^2 = 169$.

Another frequently used operation involves the summation of the product. Consider two variables, X and Y, each having n values. Then:

$$\sum_{i=1}^{n} X_i Y_i = X_1 Y_1 + X_2 Y_2 + X_3 Y_3 + \cdots + X_n Y_n$$

Continuing with the previous example, suppose there is a second variable, Y, whose five values are $Y_1 = 1$, $Y_2 = 3$, $Y_3 = -2$, $Y_4 = 4$, and $Y_5 = 3$. Then,

$$\sum_{i=1}^{n} X_i Y_i = X_1 Y_1 + X_2 Y_2 + X_3 Y_3 + X_4 Y_4 + X_5 Y_5$$

$$= (2)(1) + (0)(3) + (-1)(-2) + (5)(4) + (7)(3)$$
$$= 2 + 0 + 2 + 20 + 21$$
$$= 45$$

In computing $\sum_{i=1}^{n} X_i Y_i$, you need to realize that the first value of X is multiplied by the first value of Y, the second value of X is multiplied by the second value of Y, and so on. These products are then summed in order to compute the desired result. However, the summation of products is *not* equal to the product of the individual sums:

$$\sum_{i=1}^{n} X_i Y_i \neq \left(\sum_{i=1}^{n} X_i \right) \left(\sum_{i=1}^{n} Y_i \right)$$

In this example,

$$\sum_{i=1}^{5} X_i = 13$$

and

$$\sum_{i=1}^{5} Y_i = 1 + 3 + (-2) + 4 + 3 = 9$$

so that

$$\left(\sum_{i=1}^{5} X_i \right) \left(\sum_{i=1}^{5} Y_i \right) = (13)(9) = 117$$

However,

$$\sum_{i=1}^{5} X_i Y_i = 45$$

The following table summarizes these results:

Value	X_i	Y_i	$X_i Y_i$
1	2	1	2
2	0	3	0
3	−1	−2	2
4	5	4	20
5	7	3	21
	$\sum_{i=1}^{5} X_i = 13$	$\sum_{i=1}^{5} Y_i = 9$	$\sum_{i=1}^{5} X_i Y_i = 45$

Rule 1 The summation of the values of two variables is equal to the sum of the values of each summed variable:

$$\sum_{i=1}^{n} (X_i + Y_i) = \sum_{i=1}^{n} X_i + \sum_{i=1}^{n} Y_i$$

Thus,

$$\sum_{i=1}^{5}(X_i + Y_i) = (2+1) + (0+3) + (-1+(-2)) + (5+4) + (7+3)$$

$$= 3 + 3 + (-3) + 9 + 10$$
$$= 22$$

$$\sum_{i=1}^{5}X_i + \sum_{i=1}^{5}Y_i = 13 + 9 = 22$$

Rule 2 The summation of a difference between the values of two variables is equal to the difference between the summed values of the variables:

$$\sum_{i=1}^{n}(X_i - Y_i) = \sum_{i=1}^{n}X_i - \sum_{i=1}^{n}Y_i$$

Thus,

$$\sum_{i=1}^{5}(X_i - Y_i) = (2-1) + (0-3) + (-1-(-2)) + (5-4) + (7-3)$$

$$= 1 + (-3) + 1 + 1 + 4$$
$$= 4$$

$$\sum_{i=1}^{5}X_i - \sum_{i=1}^{5}Y_i = 13 - 9 = 4$$

Rule 3 The sum of a constant times a variable is equal to that constant times the sum of the values of the variable:

$$\sum_{i=1}^{n}cX_i = c\sum_{i=1}^{n}X_i$$

where c is a constant. Thus, if $c = 2$,

$$\sum_{i=1}^{5}cX_i = \sum_{i=1}^{5}2X_i = (2)(2) + (2)(0) + (2)(-1) + (2)(5) + (2)(7)$$

$$= 4 + 0 + (-2) + 10 + 14$$
$$= 26$$

$$c\sum_{i=1}^{5}X_i = 2\sum_{i=1}^{5}X_i = (2)(13) = 26$$

Rule 4 A constant summed n times will be equal to n times the value of the constant.

$$\sum_{i=1}^{n}c = nc$$

where c is a constant. Thus, if the constant $c = 2$ is summed 5 times,

$$\sum_{i=1}^{5}c = 2 + 2 + 2 + 2 + 2 = 10$$

$$nc = (5)(2) = 10$$

EXAMPLE

Suppose there are six values for the variables X and Y, such that $X_1 = 2, X_2 = 1, X_3 = 5, X_4 = -3, X_5 = 1, X_6 = -2$ and $Y_1 = 4, Y_2 = 0, Y_3 = -1, Y_4 = 2, Y_5 = 7$, and $Y_6 = -3$. Compute each of the following:

(a) $\sum_{i=1}^{6}X_i$ 　　　　　　　**(b)** $\sum_{i=1}^{6}Y_i$

(c) $\displaystyle\sum_{i=1}^{6} X_i^2$

(d) $\displaystyle\sum_{i=1}^{6} Y_i^2$

(e) $\displaystyle\sum_{i=1}^{6} X_i Y_i$

(f) $\displaystyle\sum_{i=1}^{6} (X_i + Y_i)$

(g) $\displaystyle\sum_{i=1}^{6} (X_i - Y_i)$

(h) $\displaystyle\sum_{i=1}^{6} (X_i - 3Y_i + 2X_i^2)$

(i) $\displaystyle\sum_{i=1}^{6} (cX_i)$, where $c = -1$

(j) $\displaystyle\sum_{i=1}^{6} (X_i - 3Y_i + c)$, where $c = +3$

Answers
(a) 4 **(b)** 9 **(c)** 44 **(d)** 79 **(e)** 10 **(f)** (13) **(g)** -5 **(h)** 65 **(i)** -4 **(j)** -5

References

1. Bashaw, W. L., *Mathematics for Statistics* (New York: Wiley, 1969).
2. Lanzer, P., *Basic Math: Fractions, Decimals, Percents* (Hicksville, NY: Video Aided Instruction, 2006).
3. Levine, D. and A. Brandwein, *The MBA Primer: Business Statistics*, 3rd ed. (Cincinnati, OH: Cengage Publishing, 2011).
4. Levine, D., *Statistics* (Hicksville, NY: Video Aided Instruction, 2006).
5. Shane, H., *Algebra 1* (Hicksville, NY: Video Aided Instruction, 2006).

A.5 Statistical Symbols

$+$	add	$\times$	multiply
$-$	subtract	$\div$	divide
$=$	equal to	$\neq$	not equal to
$\cong$	approximately equal to	$<$	less than
$>$	greater than	$\leq$	less than or equal to
$\geq$	greater than or equal to		

A.6 Greek Alphabet

Greek Letter		Letter Name	English Equivalent	Greek Letter		Letter Name	English Equivalent
A	α	Alpha	a	N	ν	Nu	n
B	β	Beta	b	Ξ	ξ	Xi	x
Γ	γ	Gamma	g	O	o	Omicron	ŏ
Δ	δ	Delta	d	Π	π	Pi	p
E	ε	Epsilon	ĕ	P	ρ	Rho	r
Z	ζ	Zeta	z	Σ	σ	Sigma	s
H	η	Eta	ē	T	τ	Tau	t
Θ	θ	Theta	th	Y	υ	Upsilon	u
I	ι	Iota	i	Φ	ϕ	Phi	ph
K	κ	Kappa	k	X	χ	Chi	ch
Λ	λ	Lambda	l	Ψ	ψ	Psi	ps
M	μ	Mu	m	Ω	ω	Omega	ō

Important Excel Skills and Concepts

B.1 Which Excel Do You Use?

While marketed as one product, Microsoft Excel versions vary and some versions do not include every Excel feature that this book discusses. The subscription-based Office 365 services add another level of confusion, and two Office 365 subscribers using the same type of computer may be using two different Excel versions.

Instructions in this book work best with Microsoft Windows Excel 2013 and 2016, and OS X Excel 2016, also known as Excel for Mac 2016. When slight variations occur, they are listed in parentheses or explanatory sentences that identify those variations. For example, a number of charting instructions begin **Design** (or **Chart Design**) ➔ **Add Chart Element** because the Design tab is called Chart Design in OS X Excel 2016. OS X Excel 2016 also does not contain several features that Chapters 2 and 17 discuss (and the book notes this when you encounter such a feature). If you plan to use OS X Excel 2016, note that this version is most like Excel 2013, not Microsoft Windows Excel 2016!

Some instructions make reference to "older Excels" and, if not otherwise specified, this means Microsoft Windows Excel 2007 and 2010 and OS X Excel 2011. These versions present chart formatting and other options in dialog boxes and not worksheet panes that newer versions use. OS X Excel 2011 also differs greatly in the way you produce many of the tabular and visual summaries that Chapter 2 discusses and, in Excel 2007, you select the **Office Button** in lieu of selecting **File**. Excel 2007 does not contain the technical improvements that later Excels contain and uses a different set of worksheet statistical functions (see Appendix D).

If you plan to use this book with Excel 2007, consider upgrading to a newer version. However, if you must use Excel 2007, make sure to read the Appendix D notes and always remember to substitute **Office Button** for **File** in any selection sequence that starts with **File**.

If you plan to use Excel 2011, also consider upgrading, but if you must use this version *and* plan to use the *Worksheet* Excel Guide instructions, download the **OS X Excel Supplement** that presents alternate instructions for many Chapter 2 Excel Guide features as well as for the selection sequences that Sections B.9 through B.10 discuss. (See Appendix C for more information about downloading online materials for this book.)

Office 365

Office 365 is the subscription-based service for Microsoft Office, including Excel. If you are an Office 365 subscriber, the version of Excel that you are using is hard to predict. If you have subscribed to Office 365 for a long time and never chose to upgrade your Office installation, you may be using an older Excel version and not one of the most current version which, at the time of publication of this book, was Excel 2016 for both Microsoft Windows and OS X Excels.

To use some of the advanced features of Excel, such as Power Pivot that Chapter 17 discusses, you may have to upgrade your Office installation or, in some cases, switch the Office 365 *plan* to which you are subscribed. (If you have a business or academic Office 365 plan, your Excel version will likely contain all of the advanced features that this book discusses.)

Which Build Number Do You Have?

The copy of the Excel version you use contains a *build number* that further identifies that copy version. Knowing the build number of the copy of Excel that you use can help determine if you have the latest updates applied to your copy of Excel as well as prove useful if you ever seek technical support. Use the following instructions to determine the exact build number for the Excel you use. (The build number is also known informally as the exact version number.)

In Excel 2016 or 2013, select **File** ➔ **Account** and, in the Account pane that appears, click the **About Excel icon**. In the dialog box that appears, note the build number that follows the words Microsoft Excel 2016 (or 2013). The Account pane may contain an **Update Options** pull-down list from which you can select **Update Now** to have Excel check for updates. If your Excel does not display the Update Options icon, use Windows Update to update Excel.

In Excel 2010, select **File** ➔ **Help** and, in the information pane, note the build number that appears under the heading "About Microsoft Excel." Click **Check for Updates** in that pane to have Excel check for updates.

In Excel 2007, click the **Office Button** and then click **Excel Options**. In the Excel options dialog box, click **Resources** in the left pane and, in the right panel, note the build number that appears under the "about Microsoft Office Excel 2007" heading. Click **Check for Updates** in the same pane to have Excel check for updates.

If you use OS X Excel, select **Excel ➔ About Excel** and in the dialog box that appears, note the build number. For both OS Excel 2011 and 2016, you check for updates by selecting **Help ➔ Check for Updates**.

B.2 Basic Operations

Open or Save a Workbook

Use **File ➔ Open** or **File ➔ Save As**.

As Section FTF.4 explains, "Excel files" are not single worksheets but workbooks that have one or more worksheets and chart sheets. **Open** and **Save As** use similar means to allow you to open or save the workbook by name while specifying the physical device or network location and folder for that workbook. Save As dialog boxes allow you to save your file in alternate formats for programs that cannot open Excel workbooks (**.xlsx** files) directly. Formats you might use include a simple text file with values delimited with tab characters, **Text (Tab delimited) (*.txt)** that saves the contents of the current worksheet as a simple text file, **CSV (Comma delimited) (*.csv)** that saves worksheet cell values as text values that are delimited with commas, or **Excel 97–2003 Workbook (.xls)** that saves the workbook in the Excel format formerly used. OS X Excels list these three choices as **Tab Delimited Text (.txt)**, **Windows Comma Separated (.csv)**, and **Excel 97–2004 Workbook (.xls)**, respectively.

Shown below is part of the Excel 2013 Save As dialog box. In all versions except OS X Excel 2016, you can also select a file format in the Open dialog box. If you cannot find a file, select **All Files (*.*)** (or **All Files** in OS X Excel 2011) to see if the file had previously been saved in an unexpected format.

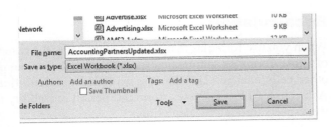

To open a new workbook, select **File ➔ New** (**New Workbook** in OS X Excel). Excel displays a new workbook with one or more blank worksheets.

Working with a Workbook

Use **Insert** (or **Insert Sheet**), **Delete**, or **Move or Copy**.
You can alter the contents of a workbook by adding a worksheet or by deleting, copying, or rearranging the worksheets and chart sheets that the workbook contains.

To perform one of these operations, right-click a sheet tab and select the appropriate choice from the shortcut menu that appears.

To add a worksheet, select **Insert**. In Microsoft Windows Excel, you also click **Worksheet** and then click **OK** in the Insert dialog box. To delete a worksheet or chart sheet, right-click the sheet tab of the worksheet to be deleted and select **Delete**. To copy or rearrange the position of a worksheet or chart sheet, right-click the sheet tab of the sheet and select **Move or Copy**. In the Move or Copy dialog box, first select the workbook and the position in the workbook for the sheet. If copying a sheet, also check **Create a copy**. Then click **OK**.

Print a Worksheet

Use **File ➔ Print**.
In Excel, you print worksheets and chart sheets, not workbooks. When you select **Print**, Excel displays a preview of the currently opened sheet in a dialog box or pane that allows you to select that sheet or other sheets from the workbook. You can adjust the print formatting of the worksheet(s) to be printed by clicking **Page Setup**. Typically, in the Page Setup dialog box, you might click the **Sheet** tab and then check or clear the **Gridlines** and **Row and column headings** checkboxes to add or remove worksheet cell gridlines and the numbered row and lettered column headings that are similar to how a worksheet is displayed onscreen.

B.3 Formulas and Cell References

An Excel **formula** is a worksheet cell entry that processes data. Formulas can compute intermediate calculations, generate a statistic, retrieve data from specific cells, or make a decision based on a logical comparison, among other things. Excel typically displays the results of a formula as the contents of the cell that contains the formula. That means that when you see the value, say 5, that a particular worksheet cell displays, you cannot determine immediately if the cell contains the numerical value 5 or a formula that results in that value. This trait of worksheets means you should always carefully review the contents of each worksheet you use. To perform this review, you can press **Crtl+`** (grave accent) to reveal all the formulas that a worksheet contains. After inspecting the formulas in a worksheet, press **Ctrl+`** a second time to restore the normal display.

To facilitate your learning, the worksheet templates and models that Excel Guide workbooks contain always have an associated "formulas" worksheet in which all formulas have already been revealed for you. You can also see formulas next to many of worksheets used in chapter figures.

Cell References

Every cell in a worksheet has its own **cell reference**, an address that identifies a cell based on the lettered column and numbered row of the cell. For example, the cell A1 is the cell in the first column and first row, A3 is the cell in in the first column and third row, and C1 is the cell in the third column and first row.

Cell references can be a **cell range** that refers to a rectangular group of cells, such as all the cells in a column that store the data for a variable. A cell range names the upper-left cell and the lower-right cell of the group, using the form *UpperLeftCell:LowerRightCell*. For example, the cell range C1:C12 refers to the first 12 cells in column C while the cell range A1:D3 refers to all the cells in columns A through D in rows 1 through 3. Cell ranges can also just name one or more columns or rows such as A:A, all the cells in column A and 4:6, all the cells in rows 4 through 6.

In workbooks that contain more than one worksheet, you append the worksheet name in the form *WorksheetName!* as a prefix to a cell reference to uniquely identify a cell or cell range. For example, the cell reference COMPUTE!B8 uniquely identifies cell B8 of the COMPUTE worksheet, and the cell reference DATA!A:A uniquely identifies all the cells in column A of the DATA worksheet. If the name of a worksheet contains spaces or special characters, such as CITY DATA_1.2, you must enclose the worksheet name in a pair of single quotes as part of the prefix, such as 'CITY DATA_1.2'!A2.

Most formulas you use contain cell references. When you enter into a formula a cell reference that does not contain a worksheet prefix, Excel assumes that the cells being referenced are in the same worksheet as the formula being entered. This book uses the helpful data entry shortcut in many Excel Guide instructions and worksheet explanations. Occasionally, an Excel feature requires that you use a worksheet prefix and instructions note these exceptions as you encounter them.

Although this book does not use them, cell references can include a workbook prefix in the form *[WorkbookName]WorksheetName!* If either the workbook or worksheet name contains spaces or special characters, you must enclose both names in a pair of single quotes. If you discover workbook prefixes in the formulas you create using the instructions in this book, you may have committed an inadvertent error when transferring data from one workbook to another. Review your work and make sure you intended to include a workbook name prefix in your formula. If you have unwanted workbook name prefixes, you may be able to eliminate them by the use of **Paste Special** that the next section explains.

Absolute and Relative Cell References

To avoid the drudgery of typing many similar formulas, you can copy a formula and paste it into all the cells in a selected cell range. For example, to copy a formula that has been entered in cell C2 down the column through row 12:

1. Right-click cell C2 and press **Ctrl+C** to copy the formula. A movie marquee–like highlight appears around cell C2.
2. Select the cell range **C3:C12**.
3. With the cell range highlighted, press **Ctrl+V** to paste the formula into the cells of the cell range.

When you perform this copy-and-paste operation, Excel adjusts these **relative cell references** in formulas so that copying the formula **=A2 + B2** from cell C2 to cell C3 results in the formula **=A3 + B3** being pasted into cell C3, the formula **=A4 + B4** being pasted into cell C4, and so on.

There are circumstances in which you do not want Excel to adjust all or part of a formula. For example, if you were copying the cell C2 formula **=(A2 + B2)/B15**, and cell B15 contained the divisor to be used in all formulas, you would not want to see pasted into cell C3 the formula **=(A3 + B3)/B16**. To prevent Excel from adjusting a cell reference, you use **absolute cell references** by inserting dollar signs ($) before the column and row references of a relative cell reference. For example, the absolute cell reference **$B$15** in the copied cell C2 formula **=(A2 + B2)/$B$15** will cause Excel to paste the formula **=(A3 + B3)/$B$15** into cell C3.

Do not confuse the use of the dollar sign symbol with the worksheet formatting operation that displays numbers as dollar currency amounts.

Recalculation

When you use formulas that refer to other cells, the results of those formulas automatically change as the values in other cells change. This process is called **recalculation**. As Section FTF.4 discusses, formulas permit reusability of worksheets through recalculation.

Worksheets that use formulas capable of recalculation are sometimes called "live" worksheets to distinguish them from worksheets that contain only text and numeric entries ("dead" worksheets). Most of the worksheets that this book uses and presents are live worksheets that serve as templates or models. A novel feature of the PHStat add-in that you can use with this book is that most worksheets the add-in constructs are "live" worksheets, too.

B.4 Entering a Formula

To enter a formula into a cell, first select the cell. You then type the equal sign (=), followed by the combination of operations and cell references that form the formula and terminate the formula. by pressing **Enter**.

For simple formulas, you use the symbols $+, -, *, /,$ and $\hat{}$ for the operations addition, subtraction, multiplication, division, and exponentiation (a number raised to a power), respectively. For example, the formula **=A2 + B2** adds the contents of cells A2 and B2 and displays the sum as the value in the cell containing the formula. To revise a formula, either retype the formula or edit it in the formula bar.

Always review and verify any formula you enter before you use its worksheet to get results. Using simple test data can also be a useful review tool, especially when a formula performs complex calculations.

Functions

You use worksheet functions in formulas to simplify certain arithmetic formulas or to gain access to advanced processing or statistical functions. For example, instead of typing **=A2 + A3 + A4 + A5 + A6**, you can use the **SUM** function to enter the equivalent, shorter formula **= SUM (A2:A6)**. Functions are entered by typing their names followed by a pair of parentheses. For almost all functions, you need to make at least one entry inside the pair of parentheses. For functions that require two or more entries, you separate entries with commas.

To use a worksheet function in a formula, either type the function as shown in the instructions in this book or select a function from one of the galleries in the Function Library group of the Formulas tab. For example, to enter the formula **= AVERAGE (A:A)** in cell C2, you could either type these 13 characters into the cell or select cell C2 and then select **Formulas → More Functions → Statistical** and click **AVERAGE** from the drop-down list and then enter **A:A** in the **Number 1** box in the Function Arguments dialog box and click **OK**.

Entering Array Formulas

An **array formula** is a formula that you enter just once but that applies to all of the cells in a selected cell range (the "array"). To enter an array formula, first select the cell range and then type the formula, and then, while holding down the **Ctrl** and **Shift** keys, press **Enter** to enter the array formula into all of the cells of the cell range. (In OS X Excel, you can also press **Command+Enter** to enter an array formula.)

To edit an array formula, you must first select the entire cell range that contains the array formula, then edit the formula and then press **Enter** while holding down **Ctrl+Shift** (or press **Command+Enter**). When you select a cell that contains an array formula, Excel adds a pair of curly braces { } to the display of the formula in the formula bar to indicate that the formula is an array formula. These curly braces disappear when you start to edit the formula. (You never type the curly braces when you enter an array formula.)

Pasting with Paste Special

While the keyboard shortcuts **Ctrl+C** and **Ctrl+V** to copy and paste cell contents will often suffice, pasting data from one worksheet to another can sometimes cause unexpected side effects. When the two worksheets are in different workbooks, a simple paste creates an external link to the original workbook that can lead to possible errors at a later time. Even pasting between worksheets in the same workbook can lead to problems if what is being pasted is a cell range of formulas. You can use **Paste Special** to avoid these complications.

To use this operation, copy the source cell range using **Ctrl+C** and then right-click the cell (or cell range) that is the target of the paste and click **Paste Special** from the shortcut menu.

In the Paste Special dialog box (shown below), click **Values** and then click **OK**. Paste Special Values pastes the current values of the cells in the first workbook and not formulas that use cell references to the first workbook.

Paste Special can paste other types of information, including cell formatting information. In some copying contexts, placing the mouse pointer over Paste Special in the shortcut menu will reveal a gallery of shortcuts to the choices presented in the Paste Special dialog box.

If you use PHStat and have data for a procedure in the form of formulas, copy your data and then use Paste Special to paste columns of equivalent *values*. (Click **Values** in the Paste Special dialog box to create the values.) PHStat will not work properly if the data for a procedure are in the form of formulas.

B.5 Formatting Cell Contents

You format the contents of worksheet cells by either making entries in the Format Cells dialog box or clicking shortcut icons in the Home tab.

To use the Format Cells dialog box method, right-click a cell or cell range and click Format Cells in the shortcut menu. In the Format Cells dialog box, select the **Number** tab. (A partial Microsoft Windows Excel dialog box is shown below; the OS X Excel dialog box is similar.)

Clicking a **Category** changes the panel to the right of the list. For example, clicking **Number** displays a panel (shown below) in which you can specify the number of decimal places to display.

When you click the **Alignment** tab of the Format Cells dialog box (partially shown below), you display a panel in which you can specify the vertical positioning of cell contents, whether cell contents are horizontally centered or left or right justified, and whether the cell contents can be wrapped to a second line if the contents are longer than the cell width.

Home Tab Shortcuts

You can also format the contents of worksheets by using shortcuts on the Home tab. In Microsoft Windows Excels, these shortcuts are divided into the groups that the following instructions name. In OS X Excels, the groups are implicit and group names are not shown on the Home tab.

Use the Font **group** shortcuts (shown below) to change the typeface, point size, color, and styling such as roman, bold, or italic of the text a cell displays or the background color of a cell. (The Font tab of the Format Cells dialog box shown above contains similar text formatting choices.)

Use the **fill icon** in the same group to change the background color for a cell (shown as yellow in the illustration below). Click the drop-down button to the right of the fill icon to display a gallery of colors from which you can select a color or click **More Colors** for more choices.

The **A icon** (not in OS X Excels) and its drop-down button offer similar choices for changing the color of the text being displayed (shown as red in the illustration).

Use the shortcuts in the **Number** group (shown below) to change the formatting of numeric values, including the formatting changes the discussion of the Format Cells dialog box mentions.

To adjust the width of a column to an optimal size, select the column and then select **Format → Autofit Column Width** in the Cells group (shown on page 625). Excel will adjust the width of the column to accommodate the width of the widest value in the column.

Many Home tab shortcuts, such as **Merge & Center**, have a drop-down list that you display by clicking the drop-down arrow at the right. For Merge & Center, this drop-down displays a gallery of related choices (shown below).

B.6 Formatting Charts

Many of the Excel Guide *Worksheet* instructions that involve charts refer you to this section so that you can correct the formatting of a chart that was just constructed. To apply any of the following corrections, you must first select the chart that is to be corrected. (If Chart Tools or PivotChart Tools appears above the Ribbon tabs, you have selected a chart.)

If, when you open to a chart sheet, the chart is either too large to be fully seen or too small and surrounded by a frame mat that is too large, click **Zoom Out** or **Zoom In**, located in the lower-right portion of the Excel window frame, to adjust the chart display.

For many chart formatting operations, instructions vary among current Excel versions. In the pairs of instructions in this section, use the first instruction if you use Excel 2013 or 2016 and use the second instruction if you use an older Excel version. Minor differences among Microsoft Windows and OS X Excels are noted in parenthetical phrases.

Changes You Most Commonly Make

To relocate a chart to its own chart sheet:

1. Click the chart background and click **Move Chart** from the shortcut menu.
2. In the Move Chart dialog box, click **New Sheet**, enter a name for the new chart sheet, and click **OK**.

To turn off the improper horizontal gridlines:

> **Design** (or **Chart Design**) → **Add Chart Element** → **Gridlines** → **Primary Major Horizontal**

> **Layout** (or **Chart Layout**) → **Gridlines** → **Primary Horizontal Gridlines** → **None**

To turn off the improper vertical gridlines:

> **Design** (or **Chart Design**) → **Add Chart Element** → **Gridlines** → **Primary Major Vertical**

> **Layout** (or **Chart Layout**) → **Gridlines** → **Primary Vertical Gridlines** → **None**

To turn off the chart legend:

> **Design** (or **Chart Design**) → **Add Chart Element** → **Legend** → **None**

> **Layout** (or **Chart Layout**) → **Legend** → **None** (or **No Legend**)

If you use Excel 2007 or Excel 2011, also select **Layout** (or **Chart Layout**) → **Data Labels** → **None** (or **No Data Labels**) and **Layout** (or **Chart Layout**) → **Data Table** → **None** (or **No Data Table**)

Chart and Axis Titles

To add a chart title to a chart missing a title:

1. Select **Design** (or **Chart Design**) → **Add Chart Element** → **Chart Title** → **Above Chart**. Otherwise, click on the chart and then select **Layout** (or **Chart Layout**) → **Chart Title** → **Above Chart**.
2. In the box that is added to the chart, select the words "Chart Title" and enter an appropriate title.

To add a title to a horizontal axis missing a title:

1. **Design** (or **Chart Design**) → **Add Chart Element** →**Axis Titles** → **Primary Horizontal**. In the new text box in the chart, replace the words Axis Title with an appropriate title.
2. **Layout** (or **Chart Layout**) → **Axis Titles** → **Primary Horizontal Axis Title** → **Title Below Axis**. In the new text box in the chart, replace the words Axis Title with an appropriate title.

To add a title to a vertical axis missing a title:

1. **Design** (or **Chart Design**) → **Add Chart Element** →**Axis Titles** → **Primary Vertical**. In the new text box in the chart, replace the words Axis Title with an appropriate title.
2. **Layout** (or **Chart Layout**) → **Axis Titles** → **Primary Vertical Axis Title** → **Rotated Title**. In the new text box in the chart, replace the words Axis Title with an appropriate title.

The word Primary will not appear as the third Layout selection for some types of charts in OS X Excel 2011.

Chart Axes

To turn on the display of the *X* axis, if not already shown:

> **Design** (or **Chart Design**) ➜ **Add Chart Element** ➜ **Axes** ➜ **Primary Horizontal**

> **Layout** (or **Chart Layout**) ➜ **Axes** ➜ **Primary Horizontal Axis** ➜ **Show Left to Right Axis** (or **Show Default Axis** or **Primary Default Axis**)

To turn on the display of the *Y* axis, if not already shown:

> **Design** (or **Chart Design**) ➜ **Add Chart Element** ➜ **Axes** ➜ **Primary Vertical**

> **Layout** (or **Chart Layout**) ➜ **Axes** ➜ **Primary Vertical Axis** ➜ **Show Default Axis**

For a chart that contains secondary axes, to turn off the secondary horizontal axis title:

> **Design** (or **Chart Design**) ➜ **Add Chart Element** ➜ **Axis Titles** ➜ **Secondary Horizontal**

> **Layout** (or **Chart Layout**) ➜ **Axis Titles** ➜ **Secondary Horizontal Axis Title** ➜ **None** (or **No Axis Title**)

For a chart that contains secondary axes, to turn on the secondary vertical axis title:

> **Design** (or **Chart Design**) ➜ **Add Chart Element** ➜ **Axis Titles** ➜ **Secondary Vertical**

> **Layout** (or **Chart Layout**) ➜ **Axis Titles** ➜ **Secondary Vertical Axis Title** ➜ **Rotated Title**

Correcting the Display of the *X* Axis

In scatter plots and related line charts, Microsoft Excel displays the *X* axis at the *Y* axis origin (*Y* = 0). When plots have negative values, this causes the *X* axis not to appear at the bottom of the chart.

To relocate the *X* axis to the bottom of a scatter plot or line chart, open to the chart sheet that contains the chart, right-click the *Y* axis, and click **Format Axis** from the shortcut menu. In the Format Axis pane click **Axis value** and, in its box, enter the value shown in the **Minimum box** in the same pane.

In older Excels, click **Axis Options** in the left pane. In the Axis Options pane on the right, click **Axis value** and in its box enter the value shown in the dimmed **Minimum box** and then click **Close**. In Excel 2011, click **Scale** in the left pane and enter the minimum value in the **Horizontal axis Crosses at** box.

Emphasizing Histogram Bars

To better emphasize each bar in a histogram, open to the chart sheet containing the histogram, right-click over one of the histogram bars, and click **Format Data Series** in the shortcut menu. In the Format Data Series pane, click the bucket icon. In the Border group, click **Solid line** (Click **Border** to reveal settings, if necessary.). From the **Color drop-down list**, select the darkest color in the same column as the currently selected (highlighted) color. Then, enter 2 (for 2 pt) as the **Width**.

In older Excels, in the Format Data Series dialog box click **Border Color** in the left pane. In the Border Color right pane, click **Solid line**. From the **Color drop-down list** select the darkest color in the same column as the currently selected (highlighted) color. Then, click **Border Styles** in the left pane. In the Border Styles right pane, enter 2 (for 2 pt) as the **Width** and then click **OK**. In Excel 2011, click **Line** in the left pane and then click the **Solid** and **Weights & Arrows** tabs to reveal similar settings.

B.7 Selecting Cell Ranges for Charts

In most cases, you can enter a cell range in an Excel dialog box in one of several ways. You can type the range (the typical way the instructions in this book tell you) or you can select a cell range using the mouse pointer and have Excel fill in the cell range for you. Likewise, most of the time you can choose to enter the cell range either using relative or absolute references (see Section B.3). The Axis Labels and Edit Series dialog boxes, associated with chart labels and data series, are exceptions to these general cases.

To enter a cell range into these two dialog boxes, you must enter the cell range as a *formula* that uses absolute cell references in the form *WorksheetName!UpperLeftCell: LowerRightCell*. (See examples below, from Microsoft Windows Excel and for the Chapter 2 Pareto chart example.) This is best done using the mouse-pointer method to enter these cell ranges. Typing the cell range, as you might normally do, will often be frustrating, as keys such as the cursor keys will not function as they do in other dialog boxes.

Selecting Non-contiguous Cell Ranges

Typically, you enter a non-contiguous cell range such as the cells A1:A11 and C1:C11 by typing the cell range of each group of cells, separated by commas—for example, **A1:A11, C1:C11**. In the dialog boxes discussed in the preceding section, you will need to select a non-contiguous cell range using the mouse pointer method. To use the mouse-pointer method with such ranges, first, select the cell range of the first group of cells and then, while holding down **Ctrl**, select the cell range of the other groups of cells that form the non-contiguous cell range.

B.8 Deleting the "Extra" Histogram Bar

As explained in "Classes and Excel Bins" on page 40, you use bins to approximate classes. One result of this approximation is that you will always create an "extra" bin that will have a frequency of zero. To delete the histogram bar associated with this extra bin, edit the cell range that Excel uses to construct the histogram.

Right-click the histogram background and click **Select Data**. In the Select Data Source dialog box in Microsoft Windows Excels:

1. Click **Edit** under the **Legend Entries (Series)** heading.
2. In the Edit Series dialog box, edit the **Series values** cell range formula to begin with the second cell of the original cell range and click OK.
3. Click **Edit** under the **Horizontal (Categories) Axis Labels** heading.
4. In the Axis Labels dialog box, edit the **Axis label range** formula to begin with the second cell of the original cell range and click **OK**.

In the Select Data Source dialog box in OS X Excels:

1. Edit the **Y values** cell range formula to begin with the second cell of the original cell range and click OK.
2. Edit the **Horizontal (Category) axis labels** [or **Category (X) axis labels**] formula.
3. In the Axis Labels dialog box, edit the **Axis label range** formula to begin with the second cell of the original cell range and click **OK**.

B.9 Creating Histograms for Discrete Probability Distributions

You can create a histogram for a discrete probability distribution based on a discrete probabilities table. For example, to create the Figure 5.3 histogram of the binomial probability distribution on page 185, open to the **COMPUTE worksheet** of the **Binomial workbook**. Select the cell range **B14:B18**, the probabilities in the Binomial Probabilities Table, and:

1. Select **Insert (or Charts)** → **Column** and select the **Clustered Column** gallery item.
2. Right-click the chart and click **Select Data** in the shortcut menu.

In the Select Data Source dialog box:

3. Click **Edit** under the **Horizontal (Categories) Axis Labels** heading. In the Axis Labels display, drag the mouse to select and enter the cell range A14:A18 with a worksheet prefix (see Section B.3), *as a formula* in the **Axis label range** box.

   In OS X Excels, in the Select Data Source display, click the icon inside the **Horizontal (Category) axis labels** [or **Category (X) axis labels**] box and drag the mouse to select and enter the same cell range, A14:A18.

4. Click **OK**.

In the chart:

5. Right-click inside a bar and click **Format Data Series** in the shortcut menu.
6. In the Format Data Series display, click **Series Options**. In the Series Options, click **Series Options**, enter **0** as the **Gap Width** and then close the display. (To see the second Series Options, you may have to first click the chart [third] icon near the top of the task pane.)

In OS X Excel 2016 there is only one Series Options label and the Gap Width setting is displayed without having to click Series Options. In the Format Data Series dialog box in OS X Excel 2011, click **Options** in the left pane to display the **Gap width** setting in the right pane.

Relocate the chart to a chart sheet and adjust the chart formatting by using the instructions in Section B.6.

Online Resources

C.1 About the Online Resources for This Book

Online resources support your study of business statistics and your use of this book. You can obtain the following resources from the student download web page or the "Tools for Success" page inside the MyStatLab course for this book.

Excel Data Workbooks The data files that are used in chapter examples, problems, or the end-of-chapter cases.

Excel Guide Workbooks Excel workbooks that contain templates or model solutions for applying Excel to a particular statistical method.

PHStat The Pearson Education statistics add-in that Sections FTF.4 and C.4 discuss separately.

Files for the Digital Cases The PDF files that support the end-of-chapter Digital Cases. Some of these PDF files include attached Excel data workbooks.

Online Topics These PDF files present additional statistical topics. This set includes the full text of two chapters, "Statistical Applications in Quality Management" and "Decision Making."

Supplemental Readings These PDF files extend the discussion of specific concepts or provide background information that some readers may find useful. (This set includes chapter "Short Takes.")

Visual Explorations Workbooks The Excel workbooks that interactively demonstrate various key statistical concepts. See Section C.3 for more information.

C.2 Accessing the Online Resources

To access resources from the student download page for this book:

1. Visit **www.pearsonhighered.com/levine**.
2. In that web page, locate this book, *Statistics for Managers Using Microsoft Excel*, eighth edition, and click the student download page link.
3. In the download page, click the links for the desired items.

Most items will cause the web browser to prompt you to save the (zip archive) that you can save and later unzip. Clicking the link for PHStat, will redirect you to the PHStat

home page, **www.pearsonhighered.com/phstat**, from which you can download PHStat.

To access resources from the MyStatLab course for this book, log into the course and in the left panel menu click **Tools for Success**. On that page, click the links for the desired items. (Using MyStatLab requires an access code.)

Downloading PHStat requires a separate access code. That access code may have been packaged with this book. If your book does not include a PHStat access code, you can purchase one at the PHStat home page.

C.3 Details of Online Resources

Data Workbooks

Throughout this book, the names of data workbooks appear in a special inverted color typeface—for example, Retirement Funds . Data workbooks are stored as **.xlsx** Excel files.

The following alphabetical list of workbooks names variables in their order of their appearance, starting with column A. Chapter references indicate the chapter or chapters that use the data file in an example or problem.

311CALLCENTER Day and abandonment rate (%) (Chapter 3)

ACCOUNTINGPARTNERS Firm and number of partners Chapter 3)

ACCOUNTINGPARTNERS2 Region and number of partners (Chapter 10)

ACCOUNTINGPARTNERS4 Region and number of partners (Chapter 11)

ACCOUNTINGPARTNERS6 Region, revenue ($millions), number of partners, number of professionals, MAS (%), southeast ($0 =$ no, $1 =$ yes), and Gulf coast southeast ($0 =$ no, $1 =$ yes)(Chapter 15)

ACT Method (online or traditional), ACT scores for condensed course, and ACT scores for regular course (Chapter 11)

ACT-ONEWAY Group 1 ACT scores, group 2 ACT scores, group 3 ACT scores, and group 4 ACT scores (Chapter 11)

ADINDEX Respondent, cola A Adindex, and cola B Adindex (Chapter 10)

AIRLINES Destination, Southwest airlines fare ($), and US Airways fare ($) (Chapter 10)

AMERICANBANKS ROE(%) and leverage ratio(%) (Chapter 11)

AMS2-1 Types of errors and frequency, types of errors and cost, and types of wrong billing errors and cost (as three separate worksheets) (Chapter 2)

AMS2-2 Days and number of calls (Chapter 2)

AMS8 Rate willing to pay ($) (Chapter 8)

AMS9 Upload speed (Chapter 9)

AMS10 Update times for email interface 1 and email interface 2 (Chapter 10)

AMS11-1 Update time for system 1, system 2, and system 3 (Chapter 11)

AMS11-2 Technology (cable or fiber) and interface (system 1, system 2, or system 3) (Chapter 11)

AMS13 Number of hours spent telemarketing and number of new subscriptions (Chapter 13)

AMS14 Week, number of new subscriptions, hours spent telemarketing, and type of presentation (formal or informal) (Chapter 14)

AMS16 Month and number of home delivery subscriptions (Chapter 16)

ANSCOMBE Data sets A, B, C, and D, each with 11 pairs of X and Y values (Chapter 13)

ATM TRANSACTIONS Cause, frequency, and percentage (Chapter 2)

ATTRACTIONS Town, ride, wait time, comments, and rating (Chapter 17)

AUDITS Year and number of audits (Chapters 2 and 16)

AUTOMAKER1 Automaker and number of complaints (Chapters 2 and 17)

AUTOMAKER2 Category and number of complaints (Chapter 2)

BANK1 Waiting time (in minutes) of 15 customers at a bank located in a commercial district (Chapters 3, 9, 10, and 12)

BANK2 Waiting time (in minutes) of 15 customers at a bank located in a residential area (Chapters 3, 10, and 12)

BANKMARKETING Age, type of job, marital status (divorced, married, or single), education (primary, secondary, tertiary, or unknown), is credit in default, mean yearly balance in account, is there a housing loan, is there a personal loan, last contact duration in seconds, number of contacts performed during this campaign, and has the client purchased a term deposit (also contains the BinaryLogisticDATA worksheet that contains recoded variables) (Chapter 17)

BARRIERS Barriers and frequency (Chapter 2)

BASEBALL Team, league ($0 =$ American, $1 =$ National) wins, earned run average, runs scored per game, saves, batting average, HRs, and WHIP (walks plus hits per inning) (Chapters 13, 14, and 15)

BASEBALLTEAMS Team, attendance, high temperature on game day, winning percentage of home team; opponent's winning percentage, game played on weekend day ($0 =$ no, $1 =$ yes), and promotion held ($0 =$ no, $1 =$ yes) (Chapter 17)

BBCOST2015 Team and fan cost index (Chapters 2, 6, and 17)

BBSALARIES Year and average major league baseball salary ($millions) (Chapter 16)

BBVALUES Team, revenue ($millions), and value ($millions) (Chapter 13)

BESTCOMPANIES Company, full-time jobs added, total worldwide revenues ($billions), and total voluntary turnover (%) (Chapters 14 and 15)

BESTFUNDS1 Fund type (short-term or long-term), 1-year return, and 3-year return (Chapters 10 and 17)

BOARDANALYSIS Director type, number before change, and number after change (Chapter 2)

BONUSES Year and bonuses ($000) (Chapter 16)

BOOKPRICES Author, title, bookstore price, and online price ($) (Chapter 10)

BRAKES Part, gauge 1, and gauge 2 (Chapter 11)

BRANDZTECHFIN Brand, brand value in 2014 ($millions), % change in brand value from 2013, region, and sector (Chapters 10 and 12)

BRANDZTECHFINTELE Brand, brand value in 2014 ($millions), % change in brand value from 2013, region, and sector (Chapter 11)

BREAKFAST Type (Continental or American), delivery time difference for early time period, and delivery time difference for late time period (Chapter 11)

BREAKFAST2 Type (Continental or American), delivery time difference for early time period, and delivery time difference for late time period (Chapter 11)

BRYNNEPACKAGING WPCT score and rating (Chapter 13)

BULBS Manufacturer ($1 = A$, $2 = B$) and length of life (hours) (Chapters 2, 10, and 12)

BUNDLE Restaurant, bundle score, and typical cost ($) (Chapter 2)

BUSINESSVALUATION Drug company name, price to book value ratio, return on equity (ROE), and growth% (Chapters 14 and 17)

BUSINESSVALUATION2 Company, ticker symbol, Standard Industrial Classification 3 (SIC3) code, Standard Industrial Classification 4 (SIC4) code, price to book value ratio, price to earnings ratio, natural log of assets (as a measure of size), return on equity (ROE), growth percentage (GS5), debt to EBITDA ratio, dummy variable indicator of SIC 4 code 2834 ($1 = 2834, 0 =$ not 2824), and dummy variable indicator of SIC 4 code 2835 $(1 = 2835, 0 = \text{not } 2835)$ (Chapter 15)

CABERNET California wine rating, Washington wine rating, California wine ranking, and Washington wine ranking (Chapter 12)

CALLCENTER Month and call volume (Chapter 16)

CANDIDATE ASSESSMENT Salary, competence rating, gender of candidate (F or M), gender of rater (F or M), rater/candidate gender (F to F, F to M, M to M, M to M), school (Private, Public), department (Biology, Chemistry, Physics), and age of rater (Chapter 17)

CARDIOGOODFITNESS Product purchased (TM195, TM498, TM798), age in years, gender (Male or Female), education in years, relationship status (Single or Partnered), average number of times the customer plans to use the treadmill each week, self-rated fitness on a 1-to-5 ordinal scale $(1 = \text{poor to } 5 = \text{excellent})$, annual household income ($), and average number of miles the customer expects to walk/run each week (Chapters 2, 3, 6, 8, 10, 11, and 12)

CARDSTUDY Upgraded $(0 = \text{no}, 1 = \text{yes})$, purchases ($thousands), and extra cards $(0 = \text{no}, 1 = \text{yes})$ (Chapter 14)

CARPRODUCTION Year, coded year, and number of units produced (Chapter 16)

CATFOOD Ounces eaten of kidney, shrimp, chicken liver, salmon, and beef cat food (Chapters 11 and 12)

CATFOOD2 Piece size $(F = \text{fine}, C = \text{chunky})$, coded weight for low fill height, and coded weight for current fill height (Chapter 11)

CDRATE Bank, 1-year CD rate, and 5-year CD rate (Chapters 2, 3, 6, and 8)

CELLPHONEACTIVITY Activity and percentage (Chapter 2)

CELLSERVICE City, AT&T rating, and Verizon rating (Chapter 10)

CEO2013 Company, CEO compensation ($millions), and return in 2013 (Chapter 2)

CEO2014 Company, CEO compensation ($millions), and return in 2014 (Chapter 13)

CEREALS Cereal, calories, carbohydrates, and sugar (Chapters 3, 13, and 17)

CHURN Customer ID, churn coded $(0 = \text{No}, 1 = \text{Yes})$, churn, calls, and visits(Chapters 14 and 17)

CIGARETTETAX State and cigarette tax ($) (Chapters 2 and 3)

COCA-COLA Year, coded year, and revenues ($billions) (Chapter 16)

COFFEE Expert and rating of coffees by brand A, B, C, and D (Chapters 10 and 11)

COFFEEEXPORTS Year and exports in thousands of 60-kg bags (Chapter 16)

COFFEESALES Coffee sales at $0.59, $0.69, $0.79, and $0.89 (Chapters 11 and 12)

COFFEESALES2 Coffee sales and price (Chapter 15)

COLLEGEDEBT Option and average debt at graduation ($) (Chapter 10)

COLLEGE FOOTBALL Head coach, school, conference, school pay of head coach, other pay, total pay, max bonus, and football net revenue (Chapters 2, 3, and 13)

COMMUNITYBANKS Institution, location, ROA(%), efficiency ratio(%), and total risk based capital(%) (Chapters 14 and 15)

CONCRETE1 Sample number and compressive strength after two days and seven days (Chapter 10)

CONCRETE2 Sample number and compressive strength after 2, 7, and 28 days (Chapter 11)

CONGESTION City, annual time waiting in traffic (hours), and cost of waiting in traffic ($) (Chapters 2 and 3)

CONGESTIONLEVEL Asia, Europe, and North America increase (%) in overall travel time compared to a free flow situation (Chapters 11 and 12)

COREAPPLIANCES Year and shipments in millions (Chapter 16)

CPI-U Year, coded year, and value of CPI-U (the consumer price index) (Chapter 16)

CREDIT SCORES City, state, and average credit score (Chapters 2 and 3)

CURRENCY Year, coded year, and exchange rates (against the U.S. dollar) for the Canadian dollar, Japanese yen, and English pound sterling (Chapters 2 and 16)

DELIVERY Customer, number of cases, and delivery time (Chapter 13)

DENSITY Ammonium percentage, density for stir rate of 100, and density for stir rate of 150 (Chapter 11)

DESKTOPLAPTOP Year and hours (Chapter 16)

DOMESTICBEER Brand, alcohol percentage, calories, and carbohydrates (Chapters 2, 3, 6, and 15)

DOWDOGS Stock and 1-year return (Chapter 3)

DOWMARKETCAP Company and market capitalization ($billions) (Chapters 3 and 6)

DOWNLOADSPEED Country and download speed (Chapter 3)

DRILL Depth, time to drill additional 5 feet, and type of hole (dry or wet) (Chapters 14 and 17)

DRINK Amount of soft drink filled in 2-liter bottles (Chapters 2 and 9)

ENERGY State and per capita kilowatt hour use (Chapter 3)

ENGINES RPM and torque (Chapter 15)

ENTREE Type and number served (Chapter 2)

ERWAITING Emergency room waiting time (in minutes) at the main facility and at satellite 1, satellite 2, and satellite 3 (Chapters 11 and 12)

ESPRESSO Tamp (inches) and time (seconds) (Chapter 13)

EUROTOURISM Country, employment in tourism 2014, and tourism establishments (Chapter 15)

EUROTOURISM2 Country, employment in tourism 2014, business travel & tourism spending 2014 (US$millions), international visitors 2014, and tourism establishments (Chapter 17)

EXAMPLE15-2 X and Y (Chapter 15)

EXAMPLE15-3 X and Y (Chapter 15)

FASTFOOD Amount spent on fast food ($) (Chapters 2, 8, and 9)

FASTFOODCHAIN Mean sales per unit ($thousands) at burger, chicken, sandwich, and snack chains (Chapters 11 and 12)

FEDRECEIPT Year, coded year, and federal receipts ($billions current) (Chapter 16)

FIFTEENWEEKS Week number, number of customers, and sales ($thousands) over a period of 15 consecutive weeks (Chapter 13)

FLYASH Fly ash percentage and strength (PSI) (Chapter 15)

FORCE Force required to break an insulator (Chapters 2, 3, 8, and 9)

FOREIGNMARKET Country, level of development (Emerging or Developed), and time required to start a business (days) (Chapter 10)

FOREIGNMARKET2 Country, region, cost to export container (US$), and cost to import container (US$) (Chapters 11 and 12)

FREEPORT Address, fair market value ($thousands), property size (acres), house size, age, number of rooms, number of bathrooms, and number of cars that can be parked in the garage (Chapter 15)

FREE SHIPPING Retailer and minimum order for free shipping ($) (Chapter 2)

FREEZER Month and shipments in thousands (Chapter 16)

FTMBA School name, program cost ($), total students per program, job offers (%), and mean starting salary ($) (Chapters 13 and 15)

FURNITURE Days between receipt and resolution of complaints regarding purchased furniture (Chapters 2, 3, 8, and 9)

GASPRICES Month and price per gallon ($) (Chapter 16)

GCFREEROSLYN Address, location (Glen Cove, Freeport, or Roslyn), fair market value ($thousands), property size (acres), age, house size (sq. ft.), number of rooms, number of bathrooms, and number of cars that can be parked in the garage (Chapter 15)

GCROSLYN Address, location (Glen Cove or Roslyn), fair market value ($thousands), property size (acres), age, house size (sq. ft.), number of rooms, number of bathrooms, and number of cars that can be parked in the garage (Chapters 14 and 15)

GDP Year and gross domestic product (Chapter 16)

GLENCOVE Address, fair market value ($thousands), property size (acres), age, house size (sq. ft.), number of rooms, number of bathrooms, and number of cars that can be parked in the garage (Chapters 14 and 15)

GLOBALINTERNETUSAGE Country, GDP per capita ($thousands), and Internet use percentage (Chapters 2 and 3)

GLOBALSOCIALMEDIA Country, GDP, and social media usage (%) (Chapters 2, 3 and 13)

GOLD Quarter, coded quarter, price ($), Q1, Q2, and Q3 (Chapter 16)

GRANULE Granule loss in Boston and Vermont shingles (Chapters 3, 8, 9, and 10)

HEATINGOIL Monthly consumption of heating oil (gallons), temperature (degrees Fahrenheit), attic insulation (inches), and ranch-style (0 = not ranch-style, 1 = ranch-style) (Chapters 14 and 15)

HEMLOCKFARMS Asking price, hot tub (0 = no, 1 = yes), rooms, lake view (0 = no, 1 = yes), bathrooms, bedrooms, loft/den (0 = no, 1 = yes), finished basement (0 = no, 1 = yes), and number of acres (Chapter 15)

HHINCOME Median home value (000), violent crime rate/100,000 residents, average commuting time in minutes, and livability score (Chapter 15)

HONDAPRICES Age in years and price ($) (Chapter 15)

HOTELAWAY Nationality and cost (British pounds sterling) (Chapter 3)

HOTELPRICES City and average price (US$) of a hotel room at a 2-star price, 3-star price, and 4-star hotel (Chapters 2 and 3)

HOUSEHOLDS ID, Gender, age, Hispanic origin (N or Y), dwelling type (AB, AH, DH, or Other), age of dwelling (years), years living at dwelling, number of bedrooms, number of vehicles kept at dwelling, fuel type at dwelling (Electric, Gas, Oil, or Other), monthly cost of fuel at dwelling ($), U.S. citizenship (N or Y), college degree (N or Y), marital status (D, M, NM, S, or W), work for pay in previous week (N or Y), mode of transportation to work (Bus, Car, Home, Subway/Rail, Taxi, Other, or NA), commuting time (minutes), hours worked per week, type of organization(GOV, NA, PP, PNP, or SE), annual earned income ($), and total annual income ($) (Chapter 17)

HOUSESALES Year, coded year, total sales (Chapter 16)

HYBRIDSALES Year and number sold (Chapter 17)

ICECREAM Daily temperature (in degrees Fahrenheit) and sales ($thousands) for 21 days (Chapter 13)

INDICES Year, change in DJIA, S&P500, and NASDAQ (Chapter 3)

INSURANCE Processing time in days for insurance policies (Chapters 3, 8, and 9)

INSURANCECLAIMS Claims, buildup (0 = buildup not indicated, 1 = buildup indicated), and excess payment ($) (Chapter 8)

INSURANCEFRAUD ID, fraud coded (0 = no, 1 = yes), fraud (No or Yes), new business coded (0 = no, 1 = yes), new business (No or Yes), and claims/year (Chapters 14 and 17)

INTERNETMOBILETIME time in minutes spent per day using the Internet from a mobile device (Chapter 9)

INTERNETMOBILETIME2 time in minutes spent per day using the Internet from a mobile device (Chapter 10)

INVOICE Number of invoices processed and amount of time (hours) for 30 days (Chapter 13)

INVOICES Amount recorded (in dollars) from sales invoices (Chapter 9)

LUGGAGE Delivery time (in minutes) for luggage in Wing A and Wing B of a hotel (Chapters 10 and 12)

MANAGERS Sales (ratio of yearly sales divided by the target sales value for that region), Wonderlic Personnel Test score, Strong-Campbell Interest Inventory Test score, number of years of selling experience prior to becoming a sales manager, and whether the sales manager has a degree in electrical engineering (No or Yes) (Chapter 15)

MCDONALDS Year, coded year, and annual total revenues ($billions) at McDonald's Corporation (Chapter 16)

MCDONALDSSTORES State and number of stores (Chapter 3)

MEDICALWIRES1 Machine type, narrow, and wide (Chapter 11)

MEDICALWIRES2 Narrow, and wide (Chapter 11)

METALS Year and the total rate of return (in percentage) for platinum, gold, and silver (Chapter 3)

MINING Day, amount stacked, and downtime (Chapter 17)

MINING2 Day; hours of downtime due to mechanical, electrical, tonnage restriction, operator, and no feed; and total hours (Chapter 17)

MMR Monthly movie revenues from 2005 to 2014 (Chapter 2)

MOBILE ELECTRONICS In-aisle sales, front sales, kiosk sales, and expert area sales (Chapter 11)

MOBILE ELECTRONICS2 Mobile payments (No or Yes), in-aisle sales, front sales, kiosk sales, and expert area sales (Chapter 11)

MOBILECOMMERCE Country and mobile commerce penetration (%) (Chapters 3 and 8)

MOBILELOYALTY Spending ($) (Chapter 3)

MOISTURE Moisture content of Boston shingles and Vermont shingles (Chapter 9)

MOLDING Vibration time (seconds), vibration pressure (psi), vibration amplitude (%), raw material density (g/mL), quantity of raw material (scoops), product length in cavity 1 (in.), product length in cavity 2 (in.), product weight in cavity 1 (gr.), and product weight in cavity 2 (gr.) (Chapter 15)

MOTIVATION Factor, mean rating by global employees, and mean rating by U.S. employees (Chapter 10)

MOVIE Title, box office gross ($millions), and DVD revenue ($millions) (Chapter 13)

MOVIE ATTENDANCE Year and movie attendance (billions) (Chapters 2 and 16)

MOVIE REVENUES Year and revenue ($billions) (Chapter 2)

MOVING Labor hours, cubic feet, number of large pieces of furniture, and availability of an elevator (Chapters 13 14, and 17)

MYELOMA Patient, before transplant measurement, and after transplant measurement (Chapter 10)

NATURAL GAS Month, wellhead price ($/thousands cu. ft.), and residential price ($/thousands cu. ft.) (Chapters 2 and 16)

NBA Team, number of wins, field goal %, 3-point field goal %, points per game for team, points per game for opponent, difference in points per game between team and opponent, rebounds per game, and turnovers per game (Chapters 14 and 17)

NBACOST Team and cost ($) (Chapters 2 and 6)

NBAVALUES Team, team code, annual revenue ($millions), and value ($millions) and 1-year change in value (%) (Chapters 2, 3 and 13)

NEIGHBOR Selling price ($thousands), number of rooms, and neighborhood location (0 = east, 1 = west) (Chapter 14)

NEWHOMESALES Month, sales in thousands, and mean price ($thousands) (Chapter 2)

OIL&GASOLINE Week, price of a gallon of gasoline ($), and price of oil per barrel, ($) (Chapter 13)

OMNIPOWER Bars sold, price (cents), and promotion expenses ($) (Chapters 14 and 17)

ORDER Time in minutes to fill orders for a population of 200 (Chapter 8)

ORGANICFOOD Customer, organic food purchaser (0 = no, 1 = yes), age, and online health wellness e-newsletters subscriber (0 = no, 1 = yes) (Chapter 14)

O-RING Flight number, temperature, and O-ring damage index (Chapter 13)

PACKAGINGFOAM1 Die temperature, 3 mm. diameter, and 4 mm. diameter (Chapter 11)

PACKAGINGFOAM2 Die temperature, 3 mm. diameter, and 4 mm. diameter (Chapter 11)

PACKAGINGFOAM3 Die temperature, die diameter, and foam density (Chapter 14)

PACKAGINGFOAM4 Die temperature, die diameter, and foam diameter (Chapter 14)

PALLET Weight of Boston shingles and weight of Vermont shingles (Chapters 2, 8, 9, and 10)

PARACHUTE1WAY Tensile strength of parachutes from suppliers 1, 2, 3, and 4 (Chapter 11)

PARACHUTE2WAY Loom and tensile strength of parachutes from suppliers 1, 2, 3, and 4 (Chapter 11)

PAYMENT Method and percentage (Chapter 2)

PEN Ad and product rating (Chapters 11, 12)

PHILLY Zip code, population, median sales price 2012 ($000), average days on market 2012, units sold 2012, median household income ($), percentage of residents with a BA or higher, and hotness (0 = not hot, 1 = hot) (Chapter 17)

PHONE Time (in minutes) to clear telephone line problems and location (1 = I, 2 = II) (Chapters 10 and 12)

PIZZAHUT Gender coded (0 = Female, 1 = Male), gender (Female or Male), price ($), and purchase (0 = student selected another pizzeria, 1 = student selected Pizza Hut) (Chapter 14)

PIZZATIME Time period, delivery time for local restaurant, and delivery time for national chain (Chapter 10)

POLIO Year and incidence rates per 100,000 persons of reported poliomyelitis (Chapter 16)

POTATO Percentage of solids content in filter cake, acidity (pH), lower pressure, upper pressure, cake thickness, varidrive speed, and drum speed setting for 54 measurements (Chapter 15)

POTTERMOVIES Title, first weekend gross ($millions), U.S. gross ($millions), and worldwide gross ($millions) (Chapters 2, 3, and 13)

PROPERTYTAXES State and property taxes per capita ($) (Chapters 2, 3, and 6)

PROTEIN Type of food, calories (in grams), protein, percentage of calories from fat, percentage of calories from saturated fat, and cholesterol (mg) (Chapter 3)

PUMPKIN Circumference and weight of pumpkins (Chapter 13)

REDANDWHITE Fixed acidity, volatile acidity, citric acid, residual sugar, chlorides, free sulfur dioxide, total sulfur dioxide, density, pH, sulphates, alcohol, wine type coded (0 = White, 1 = Red), and wine type (Red or White), quality (Chapter 14)

REDWOOD Height (ft.), breast height diameter (in.), and bark thickness (in.) (Chapters 13 and 14)

REGISTRATIONERROR Registration error, temperature, pressure, and supplier (Chapter 15)

REGISTRATIONERROR-HIGHCOST Registration error and temperature (Chapter 15)

RENTSILVERSPRING Apartment size (sq. ft.) and monthly rental cost ($) (Chapter 13)

RESTAURANTS Location (City or Suburban), food rating, decor rating, service rating, summated rating, coded location (0 = Center City, 1 = Metro Area), and cost of a meal (Chapters 2, 3, 10, 12, 13 and 14)

RESTAURANTS2 Location, food rating, decor rating, service rating, cost of a meal, popularity index, and cuisine [American (New), Chinese, French, Indian, Italian, Japanese, or Mexican] (Chapter 17)

RETIREMENT FUNDS Fund number, market cap (Small, Mid-Cap, or Large), type (Growth or Value), assets ($millions), turnover ratio, beta (measure of the volatility of a stock), standard deviation (measure of returns relative to 36-month average), risk (Low, Average, or High), 1-year return, 3-year return, 5-year return, 10-year return, expense ratio, and star rating (Chapters 2, 3, 6, 8, 10, 11, 12, and 15)

ROSLYN Address, fair market value ($thousands), property size (acres), house size (sq. ft.), age, number of rooms, number of bathrooms, and number of cars that can be parked in the garage (Chapter 15)

SECOND EXPERIMENT In-aisle sales, front sales, kiosk sales, and expert area sales (Chapter 12)

SEDANS Miles per gallon for 2014 midsized sedans (Chapters 3 and 8)

SILICONVALLEY Sales ($millions), profits ($millions), capex ($millions), employees, cash ($millions), debt ($millions), dividends ($millions), repurchases ($millions), taxes ($millions), and R & D ($millions) (Chapter 17)

SILVER Year and price of silver ($) (Chapter 16)

SILVER-Q Quarter, coded quarter, price of silver ($), Q1, Q2, and Q3 (Chapter 16)

SILVERSPRING Address, asking price ($000), assessed value ($000), taxes ($), size (thousands sq. ft.) fireplace coded (0 = no, 1 = yes), number of bedrooms, number of bathrooms, age (years), and fireplace (No or Yes) (Chapters 13, 14, and 15)

SITESELECTION Store number, profiled customers, and sales ($millions) (Chapter 13)

SMARTPHONE SALES Type, and market share percentage for the years 2010 through 2014 (Chapter 2)

SMARTPHONES Price ($) (Chapter 3)

SOCCERVALUES Team, country, revenue ($millions), and value ($millions) (Chapter 13)

SOLARPOWER Year and amount of solar power generated (megawatts) (Chapter 16)

STANDBY Standby hours, total staff present, remote hours, Dubner hours, and total labor hours (Chapters 14 and 15)

STARBUCKS Tear, viscosity, pressure, and plate gap (Chapters 13 and 14)

STEEL Error in actual length and specified length (Chapters 2, 6, 8, and 9)

STOCK PERFORMANCE Decade and stock performance (%) (Chapters 2 and 16)

STOCKINDEX Stock index and percentage change for 2009 through 2013 (Chapter 2)

STOCKPRICES2014 Date, S&P 500 value, and closing weekly stock price for GE, Discovery Communications, and Google (Chapter 13)

STUDENTSURVEY ID, gender (Female or Male), age (as of last birthday), class designation (Sophomore, Junior, or Senior), major (Accounting, CIS, Economics/Finance, International Business, Management, Retail/Marketing, Other, or Undecided), graduate school intention (No, Yes, or Undecided), cumulative GPA, current employment status (Full-Time, Part-Time, or Unemployed), expected starting salary ($thousands), number of social networking sites registered for, satisfaction with student advisement services on campus, amount spent on books and supplies this semester, type of computer preferred (Desktop, Laptop, or Tablet), text messages per week, and wealth accumulated to feel rich (Chapters 2, 3, 6, 8, 10, 11, and 12)

SUV Miles per gallon for 2014 small SUVs (Chapters 3, 6, and 8)

TABLETS Battery life of WiFi only and 3G/4G WiFi 9 to 12 inch tablets (Chapters 10 and 12)

TEABAGS Weight of tea bags in ounces (Chapters 3, 8, and 9)

TELECOM Provider, TV rating, and Phone rating (Chapter 10)

TESTRANK Rank scores and training method (0 = traditional, 1 = experimental) for 10 people (Chapter 12)

THICKNESS Thickness, catalyst, pH, pressure, temperature, and voltage (Chapters 14 and 15)

THIRTYYRRATE Thirty-year mortgage rate in New York and West Palm Beach, Florida (Chapter 10)

TIMES Get-ready times (Chapter 3)

TOYS R US Quarter, coded quarter, revenue, and the dummy variables Q1, Q2, and for quarters (Chapter 16)

TROUGH Width of trough (Chapters 2, 3, 8, and 9)

TRSNYC Year, unit value of Diversified Equity funds, and unit value of Stable Value funds (Chapter 16)

TSMODEL1 Year, coded year, and three time series (I, II, and III) (Chapter 16)

TSMODEL2 Year, coded year, and two time series (I and II) (Chapter 16)

TVREMOTE Filling time, 60, 72.5, and 85 degrees (Chapter 11)

TWITTERMOVIES Movie, Twitter activity, and receipts ($) (Chapter 13)

UNDERWRITING End-of-training exam score, proficiency exam score, and training method (classroom, courseware app, or online) (Chapter 14)

USEDCARS Car, year, age, price ($), mileage, and power (hp), fuel (mpg) (Chapter 17)

UTILITY Utilities charges ($) for 50 one-bedroom apartments (Chapters 2 and 6)

VB Time to complete program (Chapter 10)

VINHOVERDE Fixed acidity, volatile acidity, citric acid, residual sugar, chlorides, free sulfur dioxide, total sulfur dioxide, density, pH, sulphates, alcohol, and quality (Chapters 13, 14 and 15)

VLABGO Storefront and in-aisle sales (Chapters 10 and 12)

WAIT Waiting time and seating time (Chapter 6)

WALMART Quarter and Wal-Mart Stores quarterly revenues ($billions) (Chapter 16)

WARECOST Distribution cost ($thousands), sales ($thousands), and number of orders (Chapter 13)

WIP Processing times at each of two plants (1 = A, 2 = B) (Chapter 17)

WORKFORCE Year, population, and size of the workforce (Chapter 16)

YARN Side-by-side aspect and breaking strength scores for 30 psi, 40 psi, and 50 psi (Chapter 11)

Excel Guide Workbooks

Excel Guide workbooks contain templates or model solutions for applying Excel to a particular statistical method. Chapter examples and the Excel Guide *Workbook* instructions feature worksheets from these workbooks and PHStat constructs many of the same worksheets for you. Most workbooks include a **COMPUTE worksheet** (often shown in this book) and a **COMPUTE_FORMULAS worksheet** that allows you to examine all of the formulas that the worksheet uses. The Excel Guide workbooks (with chapter references) are:

Recoded (1)	**CIE sigma unknown (8)**
Random (1)	**CIE Proportion (8)**
Data Cleaning (1)	**Sample Size Mean (8)**
Summary Table (2)	**Sample Size Proportion (8)**
Challenging (2)	**Z Mean (9)**
Contingency Table (2)	**T Mean (9)**
Distributions (2)	**Z Proportion (9)**
Pareto (2)	**Pooled-Variance T (10)**
Stem-and-leaf (2)	**Separate-Variance T (10)**
Histogram (2)	**Paired T (10)**
Polygons (2)	**F Two Variances (10)**
Scatter Plot (2)	**Z Two Proportions (10)**
Time Series (2)	**One-Way ANOVA (11)**
MCT (2)	**Levene (11)**
Slicers (2)	**Two-Way ANOVA (11)**
Descriptive (3)	**Randomized Block (11)**
Quartiles (3)	**Chi-Square (12)**
Boxplot (3)	**Chi-Square Worksheets (12)**
Parameters (3)	**Wilcoxon (12)**
VE-Variability (3)	**Kruskal-Wallis Worksheets (12)**
Covariance (3)	**Simple Linear Regression (13)**
Correlation (3)	
Probabilities (4)	**Package Delivery (13)**
Bayes (4)	**Multiple Regression (14)**
Discrete Variable (5)	**Logistic Regression add-in (14)**
Binomial (5)	
Poisson (5)	**Moving Averages (16)**
Portfolio (5)	**Exponential Smoothing (16)**
Hypergeometric (5)	**Exponential Trend (16)**
Normal (6)	**Differences (16)**
NPP (6)	**Lagged Predictors (16)**
Exponential (6)	**Forecasting Comparison (16)**
SDS (7)	
CIE sigma known (8)	

Digital Cases, Online Topics, Online Chapters and Supplemental Files

These files use the Portable Document Format (PDF) that are best viewed using the latest version of Adobe Reader (**get.adobe.com/reader/**).

Visual Explorations

Visual Explorations are workbooks that interactively demonstrate various key statistical concepts. Three workbooks are add-in workbooks that are stored in the **.xlam** add-in format. Using these add-in workbooks with Microsoft Windows Excels requires the security settings discussed in Appendix D. The Visual Explorations workbooks are:

> **VE-Normal Distribution (add-in)**
> **VE-Sampling Distribution (add-in)**
> **VE-Simple Linear Regression (add-in)**
> **VE-Variability**

C.4 PHStat

PHStat is the Pearson Education statistics add-in for Microsoft Excel that simplifies the task of using Excel as you learn business statistics. PHStat comes packaged as a zip file archive that you download and unzip to the folder of your choice. The archive contains:

PHStat.xlam, the main add-in workbook.

PHStat readme.pdf   Explains the technical requirements, and setup and troubleshooting procedures for PHStat (PDF format).

PHStatHelp.chm   The integrated help system for users of Microsoft Windows Excel.

PHStatHelp.pdf   The help system as a PDF format file.

PHStatHelp.epub   The help system in Open Publication Structure eBook format.

The zip archive containing the files that comprise PHStat can be downloaded using the Section C.2 instructions (requires an access code as explained in that section). The PHStat readme file is also separately available for download as Section C.2 discusses and this separate download does not require an access code.

Configuring Microsoft Excel

Use the information and instructions in this appendix to avoid the common types of technical problems that could impede your use of Microsoft Excel with this book. Pay particular attention to this appendix if you are responsible for installing your own copy of Microsoft Excel and maintaining your own system. If you use a computer system that others maintain, such as a typical corporate computer or one you might find in an academic lab, be prepared to show this appendix to the IT person that oversees the system you use. If you plan to use PHStat, also review the PHStat readme file for any late-breaking developments that affect configuration.

D.1 Getting Microsoft Excel Ready for Use

You must have an up-to-date, properly licensed–copy of Microsoft Excel in order to work through the examples and solve the problems in this book as well as to take advantage of the Excel-related files that Appendix C discusses. Also determine if you will need to install the Analysis ToolPak and Solver add-ins that Microsoft supplies and that are *not* automatically installed with every copy of Excel. (There is no Analysis ToolPak for OS X Excel 2011.) If you plan to use PHStat, use the Section C.2 instructions to download PHStat from the PHStat home page.

  If you need to install a new copy of Microsoft Excel on a Microsoft Windows computer system, choose the 32-bit version and not the 64-bit version *even if you have a 64-bit version of a Microsoft Windows operating system.* Only install the 64-bit version if you plan to use very large sets of data, including big data collections, with Excel.

D.2 Checking for the Presence of the Analysis ToolPak or Solver Add-Ins

You will need to use the Analysis ToolPak add-in if you plan to use the *Analysis ToolPak* Excel Guide instructions. If you plan to use Excel to study logistic regression (see Section 14.7), you will need to use the Solver add-in. These Microsoft-supplied add-ins are available for all currently supported Excel versions, with the exception of OS X Excel 2011, for which no Analysis ToolPak exists.

  To check for the presence of the Analysis ToolPak or Solver add-ins in Microsoft Windows Excel:

1. Select **File ➔ Options**.

In the Excel Options dialog box:

2. Click **Add-Ins** in the left pane and look for the entry **Analysis ToolPak** (or **Solver Add-in**) in the right pane, under **Active Application Add-ins**.

3. If the entry appears, click **OK**.

4. If the entry does not appear in the **Active Application Add-ins** list, select **Excel Add-ins** from the **Manage** drop-down list and then click **Go**.

5. In the Add-Ins dialog box, check **Analysis ToolPak** (or **Solver Add-in**) in the **Add-Ins available** list and click **OK**.

If the Add-Ins available list does not include a Microsoft-supplied add-in that you need, rerun the Microsoft Office setup program to install the missing add-in.

  To check for the presence of the Analysis ToolPak or Solver add-ins in OS X Excel 2016:

1. Select **Tools ➔ Options**.

2. In the Adds-Ins dialog box, check **Analysis ToolPak** (or **Solver Add-In**) in the **Add-Ins available** list and click **OK**.

  If the Add-Ins available list does not include a Microsoft-supplied add-in that you need, click **Browse** to locate the add-in. If a message appears that states that the add-in is not currently installed on your Mac, click **Yes** to install the add-in. Then exit Excel and restart Excel.

  To check for the presence of the Solver add-in in OS X Excel 2011, follow step 1 and in the Add-Ins dialog box, check **Solver.Xlam** and then click **OK**. If the solver add-in is missing, verify that your copy of OS X Excel 2011 is up to date. (Excel 2011, as originally released, did not contain this add-in, but a subsequent update added this add-in to Excel 2011.)

D.3 Configuring Microsoft Windows Excel Security Setttings

If you plan to use PHStat, one of the Visual Explorations add-in workbooks (see Appendix C), or the logistic regression add-in (see Section EG14.7) and plan to use a Microsoft Windows Excel version, you must configure the Excel security settings to ensure that these add-ins function properly. (OS X Excel versions have no security settings to configure.)

To configure the security settings for these add-ins supplied by Pearson:

1. Select **File → Options**.

In the Excel Options dialog box (shown below):

2. Click **Trust Center** in the left pane and then click **Trust Center Settings** in the right pane.

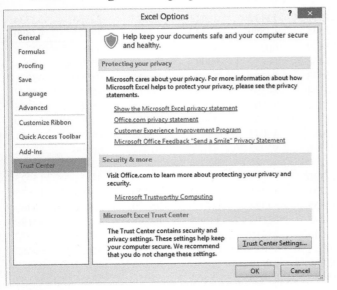

In the Trust Center dialog box:

3. Click **Add-ins** in the next left pane, and in the Add-ins right pane clear all of the checkboxes (shown below).

4. Click **Macro Settings** in the left pane, and in the Macro Settings right pane click **Disable all macros with notification** and check **Trust access to the VBA object model** (shown below).

5. Click **OK** to close the Trust Center dialog box.

Back in the Excel Options dialog box:

6. Click **OK** to finish.

On some systems that have stringent security settings, you might need to modify step 4. For such systems, in step 4, also click **Trusted Locations** in the left pane and then, in the Trusted Locations right pane, click **Add new location** to add the folder path that you chose to store the PHStat or Visual Explorations add-in files.

D.4 Opening Pearson-Supplied Add-Ins

When you open either PHStat, one of the Visual Explorations add-in workbooks, or the logistic regression add-in, Excel displays a security notice dialog box similar to the ones shown for Microsoft Windows and OS X below.

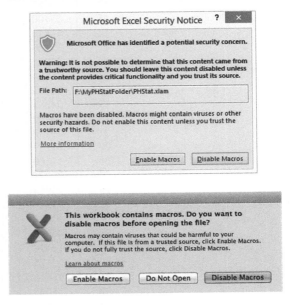

Click **Enable Macros**, which is *not* the default choice, to enable the add-in. The Pearson-supplied add-ins will add a menu to either the Add-Ins tab (Microsoft Windows Excel) or the Apple menu bar (OS X Excel).

If you are using PHStat and fail to see the PHStat menu, review the Appendix G PHStat FAQs or contact Pearson 24/7 technical support for assistance.

Tables

TABLE E.1
Table of Random
Numbers

Row	00000 12345	00001 67890	11111 12345	11112 67890	22222 12345	22223 67890	33333 12345	33334 67890
01	49280	88924	35779	00283	81163	07275	89863	02348
02	61870	41657	07468	08612	98083	97349	20775	45091
03	43898	65923	25078	86129	78496	97653	91550	08078
04	62993	93912	30454	84598	56095	20664	12872	64647
05	33850	58555	51438	85507	71865	79488	76783	31708
06	97340	03364	88472	04334	63919	36394	11095	92470
07	70543	29776	10087	10072	55980	64688	68239	20461
08	89382	93809	00796	95945	34101	81277	66090	88872
09	37818	72142	67140	50785	22380	16703	53362	44940
10	60430	22834	14130	96593	23298	56203	92671	15925
11	82975	66158	84731	19436	55790	69229	28661	13675
12	30987	71938	40355	54324	08401	26299	49420	59208
13	55700	24586	93247	32596	11865	63397	44251	43189
14	14756	23997	78643	75912	83832	32768	18928	57070
15	32166	53251	70654	92827	63491	04233	33825	69662
16	23236	73751	31888	81718	06546	83246	47651	04877
17	45794	26926	15130	82455	78305	55058	52551	47182
18	09893	20505	14225	68514	47427	56788	96297	78822
19	54382	74598	91499	14523	68479	27686	46162	83554
20	94750	89923	37089	20048	80336	94598	26940	36858
21	70297	34135	53140	33340	42050	82341	44104	82949
22	85157	47954	32979	26575	57600	40881	12250	73742
23	11100	02340	12860	74697	96644	89439	28707	25815
24	36871	50775	30592	57143	17381	68856	25853	35041
25	23913	48357	63308	16090	51690	54607	72407	55538
26	79348	36085	27973	65157	07456	22255	25626	57054
27	92074	54641	53673	54421	18130	60103	69593	49464
28	06873	21440	75593	41373	49502	17972	82578	16364
29	12478	37622	99659	31065	83613	69889	58869	29571
30	57175	55564	65411	42547	70457	03426	72937	83792
31	91616	11075	80103	07831	59309	13276	26710	73000
32	78025	73539	14621	39044	47450	03197	12787	47709
33	27587	67228	80145	10175	12822	86687	65530	49325
34	16690	20427	04251	64477	73709	73945	92396	68263
35	70183	58065	65489	31833	82093	16747	10386	59293
36	90730	35385	15679	99742	50866	78028	75573	67257
37	10934	93242	13431	24590	02770	48582	00906	58595
38	82462	30166	79613	47416	13389	80268	05085	96666
39	27463	10433	07606	16285	93699	60912	94532	95632
40	02979	52997	09079	92709	90110	47506	53693	49892
41	46888	69929	75233	52507	32097	37594	10067	67327
42	53638	83161	08289	12639	08141	12640	28437	09268
43	82433	61427	17239	89160	19666	08814	37841	12847
44	35766	31672	50082	22795	66948	65581	84393	15890
45	10853	42581	08792	13257	61973	24450	52351	16602
46	20341	27398	72906	63955	17276	10646	74692	48438
47	54458	90542	77563	51839	52901	53355	83281	19177
48	26337	66530	16687	35179	46560	00123	44546	79896
49	34314	23729	85264	05575	96855	23820	11091	79821
50	28603	10708	68933	34189	92166	15181	66628	58599

TABLE E.1
Table of Random
Numbers (*continued*)

Row	00000 12345	00001 67890	11111 12345	11112 67890	22222 12345	22223 67890	33333 12345	33334 67890
51	66194	28926	99547	16625	45515	67953	12108	57846
52	78240	43195	24837	32511	70880	22070	52622	61881
53	00833	88000	67299	68215	11274	55624	32991	17436
54	12111	86683	61270	58036	64192	90611	15145	01748
55	47189	99951	05755	03834	43782	90599	40282	51417
56	76396	72486	62423	27618	84184	78922	73561	52818
57	46409	17469	32483	09083	76175	19985	26309	91536
58	74626	22111	87286	46772	42243	68046	44250	42439
59	34450	81974	93723	49023	58432	67083	36876	93391
60	36327	72135	33005	28701	34710	49359	50693	89311
61	74185	77536	84825	09934	99103	09325	67389	45869
62	12296	41623	62873	37943	25584	09609	63360	47270
63	90822	60280	88925	99610	42772	60561	76873	04117
64	72121	79152	96591	90305	10189	79778	68016	13747
65	95268	41377	25684	08151	61816	58555	54305	86189
66	92603	09091	75884	93424	72586	88903	30061	14457
67	18813	90291	05275	01223	79607	95426	34900	09778
68	38840	26903	28624	67157	51986	42865	14508	49315
69	05959	33836	53758	16562	41081	38012	41230	20528
70	85141	21155	99212	32685	51403	31926	69813	58781
71	75047	59643	31074	38172	03718	32119	69506	67143
72	30752	95260	68032	62871	58781	34143	68790	69766
73	22986	82575	42187	62295	84295	30634	66562	31442
74	99439	86692	90348	66036	48399	73451	26698	39437
75	20389	93029	11881	71685	65452	89047	63669	02656
76	39249	05173	68256	36359	20250	68686	05947	09335
77	96777	33605	29481	20063	09398	01843	35139	61344
78	04860	32918	10798	50492	52655	33359	94713	28393
79	41613	42375	00403	03656	77580	87772	86877	57085
80	17930	00794	53836	53692	67135	98102	61912	11246
81	24649	31845	25736	75231	83808	98917	93829	99430
82	79899	34061	54308	59358	56462	58166	97302	86828
83	76801	49594	81002	30397	52728	15101	72070	33706
84	36239	63636	38140	65731	39788	06872	38971	53363
85	07392	64449	17886	63632	53995	17574	22247	62607
86	67133	04181	33874	98835	67453	59734	76381	63455
87	77759	31504	32832	70861	15152	29733	75371	39174
88	85992	72268	42920	20810	29361	51423	90306	73574
89	79553	75952	54116	65553	47139	60579	09165	85490
90	41101	17336	48951	53674	17880	45260	08575	49321
91	36191	17095	32123	91576	84221	78902	82010	30847
92	62329	63898	23268	74283	26091	68409	69704	82267
93	14751	13151	93115	01437	56945	89661	67680	79790
94	48462	59278	44185	29616	76537	19589	83139	28454
95	29435	88105	59651	44391	74588	55114	80834	85686
96	28340	29285	12965	14821	80425	16602	44653	70467
97	02167	58940	27149	80242	10587	79786	34959	75339
98	17864	00991	39557	54981	23588	81914	37609	13128
99	79675	80605	60059	35862	00254	36546	21545	78179
100	72335	82037	92003	34100	29879	46613	89720	13274

Source: Partially extracted from the Rand Corporation, *A Million Random Digits with 100,000 Normal Deviates* (Glencoe, IL, The Free Press, 1955).

TABLE E.2
The Cumulative Standardized Normal Distribution

Entry represents area under the cumulative standardized
normal distribution from $-\infty$ to Z

	Cumulative Probabilities									
Z	0.00	0.01	0.02	0.03	0.04	0.05	0.06	0.07	0.08	0.09
−6.0	0.000000001									
−5.5	0.000000019									
−5.0	0.000000287									
−4.5	0.000003398									
−4.0	0.000031671									
−3.9	0.00005	0.00005	0.00004	0.00004	0.00004	0.00004	0.00004	0.00004	0.00003	0.00003
−3.8	0.00007	0.00007	0.00007	0.00006	0.00006	0.00006	0.00006	0.00005	0.00005	0.00005
−3.7	0.00011	0.00010	0.00010	0.00010	0.00009	0.00009	0.00008	0.00008	0.00008	0.00008
−3.6	0.00016	0.00015	0.00015	0.00014	0.00014	0.00013	0.00013	0.00012	0.00012	0.00011
−3.5	0.00023	0.00022	0.00022	0.00021	0.00020	0.00019	0.00019	0.00018	0.00017	0.00017
−3.4	0.00034	0.00032	0.00031	0.00030	0.00029	0.00028	0.00027	0.00026	0.00025	0.00024
−3.3	0.00048	0.00047	0.00045	0.00043	0.00042	0.00040	0.00039	0.00038	0.00036	0.00035
−3.2	0.00069	0.00066	0.00064	0.00062	0.00060	0.00058	0.00056	0.00054	0.00052	0.00050
−3.1	0.00097	0.00094	0.00090	0.00087	0.00084	0.00082	0.00079	0.00076	0.00074	0.00071
−3.0	0.00135	0.00131	0.00126	0.00122	0.00118	0.00114	0.00111	0.00107	0.00103	0.00100
−2.9	0.0019	0.0018	0.0018	0.0017	0.0016	0.0016	0.0015	0.0015	0.0014	0.0014
−2.8	0.0026	0.0025	0.0024	0.0023	0.0023	0.0022	0.0021	0.0021	0.0020	0.0019
−2.7	0.0035	0.0034	0.0033	0.0032	0.0031	0.0030	0.0029	0.0028	0.0027	0.0026
−2.6	0.0047	0.0045	0.0044	0.0043	0.0041	0.0040	0.0039	0.0038	0.0037	0.0036
−2.5	0.0062	0.0060	0.0059	0.0057	0.0055	0.0054	0.0052	0.0051	0.0049	0.0048
−2.4	0.0082	0.0080	0.0078	0.0075	0.0073	0.0071	0.0069	0.0068	0.0066	0.0064
−2.3	0.0107	0.0104	0.0102	0.0099	0.0096	0.0094	0.0091	0.0089	0.0087	0.0084
−2.2	0.0139	0.0136	0.0132	0.0129	0.0125	0.0122	0.0119	0.0116	0.0113	0.0110
−2.1	0.0179	0.0174	0.0170	0.0166	0.0162	0.0158	0.0154	0.0150	0.0146	0.0143
−2.0	0.0228	0.0222	0.0217	0.0212	0.0207	0.0202	0.0197	0.0192	0.0188	0.0183
−1.9	0.0287	0.0281	0.0274	0.0268	0.0262	0.0256	0.0250	0.0244	0.0239	0.0233
−1.8	0.0359	0.0351	0.0344	0.0336	0.0329	0.0322	0.0314	0.0307	0.0301	0.0294
−1.7	0.0446	0.0436	0.0427	0.0418	0.0409	0.0401	0.0392	0.0384	0.0375	0.0367
−1.6	0.0548	0.0537	0.0526	0.0516	0.0505	0.0495	0.0485	0.0475	0.0465	0.0455
−1.5	0.0668	0.0655	0.0643	0.0630	0.0618	0.0606	0.0594	0.0582	0.0571	0.0559
−1.4	0.0808	0.0793	0.0778	0.0764	0.0749	0.0735	0.0721	0.0708	0.0694	0.0681
−1.3	0.0968	0.0951	0.0934	0.0918	0.0901	0.0885	0.0869	0.0853	0.0838	0.0823
−1.2	0.1151	0.1131	0.1112	0.1093	0.1075	0.1056	0.1038	0.1020	0.1003	0.0985
−1.1	0.1357	0.1335	0.1314	0.1292	0.1271	0.1251	0.1230	0.1210	0.1190	0.1170
−1.0	0.1587	0.1562	0.1539	0.1515	0.1492	0.1469	0.1446	0.1423	0.1401	0.1379
−0.9	0.1841	0.1814	0.1788	0.1762	0.1736	0.1711	0.1685	0.1660	0.1635	0.1611
−0.8	0.2119	0.2090	0.2061	0.2033	0.2005	0.1977	0.1949	0.1922	0.1894	0.1867
−0.7	0.2420	0.2388	0.2358	0.2327	0.2296	0.2266	0.2236	0.2206	0.2177	0.2148
−0.6	0.2743	0.2709	0.2676	0.2643	0.2611	0.2578	0.2546	0.2514	0.2482	0.2451
−0.5	0.3085	0.3050	0.3015	0.2981	0.2946	0.2912	0.2877	0.2843	0.2810	0.2776
−0.4	0.3446	0.3409	0.3372	0.3336	0.3300	0.3264	0.3228	0.3192	0.3156	0.3121
−0.3	0.3821	0.3783	0.3745	0.3707	0.3669	0.3632	0.3594	0.3557	0.3520	0.3483
−0.2	0.4207	0.4168	0.4129	0.4090	0.4052	0.4013	0.3974	0.3936	0.3897	0.3859
−0.1	0.4602	0.4562	0.4522	0.4483	0.4443	0.4404	0.4364	0.4325	0.4286	0.4247
−0.0	0.5000	0.4960	0.4920	0.4880	0.4840	0.4801	0.4761	0.4721	0.4681	0.4641

TABLE E.2

The Cumulative Standardized Normal Distribution (*continued*)

Entry represents area under the cumulative standardized
normal distribution from $-\infty$ to Z

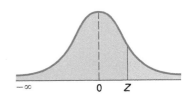

					Cumulative Probabilities					
Z	0.00	0.01	0.02	0.03	0.04	0.05	0.06	0.07	0.08	0.09
0.0	0.5000	0.5040	0.5080	0.5120	0.5160	0.5199	0.5239	0.5279	0.5319	0.5359
0.1	0.5398	0.5438	0.5478	0.5517	0.5557	0.5596	0.5636	0.5675	0.5714	0.5753
0.2	0.5793	0.5832	0.5871	0.5910	0.5948	0.5987	0.6026	0.6064	0.6103	0.6141
0.3	0.6179	0.6217	0.6255	0.6293	0.6331	0.6368	0.6406	0.6443	0.6480	0.6517
0.4	0.6554	0.6591	0.6628	0.6664	0.6700	0.6736	0.6772	0.6808	0.6844	0.6879
0.5	0.6915	0.6950	0.6985	0.7019	0.7054	0.7088	0.7123	0.7157	0.7190	0.7224
0.6	0.7257	0.7291	0.7324	0.7357	0.7389	0.7422	0.7454	0.7486	0.7518	0.7549
0.7	0.7580	0.7612	0.7642	0.7673	0.7704	0.7734	0.7764	0.7794	0.7823	0.7852
0.8	0.7881	0.7910	0.7939	0.7967	0.7995	0.8023	0.8051	0.8078	0.8106	0.8133
0.9	0.8159	0.8186	0.8212	0.8238	0.8264	0.8289	0.8315	0.8340	0.8365	0.8389
1.0	0.8413	0.8438	0.8461	0.8485	0.8508	0.8531	0.8554	0.8577	0.8599	0.8621
1.1	0.8643	0.8665	0.8686	0.8708	0.8729	0.8749	0.8770	0.8790	0.8810	0.8830
1.2	0.8849	0.8869	0.8888	0.8907	0.8925	0.8944	0.8962	0.8980	0.8997	0.9015
1.3	0.9032	0.9049	0.9066	0.9082	0.9099	0.9115	0.9131	0.9147	0.9162	0.9177
1.4	0.9192	0.9207	0.9222	0.9236	0.9251	0.9265	0.9279	0.9292	0.9306	0.9319
1.5	0.9332	0.9345	0.9357	0.9370	0.9382	0.9394	0.9406	0.9418	0.9429	0.9441
1.6	0.9452	0.9463	0.9474	0.9484	0.9495	0.9505	0.9515	0.9525	0.9535	0.9545
1.7	0.9554	0.9564	0.9573	0.9582	0.9591	0.9599	0.9608	0.9616	0.9625	0.9633
1.8	0.9641	0.9649	0.9656	0.9664	0.9671	0.9678	0.9686	0.9693	0.9699	0.9706
1.9	0.9713	0.9719	0.9726	0.9732	0.9738	0.9744	0.9750	0.9756	0.9761	0.9767
2.0	0.9772	0.9778	0.9783	0.9788	0.9793	0.9798	0.9803	0.9808	0.9812	0.9817
2.1	0.9821	0.9826	0.9830	0.9834	0.9838	0.9842	0.9846	0.9850	0.9854	0.9857
2.2	0.9861	0.9864	0.9868	0.9871	0.9875	0.9878	0.9881	0.9884	0.9887	0.9890
2.3	0.9893	0.9896	0.9898	0.9901	0.9904	0.9906	0.9909	0.9911	0.9913	0.9916
2.4	0.9918	0.9920	0.9922	0.9925	0.9927	0.9929	0.9931	0.9932	0.9934	0.9936
2.5	0.9938	0.9940	0.9941	0.9943	0.9945	0.9946	0.9948	0.9949	0.9951	0.9952
2.6	0.9953	0.9955	0.9956	0.9957	0.9959	0.9960	0.9961	0.9962	0.9963	0.9964
2.7	0.9965	0.9966	0.9967	0.9968	0.9969	0.9970	0.9971	0.9972	0.9973	0.9974
2.8	0.9974	0.9975	0.9976	0.9977	0.9977	0.9978	0.9979	0.9979	0.9980	0.9981
2.9	0.9981	0.9982	0.9982	0.9983	0.9984	0.9984	0.9985	0.9985	0.9986	0.9986
3.0	0.99865	0.99869	0.99874	0.99878	0.99882	0.99886	0.99889	0.99893	0.99897	0.99900
3.1	0.99903	0.99906	0.99910	0.99913	0.99916	0.99918	0.99921	0.99924	0.99926	0.99929
3.2	0.99931	0.99934	0.99936	0.99938	0.99940	0.99942	0.99944	0.99946	0.99948	0.99950
3.3	0.99952	0.99953	0.99955	0.99957	0.99958	0.99960	0.99961	0.99962	0.99964	0.99965
3.4	0.99966	0.99968	0.99969	0.99970	0.99971	0.99972	0.99973	0.99974	0.99975	0.99976
3.5	0.99977	0.99978	0.99978	0.99979	0.99980	0.99981	0.99981	0.99982	0.99983	0.99983
3.6	0.99984	0.99985	0.99985	0.99986	0.99986	0.99987	0.99987	0.99988	0.99988	0.99989
3.7	0.99989	0.99990	0.99990	0.99990	0.99991	0.99991	0.99992	0.99992	0.99992	0.99992
3.8	0.99993	0.99993	0.99993	0.99994	0.99994	0.99994	0.99994	0.99995	0.99995	0.99995
3.9	0.99995	0.99995	0.99996	0.99996	0.99996	0.99996	0.99996	0.99996	0.99997	0.99997
4.0	0.999968329									
4.5	0.999996602									
5.0	0.999999713									
5.5	0.999999981									
6.0	0.999999999									

TABLE E.3

Critical Values of t

For a particular number of degrees of freedom, entry represents
the critical value of t corresponding to the cumulative probability
$(1 - \alpha)$ and a specified upper-tail area (α).

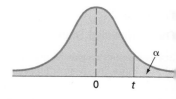

Degrees of Freedom	Cumulative Probabilities					
	0.75	0.90	0.95	0.975	0.99	0.995
	Upper-Tail Areas					
	0.25	0.10	0.05	0.025	0.01	0.005
1	1.0000	3.0777	6.3138	12.7062	31.8207	63.6574
2	0.8165	1.8856	2.9200	4.3027	6.9646	9.9248
3	0.7649	1.6377	2.3534	3.1824	4.5407	5.8409
4	0.7407	1.5332	2.1318	2.7764	3.7469	4.6041
5	0.7267	1.4759	2.0150	2.5706	3.3649	4.0322
6	0.7176	1.4398	1.9432	2.4469	3.1427	3.7074
7	0.7111	1.4149	1.8946	2.3646	2.9980	3.4995
8	0.7064	1.3968	1.8595	2.3060	2.8965	3.3554
9	0.7027	1.3830	1.8331	2.2622	2.8214	3.2498
10	0.6998	1.3722	1.8125	2.2281	2.7638	3.1693
11	0.6974	1.3634	1.7959	2.2010	2.7181	3.1058
12	0.6955	1.3562	1.7823	2.1788	2.6810	3.0545
13	0.6938	1.3502	1.7709	2.1604	2.6503	3.0123
14	0.6924	1.3450	1.7613	2.1448	2.6245	2.9768
15	0.6912	1.3406	1.7531	2.1315	2.6025	2.9467
16	0.6901	1.3368	1.7459	2.1199	2.5835	2.9208
17	0.6892	1.3334	1.7396	2.1098	2.5669	2.8982
18	0.6884	1.3304	1.7341	2.1009	2.5524	2.8784
19	0.6876	1.3277	1.7291	2.0930	2.5395	2.8609
20	0.6870	1.3253	1.7247	2.0860	2.5280	2.8453
21	0.6864	1.3232	1.7207	2.0796	2.5177	2.8314
22	0.6858	1.3212	1.7171	2.0739	2.5083	2.8188
23	0.6853	1.3195	1.7139	2.0687	2.4999	2.8073
24	0.6848	1.3178	1.7109	2.0639	2.4922	2.7969
25	0.6844	1.3163	1.7081	2.0595	2.4851	2.7874
26	0.6840	1.3150	1.7056	2.0555	2.4786	2.7787
27	0.6837	1.3137	1.7033	2.0518	2.4727	2.7707
28	0.6834	1.3125	1.7011	2.0484	2.4671	2.7633
29	0.6830	1.3114	1.6991	2.0452	2.4620	2.7564
30	0.6828	1.3104	1.6973	2.0423	2.4573	2.7500
31	0.6825	1.3095	1.6955	2.0395	2.4528	2.7440
32	0.6822	1.3086	1.6939	2.0369	2.4487	2.7385
33	0.6820	1.3077	1.6924	2.0345	2.4448	2.7333
34	0.6818	1.3070	1.6909	2.0322	2.4411	2.7284
35	0.6816	1.3062	1.6896	2.0301	2.4377	2.7238
36	0.6814	1.3055	1.6883	2.0281	2.4345	2.7195
37	0.6812	1.3049	1.6871	2.0262	2.4314	2.7154
38	0.6810	1.3042	1.6860	2.0244	2.4286	2.7116
39	0.6808	1.3036	1.6849	2.0227	2.4258	2.7079
40	0.6807	1.3031	1.6839	2.0211	2.4233	2.7045
41	0.6805	1.3025	1.6829	2.0195	2.4208	2.7012
42	0.6804	1.3020	1.6820	2.0181	2.4185	2.6981
43	0.6802	1.3016	1.6811	2.0167	2.4163	2.6951
44	0.6801	1.3011	1.6802	2.0154	2.4141	2.6923
45	0.6800	1.3006	1.6794	2.0141	2.4121	2.6896
46	0.6799	1.3002	1.6787	2.0129	2.4102	2.6870
47	0.6797	1.2998	1.6779	2.0117	2.4083	2.6846
48	0.6796	1.2994	1.6772	2.0106	2.4066	2.6822
49	0.6795	1.2991	1.6766	2.0096	2.4049	2.6800
50	0.6794	1.2987	1.6759	2.0086	2.4033	2.6778

TABLE E.3

Critical Values of *t* (*continued*)

For a particular number of degrees of freedom, entry represents the critical value of *t* corresponding to the cumulative probability $(1 - \alpha)$ and a specified upper-tail area (α).

Degrees of Freedom	Cumulative Probabilities					
	0.75	0.90	0.95	0.975	0.99	0.995
	Upper-Tail Areas					
	0.25	0.10	0.05	0.025	0.01	0.005
51	0.6793	1.2984	1.6753	2.0076	2.4017	2.6757
52	0.6792	1.2980	1.6747	2.0066	2.4002	2.6737
53	0.6791	1.2977	1.6741	2.0057	2.3988	2.6718
54	0.6791	1.2974	1.6736	2.0049	2.3974	2.6700
55	0.6790	1.2971	1.6730	2.0040	2.3961	2.6682
56	0.6789	1.2969	1.6725	2.0032	2.3948	2.6665
57	0.6788	1.2966	1.6720	2.0025	2.3936	2.6649
58	0.6787	1.2963	1.6716	2.0017	2.3924	2.6633
59	0.6787	1.2961	1.6711	2.0010	2.3912	2.6618
60	0.6786	1.2958	1.6706	2.0003	2.3901	2.6603
61	0.6785	1.2956	1.6702	1.9996	2.3890	2.6589
62	0.6785	1.2954	1.6698	1.9990	2.3880	2.6575
63	0.6784	1.2951	1.6694	1.9983	2.3870	2.6561
64	0.6783	1.2949	1.6690	1.9977	2.3860	2.6549
65	0.6783	1.2947	1.6686	1.9971	2.3851	2.6536
66	0.6782	1.2945	1.6683	1.9966	2.3842	2.6524
67	0.6782	1.2943	1.6679	1.9960	2.3833	2.6512
68	0.6781	1.2941	1.6676	1.9955	2.3824	2.6501
69	0.6781	1.2939	1.6672	1.9949	2.3816	2.6490
70	0.6780	1.2938	1.6669	1.9944	2.3808	2.6479
71	0.6780	1.2936	1.6666	1.9939	2.3800	2.6469
72	0.6779	1.2934	1.6663	1.9935	2.3793	2.6459
73	0.6779	1.2933	1.6660	1.9930	2.3785	2.6449
74	0.6778	1.2931	1.6657	1.9925	2.3778	2.6439
75	0.6778	1.2929	1.6654	1.9921	2.3771	2.6430
76	0.6777	1.2928	1.6652	1.9917	2.3764	2.6421
77	0.6777	1.2926	1.6649	1.9913	2.3758	2.6412
78	0.6776	1.2925	1.6646	1.9908	2.3751	2.6403
79	0.6776	1.2924	1.6644	1.9905	2.3745	2.6395
80	0.6776	1.2922	1.6641	1.9901	2.3739	2.6387
81	0.6775	1.2921	1.6639	1.9897	2.3733	2.6379
82	0.6775	1.2920	1.6636	1.9893	2.3727	2.6371
83	0.6775	1.2918	1.6634	1.9890	2.3721	2.6364
84	0.6774	1.2917	1.6632	1.9886	2.3716	2.6356
85	0.6774	1.2916	1.6630	1.9883	2.3710	2.6349
86	0.6774	1.2915	1.6628	1.9879	2.3705	2.6342
87	0.6773	1.2914	1.6626	1.9876	2.3700	2.6335
88	0.6773	1.2912	1.6624	1.9873	2.3695	2.6329
89	0.6773	1.2911	1.6622	1.9870	2.3690	2.6322
90	0.6772	1.2910	1.6620	1.9867	2.3685	2.6316
91	0.6772	1.2909	1.6618	1.9864	2.3680	2.6309
92	0.6772	1.2908	1.6616	1.9861	2.3676	2.6303
93	0.6771	1.2907	1.6614	1.9858	2.3671	2.6297
94	0.6771	1.2906	1.6612	1.9855	2.3667	2.6291
95	0.6771	1.2905	1.6611	1.9853	2.3662	2.6286
96	0.6771	1.2904	1.6609	1.9850	2.3658	2.6280
97	0.6770	1.2903	1.6607	1.9847	2.3654	2.6275
98	0.6770	1.2902	1.6606	1.9845	2.3650	2.6269
99	0.6770	1.2902	1.6604	1.9842	2.3646	2.6264
100	0.6770	1.2901	1.6602	1.9840	2.3642	2.6259
110	0.6767	1.2893	1.6588	1.9818	2.3607	2.6213
120	0.6765	1.2886	1.6577	1.9799	2.3578	2.6174
∞	0.6745	1.2816	1.6449	1.9600	2.3263	2.5758

TABLE E.4

Critical Values of χ^2

For a particular number of degrees of freedom, entry represents the critical value of χ^2 corresponding to the cumulative probability $(1 - \alpha)$ and a specified upper-tail area (α).

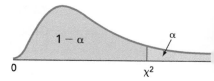

Degrees of Freedom	Cumulative Probabilities												
	0.005	0.01	0.025	0.05	0.10	0.25	0.75	0.90	0.95	0.975	0.99	0.995
	Upper-Tail Areas (α)											
	0.995	0.99	0.975	0.95	0.90	0.75	0.25	0.10	0.05	0.025	0.01	0.005
1			0.001	0.004	0.016	0.102	1.323	2.706	3.841	5.024	6.635	7.879
2	0.010	0.020	0.051	0.103	0.211	0.575	2.773	4.605	5.991	7.378	9.210	10.597
3	0.072	0.115	0.216	0.352	0.584	1.213	4.108	6.251	7.815	9.348	11.345	12.838
4	0.207	0.297	0.484	0.711	1.064	1.923	5.385	7.779	9.488	11.143	13.277	14.860
5	0.412	0.554	0.831	1.145	1.610	2.675	6.626	9.236	11.071	12.833	15.086	16.750
6	0.676	0.872	1.237	1.635	2.204	3.455	7.841	10.645	12.592	14.449	16.812	18.548
7	0.989	1.239	1.690	2.167	2.833	4.255	9.037	12.017	14.067	16.013	18.475	20.278
8	1.344	1.646	2.180	2.733	3.490	5.071	10.219	13.362	15.507	17.535	20.090	21.955
9	1.735	2.088	2.700	3.325	4.168	5.899	11.389	14.684	16.919	19.023	21.666	23.589
10	2.156	2.558	3.247	3.940	4.865	6.737	12.549	15.987	18.307	20.483	23.209	25.188
11	2.603	3.053	3.816	4.575	5.578	7.584	13.701	17.275	19.675	21.920	24.725	26.757
12	3.074	3.571	4.404	5.226	6.304	8.438	14.845	18.549	21.026	23.337	26.217	28.299
13	3.565	4.107	5.009	5.892	7.042	9.299	15.984	19.812	22.362	24.736	27.688	29.819
14	4.075	4.660	5.629	6.571	7.790	10.165	17.117	21.064	23.685	26.119	29.141	31.319
15	4.601	5.229	6.262	7.261	8.547	11.037	18.245	22.307	24.996	27.488	30.578	32.801
16	5.142	5.812	6.908	7.962	9.312	11.912	19.369	23.542	26.296	28.845	32.000	34.267
17	5.697	6.408	7.564	8.672	10.085	12.792	20.489	24.769	27.587	30.191	33.409	35.718
18	6.265	7.015	8.231	9.390	10.865	13.675	21.605	25.989	28.869	31.526	34.805	37.156
19	6.844	7.633	8.907	10.117	11.651	14.562	22.718	27.204	30.144	32.852	36.191	38.582
20	7.434	8.260	9.591	10.851	12.443	15.452	23.828	28.412	31.410	34.170	37.566	39.997
21	8.034	8.897	10.283	11.591	13.240	16.344	24.935	29.615	32.671	35.479	38.932	41.401
22	8.643	9.542	10.982	12.338	14.042	17.240	26.039	30.813	33.924	36.781	40.289	42.796
23	9.260	10.196	11.689	13.091	14.848	18.137	27.141	32.007	35.172	38.076	41.638	44.181
24	9.886	10.856	12.401	13.848	15.659	19.037	28.241	33.196	36.415	39.364	42.980	45.559
25	10.520	11.524	13.120	14.611	16.473	19.939	29.339	34.382	37.652	40.646	44.314	46.928
26	11.160	12.198	13.844	15.379	17.292	20.843	30.435	35.563	38.885	41.923	45.642	48.290
27	11.808	12.879	14.573	16.151	18.114	21.749	31.528	36.741	40.113	43.194	46.963	49.645
28	12.461	13.565	15.308	16.928	18.939	22.657	32.620	37.916	41.337	44.461	48.278	50.993
29	13.121	14.257	16.047	17.708	19.768	23.567	33.711	39.087	42.557	45.722	49.588	52.336
30	13.787	14.954	16.791	18.493	20.599	24.478	34.800	40.256	43.773	46.979	50.892	53.672

For larger values of degrees of freedom (df) the expression $Z = \sqrt{2\chi^2} - \sqrt{2(df) - 1}$ may be used and the resulting upper-tail area can be found from the cumulative standardized normal distribution (Table E.2).

TABLE E.5

Critical Values of F

For a particular combination of numerator and denominator degrees of freedom, entry represents the critical values of F corresponding to the cumulative probability $(1 - \alpha)$ and a specified upper-tail area (α).

$\alpha = 0.05$

Cumulative Probabilities = 0.95

Upper-Tail Areas = 0.05

Numerator, df_1

Denominator df_2	1	2	3	4	5	6	7	8	9	10	12	15	20	24	30	40	60	120	∞
1	161.40	199.50	215.70	224.60	230.20	234.00	236.80	238.90	240.50	241.90	243.90	245.90	248.00	249.10	250.10	251.10	252.20	253.30	254.30
2	18.51	19.00	19.16	19.25	19.30	19.33	19.35	19.37	19.38	19.40	19.41	19.43	19.45	19.45	19.46	19.47	19.48	19.49	19.50
3	10.13	9.55	9.28	9.12	9.01	8.94	8.89	8.85	8.81	8.79	8.74	8.70	8.66	8.64	8.62	8.59	8.57	8.55	8.53
4	7.71	6.94	6.59	6.39	6.26	6.16	6.09	6.04	6.00	5.96	5.91	5.86	5.80	5.77	5.75	5.72	5.69	5.66	5.63
5	6.61	5.79	5.41	5.19	5.05	4.95	4.88	4.82	4.77	4.74	4.68	4.62	4.56	4.53	4.50	4.46	4.43	4.40	4.36
6	5.99	5.14	4.76	4.53	4.39	4.28	4.21	4.15	4.10	4.06	4.00	3.94	3.87	3.84	3.81	3.77	3.74	3.70	3.67
7	5.59	4.74	4.35	4.12	3.97	3.87	3.79	3.73	3.68	3.64	3.57	3.51	3.44	3.41	3.38	3.34	3.30	3.27	3.23
8	5.32	4.46	4.07	3.84	3.69	3.58	3.50	3.44	3.39	3.35	3.28	3.22	3.15	3.12	3.08	3.04	3.01	2.97	2.93
9	5.12	4.26	3.86	3.63	3.48	3.37	3.29	3.23	3.18	3.14	3.07	3.01	2.94	2.90	2.86	2.83	2.79	2.75	2.71
10	4.96	4.10	3.71	3.48	3.33	3.22	3.14	3.07	3.02	2.98	2.91	2.85	2.77	2.74	2.70	2.66	2.62	2.58	2.54
11	4.84	3.98	3.59	3.36	3.20	3.09	3.01	2.95	2.90	2.85	2.79	2.72	2.65	2.61	2.57	2.53	2.49	2.45	2.40
12	4.75	3.89	3.49	3.26	3.11	3.00	2.91	2.85	2.80	2.75	2.69	2.62	2.54	2.51	2.47	2.43	2.38	2.34	2.30
13	4.67	3.81	3.41	3.18	3.03	2.92	2.83	2.77	2.71	2.67	2.60	2.53	2.46	2.42	2.38	2.34	2.30	2.25	2.21
14	4.60	3.74	3.34	3.11	2.96	2.85	2.76	2.70	2.65	2.60	2.53	2.46	2.39	2.35	2.31	2.27	2.22	2.18	2.13
15	4.54	3.68	3.29	3.06	2.90	2.79	2.71	2.64	2.59	2.54	2.48	2.40	2.33	2.29	2.25	2.20	2.16	2.11	2.07
16	4.49	3.63	3.24	3.01	2.85	2.74	2.66	2.59	2.54	2.49	2.42	2.35	2.28	2.24	2.19	2.15	2.11	2.06	2.01
17	4.45	3.59	3.20	2.96	2.81	2.70	2.61	2.55	2.49	2.45	2.38	2.31	2.23	2.19	2.15	2.10	2.06	2.01	1.96
18	4.41	3.55	3.16	2.93	2.77	2.66	2.58	2.51	2.46	2.41	2.34	2.27	2.19	2.15	2.11	2.06	2.02	1.97	1.92
19	4.38	3.52	3.13	2.90	2.74	2.63	2.54	2.48	2.42	2.38	2.31	2.23	2.16	2.11	2.07	2.03	1.98	1.93	1.88
20	4.35	3.49	3.10	2.87	2.71	2.60	2.51	2.45	2.39	2.35	2.28	2.20	2.12	2.08	2.04	1.99	1.95	1.90	1.84
21	4.32	3.47	3.07	2.84	2.68	2.57	2.49	2.42	2.37	2.32	2.25	2.18	2.10	2.05	2.01	1.96	1.92	1.87	1.81
22	4.30	3.44	3.05	2.82	2.66	2.55	2.46	2.40	2.34	2.30	2.23	2.15	2.07	2.03	1.98	1.94	1.89	1.84	1.78
23	4.28	3.42	3.03	2.80	2.64	2.53	2.44	2.37	2.32	2.27	2.20	2.13	2.05	2.01	1.96	1.91	1.86	1.81	1.76
24	4.26	3.40	3.01	2.78	2.62	2.51	2.42	2.36	2.30	2.25	2.18	2.11	2.03	1.98	1.94	1.89	1.84	1.79	1.73
25	4.24	3.39	2.99	2.76	2.60	2.49	2.40	2.34	2.28	2.24	2.16	2.09	2.01	1.96	1.92	1.87	1.82	1.77	1.71
26	4.23	3.37	2.98	2.74	2.59	2.47	2.39	2.32	2.27	2.22	2.15	2.07	1.99	1.95	1.90	1.85	1.80	1.75	1.69
27	4.21	3.35	2.96	2.73	2.57	2.46	2.37	2.31	2.25	2.20	2.13	2.06	1.97	1.93	1.88	1.84	1.79	1.73	1.67
28	4.20	3.34	2.95	2.71	2.56	2.45	2.36	2.29	2.24	2.19	2.12	2.04	1.96	1.91	1.87	1.82	1.77	1.71	1.65
29	4.18	3.33	2.93	2.70	2.55	2.43	2.35	2.28	2.22	2.18	2.10	2.03	1.94	1.90	1.85	1.81	1.75	1.70	1.64
30	4.17	3.32	2.92	2.69	2.53	2.42	2.33	2.27	2.21	2.16	2.09	2.01	1.93	1.89	1.84	1.79	1.74	1.68	1.62
40	4.08	3.23	2.84	2.61	2.45	2.34	2.25	2.18	2.12	2.08	2.00	1.92	1.84	1.79	1.74	1.69	1.64	1.58	1.51
60	4.00	3.15	2.76	2.53	2.37	2.25	2.17	2.10	2.04	1.99	1.92	1.84	1.75	1.70	1.65	1.59	1.53	1.47	1.39
120	3.92	3.07	2.68	2.45	2.29	2.17	2.09	2.02	1.96	1.91	1.83	1.75	1.66	1.61	1.55	1.50	1.43	1.35	1.25
∞	3.84	3.00	2.60	2.37	2.21	2.10	2.01	1.94	1.88	1.83	1.75	1.67	1.57	1.52	1.46	1.39	1.32	1.22	1.00

(*continued*)

TABLE E.5

Critical Values of F (continued)

For a particular combination of numerator and denominator degrees of freedom, entry represents the critical values of F corresponding to the cumulative probability $(1 - \alpha)$ and a specified upper-tail area (α).

$\alpha = 0.025$

Cumulative Probabilities = 0.975

Upper-Tail Areas = 0.025

Numerator, df_1

Denominator, df_2	1	2	3	4	5	6	7	8	9	10	12	15	20	24	30	40	60	120	∞
1	647.80	799.50	864.20	899.60	921.80	937.10	948.20	956.70	963.30	968.60	976.70	984.90	993.10	997.20	1,001.00	1,006.00	1,010.00	1,014.00	1,018.00
2	38.51	39.00	39.17	39.25	39.30	39.33	39.36	39.39	39.39	39.40	39.41	39.43	39.45	39.46	39.46	39.47	39.48	39.49	39.50
3	17.44	16.04	15.44	15.10	14.88	14.73	14.62	14.54	14.47	14.42	14.34	14.25	14.17	14.12	14.08	14.04	13.99	13.95	13.90
4	12.22	10.65	9.98	9.60	9.36	9.20	9.07	8.98	8.90	8.84	8.75	8.66	8.56	8.51	8.46	8.41	8.36	8.31	8.26
5	10.01	8.43	7.76	7.39	7.15	6.98	6.85	6.76	6.68	6.62	6.52	6.43	6.33	6.28	6.23	6.18	6.12	6.07	6.02
6	8.81	7.26	6.60	6.23	5.99	5.82	5.70	5.60	5.52	5.46	5.37	5.27	5.17	5.12	5.07	5.01	4.96	4.90	4.85
7	8.07	6.54	5.89	5.52	5.29	5.12	4.99	4.90	4.82	4.76	4.67	4.57	4.47	4.42	4.36	4.31	4.25	4.20	4.14
8	7.57	6.06	5.42	5.05	4.82	4.65	4.53	4.43	4.36	4.30	4.20	4.10	4.00	3.95	3.89	3.84	3.78	3.73	3.67
9	7.21	5.71	5.08	4.72	4.48	4.32	4.20	4.10	4.03	3.96	3.87	3.77	3.67	3.61	3.56	3.51	3.45	3.39	3.33
10	6.94	5.46	4.83	4.47	4.24	4.07	3.95	3.85	3.78	3.72	3.62	3.52	3.42	3.37	3.31	3.26	3.20	3.14	3.08
11	6.72	5.26	4.63	4.28	4.04	3.88	3.76	3.66	3.59	3.53	3.43	3.33	3.23	3.17	3.12	3.06	3.00	2.94	2.88
12	6.55	5.10	4.47	4.12	3.89	3.73	3.61	3.51	3.44	3.37	3.28	3.18	3.07	3.02	2.96	2.91	2.85	2.79	2.72
13	6.41	4.97	4.35	4.00	3.77	3.60	3.48	3.39	3.31	3.25	3.15	3.05	2.95	2.89	2.84	2.78	2.72	2.66	2.60
14	6.30	4.86	4.24	3.89	3.66	3.50	3.38	3.29	3.21	3.15	3.05	2.95	2.84	2.79	2.73	2.67	2.61	2.55	2.49
15	6.20	4.77	4.15	3.80	3.58	3.41	3.29	3.20	3.12	3.06	2.96	2.86	2.76	2.70	2.64	2.59	2.52	2.46	2.40
16	6.12	4.69	4.08	3.73	3.50	3.34	3.22	3.12	3.05	2.99	2.89	2.79	2.68	2.63	2.57	2.51	2.45	2.38	2.32
17	6.04	4.62	4.01	3.66	3.44	3.28	3.16	3.06	2.98	2.92	2.82	2.72	2.62	2.56	2.50	2.44	2.38	2.32	2.25
18	5.98	4.56	3.95	3.61	3.38	3.22	3.10	3.01	2.93	2.87	2.77	2.67	2.56	2.50	2.44	2.38	2.32	2.26	2.19
19	5.92	4.51	3.90	3.56	3.33	3.17	3.05	2.96	2.88	2.82	2.72	2.62	2.51	2.45	2.39	2.33	2.27	2.20	2.13
20	5.87	4.46	3.86	3.51	3.29	3.13	3.01	2.91	2.84	2.77	2.68	2.57	2.46	2.41	2.35	2.29	2.22	2.16	2.09
21	5.83	4.42	3.82	3.48	3.25	3.09	2.97	2.87	2.80	2.73	2.64	2.53	2.42	2.37	2.31	2.25	2.18	2.11	2.04
22	5.79	4.38	3.78	3.44	3.22	3.05	2.93	2.84	2.76	2.70	2.60	2.50	2.39	2.33	2.27	2.21	2.14	2.08	2.00
23	5.75	4.35	3.75	3.41	3.18	3.02	2.90	2.81	2.73	2.67	2.57	2.47	2.36	2.30	2.24	2.18	2.11	2.04	1.97
24	5.72	4.32	3.72	3.38	3.15	2.99	2.87	2.78	2.70	2.64	2.54	2.44	2.33	2.27	2.21	2.15	2.08	2.01	1.94
25	5.69	4.29	3.69	3.35	3.13	2.97	2.85	2.75	2.68	2.61	2.51	2.41	2.30	2.24	2.18	2.12	2.05	1.98	1.91
26	5.66	4.27	3.67	3.33	3.10	2.94	2.82	2.73	2.65	2.59	2.49	2.39	2.28	2.22	2.16	2.09	2.03	1.95	1.88
27	5.63	4.24	3.65	3.31	3.08	2.92	2.80	2.71	2.63	2.57	2.47	2.36	2.25	2.19	2.13	2.07	2.00	1.93	1.85
28	5.61	4.22	3.63	3.29	3.06	2.90	2.78	2.69	2.61	2.55	2.45	2.34	2.23	2.17	2.11	2.05	1.98	1.91	1.83
29	5.59	4.20	3.61	3.27	3.04	2.88	2.76	2.67	2.59	2.53	2.43	2.32	2.21	2.15	2.09	2.03	1.96	1.89	1.81
30	5.57	4.18	3.59	3.25	3.03	2.87	2.75	2.65	2.57	2.51	2.41	2.31	2.20	2.14	2.07	2.01	1.94	1.87	1.79
40	5.42	4.05	3.46	3.13	2.90	2.74	2.62	2.53	2.45	2.39	2.29	2.18	2.07	2.01	1.94	1.88	1.80	1.72	1.64
60	5.29	3.93	3.34	3.01	2.79	2.63	2.51	2.41	2.33	2.27	2.17	2.06	1.94	1.88	1.82	1.74	1.67	1.58	1.48
120	5.15	3.80	3.23	2.89	2.67	2.52	2.39	2.30	2.22	2.16	2.05	1.94	1.82	1.76	1.69	1.61	1.53	1.43	1.31
∞	5.02	3.69	3.12	2.79	2.57	2.41	2.29	2.19	2.11	2.05	1.94	1.83	1.71	1.64	1.57	1.48	1.39	1.27	1.00

TABLE E.5

Critical Values of F (continued)

For a particular combination of numerator and denominator degrees of freedom, entry represents the critical values of F corresponding to the cumulative probability $(1 - \alpha)$ and a specified upper-tail area (α).

$\alpha = 0.01$

Cumulative Probabilities = 0.99

Upper-Tail Areas = 0.01

Numerator, df_1

Denominator, df_2	1	2	3	4	5	6	7	8	9	10	12	15	20	24	30	40	60	120	∞
1	4,052.00	4,999.50	5,403.00	5,625.00	5,764.00	5,859.00	5,928.00	5,982.00	6,022.00	6,056.00	6,106.00	6,157.00	6,209.00	6,235.00	6,261.00	6,287.00	6,313.00	6,339.00	6,366.00
2	98.50	99.00	99.17	99.25	99.30	99.33	99.36	99.37	99.39	99.40	99.42	99.43	44.45	99.46	99.47	99.47	99.48	99.49	99.50
3	34.12	30.82	29.46	28.71	28.24	27.91	27.67	27.49	27.35	27.23	27.05	26.87	26.69	26.60	26.50	26.41	26.32	26.22	26.13
4	21.20	18.00	16.69	15.98	15.52	15.21	14.98	14.80	14.66	14.55	14.37	14.20	14.02	13.93	13.84	13.75	13.65	13.56	13.46
5	16.26	13.27	12.06	11.39	10.97	10.67	10.46	10.29	10.16	10.05	9.89	9.72	9.55	9.47	9.38	9.29	9.20	9.11	9.02
6	13.75	10.92	9.78	9.15	8.75	8.47	8.26	8.10	7.98	7.87	7.72	7.56	7.40	7.31	7.23	7.14	7.06	6.97	6.88
7	12.25	9.55	8.45	7.85	7.46	7.19	6.99	6.84	6.72	6.62	6.47	6.31	6.16	6.07	5.99	5.91	5.82	5.74	5.65
8	11.26	8.65	7.59	7.01	6.63	6.37	6.18	6.03	5.91	5.81	5.67	5.52	5.36	5.28	5.20	5.12	5.03	4.95	4.86
9	10.56	8.02	6.99	6.42	6.06	5.80	5.61	5.47	5.35	5.26	5.11	4.96	4.81	4.73	4.65	4.57	4.48	4.40	4.31
10	10.04	7.56	6.55	5.99	5.64	5.39	5.20	5.06	4.94	4.85	4.71	4.56	4.41	4.33	4.25	4.17	4.08	4.00	3.91
11	9.65	7.21	6.22	5.67	5.32	5.07	4.89	4.74	4.63	4.54	4.40	4.25	4.10	4.02	3.94	3.86	3.78	3.69	3.60
12	9.33	6.93	5.95	5.41	5.06	4.82	4.64	4.50	4.39	4.30	4.16	4.01	3.86	3.78	3.70	3.62	3.54	3.45	3.36
13	9.07	6.70	5.74	5.21	4.86	4.62	4.44	4.30	4.19	4.10	3.96	3.82	3.66	3.59	3.51	3.43	3.34	3.25	3.17
14	8.86	6.51	5.56	5.04	4.69	4.46	4.28	4.14	4.03	3.94	3.80	3.66	3.51	3.43	3.35	3.27	3.18	3.09	3.00
15	8.68	6.36	5.42	4.89	4.56	4.32	4.14	4.00	3.89	3.80	3.67	3.52	3.37	3.29	3.21	3.13	3.05	2.96	2.87
16	8.53	6.23	5.29	4.77	4.44	4.20	4.03	3.89	3.78	3.69	3.55	3.41	3.26	3.18	3.10	3.02	2.93	2.81	2.75
17	8.40	6.11	5.18	4.67	4.34	4.10	3.93	3.79	3.68	3.59	3.46	3.31	3.16	3.08	3.00	2.92	2.83	2.75	2.65
18	8.29	6.01	5.09	4.58	4.25	4.01	3.84	3.71	3.60	3.51	3.37	3.23	3.08	3.00	2.92	2.84	2.75	2.66	2.57
19	8.18	5.93	5.01	4.50	4.17	3.94	3.77	3.63	3.52	3.43	3.30	3.15	3.00	2.92	2.84	2.76	2.67	2.58	2.49
20	8.10	5.85	4.94	4.43	4.10	3.87	3.70	3.56	3.46	3.37	3.23	3.09	2.94	2.86	2.78	2.69	2.61	2.52	2.42
21	8.02	5.78	4.87	4.37	4.04	3.81	3.64	3.51	3.40	3.31	3.17	3.03	2.88	2.80	2.72	2.64	2.55	2.46	2.36
22	7.95	5.72	4.82	4.31	3.99	3.76	3.59	3.45	3.35	3.26	3.12	2.98	2.83	2.75	2.67	2.58	2.50	2.40	2.31
23	7.88	5.66	4.76	4.26	3.94	3.71	3.54	3.41	3.30	3.21	3.07	2.93	2.78	2.70	2.62	2.54	2.45	2.35	2.26
24	7.82	5.61	4.72	4.22	3.90	3.67	3.50	3.36	3.26	3.17	3.03	2.89	2.74	2.66	2.58	2.49	2.40	2.31	2.21
25	7.77	5.57	4.68	4.18	3.85	3.63	3.46	3.32	3.22	3.13	2.99	2.85	2.70	2.62	2.54	2.45	2.36	2.27	2.17
26	7.72	5.53	4.64	4.14	3.82	3.59	3.42	3.29	3.18	3.09	2.96	2.81	2.66	2.58	2.50	2.42	2.33	2.23	2.13
27	7.68	5.49	4.60	4.11	3.78	3.56	3.39	3.26	3.15	3.06	2.93	2.78	2.63	2.55	2.47	2.38	2.29	2.20	2.10
28	7.64	5.45	4.57	4.07	3.75	3.53	3.36	3.23	3.12	3.03	2.90	2.75	2.60	2.52	2.44	2.35	2.26	2.17	2.06
29	7.60	5.42	4.54	4.04	3.73	3.50	3.33	3.20	3.09	3.00	2.87	2.73	2.57	2.49	2.41	2.33	2.23	2.14	2.03
30	7.56	5.39	4.51	4.02	3.70	3.47	3.30	3.17	3.07	2.98	2.84	2.70	2.55	2.47	2.39	2.30	2.21	2.11	2.01
40	7.31	5.18	4.31	3.83	3.51	3.29	3.12	2.99	2.89	2.80	2.66	2.52	2.37	2.29	2.20	2.11	2.02	1.92	1.80
60	7.08	4.98	4.13	3.65	3.34	3.12	2.95	2.82	2.72	2.63	2.50	2.35	2.20	2.12	2.03	1.94	1.84	1.73	1.60
120	6.85	4.79	3.95	3.48	3.17	2.96	2.79	2.66	2.56	2.47	2.34	2.19	2.03	1.95	1.86	1.76	1.66	1.53	1.38
∞	6.63	4.61	3.78	3.32	3.02	2.80	2.64	2.51	2.41	2.32	2.18	2.04	1.88	1.79	1.70	1.59	1.47	1.32	1.00

(continued)

TABLE E.5
Critical Values of F (continued)

For a particular combination of numerator and denominator degrees of freedom, entry represents the critical values of F corresponding to the cumulative probability $(1 - \alpha)$ and a specified upper-tail area (α).

Cumulative Probabilities = 0.995

Upper – Tail Areas = 0.005

Denominator, df_2	Numerator, df_1																		
	1	2	3	4	5	6	7	8	9	10	12	15	20	24	30	40	60	120	∞
1	16,211.00	20,000.00	21,615.00	22,500.00	23,056.00	23,437.00	23,715.00	23,925.00	24,091.00	24,224.00	24,426.00	24,630.00	24,836.00	24,910.00	25,044.00	25,148.00	25,253.00	25,359.00	25,465.00
2	198.50	199.00	199.20	199.20	199.30	199.30	199.40	199.40	199.40	199.40	199.40	199.40	199.40	199.50	199.50	199.50	199.50	199.50	199.50
3	55.55	49.80	47.47	46.19	45.39	44.84	44.43	44.13	43.88	43.69	43.39	43.08	42.78	42.62	42.47	42.31	42.15	41.99	41.83
4	31.33	26.28	24.26	23.15	22.46	21.97	21.62	21.35	21.14	20.97	20.70	20.44	20.17	20.03	19.89	19.75	19.61	19.47	19.32
5	22.78	18.31	16.53	15.56	14.94	14.51	14.20	13.96	13.77	13.62	13.38	13.15	12.90	12.78	12.66	12.53	12.40	12.27	12.11
6	18.63	14.54	12.92	12.03	11.46	11.07	10.79	10.57	10.39	10.25	10.03	9.81	9.59	9.47	9.36	9.24	9.12	9.00	8.88
7	16.24	12.40	10.88	10.05	9.52	9.16	8.89	8.68	8.51	8.38	8.18	7.97	7.75	7.65	7.53	7.42	7.31	7.19	7.08
8	14.69	11.04	9.60	8.81	8.30	7.95	7.69	7.50	7.34	7.21	7.01	6.81	6.61	6.50	6.40	6.29	6.18	6.06	5.95
9	13.61	10.11	8.72	7.96	7.47	7.13	6.88	6.69	6.54	6.42	6.23	6.03	5.83	5.73	5.62	5.52	5.41	5.30	5.19
10	12.83	9.43	8.08	7.34	6.87	6.54	6.30	6.12	5.97	5.85	5.66	5.47	5.27	5.17	5.07	4.97	4.86	4.75	4.61
11	12.23	8.91	7.60	6.88	6.42	6.10	5.86	5.68	5.54	5.42	5.24	5.05	4.86	4.75	4.65	4.55	4.44	4.34	4.23
12	11.75	8.51	7.23	6.52	6.07	5.76	5.52	5.35	5.20	5.09	4.91	4.72	4.53	4.43	4.33	4.23	4.12	4.01	3.90
13	11.37	8.19	6.93	6.23	5.79	5.48	5.25	5.08	4.94	4.82	4.64	4.46	4.27	4.17	4.07	3.97	3.87	3.76	3.65
14	11.06	7.92	6.68	6.00	5.56	5.26	5.03	4.86	4.72	4.60	4.43	4.25	4.06	3.96	3.86	3.76	3.66	3.55	3.41
15	10.80	7.70	6.48	5.80	5.37	5.07	4.85	4.67	4.54	4.42	4.25	4.07	3.88	3.79	3.69	3.58	3.48	3.37	3.26
16	10.58	7.51	6.30	5.64	5.21	4.91	4.69	4.52	4.38	4.27	4.10	3.92	3.73	3.64	3.54	3.44	3.33	3.22	3.11
17	10.38	7.35	6.16	5.50	5.07	4.78	4.56	4.39	4.25	4.14	3.97	3.79	3.61	3.51	3.41	3.31	3.21	3.10	2.98
18	10.22	7.21	6.03	5.37	4.96	4.66	4.44	4.28	4.14	4.03	3.86	3.68	3.50	3.40	3.30	3.20	3.10	2.99	2.87
19	10.07	7.09	5.92	5.27	4.85	4.56	4.34	4.18	4.04	3.93	3.76	3.59	3.40	3.31	3.21	3.11	3.00	2.89	2.78
20	9.94	6.99	5.82	5.17	4.76	4.47	4.26	4.09	3.96	3.85	3.68	3.50	3.32	3.22	3.12	3.02	2.92	2.81	2.69
21	9.83	6.89	5.73	5.09	4.68	4.39	4.18	4.02	3.88	3.77	3.60	3.43	3.24	3.15	3.05	2.95	2.84	2.73	2.61
22	9.73	6.81	5.65	5.02	4.61	4.32	4.11	3.94	3.81	3.70	3.54	3.36	3.18	3.08	2.98	2.88	2.77	2.66	2.55
23	9.63	6.73	5.58	4.95	4.54	4.26	4.05	3.88	3.75	3.64	3.47	3.30	3.12	3.02	2.92	2.82	2.71	2.60	2.48
24	9.55	6.66	5.52	4.89	4.49	4.20	3.99	3.83	3.69	3.59	3.42	3.25	3.06	2.97	2.87	2.77	2.66	2.55	2.43
25	9.48	6.60	5.46	4.84	4.43	4.15	3.94	3.78	3.64	3.54	3.37	3.20	3.01	2.92	2.82	2.72	2.61	2.50	2.38
26	9.41	6.54	5.41	4.79	4.38	4.10	3.89	3.73	3.60	3.49	3.33	3.15	2.97	2.87	2.77	2.67	2.56	2.45	2.33
27	9.34	6.49	5.36	4.74	4.34	4.06	3.85	3.69	3.56	3.45	3.28	3.11	2.93	2.83	2.73	2.63	2.52	2.41	2.29
28	9.28	6.44	5.32	4.70	4.30	4.02	3.81	3.65	3.52	3.41	3.25	3.07	2.89	2.79	2.69	2.59	2.48	2.37	2.25
29	9.23	6.40	5.28	4.66	4.26	3.98	3.77	3.61	3.48	3.38	3.21	3.04	2.86	2.76	2.66	2.56	2.45	2.33	2.21
30	9.18	6.35	5.24	4.62	4.23	3.95	3.74	3.58	3.45	3.34	3.18	3.01	2.82	2.73	2.63	2.52	2.42	2.30	2.18
40	8.83	6.07	4.98	4.37	3.99	3.71	3.51	3.35	3.22	3.12	2.95	2.78	2.60	2.50	2.40	2.30	2.18	2.06	1.93
60	8.49	5.79	4.73	4.14	3.76	3.49	3.29	3.13	3.01	2.90	2.74	2.57	2.39	2.29	2.19	2.08	1.96	1.83	1.69
120	8.18	5.54	4.50	3.92	3.55	3.28	3.09	2.93	2.81	2.71	2.54	2.37	2.19	2.09	1.98	1.87	1.75	1.61	1.43
∞	7.88	5.30	4.28	3.72	3.35	3.09	2.90	2.74	2.62	2.52	2.36	2.19	2.00	1.90	1.79	1.67	1.53	1.36	1.00

$\alpha = 0.005$

TABLE E.6

Lower and Upper Critical Values, T_1, of the Wilcoxon Rank Sum Test

n_2	One-tail	Two-tail	4	5	6	7	8	9	10
	α					n_1			
4	0.05	0.10	11,25						
	0.025	0.05	10,26						
	0.01	0.02	—,—						
	0.005	0.01	—,—						
5	0.05	0.10	12,28	19,36					
	0.025	0.05	11,29	17,38					
	0.01	0.02	10,30	16,39					
	0.005	0.01	—,—	15,40					
6	0.05	0.10	13,31	20,40	28,50				
	0.025	0.05	12,32	18,42	26,52				
	0.01	0.02	11,33	17,43	24,54				
	0.005	0.01	10,34	16,44	23,55				
7	0.05	0.10	14,34	21,44	29,55	39,66			
	0.025	0.05	13,35	20,45	27,57	36,69			
	0.01	0.02	11,37	18,47	25,59	34,71			
	0.005	0.01	10,38	16,49	24,60	32,73			
8	0.05	0.10	15,37	23,47	31,59	41,71	51,85		
	0.025	0.05	14,38	21,49	29,61	38,74	49,87		
	0.01	0.02	12,40	19,51	27,63	35,77	45,91		
	0.005	0.01	11,41	17,53	25,65	34,78	43,93		
9	0.05	0.10	16,40	24,51	33,63	43,76	54,90	66,105	
	0.025	0.05	14,42	22,53	31,65	40,79	51,93	62,109	
	0.01	0.02	13,43	20,55	28,68	37,82	47,97	59,112	
	0.005	0.01	11,45	18,57	26,70	35,84	45,99	56,115	
10	0.05	0.10	17,43	26,54	35,67	45,81	56,96	69,111	82,128
	0.025	0.05	15,45	23,57	32,70	42,84	53,99	65,115	78,132
	0.01	0.02	13,47	21,59	29,73	39,87	49,103	61,119	74,136
	0.005	0.01	12,48	19,61	27,75	37,89	47,105	58,122	71,139

Source: Adapted from Table 1 of F. Wilcoxon and R. A. Wilcox, *Some Rapid Approximate Statistical Procedures* (Pearl River, NY: Lederle Laboratories, 1964), with permission of the American Cyanamid Company.

TABLE E.7

Critical Values of the Studentized Range, Q

Upper 5% Points ($\alpha = 0.05$)

Denominator, df	Numerator, df																		
	2	3	4	5	6	7	8	9	10	11	12	13	14	15	16	17	18	19	20
1	18.00	27.00	32.80	37.10	40.40	43.10	45.40	47.40	49.10	50.60	52.00	53.20	54.30	55.40	56.30	57.20	58.00	58.80	59.60
2	6.09	8.30	9.80	10.90	11.70	12.40	13.00	13.50	14.00	14.40	14.70	15.10	15.40	15.70	15.90	16.10	16.40	16.60	16.80
3	4.50	5.91	6.82	7.50	8.04	8.48	8.85	9.18	9.46	9.72	9.95	10.15	10.35	10.52	10.69	10.84	10.98	11.11	11.24
4	3.93	5.04	5.76	6.29	6.71	7.05	7.35	7.60	7.83	8.03	8.21	8.37	8.52	8.66	8.79	8.91	9.03	9.13	9.23
5	3.64	4.60	5.22	5.67	6.03	6.33	6.58	6.80	6.99	7.17	7.32	7.47	7.60	7.72	7.83	7.93	8.03	8.12	8.21
6	3.46	4.34	4.90	5.31	5.63	5.89	6.12	6.32	6.49	6.65	6.79	6.92	7.03	7.14	7.24	7.34	7.43	7.51	7.59
7	3.34	4.16	4.68	5.06	5.36	5.61	5.82	6.00	6.16	6.30	6.43	6.55	6.66	6.76	6.85	6.94	7.02	7.09	7.17
8	3.26	4.04	4.53	4.89	5.17	5.40	5.60	5.77	5.92	6.05	6.18	6.29	6.39	6.48	6.57	6.65	6.73	6.80	6.87
9	3.20	3.95	4.42	4.76	5.02	5.24	5.43	5.60	5.74	5.87	5.98	6.09	6.19	6.28	6.36	6.44	6.51	6.58	6.64
10	3.15	3.88	4.33	4.65	4.91	5.12	5.30	5.46	5.60	5.72	5.83	5.93	6.03	6.11	6.20	6.27	6.34	6.40	6.47
11	3.11	3.82	4.26	4.57	4.82	5.03	5.20	5.35	5.49	5.61	5.71	5.81	5.90	5.99	6.06	6.14	6.20	6.26	6.33
12	3.08	3.77	4.20	4.51	4.75	4.95	5.12	5.27	5.40	5.51	5.62	5.71	5.80	5.88	5.95	6.03	6.09	6.15	6.21
13	3.06	3.73	4.15	4.45	4.69	4.88	5.05	5.19	5.32	5.43	5.53	5.63	5.71	5.79	5.86	5.93	6.00	6.05	6.11
14	3.03	3.70	4.11	4.41	4.64	4.83	4.99	5.13	5.25	5.36	5.46	5.55	5.64	5.72	5.79	5.85	5.92	5.97	6.03
15	3.01	3.67	4.08	4.37	4.60	4.78	4.94	5.08	5.20	5.31	5.40	5.49	5.58	5.65	5.72	5.79	5.85	5.90	5.96
16	3.00	3.65	4.05	4.33	4.56	4.74	4.90	5.03	5.15	5.26	5.35	5.44	5.52	5.59	5.66	5.72	5.79	5.84	5.90
17	2.98	3.63	4.02	4.30	4.52	4.71	4.86	4.99	5.11	5.21	5.31	5.39	5.47	5.55	5.61	5.68	5.74	5.79	5.84
18	2.97	3.61	4.00	4.28	4.49	4.67	4.82	4.96	5.07	5.17	5.27	5.35	5.43	5.50	5.57	5.63	5.69	5.74	5.79
19	2.96	3.59	3.98	4.25	4.47	4.65	4.79	4.92	5.04	5.14	5.23	5.32	5.39	5.46	5.53	5.59	5.65	5.70	5.75
20	2.95	3.58	3.96	4.23	4.45	4.62	4.77	4.90	5.01	5.11	5.20	5.28	5.36	5.43	5.49	5.55	5.61	5.66	5.71
24	2.92	3.53	3.90	4.17	4.37	4.54	4.68	4.81	4.92	5.01	5.10	5.18	5.25	5.32	5.38	5.44	5.50	5.54	5.59
30	2.89	3.49	3.84	4.10	4.30	4.46	4.60	4.72	4.83	4.92	5.00	5.08	5.15	5.21	5.27	5.33	5.38	5.43	5.48
40	2.86	3.44	3.79	4.04	4.23	4.39	4.52	4.63	4.74	4.82	4.91	4.98	5.05	5.11	5.16	5.22	5.27	5.31	5.36
60	2.83	3.40	3.74	3.98	4.16	4.31	4.44	4.55	4.65	4.73	4.81	4.88	4.94	5.00	5.06	5.11	5.16	5.20	5.24
120	2.80	3.36	3.69	3.92	4.10	4.24	4.36	4.48	4.56	4.64	4.72	4.78	4.84	4.90	4.95	5.00	5.05	5.09	5.13
∞	2.77	3.31	3.63	3.86	4.03	4.17	4.29	4.39	4.47	4.55	4.62	4.68	4.74	4.80	4.85	4.89	4.93	4.97	5.01

(continued)

TABLE E.7

Critical Values of the Studentized Range, Q (*continued*)

Upper 1% Points ($\alpha = 0.01$)

Denominator, df	Numerator, df																		
	2	3	4	5	6	7	8	9	10	11	12	13	14	15	16	17	18	19	20
1	90.03	135.00	164.30	185.60	202.20	215.80	227.20	237.00	245.60	253.20	260.00	266.20	271.80	277.00	281.80	286.30	290.40	294.30	298.00
2	14.04	19.02	22.29	24.72	26.63	28.20	29.53	30.68	31.69	32.59	33.40	34.13	34.81	35.43	36.00	36.53	37.03	37.50	37.95
3	8.26	10.62	12.17	13.33	14.24	15.00	15.64	16.20	16.69	17.13	17.53	17.89	18.22	18.52	18.81	19.07	19.32	19.55	19.77
4	6.51	8.12	9.17	9.96	10.58	11.10	11.55	11.93	12.27	12.57	12.84	13.09	13.32	13.53	13.73	13.91	14.08	14.24	14.40
5	5.70	6.98	7.80	8.42	8.91	9.32	9.67	9.97	10.24	10.48	10.70	10.89	11.08	11.24	11.40	11.55	11.68	11.81	11.93
6	5.24	6.33	7.03	7.56	7.97	8.32	8.61	8.87	9.10	9.30	9.49	9.65	9.81	9.95	10.08	10.21	10.32	10.43	10.54
7	4.95	5.92	6.54	7.01	7.37	7.68	7.94	8.17	8.37	8.55	8.71	8.86	9.00	9.12	9.24	9.35	9.46	9.55	9.65
8	4.75	5.64	6.20	6.63	6.96	7.24	7.47	7.68	7.86	8.03	8.18	8.31	8.44	8.55	8.66	8.76	8.85	8.94	9.03
9	4.60	5.43	5.96	6.35	6.66	6.92	7.13	7.32	7.50	7.65	7.78	7.91	8.03	8.13	8.23	8.33	8.41	8.50	8.57
10	4.48	5.27	5.77	6.14	6.43	6.67	6.87	7.06	7.21	7.36	7.49	7.60	7.71	7.81	7.91	7.99	8.08	8.15	8.23
11	4.39	5.15	5.62	5.97	6.25	6.48	6.67	6.84	6.99	7.13	7.25	7.36	7.47	7.56	7.65	7.73	7.81	7.88	7.95
12	4.32	5.04	5.50	5.84	6.10	6.32	6.51	6.67	6.81	6.94	7.06	7.17	7.26	7.36	7.44	7.52	7.59	7.66	7.73
13	4.26	4.96	5.40	5.73	5.98	6.19	6.37	6.53	6.67	6.79	6.90	7.01	7.10	7.19	7.27	7.35	7.42	7.49	7.55
14	4.21	4.90	5.32	5.63	5.88	6.09	6.26	6.41	6.54	6.66	6.77	6.87	6.96	7.05	7.13	7.20	7.27	7.33	7.40
15	4.17	4.84	5.25	5.56	5.80	5.99	6.16	6.31	6.44	6.56	6.66	6.76	6.85	6.93	7.00	7.07	7.14	7.20	7.26
16	4.13	4.79	5.19	5.49	5.72	5.92	6.08	6.22	6.35	6.46	6.56	6.66	6.74	6.82	6.90	6.97	7.03	7.09	7.15
17	4.10	4.74	5.14	5.43	5.66	5.85	6.01	6.15	6.27	6.38	6.48	6.57	6.66	6.73	6.81	6.87	6.94	7.00	7.05
18	4.07	4.70	5.09	5.38	5.60	5.79	5.94	6.08	6.20	6.31	6.41	6.50	6.58	6.66	6.73	6.79	6.85	6.91	6.97
19	4.05	4.67	5.05	5.33	5.55	5.74	5.89	6.02	6.14	6.25	6.34	6.43	6.51	6.59	6.65	6.72	6.78	6.84	6.89
20	4.02	4.64	5.02	5.29	5.51	5.69	5.84	5.97	6.09	6.19	6.29	6.37	6.45	6.52	6.59	6.65	6.71	6.77	6.82
24	3.96	4.55	4.91	5.17	5.37	5.54	5.69	5.81	5.92	6.02	6.11	6.19	6.26	6.33	6.39	6.45	6.51	6.56	6.61
30	3.89	4.46	4.80	5.05	5.24	5.40	5.54	5.65	5.76	5.85	5.93	6.01	6.08	6.14	6.20	6.26	6.31	6.36	6.41
40	3.83	4.37	4.70	4.93	5.11	5.27	5.39	5.50	5.60	5.69	5.76	5.84	5.90	5.96	6.02	6.07	6.12	6.17	6.21
60	3.76	4.28	4.60	4.82	4.99	5.13	5.25	5.36	5.45	5.53	5.60	5.67	5.73	5.79	5.84	5.89	5.93	5.97	6.02
120	3.70	4.20	4.50	4.71	4.87	5.01	5.12	5.21	5.30	5.38	5.44	5.51	5.56	5.61	5.66	5.71	5.75	5.79	5.83
∞	3.64	4.12	4.40	4.60	4.76	4.88	4.99	5.08	5.16	5.23	5.29	5.35	5.40	5.45	5.49	5.54	5.57	5.61	5.65

Source: Extracted from H. L. Harter and D. S. Clemm, "The Probability Integrals of the Range and of the Studentized Range—Probability Integral, Percentage Points, and Moments of the Range," *Wright Air Development Technical Report 58–484*, Vol. 1, 1959.

TABLE E.8
Critical Values, d_L and d_U, of the Durbin-Watson Statistic, D (Critical Values Are One-Sided)[a]

| | α = 0.05 | | | | | | | | | | α = 0.01 | | | | | | | | | |
| | k = 1 | | k = 2 | | k = 3 | | k = 4 | | k = 5 | | k = 1 | | k = 2 | | k = 3 | | k = 4 | | k = 5 | |
n	d_L	d_U	d_L	d_U	d_L	d_U	d_L	d_U	d_L	d_U	d_L	d_U	d_L	d_U	d_L	d_U	d_L	d_U	d_L	d_U
15	1.08	1.36	.95	1.54	.82	1.75	.69	1.97	.56	2.21	.81	1.07	.70	1.25	.59	1.46	.49	1.70	.39	1.96
16	1.10	1.37	.98	1.54	.86	1.73	.74	1.93	.62	2.15	.84	1.09	.74	1.25	.63	1.44	.53	1.66	.44	1.90
17	1.13	1.38	1.02	1.54	.90	1.71	.78	1.90	.67	2.10	.87	1.10	.77	1.25	.67	1.43	.57	1.63	.48	1.85
18	1.16	1.39	1.05	1.53	.93	1.69	.82	1.87	.71	2.06	.90	1.12	.80	1.26	.71	1.42	.61	1.60	.52	1.80
19	1.18	1.40	1.08	1.53	.97	1.68	.86	1.85	.75	2.02	.93	1.13	.83	1.26	.74	1.41	.65	1.58	.56	1.77
20	1.20	1.41	1.10	1.54	1.00	1.68	.90	1.83	.79	1.99	.95	1.15	.86	1.27	.77	1.41	.68	1.57	.60	1.74
21	1.22	1.42	1.13	1.54	1.03	1.67	.93	1.81	.83	1.96	.97	1.16	.89	1.27	.80	1.41	.72	1.55	.63	1.71
22	1.24	1.43	1.15	1.54	1.05	1.66	.96	1.80	.86	1.94	1.00	1.17	.91	1.28	.83	1.40	.75	1.54	.66	1.69
23	1.26	1.44	1.17	1.54	1.08	1.66	.99	1.79	.90	1.92	1.02	1.19	.94	1.29	.86	1.40	.77	1.53	.70	1.67
24	1.27	1.45	1.19	1.55	1.10	1.66	1.01	1.78	.93	1.90	1.04	1.20	.96	1.30	.88	1.41	.80	1.53	.72	1.66
25	1.29	1.45	1.21	1.55	1.12	1.66	1.04	1.77	.95	1.89	1.05	1.21	.98	1.30	.90	1.41	.83	1.52	.75	1.65
26	1.30	1.46	1.22	1.55	1.14	1.65	1.06	1.76	.98	1.88	1.07	1.22	1.00	1.31	.93	1.41	.85	1.52	.78	1.64
27	1.32	1.47	1.24	1.56	1.16	1.65	1.08	1.76	1.01	1.86	1.09	1.23	1.02	1.32	.95	1.41	.88	1.51	.81	1.63
28	1.33	1.48	1.26	1.56	1.18	1.65	1.10	1.75	1.03	1.85	1.10	1.24	1.04	1.32	.97	1.41	.90	1.51	.83	1.62
29	1.34	1.48	1.27	1.56	1.20	1.65	1.12	1.74	1.05	1.84	1.12	1.25	1.05	1.33	.99	1.42	.92	1.51	.85	1.61
30	1.35	1.49	1.28	1.57	1.21	1.65	1.14	1.74	1.07	1.83	1.13	1.26	1.07	1.34	1.01	1.42	.94	1.51	.88	1.61
31	1.36	1.50	1.30	1.57	1.23	1.65	1.16	1.74	1.09	1.83	1.15	1.27	1.08	1.34	1.02	1.42	.96	1.51	.90	1.60
32	1.37	1.50	1.31	1.57	1.24	1.65	1.18	1.73	1.11	1.82	1.16	1.28	1.10	1.35	1.04	1.43	.98	1.51	.92	1.60
33	1.38	1.51	1.32	1.58	1.26	1.65	1.19	1.73	1.13	1.81	1.17	1.29	1.11	1.36	1.05	1.43	1.00	1.51	.94	1.59
34	1.39	1.51	1.33	1.58	1.27	1.65	1.21	1.73	1.15	1.81	1.18	1.30	1.13	1.36	1.07	1.43	1.01	1.51	.95	1.59
35	1.40	1.52	1.34	1.58	1.28	1.65	1.22	1.73	1.16	1.80	1.19	1.31	1.14	1.37	1.08	1.44	1.03	1.51	.97	1.59
36	1.41	1.52	1.35	1.59	1.29	1.65	1.24	1.73	1.18	1.80	1.21	1.32	1.15	1.38	1.10	1.44	1.04	1.51	.99	1.59
37	1.42	1.53	1.36	1.59	1.31	1.66	1.25	1.72	1.19	1.80	1.22	1.32	1.16	1.38	1.11	1.45	1.06	1.51	1.00	1.59
38	1.43	1.54	1.37	1.59	1.32	1.66	1.26	1.72	1.21	1.79	1.23	1.33	1.18	1.39	1.12	1.45	1.07	1.52	1.02	1.58
39	1.43	1.54	1.38	1.60	1.33	1.66	1.27	1.72	1.22	1.79	1.24	1.34	1.19	1.39	1.14	1.45	1.09	1.52	1.03	1.58
40	1.44	1.54	1.39	1.60	1.34	1.66	1.29	1.72	1.23	1.79	1.25	1.34	1.20	1.40	1.15	1.46	1.10	1.52	1.05	1.58
45	1.48	1.57	1.43	1.62	1.38	1.67	1.34	1.72	1.29	1.78	1.29	1.38	1.24	1.42	1.20	1.48	1.16	1.53	1.11	1.58
50	1.50	1.59	1.46	1.63	1.42	1.67	1.38	1.72	1.34	1.77	1.32	1.40	1.28	1.45	1.24	1.49	1.20	1.54	1.16	1.59
55	1.53	1.60	1.49	1.64	1.45	1.68	1.41	1.72	1.38	1.77	1.36	1.43	1.32	1.47	1.28	1.51	1.25	1.55	1.21	1.59
60	1.55	1.62	1.51	1.65	1.48	1.69	1.44	1.73	1.41	1.77	1.38	1.45	1.35	1.48	1.32	1.52	1.28	1.56	1.25	1.60
65	1.57	1.63	1.54	1.66	1.50	1.70	1.47	1.73	1.44	1.77	1.41	1.47	1.38	1.50	1.35	1.53	1.31	1.57	1.28	1.61
70	1.58	1.64	1.55	1.67	1.52	1.70	1.49	1.74	1.46	1.77	1.43	1.49	1.40	1.52	1.37	1.55	1.34	1.58	1.31	1.61
75	1.60	1.65	1.57	1.68	1.54	1.71	1.51	1.74	1.49	1.77	1.45	1.50	1.42	1.53	1.39	1.56	1.37	1.59	1.34	1.62
80	1.61	1.66	1.59	1.69	1.56	1.72	1.53	1.74	1.51	1.77	1.47	1.52	1.44	1.54	1.42	1.57	1.39	1.60	1.36	1.62
85	1.62	1.67	1.60	1.70	1.57	1.72	1.55	1.75	1.52	1.77	1.48	1.53	1.46	1.55	1.43	1.58	1.41	1.60	1.39	1.63
90	1.63	1.68	1.61	1.70	1.59	1.73	1.57	1.75	1.54	1.78	1.50	1.54	1.47	1.56	1.45	1.59	1.43	1.61	1.41	1.64
95	1.64	1.69	1.62	1.71	1.60	1.73	1.58	1.75	1.56	1.78	1.51	1.55	1.49	1.57	1.47	1.60	1.45	1.62	1.42	1.64
100	1.65	1.69	1.63	1.72	1.61	1.74	1.59	1.76	1.57	1.78	1.52	1.56	1.50	1.58	1.48	1.60	1.46	1.63	1.44	1.65

[a] n = number of observations; k = number of independent variables.

Source: Computed from TSP 4.5 based on R. W. Farebrother, "A Remark on Algorithms AS106, AS153, and AS155: The Distribution of a Linear Combination of Chi-Square Random Variables," *Journal of the Royal Statistical Society*, Series C (Applied Statistics), (1984), 29, p. 323–333.

TABLE E.9

Control Chart Factors

Number of Observations in Sample/Subgroup (n)	d_2	d_3	D_3	D_4	A_2
2	1.128	0.853	0	3.267	1.880
3	1.693	0.888	0	2.575	1.023
4	2.059	0.880	0	2.282	0.729
5	2.326	0.864	0	2.114	0.577
6	2.534	0.848	0	2.004	0.483
7	2.704	0.833	0.076	1.924	0.419
8	2.847	0.820	0.136	1.864	0.373
9	2.970	0.808	0.184	1.816	0.337
10	3.078	0.797	0.223	1.777	0.308
11	3.173	0.787	0.256	1.744	0.285
12	3.258	0.778	0.283	1.717	0.266
13	3.336	0.770	0.307	1.693	0.249
14	3.407	0.763	0.328	1.672	0.235
15	3.472	0.756	0.347	1.653	0.223
16	3.532	0.750	0.363	1.637	0.212
17	3.588	0.744	0.378	1.622	0.203
18	3.640	0.739	0.391	1.609	0.194
19	3.689	0.733	0.404	1.596	0.187
20	3.735	0.729	0.415	1.585	0.180
21	3.778	0.724	0.425	1.575	0.173
22	3.819	0.720	0.435	1.565	0.167
23	3.858	0.716	0.443	1.557	0.162
24	3.895	0.712	0.452	1.548	0.157
25	3.931	0.708	0.459	1.541	0.153

Source: Reprinted from *ASTM-STP 15D* by kind permission of the American Society for Testing and Materials. Copyright ASTM International, 100 Barr Harbor Drive, Conshohocken, PA 19428.

TABLE E.10

The Standardized Normal Distribution

Entry represents area under the standardized normal
distribution from the mean to Z

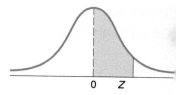

Z	.00	.01	.02	.03	.04	.05	.06	.07	.08	.09
0.0	.0000	.0040	.0080	.0120	.0160	.0199	.0239	.0279	.0319	.0359
0.1	.0398	.0438	.0478	.0517	.0557	.0596	.0636	.0675	.0714	.0753
0.2	.0793	.0832	.0871	.0910	.0948	.0987	.1026	.1064	.1103	.1141
0.3	.1179	.1217	.1255	.1293	.1331	.1368	.1406	.1443	.1480	.1517
0.4	.1554	.1591	.1628	.1664	.1700	.1736	.1772	.1808	.1844	.1879
0.5	.1915	.1950	.1985	.2019	.2054	.2088	.2123	.2157	.2190	.2224
0.6	.2257	.2291	.2324	.2357	.2389	.2422	.2454	.2486	.2518	.2549
0.7	.2580	.2612	.2642	.2673	.2704	.2734	.2764	.2794	.2823	.2852
0.8	.2881	.2910	.2939	.2967	.2995	.3023	.3051	.3078	.3106	.3133
0.9	.3159	.3186	.3212	.3238	.3264	.3289	.3315	.3340	.3365	.3389
1.0	.3413	.3438	.3461	.3485	.3508	.3531	.3554	.3577	.3599	.3621
1.1	.3643	.3665	.3686	.3708	.3729	.3749	.3770	.3790	.3810	.3830
1.2	.3849	.3869	.3888	.3907	.3925	.3944	.3962	.3980	.3997	.4015
1.3	.4032	.4049	.4066	.4082	.4099	.4115	.4131	.4147	.4162	.4177
1.4	.4192	.4207	.4222	.4236	.4251	.4265	.4279	.4292	.4306	.4319
1.5	.4332	.4345	.4357	.4370	.4382	.4394	.4406	.4418	.4429	.4441
1.6	.4452	.4463	.4474	.4484	.4495	.4505	.4515	.4525	.4535	.4545
1.7	.4554	.4564	.4573	.4582	.4591	.4599	.4608	.4616	.4625	.4633
1.8	.4641	.4649	.4656	.4664	.4671	.4678	.4686	.4693	.4699	.4706
1.9	.4713	.4719	.4726	.4732	.4738	.4744	.4750	.4756	.4761	.4767
2.0	.4772	.4778	.4783	.4788	.4793	.4798	.4803	.4808	.4812	.4817
2.1	.4821	.4826	.4830	.4834	.4838	.4842	.4846	.4850	.4854	.4857
2.2	.4861	.4864	.4868	.4871	.4875	.4878	.4881	.4884	.4887	.4890
2.3	.4893	.4896	.4898	.4901	.4904	.4906	.4909	.4911	.4913	.4916
2.4	.4918	.4920	.4922	.4925	.4927	.4929	.4931	.4932	.4934	.4936
2.5	.4938	.4940	.4941	.4943	.4945	.4946	.4948	.4949	.4951	.4952
2.6	.4953	.4955	.4956	.4957	.4959	.4960	.4961	.4962	.4963	.4964
2.7	.4965	.4966	.4967	.4968	.4969	.4970	.4971	.4972	.4973	.4974
2.8	.4974	.4975	.4976	.4977	.4977	.4978	.4979	.4979	.4980	.4981
2.9	.4981	.4982	.4982	.4983	.4984	.4984	.4985	.4985	.4986	.4986
3.0	.49865	.49869	.49874	.49878	.49882	.49886	.49889	.49893	.49897	.49900
3.1	.49903	.49906	.49910	.49913	.49916	.49918	.49921	.49924	.49926	.49929
3.2	.49931	.49934	.49936	.49938	.49940	.49942	.49944	.49946	.49948	.49950
3.3	.49952	.49953	.49955	.49957	.49958	.49960	.49961	.49962	.49964	.49965
3.4	.49966	.49968	.49969	.49970	.49971	.49972	.49973	.49974	.49975	.49976
3.5	.49977	.49978	.49978	.49979	.49980	.49981	.49981	.49982	.49983	.49983
3.6	.49984	.49985	.49985	.49986	.49986	.49987	.49987	.49988	.49988	.49989
3.7	.49989	.49990	.49990	.49990	.49991	.49991	.49992	.49992	.49992	.49992
3.8	.49993	.49993	.49993	.49994	.49994	.49994	.49994	.49995	.49995	.49995
3.9	.49995	.49995	.49996	.49996	.49996	.49996	.49996	.49996	.49997	.49997

Useful Excel Knowledge

This appendix reviews knowledge that you will find useful if you plan to be more than a casual user of Microsoft Excel. This appendix assumes that you are familiar with the important Excel skills and concepts that Appendix B discusses. If you are a first-time user of Excel, make sure to study and review Appendix B before reading and using this appendix.

F.1 Useful Keyboard Shortcuts

In Microsoft Office programs including Microsoft Excel, certain individual keys or combinations of keys held down as you press another key are shortcuts that allow you to execute common operations without having to select choices from menus or the Ribbon. As first explained in the First Things First Chapter, this book uses key names and plus signs to indicate a keystroke combination. For example, **Ctrl+C** means "while holding down the **Ctrl** key, press the **C** key."

Editing Shortcuts

Pressing **Backspace** erases typed characters to the left of the current position, one character at a time. Pressing **Delete** erases characters to the right of the cursor, one character at a time.

Ctrl+C copies a worksheet entry, and **Ctrl+V** pastes that entry into the place that the editing cursor or worksheet cell highlight indicates. Pressing **Ctrl+X** cuts the currently selected entry or object so that you can paste it somewhere else. **Ctrl+C** and **Ctrl+V** (or **Ctrl+X** and **Ctrl+V**) can also be used to copy (or cut) and paste certain workbook objects such as charts. (Using copy and paste to copy formulas from one worksheet cell to another is subject to the adjustment discussed in Appendix Section B.2.)

Pressing **Ctrl+Z** undoes the last operation, and **Ctrl+Y** redoes the last operation. Pressing **Enter** or **Tab** finalizes an entry typed into a worksheet cell. Pressing either key is implied by the use of the verb *enter* in the Excel Guides.

Formatting & Utility Shortcuts

Pressing **Ctrl+B** toggles on (or off) boldface text style for the currently selected object. Pressing **Ctrl+I** toggles on (or off) italic text style for the currently selected object. Pressing **Ctrl+Shift+%** formats numeric values as a percentage with no decimal places.

Pressing **Ctrl+F** finds a **Find what** value, and pressing **Ctrl+H** replaces a **Find what** value with the **Replace with** value. Pressing **Ctrl+A** selects the entire current worksheet (useful as part of a worksheet copy or format operation). Pressing **Esc** cancels an action or a dialog box. Pressing **F1** displays the Microsoft Excel help system.

F.2 Verifying Formulas and Worksheets

If you use formulas in your worksheets, you should review and verify formulas before you use their results. To view the formulas in a worksheet, press **Ctrl+`** (grave accent key). To restore the original view, the results of the formulas, press **Ctrl+`** a second time.

As you create and use more complicated worksheets, you might want to visually examine the relationships among a formula and the cells it uses (called the *precedents*) and the cells that use the results of the formula (the *dependents*). Select **Formulas → Trace Precedents** (or **Trace Dependents**) to examine relationships. When you are finished, clear all trace arrows by selecting **Formulas → Remove Arrows**.

After verifying formulas, you should test, using simple numbers, any worksheet that you have modified or constructed from scratch.

F.3 New Function Names

Beginning in Excel 2010, Microsoft renamed many statistical functions and reprogrammed a number of functions to improve their accuracy. Generally, this book uses the new function names in worksheet cell formulas. Table F.1 on page 657 lists the new function names used in this book, along with the place of their first use in an Excel Guide section. The table also lists the older function name identical or most similar to each new function name used in this book.

TTABLE F.1
New and Older Function
Names

New Name	First Mention	Older Name
BINOM.DIST	EG5.3	BINOMDIST
CHISQ.DIST.RT	EG11.1	CHIDIST
CHISQ.INV.RT	EG11.1	CHIINV
CONFIDENCE.NORM	EG8.1	CONFIDENCE
COVARIANCE.S	EG3.5	none*
EXPON.DIST	EG6.5	EXPONDIST
F.DIST.RT	EG10.4	FDIST
F.INV.RT	EG10.4	FINV
HYPGEOM.DIST	EG5.5	HYPERGEOMDIST
NORM.DIST	EG6.2	NORMDIST
NORM.INV	EG6.2	NORMINV
NORM.S.DIST	EG9.1	NORMSDIST
NORM.S.INV	EG6.2	NORMSINV
POISSON.DIST	EG5.4	POISSON
STDEV.S	EG3.2	STDEV
STDEV.P	EG3.2	STDEVP
T.DIST.RT	EG9.3	TDIST
T.DIST.2T	EG9.2	TDIST
T.INV.2T	EG8.2	TINV
VAR.S	EG3.2	VAR
VAR.P	EG3.2	VARP

COVARIANCE.S is a function that was new to Excel 2010. The COVARIANCE.P function (not used in this book) replaces the older COVAR function.

Alternative Worksheets

If a worksheet in an Excel Guide workbook uses one or more of the new function names, the workbook contains an alternative worksheet for use with Excel versions that are older than Excel 2010. Three exceptions to the rule are the **Simple Linear Regression 2007**, **Multiple Regression 2007**, and **Exponential Trend 2007** *workbooks*. Alternative worksheets and workbooks work best in Excel 2007.

The following Excel Guide workbooks contain alternative COMPUTE_OLDER worksheets. Numbers that appear in parentheses are the chapters in which these workbooks are first mentioned.

Parameters (3)	**CIE sigma unknown (8)**	**Separate-Variance T (10)**
Covariance (3)	**CIE Proportion (8)**	**Paired T (10)**
Hypergeometric (5)	**Z Mean workbook (9)**	**One-Way ANOVA (11)**
Normal (6)	**T mean workbook (9)**	**Chi-Square (12)**
Exponential (6)	**Z Proportion (9)**	
CIE sigma known (8)	**Pooled-Variance T (10)**	

The following Excel Guide workbooks have alternative worksheets with various names:

Descriptive (3)	CompleteStatistics_OLDER
Binomial (5)	CUMULATIVE_OLDER
Poisson (5)	CUMULATIVE_OLDER
NPP (6)	PLOT_OLDER and NORMAL_PLOT_OLDER
One-Way ANOVA (11)	TK4_OLDER
Chi-Square Worksheets (11)	ChiSquare2x3_OLDER and others
Chi-Square Worksheets (12)	ChiSquare2x3_ OLDER, Marascuilo2x3_OLDER, and others
Wilcoxon (12)	COMPUTE_ALL_OLDER
Kruskal-Wallis Worksheets (12)	KruskalWallis3_OLDER and KruskalWallis4_OLDER

Quartile Function

In this book, you will see the older QUARTILE function and not the newer QUARTILE.EXC function. In Microsoft's *Function Consistency Improvements in Excel 2010* (available at **bit.ly/1Pmu0jH**), QUARTILE.EXC is explained as being "consistent with industry best practices, assuming percentile is a value between 0 and 1, exclusive." Because there are several established but different ways of computing quartiles, there is no way of knowing exactly how the new function works.

As the COMPARE worksheet of the QUARTILES workbook illustrates, neither the new QUARTILE.EXC function or the renamed QUARTILE function QUARTILE.INC calculates quartiles using the Section 3.3 rules. Therefore, this book uses an alternate way to compute quartiles that the COMPUTE worksheet in the same workbook illustrates.

F.4 Understanding the Nonstatistical Functions

Selected Excel Guide and PHStat worksheets use a number of nonstatistical functions that either compute an intermediate result or perform a mathematical or programming operation. These functions are explained in the following alphabetical list:

CEILING(*cell, round-to value*) takes the numeric value in *cell* and rounds it to the next multiple of the *round-to value*. For example, if the *round-to value* is **0.5**, as it is in several column B formulas in the COMPUTE worksheet of the Quartiles workbook, then the numeric value will be rounded either to an integer or a number that contains a half such as 1.5.

COUNT(*cell range*) counts the number of cells in a cell range that contain a numeric value. This function is often used to compute the sample size, n, for example, in cell B9 of the COMPUTE worksheet of the Correlation workbook. When seen in the worksheets presented in this book, the *cell range* will typically be the cell range of variable column, such as **DATA!A:A**. This will result in a proper count of the sample size of that variable if you follow the Getting Started Chapter rules for entering data.

COUNTIF(*cellrange for all values, value to be matched*) counts the number of occurrences of a value in a cell range. For example, the COMPUTE worksheet of the Wilcoxon workbook uses **COUNTIF(SortedRanks!A2:A21, "Special Front")** in cell B7 to compute the sample size of the Population 1 Sample by counting the number of occurrences of the sample name Special Front in column A of the SortedRanks worksheet.

DEVSQ(*variable cell range*) computes the sum of the squares of the differences between a variable value and the mean of that variable.

FLOOR(*cell*, 1) takes the numeric value in *cell* and rounds down the value to the nearest integer.

IF(*logical comparison, what to display if comparison holds, what to display if comparison is false*) uses the *logical comparison* to make a choice between two alternatives. In the worksheets shown in this book, the IF function typically chooses from two text values, such as **Reject the null hypothesis** and **Do not reject the null hypothesis**, to display.

MMULT(*cell range 1, cell range 2*) treats both *cell range* **1** and *cell range* **2** as matrices and computes the matrix product of the two matrices. When each of the two cell ranges is either a single row or a single column, MMULT can be used as part of a regular formula. If the cell ranges each represent rows and columns, then MMULT must be used as part of an array formula (see Appendix Section B.3).

ROUND(*cell*, 0) takes the numeric value in *cell* and rounds to the nearest whole number.

SMALL(*cell range*, k) selects the *kth* smallest value in *cell range*.

SQRT(*value*) computes the square root of *value*, where *value* is either a cell reference or an arithmetic expression.

SUMIF(*cellrange for all values, value to be matched, cell range in which to select cells for summing*) sums only those rows in *cell range in which to select cells for summing* in which the value in **cell range for all values** matches the **value to be matched**. SUMIF provides a convenient way to compute the sum of ranks for a sample in a worksheet that contains stacked data.

SUMPRODUCT(*cell range 1, cell range 2*) multiplies each cell in cell range **1** by the corresponding cell in **cell range 2** and then sums those products. If **cell range 1** contains a column of differences between an X value and the mean of the variable X, and **cell range 2** contains a column of differences between a Y value and the mean of the variable Y, then this function would compute the value of the numerator in Equation (3.16) that defines the sample covariance.

TRANSPOSE(*horizontal or verticalcell range*) takes the **cell range**, which must be either a horizontal cell range (cells all in the same row) or a vertical cell range (cells all in the same column) and transposes, or rearranges, the cell in the other orientation such that a horizontal cell range becomes a vertical cell range and vice versa. When used inside another function, Excel considers the results of this function to be an *array*, not a cell range.

VLOOKUP(*lookup value cell, table of lookup values, table column to use*) function displays a value that has been looked up in a **table of lookup values**, a rectangular cell range. In the ADVANCED worksheet of the Recoded workbook, the function uses the values in the second column of **table of lookup values** (an example of which is shown below) to look up the Honors values based on the GPA of a student (the **lookup value cell**). Numbers in the first column of **table of lookup values** are implied ranges such that No Honors is the value displayed if the GPA is at least 0, but less than 3; Honor Roll is the value displayed if the GPA is at least 3, but less than 3.3; and so on:

0	No Honors
3	Honor Roll
3.3	Dean's List
3.7	President's List

Software FAQs

G.1 PHStat FAQs

What is PHStat?
PHStat is the add-in workbook that you use with Excel to help build solutions to statistical problems. With PHStat, you fill in simple-to-use dialog boxes and watch as PHStat creates a worksheet solution for you. PHStat allows you to use the Microsoft Excel statistical functions without having to first learn advanced Excel techniques or worrying about building worksheets from scratch. As a student studying statistics, you can focus mainly on learning statistics and not worry about having to fully master Excel as well.

PHStat executes for you the low-level menu selection and worksheet entry tasks that are associated with implementing statistical analysis in Microsoft Excel. PHStat creates worksheets and chart sheets that are identical to the ones featured in this book. From these sheets, you can learn real Excel techniques at your leisure and give yourself the ability to use Excel effectively outside your introductory statistics course.

Note that other add-ins that appear similar to PHStat report results as a series of text labels, hiding the details of using Microsoft Excel and leaving you with no basis for learning to use Excel effectively.

Which versions of Excel are compatible with PHStat?
PHStat is compatible with all Excel versions that Microsoft supported at the time of publication of this book. Those versions included Microsoft Windows Excels 2007, 2010, 2013, and 2016 and OS X Excels 2011 and 2016. PHStat is not compatible with mobile versions of Excel, even as most of the worksheets and chart sheets PHStat produces will be viewable in those versions.

Using PHStat with Excel 2007 will alter the contents of some worksheet formulas, as PHStat uses the older statistical functions and not the current functions that this book features when it senses Excel 2007. (See Section F.4 for more information about these differences.)

How do I obtain my own copy of PHStat?
You use an access code to download PHStat through the PHStat home page, as fully explained in Section C.2. Before downloading PHStat, download the PHStat readme file that is available (without an access code) from the PHStat home page as well as from the student download page and the MyStatLab "Tools for Success" page for this book.

How do I get PHStat ready for use?
Section D.2 explains how to get PHStat ready for use. You should also review the PHStat readme file (available for download as discussed in Appendix C) for any late-breaking news or changes that might affect this process.

When I use a particular PHStat procedure, I get an error message that includes the words "unexpected error." What should I do?
"Unexpected error" messages are typically caused by improperly prepared data. Review your data to ensure that you have organized your data according to the conventions PHStat expects, as explained in the PHStat help system.

Where can I get further news and information about PHStat? Where can I get further assistance about using PHStat?
Several online sources can provide you with news and information or provide you with assistance that supplements the readme file and help system included with PHStat.

www.pearsonhighered.com/phstat is the official PHStat home page. The page will contain late-breaking news about PHStat as well as provide a link to Pearson 24/7 Technical Support website, **247pearsoned.custhelp.com**. At that website, you can search for answers to additional questions about PHStat or get live assistance in downloading and setting up PHStat.

Follow the Twitter user @RealPHStat for news directly from the PHStat developers. Use the hashtag #PHSTAT to search Twitter community comments about PHStat.

softwareforbusstat.org is a new website that discusses using software, including PHStat and Excel, in business statistics courses. On the home page of that website, you will find links to the latest news and developments about PHStat.

How can I get updates to PHStat when they become available?
PHStat is subject to continuous improvement. When enhancements are made, a new PHStat zip archive is posted on the official web page for PHStat. If you hold a valid access code, you can download that archive and overwrite your older version. To discover which version of PHStat you have, select **About PHStat** from the PHStat menu.

G.2 Microsoft Excel FAQs

Do all Microsoft Excel versions contain the same features and functionality?
Unfortunately, features and functionality vary across currently available versions, as Section B.1 explains. This book identifies differences among versions when they are significant.

Which Microsoft Excel version should I use with this book?

Try to use the most current Excel version. Using such a version will provide you with the fullest learning experience and give you the most up-to-date practical knowledge about Excel.

What does "Compatibility Mode" in the title bar mean?

Excel displays "Compatibility Mode" when you open and use a workbook that was stored using the older **.xls** Excel workbook file format or using the **.xlsx** format in a copy of Excel that is not fully up-to-date. Compatibility Mode does not affect Excel functionality but will cause Excel to review your workbook for exclusive-to-xlsx formatting properties.

To convert a **.xls** workbook to the **.xlsx** format, use **Save As** (see Appendix B) to save (re-save) the workbook in **.xlsx** format. One quirk in Microsoft Excel is that when you convert a workbook by using **Save As**, the newly converted .xlsx workbook stays temporarily in Compatibility Mode. To avoid possible complications and errors, close the newly converted workbook and then reopen it.

Using Compatibility Mode can cause minor differences in the objects such as charts and PivotTables that Excel creates and can cause problems when you seek to transfer data from other workbooks.

What is Microsoft OneDrive?

Microsoft OneDrive is an Internet-based service that offers you online storage that enables you to access and share your files anytime and anywhere there is an Internet connection available.

You must sign in to the OneDrive service using a "Microsoft account," formerly known as a "Windows Live ID." If you use Office online or certain other special versions of Excel, you may need to sign into the OneDrive service to use Excel itself.

What is Office 365?

Office 365 is a subscription-based service that supplies you with the latest version of Microsoft Office programs for your system. Office 365 requires you to be signed in using a Microsoft account in the same way as you would sign in to use OneDrive (see previous answer). Using Office 365 gives you access to the most current versions of Microsoft Excel as they become available.

What is the Microsoft Office Store?

The Office Store is an Internet-based service that distributes enhancements to Microsoft Office programs such as Excel. In *some* Excel versions, the store can be used to add func-

tionality to Excel, such as the descriptive analytics visualizations that Section EG17.4 discusses.

In compatible Excel versions, the Insert tab contains links to the Office Store as well as the added functionality you have installed previously. In Excel 2013, the added functionality you install are called "My Apps" and the Office Store is called "Apps for Office." In Microsoft Windows Excel 2016, the added functionality you install are called "My Add-Ins" and the Office Store is called "Office Add-ins." (This use of "add-ins" should not be confused with the Excel components such as PHStat that Appendix D discusses which are also known as add-ins, but which are completely different things.)

Using the Office Store requires a Microsoft account and not all of the items in the Store are complimentary. When you use your previously installed added functionality, you must be connected to the Internet and signed into the Microsoft account you use to install that functionality.

In the Insert tab, what are Recommended PivotTables and Recommended Charts? Should I use these features?

These features display one or more "recommended" PivotTables or charts as shortcuts. Unfortunately, the recommended PivotTables can include statistical errors such as treating the categories of a categorical variable as zero values of a numerical variable and the recommended charts often do not conform to best practices.

Can I use a mobile version of Microsoft Excel such as the Microsoft Excel app for Android with this book?

You can use mobile versions of Excel to create your own data workbooks and to open and review any of the data workbooks and Excel Guide workbooks that Appendix C lists and this book uses. Because Excel Guide workbooks contain special formulas worksheets, you can inspect formulas that the workbooks use in their template and model solution worksheets. At the time of publication, mobile Excel versions did not include the capability to view formulas using the **Ctrl+`** method that Section B.3 discusses.

Should I use the charting features that mobile versions of Excel contain to create the visual summaries that this book discusses?

In some mobile versions of Excel, you can create many of the visual summaries that Chapter 2 discusses. However, you will not be able to apply the chart formatting instructions that Section B.6 discusses, so use this feature only to create preliminary summaries. Note that some chart types including "box and whisker" (boxplot in this book) create a visualization that is not identical to the visualizations in this book.

Self-Test Solutions and Answers to Selected Even-Numbered Problems

The following sections present worked-out solutions to Self-Test Problems and brief answers to most of the even-numbered problems in the text. For more detailed solutions, including explanations, interpretations, and Excel results, see the *Student Solutions Manual*.

CHAPTER 1

1.2 Small, medium, and large sizes imply order but do not specify how much the size of the business increases at each level.

1.4 (a) The number of cellphones is a numerical variable that is discrete because the outcome is a count. It is ratio scaled because it has a true zero point. **(b)** Monthly data usage is a numerical variable that is continuous because any value within a range of values can occur. It is ratio scaled because it has a true zero point. **(c)** Number of text messages exchanged per month is a numerical variable that is discrete because the outcome is a count. It is ratio scaled because it has a true zero point. **(d)** Voice usage per month is a numerical variable that is continuous because any value within a range of values can occur. It is ratio scaled because it has a true zero point. **(e)** Whether a cellphone is used for email is a categorical variable because the answer can be only yes or no. This also makes it a nominal-scaled variable.

1.6 (a) Categorical, nominal scale **(b)** Numerical, continuous, ratio scale **(c)** Categorical, nominal scale **(d)** Numerical, discrete, ratio scale **(e)** Categorical, nominal scale.

1.8 Type of data: **(a)** Numerical, continuous **(b)** Numerical, discrete **(c)** Numerical, continuous **(d)** Categorical scale. Measurement scale: **(a)** ratio scale **(b)** ratio scale **(c)** ratio scale **(d)** nominal scale.

1.10 The underlying variable, ability of the students, may be continuous, but the measuring device, the test, does not have enough precision to distinguish between the two students.

1.12 (a) Data distributed by an organization or individual **(b)** sample.

1.18 Sample without replacement: Read from left to right in three-digit sequences and continue unfinished sequences from the end of the row to the beginning of the next row:
Row 05: 338 505 855 551 438 855 077 186 579 488 767 833 170
Rows 05–06: 897
Row 06: 340 033 648 847 204 334 639 193 639 411 095 924
Rows 06–07: 707
Row 07: 054 329 776 100 871 007 255 980 646 886 823 920 461
Row 08: 893 829 380 900 796 959 453 410 181 277 660 908 887
Rows 08–09: 237
Row 09: 818 721 426 714 050 785 223 801 670 353 362 449
Rows 09–10: 406
Note: All sequences above 902 and duplicates are discarded.

1.20 A simple random sample would be less practical for personal interviews because of travel costs (unless interviewees are paid to go to a central interviewing location).

1.22 Here all members of the population are equally likely to be selected, and the sample selection mechanism is based on chance. But selection of two elements is not independent; for example, if A is in the sample, we know that B is also and that C and D are not.

1.24 (a)
Row 16: 2323 6737 5131 8888 1718 0654 6832 4647 6510 4877
Row 17: 4579 4269 2615 1308 2455 7830 5550 5852 5514 7182
Row 18: 0989 3205 0514 2256 8514 4642 7567 8896 2977 8822
Row 19: 5438 2745 9891 4991 4523 6847 9276 8646 1628 3554
Row 20: 9475 0899 2337 0892 0048 8033 6945 9826 9403 6858
Row 21: 7029 7341 3553 1403 3340 4205 0823 4144 1048 2949
Row 22: 8515 7479 5432 9792 6575 5760 0408 8112 2507 3742
Row 23: 1110 0023 4012 8607 4697 9664 4894 3928 7072 5815
Row 24: 3687 1507 7530 5925 7143 1738 1688 5625 8533 5041
Row 25: 2391 3483 5763 3081 6090 5169 0546
Note: All sequences above 5,000 are discarded. There were no repeating sequences.

(b)

089	189	289	389	489	589	689	789	889	989
1089	1189	1289	1389	1489	1589	1689	1789	1889	1989
2089	2189	2289	2389	2489	2589	2689	2789	2889	2989
3089	3189	3289	3389	3489	3589	3689	3789	3889	3989
4089	4189	4289	4389	4489	4589	4689	4789	4889	4989

(c) With the single exception of invoice 0989, the invoices selected in the simple random sample are not the same as those selected in the systematic sample. It would be highly unlikely that a simple random sample would select the same units as a systematic sample.

1.26 (a) For the third value, Apple is spelled incorrectly. The twelfth value should be Blackberry not Blueberry. The fifteenth value, APPLE, may lead to an irregularity. The eighteenth value should be Samsung not Samsun. **(b)** The eighth value is a missing value.

1.28 (a) The times for each of the hotels would be arranged in separate columns. **(b)** The hotel names would be in one column and the times would be in a second column.

1.30 Before accepting the results of a survey of college students, you might want to know, for example: Who funded the survey? Why was it conducted? What was the population from which the sample was selected? What sampling design was used? What mode of response was used: a personal interview, a telephone interview, or a mail survey? Were interviewers trained? Were survey questions field-tested? What questions were asked? Were the questions clear, accurate, unbiased, and valid? What operational definition of immediately and effortlessly was used? What was the response rate?

1.32 The results are based on an online survey. If the frame is supposed to be smartphone and tablet users, how is the population defined? This is a self-selecting sample of people who responded online, so there is an undefined nonresponse error. Sampling error cannot be determined since this is not a probability sample.

1.34 Before accepting the results of the survey, you might want to know, for example: Who funded the study? Why was it conducted? What was the population from which the sample was selected? What sampling design was used? What mode of response was used: a personal interview, a telephone interview, or a mail survey? Were interviewers trained? Were survey questions field-tested? What other questions were asked? Were the questions clear, accurate, unbiased, and valid? What was the response rate? What was the margin of error? What was the sample size? What frame was used?

1.50 (a) All benefitted employees at the university. (b) The 3,095 employees who responded to the survey. (c) Gender, marital status, and employment are categorical. Age (years), education level (years completed), and household income ($) are numerical.

CHAPTER 2

2.2 (a) Table of frequencies for all student responses:

Gender	Student Major Categories			
	A	C	M	Totals
Male	14	9	2	25
Female	6	6	3	15
Totals	20	15	5	40

(b) Table based on total percentages:

Gender	Student Major Categories			
	A	C	M	Totals
Male	35.0%	22.5%	5.0%	62.5%
Female	15.0%	15.0%	7.5%	37.5%
Totals	50.0%	37.5%	12.5%	100.0%

Table based on row percentages:

Gender	Student Major Categories			
	A	C	M	Totals
Male	56.0%	36.0%	8.0%	100.0%
Female	40.0%	40.0%	20.0%	100.0%
Totals	50.0%	37.5%	12.5%	100.0%

Table based on column percentages:

Gender	Student Major Categories			
	A	C	M	Totals
Male	70.0%	60.0%	40.0%	62.5%
Female	30.0%	40.0%	60.0%	37.5%
Totals	100.0%	100.0%	100.0%	100.0%

2.4 (a) The percentage of complaints for each automaker:

Automaker	Frequency	Percentage
General Motors	551	18.91%
Other	516	17.71%
Nissan Motors Corporation	467	16.03%
Ford Motor Company	440	15.10%
Chrysler LLC	439	15.07%
Toyota Motor Sales	332	11.39%
American Honda	169	5.80%

(b) General Motors has the most complaints, followed by Other, Nissan Motors Corporation, Ford Motor Company, Chrysler LLC, Toyota Motor Sales and American Honda.

(c) The percentage of complaints for each category:

Category	Frequency	Percentage
Powertrain	1148	42.82%
Steering	397	14.81%
Interior Electronics/Hardware	279	10.41%
Fuel/Emission/Exhaust System	240	8.95%
Airbags and Seatbelts	201	7.50%
Body and Glass	182	6.79%
Brakes	163	6.08%
Tires and Wheels	71	2.65%

(d) Powertrain has the most complaints, followed by steering, interior electronics/hardware, fuel/emission/exhaust system, airbags and seatbelts, body and glass, brakes, and, finally, tires and wheels.

2.6 (a) The percentages are 3.273, 11.656, 21.815, and 63.256. **(b)** More than 60% of the oil produced is from non-OPEC countries. More than 20% is produced by OPEC countries other than Iran and Saudi Arabia.

2.8 (a) Table of row percentages:

Influenced by Social Media	Gender		
	Male	Female	Total
Yes	33.97%	66.03%	100%
No	52.92%	47.08%	100%
Total	50%	50%	100%

Table of column percentages:

Influenced by Social Media	Gender		
	Male	Female	Total
Yes	10.47%	20.35%	15.12%
No	89.53%	79.65%	84.58%
Total	100%	100%	100%

Table of total percentages:

Influenced by Social Media	Gender		
	Male	Female	Total
Yes	5.24%	10.18%	15.41%
No	44.76%	39.82%	84.59%
Total	50%	50%	100%

(b) A higher percentage of females are influenced by social media.

2.10 Social recommendations had very little impact on correct recall. Those who arrived at the link from a recommendation had a correct recall of 73.07% as compared to those who arrived at the link from browsing who had a correct recall of 67.96%.

2.12 73 78 78 78 85 88 91.

2.14 (a) 0 but less than 5 million, 5 million but less than 10 million, 10 million but less than 15 million, 15 million but less than 20 million, 20 million but less than 25 million, 25 million but less than 30 million. **(b)** 5 million. **(c)** 2.5 million, 7.5 million, 12.5 million, 17.5 million, 22.5 million, and 27.5 million.

2.16 (a)

Electricity Costs	Frequency	Percentage
$80 but less than $100	4	8%
$100 but less than $120	7	14%
$120 but less than $140	9	18%
$140 but less than $160	13	26%
$160 but less than $180	9	18%
$180 but less than $200	5	10%
$200 but less than $220	3	6%

(b)

Electricity Costs	Frequency	Percentage	Cumulative %
$ 99	4	8.00%	8.00%
$119	7	14.00%	22.00%
$139	9	18.00%	40.00%
$159	13	26.00%	66.00%
$179	9	18.00%	84.00%
$199	5	10.00%	94.00%
$219	3	6.00%	100.00%

(c) The majority of utility charges are clustered between $120 and $180.

2.18 (a), (b)

Credit Score	Frequency	Percent (%)	Cumulative %
600 – under 610	1	0.70	0.70
610 – under 620	0	0.00	0.70
620 – under 630	2	1.40	2.10
630 – under 640	15	10.49	12.59
640 – under 650	18	12.59	25.17
650 – under 660	24	16.78	41.96
660 – under 670	22	15.38	57.34
670 – under 680	28	19.58	76.92
680 – under 690	21	14.69	91.61
690 – under 700	11	7.69	99.30
700 – under 710	1	0.70	100.00

(c) The average credit scores are concentrated between 650 and 690.

2.20 (a)

Width	Frequency	Percentage
8.310 but less than 8.330	3	6.12%
8.330 but less than 8.350	2	4.08%
8.350 but less than 8.370	1	2.04%
8.370 but less than 8.390	4	8.16%
8.390 but less than 8.410	5	10.20%
8.410 but less than 8.430	16	32.65%
8.430 but less than 8.450	5	10.20%
8.450 but less than 8.470	5	10.20%
8.470 but less than 8.490	6	12.24%
8.490 but less than 8.510	2	4.08%

(b)

Width	Percentage Less Than
8.310	0
8.330	6.12
8.350	10.20
8.370	12.24
8.390	20.40
8.410	30.60
8.430	63.25
8.450	73.45
8.470	83.65
8.490	95.89
8.51	100.00

(c) All the troughs will meet the company's requirements of between 8.31 and 8.61 inches wide.

2.22 (a)

Bulb Life (hours)	Percentage, Mfgr A	Percentage, Mfgr B
6,500 but less than 7,500	7.5%	0.0%
7,500 but less than 8,500	12.5%	5.0%
8,500 but less than 9,500	50.0%	20.0%
9,500 but less than 10,500	22.5%	40.0%
10,500 but less than 11,500	7.5%	22.5%
11,500 but less than 12,500	0.0%	12.5%

(b)

% Less Than	Percentage Less Than, Mfgr A	Percentage Less Than, Mfgr B
7,500	7.5%	0.0%
8,500	20.0%	5.0%
9,500	70.0%	25.0%
10,500	92.5%	65.0%
11,500	100.0%	87.5%
12,500	100.0%	100.0%

(c) Manufacturer B produces bulbs with longer lives than Manufacturer A. The cumulative percentage for Manufacturer B shows that 65% of its bulbs lasted less than 10,500 hours, contrasted with 92.5% of Manufacturer A's bulbs. None of Manufacturer A's bulbs lasted at least 11,500 hours, but 12.5% of Manufacturer B's bulbs lasted at least 11,500 hours. At the same time, 7.5% of Manufacturer A's bulbs lasted less than 7,500 hours, whereas none of Manufacturer B's bulbs lasted less than 7,500 hours.

2.24 (b) The Pareto chart is best for portraying these data because it not only sorts the frequencies in descending order but also provides the cumulative line on the same chart. **(c)** You can conclude that "improved regulation and oversight of global systemic risk" and "improved transparency of financial reporting and other financial disclosures" account for 49% of the most needed action to improve investor trust and market integrity.

2.26 (b) 85%. **(d)** The Pareto chart allows you to see which sources account for most of the electricity.

2.28 (b) Since energy use is spread over many types of appliances, a bar chart may be best in showing which types of appliances used the most energy. **(c)** Heating, water heating, and cooling accounted for 40% of the residential energy use in the United States.

2.30 Side-by-side highlights the increase in number of the truly independent directors, but obscures the part of the whole that independents represent. The doughnut chart highlights that the truly independent directors still do not comprise a majority of directors.

2.32 (b) Social recommendations had very little impact on correct recall.

2.34 50 74 74 76 81 89 92.

2.36 (a)

Stem Unit	100
2	1 2 2 3 5 6 6 6 7 8 8 8 8 9
3	0 1 2 2 2 4 4 4 7
4	0 4 4 7 8
5	4
6	8

(b) The results are concentrated between $200 and $370.

2.38 (c) The majority of utility charges are clustered between $120 and $180.

2.40 Property taxes seem concentrated between $1,000 and $1,500 and also between $500 and $1,000 per capita. There were more states with property taxes per capita below $1,500 than above $1,500.

2.42 The average credit scores are concentrated between 650 and 690.

2.44 (c) All the troughs will meet the company's requirements of between 8.31 and 8.61 inches wide.

2.46 (c) Manufacturer B produces bulbs with longer lives than Manufacturer A.

2.48 (b) Yes, there is a strong positive relationship between X and Y. As X increases, so does Y.

2.50 (c) There appears to be a linear relationship between the first weekend gross and either the U.S. gross or the worldwide gross of Harry Potter movies. However, this relationship is greatly affected by the results of the last movie, *Deathly Hallows, Part II*.

2.52 (a), (c) There appears to be a positive relationship between the coaches' total pay and revenue. Yes, this is borne out by the data.

2.54 (b) There is a great deal of variation in the returns from decade to decade. Most of the returns are between 5% and 15%. The 1950s, 1980s, and 1990s had exceptionally high returns, and only the 1930s and 2000s had negative returns.

2.56 (b) There was a decline in movie attendance between 2001 and 2014. During that time, movie attendance increased from 2002 to 2004 but then decreased to a level below that in 2001.

2.58

Count of Type	Star Rating					
Type	One	Two	Three	Four	Five	Grand Total
Growth	**19**	**78**	**118**	**45**	**9**	**269**
Large	9	34	56	21	7	127
Mid-Cap	6	26	39	17	1	89
Small	4	18	23	7	1	53
Value	**9**	**40**	**60**	**27**	**2**	**138**
Large	5	22	39	16	1	83
Mid-Cap	3	10	10	6	1	30
Small	1	8	11	5		25
Grand Total	**28**	**118**	**178**	**72**	**11**	**407**

Pivot Table in terms of %

Count of Type	Star Rating					
Type	One	Two	Three	Four	Five	Grand Total
Growth	**4.67%**	**19.16%**	**28.99%**	**11.06%**	**2.21%**	**66.09%**
Large	2.21%	8.35%	13.76%	5.16%	1.72%	31.20%
Mid-Cap	1.47%	6.39%	9.58%	4.18%	0.25%	21.87%
Small	0.98%	4.42%	5.65%	1.72%	0.25%	13.02%
Value	**2.21%**	**9.83%**	**14.74%**	**6.63%**	**0.49%**	**33.91%**
Large	1.23%	5.41%	9.58%	3.93%	0.25%	20.39%
Mid-Cap	0.74%	2.46%	2.46%	1.47%	0.25%	7.37%
Small	0.25%	1.97%	2.70%	1.23%	0.00%	6.14%
Grand Total	**6.88%**	**28.99%**	**43.73%**	**17.69%**	**2.70%**	**100.00%**

The value funds have a similar pattern except for the mid-cap funds, which are equally likely to have two- and three-star ratings.

Patterns of market cap conditioned on star rating:

Most of the growth funds are large-cap, followed by mid-cap and small-cap. The pattern is similar among each of the star ratings.

The largest share of the value funds is large-cap, followed by mid-cap and small-cap. The pattern is similar among all the rating categories.

2.60 Pivot table of tallies in terms of counts:

Count of Type	Star Rating					
Type	One	Two	Three	Four	Five	Grand Total
Growth	**19**	**78**	**118**	**45**	**9**	**269**
Low	1	4	7	3	1	16
Average	11	51	95	35	7	199
High	7	23	16	7	1	54
Value	**9**	**40**	**60**	**27**	**2**	**138**
Low	1	4	15	5		25
Average	5	29	41	20	2	97
High	3	7	4	2		16
Grand Total	**28**	**118**	**178**	**72**	**11**	**407**

Pivot Table in terms of %

Count of Type	Star Rating					
Type	One	Two	Three	Four	Five	Grand Total
Growth	**4.67%**	**19.16%**	**28.99%**	**11.06%**	**2.21%**	**66.09%**
Low	0.25%	0.98%	1.72%	0.74%	0.25%	3.93%
Average	2.70%	12.53%	23.34%	8.60%	1.72%	48.89%

Count of Type	Star Rating					
Type	One	Two	Three	Four	Five	Grand Total
High	1.72%	5.65%	3.93%	1.72%	0.25%	13.27%
Value	**2.21%**	**9.83%**	**14.74%**	**6.63%**	**0.49%**	**33.91%**
Low	0.25%	0.98%	3.69%	1.23%	0.00%	6.14%
Average	1.23%	7.13%	10.07%	4.91%	0.49%	23.83%
High	0.74%	1.72%	0.98%	0.49%	0.00%	3.93%
Grand Total	**6.88%**	**28.99%**	**43.73%**	**17.69%**	**2.70%**	**100.00%**

(b) Patterns of star rating conditioned on risk:

For the growth funds as a group, most are rated as three-star, followed by two-star, four-star, one-star, and five-star. The pattern of star rating is the same among the low-risk growth funds.

For the value funds as a group, most are rated as three-star, followed by two-star, four-star, one-star and five-star. Among the high-risk value funds, more are two-star than three-star.

Most of the growth funds are rated as average-risk, followed by high-risk and then low-risk. The pattern is the same among all the rating categories.

Most of the value funds are rated as average-risk, followed by low-risk and then high-risk. The pattern is the same among the three-star and four-star value funds. Among the one-star and two-star funds, there are more high risk funds than low risk funds.

(c)

Average of 3YrReturn%	Star Rating					
Type	One	Two	Three	Four	Five	Grand Total
Growth	**12.0311**	**13.8681**	**15.4837**	**17.0080**	**19.1144**	**15.1478**
Low	14.2600	14.2050	15.2071	16.7133	18.1000	15.3600
Average	12.9064	14.0775	15.6177	16.9457	19.0186	15.4263
High	10.3371	13.3452	14.8094	17.4457	20.8000	14.0587
Value	**9.9322**	**14.4315**	**15.5308**	**16.7463**	**19.4600**	**15.1418**
Low	14.2600	10.5325	14.1047	15.3620		13.7908
Average	10.6000	15.2976	16.1334	17.2985	19.4600	15.9071
High	7.3767	13.0714	14.7025	14.6850		12.6131
Grand Total	**11.3564**	**14.0591**	**15.4996**	**16.9099**	**19.1773**	**15.1458**

The three-year returns for growth and value funds are virtually the same. The return is higher for funds with higher ratings than lower ratings. This pattern holds for the growth funds for each risk level. For the low risk value funds, the return is lowest for the funds with a two-star rating.

(d) There are 16 growth funds with high risk with a rating of three.

2.62 The fund with the highest five-year return of 22.83 is a large cap growth fund that has a four-star rating and average risk.

2.64 Funds 191, 206, 213, 371, and 400 have the lowest five-year return.

2.66 The five funds with the lowest five-year return have either low or high risk and either a one-star or two-star rating.

2.68 All the stock indexes except Dow utilities spiked up in 2009 and 2013. Dow utilities spiked up in 2014 .

2.88 (c) The publisher gets the largest portion (64.8%) of the revenue. About half (32.3%) of the revenue received by the publisher covers manufacturing costs. The publisher's marketing and promotion account for the next largest share of the revenue, at 15.4%. Author, bookstore employee salaries and benefits, and publisher administrative costs and taxes each account for around 10% of the revenue, whereas the publisher after-tax profit, bookstore operations, bookstore pretax profit, and freight constitute the "trivial few" allocations of the revenue. Yes, the bookstore gets twice the revenue of the authors.

2.90 (b) The pie chart may be best since with only five categories, it enables you to see the portion of the whole in each category. **(d)** The pie chart may be best since, with only three categories it enables you to see the portion of the whole in each category. **(e)** Marketers mostly find out about new marketing agencies from calls/emails from agencies and referrals from friends and colleagues. Almost 90% believe that it is important for a marketing agency to specialize in the marketer's industry.

2.92 (a)

Dessert Ordered	Gender		Total
	Male	Female	
Yes	34%	66%	100%
No	52%	48%	100%
Total	48%	52%	100%

Dessert Ordered	Gender		Total
	Male	Female	
Yes	17%	29%	23%
No	83%	71%	77%
Total	100%	100%	100%

Dessert Ordered	Gender		Total
	Male	Female	
Yes	8%	15%	23%
No	40%	37%	77%
Total	48%	52%	100%

Dessert Ordered	Beef Entrée		Total
	Yes	No	
Yes	52%	48%	100%
No	25%	75%	100%
Total	31%	69%	100%

Dessert Ordered	Beef Entrée		Total
	Yes	No	
Yes	38%	16%	23%
No	62%	84%	77%
Total	100%	100%	100%

Dessert Ordered	Beef Entrée		Total
	Yes	No	
Yes	11.75%	10.79%	22.54%
No	19.52%	57.94%	77.46%
Total	31.27%	68.73%	100%

(b) If the owner is interested in finding out the percentage of males and females who order dessert or the percentage of those who order a beef entrée and a dessert among all patrons, the table of total percentages is most informative. If the owner is interested in the effect of gender on ordering of dessert or the effect of ordering a beef entrée on the ordering of dessert, the table of column percentages will be most informative. Because dessert is usually ordered after the main entrée, and the owner has no direct control over the gender of patrons, the table of row percentages is not very useful here. **(c)** 17% of the men ordered desserts, compared to 29% of the women; women are almost twice as likely to order dessert as men. Almost 38% of the patrons ordering a beef entrée ordered dessert, compared to 16% of patrons ordering all other entrées. Patrons ordering beef are more than 2.3 times as likely to order dessert as patrons ordering any other entrée.

2.94 (a) Most of the complaints were against the airlines.

2.96 (c) The alcohol percentage is concentrated between 4% and 6%, with more between 4% and 5%. The calories are concentrated between 140 and 160. The carbohydrates are concentrated between 12 and 15. There are outliers in the percentage of alcohol in both tails. There are a few beers with alcohol content as high as around 11.5%. There are a few beers with

calorie content as high as around 327.5 and carbohydrates as high as 31.5. There is a strong positive relationship between percentage of alcohol and calories and between calories and carbohydrates, and there is a moderately positive relationship between percentage alcohol and carbohydrates.

2.98 (c) There appears to be a moderate positive relationship between the yield of the one-year CD and the five-year CD.

2.100 (a)

Frequency (Boston)		
Weight (Boston)	Frequency	Percentage
3,015 but less than 3,050	2	0.54%
3,050 but less than 3,085	44	11.96%
3,085 but less than 3,120	122	33.15%
3,120 but less than 3,155	131	35.60%
3,155 but less than 3,190	58	15.76%
3,190 but less than 3,225	7	1.90%
3,225 but less than 3,260	3	0.82%
3,260 but less than 3,295	1	0.27%

(b)

Frequency (Vermont)		
Weight (Vermont)	Frequency	Percentage
3,550 but less than 3,600	4	1.21%
3,600 but less than 3,650	31	9.39%
3,650 but less than 3,700	115	34.85%
3,700 but less than 3,750	131	39.70%
3,750 but less than 3,800	36	10.91%
3,800 but less than 3,850	12	3.64%
3,850 but less than 3,900	1	0.30%

(d) 0.54% of the Boston shingles pallets are underweight and 0.27% are overweight. 1.21% of the Vermont shingles pallets are underweight and 3.94% are overweight.

2.102 (c)

Calories	Frequency	Percentage	Limit	Percentage Less Than
50 but less than 100	3	12%	100	12%
100 but less than 150	3	12%	150	24%
150 but less than 200	9	36%	200	60%
200 but less than 250	6	24%	250	84%
250 but less than 300	3	12%	300	96%
300 but less than 350	0	0%	350	96%
350 but less than 400	1	4%	400	100%

Cholesterol	Frequency	Percentage	Limit	Percentage Less Than
0 but less than 50	2	8%	50	8%
50 but less than 100	17	68%	100	76%
100 but less than 150	4	16%	150	92%
150 but less than 200	1	4%	200	96%
200 but less than 250	0	0%	250	96%
250 but less than 300	0	0%	300	96%
300 but less than 350	0	0%	350	96%
350 but less than 400	0	0%	400	96%
400 but less than 450	0	0%	450	96%
450 but less than 500	1	4%	500	100%

The sampled fresh red meats, poultry, and fish vary from 98 to 397 calories per serving, with the highest concentration between 150 and 200 calories. One protein source, spareribs, with 397 calories, is more than 100 calories above the next-highest-caloric food. Spareribs and fried liver are both very different from other foods sampled—the former on calories and the latter on cholesterol content.

2.104 (b) There is a downward trend in the amount filled. **(c)** The amount filled in the next bottle will most likely be below 1.894 liters. **(d)** The scatter plot of the amount of soft drink filled against time reveals the trend of the data, whereas a histogram only provides information on the distribution of the data.

2.106 (a) The percentage of downloads is 9.64% for the Original Call to Action Button and 13.64% for the New Call to Action Button. **(c)** The New Call to Action Button has a higher percentage of downloads at 13.64% when compared to the Original Call to Action Button with a 9.64% of downloads. **(d)** The percentage of downloads is 8.90% for the Original web design and 9.41% for the New web design. **(f)** The New web design has only a slightly higher percentage of downloads at 9.41% when compared to the Original web design with an 8.90% of downloads. **(g)** The New web design is only slightly more successful than the Original web design while the New Call to Action Button is much more successful than the Original Call to Action Button with about 41% higher percentage of downloads.

(h)

Call to Action Button	Web Design	Percentage of Downloads
Old	Old	8.30%
New	Old	13.70%
Old	New	9.50%
New	New	17.00%

(i) The new Call to Action Button and the New web design together had a higher percentage of downloads. **(j)** The New web design is only slightly more successful than the Original web design while the New Call to Action Button is much more successful than the Original Call to Action Button with about 41% higher percentage of downloads. However, the combination of the New Call to Action Button and the New web design results in more than twice as high a percentage of downloads than the combination of the Original Call to Action Button and the Origiunal web design.

CHAPTER 3

3.2 (a) Mean = 7, median = 7, mode = 7. **(b)** Range = 9, S^2 = 10.8, S = 3.286, CV = 46.948%. **(c)** Z scores: 0, −0.913, 0.609, 0, −1.217, 1.522. None of the Z scores are larger than 3.0 or smaller than −3.0. There is no outlier. **(d)** Symmetric because mean = median.

3.4 (a) Mean = 2, median = 7, mode = 7. **(b)** Range = 17, S^2 = 62 S = 7.874, CV = 393.7%. **(c)** 0.635, −0.889, −1.270, 0.635, 0.889. There are no outliers. **(d)** Left-skewed because mean < median.

3.6 −0.0835

3.8 (a)

	Grade X	Grade Y
Mean	575	575.4
Median	575	575
Standard deviation	6.40	2.07

(b) If quality is measured by central tendency, Grade X tires provide slightly better quality because X's mean and median are both equal to the expected value, 575 mm. If, however, quality is measured by consistency, Grade Y provides better quality because, even though Y's mean is only slightly larger than the mean for Grade X, Y's standard deviation is much smaller. The range in values for Grade Y is 5 mm compared to the range in values for Grade X, which is 16 mm.

(c)

	Grade X	Grade Y, Altered
Mean	575	577.4
Median	575	575
Standard deviation	6.40	6.11

When the fifth Y tire measures 588 mm rather than 578 mm, Y's mean inner diameter becomes 577.4 mm, which is larger than X's mean inner diameter, and Y's standard deviation increases from 2.07 mm to 6.11 mm. In this case, X's tires are providing better quality in terms of the mean inner diameter, with only slightly more variation among the tires than Y's.

3.10 (a), (b)

Spend ($)	
Mean	56.40
Median	55.35
Minimum	22.90
Maximum	108.25
Range	85.35
Variance	380.4062
Standard Deviation	19.5040
Coefficient of Variation	34.58%
Skewness	1.1078
Kurtosis	3.0651
Count	15

(c) The mean is greater than the median and the skewness statistic is positive, so the amount spent is right- or positive-skewed. **(d)** The mean amount spent is $56.40 and half the customers spent more than $55.35. The amount spent is right-skewed since there are some amounts spent that are high. The average scatter around the mean is $19.50. The difference between the largest amount spent and the smallest amount spent is $85.35.

3.12 (a), (b)

MPG	
Mean	23.15
Median	22.5
Minimum	21
Maximum	28
Range	7
Variance	3.8184
Standard Deviation	1.9541
Coeff. of Variation	8.44%
Skewness	0.9427
Kurtosis	0.3998
Count	20

MPG	Z	MPG	Z
26	1.4585	22	−0.5885
22	−0.5885	21	−1.1003
24	0.4350	22	−0.5885
22	−0.5885	21	−1.1003
26	1.4585	24	0.4350
21	−1.1003	23	−0.0768
24	0.4350	23	−0.0768
25	0.9467	22	−0.5885
28	2.4820	21	−1.1003
24	0.4350	22	−0.5885

(c) Since the mean MPG is greater than the median and the skewness statistic is positive, the distribution of MPG is right- or positive-skewed. **(d)** The mean miles per gallon of small SUVs is 23.15 and half the small SUVs achieve at least 22.5 miles per gallon. There are no outliers in the data as the largest Z score is 2.482 and the smallest Z score is −1.10. The average scatter around the mean is 1.9541 mpg. The lowest mpg is 21 and the highest is 28. The mpg of mid-sized sedans is much higher than for small SUVs. The mean miles per gallon of mid-sized sedans is 28.7083 and half the mid-sized sedans achieve at least 27 miles per gallon. The average scatter around the mean is 5.32 mpg. The lowest mpg of mid-sized sedans is 22 and the highest is 40.

3.14 (a), (b)

Mobile Commerce Penetration (%)

Mean	16.3929
Median	15
Minimum	6
Maximum	37
Range	31
Variance	44.2474
Standard Deviation	6.6519
Coefficient of Variation	40.58%
Skewness	1.1724
Kurtosis	2.1999
Count	28

Country	Mobile Commerce Penetration (%)	Z Score
Argentina	17	0.0913
Australia	15	−0.2094
Brazil	15	−0.2094
Canada	13	−0.5101
China	27	1.5946
France	12	−0.6604
Germany	20	0.5423
Hong Kong	23	0.9933
India	9	−1.1114
Indonesia	9	−1.1114
Italy	16	−0.0591
Japan	6	−1.5624
Malaysia	19	0.3919
Mexico	14	−0.3597
Philippines	11	−0.8107
Poland	14	−0.3597
Russia	8	−1.2617
Saudi Arabia	15	−0.2094
Singapore	23	0.9933
South Africa	11	−0.8107
South Korea	37	3.0979
Spain	17	0.0913
Thailand	11	−0.8107
Turkey	19	0.3919
United Arab Emirates	27	1.5946
United Kingdom	18	0.2416
United States	18	0.2416
Vietnam	15	−0.2094

The highest Z score is 3.098 and the lowest Z score is −1.5624, so there is one extreme value. **(c)** The mean is greater than the median, so Mobile Commerce penetration is right-skewed. **(d)** The mean Mobile Commerce penetration is 16.3929% and half the countries have Mobile Commerce penetration greater than or equal to 15%. The average scatter around the mean is 6.6519%. The lowest Mobile Commerce penetration is 6% in Japan and the highest Mobile Commerce penetration is 37% in South Korea.

3.16 (a), (b)

Price (USD)

Mean	159.75
Median	162
Range	33
Variance	134.5
Standard Deviation	11.5974

(c) The mean room price is $159.75 and half the room prices are greater than or equal to $162, so room price is left-skewed. The average scatter around the mean is 11.5974. The lowest room price is $141 in France and the highest room price is $174 in the United States.

3.18 (a) Mean $= 7.11$, median $= 6.68$. **(b)** Variance $= 4.336$, standard deviation $= 2.082$, range $= 6.67$, $CV = 29.27\%$.

Waiting Time	Z Score	Waiting Time	Z Score
9.66	1.222431	10.49	1.62105
5.90	−0.58336	6.68	−0.20875
8.02	0.434799	5.64	−0.70823
5.79	−0.63619	4.08	−1.45744
8.73	0.775786	6.17	−0.45369
3.82	−1.58231	9.91	1.342497
8.01	0.429996	5.47	−0.78987
8.35	0.593286		

(c) Because the mean is greater than the median, the distribution is right-skewed. **(d)** The mean and median are both greater than five minutes. The distribution is right-skewed, meaning that there are some unusually high values. Further, 13 of the 15 bank customers sampled (or 86.7%) had waiting times greater than five minutes. So the customer is likely to experience a waiting time in excess of five minutes. The manager overstated the bank's service record in responding that the customer would "almost certainly" not wait longer than five minutes for service.

3.20 (a) $[(1 + 1.053) \times (1 + (0.428)]^{1/2} - 1 = 0.7122$ or 71.22%. **(b)** $= (\$1,000) \times (1 + 0.7122) \times (1 + 0.7122) = \$2,931.63$. **(c)** The result for Facebook was better than the result for GE, which was worth $1,204.51.

3.22 (a) Platinum $= -6.89\%$ gold $= -4.41\%$ silver $= -6.65\%$. **(b)** Platinum had the least negative return. **(c)** All the metals had negative returns, whereas the three stock indices all had positive returns.

3.24 (a)

Mean of 1YrReturn%	Star Rating					
Type	One	Two	Three	Four	Five	Grand Total
Growth	**2.8416**	**6.2064**	**7.9194**	**9.2507**	**13.9111**	**7.4872**
Large	8.7433	9.5938	11.0141	11.7167	14.8043	10.7980
Mid-Cap	1.6867	6.0562	7.0326	8.7429	11.2700	6.7612
Small	−8.7050	0.0250	1.8883	3.0857	10.3000	0.7728
Value	**0.9167**	**7.1840**	**9.1857**	**10.7559**	**14.4450**	**8.4496**
Large	−0.1480	8.9514	10.7682	12.1919	11.1400	9.9080
Mid-Cap	3.8967	8.1650	10.2310	10.4350	17.7500	9.2003
Small	−2.7000	1.0975	2.6245	6.5460		2.7072
Grand Total	**2.2229**	**6.5378**	**8.3462**	**9.8151**	**14.0082**	**7.8135**

(b)

StdDev of 1YrReturn%	Star Rating					
Type	One	Two	Three	Four	Five	Grand Total
Growth	**$7.9517**	**$5.2576**	**$5.1226**	**$4.5287**	**$4.0665**	**$5.6128**
Large	$2.0218	$3.5057	$3.5888	$4.0362	$4.2169	$3.7788
Mid-Cap	$5.1351	$4.3353	$4.0308	$1.8247	#DIV/0!	$4.1694
Small	$6.2933	$3.2039	$3.9359	$4.5672	#DIV/0!	$4.9720
Value	**$8.8806**	**$4.4291**	**$4.1795**	**$2.8695**	**$4.6740**	**$5.0438**
Large	$10.4456	$3.3042	$2.4800	$1.5642	#DIV/0!	$4.3836
Mid-Cap	$8.6339	$3.4190	$2.7058	$2.4363	#DIV/0!	$4.3065
Small	#DIV/0!	$2.8250	$3.8583	$2.5242		$3.8402
Grand Total	**$8.1461**	**$4.9947**	**$4.8506**	**$4.0328**	**$3.9320**	**$5.4395**

(c) The mean one-year return of small cap funds is much lower than mid-cap and large funds. Five star funds for all market cap categories show the highest mean one-year returns. The mean one-year returns for all combinations of type and market cap rises as the star rating rises, consistent to the mean one-year returns for all growth and value funds.

The standard deviations of the one-year return for large cap and mid-cap value funds vary greatly among star rating categories, with four star funds showing the lowest standard deviation and one star funds showing the highest. In contrast, the standard deviation of the one-year return for large cap growth funds varies much less.

3.26 (a)

Mean of 1YrReturn%	Star Rating					
Type	One	Two	Three	Four	Five	Grand Total
Growth	**2.8416**	**6.2064**	**7.9194**	**9.2507**	**13.9111**	**7.4872**
Low	8.6700	10.6850	11.5286	13.8000	11.2700	11.5488
Average	6.9991	7.5802	8.9641	9.9846	14.1757	8.8636
High	−4.5243	2.3813	0.1375	3.6314	14.7000	1.2115
Value	**0.9167**	**7.1840**	**9.1857**	**10.7559**	**14.4450**	**8.4496**
Low	8.6700	5.8475	11.6980	13.2740		10.9560
Average	4.4280	8.7093	8.7637	10.5560	14.4450	9.0106
High	−7.5200	1.6286	4.0900	6.4600		1.1325
Grand Total	**2.2229**	**6.5378**	**8.3462**	**9.8151**	**14.0082**	**7.8135**

(b)

StdDev of 1YrReturn%	Star Rating					Grand Total
	One	**Two**	**Three**	**Four**	**Five**	
Growth	**$7.9517**	**$5.2576**	**$5.1226**	**$4.5287**	**$4.0665**	**$5.6128**
Low	#DIV/0!	$1.1001	$3.5158	$1.0633	#DIV/0!	$2.6660
Average	$4.6952	$4.8491	$4.0607	$3.6713	$4.5498	$4.4343
High	$7.2317	$4.4523	$4.3376	$4.8285	#DIV/0!	$5.6220
Value	**$8.8806**	**$4.4291**	**$4.1795**	**$2.8695**	**$4.6740**	**$5.0438**
Low	#DIV/0!	$3.2025	$2.0166	$1.3177		$3.1582
Average	$7.5990	$3.4779	$4.3269	$2.6492	$4.6740	$4.1966
High	$5.6854	$4.1821	$2.5124	$2.0930		$5.8365
Grand Total	**$8.1461**	**$4.9947**	**$4.8506**	**$4.0328**	**$3.9320**	**$5.4395**

(c) The mean one-year return of high risk funds is much lower than the other risk categories except for five star funds. In the average and high risk categories, five star funds have the highest mean one-year return whereas in low risk funds four star funds have the highest mean one-year return. The mean one-year returns for high risk growth and value funds are much lower than the means for the other risk categories.

The standard deviations of the one-year return for average risk funds show the most consistency across star rating categories and the standard deviations of the one-year return for low risk funds are the lowest across categories. The standard deviations of the one-year return for high risk value funds declines as the star rating increases. They also vary greatly among star rating categories, with four star funds showing the lowest standard deviation and one star funds showing the highest. In contrast, the standard deviation of the one-year return for large cap growth funds varies much less.

3.28 (a) 4, 9, 5. **(b)** 3, 4, 7, 9, 12. **(c)** The distances between the median and the extremes are close, 4 and 5, but the differences in the tails are different (1 on the left and 3 on the right), so this distribution is slightly right-skewed. **(d)** In Problem 3.2 (d), because mean = median, the distribution is symmetric. The box part of the graph is symmetric, but the tails show right-skewness.

3.30 (a) −6.5, 8, 14.5. **(b)** −8, −6.5, 7, 8, 9. **(c)** The shape is left-skewed. **(d)** This is consistent with the answer in Problem 3.4 (d).

3.32 (a), (b) Minimum = 6 Q_1 = 11 Median = 15 Q_3 = 19 Maximum = 37 Interquartile range = 8 **(c)** the boxplot is right skewed.

3.34 (a), (b) Minimum = 21 Q_1 = 22 Median = 22.5 Q_3 = 24 Maximum = 28 Interquartile range = 2 **(c)** The boxplot is right skewed

3.36 (a) Commercial district five-number summary: 0.38 3.2 4.5 5.55 6.46. Residential area five-number summary: 3.82 5.64 6.68 8.73 10.49. **(b)** Commercial district: The distribution is left-skewed. Residential area: The distribution is slightly right-skewed. **(c)** The central tendency of the waiting times for the bank branch located in the commercial district of a city is lower than that of the branch located in the residential area. There are a few long waiting times for the branch located in the residential area, whereas there are a few exceptionally short waiting times for the branch located in the commercial area.

3.38 (a) Population mean, μ = 6. **(b)** Population standard deviation, σ = 1.673, population variance, σ^2 = 2.8.

3.40 (a) 68%. **(b)** 95%. **(c)** Not calculable, 75%, 88.89%. **(d)** $\mu - 4\sigma$ to $\mu + 4\sigma$ or −2.8 to 19.2.

3.42 (a) Mean = $\dfrac{17,839.2}{51}$ = 349.7882, variance = $\dfrac{1,481,386.413}{51}$ = 29,046.7924, standard deviation = $\sqrt{29,046.7924}$ = 170.4312 **(b)**, 9.8%, 92.84%, and 96.08% of these states have mean per capita energy consumption within 1, 2, and 3 standard deviations of the mean, respectively. **(c)** This is different from 68%, 95%, and 99.7%, according to the empirical rule.

3.44 (a) Covariance = 65.2909, **(b)** r = +1.0. **(c)** there is a perfect positive relationship.

3.46 (a) $\text{cov}(X, Y) = \dfrac{\sum\limits_{i=1}^{n}(X_i - \overline{X})(Y_i - \overline{Y})}{n-1} = \dfrac{800}{6} = 133.3333.$

(b) $r = \dfrac{\text{cov}(X, Y)}{S_X S_Y} = \dfrac{133.3333}{(46.9042)(3.3877)} = 0.8391.$

(c) The correlation coefficient is more valuable for expressing the relationship between calories and sugar because it does not depend on the units used to measure calories and sugar. **(d)** There is a strong positive linear relationship between calories and sugar.

3.48 (a) $\text{cov}(X, Y)$ = 44,624,302,512,751.7 **(b)** r = 0.8388 **(c)** There is a positive linear relationship between the coaches' total pay and revenue.

3.64 (a) Mean = 43.89, median = 45, 1st quartile = 18, 3rd quartile = 63. **(b)** Range = 76, interquartile range = 45, variance = 639.2564, standard deviation = 25.28, CV = 57.61%. **(c)** The distribution is right-skewed. **(d)** The mean approval process takes 43.89 days, with 50% of the policies being approved in less than 45 days. 50% of the applications are approved between 18 and 63 days. About 59% of the applications are approved between 18.6 and 69.2 days.

3.66 (a) Mean = 8.421, median = 8.42, range = 0.186, S = 0.0461. The mean and median width are both 8.42 inches. The range of the widths is 0.186 inch, and the average scatter around the mean is 0.0461 inch. **(b)** 8.312, 8.404, 8.42, 8.459, 8.498. **(c)** Even though the mean = median, the left tail is slightly longer, so the distribution is slightly left-skewed. **(d)** All the troughs in this sample meet the specifications.

3.68 (a), (b)

	Bundle Score	Typical Cost ($)
Mean	54.775	24.175
Median	62	20
Mode	75	8
Standard Deviation	27.6215	328.6096
Sample Variance	762.9481	18.1276
Range	98	83
Minimum	2	5
Maximum	100	88
First Quartile	34	9
Third Quartile	75	31
Interquartile Range	41	22
CV	50.43%	74.98%

(c) The typical cost is right-skewed, while the bundle score is left-skewed. **(d)** $r = 0.3465$. **(e)** The mean typical cost is $24.18, with an average spread around the mean equaling $18.13. The spread between the lowest and highest costs is $83. The middle 50% of the typical cost fall over a range of $22 from $9 to $31, while half of the typical cost is below $20. The mean bundle score is 54.775, with an average spread around the mean equaling 27.6215. The spread between the lowest and highest scores is 98. The middle 50% of the scores fall over a range of 41 from 34 to 75, while half of the scores are below 62. The typical cost is right-skewed, while the bundle score is left-skewed. There is a weak positive linear relationship between typical cost and bundle score.

3.70 (a) Boston: 0.04, 0.17, 0.23, 0.32, 0.98; Vermont: 0.02, 0.13, 0.20, 0.28, 0.83. **(b)** Both distributions are right-skewed. **(c)** Both sets of shingles did well in achieving a granule loss of 0.8 gram or less. Only two Boston shingles had a granule loss greater than 0.8 gram. The next highest to these was 0.6 gram. These two values can be considered outliers. Only 1.176% of the shingles failed the specification. Only one of the Vermont shingles had a granule loss greater than 0.8 gram. The next highest was 0.58 gram. Thus, only 0.714% of the shingles failed to meet the specification.

3.72 (a) The correlation between calories and protein is 0.4644. **(b)** The correlation between calories and cholesterol is 0.1777. **(c)** The correlation between protein and cholesterol is 0.1417. **(d)** There is a weak positive linear relationship between calories and protein, with a correlation coefficient of 0.46. The positive linear relationships between calories and cholesterol and between protein and cholesterol are very weak.

3.74 (a), (b)

Property Taxes per Capita ($)

Mean	1,332.2353
Median	1,230
Standard deviation	577.8308
Sample variance	333,888.4235
Range	2,479
First quartile	867
Third quartile	1,633
Interquartile range	766
Coefficient of variation	43.37%

(c), (d) The distribution of the property taxes per capita is right-skewed, with a mean value of $1,332.24, a median of $1,230, and an average spread around the mean of $577.83. There is an outlier in the right tail at $2,985, while the standard deviation is about 43.37% of the mean. Twenty-five percent of the states have property tax that falls below $867 per capita, and 25% have property taxes that are higher than $1,633 per capita.

3.76 (a), (b)

Abandonment Rate in % (7:00 AM–3:00 PM)

Mean	13.8636
Median	10
Mode	9
Standard Deviation	7.6239
Sample Variance	58.1233
Range	29
Minimum	5
Maximum	34
First Quartile	9
Third Quartile	20
Interquartile Range	11
CV	54.99%

(c) The data are right-skewed.

(d) $r = 0.7575$

(e) The mean abandonment rate is 13.86%. Half of the abandonment rates are less than 10%. One-quarter of the abandonment rates are less than 9% while another one-quarter are more than 20%. The overall spread of the abandonment rates is 29%. The middle 50% of the abandonment rates are spread over 11%. The average spread of abandonment rates around the mean is 7.62%. The abandonment rates are right-skewed.

3.78 (a), (b)

Average Credit Score

Mean	664.0280
Median	665
Mode	649
Standard Deviation	18.8739
Sample Variance	356.2246
Range	93
Minimum	609
Maximum	702
Count	143
First Quartile	649
Third Quartile	678
Interquartile Range	29
CV	2.84%

(c) The data are symmetrical. **(d)** The mean of the average credit scores is 664.028. Half of the average credit scores are less than 665. One-quarter of the average credit scores are less than 649 while another one-quarter is more than 678. The overall spread of average credit scores is 93. The middle 50% of the average credit scores spread over 29. The average spread of average credit scores around the mean is 18.8739.

CHAPTER 4

4.2 (a) Simple events include selecting a red ball. **(b)** Selecting a white ball. **(c)** The sample space consists of the 12 red balls and the 8 white balls.

4.4 (a) 0.6. **(b)** 0.10. **(c)** 0.35. **(d)** 0.90.

4.6 (a) Mutually exclusive, not collectively exhaustive. **(b)** Not mutually exclusive, not collectively exhaustive. **(c)** Mutually exclusive, not collectively exhaustive. **(d)** Mutually exclusive, collectively exhaustive.

4.8 (a) Is a male. **(b)** Is a male and feels tense or stressed out at work. **(c)** Does not feel tense or stressed out at work. **(d)** Is a male and feels tense or stressed out at work is a joint event because it consists of two characteristics.

4.10 (a) A marketer who plans to increase use of LinkedIn. **(b)** A B2B marketer who plans to increase use of LinkedIn. **(c)** A marketer who does not plan to increase use of LinkedIn. **(d)** A marketer who plans to increase use of LinkedIn and is a B2C marketer is a joint event because it consists of two characteristics, plans to increase use of LinkedIn and is a B2C marketer.

4.12 (a) $579/746 = 0.7761$. **(b)** $336/746 = 0.4504$. **(c)** $660/746$. **(d)** The probability of saying that analyzing data is critical *or* is a manager includes the probability of saying that analyzing data is critical plus the probability of being a manager minus the joint probability of saying that analyzing data is critical *and* is a manager.

4.14 (a) 0.1541. **(b)** 0.1018. **(c)** 0.5524. **(d)** 1.00.

4.16 (a) 0.33. **(b)** 0.33. **(c)** 0.67. **(d)** Because $P(A|B) = P(A) = 1/3$, events A and B are independent.

4.18 0.50.

4.20 Because $P(A \text{ and } B) = 0.20$ and $P(A)P(B) = 0.12$, events A and B are not independent.

4.22 (a) 0.7703. **(b)** 0.5402. **(c)** 0.6346, which is not equal to $P(\text{Increased use of LinkedIn}|\text{B2B}) = 0.7703$. Therefore increased use, of LinkedIn and business focus are not independent.

4.24 (a) $324/410 = 0.7902$ **(b)** $86/410 = 0.2098$ **(c)** $255/336 = 0.7589$ **(d)** $81/336 = 0.2411$.

4.26 (a) 0.0417. **(b)** 0.0375. **(c)** Because $P(\text{Needs warranty repair} \mid \text{Manufacturer based in the United States}) = 0.0417$ and $P(\text{Needs warranty repair}) = 0.04$, the two events are not independent.

4.28 (a) 0.0045. **(b)** 0.012. **(c)** 0.0059. **(d)** 0.0483.

4.36
(a)

Ask for Pay Raise	Generation		Total
	Baby Boomers	Millennials	
Yes	225	340	565
No	275	160	435
Total	500	500	1,000

(b) Asking for a pay raise; being a baby boomer and asking for a pay raise. **(c)** 0.565. **(d)** 0.225. **(e)** They are not independent because baby boomers and millennials have different probabilities of asking for a pay raise.

4.38 (a) 0.14. **(b)** 0.19. **(c)** 0.765. **(d)** 0.225. **(e)** 0.29.

4.40 (a) 0.3785. **(b)** 0.3333. **(c)** 0.4881. **(d)** 0.2188. **(e)** 0.1716. **(f)** 0.3333. **(g)** B2C firms are more likely to use marketing analytics.

CHAPTER 5

5.2 (a)
$$\mu = 0(0.10) + 1(0.20) + 2(0.45) + 3(0.15) + 4(0.05) + 5(0.05) = 2.0.$$
(b)
$$\sigma = \sqrt{\begin{array}{l}(0-2)^2(0.10) + (1-2)^2(0.20) + (2-2)^2(0.45) + \\ (3-2)^2(0.15) + (4-2)^2(0.05) + (5-2)^2(0.05)\end{array}} = 1.183.$$

5.4 (a)

X	$P(X)$
$\$ - 1$	21/36
$\$ + 1$	15/36

(b)

X	$P(X)$
$\$ - 1$	21/36
$\$ + 1$	15/36

(c)

X	$P(X)$
$\$ - 1$	30/36
$\$ + 4$	6/36

(d) $-\$0.167$ for each method of play.

5.6 (a) 2.1058. **(b)** 1.4671.

5.8 (a) $E(X) = \$66.20$; $E(Y) = \$63.01$. **(b)** $\sigma_X = \$57.22$; $\sigma_Y = \$195.22$. **(c)** Based on the expected value criteria, you would choose the common stock fund. However, the common stock fund also has a standard deviation more than three times higher than that for the corporate bond fund. An investor should carefully weigh the increased risk. **(d)** If you chose the common stock fund, you would need to assess your reaction to the small possibility that you could lose virtually all of your entire investment.

5.10 (a) 0.40, 0.60. **(b)** 1.60, 0.98. **(c)** 4.0, 0.894. **(d)** 1.50, 0.866.

5.12 (a) 0.2615. **(b)** 0.0222. **(c)** 0.4015. **(d)** $\mu = 3.18$, $\sigma = 1.2225$. **(e)** That each 30 to 34-year-old in the United States owns a tablet or does not own a tablet and that each person is independent of all other persons.

5.14 (a) 0.5987. **(b)** 0.3151. **(c)** 0.9885. **(d)** 0.0115.

5.16 (a) 0.5574. **(b)** 0.0055. **(c)** 0.9171. **(d)** $\mu = 2.469$, $\sigma = 0.6611$.

5.18 (a) 0.2565. **(b)** 0.1396. **(c)** 0.3033. **(d)** 0.0247.

5.20 (a) 0.0337. **(b)** 0.0067. **(c)** 0.9596. **(d)** 0.0404.

5.22 (a)
$$\begin{aligned} P(X < 5) &= P(X = 0) + P(X = 1) + P(x = 2) + P(X = 3) \\ &\quad + P(X = 4) \\ &= \frac{e^{-6}(6)^0}{0!} + \frac{e^{-6}(6)^1}{1!} + \frac{e^{-6}(6)^2}{2!} + \frac{e^{-6}(6)^3}{3!} + \frac{e^{-6}(6)^4}{4!} \\ &= 0.002479 + 0.014873 + 0.044618 + 0.089235 + 0.133853 \\ &= 0.2851.\end{aligned}$$
(b) $P(X = 5) = \dfrac{e^{-6}(6)^5}{5!} = 0.1606$.
(c) $P(X \geq 5) = 1 - P(X < 5) = 1 - 0.2851 = 0.7149$.
(d) $P(X = 4 \text{ or } X = 5) = P(X = 4) + P(X = 5) = \dfrac{e^{-6}(6)^4}{4!} + \dfrac{e^{-6}(6)^5}{5!}$
$$= 0.2945.$$

5.24 (a) 0.1119. **(b)** 0.8881. **(c)** 0.6430.

5.26 (a) 0.0369. **(b)** 0.1217. **(c)** 0.8414. **(d)** 0.1586.

5.28 (a) 0.3296. **(b)** 0.8984. **(c)** Because Ford had a higher mean rate of problems per car than Toyota, the probability of a randomly selected Ford having zero problems and the probability of no more than two problems are both lower than for Toyota.

5.34 (a) 0.67. **(b)** 0.67. **(c)** 0.3325. **(d)** 0.0039. **(e)** The assumption of independence may not be true.

5.36 (a) 0.0461. **(b)** 0.5843.

5.38 (a) 0.0060. **(b)** 0.2007. **(c)** 0.1662. **(d)** Mean = 4.0, standard deviation = 1.5492. **(e)** Since the percentage of bills containing an error is lower in this problem, the probability is higher in (a) and (b) of this problem and lower in (c).

5.40 (a) 9.4. **(b)** 2.2320 **(c)** 0.1700. **(d)** 0.0381. **(e)** 0.9879.

5.42 (a) 0.0000. **(b)** 0.0054. **(c)** 0.7604. **(d)** Based on the results in (a)–(c), the probability that the Standard & Poor's 500 Index will increase if there is an early gain in the first five trading days of the year is very likely to be close to 0.90 because that yields a probability of 76.04% that at least 37 of the 42 years the Standard & Poor's 500 Index will increase the entire year.

5.44 (a) The assumptions needed are (i) the probability that a questionable claim is referred by an investigator is constant, (ii) the probability that a questionable claim is referred by an investigator approaches 0 as the interval gets smaller, and (iii) the probability that a questionable claim is referred by an investigator is independent from interval to interval. **(b)** 0.1277. **(c)** 0.9015. **(d)** 0.0985.

CHAPTER 6

6.2 (a) 0.9089. **(b)** 0.0911. **(c)** +1.96. **(d)** −1.00 and +1.00.

6.4 (a) 0.1401. **(b)** 0.4168. **(c)** 0.3918. **(d)** +1.00.

6.6 (a) 0.9599. **(b)** 0.0228. **(c)** 43.42. **(d)** 46.64 and 53.36.

6.8 (a) $P(34 < X < 50) = P(-1.33 < Z < 0) = 0.4082$. **(b)** $P(X < 30) + P(X > 60) = P(Z < -1.67) + P(Z > 0.83) = 0.0475 + (1.0 - 0.7967) = 0.2508$. **(c)** $P(Z < -0.84) \cong 0.20$, $Z = -0.84 = \frac{X - 50}{12}, X = 50 - 0.84(12) = 39.92$ thousand miles, or 39,920 miles. **(d)** The smaller standard deviation makes the absolute Z values larger. **(a)** $P(34 < X < 50) = P(-1.60 < Z < 0) = 0.4452$. **(b)** $P(X < 30) + P(X > 60) = P(Z < -2.00) + P(Z > 1.00) = 0.0228 + (1.0 - 0.8413) = 0.1815$. **(c)** $X = 50 - 0.84(10) = 41.6$ thousand miles, or 41,600 miles.

6.10 (a) 0.9878. **(b)** 0.8185. **(c)** 86.16%. **(d)** Option 1: Because your score of 81% on this exam represents a Z score of 1.00, which is below the minimum Z score of 1.28, you will not earn an A grade on the exam under this grading option. Option 2: Because your score of 68% on this exam represents a Z score of 2.00, which is well above the minimum Z score of 1.28, you will earn an A grade on the exam under this grading option. You should prefer Option 2.

6.12 (a) 0.0843. **(b)** 0.1574. **(c)** 0.0186. **(d)** 72.3425.

6.14 With 39 values, the smallest of the standard normal quantile values covers an area under the normal curve of 0.025. The corresponding Z value is −1.96. The middle (20th) value has a cumulative area of 0.50 and a corresponding Z value of 0.0. The largest of the standard normal quantile values covers an area under the normal curve of 0.975, and its corresponding Z value is +1.96.

6.16 (a) Mean = 23.15, median = 22.5, S = 1.9541, range = 7, 6S = 11.7246, interquartile range = 2.0, 1.33 (1.9541) = 2.5990. The mean is slightly more than the median. The range is much less than 6S, and the interquartile range is less than 1.33S. **(b)** The normal probability plot appears to be right skewed. The skewness statistic is 0.9427 The kurtosis is 0.3998, indicating some departure from a normal distribution.

6.18 (a) Mean = 1,332.2353, median = 1,230, S = 577.8308, range = 2,479, 6S = 6(577.8308) = 3,466.9848, interquartile range = 766, 1.33(577.8308) = 768.5150. The mean is greater than the median. The range is much less than 6S, and the interquartile range is

approximately equal to 1.33S. **(b)** The normal probability plot appears to be right skewed. The skewness statistic is 0.9183 The kurtosis is 0.5395, indicating some departure from a normal distribution.

6.20 (a) Interquartile range = 0.0025, S = 0.0017, range = 0.008, 1.33(S) = 0.0023, 6(S) = 0.0102. Because the interquartile range is close to 1.33S and the range is also close to 6S, the data appear to be approximately normally distributed. **(b)** The normal probability plot suggests that the data appear to be approximately normally distributed.

6.22 (a) Five-number summary: 82 127 148.5 168 213; mean = 147.06, mode = 130, range = 131, interquartile range = 41, standard deviation = 31.69. The mean is very close to the median. The five-number summary suggests that the distribution is approximately symmetric around the median. The interquartile range is very close to 1.33S. The range is about $50 below 6S. In general, the distribution of the data appears to closely resemble a normal distribution. **(b)** The normal probability plot confirms that the data appear to be approximately normally distributed.

6.24 (a) 0.1667. **(b)** 0.1667. **(c)** 0.7083. **(d)** Mean = 60, standard deviation = 34.641

6.26 (a) 0.1667. **(b)** 0.1667. **(c)** 0.3333. **(d)** Mean = 21, standard deviation = 1.7321

6.34 (a) 0.4772. **(b)** 0.9544. **(c)** 0.0456. **(d)** 1.8835. **(e)** 1.8710 and 2.1290.

6.36 (a) 0.0228. **(b)** 0.1524. **(c)** $275.63. **(d)** $224.37 to $275.63.

6.38 (a) Waiting time will more closely resemble an exponential distribution. **(b)** Seating time will more closely resemble a normal distribution. **(c)** Both the histogram and normal probability plot suggest that waiting time more closely resembles an exponential distribution. **(d)** Both the histogram and normal probability plot suggest that seating time more closely resembles a normal distribution.

6.40 (a) 0.4129. **(b)** 0.3745. **(c)** 0.1003. **(d)** $5,057.46. **(e)** $5,204.01 and $6,771.99.

CHAPTER 7

7.2 (a) Virtually 0. **(b)** 0.1587. **(c)** 0.0139. **(d)** 50.195.

7.4 (a) Both means are equal to 6. This property is called unbiasedness. **(c)** The distribution for n = 3 has less variability. The larger sample size has resulted in sample means being closer to μ. **(d)** Same answer as in (c).

7.6 (a) When n = 4, because the mean is larger than the median, the distribution of the sales price of new houses is skewed to the right, and so is the sampling distribution of $\bar{X}$ although it will be less skewed than the population. **(b)** If you select samples of n = 100, the shape of the sampling distribution of the sample mean will be very close to a normal distribution, with a mean of $345,800 and a standard error of the mean of $9,000. **(c)** 0.9964. **(d)** 0.3039.

7.8 (a) 0.8413. **(b)** 18.0364. **(c)** To be able to use the standardized normal distribution as an approximation for the area under the curve, you must assume that the population is approximately symmetrical. **(d)** 17.5182.

7.10 (a) 0.40. **(b)** 0.0704.

7.12

(a) $\pi = 0.501, \sigma_p = \sqrt{\frac{\pi(1-\pi)}{n}} = \sqrt{\frac{0.501(1-0.501)}{100}} = 0.05$

$P(p > 0.55) = P(Z > 0.98) = 1.0 - 0.8365 = 0.1635$.

(b) $\pi = 0.60, \sigma_p = \sqrt{\frac{\pi(1-\pi)}{n}} = \sqrt{\frac{0.6(1-0.6)}{100}} = 0.04899$

$P(p > 0.55) = P(Z > -1.021) = 1.0 - 0.1539 = 0.8461.$

(c) $\pi = 0.49, \sigma_p = \sqrt{\dfrac{\pi(1-\pi)}{n}} = \sqrt{\dfrac{0.49(1-0.49)}{100}} = 0.05$

$P(p > 0.55) = P(Z > 1.20) = 1.0 - 0.8849 = 0.1151.$

(d) Increasing the sample size by a factor of 4 decreases the standard error by a factor of 2.

(a) $P(p > 0.55) = P(Z > 1.96) = 1.0 - 0.9750 = 0.0250.$

(b) $P(p > 0.55) = P(Z > -2.04) = 1.0 - 0.0207 = 0.9793.$

(c) $P(p > 0.55) = P(Z > 2.40) = 1.0 - 0.9918 = 0.0082.$

7.14 (a) 0.8186. **(b)** 0.6372. **(c)** 0.3264. **(d) (a)** 0.9656. **(b)** 0.9312. **(c)** 0.1814.

7.16 (a) 0.7416. **(b)** The probability is 90% that the sample percentage will be contained between 0.1263 to 0.2137. **(c)** The probability is 95% that the sample percentage will be contained between 0.1179 to 0.2221.

7.18 (a) 0.1379. **(b)** 0.0073. **(c)** Increasing the sample size by a factor of 5 decreases the standard error by a factor of more than 2. The sampling distribution of the proportion becomes more concentrated around the true proportion of 0.30 and, hence, the probability in **(b)** becomes smaller than that in **(a)**.

7.24 (a) 0.4999. **(b)** 0.00009. **(c)** 0. **(d)** 0. **(e)** 0.7518.

7.26 (a) 0.8944. **(b)** 4.617; 4.783. **(c)** 4.641.

7.28 (a) 0.0087. **(b)** 0.3520. **(c)** 0.6480.

CHAPTER 8

8.2 $114.68 \le \mu \le 135.32.$

8.4 Yes, it is true because 5% of intervals will not include the population mean.

8.6 (a) You would compute the mean first because you need the mean to compute the standard deviation. If you had a sample, you would compute the sample mean. If you had the population mean, you would compute the population standard deviation. **(b)** If you have a sample, you are computing the sample standard deviation, not the population standard deviation needed in Equation (8.1). If you have a population and have computed the population mean and population standard deviation, you don't need a confidence interval estimate of the population mean because you already know the mean.

8.8 Equation (8.1) assumes that you know the population standard deviation. Because you are selecting a sample of 100 from the population, you are computing a sample standard deviation, not the population standard deviation.

8.10 (a) $\bar{X} \pm Z \cdot \dfrac{\sigma}{\sqrt{n}} = 7{,}500 \pm 1.96 \cdot \dfrac{1{,}000}{\sqrt{64}}; \ 7{,}255 \le \mu \le 7{,}745.$

(b) No, since the confidence interval does not include 8,000 hours the manufacturer cannot support a claim that the bulbs have a mean of 8,000 hours. **(c)** No. Because σ is known and $n = 64$, from the Central Limit Theorem, you know that the sampling distribution of $\bar{X}$ is approximately normal. **(d)** The confidence interval is narrower, based on a population standard deviation of 800 hours rather than the original standard deviation of 1,000 hours. $\bar{X} \pm Z \times \dfrac{\sigma}{\sqrt{n}} = 7{,}500 \pm 1.96 \times \dfrac{800}{\sqrt{64}},$

$7{,}304 \le \mu \le 7{,}696.$ No, since the confidence interval does not include 8,000 the manufacturer cannot support a claim that the bulbs have a mean life of 8,000 hours.

8.12 (a) 2.2622. **(b)** 3.2498. **(c)** 2.0395. **(d)** 1.9977. **(e)** 1.7531.

8.14 $-0.12 \le \mu \le 11.84$, $2.00 \le \mu \le 6.00$. The presence of the outlier increases the sample mean and greatly inflates the sample standard deviation.

8.16 (a) $82 \pm (1.9890)(9)/\sqrt{84}$; $80.05 \le \mu \le 83.95.$ **(b)** You can be 95% confident that the population mean amount of one-time gift is between $80.05 and $83.95.

8.18 (a) $6.31 \le \mu \le 7.87.$ **(b)** You can be 95% confident that the population mean amount spent for lunch at a fast-food restaurant is between $6.31 and $7.87.

8.20 (a) $22.24 \le \mu \le 24.06.$ **(b)** You can be 95% confident that the population mean miles per gallon of 2015 small SUVs is between 22.24 and 24.06. **(c)** Because the 95% confidence interval for population mean miles per gallon of 2015 small SUVs does not overlap with that for the population mean miles per gallon of 2015 family sedans, you can conclude that the population mean miles per gallon of 2015 small SUVs is lower than that of 2015 family sedans.

8.22 (a) $31.12 \le \mu \le 54.96.$ **(b)** The number of days is approximately normally distributed. **(c)** No, the outliers skew the data. **(d)** Because the sample size is fairly large, at $n = 50$, the use of the t distribution is appropriate.

8.24 (a) $13.81 \le \mu \le 18.97.$ **(b)** That the population distribution is normally distributed. **(c)** The boxplot and the skewness and kurtosis statistics indicate a right skewed distribution due to the outlier from the Republic of Korea.

8.26 $0.19 \le \pi \le 0.31.$

8.28 (a)

$$p = \dfrac{X}{n} = \dfrac{135}{500} = 0.27, p \pm Z\sqrt{\dfrac{p(1-p)}{n}} = 0.27 \pm 2.58\sqrt{\dfrac{0.27(0.73)}{500}};$$

$0.2189 \le \pi \le 0.3211.$ **(b)** The manager in charge of promotional programs can infer that the proportion of households that would upgrade to an improved cellphone if it were made available at a substantially reduced cost is somewhere between 0.22 and 0.32, with 99% confidence.

8.30 (a) $0.2328 \le \pi \le 0.2872.$ **(b)** No, you cannot because the interval estimate includes 0.25 (25%). **(c)** $0.2514 \le \pi \le 0.2686.$ Yes, you can, because the interval is above 0.25 (25%). **(d)** The larger the sample size, the narrower the confidence interval, holding everything else constant.

8.32 (a) $0.8505 \le \pi \le 0.8907.$ **(b)** $0.3610 \le \pi \le 0.4193.$ **(c)** It appears that more people are connected to friends from the past than to people they have never met in person.

8.34 $n = 35.$

8.36 $n = 1{,}041.$

8.38 (a) $n = \dfrac{Z^2\sigma^2}{e^2} = \dfrac{(1.96)^2(400)^2}{50^2} = 245.86.$ Use $n = 246.$

(b) $n = \dfrac{Z^2\sigma^2}{e^2} = \dfrac{(1.96)^2(400)^2}{25^2} = 983.41.$ Use $n = 984.$

8.40 $n = 97.$

8.42 (a) $n = 107.$ **(b)** $n = 62.$

8.44 (a) $n = 246.$ **(b)** $n = 385.$ **(c)** $n = 554.$ **(d)** When there is more variability in the population, a larger sample is needed to accurately estimate the mean.

8.46 (a) $0.4135 \leq \pi \leq 0.5265$. **(b)** $0.2768 \leq \pi \leq 0.3832$.
(c) $0.3641 \leq \pi \leq 0.4759$. **(d) (a)** $n = 2,393$, **(b)** $n = 2,124$,
(c) $n = 2,140$.

8.48 (a) If you conducted a follow-up study, you would use $\pi = 0.33$ in the sample size formula because it is based on past information on the proportion. **(b)** $n = 944$.

8.54 (a) PC/laptop: $0.8923 \leq \pi \leq 0.9277$.
    Smartphone: $0.7752 \leq \pi \leq 0.8248$.
       Tablet: $0.4391 \leq \pi \leq 0.5009$.
   Smart watch: $0.0723 \leq \pi \leq 0.1077$.
(b) Most adults have a PC/laptop. Many adults have a smartphone. Some adults have very few have a smartwatch a tablet computer.

8.56 (a) $40.88 \leq \mu \leq 52.12$. **(b)** $0.6760 \leq \pi \leq 0.9240$. **(c)** $n = 25$.
(d) $n = 267$. **(e)** If a single sample were to be selected for both purposes, the larger of the two sample sizes ($n = 267$) should be used.

8.58 (a) $3.19 \leq \mu \leq 9.21$. **(b)** $0.3242 \leq \pi \leq 0.7158$. **(c)** $n = 110$.
(d) $n = 121$. **(e)** If a single sample were to be selected for both purposes, the larger of the two sample sizes ($n = 121$) should be used.

8.60 (a) $0.2562 \leq \pi \leq 0.3638$. **(b)** $3.22 \leq \mu \leq \$3.78$.
(c) $\$17,581.68 \leq \mu \leq \$18,418.32$.

8.62 (a) $\$36.66 \leq \mu \leq \$40.42$. **(b)** $0.2027 \leq \pi \leq 0.3973$.
(c) $n = 110$. **(d)** $n = 423$. **(e)** If a single sample were to be selected for both purposes, the larger of the two sample sizes ($n = 423$) should be used.

8.64 (a) $0.4643 \leq \pi \leq 0.6690$. **(b)** $\$136.28 \leq \mu \leq \$502.21$.

8.66 (a) $8.41 \leq \mu \leq 8.43$. **(b)** With 95% confidence, the population mean width of troughs is somewhere between 8.41 and 8.43 inches.
(c) The assumption is valid as the width of the troughs is approximately normally distributed.

8.68 (a) $0.2425 \leq \mu \leq 0.2856$. **(b)** $0.1975 \leq \mu \leq 0.2385$. **(c)** The amounts of granule loss for both brands are skewed to the right, but the sample sizes are large enough. **(d)** Because the two confidence intervals do not overlap, it appears that the mean granule loss of Boston shingles is higher than that of Vermont shingles.

CHAPTER 9

9.2 Because $Z_{STAT} = +2.21 > 1.96$, reject H_0.

9.4 Reject H_0 if $Z_{STAT} < -2.58$ or if $Z_{STAT} > 2.58$.

9.6 p-value $= 0.0456$.

9.8 p-value $= 0.1676$.

9.10 H_0: Defendant is guilty; H_1: Defendant is innocent. A Type I error would be not convicting a guilty person. A Type II error would be convicting an innocent person.

9.12 H_0: $\mu = 20$ minutes. 20 minutes is adequate travel time between classes. H_1: $\mu \neq 20$ minutes. 20 minutes is not adequate travel time between classes.

9.14 (a) $Z_{STAT} = \dfrac{7{,}250 - 7{,}500}{\dfrac{1{,}000}{\sqrt{64}}} = -2.0$. Because $Z_{STAT} = -2.00$

< -1.96, reject H_0. **(b)** p-value $= 0.0456$. **(c)** $7{,}005 \leq \mu \leq 7{,}495$.
(d) The conclusions are the same.

9.16 (a) Because $-2.58 < Z_{STAT} = -1.7678 < 2.58$, do not reject H_0.
(b) p-value $= 0.0771$. **(c)** $0.9877 \leq \mu \leq 1.0023$. **(d)** The conclusions are the same.

9.18 $t_{STAT} = 2.00$.

9.20 ± 2.1315.

9.22 No, you should not use a t test because the original population is left-skewed, and the sample size is not large enough for the t test to be valid.

9.24 (a) $t_{STAT} = (3.57 - 3.70)/(0.8/\sqrt{64}) = -1.30$. Because $-1.9983 < t_{STAT} = -1.30 < 1.9983$ and p-value $= 0.1984 > 0.05$, do not reject H_0. There is insufficient evidence that the population mean waiting time is different from 3.7 minutes. **(b)** Because $n = 64$, the sampling distribution of the t test statistic is approximately normal. In general, the t test is appropriate for this sample size except for the case where the population is extremely skewed or bimodal.

9.26 (a) $-1.9842 < t_{STAT} = 1.25 < 1.9842$, do not reject H_0. There is insufficient evidence that the population mean spent by Amazon Prime customers is different from $1,475. **(b)** p-value $= 0.2142 > 0.05$. The probability of getting a t_{STAT} statistic greater than $+1.25$ or less than -1.25, given that the null hypothesis is true, is 0.2142.

9.28 (a) Because $-2.1448 < t_{STAT} = 1.6344 < 2.1448$, do not reject H_0. There is not enough evidence to conclude that the mean amount spent for lunch at a fast-food restaurant, is different from $6.50. **(b)** The p-value is 0.1245. If the population mean is $6.50, the probability of observing a sample of fifteen customers that will result in a sample mean farther away from the hypothesized value than this sample is 0.1245. **(c)** The distribution of the amount spent is normally distributed. **(d)** With a sample size of 15, it is difficult to evaluate the assumption of normality. However, the distribution may be fairly symmetric because the mean and the median are close in value. Also, the boxplot appears only slightly skewed so the normality assumption does not appear to be seriously violated.

9.30 (a) Because $-2.0096 < t_{STAT} = 0.114 < 2.0096$, do not reject H_0. There is no evidence that the mean amount is different from 2 liters.
(b) p-value $= 0.9095$. **(d)** Yes, the data appear to have met the normality assumption. **(e)** The amount of fill is decreasing over time so the values are not independent. Therefore, the t test is invalid.

9.32 (a) Because $t_{STAT} = -5.9355 < -2.0106$, reject H_0. There is enough evidence to conclude that mean widths of the troughs is different from 8.46 inches. **(b)** The population distribution is normal. **(c)** Although the distribution of the widths is left-skewed, the large sample size means that the validity of the t test is not seriously affected. The large sample size allows you to use the t distribution.

9.34 (a) Because $-2.68 < t_{STAT} = 0.094 < 2.68$, do not reject H_0. There is no evidence that the mean amount is different from 5.5 grams.
(b) $5.462 \leq \mu \leq 5.542$. **(c)** The conclusions are the same.

9.36 p-value $= 0.0228$.

9.38 p-value $= 0.0838$.

9.40 p-value $= 0.9162$.

9.42 2.7638.

9.44 -2.5280.

9.46 (a) $t_{STAT} = 2.7325 > 1.6694$, reject H_0. There is evidence that the population mean bus miles is greater than 3,013 miles.
(b) p-value $= 0.0041 < 0.05$. The probability of getting a t_{STAT} statistic greater than 2.7325 given that the null hypothesis is true, is 0.0041.

9.48 (a) $t_{STAT} = (23.05 - 25)/(16.83/\sqrt{355}) = -2.1831$. Because $t_{STAT} = -2.1831 > -2.3369$, do not reject H_0. p-value $= 0.0148 > 0.01$, do not reject H_0. **(b)** The probability of getting a sample mean of 23.05 minutes or less if the population mean is 25 minutes is 0.0148.

9.50 (a) $t_{STAT} = 2.0367 < 2.3721$, do not reject H_0. There is insufficient evidence that the population mean one-time gift donation is greater than $80. **(b)** The probability of getting a sample mean of $82 or more if the population mean is $80 is 0.0224.

9.52 $p = 0.22$.

9.54 Do not reject H_0.

9.56 (a) $Z_{STAT} = 0.9119$, p-value $= 0.1809$. Because $Z_{STAT} = 0.9119 < 1.645$ or p-value $= 0.1809 > 0.05$, do not reject H_0. There is no evidence to show that more than 26% of students at your university use the Chrome web browser. **(b)** $Z_{STAT} = 1.8238$, p-value $= 0.0341$. Because $Z_{STAT} = 1.8238 > 1.645$, or p-value $= 0.0341 < 0.05$, reject H_0. There is evidence to show that more than 26% of students at your university use the Chrome web browser. **(c)** The sample size had a major effect on being able to reject the null hypothesis. **(d)** You would be very unlikely to reject the null hypothesis with a sample of 20.

9.58 H_0: $\pi = 0.45$; H_1: $\pi \neq 0.45$. Decision rule: If $Z_{STAT} > 1.96$ or $Z_{STAT} < -1.96$, reject H_0.

$$p = \frac{215}{406} = 0.5296$$

Test statistic:

$$Z_{STAT} = \frac{p - \pi}{\sqrt{\dfrac{\pi(1 - \pi)}{n}}} = \frac{0.5296 - 0.45}{\sqrt{\dfrac{0.45(1 - 0.45)}{406}}} = 3.2222.$$

Because $Z_{STAT} = 3.2222 > 1.96$ or p-value $= 0.0013 < 0.05$, reject H_0 and conclude that there is evidence that the proportion of all talent acquisition professionals who report competition is the biggest obstacle to attracting the best talent at their company is different from 45%.

9.60 (a) H_0: $\pi \geq 0.42$. H_1: $\pi < 0.42$.
(b) $Z_{STAT} = -0.4052 > -1.645$; p-value $= 0.3427$. Because $Z_{STAT} = -0.4052 > -1.645$ or p-value $= 0.3427 > 0.05$, do not reject H_0. There is insufficient evidence that the percentage is less than 42%.

9.70 (a) Concluding that a firm will go bankrupt when it will not. **(b)** Concluding that a firm will not go bankrupt when it will go bankrupt. **(c)** Type I. **(d)** If the revised model results in more moderate or large Z scores, the probability of committing a Type I error will increase. Many more of the firms will be predicted to go bankrupt than will go bankrupt. On the other hand, the revised model that results in more moderate or large Z scores will lower the probability of committing a Type II error because few firms will be predicted to go bankrupt than will actually go bankrupt.

9.72 (a) Because $t_{STAT} = 3.3197 > 2.0010$, reject H_0. **(b)** p-value $= 0.0015$. **(c)** Because $Z_{STAT} = 0.2582 < 1.645$, do not reject H_0. **(d)** Because $-2.0010 < t_{STAT} = -1.1066 < 2.0010$, do not reject H_0. **(e)** Because $Z_{STAT} = 2.3238 > 1.645$, reject H_0.

9.74 (a) Because $t_{STAT} = -1.69 > -1.7613$, do not reject H_0. **(b)** The data are from a population that is normally distributed. **(d)** With the exception of one extreme value, the data are approximately normally distributed. **(e)** There is insufficient evidence to state that the waiting time is less than five minutes.

9.76 (a) Because $t_{STAT} = -1.47 > -1.6896$, do not reject H_0. **(b)** p-value $= 0.0748$. If the null hypothesis is true, the probability of obtaining a t_{STAT} of -1.47 or more extreme is 0.0748. **(c)** Because $t_{STAT} = -3.10 < -1.6973$, reject H_0. **(d)** p-value $= 0.0021$. If the null hypothesis is true, the probability of obtaining a t_{STAT} of -3.10 or more extreme is 0.0021. **(e)** The data in the population are assumed to be normally distributed. **(g)** Both boxplots suggest that the data are skewed slightly to the right, more so for the Boston shingles. However, the very large sample sizes mean that the results of the t test are relatively insensitive to the departure from normality.

9.78 (a) $t_{STAT} = -3.2912$, reject H_0. **(b)** p-value $= 0.0012$. The probability of getting a t_{STAT} value below -3.2912 or above $+3.2912$ is 0.0012. **(c)** $t_{STAT} = -7.9075$, reject H_0. **(d)** p-value $= 0.0000$. The probability of getting a t_{STAT} value below -7.9075 or above $+7.9075$ is 0.0000. **(e)** Because of the large sample sizes, you do not need to be concerned with the normality assumption.

CHAPTER 10

10.2 (a) $t = 3.8959$. **(b)** $df = 21$. **(c)** 2.5177. **(d)** Because $t_{STAT} = t_{STAT} = 3.8959 > 2.5177$, reject H_0.

10.4 $3.73 \leq \mu_1 - \mu_2 \leq 12.27$.

10.6 Because $t_{STAT} = 2.6762 < 2.9979$ or p-value $= 0.0158 > 0.01$, do not reject H_0. There is no evidence of a difference in the means of the two populations.

10.8 (a) Because $t_{STAT} = 2.8990 > 1.6620$ or p-value $= 0.0024 < 0.05$, reject H_0. There is evidence that the mean amount of Walker Crisps eaten by children who watched a commercial featuring a long-standing sports celebrity endorser is higher than for those who watched a commercial for an alternative food snack. **(b)** $3.4616 \leq \mu_1 - \mu_2 \leq 18.5384$. **(c)** The results cannot be compared because (a) is a one-tail test and (b) is a confidence interval that is comparable only to the results of a two-tail test.

10.10 (a) H_0: $\mu_1 = \mu_2$, where Populations: $1 =$ Southeast, $2 =$ Gulf Coast. H_1: $\mu_1 \neq \mu_2$. Decision rule: $df = 28$. If $t_{STAT} < -2.0484$ or $t_{STAT} > 2.0484$, reject H_0.

Test statistic:

$$S_p^2 = \frac{(n_1 - 1)(S_1^2) + (n_2 - 1)(S_2^2)}{(n_1 - 1) + (n_2 - 1)}$$

$$= \frac{(10)(42.2617^2) + (18)(35.5486^2)}{10 + 18} = 1,450.2563$$

$$t_{STAT} = \frac{(\overline{X}_1 - \overline{X}_2) - (\mu_1 - \mu_2)}{\sqrt{S_p^2\left(\dfrac{1}{n_1} + \dfrac{1}{n_2}\right)}}$$

$$= \frac{(48.3636 - 28.5789) - 0}{\sqrt{1,450.2563\left(\dfrac{1}{11} + \dfrac{1}{19}\right)}} = 1.3713.$$

Decision: Because $-2.0484 < t_{STAT} = 1.3713 < 2.0484$, do not reject H_0. There is not enough evidence to conclude that the mean number of partners between the Southeast and Gulf Coast is different. **(b)** p-value $= 0.1812$. **(c)** In order to use the pooled-variance t test, you need to assume that the populations are normally distributed with equal variances.

10.12 **(a)** Because $t_{STAT} = -4.1343 < -2.0484$, reject H_0. **(b)** p-value = 0.0003. **(c)** The populations of waiting times are approximately normally distributed. **(d)** $-4.2292 \leq \mu_1 - \mu_2 \leq -1.4268$.

10.14 **(a)** Because $t_{STAT} = -2.1814 > 2.0484$, reject H_0. There is evidence of a difference in the mean time to start a business between developed and emerging countries. **(b)** p-value = 0.0377. The probability that two samples have a mean difference of 12.5733 or more is 0.0377 if there is no difference in the mean time to start a business between developed and emerging countries. **(c)** You need to assume that the population distribution of the time to start a business of both developed and emerging countries is normally distributed. **(d)** $0.7664 \leq \mu_1 - \mu_2 \leq 24.3802$.

10.16 **(a)** Because $t_{STAT} = -2.1554 < -2.0017$ or p-value = 0.03535 <0.05, reject H_0. There is evidence of a difference in the mean time per day accessing the Internet via a mobile device between males and females. **(b)** You must assume that each of the two independent populations is normally distributed.

10.18 $df = 19$.

10.20 **(a)** $t_{STAT} = (-1.5566)/(1.424/\sqrt{9}) = -3.2772$. Because $t_{STAT} = -3.2772 < -2.306$ or p-value = 0.0112 < 0.05, reject H_0. There is enough evidence of a difference in the mean summated ratings between the two brands. **(b)** You must assume that the distribution of the differences between the two ratings is approximately normal. **(c)** p-value = 0.0112. The probability of obtaining a mean difference in ratings that results in a test statistic that deviates from 0 by 3.2772 or more in either direction is 0.0112 if there is no difference in the mean summated ratings between the two brands. **(d)** $-2.6501 \leq \mu_D \leq -0.4610$. You are 95% confident that the mean difference in summated ratings between brand A and brand B is somewhere between −2.6501 and −0.4610.

10.22 **(a)** Because $t_{STAT} = -7.476 < 2.0739$ reject H_0. There is evidence to conclude that the mean rating at AT&T is lower than at Verizon Wireless **(b)** You must assume that the distribution of the differences between the ratings is approximately normal. **(d)** The confidence interval is from 4.2099 to 7.4423.

10.24 **(a)** Because $t_{STAT} = 1.8425 < 1.943$, do not reject H_0. There is not enough evidence to conclude that the mean bone marrow microvessel density is higher before the stem cell transplant than after the stem cell transplant. **(b)** p-value = 0.0575. The probability that the t statistic for the mean difference in microvessel density is 1.8425 or more is 5.75% if the mean density is not higher before the stem cell transplant than after the stem cell transplant. **(c)** $-28.26 \leq \mu_D \leq 200.55$. You are 95% confident that the mean difference in bone marrow microvessel density before and after the stem cell transplant is somewhere between −28.26 and 200.55. **(d)** That the distribution of the difference before and after the stem cell transplant is normally distributed.

10.26 **(a)** Because $t_{STAT} = -9.3721 < -2.4258$, reject H_0. There is evidence that the mean strength is lower at two days than at seven days. **(b)** The population of differences in strength is approximately normally distributed. **(c)** $p = 0.000$.

10.28 **(a)** Because $-2.58 \leq Z_{STAT} = -0.58 \leq 2.58$, do not reject H_0. **(b)** $-0.273 \leq \pi_1 - \pi_2 \leq 0.173$.

10.30 **(a)** $H_0: \pi_1 \leq \pi_2$. $H_1: \pi_1 > \pi_2$. Populations: 1 = VOD D4 + 2 = general TV. **(b)** Because $Z_{STAT} = 8.9045 > 1.6449$ or p-value = 0.0000 < 0.05, do not reject H_0. There is evidence to conclude that the population proportion of those who viewed the brand on VOD D4 were more likely to visit the brand website. **(c)** Yes, the result in **(b)** makes it appropriate to claim that the population proportion of those who viewed the brand on VOD D4 were more likely to visit the brand website than those who viewed the brand on general TV.

10.32 **(a)** $H_0: \pi_1 = \pi_2$. $H_1: \pi_1 \neq \pi_2$. Decision rule: If $|Z_{STAT}| > 2.58$, reject H_0.

Test statistic: $\bar{p} = \dfrac{X_1 + X_2}{n_1 + n_2} = \dfrac{278 + 316}{376 + 376} = 0.79$

$$Z_{STAT} = \frac{(p_1 - p_2) - (\pi_1 - \pi_2)}{\sqrt{\bar{p}(1 - \bar{p})\left(\dfrac{1}{n_1} + \dfrac{1}{n_2}\right)}} = \frac{(0.7394 - 0.8404) - 0}{\sqrt{0.79(1 - 0.79)\left(\dfrac{1}{376} + \dfrac{1}{376}\right)}}.$$

$Z_{STAT} = -3.4015 > 2.58$, reject H_0. There is evidence of a difference in the proportion of organizations with recognition programs between organizations that have between 500 and 2,499 employees and orgnizations that have 2,500+ employees **(b)** p-value = 0.0007. The probability of obtaining a difference in proportions that gives rise to a test statistic below -3.4015 or above $+3.4015$ is 0.0007 if there is no difference in the proportion based on the size of the organization. **(c)** $-0.1770 \leq (\pi_1 - \pi_2) \leq -0.0251$. You are 99% confident that the difference in the proportion based on the size of the organization is between 2.51%and 17.7%.

10.34 **(a)** Because $Z_{STAT} = 4.4662 > 1.96$, reject H_0. There is evidence of a difference in the proportion of co-browsing organizations and non-co-browsing organizations that use skills-based routing to match the caller with the *right* agent. **(b)** p-value = 0.0000. The probability of obtaining a difference in proportions that is 0.2586 or more in either direction is 0.0000 if there is no difference between the proportion of co-browsing organizations and non-co-browsing organizations that use skills-based routing to match the caller with the *right* agent.

10.36 **(a)** 2.20. **(b)** 2.57. **(c)** 3.50.

10.38 **(a)** Population B: $S^2 = 25$. **(b)** 1.5625.

10.40 $df_{numerator} = 24$, $df_{denominator} = 24$.

10.42 Because $F_{STAT} = 1.2109 < 2.27$, do not reject H_0.

10.44 **(a)** Because $F_{STAT} = 1.2995 < 3.18$, do not reject H_0. **(b)** Because $F_{STAT} = 1.2995 < 2.62$, do not reject H_0.

10.46 **(a)** $H_0: \sigma_1^2 = \sigma_2^2$. $H_1: \sigma_1^2 \neq \sigma_2^2$.

Decision rule: If $F_{STAT} > 2.8664$, reject H_0.

Test statistic: $F_{STAT} = \dfrac{S_1^2}{S_2^2} = \dfrac{(42.2617)^2}{(35.5486)^2} = 1.4134$.

Decision: Because $F_{STAT} = 1.4134 < 2.8664$, do not reject H_0. There is insufficient evidence to conclude that the two population variances are different. **(b)** p-value = 0.5021. **(c)** The test assumes that each of the two populations is normally distributed. **(d)** Based on (a) and (b), a pooled-variance t test should be used.

10.48 **(a)** Because $F_{STAT} = 1.9078 < 5.4098$ or p-value = 0.4417 > 0.05, do not reject H_0. There is insufficient evidence of a difference in the variability of the battery life between the two types of tablets. **(b)** p-value = 0.4417. The probability of obtaining a sample that yields a test statistic more extreme than 1.9078 is 0.4417 if there is no difference in the two population variances. **(c)** The test assumes that each of the two populations are normally distributed. The boxplots appear left-skewed especially the 3G/4G/WiFi tablets. **(d)** Based on (a) and (b), a pooled-variance *t* test should be used. However, because of the skewness and kurtosis in the 3G/4G/WiFi tablets, the validity of either a pooled-variance or separate-variance t test is in doubt.

10.50 Because $F_{STAT} = 2.197 < 3.6669$, or p-value = 0.2252 > 0.05, do not reject H_0. There is insufficient evidence of a difference in the variance of the mortgage rate in the two cities.

10.58 (a) Because $F_{STAT} = 1.1942 < 1.6885$, or p-value $= 0.4938 > 0.05$, do not reject H_0. There is not enough evidence of a difference in the variance of the salary of Black Belts and Green Belts. **(b)** The pooled-variance t test. **(c)** Because $t_{STAT} = 3.9806 > 1.654$ or p-value $= 0.0001 < 0.05$, reject H_0. There is evidence that the mean salary of Black Belts is greater than the mean salary of Green Belts.

10.60 (a) Because $F_{STAT} = 2.25 > \ = 1.6854$, reject H_0. There is evidence to conclude that there is a difference between the variances in the online time per week between women and men. **(b)** It is more appropriate to use a separate variance t test. Using the separate variance t test, because $t_{STAT} = -36.6113 < -1.9739$, reject H_0. There is enough evidence of a difference in the mean online time per week between women and men. **(c)** Because $F_{STAT} = 1.7778 > 1.6854$, reject H_0. There is evidence to conclude that there is a difference between the variances in the time spent playing games between women and men. **(d)** Using the separate-variance t test, because $t_{STAT} = -48.0 < -2.603$, reject H_0. There is evidence of a difference in the mean time spent playing games. between women and men.

10.62 (a) Because $t_{STAT} = 3.3282 > 1.8595$, reject H_0. There is enough evidence to conclude that the introductory computer students required more than a mean of 10 minutes to write and run a program in VB.NET **(b)** Because $t_{STAT} = 1.3636 < 1.8595$, do not reject H_0. There is not enough evidence to conclude that the introductory computer students required more than a mean of 10 minutes to write and run a program in VB.NET **(c)** Although the mean time necessary to complete the assignment increased from 12 to 16 minutes as a result of the increase in one data value, the standard deviation went from 1.8 to 13.2, which reduced the value of t statistic. **(d)** Because $F_{STAT} = 1.2308 < 3.8549$, do not reject H_0. There is not enough evidence to conclude that the population variances are different for the Introduction to Computers students and computer majors. Hence, the pooled-variance t test is a valid test to determine whether computer majors can write a VB.NET program in less time than introductory students, assuming that the distributions of the time needed to write a VB.NET program for both the Introduction to Computers students and the computer majors are approximately normally distributed. Because $t_{STAT} = 4.0666 > 1.7341$, reject H_0. There is enough evidence that the mean time is higher for Introduction to Computers students than for computer majors. **(e)** p-value $= 0.000362$. If the true population mean amount of time needed for Introduction to Computer students to write a VB.NET program is no more than 10 minutes, the probability of observing a sample mean greater than the 12 minutes in the current sample is 0.0362%. Hence, at a 5% level of significance, you can conclude that the population mean amount of time needed for Introduction to Computer students to write a VB.NET program is more than 10 minutes. As illustrated in (d), in which there is not enough evidence to conclude that the population variances are different for the Introduction to Computers students and computer majors, the pooled-variance t test performed is a valid test to determine whether computer majors can write a VB.NET program in less time than introductory students, assuming that the distribution of the time needed to write a VB.NET program for both the Introduction to Computers students and the computer majors are approximately normally distributed.

10.64 From the boxplot and the summary statistics, both distributions are approximately normally distributed. $F_{STAT} = 1.056 < 1.89$. There is insufficient evidence to conclude that the two population variances are significantly different at the 5% level of significance. $t_{STAT} = -5.084 < -1.99$. At the 5% level of significance, there is sufficient evidence to reject the null hypothesis of no difference in the mean life of the bulbs between the two manufacturers. You can conclude that there is a significant difference in the mean life of the bulbs between the two manufacturers.

10.66 (a) Because $Z_{STAT} = -3.6911 < -1.96$, reject H_0. There is enough evidence to conclude that there is a difference in the proportion of men and women who order dessert. **(b)** Because $Z_{STAT} = 6.0873 > 1.96$, reject H_0. There is enough evidence to conclude that there is a difference in the proportion of people who order dessert based on whether they ordered a beef entree.

10.68 The normal probability plots suggest that the two populations are not normally distributed. An F test is inappropriate for testing the difference in the two variances. The sample variances for Boston and Vermont shingles are 0.0203 and 0.015, respectively. Because $t_{STAT} = 3.015 > 1.967$ or p-value $= 0.0028 < \alpha = 0.05$, reject H_0. There is sufficient evidence to conclude that there is a difference in the mean granule loss of Boston and Vermont shingles.

CHAPTER 11

11.2 (a) $SSW = 150$. **(b)** $MSA = 15$. **(c)** $MSW = 5$. **(d)** $F_{STAT} = 3$.

11.4 (a) 2. **(b)** 18. **(c)** 20.

11.6 (a) Reject H_0 if $F_{STAT} > 2.95$; otherwise, do not reject H_0. **(b)** Because $F_{STAT} = 4 > 2.95$, reject H_0. **(c)** The table does not have 28 degrees of freedom in the denominator, so use the next larger critical value, $Q_\alpha = 3.90$. **(d)** Critical range $= 6.166$.

11.8 (a) H_0: $\mu_A = \mu_B = \mu_C = \mu_D$ and H_1: At least one mean is different.

$$MSA = \frac{SSA}{c-1} = \frac{8,275,375.875}{3} = 2,758,458.625.$$

$$MSW = \frac{SSW}{n-c} = \frac{17,385,053.9}{36} = 482,918.1639.$$

$$F_{STAT} = \frac{MSA}{MSW} = \frac{2,758,458.625}{482,918.1639} = 5.7121.$$

Because the p-value is 0.0026 and $F_{STAT} = 5.7121 > 2.8663$, reject H_0. There is sufficient evidence of a difference in the mean import cost across the four global regions. **(b)** Critical range $= Q_\alpha \sqrt{\dfrac{MSW}{2} \left(\dfrac{1}{n_j} + \dfrac{1}{n_{j'}} \right)}$

$$= 3.79 \sqrt{\frac{482,918.1639}{2} \left(\frac{1}{10} + \frac{1}{10} \right)} = 219.754.$$

From the Tukey-Kramer procedure, there is a difference in the mean import cost between the East Asia and Pacific region and Eastern Europe and Central Asia and Latin America and the Caribbean. None of the other regions are different. **(c)** ANOVA output for Levene's test for homogeneity of variance:

$$MSA = \frac{SSA}{c-1} = \frac{1,465,749.275}{3} = 488,583.0917$$

$$MSW = \frac{SSW}{n-c} = \frac{9,256,342.0}{36} = 257,120.6111$$

$$F_{STAT} = \frac{MSA}{MSW} = \frac{488,583.0917}{257,120.6111} = 1.9002$$

Because p-value $= 0.1470 > 0.05$ and $F_{STAT} = 1.9002 < 2.8663$, do not reject H_0. There is insufficient evidence to conclude that the variances in the import cost are different. **(d)** From the results in (a) and (b), the mean import cost for the East Asia and Pacific region is lower than for Eastern Europe and Central Asia and Latin America and the Caribbean.

11.10 (a) Because $F_{STAT} = 12.56 > 2.76$, reject H_0. **(b)** Critical range = 4.67. Advertisements A and B are different from Advertisements C and D. Advertisement E is only different from Advertisement D. **(c)** Because $F_{STAT} = 1.927 < 2.76$, do not reject H_0. There is no evidence of a significant difference in the variation in the ratings among the five advertisements. **(d)** The advertisements underselling the pen's characteristics had the highest mean ratings, and the advertisements overselling the pen's characteristics had the lowest mean ratings. Therefore, use an advertisement that undersells the pen's characteristics and avoid advertisements that oversell the pen's characteristics.

11.12 (a)

Source	Degrees of Freedom	Sum of Squares	Mean Squares	F
Among groups	4	13,918.573	3,479.6432	2.188
Within groups	179	284,671.467	1,590.3433	
Total	183	298,590.040		

(b) Since $F_{STAT} = 2.188 < 2.45$, do not reject H_0. There is insufficient evidence of a difference in the mean LPI score of the different groups.

(c) Since there was no significant difference among the groups, none of the critical ranges were significant.

11.14 (a) Because $F_{STAT} = 9.9637 > 3.1013$, reject H_0. **(b)** Critical range = 5.3918 (using 90 degrees of freedom). Asia is different from Europe and North America **(c)** The assumptions are that the samples are randomly and independently selected (or randomly assigned), the original populations of distances are approximately normally distributed, and the variances are equal. **(d)** Because $F_{STAT} = 1.01 < 3.1013$, do not reject H_0. There is insufficient evidence of a difference in the variation in the mean congestion level among the continents.

11.16 (a) 40. **(b)** 60 and 55. **(c)** 10. **(d)** 10.

11.18 Because $F_{STAT} = 6.00 > 3.35$, reject H_0. **(b)** Because $F_{STAT} = 5.50 > 3.35$, reject H_0. **(c)** Because $F_{STAT} = 1.00 < 2.73$, do not reject H_0.

11.20 $df_B = 4$, $df_{TOTAL} = 44$, $SSA = 160$, $SSAB = 80$, $SSE = 150$, $SST = 610$, $MSB = 55$, $MSE = 5$. For A: $F_{STAT} = 16$. For B: $F_{STAT} = 11$. For AB: $F_{STAT} = 2$.

11.22 (a) Because $F_{STAT} = 3.4032 < 4.3512$, do not reject H_0. **(b)** Because $F_{STAT} = 1.8496 < 4.3512$, do not reject H_0. **(c)** Because $F_{STAT} = 9.4549 > 4.3512$ reject H_0. **(e)** Die diameter has a significant effect on density, but die temperature does not. However, the cell means plot shows that the density seems higher with a 3 mm die diameter at 155 C but that there is little difference in density with a 4 mm die diameter. This interaction is not significant at the 0.05 level of significance.

11.24 (a) H_0: There is no interaction between filling time and mold temperature. H_1: There is an interaction between filling time and mold temperature.

Because $F_{STAT} = \dfrac{0.1136}{0.05} = 2.27 < 2.9277$ or the p-value =

0.1018 > 0.05, do not reject H_0. There is insufficient evidence of interaction between filling time and mold temperature. **(b)** $F_{Stat} = 9.0222 > 3.5546$, reject H_0. There is evidence of a difference in the warpage due to the filling time. **(c)** $F_{Stat} = 4.2305 > 3.5546$, reject H_0. There is evidence of a difference in the warpage due to the mold temperature. **(e)** The warpage for a three-second filling time seems to be much higher at 60°C and 72.5°C but not at 85°C.

11.26 (a) $F_{STAT} = 0.1523$, p-value = $0.9614 > 0.05$, do not reject H_0. There is not enough evidence to conclude that there is an interaction

between the brake discs and the gauges. **(b)** $F_{STAT} = 7.7701$, p-value is virtually $0 < 0.05$, reject H_0. There is sufficient evidence to conclude that there is an effect due to brake discs. **(c)** $F_{STAT} = 0.1465$, p-value = $0.7031 > 0.05$, do not reject H_0. There is inadequate evidence to conclude that there is an effect due to the gauges. **(d)** From the plot, there is no obvious interaction between brake discs and gauges. **(e)** There is no obvious difference in mean temperature across the gauges. It appears that Part 1 has the lowest, Part 3 the second lowest, and Part 2 has the highest average temperature.

11.36 (a) Because $F_{STAT} = 0.0111 < 2.9011$, do not reject H_0. **(b)** Because $F_{STAT} = 0.8096 < 4.1491$, do not reject H_0. **(c)** Because $F_{STAT} = 5.1999 > 2.9011$, reject H_0. **(e)** Critical range = 3.56. Only the means of Suppliers 1 and 2 are different. You can conclude that the mean strength is lower for Supplier 1 than for Supplier 2, but there are no statistically significant differences between Suppliers 1 and 3, Suppliers 1 and 4, Suppliers 2 and 3, Suppliers 2 and 4, and Suppliers 3 and 4. **(f)** $F_{STAT} = 5.6998 > 2.8663$ (p-value = $0.0027 < 0.05$). There is evidence that the mean strength of suppliers is different. Critical range = 3.359. Supplier 1 has a mean strength that is less than suppliers 2 and 3.

11.38 (a) Because $F_{STAT} = 0.075 < 3.68$, do not reject H_0. **(b)** Because $F_{STAT} = 4.09 > 3.68$, reject H_0. **(c)** Critical range = 1.489. Breaking strength is significantly different between 30 and 50 psi.

11.40 (a) Because $F_{STAT} = 0.1899 < 4.1132$, do not reject H_0. There is insufficient evidence to conclude that there is any interaction between type of breakfast and desired time. **(b)** Because $F_{STAT} = 30.4434 > 4.1132$, reject H_0. There is sufficient evidence to conclude that there is an effect due to type of breakfast. **(c)** Because $F_{STAT} = 12.4441 > 4.1132$, reject H_0. There is sufficient evidence to conclude that there is an effect due to desired time. **(e)** At the 5% level of significance, both the type of breakfast ordered and the desired time have an effect on delivery time difference. There is no interaction between the type of breakfast ordered and the desired time.

11.42 Interaction: $F_{STAT} = 0.2169 < 3.9668$ or p-value = $0.6428 > 0.05$. There is insufficient evidence of an interaction between piece size and fill height. Piece size: $F_{STAT} = 842.2242 > 3.9668$ or p-value = $0.0000 < 0.05$. There is evidence of an effect due to piece size. The fine piece size has a lower difference in coded weight. Fill height: $F_{STAT} = 217.0816 > 3.9668$ or p-value = $0.0000 < 0.05$. There is evidence of an effect due to fill height. The low fill height has a lower difference in coded weight.

CHAPTER 12

12.2 (a) For $df = 1$ and $\alpha = 0.05$, $\chi_{\alpha}^2 = 3.841$. **(b)** For $df = 1$ and $\alpha = 0.025$, $\chi^2 = 5.024$. **(c)** For $df = 1$ and $\alpha = 0.01$, $\chi_{\alpha}^2 = 6.635$.

12.4 (a) All $f_e = 25$. **(b)** Because $\chi_{STAT}^2 = 4.00 > 3.841$, reject H_0.

12.6 (a) H_0: $\pi_1 = \pi_2$. H_1: $\pi_1 \neq \pi_2$. **(b)** Because $\chi_{STAT}^2 = 79.29 > 3.841$, reject H_0. There is evidence to conclude that the population proportion of those who viewed the brand on general TV was different from those who viewed the brand on VOD D4+. p-value = 0.0000. The probability of obtaining a test statistic of 79.29 or larger when the null hypothesis is true is 0.0000. **(c)** You should not compare the results in (a) to those of Problem 10.30 (b) because that was a one-tail test.

12.8 (a) H_0: $\pi_1 = \pi_2$. H_1: $\pi_1 \neq \pi_2$. Because $\chi_{STAT}^2 = (278 - 297)^2/297 + (98 - 79)^2/79 + (316 - 297)^2/297 + (60 - 79)^2/79 =$

$11.5702 > 6.635$, reject H_0. There is evidence of a difference in the proportion of organizations with 500 to 2,499 employees and organizations with 2,500+ employees with respect to the proportion that have employee recognition programs. **(b)** p-value $= 0.0007$. The probability of obtaining a difference in proportions that gives rise to a test statistic above 11.5702 is 0.0000 if there is no difference in the proportion in the two groups. **(c)** The results of (a) and (b) are exactly the same as those of Problem 10.32. The χ^2 in (a) and the Z in Problem 10.32 (a) satisfy the relationship that $\chi^2 = 11.5702 = Z^2 = (3.4015)^2$, and the p-value in (b) is exactly the same as the p-value computed in Problem 10.32 (b).

12.10 (b) Since $\chi^2_{STAT} = 19.9467 > 3.841$, reject H_0. There is evidence that there is a significant difference between the proportion of co-browsing organizations and non-co-browsing organizations that use skills-based routing to match the caller with the *right* agent. **(c)** p-value is virtually zero. The probability of obtaining a test statistic of 19.9467 or larger when the null hypothesis is true is 0.0000. **(d)** The results are identical since $(4.4662)^2 = 19.9467$.

12.12 (a) The expected frequencies for the first row are 20, 30, and 40. The expected frequencies for the second row are 30, 45, and 60. **(b)** Because $\chi^2_{STAT} = 12.5 > 5.991$, reject H_0.

12.14 (a) Since the calculated test statistic 46.4046 is greater than the critical value of 7.8147, you reject H_0 and conclude that there is evidence of a difference among the age groups in the proportion smartphone owners who have reached the maximum amount of data they are allowed to use as part of their plan, at least on occasion. **(b)** p-value $= 0.0000$. The probability of obtaining a data set that gives rise to a test statistic of 46.4046 or more is 0.0000 if there is no difference in the proportion who have reached the maximum amount of data they are allowed to use as part of their plan, at least on occasion. **(c)** There is a significant difference between 18- to 29-year-olds and 50- to 64-years-olds and those 65 and older. There is a significant difference between 30- to 49-year-olds and 50- to 64-years-olds and those 65 and older.

12.16 (a) H_0: $\pi_1 = \pi_2 = \pi_3$. H_1: At least one proportion differs.

Observed Frequencies

Investing?	Global Region			
	NA	E	A	Total
Yes	100	132	142	374
No	100	68	58	226
Total	200	200	200	600

Expected Frequencies

Investing?	Global Region			
	NA	E	A	Total
Yes	124.6667	124.6667	124.6667	374
No	75.3333	75.3333	75.3333	226
Total	200	200	200	600

Data

Level of Significance	0.05
Number of Rows	2
Number of Columns	3
Degrees of Freedom	2

Results

Critical Value	5.9915
Chi-Square Test Statistic	20.5007
p-Value	0.0000
Reject the null hypothesis	

Since $20.5007 > 5.9915$, reject H_0.

There is a significant difference among global regions with respect to the proportion of organizations that are investing heavily in analytics and big data technologies **(b)** p-value $= 0.0000$. The probability of a test statistic greater than 20.5007 is 0.0000. **(c)**

Level of Significance	0.05
Square Root of Critical Value	2.4477

Sample Proportions

Group 1	0.50
Group 2	0.66
Group 3	0.71

Marascuilo Table

Proportions	Absolute Differences	Critical Range	
|Group 1 − Group 2|	0.16	0.1192	Significant
|Group 1 − Group 3|	0.21	0.1169	Significant
|Group 2 − Group 3|	0.05	0.1135	Not significant

North America is different from Europe and Asia.

12.18 (a) Because $\chi^2_{STAT} = 9.0485 > 5.9915$, reject H_0. There is evidence of a difference in the percentage who use their cellphones while watching TV between the groups. **(b)** p-value $= 0.0108$. **(c)** Group 1 versus group 2: $0.0215 < 0.0788$. Not significant. Group 1 versus group 3: $0.0905 > 0.0859$ significant. Group 2 versus group 3: $0.0691 > 0.06457$ significant. The rural group is different from the urban and suburban groups.

12.20 $df = (r − 1)(c − 1) = (3 − 1)(4 − 1) = 6$.

12.22 $\chi^2_{STAT} = 92.1028 > 16.919$, reject H_0 and conclude that there is evidence of a relationship between the type of dessert ordered and the type of entrée ordered.

12.24 H_0: There is no relationship between the frequency of posting on Facebook and age. H_1: There is a relationship between the frequency of posting on Facebook and age.

f_o	f_e	$(f_o − f_e)$	$(f_o − f_e)^2/f_e$
20	8.895459	11.10454	13.8622
28	13.83738	14.16262	14.4955
32	19.43823	12.56177	8.1179
32	26.35692	5.643083	1.2082
22	27.83949	−5.83949	1.2249
16	34.59345	−18.5935	9.9937
6	25.03907	−19.0391	14.4768
22	17.90496	4.095037	0.936574
37	27.85216	9.147835	3.004538
46	39.12566	6.87434	1.207815
69	53.05174	15.94826	4.794318
66	56.0359	9.964097	1.771779
59	69.63041	−10.6304	1.622935
15	50.39916	−35.3992	24.86352
9	13.34319	−4.34319	1.413702
14	20.75607	−6.75607	2.199092
31	29.15734	1.842661	0.116451
35	39.53537	−4.53537	0.520284
47	41.75924	5.24076	0.657712
56	51.89018	4.10982	0.325507
42	37.55861	4.441394	0.525205
2	10.5491	−8.5491	6.928282
4	16.40971	−12.4097	9.384747
7	23.05174	−16.0517	11.1774
17	31.2566	−14.2566	6.502647

f_o	f_e	$(f_o - f_e)$	$(f_o - f_e)^2/f_e$
28	33.01478	−5.01478	0.761721
61	41.02429	19.97571	9.726655
66	29.69377	36.30623	44.39121
1	3.307286	−2.30729	1.609649
1	5.144667	−4.14467	3.339043
2	7.227033	−5.22703	3.78051
7	9.799366	−2.79937	0.79969
6	10.35058	−4.35058	1.828646
18	12.86167	5.138332	2.052801
23	9.309398	13.6906	20.13369

Decision rule: If $\chi^2_{STAT} > 42.9798$, reject H_0.

Test statistic: $\chi^2_{STAT} = \sum_{\text{all cells}} \dfrac{(f_o - f_e)^2}{f_e} = 229.7554$.

Decision: Because $\chi^2_{STAT} = 229.7554 > 42.9798$ reject H_0. There is evidence to conclude that there is a relationship between the frequency of Facebook posts and age.

12.26 Because $\chi^2_{STAT} = 38.021 > 21.0261$ reject H_0. There is evidence of a relationship between identified main opportunity and geographic region.

12.28 (a) 31. (b) 29. (c) 27. (d) 25.

12.30 40 and 79.

12.32 (a) The ranks for Sample 1 are 1, 2, 4, 5, and 10. The ranks for Sample 2 are 3, 6.5, 6.5, 8, 9, and 11. (b) 22. (c) 44.

12.34 Because $T_1 = 22 > 20$, do not reject H_0.

12.36 (a) The data are ordinal. (b) The two-sample t test is inappropriate because the data can only be placed in ranked order. (c) Because $Z_{STAT} = -2.2054 < -1.96$, reject H_0. There is evidence of a significant difference in the median rating of California Cabernets and Washington Cabernets.

12.38 (a) $H_0: M_1 = M_2$, where Populations: $1 =$ Wing A, $2 =$ Wing B. $H_1: M_1 \neq M_2$.

Population 1 sample: Sample size 20, sum of ranks 561

Population 2 sample: Sample size 20, sum of ranks 259

$\mu_{T_1} = \dfrac{n_1(n+1)}{2} = \dfrac{20(40+1)}{2} = 410$

$\sigma_{T_1} = \sqrt{\dfrac{n_1 n_2(n+1)}{12}} = \sqrt{\dfrac{20(20)(40+1)}{12}} = 36.9685$

$Z_{STAT} = \dfrac{T_1 - \mu_{T_1}}{S_{T_1}} = \dfrac{561 - 410}{36.9685} = 4.0846$

Decision: Because $Z_{STAT} = 4.0846 > 1.96$ (or p-value = 0.0000 < 0.05), reject H_0. There is sufficient evidence of a difference in the median delivery time in the two wings of the hotel.

(b) The results of (a) are consistent with the results of Problem 10.65.

12.40 (a) Because $Z_{STAT} = 1.7671 < 1.96$, do not reject H_0. There is insufficient evidence to conclude that there is a difference in the median brand value between the two sectors. (b) You must assume approximately equal variability in the two populations. (c) using the pooled-variance t test you rejected the null hypothesis and the separate-variance t test did not allow you to reject the null hypothesis and conclude in Problem 10.17 that the mean brand value is different between the two sectors. In this test,

using the Wilcoxon rank sum test with large-sample Z approximation did not allow you to reject the null hypothesis and conclude that the median brand value differs between the two sectors.

12.42 (a) Because $-1.96 < Z_{STAT} = 0.803 < 1.96$ (or the p-value = 0.4220 > 0.05), do not reject H_0. There is not enough evidence to conclude that there is a difference in the median battery life between Wi-Fi-only and 3G/4G/Wi-Fi tablets. (b) You must assume approximately equal variability in the two populations. (c) Using the pooled-variance t-test, you do not reject the null hypothesis $(t = -2.1098 < t_{STAT} = -0.6721 < 2.1098; p\text{-value} = 0.5106 > 0.05)$ and conclude that there is insufficient evidence of a difference in the mean battery life between the two types of tablets in Problem 10.11 (a).

12.44 (a) Decision rule: If $H > \chi^2_U = 15.086$, reject H_0 (b) Because $H = 13.77 < 15.806$, do not reject H_0.

12.46 (a) $H = 13.517 > 7.815$, p-value = 0.0036 < 0.05, reject H_0. There is sufficient evidence of a difference in the median waiting time in the four locations. (b) The results are consistent with those of Problem 11.9.

12.48 (a) $H = 19.3269 > 9.488$, reject H_0. There is evidence of a difference in the median ratings of the ads. (b) The results are consistent with those of Problem 11.10. (c) Because the combined scores are not true continuous variables, the nonparametric Kruskal-Wallis rank test is more appropriate because it does not require that the scores are normally distributed.

12.50 (a) Because $H = 20.3221 > 7.815$ or the p-value is 0.0001, reject H_0. There is sufficient evidence of a difference in the median cost associated with importing a standardized cargo of goods by sea transport across the global regions. (b) The results are the same.

12.56 (a) Because $\chi^2_{STAT} = 0.412 < 3.841$, do not reject H_0. There is insufficient evidence to conclude that there is a relationship between a student's gender and pizzeria selection. (b) Because $\chi^2_{STAT} = 2.624 < 3.841$, do not reject H_0. There is insufficient evidence to conclude that there is a relationship between a student's gender and pizzeria selection. (c) Because $\chi^2_{STAT} = 4.956 < 5.991$, do not reject H_0. There is insufficient evidence to conclude that there is a relationship between price and pizzeria selection. (d) p-value = 0.0839. The probability of a sample that gives a test statistic equal to or greater than 4.956 is 8.39% if the null hypothesis of no relationship between price and pizzeria selection is true.

12.58 (a) Because $\chi^2_{STAT} = 11.895 < 12.592$, do not reject H_0. There is not enough evidence to conclude that there is a relationship between the attitudes of employees toward the use of self-managed work teams and employee job classification. (b) Because $\chi^2_{STAT} = 3.294 < 12.592$, do not reject H_0. There is insufficient evidence to conclude that there is a relationship between the attitudes of employees toward vacation time without pay and employee job classification.

CHAPTER 13

13.2 (a) Yes. (b) No. (c) No. (d) Yes.

13.4 (a) The scatter plot shows a positive linear relationship.
(b) For each increase in alcohol percentage of 1.0, mean predicted mean wine quality is estimated to increase by 0.5624.
(c) $\hat{Y} = 5.2715$.
(d) Wine quality appears to be affected by the alcohol percentage. Each increase of 1% in alcohol leads to a mean increase in wine quality of a little more than half a unit.

13.6 (b) $b_0 = -23,147.8207$, $b_1 = 2.5819$. **(c)** For each increase of $1,000 in tuition, the mean starting salary is predicted to increase by $2,582.90. **(d)** $107,757.15 **(e)** Starting salary seems higher for those schools that have a higher tuition.

13.8 (b) $b_0 = -841.8773$, $b_1 = 7.7876$. **(c)** For each additional million-dollar increase in revenue, the mean value is predicted to increase by an estimated $7.7876 million Literal interpretation of b_0 is not meaningful because an operating franchise cannot have zero revenue. **(d)** $1,105.011 million. **(e)** That the value of the franchise can be expected to increase as revenue increases.

13.10 (b) $b_0 = 3.0532$, $b_1 = 0.1489$. **(c)** For each increase of $1 million of box office gross, the predicted DVD revenue is estimated to increase by $0.1489 million. **(d)** $17.9404 million. **(e)** You can conclude that the mean predicted increase in DVD sales is $148,900 for each million-dollar increase in movie gross.

13.12 $SST = 40$, $r^2 = 0.90$. 90% of the variation in the dependent variable can be explained by the variation in the independent variable.

13.14 $r^2 = 0.75$. 75% of the variation in the dependent variable can be explained by the variation in the independent variable.

13.16 (a) $r^2 = \dfrac{SSR}{SST} = \dfrac{21.8677}{64.0000} = 0.3417$, 34.17% of the variation in wine quality can be explained by the variation in the percentage of alcohol.

(b) $S_{YX} = \sqrt{\dfrac{SSE}{n-2}} = \sqrt{\dfrac{\sum\limits_{i=1}^{n}(Y_i - \hat{Y}_i)^2}{n-2}} = \sqrt{\dfrac{42.1323}{48}} = 0.9369$.

(c) Based on (a) and (b), the model should be somewhat useful for predicting wine quality.

13.18 (a) $r^2 = 0.6364$. 63.64% of the variation in starting salary can be explained by the variation in tuition. **(b)** $S_{YX} = 18,245.4459$. **(c)** Based on (a) and (b), the model should be very useful for predicting the starting salary.

13.20 (a) $r^2 = 0.9592$, 95.92% of the variation in the value of a baseball franchise can be explained by the variation in its annual revenue. **(b)** $S_{YX} = 118.8687$. **(c)** Based on (a) and (b), the model should be very useful for predicting the value of a baseball franchise.

13.22 (a) $r^2 = 0.279$, 27.97% of the variation in DVD revenue can be explained by the variation in box office gross. **(b)** $S_{YX} = 25.2987$. The variation of DVD revenue around the prediction line is $25.2987 million. The typical difference between actual DVD revenue and the predicted DVD revenue using the regression equation is approximately $25.2987 million. **(c)** Based on (a) and (b), the model may only be somewhat useful for predicting DVD revenue. **(d)** Other variables that might explain the variation in DVD revenue could be the amount spent on advertising, the timing of the release of the DVDs, and the type of movie.

13.24 A residual analysis of the data indicates a pattern, with sizable clusters of consecutive residuals that are either all positive or all negative. This pattern indicates a violation of the assumption of linearity. A curvilinear model should be investigated.

13.26 There does not appear to be a pattern in the residual plot. The assumptions of regression do not appear to be seriously violated.

13.28 Based on the residual plot, the assumption of equal variance appears to be violated.

13.30 Based on the residual plot, there is no evidence of a pattern.

13.32 (a) An increasing linear relationship exists. **(b)** There is evidence of a strong positive autocorrelation among the residuals.

13.34 (a) No, because the data were not collected over time. **(b)** If data were collected at a single store had been selected and studied over a period of time, you would compute the Durbin-Watson statistic.

13.36 (a)

$$b_1 = \frac{SSXY}{SSX} = \frac{201,399.05}{12,495,626} = 0.0161$$

$$b_0 = \bar{Y} - b_1\bar{X} = 71.2621 - 0.0161(4,393) = 0.4576.$$

(b) $\hat{Y} = 0.458 + 0.0161X = 0.4576 + 0.0161(4,500) = 72.9867$, or $72,908. **(c)** There is no evidence of a pattern in the residuals over time.

(d) $D = \dfrac{\sum\limits_{i=2}^{n}(e_i - e_{i-1})^2}{\sum\limits_{i=1}^{n} e_i^2} = \dfrac{1,243.2244}{599.0683} = 2.08 > 1.45$. There is no evidence of positive autocorrelation among the residuals. **(e)** Based on a residual analysis, the model appears to be adequate.

13.38 (a) $b_0 = -2.535$, $b_1 = 0.06073$. **(b)** $2,505.40. **(d)** $D = 1.64 > d_U = 1.42$, so there is no evidence of positive autocorrelation among the residuals. **(e)** The plot shows some nonlinear pattern, suggesting that a nonlinear model might be better. Otherwise, the model appears to be adequate.

13.40 (a) 3.00. **(b)** ± 2.1199. **(c)** Reject H_0. There is evidence that the fitted linear regression model is useful. **(d)** $1.32 \leq \beta_1 \leq 7.68$.

13.42 (a) $t_{STAT} = \dfrac{b_1 - \beta_1}{S_{b_1}} = \dfrac{0.5624}{0.1127} = 4.9913 > 2.0106$. Reject H_0. There is evidence of a linear relationship between the percentage of alcohol and wine quality **(b)** $b \pm t_{\alpha/2}S_{b_1} = 0.5624 \pm 2.0106(0.1127)$ $0.3359 \leq \beta_1 \leq 0.7890$.

13.44 (a) $t_{STAT} = 7.8275 > 2.0301$; reject H_0. There is evidence of a linear relationship between tuition and starting salary. **(b)** $1.913 \leq \beta_1 \leq 3.2527$.

13.46 (a) $t_{STAT} = 25.6493 > 2.0484$ or because the p-value is 0.0000, reject H_0 at the 5% level of significance. There is evidence of a linear relationship between annual revenue and franchise value. **(b)** $7.1656 \leq \beta_1 \leq 8.40951$.

13.48 (a) $t_{STAT} = 3.7344 > 2.0281$ or because the p-value $= 0.0002 < 0.05$; reject H_0. There is evidence of a linear relationship between box office gross and sales of DVDs. **(b)** $0.068 \leq \beta_1 \leq 0.2297$.

13.50 (a) (% daily change in SPXL) $= b_0 + 3.0$ (% daily change in S&P 500 index). **(b)** If the S&P 500 gains 10% in a year, SPXL is expected to gain an estimated 30%. **(c)** If the S&P 500 loses 20% in a year, SPXL is expected to lose an estimated 60%. **(d)** Risk takers will be attracted to leveraged funds, and risk-averse investors will stay away.

13.52 (a), (b) First weekend and U.S. gross: $r = 0.7284$, $t_{STAT} = 2.6042 > 2.4469$, p-value $= 0.0404 < 0.05$. reject H_0. At the 0.05 level of significance, there is evidence of a linear relationship between first weekend sales and U.S. gross. First weekend and worldwide gross: $r = 0.8233$, $t_{STAT} = 3.5532 > 2.4469$, p-value $= 0.0120 < 0.05$. reject H_0. At the 0.05 level of significance, there is evidence of a linear relationship between first weekend sales and worldwide gross. U.S. gross and worldwide gross: $r = 0.9642$, $t_{STAT} = 8.9061 > 2.4469$, p-value $= 0.0001 < 0.05$. Reject H_0. At the 0.05 level of significance, there is evidence of a linear relationship between U.S gross and worldwide gross.

13.54 (a) $r = 0.0305$. There is an insignificant linear relationship between social media networking and the GDP per capita. **(b)** $t_{STAT} = 0.1645$, p-value $= 0.8705 > 0.05$. Do not reject H_0. At the 0.05 level of significance, there is insufficient evidence of a linear relationship between social media networking and the GDP per capita. **(c)** There does not appear to be a linear relationship.

13.56 (a) $15.95 \leq \mu_{Y|X=4} \leq 18.05$. **(b)** $14.651 \leq Y_{X=4} \leq 19.349$. **(c)** The intervals in this problem are wider than in Problem 13.55 because they involve X values that are different from the mean.

13.58 (a) $\hat{Y} = -0.3529 + (0.5624)(10) = 5.2715$ $\hat{Y} \pm t_{\alpha/2}S_{YX}\sqrt{h_i}$
$$= 5.2715 \pm 2.0106(0.9369)\sqrt{0.0249}$$
$$4.9741 \leq \mu_{Y|X=10} \leq 5.5690.$$

(b) $\hat{Y} \pm t_{\alpha/2}S_{YX}\sqrt{1 + h_i}$
$$= 5.2715 \pm 2.0106(9,369)\sqrt{1 + 0.0249}$$
$$3.3645 \leq Y_{X=10} \leq 7.1786.$$

(c) Part (b) provides a prediction interval for the individual response given a specific value of the independent variable, and part (a) provides a confidence interval estimate for the mean value, given a specific value of the independent variable. Because there is much more variation in predicting an individual value than in estimating a mean value, a prediction interval is wider than a confidence interval estimate.

13.60 (a) $\$101,067.77 \leq \mu_{Y|X=500} \leq \$113,246.53$. **(b)** $\$69,619.72 \leq Y_{X=500} \leq \$144,694.58$. **(c)** You can estimate a mean more precisely than you can predict a single observation.

13.62 (a) $1,059.9199 \leq \mu_{Y|X=250} \leq 1,150.102$. **(b)** $857.3797 \leq Y_{X=250} \leq 1,352.642$. **(c)** Because there is much more variation in predicting an individual value than in estimating a mean, the prediction interval is wider than the confidence interval.

13.74 (a) $b_0 = 24.84$, $b_1 = 0.14$. **(b)** For each additional case, the predicted delivery time is estimated to increase by 0.14 minute. The interpretation of the Y intercept is not meaningful since the number of cases delivered cannot be 0. **(c)** 45.84. **(d)** No, 500 is outside the relevant range of the data used to fit the regression equation. **(e)** $r^2 = 0.972$. **(f)** There is no obvious pattern in the residuals, so the assumptions of regression are met. The model appears to be adequate. **(g)** $t_{STAT} = 24.88 > 2.1009$; reject H_0. **(h)** $44.88 \leq \mu_{Y|X=150} \leq 46.80$. $41.56 \leq Y_{X=150} \leq 50.12$. **(i)** The number of cases explains almost all of the variation in delivery time.

13.76 (a) $b_0 = 276.848$, $b_1 = 50.8031$. **(b)** For each additional 1,000 square feet in the size of the house, the mean assessed value is predicted to increase by $\$50,803.10$. The estimated selling price of a house with a 0 size is $\$276,848$ thousand. However, this interpretation is not meaningful because the size of the house cannot be 0. **(c)** $\hat{Y} = 378.4542$ thousand dollars. **(d)** $r^2 = 0.3273$. So 32.73% of the variation in assessed value is explained by the variation in size. **(e)** Neither the residual plot nor the normal probability plot reveals any potential violation of the linearity, equal variance, and normality assumptions. **(f)** $t_{STAT} = 3.6913 > 2.0484$, p-value is 0.0009. Because p-value < 0.05, reject H_0. There is evidence of a linear relationship between assessed value and size. **(g)** $22.6113 \leq \beta_1 \leq 78.9949$. **(h)** The size of the house is somewhat useful in predicting the assessed value, but since only 32.73% of the variation in assessed value is explained by variation in size, other variables should be considered.

13.78 (a) $b_0 = 12.8829$, $b_1 = -0.2687$. **(b)** For each additional point on the leverage ratio, the predicted ROE is estimated to decrease by 0.2687. For a leverage ratio of 0, the predicted mean ROE is 12.8829. **(c)** 10.4645. **(d)** $r^2 = 0.0449$. **(e)** There is no obvious pattern in the residuals, so the assumptions of regression are met. The model appears to be

adequate. **(f)** $-2.0687 < t_{STAT} = -1.0394 > 2.0687$; do not reject H_0. **(g)** $9.5192 \leq \mu_{Y|X=9} \leq 11.4098$, $5.8397 \leq Y_{X=9} \leq 15.08939$. **(h)** $-0.8035 \leq \beta_1 \leq 0.2661$. **(i)** There is virtually no relationship between leverage ratio and ROE.

13.80 (a) There is no clear relationship shown on the scatter plot. **(c)** Looking at all 23 flights, when the temperature is lower, there is likely to be some O-ring damage, particularly if the temperature is below 60 degrees. **(d)** 31 degrees is outside the relevant range, so a prediction should not be made. **(e)** Predicted $Y = 18.036 - 0.240X$, where $X =$ temperature and $Y =$ O-ring damage. **(g)** A nonlinear model would be more appropriate. **(h)** The appearance on the residual plot of a nonlinear pattern indicates that a nonlinear model would be better. It also appears that the normality assumption is invalid.

13.82 (a) $b_0 = -742.7832$, $b_1 = 11.5518$. **(b)** For each additional million-dollar increase in revenue, the franchise value will increase by an estimated 11.5518 million. Literal interpretation of b_0 is not meaningful because an operating franchise cannot have zero revenue. **(c)** $\$989.9823$ million. **(d)** $r^2 = 0.8548$. 85.48% of the variation in the value of an NBA franchise can be explained by the variation in its annual revenue. **(e)** There does not appear to be a pattern in the residual plot. The assumptions of regression do not appear to be seriously violated. **(f)** $t_{STAT} = 12.8391 > 2.0484$ or because the p-value is 0.0000, reject H_0 at the 5% level of significance. There is evidence of a linear relationship between annual revenue and franchise value. **(g)** $913.1332 \leq \mu_{Y|X=150} \leq 1,066.831$. **(h)** $574.183 \leq Y_{X=150} \leq 1,405.782$. **(i)** The strength of the relationship between revenue and value is higher for NBA franchises than for European soccer teams but lower than for Major League Baseball teams.

13.84 (a) $b_0 = -2,629.222$, $b_1 = 82.472$. **(b)** For each additional centimeter in circumference, the weight is estimated to increase by 82.472 grams. **(c)** 2,319.08 grams. **(d)** Yes, since circumference is a very strong predictor of weight. **(e)** $r^2 = 0.937$. **(f)** There appears to be a nonlinear relationship between circumference and weight. **(g)** p-value is virtually $0 < 0.05$; reject H_0. **(h)** $72.7875 \leq \beta_1 \leq 92.156$.

13.86 (a) The correlation between compensation and stock performance is 0.1026. **(b)** $t_{STAT} = 1.4255$; p-value $= 0.1556 > 0.05$. The correlation between compensation and stock performance is not significant, only 10.26% of the variation in compensation can be explained by return. **(c)** The small correlation between compensation and stock performance was surprising (or maybe it shouldn't have been!).

CHAPTER 14

14.2 (a) For each one-unit increase in X_1, you estimate that the mean of Y will decrease 2 units, holding X_2 constant. For each one-unit increase in X_2, you estimate that the mean of Y will increase 7 units, holding X_1 constant. **(b)** The Y intercept, equal to 50, estimates the value of Y when both X_1 and X_2 are 0.

14.4 (a) $\hat{Y} = 1.8508 - 0.0170X_1 + 0.0194X_2$. **(b)** For a given capital adequacy, for each increase of 1% in efficiency ratio, ROA decreases by 0.0170%. For a given efficiency ratio, for each increase of 1% in capital adequacy, ROA increases by 0.0194% **(c)** $\hat{Y} = 1.1211$ **(d)** $1.0813 \leq \mu_{Y|X} \leq 1.1608$. **(e)** $0.6322 \leq Y_X \leq 1.6099$ **(f)** The interval in (e) is narrower because it is estimating the mean value, not an individual value. **(g)** The model uses both the efficiency ratio and capital adequacy to predict ROA. This may produce a better model than if only one of these independent variables is included.

14.6 (a) $\hat{Y} = -89.2061 + 25.878X_1 + 31.818X_2$. **(b)** For a given amount of voluntary turnover, for each increase of \$1 billion in worldwide revenue, the mean number of full-time jobs added is predicted to increase by 25.878. For a given \$1 billion in worldwide revenue, for each increase of 1% in voluntary turnover, the mean number of full-time jobs added is predicted to increase by 31.8184. **(c)** The Y intercept has no meaning in this problem. **(d)** Holding the other independent variable constant, voluntary turnover has a higher slope than worldwide revenue

14.8 (a) $\hat{Y} = 532.2883 + 407.1346X_1 - 2.8257X_2$, where $X_1 =$ land area, $X_2 =$ age. **(b)** For a given age, each increase by one acre in land area is estimated to result in an increase in the mean fair market value by \$407.1346 thousands. For a given land area, each increase of one year in age is estimated to result in a decrease in the mean fair market value by \$2.8257 thousands. **(c)** The interpretation of b_0 has no practical meaning here because it would represent the estimated fair market value of a new house that has no land area. **(d)** $\hat{Y} = \$478.6577$ thousands. **(e)** $446.8367 \leq \mu_{Y|X} \leq 510.4788$. **(f)** $307.2577 \leq Y_X \leq 650.0577$.

14.10 (a) $MSR = 15$, $MSE = 12$. **(b)** 1.25. **(c)** $F_{STAT} = 1.25 < 4.10$; do not reject H_0. **(d)** 0.20. 20% of the variation in Y is explained by variation in X. **(e)** 0.04.

14.12 (a) $F_{STAT} = 97.69 > 3.89$. Reject H_0. There is evidence of a significant linear relationship with at least one of the independent variables. **(b)** p-value $= 0.0001$. **(c)** $r^2 = 0.9421$. 94.21% of the variation in the long-term ability to absorb shock can be explained by variation in forefoot-absorbing capability and variation in midsole impact. **(d)** $r^2_{adj} = 0.9325$.

14.14 (a) $F_{STAT} = 70.4989 > 3.00$; reject H_0. **(b)** p-value $= 0$. **(c)** $r^2 = 0.4184$. 41.84% of the variation in ROA can be explained by variation in efficiency ratio and variation in risk-based capital. **(d)** $r^2_{adj} = 0.4125$.

14.16 (a) $F_{STAT} = 5.2073 > 3.13$. Reject H_0. There is evidence of a significant linear relationship. **(b)** p-value $= 0.0075$. **(c)** $r^2 = 0.1152$. 11.52% of the variation in full-time jobs added can be explained by variation in worldwide revenue and variation in full-time voluntary turnover. **(d)** $r^2_{adj} = 0.0931$.

14.18 (a) – **(e)** Based on a residual analysis, there is no evidence of a violation of the assumptions of regression.

14.20 (a) There is no evidence of a violation of the assumptions **(b)** Since the data are not collected over time, the Durbin-Watson test is not appropriate. **(c)** They are valid

14.22 (a) The residual analysis reveals no patterns. **(b)** Since the data are not collected over time, the Durbin-Watson test is not appropriate. **(c)** There are no apparent violations in the assumptions.

14.24 (a) Variable X_2 has a larger slope in terms of the t statistic of 3.75 than variable X_1, which has a smaller slope in terms of the t statistic of 3.33. **(b)** $1.46824 \leq \beta_1 \leq 6.53176$. **(c)** For $X_1 : t_{STAT} = 3.33 > 2.1098$. Reject H_0. There is evidence that X_1 contributes to a model already containing X_2. For $X_2 : t_{STAT} = 3.75 > 2.1098$. Reject H_0. There is evidence that X_2 contributes to a model already containing X_1. Both X_1 and X_2 should be included in the model.

14.26 (a) 95% confidence interval on $\beta_1 : b_1 \pm t S_{b_1}$, -0.017 ± 1.98 (0.0017), $-0.0204 \leq \beta_1 \leq -0.0136$. **(b)** For $X_1 : t_{STAT} = b_1 / S_{b_1} = -0.017/0.0017 = -9.7452 < -1.98$. Reject H_0. There is evidence that X_1 contributes to a model already containing X_2. For $X_2 : t_{STAT} = b_2 / S_{b_2} = 0.0194/0.0048 = 4.0071 > 1.98$. Reject H_0. There is evidence that X_2 contributes to a model already containing X_1. Both X_1 (efficiency ratio) and X_2 (total risk-based capital) should be included in the model.

14.28 (a) $7.9983 \leq \beta_1 \leq 43.7628$. **(b)** For $X_1 : t_{STAT} = 2.8795 > 1.9901$. Reject H_0. There is evidence that X_1 contributes to a model already containing X_2. For $X_2 : t_{STAT} = 1.6899 < 1.9901$. Do not reject H_0. There is insufficient evidence that X_2 contributes to a model already containing X_1. Only X_1 total worldwide revenues should be included in the model.

14.30 (a) $274.1702 \leq \beta_1 \leq 540.0990$. **(b)** For $X_1 : t_{STAT} = 6.2827$ and p-value $= 0.0000$. Because p-value < 0.05, reject H_0. There is evidence that X_1 contributes to a model already containing X_2. For $X_2 : t_{STAT} = -4.1475$ and p-value $= 0.0003$. Because p-value < 0.05 reject H_0. There is evidence that X_2 contributes to a model already containing X_1. Both X_1 (land area) and X_2 (age) should be included in the model.

14.32 (a) For X_1: $F_{STAT} = 1.25 < 4.96$; do not reject H_0. For X_2: $F_{STAT} = 0.833 < 4.96$; do not reject H_0. **(b)** 0.1111, 0.0769.

14.34 (a) For X_1: $SSR(X_1|X_2) = SSR(X_1 \text{ and } X_2) - SSR(X_2) = 8.6048 - 2.809 = 5.7958$, $F_{STAT} = \dfrac{SSR(X_1|X_2)}{MSE} = \dfrac{5.7958}{11.9615/196} = 95.01 > 3.897$. Reject H_0. There is evidence that X_1 contributes to a model already containing X_2. For X_2: $SSR(X_2|X_1) = SSR(X_1 \text{ and } X_2) - SSR(X_1) = 8.6048 - 7.6249 = 0.9799$, $F_{STAT} = \dfrac{SSR(X_2|X_1)}{MSE} = \dfrac{0.9799}{11.9615/196} = 16.06 > 3.897$.

Reject H_0. There is evidence that X_2 contributes to a model already containing X_1. Because both X_1 and X_2 make a significant contribution to the model in the presence of the other variable, both variables should be included in the model.

(b) $r^2_{Y1.2} = \dfrac{SSR(X_1|X_2)}{SST - SSR(X_1 \text{ and } X_2) + SSR(X_1|X_2)}$

$= \dfrac{5.7958}{20.5663 - 8.6048 + 5.7958} = 0.3264$.

Holding constant the effect of the total risk based capital, 32.64% of the variation in ROA can be explained by the variation in efficiency ratio.

$r^2_{Y2.1} = \dfrac{SSR(X_2|X_1)}{SST - SSR(X_1 \text{ and } X_2) + SSR(X_2|X_1)}$

$= \dfrac{0.9799}{20.5663 - 8.6048 + 0.9799} = 0.0757$

Holding constant the effect of efficiency ratio 7.57% of the variation in ROA can be explained by variation in the total risk-based capital.

14.36 (a) For X_1: $F_{STAT} = 8.29 > 3.967$. Reject H_0. There is evidence that X_1 contributes to a model containing X_2. For X_2: $F_{STAT} = 2.8557 < 3.967$. Do not reject H_0. There is insufficient evidence that X_2 contributes to a model already containing X_1. Because only X_1 makes a significant contribution to the model in the presence of the other variable, only X_i should be included in the model. **(b)** $r^2_{Y1.2} = 0.0939$. Holding constant the effect of full-time voluntary turnover, 9.39% of the variation in full-time jobs added be explained by the variation in total worldwide revenue . $r^2_{Y2.1} = 0.0345$. Holding constant the effect of total worldwide revenue, 3.45% of the variation in full-time jobs created can be explained by the variation in full-time voluntary turnover.

14.38 (a) Holding constant the effect of X_2, for each increase of one unit of X_1, Y increases by 4 units. **(b)** Holding constant the effect of X_1, for each increase of one unit of X_2, Y increases by 2 units. **(c)** Because $t_{STAT} = 3.27 > 2.1098$, reject H_0. Variable X_2 makes a significant contribution to the model.

14.40 (a) $\hat{Y} = 243.7371 + 9.2189X_1 + 12.6967X_2$, where $X_1 =$ number of rooms and $X_2 =$ neighborhood (east $= 0$). **(b)** Holding constant the effect of neighborhood, for each additional room, the mean selling price is estimated to increase by 9.2189 thousands of dollars, or \$9,218.9. For a given number of rooms, a west neighborhood is estimated to increase the mean selling price over an east neighborhood by 12.6967 thousands of dollars, or \$12,696.7. **(c)** $\hat{Y} = 326.7076$, or \$326, 707.6. $309,560.04 \le Y_X \le 343,855.1$. $321,471.44 \le \mu_{Y|X} \le 331,943.71$. **(d)** Based on a residual analysis, the model appears to be adequate. **(e)** $F_{STAT} = 55.39$, the p-value is virtually 0. Because p-value < 0.05, reject H_0. There is evidence of a significant relationship between selling price and the two independent variables (rooms and neighborhood). **(f)** For X_1: $t_{STAT} = 8.9537$, the p-value is virtually 0. Reject H_0. Number of rooms makes a significant contribution and should be included in the model. For X_2: $t_{STAT} = 3.5913$, p-value $= 0.0023 < 0.05$. Reject H_0. Neighborhood makes a significant contribution and should be included in the model. Based on these results, the regression model with the two independent variables should be used. **(g)** $7.0466 \le \beta_1 \le 11.3913$. **(h)** $5.2378 \le \beta_2 \le 20.1557$. **(i)** $r^2_{adj} = 0.851$. **(j)** $r^2_{Y1.2} = 0.825$. Holding constant the effect of neighborhood, 82.5% of the variation in selling price can be explained by variation in number of rooms. $r^2_{Y2.1} = 0.431$. Holding constant the effect of number of rooms, 43.1% of the variation in selling price can be explained by variation in neighborhood. **(k)** The slope of selling price with number of rooms is the same, regardless of whether the house is located in an east or west neighborhood. **(l)** $\hat{Y} = 253.95 + 8.032X_1 - 5.90X_2 + 2.089X_1X_2$. For $X_1 X_2$, p-value $= 0.330$. Do not reject H_0. There is no evidence that the interaction term makes a contribution to the model. **(m)** The model in (b) should be used. **(n)** The number of rooms and the neighborhood both significantly affect the selling price, but the number of rooms has a greater effect.

14.42 (a) Predicted time $= 8.01 + 0.00523$ Depth $- 2.105$ Dry. **(b)** Holding constant the effect of type of drilling, for each foot increase in depth of the hole, the mean drilling time is estimated to increase by 0.00523 minutes. For a given depth, a dry drilling hole is estimated to reduce the drilling time over wet drilling by a mean of 2.1052 minutes. **(c)** 6.428 minutes, $6.210 \le \mu_{Y|X} \le 6.646$, $4.923 \le Y_X \le 7.932$. **(d)** The model appears to be adequate. **(e)** $F_{STAT} = 111.11 > 3.09$; reject H_0. **(f)** $t_{STAT} = 5.03 > 1.9847$; reject H_0. $t_{STAT} = -14.03 < -1.9847$; reject H_0. Include both variables. **(g)** $0.0032 \le \beta_1 \le 0.0073$. **(h)** $-2.403 \le \beta_2 \le -1.808$. **(i)** 69.0%. **(j)** 0.207, 0.670. **(k)** The slope of the additional drilling time with the depth of the hole is the same, regardless of the type of drilling method used. **(l)** The p-value of the interaction term $= 0.462 > 0.05$, so the term is not significant and should not be included in the model. **(m)** The model in part (b) should be used. Both variables affect the drilling time. Dry drilling holes should be used to reduce the drilling time.

14.44 (a) $\hat{Y} = 1.2604 - 0.0071X_1 + 0.0541X_2 - 0.0006X_1X_2$, where $X_1 =$ efficiency ratio, $X_2 =$ total risk-based capital, p-value $= 0.1037 > 0.05$. Do not reject H_0. There is not enough evidence that the interaction term makes a contribution to the model. **(b)** Because there is insufficient evidence of any interaction effect between efficiency ratio and total risk-based capital, the model in Problem 14.4 should be used.

14.46 (a) The p-value of the interaction term $= 0.0347 < 0.05$, so the term is significant and should be included in the model. **(b)** Use the model developed in this problem.

14.48 (a) For $X_1 X_2$, p-value $= 0.2353 > 0.05$. Do not reject H_0. There is insufficient evidence that the interaction term makes a contribution to the model. **(b)** Because there is not enough evidence of an interaction effect between total staff present and remote hours, the model in Problem 14.7 should be used.

14.50 Holding constant the effect of other variables, the natural logarithm of the estimated odds ratio for the dependent categorical response will increase by 2.2 for each unit increase in the particular independent variable.

14.52 0.4286.

14.54 (a) ln(estimated odds ratio) $= -6.9394 + 0.1395X_1 + 2.7743X_2 = -6.9394 + 0.1395(36) + 2.7743(0) = -1.91908$. Estimated odds ratio $= 0.1470$. Estimated Probability of Success $=$ Odds Ratio/$(1 +$ Odds Ratio$) = 0.1470/(1 + 0.1470) = 0.1260$. **(b)** From the text discussion of the example, 70.2% of the individuals who charge \$36,000 per annum and possess additional cards can be expected to purchase the premium card. Only 12.60% of the individuals who charge \$36,000 per annum and do not possess additional cards can be expected to purchase the premium card. For a given amount of money charged per annum, the likelihood of purchasing a premium card is substantially higher among individuals who already possess additional cards than for those who do not possess additional cards. **(c)** ln(estimated odds ratio) $= -6.9394 + 0.13957X_1 + 2.7743X_2 = -6.9394 + 0.1395(18) + 2.7743(0) = -4.4298$. Estimated odds ratio $= e^{-4.4298} = 0.0119$. Estimated Probability of Success $=$ Odds Ratio/$(1 +$ Odds Ratio$) = 0.0119/(1 + 0.0119) = 0.01178$. **(d)** Among individuals who do not purchase additional cards, the likelihood of purchasing a premium card diminishes dramatically with a substantial decrease in the amount charged per annum.

14.56 (a) ln(estimated odds) $= -47.4723 + 1.3099$ fixed acidity $+ 90.5722$ chlorides $+ 9.777$ pH. **(b)** Holding constant the effect of chlorides and pH, for each increase of one point in fixed acidity, ln(estimated odds) increases by an estimate of 1.3099. Holding constant the effect of fixed acidity and pH, for each increase of one point in chlorides, ln(estimated odds) increases by an estimate of 90.5722. Holding constant the effect of fixed acidity and chlorides, for each increase of one point in pH, ln(estimated odds) increases by an estimate of 9.777. **(c)** 0.3686. **(d)** Deviance $= 54.456$, p-value $= 1.0000$, do not reject H_0, so model is adequate. **(e)** For fixed acidity: $Z_{STAT} = 3.17 > 1.96$, reject H_0. For chlorides: $Z_{STAT} = 4.00 > 1.96$, reject H_0. For pH: $Z_{STAT} = 3.29 > 1.96$, reject H_0. Each variable makes a significant contribution to the model. **(f)** Fixed acidity, chlorides, and pH are all important factors in distinguishing between white and red wines.

14.58 (a) ln(estimated odds) $= -0.6048 + 0.0938$ claims/year $+ 1.8108$ new business **(b)** Holding constant the effects of whether the policy is new, for each increase of the number of claims submitted per year by the policy holder, ln(odds) increases by an estimate of 0.0938. Holding constant the number of claims submitted per year by the policy holder, ln(odds) is estimated to be 1.8108 higher when the policy is new as compared to when the policy is not new. **(c)** ln(estimated odds ratio) $= 1.2998$. Estimated odds ratio $= 3.6684$ Estimated probability of a fraudulent claim $= 0.7858$ **(d)** The deviance statistic is 119.4353 with a p-value $= 0.0457 < 0.05$. Reject H_0. The model is not a good fitting model. **(e)** For claims/year: $Z_{STAT} = 0.1865$, p-value $= 0.8521 > 0.05$. Do not reject H_0. There is insufficient evidence that the number of claims submitted per year by the policy holder makes a significant contribution to the logistic regression model. For new business: $Z_{STAT} = 2.2261$, p-value $= 0.0260 < 0.05$. Reject H_0. There is sufficient evidence that whether the policy is new makes a significant contribution to the logistic model regression. **(f)** ln(estimated odds) $= -1.0125 + 0.9927$ claims/year **(g)** ln(estimated odds) $= -0.5423 + 1.9286$ new business **(h)** The deviance statistic for (f) is 125.0102 with a p-value $= 0.0250 < 0.05$. Reject H_0. The model is not a good fitting model. The deviance statistic for (g) is 119.4702 with a p-value $= 0.0526 > 0.05$. Do not reject H_0. The model is a good fitting model. The model in **(g)** should be used to predict a fraudulent claim.

14.60 (a) ln(estimated odds) $= 1.252 - 0.0323$ Age $+ 2.2165$ subscribes to the wellness newsletters. **(b)** Holding constant the effect of subscribes to the wellness newsletters, for each increase of one year in age, ln(estimated odds) decreases by an estimate of 0.0323. Holding constant the effect of age, for a customer who subscribes to the wellness newsletters, ln(estimated odds) increases by an estimate of 2.2165. **(c)** 0.912. **(d)** Deviance $= 102.8762$, p-value = 0.3264. Do not reject H_0 so model is adequate. **(e)** For Age: $Z = -1.8053 > -1.96$, Do not reject H_0. For subscribes to the wellness newsletters: $Z = 4.3286 > 1.96$, Reject H_0. **(f)** Only subscribes to wellness newsletters is useful in predicting whether a customer will purchase organic food.

14.72 (a) $\hat{Y} = -3.9152 + 0.0319X_1 + 4.2228X_2$, where $X_1 =$ number cubic feet moved and $X_2 =$ number of pieces of large furniture. **(b)** Holding constant the number of pieces of large furniture, for each additional cubic foot moved, the mean labor hours are estimated to increase by 0.0319. Holding constant the amount of cubic feet moved, for each additional piece of large furniture, the mean labor hours are estimated to increase by 4.2228. **(c)** $\hat{Y} = 20.4926$. **(d)** Based on a residual analysis, the errors appear to be normally distributed. The equal-variance assumption might be violated because the variances appear to be larger around the center region of both independent variables. There might also be violation of the linearity assumption. A model with quadratic terms for both independent variables might be fitted. **(e)** $F_{STAT} = 228.80$, p-value is virtually $0 < 0.05$, reject H_0. There is evidence of a significant relationship between labor hours and the two independent variables (the amount of cubic feet moved and the number of pieces of large furniture). **(f)** The p-value is virtually 0. The probability of obtaining a test statistic of 228.80 or greater is virtually 0 if there is no significant relationship between labor hours and the two independent variables (the amount of cubic feet moved and the number of pieces of large furniture). **(g)** $r^2 = 0.9327$. 93.27% of the variation in labor hours can be explained by variation in the number of cubic feet moved and the number of pieces of large furniture. **(h)** $r^2_{adj} = 0.9287$. **(i)** For X_1: $t_{STAT} = 6.9339$, the p-value is virtually 0. Reject H_0. The number of cubic feet moved makes a significant contribution and should be included in the model. For X_2: $t_{STAT} = 4.6192$, the p-value is virtually 0. Reject H_0. The number of pieces of large furniture makes a significant contribution and should be included in the model. Based on these results, the regression model with the two independent variables should be used. **(j)** For X_1: $t_{STAT} = 6.9339$, the p-value is virtually 0. The probability of obtaining a sample that will yield a test statistic greater than 6.9339 is virtually 0 if the number of cubic feet moved does not make a significant contribution, holding the effect of the number of pieces of large furniture constant. For X_2: $t_{STAT} = 4.6192$, the p-value is virtually 0. The probability of obtaining a sample that will yield a test statistic greater than 4.6192 is virtually 0 if the number of pieces of large furniture does not make a significant contribution, holding the effect of the amount of cubic feet moved constant. **(k)** $0.0226 \le \beta_1 \le 0.0413$. **(l)** $r^2_{Y1.2} = 0.5930$. Holding constant the effect of the number of pieces of large furniture, 59.3% of the variation in labor hours can be explained by variation in the amount of cubic feet moved. $r^2_{Y2.1} = 0.3927$. Holding constant the effect of the number of cubic feet moved, 39.27% of the variation in labor hours can be explained by variation in the number of pieces of large furniture. **(m)** Both the number of cubic feet moved and the number of large pieces of furniture are useful in predicting the labor hours, but the cubic feet moved is more important.

14.74 (a) $\hat{Y} = 257.9033 + 53.3606X_1 + 0.2521X_2$, where $X_1 =$ house size and $X_2 =$ age. **(b)** Holding constant the age, for each additional thousand square feet in the size of the house, the mean assessed value is estimated to increase by 53.3606 thousand dollars.

Holding constant the size of the house, for each additional year in age, the assessed value is estimated to increase by 0.2521 thousand dollars. **(c)** $\hat{Y} = 378.4093$ thousand dollars. **(d)** Based on a residual analysis, the model appears to be adequate. **(e)** $F_{STAT} = 6.6459$, the p-value $= 0.0045 < 0.05$, reject H_0. There is evidence of a significant relationship between assessed value and the two independent variables (size of the house and age). **(f)** The p-value is 0.0045. The probability of obtaining a test statistic of 6.6459 or greater is virtually 0 if there is no significant relationship between assessed value and the two independent variables (size of the house and age). **(g)** $r^2 = 0.3299$. 32.99% of the variation in assessed value can be explained by variation in the size of the house and age. **(h)** $r^2_{adj} = 0.2803$. **(i)** For X_1: $t_{STAT} = 3.3128$, the p-value is 0.0026. Reject H_0. The size of the house makes a significant contribution and should be included in the model. For X_2: $t_{STAT} = 0.3203$, p-value $= 0.7512 > 0.05$. Do not reject H_0. Age does not make a significant contribution and should not be included in the model. Based on these results, the regression model with only the size of the house should be used. **(j)** For X_1: $t_{STAT} = 3.3128$. The probability of obtaining a sample that will yield a test statistic farther away than 3.3128 is 0.0026 if the house size does not make a significant contribution, holding age constant. For X_2: $t_{STAT} = 0.3203$. The probability of obtaining a sample that will yield a test statistic farther away than 0.3203 is 0.7512 if the age does not make a significant contribution holding the effect of the house size constant. **(k)** $20.3109 \le \beta_1 \le 86.4104$. You are 95% confident that the assessed value will increase by an amount somewhere between \$20.3109 thousand and \$86.4104 thousand for each additional thousand square foot increase in house size, holding constant the age of the house. In Problem 13.76, you are 95% confident that the assessed value will increase by an amount somewhere between \$22.6113 thousand and \$78.9949 thousand for each additional 1,000 square foot increase in house size, regardless of the age of the house. **(l)** $r^2_{Y1.2} = 0.2890$. Holding constant the effect of the age of the house, 28.9% of the variation in assessed value can be explained by variation in the size of the house. $r^2_{Y2.1} = 0.0038$. Holding constant the effect of the size of the house, 0.38% of the variation in assessed value can be explained by variation in the age of the house. **(m)** only the size of the house should be used to predict assessed value.

14.76 (a) $\hat{Y} = 694.9557 + 8.6059X_1 + 2069X_2$, where $X_1 =$ assessed value and $X_2 =$ age. **(b)** Holding age constant, for each additional \$1,000 in assessed value, the taxes are estimated to increase by a mean of \$8.61 thousand. Holding assessed value constant, for each additional year, the taxes are estimated to increase by \$2.069 **(c)** $\hat{Y} = \$4,240.542$. **(d)** Based on a residual analysis, the errors appear to be normally distributed. The equal-variance assumption appears to be valid. **(e)** $F_{STAT} = 22.0699$, p-value $= 0.0000 < 0.05$, reject H_0. There is evidence of a significant relationship between taxes and the two independent variables (assessed value and age). **(f)** p-value $= 0.0000$. The probability of obtaining an F_{STAT} test statistic of 22.0699 or greater is virtually 0 if there is no significant relationship between taxes and the two independent variables (assessed value and age). **(g)** $r^2 = 0.6205$. 62.05% of the variation in taxes can be explained by variation in assessed value and age. **(h)** $r^2_{adj} = 0.5924$. **(i)** For X_1: $t_{STAT} = 6.5271$, p-value $= 0.0000 < 0.05$. Reject H_0. The assessed value makes a significant contribution and should be included in the model. For X_2: $t_{STAT} = 0.3617$, p-value $= 0.7204 > 0.05$. Do not reject H_0. The age of a house does not make a significant contribution and should not be included in the model. Based on these results, the regression model with only assessed value should be used. **(j)** For X_1: p-value $= 0.0000$. The probability of obtaining a sample that will yield a test statistic greater than 6.5271 is 0.0000 if the assessed value does not make a significant contribution, holding age constant. For X_2: p-value $= 0.7204$. The probability of obtaining a sample that will yield a test statistic greater than 0.3617 is 0.7204 if the age of a house does not make a significant contribution, holding the effect of the assessed value constant. **(k)** $5.9005 \le \beta_1 \le 11.3112$. You are 95% confident that the mean taxes will increase by an amount somewhere between \$5.90 and \$11.31 for each additional \$1,000 increase in the assessed value, holding constant the age. In Problem 13.77, you are 95% confident that the mean taxes will increase by an amount somewhere between \$5.91 and \$11.07 for each additional \$1,000 increase in assessed value, regardless of the age. **(l)** $r^2_{Y1.2} = 0.6121$. Holding constant the effect of age, 61.21% of the variation in taxes can be explained by variation in the assessed value. $r^2_{Y2.1} = 0.0048$. Holding constant the effect of the assessed value, 0.48% of the variation in taxes can be explained by variation in the age. **(m)** Based on your answers to (b) through (k), the age of a house does not have an effect on its taxes.

14.78 (a) $\hat{Y} = 153.2356 - 17.2233X_1 - 4.2779X_2$, where $X_1 =$ ERA and $X_2 =$ league (American $= 0$ National $= 1$). **(b)** Holding constant the effect of the league, for each additional earned run, the number of wins is estimated to decrease by 17.2233. For a given ERA, a team in the National League is estimated to have 4.2779 fewer wins than a team in the American League. **(c)** 75.7307 wins. **(d)** Based on a residual analysis, there is no pattern in the errors. There is no apparent violation of other assumptions. **(e)** $F_{STAT} = 18.4172 > 3.35$, p-value $= 0.0000$ < 0.05, reject H_0. There is evidence of a significant relationship between wins and the two independent variables (ERA and league). **(f)** For X_1: $t_{STAT} = -6.0187 < -2.0518$, the p-value $= 0.0000$. Reject H_0. ERA makes a significant contribution and should be included in the model. For X_2: $t_{STAT} = -1.7649 > -2.0518$, p-value $= 0.0889 > 0.05$. Do not reject H_0. The league does not make a significant contribution and should not be included in the model. Based on these results, the regression model with only the ERA as the independent variable should be used. **(g)** $-23.0949 \leq \beta_1 \leq -11.3517$. **(h)** $-9.2512 \leq \beta_2 \leq 0.6954$. **(i)** $r^2_{adj} = 0.5457$. 54.57% of the variation in wins can be explained by the variation in ERA and league after adjusting for number of independent variables and sample size. **(j)** $r^2_{Y1.2} = 0.5730$. Holding constant the effect of league, 57.3% of the variation in number of wins can be explained by the variation in ERA. $r^2_{Y2.1} = 0.1034$. Holding constant the effect of ERA, 10.34% of the variation in number of wins can be explained by the variation in league. **(k)** The slope of the number of wins with ERA is the same, regardless of whether the team belongs to the American League or the National League. **(l)** For X_1X_2: $t_{STAT} = 0.0732 < 2.0555$ the p-value is $0.9422 > 0.05$. Do not reject H_0. There is no evidence that the interaction term makes a contribution to the model. **(m)** The model with one independent variable (ERA) should be used.

14.80 The r^2 of the multiple regression is very low, at 0.0645. Only 6.45% of the variation in thickness can be explained by the variation of pressure and temperature. The F test statistic for the model including pressure and temperature is 1.621, with p-value $= 0.2085$. Hence, at a 5% level of significance, there is not enough evidence to conclude that pressure and/or temperature affect thickness. The p-value of the t test for the significance of pressure is $0.8307 > 0.05$. Hence, there is insufficient evidence to conclude that pressure affects thickness, holding constant the effect of temperature. The p-value of the t test for the significance of temperature is 0.0820, which is also > 0.05. There is insufficient evidence to conclude that temperature affects thickness at the 5% level of significance, holding constant the effect of pressure. Hence, neither pressure nor temperature affects thickness individually.

The normal probability plot does not suggest any potential violation of the normality assumption. The residual plots do not indicate potential violation of the equal variance assumption. The temperature residual plot, however, suggests that there might be a nonlinear relationship between temperature and thickness.

The r^2 of the multiple regression model that includes the interaction of pressure and temperature is very low, at 0.0734. Only 7.34% of the variation in thickness can be explained by the variation of pressure, temperature, and the interaction of the two. The F test statistic for the model

that includes pressure and temperature and their interaction is 1.214, with a p-value of 0.3153. Hence, at a 5% level of significance, there is insufficient evidence to conclude that pressure, temperature, and the interaction of the two affect thickness. The p-value of the t test for the significance of pressure, temperature, and the interaction term are 0.5074, 0.4053, and 0.5111, respectively, which are all greater than 5%. Hence, there is insufficient evidence to conclude that pressure, temperature, or the interaction individually affects thickness, holding constant the effect of the other variables.

The pattern in the normal probability plot and residual plots is similar to that in the regression without the interaction term. Hence the article's suggestion that there is a significant interaction between the pressure and the temperature in the tank cannot be validated.

14.82 $b_0 = 18.2892$ (die temperature), $b_1 = 0.5976$, (die diameter), $b_2 = -13.5108$. The r^2 of the multiple regression model is 0.3257 so 32.57% of the variation in unit density can be explained by the variation of die temperature and die diameter. The F test statistic for the combined significance of die temperature and die diameter is 5.0718 with a p-value of 0.0160. Hence, at a 5% level of significance, there is enough evidence to conclude that die temperature and die diameter affect unit density. The p-value of the t test for the significance of die temperature is 0.2117, which is greater than 5%. Hence, there is insufficient evidence to conclude that die temperature affects unit density holding constant the effect of die diameter. The p-value of the t test for the significance of die diameter is 0.0083, which is less than 5%. There is enough evidence to conclude that die diameter affects unit density at the 5% level of significance holding constant the effect of die temperature. After removing die temperature from the model, $b_0 = 107.9267$ (die diameter), $b_1 = -13.5108$. The r^2 of the multiple regression is 0.2724. So 27.24% of the variation in unit density can be explained by the variation of die diameter. The p-value of the t test for the significance of die diameter is 0.0087, which is less than 5%. There is enough evidence to conclude that die diameter affects unit density at the 5% level of significance. There is some lack of equality in the residuals and some departure from normality.

CHAPTER 15

15.2 (a) Predicted HOCS is 2.8600, 3.0342, 3.1948, 3.3418, 3.4752, 3.5950, 3.7012, 3.7938, 3.8728, 3.9382, 3.99, 4.0282, 4.0528, 4.0638, 4.0612, 4.045, 4.0152, 3.9718, 3.9148, 3.8442, and 3.76. **(c)** The curvilinear relationship suggests that HOCS increases at a decreasing rate. It reaches its maximum value of 4.0638 at GPA $= 3.3$ and declines after that as GPA continues to increase. **(d)** An r^2 of 0.07 and an adjusted r^2 of 0.06 tell you that GPA has very low explanatory power in identifying the variation in HOCS. You can tell that the individual HOCS scores are scattered widely around the curvilinear relationship.

15.4 (a) $\hat{Y} = -5.1583 - 21.534X_1 + 3.9723X_2$ where $X_1 =$ alcohol % and $X_2 =$ carbohydrates. $F_{STAT} = 2,340.3357$ p-value $= 0.0000 < 0.05$, so reject H_0. At the 5% level of significance, the linear terms are significant together. **(b)** $\hat{Y} = 11.1239 + 14.6586X_1 + 4.6379X_2 + 0.5184X_1^2 - 0.0237X_2^2$, where $X_1 =$ alcohol % and $X_2 =$ carbohydrates. **(c)** $F_{STAT} = 1,204.3006$ p-value $= 0.0000 < 0.05$, so reject H_0. At the 5% level of significance, the model with quadratic terms are significant. $t_{STAT} = 2.4266$, and the p-value $= 0.0164$. Reject H_0. There is enough evidence that the quadratic term for alcohol % is significant at the 5% level of significance. $t_{STAT} = -1.4681$, p-value $= 0.1441$. Do not reject H_0. There is insufficient evidence that the quadratic term for carbohydrates is significant at the 5% level of significance. Hence, since the quadratic term for alcohol is significant, the model in **(b)** that includes this term is better. **(d)** The number of calories in a beer depends quadratically on the alcohol percentage but linearly on the number of carbohydrates. The alcohol percentage and number of carbohydrates explain about 96.92% of the variation in the number of calories in a beer.

15.6 (b) price $= 17,429.2098 - 1,797.0198$ age $+ 62.843$ age^2. **(c)** $17,429.2098 - 1,797.0198(5) + 62.843(5)^2 = \$10,015.19$. **(d)** There are no patterns in any of the residual plots. **(e)** $F_{STAT} = 363.0192 > 3.18$. Reject H_0. There is a significant quadratic relationship between age and price. **(f)** p-value $= 0.0000$. The probability of $F_{STAT} = 363.0192$ or higher is 0.0000. **(g)** $t_{STAT} = 5.9707 > 2.0281$. Reject H_0. **(h)** The probability of $t_{STAT} = 5.9707$ or higher is 0.0000. **(i)** $r^2 = 0.9528$. 95.28% of the variation in price can be explained by the quadratic relationship between age and price. **(j)** adjusted $r^2 = 0.9501$. **(k)** There is a strong quadratic relationship between age and price.

15.8 (a) 215.37. **(b)** For each additional unit of the logarithm of X_1, the logarithm of Y is estimated to increase by 0.9 unit, holding all other variables constant. For each additional unit of the logarithm of X_2, the logarithm of Y is estimated to increase by 1.41 units, holding all other variables constant.

15.10 (a) $\hat{Y} = -174.371 + 108.4346\sqrt{X_1} + 24.4253\sqrt{X_2}$, where $X_1 =$ alcohol % and $X_2 =$ carbohydrates. **(b)** The normal probability plot suggests that the errors are slightly right-skewed. However, because of the large sample size, the validity of the results is not seriously impacted. The residual plots of the square-root transformation of alcohol percentage and carbohydrates do not show any major patterns. **(c)** $F_{STAT} = 1,580.3768$. Because the p-value is 0.0000, reject H_0 at the 5% level of significance. There is evidence of a significant linear relationship between calories and the square root of the percentage of alcohol and the square root of the number of carbohydrates. **(d)** $r^2 = 0.9533$. So 95.33% of the variation in calories can be explained by the variation in the square root of the percentage of alcohol and the square root of the number of carbohydrates. **(e)** Adjusted $r^2 = 0.9527$. **(f)** The model in Problem 15.4 is slightly better because it has a higher r^2.

15.12 (a) Predicted $\ln(\text{Price}) = 9.7435 - 0.1065$ Age. **(b)** \$10,005.20. **(c)** Because there is a lack of equal variance in the residuals, the model is not adequate. **(d)** $t_{STAT} = -19.0145 < -2.0262$; reject H_0. **(e)** 90.72%. 90.72% of the variation in the natural log of price can be explained by the age of the auto. **(f)** 90.47%. **(g)** Choose the model from Problem 15.6. That model has a higher adjusted r^2 of 95.01%.

15.14 1.25.

15.16 $R_1^2 = 0.0681$, $VIF_1 = \dfrac{1}{1-0.0681} = 1.073$, $R_2^2 = 0.0681$, $VIF_2 = \dfrac{1}{1-0.0681} = 1.073$. There is no evidence of collinearity.

15.18 $VIF = 1.0069 < 5$. There is no evidence of collinearity.

15.20 $VIF = 1.0105$. There is no evidence of collinearity.

15.22 (a) 35.04. **(b)** $C_p > 3$. This does not meet the criterion for consideration of a good model.

15.24 Let $Y =$ assessed value, $X_1 =$ size, $X_2 =$ fireplace (0 = no 1 = yes), and $X_3 =$ number of bedrooms. $X_4 =$ number of bathrooms. Based on a full regression model involving all of the variables, all the VIF values (2.3355, 1.1873, 1.9885, and 1.4428, respectively) are less than 5. There is no reason to suspect the existence of collinearity. Based on a best-subsets regression and examination of the resulting C_p values, the best models appear to be a model with variables X_1 and X_2, which has $C_p = 1.1712$, and the regression model with only X_1. Based on a stepwise regression analysis with all the original variables, only variable X_1 makes a significant contribution to the model at the 0.05 level. Thus, the best model is the model using the size of the house (X_1) as the

independent variable. A residual analysis shows no strong patterns. The final model is $\hat{Y} = 276.848 + 508,031X_1$, $r^2 = 0.3273$, $r^2_{adj} = 0.3033$. Overall significance of the model: $F_{STAT} = 13.326$, $p < 0.001$.

15.30 (a) An analysis of the linear regression model with all of the three possible independent variables reveals that the highest VIF is only 1.06. A stepwise regression model selects only the supplier dummy variable for inclusion in the model. A best-subsets regression produces only one model that has a C_p value less than or equal to $k + 1$ which is the model that includes pressure and the supplier dummy variable. This model is $\hat{Y} = -31.5929 + 0.7879X_2 + 13.1029X_3$. This model has $F = 5.1088$ with a p-value $= 0.027$. $r^2 = 0.4816$, $r^2_{adj} = 0.3873$. A residual analysis does not reveal any strong patterns. The errors appear to be normally distributed.

15.32 (a) Best model: $C_p = 2.1558$, predicted fair market value $= 260.6791 + 362.8318$ land $+ 0.1109$ house size (sq ft)$- 1.7543$ age. **(b)** The adjusted r^2 for the best model in 15.32(a), 15.33(a), and 15.34(a) are, respectively, 0.8242, 0.9047, and 0.8481. The model in 15.33(a) has the highest explanatory power after adjusting for the number of independent variables and sample size.

15.34 (a) Predicted fair maket value $= 145.1217 + 149.9337$ land $+ 0.0913$ house size (sq. ft.). **(b)** The adjusted r^2 for the best model in 15.32(a), 15.33(a), and 15.34(a) are, respectively, 0.8242, 0.9047, and 0.8481. The model in 15.33(a) has the highest explanatory power after adjusting for the number of independent variables and sample size.

15.36 Let $Y =$ fair market value, $X_1 =$ land area, $X_2 =$ interior size, $X_3 =$ age, $X_4 =$ number of rooms, $X_5 =$ number of bathrooms, $X_6 =$ garage size, $X_7 = 1$ if Glen Cove and 0 otherwise, and $X_8 = 1$ if Roslyn and 0 otherwise. **(a)** The VIFs of X_2, X_3, and X_7 are greater than 5. Dropping X_2 with the largest VIF, X_3 still has a VIF greater than 5. After dropping X_2 and X_3, all remaining VIFs are less than 5 so there is no reason to suspect collinearity between any pair of variables. The following is the multiple regression model that has the smallest $C_p(4.3211)$ and the highest adjusted $r^2(0.6815)$:

Fair Market Value $= 49.2379 + 579.0105$ Land $+ 109.5767$ Baths $+ 48.2282$ Garage $+ 213.2326$ Roslyn

The individual t test for the significance of each independent variable at the 5% level of significance concludes that only property size, baths, and the dummy variable Roslyn are significant given that the others are in the model. The following is the multiple regression result for the model chosen by stepwise regression:

Fair Market Value $= 30.3016 + 611.6910$ Land $+ 130.7788$ Baths $+ 214.2567$ Roslyn

All the variables are significant individually at the 5% level of significance. Combining the stepwise regression and the best-subsets regression results along with the individual t test results, the most appropriate multiple regression model for predicting the fair market value is the stepwise regression model. **(b)** The estimated fair market value in Roslyn is \$214.2567 thousands above Glen Cove or Freeport for two otherwise identical properties.

15.38 In the multiple regression model with catalyst, pH, pressure, temperature, and voltage as independent variables, none of the variables has a VIF value of 5 or larger. The best-subsets approach showed that only the model containing X_1, X_2, X_3, X_4, and X_5 should be considered, where $X_1 =$ catalyst, $X_2 =$ pH, $X_3 =$ pressure, $X_4 =$ temp, and $X_5 =$ voltage. Looking at the p-values of the t statistics for each slope coefficient of the model that includes X_1 through X_5 reveals that pH level is not significant at the 5% level of significance (p-value $= 0.2862$). The multiple regression model with pH level deleted shows that all coefficients are significant individually at the 5% level of significance. The best linear model is determined to be $\hat{Y} = 3.6833 + 0.1548X_1 - 0.04197X_3 - 0.4036X_4 + 0.4288X_5$. The overall model has $F = 77.0793$, with a p-value that is virtually 0. $r^2 = 0.8726$, $r_{adj}^2 = 0.8613$. The normal probability plot does not suggest possible violation of the normality assumption. A residual analysis reveals a potential nonlinear relationship in temperature. The p-value of the squared term for temperature (0.1273) in the following quadratic transformation of temperature does not support the need for a quadratic transformation at the 5% level of significance. The p-value of the interaction term between pressure and temperature (0.0780) indicates that there is not enough evidence of an interaction at the 5% level of significance. The best model is the one that includes catalyst, pressure, temperature, and voltage, which explains 87.26% of the variation in thickness.

15.40 Best subset regression produced several models that had $C_p \le k + 1$. They were $X_2X_3 = 2.4346$, $X_1X_2X_3 = 4.0605$, $X_2X_3X_4 = 3.535$, $X_2X_3X_5 = 3.5252$, and $X_1X_2X_3X_4 = 4.0459$. Stepwise regression produced a model that included only X_2 (median home value) and X_3 (violent crime rate). Since X_2 (median home value) and X_3 (violent crime rate) were included in all the models with low C_p, this model was chosen for further analysis. The residual plot for the violent crime variable in this model indicated a curvilinear relationship, so a curvilinear term was added to the model. However, this was not significant (p-value = 0.7427), so the model with median home value and violent crime rate was selected. The model is

Median Household Income $= 82,994.1964 + 0.0517$ Median
home value ($000) -155.5687
Violent crime/100,000 residents

The r^2 of this model is 0.5671, meaning that 56.71% of the variation in median household income can be explained by variation in median household income and variation in violent crime. Each of these independent variables is highly significant ($t = 3.103$, p-value = 0.0052 and $t = -3.8659$, p-value = 0.0008, respectively). 30.44% of the variation in median household income can be explained by variation in the median home value, holding constant the violent crime rate. 40.45% of the variation in median household income can be explained by variation in the violent crime rate, holding constant the median home value.

CHAPTER 16

16.2 (a) 1988. **(b)** The first four years and the last four years.

16.4 (b), (c), (e)

Year	Hours Per Day	MA(3)	ES($W = 0.5$)	ES($W = 0.25$)
2008	2.2	#N/A	2.2000	2.2000
2009	2.3	2.3000	2.2500	2.2250
2010	2.4	2.4333	2.3250	2.2688
2011	2.6	2.5000	2.4625	2.3516
2012	2.5	2.4667	2.4813	2.3887
2013	2.3	2.4000	2.3906	2.3665
2014	2.4	#N/A	2.3953	2.3749

(d) $W = 0.5$: $\hat{Y}_{2015} = E_{2014} = 2.3953$; $W = 0.25$: $\hat{Y}_{2015} = E_{2014} = 2.3749$. **(f)** The exponentially smoothed forecast for 2015 with $W = 0.5$ is slightly higher than that with $W = 0.25$. A smoothing coefficient of $W = 0.25$ smooths out the hours more than $W = 0.50$.

16.6 (b), (c), (e)

Decade	Performance (%)	MA(3)	ES($W = 0.5$)	ES($W = 0.25$)
1830s	2.8	#N/A	2.8000	2.8000
1840s	12.8	7.4000	7.8000	5.3000
1850s	6.6	10.6333	7.2000	5.6250
1860s	12.5	8.8667	9.8500	7.3438
1870s	7.5	8.6667	8.6750	7.3828
1880s	6.0	6.3333	7.3375	7.0371
1890s	5.5	7.4667	6.4188	6.6528
1900s	10.9	6.2000	8.6594	7.7146
1910s	2.2	8.8000	5.4297	6.3360
1920s	13.3	4.4333	9.3648	8.0770
1930s	−2.2	6.9000	3.5824	5.5077
1940s	9.6	8.5333	6.5912	6.5308
1950s	18.2	12.0333	12.3956	9.4481
1960s	8.3	11.0333	10.3478	9.1611
1970s	6.6	10.5000	8.4739	8.5208
1980s	16.6	13.6000	12.5370	10.5406
1990s	17.6	11.2333	15.0685	12.3055
2000s	−0.5	#N/A	7.2842	9.1041

(d) $\hat{Y}_{2010} = E_{2000} = 7.2842$ **(e)** $\hat{Y}_{2010} = E_{2000} = 9.1041$. **(f)** The exponentially smoothed forecast for the 2010s with $W = 0.5$ is lower than that with $W = 0.25$. **(g)** According to the exponential smoothing with $W = 0.25$, there appears to be a general upward trend in the performance of the stocks in the past.

16.8 (b), (c), (e)

Year	Audits	MA(3)	ES($W = 0.5$)	ES($W = 0.25$)
2001	3305	#N/A	3305.0000	3305.0000
2002	3749	3461.3333	3527.0000	3416.0000
2003	3330	3821.6667	3428.5000	3394.5000
2004	4386	4191.6667	3907.2500	3642.3750
2005	4859	4507.0000	4383.1250	3946.5313
2006	4276	4186.3333	4329.5625	4028.8984
2007	3424	3784.6667	3876.7813	3877.6738
2008	3654	3616.3333	3765.3906	3821.7554
2009	3771	3625.0000	3768.1953	3809.0665
2010	3450	3630.0000	3609.0977	3719.2999
2011	3669	3736.0000	3639.0488	3706.7249
2012	4089	4199.6667	3864.0244	3802.2937
2013	4841	#N/A	4352.5122	4061.9703

(d) $W = 0.5$: $\hat{Y}_{2015} = E_{2014} = 4,352.5122$; $W = 0.25$: $\hat{Y}_{2015} = E_{2014} = 4061.9703$. **(f)** The exponentially smoothed forecast for 2014 with $W = 0.5$ is higher than that with $W = 0.25$.

16.10 (a) The Y intercept $b_0 = 4.0$ is the fitted trend value reflecting the real total revenues (in millions of dollars) during the origin, or base year, 1994. **(b)** The slope $b_1 = 1.5$ indicates that the real total revenues are increasing at an estimated rate of $1.5 million per year. **(c)** Year is 1996, $X = 1998 - 2014 = 4$, $\hat{Y}_5 = 4.0 + 1.5(4) = 10.0$ million dollars. **(d)** Year is 2015, $X = 2015 - 1994 = 21$, $\hat{Y}_{20} = 4.0 + 1.5(21) = 35.5$ million dollars. **(e)** Year is 2018, $X = 2018 - 1994 = 24$, $\hat{Y}_{23} = 4.0 + 1.5(24) = 40$ million dollars.

16.12 (b) Linear trend: $\hat{Y} = 92.07 + 5.3757X$, where X is relative to 2000. **(c)** Quadratic trend: $\hat{Y} = 77.8553 + 11.9363X - 0.4686X^2$, where X is relative to 2000. **(d)** Exponential trend: $\log_{10}\hat{Y} = 1.9476 + 0.0207X$, where X is relative to 2000. **(e)** Linear trend:

$\hat{Y}_{2015} = 92.07 + 5.3757(15) = 172.7055$

$\hat{Y}_{2016} = 92.07 + 5.3757(16) = 178.0812$

Quadratic trend: $\hat{Y}_{2015} = 77.8553 + 11.9363(15) - 0.4686(15)^2$
$= 151.46$

$\hat{Y}_{2016} = 77.8553 + 11.9363(16) + (-0.4686)(16)^2 = 148.87$

Exponential trend: $\hat{Y}_{2015} = 10^{1.9476 + 0.0207(15)} = 181.18$

$\hat{Y}_{2016} = 10^{1.9476 + 0.0207(16)} = 189.73$

(f) The quadratic and exponential trend models fit the data better than the linear trend model and, hence, either forecast should be used.

16.14 (b) $\hat{Y} = 289.9030 + 67.4570X$ where $X =$ years relative to 1978. **(c)** $X = 37$, $\hat{Y} = 2,785.814$ billion $X = 38$ $\hat{Y} = 2,853.271$ billion **(d)** There is an upward trend in federal receipts between 1978 and 2014. The trend appears to be linear.

16.16 (b) Linear trend: $\hat{Y} = -2,548.4615 + 937.8462X$, where X is relative to 2002. **(c)** Quadratic trend: $\hat{Y} = 2,638.7912 - 1,891.5644 + 235.7842X^2$, where X is relative to 2002. **(d)** Exponential trend: $\log_{10}\hat{Y} = 2.4183 + 0.1170X$, where X is relative to 2002. **(e)** Linear trend: $\hat{Y}_{2015} = 9,643.538$ million KWh $\hat{Y}_{2016} = 10,581.38$ million KWh Quadratic trend: $\hat{Y}_{2015} = 17,895.99$ million KWh

$\hat{Y}_{2016} = 22,370.6$ millions of KWh

Exponential trend: $\hat{Y}_{2015} = 8,684.42$ million KWh
$\hat{Y}_{2016} = 10^{2.5659 + 0.0747(12)} = 11,368.34$ million KWh.

16.18 (b) Linear trend: $\hat{Y} = 2.0718 + 0.1250X$, where X is relative to 2000. **(c)** Quadratic trend: $\hat{Y} = 2.1391 + 0.0962X - 0.0019X^2$, where X is relative to 2000. **(d)** Exponential trend: $\log_{10}\hat{Y} = 0.3329 + 0.0183X$, where X is relative to 2000. All the models appear to fit the data equally, so choose the linear model because it is simplest.
(f) The forecast using the linear model is:
Linear trend: $\hat{Y}_{2016} = 4.072$ millions

16.20 (b) There has been an upward trend in the CPI in the United States over the 50-year period.
(c) Linear trend: $\hat{Y} = 16.2012 + 4.4953X$. **(d)** Quadratic trend: $\hat{Y} = 19.4054 + 4.0948X + 0.0087X^2$. **(e)** Exponential trend: $\log_{10}\hat{Y} = 1.570 + 0.0186X$. **(f)** Choose the linear model because it is simplest. **(g)** Linear trend:
For 2015: $\hat{Y}_{2015} = 240.9661$
For 2016: $\hat{Y}_{2016} = 245.9614$

16.22 (a) For Time Series I, the graph of Y versus X appears to be more linear than the graph of log Y versus X, so a linear model appears to be more appropriate. For Time Series II, the graph of log Y versus X appears to be more linear than the graph of Y versus X, so an exponential model appears to be more appropriate.
(b) Time Series I : $\hat{Y} = 100.0731 + 14.9776X$, where $X =$ years relative to 2003

Time Series II: $\hat{Y} = 10^{1.9982 + 0.0609X}$, where $X =$ years relative to 2003.

(c) $X = 12$ for year 2015 in all models. Forecasts for the year 2015:
Time Series I: $\hat{Y} = 100.0731 + 14.9776(12) = 279.8045$
Time Series II: $\hat{Y} = 10^{1.9982 + 0.0609(12)} = 535.6886$.

16.24 $t_{STAT} = 2.40 > 2.2281$; reject H_0.

16.26 (a) $t_{STAT} = 1.60 < 2.2281$; do not reject H_0.

16.28 (a)

	Coefficients	Standard Error	t Stat	P-value
Intercept	95.3171	42.4806	2.2438	0.0551
YLag1	0.0540	0.3112	1.7352	0.1209
YLag2	−0.2600	0.3562	−0.7298	0.4863
YLag3	0.0643	0.2975	0.2160	0.8344

Since the p-value $= 0.8344 > 0.05$ level of significance, the third-order term can be dropped.

(b)

	Coefficients	Standard Error	t Stat	P-value
Intercept	76.2264	34.8522	2.1871	0.0536
YLag1	0.7059	0.2843	2.4827	0.0324
YLag2	−0.2499	0.2947	−0.8480	0.4163

Since the p-value $= 0.4163 > 0.05$, the second-order term can be dropped.

(c)

	Coefficients	Standard Error	t Stat	p-value
Intercept	51.9983	30.9242	1.6815	0.1185
YLag1	0.6302	0.2343	2.6892	0.0197

Since the p-value $= 0.0197 < 0.05$ the first-order term cannot be dropped.
(d) The most appropriate model for forecasting is the first-order autoregressive model:

$\hat{Y}_{2015} = 51.9983 + 0.6302Y_{2014} = 160.96$ \$000.

$\hat{Y}_{2016} = 51.9983 + 0.6302\hat{Y}_{2015} = 153.44$ \$000.

16.30
(a) Since the p-value $= 0.4653 > 0.05$ level of significance, the third-order term can be dropped.
(b) Since the p-value $= 0.9739 > 0.05$ level of significance, the second-order term can be dropped.
(c) Since the p-value is 0.0000, the first-order term is significant.
(d) The most appropriate model for forecasting is the first-order autoregressive model:
$\hat{Y}_{2016} = 0.0355 + 1.0394Y_{2015} = \$4.453$ million.

16.32 (a) 2.121. **(b)** 1.50.

16.34 (a) The residuals in the linear, quadratic, and exponential trend model show strings of consecutive positive and negative values.
(b), (c)

	Linear	Quadratic	Exponential	AR1
S_{YX}	3,871.6310	2,314.8400	3,789.5293	460.8646
MAD	2,751.11	1,685.3551	1,623.5791	305.8783

(d) The residuals in the three trend models show strings of consecutive positive and negative values. The autoregressive model performs well for the historical data and has a fairly random pattern of residuals. It has the smallest values in MAD and S_{YX}. The autoregressive model would be the best model for forecasting.

16.36 (b), (c)

	Linear	Quadratic	Exponential	AR1
Syx	31.9700	32.1210	32.9932	32.6210
MAD	22.4162	24.0834	22.3892	24.7721

(d) The residuals in the three trend models show strings of consecutive positive and negative values. The autoregressive model has a fairly random pattern of residuals. There is very little difference in MAD and S_{YX} between the models. The fact that the autoregressive model has a random pattern in the residuals, the autoregressive model would be the best model for forecasting.

16.38 (b), (c)

	Linear	Quadratic	Exponential	AR1
Syx	0.1223	0.1203	0.1151	0.1306
MAD	0.0896	0.0901	0.0912	0.0963

(d) The residuals in the linear, quadratic, and exponential trend models show strings of consecutive positive and negative values. The autoregressive model has a fairly random pattern of residuals. The MAD and S_{YX} values are similar in all the models. The autoregressive model would be the best model for forecasting due to its fairly random pattern of residuals.

16.40 (a) $\log \hat{\beta}_0 = 2, \hat{\beta}_0 = 100$. This is the fitted value for January 2009 prior to adjustment with the January multiplier.
(b) $\log \hat{\beta}_1 = 0.01, \hat{\beta}_1 = 1.0233$. The estimated monthly compound growth rate is 2.33%. **(c)** $\log \hat{\beta}_2 = 0.1, \hat{\beta}_2 = 1.2589$. The January values in the time series are estimated to have a mean 25.89% higher than the December values.

16.42 (a) $\log \hat{\beta}_0 = 3.0, \hat{\beta}_0 = 1,000$. This is the fitted value for the first quarter of 2011 prior to adjustment by the quarterly multiplier.
(b) $\log \hat{\beta}_1 = 0.1, \hat{\beta}_1 = 1.2589$. The estimated quarterly compound growth rate is $(\hat{\beta}_1 - 1)100\% = 25.89\%$.
(c) $\log \hat{\beta}_3 = 0.2, \hat{\beta}_3 = 1.5849$.

16.44 (a) The retail industry is heavily subject to seasonal variation due to the holiday seasons and so are the revenues for Toys R Us.
(b) There is obvious seasonal effect in the time series.
(c) $\log_{10}\hat{Y} = 3.6398 + 0.0020X - 0.3635Q_1 - 0.3640Q_2 - 0.3411Q_3$.
(d) $\log_{10}\hat{\beta}_1 = 0.0020$. $\hat{\beta}_1 = 1.0046$. The estimated quarterly compound growth rate is $(\hat{\beta}_1 - 1)100\% = 0.46\%$.
(e) $\log_{10}\hat{\beta}_2 = -0.3635$. $\hat{\beta}_2 = 0.4330$. $(\hat{\beta}_2 - 1)100\% = -56.70\%$. The 1st quarter values in the time series are estimated to have a mean 57.30% below the 4th quarter values. $\log_{10}\hat{\beta}_3 = -0.3640$. $\hat{\beta}_3 = 0.4325$. $(\hat{\beta}_3 - 1)100\% = -56.75\%$.

The 2nd quarter values in the time series are estimated to have a mean 56.75% below the 4th quarter values. $\log_{10}\hat{\beta}_4 = -0.3411$. $\hat{\beta}_4 = 0.4559$. $(\hat{\beta}_4 - 1)100\% = -54.41\%$.

The 3rd quarter values in the time series are estimated to have a mean 54.41% below the 4th quarter values. **(f)** Forecasts for the last three quarters of 2014 and all of 2015 are 2,624.8108, 2,779.4253, 6,124.2936, 2,664.1336, 2,672.7110, 2,830.6684, and 6,236.0559 millions

16.46 (b)

	Coefficients	Standard Error	t Stat	P-value
Intercept	2.2545	0.0246	91.8251	0.0000
Coded Month	−0.0010	0.0006	−1.6812	0.1063
M1	−0.2146	0.0295	−7.2778	0.0000
M2	−0.1697	0.0294	−5.7804	0.0000
M3	0.0335	0.0292	1.1465	0.2634
M4	−0.1720	0.0291	−5.9014	0.0000
M5	−0.0982	0.0290	−3.3818	0.0026

	Coefficients	Standard Error	t Stat	P-value
M6	0.0662	0.0290	2.2853	0.0318
M7	−0.0623	0.0289	−2.1560	0.0418
M8	−0.0256	0.0288	−0.8858	0.3849
M9	0.0912	0.0288	3.1651	0.0043
M10	0.0243	0.0288	0.8449	0.4069
M11	−0.0506	0.0288	−1.7605	0.0916

(c) $\hat{Y}_{135} = 165.68$. **(d)** Forecasts for the last four months of 2014 are 205.8022, 176.0334, 147.7968 161.254. **(e)** −0.23%. **(f)** 0.8664 $(\hat{\beta}_8 - 1)\,100\% = -13.36\%$. The July values in the time series are estimated to have a mean 13.36% below the December values.

16.48 (b)

	Coefficients	Standard Error	t Stat	P-value
Intercept	0.8790	0.0540	16.2773	0.0000
Coded Quarter	0.0141	0.0016	8.9055	0.0000
Q1	0.0585	0.0567	1.0325	0.0382
Q2	0.0061	0.0566	0.1087	0.9140
Q3	0.0101	0.0565	0.1783	0.8594

(c) 3.3%, after adjusting for the seasonal component. **(d)** 14.42% above the fourth-quarter values. **(e)** Last quarter, 2014: $\hat{Y}_{35} = \$30.4705$.
(f) 2015: 36.1638, 32.9739, 34.3685, 34.6857

16.60 (b) Linear trend: $\hat{Y} = 173,913.2560 + 2,447.1528X$, where X is relative to 1984.
(c) 2015: $\hat{Y}_{2015} = 249,774.994$ thousands
2016: $\hat{Y}_{2016} = 252,722.146$.
(d) (b) Linear trend: $\hat{Y} = 116,213.625 + 1,485.8831X$, where X is relative to 1984. **(c)** 2015: $\hat{Y}_{2015} = 162,276$ thousands.
2016: $\hat{Y}_{2016} = 163,761.883$ thousands.

16.62 Linear trend: $\hat{Y} = -2.8167 + 0.7383X$, where X is relative to 1975.

	Coefficients	Standard Error	t Stat	P-value
Intercept	−2.8167	0.6187	−4.5529	0.0001
Coded Yr	0.7383	0.0273	27.0421	0.0000

(c) Quadratic trend: $\hat{Y} = 0.9724 + 0.1400X + 0.0153X^2$, where X is relative to 1975.

	Coefficients	Standard Error	t Stat	P-value
Intercept	0.9724	0.3106	3.1303	0.0034
Coded Yr	0.1400	0.0369	3.7995	0.0005
Coded Yr Sq	0.0153	0.0009	16.7937	0.0000

Exponential trend: $\log_{10}\hat{Y} = 0.1895 + 0.0362X$, where X is relative to 1975.

	Coefficients	Standard Error	t Stat	P-value
Intercept	0.1895	0.0234	8.1064	0.0000
Coded Yr	0.0362	0.0010	35.0857	0.0000

AR(3): $\hat{Y}_i = 0.4954 + 1.2924Y_{i-1} - 0.7386Y_{i-2} + 0.4769_{i-3}$

	Coefficients	Standard Error	*t* Stat	*P*-value
Intercept	0.4954	0.1875	2.6428	0.0125
YLag1	1.2924	0.1774	7.2852	0.0000
YLag2	−0.7386	0.2708	−2.7272	0.0102
YLag3	0.4769	0.1905	2.503	0.0174

Test of A_3: *p*-value $= 0.0174 < 0.05$. Reject H_0 that $A_3 = 0$. Third-order term cannot be deleted. A third-order autoregressive model is appropriate.

	Linear	Quadratic	Exponential	AR3
Syx	1.9932	0.6879	3.0371	0.6194
MAD	1.6967	0.4338	1.6667	0.4390

(h) The residuals in the first three models show strings of consecutive positive and negative values. The autoregressive model performs well for the historical data and has a fairly random pattern of residuals. It also has the smallest values in the standard error of the estimate and *MAD*. Based on the principle of parsimony, the autoregressive model would probably be the best model for forecasting.

(i) $\hat{Y}_{2015} = \$28.3149$ billions.

Index

Credits

Front matter
Page vi, Courtesy of David Levine

First Things First
Page 1, Wallix/iStock/Getty Images; page 2, Excerpt from Ticket Pricing Puts 'Lion King' Atop Broadway's Circle Of Life by Patrick Healy. Published by The New York Times © 2014.

Chapter 1
Pages 12 and 26, Haveseen/YAY Micro/AGE Fotostock

Chapter 2
Pages 32 and 73, Scanrail/123RF

Chapter 3
Pages 95 and 130, Gitanna/Fotolia

Chapter 4
Pages 141 and 161, Blue Jean Images/Collage/Corbis

Chapter 5
Pages 166 and 182, Hongqi Zhang/123RF

Chapter 6
Pages 189 and 210, Cloki/Shutterstock; screen image from The Adventures of Dirk "Sunny" Lande appears courtesy of Waldowood Productions.

Chapter 7
Pages 216 and 231, Bluecinema/E+/Getty Images

Chapter 8
Pages 237 and 261, Mark Hunt/Huntstock/Corbis

Chapter 9
Pages 270 and 300, Ahmettozar/iStock/Getty Images

Chapter 10
Pages 307 and 337, Echo/Cultura/Getty Images

Chapter 11
Pages 348 and 375, Paul Morris/Bloomberg/Getty Images

Chapter 12
Pages 386 and 418, Vibrant Image Studio/Shutterstock

Chapter 13
Pages 427 and 464, Hero Images/Hero Images/Corbis

Chapter 14
Pages 475 and 509, Maridav/123RF

Chapter 15
Pages 521 and 544, Antbphotos/Fotolia

Chapter 16
Pages 553 and 589, Stylephotographs/123RF

Chapter 17
Pages 598 and 608, Courtesy of Sharyn Rosenberg

Online Chapter 18
Pages 18-1 and 18-31, Zest_marina/Fotolia; Figure 18.9, From The Deming Route to Quality and Productivity: Road Maps and Roadblocks by William W. Scherkenbach. Copyright by CEEP Press Books. Used by permission of CEEP Press Books.

Online Chapter 19
Pages 19-1 and 19-22, Ken Mellott/Shutterstock

Appendix E
Table E.09, From ASTM-STP 15D. Copyright by ASTM International. Used by permission of ASTM International.

Appendix F
Excerpt from Microsoft Corporation, Function Improvements In Microsoft Office Excel 2010. Published by Microsoft Corporation.

Credits

The Cumulative Standardized Normal Distribution

Entry represents area under the cumulative standardized
normal distribution from $-\infty$ to Z

Z	Cumulative Probabilities									
	0.00	0.01	0.02	0.03	0.04	0.05	0.06	0.07	0.08	0.09
−6.0	0.000000001									
−5.5	0.000000019									
−5.0	0.000000287									
−4.5	0.000003398									
−4.0	0.000031671									
−3.9	0.00005	0.00005	0.00004	0.00004	0.00004	0.00004	0.00004	0.00004	0.00003	0.00003
−3.8	0.00007	0.00007	0.00007	0.00006	0.00006	0.00006	0.00006	0.00005	0.00005	0.00005
−3.7	0.00011	0.00010	0.00010	0.00010	0.00009	0.00009	0.00008	0.00008	0.00008	0.00008
−3.6	0.00016	0.00015	0.00015	0.00014	0.00014	0.00013	0.00013	0.00012	0.00012	0.00011
−3.5	0.00023	0.00022	0.00022	0.00021	0.00020	0.00019	0.00019	0.00018	0.00017	0.00017
−3.4	0.00034	0.00032	0.00031	0.00030	0.00029	0.00028	0.00027	0.00026	0.00025	0.00024
−3.3	0.00048	0.00047	0.00045	0.00043	0.00042	0.00040	0.00039	0.00038	0.00036	0.00035
−3.2	0.00069	0.00066	0.00064	0.00062	0.00060	0.00058	0.00056	0.00054	0.00052	0.00050
−3.1	0.00097	0.00094	0.00090	0.00087	0.00084	0.00082	0.00079	0.00076	0.00074	0.00071
−3.0	0.00135	0.00131	0.00126	0.00122	0.00118	0.00114	0.00111	0.00107	0.00103	0.00100
−2.9	0.0019	0.0018	0.0018	0.0017	0.0016	0.0016	0.0015	0.0015	0.0014	0.0014
−2.8	0.0026	0.0025	0.0024	0.0023	0.0023	0.0022	0.0021	0.0021	0.0020	0.0019
−2.7	0.0035	0.0034	0.0033	0.0032	0.0031	0.0030	0.0029	0.0028	0.0027	0.0026
−2.6	0.0047	0.0045	0.0044	0.0043	0.0041	0.0040	0.0039	0.0038	0.0037	0.0036
−2.5	0.0062	0.0060	0.0059	0.0057	0.0055	0.0054	0.0052	0.0051	0.0049	0.0048
−2.4	0.0082	0.0080	0.0078	0.0075	0.0073	0.0071	0.0069	0.0068	0.0066	0.0064
−2.3	0.0107	0.0104	0.0102	0.0099	0.0096	0.0094	0.0091	0.0089	0.0087	0.0084
−2.2	0.0139	0.0136	0.0132	0.0129	0.0125	0.0122	0.0119	0.0116	0.0113	0.0110
−2.1	0.0179	0.0174	0.0170	0.0166	0.0162	0.0158	0.0154	0.0150	0.0146	0.0143
−2.0	0.0228	0.0222	0.0217	0.0212	0.0207	0.0202	0.0197	0.0192	0.0188	0.0183
−1.9	0.0287	0.0281	0.0274	0.0268	0.0262	0.0256	0.0250	0.0244	0.0239	0.0233
−1.8	0.0359	0.0351	0.0344	0.0336	0.0329	0.0322	0.0314	0.0307	0.0301	0.0294
−1.7	0.0446	0.0436	0.0427	0.0418	0.0409	0.0401	0.0392	0.0384	0.0375	0.0367
−1.6	0.0548	0.0537	0.0526	0.0516	0.0505	0.0495	0.0485	0.0475	0.0465	0.0455
−1.5	0.0668	0.0655	0.0643	0.0630	0.0618	0.0606	0.0594	0.0582	0.0571	0.0559
−1.4	0.0808	0.0793	0.0778	0.0764	0.0749	0.0735	0.0721	0.0708	0.0694	0.0681
−1.3	0.0968	0.0951	0.0934	0.0918	0.0901	0.0885	0.0869	0.0853	0.0838	0.0823
−1.2	0.1151	0.1131	0.1112	0.1093	0.1075	0.1056	0.1038	0.1020	0.1003	0.0985
−1.1	0.1357	0.1335	0.1314	0.1292	0.1271	0.1251	0.1230	0.1210	0.1190	0.1170
−1.0	0.1587	0.1562	0.1539	0.1515	0.1492	0.1469	0.1446	0.1423	0.1401	0.1379
−0.9	0.1841	0.1814	0.1788	0.1762	0.1736	0.1711	0.1685	0.1660	0.1635	0.1611
−0.8	0.2119	0.2090	0.2061	0.2033	0.2005	0.1977	0.1949	0.1922	0.1894	0.1867
−0.7	0.2420	0.2388	0.2358	0.2327	0.2296	0.2266	0.2236	0.2206	0.2177	0.2148
−0.6	0.2743	0.2709	0.2676	0.2643	0.2611	0.2578	0.2546	0.2514	0.2482	0.2451
−0.5	0.3085	0.3050	0.3015	0.2981	0.2946	0.2912	0.2877	0.2843	0.2810	0.2776
−0.4	0.3446	0.3409	0.3372	0.3336	0.3300	0.3264	0.3228	0.3192	0.3156	0.3121
−0.3	0.3821	0.3783	0.3745	0.3707	0.3669	0.3632	0.3594	0.3557	0.3520	0.3483
−0.2	0.4207	0.4168	0.4129	0.4090	0.4052	0.4013	0.3974	0.3936	0.3897	0.3859
−0.1	0.4602	0.4562	0.4522	0.4483	0.4443	0.4404	0.4364	0.4325	0.4286	0.4247
−0.0	0.5000	0.4960	0.4920	0.4880	0.4840	0.4801	0.4761	0.4721	0.4681	0.4641

The Cumulative Standardized Normal Distribution (*continued*)

Entry represents area under the cumulative standardized
normal distribution from $-\infty$ to Z

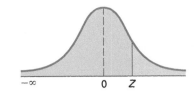

Z	0.00	0.01	0.02	0.03	0.04	0.05	0.06	0.07	0.08	0.09
					Cumulative Probabilities					
0.0	0.5000	0.5040	0.5080	0.5120	0.5160	0.5199	0.5239	0.5279	0.5319	0.5359
0.1	0.5398	0.5438	0.5478	0.5517	0.5557	0.5596	0.5636	0.5675	0.5714	0.5753
0.2	0.5793	0.5832	0.5871	0.5910	0.5948	0.5987	0.6026	0.6064	0.6103	0.6141
0.3	0.6179	0.6217	0.6255	0.6293	0.6331	0.6368	0.6406	0.6443	0.6480	0.6517
0.4	0.6554	0.6591	0.6628	0.6664	0.6700	0.6736	0.6772	0.6808	0.6844	0.6879
0.5	0.6915	0.6950	0.6985	0.7019	0.7054	0.7088	0.7123	0.7157	0.7190	0.7224
0.6	0.7257	0.7291	0.7324	0.7357	0.7389	0.7422	0.7454	0.7486	0.7518	0.7549
0.7	0.7580	0.7612	0.7642	0.7673	0.7704	0.7734	0.7764	0.7794	0.7823	0.7852
0.8	0.7881	0.7910	0.7939	0.7967	0.7995	0.8023	0.8051	0.8078	0.8106	0.8133
0.9	0.8159	0.8186	0.8212	0.8238	0.8264	0.8289	0.8315	0.8340	0.8365	0.8389
1.0	0.8413	0.8438	0.8461	0.8485	0.8508	0.8531	0.8554	0.8577	0.8599	0.8621
1.1	0.8643	0.8665	0.8686	0.8708	0.8729	0.8749	0.8770	0.8790	0.8810	0.8830
1.2	0.8849	0.8869	0.8888	0.8907	0.8925	0.8944	0.8962	0.8980	0.8997	0.9015
1.3	0.9032	0.9049	0.9066	0.9082	0.9099	0.9115	0.9131	0.9147	0.9162	0.9177
1.4	0.9192	0.9207	0.9222	0.9236	0.9251	0.9265	0.9279	0.9292	0.9306	0.9319
1.5	0.9332	0.9345	0.9357	0.9370	0.9382	0.9394	0.9406	0.9418	0.9429	0.9441
1.6	0.9452	0.9463	0.9474	0.9484	0.9495	0.9505	0.9515	0.9525	0.9535	0.9545
1.7	0.9554	0.9564	0.9573	0.9582	0.9591	0.9599	0.9608	0.9616	0.9625	0.9633
1.8	0.9641	0.9649	0.9656	0.9664	0.9671	0.9678	0.9686	0.9693	0.9699	0.9706
1.9	0.9713	0.9719	0.9726	0.9732	0.9738	0.9744	0.9750	0.9756	0.9761	0.9767
2.0	0.9772	0.9778	0.9783	0.9788	0.9793	0.9798	0.9803	0.9808	0.9812	0.9817
2.1	0.9821	0.9826	0.9830	0.9834	0.9838	0.9842	0.9846	0.9850	0.9854	0.9857
2.2	0.9861	0.9864	0.9868	0.9871	0.9875	0.9878	0.9881	0.9884	0.9887	0.9890
2.3	0.9893	0.9896	0.9898	0.9901	0.9904	0.9906	0.9909	0.9911	0.9913	0.9916
2.4	0.9918	0.9920	0.9922	0.9925	0.9927	0.9929	0.9931	0.9932	0.9934	0.9936
2.5	0.9938	0.9940	0.9941	0.9943	0.9945	0.9946	0.9948	0.9949	0.9951	0.9952
2.6	0.9953	0.9955	0.9956	0.9957	0.9959	0.9960	0.9961	0.9962	0.9963	0.9964
2.7	0.9965	0.9966	0.9967	0.9968	0.9969	0.9970	0.9971	0.9972	0.9973	0.9974
2.8	0.9974	0.9975	0.9976	0.9977	0.9977	0.9978	0.9979	0.9979	0.9980	0.9981
2.9	0.9981	0.9982	0.9982	0.9983	0.9984	0.9984	0.9985	0.9985	0.9986	0.9986
3.0	0.99865	0.99869	0.99874	0.99878	0.99882	0.99886	0.99889	0.99893	0.99897	0.99900
3.1	0.99903	0.99906	0.99910	0.99913	0.99916	0.99918	0.99921	0.99924	0.99926	0.99929
3.2	0.99931	0.99934	0.99936	0.99938	0.99940	0.99942	0.99944	0.99946	0.99948	0.99950
3.3	0.99952	0.99953	0.99955	0.99957	0.99958	0.99960	0.99961	0.99962	0.99964	0.99965
3.4	0.99966	0.99968	0.99969	0.99970	0.99971	0.99972	0.99973	0.99974	0.99975	0.99976
3.5	0.99977	0.99978	0.99978	0.99979	0.99980	0.99981	0.99981	0.99982	0.99983	0.99983
3.6	0.99984	0.99985	0.99985	0.99986	0.99986	0.99987	0.99987	0.99988	0.99988	0.99989
3.7	0.99989	0.99990	0.99990	0.99990	0.99991	0.99991	0.99992	0.99992	0.99992	0.99992
3.8	0.99993	0.99993	0.99993	0.99994	0.99994	0.99994	0.99994	0.99995	0.99995	0.99995
3.9	0.99995	0.99995	0.99996	0.99996	0.99996	0.99996	0.99996	0.99996	0.99997	0.99997
4.0	0.999968329									
4.5	0.999996602									
5.0	0.999999713									
5.5	0.999999981									
6.0	0.999999999									

They Call Me Black

CHARVETTE YVONNE JONES, EdS

Print information available on the last page

Rev. date: 04/05/2016

To order additional copies of this book, contact:
Xlibris
1-888-795-4274
www.Xlibris.com
Orders@Xlibris.com

THEY CALL
ME
BLACK

BEING BLACK SERIES

CHARVETTE YVONNE JONES, EDS
ILLUSTRATED BY JEFF MEYER

This book is dedicated to my daughter

SeaAira Sybri` Smith

I am black!
That's a fact,
and there is no denying that!

Black is beautiful
and that is the truth.

I come in many, different
colors, tints, and hues.

I am the color of the night
shining bright with little specks of light.

I am the pupil in your eyes
that keeps you bright and wise!

I am the darkness that comes
before a surprise!

I am the sunset ahead of the sunrise!

I am the licorice
that gives you endurance!

I am the candy bars
that keep you reaching for the stars!

I am the jelly beans
that make you sing!

I am what starts all dreams!

I am the coffees and teas
that keeps you moving with ease!

Yes, yes, I am everything!

You see, I'm the beginning and the ending.

I love everyone,
that's why I'm always befriending.

I am the chalkboards filled with knowledge that prepares everyone for college!

I am the crayons used to outline a picture
which helps everyone remember!

I am the paint used to make a statement
when everyone needs to pay attention!

I am strong and powerful,
mighty and able!
If anyone is ever doubtful,
I will prove that I am unstoppable!

Therefore, I have no problem when,
They Call Me Black!

CPSIA information can be obtained
at www.ICGtesting.com
Printed in the USA
BVHW022000180720
583904BV00017B/190

9 781514 482131